Fahrenheit/Celsius

-40°F = -40°C	120°F = 49°C	320°F = 160°C
-30°F = -34°C	125°F = 52°C	330°F = 166°C
-20°F = -29°C	130°F = 54°C	340°F = 171°C
-10°F = -23°C	135°F = 57°C	350°F = 177°C
- 5°F = -21°C	140°F = 60°C	360°F = 182°C
0°F = -18°C	145°F = 63°C	370°F = 188°C
5°F = -15°C	150°F = 66°C	380°F = 193°C
10°F = -12°C	155°F = 68°C	390°F = 199°C
15°F = - 9°C	160°F = 71°C	400°F = 204°C
20°F = - 6°C	165°F = 74°C	410°F = 210°C
25°F = - 4°C	170°F = 77°C	420°F = 216°C
30°F = - 1°C	175°F = 79°C	430°F = 221°C
32°F = 0°C	180°F = 82°C	440°F = 227°C
35°F = 2°C	185°F = 85°C	450°F = 232°C
40°F = 4°C	190°F = 88°C	460°F = 238°C
45°F = 7°C	195°F = 91°C	470°F = 243°C
50°F = 10°C	200°F = 93°C	480°F = 249°C
55°F = 13°C	205°F = 96°C	490°F = 254°C
60°F = 16°C	210°F = 99°C	500°F = 260°C
65°F = 18°C	212°F = 100°C	510°F = 266°C
70°F = 21°C	220°F = 104°C	520°F = 271°C
75°F = 24°C	230°F = 110°C	530°F = 277°C
80°F = 27°C	240°F = 116°C	540°F = 282°C
85°F = 29°C	250°F = 121°C	550°F = 288°C
90°F = 32°C	260°F = 127°C	560°F = 293°C
95°F = 35°C	270°F = 132°C	570°F = 299°C
100°F = 38°C	280°F = 137°C	580°F = 304°C
105°F = 41°C	290°F = 143°C	590°F = 310°C
110°F = 43°C	300°F = 149°C	600°F = 316°C
115°F = 46°C	310°F = 154°C	

CLASSICAL COOKING THE MODERN WAY

Eugen Pauli
Restaurateur, Food and Catering Consultant

EDITED BY

Marjorie S. Arkwright, R.D.
Director of Foodservice, University of Illinois

CBI PUBLISHING COMPANY, INC.
51 Sleeper Street
Boston, Massachusetts 02210

Acknowledgments

Color illustrations are reprinted from the European editions through the courtesy of the following sources:

F. Waldvogel, "Piltze," vol. 1 and 2 (Zurich: Silva-Verlag).
Katinka Moster ("Das grosse Reader's Digest Kochbuch"), Foto Teubner-Studio, Fussen.
Howeg, Cooperative d'achat pour l'industrie suisse l'hotellerie et de la restaurant.
Rundshau: Hotel & Gastgewerb (Zurich: Forster-Verlag AG).
Union Suisse du commerce de fromage S.A., Berne.
H. P. Pellaprat, "Die feine Kuche" (Castagnola; Edizioni Rene Kramer S.A.).
Centrale de propagande de l'industrie laitiere suisse (Pierrot Ice Cream), Berne.
H. Tschumper (Haco AG, Gumligen).
Hotellerie (Lucerne: Edition Union Helvetica).

English translation by Peter C. March *and* Monroe S. Levine
Drawings by Beatrice Thommen *and* Yvonne Escher
Designed by Amato Prudente

***Previously published in French and German under the titles:* Technologie Culinaire *and* Lehrbuch der Küche.**

Copyright © 1979 by CBI Publishing Company, Inc.

All rights reserved. No part of this book may be reproduced in any form without written permission from the publisher.

Printed in the United States of America

Library of Congress Cataloging in Publication Data

Pauli, Eugen.
Classical cooking the modern way.
"Previously published in French and German under the titles: *Technologie culinaire* and *Lehrbuch der küche*."
"The first English language edition . . . is based on the seventh German and the first French editions."
Includes index.
1. Cookery. 2. Food service. I. Arkwright, Marjorie S. II. Title.
TX652.P35 642'.5 78-24208
ISBN 0-8436-2074-9

In memory of my father and to all those entering the foodservice profession.

Contents

Foreword

To follow the history of mankind is to follow man's quest to assuage his hunger through the production and preparation of food. In the beginning, these activities were necessary for survival, but as civilizations grew and life became more complex, a greater degree of sophistication developed in man's eating habits.

Among the first printed volumes we find works dealing with all aspects of food, including the written recipes which had been transmitted orally from generation to generation. Indeed, the library of the School of Hotel Administration at Cornell has several volumes of incunabula devoted to foods, food preparation, and foodservice. These books illustrate man's interest in eating and in refining his earlier tastes.

In 1902 Auguste Escoffier revolutionized the culinary world with his "Guide Culinaire." This was to become the "bible" for chefs and cooks for the next fifty years.

Since that time a plethora of books have been published concerning almost every phase of food preparation for home use, commercial use, and educational use. Many of these books have offered vital additions to man's knowledge and growth and have provided the necessary information to make life more enjoyable.

Now, we have a new book—a well-written, beautifully illustrated volume that is certain to have a strong impact on the culinary arts. This book is most informative and will be of considerable assistance to those schools and colleges in the United States offering courses in the field of hospitality. A valuable reference source for instructors in foodservice, classical cooking the modern way will undoubtedly prove to be a very worthwhile text for the student as well.

We congratulate Mr. Pauli on an outstanding contribution to the culinary world.

Robert A. Beck
Dean, School of Hotel Administration
Cornell University
Ithaca, New York
April 1978

Preface

The first English language edition of *Classical Cooking the Modern Way* is based on the seventh German and the first French editions. It is designed to be used as a text by students preparing for careers in the foodservice industry and as a useful reference for persons actively engaged in the planning, production, and service of food.

This is no ordinary cookbook, but rather a manual which covers the *basic principles of kitchen management and cookery.* It is probably the only work in existence that deals both with kitchen management, that is, the organization which is prerequisite to cooking, and the whole field of cookery.

The fundamental principles of cooking contained in this volume are based on classical French cookery (Escoffier) and on the latest developments and trends in the foodservice industry. A unique feature is the description and illustration of all the basic forms of food preparation. The graphic presentation of these fundamental principles makes it possible for cooks, waiters, caterers, or hotel managers to grasp the essentials easily and quickly. The book should also be of considerable interest to persons in a wide range of related professions and industries, such as kitchen designers, architects, and personnel in the meat and food industries.

Special thanks are due to Peter C. March and Monroe S. Levine for undertaking the immense task of translating the work into English. My deepest thanks go to Marjorie S. Arkwright for the enormous work of adapting and editing the English version. I should also like to thank the publishers, CBI Publishing Company, Inc., for their generous cooperation in preparing this English language edition for publication.

May every reader benefit from it and derive full satisfaction in the pursuit of his chosen profession.

Eugen Pauli
Aarau, Switzerland
March, 1978

PART I

GENERAL THEORY

Specialized Professional Knowledge 1

1.1 The Ethics of the Profession

There is a set of sustaining attitudes, values, behaviors, and expectancies that characterizes foodservice as a vocation. Their purpose is to facilitate the long journey from beginner to expert, to ensure transmission of the art and science of quality foodservice to the next generation, and to provide a personal work life that is satisfying and meaningful.

The traditional method of training the inexperienced in this field has always been through some form of apprenticeship. The competent professional at the work place is the model who in ongoing activities demonstrates what is to be done; the beginner observes and imitates the behavior, work style, and attitudes being modeled. At its best this on-the-job education is also an interactive process of active participants: the experienced and the inexperienced, the skilled and the less skilled, the expert and the novice. The advantages of learning by doing have long been recognized, and there is increasing evidence that modeling, intentional or otherwise, is a particularly potent teaching method. In-service learning is also powerfully enhanced when the teacher-learner relationship is continous and based on mutual trust and respect. Small wonder then that apprenticeship type training has persisted and continues to be expected at each level of induction into the foodservice profession.

Practical experiences and in-service training will continue to be necessary, but no longer are they sufficient for the vocational education of aspiring foodservice students. Modern research has produced new scientific knowledge and technologies. Their sophistication and sheer number demand a more structured approach. No longer is "know how" sufficient; one must also know "why." Basic facts and principles have become the most creative tools available to us in our craft. Their acquisition is therefore imperative.

The valuing of excellence and the desire for its continuance provide both the goal and motivation to learn and pass along one's skills and high standards to each new wave of beginners. In foodservice this professional cycle calls for a progressive and developmental teacher-learner relationship. Discipline and the acceptance of discipline are demanded to build character and the self-discipline so essential to attainment of complex and aesthetic skills and to the development of competency. The responsibilities are reciprocal and compelling. In the climb toward excellence, however, personal and professional attributes cannot be separated. The most competent and creative foodservice person is not a machine, a wind-up toy professional, but a complete human being. Thus, his or her general education as a human being is as important in this world of burgeoning technology and mass production as is his or her professional preparation. One of the benchmarks of the true professional in this field is the ability to maintain a balance, a sense of proportion, between human and technical values.

In summary: a successful and self-actualizing career in foodservice depends upon one's natural ability, upon acceptance of discipline and successful transformation to self-discipline, upon growth of character, and upon opportunities for good on-the-job guidance and learning in addition to both general and vocational education. The beginner is often given much needed support and confidence by a more experienced colleague who offers friendship and counsel. It is expected that the trainee will in time become such a confidant to another beginner. There is also an ethical commitment to pass along to others the traditional skills, attitudes, and goals of one's profession and to contribute creatively to this heritage wherever possible and in such a manner that the balance between human and technical values is ensured. Failure to meet these commitments could trigger a disastrous shortage of personnel in the hotel and restaurant trades and usher in a new era in which the delights of the palate are standardized and mass-produced out of existence.

Each serious student of foodservice who accepts this challenge will discover that it provides both the goal and the stimulus for development within the profession. This is how, also why, foodservice can be and is such an intrinsically satisfying career.

1.2 Sanitation

1.2.1 Basic Principle

Good health is one of life's most precious gifts. High standards of sanitation are strategic to good physical and mental health. The National Sanitation Foundation, a nonprofit organization in Ann Arbor, Michigan, brings into focus the importance of sanitation in these words:

> **Sanitation is a way of life. It is the quality of living that is expressed in the clean home, the clean farm, the clean business and industry, the clean neighborhood, the clean community. Being a way of life it must come from within the people; it is nourished by knowledge and grows as an obligation and an ideal in human relations.[1]**

The Foundation places particular emphasis on the importance of thorough knowledge and practice of high standards of sanitation in the foodservice industry. In any foodservice operation, the primary objective is to serve food that is safe, wholesome, attractive, and nutritious in an environment that is safe and clean. This objective can be achieved only if everyone who works in foodservice assumes his individual responsibility. Each foodservice worker must know and practice high standards of sanitation to protect the consumer from health hazards and illness.

1.2.2 Legal Background

The laws pertaining to sanitation and safety in foodservice are established and enforced by national, state, and local government agencies.

The United States Department of Health, Education, and Welfare and the United States Department of Agriculture are two federal agencies concerned with promoting a high level of health for every individual. These departments are also concerned with the sanitation aspects of food protection.

The Public Health Service and the Food and Drug Administration, divisions of the United States Department of Health, Education, and Welfare, are engaged in activities that promote high standards of sanitation in the foodservice industry. By providing educational and technical services to states and municipalities, the United States Public Health Service has encouraged adoption of uniform codes and ordinances which regulate foodservice operations. The

1. National Sanitation Foundation, Ann Arbor, Michigan.

provisions in these codes and ordinances have, in principle, two main goals:

- the protection of the consumer from contaminated foods and goods.
- the protection of the consumer from fraud in the food industry (regulating inspections, providing for the sale of only unadulterated, wholesome, properly labeled foods).

1.2.3 Regulations and Standards

The execution of the food controls is the responsibility of each state. Food analysts and inspectors are responsible for the application of the laws of sanitation. Foods, facilities, equipment, and utensils are covered by the sanitation controls. Dietitians and foodservice managers are responsible for developing and implementing educational programs for foodservice personnel that will promote high standards of sanitation in their respective establishments.

1.2.4 Basic Principles of Microbiology

A knowledge of the principles of microbiology is basic to an understanding of food sanitation. Microorganisms are organisms so small that they can only be seen through a microscope. They consume food, give off waste, and multiply. Some are harmless, some are beneficial, and others are very dangerous.

Microorganisms can cause food spoilage and food-borne illnesses. Those that cause food spoilage are yeasts, bacteria, and molds. Most food-borne illnesses are caused by bacteria; however, viruses, trichinae, and protozoa can also cause food-borne illnesses.

It is important for foodservice managers, dietitians, and all food handlers to understand the conditions that cause food spoilage and food-borne illnesses. They must also know how to prevent contamination of foods during processing, transporting, storing, preparing, and serving.

To prevent food-borne illnesses and food spoilage, it is the responsibility of management to develop and carry out educational programs for foodservice personnel emphasizing:

- Effective control of food temperatures during storage, cooking, and holding.
- Protection of food from microorganisms, roaches, flies, rodents, and pests.
- Protection of food from poisonous substances such as chemicals and poisonous materials.
- Good health, personal hygiene, and safe food handling practices.

Microorganisms are classified into the following groups:

Bacteria

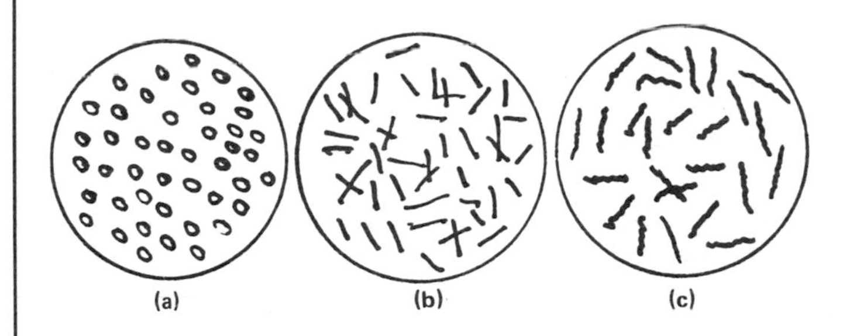

FIGURE 1-1
(a) round bacteria, "cocci." (b) rod-shaped bacteria, rods without spores, and spore bacilli. (c) spiral-shaped bacteria, spirilla.

Most bacteria are harmless for human beings, and can even be useful. Some types are important in the production of certain foods, such as sour milk, yoghurt, sauerkraut, and sour dough.

Bacteria *reproduce* by splitting into two parts (mitosis). The splitting of the cells proceeds very quickly (one to four divisions per hour) when there is adequate nourishment and when the temperature is between 90°F. (32°C.) and 105°F. (41°C.). Thus, assuming a doubling of numbers every fifteen minutes, approximately one million bacteria could be produced in five hours. Bacteria need moisture, food, and heat for growth. Some bacteria require oxygen; others, thrive better without air.

The various kinds of bacteria differ in their food requirements. Dry foods, such as sugar, flour, rice, and dry pastries, do not have sufficient moisture for bacterial multiplication. Acid foods, such as citrus foods and tomatoes, and items prepared with acid ingredients are the foods least preferred by bacteria. Most bacteria prefer nonacidic, protein-rich foods such as milk, milk products, eggs, meat, poultry, fish, glazes, and creams.

Bacterial contamination of foods can be retarded through constant and effective control of the temperature of food. Most bacteria develop best between 50°F. (10°C.) and 120°F. (49°C.). Bacteria practically stop growing and multiplying at temperatures above 165°F. (74°C.) and below 40°F. (4°C.). While all bacteria cannot be killed by cold temperatures, their growth can be arrested. The most suitable temperature for disease-producing organisms, pathogens, is body temperature, 98.6°F. (37°C.). *Pathogenic agents* can be transmitted by food and can be very dangerous to humans. The food can be contaminated by contact with dirty hands, soiled clothes and towels, dirty tables and utensils, dirty containers and machinery. Contamination of food may also result from contact with household pets, rats, mice, flies, cockroaches, insects, and polluted water. Diseases transmitted in this way include typhoid fever, salmonellosis, dysentery, cholera, jaundice, tuberculosis, and diptheria.

Bacteria can be destroyed by:

- the use of high temperatures, boiling water, 212°F. (100°C.); steam-cleaning tables, utensils, containers, and machines. Immersion in 180°F. (82°C.) for ten seconds will destroy most pathogens.
- the application of heat when cooking (pasteurization) or by sterilizing foods.
- the use of chemical compounds, such as chlorine, iodine, or quaternary ammonium to clean and sanitize equipment and utensils. The following amounts in 10 gallons (45 liters) of water will provide a safety level: 4 ounces (113 grams) iodine-type disinfectant; 2¼ ounces (64 grams) 5½% sodium hypochlorite.

Molds

Molds, a form of life called fungi, are made up of many cells that require air and moisture for growth. Different types of molds are different colors—white, blue, green, pink, and black. As molds develop, the growth resembles cobwebs or fine threads, and the powdery substance is easily visible. Some molds, like some bacteria, may be helpful to mankind; others may cause problems. Certain molds are used for penicillin, aureomycin, and terramycin—all well-known antibiotics.

Molds can grow on practically all foods—on sweet, sour, bitter, and even relatively dry foods. Some give a special flavor to foods such as bleu cheese, Roquefort, and Camembert. Molds, however, can cause food spoilage which can be detected by the fuzzy growth and an unpleasant odor and a musty flavor. Some molds produce wastes which can be classified among the most lethal poisons (aflatoxins) and can cause dangerous liver malfunctions. The formation of molds in foods can be prevented by controlling storage conditions and by avoiding long storage periods. (See page 9.)

Most molds reproduce by the formation of spores, which are very lightweight and can be found almost everywhere, particularly in the soil. They may be carried by air currents, insects, animals, and people. Mold and mold spores can be destroyed by the same methods used to eliminate bacteria.

Yeasts

Yeasts are one-celled organisms that absorb food and moisture and multiply by germinating. Yeast cells are important in fermentation and leavening processes. Whenever yeast cells are combined with warm temperatures, air, moisture, and sugar, they multiply and grow. Yeasts are important in making breads, wines, and alcoholic beverages and are also used as vitamin B_{12} supplements.

Yeast cells are very light and are often in the air. When these cells come in contact with food and start breaking down the starches and sugars, the food usually spoils. The spoilage can generally be identified by the alcoholic odor and the presence of bubbles. Although some types of yeast may cause skin infections, yeasts are usually considered harmless to humans and are destroyed by high temperatures.

Viruses

Viruses are not independent organisms and cannot reproduce in food. The viruses, however, may be transmitted to human beings through food. For example, the viruses responsible for jaundice and polio can be transmitted if the food has been infected with these viruses by people.

1.2.5 Food Spoilage

Food is very perishable, and because of its delicacy, it is susceptible to spoilage. The U. S. Public Health Food Service Ordinance and Code states:

> Food used in foodservice operations shall be from a source approved, or considered satisfactory by the health authority and which is in compliance with applicable state and local laws and regulations. Food from such sources shall have been protected from contamination and spoilage during subsequent handling, packaging, and storage, and while in transit.[2]

Causes of food spoilage:

- presence of bacteria and molds that produce toxins and break down sugars
- contamination by insects and pests
- chemical reactions that cause rancidity when foods with high fat content have been overexposed to light; metallic tastes that develop when canned foods have been stored too long
- chemical reactions in canned foods causing leaks and bulges in the cans

1.2.6 Personal Hygiene

Top management and the professional foodservice staff are responsible for determining the standards of sanitation for the foodservice establishment. These standards and the methods of achieving them should be emphasized in an educational program for all the foodservice personnel. Persons who are knowledgeable about sanitation should plan and implement the program. Throughout these sessions, employees should be made aware of their individual roles in the total sanitation program.

Many food-borne illnesses are traced to human contamination of food. These illnesses are frequently caused by employees who are ill or who are careless about their own personal hygiene and food handling practices. Each employee must understand the principles of sanitation and the causes of food contamination. Furthermore, he must know what he can do to prevent contamination of food. Proper techniques of handling food, the importance of good health, and good personal hygiene habits should be stressed through continuous training. The educational program should bring into focus the role of each food handler in protecting his own health and the well-being of customers.

Visual aids such as films, posters, and other educational materials are effective tools for stimulating interest in good sanitation and reinforcing proper sanitation techniques. Such materials are available through state and federal agencies and through many commercial companies. Other sources include the National Sanitation Foundation, The National Restaurant Association, the Communicable Disease Center in Atlanta, Georgia, and educational film companies.

The health of employees, their personal hygiene habits, and their food handling practices reflect the standards of sanitation in the production, manufacture, preparation, storage, packaging, distribution, and selling of food. Training and follow-up supervision by qualified staff members must be continuous and constant to ensure a safe and sanitary foodservice.

Carelessness as related to body cleanliness or food handling practices can lead to serious illness. Bacteria are present everywhere—on skin, in mouths, on hands, in hair, in body discharges, on clothing, and on utensils and equipment. Organisms can be passed from the careless worker to the food or utensils and then to the consumer.

Persons who work with food must be in good physical condition. Annual physical examinations, semi-annual dental checkups, regular eye examina-

2. Treva Richardson, *Sanitation for Foodservice Workers*, (Boston: CBI Publishing Company, Inc., 1974) p. 38 (1).

tions, and sufficient rest are extremely important to maintain good health. Underweight or overweight conditions should be avoided or corrected. Well-balanced, nourishing meals are necessary to maintain proper weight and good health. While these are practices that everyone should observe, they are especially important for the foodservice worker who is responsible for protecting his own health as well as that of others. In addition to these general practices, every foodservice worker is responsible for adhering to very rigid standards of cleanliness and personal hygiene.

- *A clean body* is the foundation for cleanliness and good appearance. A daily bath, clean teeth, clean and well-groomed hair, and skin free from blemishes are essential for cleanliness. The use of effective deodorants, dental floss, and mouth astringents will aid in avoiding body odors which are offensive to co-workers and customers.
- *Clean hands* with short well-manicured fingernails must be kept immaculate. Hands should be washed thoroughly with soap and water in a hand sink, (sinks for washing dishes or utensils or for the preparation of food should not be used for hand washing), and dried carefully before handling food or equipment, after using toilet facilities, after handling any soiled or contaminated objects, after smoking, and after eating. Disposable towels, or a mechanical dryer should be used for drying hands. *Communal towels must not be used.* The use of communal towels poses serious danger of contaminating the hands with bacteria. Jewelry, watches, and nail polish should not be worn in foodservice areas. Jewelry may catch on equipment and cause injury. Pieces of jewelry may break and get into the food causing injury to the customer. Nail polish may chip off and fall into the food.
- *Clothing* including uniforms, aprons, undergarments, and hose must be clean and changed daily. Comfortable and carefully-fitted shoes that are in good repair should be worn to prevent discomfort, fatigue, and accidents. Hair nets and/or caps must be worn to protect the food and work surfaces from contact with hair.
- *People with communicable diseases* should not work with food. Germs may be spread by discharges from the respiratory tract and from the intestinal tract. Mumps, meningitis, measles, and the common cold are infections that can be spread by discharges from the nose and throat. Typhoid fever, dysentery, and diarrhea are but a few infections that are associated with intestinal discharges.
- *Disposable tissues* should be used only once and then discarded. Germs can be transferred directly and indirectly. Hands should be washed thoroughly after coughing, sneezing, or using tissues.
- *People suffering from eczema,* other skin diseases, sores, or infected wounds should not work with food.

1.2.7 General Sanitation Practices

Foodservice personnel must observe certain practices when working in foodservice areas to protect the consumer as well as themselves.

Food should be handled, whenever possible, with spoons, tongs, or forks. A clean spoon or fork should be used to taste food and the utensil should never be put back into the food after it has touched the mouth. Food should never be tasted with the fingers, and hands should never be put into a bin where ice is stored. Plastic gloves are recommended for mixing foods, making sandwiches, arranging or dispensing food. Gloves should be replaced after handling raw poultry or meat, after handling any soiled objects, after work has been interrupted, and whenever a glove is torn or punctured. When working with a meat slicer or other equipment, gloves should be removed. The glove may catch on the machine and cause injury.

Hands should be kept away from the areas of dishes, glassware, and silverware that come in contact with the mouth. Plates should be held by placing the palm of the hand underneath the plate with the fleshy part of the thumb on the edge of the plate. Cups should be lifted by the handle; glassware should be held at the base of the glass; and only the handles of silverware should be touched.

Household pets (cats, dogs, birds, and fish) should be kept out of all foodservice areas. Animals should never be touched by anyone when working with food.

Garbage and trash need to be moved from foodservice areas at regular intervals throughout the day and should be stored in a separate room—refrigerated if possible. Mechanical disposal units and compactors should be cleaned frequently.

Pest control is important for safe sanitation. Clean equipment and good maintenance, elimination of breeding areas, and the assistance of qualified pest control operators are required to eliminate insects and rodents. Consultation with pest control experts is necessary before using any pesticides, poisons, or chemicals in a foodservice area. Foodservice personnel need to be trained to read all labels and to follow proper procedures so that food, utensils, and equipment will not be contaminated with poisonous materials.

Soiled dishes, glassware, silverware, linen, and utensils may be contaminated with disease organisms from users. Unless this ware is handled carefully, employees may pick up the germs on their own hands and transfer them to their mouths or to customers. Soiled items must be handled with the same care used for clean utensils. After handling dishes and utensils used by others, it is extremely important to wash hands thoroughly with soap and water.

1.2.8 Food Sanitation

The kitchen is *the most important area of the operation from the point of view of sanitation. Absolute cleanliness in the processing and storage of food* are rules that should be followed at all times. The following practices must be observed in handling the various types of food:

Milk and cream are very perishable and must be stored in the original containers (not plastic) or in containers that have been sanitized. Milk products should be refrigerated at a temperature of 40°F. (4°C.).

Butter or margarine should be covered and stored in the refrigerator at 40°F. (4°C.).

Fats and cooking oils should be stored at low temperatures in closed containers that are protected from exposure to light and air to prevent rancidity.

Eggs must be kept refrigerated. Fresh eggs should be stored between 33°F. and 45°F. (−.6°C. and 7°C.). Frozen eggs should be held at 0°F. to 20°F. (−.18°C. to −6°C.).

Fruits and vegetables should be stored at 50°F. (10°C.) and should be thoroughly washed before using. Control of humidity and proper covering of the products will reduce losses.

Potatoes and vegetables should be peeled as near to the cooking time as possible. Prolonged soaking in cold water leads to a loss of nutrients.

Canned foods should be stored in areas that are cool, dry, and well-ventilated. A temperature of 60°F. (16°C.) is recommended to retain maximum quality while humidity control is necessary to prevent rusting of cans. Food in cans with bulged lids, dents, or leaks should not be used. Canned foods that have been opened should be transferred to containers that can be covered.

Meat glazes are made from ingredients which provide good growing conditions for bacteria. Extreme cleanliness is necessary while glazes are being prepared. Meat glazes should be heated to 185°F. (85°C.) for at least one minute and then quickly cooled to below 40°F. (4°C.). All utensils used in the preparation of glazes should be thoroughly cleaned and sterilized with disinfectant or boiling water.

Cream-filled pastries and custards are highly perishable. After preparation, these products should be refrigerated immediately. Only freshly prepared custards and cream-filled pastries should be served.

Sandwiches and canapes prepared with meats, poultry, fish, eggs, or salad dressings must be refrigerated at 40°F. (4°C.). Counter tops and equipment used for sandwich preparation should be sanitized and hands should be carefully washed.

Fresh meat, products containing meat, fish, and other seafoods must be prepared and stored with caution. Pork should be cooked to 150°F. (66°C.). Cooked foods should not be held at room temperature. They should be stored in shallow pans at 35°F. (2°C.); 40°F. (4°C.) is the upper limit. Ground meat and similar raw meat products spoil very quickly and should be kept no longer than one day. A greasy layer on the meat, an unpleasant odor, changes in color, and the formation of mold are all typical signs of spoilage in meat or meat products. When in doubt, throw it out!

Fresh mushrooms (except cultivated mushrooms and chanterelles) can be used only after an expert has examined the variety carefully and found them to be edible. Some types are highly toxic. Mushrooms showing signs of decay may harbor poisons and these should never be used.

Frozen products should be stored at 0°F. (-18°C.) and should always be thawed at refrigrerator temperature 40°F. (4°C.). Thawing at room temperature is dangerous.

The U.S. Public Health Service states:

> All food, while being stored, prepared, displayed, served, or sold at food service establishments, shall be protected from contamination. All perishable food shall be stored at such temperatures as will protect against spoilage. All potentially hazardous food shall be maintained at safe temperatures 45°F. (7°C.) or below, or 140°F. (60°C.) or above, except during necessary periods of preparation and service.[3]

1.2.9 Sanitation of the Utensils, Equipment, and Premises

All utensils and equipment that come into contact with food, and areas in which food is processed, *especially the kitchen,* must be kept clean at all times, by following a well-planned system.

The kitchen must be cleaned at least once a day. *Floors, ceilings, and walls* should have smooth, hard surfaces for easy maintenance. Damaged surfaces such as crevices, splits, and holes are hiding places for bacteria, vermin, and insects. These surfaces should be repaired and carefully maintained to block the entrances and eliminate the hiding and breeding places for such pests. Floors should be mopped after every service and must be thoroughly washed each day. *Floor drains* facilitate cleaning and washing equipment and floors. The kitchen should be equipped with effective *ventilation and lighting systems.*

Refrigerators and freezers require regular inspections. Routine checks of motors, condensers, coils, and all mechanical parts and frequent defrosting are essential for good maintenance. The shelving and accessories should be removed and cleaned regularly. Inside walls and floors should be properly cleaned once a week. Before restocking, the refrigerator should be thoroughly dry.

Storerooms should be equipped with temperature and humidity controls that will provide optimum conditions for holding various food products. Dry storage areas must be well-ventilated, cool, and clean. A systematic plan for the organization and arrangement of the storeroom will facilitate cleaning.

Machines and other equipment should be sanitized with a suitable disinfectant at regular intervals. Dishwashing machines, food mixers, grinders, slicers, steamers, ranges, ovens, and other equipment must be cleaned daily or after each use.

Kitchen utensils, containers, knives, and tools constructed of noncorrosive metals (alloys of iron, nickel, and chrome) are durable, easy to clean, and resistant to chemical reactions with foods. Utensils must be fabricated in such a way that there are no traces of poisonous metals such as zinc or lead that could come in contact with food. At one time copper and brass were commonly used for cooking utensils. The weight and upkeep of equipment made from these materials have made them unsatisfactory for institution use. Enamelware chips and cracks easily and is not suitable for heavy duty kitchen equipment. Only plastic containers that have been officially certified for use with foods can be used.

Work tables and work surfaces constructed of stainless steel, rubber, or plastic without seams are easily cleaned, nontoxic, and nonabsorbent. Wooden cutting boards should be replaced with hard rubber, plastic, or fiberglass.

Deep-fat fryers. The oil should be drained from deep-fat fryers each day. The fryer should then be scrubbed and cleaned with detergents or baking soda and rinsed thoroughly. Oil or shortening should be

3. U.S. Department of Health, Education, and Welfare, *Food Sanitation Manual,* Public Health Service Publication #934, p. 42, 1962.

changed frequently to prevent the accumulation of acid products which affect the quality of the oil and products fried in oil.

Grills and roasting spits should be cleaned after each use. The heating surface should be brushed with a steel brush to remove any carbonized material.

Fish tanks. The systems for oxygenating and for circulating the water in fish tanks require daily inspection. The condition of the fish should be checked daily. Tanks should be cleaned at least once a week and filled with fresh water.

Restrooms must be cleaned as often as is necessary during the day. They should be well-ventilated. The walls and floors of the restrooms must have hard, smooth, easy-to-clean surfaces.

Hand-basins should be available in the restrooms, dressing rooms, and kitchens. Each should be equipped with hot and cold running water, liquid soap, and *single-use towels* (paper or roller towels). The hand-basins and toilets should be cleaned frequently throughout the day.

Trash containers must be washed and disinfected inside and outside. The areas where they are stored must be cleaned and sanitized daily.

Packing cases may be dangerous sources of bacteria. Vermin (cockroaches, beetles, and moths) find their way into the kitchen in suppliers' packing cases. Such cases should be stored in an area outside the kitchen until they can be unpacked and removed.

Soiled laundry should be stored in laundry carts or containers outside the kitchen.

1.3 Safety

Safety is a major responsibility of all foodservice personnel. Accident prevention should be practiced according to the old principle, "prevention is better than cure."

Management must organize for safety. The Occupational Safety and Health Act of 1970 became effective in 1971. Through this act, management is legally responsible to protect its employees as well as the public. The act requires each employer to comply with provisions of the law and provide a place of employment that is safe and free from hazards that may cause physical injuries or fatalities.

Every foodservice establishment should develop an overall safety program that includes firm safety policies and procedures, safety education for staff and employees, and kitchen equipment with built-in safety features. Such a program is necessary to reduce the number of accidents which cause suffering to the injured; financial loss to the institution due to cost of temporarily replacing injured personnel, high insurance costs and legal fees, and the loss of business and goodwill through customer injuries on the premises.

The following steps to safety are the responsibility of management:

- arrange for inspections by qualified safety inspectors.
- follow through on removing and/or correcting potential safety hazards.
- furnish written reports of all accidents.
- provide continuous training programs and supervision by qualified staff that include teaching and enforcing safety procedures.
- keep all equipment, machines, physical structures, and surfaces in good repair.
- specify non-slip materials for floors when planning or remodeling foodservice facilities.
- provide uniform and adequate lighting on work surfaces, in corridors, and at entrances and exits.
- keep all electric wiring in good repair. Electric wires and cords must be properly insulated; electric equipment should be grounded properly; light bulbs should be protected with a guard; electric switches should be located so they can be reached easily in case of an emergency.
- keep correct type of fire extinguishing equipment in appropriate locations, and provide a regular maintenance program for the equipment.
- provide equipment required for safety, including: safe ladders for specific uses; special containers, plainly marked, for broken glass; storage racks for knives and sharp tools; covered containers for trash and refuse.

- keep emergency telephone numbers for police, ambulances, and hospitals posted near the telephone.
- keep first aid supplies available.
- keep exits clearly marked.

The most frequent injuries are the result of accidents caused by burns, cuts, and falls. To avoid such accidents, employees should be aware of specific rules and procedures. These include:

Prevention of Burns

- know the emergency procedures for reporting fires.
- know the location of fire extinguishers and fire exits and know how to use them.
- keep the hoods over ranges and cooking equipment clean and free of accumulated grease.
- keep oven doors closed except when loading and unloading the oven.
- open and ventilate gas ovens a few minutes before lighting.
- keep ranges, fryers, griddles, and broilers clean and free from accumulated grease.
- use only dry pads to move hot pans or cooking utensils.
- use long-handled hooks to open covers of steam kettles. Stir contents with long-handled paddles.
- stand back from equipment when opening doors of pressure steamers and lids of steam-jacketed kettles.
- lift lids on the side of the pan opposite you to allow steam to escape.
- keep handles of pans out of the aisle and away from the direct source of heat, such as over an open flame or burner.
- open valves of steam-jacketed kettles and urns slowly to avoid splashing hot water and steam.
- close all valves and spigots before filling urns or kettles.
- get assistance when moving heavy containers and hot food.
- warn others about hot pans or hot china.
- avoid over-filling pans and containers with hot foods and liquids.
- wear clean uniforms that fit properly. Loose sleeves and apron strings may catch on equipment or touch a source of heat. Wear shoes with closed toe and heel for protection from spills of hot foods and liquids.
- strike matches in a direction away from you.
- avoid spattering liquids into hot fat.
- keep supply of salt in appropriate place to extinguish fires in oven or on stove tops.
- keep supply of baking soda in appropriate place to extinguish fires in fryers.
- keep fire doors closed.
- keep exits, fire doors, and fire escapes free of obstacles and equipment. Use these only as directed for emergencies.
- smoke only in designated areas and never leave a burning cigarette unattended.
- do not handle electrical equipment with wet hands or while standing in water.
- report defective electrical wiring.

Prevention of Cuts

- learn the complete instructions for operating meat slicers, food grinders, or food choppers. Always read directions.
- keep blades of knives and slicers sharp.
- store knives in safe holders or racks when not in use. Knives should never be left in a sink or in an area where they cannot be seen.
- never try to catch a falling knife. Move out of its path and let it fall.
- select the appropriate knife for the specific cutting or boning task.
- use knives for cutting and chopping. Never use a knife to open lids, cans, or other containers.
- hold knives and sharp tools by the handles.
- use a cutting board. Cut away from your body.
- be attentive to the job when using a knife.
- turn switch to "off" position before cleaning or adjusting a machine. Do not remove food from a machine until the machine stops.
- check switches of electrical equipment and appliances and be sure that they are in the "off" position before plugging the electric cord into the outlet.

- dispose of chipped and broken china and glassware. Place them in a container that has no other use. Do not put in waste baskets, trash, or garbage receptacles. Sweep broken glass or china into a dustpan. Use disposable towels and cloths to pick up slivers of glass and china.
- use the proper tool to open crates, boxes, cans, and bottles. Remove nails, staples, and wires and put them in a disposable container.
- drain the water from the sink before removing broken glass or china.
- turn the switch of mixers, slicers, and other equipment to the "off" position when the task is completed.
- keep hands away from the edge of the cutting blade while cleaning a slicer. Always keep the switch in the "off" position and the blade closed when the slicer is not in use.
- use safety guards when using equipment.
- lock the bowls, containers, and attachments in place before starting equipment.

Prevention of Falls

- stand on a safe ladder—not chairs, stools, or boxes—to clean coffee urns, deck ovens, and hoods.
- keep floors and stairs free of grease, spills, and wet spots.
- keep floors, stairways, and traffic lanes free of boxes, cleaning equipment, and other obstructions.
- stack carts and trucks no higher than eye level.

First Aid

First aid is defined as the immediate care given to the victim of an injury or a sudden illness. The person who administers first aid knows that his knowledge of and skill in first aid techniques can mean the difference between life and death, between temporary and permanent disability, and between rapid recovery and long hospitalization. Everyone feels obliged to help those who have met emergencies, particularly those who are helpless.[4]

4. The American National Red Cross, *Advanced First Aid and Emergency Care,* p. 17.

Basic Principle

The first-aider must think quickly and then act. A physician should be notified whenever a serious accident occurs. Only persons who are qualified should be permitted to administer first aid. The first-aider should check the victim's respiration and pulse; take the necessary action; and have someone arrange for assistance needed, such as a physician, the police, an ambulance, the fire department, or the rescue squad.

Bleeding

Bleeding rarely represents an immediate threat to the life of the patient; however, severe bleeding from wounds may be fatal. If excessive bleeding occurs, the patient should be positioned so that the wound is elevated above the level of the heart until medical assistance can be arranged. The wound should be covered with a clean compress and pressure should be applied with the palm of the hand. The compress can be held in place by use of a pressure pad placed over the compress and tied directly over the pad.

Wounds

A wound is an internal or external break in the skin, tissue, or mucous membrane. Open wounds should be covered with a clean compress. Ointments should not be applied. Cleansing wounds and removal of foreign objects should be left to a physician. Infections may develop following an injury. Symptoms of infection include:

- redness of the affected area
- fever and chills
- pain
- red streaks emanating from the wound
- swollen lymph glands

If such symptoms develop, the person should be referred to a physician at once.

Burns

Burns are injuries caused by heat, radiation, or chemical agents. The degree of burn is usually classified by the depth of the burn. The classifications and their symptoms are:

- first degree burns—redness or discoloration
- second degree burns—formation of blisters
- third degree burns—destruction of cells

First degree burns seldom require medical attention. Pain will be relieved by submerging the area in cold water. The area should be covered by a clean dry cloth or gauze.

Second and third degree burns require medical care, and the first aid treatment is the same for severe second degree burns as that required for third degree burns.

First aid treatment for these burns:

- obtain medical assistance.
- cover the burned areas with a sterile cloth.
- avoid use of ointments, salt, spray, or home remedies.
- elevate burned feet or legs.
- apply cold packs, not ice water, to burned areas.
- elevate burned arm above heart level.
- keep person with facial burns sitting up and observe breathing.
- avoid breaking blisters or removing shreds of skin.
- give solution of salt and soda water to victim if he is not vomiting (one teaspoon salt and ½ teaspoon baking soda per quart of water). Allow victim to sip 4 ounces each 15 minute period.[5]

Chemical Burns

Should a corrosive agent get into the eye, the eyelid should be opened fully. The eye should be washed immediately with large amounts of water. Skin that has been burned by chemicals should be washed at once with large quantities of water for 10 or 15 minutes. Clothing should be removed from burned areas immediately. Burned areas may be covered with a sterile bandage.

Poisoning

A poison is a solid, liquid, or gas substance that causes injury or illness on contact with body surfaces or when swallowed or inhaled. Medical aid should be summoned for the victim as quickly as possible. In the meantime, first aid should be administered to dilute the poison, to induce vomiting (except when acids or alkalis have been swallowed), and to maintain respiration.

The label of the poison should be read and the antidote prescribed should be given to the victim. The label should be given to the physician. Persons who have swallowed roach powder, drugs, or other noncorrosive poisons should be given three or four glasses of water. If this does not induce vomiting, the blunt end of a spoon or a finger should be inserted into the back of the victim's mouth. Medicinal charcoal mixed with water will absorb poison and may be given to the victim; however, the stomach should be flushed or vomiting induced within a short period after the charcoal is swallowed. Victims who are semiconscious should be given artificial respiration, and no attempt should be made to give them liquids.

If acids, alkalis, or other corrosive poisons have been swallowed, milk or water should be given to the victim, and vomiting should not be induced. The victim should be treated for shock, kept from chilling, and should be given artificial respiration if necessary.[6] A cloth should be placed over the mouth of the victim before resuscitation is started. This is necessary for the protection of the individual administering the resuscitation.

Foreign Objects

In the eye. Foreign objects such as dust, particles of carbon, or sand are irritating to the eye or may damage the eye. These precautions should be followed in administering first aid:

- consult a physician immediately if a substance is embedded in the area of the eyeball.
- avoid rubbing the eye.
- wash hands thoroughly before examining the eye.

If an object is embedded under the upper eyelid, pull the upper lid forward and down. Place a matchstick on top of the cartilage parallel to the edge of the eyelid. The eyelid can then be rolled back over the

5. The American National Red Cross, *Advanced First Aid and Emergency Care,* pp. 139-140.

6. The American National Red Cross, *Advanced First Aid and Emergency Care,* pp. 99-100.

matchstick while the patient looks downward. The foreign object can be removed with the corner of a clean handkerchief. The eye should be flushed with water from an eye dropper.

In the throat. Foreign objects can often be expelled by coughing; however, if the victim shows signs of distress, the following techniques should be used immediately:

- send for help and start administering first aid.
- tilt the victim's head back, grasp the victim's tongue with a clean cloth or napkin; pull the tongue forward as far as possible; use the middle and index fingers like tweezers; grasp the obstruction and pull it out.

If the object still cannot be extracted, use the Heimlich Maneuver:[7]

- seek prompt medical attention.
- wrap your arms above the victim's waist from behind. Make a fist with one hand and place the thumb-side against the victim's abdomen between the navel and the rib cage.
- clasp the fist with your free hand and press it in with a quick upward thrust. Repeat several times if necessary.
- restore breathing with artificial respiration after the obstruction has been removed, if necessary.

1.4 Recipe Book and File

Standardized recipes. The food production system is the key to wholesome and palatable food, controlled food costs, and satisfied clientele.

Standardized recipes are one of the most important tools for assuring high quality food production. A standardized recipe is one that has been tested and developed to meet the needs of the specific establishment. The available equipment, the skills of the foodservice personnel, and the food budget must be considered. The yield is calculated for an exact quantity based on the predicted number of portions required and the specific portion size.

The recipe is tested several times until at least three trials have produced a product of the desired quality and quantity. Recipes may be recorded on either standard size sheets or cards.

The beginner's curriculum includes building a file of standardized recipes. Similar files should be maintained for members of the food production staff.

A standardized format should be used for recording all recipes. The form may be on sheets that are 8½ inches by 11 inches or on cards 5 inches by 8 inches. The format of the recipe sheet or card should be designed to meet the organization's needs.

Whether a recipe book or a recipe file system is selected, duplicates should be in the manager's office, the kitchen supervisor's office, and in the kitchen.

A recipe rack to which the recipe can be attached and placed over the cook's work station is a convenience that will keep the recipe available and clean.

Recipe book. A loose-leaf notebook might be used so that additional recipes can be inserted in the correct place. *Advantages*: convenient and a minimum of space required. *Disadvantages*: it is not as clear-cut and more time is required to locate recipes than with a card file.

Recipe file. Individual recipe cards are classified, numbered, and filed in a standard size box under headings such as soups, meats, vegetables, and salads. Colored cards may be used to separate the sections. The recipe cards should be laminated or placed in transparent plastic sleeves to protect the recipes. *Advantages*: recipe cards are easy to locate; recipes can be kept clean; recipe cards can be corrected or revised easily. *Disadvantages*: files require more storage space; individual cards may be lost.

Index. A chronological index is indispensable for either a recipe book or file. The index should be divided into main and subgroups as it is in this book.

7. Fireman's Fund American Life Insurance Company. San Francisco, California.

The main groups are annotated on the colored section cards with their reference number (decimal) and description. The subgroups are marked with their reference numbers on each of the recipe cards. The system of reference numbers and descriptions then appears again in the index.

Example of index for Hungarian Goulash (taken from this book):

17	= Entree	*(main group)*
17.1	= Sauteing	*(subgroup 1 of the entrees)*
17.2	= Broiling	*(subgroup 2 of the entrees)*
17.3	= Braising	*(subgroup 3 of the entrees)*
17.4	= Stewing/Simmering	*(subgroup 4 of the entrees)*
17.4.1	= Stewed white meats	*(subgroup 1 of stewing)*
17.4.2	= Stewed red meats	*(subgroup 2 of stewing)*

Recipe sheet or card. The format is, in principle, the same for both. The following information should be included:

- exact title or description of the recipe
- text for the menu
- file number
- name of the establishment
- chef's name
- tester's name
- date of standardization and/or revision
- portion size
- number of portions (yield)
- ingredients
- weight or measure of each ingredient
- equipment to be used (pan size)
- preparation procedures
- time and temperature for cooking or baking
- method or suggestions for serving and garnishes
- comments

The recipe sheet example for Hungarian Goulash is arranged as follows:

17.4.2.1

17	= Entree	*(main group)*
17.4	= Stewing/Simmering	*(subgroup 4 of the entrees)*
17.4.2	= Stewed red meats	*(subgroup 2 under stewing)*
17.4.2.1	= Hungarian Goulash	*(final recipe number)*

1.5 Menu Book

The beginning cook and the trained cook should keep menu books. A collection of important menus is a good reference that may be very useful in planning menus. A loose-leaf book is recommended for classification of the individual menus. Two copies of the book, one for the kitchen and one for the office, will simplify menu planning. See menu planning on page 189.

Index. An index, divided into main and subgroups, should be included in the menu book. Colored pages which can be annotated are used to separate the sections. The individual menus are arranged in chronological order with main and subgroups.

Example of Index

1	Menus for the day	*(main group)*
1.1	Menus including meat	*(subgroup 1 of daily menus)*
1.2	Menus including fish	*(subgroup 2 of daily menus)*
1.3	Menus including poultry	*(subgroup 3 of daily menus)*
1.4	Menus including game	*(subgroup 4 of daily menus)*
1.5	Menus for vegetarians	*(subgroup 5 of daily menus)*
1.6	Drive-in lunches	*(subgroup 6 of daily menus)*
1.7	Menus for calorie watchers	*(subgroup 7 of daily menus)*

Text for Menu	**Hungarian Goulash (Gulyas)** The classical Hungarian Goulash with beef, paprika, and potatoes. Fiery, warm, and tender.	**File No.:** 17.4.2.1 **Yield:** 10 portions

Establishment: Old Post Inn, Worthing   **Tester:** M. Smith

Chef: E. Ruch   **Date tested:** August 14, 1976

Ingredients	U.S. Weight or Volume	Metric Weight or Volume	Procedure
Pork fat	4 ounces	113.4 grams	1. Simmer the fat, meat, and onion.
Rump steak, cut into 2 ounce pieces	4-1/2 pounds	2.7 kilograms	2. Stir until a light glaze is formed.
Onion, chopped	1-3/4 pounds	795 grams	
Water	1 pint	1/2 liter	3. Add the water and wine and simmer until liquid is reduced.
Red wine	1 cup	2 deciliters	
Paprika, sweet	2 ounces	57 grams	4. Add paprika, tomatoes, and salt.
Tomatoes, peeled and diced	1-1/4 pounds	566 grams	5. Cover and cook for 70 minutes.
Salt	1 tablespoon	14 grams	
Potatoes, raw and diced	1-1/2 pounds	681 grams	6. Add the potatoes and cook until soft. Note: Cook potatoes separately for a la carte.

FIGURE 1-2
Example of a Recipe Card or Sheet

2 Menus for holidays *(main group)*
2.1 New Year's Day *(subgroup 1 of holiday menus)*
2.2 Mardi Gras *(subgroup 2 of holiday menus)*
2.3 Palm Sunday *(subgroup 3 of holiday menus)*
2.4 Good Friday *(subgroup 4 of holiday menus)*
2.5 Easter *(subgroup 5 of holiday menus)*
2.6 Ascension *(subgroup 6 of holiday menus)*
2.7 Whitsuntide *(subgroup 7 of holiday menus)*
2.8 Mother's Day *(subgroup 8 of holiday menus)*
2.9 Thanksgiving *(subgroup 9 of holiday menus)*
2.10 Christmas *(subgroup 10 of holiday menus)*
3 Menus for banquets *(main group)*

3.1	Smaller banquets (up to 20 persons)	*(subgroup 1 of banquet menus)*
3.2	Larger banquets (over 20 persons)	*(subgroup 2 of banquet menus)*
3.3	Special banquets	*(subgroup 3 of banquet menus)*
4	Buffets	*(main group)*
4.1	Cold buffets	*(subgroup 1 of buffets)*
4.2	Hot buffets	*(subgroup 2 of buffets)*
4.3	Mixed buffets	*(subgroup 3 of buffets)*
4.4	Brunch buffets	*(subgroup 4 of buffets)*

Menu forms. Menu forms should be designed to meet the needs of the particular foodservice. The form should be of sufficient size to include menus that are to be prepared on a specific day. Guides are frequently printed on the menu form to facilitate planning and checking. The following points should be included:

- menu number
- name of establishment
- name of chef
- date
- text for menu
- text number
- number of portions prepared
- number of portions sold
- retail price
- notes

FIGURE 1-3
Example of a Menu Sheet

Menu Number: 1.1.1.37	
Establishment: Old Post Inn, Worthing	**Portions prepared:** 50
Chef: E. Baker	**Portions sold:** 31
Date: January 15, 1977	**Retail price including service:** $5
Menu	**Recipe Numbers** (or special information)
Soup bonne femme style *Potage bonne femme*	12.2.2.1
Hungarian Goulash *Goulache hongroise*	17.4.2.1
Salad *Salade*	Tomatoes and chicory Italian dressing
Caramel Custard with whipped cream *Creme caramel Chantilly*	27.1.2
Note: Cook the potatoes separately and specify on the menu; otherwise, it is difficult to use the leftovers.	

Example of Sheet of Menu Book. The layout would be as follows for this menu of the day:

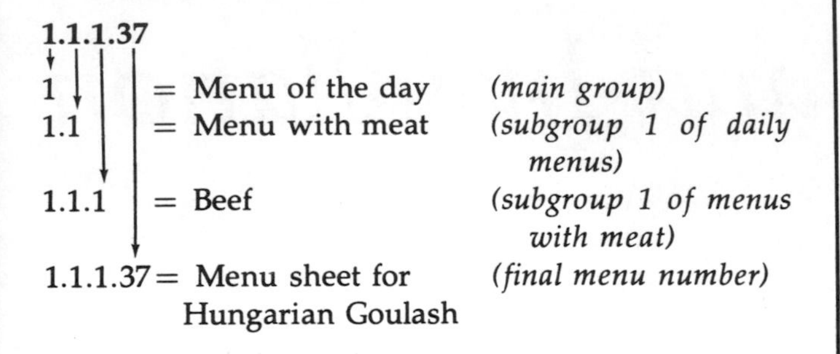

1.6 Kitchen Utensils

Stainless steel, aluminum, glass, porcelain, and plastic are materials used in the construction of the following utensils:

Boning knife
Bread knife
Brush
Butcher's knife
Canneler knife
Can opener
Carving knife
Cheese knife
Cherry pitting tool
Chopper
Clam knife
Cleaver
Cutlet bat
Dough cutter
Dough rolling pin
Dressing needle
Egg cutter
Filleting knife (for fish)
Fish slicer
Fish scissors
Fish and sausage fork
Flour brush
Flour scoop
French or chef's knife
Fruit knife
Ice cream dipper
Kitchen knife
Knife with serrated edge
Ladle
Larding knife
Larding needle
Large and small ladles
Lemon knife
Lemon grater
Meat fork
Meat saw
Nutmeg grater
Olive pitting tool
Oyster knife
Palette knife
Paring/peeling knife
Pastry bag
Pastry knife
Pastry tubes
Poultry secateurs
Skimmer
Small mosaic decoration dough cutter
Spatula
Steel
Truffle cutter
Whisk/whip
Wooden spatula
Vegetable slicer (mandolin)

2 The Kitchen: Organization and Installation

Foodservice organizations vary in terms of function and size, and each must have its own organizational structure. The needs and sizes of food production units in restaurants, hotels, hospitals, extended care facilities, and colleges and universities will differ; the organization systems, however, are much the same.

The location of the foodservice department in the organizational structure of the facility is significant. The department should be close to top management because of its complex nature and importance. Management may be the responsibility of the owner, a dietitian, or a food and beverage manager.

2.1 Kitchen Staff

The kitchen staff is a working team of trained cooks and beginners who produce and complete dishes under the management of the chef or food production manager. *The structure* and *size of the staff,* as well as its *functions,* are usually determined by the following factors:

- size of the establishment
- type of establishment
- organization of the establishment
- equipment available
- foods and dishes to be offered

The allocation of duties depends on the type of kitchen organization chosen and, in the final analysis, determines the following:

- tour rotas
- duty schedules

It is erroneous to assume that the need for organizational structure and allocation of duties applies only to large kitchens. Small establishments must also organize their kitchens and allocate duties to be successful. Even a kitchen with four or five cooks may classify the kitchen staff and allocate the duties as related to preparation and finishing. In addition to the kitchen organization, the functions of each staff member, the correct allocation of duties, and *personnel management* are *very important.*

2.1.1 Ranks

The rank of those in the profession is, in principle, the same for both conventional and modern kitchens. *Only the duties and functions* of the cooks differ. In the cooking profession there are the following ranks:

Executive Chef (with diploma or certificate)*****
This is the highest level possible. The Executive Chef is in charge of the kitchens of large establishments. He has the overall responsibility for the preparation and service of food in accordance with the standards and practices of the company or facility. He plans menus, meets with management and department heads, and coordinates all kitchen functions.

Head Chef*****
This title can be used only by those who have professional cooks working for them. The Head Chef is the person in authority in the kitchen.

Sous-Chef****
The Sous-Chef, second in command, is responsible for the physical aspect of the kitchen operations, including supervision of the kitchen staff as well as the preparation and service of the food. This individual is sometimes responsible for training beginners.

Chef Steward****
This position of Chef Steward is used in medium-sized establishments for economic reasons. The person in this role functions as a chef and purchases the food and supplies. In the absence of the Chef Steward, the Sous-Chef or Second Cook is in charge. The Chef Steward acts in a supervisory role during meal hours and banquet service.

Working Chef***
The Working Chef is in charge of the kitchen in smaller foodservice operations. In addition to performing the regular duties of chef, the Working Chef is responsible for a station or part of a station. Tasks may include: preparing the soups, entrees, and sauces; cutting the meat; assisting at stations; and preparing special dishes.

Chef's Assistant***
An administrative technically-qualified member of the staff.

Chef de Partie***
This person is in charge of a department or section such as fry station, broil station, or roasting station. One or more assistants report to the Chef de Partie.

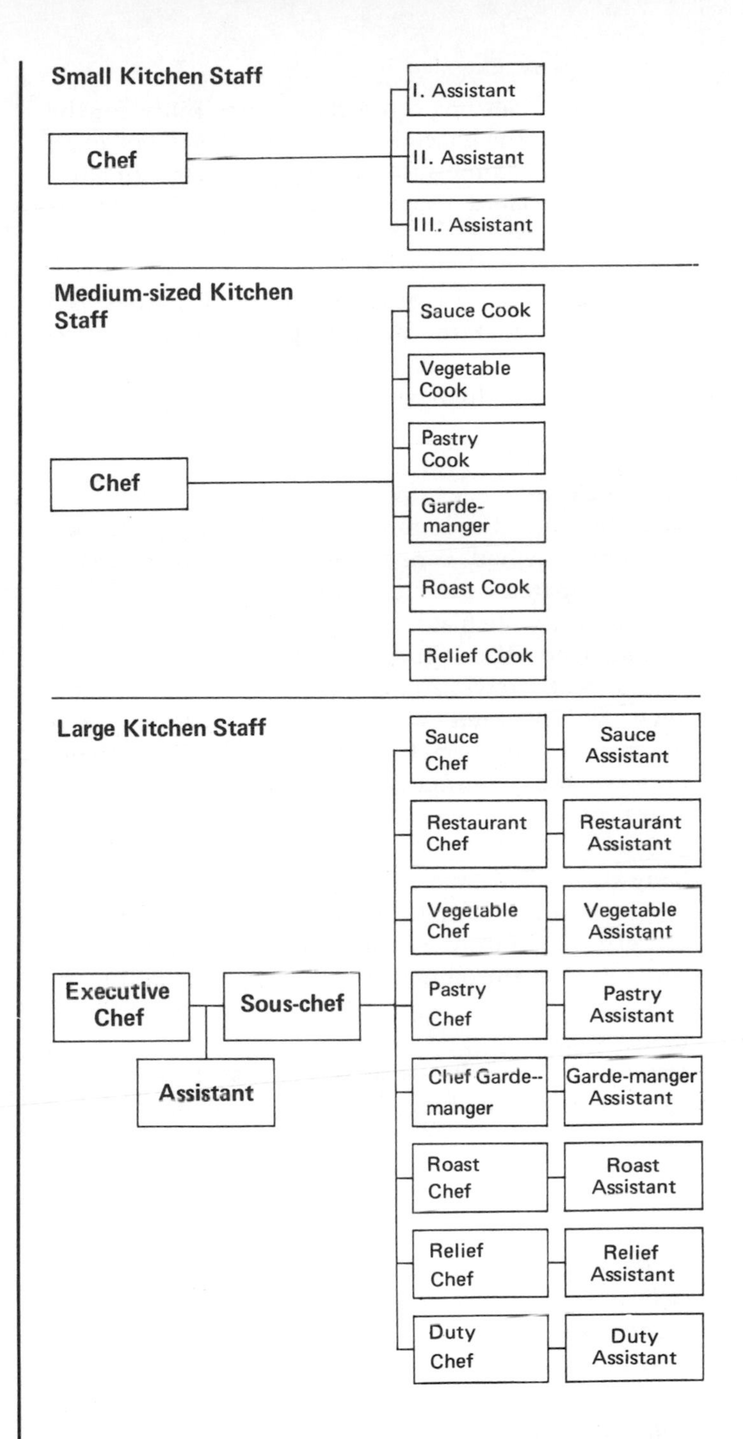

FIGURE 2-1
Diagram of a Conventional Kitchen Staff

Night Chef***
The Night Chef has complete responsibility for the kitchen after the Executive Chef and Sous-Chef go off duty. At other times, the Night Chef acts as an alternate for the Garde-Manger.

Banquet Chef***
The Banquet Chef is responsible for all parties and banquets. Under the direct supervision of the Executive Chef, the Banquet Chef is responsible for all the stations to which party or banquet work has been assigned.

Second Cook**
The Second Cook prepares all soups, stocks, bouillons, jellied consommes, and sauces. Other items prepared by the individual in this position are: boiled meats, such as boiled beef, corned beef, boiled and sauteed fish; all braised dishes, such as pot roast, Swiss steak, stews, and goulash; all creamed dishes, such as creamed chipped beef, chicken, and mushrooms; all special a la carte and chafing dish orders, such as seafood Newburg, chicken a la king, and breast of chicken in wine sauce.

Soup Cook**
The jobs of the Soup Cook and the Second Cook are sometimes combined. The Soup Cook prepares all soup stocks, consommes, bouillons, and fish stocks.

Broiler Cook**
The Broiler Cook broils steaks, chops, chicken, fish, kabobs, and tomatoes. Frequently the broiler and roast stations are combined. The cook assigned to this role must have expertise for both jobs.

Fry Cook**
The Fry Cook's work includes deep-fat frying, preparing eggs, omelets, fritters, potatoes, au gratin dishes, and crepes. Vegetables are cooked at this station if there is no Vegetable Cook on the staff.

Vegetable Cook**
The Vegetable Cook, responsible to the Chef, directs the cleaning, preparation, and cooking of all vegetables.

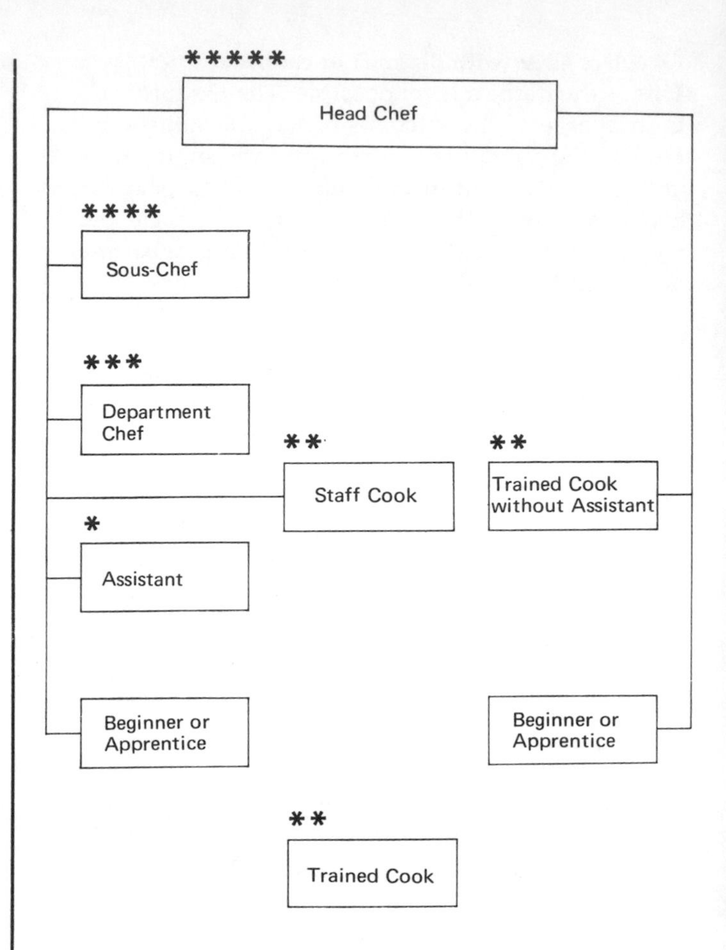

FIGURE 2-2
Diagram of Kitchen Ranks

Cook's Assistant*
The Cook's Assistant helps prepare and serve the food.

Relief or Swing Cook**
The Swing Cook relieves the cooks on major stations. Duties include stocking supplies for menus, planning and completing work required for the following day's menu, and maintaining the routine of the day.

Garde-Manger* (Cold Meat Department)**
The Garde-Manger supervises the cold meat department, the breading of meats, fish, and seafood. Other foods prepared in this department include: meat,

fish, and seafood salads; salad dressings and cold sauces; appetizers, canapes, and sandwiches. All cold foods for buffet service are prepared and decorated by the Garde-Manger.

Pastry Chef**

The pastry department is under the supervision of the Pastry Chef. Duties of this position include planning dessert menus, requisitioning materials and supplies, scheduling the work of assistants, decorating cakes and pastries, and testing and costing recipes.

Assistant Pastry Chef**

The Assistant Pastry Chef, under the direct supervision of the Pastry Chef, is in complete charge of pastry production. All cakes, pies, puddings, cookies, and pastries on the dessert menu are prepared by the Assistant Pastry Chef.

Baker**

The Head Baker has complete responsibility for the bakery department including the production of breads, rolls, and hot breads.

Baker's Assistant*

The Baker's Assistant weighs ingredients, prepares baking sheets and pans, and keeps the bakeshop clean and orderly.

Other Occupations

Additional jobs include Assistant Cook, Butcher, Fish Butcher, Chicken Butcher, Sandwich Maker, Salad Maker, Pantry Worker, Cake Decorator, and Food Checker.

2.1.2 Functions

Each department in the kitchen has different areas of responsibility. *The classical divisions overlap, however, when the work is separated into two areas, namely, preparation and finishing.* For example, it is possible that in a kitchen used for preparation the vegetable cook prepares pan-fried or deep-fried foods, and that in a finishing kitchen a roast cook finishes and serves vegetable dishes. *It is important, however, that in any duty schedule, no cook should serve in the same function for too long.* In a preparation and finishing kitchen, a cook is assigned according to the department requirements, and at the same time, he retains his normal rank. (When this system is used, the conventional names for the different departments are replaced by the title of the overall function.)

The duties of the different positions of the classical French and preparation and finishing kitchens are shown in Figures 2-3 and 2-4.

2.1.3 Allocation of Duties

As has been mentioned in section 2.1, a small kitchen may also be separated into preparation and finishing. The *preparation section* is responsible for producing pre-prepared sauces, brown sauce, sauce base, white sauce, and for preparing precooked pasta and vegetables.

The modern kitchen with a preparation section and a finishing section does not necessarily imply two separate kitchens. In the modern kitchen the preparation of food can be completed without interruption. The chefs can work more rationally and have working hours which are comparable to those in industry. The finishing chefs can concentrate on the orders as they come into the finishing section. Depending upon the type of kitchen, it is possible to assign the chefs who are in the preparation section to the finishing section during peak hours. This system offers great flexibility in the use of professional staff and unskilled labor. This is becoming increasingly necessary because of the continued shortage of qualified staff and high labor costs. For example, not only would it be illogical to have a department chef peeling carrots by hand, when this could be done faster with machines and unskilled labor, but also the talents and skills of an expert would be lost. The division into preparation and finishing sections, however, poses disadvantages for certain types of kitchens. Those catering for table d'hote (fixed menu) and banquets require a maximum of labor at peak periods. These kitchens will continue to give preference to the conventional system.

FIGURE 2-3
Diagram of the Duties of the Different Positions of the Classical French Kitchen

Positions	Duties
Head Chef	Manager of the kitchen and kitchen staff.
Chef's Assistant	Administrative and technical kitchen duties, recipe development, and costing.
Sauce Cook	Prepares fish, sauteed dishes, stews, hot hors d'oeuvre, hot entrees, and sauces. (In addition, serves as the deputy head chef where there is no sous-chef.)
Garde-Manger	Processes raw meat, cold dishes, forcemeat, pies, galantines, and cold hors d'oeuvre.
Vegetable Cook	Prepares soups, vegetables, pasta, and foods made of flour, eggs, and cheese.
Roast Cook	Prepares items roasted in the oven and on the spit, deep-fried and grilled foods, baked potato dishes, and gravies.
Restaurant Cook	Prepares a la carte dishes which must be prepared a la minute.
Pastry Cook	Prepares all basic desserts, hot desserts, cold desserts, frozen desserts, and hot and cold pastries.
Relief Cook	Replaces the department chef positions.
Duty Cook	Assumes overall responsibility during a tour of duty. Carries out the extra work of chefs in their absence.
Staff Cook	Prepares the food for the staff.
Assistants	Assist according to their individual skills.

2.1.3.1 Diagrams Showing Allocation of Duties

The following three basic diagrams illustrate the organizational structure for three different types of kitchens.

Figure 2-5 applies to a medium-sized establishment offering many different items on the menu and various portion sizes. There are no preparation and finishing sections, and the work is, therefore, carried out according to the conventional principles for the allocation of duties.

Figure 2-6 applies to a medium-sized establishment with a standardized menu and standard portions.

Figure 2-7 represents a large establishment which is standardized both in terms of menu and portion size. Irrespective of the way in which duties are allocated, the principles of recipe development and menu planning, as described in sections 1.4, 1.5, and 5.1.1 should be observed.

Only through organization in the kitchen, including recipe specification, menu planning, tour rotas, and duty schedules, can a uniform quality of food preparation and economic kitchen management be achieved. Figure 2-6 demonstrates that two separate kitchens are not required to effect the division into preparation and finishing. It is possible to allocate almost all the kitchen staff to the finishing section

FIGURE 2-4
Diagram of the Responsibilities of the Various Departments in the Preparation and Finishing Kitchen

Position	Duties
→ *Head Chef*	Responsible for the preparation and finishing kitchens. Replaces any absent department chef.
→ *Preparation Kitchen*	
1st Department Chef	Responsible for the preparation kitchen, and for preparation of all meat, fish, and sauce dishes.
2nd Department Chef	Responsible for preparing soups, vegetables, pasta, foods made from flour, eggs or cheese, and for deep-fat fried foods.
Assistants	Assist chefs.
→ *Finishing Kitchen*	
1st Department Chef	Responsible for the finishing kitchen, and for the preparation of a la minute and grilled items.
2nd Department Chef	Responsible for finishing and serving vegetables, pasta, foods made from flour, eggs or cheese, and for deep-fried foods.
Assistants	Responsible for finishing and serving cold dishes, salads, and desserts.

during peak hours, and at the same time avoid having any one cook assigned to the same work for too long. Alternating the cooks from a preparation tour to a finishing tour every week or two assures an all-round training experience equivalent to that provided in a conventional kitchen. In addition to the conditions necessary for the correct functioning of such a kitchen, *the importance of teamwork should be stressed.* These diagrams cannot be applied without first analyzing the allocation of the duties in the specific kitchen.

2.2 Mise en Place

Mise en place is merely organizing and completing in advance all the preliminary tasks involved in the preparation of a meal. Whether the mise en place is carried out for a conventional kitchen, a preparation kitchen, or a finishing kitchen, preliminary work must be completed methodically and carefully before further work in the kitchen can be executed. When observing the work of the various cooks on the kitchen staff, it is easy to recognize those who have the ability to organize their work in conjunction with a correct mise en place. When a kitchen is properly organized, the routine mise en place for the various departments is in written form. Department chefs or cooks should be able to give the assistant exact instructions for the daily mise en place on the basis of the recipe and the menu plans. The saying, "A good mise en place is half the cooking," applies to small kitchens as well as to large preparation and finishing kitchens. The aim of an exact mise en place is to complete all the preparatory operations before the actual cooking begins. The cooking process is then simplified and unexpected orders may be filled easily

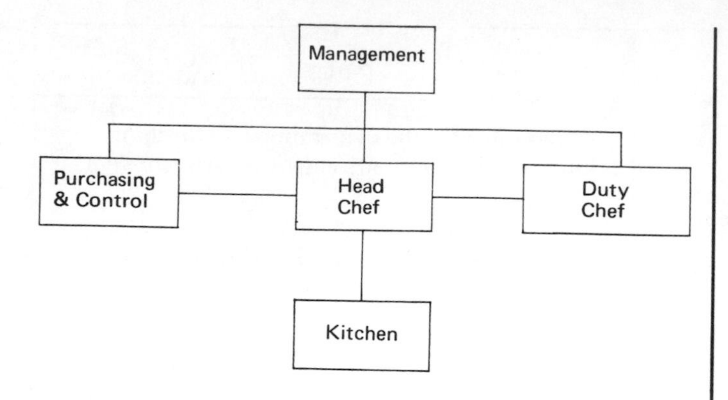

FIGURE 2-5
Organization Chart for a Conventional Kitchen

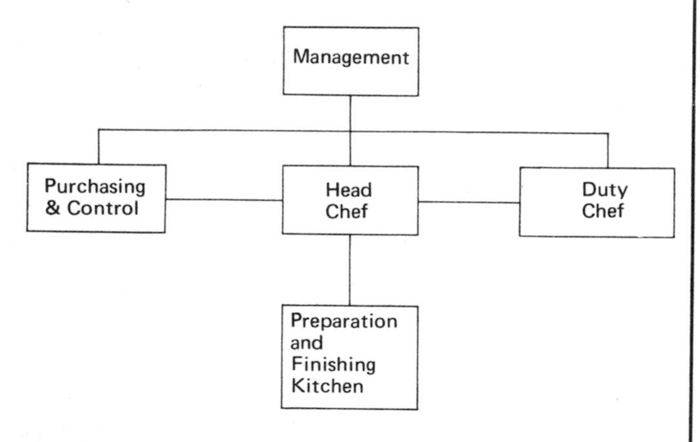

FIGURE 2-6
Organization Chart for a Combined Preparation and Finishing Kitchen

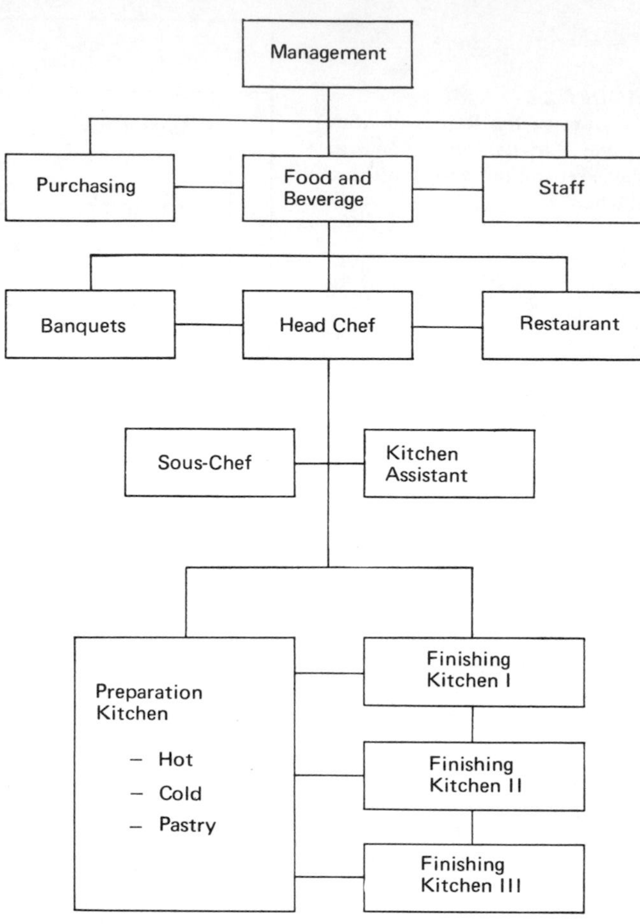

FIGURE 2-7
Organization Chart for a Separate Preparation and Finishing Kitchen

and promptly. *Before the service begins,* each member of the cooking staff should allow himself sufficient time to check his mise en place thoroughly. Only in this way can a service be completed in an organized manner. The mise en place should also include a number of reserve items, and the quality of these should be as good as the quality of the original menu items. Such a plan will prevent dissatisfaction among the guests and will reduce staff frustrations. It is not without reason that a professional French cook once said, "The best cook isn't the one who cooks best, but the one who keeps something just as good in reserve." Cleaning and closing the area are also a part of the mise en place. Inventorying supplies on hand, planning and ordering food for reserves, preparing food items in advance, and clearing and cleaning all foodservice areas are duties that must be completed each day. Each of these functions is dependent on the other, and a complete interaction of all the functions is necessary to experience a complete mise en place. The general term, large mise en place, today means everything from arranging the utensils and linen to preparing a goulash in the preparation kitchen. It should be remembered that the mise en place for the finishing kitchen includes taking pre-prepared food and ingredients from the preparation kitchen. The following classifications for the mise en place applicable to the various positions and departments are diagrammatic and must be adapted for each individual kitchen.

Mise en place of the Cooks' Tools, Cooking Utensils, and Linen
Regardless of the positions and departments, the cooks' tools, cooking utensils, and linen include the following:

Various kitchen knives, meat forks, sharpening steels, paring knives, serrated-edged knives, spatulas, tongs, whips, and skimming ladles and spoons, strainers, graters, colanders, forks, meat hooks, measuring devices such as cups, spoons, ladles, and scoops.

Various saucepans, stock pots, braising pans, saute pans, roasting pans, baking pans, sheet pans, counter pans, omelet pans, pie pans, forks, spoons, storage containers, china caps, lids, and molds.

Kitchen aprons, towels, dishtowels, range cloths, straining cloths, dishcloths, sponges, and cleaning products and equipment.

General Mise en Place Duties
These duties differ according to the kitchen and department but usually include the preparing and/or the assembling of chopped and peeled onions, whole and chopped parsley, eggs, butter, fats, oil, vinegar, red and white wine, Mediterranean and sweet wines, cognac, bouquet garni, mirepoix (diced vegetables), spices, lemons, and flour.

Mise en Place for the Preparation Kitchen
The mise en place for the preparation kitchen includes preparation of the same items as the general mise en place for a conventional kitchen. The items include bread crumbs, grated cheese, stocks, sauces, raw meat, poultry, game, fish, crustaceans and mollusks, vegetables, potatoes, pasta, pastries, fillings, glazes, and sauces, and creams for desserts. Operational duties that are part of the mise en place in the preparation kitchen are cleaning and organizing the refrigerators; replenishing the fish chest with ice; and preparing leftover foods.

Mise en Place for the Finishing Kitchen
In addition to the general duties, the mise en place for the finishing kitchen consists of checking and adjusting the seasonings of the partially and wholly cooked items from the preparation kitchen. Preparation of the ingredients and dishes should be completed if possible and then the items should be placed in the thermostatically-controlled heating cabinets, or refrigerators, or freezers, or bains-marie. These items and dishes include: soups and gravies; fish, crustaceans and mollusks; meat, poultry, and game; potatoes and pastas; vegetables; salads and aspics; sauces, such a mayonnaise, tartar, vinaigrette; cold entrees and garnishes; glazes and ice specialties; pastries and biscuits; and desserts.

2.3 Kitchen Organization

The organization of the kitchen depends on the following:

- type of establishment
- size of establishment
- the type and method of customer service, and
- extent of the menu

After this information has been provided, the kitchen can be planned in one of the following ways:

- conventional
- combined preparation and finishing
- separate preparation and satellite, or
- convenience food

In selecting one of these types of kitchens, consideration should be given to:

- number of meals to be prepared at each meal period

- type of service
- customer prices
- system for serving the meals
- serving times for hot meals
- serving times for cold meals

After determination of these factors, it should be possible to select a kitchen plan that is practical and of the appropriate size. The kitchen plan must also provide:

- flexibility related to the location and the size of the rooms
- efficient work flow
- provision for receiving incoming goods
- supplies/storeroom
- adequate refrigeration
- preparation kitchen (hot, cold, pastry)
- finishing kitchen
- sufficient service area
- warewashing
- scullery
- secure flatware storage

The kitchen staff can be efficient only if the work flow has been properly planned. Figures 2-8 through 2-11 indicate the correct basic arrangement of the various areas and show the relationship of one part of the kitchen to another.

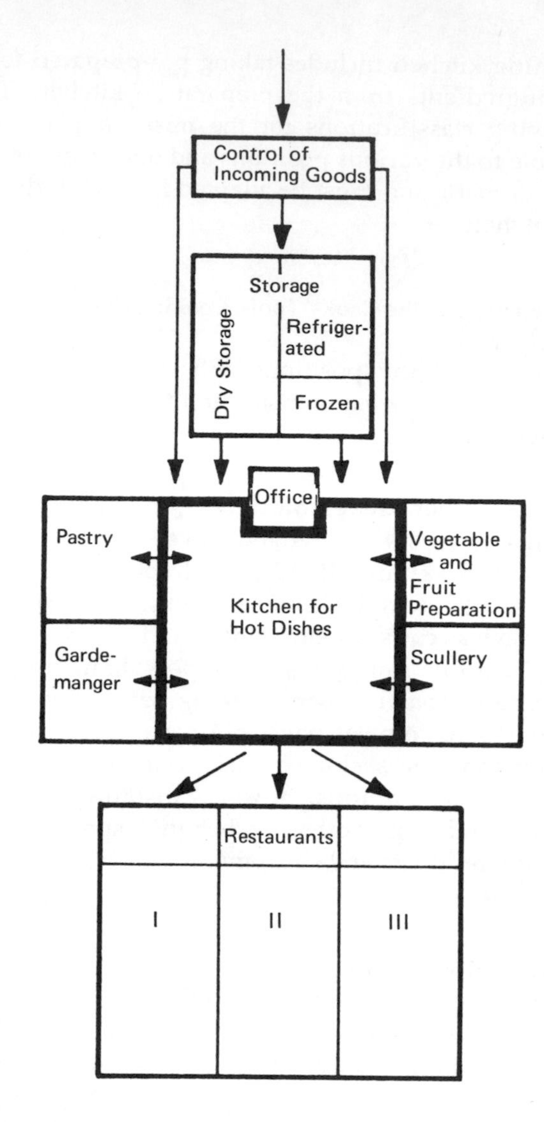

FIGURE 2-8
Diagram of Conventional Kitchen I

2.3.1 The Functions of the Kitchen

Kitchens can be grouped into four main types, reflecting various demands. They are:

Conventional kitchen. For small table d'hote and banquet kitchens which have flexible standards for menus and portions. *Arrangement:* All departments are grouped together in blocks. Both preparation and finishing are carried out in the same areas. All hot dishes are served at one counter in the kitchen. (See Fig. 2-8.)

Combined Preparation and Finishing Kitchen. This is primarily of interest to the medium-sized establishment, open year-round, where a certain amount of standardization of the menu and the portion size is possible. The advantage of this system is that cooks may be assigned to both sections. *Arrangement:* In principle, preparation and finishing are separated into two blocks. Whether these blocks are totally or partially separated, depends on the type of establishment. Each block should accommodate all

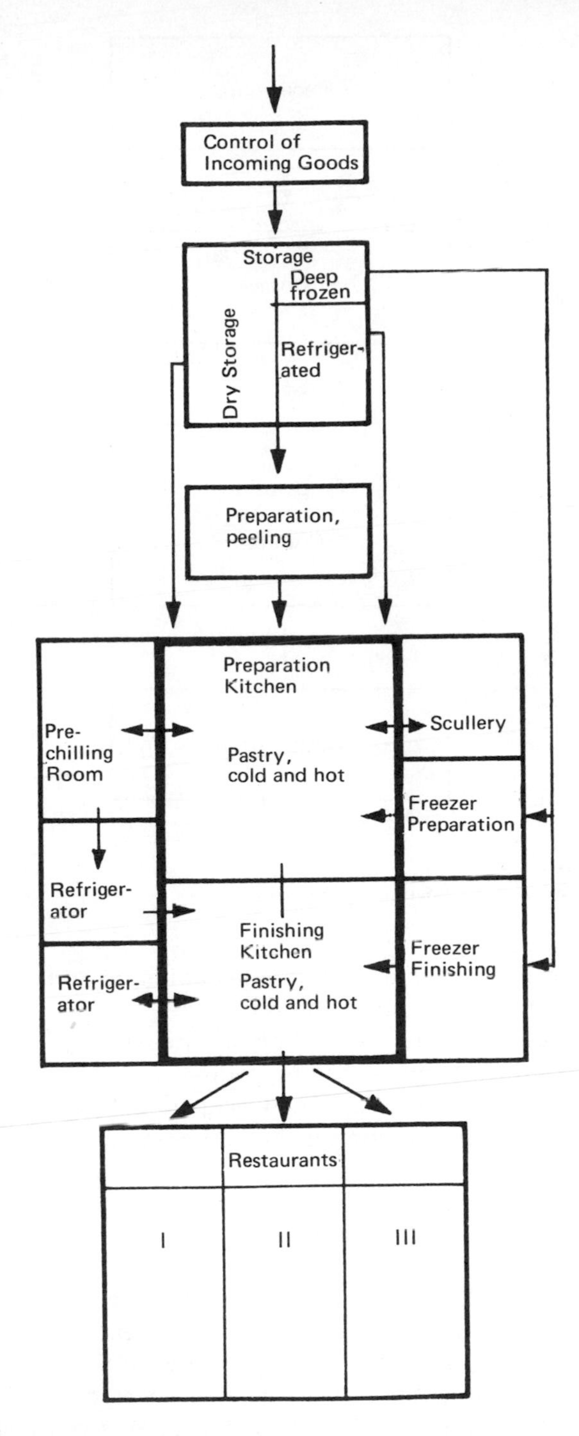

FIGURE 2-9
Diagram of a Combined Preparation and Finishing Kitchen II

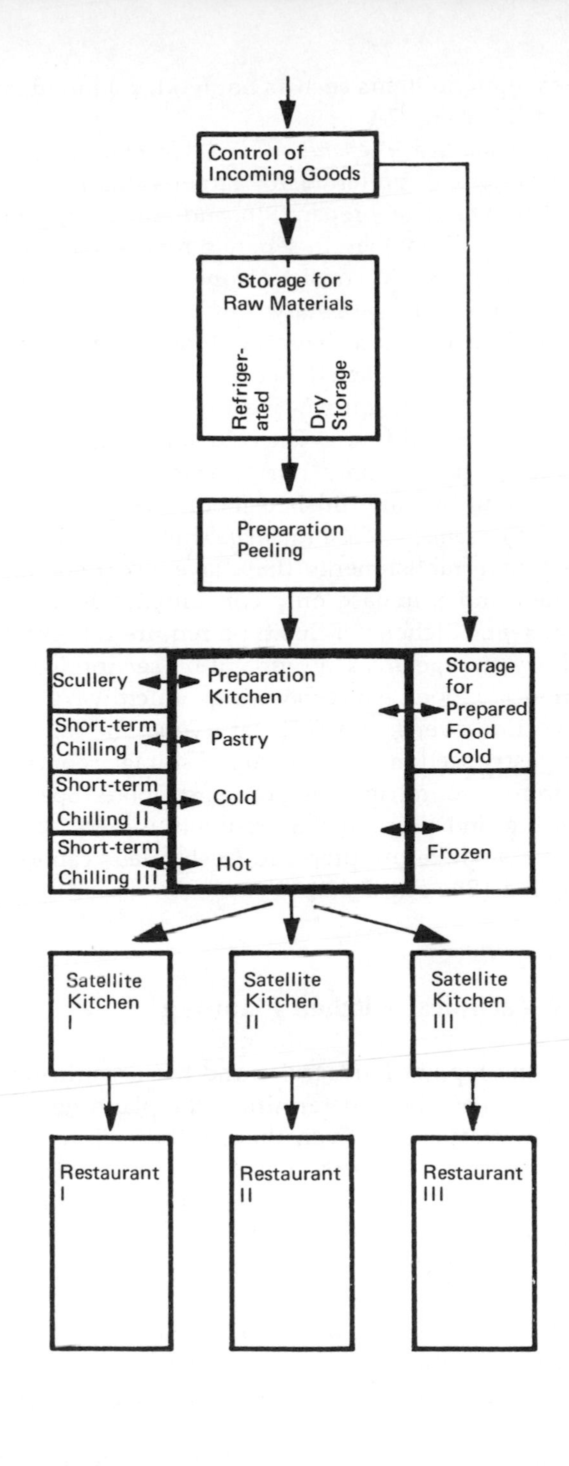

FIGURE 2-10
Diagram of a Separated Preparation and Finishing Kitchen III

types of menu items such as hot food, cold food, and pastry. (See Fig. 2-9.)

Separated Preparation and Finishing Kitchens. This system is preferred for larger establishments. *Arrangement:* The preparation and finishing blocks (satellite kitchens) are in separate rooms. Each satellite kitchen should consist of one room housing all the departments necessary for the dishes on the menu. Usually these have no large ranges, frying pans, or steam-jacketed kettles. Instead, there are grills and griddles, microwave and convection ovens, bains-marie, and fryers. The cold and pastry sections generally include only refrigerators for storage of partially and totally finished foods. (See Fig. 2-10.)

Convenience Food Kitchen. This system is of interest to establishments that have no preparation kitchen and purchase only convenience foods. *Arrangement:* Kitchens of this type require refrigerated and dry storage areas, a preparation section for convenience foods incorporating microwave and convection ovens, and deep-fat fryers. The cold food and pastry section consists only of storage rooms and equipment for refrigerating prepared foods. Space for washing and preparing ingredients is necessary in locations where pre-prepared fresh salads cannot be supplied. (See Fig. 2-11.)

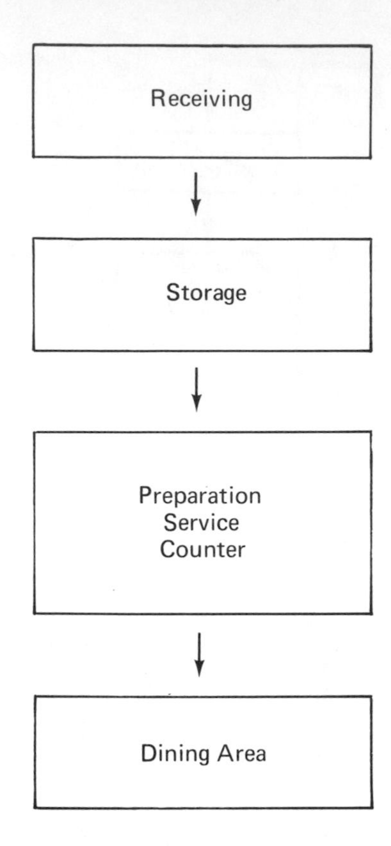

FIGURE 2-11
Diagram of a Convenience Food Kitchen IV

2.3.2 Technical Kitchen Planning

After the type of foodservice and the organizational structure have been determined, the planning of the kitchen may begin. Even though the architect may have expertise in kitchen planning, a professional kitchen planner should also be assigned to the job. The following are several additional decisions that need to be made:

- optimum size ratio between the individual rooms
- proper positioning of the equipment in work areas
- good illumination of the working and cooking surfaces
- good ventilation for both the hot and cold sections
- working diagrams for the utilities, water, and waste installation
- equipment that conforms to sanitation codes
- materials for non-slip floors
- washable wall and ceiling surfaces
- conformance to building codes
- conformance to OSHA (Occupational Safety and Health Administration) and other safety standards

The professional kitchen consultant or designer is responsible for translating the specified requirements into building and installation plans. He is also responsible for reconciling the technical requirements of the building, sanitation, heating, ventilation, refrigeration, and utility installation with the relevant official regulations. The state or local codes and standards for foodservice establishments must also be met. Only by seriously planning the kitchen in conjunction with the demands and desires of the pro-

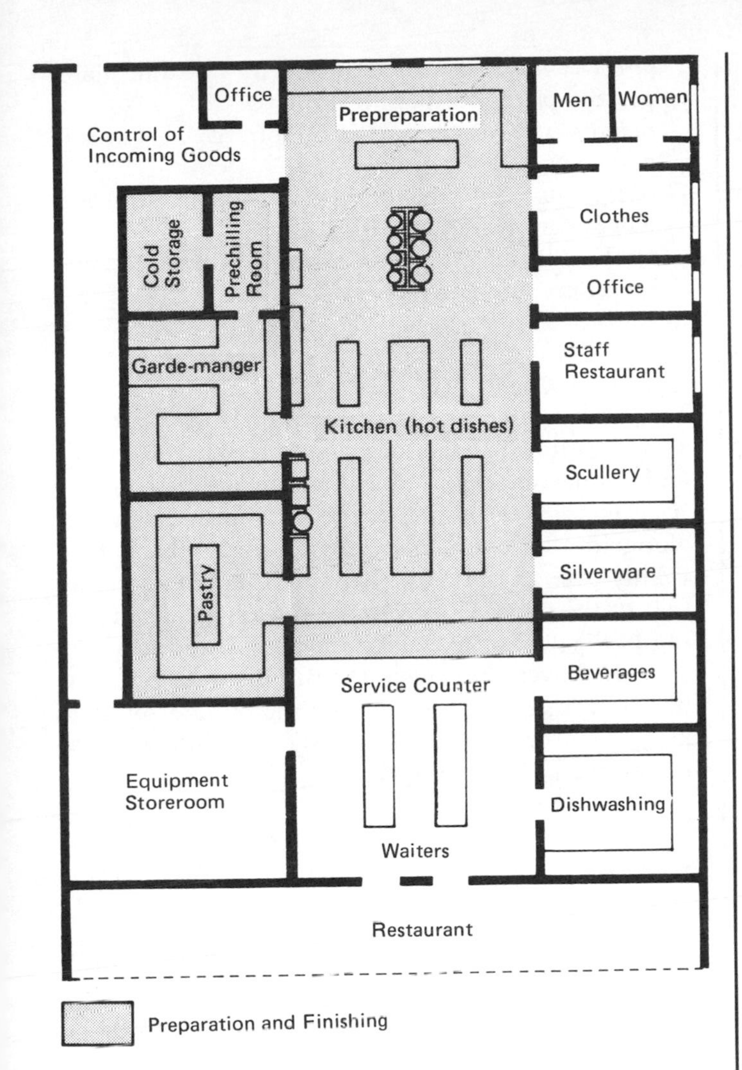

FIGURE 2-12
Conventional Kitchen I, Design and Layout

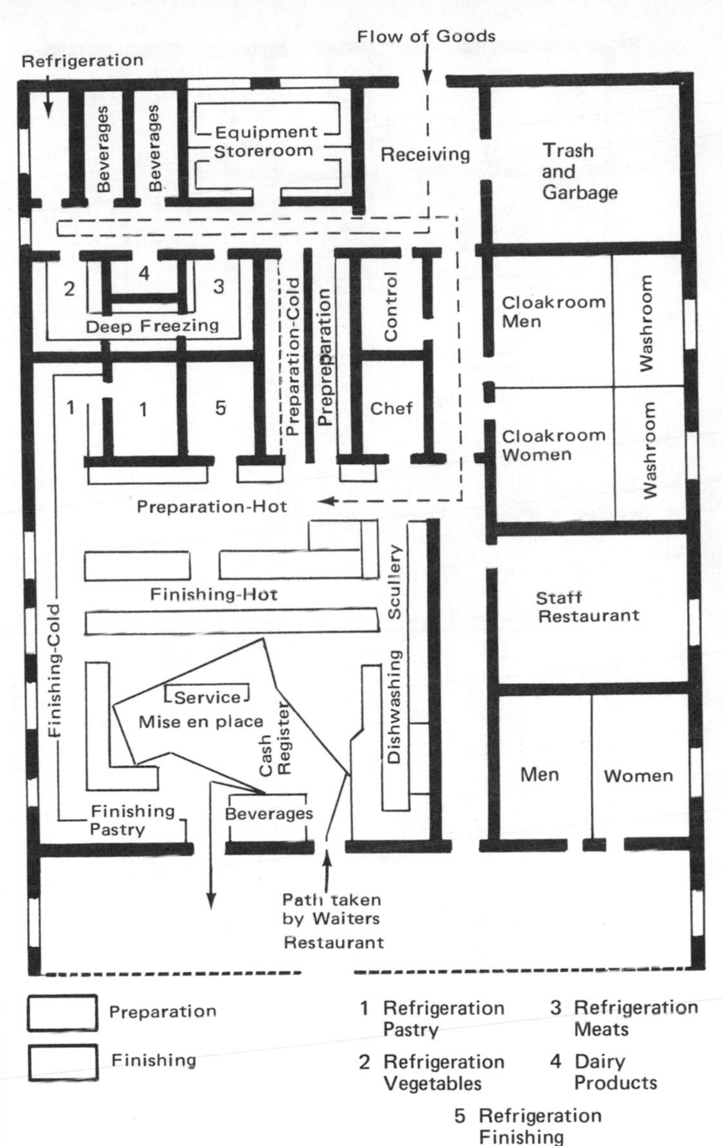

FIGURE 2-13
Preparation and Finishing Kitchen II, Design and Layout

fessional staff can their needs be developed into a kitchen that functions efficiently and economically. Independent foodservice designers and the planning departments of the foodservice equipment distributors can recommend building contractors, professional foodservice personnel, and architects who are qualified to assist with the planning.

Basic research and a professional kitchen planner are essential in developing kitchen designs and layouts. (See Figures 2-12, 2-13, 2-14, 2-15.)

2.3.3 Heating Methods and Equipment

The following heating methods can be used either directly or indirectly in the cooking process. (See Fig. 2-16.) The different types of heat are defined by these criteria:

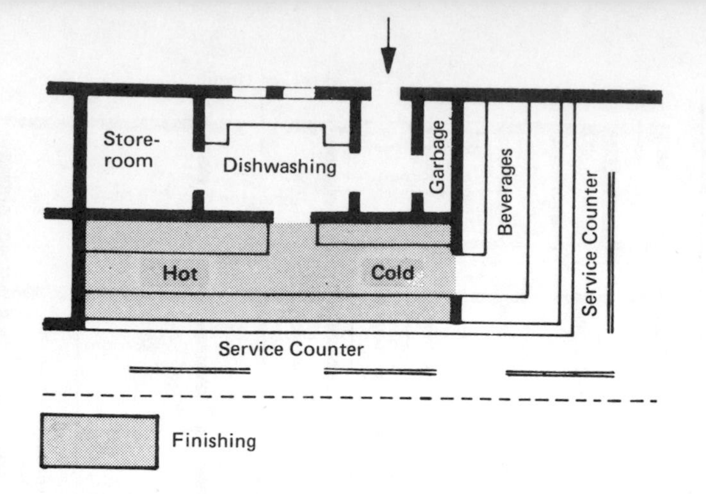

FIGURE 2-14
Satellite Kitchen III, Design and Layout

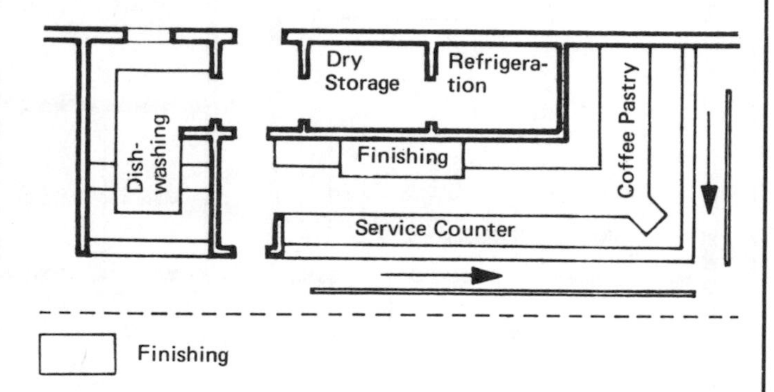

FIGURE 2-15
Fast Food Kitchen IV, Design and Layout

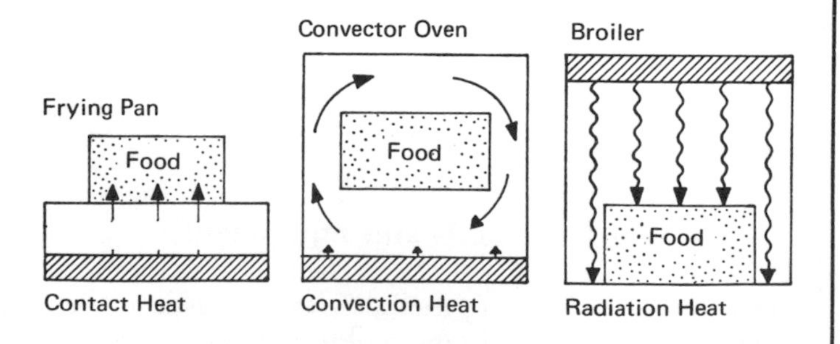

FIGURE 2-16
Frying Pan; Convector Oven; Broiler

- *direct contact:* heat conducted by fire, hot plate, griddle plate, pot/pan, or grill
- *radiation:* heat conducted by infrared heat or microwaves
- *convection:* heat conducted by hot air, dry and wet steam, water, and oil
- *combination of the above methods:* direct contact, radiation, and convection

Convection Oven

This oven operates on the principle of forced-air convected heat. It is used for primary cooking, roasting, and baking, as well as reheating prepared foods. The heat is introduced in chambers above, below, or alongside the oven cavity. A fan forces the hot air evenly over all the food, therefore it is not necessary to turn the trays. This oven has the advantage of saving both space and cooking time compared to a conventional oven. However, the turbulent air limits its use with soft, fluffy foods (meringue) and tends to make food dry out more quickly than in a conventional oven. (See Fig. 2-17.)

Steamer

There are three types of steamers: high pressure—15 psi; low pressure—5 psi; and atmospheric—using a convection principle with no pressure. Depending on the model, steamers will generate their own steam from an outside source. It is important that the steam be injected directly into the chamber. Depending on the food, the cooking time required for food cooked in a steamer may be reduced by a half to two-thirds. For those foods which are best cooked in moist heat, steaming is a fast method of cooking. However, it is not suitable for steaming items of irregular size. (See Fig. 2-18.)

Microwave Oven

This type of oven generates energy in the form of short microwaves. The heat is not conducted from a heat source, but developed inside the food itself by an electro-magnetic field. This field sets the molecules in the food in violent motion so that they

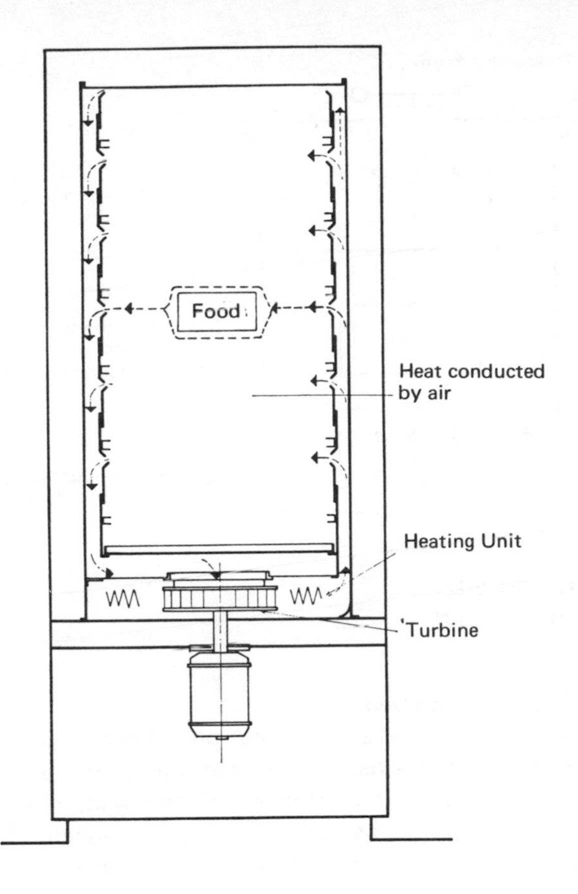

FIGURE 2-17
Automatic Convection Oven

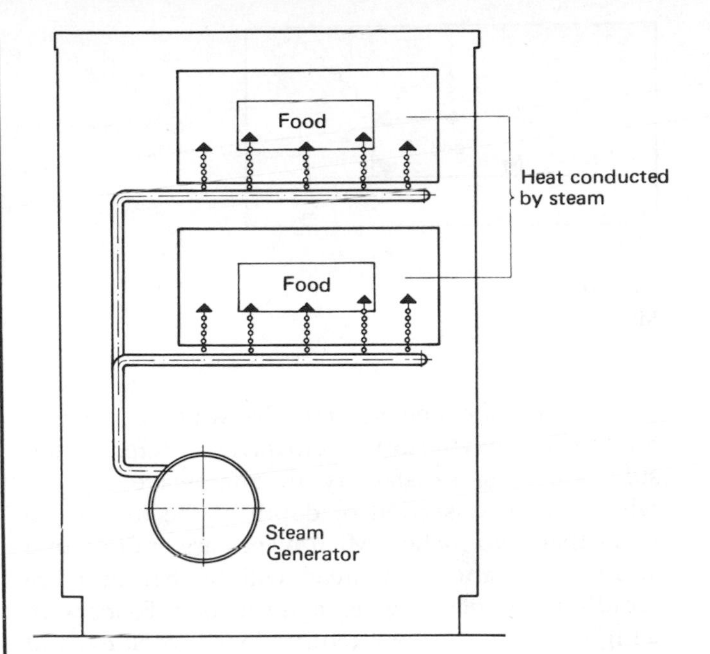

FIGURE 2-18
Steamer

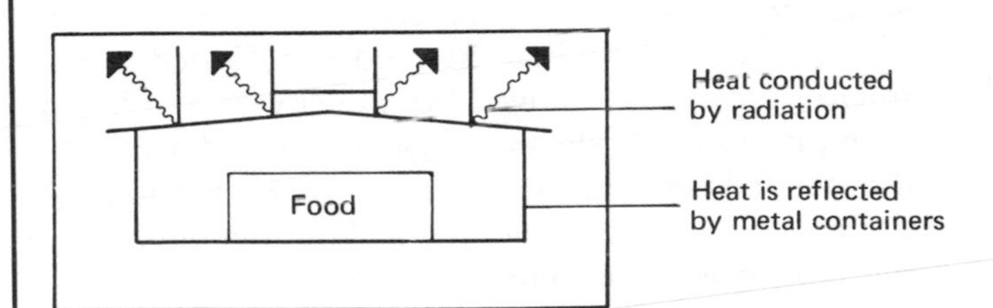

FIGURE 2-19
Microwave Oven

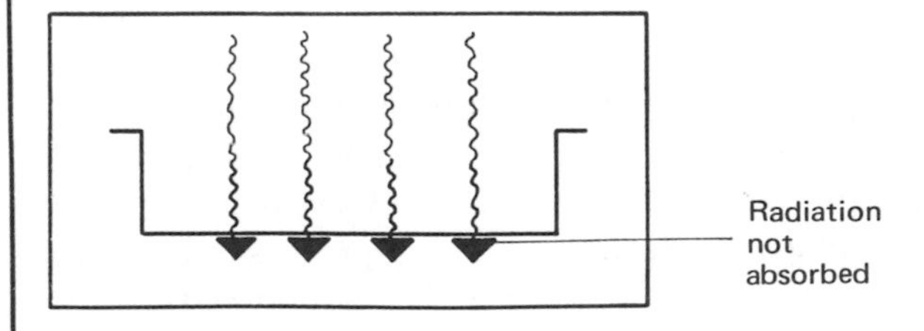

FIGURE 2-20
Microwave Oven

repeatedly collide with each other. This *friction* results in heat, which cooks the food very quickly. Because the heat is created internally, the food is neither encrusted by heat nor does its color change. Metal utensils or containers should never be used in a microwave oven.

Microwave ovens find their best use in reheating prepared items or in cooking specialties. Because of the technical principle, the oven cavity is small, therefore it is not recommended for the preparation of large quantities of food. (See Figures 2-19 and 2-20.) Microwaves pass through glass, porcelain, plastics, paper, and similar low-moisture materials without creating heat in them. (See Fig. 2-21.) Most food, depending on the moisture content, will absorb microwaves to some extent and are heated in this way.

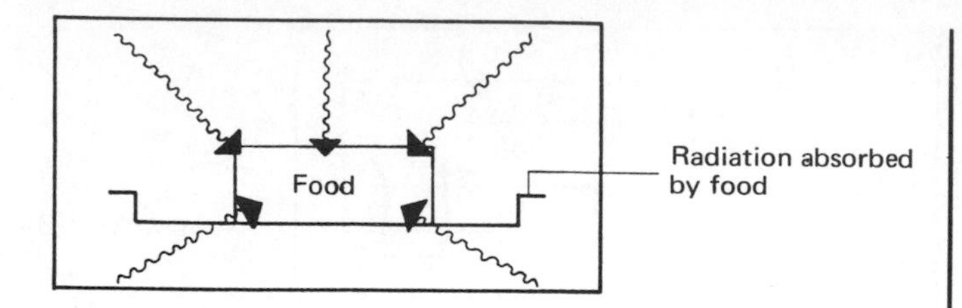

FIGURE 2-21
Microwave Oven

Since the density and the water content of foods vary, they absorb microwaves differently. Results are most satisfactory in microwave cooking when the cross section or depth of the food is no more than two inches. Microwaves are emitted in a steady flow and thin areas will be heated more rapidly than thicker sections of the food. Foods with a high moisture content require longer cooking, and unless these foods are uniform in size, it will be difficult to have a uniform temperature and degree of doneness in the product.

Frozen food products contain many ice crystals which the microwaves transform into steam. Best results are achieved when the food is defrosted in the microwave oven, removed from the oven cavity, and then put back into the microwave oven and heated to the desired serving temperature. This assures more uniform cooking and avoids cooking the outside of the food before the center thaws.

Pressure Fryer

This fryer is heat sealed. The steam pressure is produced by the food itself during deep-fat frying. This process, known as broasting, is suitable for fresh and frozen pieces of chicken and turkey. Advantages of these pressure fryers are increased tenderness, flavor, and moisture content in the product while the cooking time is reduced to less than half the conventional time. These fryers should not be used to cook small quantities of food, because there is not enough moisture given off in the cooking process to build up the necessary steam pressure. Pressure fryers are not suitable for foods with a high moisture content, such as vegetables and potatoes. (See Fig. 2-22.)

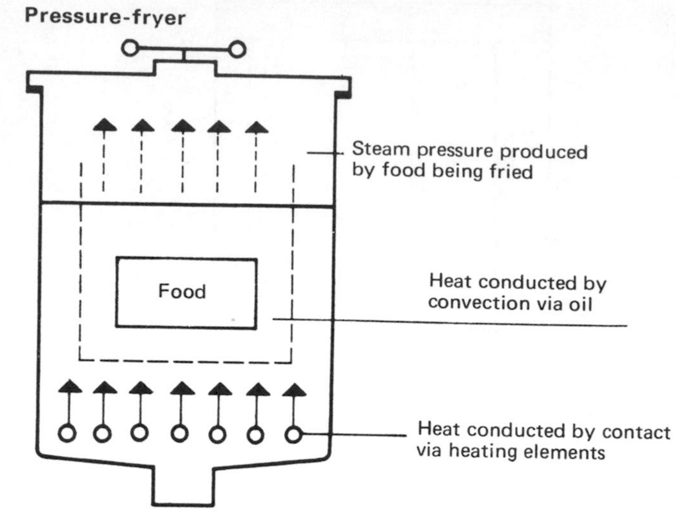

FIGURE 2-22
Pressure Fryer

Regeneration Oven

These ovens are used to heat pre-plated meals or individual portions. Some manufacturers use heat transmitted by radiation (infrared); and others use heat conducted by convection. Both systems, however, are nothing more than heating processes. They are generally used for banquets, self-service restaurants, and convenience food kitchens. (See Fig. 2-23.)

The advantages of these ovens are:

- food preparation can be scheduled during slow periods.
- food can be prepared and portioned more carefully during slack periods.
- ovens can be located near the point of service where food may be heated quickly and served to the customer at the proper serving temperature.

There are some disadvantages in the use of these ovens. These include:

- menu selections are limited.
- equipment and dishware represent a high financial investment.
- limited flexibility in portion sizes as these must be predetermined.

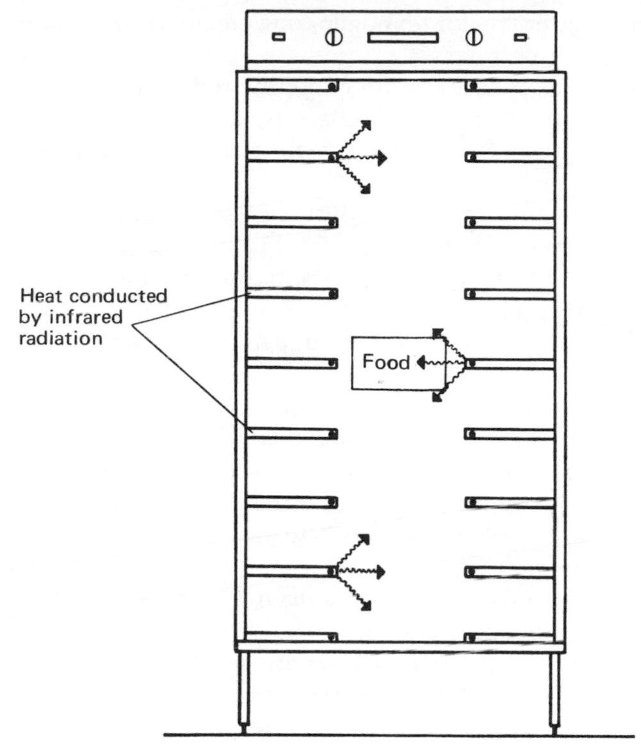

FIGURE 2-23
Regeneration Oven

Combimat

The microwave-convection oven is equipped with microwave energy and forced-air convection heating devices. Food can be cooked much faster than in a conventional type oven.The oven may also be used for roasting and baking. (See Fig. 2-24.)

The advantages of the microwave-convection oven are:

- cooking, baking, and roasting times are reduced.
- the microwave energy and forced-air heating devices can be applied simultaneously or separately.

The disadvantages are:

- fats and oils used on foods will burn at high temperatures.
- it is difficult to retain the red color in the interior of roasted meats.

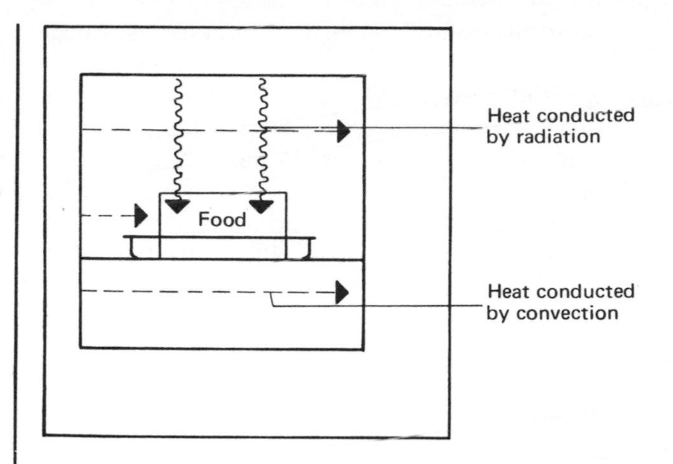

FIGURE 2-24
Combimat

2.3.4 Kitchen Equipment

Roasting, Boiling, and Deep-Fat Frying Equipment

Bain-marie: heated by radiation, steam, or hot water; thermostatically-controlled; available in sizes which conform to official norms

Broiler: high temperature top heat via infrared; gas or electric-powered

Deep-fat fryer: heated electrically or with gas, sometimes equipped with automatic fat filter

Fry pan: fixed or tilting

Griddle: independent or built-in units; thermostatically-controlled hot plates with drip pans for excess fat

Grill: bottom, top, or top and bottom contact heat; direct or indirect infrared heat

Infrared oven: available as baking or reheating oven

Microwave oven: for all heating procedures (see page 32, heating and preparation systems)

Pizza oven: heated electrically or by gas; to heat fresh or frozen pizza

Pressure cooker: for all pressure steam cooking methods

Pressure fryer: a deep-fat fryer with a hermetic seal; steam pressure is produced by the moisture from the foods being fried; recommended for large quantities of food, particularly poultry (see page 34.)

Roasting spit: thermostatically-controlled; preferably a horizontal spit with lateral heating (see also basic roasting principles on page 255.)

Steamer: For all pressure steam methods (see page 32), heating and preparation systems

Steam-jacketed kettle: fixed or tilting, heated either by heat radiation, or direct or indirect steam heating

Toaster: for toasting bread or buns

Toaster, conveyor: conveyor type model for toasting bread or rolls using either electricity or gas

Chilling/Freezing Equipment

Blast freezer: for fast-freezing raw products, prepared dishes, and prepared meals

Ice cream freezer: either horizontal or vertical, continuous or batch production

Ice machines: for making ice cubes, cracked ice, and snow

Refrigerators: reach-in and walk-in

Soft-freeze machine: for making soft-freeze

Storage freezers: reach-in and walk-in

Kitchen Machines

Blender: for chopping fruits, vegetables, or nuts; for whipping or pureeing food; for mixing cocktails; for making dressings; and for emulsifying small quantities of sauces and creams

Bread slicer: semi- or fully-automatic machine with a revolving knife that slices bread. The thickness of the slice may be varied

Compactor: for grinding disposables, and glass and metal containers

Food chopper: for preparing forcemeat, vegetable and fish forces, and meat stuffings

Food mill: for making soups, purees, and jams

Fruit and vegetable press: for making fruit and vegetable juices

Grating machine: for making almond or hazelnut mixtures, for grating cheese, and for making bread crumbs

Grinder: for grinding meat and vegetables

Homogenizer: for homogenizing creams, sauces, and glazing mixes

Meat chopper/slicer: for chopping red meat, poultry, game, or meat for tartare

Meat saw: for sawing bones, and frozen and dehydrated products

Meat tenderizer: for tenderizing steaks and cutlets

Mechanical pastry roller: for rolling all kinds of pastry dough, pie crusts, pasta, and for making crescents

Mixer, food: for making doughs, fillings, sauces, and creams

Pot and utensil washer: for automatic cleaning of utensils, saucepans, pots, and bowls

Roller machine: cylindrical marble rollers for grinding almonds to paste, for making marzipan, and for emulsifying fine creams and semi-liquid dough

Salad draining machine: for drying fresh lettuce, vegetables, and potatoes

Scales: semi- or fully-automatic mechanical or electrical portable or stationary scales. Some commercial models can be connected to portioning and cutting machines

Sealing apparatus: for sealing plastic boiling bags used for prepared dishes and meals

Silver polishing machine: for deoxidizing and polishing silverware

Slicing machine: for slicing meat, vegetables, and cheese

Vegetable cutter: for making uniform strips, sticks, or cubes of vegetables, bread, or potatoes in various sizes and thicknesses

Vegetable peeler: for peeling potatoes and vegetables

Vegetable washing machine: for cleaning vegetables and potatoes

Vertical cutter/mixer: for cutting, chopping, blending, kneading, grinding, and liquifying; for making creams, sauces, salads, and various kinds of dough

2.3.5 Gastro-Norm

The subject of Gastro-Norm was discussed in detail in a report published in the *Foodservice Equipment*

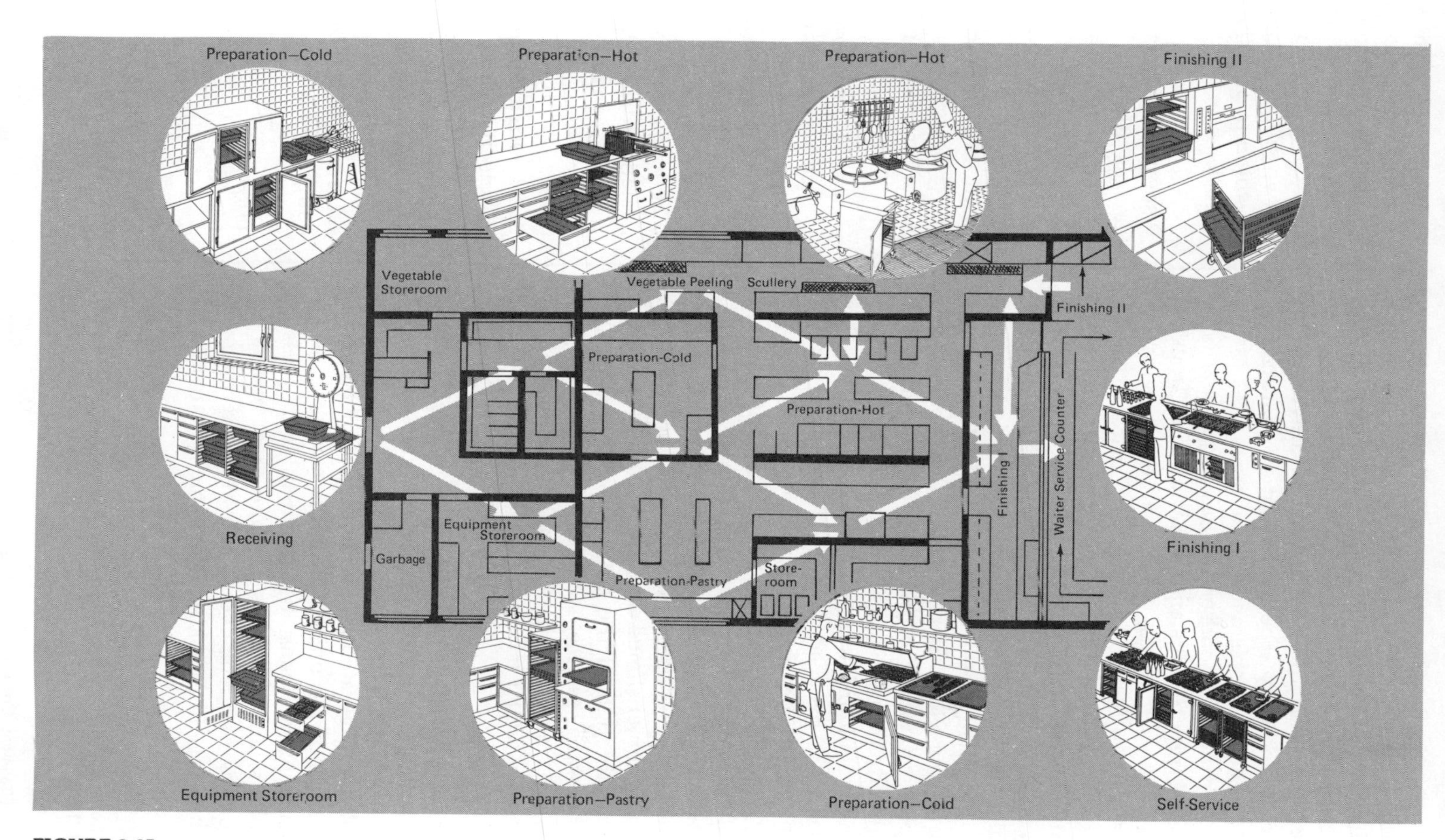

FIGURE 2-25
Gastro-Norms

Dealer. The United States, known for its leadership in technological matters, lags behind the rest of the world in one basic scientific area: failure to adopt the metric system of weights and measures. The increases in world trade is making a conversion to metrics a necessity. The matters of standardization will pose many problems in some areas.

Fortunately, foodservice has its standards in place. The impetus for standardization came from the Swiss. Representatives of several foodservice organizations in Switzerland met in Zurich to sign a document that would standardize dimensions for "all movable inserts for food, dishes, and utensils such as pans, trays, wire racks, drawers, screens and trolleys, and also for kitchen equipment and refrigerators.

Originally the representatives had planned to create a new Swiss Standard. But these plans were dropped in favor of the basic size of 530 mm × 325 mm already in use with standard American pans."[1] The new standard was named Gastro-Norm. This standard has been adopted by foodservice groups and manufacturers throughout Europe.

Antonio Trippi, a Swiss Hotel Association consultant, points out that this dimensional standardization provides for a uniform system throughout the entire foodservice. The food can remain in uniformly dimensioned containers from the time it is received throughout the entire operation (preparation, finishing, service, storage).

The standardization has many applications in foodservice which include:

- standard packages as well as various combinations of trays and pans will fit standard carts and racks
- Gastro-Norm trays, pans, and sheets will fit steam tables, refrigerated and heated drawers and cabinets, sandwich units, and bains-marie
- Gastro-Norm pans fit steamers and pressure cookers, and the trays become exact inserts for proofing cabinets, ovens, and heated/refrigerated cabinets. After cooking, the same containers may be moved to the service area since the transport, preparation, storage, and handling are all based on the same common denominator
- dishwashing racks are standardized, 500 mm × 500 mm (20 in × 20 in), with guide rails on two sides extending to 530 mm. Dishware can be stored in or delivered to the serving areas in these racks.

1."A Look at Gastro-Norm Today," *Foodservice Equipment Dealer,* April, 1975.

It should be remembered that use in all standard 2/1 devices (the 2/1 module corresponds to the 20 in × 24 in pan) can always be achieved by retaining the dimension of the 530 mm in one direction.The shapes and dimensions for pans in the Gastro-Norm system are illustrated in Fig. 2-26 from the British Standards Institution, London.

Several advantages of the Gastro-Norm standards for the operator:

- speeds up operating procedures
- increases stacking volume in small areas
- simplifies internal transportation systems
- reduces working distances for staff and employees
- allows universal usage of the transport and storage units
- reduces labor costs
- standardizes service ware
- permits interchangeability of units

Standardized Equipment

All inserts standardized to Gastro-Norm dimensions can be stacked, and the overall measurements are such that numerous combinations of the various sizes are possible. Standardized bowls and trays are usually made of top-grade stainless steel. This material is unaffected by heat and cold and can withstand rough treatment. When serving meals, similar units made from different materials (silver, glass, porcelain) may also be used individually or combined.

Applications

Cooking equipment (pressure cooking equipment, microwave units, fryers, convection ovens, ovens,

FIGURE 2-26
Gastro-Norms

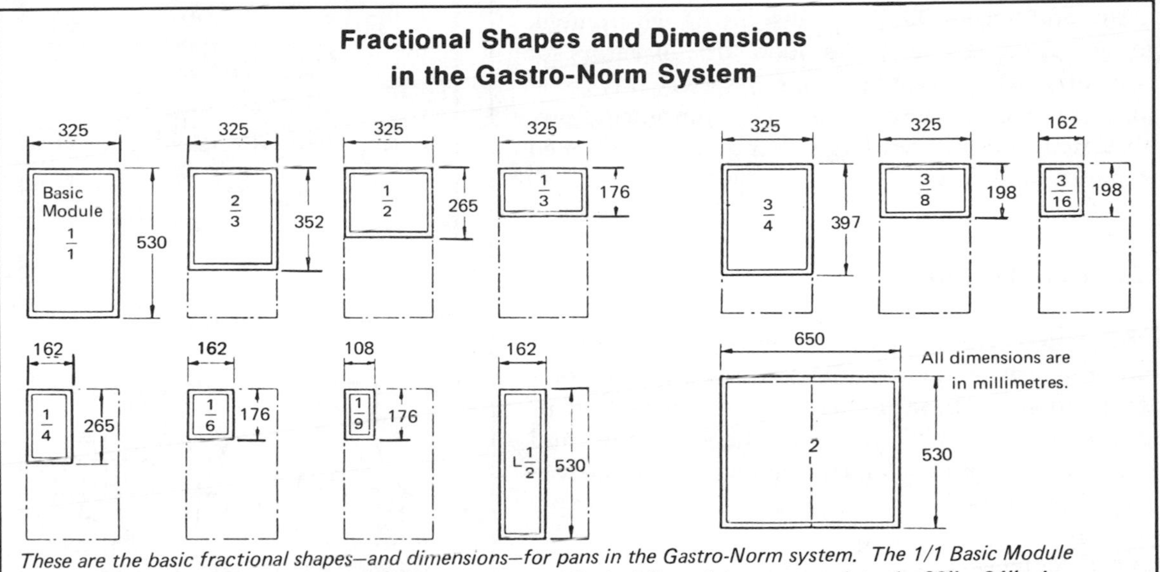

These are the basic fractional shapes—and dimensions—for pans in the Gastro-Norm system. The 1/1 Basic Module (325 mm x 530 mm) corresponds to our 12" x 20" pan, while the 2/1 module corresponds to the 20" x 24". As shown, overall dimensions include flanged lips.

Flanged Container Specifications

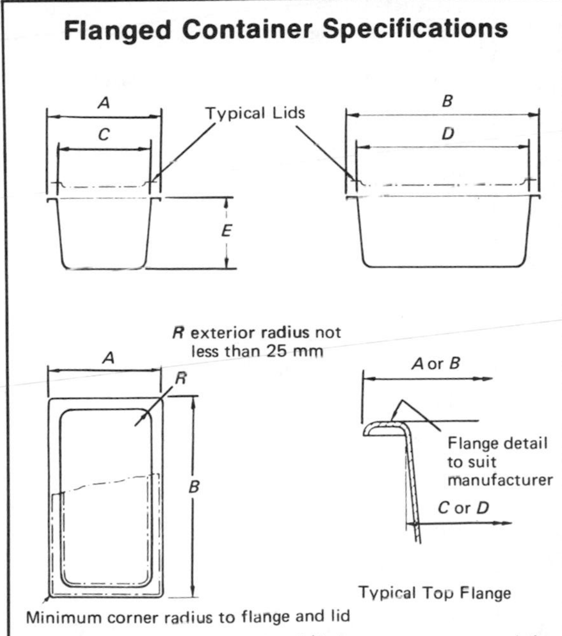

Tolerance dimensions for the 1/1 size must not exceed the 325 mm (a) or 530 mm (b), nor be less than −2 mm. The C dimension is 298-mm, the D is 503 mm. The depth (E) is 200.

Non-Flanged Container Specifications

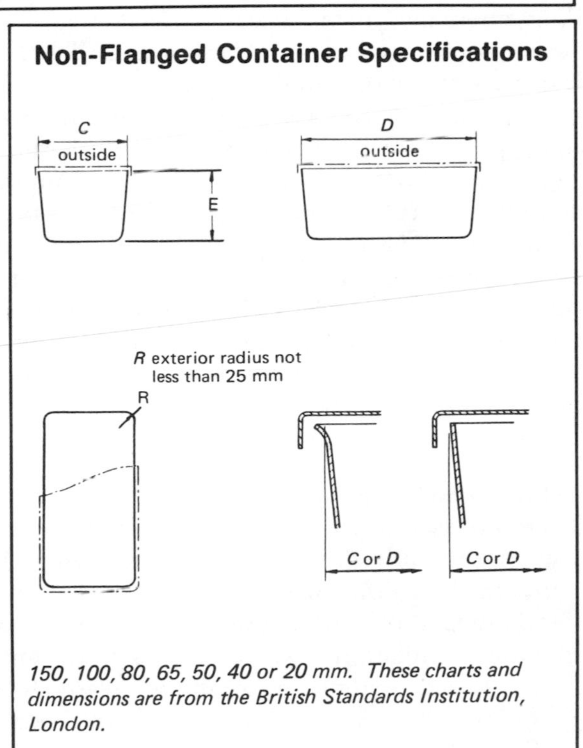

150, 100, 80, 65, 50, 40 or 20 mm. These charts and dimensions are from the British Standards Institution, London.

broilers), walk-in and reach-in refrigerators and freezers, built-in drawers and cupboard units, bains-marie and steam tables, transporting equipment, storage units, storage racks, food lifts, elevators for food carts, self-service buffets, self-service trays, sections of menus which can be combined, prefabricated units for large banquets, portioned prepared food trays.

2.3.6 Refrigeration

Refrigerated storage requirements are increasing with the use of more perishable, frozen, and prepared foods. These foods require storage temperatures that will preserve their quality and nutritive value and safeguard against loss from bacterial growth.

2.3.6.1 Refrigeration Principles

Fundamentally, cold is created by removing heat. The principle of mechanical refrigeration is based upon the evaporation of a liquid refrigerant inside a sealed circuit and the recondensation into a liquid. In order to evaporate, the gas removes the heat from the chilling compartment. Every refrigeration and deep-freezing plant should be equipped with an automatic defrosting device. The ice that forms around the cooling element acts as insulation, delaying or even obstructing the transfer of the heat and stopping its passage to the compressor. Each refrigerated area should be equipped with a thermostat to control its temperature. (See Fig. 2-27.)

Refrigeration Equipment

There are basically two types of compressors for refrigeration equipment: air-cooled and water-cooled. Air-cooled equipment must be installed in a well-ventilated room to insure the fresh flow of air. An automatic ventilation system can act as an aid. Water-cooled equipment requires relatively little space, but the water consumption is in direct ratio with its performance. The choice of one or the other of these two systems cannot be made until the local

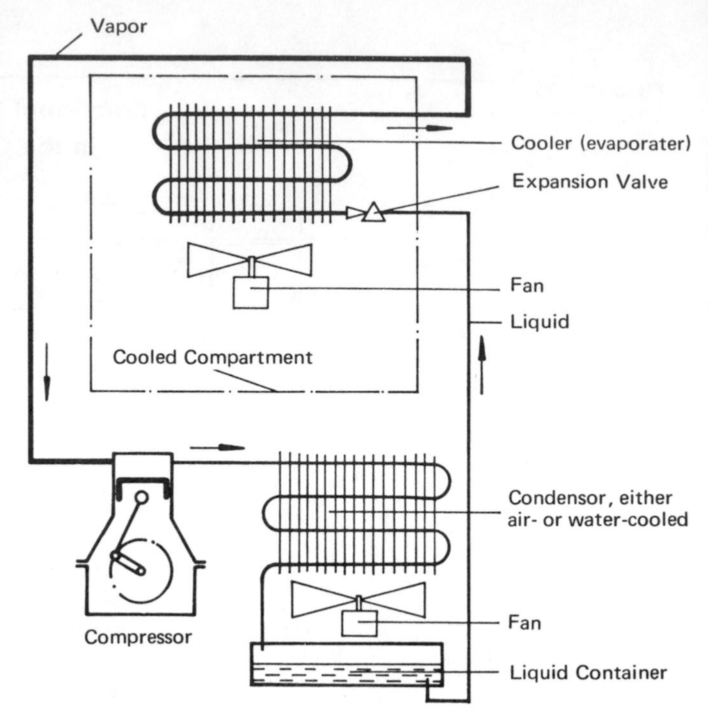

FIGURE 2-27
Functional Diagram of Refrigeration Technique

conditions have been thoroughly examined. Most compressors today are either partially or totally hermetically sealed, so that the electric motors rarely need servicing.

Refrigerated Areas

The design of refrigerated areas is dependent upon the type of establishment: hotel, restaurant, canteen, retirement home, children's home, hospital, college or university, or school foodservice. Each of these has its own specific requirements, and these must be considered when planning the size of the rooms, the length of time the goods will be stored, and the cooling procedure to be used—fast chilling, blast-freezing, and/or frozen storage.

Large establishments must have two zones:

Zone 1: storerooms and a freezer with large doors to accommodate forklift trucks with pallets.
Zone 2: refrigerators for daily use located near the following: kitchen, pastry department, ice cream department, garde-manger, and buffet.

FIGURE 2-28
Diagram of Walk-in Refrigerators/Freezers

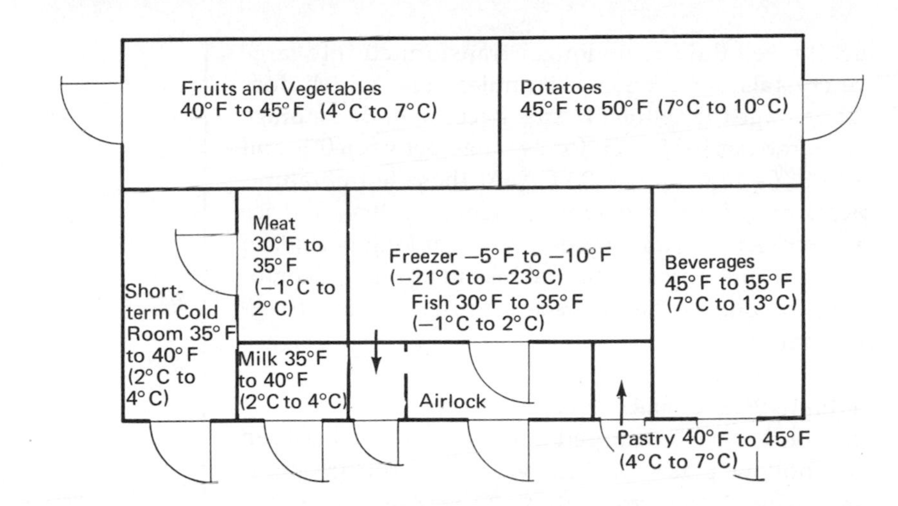

Refrigerators and freezers should be constructed in blocks, possibly placing the freezer in the center. This type of construction offers advantages from the technical and insulation standpoint, and in terms of construction and costs. The storage rooms for fruit, potatoes, and vegetables should be equipped with humidifiers, and those for meat with a dehumidifier.

Storeroom Temperatures and Humidity

	Temperature °F.	°C.	*Relative humidity in %*
Meat and sausages	30 to 35	−1 to 2	70 to 75
Fish in ice in the refrigerator	30 to 35	−1 to 2	80 to 100
Milk, butter, cream	35 to 40	2 to 4	75
Eggs	33 to 45	1 to 7	75 to 85
Fruits and vegetables	40 to 45	4 to 7	80 to 90

Diagram for Walk-in Refrigerators/Freezers
Walk-ins should be long and narrow so that there is sufficient wall space for racks and standardized trays and shelves. Because of humidity requirements, only meat and meat products should be stored in the meat refrigerator. The short-term refrigerator space must be large. Foods such as milk, cheese, fish, and pastry should always be stored separately, if possible, so that the odor of one does not transfer to another. Shelving dimensions should correspond to accepted norms. (See Fig. 2-28.) The operational system must be determined before planning the walk-ins. These details will be necessary for calculating capacity and performance.

Refrigerators and Standardized Refrigerated Units
All modern refrigerators, refrigerated units, and refrigerated chests are standardized according to the accepted norms. All these units may be fitted with drawers to accommodate the standardized inserts for the safe storage of food. The fan-cooling system is absolutely necessary to achieve sufficient airflow in these very compact units.

2.3.6.2 Food Freezing Processes

Freezing refers to the process of preserving fresh or prepared food by quickly reducing the temperature of the food to 0°F. to −5°F. (−18°C. to −21°C.). The technology associated with fast-freezing has made considerable advances. Research proves that fast-frozen food maintains freshness and taste much longer than when it is preserved any other way. Formerly, food was frozen slowly at 23°F. to 10°F. (−5°C. to −12°C.). This resulted in the cell fluid turning into ice crystals. Today, low temperatures—between −40°F. and −50°F. (−40°C. and −45°C.)—are used. With this fast-freezing process, known as *blast freez-*

ing, the cell fluid is no longer transformed into large ice crystals. It becomes a granular mass which does not damage the cellular tissue. Recommended storage temperatures for frozen foods range between 0°F. and −10°F. (−18°C. and −23°C.). At these temperatures meat, fish, fruit, vegetables, game, poultry, and ice cream products can be preserved over long periods of time without any substantial loss in aroma, flavor, or vitamin content. There are four different blast freezing methods:

Multiple-Plate Contact Process

The food is first wrapped and then placed between two hollow plates within which the refrigerant is circulating. If the temperature of the plates is roughly −40°F. to −60°F. (−40°C. to −51°C.), the temperature of a food product measuring two inches across can be reduced to −5°F. (−21°C.) in less than two hours.

Tunnel Process

The food is placed in a tunnel and subjected to a current of air at −30°F. to −50°F. (−34°C. to −45°C.). The ice-cold air must be circulated by fans so that the surface temperature of the food drops quickly but uniformly.

Blast-Freezer Process

This involves a small freezing chamber. Besides the cooling unit itself, two powerful fans are built into the rear. The conditions are the same as in the freezing tunnel. The standardized cart, which is fitted with metal gratings, is filled with flat plastic bags containing prepared meals. Its high performance within a very small space makes it possible to reduce the temperature of the products to −5°F. (−21°C.) within 20 to 30 minutes. (See Fig. 2-29.)

Liquid Nitrogen Spraying Process

Spraying the food with liquid nitrogen at −110°F. to −180°F. (−79°C. to −118°C.) makes it possible to freeze food products very quickly. Conventional deep-freezing equipment can finish the job. This rather expensive method of shock-freezing results in an improvement in the quality of certain foods such as bakery products, delicate fish, prepared meals, and meat portions. The process can be used in conjunction with specially constructed freezing tunnels and chambers.

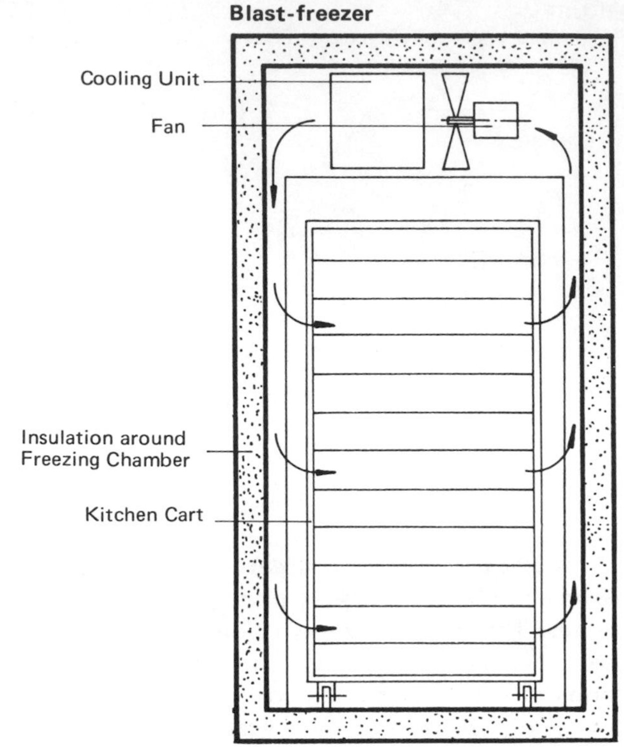

FIGURE 2-29
Blast-Freezer

2.3.6.3 Equipment for Making and Handling Sherbet and Ice Cream

Ice cream and sherbets are made from mixes frozen by mechanical freezers which have a stirring mechanism that whips air into the products as they freeze. If a commercial ice cream mix is used, the only equipment needed will be a freezer and hardening cabinets. (See Fig. 2-30.)

The ice cream should freeze fast enough to develop fine crystals, and the beating should be sufficient to retain the fine texture. Fast hardening at low temperatures is also necessary to maintain a fine texture.

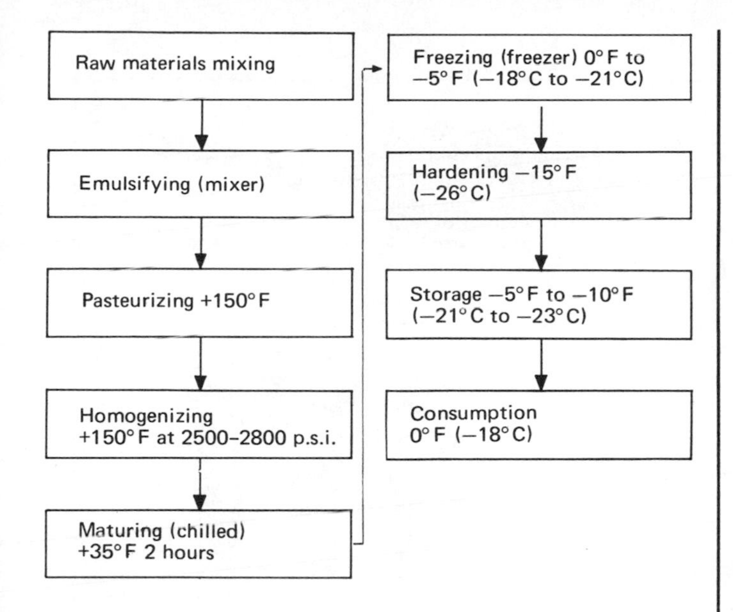

FIGURE 2-30
Diagram of Ice Cream Manufacture

2.4 Kitchenware—Pots and Pans

(See Fig. 2-31.)

1. Fry pan
2. Sauteuse (small saute pan)
3. Griddle pan
4. Stewing and boiling pot
5. Sautoir (large saute pan)
6. Round stewing and roasting pot
7. Low stock pot
8. Double-size stock pot
9. Roasting pan
10. Braziere
11. Bain-marie, sauce and soup container
12. Oblong fish kettle

2.5 Materials for the Manufacture of Kitchenware

Materials for foodservice equipment should be appropriate for the specific use. The materials used to fabricate foodservice equipment must meet certain minimum requirements as established by the Joint Committee on Food Equipment Standards:

> Only such materials shall be used on the construction of foodservice equipment/or appurtenances, as will withstand normal wear, penetration of vermin, the corrosive action of foods or beverages, cleaning compounds and such other elements as may be found in the use environments and will not impart an odor, color or taste to the food.[2]

The basic materials most commonly used in the manufacture of today's equipment are either ferrous, such as iron or steel, or nonferrous, such as aluminum or fiberglass. The material selected will affect the durability, the maintenance, the appearance, the weight, the sanitation, and the cost of the equipment.

Metals are used for structural features of kitchens and dining areas, for equipment, and for utensils. Some of the materials used extensively today include aluminum, cast iron, copper, glass, porcelain, ceramics, silver, stainless steel, and plastics.

Aluminum is a lightweight metal that is less expensive than some materials. It has high thermal and electrical conductivity and is relatively easy to clean. It is used for steam-jacketed kettles, food carts, cooking and baking pans, trays, and utensils.

Foods with high acid and/or alkali content attack pure aluminum. The discoloration in the metal is easily removed with fine steel wool or an aluminum cleaner. Copper scouring pads will scratch aluminum and should not be used.

The surface of aluminum can be treated to be more resistant to corrosion, discoloration, and marring. This treatment is called anodizing. Anodized aluminum is lightweight and durable, and it is suitable for portable equipment such as carts, trucks, dollies, and for storage shelves and cabinets.

Cast iron is used for large pieces of equipment such as ranges and ovens. It is also used for griddles and fry pans.

---

2. Standards—Food Service Equipment, National Sanitation Foundation, Standard 2, revised 1973.

FIGURE 2-31
Kitchenware—Pots and Pans

Copper kitchenware was very popular in the kitchens of early days. Even today copper-clad kitchenware is used both in the home and in institution kitchens. Traditional cooks have been reluctant to give up their shining copper kitchenware because of its high conductivity, its attractive appearance, and its resistance to corrosion.

Copper-clad cooking utensils must be lined with stainless steel or aluminum to prevent reactions of foodstuffs with the copper. The high initial costs, the heavy weight, the cost of replacing the linings, and the maintenance costs have limited the use of copper-clad utensils in today's institution kitchens. These utensils are frequently used for display cooking and decorative purposes.

Glass, porcelain, and ceramics have limited use for commercial kitchen equipment. They are often used as protective linings in equipment to prevent absorption of odors and flavors and metallic contamination. Glass is hard and resistant to acids and very high temperatures. The materials are easily cleaned and attractive.

Silver is a precious metal and its cost makes it prohibitive for use in commercial foodservice. Silver plate is also costly; however, it is occasionally used for flatware such as knives, forks, spoons and for holloware including coffee servers, tea pots, pitchers, and sugar bowls. These items, often referred to as hotel silver, are covered with a thick layer of silver plating.

Steel—stainless steel is a noncorrosive metal which is used more extensively than any other in the foodservice industry. Alloys of iron, nickel, and chromium are combined with steel and used for the manufacture of all kinds of equipment. Manufacturers may use different trade names, but stainless steel is the one most generally known in foodservice. It is made of approximately 70 percent steel, 20 percent chrome, and 10 percent nickel. Manufacturers may vary the formula slightly, but the important elements of the alloys are very similar.

Stainless steel has many outstanding qualities that make its use important in foodservice. Its strength, attractive appearance, permanence, smooth hard surface, and high weldability make it particularly suitable for fabricated equipment, serving counters, heavy duty equipment, tables, and machines. It is also used for kitchen utensils, pans, inserts for serving, counters, and tableware. Pans made of polished stainless steel are not recommended for certain uses such as the preparation of omelets. The food tends to stick to the fine pores of the metal. Other important features are its resistance to stain, scratches, and corrosion, ease of cleaning, availability of different finishes ranging from dull to bright. It is resistant to any chemical reaction with foodstuffs and may be used for all food preparation processes at any temperature. These characteristics are particularly significant for the foodservice industry where sanitation and safety are of utmost importance.

Plastics are lightweight and have only limited use in the kitchen. There are two main groups: thermosetting and thermoplastic. The former is harder and more resistant to heat; the latter, softer and less heat resistant. At temperatures between 175°F. and 210°F. (82°C. and 99°C.) plastic tends to lose its shape and may even melt. Plastics are most useful for storage and in the garde-manger. Since the material is fairly soft, it should not be cleaned with scouring products. Kitchen utensils made of hard metals should not be used with plastics.

2.6 Kitchen Equipment—Accessories

Materials recommended: stainless steel, aluminum, and plastic
Materials to be avoided: copper and bronze

Baking trays
Bains-marie, sauce and soup containers
Can openers
China caps
Colanders
Container and pan lids
Cutting boards
Deep-frying baskets
Deep-frying pans
Egg slicers
Fish kettles
Fry pans

Funnels
Graters
Juice extractors
Meat hooks
Meat trays
Measuring cups
Measuring spoons
Mixing bowls
Mortars
Mold pans
Omelet pans
Pastry tubes
Pate molds
Pitchers
Pudding pans
Ravioli boards
Roasting pans
Roasting and stewing pots
Saucepans with handles
Saute pans
Sauce pots, shallow and deep
Scales: ingredient, portion
Sieves
Skimmers
Spice containers
Spider (wiremesh skimmer for deep frying)
Spring form pans
Stock pots
Storage bins and containers
Strainers
Sugar sprinklers
Thermometers: candy, meat
Vegetable slicers
Whips

2.7 Technical Kitchen Terms

Abattis	Poultry giblets
Aiguillettes	Fine slices of meat
Annoncer	To announce: call an order
Appareil	A ready mix
Aromate	Special flavoring agents (spices)
Arroser	To baste a roast
Aspic	Gelatin base for desserts, or hors d'oeuvres, or salads
Assaisonner	To season food
Bain-marie	Waterbath: extended to mean special saucepans for sauces or creams
Barder	Barding: covering poultry or game with bacon slices before roasting (see page 237)
Baron	A single roast consisting of the legs and half-saddle of lamb
Barquettes	Boats
Beurrer	To butter
Beurre manie	Butter with flour, kneaded butter
Biscotte	Crisp toast, zwieback
Blanchir	To blanch (see page 265)
Blinis	Russian buckwheat—flour griddle cakes spread with caviar
Bordure	Ring of aspic/jelly, hot rice
Bouquet Garni	A small bunch of vegetables and herbs (see page 291)
Braiser	To braise, stew (pages 272, 275)
Brider	To truss: tying up poultry, meat, or game prior to cooking (see pages 234, 236)
Brunoise	Diced vegetables
Canapes	Small pieces of toast spread with different meat or fish pastes
Cannele	Fluted, grooved: e.g., a fluted icing tube
Caramel	Burned sugar. Caramelizing means pouring over with liquid sugar
Carcasse	Skeleton of poultry
Cassolette	French-style small porcelain bowl
Cassonade	Powdered sugar
Chapelure	Dried bread crumbs
Chaud-froider	Coating cold fish or meat with a gelatin sauce
Chemiser	Coating the inside of a mold with aspic jelly or an ice dessert with ice cream
Chiffonade	Finely shredded leaves
Chinois	China cap, conical strainer

Ciseler	Making small cuts or incisions; especially on the back of fish to hasten its cooking
Clarifier	To clarify a liquid: consomme, butter
Cocotte	Round or oval shaped dish in which certain foods are cooked and served
Coller	To stick; to become firm with the addition of flour or gelatin
Colorer	To color, tint, or mix in a color
Concasser	To chop coarsely with a knife; to crush in a mortar
Convenience food	Partially or completely processed raw food
Corser	To make a liquid stronger by boiling it down quickly
Coulis	Liquid purees of meat or fish made without flour
Coquille	Fireproof porcelain, tempered glass, or metal dishes in the form of a shell
Coral	Lobster or rock lobster eggs
Court-bouillon	Stock for poaching fish, sweetbread (see page 361)
Croustadine	Puff pastry baked into various shapes
Croquant	Crisp, crusty, crunchy
Croustade	Dish prepared with pastry or puff pastry, butter
Croutons	Diced or small slices of bread fried in butter
Darioles	Conical-shaped mold
Darne	Center section of large fish (salmon, sturgeon, etc.) (see page 226)
Dauphine-masse	Mixture of potato and puff pastry for frying
Decanter	To decant; transfer a liquid from one bottle to another to separate the sediment from the liquid
Decorer	To decorate a cake, a ham, or an aspic
Decortiquer	Remove the rind or shell of a lobster
Deglacer	Dissolve or dilute the concentrated juices in the pan in which meat, poultry, fish, or game has been roasted or braised
Degorger	Clean parts of fish such as the brain, roe, etc., in fresh running water
Degraisser	To remove excess fat from boiling stock, or to cut the fat from pieces of meat
Demouler	To remove from a mold
Deplumer	To pluck a fowl
Desosser	Remove the meat from the bone
Dessecher	To dry out
Dresser	To dress; to dish up food
Duchesse	A term given to various preparations, especially a method of preparing potatoes
Egoutter	To drain, to drip
Emincer	To cut into small slices
Entree	The third course (French)
Entremets	Desserts
Escalope	Thinly cut slices of meat or fish
Escaloper	To cut into uniform slices
Espagnole	Basic brown sauce (now out-of-date)
Etuver	To cook food in a covered pan without adding liquid (see page 277)
Etamine	Sieve, strainer, or cloth
Faisande	The term for high or gamy taste, when referring to game
Farcir	To stuff meat, poultry, and vegetables
Fariner	To coat, dust, or dredge with flour
Ficeler	To dress using string; to bind or tie with string
Fileter	To fillet (see pages 227, 229)
Flamber	To singe, to hold over the flame, to pass through the flame, to blaze
Flanquer	To garnish

Fleurons — Cuts of puff pastry
Foncer — To line a pan or mold with vegetables or with dough
Fond — Stock for soups or sauces
Fouetter — To beat with a wire whip; to stir
Frapper — To place food or drinks in a mixture of salt and ice
Frire — To fry
Frivolites — Hors d'oeuvres, consisting of little tarts, boats, and creams
Frotter — To rub, rub out, rub in
Fruits de mer — All kinds of seafood, crustaceans, and mollusks
Fumer — To smoke
Fumet — Rich liquid prepared by cooking foods in stock or wine
Galantine — Boned poultry or game cooked in a gelatin stock and pressed into a mold (pages 497, 498)
Galettes — A broad thin cake. There are many types, such as galettes of potatoes, sea biscuits, or galette des Rois (Twelfth-night cake)
Garnir — To garnish; to present a dish in an appealing way
Garniture — The vegetables and starch served with meat, fish, or poultry; the solid foods in soups or sauces; garnishes
Genoise — Italian sponge cake
Glacer — To coat cakes with a sugar glaze; to freeze a liquid until it turns to ice; to steam vegetables until the cooked juice glazes the vegetable; to glaze roasted meats with the reduced meat stock (see pages 274, 276)
Glace de viande — Thickened stock from bones, meat, essence, or extract
Gouter — To taste
Gratiner — To prepare a crust on the top of the food (see page 270)
Gril — Grill
Griller — To grill; to broil
Grenadin — Thick veal cutlets criss-crossed with strips of bacon and glazed
Grosse piece — The main course of a menu
Hatelet — Wooden or metal skewers used for grilling
Hors-d'oeuvre — Hot or cold dish at the beginning of a meal
Infusion — To steep herbs, tea, coffee, or other ingredients in boiling liquid until the liquid absorbs the aroma and flavor
Julienne — Meat or vegetables cut into long thin pieces
Jus — Natural juice of roasted meat
Konvectomat — Convectomat, convection oven (see page 33)
Liaison — To thicken a liquid, sauce, or broth
Lier — Thickening agent for soups and sauces
Macedoine — A mixture of vegetables or fruit
Macerer — To cure: to infuse meat with spices by soaking it over a long period in wine, vinegar, oil, or lemon juice
Mariner — To marinate; to place in a marinade
Marinade — The liquid used for marinating
Marmite — Stock pot for meat or soup
Masquer — To mask; to coat a dish with a sauce
Matelote — Sailor's dish, made with fish or veal with red wine
Meler — To mix different foods
Mignonettes — Small or finely cut
Mijoter — To cook slowly, simmer
Mirepoix — Vegetables diced for soups, sauces, and roasts (see page 291)
Monter — To whip up: e.g., a sauce or whites of eggs
Mouiller — To steep; to moisten; to soak
Mousseline — A fine cheesecloth

Nageoires	Fins of fish
Napper	Coating foods evenly with sauce or jelly
Paner	To coat meats, fish, or potatoes with bread crumbs
Papillote	Paper frills
Parer	To trim meat or fish
Parures	The trimmings of meat or fish
Parfumer	To flavor a dish; to add an aroma
Passer	To strain, to puree
Paupiettes	Stuffed slices of meat
Pie	A baked dish consisting of fruit or meat filling with either a bottom pastry crust, or a top pastry crust, or both top and bottom crusts
Piler	To pound; to crush
Piquer	To lard meat or poultry
Pocher	To poach (see page 265)
Poeler	To simmer under a cover in the oven (see page 276)
Preparer	To prepare
Praline	Candy made from almond or hazelnut paste with burned sugar
Printaniere	Spring vegetables
Profiterolles	Small puffs made of cream puff paste and filled with creams, cheese mixtures, custards, and other savory fillings
Pulpe	A moist paste of pulp of fruits or vegetables
Puree	Foodstuffs reduced to a smooth consistency by mashing or blending
Quartiers	Quarters of vegetables, fruit, or meat
Quenelles	Dumplings of meat, fish, poultry or game
Quiche	Bacon and cheese custard pie or tart
Ready food	Ready prepared meals, dishes (see page 278)
Rechauffer	To warm up; to reheat
Reduire	To reduce a liquid; to boil down
Releve	Main dish
Relever	To improve the taste by adding spices
Remouillage	Stock pot gravy (see page 296)
Revenir	(faire revenir) Slightly brown ingredients in butter or fat
Rissoler	To brown potatoes in butter or fat
Roux	Brown or white mixture of butter or fat and flour (see page 291)
Royale	Poached egg and milk custard
Saisir	(faire saisir) To expose meat suddenly to heat
Saignant	Bloody; underdone meat
Salpicon	Small diced meats, vegetables, or fruits bound with a sauce
Saucer	To sauce
Saumure	Brined, pickled
Saupoudrer	To dust with flour, pepper, or salt
Sorbetiere	Container for ice cream, sherbets, and ice
Souffle	A light, sweet or savory dish served hot or cold
Souffler	To puff up
Steamer	Steamer, pressure cooker
Supreme	(Sauce) A thickened rich sauce of cream and butter. It may also mean one half breast of chicken, e.g., Supreme de Volaille
Tampon	Base made of baked bread, rice, or fat
Tartelette	A small tart, tartlet
Tourne	To curdle, e.g., milk, mayonnaise
Trancher	To cleave; to carve; to cut into slices
Tremper	To soak, to steep
Troncons	Pieces of small fish or the tail of large fish (see page 226)
Zeste	Thin peel of lemon, or orange, or citron

3 Foods

All phases of marketing, the composition, and the method of handling materials used in the various fields of foodservice by the manager or dietitian, the chef or the cook, and the buyer are discussed in this chapter. The various categories of food will differ in their standards, grades, market forms (fresh, frozen, dehydrated, smoked, canned), units of purchase, costs, storage requirements (see Table 3-1), and federal and legal regulations. These differences must be known by those responsible for the purchase and preparation of food. The basic principles of the food laws and of sanitation are explained in the sections Sanitation/Legal Background (See pages 4,5).

Categories
There are five main groups:

- *Meat, fish, and poultry*
- *Eggs and dairy products*
- *Edible fats and oils (animal and vegetable)*
- *Grains, fruits, and vegetables*
- *Beverages*

3.1 Purchasing

Supervision of Purchasing
Purchasing refers to the task of obtaining the necessary goods in the right quality and quantity at the right time, in the right place, and at the most economical price. With purchasing so defined, and with the aim of bringing about a noticeable cost saving, while at the same time providing the best possible service, careful supervision of the most important elements of the purchasing function can be achieved.

Control of the Requirements
The two extremes that must be avoided are the "hand-to-mouth-method," or emergency buying; and buying excessive quantities of goods. Huge stocks of rarely used goods increase operating costs through storage costs (rent, interest, depreciation) and through losses caused by waste and theft. These costs can exceed any savings made by purchasing large quantities of one item.

The control of the requirements must be based upon three premises:

- purchase of the food at the right time
- purchase of the right kind and quantity of food for the intended use
- purchase of the food at the right price.

Obtaining the Merchandise at the Right Time
Planning the requirements in relation to time of need necessitates asking the following questions: What in-

ventory level should be established as the reorder point? What security margin is required? This margin is calculated by determining the maximum number of days a delivery could be delayed. This number is multiplied by the maximum number of units required per day. For example, if the deliveries might be delayed for as many as five days and four cases of the specific item are used each day, the security margin required would be twenty cases. Available storage space will influence the inventory level at which reordering is necessary. Therefore, the maximum quantity that can be stored, the average consumption over a given period of time, and the margin of safety must be known for every product used. After this information is determined, a reordering cycle can be calculated for each product.

Purchasing at the Right Price

In the foodservice industry, the price at the point of delivery is the critical factor. The purchasing calculation is, therefore, greatly affected by the services provided by the supplier. Transportation costs (including insurance), warehouse charges, and interest and bank charges must be added to the cost of the goods. If the goods are purchased directly at the supplier, then the transport costs are one's own responsibility and usually have to be paid in cash. If the supplier gives credit, then this represents *a saving in interest and should not be underestimated.* If one transports the goods oneself, then the cost of fuel, auto insurance, and depreciation costs of the vehicle must be considered in calculating the cost per mile. The time involved (wages) and the risk of losing the goods are not included in the calculation. The "cheap" supplier is, therefore, not always the most favorable supplier, nor necessarily the one representing the best value for money!

Optimal Supply. In order to achieve optimal supply, it is best to use the "ABC analysis." The most important article in terms of turnover is placed first on the list of all articles which are purchased. The second most important article takes the second place, and so on until a list of all articles which are consumed or sold is complete. The list is then divided into three groups (A, B, and C). Group A contains the first 10 percent of the listed articles, group B the next 20 percent, and group C the remainder.

If the percentage share of each article of the overall turnover is added to the table, one obtains an extremely interesting and informative purchasing aid. For example, one discovers that 50 percent of total turnover is accounted for by 10 percent of all the articles, or that 20 percent of all the articles makes up the last percentage point of turnover! "Optimal supply" seen in the light of the "ABC analysis" becomes "optimal supply for the storeroom or warehouse." The quantity ordered of each article necessary for optimal supply of the storeroom is fixed as a function of the purchase price, the requirement over a given period of time, the transport, warehousing, storage costs, and the bank charges. In this way, the optimal quantity to be ordered can be fixed.

Maintaining an Analysis of the Various Markets

A knowledge of the market is increasingly important today, not only among the prospective clients, but also the market where the goods are obtained. Only profound knowledge of these markets can protect one from losses. Good suppliers provide their clients with reliable, objective information, and not just brand advertising.

Supervision of the Ordering of Goods

Purchasing is an important and challenging function. The buyer for an institution must be knowledgeable about marketing. He must know the kinds and forms of foods available for the specific need, the quantities required, the standards of foods, market trends, and he must have a knowledge of contracts and their legal requirements. The buyer must be well-qualified for the position. He must maintain a high standard of ethics with companies and their sales representatives. Very often it is the director or the manager of the foodservice who assumes responsibility for purchasing certain sectors such as wine, spirits, and meat. What purchasing alternatives exist? It is important that the buyer not be influenced by cheap prices or other decoys. Merchandise with guaranteed quality (particularly important in the cases of wines and meat), financial soundness, good and dependable service, and sufficient capacity on the part of the supplier increase the quantitative and qualitative rating the supplier receives when various firms are under consideration. The most important criterion is the quality of the goods. The prices and conditions should only be of secondary importance. The terms of delivery and of payment are very important when making a choice of suppliers. Buying from a wide variety of sources (many suppliers, many small deliveries) in the long run overworks the purchasing office and leads to many deliveries of single articles.

Control of Deliveries
The acceptance of merchandise (i.e., control of deliveries) consists of checking products at entry and storing them or transferring them to the appropriate section of the establishment. First of all, one verifies that an order was made out for the goods which have been delivered and that the delivery conforms with the order in terms of products and quantity. Once the delivery note has been signed, the inventory card must be completed. It is then possible to check the inventory of any product in stock in the storeroom.

Control of the Quality
The checking of quality in the food trade is normally possible only when the merchandise is being used. For this reason, signing the delivery note does not prejudice subsequent claims on a delivery that was not in order. It should be remembered, however, that when a complaint is made, a sample of the objectionable merchandise should accompany the complaint, so that the claim for compensation can be documented. It is quite evident that such an extensive purchasing organization is not suitable for every establishment. Nevertheless, it does seem that in this particular field improvements are necessary for a number of establishments.

Control of Quantities
The quantities of food to be prepared must be checked against the recipe and a quantity table, which should be clearly displayed in every kitchen. (See pages 262, 263.) Accurate scales are needed in all departments for exact portion control. The menu plans will also aid in determining the quantities of food to be prepared. (See pages 186-189.) When these controls are used, there will be a minimum of leftovers.

Control of the Losses
Losses are caused by poor purchasing practices as related to quality and quantity controls and inadequate supervision. Usually the accounting department identifies the losses at the time the monthly or annual calculation of gross profit is completed. To avoid losses, recheck the calculation and make a daily calculation of the kitchen's gross profit.

3.2 Fish, Meats, and Poultry

Fish, meats, and poultry are used in large quantities in every foodservice. They have a high nutritional value and they are satisfying when prepared properly. These categories of food are very expensive, and a great deal of care is necessary in appropriate preparation and usage. Nutrition based solely upon meat is a health hazard. Inappropriate methods of preparation are costly. A complete knowledge of the characteristics and peculiarities of the raw materials is essential to insure high standards of quality. All raw materials derived from animals belong in this group of foods. There are several different types which vary greatly in terms of their characteristics and their mode of preparation.

3.2.1 Fish—Poissons

Fish are divided into the following main groups:

- *Freshwater Fish—Poissons d'eau douce*
- *Saltwater fish—Poissons de mer*

Both groups are then broken down into families.

Typical signs of good quality. Fresh fish have bright clear eyes, reddish-pink gills that are free from odor or slime, bright-colored scales adhering tightly to the skin, and firm flesh that is free from objectionable odors. Fish usually have less flavor immediately preceding and following the spawning period.

Preservation. Fresh fish and seafood deteriorate rapidly, and these procedures should be followed immediately after fish are received:

- Pack in ice or store in a refrigerator at 35°F. to 40°F. (2°C. to 5°C.).
- Store in the original moistureproof wrapper.
- Keep fish no longer than one or two days before cooking.

Specialized factories in the fishing harbors conserve fish by the following methods:

- Marinating: herrings
- Smoking: eel, bloaters, salmon, plaice, sprats
- Salting: herring, sardines
- Freezing: most kinds of fish
- Drying: cod, mackerel

Fish tanks used to store live fish require water that is properly circulated and oxygenated. The temperature of the water should be constant at 40°F. to 55°F. (5°C. to 13°C.). The fish tank must be kept clean.

3.2.1.1 Freshwater Fish—Poissons d'eau douce

The Eel Family

EEL—ANGUILLE

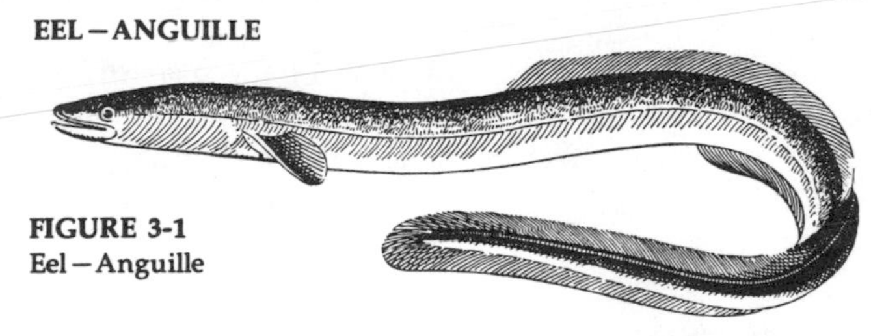

FIGURE 3-1
Eel—Anguille

Origin and occurrence: The eel, a migratory fish, leaves the sea when young and heads for fresh water, where it grows to a maximum length of 5 feet. It then returns to the sea for spawning. It stays there and may grow to a length of 8 feet.

Species and description: The eel is a snake-like fish, and belongs to the family of bonefish. (See illustration on page 140.)
Quality characteristics: The fat content of eel is high, and therefore it is less easy to digest. Medium-sized eels have a pleasant taste. Eels from ponds have an undesirable taste, and they should be kept in a fish tank with flowing water before killing.
Usage: The eel should be skinned before preparation. (See Fig. 7-11.) Fresh eel may be used for eel soup, or it may be deep-fat fried, marinated, or served cold in aspic. Smoked eels are also on the market.

The Perch Family

PERCH—PERCHE

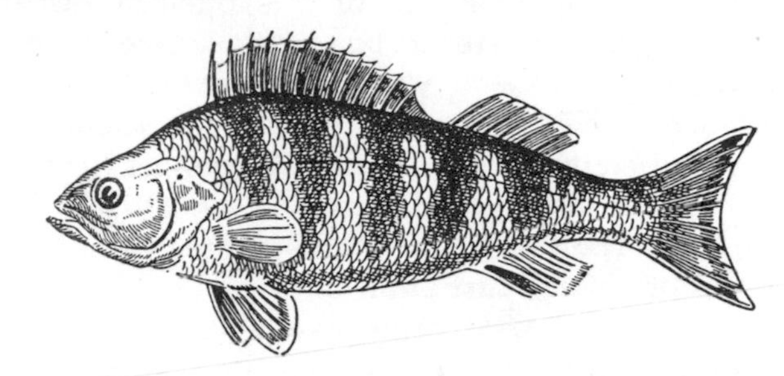

FIGURE 3-2
Perch—Perche

Origin and occurrence: Perch is both a freshwater and saltwater fish, and it is known as a tough hunter.
Species and description: This member of the perch family grows to a length between 10 and 15 inches, and can weigh over two pounds. Its head is conical, its skin is very scaly, and it has sharp fins. The fins on the back are a violet color, while those on the belly are reddish-yellow. The back is dark green with black vertical stripes. There is a characteristic dark spot immediately behind the first dorsal fin.
Quality characteristics: When cooked, the flesh is firm, white, and it has a very delicate flavor.
Usage: Small perch are usually deep-fat fried and served whole. Larger perch are filleted and prepared in various ways—steamed, deep-fat fried, pan-fried with lemon or with almonds.

PIKE-PERCH—SANDRE

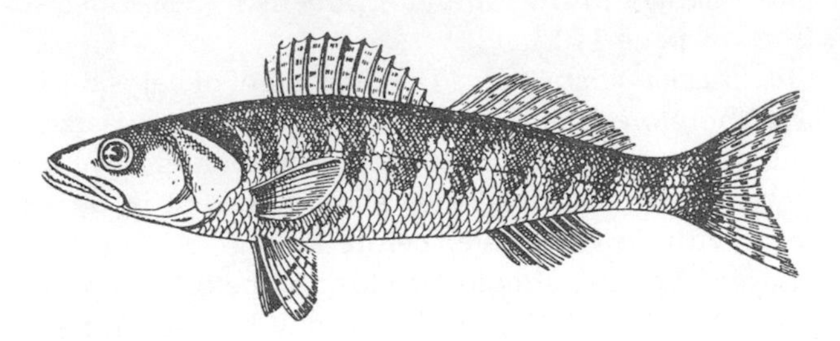

FIGURE 3-3
Pike-perch—Sandre

Origin and occurrence: Although pike-perch originated in Eastern Europe, it is now flourishing in several of the European rivers. The fish requires water with a very low salt content. It is found in Austria and Hungary, where it bears the name *Fogash* (French *Fogas*).
Species and description: The pike-perch belongs to the perch family. It is quite thin and ranges from 15 to 20 inches in length, although some 30-inch fish have been reported. Its back is dark green with shiny white sides. **(See illustration on page 140.)**
Quality characteristics: The pike-perch spawns between April and July. Its flesh is white, soft and delicate, juicy and tasty. Pike-perch is better fresh than frozen, although there is more of the latter on the market since it is imported from Eastern Europe.
Usage: All of the basic preparations can be applied without affecting the taste.

The Pike Family

PIKE—BROCHET

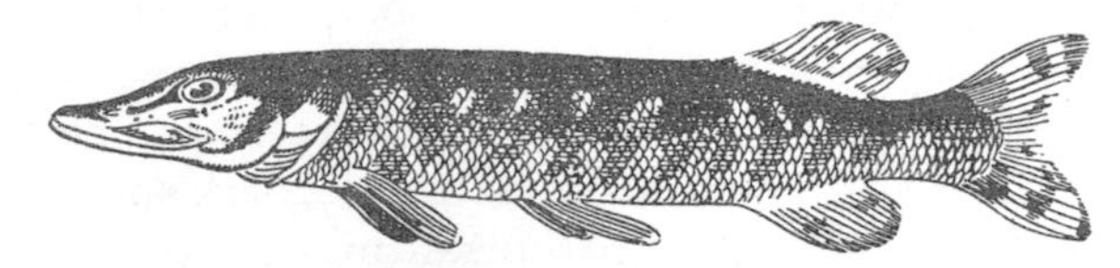

FIGURE 3-4
Pike—Brochet

Origin and occurrence: Pike is found in rivers, lakes, and large ponds.
Species and description: It is a noble fish, one of the bonefish, a tough hunter, and for the most part, feeds on smaller fish. It sometimes reaches a length of 4 feet and a weight of 65 pounds. The body is long and thin and the head wide and flat. One-year-old fish are called jack. **(See illustration on page 140.)**
Quality characteristics: The flesh of a pike is tender and tasty and at its best when the fish is two years old and weighs 4 to 6 pounds. Older pike are less tender and their flesh is full of fine needle-like bones.
Usage: Pike weighing less than one pound is usually pan-fried. Otherwise, it should be steamed, simmered, boiled, or deep-fat fried to preserve the delicacy of the fish. The flesh of older pike is generally used for fish stuffing.

The Salmon Family (Salmonidae)

GRAYLING—OMBRE

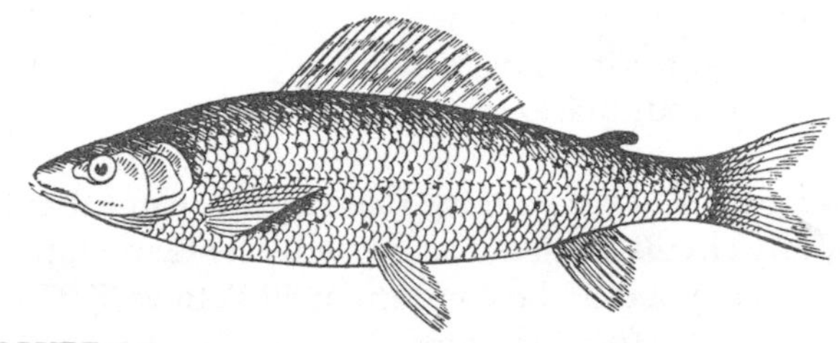

FIGURE 3-5
Grayling—Ombre

Origin and occurrence: Grayling is found in rivers and streams throughout the northern hemisphere.
Species and description: A member of the salmonidae family, grayling resembles trout and it may reach a length of 16 inches.
Quality characteristics: The flesh of the grayling is very delicate and moist and has the flavor of thyme.
Usage: For pan-frying, steaming, poaching, and grilling.

GOLDEN TROUT (SAIBLING)—OMBRE CHEVALIER

Origin and occurrence: Several varieties of the fish are found in lakes north of the Alps, in lakes throughout Northern Europe, and in North America.
Species and description: The golden trout is a mem-

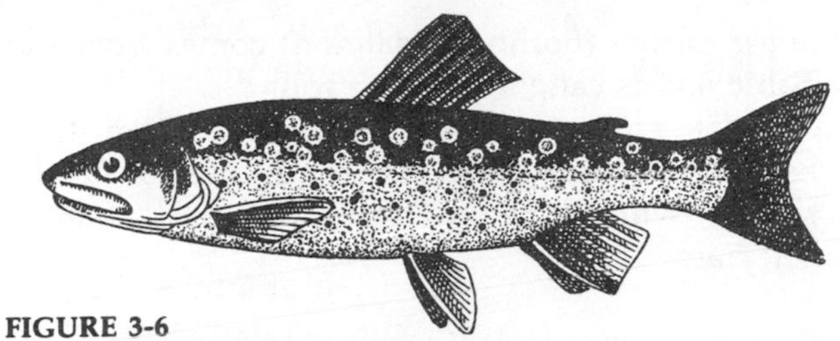

FIGURE 3-6
Golden Trout (Saibling)—Ombre chevalier

ber of the salmonidae family. The colors of the fish vary according to age, sex, and region.
Quality characteristics: The flesh of golden trout is delicious, and it is popular on many menus.
Usage: Golden trout is usually prepared by the same methods used for preparing river trout; however, methods of preparation vary in different regions.

LAKE TROUT—TRUITE DE LAC

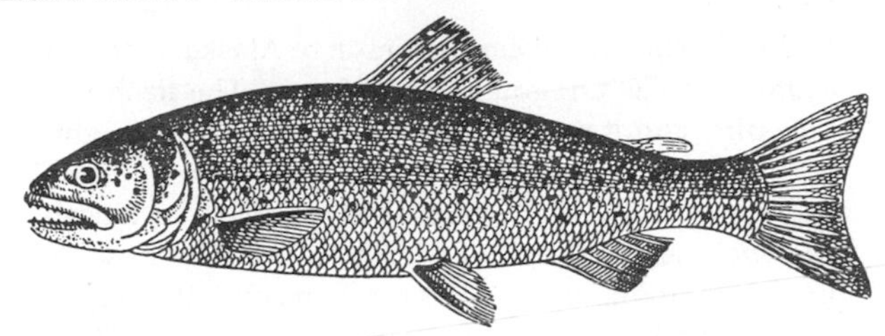

FIGURE 3-7
Lake Trout—Truite de lac

Origin and occurrence: Those in lakes constitute a variation of the river trout. The trout found in arctic seas is referred to as ocean trout.
Species and description: Like all other types of trout, this species belongs to the salmonidae group, and is a migrating fish, which swims up rivers in order to spawn. The fish grows up to 4 feet in length; its back is a gray-blue to black color and is covered with many light yellow and red spots.
Quality characteristics: Lake trout, which are neither too old nor too large, have flesh which is relatively easy to digest.
Usage: The fish is best when boiled, poached, pan-fried (a la meuniere), or grilled.

RAINBOW TROUT—TRUITE ARC-EN-CIEL

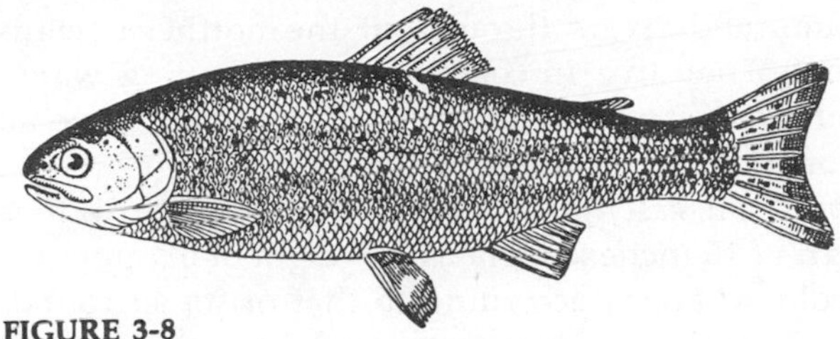

FIGURE 3-8
Rainbow Trout—Truite arc-en-ciel

Origin and occurrence: The rainbow trout, a native of the Pacific slope of the Sierras from California to Alaska, is now found throughout the United States and Europe. It prefers clear, cool, unpolluted water. Because of its voracity and resistance to illnesses (for example, furuncles), it has established itself among many fish breeders.
Species and description: The various types of trout form a special group within the large salmonidae family. Wild rainbow trout grow up to two feet in length. They normally come from the breeders in a size suitable for one portion. The rainbow trout is easily identified by the reddish band or rainbow which runs from head to tail on each side of the fish. The back dorsal fin and the tail are covered with a multitude of black spots.The brightness of color will vary depending on the environmental and feeding conditions.
Quality characteristics: The quality of the flesh is dependent upon the type of food consumed by the fish. All types of trout are noble fish and are known for their excellent eating quality.
Usage: The fish should be cooked immediately after killing and cleaning. The forms of preparation are: boiling, deep-fat frying, and pan-frying (a la meuniere).

RIVER TROUT—TRUITE DE RIVIERE

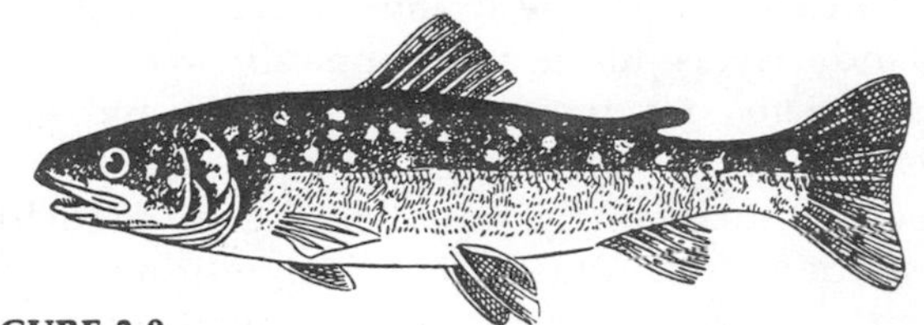

FIGURE 3-9
River Trout—Truite de riviere

Origin and occurrence: River trout is found in streams and rivers throughout the northern hemisphere. They live in cold, clear, fast-flowing water. River trout can become ocean trout if they have an opportunity to migrate out to sea.
Species and description: River trout can grow to a length of 15 inches and reach a weight of 6½ pounds. Its color changes according to that of its surroundings. The skin is mostly spotted, and the back is olive-green to black. The scales are very small. Not only does the color adapt itself to the local surroundings, but also to the quality of the flesh. This is the reason the fish is given different names, i.e., wood trout, mountain trout, or stone trout. They all belong to the same species. (See illustration on page 140.)
Quality characteristics: Stone and mountain trout have a delicate, white, easily digestible flesh. However, any trout that feed on the bottom of shallow water have a matt white or slightly reddish flesh characterized by a mossy taste.
Usage: Live trout are especially good for boiling. Trout which have been stored are better pan-fried (a la meuniere).

SALMON – SAUMON

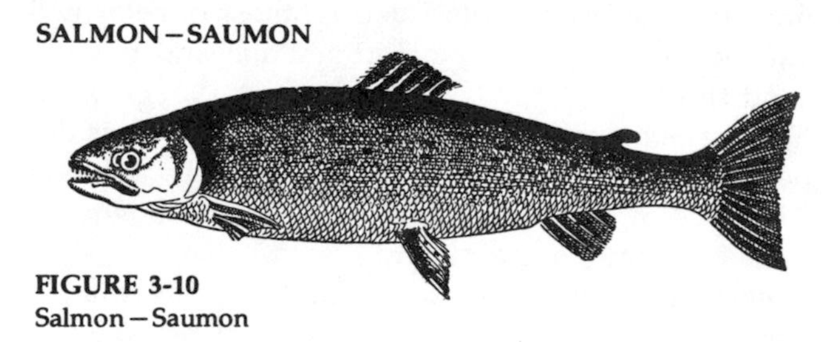

FIGURE 3-10
Salmon – Saumon

Origin and occurrence: The fish industry divides salmon into four groups:

- *River salmon* from the Rhine, Loire, Scottish, and Islandic rivers. Rhine and Loire salmon are highly appreciated for their fine pink flesh and good taste. In recent years these types of salmon have become increasingly rare because of industrial pollution. Today the catch is insignificant.
- *Norwegian and Swedish salmon* are available on the market from spring until autumn.
- *Silver salmon* (Bornholm salmon) comes from the Baltic and is caught the year round.
- *American salmon* (real salmon) is found from Alaska to California. There are five species of Pacific salmon which live in North American waters. They are:[1]

Chinook salmon or *king salmon* is the largest of the Pacific salmon, averaging 20 pounds. It has a blue-green back marked with dark spots and silvery sides. The flesh, rich in oils, ranges from dark salmon red to white in color. It breaks into large flakes and is especially good in salads.
Chum salmon grows to an average length of 3 feet and weighs about 10 pounds. It is found in the Sacramento River and in Puget Sound. The flesh has less color and less oil than the other species.
Coho or *silver salmon,* a favorite with sportsmen, weighs from 6 to 12 pounds and is 2 to 3 feet in length. Coho is abundant in Alaska and Puget Sound. Its flesh is a deep salmon color and it breaks into large flakes.
Pink or *humpback salmon,* common to Alaska, is found as far south as Oregon and California. The flesh is a pale pink and it ranges from 3 to 6 pounds in weight. It is used in soups, entrees, and sandwiches.
Sockeye or *red salmon* averages about 2 feet in length and weighs between 3 and 5 pounds. The flesh is firm, rich in oil, and is a deep red in color. It is suitable for salads and cold entrees.

Species and description: The spawning period of the salmon lasts from October to December. In the spring the fish leaves the sea and swims upstream to the river to spawn. Some of the fish then return to the sea. The flesh of fish going upstream to spawn is red and fatty, while that of fish returning to the sea after spawning is rather white and of poor quality. After spawning, some American varieties die from exhaustion or from fungus disease, and thus create food for the young salmon. The young fish remain in the upper reaches of the rivers for 1 to 2 years and then they migrate to the sea. Salmon are approximately 5 to 6 feet long and weigh 44 pounds. They have a longish

1. *Food Fish Facts No. 8,* Chicago: National Marine Fisheries Service.

round shape, a relatively small pointed head, a blue-green back, silvery sides with colored spots, and a shiny white belly. The male fish (milter) have a hook-shaped appendix on the lower jaw and are, therefore, called *hook salmon*. They are preferred over the female fish.

Quality and characteristics: Fish weighing between 15 and 30 pounds are the best quality.

Usage: Fresh salmon is usually grilled or poached in a court bouillon.

Smoked salmon: The fish is salted and then smoked when cold. It is cut into sides weighing 3 to 9 pounds, and it is packed in long hampers for shipment. On arrival, smoked salmon must be unpacked and hung. During the night the cut sides should be laid on marble or stone. Smoked salmon should never be stored in the refrigerator, because it turns soft and can no longer be cut.

Canned salmon: This fish is not sterilized, therefore, it does not have the keeping-quality of regular canned food. It must be stored in a very cool place.

SALMON TROUT—TRUITE SAUMONEE

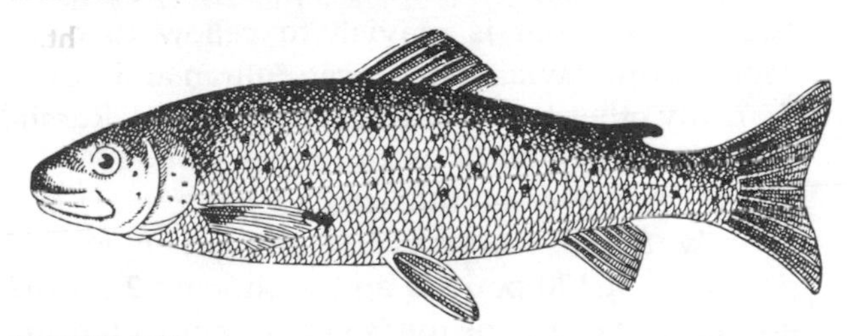

FIGURE 3-11
Salmon Trout—Truite saumonee

Origin and occurrence: This fish is either a cross between trout and salmon, or a variety of salmon. Salmon trout is found in rivers and lakes.

Species and description: The salmon trout, which is similar to salmon, differs from the river trout in that it has a pointed head. It is up to 2½ feet long and can weigh 17½ pounds.

Quality characteristics: The flesh is pink in hue and has a pleasant flavor.

Usage: Salmon trout is normally prepared like salmon, either poached in a court bouillon, grilled, or fried.

WHITEFISH—FERA

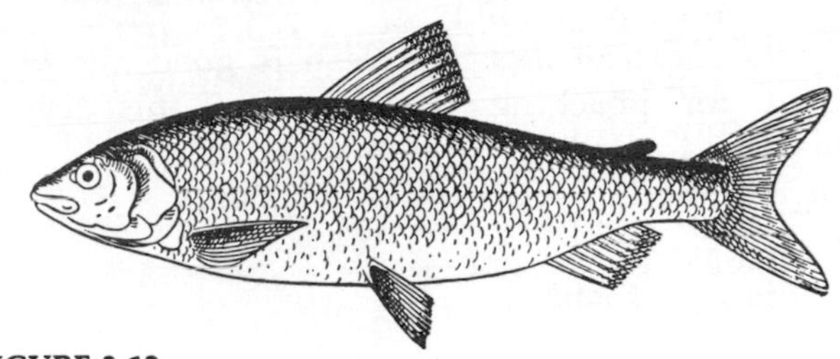

FIGURE 3-12
Whitefish—Fera

The whitefish types can be grouped by size: large (mostly found near banks), medium, small, and dwarf.

Origin and occurrence: Almost all the lakes contain whitefish.

Species and description: The whitefish varieties belong to the salmonidae family. This fish is recognized by the small fat fin at the tail end of the fish. (See illustration on page 140.)

Quality characteristics: Whitefish have a white, tasty flesh which is rather dry.

Usage: The best way to prepare medium or large whitefish is pan-frying (a la meuniere). Butter should be added to compensate for the lack of fat in the flesh. Small whitefish and dwarf whitefish are best deep-fat fried.

The Soft-Finned Family

EEL-POUT (BURBOT)—LOTTE

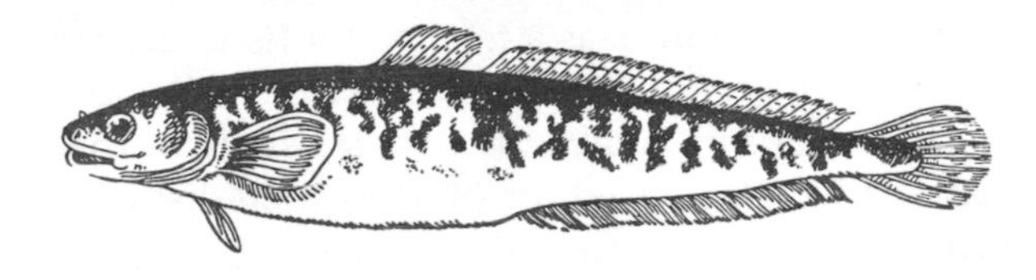

FIGURE 3-13
Eel-pout (Burbot)—Lotte

Origin and occurrence: Eel-pout is found in shallow waters north of 40° latitude.

Species and description: Classified in the family of soft-finned fish, eel-pout has a rather wide, flat head, a narrow body, and soft fins. Like the eel, it has no

scales, and for this reason, is usually skinned. (See illustration on page 140.)
Quality characteristics: Its flesh is good and well-suited for poaching. The liver of this fish is considered a delicacy by connoisseurs.
Usage: Fried or poached (en matelote).

The Sturgeon Family

STURGEON–ESTURGEON

FIGURE 3-14
Sturgeon–Esturgeon

Origin and occurrence: The different variations of this fish include the sterlet and hausen which are most frequently found in the Black and Caspian Seas and in the rivers flowing into them.
Species and description: The *sterlet,* a prize breed in Russia, measures up to 5 feet in length and can weigh a maximum of 330 pounds. The *sturgeon* grows up to 6 feet in length and weighs 440 pounds. The *hausen,* the largest fish in the sturgeon family, grows as large as 13 feet in length and weighs up to 3,000 pounds. The fish has a gray-blue back, silver-gray sides, and whitish belly. The mouth opens like a shovel and underneath are four beard strings. Since it is born in fresh water, it counts as a freshwater fish. The roe of the different types of sturgeon is used to make caviar. From the hausen is taken the isinglass (from the air bladder) which is used for binding cold dishes. The spine-marrow is called *vesiga,* which, after drying, is used to make Russian fish pies and pates.
Quality characteristics: The flesh has a good flavor.
Usage: Sturgeon is sold smoked, salted, and fresh. The main consumers are the Russians and those living in adjacent countries.

CAVIAR–CAVIAR

Origin and occurrence: Caviar is the salted roe (fish eggs) of various species of the sturgeon family in the Black and Caspian Seas. The roe is removed as soon as the fish is caught. It is prepared by removing the cellular tissue around the roe, pressing it through a hemp sieve, and salting the roe. Until 1953, the Russian town of Astrachan, on the Caspian Sea, was the center of the caviar trade. At that time, Iran withdrew the fishing concessions which it had previously granted Russia and set up its own trading organization in Bender Pehlevi. Europe and America obtain most of their caviar from there.
Species and description: Caviar is classified according to the type of sturgeon:

- *Beluga (hausen),* the largest variety of sturgeon, produce up to 350 pounds of eggs. The silver-gray coarse caviar obtained from this fish is of first class quality, and it is preferred in the West.
- *Schip (Russian name for sturgeon)* reaches a weight of 175 pounds and produces a medium quantity of up to 25 pounds of second class caviar.
- *Osetrova* is a kind of sturgeon weighing roughly 440 pounds and containing up to 45 pounds of eggs. This caviar is grayish to yellow in color. More of this caviar is produced in Iran and Russia than any other types. Mainly consumed in Russia, Osetrova is seldom found in other markets.
- *Seruga* comes from the smallest, but most frequently found sturgeon, weighing between 25 pounds and 120 pounds and producing 2½ to 12 pounds of caviar. The roe is very fine-textured and has an excellent flavor.
- *Botarga* is the so-called *Ketarogen,* which is not made from sturgeon, but from the roe of salmon, pike-perch, grayling, and tuna. Botarga caviar is red and very coarse. It is used for garnishing and for decorative purposes.

Quality characteristics: The larger the individual egg and the lighter its silver-gray color, the more valuable the caviar. The egg should be glassy, well-rounded and dry, uniform in size and color, and it should have a mild taste which is neither salty nor bitter. Caviar spoils quickly, and for this reason it must be kept on ice. Caviar packed in cans should be refrigerated.

- *Mallossal* caviar is only slightly salted and is considered a special delicacy since the taste of salt is not evident. This caviar, which contains 3 to 4 percent salt, keeps only a limited time.
- *Salt-barrel caviar* contains 10 to 12 percent salt. Although the salt prolongs the shelf life, it does lower the quality and affects the taste. This type of caviar is rare.

Usage: The nutritional value of caviar is high because of its fat and protein content, but the main reason for its use is pure enjoyment. Caviar is served either in ice or over ice as an hors-d'oeuvre. It may be used for garnishing, on toast, as a canape, or in cold sauces. Caviar butter may be prepared by mixing five parts butter to one part caviar and forcing the mixture through a sieve. Salt-barrel caviar is the most suitable for this use.

The Whitefish Family (Cyprinidae)

BARBEL—BARBEAU

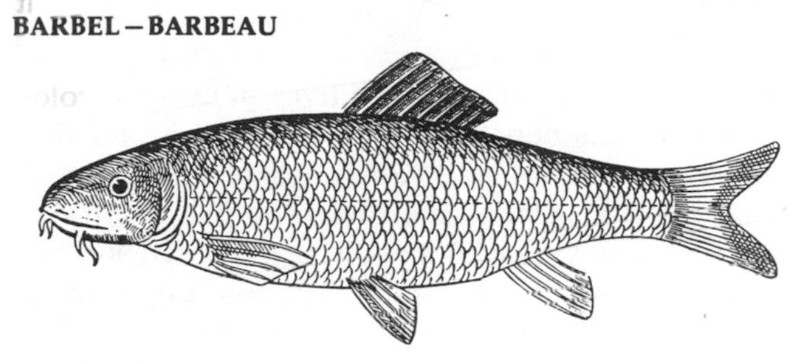

FIGURE 3-15
Barbel—Barbeau

Origin and occurrence: Barbel lives near the bottom of European rivers.
Species and description: Barbel is one of the carp species, and it can grow up to 28 inches and weigh up to 9 pounds. The body is thin, and the back is an olive-green color. (See illustration on page 140.)
Quality characteristics: The full-flavored flesh ranks low in eating quality because it is very bony. The roe should not be eaten during the spawning period from May to June.
Usage: When this fish is served, it is best deep-fat fried.

CARP—CARPE

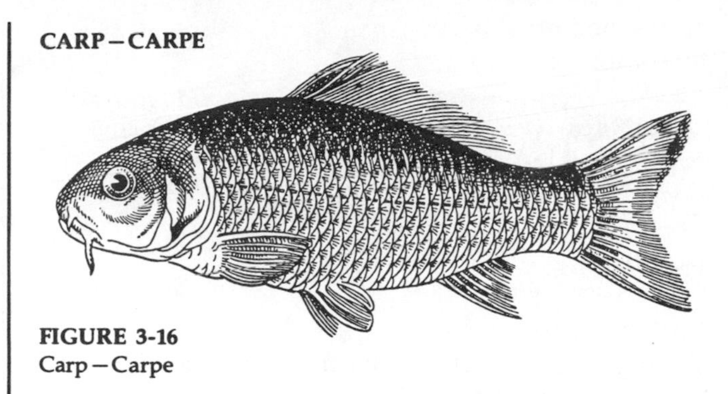

FIGURE 3-16
Carp—Carpe

Origin and occurrence: A European fish that has been introduced all over North America. It is found in running or stagnant water and in special breeding ponds.
Species and description: Classified as a bonefish, carp can reach a length of over 3½ feet and weigh up to 33 pounds. There are pond and river varieties; the three types of pond carp are:

- *mirror carp* with large shiny scales scattered along the line running down the center of the sides of the fish.
- *scale carp* with regular scales
- *leather carp* which has no scales

The body of *river carp* is somewhat longer. This type of carp has no commercial value. (See illustration on page 140.)
Quality characteristics: The flesh is soft and easily digested and is at its best in winter. All pond carp should be kept in fresh flowing water for some time before killing to eliminate the muddy flavor. Medium-sized carp are best, especially mirror carp. The *soft roe of carp (Laitance de carpe)* is a delicacy.
Usage: Fresh carp are usually stewed or boiled.

CHUB—CHEVAINE
Origin and occurrence: Chub lives in rivers and streams.
Species and description: Since it is a member of the carp family, it is a whitefish. It grows to 16 inches in length. (See illustration on page 140.)

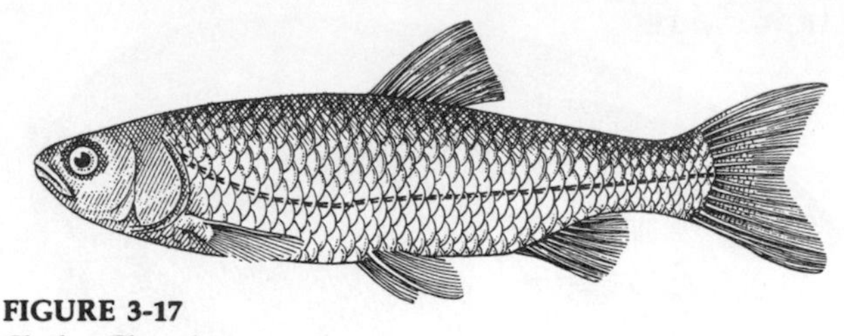

FIGURE 3-17
Chub – Chevaine

Quality characteristics: The flesh is good, but contains many bones.
Usage: It is usually deep-fat fried.

DACE – VANGERON

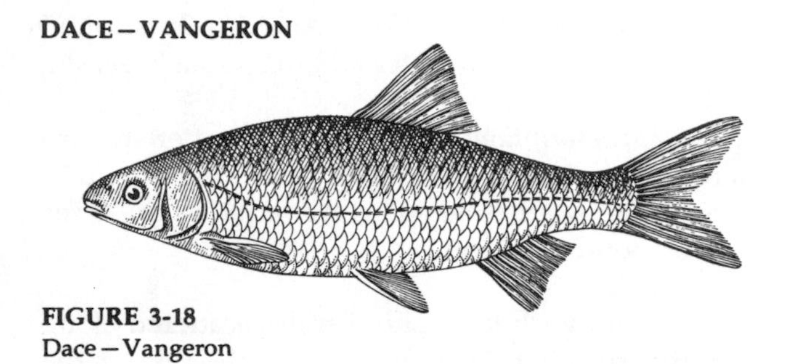

FIGURE 3-18
Dace – Vangeron

Origin and occurrence: Dace is found in the inland waters of northern and central Europe as well as throughout North America.
Species and description: It is a small to medium-sized whitefish belonging to the carp family. It can grow to 12 inches in length and weigh 3½ pounds. The back is olive-green, the belly white, and the fins a reddish color.
Quality characteristics: The flesh has a good flavor and, although full of bones, it is generally well-liked.
Usage: It is best deep-fat fried.

NEZ-NASLING (BROAD-SNOUT) – NEZ

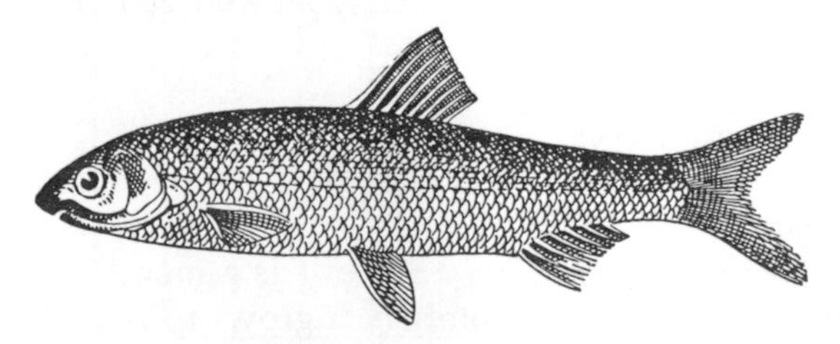

FIGURE 3-19
Nez – Nasling (broad snout) – Nez

Origin and occurrence: The nez-nasling lives in the Rhine and Danube, but is also found in streams and other rivers of Europe.
Species and description: This fish belongs to the carp family (whitefish). The back is blackish-green and the sides and belly are silver-white.
Quality characteristics: The bony and undesirable flavor make this an unsatisfactory food product.
Usage: It is used for simple dishes, either deep-fat fried or stewed.

TENCH – TANCHE

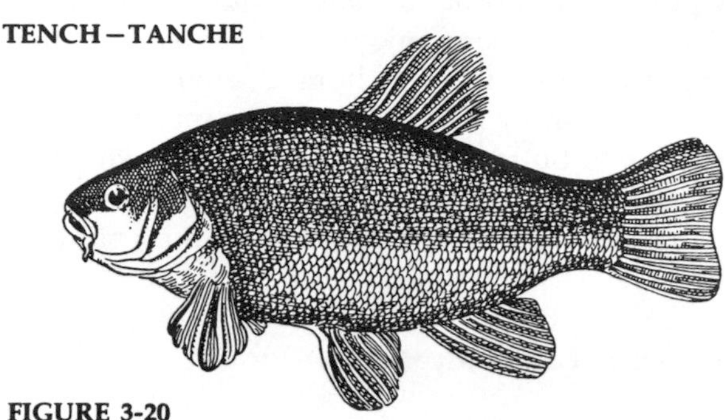

FIGURE 3-20
Tench – Tanche

Origin and occurrence: Tench lives in either slowly-running or stagnant water and in breeding ponds.
Species and description: A member of the whitefish family, it is similar to the carp. The fish is covered with tiny scales. The back is olive-green in color, and the sides and belly are lighter. The fins are rounded. The male is recognized by the larger belly fins. The mouth has two beard strings. (See illustration on page 140.)
Quality charactersitics: The flesh is delicate, oily, and has a good flavor. Tench taken from muddy water may have an unpleasant taste. It must be kept in clear running water for several days before being killed to improve the flavor. The average size marketed is about 1½ pounds and 10 to 12 inches in length. They can, however, reach a length of 20 inches and weigh 6½ pounds.
Usage: Tench is usually boiled or stewed.

The Wels Family

SHEAT-FISH (WELS) – SILURUS GLANIS

Origin and occurrence: This catfish type is found in the rivers and lakes of central Europe. This, next to the sturgeon, is the largest river fish in Europe, weighing 300 to 400 pounds.

Species and description: This fish is classified under the wels species. It is frequently 10 feet in length, has a fat body, a flattened head with two long and four short beard strings, and is brown in color. It is a fish which lives in the bottom of rivers and lakes and feeds on fish, crabs, and frogs. It has even been known to eat water birds. (See illustration on page 140.)

Quality characteristics: Young sheat-fish have a good flavor.

Usage: Fillets may be sauteed, deep-fat fried, or stewed.

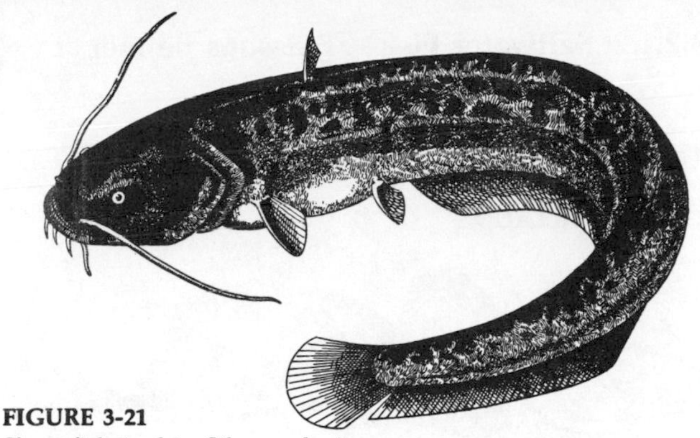

FIGURE 3-21
Sheat-fish (wels)—Silurus glanis

Freshwater Fish Spawning Periods:

(Spawning periods can be delayed especially in higher altitudes.)

— = spawning period	January	February	March	April	May	June	July	August	September	October	November	December
Bream				—	—	—						
Carp					—	—						
Chub					—	—						
Eel (migration to sea)									X	X		
Eel-pout	—											—
Golden trout											—	—
Grayling			—	—	—							
Lake trout											—	—
Nez-Nasling (broad snout)				—	—	—						
Perch					—	—						
Pike			—	—	—							
Rainbow trout			—	—	—	—						
Roach				—	—							
Rudd				—	—	—						
Salmon											—	—
Salmonide family								—	—			
Sheat-fish					—	—						
Tench					—	—						
Trout	—									—	—	—

FIGURE 3-22
Freshwater Fish Spawning Periods

3.2.1.2 Saltwater Fish — Poissons de mer

The Cod Family

COD — CABILLAUD

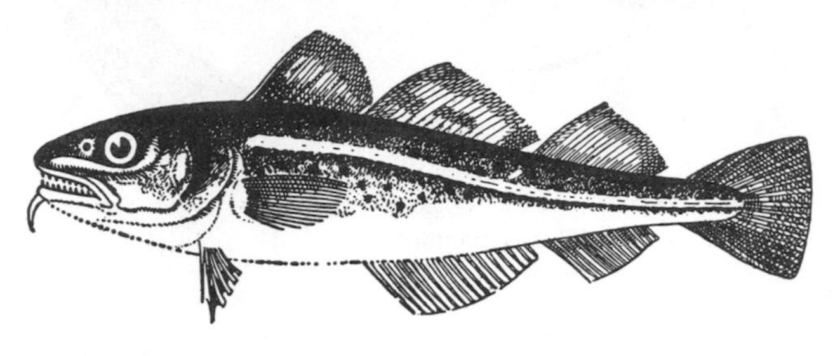

FIGURE 3-23
Cod — Cabillaud

Origin and occurrence: It is found in Atlantic waters from Virginia to the Arctic, but most abundant in the Gulf of St. Lawrence, off Newfoundland. When dried, it is a *stockfish,* and when dried and salted a *salted cod.*
Species and description: It belongs to the cod family and has long been recognized for its value as a food and as an important resource in world trade. As an inveterate hunter, cod lives off other fish. It is also a very fertile fish. Each female produces some nine million eggs over the spawning period. The cod has a strong stubby head with protruding upper jaws and long beard strings. The light-colored lateral line extending along the sides is a typical characteristic. It can reach a length of 5 feet.
Quality characteristics: Its flaky, grayish-white flesh is rather fragile.
Usage: Fresh cod is usually boiled or poached. Dried or salted cod is soaked in water and then boiled in a court bouillon and garnished with parsley and hard-cooked eggs and served with a sauce. Cod is found on the market in fresh, frozen, and dried forms. Practically all of the fish portions and sticks on the market are produced from domestic and imported cod.

HADDOCK — AIGREFIN

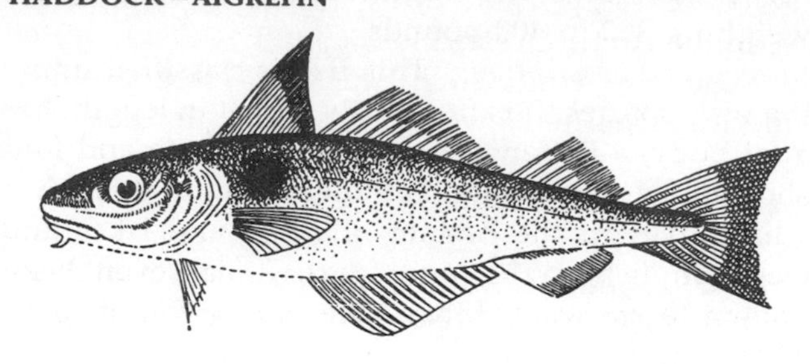

FIGURE 3-24
Haddock — Aigrefin

Origin and occurrence: This fish is a member of the cod family, and it lives in the North Atlantic and the North Sea.
Species and description: Haddock belongs to a large group known as groundfish. The back is grayish-brown, the belly white. Above the lateral fin, there is a black spot, and the line down the middle of both sides is jet black. Commercially, haddock are landed in two market categories, "scrod" which weighs 1½ to 2½ pounds and "large" which weighs more than 2½ pounds.
Quality characteristics: The flesh is white, tender, and firm, with a mild and pleasing flavor. It is rich in protein and low in fat.
Usage: It is suitable for stewing, sauteing, and deep-fat frying; for making fish salads, marinades, and for smoking.

WHITING — MERLAN

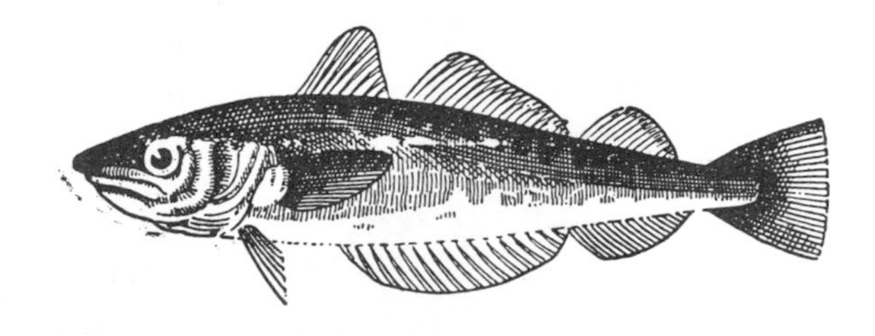

FIGURE 3-25
Whiting — Merlan

Origin and occurrence: The whiting is found between the Arctic Ocean and the Black Sea. It is abundant on the continental shelf of eastern North America from the Newfoundland Bank to Cape Hatteras.
Species and description: Whiting, a member of the cod family, has two dorsal fins and one anal fin, while cod, haddock, and pollack have three dorsal and two anal fins. Although it can grow to 20 inches, it is rarely longer than 12 inches or heavier than 5 pounds. It is light-colored with a black dot at the base of the lateral fin. It has a silvery line along its sides.
Quality characteristics: The flesh of whiting is tender, lean, and flaky. The fish is very fragile and cannot tolerate the pressure of iceblocks.
Usage: Whiting adapt readily to poaching, steaming, deep-fat frying, sauteing, broiling, or baking. The flesh is also used in the manufacture of fish stuffings.

The Herring Family

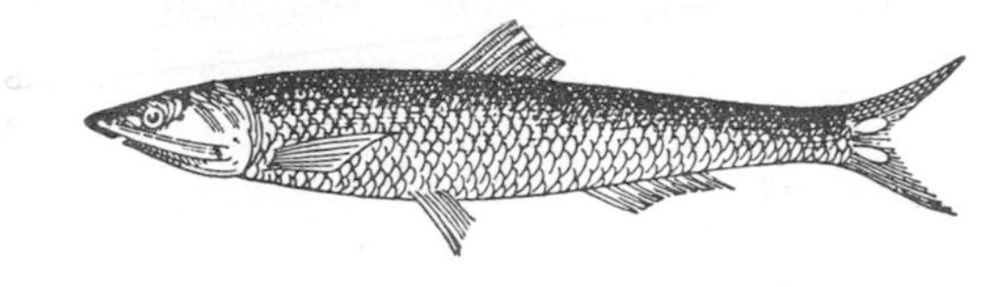

FIGURE 3-26
Anchovy – Anchois

ANCHOVY – ANCHOIS
Origin and occurrence: It is caught in the North Sea, the Atlantic, and along the Mediterranean coasts, chiefly in winter.
Species and description: A member of the herring family, this small sea fish grows to a length of about 6 inches. Its projecting snout and large mouth distinguish it from the sardine.
Quality and characterisitics: A good anchovy is selected by size. It has a pleasant, fresh, and aromatic taste. Its flesh should be pink without oil. Its freshness can be determined by the color of its back. It turns from a beautiful green when fresh to a dark greenish-blue and then to almost black.
Usage: Anchovy fillets, anchovy rings, and paste are made from these fish. They can also be used for garnishings, sandwiches, and anchovy butter.

HERRING – HARENG

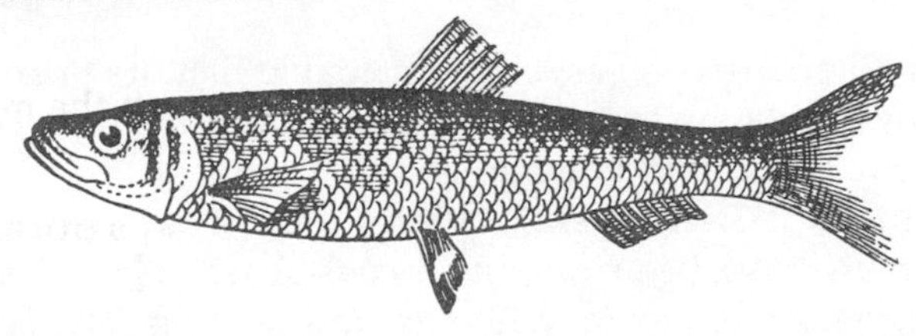

FIGURE 3-27
Herring – Hareng

Origin and occurrence: The herring lives in large schools in the Arctic Ocean, in the North Atlantic as far south as the Bay of Biscay, and in the North Sea and the Baltic. When spawning, herring migrates to warmer waters, and it is during this period that it is caught.
Species and description: The herring can be 16 inches long. It is a thin fish with silver scales, a blue-gray back, bluish sides, and a shiny, silver-white belly. In Norway, cases have been reported where herring have lived as long as 15 years. The five main types of herring are:

- *Norwegian herring* is a large fish usually over 12 inches long. Spawning is in the spring. Norwegian herring is caught the year round.
- *Scottish herring* is caught from the beginning of the summer through the fall.
- *Skagerrak herring* is caught in the fall and winter.
- *Yarmouth herring* is caught from October to December.
- *Iceland herring,* caught off the north of Iceland from July to September, is the largest and fattest.

Quality characteristics: The sea or fall herring is lean but flavorful. The coastal or spring herring is fat, but less desirable in taste. The following two groups of fish are distinguishable by age:

- *White (Matje) herring* is the virgin herring in which the roe and the milt have not yet formed (usually occur after two years). "Matje" means girl in Dutch, and in the context of the herring indicates that the fish is not yet sexually mature.

- *Full herring* is herring that is caught with the milt and roe before spawning.

The herring is an especially valuable fish. Its price is low in relation to its high fat and protein content. The flesh of the fish is white and delicate.

Usage: *"Green (fresh) herrings"* are those herrings which have been caught in coastal waters, and are primarily suited for sauteing and grilling. The surplus herring catch finds its way to the fish processor, where it is preserved in many different ways. The well-known methods of preserving herrings are:

- *Bismark herrings* have had the heads and bones removed and the flesh has been marinated in a mild vinegar solution seasoned with pepper, mustard seeds, bay leaves, and onions.
- *Collared herrings* are the skinned and pickled fillets rolled in black pepper, paprika, onions, and pickles. They are put on wooden skewers and placed in a mild vinegar solution.
- *Fried herrings* are made from green herrings that have had the head and guts removed and have been placed in vinegar. Fried collared herrings are made in the same way, except they are rolled before frying.
- *Bloaters* or *kippers* are salted and smoked herrings.

SARDINE—SARDINE

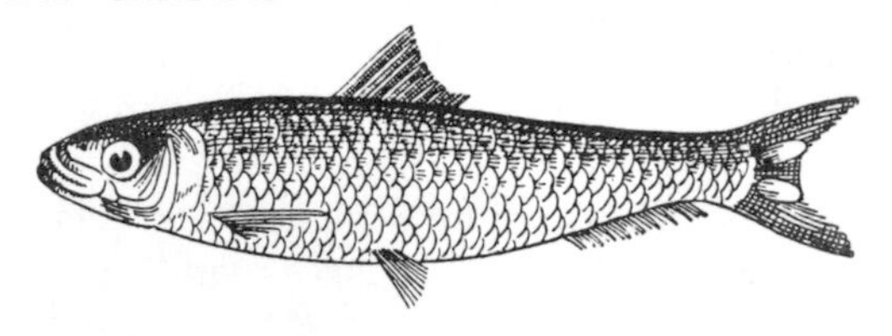

FIGURE 3-28
Sardine—Sardine

Origin and occurrence: The name "sardine" probably originated from the fact that tiny fish were first found around the island of Sardinia in the Mediterranean. The Maine sardine is a member of the Atlantic herring family.

Species and description: The sardine belongs to the herring family and is very similar to the herring, although considerably smaller. It reaches a length of 9 inches. A sardine is, in reality, a young *Pilchard,* a small fish from the herring family which is 9 to 10 inches long. The back is bluish-green, the belly white. The scales are fairly large. The only true sardines available on the market are those with a maximum length of 5 to 6 inches.

Quality characteristics: Sardines are rich in protein. They also contain iron, calcium, and phosphorus. Sardines are usually boiled and packed in oil, usually olive oil. The type of oil should be specified on the label. Maine sardines are packed in various types of oil and also in tomato and mustard sauces.

Usage: In coastal regions the sardine, or pilchard, is prepared fresh in many different ways including sauteing and grilling.The sardines which are 5 to 6 inches long are separated for use in the canning factories.

SPRAT—ESPROT

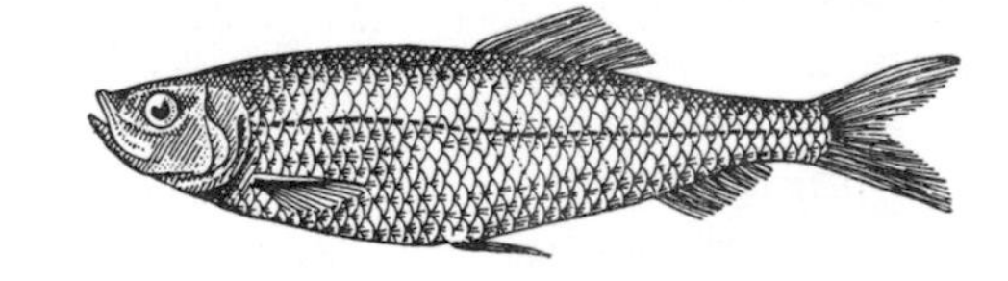

FIGURE 3-29
Sprat—Esprot

Origin and occurrence: The most important fishing grounds are off the Norwegian coast, in those parts of the North Sea bordering England, Belgium, Holland, Germany, and in the Baltic.

Species and description: The sprat belongs to the herring family and resembles a sardine. The maximum length is 7 inches. The back is darkish-blue in color, and the sides and belly are white.

Quality characteristics: The main catches occur during the winter months. The quality is best during November and December.

Usage: Sprats are usually smoked. The fresh fish are marinated with salt, sugar, spices, and herbs under controlled temperatures while they undergo a ripening process. Afterwards, they are packed in glass jars, cans, or small barrels. As semi-preserved, they are not sterilized and will keep for only a limited period of time.

The Mackerel Family

MACKEREL—MAQUEREAU

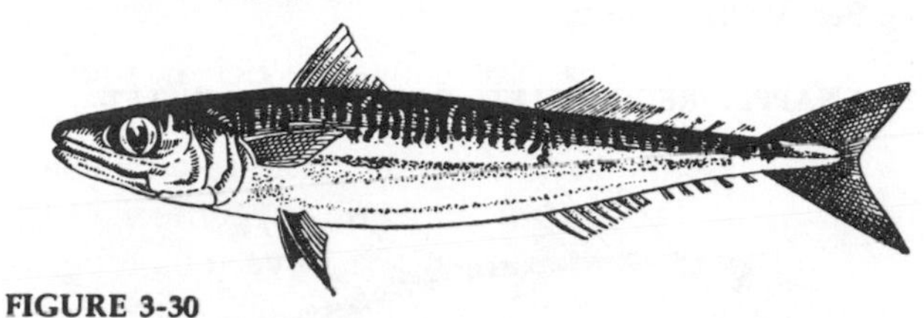

FIGURE 3-30
Mackerel—Maquereau

Origin and occurrence: This fish lives along the western European coasts and most are caught near the Scilly Isles off Cornwall, England, and the Iberian peninsula. They are hunting fish and swim deep down in the sea during the winter. In spring, they are found along the coast of the Gulf of Mexico from Florida to Texas. On the Pacific coast they range from San Diego, California, to the Galapagos Islands. During the spring, they are caught along with the herrings in large numbers by trawling nets.
Species and description: The mackerel is a very fast fish with a torpedo-shaped body, small scales, and changing colors, with green and blue predominating. Black zebra-like stripes cover the back and halfway down the sides. The lower half of the fish is white. Mackerel grow to a maximum length of 2 feet. The average size found on the market is 10 to 12 inches.
Quality characteristics: The reddish flesh of mackerel is of high quality in texture and flavor. Fresh mackerel is available only for a limited time because of the short fishing season. The fish are preserved to utilize the very large catches.
Usage: Fresh mackerel should be sauteed or grilled. Otherwise fillets of mackerel are preserved in oil, marinated, or prepared in sauce. Mackerel can also be cold or hot-smoked.

TUNA (TUNNY)—THON

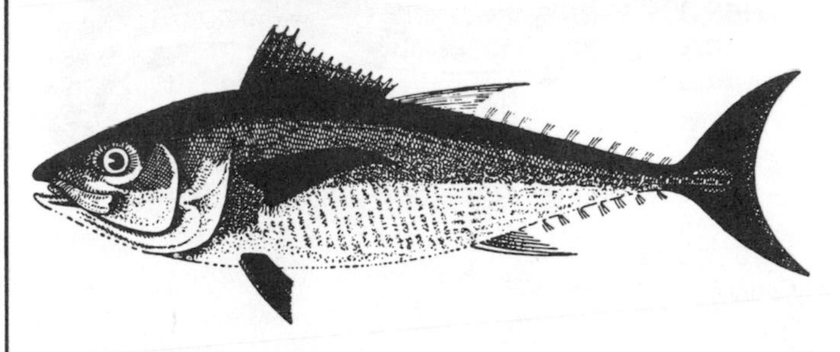

FIGURE 3-31
Tuna (tunny)—Thon

Origin and occurrence: The major seas are the home of the tuna fish, where, in springtime, it spawns along the coastlines. During this season, tuna is caught in huge numbers. It is also found in areas where herring is caught.
Species and description: Tuna, a member of the mackerel family, is a hunting fish. It grows to a length of 10 feet and to a maximum weight of one-half ton. The back is dark blue, and the sides are gray with silvery spots. Tuna are very strong, and they often break heavy-duty netting. For this reason they are difficult to catch.
Quality characteristics: The reddish flesh of the tuna is excellent, and it is prepared while still fresh in the fishing areas. The mode of preparation is similar to that of veal or young beef. In Germany, tuna is consumed either fresh or smoked. Italy, which constitutes one main fishing area, exports high quality *tonno* which is usually poached in olive oil. The United States, Portugal, Spain, Yugoslavia, France, and more recently, Peru and Japan also can tuna in oil. "White" meat is generally the preferred quality and this is achieved by blanching and cooking the fish in oil. Albacore has the lightest meat of all tuna.
Usage: Fresh tuna is sauteed, deep-fat fried, smoked or canned. Today tuna ranks as the number one seafood in the United States. Over a billion cans are consumed annually. It is available in solid-pack, chunk-style, or grated.

The Sea-Eel Family

CONGER EEL—CONGRE

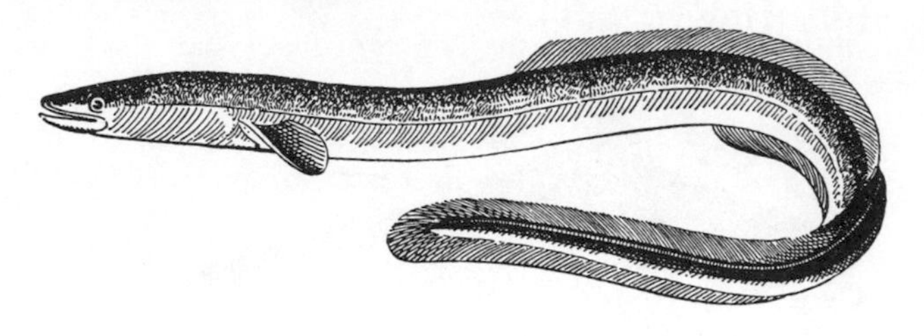

FIGURE 3-32
Conger eel—Congre

Origin and occurrence: This is strictly a marine fish found in Europe and America.
Species and description: The conger eel is a snake-like fish belonging to the family of bonefish. It lives in coastal waters, where it grows to a length of 8 or 10 feet, and it weighs about 85 pounds.
Quality characteristics: The flesh is full of bones and has little appeal for food.
Usage: The conger eel is rarely available at fish markets. It has limited use unless smoked.

The Gray Mullet Family

GRAY MULLET—MEUILLE

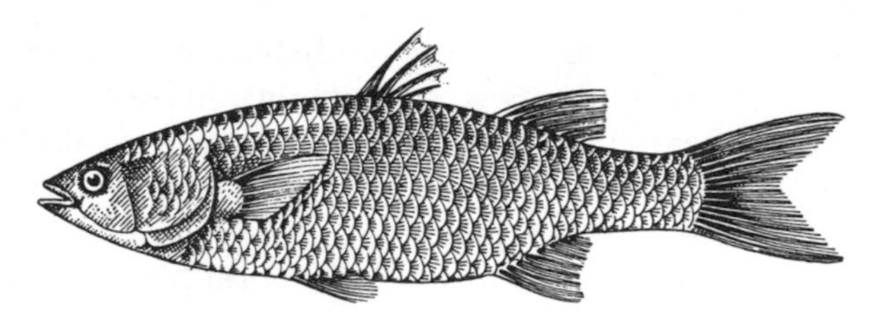

FIGURE 3-33
Gray Mullet—Meuille

Origin and occurrence: This fish is found along the Mediterranean and as far north as the English and Norwegian coastlines. It swims up river estuaries with the incoming tide.
Species and description: Gray mullet belongs to the salmonidae family, and reaches a length of approximately 16 inches. Although similar to the freshwater grayling, it has a fuller belly, a longer body, and large round scales. The mouth is wide and blunt. Very fine teeth line the edges of the jaws. The lower jaw has a hook-shaped prolongation which locks into the upper lip.
Quality characterisitcs: The flesh has a distinctive, savory flavor.
Usage: Favorite cooking methods for this fish are boiling, sauteing, grilling, and deep-fat frying.

The Sea-Mullet Family

RED SNAPPER/RED MULLET—ROUGET/SURMULLET

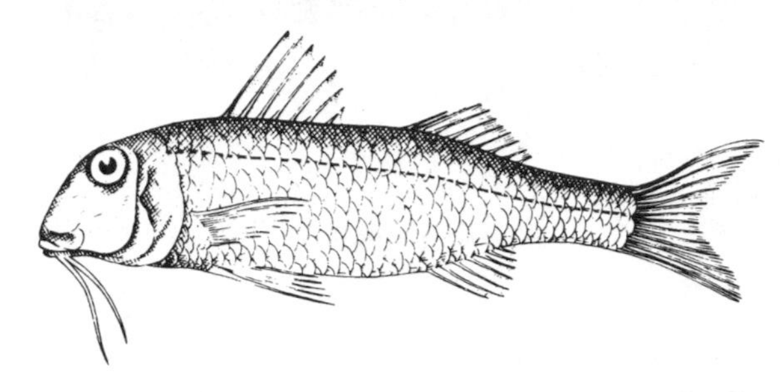

FIGURE 3-34
Red Snapper/Red Mullet—Rouget/Surmullet

Origin and occurrence: It is found along the Mediterranean coasts of France and Italy, together with their respective islands, and in the Gulf of Mexico and the South Seas.
Species and description: This fish belongs to the sea-mullet family and grows to an approximate length of 12 inches. Because it has no gall bladder, it is called the "snipe of the sea."
Quality characteristics: The flesh is white, delicate, and fine flavored.
Usage: Red snapper adapts to sauteing and grilling. Since it has no gall bladder, it is often prepared without removing the entrails.

The Hake Family

HAKE—COLIN

Origin and occurrence: Hake, also called sea-pike, is caught on both sides of the Atlantic Ocean and in the

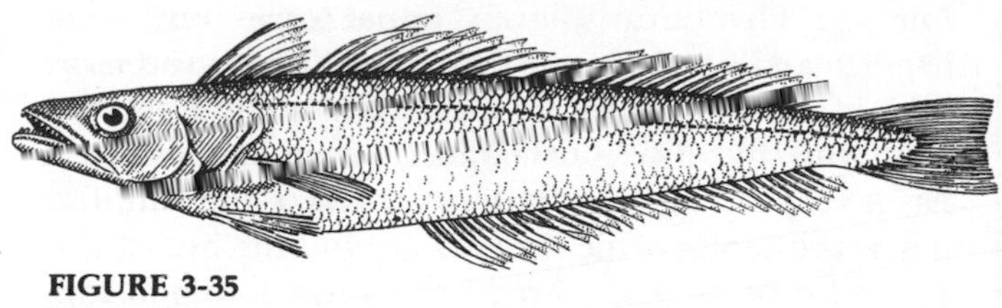

FIGURE 3-35
Hake—Colin

colder waters of the Southern Hemisphere.
Species and description: Hake is a thin fish with a pointed head. The lower jaw juts out somewhat. The back is gray-black with black spots. The sides are silvery-white and have a black line running the length of the fish. Although hake do grow to over 3 feet in length, the commercial size is between 1½ and 2½ feet.
Quality characteristics: The flesh is fine and white, and very sensitive to pressure, therefore, it should be covered with only a light layer of ice.
Usage: Hake may be prepared in several ways. The preferred method is to saute thin slices of the fish. It is abundant and inexpensive, and for this reason, it is often used in medium-sized establishments. Poached fillet of hake is also very good.

The Flatfish Family

BRILL—BARBUE

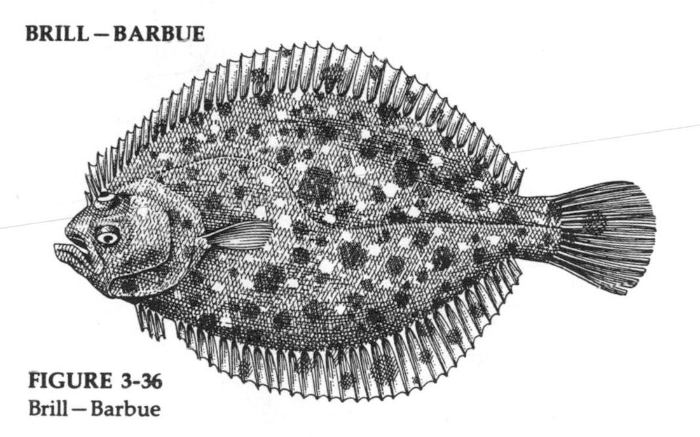

FIGURE 3-36
Brill—Barbue

Origin and occurrence: Brill are found along the coasts of the North Sea and the Baltic.
Species and description: The fish has an elliptical body and smooth skin. It grows to a length of 12 to 20 inches. The gray-brown upper side is covered with orange-colored spots.
Quality characteristics: The white, tasty flesh is highly prized.
Usage: The fish is best poached or deep-fat fried, since the flesh is too fragile for other preparations.

FLOUNDER—FLET

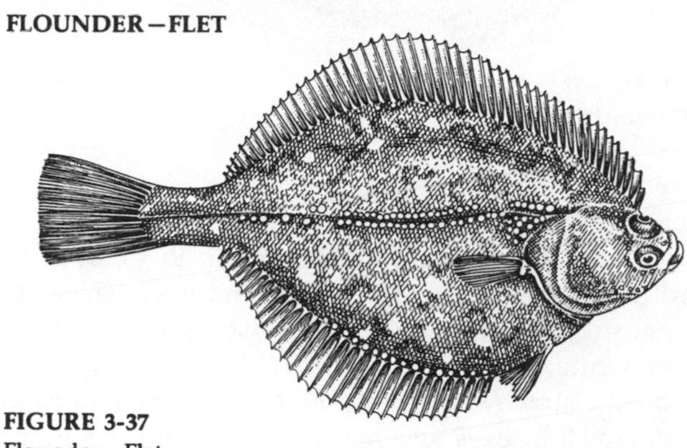

FIGURE 3-37
Flounder—Flet

Origin and occurrence: This fish, caught both in the North Sea and the Baltic, prefers the less salty Baltic. It migrates up rivers along the coasts bordering these two areas. It also is found along the Atlantic coast from the Gulf of St. Lawrence to New Jersey and in the Pacific from California to Alaska.
Species and description: The flounder, a very thin flatfish, grows up to 20 inches in length and weighs from ½ to 4½ pounds. The skin is brown with red and yellow spots on the top side. The belly is a yellowish-white color.
Quality characteristics: The good-flavored white flesh is similar to that of halibut.
Usage: Flounder is considered one of the finest edible fish. When fresh, it is suitable for poaching or deep-fat frying. It is also smoked.

HALIBUT—FLETAN

Origin and occurrence: Halibut is found in the Arctic Ocean, and is caught off Greenland, Iceland, and in the Barents Sea.
Species and description: Halibut, a very large member of the flatfish family, may grow to 6 feet in length

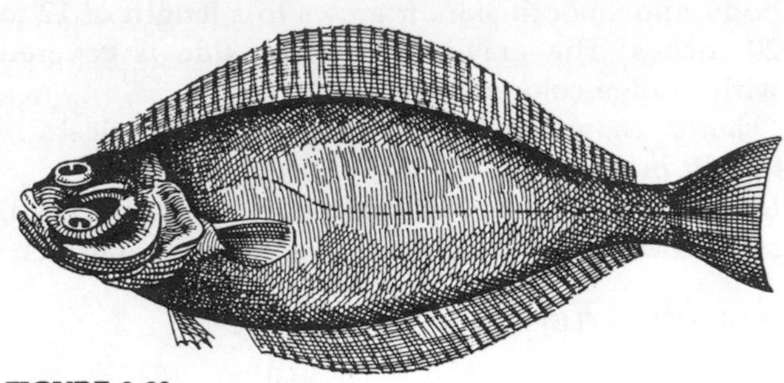

FIGURE 3-38
Halibut—Fletan

and weigh over 300 pounds. There are four commercial sizes: (a) 3¼ pounds to 6½ pounds, (b) 9 pounds to 18 pounds, (c) 22 pounds to 44 pounds, and (d) 55 pounds to 110 pounds and over. The head is pointed, the upperside is grayish-brown, and the belly white.

Quality characteristics: The flesh is white and mild in flavor. It freezes well and is suitable for use in institutional foodservice.

Usage: Similar to other large fish, halibut must be filleted or cut into slices before it is poached or deep-fat fried. All varieties of flatfish should be poached carefully and slowly over moderate heat to avoid overcooking and loss of protein.

LEMON SOLE, DAB—LIMANDE

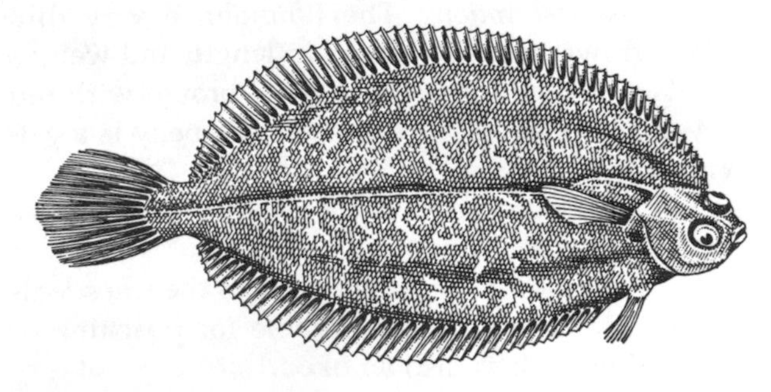

FIGURE 3-39
Lemon Sole, Dab—Limande

Origin and occurrence: This fish ranges from southern California to Alaska with the greatest abundance off the coast of New England.

Species and description: Lemon sole, a flatfish, resembles Plymouth sole in appearance, but it is heavier and has stronger fins. The skin of the lemon sole is more difficult to remove than that of the Plymouth sole. (See illustration on page 226.) This fish has a small head, a smooth skin, and a line running down the center which curves around the breast fin. The color of the fish is reddish-brown to blood red, with light and dark marbling. It grows to a length of 15 inches.

Quality characteristics: The flesh of the lemon sole has an excellent taste, but it is rather fragile and difficult to fillet.

Usage: Lemon sole may be deep-fat fried, sauteed, or poached.

PLAICE—PLIE

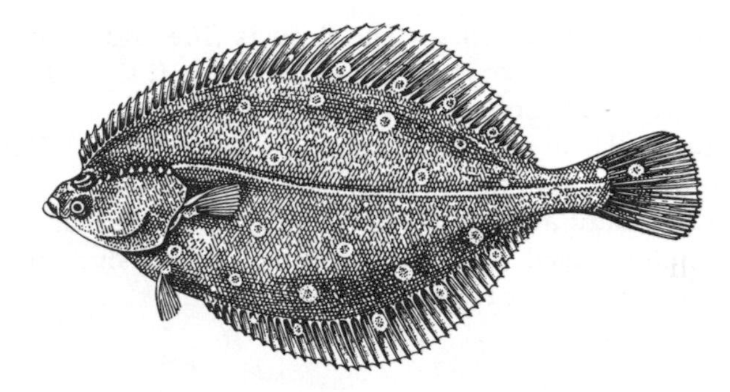

FIGURE 3-40
Plaice—Plie

Origin and occurrence: Plaice are found in the North Sea, the Baltic, the Barents Sea, and in the Atlantic. The flatfish family comprises some 200 different species, and each is called flounder or plaice.

Species and description: A member of the flatfish family, plaice do grow to 3 feet, but the smaller ones are preferred. The body is elliptical, the skin smooth. The upper side is gray-brown with round, reddish-yellow dots. The belly is yellowish-white.

Quality characteristics: Plaice are usually consumed when fresh. There are three commercial sizes: large (15 to 19 inches, weighing over 2 pounds), medium (10 to 13 inches, approximately ½ to ¼ pound), and sauteing plaice, which are the smallest. The flesh is very tasty.

Usage: It is usually filleted and poached or sauteed.

PLYMOUTH SOLE—SOLE

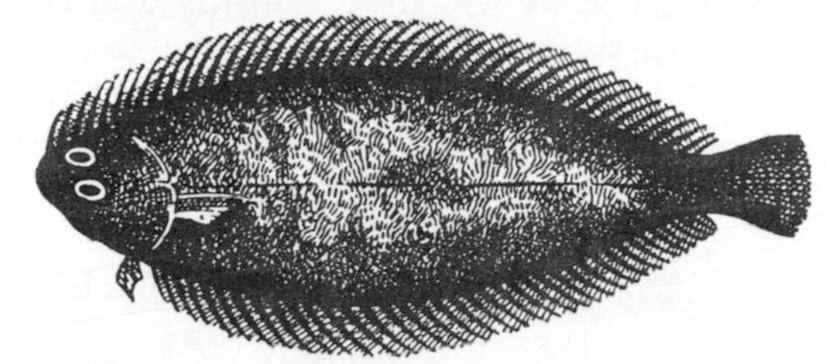

FIGURE 3-41
Plymouth Sole—Sole

Origin and occurrence: Sole live in all coastal waters off Europe, to the west of the Baltic Sea, and in some variation in all temperate and tropical seas.
Species and description: Plymouth sole is a member of the flatfish family, and grows to a length of 15 inches. It has a thin, flat body. The upper side is brown with small scales, and the belly is white.
Quality characteristics: Sole is one of the most esteemed of European fishes. The flesh of the Plymouth sole is the best and most delicious of all saltwater fish. Those coming from the ocean or the English Channel, usually called *Ostend soles,* are a light reddish-gray on the top side, have a great deal of flesh, and are preferred over the darker sole from the North Sea and Italian waters. The skin is easily removed.
Usage: Plymouth sole may be prepared in many different ways. Large sections of cookbooks are devoted to preparation ideas for Plymouth sole.

SAND DAB—CARRELET

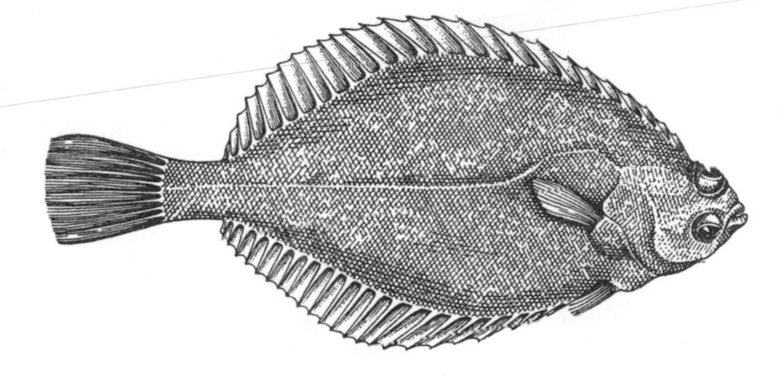

FIGURE 3-42
Sand Dab—Carrelet

Origin and occurrence: The main fishing areas are the Atlantic Ocean, the North Sea, and the Baltic.
Species and description: The sand dab is a flatfish also known as *Torbay sole.* Its body is thinner than that of the turbot, and it has small scales instead of the stone-like bony areas. The belly is glassy.
Quality characteristics: Sand dab is cheaper than turbot, but its flesh is lean, white, and tender.
Usage: It is good boiled, poached, or pan-fried.

TURBOT—TURBOT

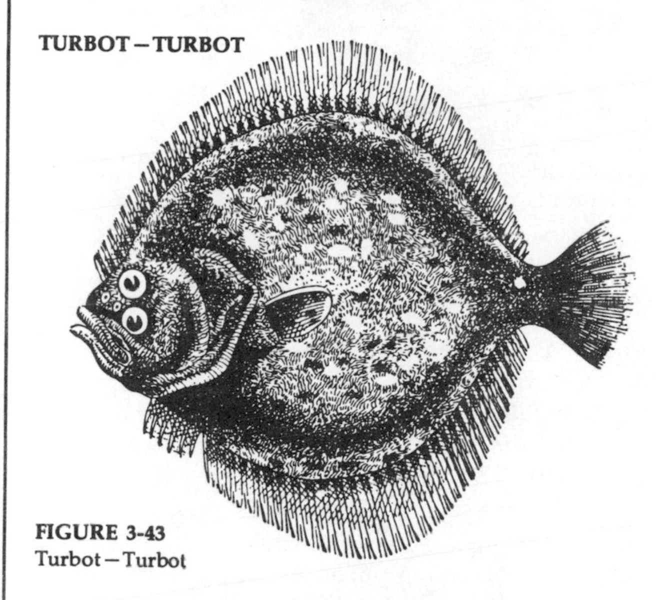

FIGURE 3-43
Turbot—Turbot

Origin and occurrence: Turbot lives in the Atlantic, in the North Sea, and in the Baltic.
Species and description: Turbot is a flatfish. Small turbots are called *turbotin.* In the North Sea and in the Baltic, turbot grows to a length of 15 inches, and in the Atlantic to 5 feet. Stone-like bony patches on the outside account for its characteristic appearance. The color is variegated brown with light specks. The belly is white. North Sea and Baltic turbot are rather dark, while those from the Atlantic are light in color.
Quality characteristics: Turbot is one of the favorite saltwater fish. The flesh is snow-white, very firm, and keeps well. It is at its best between April and September. The light-colored, medium-sized turbot from the Atlantic, also known as "Bologne turbot," is better than the darker variety from the North Sea and Baltic Sea.
Usage: Turbot is usually boiled, grilled, or poached.

The Ray Family

SKATE—RAIE

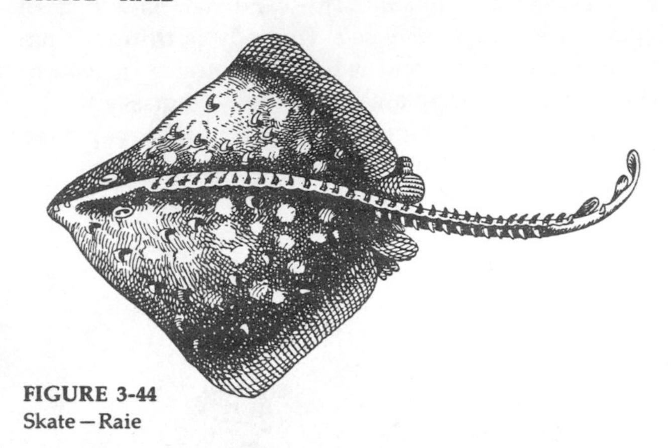

FIGURE 3-44
Skate—Raie

Origin and occurrence: The skate lives near the bottom of coastal waters and in the open sea. It is caught along the coast.
Species and description: Skate is a cartilaginous fish with a flat, disc-like body and usually a long, whip-shaped tail. The breast fins are merged with the body. There are several varieties of skates. Of the two main kinds (*stingrays* and *smooth skates*), the former is preferable for cooking purposes. The entire body of the stingray is covered with little thorn-like spines with large spines near the eyes and on the back and tail. It grows to a length of about 2½ feet. The smooth skate has a smooth skin, few spines, and a long, pointed jaw. Skates up to 10 feet long are not uncommon.
Quality characteristics: Only the wing-shaped sides of the body and the breast fins are usable for culinary purposes, therefore, there is a high proportion of waste. When fresh, skates are considered a real delicacy in France, Belgium, Holland, and Switzerland. The French term for stingrays is *Raie bouclee.*
Usage: Skate must be prepared while fresh, and the sauteing method of preparation is especially suitable. Before cooking, the fish must be properly brushed. After cooking, the skin should be removed, because it is often full of sand. It should be filleted before sauteing. Smoked skate is also very good.

3.2.2 Crustaceans, Shellfish and Mollusks—Crustaces, coquillages et mollusques

3.2.2.1 Crustaceans—Crustaces

The crustacean species consists of various types of lobsters, barnacles, shrimps, and crabs. They are characterized by their five pairs of jointed legs. The front pair is equipped with pincers or claws. The body is enclosed by a calcium secretion (hardened shell) which is shed from time to time during growth.

CRAB—CRABE

FIGURE 3-45
Crab—Crabe

Origin and occurrence: There are many different varieties, including the *spider crab, hermit crab, and fiddler crab.* In the United States three species of crabs dominate the fisheries. The *blue crab* from Atlantic waters contributes the largest share. The *dungeness crab* and the *king crab* from the Pacific coast and Alaska are also of major importance to the fishing industry. Soft-shell crabs are molting blue crabs that have shed their hard shells. Snow crabs, belonging to the family of spider crabs, are a new resource for crab meat. Crab lives along sea coasts, where it is caught in nets, pots, and various types of gear.
Species and description: These crabs belong to the short-tailed crustacean family.
Quality characteristics: The meat is fairly coarse in texture, rather tough, very perishable, and full of good flavor.
Usage: Crabs are cooked by steaming or boiling for hot and cold dishes. Soft-shell crabs may be sauteed or deep-fat fried. In the canning industry, crabs are processed into crab meat and crab extract. The canned meat may be used interchangeably in recipes specifying cooked crab meat.

CRAYFISH—ECREVISSE

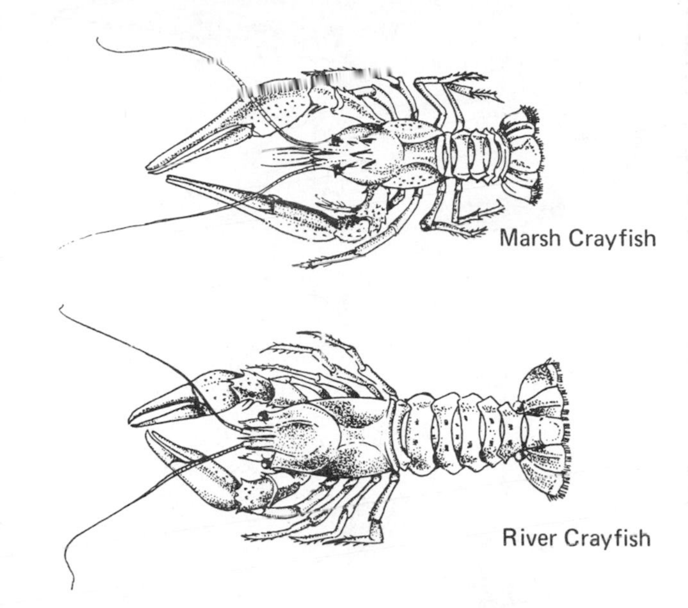

FIGURE 3-46
Crayfish—Ecrevisse (Marsh and River)

Origin and occurrence: Crayfish live in shallow, calcium-rich rivers, ponds, and lakes.
Species and description: A member of the crustacean family, the *river crayfish,* found in freshwater, is considered a "noble" crayfish. It is blackish-brown in color. There is also the *Galician pond* or *marsh crayfish.* This crayfish has a bluish-green color. The lower part of the pincers is white.
Quality characteristics: The noble crayfish tastes considerably better than the Galician crayfish. Crayfish are classified by size as soup crayfish, small, medium, large, and giant crayfish. The taste of its meat depends on the cleanliness of the water and the type of food the crayfish has been eating. Crayfish taste best during the summer months from May to August. The meat is juicy, delicate, and has a distinct sweet taste.
Usage: Only the tails of crayfish are marketed. There are hot and cold crayfish dishes which are complete in themselves. Crayfish are also used as garnishes for fish dishes and with hors-d'oeuvres.

LOBSTER—HOMARD

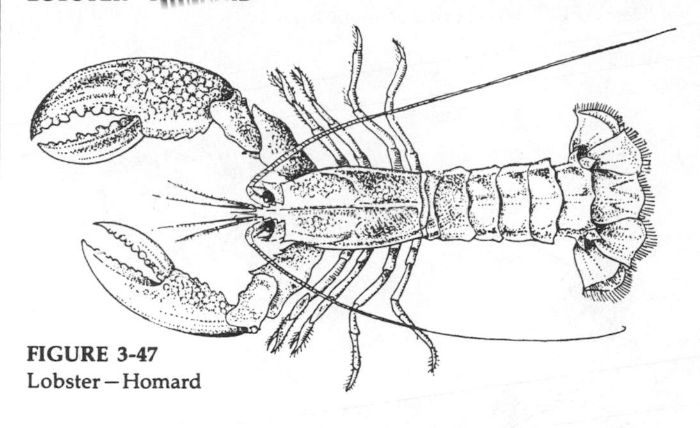

FIGURE 3-47
Lobster—Homard

Origin and occurrence: Lobster is found off the coast of the state of Maine in the United States; besides the Atlantic, it is found in the North Sea and the Mediterranean, but not in the Baltic Sea.
Species and description: Lobster belongs to the crustacean family. It is similar to a crayfish and has two pincers. It can grow to a length of 20 inches and weigh 4 pounds.
Quality characteristics: Lobster is a delicacy that is sold alive, boiled, or preserved. Beside the Maine lobster, the dark brown Swedish and Norwegian lobsters represent the best quality. Live lobsters must be protected against the heat and cold, and should be kept moist during transportation. The tail of a live lobster should be curled up tight and should also be elastic. Lobsters, like crayfish, are killed by plunging them into a container of boiling water. Cooked lobster meat and opened cans of lobster are highly perishable and must be consumed quickly. Dead lobsters develop a fish toxin and must not be used.
Usage: Lobster is used for hot and cold dishes. To cut a lobster, see pages 230, 231.

SCAMPO LOBSTER—SCAMPO/LANGOUSTINE

Origin and occurrence: Scampo is the popular Italian term for the Norwegian lobster found in the Mediterranean, and frequently along Danish and Norwegian coasts.

FIGURE 3-48
Scampo Lobster—Scampo/langoustine

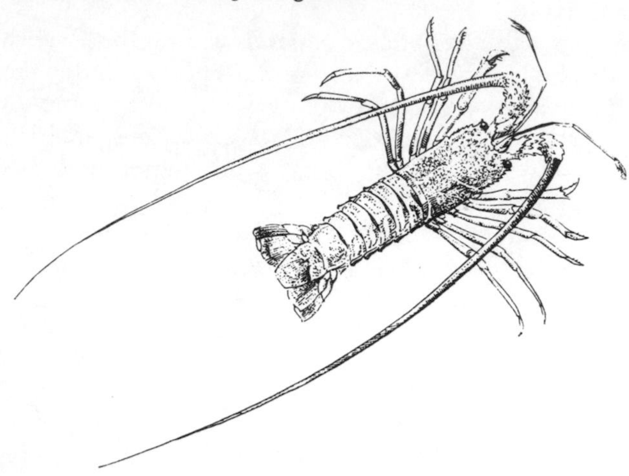

Species and description: A type of small lobster, scampo is pink in color and grows to about 8 inches in length.
Quality characteristics: The meat corresponds to that of lobster.
Usage: It is usually deep-fat fried, grilled, or boiled.

SHRIMP—CREVETTE
Origin and occurrence: Shrimps are found along all sandy coastlines.
Species and description: A shrimp is a small sea creature belonging to the long-tailed crustacean family. It has a slightly compressed body with long feelers and ten feet, but it does not have pincers. Shrimps grow to between 1½ and 3½ inches. The common varieties are: white or common; brown or grooved; pink or coral; red or royal. Prawns are large shrimp, and the term usually refers to jumbo Gulf shrimp.
Quality characteristics: The meat is tasty, but very perishable. This is the reason fresh shrimps are only obtainable near the coast. In most cases they are boiled directly on board the fishing boats.
Usage: Shrimps are available in most areas of the United States either raw or cooked, peeled or unpeeled, and fresh or frozen. After boiling, the shrimps' tails are removed from their shells and either deep-frozen or sterilized in cans or jars. They can then be used in many different ways as hors-

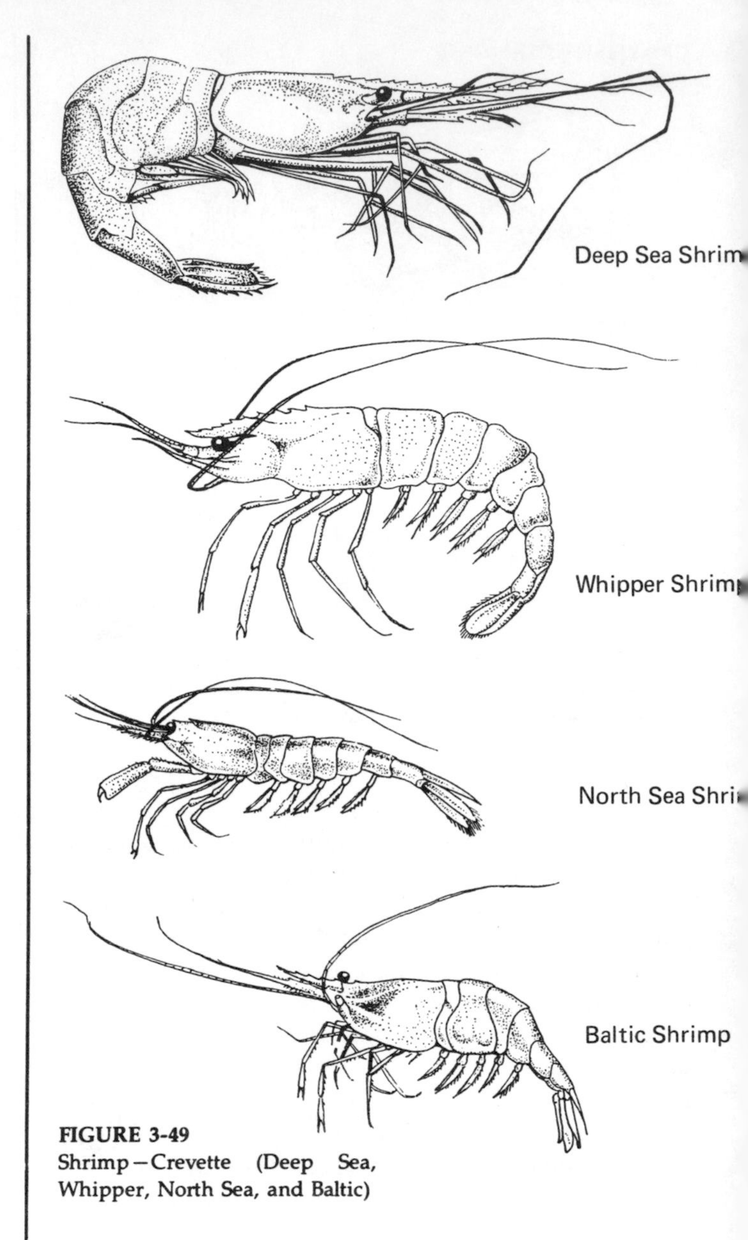

FIGURE 3-49
Shrimp—Crevette (Deep Sea, Whipper, North Sea, and Baltic)

d'oeuvres, garnishes, soups, salads, and deep-fat fried.

SPINY LOBSTER (ROCK LOBSTER)—LANGOUSTE
Origin and occurrence: Spiny lobsters are most frequently found in the Mediterranean, but also along the coast of England, Ireland, South West Africa

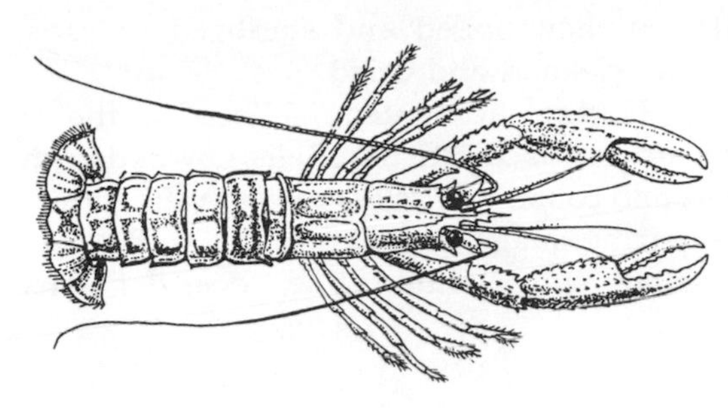

FIGURE 3-50
Spiny Lobster (Rock Lobster)—Langouste

(Cape crawfish), the Pacific coast of the United States, the east coast of Florida, and the Gulf of Mexico.
Species and description: The spiny lobster is a crustacean with long feelers, spines over the head and breast, but without pincers. It is reddish-violet in color with yellow speckles. It can grow to about 20 inches in length and weigh 13 pounds.
Quality characteristics: While still alive or when cooked, the strong tail of the spiny lobster must be curled. Those with stretched tails are not good. Since there are no claws, the spiny lobster tail is the main edible portion. The tail is removed, cleaned, and washed. It is then frozen either raw or cooked. The spiny lobster becomes red when boiled. The meat is very tasty, but drier than that of lobster.
Usage: Spiny lobster can be used for both hot and cold dishes. When boiling for cold dishes, the body must be fixed on to a piece of wood. For hot dishes, the lobster should be plunged, head first, into boiling water.

3.2.2.2 Mollusks—Coquillages et Mollusques

Mollusks have no vertebrae. Most live in the sea, although some do live in fresh water or on the land.

MUSSELS—MOULES
Origin and occurrence: Beside the *scallop* and *the clam* (*Coquille St. Jacques*), the *sea mussel* is the most important edible mussel. It is found along the European and American coasts. Mussels are bred along the Dutch coast, and form huge natural banks in the shallows between the East Fresian Islands and the mainland.
Species and description: Mussels are mollusks with two shells (bivalve) that open. They live under the water. *Sea mussels* are oval, dark blue to lilac-brown in color, and inside whitish-blue. *Clams* are flat, sometimes larger than oysters and have attractive grooved shells.
Quality characteristics: Mussels must always be closed, have a fresh sea smell, and should open only when exposed to heat. The color should be uniform. Live mussels should be clean and free from sand when sold. When purchasing mussels, at least half should be over two inches long.
Usage: When cold, mussels may be marinated or served in a jelly. Hot, they are eaten plain or may be used as a garnish for fish dishes, and fish pies. Mussels must be properly cleaned to be completely free of sand.

OYSTER—HUITRE

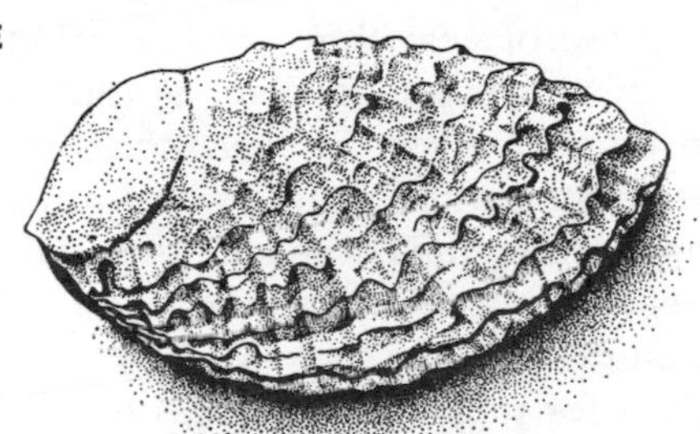

FIGURE 3-51
Oyster—Huitre

Origin and occurrence: Oysters exist along all the coasts of Europe and the United States, and are appreciated as a great delicacy. Normally they grow in large numbers on rocks, supporting piles, and other objects. At river estuaries, so-called artificial oyster beds are laid out. A good flow of fresh water into these oyster beds improves the taste of the oysters. The best known oysters come from the Baltic, the Dutch coast, from Whitstable, Triest, Venice, and, of course, the Atlantic coast of the United States.
Species and description: Oysters are mollusks. The lower shell has a concave, bowl-like shape while the upper shell is flatter. Outside the shells are rough, inside smooth. The age of the oyster can be seen by the number of layers on the shell.

Quality characteristics: Oysters are of commercial interest when over three to four years and are caught from September to April. All months with an "r" in their name are considered good months for oysters. Oysters gathered between May and August are rather tasteless and spoil easily. Oysters are identified by the surface of the oyster bed—whether it is rock, sand, or clay. Rock oysters are the best. When sold, the country of origin is normally quoted. In Europe, English oysters are considered to be the best. Oysters taken from the Atlantic, from Canada to Texas, are known as Eastern oysters. The Olympia, a small delicately flavored oyster, is found in Puget Sound. The giant Japanese oyster is taken from the waters of the Pacific. Size and uniformity are the criteria for the classification of oysters: imperial, first class, and second class. These categories are also expressed in zeroes: two zeroes refers to the imperial oysters, four refers to the first class, and six to the second class. Oysters vary in size, texture, and flavor according to the time of year they are harvested. When buying, the oysters must be alive, as indicated by a tightly-closed shell. *Oysters in open shells are dead and unfit to eat.* In the United States oysters must come from beds approved by the United States Public Health Service.
Usage: Oysters are a nutritious delicacy. They are consumed raw or cooked. They are used in soups, as filling for pies, in stews, and in stuffings. They may be served raw on the half shell, as appetizers, baked on the half shell, or deep-fat fried. The oyster stew from Boston is known all over the world.

SNAIL—ESCARGOT
Origin and occurrence: The two main types of edible snails are the *land snails* and the *marsh snails.* The former are bred in Europe, while the latter are found in stagnant water in Europe and North America.
Species and description: Snails are mollusks. They differ from mussels in that they are not bivalve and they have a head.
Quality characteristics: Snails seal themselves in during the fall season just before the first frosts. They are at their prime at this time. Snail canning factories purchase land snails throughout the summer and keep them until the fall in so-called snail farms. The snails are then boiled and sterilized in cans. The shells are cleaned and dried.
Usage: During the winter snail season, the canned snails are put back into the shells, covered with herb butter, and consumed as *Burgundy Snails.* Other ways of preparing snails include: on the spit, as a salad, marinated with white wine, deep-fat fried, or sauteed.

TURTLE—TORTUE
Origin and occurrence: There are two varieties—the land *tortoise* (terrapin) and the aquatic *turtle.* More often used for cooking purposes, turtles are found in the seas throughout the hot and sub-tropical regions of the world.
Species and description: Zoologically, tortoises and turtles belong to the reptile family. They have very strong protective shells on the back and the breast. The back is used for tortoise-shell articles.
Quality characteristics: The meat is a delicacy. Turtle meat and fat are dried or frozen at the location of the catch.
Usage: Turtles are used for making soup. They can also be made into stews or fricassees, if prepared immediately after the turtle is caught.

3.2.3 Meat

The term "meat" as used in this text refers to fresh meat only—all animals or parts of animals used as food for human consumption. This includes muscles with the attached tissues, fat, fresh blood, and glandular meats (edible organs and glands). Glandular meats include the tongue, kidney, heart, brain, liver, and pancreas (sweetbread), and the walls of the stomach (tripe). With the exception of chilling, these have not been prepared, processed, preserved nor undergone any other type of treatment.

Frozen Meat
Frozen meat refers to meat that has been preserved through storage at low temperatures. Storing meats at temperatures ranging from 0°F. to 32°F. (-18°C. to 0°C.) inhibits the activity of enzymes and bacteria.

TABLE 3-1. Storage Time Chart*
(Maximum Storage Time Recommendations for Fresh, Cooked, and Processed Meats†)

Meat	Refrigerator (38° to 40°F) (3° to 4°C)	Freezer (at 0°F or lower) (−18°C or lower)
Beef (fresh)	2 to 4 days	6 to 12 months
Veal (fresh)	2 to 4 days	6 to 9 months
Pork (fresh)	2 to 4 days	3 to 6 months
Lamb (fresh)	2 to 4 days	6 to 9 months
Ground beef, veal, and lamb	1 to 2 days	3 to 4 months
Ground pork	1 to 2 days	1 to 3 months
Variety meats	1 to 2 days	3 to 4 months
Luncheon meats	1 week	not recommended
Sausage, fresh pork	1 week	60 days
Sausage, smoked	3 to 7 days	
Sausage, dry and semi-dry (unsliced)	2 to 3 weeks	
Frankfurters	4 to 5 days	
Bacon	5 to 7 days	
Smoked hams, whole	1 week	60 days
Smoked ham, slices	3 to 4 days	
Beef, corned	1 week	2 weeks
Leftover cooked meat	4 to 5 days	2 to 3 months
Frozen combination foods		
Meat pies (cooked)	--	3 months
Swiss steak (cooked)	--	3 months
Stews (cooked)	--	3 to 4 months
Prepared meat dinners	--	2 to 6 months

* *Lessons on Meat,* National Live Stock and Meat Board.
† The range in time reflects recommendations for maximum storage time from several authorities. For top quality, fresh meats should be used in two or three days, ground meat and variety meats should be used in 24 hours.

The lower the temperature, the longer the meat can be stored without affecting the quality. Lean meats properly wrapped in good quality paper and stored at zero or lower temperatures will keep well for six to eight months.[2] The maximum storage times for fresh, cooked, and processed meats are shown in Table 3-1.

Processed Meats

These are foods which have been treated with various methods of preservation and/or cooking such as salting, smoking, drying, roasting, boiling, and canning. Sausages, canned meats, meat marinades, meat pies, meat pates, hams, and bacon are a few examples.

2. *Lessons on Meat,* 4th ed. (Chicago: National Livestock and Meat Board, 1974) p. 60.

All food products derived from meat, even though no longer in the form of tissue structure, are subject to government regulations.

Keeping Quality

The following factors determine the keeping quality of the meat:

- the species of animal
- the quality of the animal feed
- the health of the animal
- the treatment before slaughtering
- the sanitation in slaughterhouse, packing plant, and foodservice facility
- the bleeding and skinning processes
- the chilling process of the slaughtered carcass
- the sanitation, temperature, and the condition of meat cutting and processing areas
- the sanitation of equipment and implements or utensils
- the conditions of the distribution system
- the temperature controls of all work, distribution, and storage areas

Beef and mutton dry out on the surface easily and quickly and, for this reason, keep longer than veal or pork. On the other hand, the surface fat may become rancid when exposed to light and oxygen.

Any form of moisture which is in contact with meat impairs its appearance and reduces the keeping quality.

Recommended temperatures and storage times for fresh, cooked, and processed meats are shown in Table 3-1. Microorganisms that can cause food-borne illnesses and infections grow at temperatures between 40°F. and 140°F. (4°C. to 60°C.). Since meat serves as a good medium for growth of organisms, storage temperatures should be below 40°F. (4°C.). Storage at temperatures between 30°F. and 32°F. (−3°C. and 0°C.) is the most effective for controlling the quality of meat. At this temperature the development of molds and bacteria will be inhibited for a limited period of time. Meat that is to be stored for a longer period should be stored at 0°F. (−18°C.) or lower. It should be wrapped tightly in a good quality paper that is greaseproof, vaporproof, and moistureproof. The drugstore method of wrapping provides the best air seal. (See Fig 3-51A.)

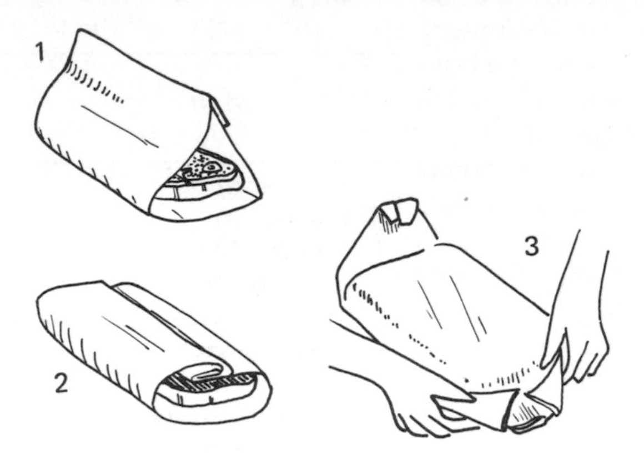

FIGURE 3-51A
Drugstore Wrap

The drugstore or lock-seal wrap is made by placing the food on the center of a sheet of paper large enough so that the ends can be brought together and folded as shown in drawing (1). The paper is folded down taut against the food making an interlocking seam as shown in drawing (2). The package is then turned over so that the seam lies on the table. A pleat fold is then made on one open end and another fold is made before pressing the folded end against the package. The package is then turned so the folded end is braced against the body as shown in drawing (3). Excess air is pressed out of the package, and the other open end is folded. The package is then sealed with freezer tape.

Composition of Meat

The gross structure of carcasses and cuts of animals consists of the edible lean or muscular tissue, the fat in and around the muscles, the bones, and the connective tissue, or gristle, that binds the muscle fibers together. The muscle tissue, the most important meat constituent, contains about 70 percent water, 20 percent protein, 9 percent fat, and 1 percent ash. As the animal is fattened, some of the water and protein of the lean is replaced by fat in the form of marbling. Marbling is the fine network or veins of fat in the muscle fibers. Marbling increases the palatability, juiciness, and tenderness of the meat. Connective tissue contributes to the toughness of the meat. The greater the content of connective tissues, the tougher the meat. The bone aids in identifying the age of the animal and the cut of the meat. Nitrogenous extractives are also found in lean meat. The extractives and the fat are largely responsible for the aroma and flavor of the meat.

The composition of the meat is directly dependent upon the condition of the animal at the moment of slaughtering. Careless handling at this stage may cause spoilage. Meat has a very high moisture content and, therefore, microorganisms can thrive unless high standards of sanitation, cleanliness, temperature, and humidity controls are maintained.

Preparation of Meat

Meat cutting requires skill. The meat cutter must know something of the anatomy of animals and the methods of fabrication. The ability to identify the characteristics of the muscles and the tissues between them, the shape and type of bones, and the location of the layers of fat will help the meat cutter perform his tasks. An understanding of preparation methods for the various cuts of meat is necessary for the person preparing the meat. Proper use of tools and equipment and a knowledge of safety and sanitation practices will protect both the worker and the consumer.

Slaughtered Meat

This term refers to the meat of hogs, cattle, and sheep. Dependent upon the quality, the percentage of bone should not exceed 20 to 25 percent of the carcass weight. Meat carcasses must be thoroughly chilled after slaughtering. To preserve the quality and wholesomeness, meat should be packaged in airproof and moistureproof containers.

Meat Inspection and Grading

Federal inspection and grading provide protection and many benefits to consumers, farmers, processors, and distributors. Meat inspection is a federal requirement in every packinghouse or processing plant in the United States. Rigid standards of processing under sanitary conditions are enforced. Federally inspected meat is marked with a round stamp which reads, "US Insp'd and P'S'D" (United States Inspected and Passed), and indicates fitness for human consumption. (See Fig. 3-52.)

Grading is a voluntary process. A packer may choose whether he wants meat in his plant federally graded. The United States Department of Agriculture through its Federal Grading Branch provides uniform standards to help the producers, packers, distributors, and consumers measure the differences between grades for price/quality comparisons. After the grade has been determined, the official shield identifying the specific grade is stamped with a roller device over the full length of the carcass. USDA initials and the designated grade appear inside the shield. (See Fig 3-53.)

Determining the Quality of Beef

The color of young top-quality lean beef should be bright cherry red. The meat of more mature beef will be a darker shade of red. The sirloin and shortloin should be sheathed with a thick layer of light-colored fat. Top quality beef will be marbled with veins of light-colored fat throughout the tender muscles. The meat should be "aged" for ten to fourteen days before cooking, especially meats that are to be used for roasts or steaks. Meat that is to be boiled requires only four to eight days of "aging."

The wholesale primal loin is composed of two subprimals, the sirloin and the shortloin. The wholesale weight of the sirloin subprimal approximates 5 percent of the live weight and 8 percent of the carcass weight. The sirloin may be cut into steaks that will equal about 3 percent of the live weight and 5 percent of the carcass weight. The top sirloin muscle may be stripped out and used as a boneless top sirloin roast or cut into top sirloin steaks. The wholesale weight of the shortloin subprimal equals about 4 percent of the live weight and 7 percent of the carcass weight. Steaks from the shortloin are porterhouse, T-bone, top-loin, or club. In another method of fabrication, the tenderloin muscle is removed from inside the shortloin and process as a fillet or cut in-

FIGURE 3-52
U.S. Government Inspection Stamps

This inspection stamp appears on meat products that have passed federal inspection standards. The number indicates the official number assigned to the processor.

U.S.
INSPECTED
AND PASSED BY
DEPARTMENT OF
AGRICULTURE
EST. 38

This mark appears on every processed meat or meat product that has been federally inspected.

INSPECTED
FOR WHOLESOMENESS
BY
U.S.
DEPARTMENT OF
AGRICULTURE
P-42

Assurance of Wholesomeness

Assurance of the Quality or Grade of Poultry

These marks are used on fresh or frozen poultry or processed poultry products that have been federally inspected and graded.

Courtesy U.S. Department of Agriculture

to steaks including the chateaubriand, filet mignon, tournedo, and tenderloin tip.[3]

There are two kinds of grading for beef. One is Quality Grading, the other is Yield Grading. (See Figs. 3-53 and 3-53A.) Quality Grading is based on palatability characteristics: tenderness, juiciness, and flavor. Yield Grading measures the amount of meat a carcass yields. The Yield Grades are numbered from 1 to 5. Yield Grade No. 1 has the greatest percentage of meat compared to fat and bone on the carcass and Yield Grade No. 5 has the lowest percentage. All graded beef will be graded for both quality and yield.[4]

There are eight "quality" grades for beef. Each is a measure of a distinct level of quality—*USDA Prime, USDA Choice, USDA Good, USDA Standard, USDA Commercial, USDA Utility, USDA Cutter,* and *USDA Canner.*

USDA Prime, the highest grade, is produced in limited quantities for use in fine hotels, restaurants, and specialty stores. This beef is well-marbled which

3. John R. Romans and P. Thomas Ziegler, *The Meat We Eat,* 10th ed. (Danville, Ill.: The Interstate Printers and Publishers, Inc., 1974), pp. 456, 461, 466.

4. *Background Report on Beef Grading* (Chicago: National Live Stock and Meat Board, 1976), pp. 7-8.

FIGURE 3-53
Stamps of U.S. Grades for Meat Quality and Yields (Courtesy of U.S. Department of Agriculture.)

enhances both flavor and juiciness. It has a thick covering of firm creamy white fat, and it is most suitable for aging. The USDA standards were revised in 1976, which resulted in reducing the marbling requirements in Prime and Choice grades. Consumers are now getting leaner beef than under the previous standards.

USDA Choice is generally the most popular grade in retail markets. The meat is tender, juicy, and well-marbled with less fat than Prime.

Both USDA Good and Standard are considered to be "economy beef." Some markets may sell this quality of beef under a brand name rather than under the USDA grade name. There is less shrinkage because of the lower fat content. *Good* is quite tender but lacks the flavor and tenderness of *Prime* and *Choice*.

USDA Standard has as a high proportion of lean meat and a small amount of fat. It lacks the flavor and tenderness of the higher grades.

USDA Commercial is produced from mature animals. It has a rich, full flavor but requires long, slow cooking to make it tender.

USDA Utility, Cutter, and Canner grades lack the palatability characteristics of the higher grades. These grades are wholesome, nutritious, and economical and are suitable for ground and manufactured items.

Determining the Quality of Veal

A *vealer* is defined by the United States Department of Agriculture as an immature bovine animal three months of age, or younger, that has been fed on milk or milk replacements. The color of its lean meat is light grayish pink. A *calf* is defined as an immature bovine animal, three to eight months of age that has been fed in part, or wholly, on feeds other than milk. The typical color of the lean meat of the calf is grayish red.

Veal has a high moisture content and a very thin covering of fat, therefore, it has a short storage life and should be refrigerated at temperatures between 30°F. and 36°F. (−3°C. and 2°C.) for no longer than five or six days. The same method used for cutting beef into retail cuts is used for cutting veal. (See Figures 3-56 and 3-61.) The name of the retail cut is preceded by the term veal to differentiate it from beef, lamb, and pork. Veal kidneys should be completely embedded in fat. The flesh of top quality veal is firm, smooth, and fine-grained. The fat is somewhat soft and pliable, and the rib bones are a bright red color. The best veal is delicately flavored. The meat of the very lightweight animals has a tendency to be watery and lacks flavor while the very heavyweight veal or calf may lack the delicate flavor of top quality veal. The grade of veal is determined by a composite evaluation of conformation and quality. The depth and thickness of flesh, the amount of feathering (fat which is interlaced with lean between the ribs), the amount and type of kidney and pelvic fat, the amount and quality of external fat, and the texture of the lean flesh are factors that influence the evaluation.[5] The USDA Grades for veal are: *USDA Prime, USDA Choice, USDA Good, USDA Standard,* and *USDA Utility.*

5. Romans and Ziegler, *The Meat We Eat*, pp. 456 and 461.

Determining the Quality of Pork

Pork ranks next to beef in the quantity consumed by the American public. Grades are based on quality of the meat and on carcass yields of the four lean cuts identified as ham, loin, picnic, and Boston butt.

The flesh should be whitish pink in color, fine-textured, and firm with fat distributed throughout. Pork should be hung three to four days before use. The four grades based on expected yields of the four lean cuts are: *USDA No. 1, USDA No. 2, USDA No. 3, USDA No. 4,* and *USDA Utility.*

Determining the Quality of Mutton and Lamb

The flesh of sheep between three and five months is called *baby lamb;* from five months to a year it is called *lamb. Mutton* is the term used for flesh from sheep over twenty months.

Lamb carcasses usually weigh between 35 and 65 pounds. The flesh of lamb is lighter in color than that of beef. Mutton flesh is darker. The lean meat of good quality lamb and mutton has a fine, velvet-like texture; the fat is very firm, brittle, and white. The cut surface of the bones is porous and a reddish color.

Lamb and mutton are good sources of phosphorous which is important in its reactions with other nutrients to produce energy and to build and repair tissues.

Lamb and mutton are graded on quality and yield. The USDA standards for quality are based on conformation, color and firmness of lean and fat, and texture or grain of flesh. The yield grades reflect differences in the yields of boneless, closely trimmed retail cuts, and in the over-all fatness of carcasses and cuts. Yield grade 1 represents the highest yield of retail cuts and grade 5 represents the lowest yield.[6]

The quality grades for lamb and yearling mutton are *US Prime, US Choice, US Good, US Utility,* and *US Cull.* For mutton the grades are *US Choice, US Good, US Utility* and *US Cull.* Prime and Choice are the grades used most extensively in institutions.

6. U.S. Department of Agriculture, Consumer and Marketing Service Livestock Division, *Institutional Meat Purchase Specifications for Fresh Lamb and Mutton—Series 200* (Washington, D.C., November 1968).

Some of the best quality lamb comes from New Zealand and Australia. Kirton and Jury have reviewed the grading of New Zealand lamb and mutton carcasses for export (Proc. N.Z. Soc. Animal Prod. 30:130,1970). They reported that overfat lambs were "hidden amongst the Primes." The authors concluded that the New Zealand Prime grade should be divided into two grades, one grade to include the overfat carcasses and the other the leaner, better cutting carcasses. The study is of significance in the United States, as the adoption of these recommendations would perhaps result in the importation of leaner and better yielding carcasses.

3.2.3.1 Sausages—Charcuterie

Sausage is one of the oldest processed foods. Over the centuries secret formulas for combinations of meat, spices, herbs, and other ingredients have been handed down from charcutiers, chefs, and families throughout the world developing sausage making into an art rather than a science.

Today there are over 250 varieties available in the United States alone. Sausage production has become very profitable in the meat packing industry. Over 3.8 billion pounds of sausage products are processed in federally inspected plants each year. This is equivalent to 18.4 pounds per person annually.[7]

Federal meat inspection regulations control the ingredients that can be used in sausage products. Only meats that have been federally inspected and approved should be used. The inspection stamp of wholesomeness should be on the products or their packaging.

The differences in the varieties depends on the kind of meat and ingredients used, the combination of the ingredients, the coarseness of the grind, the type of casing, the shape, and whether the product is raw, cooked, dried, smoked, canned, or pickled. Pork, veal, and beef are the meats used in sausages. Fat back, trimmings, jowls, and the lean meat from pork; shoulders, and shanks from veal; and boneless chucks, plate, shank, briskets, heart, liver, and blood of beef are all suitable for sausage products. Federal

7. Romans and Ziegler, *The Meat We Eat,* p. 531.

regulations permit the addition of liquid, fat, additives, and extenders in specified amounts.

The spices, whether in liquid or dry form, should be of excellent quality. Natural spices should be sterilized to prevent bacteria contamination of the meat. Ground pepper, peppercorns, paprika, red pepper, cardamon, cinnamon, and sage are but a few of the spices used. Onions, garlic, parsley, capers, pistachio, truffles, and anchovies are added in varying amounts to import special flavors to many varieties.

Adequate equipment and general conditions such as temperature and humidity controls, refrigeration, and storage facilities are necessary for efficient high quality sausage production. After the sausage is prepared it is stuffed mechanically into a casing. Natural casings are the intestines of cattle, hogs, and sheep. The stomach and bladder are also used to encase some sausage products. While natural casings are generally preferred, synthetic and collagen casings are widely used. The method of sausage production will, in some instances, influence the type of casing.

The classifications generally recognized are:

Fresh sausage is ground raw meat, such as pork sausage, in the form of links or patties or in bulk;

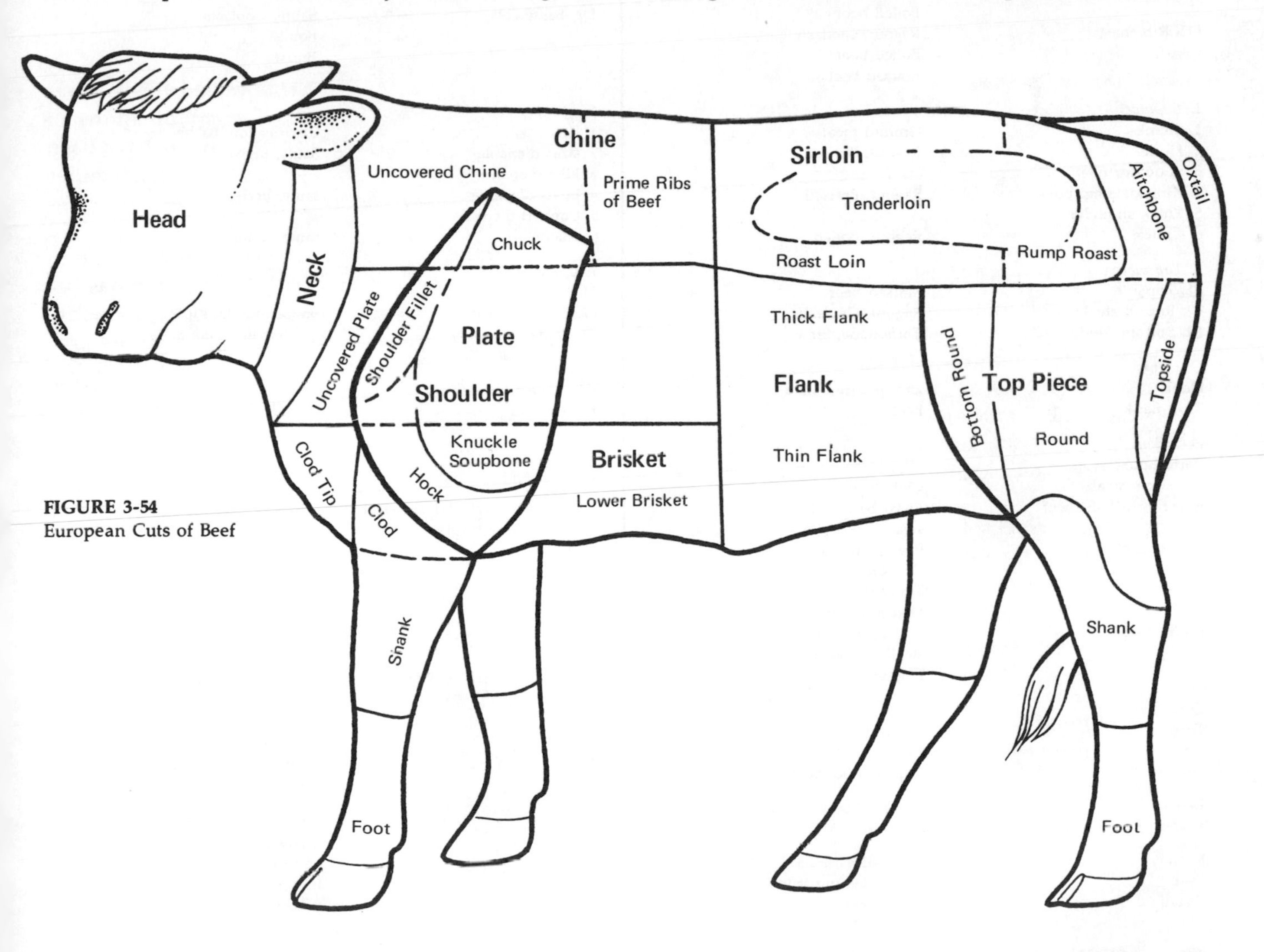

FIGURE 3-54
European Cuts of Beef

3.2.3.2 Beef

Name of cut	*Usage*
A. Neck	Ground meat
B. Brisket	
B1. Clod tip	
B2. Clod	Boiled beef
B3. Lower brisket	
C. Plate	
C1. Plate	
C2. Uncovered plate	Boiled beef
D. Chine	
D1. Prime ribs of beef	English roast beef Braised beef Boiled beef
D2. Rib roast	Ragout, Goulash Boiled beef Braised beef
E. Shoulder	
1. Shank	Ground meat
2. Hock	Ragout, Braised
3. Shoulder fillet	
4. Knuckle soup bone	Ragout, Braised
5. Thick shoulder	
6. Chuck	Ragout, Boiled
F. Top piece	
F1. Topside	Braised beef
F2. Round steak	Ragout, Goulash
F3. Bottom round	Carbonade, Stew
G. Flank	
Flank	2nd quality boiled
Thin flank	beef
H. Sirloin	
Porterhouse steak, T-bone steak,	Club steak
Roast loin/Roast beef	Roast beef; Sirloin steak
Tenderloin	Roast; Châteaubriand; Tenderloin steak; Tournedos; Filet mignon
Rump roast	Braised beef; Rump steak; Carbonade; Ragout
Other cuts	
Tongue	Salted, Smoked
Muzzle	Salad
Stomach	Tripes: Modern style/
Liver	Slivers/Slices/ Dumplings
Kidneys	Small slices/Braised
Feet	For thickening sauces
Oxtail	Soup/Stew

Boeuf: *Quartier de devant*

Denomination	*Emploi*
A. Cou	Hache
B. Poitrine	
B1. Pointe de grumeau	
B2. Grumeau	Bouilli
B3. Os blanc	
C. Cotes	
C1. Cote plate	
C2. Cote plate decouverte	Bouilli
D. Train de cotes	
D1. Cote couverte	Roti saignant Braise Bouilli
D2. Basse cote	Saute, Goulache Bouilli Braise
E. Epaule	
1. Jarret	Clarification, hache
2. Gras d'epaule	Saute, braise
3. Filet d'epaule	
4. Epais d'epaule	saute, braise
5. Couvert d'epaule	
6. Palette	saute, bouilli
F. Cuisse	
F1. Coin	
F2. Tranche ronde	Braise, bouilli, saute
F3. Fausse tranche	carbonnade, estouffade
G. Flanc	
Epais du prin	Bouilli
Flanchet du prin	2^{e} qualite
H. Aloyau	
Porterhouse steak, T-bone steak, Clubsteak	
Faux-filet (Roastbeef)	Roti saignant
Filet	Roti saignant, Chateaubriand, Beefsteak, Tournedos, Filet mignon
Rumpsteak (Culotte)	Braise, Rumpsteak, Carbonnade, Saute
Divers	
Langue	salee, fumee
Museau	salade
Estomac	tripes: a la mode/ gras-double
Foie	emince/en tranche/ quenelles
Rognons	eminces/braises
Pieds	liaison pour sauces
Queue	potage/ragout

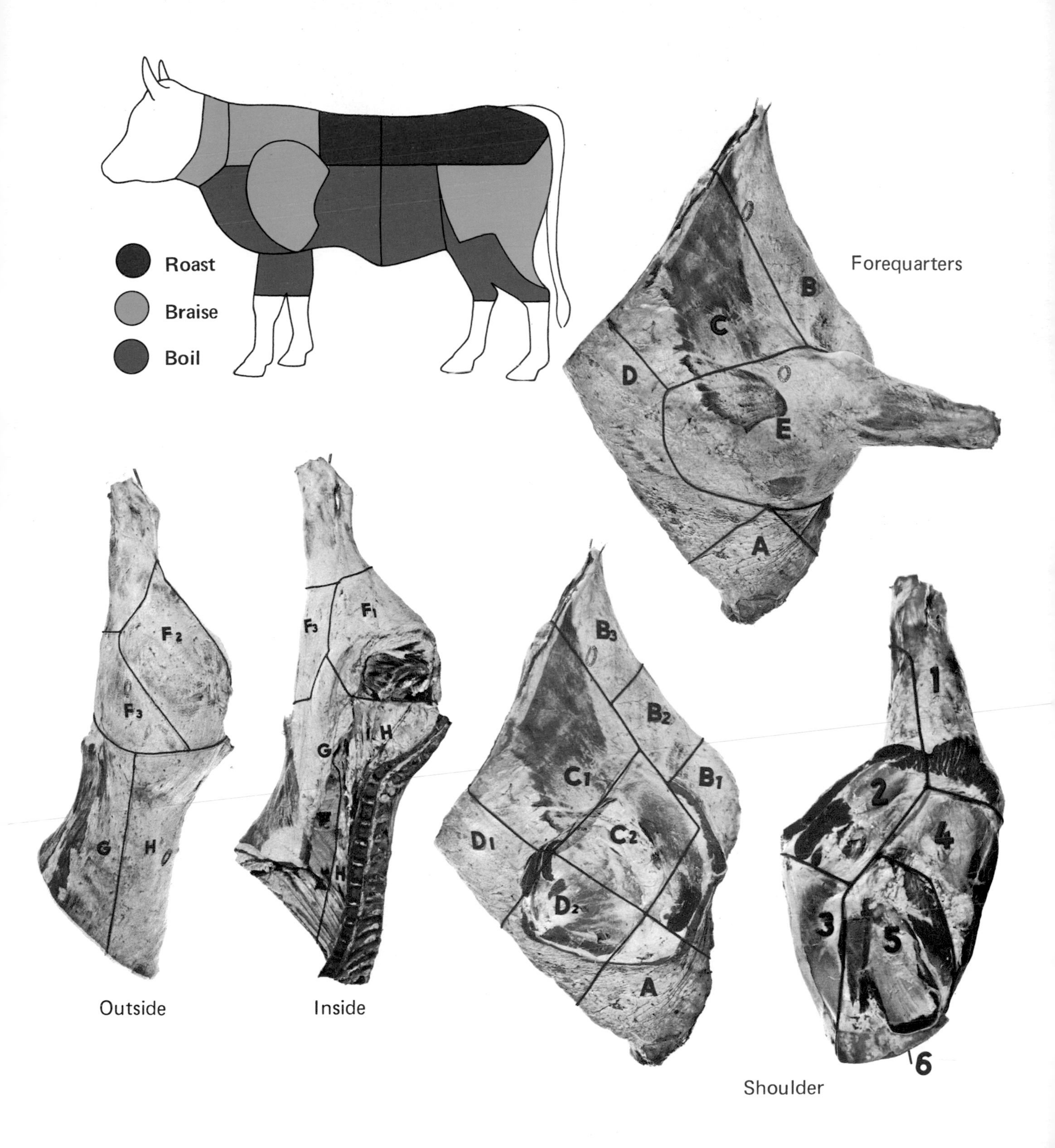

Roast
Braise
Boil
Forequarters
B
C
D
E
A
F2
F3
F1
F3
G
H
G
H
B3
B2
C1
B1
D1
C2
D2
A
1
2
4
3
5
6
Outside
Inside
Shoulder

3.2.3.3 Veal — Veau

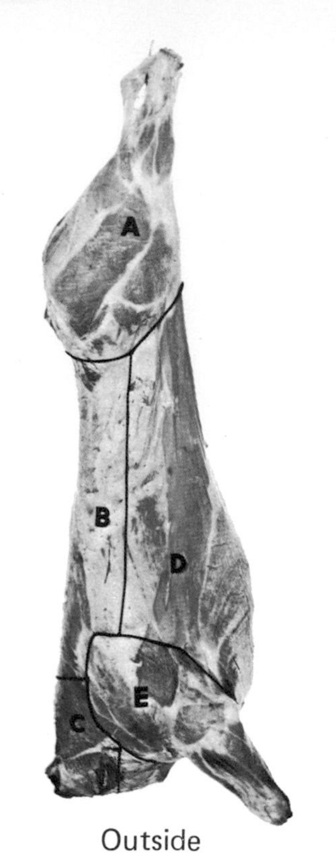

Outside

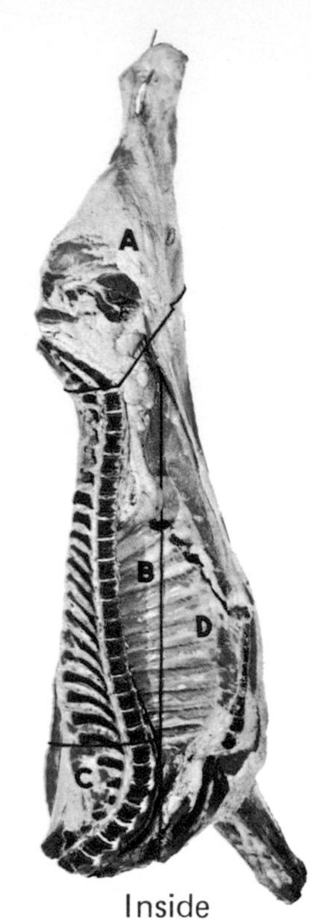

Inside

Name of cut	*Usage*
A. Leg	
Rump roast	Roast, Cutlets, Sliced
Heal of round	Roast
Round roast	Roast, sliced
Top round	Roast, Scallops, Sliced
Shank	Osso buco, Ragout
B. Saddle/back	*Orlov*
Loin	Roast, Steaks, Chops Veal kidney chops
Filet	Roast, Piccata, Sliced
Rib	Roast, Cutlets
C. Neck	Roll roast, Ragout
D. Breast	Roast, Cuts, Ragout Fricassee
E. Shoulder	
Shank	Osso buco, Ragout
Arm	Roast, Ragout
Blade	Ragout
Other cuts	
Head	Boiled, Turtle style, With vinaigrette sauce
Ruffle	Deep-fat fried/ Busecca style
Brains	Poached/Deep- fat fried
Tongue	Boiled
Sweetbreads	Braised/Poached/ As stuffing
Liver	In thin slices
Kidneys	Thin slices, Grilled
Feet	Braised/Deep-fat fried/For calves' foot jelly.

Denomination	*Emploi*
A. Cuisseau	
Noix	Roti, escalopes, emince
Longe	Roti
Quasi	Roti, emince
Noix patissiere	Roti, escalopes, emince
Jarret	Osso buco, saute
B. Selle, carre	Orlov
Filet	Roti, steak, escalopes, rognonnade
Filet mignon	Roti, piccata, emince
Cotelettes	Roti, cotelettes
C. Cou	Roulade, roti, saute
D. Poitrine	Roti, tendrons, saute, fricassee
E. Epaule	
Jarret	Osso buco, saute
Epais d'epaule	Roti, saute
Palette	Saute
Divers	
Tete	bouillie, Tortue/ Vinaigrette
Fraise	Frite/Busecca
Cervelle	poche/frit
Langue	bouillie
Ris de veau	brasie/poche/farce
Foie	emince/en tranche
Rognons	eminces/grilles
Pieds	braises/frits/pour gelee

3.2.3.4 Pork — Porc

 Roast

 Glaze

 Boil

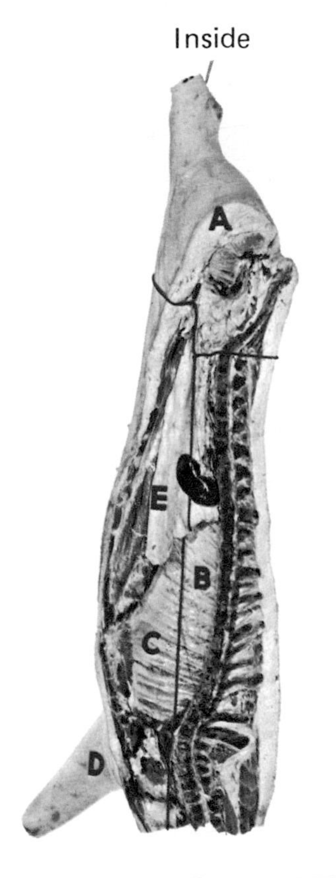

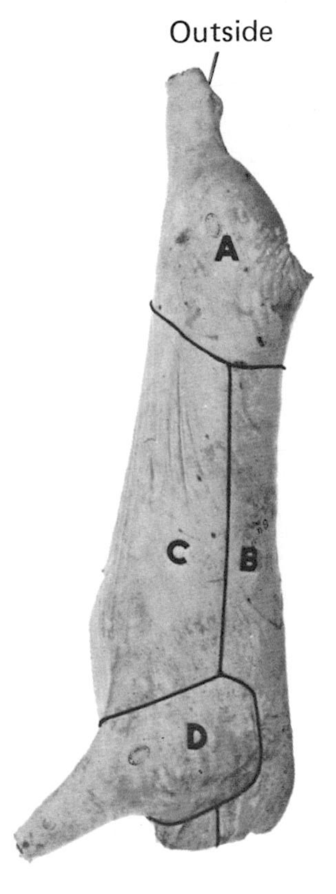

Name of cut	*Usage*
A. Ham	In brine, Smoked
Roast	Roast, Cutlet
Top round	Roast, Cutlet
Butt	Roast
B. Loin	Cured chops, Smoked, Glazed
Loin	Roast, Steaks
Filet	Roast, Mignons Thin slices
Rib	Roast, Chops
Neck	Roast, Ragout
Head	In brine
C. Spare ribs	Salted lean bacon, Smoked
D. Shoulder	Roast, Stews, Smoked
E. Belly	Lard
Other cuts	
Tongue	In brine, Boiled
Brains	Poached
Liver and kidneys	In thin slices/Sliced
Feet/trotters	Salted and boiled, Braised
Shank	Glazed, Salted
Ears, muzzle, tail	Salted

Denomination	*Emploi*
A. Jambon	Sale, fume
Noix	Roti, escalopes
Noix patissiere	Roti, escalopes
Longe	Roti
B. Carre	Sale, fume, glace
Filet	Roti, steak
Filet mignon	Roti, mignons, emince
Cotelettes	Roti, cotelettes
Cou	Roti, saute, civet
Tete	Sale (Gnagi)
C. Poitrine	Lard maigre sale, fume
D. Epaule	Ròti, saute, fume
E. Panne	Graisse
Divers	
Langue	salee et bouillie
Cervelle	poche
Foie et rognons	eminces/en tranche
Pieds	sales et bouillis, braises
Jarrets	glaces, sales
Oreilles, Museau, Queue	sale de porc (Gnagi)

3.2.3.5 Lamb/Mutton – Agneau/Mouton

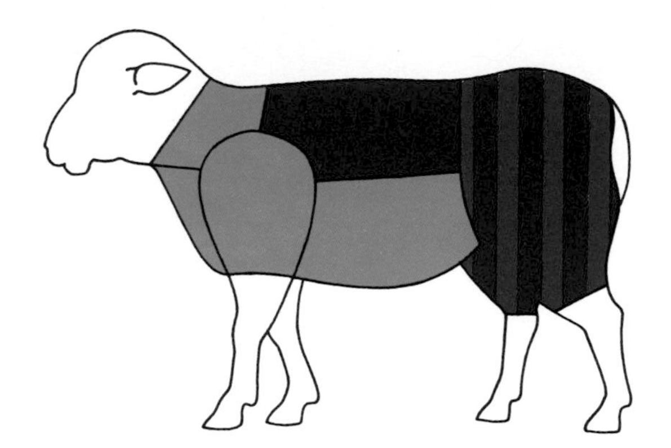

Roast

Glaze

Boil

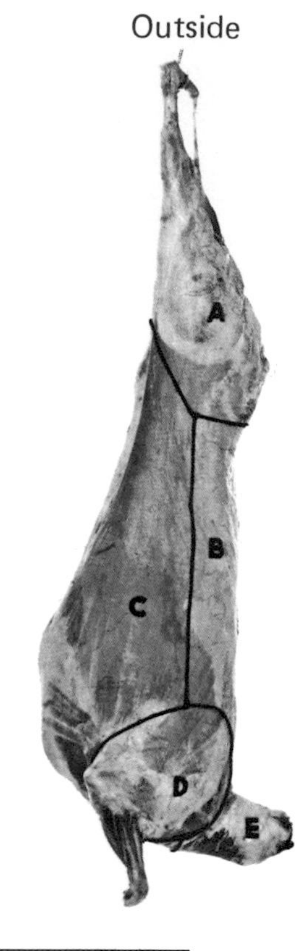

Name of cut	*Usage*
A. Leg	Roast, Braise, Boil
B. Saddle/rack	Whole, and saddle with legs (Baron)
Loin	Roast, Chops
Rib chops	Roast, Cutlets
C. Breast	Ragout, Irish stew, Curry, Epigrammes
D. Shoulder	Ragout, Irish stew, Curry, Rolled and boiled/roast
E. Neck	Ragout, Irish stew, Curry
Other cuts	
Liver	Slivered/Sliced
Kidneys	Grilled/Sliced
Feet	Stuffed

Denomination	*Emploi*
A. Gigot	Roti, braise, bouilli
B. Selle, carre	Entier et baron
Filet	Roti, chops
Cotelettes	Roti, cotelettes
C. Poitrine	Saute, irish stew, curry, epigrammes
D. Epaule	Saute, irish stew, curry, ballotine farcie et rotie
E. Cou	navarin, irish stew, curry
Divers	
Foie	emince/en tranche
Rognons	grilles/eminces
Pieds	farcis

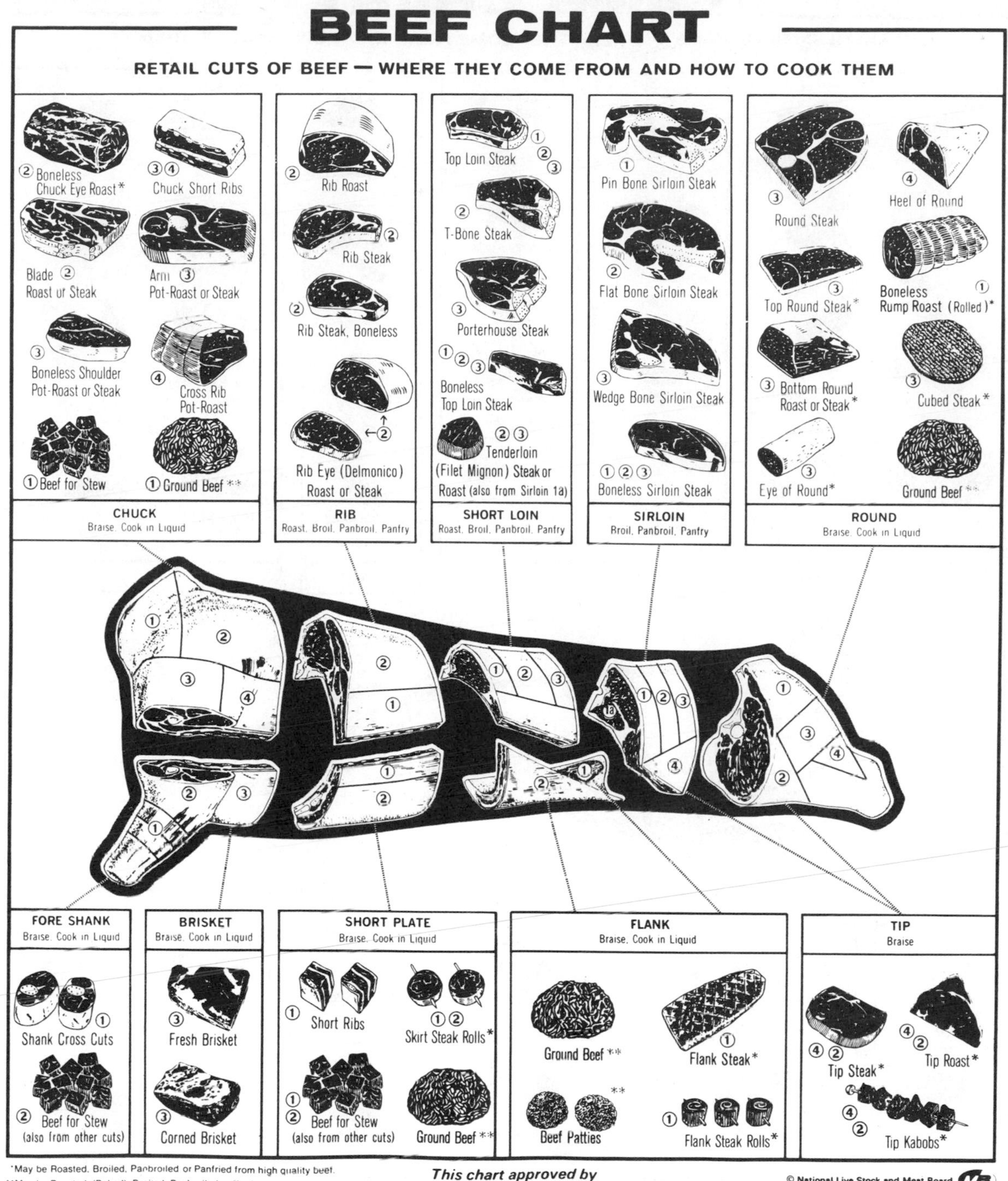

FIGURE 3-55 U.S. Beef Chart
Figures 3-55 to 3-58 courtesy of the National Live Stock and Meat Board, Chicago.

LAMB CHART

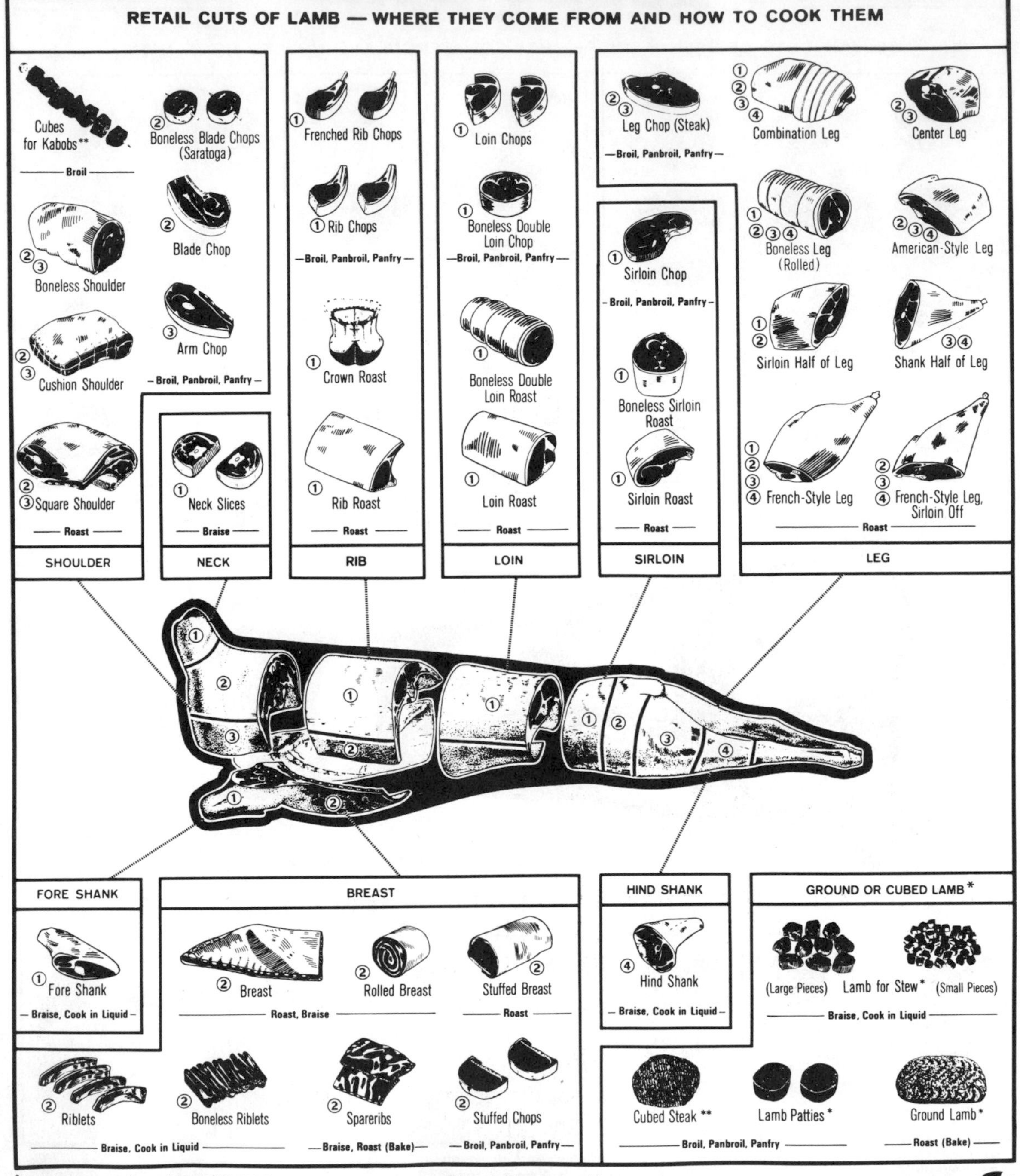

* Lamb for stew or grinding may be made from any cut.
**Kabobs or cube steaks may be made from any thick solid piece of boneless Lamb.

This chart approved by
National Live Stock and Meat Board

© National Live Stock and Meat Board

FIGURE 3-56
U.S. Lamb Chart

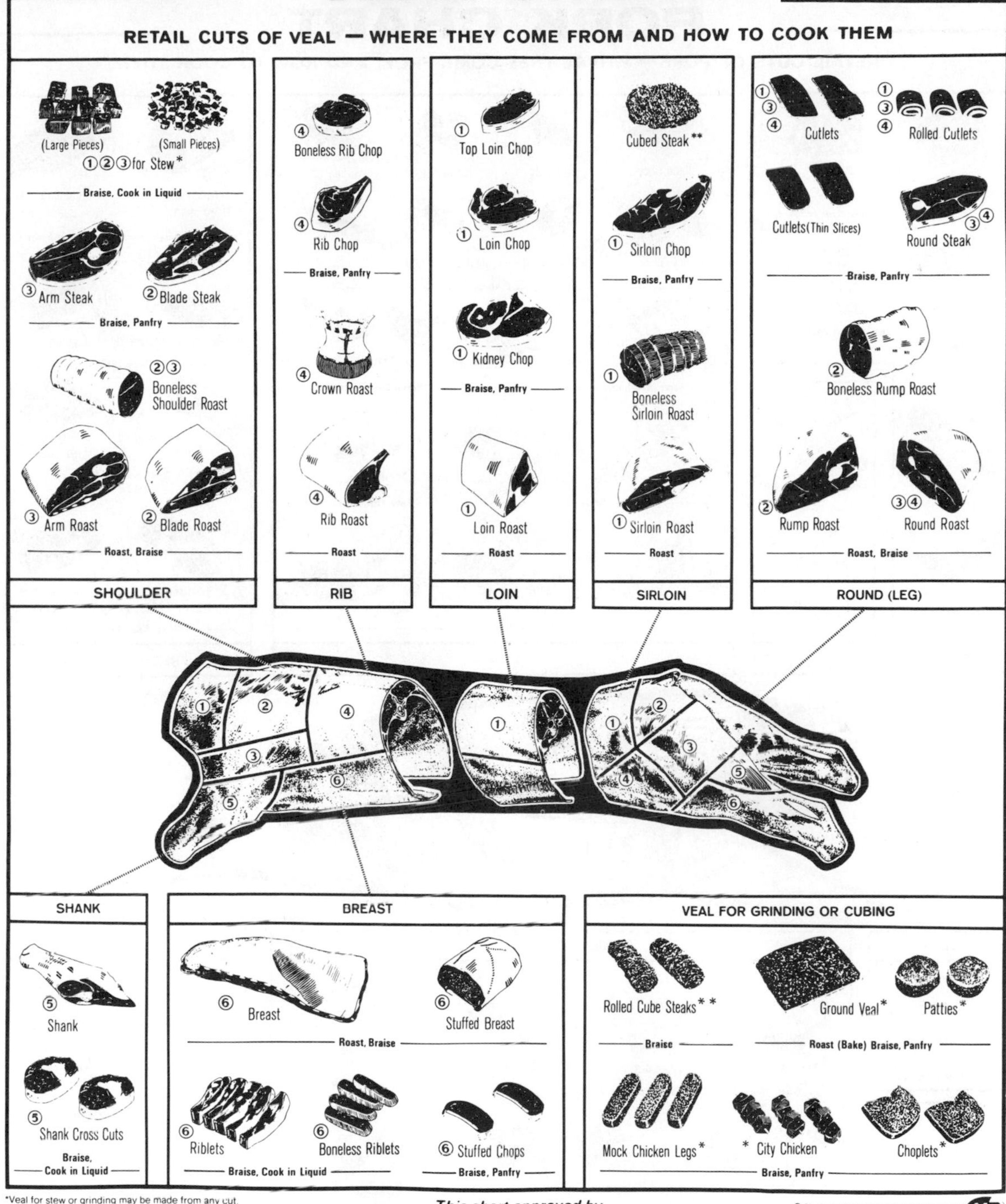

FIGURE 3-57
U.S. Veal Chart

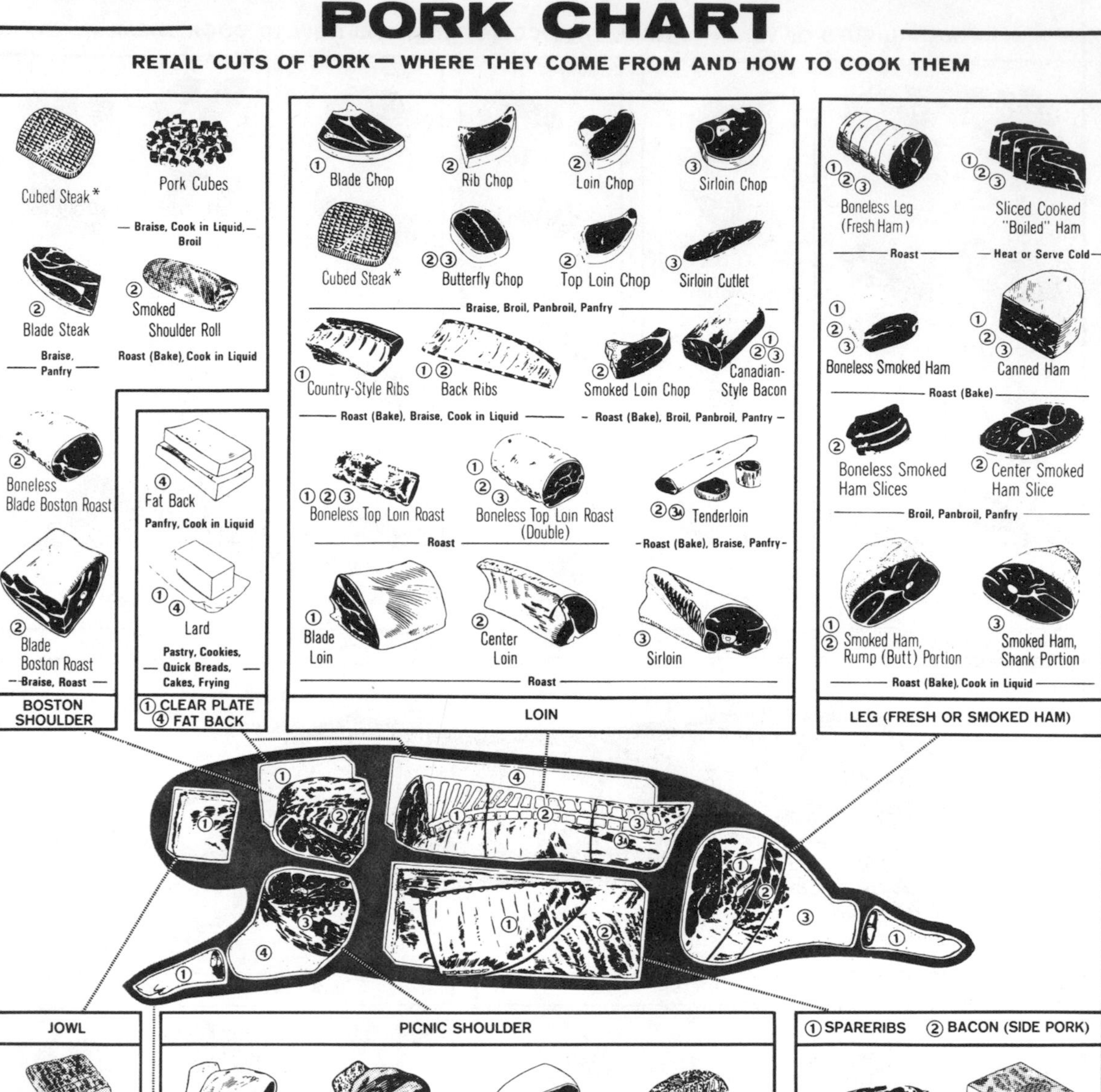

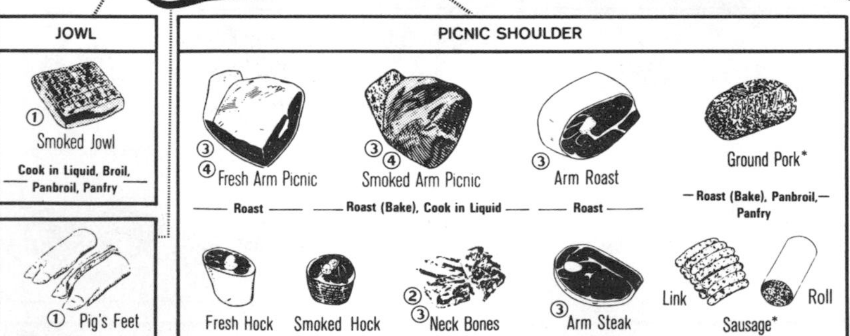

① Spareribs

② Slab Bacon

① Salt Pork

Bake, Broil, Panbroil, Panfry, Cook in Liquid

② Sliced Bacon

Bake, Broil, Panbroil, Panfry

*May be made from Boston Shoulder, Picnic Shoulder, Loin or Leg.

This chart approved by
National Live Stock and Meat Board

© National Live Stock and Meat Board 

FIGURE 3-58
U.S. Pork Chart

Mettwurst is a very fine stuffing made from lean and fat pork. Beef is added to Holsteiner and Berlin Mettwurst and frequently to country-style sausage. These products are highly perishable and should be thoroughly cooked before eating.

Smoked and/or cooked sausages may be made from pork, beef, and veal. Braunschweiger, liver sausage, frankfurters, and bologna are typical examples of this group. Dependent upon the particular variety, the sausage is stuffed into a casing and cooked in water at 160°F. (70°C.) to an internal temperature of 100°F. (38°C.).

Dry and semi-dry sausages are made from pork, beef, or a combination of pork and beef. The uncooked, highly-seasoned sausage is stuffed into a casing. Some are dried and smoked, others are only dried. Salami, Thuringer, and Cervelat are well-known varieties. Salami is a hard, raw sausage. Its name comes from the Italian *salame*—salted meat. Formerly, real salami was made from donkey meat and was merely dried in the air without smoke. Today salami is generally made from pork or from mixtures of lean pork, beef, and bacon fat. In Italy after the sausages are prepared, they are dipped in a hot flour and water mixture and dried. This leaves a white protective coating around the sausage.

Storage of sausage affects the keeping quality. Fresh sausage is highly perishable and should be refrigerated. Smoked and cooked sausages should be held for four to five days under refrigeration. Semi-dry sausages are perishable and should be refrigerated or stored in a well-ventilated, dry room at 50°F. (10°C.) or lower. Sausages are sensitive to changes in temperature and to surrounding odors. When removed from the refrigerator, sweating occurs, and this is an ideal condition for the development of molds.

3.2.4 Poultry—Volaille

The word poultry refers to the different kinds of domestic and battery-reared fowls which are commercially sold, such as chickens, geese, ducks, turkeys, and pigeons. All other varieties come under the classification of game birds. In the hotel and restaurant trade in France, poulard is referred to as *volaille.*

Origin and occurrence: The *Bresse chicken* is considered to represent the finest quality. It is named after a district in the Saone, Loire, and Ain departments in France. Because of the climate, breeding, and fodder used, the quality is unsurpassed. The *Brussels chicken,* from the Malines race, is bred in Belgium. It has a somewhat heavier bone structure and is less fat than the Bresse chickens. The *Houdan chicken* is battery-reared in Holland. The *Styrian chickens* are bred in Styria, a part of Austria. Their meat is excellent. The legs of these chickens are usually yellow.

Spring chickens are young chickens or cocks weighing 1¼ to 2 pounds and they are primarily supplied by the United States, Hungary, Rumania, Poland, and Yugoslavia. The consumption of poultry has increased rapidly in recent years. This increase has resulted from improved production and marketing procedures, year round availability, moderate costs, and the wide variety of poultry products on the market. Due to the improved methods of processing, freezing, packaging, grading, and distributing, poultry products are available throughout the year, and there is very little fluctuation in price. Immediately after slaughter, poultry should be chilled to 40°F. (5°C.) and then frozen by rapid freezing and stored at 0°F. to −5F. (−18°C. to −20°C.). The main suppliers of frozen chicken are the United States, Denmark, Holland, and France.

Quality Characteristics: According to United States federal regulations, all poultry must be inspected for wholesomeness before and after slaughter. The approval stamp is attached to the wing or to the package. After inspection the poultry may be graded by a technically trained government grader. Grading service is provided on a voluntary basis to processors and others who request it.

Indicating quality, United States grades apply to the five kinds of poultry: chicken, turkey, duck, goose, and guinea. The highest quality grade is U.S. Grade A. Grade A poultry is:

- fully fleshed and meaty
- well finished with no defects
- attractive overall appearance

U.S. Grade B and U.S. Grade C are the other official grades; these grades, however, are seldom found on the retail market. The grade shield may be found on all types of chilled or frozen poultry or poultry parts.

Poultry meat is no different from that derived from mammals. It is, however, generally appreciated for its good taste. White meat from young poultry is easy to digest. It contains animal proteins, fat, vitamins, and minerals (iron, phosphorous). The two groups within the poultry family are:

- *poultry with white meat:* chicken and turkey
- *poultry with dark meat:* duck, goose, guinea, and pigeon

The color of the meat has no effect on its quality.

Quality Determination. It is the class (age) of the bird, not the grade, that indicates the tenderness of the bird. Young birds are more tender than old ones. Young tender classes are best for barbecuing, frying, broiling, or roasting:

- Young chickens may be labeled—young chicken, broiler, fryer, roaster, or capon.
- Young turkeys may be labeled—young turkey, fryer, roaster, young hen, or young tom.
- Young ducks may be labeled—duckling, young duckling, broiler duckling, fryer duckling, or roaster duckling.

Mature, less tender meated classes are suitable for stewing or baking:

- Mature chickens may be labeled—mature chicken, old chicken, hen, stewing chicken, or fowl.
- Mature turkeys may be labeled—mature turkey, yearling turkey, or old turkey.
- Mature ducks, geese, and guineas may be labeled —mature or old.[8]

8. U.S., Department of Agriculture, *How to Buy Poultry*. Agricultural Marketing Service, Home and Garden Bulletin No. 157, 1968.

The eating quality of young poultry is superior to that of other birds. The characteristics of young poultry are:

- *poultry with white meat*—supple, not bony breastbones, strong feet, sharp claws, bright red comb, smooth skin on the legs.
- *poultry with dark meat*—soft and supple gullet. The same is true of the tip of the breastbone of geese and ducks. It is more difficult to check this, because the lower part of the body is covered with a thick layer of fat which hardens when slightly chilled and responds slightly to finger pressure.

Storage: Fresh poultry should always be stored in a refrigerator at a temperature of 34°F. to 38°F. (1°C. to 3°C.) with 70 to 75 percent humidity. The quality of *frozen poultry* that has been properly handled is equivalent to that of fresh poultry. Inadequate storage practices will affect the quality of the meat. Over longer periods of storage, the temperature should be kept at 0°F. to −5°F. (−18°C. to −20°C.). Poultry should be prepared immediately after thawing. It should not be refrozen.

Usage: Poultry can be prepared in the following ways: boiled (poached), roasted, grilled, deep-fat fried, stewed, sauteed, poeler, on the spit. The following points should be remembered:

For boiling: chickens weighing 2 pounds or more, or stewing chickens.
For steaming: chickens weighing 2 pounds or more, but not stewing chickens.
For roasting: all kinds of poultry from the largest to the smallest, excluding stewing chickens.
For roasting on the spit and grilling: only tender poultry.

United States legislation requires that all meat and poultry sold for public consumption must be federally and/or state inspected. (Federal Meat Inspection Act of 1906, the Wholesome Meat Act of 1967, and the Poultry Products Inspection Act of 1968.)

Species	Description	Usage	Average Weight	Season
Poultry with White Meat				
Chick – Poussin	The smallest variety of poultry, age one month.	Roasting	10 to 14 ozs.	Spring
Cockerel – Coq vierge	Between a chick and spring chicken. Both sexes are used.	Roasting and grilling	10 to 16 ozs.	Spring
Spring Chicken – Poulet de grain	Roosters and hens, usually under ten weeks old. Sleek skin, supple breastbone.	Roasting, grilling, and deep-fat frying	1-1/4 to 2 lbs.	Summer
Chicken – Poulet reine	Roosters and hens; use of special feed gives good meat and fat layer. Skin sleek and smooth, supple breastbone.	Roasting, grilling, and on the spit	2-1/4 to 4 lbs.	Summer, fall
Poularde – Poularde	Specially bred hens: France – poularde de Bresse; Belgium – poularde de Bruxelles; Holland – poularde de Houdan.	Roasting, poeler, and grilling	4 to 6-1/2 lbs.	Fall, winter
Capon – Chapon	A surgically unsexed male chicken (usually under eight months of age) that is tender-meated with soft, pliable, smooth-textured skin.	Same as the poularde	5 to 6-1/4 lbs.	Fall, winter
Hen – Poule	A mature female chicken or fowl (usually over ten months old) with a non-flexible breast-bone. The meat is less tender than that of a rooster.	May be used in many ways: chicken soup, chicken with rice, or fricassee	3-1/4 to 5-1/2 lbs.	Year round
Young Turkey – Dindonneau	A young turkey with white meat, which is, however, drier than that of the poularde. Strong sinews run through the legs of male and female turkeys and must be carefully removed when cleaning the birds.	Most suitable for roasting and poeler	4-1/2 lbs.	Fall
Turkey – Dinde/Dindon	Turkeys scratch for their food. They originated in North America, where they were domesticated by the Indians. Turkeys are in demand in England and North America. Apart from those bred in the U.S., the main suppliers are Argentina, Poland, and Hungary. The turkey has both light and dark meat and little fat.	Smaller turkeys may be roasted or poeler. Larger birds are boned and rolled.	6 to 12 lbs. 11 to 24 lbs.	Winter

FIGURE 3-59
The Different Types of Poultry

Species	Description	Usage	Average Weight	Season
Poultry with Dark Meat				
Guinea fowl – Pintade	Beside the poularde, the guinea fowl is the most suitable variety of poultry. Its meat is excellent and, after the hunting season, serves as a good replacement for game birds. The breastbone should be supple and the claws sharp.	Grilled or poeler and used for ballottines, galantines, and terrines (cold meat loaves).	1-1/2 to 2-1/4 lbs.	Fall, spring
Duckling – Caneton *Duck – Canard*	The Long Island duckling is best known in the U.S. Nantes duck is famous in France, where the excellent Rouen duck (caneton rouennais) is also bred. This variety is especially suitable for roasting "rare." To keep the blood in the duck, it is not slaughtered, but strangled. Young ducks can be recognized by the soft gullet and breastbone.	Roasting, braising	3 to 3-3/4 lbs. 3-1/4 to 5-3/4 lbs.	August February
Gosling – Oison *Goose – Oie*	There are two types – fattened goose and fattened gosling. Goose meat is tasty only during the first year. Fattened gosling should be no older than 5 months. Their weight is approximately 9 lbs. The gullet of young geese can be depressed easily, the webbing of the feet easily torn, and the claws are pointed, but soft. The beak can be snapped back easily.	The goose liver is a special delicacy. It can be prepared in many ways (terrines, loaves, and pies). Geese may be roasted, braised, and stuffed. They are also cut in sections – breast, drumstick.	4-1/2 to 9 lbs. 9 to 13-1/2 lbs.	September January
Young Pigeon – Pigeonneau *Pigeon – Pigeon*	Pigeons are considered as dark meat poultry, although young birds have tender, white meat. The meat of older birds is red, and can only be used for boiling in soups. The breast should be meaty, the skin smooth, firm, and without colored streaks. Dull, sunken eyes and patchy, hanging wings are signs of excess storage.	Roasting, stuffed, or grilled	1-1/4 to 1-3/4 lbs.	Fall

FIGURE 3-59 (continued)

3.2.5 Game—Gibier

3.2.5.1 Game Animals—gibier de poil

Game is the name used for the meat of the wild animal. Game beasts include the following species: deer (venison), hare, red deer, chamois, wild boar, and wild rabbit. The quality of the meat of game beasts is equivalent to that of slaughtered animals. It is tender, soft, and easily digested; its nutritional value compares with that of slaughtered meat. It is at its best during the fall hunting season. If game is to be frozen, it should not be skinned, and should be stored in a vacuum to prevent drying. When butchering game, especially if it is to be used for marinated game stews, the bones should be cut with a meat saw so that the bones will not splinter. Pieces or splinters of bone in food can cause serious injury.

RED DEER—CERF

Species and description: The male red deer, weighing between 350 and 500 pounds, can be recognized by his antlers. Red deer, as it is known in Germany, live together in herds. In Switzerland, wild red deer are only found in the mountains of the canton of Graubunden. Other varieties of deer are found throughout the world.

Quality characteristics: Animals weighing up to 75 pounds are classified as calf deer and their meat is equivalent to veal. Those weighing 75 pounds to 100 pounds are known as brockets and correspond to the meat of young bulls. The meat of red deer weighing over 130 pounds is similar to that of beef. The meat from young red deer is very tender.

Usage: The saddle may be used for chops and the leg for cutlets. It can be used for braising and for game stews (pfeffer). It is particularly important that the meat of older animals is stored properly.

CHAMOIS—CHAMOIS

Species and description: Chamois is a member of the hoofed game group and usually lives in the mountains (Alps). During the summer, the fur is rusty red with black streaks on the back, and in the winter, it is dark brown. Both sexes carry horns which point backwards.

Quality characteristics: The meat of young chamois is very tasty, but that of older animals is rather tough and leaves a peculiar aftertaste. Young chamois have thin legs; those of older animals are very bony and covered with hair.

Usage: Legs can be marinated and braised. Generally the whole chamois is used to make ragout (pfeffer).

DEER—CHEVREUIL

Species and description: Deer live in herds in the woods. The male animals carry antlers with two beams, that have one or more tines. The females are as large as the males, but carry no antlers. After an animal has been shot, the entrails are removed but it is not skinned. The weight of the animal once cleaned is between 30 pounds and 50 pounds.

Quality characteristics: The meat of animals three

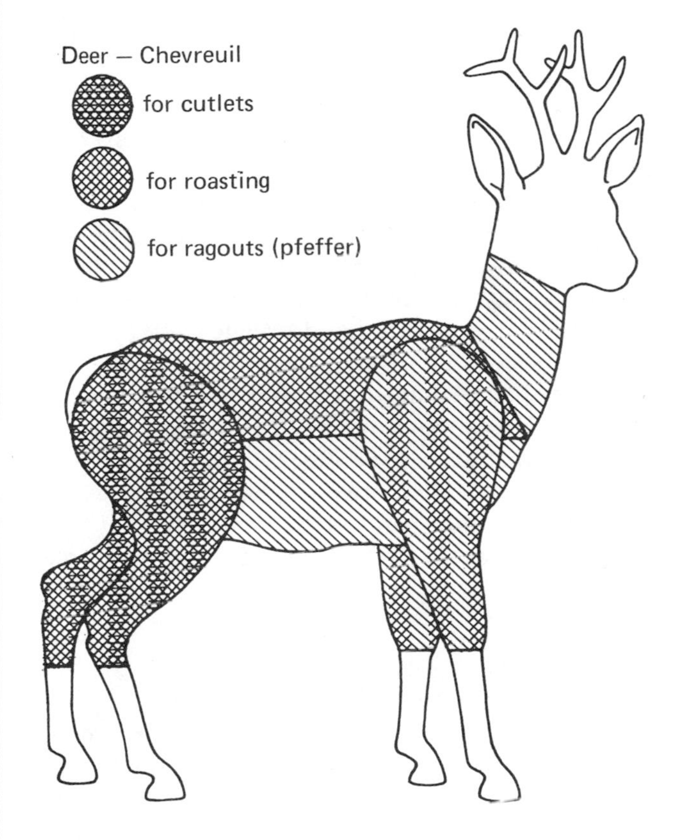

FIGURE 3-60
Deer—Chevreuil

years and younger is tasty and tender, but that of older animals is tough and less easily digestible.
Usage: Since the meat is generally lean, the leg and saddle must be larded before roasting and should be cooked to the medium or rare stage. Marinating the leg and saddle for approximately two hours tenderizes the meat. The remaining parts, which are suitable for ragouts (pfeffer), should be marinated for four to six days in a good red wine marinade.

WILD RABBIT—LAPEREAU
Species and description: Wild rabbits are found in France, England, United States, and Australia where they are sometimes so widespread that they become pests. The fur is grayish in color and the body smaller than the domesticated rabbit.
Quality characteristics: The meat is rather dry.
Usage: Pies and hasenpfeffer.

HARE—LIEVRE
Species and description: Hare is a rodent that likes seedlings and cabbage. The male is known as a buck, the female a doe.
Quality characteristics: Hares weigh between 6½ and 13 pounds. The best quality meat comes from hares that are 3 to 8 months old. They are fattest in November and December. A young hare has long legs and soft ears that bend and tear easily. Their breastbones can be pressed inward easily. The meat is quite light and grayish red; that of older animals is dark red. Hares that have been recently killed have clear eyes that glaze over after two days and dry out after eight days. Meat of young hares is very tender, while that of older hares is usually dry.
Usage: Hare keeps very well when hung by its feet, unskinned.

Hare is cut up as follows:	*Possible uses.*
Saddle—rable	Fresh or marinated, with the nerves removed, larded, and roasted to the rare stage.
Leg—cuissot	Prepared like a saddle or used in hasenpfeffer, ragout.
Neck, breast—cou, poitrine Foreleg—epaules	Marinated with red wine and mirepoix, or used in hasenpfeffer.

WILD BOAR—SANGLIER
Species and description: Wild boar weigh a maximum of 450 pounds. Males are called tuskers; females wild sows.
Quality characteristics: There are three quality groups:

- young animals, weighing up to 65 pounds, have yellowish-brown coloring
- medium animals, weighing 65 to 80 pounds, have blackish-brown coloring
- old animals, weighing over 80 pounds, have tough, wiry hair and tusks

Usage: Connoisseurs appreciate the meat of young wild boar (*marcassins*), especially the saddle and legs. The remaining meat may be used for ragout. Generally, wild boar is prepared by the same methods as used for venison and deer.

3.2.5.2 Game birds—Gibier de plume

Game birds can be hunted in most countries, but usually only during the official hunting season. Game birds include: wildfowl (capercaille, black grouse, pheasant, hazel-hen, partridge, grouse, rock partridge, quail), wild pigeon, waterfowl, (surface-feeding ducks, diving ducks, wild ducks, wild geese), snipe, and thrush.
Quality characteristics and keeping: The meat of game birds is leaner than that of domestic poultry and is easily digested. Compared with domestic poultry it has a "gamy taste." All game birds must be hung for a few days in an airy place before plucking. This is called "gaming." During this period a distinctive "high taste" develops. The muscles loosen and the meat becomes tender. Game birds deteriorate

quickly after this stage. Wild duck and other waterfowl are very perishable and should not be hung.
Signs of age: Young fowl have soft, smooth-textured, pliable skin; flexible breastbone cartilage; and tender flesh. The meat of older birds is less tender and somewhat darker with firmer breastbone cartilage.
Usage: Young birds are usually broiled, sauteed, barbecued, or roasted. Older birds are stewed, braised, or used in combination dishes.The meat of game birds is quite lean and should be barded (see Fig. 7-35) to prevent excessive browning and drying in the early stages of the cooking process.

SNIPE – BECASSINE/WOODCOCK – BECASSE
Origin and occurrence: There are two types of snipe: the *woodcock* which is the same size as the partridge, and the *marsh snipe*, which is smaller. The former lives in woods, while the latter lives in marshes and moors. The hunting season is usually between September and mid-April.
Species and description: The woodcock is a migratory bird. It has brownish-yellow plumage and a long pointed beak. The marsh snipe is related to the woodcock, and it also has a long pointed beak which appears to be split because it is so flat. It has bare legs and a yellow stripe on its back. There are three sizes of marsh snipe (large, common, and small). Large ones are about the size of a partridge, the small ones are the size of a lark. Connoisseurs consider the woodcock to be the finest of all game birds. Its meat is very tender with a gamy taste and has the advantage of keeping longer than the other types. It is considered to have reached the appropriate degree of maturity when it takes on the gamy taste, without being excessively so.
Storage: The unplucked bird should hang in a cool, dry place.
Usage: Snipe can be roasted or braised. They may be used for hot or cold dishes.The entrails are a specialty – snipe tidbits – when prepared in the following way: the intestines, heart, and liver, and an equal amount of bacon are simmered with shallots, parsley, finely chopped lemon peel, and butter. Season to taste with salt, pepper, nutmeg, a little brandy, and red wine. The mixture may be bound with bread crumbs. When cold, the mixture is blended with the yolk of one egg, spread on toast, and heated before using (as garnish for roasts and salmis).

QUAIL – CAILLE
Origin and occurrence: The European quail are migratory birds which cross the Sahara, spend the winter in the northern regions of tropical Africa, and return in May to central Europe. The hunting season is in September and October. In Italy, Spain, Greece, and southern Russia, quail are caught with nets. In Britain, quail are protected and cannot be hunted. The American varieties have short wings and can fly only short distances. The best known species is the bob-white.
Species and description: Quail is a member of the wildfowl family and it is the smallest of the game birds. It is approximately 8 inches long. The plumage is brown with a yellow fleck on the crown of the head and above each eye. The legs are covered with yellowish-red feathers. The meat of quail is excellent.
Storage: The bird should be hung unplucked.
Usage: Quail is used both in hot and cold dishes. The best methods for cooking quail are: roasting on a spit; poaching in a rich veal stock, or poeler.

WILD DUCK – CANARD SAUVAGE
Origin and occurrence: Wild duck is a waterfowl found in many different areas.
Species and description: The meat of young ducks, especially teal, is a delicacy. Older birds are tough and usually have an oily taste. Young birds have a flexible breastbone, and webbed feet which tear easily.
Storage: Wild duck should be drawn as soon as possible after the bird is shot and chilled quickly.

PHEASANT – FAISAN
Origin and occurrence: Pheasant is the most important quarry for wildfowl hunters. It originally came from the banks of the Black Sea and Asia, but it is found almost everywhere. Exporting countries are Hungary, Rumania, Czechoslovakia, and Denmark.
Species and description: Pheasant is a wildfowl. There are two kinds – those with and those without

collars. The hunted or nobel pheasant does not have a collar. Male birds have a brightly-colored plumage. The female pheasant has a short tail and its plumage is less brilliant than that of a cock. The distinctive feature of the cock-pheasant is the shape and the length of its tail. A young pheasant has gray legs with short, stubby spurs and a soft, flexible breastbone. The pheasant is one of the meatiest birds for its size. It weighs from one to two pounds in the carcass and most of the meat is on the breast.

Storage: Pheasant should be hung in a cold dry place for a few days before it is plucked. This gives the bird its special "gamy" taste. The correct degree of maturity and "gaminess" is reached when a fatty oil starts to come out around the beak.

Usage: Pheasant may be roasted, braised, or prepared as salmis. Older birds may be made into a souffle.

PARTRIDGE—PERDREAU

Origin and occurrence: Partridge, which is classified as wildfowl, is usually hunted from the end of August until January. Partridges live in northern, central, and eastern Europe and in North America.

Species and description: Partridge is somewhat larger than pigeon. The younger bird has yellowish legs that are plump and close to the feet. It has a dark pointed beak, and the feathers are tapered. The older partridge has grayish to grayish-yellow legs and a grayish-brown plumage. The feathers of the male bird are brightly colored. Partridges live in groups or coveys.

Storage: The entrails of partridges are removed immediately after the bird has been killed; the bird is then hung with its feathers.

Usage: Young birds are roasted while the mature birds are made into pies and game loaves.

3.3 Foods Derived from Animal Sources

3.3.1 Dairy Products—Produits Latiers

3.3.1.1 Milk—Lait

Milk refers to the lacteal secretion obtained from different animals. The milk of many species of animals is used in different parts of the world. In the United States, however, the cow furnishes almost all the milk that is marketed.

Milk appears on today's market in many forms to meet the demands of consumers. In recent years products have been developed to improve keeping quality, to facilitate distribution, to provide for maximum use of all by-products, and to preserve surplus. State and local governments usually determine the standards of composition for all fluid milk products. These governments also are responsible for the sanitation controls. The federal government, however, establishes the standards of identity for evaporated milk, condensed milk, and nonfat dry milk.

Quality specifications for milk are based on flavor, odor, appearance, sediment content, and bacterial count. In appearance it should be smooth and free of any curds, ropiness, or foreign materials. It should have a fresh and sweet odor and taste. Quality milk is high in nutritive value and has good keeping quality.

Average Composition of Milk

Specific gravity, approximately	1.033
Dry solids, approximately	12.75%
of which fat content, approximately	3.7%
total protein content, approximately	3.6%
milk sugar, approximately	4.7%
minerals, approximately	.7%
plus vitamins and enzymes	

(See Fig. 3-61.)

WHOLE MILK—LAIT ENTIER

The composition of milk varies between cows and between seasons of the year. Although minimum standards of the composition of milk are established by the individual states, many states define whole milk as milk that contains not less than 3.25 percent milk fat and not less than 8.25 percent milk solids—not fat.[9]

Almost all of the whole fluid milk marketed in the United States is pasteurized and homogenized.

9. *New Knowledge of Milk,* 3rd ed. (Chicago: The National Dairy Council, 1968), p. 9.

Raw milk, or milk that has not been subjected to heat treatment, should be heated or pasteurized before it is consumed.

CERTIFIED MILK—LAIT SPECIALE

Certified milk, available in only a few areas, originated in 1893 to fulfill the need for safe milk. The certification label on the container means that the raw or pasteurized milk has been produced and distributed under conditions that conform with the standards for cleanliness established by the American Association of Medical Milk Commissions. Certified milk is usually pasteurized; however, it may be raw and it may be homogenized. It may also be fortified with vitamin D.

PASTEURIZED MILK—LAIT PASTEURISE

Milk is pasteurized by heating it to 145°F. (63°C.) and holding it at this temperature for 30 minutes or by holding it at 161°F. (71°C.) continuously for 15 seconds in equipment that is safe and sanitary. The milk is promptly lowered to 45°F. (7°C.). Pasteurization destroys all pathogenic organisms in the milk without significantly changing the flavor, odor, or nutritive value. The keeping quality of milk is also improved through pasteurization.

ULTRA-HEAT-TREATED MILK—LAIT UPERISE

A new process has been developed for treating this milk (UHT = ultra-heat treated). The milk is heated to 285°F. (140°C.) to 300°F. (149°C.) for a few seconds to destroy the bacteria and then immediately cooled. This milk will keep for approximately four months if it is protected from the light. Otherwise the conditions are the same as for pasteurized milk.

SKIM MILK—LAIT ECREME

Skim milk is milk from which the fat has been removed. The fat content is usually 1 percent, although the standards established by various states range from 8 percent to 9.25 percent for the minimum total solids. Skim milk is pasteurized. With the exception of the milk fat and the vitamin A in the milk fat, the other nutrients in milk, protein, lactose, minerals, and water soluble vitamins, B_1 and B_2, are found in skim milk. Skim milk is frequently fortified with a concentrate of water-soluble vitamin A and vitamin D to replace the vitamins removed with the fat of the whole milk.

Two percent milk, made from skim or whole milk, contains 2 percent milk fat. It is frequently fortified with vitamins and milk solids—not fat.

MIXED MILK DRINKS—BOISSONS MELANGEES AU LAIT

A flavored milk drink is made of pasteurized and homogenized skim or partially skim milk. Syrups or powders with flavoring agents and sugar are added. Chocolate dairy drink consists of *skim or partially skim milk* flavored with chocolate powder or syrup.

Chocolate milk is pasteurized *whole milk* flavored with sugar and chocolate syrup or powder. Its milk fat content is the same as that of whole milk.

SOUR MILK—LAIT AIGRE

Sour milk is pasteurized whole milk which is soured through the influence of lactic acid building bacteria present in the milk or as a result of adding pure cultured bacteria, vinegar, or lemon juice to heated milk. *Buttermilk* may be either a churned or cultured product. Most buttermilk today is not the by-product from churning cream into butter. Most of the cultured buttermilk is made of pasteurized fresh fluid skim milk cultured with streptococcus lactic and incubated at 68°F. (20°C.) to 72°F. (22°C.).[10]

YOGHURT—YOGHOURT

Yoghurt is usually manufactured from fresh, partially pasteurized and homogenized skim milk which has been enriched with added milk solids—not fat.

The mixture is inoculated and incubated at 105°F. (41°C.) to 115°F. (46°C.). The yoghurt coagulates within a two hour period. The acidifying process is stopped by immediately lowering the temperature to 35°F. (2°C.) to 40°F. (4°C.). The finished product is fine-textured, smooth, semi-solid clabbered milk which contains between 11 and 12 percent solids. Fruit concentrates, jams and whole fruits are

10. *Ibid.*, p. 12.

FIGURE 3-61
Nutrient Content of Milk

Protein.
Content: 3.6% (Casein 3.0%, whey protein 0.6%)
Milk protein contains all the essential amino acids and serves as important function in the process of building the body's cells.

Milk Fat:
Content: 3.7%
Milk fat is easily digested, contains many vital substances, such as essential fatty acids and vitamins; it is an important source of energy and serves as a protection for certain vital organs.

Milk Sugar:
Content: 4.7%
Milk sugar (and therefore milk) provides energy and is necessary for the proper functioning and regulating of certain vital organs and the nervous system.

Minerals:
Content: 0.7%
Milk is rich in calcium and phosphorus. These minerals are necessary in human nutrition for building bony structures and for metabolic processes. Calcium is also needed for developing teeth, for muscle contraction, and blood coagulation.

Vitamins
Milk fat contains the vitamins A, D, and E which are soluble in fat. Milk whey contains vitamins of the B complex and C and these are soluble in water.

added to the yoghurt. A frozen yoghurt product is also available in varied flavors. Yoghurt can also be made from whole milk with 3.5 percent fat content.

CONCENTRATED MILKS
Fresh, frozen, condensed, evaporated, and dried *concentrated milks* are available on today's market. Varying amounts of water are removed under controlled conditions. The milk may be reconstituted by adding the appropriate quantity of water.

COTTAGE CHEESE—SERE DE LAIT
Cottage cheese may be made from fresh pasteurized skim milk, sour milk, or reconstituted nonfat dry milk. A combination of lactic acid starter and rennet is used in varying amounts to initiate the coagulation. The milk is further coagulated at temperatures from 70°F. (21°C.) to 90°F. (32°C.) for several hours. Cottage cheese has a mild acid flavor. It is used for salads, with fruits, vegetables, dips, desserts, and pastries.

3.3.1.2 Cream—Creme

Cream is that part of whole unhomogenized milk that rises to the surface. The fat particles are large and less dense than milk. Cream is produced under the same conditions as milk. The United States Food and Drug Administration has standards of identity for each of the various types of cream if they are shipped in interstate commerce. These standards give minimum milk fat requirements for each type of cream.

HEAVY CREAM—CREME ENTIERE
Heavy cream or whipping cream must have at least 36 percent milk fat. It is pasteurized homogenized cream. The stability and volume of the cream are usually increased if the cream has been allowed to stand for 24 hours or longer. Air is incorporated into the cream with whipping and the volume may be increased by 80 to 100 percent. To whip cream the utensils should be cold, and the cream should be 35°F. (2°C.) to 40°F. (4°C.). Cream should not be overwhipped as the product may become grainy and may produce butter.

SOUR CREAM—CREAM AIGRE
Sour cream must contain a minimum of 18 percent milk fat. It is made by adding about .2 percent lactic acid bacteria culture to pasteurized and homogenized full cream or half-and-half cream. The cream is matured for 24 hours at 68°F. (20°C.). Sour cream is used for cooking game and pfeffers. It is used in dips, soups, sauces, salads, and desserts.

HALF-AND-HALF CREAM—DEMI-CREME
Half-and-half or coffee cream is a mixture of homogenized milk and cream. The federal standards require a *minimum of 10.5 percent milk fat.*

ICE CREAM—CREME GLACEE
Ice cream products are made of cream, milk, condensed milk, syrup, fresh or frozen or dried fruits, fruit juices and purees, chocolate, sugar, and stabilizers. The mixture is pasteurized (with the exception of some sherbets and ices) and then homogenized. Federal standards state that plain ice cream must contain a minimum of 10 percent milk fat and that the maximum content of stabilizers used is .50 percent. The milk fat content of dairy ice cream with fruit, fruit juices, nuts, or chocolate must be a minimum of 8 percent.

3.3.1.3 Butter—Beurre

The origin of butter dates back to ancient times. The early nomadic people used the milk of cows, ewes, goats, and camels to prepare butter. The Aryans introduced butter to the people of India who considered it a sacred food. According to history, the Scythians brought butter to the Greeks, and from then on its use spread very rapidly throughout the world.

The United States Department of Agriculture defines butter as "the food product usually known as butter, and which is made exclusively from milk or cream, or both, with or without common salt, and with or without additional coloring matter, and containing not less than 80 percent by weight of milk fat, all tolerances having been allowed for."[11] The United States Department of Agriculture has established grades for butter; however, grading is not compulsory. A manufacturer may request inspection and grading. The USDA grade shield (AA, A or B) indicates that the butter has been tested and graded in accordance with the federal specifications for each grade.

Nomenclature and Characteristics of United States Grades of Butter[12]

United States Grade AA Butter or United States 93 Score:

- a delicate sweet flavor, with a highly pleasing aroma;
- manufactured from high-quality fresh sweet cream;
- has a smooth, creamy texture, and good spreadability;
- has completely dissolved salt blended in the right amount.

United States Grade A Butter or United States 92 Score:

- has a pleasing flavor;
- is manufactured from fresh cream;
- is fairly smooth in texture;
- rates close to the top grade.

United States Grade B Butter or United States 90 Score:

- may have a slightly acid flavor;
- is usually made from selected sour cream;
- is readily acceptable to many consumers.

United States Grade C Butter or United States 89 Score:

- malty, scorched, or stale flavor;
- uneven color.

11. U.S. Department of Agriculture, *United States Standards for Grades of Butter.* Reprinted from Federal Register of January 28, 1960.

12. U.S. Department of Agriculture, Home and Garden Bulletin, *How to Buy Dairy Products.* 1974.

Average Composition of Butter

Milk fat	81.3%
Milk solids	1.0%
Salt	2.3%
Moisture	15.3%

Butter is sold in one pound, one-half pound, and one-fourth pound packages. Ready-cut table butter is also available. It is cut 48, 60, 72, or 90 pieces per pound. The butter is arranged on parchment paper and packed in layers in 5 pound units. It is also packed with individual cuts on a paper server for use in butter dispensers. *Sweet butter* is unsalted butter made from sweet cream. *Clarified butter,* or *ghee,* is melted butter with the milk solids removed. Butter should be refrigerated at 35°F. (2°C.) in its original package or in a covered container, or it may be frozen and stored at 0°F. (−18°C.).

3.3.1.4 Cheese — Fromage

Cheese may be defined as "the concentration of all or part of the components of milk obtained through the coagulation of the major milk protein, casein, by suitable enzymes, and/or by acid produced by bacteria. The curd, separated from the whey, is used at once in unripened cheese. In the cheese, the curd is ripened by the action of beneficial bacteria, molds, yeasts, and enzymes."[13]

Natural cheese is made by separating most of the milk solids from the milk by curdling with either a bacterial culture or rennet or both and separating the curd from the whey by heating, agitating, and pressing. Most cheeses made in the United States are made from whole cow's milk; however, some are made from both milk and cream, some from skim milk, and others from whey or combinations of these products.

The distinctive characteristics such as flavor, texture, aroma, and consistency of the various cheeses are due to:

- the kind of milk used
- the type of bacteria or molds used in ripening
- the method used for curdling the milk and for cutting, cooking, and forming the curd
- the amount of salt or seasonings added
- the conditions of the ripening process such as temperature, humidity, and length of time.[14]

All natural cheese should be stored in the original wrapper or covering at refrigerated temperatures. The cut surface of cheese should be covered with aluminum foil, wax paper, or plastic wrapping material to protect the surface from drying. Large pieces that are to be stored over a long period of time may be dipped in melted paraffin. Cheese that has become hard or dried out may be grated and refrigerated in a tightly sealed container.

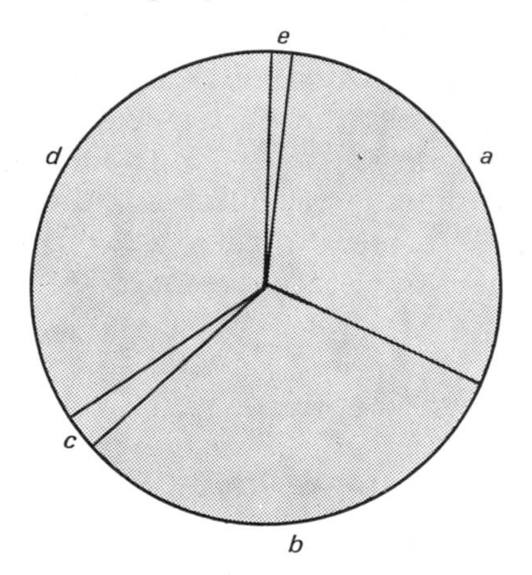

Cheese constituents:

(a) 30% Protein
(b) 31% Milk fat
(c) 2% Minerals
(Calcium, phosphorus, copper, and practically all the valuable trace elements)
(d) 36% Water
(e) 1% Salt
+ the vitamins A, D, E, K, the provitamin A, carotene, and vitamins belonging to the B-complex

FIGURE 3-62
Composition of Emmentaler Cheese

13. *Newer Knowledge of Cheese,* 2nd ed. (Chicago: The National Dairy Council, 1967), p. 9.

14. U.S. Department of Agriculture, *Home and Garden Bulletin,* No. 193, *How to Buy Cheese,* September, 1971.

The Best Known Types of Cheese

Type	Origin
Cream cheeses	
Cream cheese	United States, Europe
Pot cheese	United States
Cambridge	England
Fontainebleau	France
Petit Suisse/Petit Gervais	France
Straccino	Italy
Full fat cheeses	
Appenzeller	Switzerland
Swiss—Emmentaler	Switzerland
Gruyere—Greyerzer	Switzerland
Hobel cheese	Switzerland
Raclette cheese	Switzerland
Tete de Moine	Switzerland
Mont d'Or Vacherin	Switzerland
Bleu d'Auvergne	France
Brie	France
Camembert	France
Reblochon	France
Roquefort	France
Cheddar	England
Chester	England
Gloucester	England
Stilton	England
Bel Paese	Italy
Gorgonzola	Italy
Brick	United States
Blue	United States, Denmark
Liederkranz	United States
Havarti	Denmark
Edamer	Holland
Gouda	Holland
Munster—Munster	Alsace (France)
Limburger—Limburg	Germany
Tilsiter—Tilsit	Various countries
¾ fat cheeses	
Sbrinz (grating cheese)	Switzerland
Parmesan	Italy
Romano	Italy
Cheshire	England
¼ fat-lean cheeses	
Herb cheese—aux herbes	Switzerland
Caraway cheese—au cumin	Switzerland
Special products	
Yoghurt cheese	
Cottage cheese	
Sour milk cheese	
Schabzieger	
Ewe's cheese	
Goat's milk cheese	
Goat's whey cheese	

Except for soft unripened cheeses, such as cottage and cream cheese, the flavor and texture of cheese are best when served at room temperature. Cheese should usually be removed from the refrigerator about an hour before serving.

Vitamins have many important functions in the human body. Even slight deficiencies affect the proper functioning and lead to impaired health. For example, a 3½ ounce serving of cheese covers 33 percent of the daily requirement for vitamin A and 30 percent of that for vitamin D. Cheese is particularly rich in vitamins since those vitamins contained in the milk remain virtually unchanged.

Usage of the Most Important Types of Cheeses

Usage	Types of cheese
Breakfast	Milder cheeses: mild Emmentaler, Tilsiter, Camembert, or Carre frais
Cheese for melting (grilled cheese sandwiches, meat, Cordon-bleu, gratin, and vegetables)	In Europe Gruyere or Emmentaler are generally used. Tilsiter (especially mild), Raclette cheese, Appenzeller are used for

	certain specialties. When cheese is to be melted, a mature cheese should be used.
Cheese/egg mixtures for cheese cakes, cheese tarts, souffles, and toasted cheese	Classical grated cheese mixtures: *Strong:* ⅔ Gruyere, ⅓ Sbrinz *Medium:* ⅓ Gruyere, ⅓ Emmentaler, ⅓ Sbrinz *Mild:* ⅔ Emmentaler, ⅓ Sbrinz
Grated cheese for flavoring sauces and for serving on pasta, rice, and corn	Sbrinz has a strong flavor, and it does not become stringy when melted. If some stringiness is desired: Gruyere or Emmentaler (for grilled meat and pasta, Schabzieger may also be used).
Fondue	The usual mixture is: ⅔ Gruyere, ⅓ Emmentaler, and sometimes a little Fribourg Vacherin, and Appenzeller.
Cheese salad	Emmentaler and Gruyere are best for cheese salads. Tilsiter spiced with herbs is good for mild cheese salads. Appenzeller is used for a stronger country salad. Many other kinds of cheese, including soft cheeses, can be diced and served in cheese salad.
Cheese dishes, cheese platters, sandwiches	Strong cheese such as Gruyere, Emmentaler, well-matured Tilsiter or Appenzeller, and Sbrinz.
Dessert	Emmentaler, Gruyere, Tilsiter, Appenzeller, Sbrinz, Camembert, Vacherin, Tete de Moine, Swiss, Brie, Romadour, Reblochon, Roquefort, Bel Paese, Gorgonzola, and Edam.

3.3.2 Eggs—Oeufs

Eggs are a versatile and highly nutritious food. Fresh eggs and processed eggs are available on the market in several different forms. The buyer needs to know the products available, the most suitable uses for each product, and the standards of quality for each product.

Composition of Eggs and Their Nutritional Value

The shell constitutes the outer surface of the egg. A thin membrane made up of the inner and outer layer is on the inside of the shell. The air cell at the large end of the egg forms as moisture is lost. The size of the air cell denotes the age of the egg. The egg white is composed of three layers. Next to the shell is a thin, soft, white layer; the layer next to it is thick, viscous, and white; and a thin white layer surrounds the yolk and separates it from the thick white. The chalazae are strands of white substance on each side of the yolk which keep the yolk near the center of the egg. The yolk is made up of layers and is separated from the white by a very thin membrane.

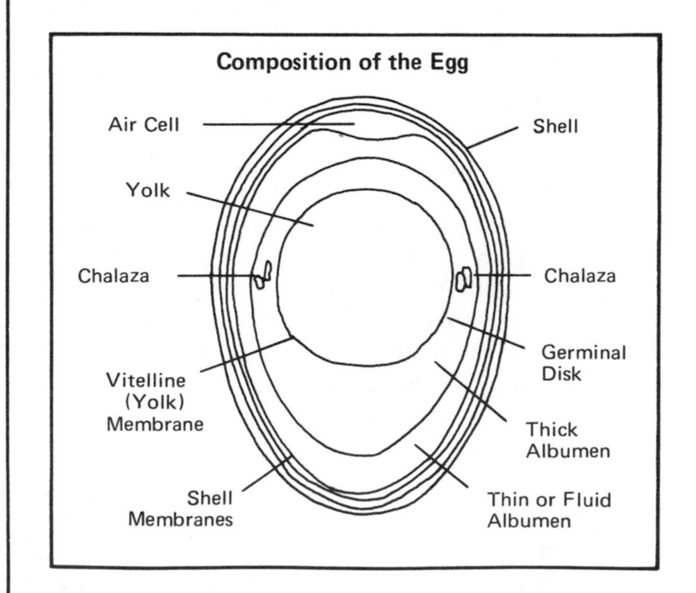

FIGURE 3-63
Composition of the Egg

Each nutrient required by man is found in the egg (water, protein, fat, minerals, vitamin A, Thiamin (B_1), Riboflavin (B_2), and vitamin D, and niacin). Lecithin, which contains phosphorus, is found in the egg yolk. There are approximately 74 calories in a whole egg.

Grades

Grade refers to the interior quality of the egg and the condition and appearance of the shell. The three consumer grades are *United States Grade AA (or Fresh Fancy), United States Grade A,* and *United States Grade B.*

Fresh Fancy Quality (or Grade AA) eggs are produced under the United States Department of Agriculture Control Program. These eggs reach the market quickly under strictly controlled conditions, guaranteeing the consumer a fresh and premium quality product. These eggs are especially good for frying, poaching, cooking in the shell, and for uses where appearance is important. Grade B eggs are suitable for most cooking and baking purposes, for scrambling, omelets, and where appearance is not significant.

Quality is based on the cleanliness, shape, and texture of the shell. The color of the eggshell varies with species and breeds of poultry, and it has no effect on the grade, quality, or nutritional value of the egg. The interior quality is based on the condition of the white and the yolk and the size of the air cell. Top quality eggs have a clean, fine textured, unbroken shell, a very small air cell, a thick and firm white with a yolk that is high, firm, and well-centered. Candling is the process used for checking quality. In this process the eggs are held in front of a light to examine the condition of the shell, the yolk, the white, the germ, and the size of the air cell. The presence of blood spots or meat spots can also be detected and eggs with such defects are sorted out. This time-consuming hand candling operation is being replaced with electronic equipment that can scan or flash candle thousands of eggs per hour. A new method of judging quality based on Haugh Units is more accurate and objective. Random samples are taken from eggs of a single flock. The eggs are broken out on a flat surface and a Haugh meter measures the height of the thick albumen. The other interior and exterior qualities are also evaluated. The eggs in the lot are scored on the basis of the sampling. A score of 72 based on Haugh Units places the lot from which the samples were taken into Grade AA quality.

Egg grading is not mandatory; the Department of Agriculture grading service is provided on a voluntary basis. The service must be requested and paid for by the producer or distributor. The United States grade shield on a carton or case of eggs certifies that the eggs meet federal standards and have been graded for quality under federal-state supervision. In addition to being marked with the United States Grade Shield, cases and cartons of eggs that score Grade A or above may have another label which states, "Produced and Marketed under Federal-State Quality Control Program." Examples of these labels are shown in Figure 3-64

Sample grade labels for shell eggs.
Courtesy, U.S. Department of Agriculture.

FIGURE 3-64
U.S. Grade Shields for Shell Eggs (Courtesy of U.S. Department of Agriculture.)

Size and Price

Eggs are marketed by size, based on the minimum weight of a dozen eggs in the shell. These classifications are:

Jumbo	30 ounces/dozen
Extra Large	27 ounces/dozen
Large	24 ounces/dozen
Medium	21 ounces/dozen
Small	18 ounces/dozen
Peewee	15 ounces/dozen

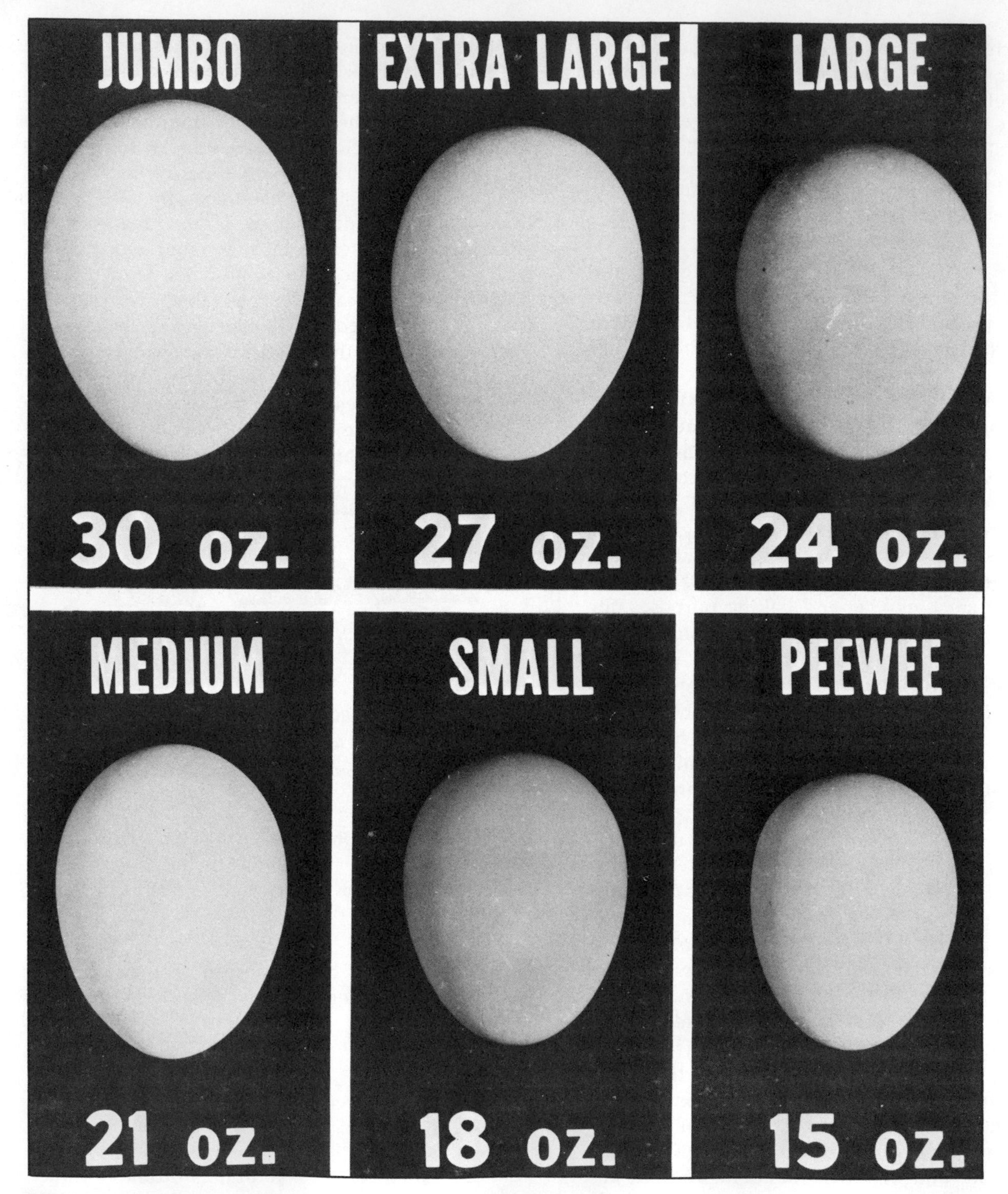

FIGURE 3-65
Minimum Weight per Dozen of the Different Sizes of Eggs (Courtesy of U.S. Department of Agriculture.)

The size is usually indicated on the grade shield, although size and quality are entirely different. Large eggs may be either high or low quality; high quality eggs may be either large or small.

Egg prices vary by size within the same grade. The amount of price variation is influenced by the supply. Constant price fluctuations pose problems in knowing which size to buy. The Department of Agriculture suggests that if less than a 7 cents difference exists between one size and the next smaller size in the same grade, the larger size is the better buy. Some foodservices have limitations on the sizes they buy for specific purposes. Uniformity in size is important for eggs that are served in a cafeteria or for table d'hotel service. If shell eggs are used for baking and general cooking, more standardization of products is experienced if recipes specify weight or measures rather than quantity.

Egg Products

The term egg products refers to liquid, frozen, and dehydrated eggs that are obtained by breaking and processing shell eggs. Included in the products are egg whites, egg yolks, mixed whole eggs, and blends of whole eggs and yolks. Sugar, salt, or corn syrup are sometimes added to improve the physical consistency and functional properties. Egg products are convenient to use, require less storage space, and have a longer shelf life than that of shell eggs. Liquid or frozen eggs packed in milk cartons are convenient for use in restaurants and institutions. Bakeries are the largest users of frozen whole eggs and frozen egg whites.

Dehydrated eggs are obtained by removing the water from the same egg products. Chief users of dried egg products are cake mix manufacturers, candy manufacturers, and manufacturers of meringue powders.

Other commercially produced egg products are hard-cooked eggs that are marketed in frozen form, scrambled egg mixes, and dietary foods. Egg products are processed under a strict inspection system under the direction of the United States Department of Agriculture. All products are pasteurized. Pasteurization is important to control Salmonella infection.

3.4 Edible Fats and Oils—Graisşes de huiles comestibles

Two main groups are defined according to their origin:

- animal fats
- vegetable fats and oils

Edible Fats and Oils

Animal Origin		*Vegetable Origin*	
Milk Fats	Body Fats	Fruit Oils	Seed Fats and Oils
Butter	Lard Suet Chicken fat	Olive Oil Palm Oil	Coconut Oil Palm Nut Oil Peanut Oil Sunflower Oil Soybean Oil Rapeseed Oil Sesame Oil Cottonseed Oil Poppyseed Oil

Labeling. The Food and Drug Administration requires that certain information be specified on the labels which identify fats and oils. The information must include the common legal name of the product; the ingredients used in the product or the standard of identity; any preservatives, additives, or artificial flavors or colors; the net weight or quantity of the product in the container. If the product contains a combination of oils or fats, the specific oils or fats must be listed on the label.

3.4.1 Animal Fats

Lard is fat rendered from the fat tissues of hogs. The quality of the lard depends on the parts of the hog from which the fat was obtained and on the method of processing. Leaf lard is the highest quality lard; it comes from the abdominal cavity. Pork fat from other sources must be labeled "rendered pork fat."

Moisture rendering is the best process for extracting lard. Lard obtained by this process is known as "kettle-rendered" lard.

Beef Fats. The highest quality beef fats come from the abdominal cavities of cattle. Suet fats have limited use in foodservices. These fats may be refined and hydrogenated (a process used to harden liquid oils. Hydrogen is added to the unsaturated carbons joined by double bonds. The process improves the plasticity of the fat, removes objectionable odors and flavors, raises the melting point, and improves the keeping quality).

3.4.2 Vegetable Fats and Oils.

Most vegetable oils originate from the seeds of plants; there are, however, some exceptions. Olive oil comes from the meat of olives, and palm oil comes from the nut of the palm. The vegetable oils are easy to handle because they are in liquid form and require no melting.

Storage. Fats and oils may become rancid when in contact with light, moisture, and high temperatures. They should be stored in airtight containers in an area that is dark, dry, and below 70°F. (21°C.).

Processing. The method used for processing the oil differs with the various fruits, seeds, and grains. After cleaning and crushing, the oil is extracted by a *cold press treatment* or a *hot press treatment* depending on the fruit or seed. The cold press treatment is used for olive oil, coconut oil, and sunflower oil. The temperature in the press of the cold press method does not exceed 120°F. (49°C.). In the hot press treatment, the oil in the plant cells is preheated to approximately 175°F. (80°C.). Oils processed by this method are thinner and easier to extract. Oils produced by the cold press method are usually more expensive. After the initial pressing, additional oil is extracted from further pressings. *Refining* is the process used to remove any foreign particles and off-flavors and odors from the oil.

Some Important Vegetable Fats and Oils

COCONUT OIL – GRAISSE DE COCO

Coconut oil is extracted from the copra, the dried white meat from the nut of the coconut palm tree. These trees are found along tropical and subtropical coastlines.

PEANUT OIL – HUILE D'ARACHIDES

Peanut oil is made from the fruit of the peanut plant, which is an annual herb-like species. Peanuts are found in all the tropical regions of the world.

RAPESEED OIL – HUILE DE COLZE

Rapeseed is the only oil plant which is cultivated in any quantity in the temperate areas of Europe. The oil made from this plant is used for brushing loaves of bread before baking and for green salads.

OLIVE OIL – HUILE D'OLIVE

Olive oil is obtained by crushing and pressing the ripe fruits of the olive tree. These trees are grown in the Mediterranean regions, Australia, China, and California. Having a very pronounced fruity taste, olive oil of the first pressing is the highest quality, and it is known as virgin oil or *huile vierge.*

PALM OIL, PALM NUT OIL – HUILE DE PALME, HUILE DE PALMISTE

Both oils come from the fruit of the oil palm – the palm oil from the flesh of the fruit, palm nut oil from the kernel.

SESAME OIL – HUILE DE SESAME

Sesame oil has been used as a cooking oil for thousands of years. It is also used as a salad oil and for making margarine. The sesame plant is an annual aromatic herb. Sesame oil has a very high content of the essential fatty acids.

SOYBEAN OIL – HUILE DE SOJA

Soybean oil comes from the seeds of soya beans, a plant originating in China. It is now cultivated in other countries, chiefly in the United States and in Brazil.

SUNFLOWER OIL – HUILE DE TOURNESOL

This oil comes from sunflower seeds. Originating in Mexico, the sunflower reached Europe and has spread throughout Spain, France, and the East. The USSR is the world's largest producer today. Other major cultivation areas are South America, southeastern Europe, and Africa.

Other oil fruits

There are many other oil plants in the world; the oil derived from their fruits include: hemp oil, poppyseed oil, corn oil, wheat oil, linseed oil, and safflower oil.

3.4.3 Margarine

Margarine is a widely used product manufactured from one or more of the various approved animal or vegetable fats and other ingredients. The manufacturing process must comply with the quality and health controls of federal and state pure food laws and the Federal Standard. The product must be labeled oleomargarine or margarine. Oleo means beef fat and at one time most margarines were produced from the olein fats of beef. Today soy oil is used more than any other fat. Margarine is also made from coconut oil, palm nut oil, sunflower oil, and/or palm oil. It is suitable for use as a spread, for baking, roasting, simmering, and for making sauces. Margarines differ from each other in flavor, texture, melting points, and other physical characteristics.

The Manufacture of Margarine

Margarine must by law contain 90 percent fat. It also contains 17 to 18½ percent pasteurized skim milk. It usually contains 1½ to 3 percent salt; however, salt-free margarine is available. Margarine may be graded and the grades are similar to those of butter. The color should be a light yellow; the flavor and odor should be fresh and pleasing. Margarines should be stored at refrigerated temperatures.

3.5 Plant foods

Plant foods are nutritious and inexpensive. High quality fruits and vegetables are available in both fresh and frozen form throughout the year. Rich in minerals and vitamins, carbohydrates, and proteins,

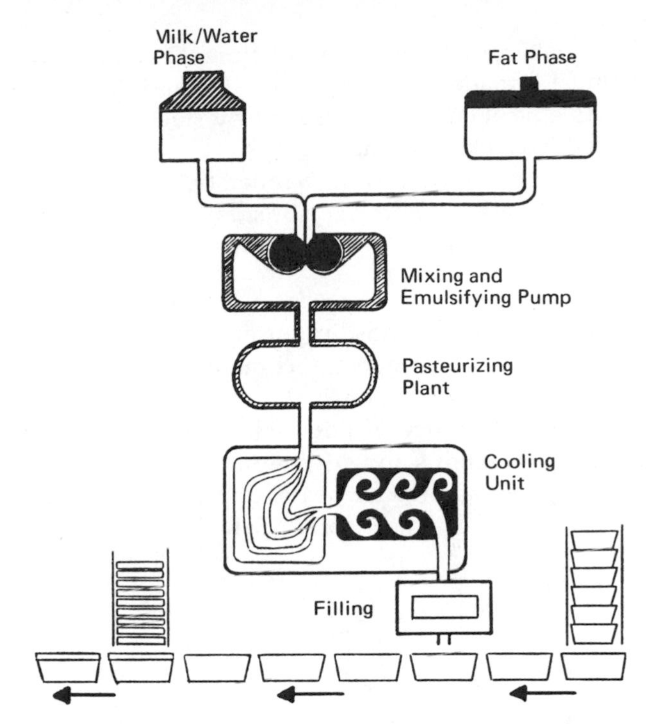

FIGURE 3-66
The Manufacture of Margarine

plant foods assist in the performance of many body functions and are essential in human diets. Fresh fruits and vegetables are perishable and should be prepared, stored, and/or preserved promptly after harvesting to avoid loss of nutrients and to assure maximum eating quality. Baking, steaming, and simmering are the basic cooking methods recommended for minimum loss of nutrients. Freezing fresh fruits and vegetables at 32°F. (0°C.) or lower for a limited period of time is the best method of preserving their nutrients.

3.5.1 Cereals—Cereales

OATS—AVOINE

Oats and other preparations of rolled oats are popular breakfast foods in many countries. The outer husk is removed from the kernel of the grain, leaving the groat. Scotch or regular oatmeal is made by steaming the groats for a long period of time. Quick-cooking oatmeal is made by cutting, pressing, and drying the groats. "Steel cut" groats are cut by steel cutters and resemble cracked wheat.

Usage: Oats, processed into rolled oats, are used for breakfast cereals, porridge, breads, muffins, cakes, cookies, and desserts.

WHEAT – FROMENT

Wheats produce the most important of all cereal grain foods grown in temperate climates. Next to rice, wheat is used more extensively than any other grain. Wheat is the source of flour which is produced by grinding the grains and sifting out the chaff. Wheats are classified as bread wheats, durum wheat, emer, rivet, or English wheat. Bread wheats include hard wheats and soft wheats. The hard wheats are the source of the highest quality bread flours because of the high protein content and the high proportion of gluten (the substance in which the starch granules are embedded). In contrast to hard wheats, the soft wheat is high in starch content and mealy in texture. The air pockets between the grains give the wheat a soft floury appearance. Soft wheats are used to make the highly refined flour used in the preparation of cakes, pastries, and biscuits. Durum, which is amber in color, also contains a high proportion of gluten. It is largely used for the manufacture of semolina which is then made into pasta products (noodles, macaroni, and spaghetti). Flours made from emer wheat or from rivet or English wheat are inferior in quality to those milled from the bread wheats, and therefore, these are generally used as food for livestock.

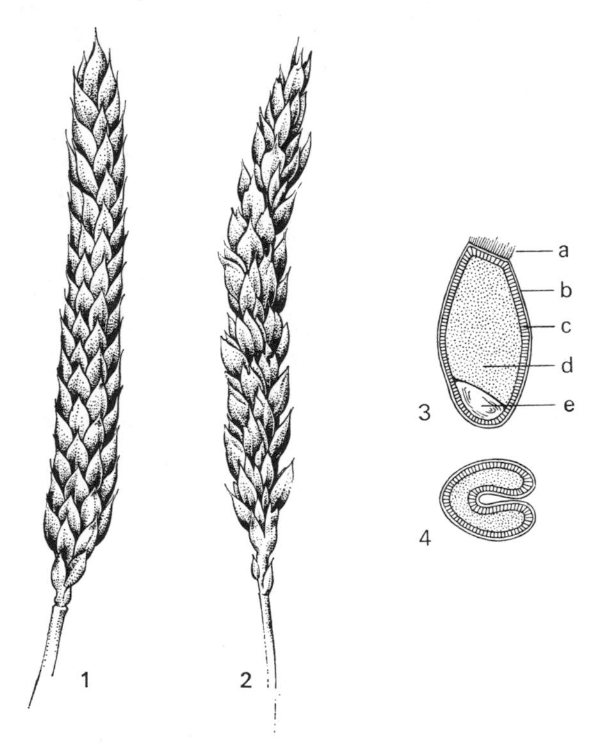

1 Hybrid Wheat
2. Natural Wheat
3 Longitudinal Section of a Grain of Wheat
4 Cross-section

3 (a) Brush
(b) Pericarp
(c) Bran
(d) Endosperm
(e) Germ

FIGURE 3-67
Wheat – Froment

Buckwheat is an herb with a triangular shaped seed. Although buckwheat is not a cereal, the seeds can be ground into a flour-like substance which is called buckwheat flour. This flour is used to make griddle cakes and Russian blinis.

CORN – MAIS

The only cereal crop that is American in origin is corn. In the United States, the world's largest producer, corn is grown as food for both people and livestock. Although the United States uses most of its corn for feeding livestock, it is a staple food for the people of South America, eastern Africa, and southeastern Europe. Corn has a high starch content and contains traces of carotene and copper. In addition to its use as a vegetable, corn is ground into a meal and used for cornmeal, corn flour, cornstarch, hominy grits, and corn oil.

MILLET – MILLET

The most widely-grown millets are sorghum, finger millet, and bulrush millet. Nutritionally, millets have a higher content of minerals than most other grains. This grain is made into golden millet, millet flakes, millet semolina, millet meal, sorghum, and beer.

BARLEY – ORGE

There are two types of barley: two-rowed barley and six-rowed barley. Most of the barley grown in the

British Isles is the two-row variety, and the seedlings are dried and used to produce malt for making beer. Pearl barley, used in soups and stews, is made by removing the husks and polishing the grains.

RICE—RIZ

Origin: The history of rice has been traced to a plant called "Newaree" which was grown in India as early as 3000 B.C. The word "rice" in Chinese means "agriculture" or "culture." Although rice originated in Asia, the largest exporter of rice today is the United States. Other rice producers are India, Java, Australia, Thailand, Italy, and France.

Types: There are 7,000 or more known varieties of rice. These varieties can be classified into three main groups: long, medium, and short grain. Long grain rice tends to separate and is light and fluffy when cooked. It is usually preferred for steamed rice, soups, salads, and for chicken, fish, and meat combinations. Short and medium grain rice are moist and tender when cooked. The particles of rice cling together. The flavor of these varieties are preferred by many persons, and they are especially popular for food items that require a tender easily molded rice, such as rice rings, croquettes, loaves, puddings, and desserts.

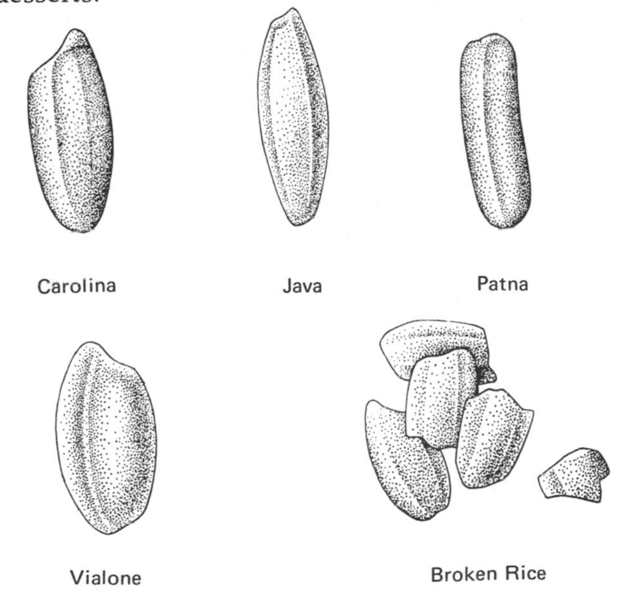

FIGURE 3-68
Rice—Riz

Parboiled or converted rice is steamed before it is milled. The process aids in retaining the vitamins and minerals. Precooked rice is usually fortified with additional vitamins. It has been milled and cooked and the moisture has been removed through a dehydration process. This instant type rice is easily and quickly prepared by restoring the moisture with boiling water.

Usage: The following rice dishes are well-known: soup caroline, risotto, creole rice, pilau rice, Indian rice, jambalaya, and rice pudding.

RYE—SEIGLE

The grain of rye is similar in composition to that of wheat. It is made into rye flour. In Europe, its chief use is for making black bread. Rye is used for making rye bread and whisky in America.

3.5.2 Leguminous Plants—Legumineaux

Quality characteristics: Leguminous plants contain important nutrients; in fact, they are the best source of plant protein. In addition, they contain carbohydrates, potassium, and phosphorus. Good legumes must be whole and shiny. Wrinkled surfaces indicate improper or excessive storage. Legumes in this condition will not become soft when cooked.

Usage: Legumes may be prepared in many ways as vegetables, salads, soups, and in combinations with other foods. Legumes are available in whole, split, or ground form.

DRIED BEANS—HARICOTS SECS

These beans are the mature, shelled, and dried garden variety. The best known type for cooking purposes is the round white *Brittany bean* or, in the United States, the *navy* or *Boston bean.* Other well-known types include: the large flat *Soissons-bean;* the long, light-green *lima bean;* the *ballet-bean;* the brown *quail-bean;* and the Italian *Borlotti-bean* for minestrone soup.

LENTILS—LENTILLES

These are produced in Chile, Italy, Rumania, and Egypt. The best variety is the light-green, flat lentil.

PEAS – POIS

There are two types: yellow peas (e.g. Victoria) and green peas (e.g. Saint-Germain).

3.5.3 Ground Products and Starches — Produits Moulus et Amidons

Quality and characteristics: All flour products must be kept in dry, clean, light, and well-ventilated storerooms. Flour responds to changes in humidity and it absorbs moisture very quickly. Unless properly stored, flour products may become moldy or rancid. These products are then attractive to many types of insects. These include:

- *The flour moth.* The eggs of the flour moth are sometimes in the filaments of the flour where they develop into caterpillars (flour worms) and moths that are grayish-yellow in color.
- *The flour mite.* Related to the spider, the flour mite grows to a length of about .06 inches. This insect which is hardly visible is found only in flour that has a high moisture content.
- *The flour beetle.* This small reddish-brown to black beetle is approximately ½ inch in length.

CRACKER CRUMBS – BRISURES

Dried biscuit and cracker fragments are crushed and sieved, and used for lining pastry molds, for au gratins, and for making cakes and puddings.

DUNST – CENDREE

A type of flour ground to a degree of fineness between that of semolina and flour. It is primarily used for making pasta.

BRAN – EGRUGE

The product comes from the remnants of ground cereals. It is used for baking whole-grain bread and crisp wafers.

FLOUR – FARINE

There are three types of flours: *baking flours, soup flours,* and *starches and binding flours.*

Baking flours. These include wheat flour and rye flour. Of all the different types of flour derived from the wheat grain, the only kinds used in good cooking are white flour, wheat flour, and premium flour. These are obtained from the lightest, middle part of the grain. Good, glutenous white flour is clinging, and the fineness of the particles is apparent. It should smell fresh and on tasting should only taste sweet after chewing for a time. Pastries made from good white flour should quickly form a crust on the outside, and should not remain greasy. White flour is used in the kitchen for soups, sauces, and pastries. The flour should be passed through a sieve before use, in order to remove possible filaments, insects, and lumps.

Soup flours. Products made from rice flour, oat flour, barley flour, green rye flour, bean flour, and pea flour.

Starch and binding flour. Practically the only starches (carbohydrates) used are those from cereals and from leguminous, bulbed or root plants. For example: *wheat starch, rice starch, cornstarch (corn flour), potato starch (fecula). Arrowroot starch* is especially used for children's food.

FLAKES – FLOCONS

Oats, rice, and corn can be made into flakes. The raw grains are first cleaned and then treated under vacuum, which breaks up the starch and makes it digestible. The vacuum-treated grains are then dried and hulled or husked in a suitable machine. Finally, they are crushed between rollers into flakes. *Oatflakes* are produced by the above process from broken oat grains and are used for soups, health foods, Birchermuesli, porridge, and popcorn.

GRUEL – GRUAU

These are broken oat, rice, or barley grains that are mostly used for porridge.

POT BARLEY – ORGES MONDES

These are cleaned and polished round barley or wheat grains that are used for soups and desserts, and the best varieties are used as food for the sick.

PEARL TAPIOCA – PERLES DE JAPON

This is prepared by washing the starch from the tubers of the cassava plant. The starch is dried in the form of small round balls or flakes. During cooking they swell to the size of peas and become glassy and transparent.

SAGO – SAGOU

The sago palm, in the countries of southeast Asia, is the most important source of sago. The pith is scooped from the logs of the tree and the starch from the pith is washed and dried. When dried at this stage, the starch is used for sago flour. When producing pearl sago, a wet starch paste is pressed through a fine sieve and the grains are dried on an oscillating hot plate. The grains are white or slightly yellow, and they have no taste and no odor.

SEMOLINA – SEMOULE

Semolina is made from flour milled from durum wheat. It is available in fine, medium, and rough forms. Good semolina should be yellowish-white (slightly creamy) and dry. A special hard, glutenous wheat semolina is used for making pasta. Semolina is used for soups, gnocchis, puddings, and dietary dishes.

TAPIOCA – TAPIOCA

The Brazilian cassava root and certain Indian palms are the source of tapioca and tapioca flour. These products are used for fruit fillings and sauces.

3.5.3.1 Bread – Pain

Ordinary bread is made from wheat flour, and it is designated according to the type of wheat flour used; e.g. *white bread, whole-wheat bread, graham bread, stone-ground bread, crisp wafers and pumpernickel* are all specially prepared whole meal breads. *Diet breads* and *bread for diabetics* are prescribed according to the illness in question.

Storage

Bread products should be stored in well-ventilated, cool, and clean areas. Bread refrigerated at 40°F. (4°C.) will stale more quickly than bread stored at room temperature. Freezing is the most effective method of retaining the flavor, freshness, aroma, and moisture of bread products. Before freezing the bread should be thoroughly cooled and then securely wrapped in moisture-vaporproof bags, sealed, labeled, and dated.

Spoilage

Bread may be stored in the refrigerator to inhibit mold growth, particularly during hot weather. Mold may occur if bread is not cooled sufficiently before wrapping or if it is stored in a humid atmosphere, or at a high temperature, or in a poorly ventilated area. The potato mold may develop in breads with a low acid content if the temperature of the storage area is over 70°F. (21°C.).

Four stages of making white bread:

- *dough preparation:* Sifted wheat flour is mixed into a dough with water and salt. To these ingredients yeast is added. (Sugar and butter are other ingredients frequently included in bread formulas. Sugar, in controlled amounts, increases the fermentation and shortening improves the flavor.) The dough is thoroughly mixed or kneaded to develop the gluten.
- *fermentation:* The dough should be placed in a warm and rather humid place and allowed to rise until double in bulk. It is usually desirable to punch the dough down and let it rise a second time.
- *dividing and shaping:* After the dough has risen, it is divided. It should then be allowed to rest about 10 minutes so that it will be more pliable and easy to handle. The dough is then shaped into loaves or rolls.
- *proofing and baking:* Bread products should double in bulk during the proofing period. The bread will continue to rise during the baking period. It should be baked 30 to 50 minutes depending upon the size and shape of the loaf. Bake the bread in an oven at 390°F. to 480°F. (199°C. to 248°C.).

Baking Process

The dough rises rapidly during the early stages of baking. The expansion of the carbon dioxide gas and the enzymatic activity increase at a rapid rate.

Dough Leavening Agents

Yeast. Yeasts are unicellular plant organisms which can only be seen with a microscope. They reproduce by budding. They live primarily on sugars, which

they convert into alcohol and carbon dioxide gas. In this way, these organisms can be used for raising dough and for the manufacture of beer, wine, and brandy.
Storage. Wrap yeast in a damp cloth and store in the refrigerator.
Baking Powder. The various kinds of baking powder consist of these substances: sodium carbonate, tartar, and starch. In a chemical reaction they produce carbon dioxide, which results in the raising of the dough.
Storage. Dry.
Salt of Hartshorn (ammonium carbonate). This substance is developed when heating carbon dioxide and ammonium hydroxide (a solution of ammonia gas in water is ammonium hydroxide). The salt consists primarily of ammonium bicarbonate and can be manufactured by a number of different processes. Formerly, it was produced by dry distillation of hartshorn.
Storage. Salt of hartshorn must be stored in hermetically sealed cans in a cool place.
Potash. Potassium carbonate, in contact with acids, produces carbon dioxide. In spice cookies, the acids (formic acid) present in the honey activate the potash.
Alcohol. Brandy, kirsch, and rum.
Egg White. Stiffly beaten egg whites.

Cakes, Pies, and Cookies

In addition to wheat flour, other ingredients, especially milk, butter, margarine, sugar, nuts, spices, honey, and fruit are used for making fine baked goods. The more milk and fats (butter) used, the finer and more delicate the resulting product. Yeast, baking powder, salt of hartshorn, honey, and alcohol can all be used for raising the dough.

3.5.3.2 Pasta – Pates

Manufacture. Pastas are made with wheat flour products and water. Usually a very finely ground hard wheat semolina is used in industrial production. The high gluten content of the hard wheat flours helps retain the shape, texture, and form of the pastas during cooking. According to government standards, *egg noodles* must contain 5.3 percent egg in the finished product. Pastas are pressed through a die into the desired shape while still soft and then thoroughly dried so that all the moisture is evaporated.
Nutritional content. Pastas have a very high carbohydrate (starch) content. Pastas are usually combined with other foods such as cheese, meats, vegetables, and sauces which provide additional nutrients.
Storage. Pastas must be stored in light, dry, and well-ventilated areas. Exposure to humidity causes them to mold, and appropriate storing should eliminate the problem of flour mites.
Cooking. Pastas should be cooked in a large quantity of rapidly boiling water, 2 gallons (7.6 liters) of water per pound (.5 kilogram) of pasta. The pasta should be immersed into the water gradually so that the boiling temperature can be maintained. All pastas should be cooked *al dente,* meaning "to the teeth." This denotes a slight resistance to the bite and a chewy, firm texture with no taste of raw flour. When the al dente stage is reached, the pasta should be rinsed in cold water and drained. It should be dipped in hot water before serving. Depending on the recipe, the pasta is mixed with butter, spices, or sauce. The cooking time of pastas varies from 5 to 15 minutes depending on the variety.
Usage. Pasta is used as an hors d'oeuvre or as a side dish with meat dishes or as a main course.

3.5.4 Vegetables – Legumes

The term vegetables refers to all plants or parts of plants that are eaten in raw, boiled, or preserved form. Vegetables are important for their nutritional value. Cereals, spices, and fruit are not classed as vegetables.

Species and Description

- *preserved vegetables* mean vegetables which have been prepared and preserved. These include all canned vegetables, dried vegetables, deep-frozen vegetables, and those which have been preserved with salt and vinegar.

- *canned vegetables* are those which have been processed and sterilized in cans or jars to preserve them.
- *fresh vegetables* are divided into these categories:

Root and Tuber Vegetables—Legumes a racines: Fennel, Jerusalem artichoke, carrot, potato, celery root (celeriac), nettle root, kohlrabi, rutabaga, horseradish, beet, salsify, and turnip
Stem Vegetables—Legumes a cotes: Cardoon, asparagus, and celery
Leafy Vegetables—Legumes a feuilles: Swiss chard, sorrel, and spinach
Salad Vegetables—Legumes salades: Endive, lettuce, chicory, watercress, and mustard
Cabbages—Choux: Cauliflower, green cabbage, brussels sprouts, red cabbage, broccoli, white cabbage, savoy cabbage, and kale
Fruit and Seed Vegetables—Legumes a graines et a fruits: Artichoke, eggplant, beans, peas, cucumbers, shell beans, corn, tomato, and zucchini
Bulbous Vegetables—Oignons: Garlic, leek, dwarf onion, shallot, and onion

Quality characteristics. Vegetables should be uniform in size and shape, crisp, firm, free of defects, mechanical damage, and decay. They should have a fresh appearance and a bright color. Vegetables are important for their minerals, vitamins, trace elements, and essential oils. They are highly versatile in terms of preparation and provide variety to the menu.
Storage. Vegetables are very perishable and require careful handling. Most vegetables require low storage temperatures and high humidity; however, there are some exceptions. All vegetables should be inspected on receipt and stored promptly at the recommended temperature and humidity. Most vegetables have a limited keeping period and should be used soon after purchase.
Seasons. Fresh vegetables are available throughout the year; however, they are at their peak during their season of the year. Vegetables purchased out of season will most likely be high in price and not of the best quality. Vegetables will most likely be of superior quality and lower in price during the time they are in season. (See seasonal chart, section 3.5.11.)
The vegetables and their seasons:

- *spring vegetables:* Spinach, spring lettuce, carrots, lettuce, dandelions, lamb's lettuce, radishes, sorrel, asparagus
- *summer vegetables:* Artichokes, eggplant, beans, peas, cucumbers, cabbages, lettuce, tomatoes, zucchini
- *fall vegetables:* Cardoons, potatoes, cabbages, leeks, parsnips, celery, and all types of bulbous vegetables
- *winter vegetables:* Rutabaga, endive, celery root (celeriac), beets, brussels sprouts, salsify, turnips

Usage. Vegetables provide flavor, texture, and color to the menu. They are the source of many essential nutrients that are not present in adequate amounts in other foods. They are one of the major sources of vitamins A and C in the diet. Both cooked and raw vegetables are good sources of fiber, or bulk, and many vegetables may be used in quite generous amounts in low caloric weight reduction diets.
Methods of Cooking Vegetables. Blanching preceding further preparation: boiling, steaming, sauteing, deep-fat frying, gratinating, glazing, simmering, and grilling.
Artichoke—Artichaut. A thistle-like flowering plant, artichokes are culinary delicacies. The reddish or blue-brown varieties are superior to the green varieties. The base of the flower and the lower thicker part of the leaves are fleshy and flavorful. They are used for both hot and cold specialty dishes. France is the home of the artichoke, although Spain, United States, and Italy also supply good quality artichokes.
Asparagus—Asperge. A luxury vegetable which is in season from April to June. The young asparagus shoots with their purple tips or green tips are superior to mature tough and woody asparagus. Among the canned asparagus, the tender California variety is well-known.
Beans (fresh)—Haricots (frais). The approximately

fifty different varieties are divided into three categories. These are: the young, *string (snap) bean*, which should contain few, if any, seeds; the larger, light green *French bean* with immature seeds; and the tender light green *runner bean*. Each variety should be well-formed, firm, tender, and free of defects. Beans come onto the market from early summer until October. Matured beans are shelled and used as seeds or as a dry vegetable.

Beets—Betterave. Beets are round or long-shaped root tubers and the interior of the young beets is deep red. The interior texture of mature beets is stringy and the color is often a pale pink. Beets are prepared in different ways for vegetables, for salads, for garnishes, and for soups.

Black Salsify—Salsifis. This long, fleshy, root, ½ inch (1.2 centimeters) to 1 inch (2.5 centimeters) thick with a black skin and white flesh, is eaten as a boiled vegetable. When snapped in two, good fresh black salsify should contain milky juice; older black salsify is woody and spongy. The young leaves are sometimes eaten in salads. Although originally from southern European countries, black salsify is now grown all over Europe and in the United States.

Broccoli—Broccoli. The term "broccoli" usually refers to sprouting broccoli rather than heading broccoli. The latter is very similar to cauliflower. The plant forms a head, looser than cauliflower, of green buds and a thick fleshy stalk.

Brussels Sprouts—Choux de Bruxelles. Brussels sprouts are a variety of cabbage. The small, firmly-closed green sprouts grow along the stalks. Brussels sprouts are available throughout the year but are most abundant from September to February. They may be boiled, baked, steamed, or French-fried.

Green Cabbage—Choux verts. This variety of cabbage does not form a head. The leaves are dark green and very curly and wrinkled. It is generally used for vegetable soup.

Savoy Cabbage—Chou frise. This cabbage is easily identified by the crinkling of the tissues through the greenish-yellow leaves. The heads are loosely formed with a softer and more widely opened bud than green cabbage, and the flavor is milder.

White Cabbage—Chou blanc. United States standards for cabbage provide for two grades: U.S. 1 and U.S. Commercial. The heads of cabbage should be firm or hard with leaves that are tightly closed and finely ribbed. The weight of cabbage heads ranges from 1 to 9 pounds (.5 to 5 kilograms).

Cardoons—Cardon (Carde). A French vegetable consisting of a bundle of veined leaves. The center leaves are very tender. This vegetable, in season in the fall and the winter, grows to a height of 4½ feet (135 centimeters). Cardoons are also cultivated in other parts of the world.

Carrot—Carotte. Young, tender carrots are available in spring and early summer. The small ones, which are stumpy at the bottom, are the best quality. The carrot is a versatile vegetable and is good when served raw or cooked, alone, or in combination with other foods. Carrots add color, texture, and flavor to many foods and have a high sugar content. They are a rich source of vitamin A.

Cauliflower—Chou-fleur. Cauliflower is a popular vegetable available throughout the year. The large flower should be firm, white in color, and surrounded by green leaves. The so-called Paris cauliflower with its large flower and also the Dutch cauliflower are good varieties. Cauliflower became an important crop in the United States in about 1920. Coast areas, such as parts of the Pacific Coast and Long Island, New York, and high altitudes in Colorado are important production centers. The peak of the marketing season is October, and there are relatively large supplies in September and November. The supply is lower from May through August.

Celeriac—Celeri-rave. Celeriac is grown all over Europe, but is rare in the United States. Closely related to celery, the stem is the edible part of celery, whereas the part of celeriac that is eaten is the swollen base of the stem. It may be boiled and eaten as a vegetable. It is also used in soups, stews, and salads. If the skins are properly cleaned, they can be used in soups. Medium-sized celeriacs are preferred. The large ones are often hollow and spongy.

Celery Stalks—Celeri en branche. Celery belongs to the Unbelliferae family, frequently referred to as the parsley family. The characteristic flavor and odor of the plants of this family are the result of the volatile oils found in the stems, leaves, and seeds. Celery varieties are classified by color, *green* and *golden*, and by types within the colors. The types of *green* celery are Utah, crystal, and various types of Pascal. The *golden* varieties are divided into Golden Self-Blanching, Golden Plume, and other types. The leaf stalks grow together in a tight bunch; the inner part, the heart, is especially tender. Celery is used as an appetizer, a salad, and a vegetable. It is also used in soups, sauces, stuffings, and relishes. The seeds are also used for flavoring.

Chicory—Chicoree. There are various types of chicory, all of which are used as salads. Some varieties are grown for their large roots. These are dried, roasted, ground, and blended with some coffees. The best known salad varieties are:

- Broad-leafed Endive—Chicoree scarol
- Chicory—Endive de Bruxelles
- Endive—Chicoree frisee
- Red Chicory—Barbe-de-Capucin

Chinese Artichokes—Crosnes du Japon. A small delicate spiral-shaped tuber which is usually served *a la creme.* Originally this was an oriental vegetable, but it is now grown in most warm climates.

Chinese Cabbage—Chou de chine. This variety has a very long, tightly-closed head, and the flavor is similar to that of celery. It is used in soups and salads.

Cress—Cresson. There are two types of cress:

- *Watercress—Cresson de fontaine.* This cress grows best in running water. It also grows in ditches and along streams, but it is usually cultivated for commercial purposes. It has a very high mineral content, primarily iron, and it is rich in Vitamins A and C. It is used raw in salads, and in soups, sandwiches, sauces, and as a garnish.
- *Garden Cress—Cresson de jardin.* This is similar to watercress, although less spicy in taste. It is cultivated in gardens and is native to Europe. It is used in the same way as water cress. This cress wilts very quickly and, therefore, should be prepared just before using.

Cucumber—Concombre. There are two types of cucumber: those which have been grown in hothouses, known as indoor or long cucumbers, and those grown out-of-doors, known as outdoor or ridge cucumbers. Cucumbers are used for soups, salads, and as vegetables and garnishes. Young cucumbers are sterilized together with herbs and sugar in vinegar, and are sold under one of the following names according to their size, cut, and method of preparation: *gherkins, delicatessen pickles, spiced pickles, mustard pickles, dill pickles,* and *sweet pickles.* The main producers are the United States, Holland, Belgium, Germany, and Israel.

Eggplant—Aubergine. This is a long or round fruit from the Solanaceae family, violet in color, and better known as eggplant in the United States. Eggplant is eaten as a cooked vegetable and is at its peak in the summer and fall.

Fennel—Fenouil. In its prime in summer and winter, the fruit of fennel is a tightly closed leafy bulb which grows in southern climates and has a characteristic fine anise aroma. The leaves are used in sauces, soups, and salads. The fleshy bulbous stem is eaten raw or cooked as a vegetable.

Garlic—Ail. A round-shaped bulb formed by several individual cloves enclosed within the skin of the bulb. It is used for seasoning hot dishes, or for cold dishes, salads, dressings, and sauces.

Jerusalem Artichoke—Topinambour. This artichoke is an irregularly-shaped tuber, often covered with wart-like spots. It is about the size of a potato with a high water content, an earthy odor, and a faint taste of turnips. The tubers can be boiled, baked, and used in soups and stews.

Kohlrabi—Chou-rave. Kohlrabi can be distinguished from other tuber-forming vegetables by the bulb-like thickening of the stem 1 to 3 inches (2.5 to 7.5 centimeters) above the ground. This is the edible portion of the plant, and it is usually yellow-green or violet in color. The plant is harvested when the bulb-like part is 2 or 3 inches (5 to 7.5 centimeters) in diameter. It grows larger but it is then too woody and tough for eating. The name, "rabi," means turnip. This bulb-like part may be eaten raw or as a cooked vegetable. The young leaves may also be used as a salad or they may be steamed.

Lamb's Lettuce—Mache/Doucette. This is a valerian plant generally used as a salad. Today it is often cultivated, but also grows wild. Its main season is winter. This plant should not be confused with rampion which is used chiefly for its roots.

Leek—Poireau. The common leek grows from a bulbous root into a long, tightly-closed leaf stalk which is green at the top where the leaves are separated. The blanched, elongated bulb is used as a vegetable and for seasoning in soups, sauces, and stews.

Lettuce—Laitue. There are several varieties of lettuce which can be classified as salad vegetables. The best known are:

- Looseleaf or Bunching Lettuce—Laitue a tondre (couper) (open, loosely branched varieties that do not form a head)
- Butterhead Lettuce—Laitue pommee (soft pliable leaves with a buttery flavor. Boston and Bibb are principal types of the variety.)
- Cos Lettuce or Romaine – Laitue romaine (elongated, stiff-leaved)
- Crisphead Lettuce—Crisphead lettuce (often but incorrectly called Iceberg)
- Stem Lettuce—Stem lettuce (the seedstalk is the edible part of this lettuce. It is an ingredient in many Chinese dishes.)

All varieties of lettuce are a basic ingredient of most salads. The popularity of tossed salad has increased the demand for cos varieties. Characteristics of good quality: medium to light green color; firm but not hard heads; fresh and tender leaves. Almost all varieties are cultivated in hothouses and are available on most markets throughout the year. The season is at its peak from June to October.

Onion—Oignon. The real, large onion is round, slightly flattened or pear-shaped, and it contains a milky juice. Onions should be firm and dry with small necks. Avoid onions with thick woody centers in the neck or with fresh sprouts.

Parsnip—Panais. This is a hybrid between the carrot and parsley roots. Parsnips are shaped like carrots. The flesh is fine-grained, tender, and white. They have a sweet, nutty, spicy flavor similar to that of celery. The roots are usually used for seasoning, while the tubers are used for vegetable soup and as a vegetable.

Green Peas—Petits pois. These are the immature *shelled peas.* These peas are considered the finest flavored. They should be picked when young and shelled while fresh just before cooking. Mature peas are ripened for use as dried peas. When dried, they may be used as seeds or for yellow pea soup.

Sugar (snow) Peas—Pois mange-tout. An immature pea with a tender shrunken pod. Both pea and pod can be eaten. The pod should be green and tender. The peak seasons are spring and summer. Mature peas are podded and dried as green peas.

Potato—Pomme de terre. The potato tuber is an enlarged part of the ground stem. The potato has liberal amounts of water, carbohydrates, protein, minerals, and vitamins.

The types of potatoes generally found on the United States market are classified by their shape and skin color. Potatoes are long or round and their skin color may be white, red, or russet. The principal varieties of each of these types are the Russet Burbank

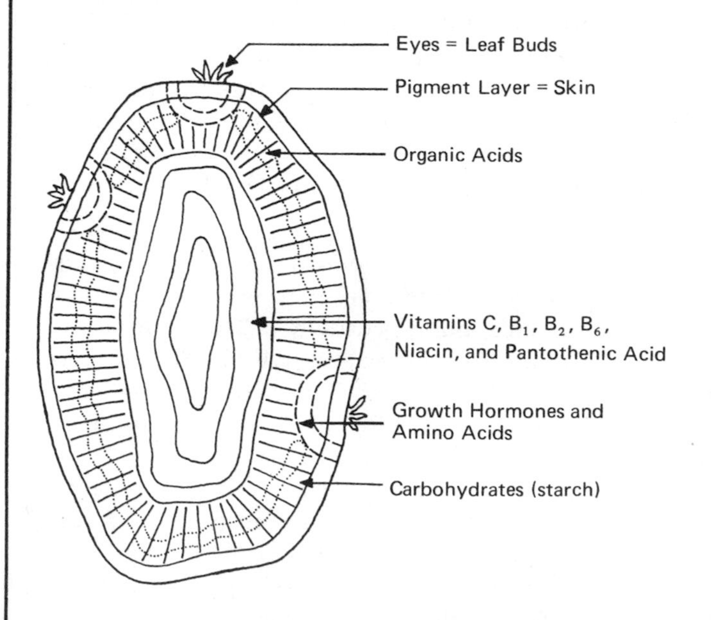

FIGURE 3-69
Potato—Pomme de Terre

:epe – *Bolet Cepe* (edible)

Devil's Boletus – *Bolet de satan* (poisonous)

ed-Staining Inocybe – *Inocybe lobee* (very poisonous)

St. George's Mushroom – *Mousseron de la St. Georges* (edible)

Common Morel – *Morille ronde* (edible)

Gyromitra – *Gyromitre esculenta* (edible, conditionally)

Conical Morel – *Morille pointue* (edible)

Saffron Milk Cap – *Lactaire delicieux* (edible)

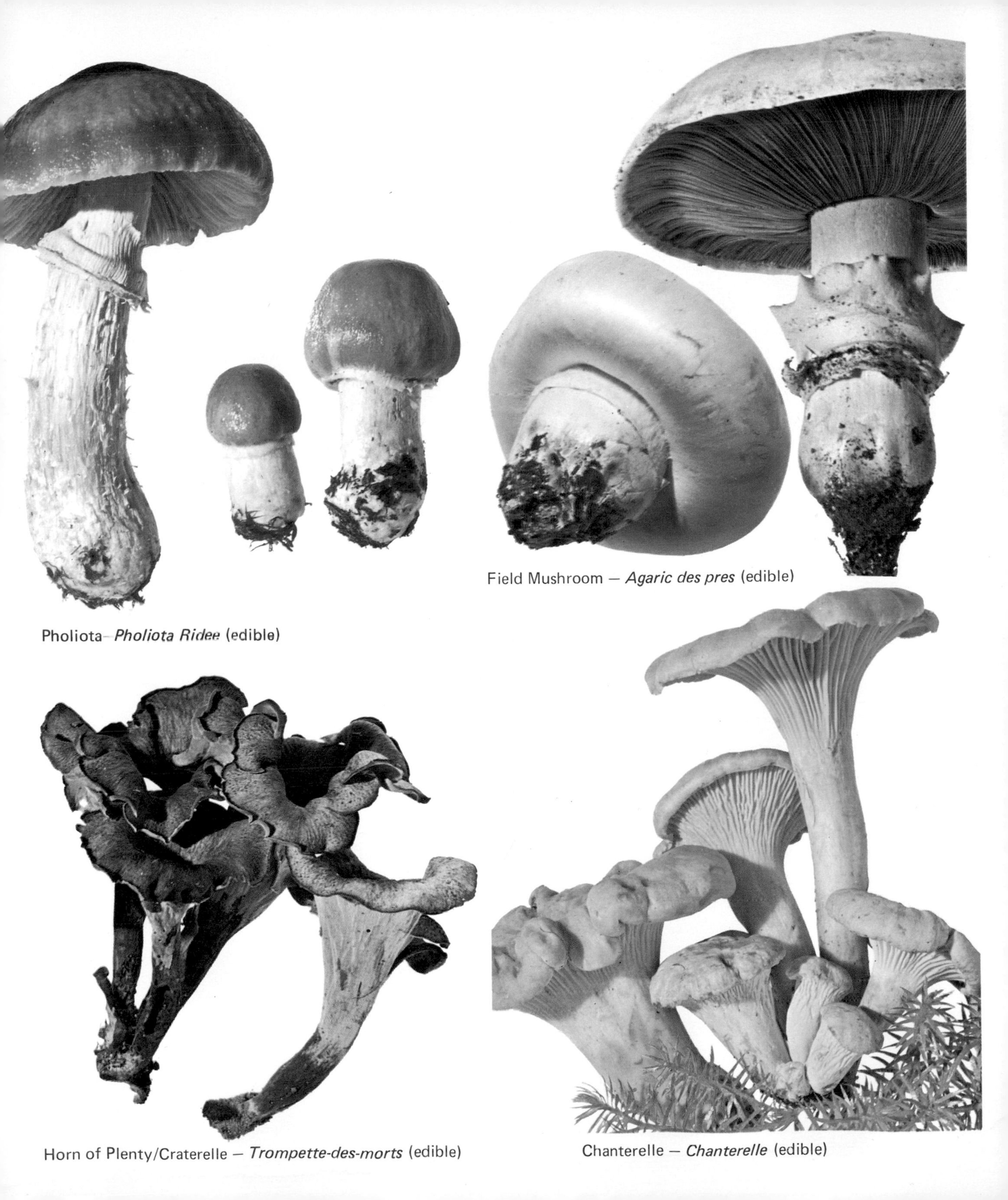

Field Mushroom — *Agaric des pres* (edible)

Pholiota– *Pholiota Ridee* (edible)

Horn of Plenty/Craterelle — *Trompette-des-morts* (edible)

Chanterelle — *Chanterelle* (edible)

Panther Cap – *Amanite panthere* (very poisonous)

Tawny Grisette (Grey Amanita) – *Amanite vineuse* (edible)

Death Cap – *Amanite phalloide* (deadly poisonous)

Tiger Tricholoma – *Tricholome tigre* (very poisonous)

(long russet), the White Rose (long white), the Katahdin (round white), and Red Pontiac (round red). Other varieties are available at different times of the year. The Norgold Russet (a long to blocky shape and a light russet color) and the Norland (a round red) are but a few varieties that are becoming increasingly popular.

Potatoes may also be classified by their use. There are "new" potatoes, general purpose potatoes, and baking potatoes. "New" potatoes are best when boiled. Because of their immaturity, they may be skinned easily and they remain firm when cooked. General purpose potatoes, both round and long types, are used for boiling, frying, and baking. These potatoes are available the year-round, and they are used more than any other type. Potatoes grown specifically for their baking qualities are quite dry and mealy. The best known variety for this use is the Russet Burbank.

The United States Department of Agriculture provides a voluntary grading service as a guide to the purchase of quality potatoes. The grade standards have been revised recently, and now the U.S. Extra No. 1 is the premium grade. In this grade, the tolerance for defects is very low. The next grade is U.S. No. 1. Minimum sizes and weights of the potatoes are also specified in the grades. Potatoes should be firm, well-shaped, smooth, free from bruises, cuts, sprouts, and decay.

It is important to store potatoes in a cool, 45°F. to 50°F. (7°C. to 10°C.), well-ventilated, dark area.

Rampion—Raiponce. This is a variety of European bellflower with thick, fleshy roots that can be eaten raw or prepared like black salsify. The leaves are used in salads or cooked as a vegetable.

Red Cabbage—chou rouge. This cabbage is identified by its red or purple color. The heads are very firm and compact.

Rutabaga—Chou-navet. A round-shaped root vegetable, rutabagas are both white-fleshed and yellow-fleshed; however, commercially, rutabagas are most always yellow-fleshed. Rutabagas are usually eaten as a cooked vegetable.

Sauerkraut—Choucroute. This is finely-shredded white cabbage mixed with salt and preserved over a long period in barrels or jars where it undergoes an acidic fermentation. Sauerkraut prepared with vinegar bacteria is artificially acidified and of poorer quality.

Shallot—Echalote. Every part of this mild and aromatic plant is edible. The crisp green stalks and the small elongated bulb are chopped and used in salads, soups, and meat dishes. They are excellent in fine sauces and for pickles.

Sorrel—Oseille. A spring vegetable similar to spinach, sorrel is used as a vegetable and for soup. The young tender vegetable has a pleasant acid taste.

Spinach—Epinards. This is a popular vegetable which is primarily available in spring and the fall, although it can be obtained throughout the year. Good spinach should be a deep green color with tender young leaves, not stalks. After the seedstalk develops, the spinach is tough, discolored, and bitter. Spinach must be dry and the leaves separated for storage.

Spring Onion—Petit oignons. A small white or silver onion which is used as a garnish for sauces, fish, meat, and vegetables.

Squash (Zucchini)—Courgettes. This vegetable, originally from Italy, is a relative of the pumpkin. The young vegetables up to 6 inches (15 centimeters) are sold as *zucchini.* They are usually dark green or green and white striped. These squash are delicately flavored and are used as vegetables, in soup, or as an hors d'oeuvre.

Sweet Corn. Corn is the only cereal crop that has an American origin. It is now grown in most countries throughout the world. It is used as food for both humans and animals. There are many different types of corn. Sweet corn has a sweeter taste than most varieties and is preferred for humans. The cob should be filled with plump and milky kernels and covered with husks that are soft, tender, and green. The grains should be yellow or white, soft, and sweet. Sweet corn is used fresh, frozen, and canned.

Swiss Chard—Cote de blette. Swiss chard, or seakale beet, is grown for its foliage. It has a broad, white-leaf stalk. The young, tender leaves have a milder flavor than spinach. The white stems are prepared like celery or asparagus.

Tomato—Tomate. The tomato is a vegetable by cul-

Illustrations on pages 119—122 reprinted by permission from F. Waldvogel, "Pilze," vol. 1 and 2 (Zurich: Silva-Verlag)

tivation and use, but botanically it is a fruit. It is native to South America and was brought to Europe and North America by the early Spanish explorers. It is available throughout the year, but is at its prime in summer and fall. Good tomatoes are firm, large, and bright red with a smooth skin. Tomatoes are rich in vitamins A and C. In the United States, the small cherry tomato and the pear tomato are very small tomatoes that may be either red or yellow. They are attractive in salads and as garnishes. There is also a green variety that is ripe in spite of its color.

Turnip—Navet. This is a smooth root tuber which is round or oblong in shape. The flavor is slightly bitter. Young, firm vegetables should be chosen. They are good in stews, casseroles, salads, and as a vegetable. Turnips are available throughout the year but are at their prime between June and February. The mild, oblong Parisian-type turnip is particularly good.

3.5.5 Mushrooms—Champignons

Mushrooms, the fruits of higher fungi, belong to the sub-kingdom Thallophyta. All Thallophyta, algae, fungi, and bacteria, are characterized by their lack of true roots, stems, or leaves.

Most mushrooms are saprophytes, "plants deriving all of their nourishment from the bodies of decaying, dead organisms."[15] They grow wild in the woods and meadows, and their food source is from the organic matter in dead leaves, soil, and rotting logs. The mushroom plant consists of the sporophore and the mycelium. The sporophore is the reproduction portion of the plant. This fruiting body, commonly known as the mushroom, has a stalk and a cap with knifeblade-like gills on the undersurface from which spores are produced and shed. The mycelium is the underground vegetative portion of the plant. It originates from the spores and forms an extensive underground network of filaments, known to commercial growers as "spawn." The fruit-bodies, or mushrooms, are formed on the mycelium.[16] There are many species and varieties of mushrooms; however, most mushroom experts agree that the *agaricus bisporous* is the only mushroom cultivated in either the United States or Europe. The *agaricus campestris* is the ordinary field mushroom.[17] It is often difficult to distinguish between edible and poisonous mushrooms. The commercially cultivated mushrooms are always safe. Mushrooms can be grown in cellars, caves, and tunnels. They require an even temperature for growth.

Quality Characteristics and Composition. Mushrooms should be fresh in appearance. The gills, the fluted formation on the undersurface of the cap, should be tight and free of open veils and should be light-colored. Black or dark brown gills are a sign of age. The mushrooms should be white or cream-colored and should be free of dirt, wilting, and pitting. The composition of a 3.5 ounce (100 gram) uncooked edible portion of mushrooms includes: 90 percent water; 2.7 grams protein; 4.4 grams carbohydrate; 28 calories. In addition, there are small amounts of fat, phosphorus, potassium, and trace minerals.

Storage. Fresh mushrooms are very perishable and should be refrigerated at 32°F. (0°C.) to keep in prime condition. They should not be washed until just before preparing. Mushrooms can be preserved by drying, canning, pickling, or processing into mushroom extract.

Cooking Methods. Mushrooms can be boiled, steamed, or sauteed.

Usage. Mushrooms may be used as a main dish, a garnish, an hors d'oeuvre, in sauces, and in salads. Black truffles (Perigord) are used as garnishes and for decorating cold dishes.

3.5.5.1 Edible Mushrooms

BAY BOLETA—BOLET BAI BRUN. BOLETUS BADIUS (EDIBLE)

The cap grows to a diameter of 4½ inches (11.2 centimeters) and is chestnut-brown in color. When dry,

15. Clarice Sackett, *Fruit and Vegetable Facts and Pointers: Mushrooms*, 4th rev. ed. (Washington, D.C.: United Fresh Fruit and Vegetable Association, 1975), p. 2.
16. Ibid.
17. Ibid.

it is matt and velvety; when wet, it is slimy and shiny. The thick stalk is stringy and lighter in color than the cap. The flesh is yellowish-white, firm, and turns blue when broken near the pores.
Occurrence. Found in pine forests and occasionally in deciduous woods. This variety avoids chalky soil.
Usage. These mushrooms are steamed with herbs and served with a cream sauce.

CEPE – BOLET-CEPE. BOLETUS EDULIS (EDIBLE)

The cap of the young cepe is roundish, rimmed, and moist, and it sits on the stout stalk like a hat. (See page 119.) It can grow to a diameter of 10 inches (25 centimeters); it is smooth and bare and shaped like a cushion. This mushroom becomes slimy with age and when exposed to damp weather. The color varies, depending on the locality: white, light or dark brown, or reddish-brown. The edges are lighter in color. The pores are first white, then yellowish-green, and finally olive-green. They are separated from the stalk, or at least very short at that point. When mature, the pores are up to 1 inch (2.5 centimeters) long. The stalk, first round and later cylindrical, is white to pale brown with a fine network of raised white veins toward the top. The flesh is white, with a wine-red area underneath the skin of the cap in older specimens. The taste is mild, similar to that of nuts.
Occurrence. It is found in sparse deciduous and pine forests, and in meadows.
Possibilities of confusion with other varieties. The brownish-black-capped cepe is found in southern climates in sparse oak and beech forests. It has a dark-brown velvety cap and saffron-colored stalk.
Usage. It is best when steamed with herbs and served with a cream sauce.

CHANTERELLE – CHANTERELLE. CANTHARELLUS CARUNCOPIOIDES (EDIBLE)

The cap, growing to a width of over 3 inches (7.5 centimeters), is humped and then spreads out and deepens. (See page 121.) The edge of the cap is irregular, ragged, indented, and wavy. It is the color of egg yolk, but fades after exposure to rain. The gills are like folds that divide and practically form a network running down to the point where the stalk gradually replaces the cap. The flesh of the stalk is firm, thinner at the bottom, and can be split into long fibers. The flesh of the cap is white, yellowish towards the edges, and it has a slight peppery taste and an aroma that is similar to that of apricots.
Occurrence. Found in the woods from June through autumn, chanterelles are often found in clumps.
Possibilities of confusion with other varieties. The violet-scaled chanterelle has a thick, violet, scaly skin which later becomes loose and often disappears. This variety is less irregular when fully grown, and the gills are thicker and less intricate. It is usually found in beech woods in mountainous areas. The corn-colored chanterelle has a cap that is almost white. The gills and stalk are the color of egg yolk; the mushroom, as a whole, is more stumpy and the flesh firmer. It is usually found in beech woods that have a chalky soil.
Usage. Chanterelles may be simmered in butter, with herbs, or served in cream sauce or Greek style.

COMMON MOREL – MORILLE RONDE. MORCHELLA ESCULENTA (EDIBLE)

The cap is conical and the color is ochre-yellow to dark brown, or olive to brown. (See page 120.) It is pitted with irregular cavities up to ½ inch (1.2 centimeters) wide. The folds between these cavities are often uneven, and in older plants they are rust colored (not black!). The stalk is thick, often grooved or folded, and the base is sometimes very wide. The point is powdery with a white to yellow color.
Occurrence. The common morel is found on sandy river banks; in sunny damp meadows which are protected from the wind and located near ash trees; near stacked wood; in fruit gardens, woods, and parks. This morel is in season in April and May.
Usage. Used only in dried form, these morels may be sauteed in butter, with herbs or served in a brown sauce with meat dishes, or as creamed morels (morilles a la creme).

CONICAL MOREL – MORILLE POINTUE. MORCHELLA CONICA (EDIBLE)

The cap is mitre-shaped, always pointed, and a pale whitish-gray-yellow-brown color. (See page 120.) The folds are thick, fluffy, and matted. The cap on older plants is brown or black. The folds curve regularly from top to bottom of the cap. The transversal folds lie deeper, and the longitudinal cavities are narrow. The stalk is smooth and pale. The top is very fragile with a fine smooth texture.

Occurrence: This morel grows in moss in mountain woods, in woody meadows, and on old burned patches of ground. It is in season from April to the end of July.

Usage. These may be sauteed in butter with herbs, or they may be creamed.

CULTIVATED MUSHROOM–CHAMPIGNON DE COUCHE. AGARICUS BISPORUS (EDIBLE)

This mushroom is a whitish-brown color with a thick stalk. The meat changes in color from white to slightly red. The cap is 2 to 4 inches (5 to 10 centimeters) in diameter, curved with small scales, and it varies from white to light-brown.

Odor. Faint, nut-like, pleasant. The cultivated mushroom, considered to be one of the greatest delicacies among mushrooms, is grown in dark places in soil that has been enriched with horse manure. It requires a constant temperature between 57°F. and 64°F. (15°C. and 18°C.), and a quality spawn is essential. Cleanliness and sanitation are necessary to prevent infestation of insects and vermin.

Occurrence: Although originally cultivated in France, this mushroom is grown in many European and North American areas, and in the Far East (especially Taiwan).

Usage. These mushrooms may be served whole or sliced, in cream sauce, provence style, with herbs, as a puree, and for hors d'oeuvres, and with cocktail sauce. They are also used as garnishes.

FIELD MUSHROOMS–AGARIC DES PRES. AGARICUS CAMPESTRIS (EDIBLE)

The cap of this mushroom grows to 6 inches (15 centimeters) in diameter. (See page 121.) It varies from white to brown in color; from a silky smooth surface to one that is covered with fibrous scales; from a shape that is round when young to one that is flattened and spread out when older. The rim of the cap hangs over the gills, which are free, close to one another, and quite full. Initially they are light pink, soon turning purplish brown, and finally brown to black. The stalks are quite short and silky smooth with a brown base. There is never a volva. The ring is split at the edges and hangs slightly. The flesh is white but turns to a meat-red color when broken. The flavor is spicy and excellent.

Occurrence. It is found in meadows, pastures, and gardens from June to autumn.

Possibilities of confusion with other varieties. This variety is confused with the carbolic champignon. When rubbed or cooked, this mushroom smells strongly of carbolic acid or ink, and the flesh from the base of the stalk turns an intensive yellow color.

GYROMITRA–GYROMITRE ESCULENTA (EDIBLE CONDITIONALLY)

The cap is irregular, with thick, indented, waxy, brown folds which are very fragile. (See page 120.) The appearance is similar to that of brains. The interior is grayish-white, fine in texture, and pocketed. The stalk is short, fat, and shaped in folds. Initially the stalk is solid, but subsequently it becomes hollow. The flavor is very strong.

Occurrence. A scarce variety, Gyromitra, are found in sandy, non-chalky pine forests, in clearings, burned areas, and in areas where logs are stacked. These are imported to the United States from Europe.

Poisonous. Boil for 5 to 10 minutes and dispose of the water which contains the water-soluble poison. In Central Europe these mushrooms are sorted according to size, strung on threads, and dried over heat.

Usage. These are dried and used like morels.

HORN OF PLENTY/CRATERELLE–TROMPETTE-DES-MORTS. CRATERELLUS CORNUCOPIOIDES (EDIBLE)

The cap can reach a width of 3 inches (7.5 centimeters) and is grayish-brown. (See page 121.) It consists of thin, irregular-shaped, wavy-sided funnels with crinkled edges. The gills are a dirty yellow, which turn to gray, and they run down the stalk. The stalk itself is hollow, yellowish, and often flattened and grooved. The flesh is yellowish, with a strong and sometimes earthy smell and taste.

Occurrence. These are often found in masses in fir tree forests, in moss, and near bilberry bushes.

Usage. These are usually dried and used in sauces and as a substitute for truffles.

PHOLIOTA – PHOLIOTA RIDEE. PHOLIOTA CAPERATA (EDIBLE) E)

The cap is up to 4 inches (10 centimeters) wide, initially bell-shaped and then slanted outwards. (See page 121.) It is straw-yellow to ochre-brown, and rimmed with white in the middle. The rim is shrivelled, torn, and pitted. The gills are often wrinkled and close to each other; they are initially a pale yellowish color, then later turn to rusty-brown. The edges of the gills are white and notched. The stalk is first silky white, strong and firm, but later becomes fibrous below the ring. Above the ring it is white and flaky. The flesh is whitish-yellow and usually permeated with water. It is mild and tender. The smell is spicy and the flavor good.
Occurrence. These mushrooms are found in the moss in spruce and pine forests and occasionally under deciduous trees.
Usage. They may be sauteed or stewed.

ST. GEORGE'S MUSHROOM – MOUSSERON DE LA ST. GEORGES. TRICHOLOMA GEORGII (EDIBLE)

The cap grows up to 6 inches (15 centimeters) wide, first hemispherical and then flattens out; the edge is rolled inwards; the color is white to ochre-yellow, and it sometimes splits open. The gills are thin and narrow, and very close together. (See page 119.) They can either grow right up to the stalk, or be separated from it. They are fragile. The thick stalk is the same color as the cap. The flesh is white and the odor resembles that of flour.
Occurrence. This variety is found in fields and meadows from the end of April until June. It tends to grow in groups, even in circles, or in so-called fairy rings.
Possibilities of confusion with other varieties. This excellent edible mushroom occurs in many different forms and colors. It is usually identified by its odor. It is possible to confuse it with the poisonous red-staining inocybe, which also appears in the spring.
Usage. These mushrooms may be prepared by the same methods suggested for cepes.

SAFFRON MILK CAP/ORANGE AGARIC – LACTAIRE DELICIEUX. LACTARIUS DELICIOSUS (EDIBLE)

The cap can grow to 4 inches (10 centimeters) in diameter and is between a reddish or yellowish-orange with dark concentric circles. (See page 120.) It is sticky and slimy and has a tightly curled rim. Later on it becomes funnel-shaped and frequently has green spots. The gills reach down the stalk. They are orange-red and delicate. If damaged, green spots develop. The stalk is firm and solid when young, and later it becomes hollow, and is the same color as the cap. The flesh is fragile and white, but when broken open, it releases an orange-colored milk which turns carrot-red. The flavor is usually mild, but it can be bitter and spicy, especially in dry areas.
Occurrence. Very frequently these are found in damp pine forests and in fields.
Usage. These may be deep-fat fried, sauteed, stewed, or used in mixed mushroom dishes.

TAWNY GRISETTE – AMANITE VINEUSE. AMANITA SPISSA, EXCELSA (EDIBLE)

The cap is curved initially in a hemispherical shape which later flattens. It is about 3 to 5 inches (7.5 to 12.5 centimeters) wide, grayish-brown with flaky gray remnants. (See page 122.) The rim is smooth and moist. The gills are white and closely bunched. The solid stalk is cylindrical with a white hanging ring. The ring, high up on the stem, is white; beneath the ring, it is gray. The flesh is white and mild.
Occurrence. It is found in deciduous and evergreen woods from spring to autumn.
Possibilities of confusion with other varieties. It is sometimes confused with the poisonous panther cap. (See page 122.); however, the latter has a sack-shaped volva and white scales on the cap.
Usage. These mushrooms are best when stewed with onions and herbs.

BLACK TRUFFLE – TRUFFE DU PERIGORD. TUBER MELNOSPORUM (EDIBLE)

Black truffles are ½ to 3 inches (1.2 to 7.5 centimeters) wide, dark brown to black in color, and covered with small warts. (See page 128.) They are shaped like a tuber and pitted with cavities. The flesh is marbled with black veins, and it has a strong and aromatic odor.

Occurrence. These truffles are found in France below the soil surface and usually under oak trees in deciduous woods. They are ripe from November to March. The Perigord truffle is the favorite of all truffles and is very expensive.
Usage. Raw truffles are used in soups, sauces, salads, and meat dishes. They may be sauteed in butter or simmered in wine. They are a choice garnish or decoration for many dishes.

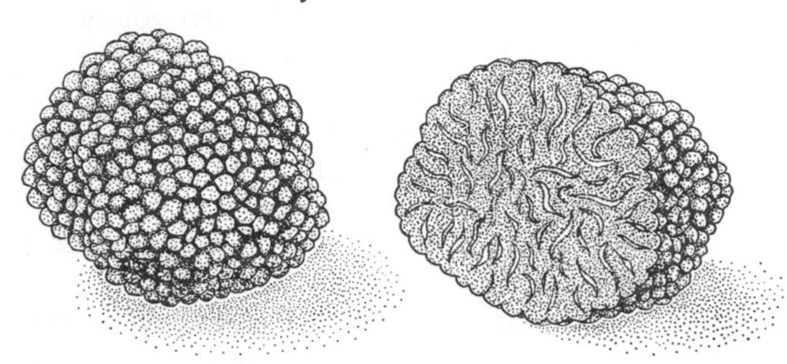

FIGURE 3-70
Black Truffle—Truffle du Perigord

SUMMER TRUFFLE—TRUFFE D'ETE. TUBER AESTIVUM (EDIBLE)

Shaped like a tuber, these truffles are 1 to 4 inches (2.5 to 10 centimeters) wide and are usually covered with bumps. They are blackish-brown with a thick skin and large warts. The flesh varies from grayish-white to yellowish-brown, with light colored veins.
Occurrence. This variety is found from August to March in deciduous woods. It grows 1 to 6 inches (2.5 to 15 centimeters) below the surface of the soil, and is found in Italy, France, Switzerland, and Germany.
Usage. Raw truffles are used for salads and garnishes. They may be sauteed or stewed with spices.

WHITE TRUFFLE—TRUFFE BLANCHE. CHOIROMYCES MAEANDRIFORMIS (EDIBLE)

This mushroom is 2 to 3 inches (5 to 7.5 centimeters) wide, usually the size of a duck's egg, and it can grow much larger. It is round and similar to a potato, but covered with large bumps. The skin is like leather, firm, smooth, and without warts. Initially it is grayish-white, with cracks, and then turns yellowish-brown.
Occurrence. These are grown in Italy, in Piedmont, and in Central Europe. They are on the market from July to September.
Usage. Raw white truffles are used for salads and hors d'oeuvres. They may be sauteed and used in a casserole and as a seasoning.

3.5.5.2 Poisonous Mushrooms (Toadstools)

DEATH CAP—AMANITE PHALLOIDE. AMANITA PHALLOIDES (DEADLY POISONOUS)

The cap, which grows to a width of 5 inches (12.5 centimeters), is a light or dark olive-brown with dark fibers radiating out to the rim. (See page 122.) When dry, the cap has a silky sheen, when damp it becomes sticky. The gills are pure white, with a greenish shimmer. They are quite close together and free. The thin long stalk is bulbous at the base and is white with pale green lateral bands. The stem has a large hanging ring which is enclosed in a wavy volva. The flesh is white and when young it has a faint but pleasant odor that develops into a repugnant smell. This is the most dangerous of all varieties.
Occurrence. This variety is found in deciduous forests, especially under oak trees, from July to September.
Possibilities of confusion with other varieties. The majority of deaths caused by eating mushrooms can be traced to this variety. It can be confused with the green Russula varieties and the rusty-striped Tricholoma portentosum. Neither of these possess a ring or a volva.

DESTROYING ANGEL—AMANITE VIREUSE. AMANITA VIROSA (DEADLY POISONOUS)

The cap, as wide as 4 inches (10 centimeters), is conical or bell-shaped; it is white, although when old the center turns to an ivory color. It is sticky and slimy in wet weather. The gills are white, free, and narrow near the rim of the cap. The stalk is slim with fine streaks above the tattered ring. Shreds hang from the margin of the cap. The thin volva surrounds the base. The flesh is white and has an unpleasant chlorine odor.
Occurrence. This variety is found throughout damp woods.
Possibilities of confusion with other varieties. Similar

to the Amanita verna, the cap of the virosa, however, is bell-shaped with a ragged margin and the ring is tattered. Both are found in the same localities.

DEVIL'S BOLETUS—BOLET DE SATAN. BOLETUS SATANAS (POISONOUS)

The cap, a firm, thick, spongy mass, grows to 10 inches (25 centimeters) in width. (See page 119.) It is yellowish-white, with a greenish tint. This changes to an ochre-yellow, smooth texture, and during dry periods it splits open. The tubes can be either free or fixed. Originally yellow, these tubes are blood-red to orange-yellow at their pores. Broken or pressed areas turn blue-green. The stalk is short and bulging; the upper part is yellow, the middle carmine red. There is a delicate red network over the upper part of the stalk. The flesh is whitish and firm, although it later becomes spongy. The odor of older fungi is unpleasant. Devil's Boletus is very poisonous!
Possibilities of confusion with other varieties. Young specimens can be mistaken for cepes.

FOOL'S MUSHROOM—AMANITE PRINTANIERE. AMANITA VERNA (DEADLY POISONOUS)

The cap, growing to 4 inches (10 centimeters) in width, is white or slightly ochre-colored in the center. It is sticky when wet, otherwise shiny. The gills are free, pure white, and run to the rim of the cap. The thin stalk tapers upwards, and is slightly flaky beneath the hanging ring. The tight ring is finely streaked and attached high on the stalk. The thin volva hugs the bulbous base. The flesh is white and soft, and in older specimens the odor is very offensive.

PANTHER CAP—AMANITE PANTHERE. AMANITA PANTHERINA (VERY POISONOUS)

The cap grows up to 5 inches (12.5 centimeters) wide and is colored from grayish-yellow to brown and is darker in the center. (See page 122.) The rim is skirted. The cap is covered with small pure white flakes in concentric circles. The gills are shining white and set close together, and the edge is striated. The stem is white and the upper part, above the hanging, heavily-fringed ring, is smooth (without streaks). The bulbous base of the stalk stands in a tightly-fitting volva, and bears two or three circular ridges.
Occurrence. This mushroom is found in deciduous and pine forests.
Possibilities of confusion with other varieties. The panther cap cannot be confused with the circular-shaped gray amanita (tawny grisette). (See page 122.) These gray amanita have grayish scales on the cap, a smooth or slightly skirted rim, and a streaked ring. The stem has a club-shaped base but there is no volva. The tawny grisette is not poisonous.

RED-STAINING INOCYBE—INOCYBE LOBEE. INOCYBE PATOUILLARDII (VERY POISONOUS)

The cap is white and 1 to 3 inches (2.5 to 7.5 centimeters) in diameter. (See page 119.) When the mushroom is young, the rim of the cap is rolled inwards. Later, the cap turns yellowish-brown and opens into a conical or bell-shape, with streaks radiating from the center. The stalk is stout and white with reddish spots. The gills are free, set close together, and uneven. Initially white, they later turn to a rusty tinge. The flesh is firm, fibrous, and white, and becomes red with age or on contact with the air. Parts which are broken or pressed turn red. The mushroom has an acid odor and only a faint taste.
Occurrence. This mushroom grows in groups in deciduous woods during spring and summer.
Possibilities of confusion with other varieties. It may be confused with the St. George's mushroom or the Pholiota (pholiota capera).

TIGER TRICHOLOMA—TRICHOLOME TIGRE. TRICHOLOMA TIGRINUM (VERY POISONOUS)

The cap can grow to 6 inches (15 centimeters) wide. It is grayish in color with violet shading and dark gray-brown scales. (See page 122.) The cap is initially bell-shaped and gradually slants irregularly outwards. It is firm and fleshy, and turned inwards at the edges. The gills are dirty white, with a greenish tinge, dense and almost free at the stem, and often with water droplets at the edges of the gills. The compact stalk is 1¼ inches (3.1 centimeters) wide; its base is club-shaped. Water droplets often collect at the top of the stalk. The flesh is whitish with the exception of the gray area under the skin of the cap. The base of the stalk is whitish to a light ochre color. It has a faint "floury" odor. The taste is mild to bitter.

Occurrence: This variety is found in groups in chalky soils in hilly areas.
Possibilities of confusion with other varieties. Unless the scales on the cap are properly developed, it is difficult to identify this variety. It is easily confused with the Pholiota, although the robust nature of the fungus is different. The poison of the tiger tricholoma causes serious stomach and intestinal disorders.

3.5.6 Fruit—Fruit

Fruit, in food terminology, is the collective term for all edible fruits of cultivated or wild plants and for certain kinds of seed nucleii (nuts, almonds). Most fruits may be eaten raw.
Species and description. The fresh produce market generally divides fruit into the following groups:

- *Berries—Baies:* Blackberries, strawberries, blueberries, raspberries, currants, cranberries, gooseberries, and wine and table grapes
- *Citrus Fruits—Agrumes:* Oranges, grapefruits, kumquats, limes, mandarins, and lemons
- *Exotic Fruits—Fruits du midi:* Pineapples, avocados, bananas, dates, figs, pomegranates, persimmons, mangoes, melons, olives, okra (also used as vegetable), papayas, passion fruit, pistachios, peanuts, and sultanas
- *Hard-shelled Fruits—Fruits a coque:* Hazelnuts, chestnuts, almonds, and walnuts
- *Seed Fruits—Fruits a pepins:* Apples, pears, and quinces
- *Stone Fruits—Fruits a noyau:* Apricots, cherries, peaches, and plums

Quality characteristics. Fruits differ in quality and flavor, texture, and appearance. They are usually priced according to their quality and size. United States grade standards have been established for most fresh and processed fruits. The top grades of fresh fruits may be either U.S. Fancy or U.S. No. 1. The grade standards for frozen and canned fruits are U.S. Grade A or Fancy for fruit with excellent color, uniform weight, size, and shape with few or no blemishes. U.S. Grade B canned fruits are very good quality and only slightly less perfect than Grade A. U.S. Grade C canned fruits may contain some broken and uneven pieces. These fruits are good and wholesome and particularly suitable for jam, frozen desserts, puddings, gelatin salads, and desserts.
Storage. Fresh fruits are highly perishable and should be purchased only for the specific use and quantity needed. They should be stored in well-ventilated areas and at the proper temperature. Nuts are perishable and only the current year's crop should be purchased. Canned fruits should be stored in a well-ventilated area no warmer than 75°F. (25°C.). To maintain the quality of frozen fruits, they should be stored at 0°F. (−18°C.). Nutmeats should be stored in airtight containers at refrigerated temperatures.
Usage. Fresh, canned, and frozen fruits are used for salads, sauces, garnishes, desserts, and other dishes. Fruit is an important and economical food in terms of its nutritional value. Most fruits contain carbohydrates, minerals, and vitamins.
Classification of fresh fruits. All domestic and imported varieties of fresh fruit can be classified as follows:

- *Cooking Fruit:* Ripe, clean, and undamaged fruit suitable for cooking, drying, or preserving
- *Fallen or Damaged Fruit:* Any fruit which is not ripe, overripe, or damaged
- *Table Fruit:* Completely ripe, undamaged, and clean fruit which corresponds to the accepted standard for the variety in terms of size and color.

Almond—Amande. Almonds may be classified as *sweet almond, bitter almond,* and *shell almond;* the sweet and bitter almond are, however, the two varieties of economic value. Grown for its edible nuts, the sweet almond is used for snacks, desserts, and garnishes, and is used by confectioners and bakers.

The bitter almond is used for flavoring and in cosmetic skin preparations. The kernels and the crude oil of the bitter almond contain prussic acid (HCN, a poisonous acid); however, the bitter flavor tends to deter anyone from eating these almonds in

FIGURE 3-71
Almond — Amande

amounts that would cause poisoning. The term "mixed" means that about one percent of bitter almonds is added to sweet almonds to give a spicy flavor.

Originally from southern France and Italy, shell almonds have a brittle shell, and are served on many fruit trays as a dessert.

Apple — Pomme. The cultivated apple of commercial value is of the genus *Malus* and of the species *sylvestris.* Apples have been grown for at least 3,000 years, and until the twentieth century, they were about the only fresh fruit available during the winter months. Although there are innumerable varieties of apples, only seventeen or eighteen varieties represent most of the commercial production in the United States. More *Delicious* apples are produced than any other variety. *McIntosh* ranks second, and *Golden Delicious,* third. Other well-known varieties in the United States are Rome Beauty, Jonathan, Winesap, Baldwin, Stayman, York, Astrachan, Starr, Newton, Northern Spy, and Rhode Island Greening.[18]

The flavor of apples is a combination of sweetness, acidity, bitterness, and the aroma. There is a great variation in these qualities that affects the flavor. There is also a difference in the texture. Some varieties are soft and mealy; others are crisp and hard.

18. R. A. Seeley, *Fruit and Vegetable Facts and Pointers: Apples,* 3rd ed. (Washington, D.C.: United Fresh Fruit and Vegetable Association), p. 1, 12.

Apples are eaten out of the hand peeled or unpeeled; in compotes and salads, as baked, spiced, pickled, fried, or candied; in pies, cobblers, strudels, pastries, and pudding; in chutney, mincemeat, jellies and jams. Apples are made into cider and vinegar. They are used as a garnish for many dishes and are available in canned, dried, and frozen form.

The storage requirements of apples differ with the variety. The fruit must be carefully handled and stored under conditions compatible to their own needs. Storerooms should be well-ventilated and the temperature for most varieties is 30°F. to 32°F. (−1°C. to 0°C.) at 80 to 90 percent relative humidity.[19]

Apricot — Abricot. The apricot varies in color from pale yellow to deep orange with a red blush. The fruit is slightly flattened with a smooth surface and has a smooth flat kernel. It grows in areas with warm or temperate climate. Apricots are used for table fruit, baking, stewing, compotes, salads, and garnishes. They are excellent in preserves and pastries. Apricots are canned, dried, and frozen.

Avocado — Avocado. (See illustrations on page 142.) The avocado is a tasty tropical fruit grown in the United States, Central America, South Africa, Israel, and Italy. When ripe, avocados are cut in half, the stone is removed, and the fruit is eaten plain or served as a cocktail, entree, salad, main dish, or dessert. The best varieties are those with a small kernel and weighing 7 to 10 ounces (198 to 283 grams). Avocados are rich in protein, fat, and vitamins A and B.

Banana — Banane. Bananas are grown in hot, humid, tropical climates; Equador is the leading supplier. Bananas ripen after they are harvested and develop their best eating qualities during the ripening process. They should be stored at 60°F. to 70°F. (15°C. to 20°C.) and should never be refrigerated. Ripe bananas are golden-yellow. Black spots on the skin indicate that the fruit is overripe; however, these bananas may be used in cakes, pie fillings, breads, and puddings.

Blackberry — Murel meuron. The many varieties of blackberries grow on bushes in shady woods and in

19. Ibid., p. 26.

sunny groves. The berries should be black, fresh, dry, and free of mold, and they are at their peak in June. They may be eaten fresh or canned, and are used in compotes, desserts, yoghurt, jam, jelly, syrup, and sherbet.

Blueberry—Myrtille. The blueberry bush, common throughout Europe and the United States, bears pea-sized berries, bluish-black in color and very juicy. Blueberries grow in dry woods in central Europe, in the pre-Alpine regions in Europe, and in North America. Most of the blueberries that reach the fresh food market are cultivated. At their peak in June and July, blueberries are available from May through August. Fresh blueberries are eaten as a dessert with cream, as blueberry pie, and blueberry muffins. They can be made into conserve, jelly, and a topping or syrup to serve over ice cream or pancakes.

Cherry—Cerise. Cherries originated in Persia. Like all stone fruits, cherries can be stored for only one or two days. There are many varieties of cherries but of all the species, only the sour or pie cherry and the sweet cherry have been domesticated. Bing, Royal Ann, and Lambert are three of the popular sweet cherries grown in the United States. The sour cherries are: Montmorency, which is the most popular of cherries grown in America; Early Richmond, a dark red cherry which is good for all cooking purposes; and the English Morello, a very dark red cherry and excellent for all culinary uses. Cherries are used for table fruit, in pies, pastries, cakes, tarts, jams, and jellies.

Chestnut—Marron. Chestnuts found their way from Persia to Greece and Rome and from there to the Alps. The shiny chestnuts are especially suitable for cooking purposes since they are easy to peel. The skin of the gray-flocked chestnuts is more difficult to remove. Chestnuts are used in stuffings or combined with vegetables, such as cabbage and brussels sprouts.

Cranberry—Airelle rouge. The fruit of a wild, low, evergreen bush, cranberries are native to the peat and bog areas of North America, Europe, and Asia. The large American cranberry, native to America, is exported in large quantities. The acid taste changes after cooking to a delicate and pleasing one. Maturity is indicated by color which ranges from bright red to almost black. Cranberries are used in jams, jellies, cakes, relishes, ices, salads, and for making fruit juices. They are a good accompaniment with game dishes. November is the peak month for cranberries in the United States, and large amounts are used at Thanksgiving and Christmas with the traditional roast turkey.

Currants—Groseille a grappe. These are the berries of the currant bush. There are three main varieties: *red, white,* and *black currants.* The latter are also known as *cassis. Blanc de cassis,* a French aperitif, should not be confused with the black currant (cassis). Currants are grown in Germany, England, Switzerland, and in sub-tropical countries. The berries can be eaten fresh, canned, or they may be processed into syrup. They are used in many different ways for desserts, ice cream, sherbet, sauces, and jellies.

Date—Datte. This is the fruit of the date palm. Dates are usually classified into three types: the soft dates generally sold in pressed masses and eaten raw or used in making candies; the semi-dry date from North Africa with the fruit still attached to the strand; and dry dates, which are quite hard, are important in the diets of the Arab countries. The world's most popular date, "Deglet Noor," is a semi-dry date. Good quality dates are fat and full with a soft interior flesh. The main exporting countries are Iraq, North Africa, and Egypt. Dates are eaten as a confection and are used for making pastries and desserts.

Fig—Figue. The fig tree is one of the most important commercially grown plants in the Mediterranean countries. It is also found in California. The *Smyrna figs* which come from Turkey are very well-known. Greece supplies the *Calmata figs* (fan-shaped) and also cheaper varieties. The California varieties are: Calimyrna, Black Mission, and Kadota. Figs are extremely perishable and must be handled carefully and cooled immediately after harvesting. Figs are eaten fresh, canned, or dried, and are used for desserts and for garnishes.

Gooseberry—Groseille verte. This berry of the gooseberry bush exists in some 500 varieties. The fruits are also classified according to color (red, yellow, green, and white). They are grown in Europe, North Africa, and Western Asia. Ripe gooseberries are used as table fruit and for tarts and jam. Unripe

gooseberries may be made into an excellent compote.
Grape—Raisin. The grape is a member of the vine family and the most important species for dessert and wine grapes is the *Vitis vinifera.* Grape growing is the world's largest fruit industry. Grapes are grown throughout the world, except in regions with extremely cold temperatures. Depending on their use, grapes are classified into five groups: table grapes, raisin grapes, wine grapes, juice grapes, and canning grapes. The following *European types* are well-known table grapes: Thompson seedless, Emperor, Tokay, Ribier, and Red Malaga. The *American types* are Concord, Niagara, Catawba, and Delaware. In the United States, Emperor, Thompson seedless, Tokay, Cardinal, and Ribier are well-known table grapes. Grapes used for dry wine must be of high quality and moderate sugar content; those used for sweet wine should have a high sugar content and moderately low acidity. Most grape juice and jellies are made from Concord grapes. Most varieties should be stored at 30°F. (−1°C.) and at a relative humidity of 90 to 95 percent.
Grapefruit—Pamplemousse. This citrus fruit grows chiefly in tropical or sub-tropical countries. In Europe, the very juicy, white-fleshed Jaffa grapefruit from Israel is best known. In the United States, grapefruit is available throughout the year, with the most abundant supplies from January through May. While Florida is the major producer of grapefruit in the United States, other states known for their grapefruit are Texas, California, and Arizona.

There are several varieties of grapefruit, but the principal distinctions are between those that are "seedless" (few or no seeds) and the "seeded," and those with differences in the color of the flesh. The white-flesh grapefruit is most common, but the pink-flesh varieties are becoming more popular.[20]

Grapefruit is used for juice, appetizers, salads, cocktails, garnishes, desserts, and sherbets.
Hazelnut and Walnut—Noisette et Noix. Hazelnuts are grown in large quantities in the areas along the coasts of the Black Sea and the Mediterranean; they are also grown in the United States. Those from Italy and the eastern Mediterranean countries are sold as *Levantine nuts.* Walnuts are found in many varieties all over the world. The thin-shelled types are best for desserts. Green, unripe walnuts are often pickled. Hazelnuts and walnuts are perishable and may easily become rancid or infected with insects. Only nuts from the current year's crop should be purchased and they should be purchased in limited quantities and for the specific use, such as whole, chopped, or broken. Hazelnuts and walnuts are eaten out of hand, in salads, pastries, and desserts. Nuts in the shell are sometimes served as a dessert.
Kiwi Berries. These berries are an exotic tropical fruit grown commercially only in New Zealand. The vines also grow naturally on the fringes of forests in the Yangtze Valley of China. The kiwi is the size and shape of a lime. It has a brown, fuzzy, thin skin. The outer flesh is a light translucent chartreuse and the center is white with tiny edible seeds. The delicate flavor is often described as a composite of the gooseberry, strawberry, banana, and peach. They are eaten out of hand, in fruit salads, on ice cream, and as garnishes.
Kumquat—Cumquat. (See illustration on page 142.) This is a type of dwarf orange which comes from China. The Chinese kumquat grows on a small evergreen shrub with dark green leaves. They are also grown in California. Unlike other citrus fruits, they are eaten with the skin. Good kumquats are firm, bright, and glossy. They may be sliced for salads and compotes, ground with cranberries for a relish, pickled, or made into preserves. Preserved kumquats are a good accompaniment with pork, poultry, and game.
Lemon—Citron. Southern Asia is the home of the lemon, although it is grown in the Mediterranean countries, California, and Florida. Lemons that are to be exported are picked when green, and then stored in hothouses for two or three weeks at 120°F. (49°C.) until the skin turns yellow. The common lemon has a thin skin, and it is fleshy and juicy. The thin-skinned lemon, known as the *Premiere fleur,* is available from the late fall to January.
Lime—Limon (lime). (See illustration page 142.) This citrus fruit has the appearance of a small lemon;

20. United States Department of Agriculture, *How to Buy Fresh Fruits.* Consumer and Marketing Service, Home and Garden Bulletin No. 141, 1967.

however, it has a thin green skin. Although originally from the Himalayan valleys, it is now cultivated in America, Asia, and Africa. The lime is largely used for *lime juice* to enhance the flavor of foods, or as an additive in drinks. Lime juice is sometimes mixed with beer, used in cocktails, and made into sherbet.

Mango—Mango. (See illustration page 142.) Mangoes are one of the most popular fruits of the tropics. They grow on Magnifera or mango trees in all areas near the equator. There are green and yellow to orange varieties. Mangoes are best when eaten fresh. The fruit is cut in half, the kernel removed, and the flesh eaten out of the skin with a spoon. Mangoes may also be used in salads, fruit cups, and desserts.

Mango chutney is the preserved product made from the unripe fruit and served with oriental dishes, particularly curry.

Melon—Melon. Most melons belong to the Cucurbitaceae family which includes pumpkins, squashes, watermelon, and muskmelons. There are many varieties of cantaloupe. Hales Best is the most important commercial variety in the United States and the Bender and Hearts of Gold are other excellent melons. The characteristics of good cantaloupe are thick, sweet, and juicy flesh with a rich aroma. California is the main source of cantaloupes in the United States. Most cantaloupes are eaten fresh as appetizers or desserts. They are also used in salads, compotes, ice cream, toppings, and some are pickled.[21]

Honeydew melons are related to the cataloupe. They have a smooth, light green to yellow rind. The flesh should be thick, fine-textured, and juicy with a sweet flavor.

Persian melons are similar in exterior appearance to the cantaloupe. The dark green rind is covered with a fine netting. The thick orange flesh is sweet, juicy, and rich in flavor.

Crenshaw melons are a late variety. They have a smooth rind mottled with gold and green color with very little ribbing and netting. The flavor of this melon is rich, sweet, and mellow.

Casaba melons are another late variety. The rind is deeply furrowed and the flesh is soft and white with a delicate sweet flavor.

Watermelon is especially popular during the summer months. There are many varieties, but the Charleston Gray ranks as the most popular on the United States markets. The melon, about 24 inches (60 centimeters) long and weighing up to 35 pounds (15 kilograms), has a grayish-green rind with darker green veins. The bright red flesh is crisp, sweet, and rich in flavor. The seeds are black. Other important varieties of watermelon are Black Diamond (Cannonball or Florida Giant), Jubilee, Klondike, and Congo. Seedless varieties have been developed. They are round and weigh between 8 and 10 pounds (3.6 to 4.5 kilograms).[22]

Okra—Ladyfinger. (See illustration page 142.) Okra is a type of pod, similar to the paprika. Okra grows to a length of 1¼ to 2 inches (3 to 5 centimeters), and is produced in Africa, Greece, and Turkey. Okra is quite mucilaginous and is used in soups, salads, stews, and as a vegetable.

Olive—Olive. The fruit of the olive plant is used as a food and as a source of edible oil. The flesh contains about 22 percent oil, and the seed also has a high oil content. Although the olive originated in the Mediterranean region with Spain, France, and Italy important producers, the tree is also grown in China, southern Australia, and the United States. The fruit is a drupe. It contains a single hard seed surrounded by firm flesh, and the skin changes from green to dark blue or purple when ripe. The fruits are picked when ripe or when fully grown, and are then processed and packed in a brine. Fresh olives can be processed into ripe, green, Sicilian-style green or salt-cured, or oil-coated olives.

Orange—Orange. The word *orange* is derived from the Arabian word *naranj* and the Persian *narong*. The term *orangus* was later used for sour oranges, and is supposedly the basis for the modern word, orange.

Oranges are divided into sour oranges and sweet oranges. The sour orange is important in this

21. United Fresh Fruit and Vegetable Association, *Cantaloupes* (Washington, D.C.)

22. United Fresh Fruit and Vegetable Association, *Watermelons* (Washington, D.C.)

country as a rootstock and in Spain and other countries for its bitter or sour fruits. The sweet orange species is grown in the United States and elsewhere for commercial use.

The sweet orange can be divided into four varieties, the *common* orange such as the Valencias from Florida and California; the *blood* or pigmented orange such as the Ruby; the *acidless* orange grown in some Mediterranean areas; and the *navel* orange such as the Washington navel of California.

Good quality oranges have a fine textured skin and good color for the specific variety. They are firm and heavy for the size. Sweet oranges are used as a table fruit and for juice; in salads, desserts, and as garnishes. The skin of the bitter orange is suitable for confections, particularly in the form of candied orange peel. Oranges are grown in the Mediterranean countries and in California, Arizona, Texas, Florida, and Washington.

Papaya—Papaya. (See illustrations page 142.) The papaya is native to tropical America; however, it is also grown in Africa, Sri Lanka, India, Malaya, and Australia. It is spherical to oblong in shape with a thin smooth skin that turns from green to yellow or orange when ripe. The flesh, yellow to orange in color, has a sweet delicate flavor. Black seeds are packed in the center of the fruit and must be removed before eating. Papaya is cut into slices or served with cocktails, drinks, or as a garnish for meat. It is often served at breakfast. The juice of unripe papaya contains an enzyme which is an excellent natural meat "tenderizer" and is sold commercially for this purpose.

Passion Fruit—Passionfruit. (See illustration page 142.) The fruit of several varieties of the passionflower. It has a yellow to brownish-yellow hard skin. This tropical creeper flourishes most frequently in South America and in other tropical and sub-tropical areas of Africa and the Far East. The juice of the fruit is drunk pure or mixed as a soft drink, or added to punches. The pulp is used in ice cream and dessert recipes and is used for jam.

Peach—Peche. The peach is a small to moderately-sized deciduous tree that grows to a height of 30 feet (900 centimeters). The fruit is a derivative from persica, the species name. China is the original home of the peach but it is now grown in central Europe and in the United States. The fruit is one of the finest table fruits. Good peaches are quite firm with a velvety skin and yellow color.

There are many varieties of peaches in the United States, but the general classifications are: *freestones* (flesh readily separates from the pit) and *clingstone* (flesh clings tightly to the pit). Freestones are used for freezing and eating fresh; clingstones are used primarily for canning.[23] Peaches are used for hot and cold dishes, garnishes, and desserts.

Peanut—Arachide—cacahuete. Peanuts are of South American origin, but today they are an important crop all over the tropics and in India, Africa, and America. The plant is a bushy annual. After pollination, the short flower stalks lengthen downwards and push the fruits, which are on the end of the stalks, into the ground, where they ripen 2 to 3 inches (5 to 7.5 centimeters) below the surface. A neutral-tasting oil, pressed out of the groundnuts, is used as cooking and salad oil and for making margarine. The peanuts, containing 40 to 50 percent oil, are pressed. The residue left after extracting the oil is used for animal feed.

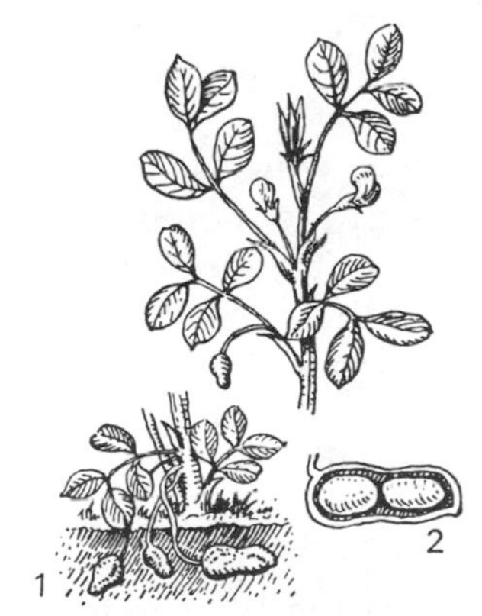

FIGURE 3-72
Peanut—Arachide (cacahuete)

23. United States Agricultural Marketing Service, Home and Garden Bulletin No. 141, October, 1967.

Pear—Poire. Pears are of the genus Pyrus which includes 20 to 25 species native to Europe, Asia, and northern Africa. Commercial varieties in the United States are derived from *Pyrus communis* varieties of Europe. In the United States, the pear growing centers are in the dry valleys of Oregon, Washington, and California. Of the 3,000 varieties known in the United States, only a few are of commercial value. The Bartlett pear is now the world's leading commercial variety. It is on the market from July until October. This pear is yellow when ripe, the flesh is white, and the flavor is sweet with a rich muscatel flavor.

The Beurre d'Anjou is the principal winter pear and is on the market from October to May. The Anjou is yellowish-white in color, juicy, and it has a spicy sweet flavor.

The Bosc pear is another popular winter pear which is known for its unique shape and color. This variety has a long tapering neck and its skin is dark yellow with an overlay of brownish russet. The flesh of the Bosc is yellowish-white and very juicy. It is a popular dessert pear. Other well-known varieties include the Comice, Kieffer, Hardy, Clapp, and Seckel. Fresh pears are eaten out of the hand; in salads and compotes; they may be stewed, baked, glazed, and pickled. Great quantities of pears are canned and some are dried.[24]

Persimmon—Kaki. Persimmon, which is a delicacy, grows on the persimmon tree in Italy, southern Europe, and the United States. The region around Naples, Emilia, and the Ligurian coast are well-known as exporters of this special fruit. The yellowish-red fruits, which have the appearance of tomatoes, are ripe in the late fall. The fruit is eaten fresh, dried, or stewed.

Pineapple—Ananas. The pineapple, belonging to the orchid family, comes from the West Indies and Central America and flourishes in the tropics. The main areas of cultivation are Hawaii, California, Jamaica, Mexico, Puerto Rico, and the Canary Islands. In Europe, pineapples are grown in hothouses, but these are inferior in both taste and aroma. The pineapple is a multiple fruit. All parts of the flower, including the axis, bracts, sepals, petals, and ovaries, coalesce and become very fleshy and aromatic. The fruit's aroma comes from the pineapple ether. Fully ripe, mature pineapples are golden yellow or reddish brown, firm, and heavy. The eyes or pips are glossy, and the leaves can be pulled out easily. Pineapple is used in many different ways as dessert, in fruit bowls, in salads, and as a garnish.

Pistachio—Pistache. These small, green, almond-like kernels are from a small tree of the cashew family. They grow in the Mediterranean countries and in Asia Minor. The main trade brands are: Tunis, Aleppo, and Sicily. The nuts are used for decorating cakes, ice cream, desserts, for cold meat pies, galatines, and delicatessen sausages. They are also eaten salted and as a confectionary.

FIGURE 3-73
Pistachio—Pistache

Plum—Pruneau. An excellent table fruit, plums are also good in pies, puddings, cakes, tarts, jellies, and jams. They may be stewed, poached, and served in salads and compotes.

Pomegranate—Grenade. The fruit of the pomegranate tree has a hard brownish to red-colored shell

24. United Fruit and Vegetable Association, *Pears* (Washington, D.C.)

and is the size of an apple. It is cultivated in Cyprus, the Canary Islands, North Africa, Sicily, and Spain. A light-colored, sweet, juicy, and wine-like layer of fruit flesh surrounds numerous seeds. This is eaten fresh, or made into syrup, ices, and sherbets.

Quince—Coing. Originally grown in the Kydone district of Crete, the quince was brought to Central Europe by the Romans. There are both apple and pear-shaped quinces. The ripe, golden fruit have a greenish felt-like cover, and although hard and very acid, the flesh turns dull pink when cooked with sugar. It makes a delicious jelly.

Raisin—Raisin de Corinthe. These are dried vine berries, coming from southern Europe, Asia Minor, South Africa, Australia, and the United States in various sizes and colors. The best known variety is the *Smyrna raisin;* it is the real raisin and is large, yellow-skinned, with or without seeds. The *Malaga raisin* is large, blue in color, and excellent in flavor. The *Sultana* raisin is either light yellow or blue. The fine sultana is small, light yellow in color with a delicate skin. The *Corinthian raisin* is a small, almost black, dried grape with a pleasant taste. Raisins must be kept dry and cool in closed containers.

Raspberry—Framboise. This is the fruit of the raspberry bush which grows both wild in the woods and cultivated in gardens. There are three groups of cultivated raspberries in North America. These are: red raspberries, black raspberries or blackcaps, and purple canes. Raspberries are usually consumed fresh or as a jelly, jam, or syrup. They are also used in bavarians, pies, mousse, punch, and ices. Raspberry juice is fermented and distilled and sold as a brandy. These berries are in season in June and July.

Strawberry—Fraise. The strawberry, king of all berries, is a favorite fruit throughout the world. It is an aggregate fruit, since the bottom of the flower develops into an aromatic, sweet berry-like structure on which the actual fruits, in the form of seedlings, are attached. *Wild strawberries* abound in Europe, and the *ever-bearing strawberry* is derived from them. The large garden strawberry and the large *Chile or giant strawberry* are of the same origin. The cultivated strawberry is native to America. Strawberries are used in desserts, jams, as breakfast fruit, and as garnishes.

Tangerine (mandarin orange)—Mandarine. A somewhat flattened orange-like fruit, the tangerine has loose skin that is easily peeled from the fleshy part of the fruit. Good quality tangerines are smooth-skinned, shiny, segmented, and not too small. They are used as table fruit and for special desserts. Tangerines and oranges belong to the citrus family, and originally came from southern China, Burma, and the southern regions of the Himalayas. Today the chief areas of production are southeastern United States, Central America, and the Mediterranean countries. The California/Arizona tangerine varieties are divided into four categories: Mandarins, lighter in color than other varieties, have a mild sweet flavor; tangelos, a cross between a grapefruit and tangerine, combine the best of both fruits for a tangy and sweet flavor; tangerines are a brighter orange color than any of the varieties; and temple oranges, larger than the others, have a sweet-tart distinctive flavor. Tangerines should be stored in well-ventilated areas at approximately 45°F. (7°C.).

3.5.7 Sugar—Sucre

Sugar is an energy-producing food. The basic unit of all carbohydrates is simple sugar. There are two types of raw sugar:

- sugar obtained from sugar cane
- sugar obtained from sugar beet

The two types vary only slightly in their cooking qualities. After processing in a sugar factory, a refined sugar is derived, from which the various commercial products are manufactured.

Corn Syrup—Glucose and dextrose. Glucose, as well as fructose, is found in honey and in the juice of most sweet fruits, such as grapes, cherries, and plums. This sugar is generally extracted from potato or cornstarch by boiling the starch with dilute sulphuric acid. The action of the acids or enzymes changes the cornstarch

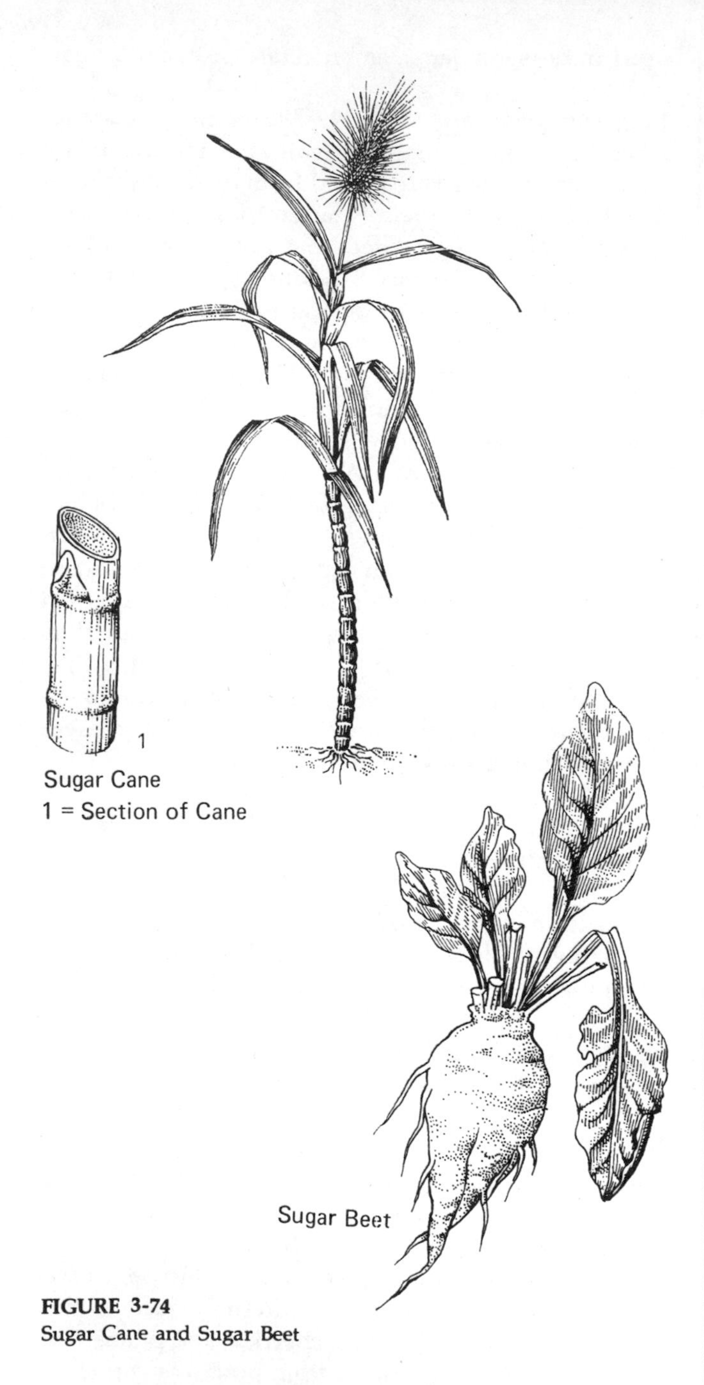

FIGURE 3-74
Sugar Cane and Sugar Beet

to glucose. Clucose is used in the manufacture of candies and jam (fondant).

Invert Sugar. When sucrose is hydrolyzed or inverted, equal parts of glucose and fructose are formed, and this product is called *invert sugar.*

Molasses. Sulfured molasses is the term used to describe the syrup which is a by-product of the manufacture of the sugar. It is a brown or brownish-black mass. The molasses, remaining after sugar is extracted from the sugar beet, is too bitter for human consumption. It is used for making alcohol. Sugar cane molasses is an unsulfured molasses made from the sun-ripened sugar cane. It can be used as a syrup or in the manufacture of imitation honey.

Maltose—Malt sugar. Maltose is available in sugar or syrup form. Real malt products are made from germinated barley using the so-called maltin-process. The barley starch is converted into malt sugar by diastasis. Maltose has a distinct flavor and may be used for making many yeast products, such as breads and rolls.

Lactose. Lactose is a sugar found in milk and is derived by evaporation of the whey and subsequent crystallization and purification of the sugar. It is also called milk sugar.

Vanilla sugar. Vanilla sugar is made by keeping one or two vanilla beans in a closed container with two cups of sugar. It originally consisted of the vanilla crystals which formed when vanilla was stored in closed barrels.

Caramelized sugar. If sugar is heated to between 350°F. and 400°F. (177°C. and 204°C.), the sucrose breaks down, gives off water, and forms a brown viscous mass known as *caramelized sugar.* When the caramel is dissolved in diluted alcohol or water, a dark-brown liquid with a definite odor and a bitter flavor is formed. It is a very strong coloring agent, and it is used to color and flavor many different kinds of foods and candies.

Artificial Sweeteners

Saccharin. Saccharin is a white crystalline compound extracted from coal tar. Chemically pure saccharin is about 550 times sweeter than sugar. The commercial product is the soluble powder pressed into tablets which are about 110 times sweeter than sugar crystals.

Cyclamates. Cyclamates used alone or in combination with saccharin must be labeled as drugs and

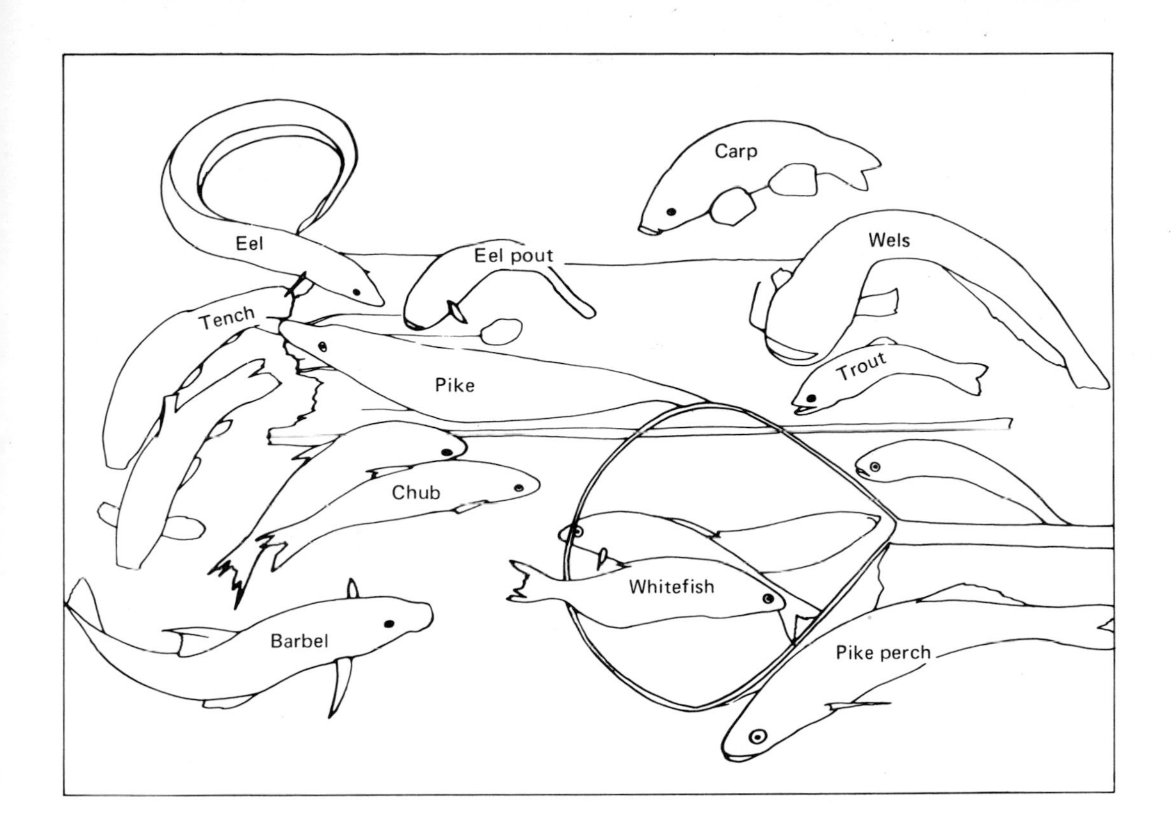

Key to Illustration of Freshwater Fish

Key to Illustration of Exotic Fruits

Exotic Fruits

1 Avocado	5 Kumquat
2 Okra (Lady's Fingers)	6 Ginger
3 Papaya	7 Mango
4 Passion Fruit	8 Lime

should be used only under a physician's order. They are extracted from a chemical substance. Although somewhat less sweet than saccharin, cyclamates can withstand cooking, which saccharin cannot. The manufacturer's directions should be followed when used in baking. Neither saccharin nor cyclamate has any nutritional value.

3.5.8 Spices—Epices

Spices are aromatic substances obtained from the dried parts of plants such as the roots, shoots, fruits, leaves, and bark. These substances are marketed as whole or ground spices, whole or crushed herbs, seeds, and blends of spices, herbs, and seasonings. The aromatic substances which give the spice its particular aroma and flavor are the etheric oils. This flavor of the essential oil or flavoring compound will vary depending on the quality and freshness of the spice. The oils of spices are volatile and the flavors may be lost rapidly if the spices are stored in open containers or in warm or humid areas.

Forms and Usage

- *fresh herbs:* Many herbs may be used in the fresh form. The plants are cleaned and washed. Such plants as parsley, chives, and chervil are usually chopped and added to or sprinkled over salads, soups, and other foods. The stalks are frequently used in bouquet garni.
- *dried herbs and spices:* Whole leaves, twigs, seeds, or finely chopped root vegetables are often used in foods that are to be cooked for a long period of time. These spices and herbs should be added at the beginning of the cooking. The spices can be removed only if they are wrapped and tied in a piece of cheesecloth.
- *ground spices:* Ground spices release their flavors quickly. When they are to be used in a dish that requires a long cooking time, they should be added at the end of the cooking period. Ground spices must be stored in airtight containers in a cool, dry place. Containers should be tightly closed after each use to avoid loss of the volatile oils.

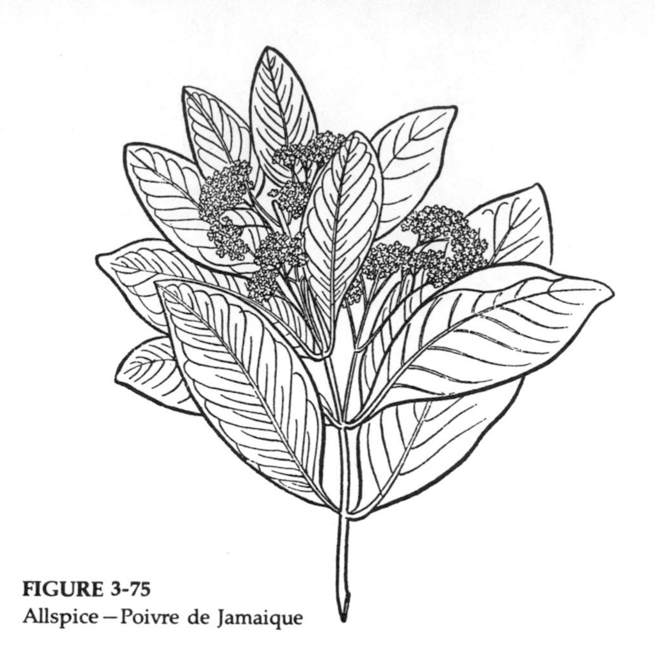

FIGURE 3-75
Allspice—Poivre de Jamaique

Allspice—Poivre de Jamaique
Origin: Allspice is produced from the berries of a small tropical evergreen tree that grows in Jamaica. It is also grown in Mexico, the Antilles Islands, and South America.
Form and characteristics: Allspice is also known as *pimento, pimenta,* and *Jamaica pepper.* The red or dark brown to yellowish berries are about ¼ inch (.6 centimeter) in diameter, and contain dark brown seeds. The odor and flavor are reminiscent of several spices—cloves, nutmeg, and cinnamon.
Usage: The spice is used in the preparation of sausages, fish, pickles, relishes, and desserts.

Anise—Anis (Pimpinella anisum). The herb anise should not be confused with the vegetable anise or with star anise. The vegetable can be distinguished by its bulb. The star anise is from a tree belonging to the magnolia tree of China.
Origin: This herb is thought to be native to the Orient, but it has been long established in Mexico, Spain, Morocco, Mediterranean countries, Yugoslavia, Turkey, and Russia. (See illustration p. 176.)
Form and characteristics: A plant of the parsley family, it is similar to burnet. The plant grows to a height

FIGURE 3-76
Anise—Anis (Pimpinella anisum)

of 18 inches (45 centimeters). It has fine leaves and clusters of small white flowers. The seeds, used for flavoring, are small, hard, and a greenish-brown color. The Spanish Malaga aniseed, with large, green-tinged seeds, and very sour, is the best variety. The Russian aniseed is superior for its aroma.
Usage: Aniseed is a raw material for the liqueur industry. The liqueur, anisette, and other beverages are flavored with anise. The oil of anise is used in cough medicines. Aniseeds are added to pastries, cookies, breads, candies, and pickles. The oils are very volatile and, therefore, the seeds should be stored in sealed tins. Anise is marketed as aniseseed, ground anise, and oil of anise.

Artemisia (Wormwood)—Armoise
Origin: Wormwood belongs to the daisy family and it is a native of Europe.
Form and characteristics: A perennial herb, it grows to a height of 3 feet (90 centimeters) with grayish-green, silk-like stems and leaves, and aromatic flowers.
Usage: Wormwood is used in the preparation of roast goose and eel dishes. It is also used for making absinthe liqueur and vermouth wine. With the stalks removed, it can be boiled or simmered with food.

FIGURE 3-77
Artemisia (wormwood)—Armoise

Basil—Basilic
Origin: A native of East Asia and central Europe, basil belongs to the mint family. (See illustration on pages 175, 176.)

FIGURE 3-78
Basil—Basilic

Origin: The bay laurel, an evergreen shrub or tree, is native to the Mediterranean countries, especially Italy, Dalmatia, Crete, Greece, and Turkey. The leaves of this tree are dried and used for bay leaves. (See illustration page 176.)
Form and characteristics: The bay leaves, dark green in color, are approximately 2 to 4 inches (5 to 10 centimeters) in length. The color turns to an olive-green as the leaves dry. The pungent flavor and distinct aroma make this an ideal herb for many dishes.
Form and characteristics: This annual plant grows to a height of 18 inches (45 centimeters). The flowers and leaves have long been used as a culinary herb.
Usage: The leaves add flavor to fish and meat dishes, soups, sauces, salads, tomato products, and pickles. The herb can be boiled or simmered with food.
Usage: Bay leaf is used for oxtail soup, meat stews, roast wild boar, leg and rib of lamb, minced or ground meat, hasenpfeffer, carp in beer, marinated herrings, soups, sauces, and tomato dishes. Bay leaves should be washed carefully before using.

FIGURE 3-79
Bay Leaf—Laurier

FIGURE 3-80
Borage—Bourrache

Borage—Bourrache
Origin: Borage, originally from the Mediterranean area, is now cultivated as a garden herb. (See illustration p. 175.)
Form and characteristics: This herb-like plant has blue flowers with hairy leaves and stems.
Usage: The fresh, young leaves of borage are used to flavor salads, the blue flowers to color vinegar. Dried borage can be used to season cabbage by simmering it with the vegetable.

Burnet—Pimprenelle
Origin: Burnet is grown in Germany and central Europe. (See illustration p. 175.)
Form and characteristics: A plant of the rose family with clustered flowers, burnet grows wild. There are over 200 varieties. In addition to oils, the plant contains bitter essences. When crushed, the leaves have a taste similar to that of cucumber. The roots are 4 to 8 inches (10 to 20 centimeters) long, yellow on the inside, and a brown to grayish-yellow on the outside.
Usage: Burnet is used for seasoning in soups, sauces, and vegetable and fish dishes. The young leaves can be used in salads; the dried roots are used as a drug.

FIGURE 3-81
Burnet—Pimprenelle

Caper—Capre
Origin: Mediterranean countries, Spain, Italy, and Majorca.
Form and characteristics: Capers are the buds of the caper bush. They are similar to the buds of the marsh marigold and the nasturtium. The fruits are sorted according to size, the smallest being the best quality and the largest the inferior. They are stored and shipped in brine, then drained and preserved in vinegar in the country where they are to be packed in consumer units. They are available in the following qualities: "Nonpareilles" (small), "Surfines" (medium), "Capucines" (large).
Usage: Capers are used in meat balls, stews, meat pies, tartare-steaks, salads, sauces, and pickled herring. Capers should not be cooked with the food, but added to the finished product.

Caraway—Carum carvi
Origin: This plant has been grown for its seeds since very early times. Generally believed that it originally came from Asia Minor, caraway is cultivated from

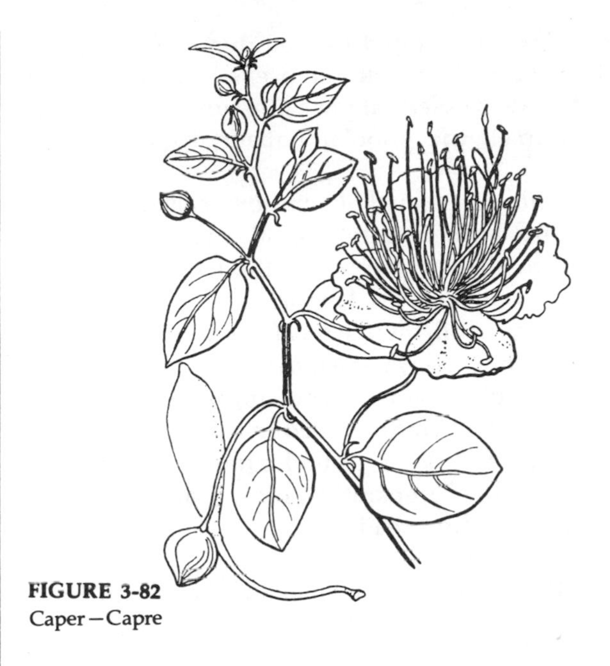

FIGURE 3-82
Caper—Capre

Europe to Siberia, northern Persia, and the Himalayas. (See illustration p. 176.)
Form and characteristics: The many-branched hollow-stemmed biennial herb grows up to two feet high (60 centimeters) and has small white flowers. The fruit (seed), approximately 1/8 inch long is grayish-brown when ripe and each carpel has five thin ridges.

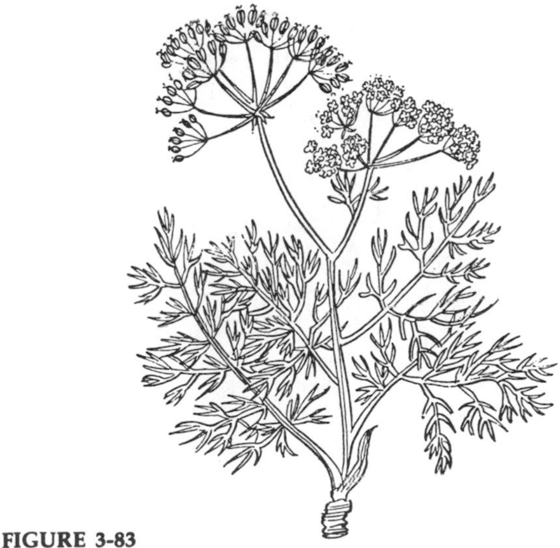

FIGURE 3-83
Caraway—Carum Carvi

Usage: Caraway, added to food during cooking, is used in rye bread, sauerkraut, beef stews, soups, and candy. Caraway seed, along with cumin and anise, gives kummel, the popular liqueur, its distinctive flavor.
Note: Although *cumin (cuminum cyminum)* and *caraway* are both members of the parsley family, there is a distinct difference in the flavor. The Germans call both seeds *kummel,* the Spanish call caraway *carvi,* and their word for cumin is *comino.* The French, however, named caraway, *cumin de pres* or *carvi,* and both caraway and cumin are known as cumin in France. Cumin is used in curry powder and chili powder. Whole or ground cumin is used commercially in the preparation of sausages, pickles, cheese, meats, and breads.

Cayenne Pepper—Cayenne. (See Red Pepper p. 157)

Chervil—Cerfeuil

Origin: Chervil is native to western Asia, Russia, and Caucasus. (See illustration p. 176.)
Form and characteristics: Chervil is grown as a garden plant with very aromatic curled leaves and hemlock-like flowers. It has the flavor of mild parsley.

FIGURE 3-84
Chervil—Cerfeuil

Usage: Fresh chervil is used in soups and salads. Dried chervil is used for seasoning in sauces and with roast lamb.

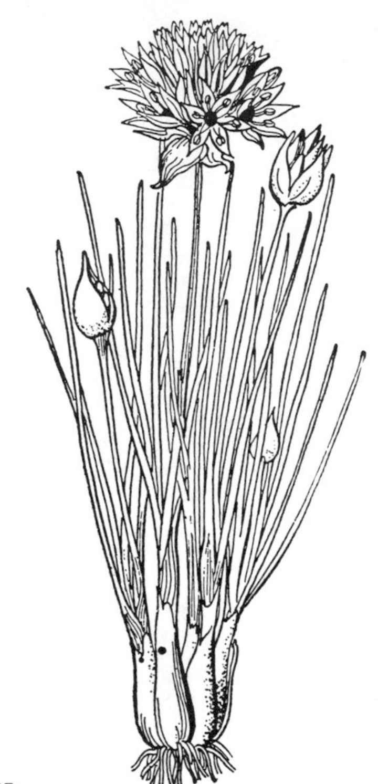

FIGURE 3-85
Chives—Ciboulette

Chives—Ciboulette
Origin: Chives are widespread in Europe, the United States, Russia, and Japan. (See illustration p. 175.)
Form and characteristics: Chives are primarily a garden plant, related to leeks, with bright green, tuber-shaped, mild-flavored leaves, and reddish-blue clusters of flowers. Chives are often grown as potted plants.
*Usage:*The leaves are chopped and used for garnishes and in salads, fish dishes, soups, cream cheese, and omelets.

Cinnamon—Cannelle
Origin: Cinnamon is ground from the dried bark of trees in the evergreen or "cinnamomum" family. The

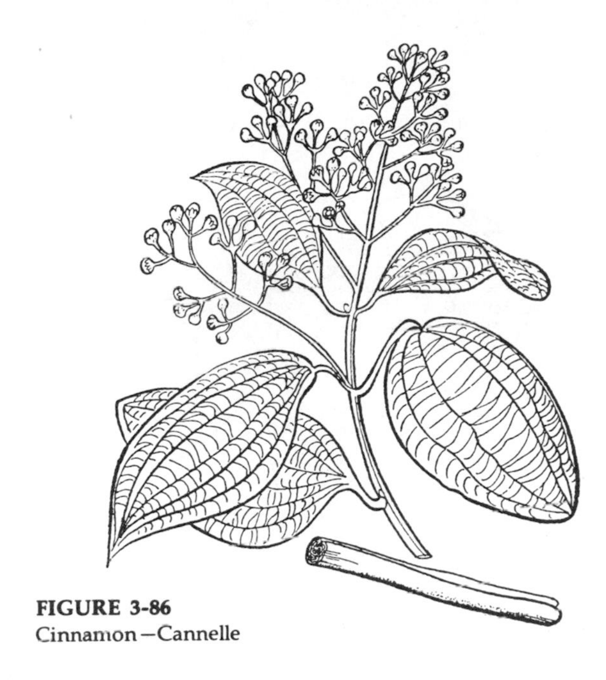

FIGURE 3-86
Cinnamon—Cannelle

true cinnamon *(cinnamomum zeylanicum)* is imported from Seychelles and Sri Lanka. It is known as the "Ceylon cinnamon." Most of the cinnamon used in the United States is derived from the trees of the *cinnamomum cassia* family. The term "cassia" is used to identify this cinnamon that is native to China, Indonesia, and Indo-China. (See illustration p. 176.)
Form and characteristics: The cultivated Ceylon cinnamon tree resembles an evergreen laurel bush and reaches a height of approximately 30 feet (900 centimeters). In Sri Lanka, the tree is pruned back to a height of 6 feet (180 centimeters) so that the plant will produce a maximum number of branches. The outer bark is yellowish-brown, and it is removed from the tree after two years of growth. The shoots are cut off close to the ground and the bark is pulled off in two strips. The outer skin of the bark is scraped off, and the pale brown strips are placed concentrically inside one another and slowly dried into "quills." The thinnest varieties are the best. The quality diminishes with increased thickness. The flavor of this bark is milder and the color lighter than the bark of the cassia tree. Most countries use Ceylon cinnamon; however, cinnamon from cassia type trees which have a higher oil content are in greater demand in the United States. The higher the oil content, the stronger the flavor and aroma. The Saigon cinnamon, highest oil content of all types, is the finest quality of cassia cinnamons.
Usage: Cinnamon may be ground for use in pastries, breads, puddings, cakes, candies, and cookies. Stick cinnamon is used for preserved fruits, pickles, and fruit soups, compotes, and hot beverages. Oil of cinnamon, distilled from broken bark, is used for flavoring and for medicinal purposes.

Coriander—Coriandre
Origin: Mediterranean area, Morocco, southern France, and the Orient. (See illustration p. 176.)
Form and characteristics: Coriander is a solid-stemmed plant approximately 2 feet (60 centimeters) high with white flowers. It is a member of the parsley family. The dried fruits, which are about the size of small peppercorns, are rippled on the outside, and a reddish-brown color. The plant is susceptible to damage by beetles.
Usage: Ground coriander is used in gingerbread, cakes, pastries, and curry powder. The whole seeds are used in pickles.

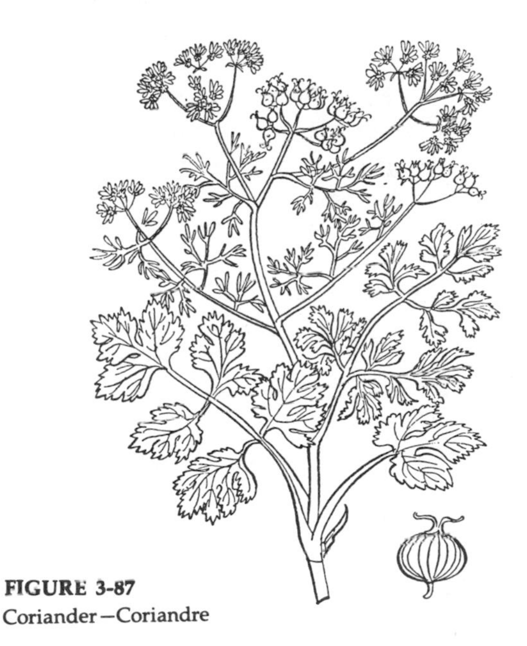

FIGURE 3-87
Coriander—Coriandre

FIGURE 3-88
Clove—Clou de Girofle

FIGURE 3-89
Curry—Curry

Clove—Clou de Girofle
Origin: Cloves are the dried, unopened flower buds of a tropical tree which is native to Indonesia. These trees are grown commercially on Zanzibar, Madagascar, and Pemba. These countries are leading producers and exporters.
Form and characteristics: The source of the word clove is from the French word *clou* which means spike or nail. Zanzibar and Pemba alone have half a million 40 foot (12 meters) clove trees, which are bright crimson during the flowering season. The bright red flower buds are broken off the trees with bamboo poles and dried either in the sun or near a fire. The nail-shaped clove is dark brown. The clove is characterized by its spicy aroma and strong pungent flavor.
Usage: Whole cloves are used in marinades, leg of lamb, red cabbage, game of all kinds, meat stews, soups, hasenpfeffer, carp in beer, eels in beer, marinated herrings, pickles, and mustard fruits. Ground cloves are used in fruit cakes, gingerbread, honey cakes, pepper cakes, hot punches, cookies, and breads.

Curry—Curry
Origin: India produces curry.
Form and characteristics: Curry is a blend of several ground spices according to traditional and jealously guarded formulas. The main spices include turmeric, coriander, ginger, fenugreek, caraway, pepper, and paprika. The curry should have a sweet, well-blended, and mild flavor. It should be a bright, rich yellow color.
Usage: Curry powder is used in curried rice, chicken curry, curry sauce, eggs, vegetables, and fish dishes. The flavor of many foods can be enhanced by the addition of curry.

Dill—Aneth
Origin: A native of Europe, dill is also grown in the United States and the West Indies.
Form and characteristics: Dill is a German garden plant, similar in form and taste to that of caraway. A parchment-like skin is found on each side of the seed. It is available as dill seed or dill weed.
Usage: It is used for pickling, in salads, sauerkraut, soups, and sauces. Dill should be added after cooking!

Garlic—Ail
Origin: Garlic is derived from a plant which grows in Central Asia and the Mediterranean countries.
Form and characteristics: This onion-like growth consists of a bulb surrounded by several layers of

FIGURE 3-90
Dill—Aneth

skin. Each bulb is made up of several smaller white or purplish colored cloves that are enclosed in a membrane. The most distinctive characteristic of garlic is its odor. Dehydrated garlic is marketed as instant garlic powder, instant minced garlic, and garlic salt.
Usage: Garlic is used in meat dishes, soups, salads, dressings, pasta dishes, sauces, pickles, and goulash.

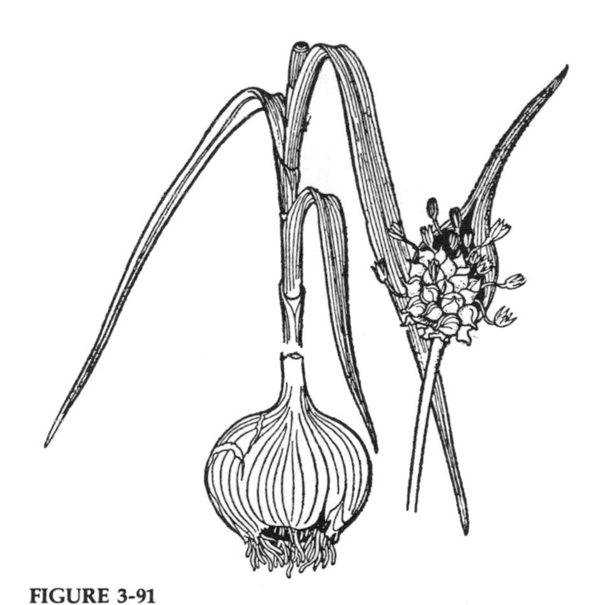

FIGURE 3-91
Garlic—Ail

FIGURE 3-92
Ginger—Gingembre

Ginger—Gingembre
Origin: The ginger plant is a native of Asia. It is grown in Japan, China, India, Jamaica, and Africa. (See illustration page 176.)
Form and characteristics: Ginger is produced from herb-like plants with leaves similar to reeds. The ginger used for food comes from the rhizome (root). The roots of the young plants (10 months old) are used for the best quality crystallized ginger. The flavor is pungent and spicy. Ground ginger is produced from the more mature rhizomes. It is a yellowish-brown color.
Usage: Ground ginger is used as a spice in pickles, stews, eggs, mustard, fruits, fruit cakes, ice cream, pepper cakes, ginger milk, and Vermouth. Candied ginger is used as a garnish and in pastries and confectionery. Fresh green ginger is used in many Oriental and Polynesian dishes and in marmalades and confections. Ginger is also used in making gingerale and ginger beer.

Horseradish—Raifort
Origin: Horseradish is a member of the wallflower family. It is a perennial herb that originated in central

FIGURE 3-93
Horseradish—Raifort

Europe and Asia. It is now cultivated throughout Europe and the United States.
Form and characteristics: The brownish-yellow root is approximately 18 inches (45 centimeters) long. The interior of the root is an off-white color. The distinctive flavor is very strong and pungent. The root is peeled and grated and simmered with vinegar and milk.
Usage: Fresh horseradish is grated for sauces and for fish and meat dishes. It is available in fresh or dehydrated form.

Juniper—Genievre
Origin: The juniper plant is grown in Italy, Czechoslovakia, and Rumania. (See illustration page 176.)
Form and characteristics: The juniper is a small evergreen shrub or tree belonging to the cypress family. The blue-black fruits are about the size of peas, and they are picked the second season the berries appear. Italy, where the berries are handpicked, produces the finest quality.
Usage: Juniper berries are used to flavor sauerkraut, roast wild boar, gin, liqueurs, and cordials. The berries should be cooked with the food.

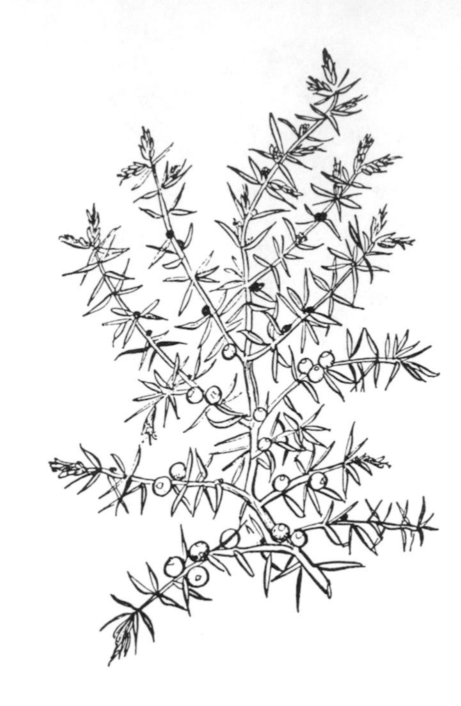

FIGURE 3-94
Juniper—Genievre

FIGURE 3-95
Lovage—Liveche

Lovage—Liveche
Origin: The Levisticum officinale is naturalized in Europe. The Scotch lovage is a native plant in northern England. (See illustration page 175.)

Form and characteristics: This herb garden plant grows about 6 feet (180 centimeters) high with clusters of aromatic yellow flowers. The stem and roots are used as an herb.
Usage: The herb is used in roasts, soups, and sauces. It should be cooked with the food. The plant is also used as a vegetable. The young stems may be candied.

Mace—Macis
Origin: Mace is a product of the nutmeg tree that is native to the Molucca Islands in Indonesia.
Form and characteristics: See nutmeg. Mace is the reddish-yellow coating around the nutmeg called aril. The mace, a highly aromatic spice with a taste more delicate than that of the nutmeg, is best when it is thin and brittle and reddish-yellow in color.
Usage: Mace is used in the preparation of pickles, preserves, sauces, pound cakes, breads, puddings, and pastries. It is used in large quantities in the meat-processing industry.

FIGURE 3-96
Mace—Macis

Marjoram—Marjolaine
Origin: The sweet or knotted marjoram is the best known, and it is native to the Mediterranean region. It is also grown in Britain, Germany, France, and Czechoslovakia. (See illustration pages 175, 176.)

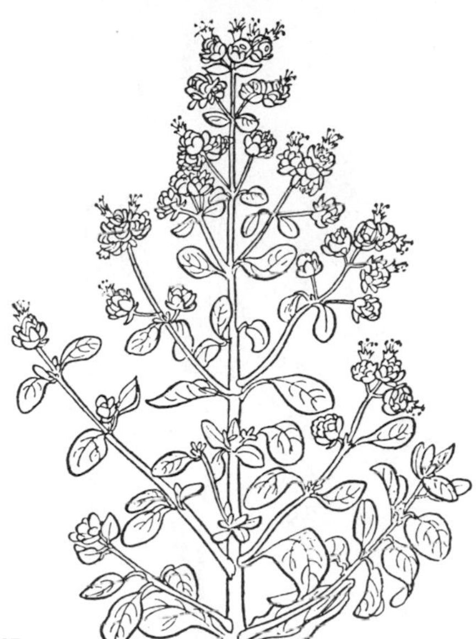

FIGURE 3-97
Marjoram—Marjolaine

Form and characteristics: They are small plants with light rose flowers. The plants are often cut after flowering and dried. The leaves are a gray-green color, and they are sold as marjoram leaves or ground marjoram.
Usage: Marjoram is used for seasoning potato soup, stuffed goose, liver dumplings, snails in sauce, roast rabbit, ham and meat dumplings, and herb sauces. The leaves lose their color unless stored in sealed containers.

Mint/Peppermint—Menthe
Origin: Peppermint is cultivated throughout Europe and the United States. Spearmint, a native of Europe, is cultivated throughout England and the United States. (See illustration page 175.)
Form and characteristics: Peppermint can be identified by its characteristic odor, its short leaves, and its flowers. The spear-shaped leaves of spearmint are spicy and contain menthol. The plant has spikes of lilac-colored flowers with stamens that extend beyond the corolla. The most popular variety is English spearmint with its red stem.
Usage: Peppermint is used in liqueurs, cordials, candies, and beverages. It is also used for oil of peppermint. Spearmint is used as a flavoring for lamb,

FIGURE 3-98
Mint/Peppermint—Menthe

vegetables, fruit soups, potatoes, and for mint sauce and mint ice cream.

Nutmeg—Noix de muscade
Origin: The nutmeg tree is a native of the Moluccas (Spice Islands) in Indonesia. It is also grown in the West Indies, Banda Isles, and Papua.
Form and characteristics: The nutmeg tree averages between 32 and 38 feet (9 to 12 meters) in height. The fruit is similar to the peach. Between the fleshy outside skin and the kernel itself, there is a reddish-yellow seed coating (mace). Nutmeg is the kernel or seed of the fruit, and its flavor is sweet and spicy. There are approximately 60 large nuts or 150 very small nuts in 1 pound (.45 kilogram). Nutmeg may be purchased in whole or ground form. Whole nutmeg may be grated as needed.
Usage: Nutmeg is used extensively in custards, eggnogs, and cream puddings and desserts. It is also used in aspics, meat pies, soups, fried brains, shelled vegetables, chicken soups, chicken fricassee, breast of veal, mushroom dishes, and spinach.

FIGURE 3-99
Nutmeg—Noix de muscade

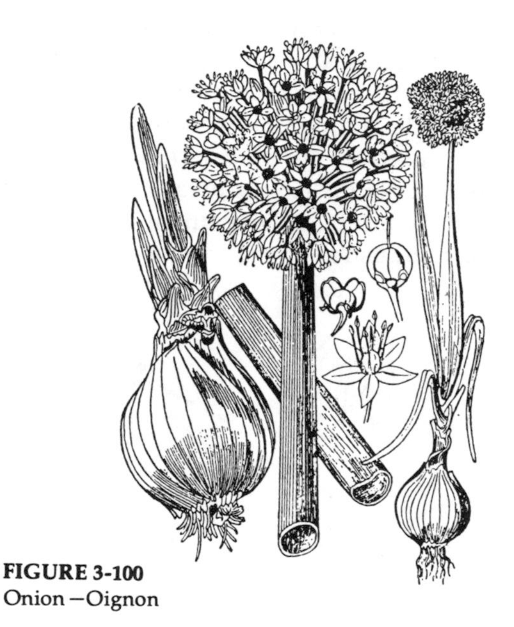

FIGURE 3-100
Onion—Oignon

Onion—Oignon
Origin: Holland, Egypt, United States, Italy, and Bermuda are the main producers.
Form and characteristics: A leek-like, 2½ foot (75 centimeters) tall plant with a bulb, a hollow stalk, and whitish-green clumps of flowers. Onions which are allowed to grow to full size may be dried and processed into instant chopped onions, instant onion powder, onion salt, and onion flakes.
Usage: Spring onions are used in salads and as garnishes. Dehydrated onions are a convenient form to use in the preparation of soups, stews, meat dishes, sauces, and dressings.

FIGURE 3-101
Oregano—Oregano

Oregano—Oregano
Origin: Oregano grows in Mexico, Italy, and the United States. (See illustration page 176.)
Form and characteristics: Oregano, a member of the mint family, has a strong, aromatic, and pleasant taste. The dried leaves are a dull green color.
Usage: This herb is used to season Mexican and Italian dishes such as pizza and pastas. It is an ingredient in chili powder.

Paprika—Paprika
Origin: Spain, Southern France, Italy, Yugoslavia, and Hungary. (See illustration page 175.)
Form and characteristics: Paprika is produced from the sweet pepper *(Gapsicum annum)*. The bright red fruits are conical-shaped and 2 to 3 inches (5 to 7.5 centimeters) long. The rather flat yellow seeds are inside the fruit. The peppers are eaten as a vegetable, as pickles, and in salads. The red peppers are ground after the seeds and membranes are removed. Spanish-grown paprika is a brilliant red color with a sweet mild flavor. Hungarian paprika is dark red with a pungent flavor.
Usage: Paprika is used to add color to foods. It is used in risotto, Hungarian goulash, carp with paprika, and on canapes.

FIGURE 3-102
Paprika—Paprika

Parsley—Persil
Origin: Parsley is native to the Mediterranean countries. (See illustration page 175.)
Form and characteristics: A small garden herb, the leaves are usually curled, crisp, and bright green. The plant can be harvested several times a year. The characteristic odor is due to the presence of volatile oils in the stems and leaves. The leaves may be dried.
Usage: When fresh, the herb is used with fish, meat, vegetables, salads, soups, and for garnishing all dishes. Dried leaves of parsley are excellent for seasoning and garnishing. When dried or preserved in brine, parsley loses its aroma.

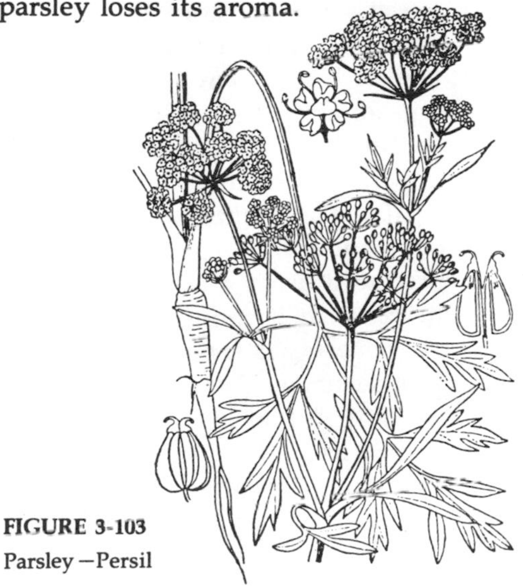

FIGURE 3-103
Parsley—Persil

FIGURE 3-104
Pepper—Poivre

Pepper—Poivre
Origin: Black pepper is obtained from the Piper Nigrum vine which is native to southeast Asia, chiefly on the Malabar coast, Borneo, Java, and Sumatra. (See illustration page 176.)
Form and characteristics: The Piper Nigrum is a climbing plant that forms its fruits on long hanging spikes. The fruits, called peppercorns, turn a red color when ripe. Pepper is available as whole black pepper, ground black pepper, coarse ground black pepper, whole white pepper, and ground white pepper.
Black pepper is the unripe peppercorn that is sun-dried until the outer skin becomes wrinkled and changes to a black color. It has a stronger and more pungent flavor than that of white pepper. The best quality comes from the Malabar coast, where the peppercorns are properly sieved and cleaned. Black pepper from Borneo (Sarawak) and Indonesia is inferior to the Malabar standard.
White pepper is produced from the mature peppercorn of the same plant. It is fermented after the harvest and the outer covering is separated from the seed. The small white seeds are dried. The flavor is hotter but less pungent than that of black pepper.
Usage: Whole peppercorns are used to flavor soups, meats, and pickles. Ground pepper is used to season foods. White pepper is often preferred for light-colored foods.

Poppy—Pavot
Origin: The poppy plant comes from the Far East and the Netherlands.
Form and characteristics: Poppy seeds are from the perennial poppy plant which grows to a height of about 5 feet (150 centimeters). Poppies are cultivated for the seeds in the fruit capsule which contain oil. Immature capsules contain the milk juice, which is the source of opium. The ripe dried seeds have a crunchy mint-like flavor.
Usage: When dried, poppy seeds are used on bread and rolls, cakes, cookies, in salads and mild dishes such as cabbage and noodles, and in fillings for pastries.

Poppy — Pavot

1 Longitudinal section of the seed capsule
 (a) Empty seed chamber
 (b) Filled seed chamber
2 Seed capsule (cross-section)
3 Whole seed capsule

FIGURE 3-105
Poppy—Pavot

FIGURE 3-106
Red Pepper—Chilli

Red Pepper—Chilli
Origin: This Capsicum plant is native to tropical America and is also grown in Africa, West Indies, and Japan.
Form and characteristics: The fruits of the Capsicum plants are bright red in color and vary in size and shape. The fruits are usually sun-dried and cayenne pepper is made from the powdered dried fruits. Red pepper is a very strong spice.
Usage: Red peppers are an essential ingredient in tabasco sauce and in curry powder. It can be used with other spices for pickling and marinating.

Rosemary—Romarin
Origin: Rosemary is a native of the Mediterranean area. (See illustration page 175.)
Form and characteristics: Rosemary is a tall bushy shrub with silvery green leaves, resembling pine needles, and violet flowers. The herb is available as rosemary leaves or ground rosemary.
Usage: Fresh or dried rosemary is used to flavor meat and poultry dishes and salads. It is also used in stews and soups.

Form and characteristics: The three stigmas of the crocus-like flower are the only part of the plant used in the production of saffron. They are picked by hand and carefully sorted by color, which varies from yellow to red. Saffron gives a strong yellow coloring to foods. It has a distinctive mild bitter-sweet flavor. It is a very expensive spice.
Usage: Saffron is used for sauces, soups, rice dishes, potato dishes, breads, and for pastries.

FIGURE 3-107
Rosemary—Romarin

Saffron—Safran
Origin: A member of the iris family, saffron is a native of Asia. It is also grown in Spain, France, and Italy.

Sage—Sauge
Origin: Sage, a native of Europe, is grown in Britain and the United States.
Form and characteristics: Sage is a garden plant that grows about 3 feet (90 centimeters) tall and has blue flowers and grayish-green leaves. Fresh and dried sage is sold in bunches, although the leaf is the only part of the plant used. The flavor is spicy and somewhat bitter.
Usage: Poultry seasoning, stuffings.

FIGURE 3-108
Saffron—Safran

FIGURE 3-109
Sage—Sauge

Savory—Sariette
Origin: Summer savory was originally grown as a garden herb in the Mediterranean countries. (See illustration p. 175.)
Form and characteristics: This very fragrant herb has spicy leaves and pale-colored lilac flowers.

FIGURE 3-110
Savory—Sariette

Usage: Fresh or dried savory is used in beans, sauerkraut, sausages, stuffings, vegetables, soups, and roast lamb. It should be cooked with the food.

Tarragon—Estragon
Origin: The plant is native to Europe and was grown as a garden plant in Russia and Mongolia. (See illustration p. 175.)
Form and characteristics: A perennial herb with long, thin, olive-green leaves and small, button-shaped flowers.
Usage: The leaves are used in pickles, soups, salads, and sauces, and for making tarragon vinegar.

Thyme—Thym
Origin: Thyme, originally a Mediterranean plant, is now grown in France, Spain, Yugoslavia, Czechoslovakia, Great Britain, and the United States. (See illustration pages 175, 176.)
Form and characteristics: This herb is from a low-growing plant with small, aromatic, rolled-up

FIGURE 3-111
Tarragon—Estragon

leaves and reddish-lilac labiated flowers.
Usage: Thyme is used as a seasoning in roast rabbit, roast game, game stews, ragouts, stuffed duckling, venison pie, hasenpfeffer, sauces, roasts, and soups. This herb should be cooked with the food.

FIGURE 3-112
Thyme—Thym

FIGURE 3-113
Turmeric—Curcuma

Turmeric—Curcuma
Origin: Turmeric is grown in East Asia, India, Africa, and Australia.
Form and characteristics: This belongs to the ginger family. The flavor is mild and sweet, and it has a strong aroma. The roots have a distinctive yellow color due to the pigment called curcumin.
Usage: Ground turmeric is one of the main ingredients in curry powder and in mustard. It is imported by Sweden and England for making their well-known sauces. It is also used to produce a yellow dye used in India.

Vanilla—Vanille
Origin: Vanilla is produced from an orchid type plant native to Central America. The plant has been transplanted to other parts of the world. Madagascar is the major producing country today.
Form and characteristics: The vanilla beans from Madagascar are cured by dipping them in boiling water and drying slowly. The cured pods should be black in color. They are packed in airtight boxes or tins. The vanilla from this area, formerly called the Bourbon Islands, is known as Bourbon vanilla. This and the vanilla from Mexico are superior in quality. A more economical and efficient method of curing has been developed. The harvested beans are ground

RIGHT:
Key to illustration (page 175) of Herbs and Spices Used for Cooking

Herbs and Spices Used for Cooking

1	Garden Peppermint	10	Winter Savory
2	English or Red Peppermint	11	Lemon Melissa
3	Chives	12	Tarragon
4	Burnet	13	Savory
5	Marjoram	14	Rosemary
6	Borage	15	Parsley
7	Lavender	16	Sage
8	Thyme	17	Basil
9	Oregano	18	Lovage

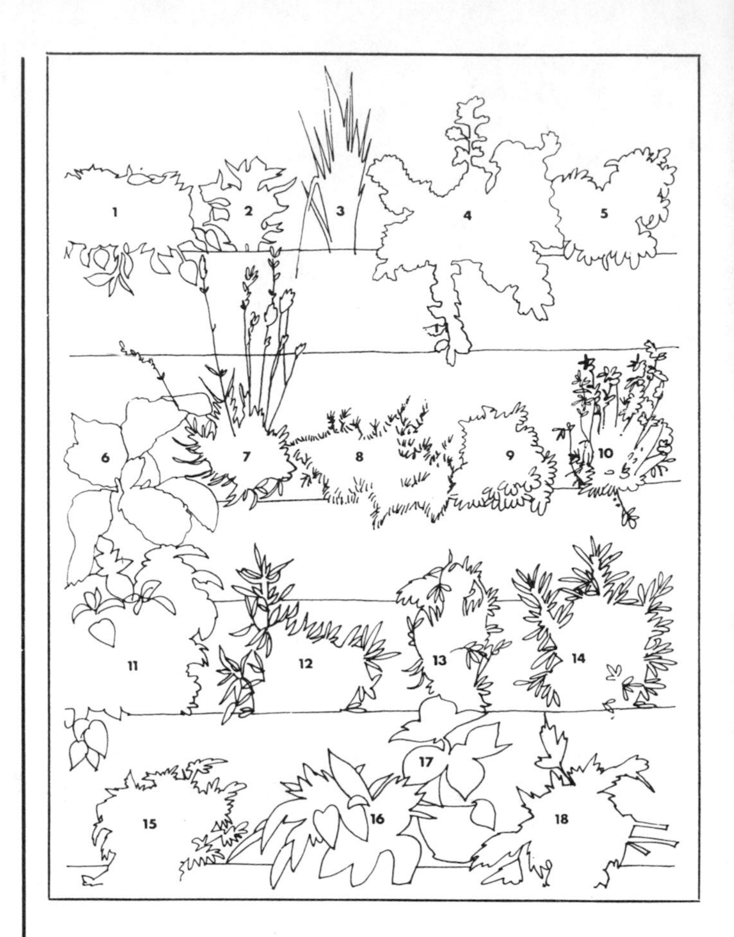

FIGURE 3-114
Vanilla—Vanille

without drying. They are cured in a brine and then dehydrated. Imitation vanilla extracts are made from a colorless crystalline synthetic compound called vanillin. Pure vanilla extract is superior to imitation vanilla.

Usage: Vanilla beans or vanilla extract are used to flavor creams and desserts, cold fruit soups, compotes, cookies and cakes, tarts, rice pudding, ice cream, burnt almonds, and candies. The pod of the vanilla bean should be slit open, cooked with the food, and removed before serving.

3.5.9 Condiments—Condiments

Glutamate. A sodium salt of glutamic acid is derived from protein. It is a spicing ingredient which enhances the taste of the food.

Mustard—Moutarde. This is a ground product derived from the mustard seed. It is sold either in powdered form or as table mustard. English-style, which is the strongest, and French-style mustards are the most popular varieties. German-style mustard is mild and Austrian-style mustard, sweet. Jamaican and Chinese-style mustards are fiery. Table mustard is prepared from vinegar, wine, water, salt, garlic, horseradish, sugar, and spices.

Salt—Sel

- *Brine Salt.* Deep holes, 450 to 900 feet (135 to 270 meters), are bored into the earth so that the salt strata dissolves in the ground water. The brine is then pumped to the surface, purified, and evaporated.

- *Kitchen Salt—Sel de cuisine.* Salt is a white, crystalline substance, sodium chloride, that is found in natural beds in sea water. It is added to food to improve flavor. All varieties of kitchen salt come either directly or indirectly from the sea. There are different kinds of salt, depending upon the method of extraction.
- *Rock Salt.* This salt is extracted by natural evaporation of sea water. It is a nonedible, unrefined salt that is used in freezing ice cream or as a base for heating oysters on the half shell.
- *Saltpeter.* This is sodium nitrate used in some meat processing. The chemical gives a red color to the meat.
- *Sea Salt.* This salt is known as Kosher or coarse salt. It is a coarse grained salt that is sometimes sprinkled over pretzels or rolls before baking or over meats just before serving. It is very flavorful but should be used sparingly.
- *Table Salt.* This consists of especially small salt crystals or finely ground salt. For some cooking purposes, coarse salt crystals may be dried slowly in the oven and then ground. Good salt should dissolve completely in water. The reddish *commercial salt* contains iron oxide and carbon, and should not be permitted in the kitchen. Iodized salt is table salt to which a very small quantity of potassium iodide has been added.

Vinegar—Vinaigre. Comestible vinegar is a condiment or a dilute solution of acetic acid which is extracted from wine, fermented fruits or grains, or other alcoholic liquids. The strength of vinegar is specified by the percent of acid. There are four different varieties of vinegar:

- *Fermentation vinegar* is formed naturally by the action of vinegar bacteria on dilute alcohol.
- *Flavored vinegars* are made of a cider vinegar to which herbs, spices, or honey are added.
- *Lemon vinegar* is made up of equal parts of well-flavored vinegar and lemon juice.
- *Vinegar essence* is manufactured in several different ways, including purely chemical processes.

3.5.10 Cooking Aids—Produits auxiliaires

Agar—Agar. A vegetable substance extracted from red seaweed which is gathered by divers off the coasts of Sri Lanka, Japan, and California. The salt is removed by repeated washing in clear fresh water. The seaweed is then cooked to yield a solution which is bleached, filtered, and poured into molds. When cool the gelatin-like mass is cut into strips or slabs. It is also available in powdered form. Good agar dissolves in hot water and is colorless. Its jellifying capacity is eight times as strong as that of ordinary gelatin.
Usage: It is used for gelatin products that require a strong jellifying power.
Candied Fruits—Fruits confits. Fruits that have been preserved in sugar. They are used in cakes and as garnishes for desserts and pastries.

- *Candied Lemon Peel.* The peel of lemon is candied and used in cakes and pastries.
- *Candied Orange Peel.* The peel of the orange is candied for use in cakes and pastries.

Food Coloring—Colorants. Coloring agents used in cooking or baking. They are made from plants, flowers, fruits, and officially approved synthetic colors.
Gelatin—Gelatine. Gelatin is made from bones, connective tissue, and skins of animals. The calcium is removed with dilute hydrochloric acid. The remaining substance is soaked in cold water for a period of time, and then heated to 100°F. to 140°F. (38°C. to 60°C.). The liquid is then partially evaporated, defatted, and coagulated on stone or glass plates and poured into special molds. The solid blocks are cut into slices and dried on wire nets. Gelatin is marketed as plain, unflavored gelatin and may be purchased in sheets, granules, powder, or flakes. The quality of gelatin depends on the method of processing and manufacturing. Good quality gelatin is odorless and tasteless and it produces a strong, soft, and tender gel.

Honey—Miel. The general term honey refers to the mature, sweet substance which bees gather from the nectar of flowers or from other natural plant secretions and store in the honeycombs. Honey is marketed in two basic forms: extracted and comb. Extracted honey has been removed from the comb by centrifuge, and it is sold in either liquid or crystallized form. The latter forms are creamed, candied, or spread. The light-colored May and blossom honeys, or even the honey that is made primarily from the blossom of linden trees, are superior to the darker forest honey. Honey should be stored in a dry place at room temperature.
Imitation Honey—Miel artificiel. Products which contain sugar and are similar to honey in terms of appearance and consistency, should be labeled as "imitation honey" specifying the actual ingredients. Glucose is the main ingredient in imitation honey.
Marzipan—Massepain. This is a dry-rubbed mixture of almonds and sugar. The addition of a small amount of bitter almonds will give a special aroma to the mixture. Marzipan is used for confections, pastries, and for decorative purposes.
Mock Marzipan—Persipan. A substitute for marzipan. Apricot, peach, and other fruit kernels are substituted for almonds.
Nougat—Nougat. This is a confection made from roasted almonds or hazelnuts, honey, and sugar. There are many distinctive flavored nougats due to the varying flavors of honey. There are hard, soft, white, and colored nougats. Nougat noir (black nougat) is a nougat to which powdered chocolate has been added. White nougats are usually made commercially. Nougats from Montelimar (France) are known throughout the world.
Recipe: Dry 1 pound (454 grams) of almonds or hazelnuts in the oven. Clean and crush into small pieces. Caramelize 14 ounces (390 grams) of sugar in a copper pan and acidify with a little lemon juice. Add the almonds and mix in using a wooden spoon. Press the warm mixture into forms or roll the nougat into a thin sheet on an oiled marble surface, and form or cut into desired shapes.
Usage: Ground nougat is used for nougat ice cream.
Pectin—Pectin. A substance from the fibrous parts of most fruits.
Usage: Pectin is used to jellify cooked fruits and juices used in the preparation of jellies, jams, and preserves.
Sturgeon Bone Marrow — Vesiga du grand esturgeon. This is the spinal marrow taken from the hausen variety of sturgeon. The blood is removed by bathing in salted water. The filaments are then dried and plaited together in groups of 15 to 20, and sold in this form. In Russia, this marrow is used for making *pirok.*

3.5.11 Seasonal Calendar

The following fresh foods are generally at their peak during the months indicated:

Almond	July-November
Anchovy	October-May
Apple	September-April
Apricot	May-September
Artichoke	January-September
Banana	January-December
Barbel	October-March
Beans	May-October
Beef	January-December
Bilberry	June-September
Blackberry	June-September
Black Truffle	November-April
Blue Char	May-November
Boston Lettuce	June-October
Bream	July-October
Broccoli	October-March
Brussels Sprouts	September-March
Burbot	January-December
Cabbage	January-December
Cardoon	October-March
Carp	January-December
Carrot	May-November
Cauliflower	July-May
Caviar	January-December
Celery (root)	September-February
Chamois	July-September
Chanterelle	July-September
Cherry	May-August
Chestnut	January-December

Chicken	January-December
Chicory	April-October
Chives	March-November
Chub	February-August
Clams	August-April
Cod	January-December
Conical Morel	April-May
Corn	August-September
Crab	September-March
Cranberry	September-October
Crayfish	May-September
Cucumber	June-November
Duck	March-October
Eel	January-December
Eel-pout	January-December
Eggplant	July-October
Endive	April-October
Field Mushroom	July-October
Fig (green)	July-November
Frogs' Legs	March-October
Golden Trout	February-October
Goose	January-December
Gooseberry	June-August
Goose Liver	October-April
Grapes (fresh)	September-October
Grouse	October-November
Guinea-fowl	March-October
Haddock	January-December
Hare	September-March
Hausen	May-December
Hazel-grouse	September-January
Hazelnut	January-December
Herring	May-January
Lake Trout	February-August
Lamb	March-June
Leek	January-December
Lettuce	June-October
Lobster	April-September
Mackerel	April-December
Melon	June-October
Morel	April-May
Mushroom (cultivated)	January-December
Mussel	August-April
Mutton	January-December
Nectarine	July-October
New Potatoes	June-July
Nut	September-April
Onion	January-December
Orange	October-July
Oyster	September-April
Parsley	January-December
Partridge	September-March
Pea	May-August
Peach	July-October
Pear	July-February
Perch	January-September
Pheasant	November-February
Pigeon	January-December
Pike	July-April
Pike-perch	January-December
Pineapple	January-December
Plaice	April-November
Plum	August-October
Pork	January-December
Potato	January-December
Quail	May-October
Quince	October-January
Rabbit	January-December
Radish	February-September
Raspberry	July-October
Ray	January-December
Red Cabbage	August-December
Red Currant	June-August
Red Deer	September-March
Reindeer	December-May
Rhubarb	May-September
Rock Lobster	February-October
Romaine Lettuce	April-November
Rutabaga	May-September
Salmon	August-March
Salmon-trout	February-October
Salsify	December-March
Sardine	June-October
Sauerkraut	October-April
Savoy Cabbage	July-October
Scallops	January-June

Shrimp	March-September
Snail	October-April
Snipe	August-March
Snow Grouse	October-March
Sole	January-December
Sorrel	March-July
Sour Cherry	May-August
Spring Chicken	January-December
Spring Lamb	March-June
Strawberry	May-August
Sturgeon	May-October
Summer Truffle	June-August
Tench	July-March
Tomato	January-December
Trout	February-November
Tuna	May-October
Turbot	January-December
Turkey	January-December
Veal	January-December
Venison	September-March
Walnut	August-September
Watermelon	August-December
Whitebait	February-August
Whitefish	May-November
White Truffle	July-September
Wild Boar	January-December
Wild Duck	August-April
Wild Rabbit	September-April

3.6 Beverages

Beverages as described here have little or no food value. They contain substances which have either a stimulating or a calming effect on the brain and nerves. Included in these substances are caffeine, theine, alcohol, nicotine, and opium. All stimulants must undergo fermentation, low or high temperature roasting (coffee), or distillation (alcohol).

3.6.1 Coffee—Cafe

Coffee originally came from the mountainous Kaffa region in Ethiopia and the coffee tree was transplanted from there to Arabia. Pilgrims travelling to Mecca in the seventeenth century brought the first fertile beans to East India, the Dutch to Dutch East India in 1696 and, soon afterwards, to the West Indies. The earliest recorded evidence of coffee plantations in Brazil dates back to 1727. The French were highly successful in establishing coffee plantations on Haiti and Santo Domingo. Today coffee is cultivated in South America, Central America, West Indies, Asia, and Africa. The Mohammedan religion prohibits the consumption of alcoholic drinks; however, coffee is in great demand, and drinking has become a habit throughout all Arab countries. In Turkey, the first coffee houses opened in Constantinople in the middle of the 16th century. At the siege of Vienna in 1683, the Turks fled, leaving 500 sacks of coffee among the booty for the victors. Thus, the first coffee houses opened in Vienna, and, as time went by, coffee drinking became a custom throughout the world.

Coffee Varieties. Coffee beans are classified according to their origin, method of preparation, size, and ripeness. There are considerable differences in terms of shape, color, purity, consistency, reaction upon roasting, and brewing. The different varieties of coffee are, in some cases, named after the producing country, in other cases, after the port of shipment.

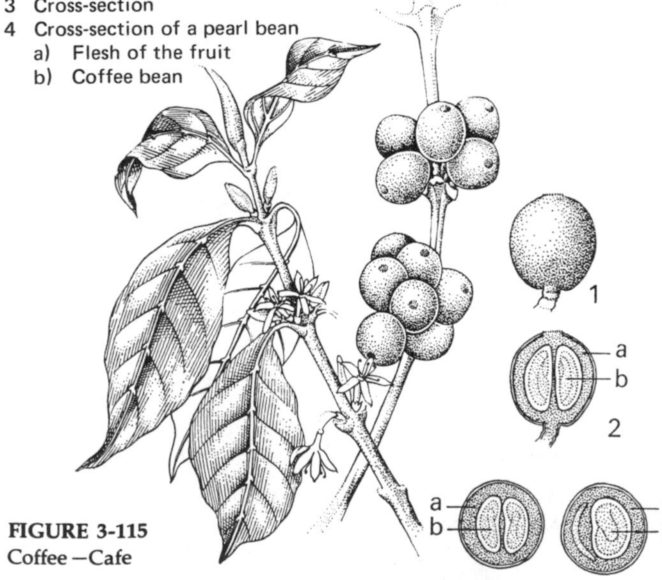

FIGURE 3-115
Coffee—Cafe

Leading Producers of Commercial Coffees:

South America	Brazil (Brasil, Santos, Parana, Rio, Bahia, Minas), Columbia, Venezuela (Caracas)
Central America	Guatemala, Costa-Rica, Salvador, Mexico, Nicaragua
West Indies	Haiti, Santo Domingo, Cuba
Asia	Western India (Malabar coast), Java, Sumatra, Celebes
Africa and Arabia	East Africa (Kenya, Uganda, Ethiopia); West Africa (Angola); Arabia: Yemen (Arabian Mocca, port of shipment: Hodeida)

Cultivation of Coffee. Growing wild, the coffee tree, with its 3 to 4 inch (7.5 to 10 centimeters) long, dark, evergreen leaves similar to bay leaves, reaches a height of 20 to 24 feet (600 to 720 centimeters), but in plantations it is cultivated in bushes about 7 to 9 feet (210 to 270 centimeters) tall. The trees are pruned to keep the height within the reach of the pickers. The flowers are white and have a fragrance similar to that of jasmine. The bush flowers two or three times a year and the blossoms, the ripe and the unripe fruits often appear on the bush at the same time. The ripe fruits look like cherries, and are a dark red to bluish-black, depending upon the variety. The flesh of each berry holds two beans, which are surrounded by a silvery skin and a horn shell. After the shell has been removed, the contents are referred to as shelled coffee. The size of the coffee bean contained in the fruit varies between 1/6 to 2/3 inch (.4 to 1.6 centimeters) long, 1/10 to 1/3 inch (.2 to .8 centimeter) wide, and 1/10 to 1/7 inch (.2 to .3 centimeter) thick. If the fruit produces only one bean, then it is round or roller-shaped and is known as *pearl coffee.* These pearl beans are removed and sold separately. Their quality is not superior to that of normal coffee beans.

Processing of the Coffee Berries

- *Dry process.* Unwashed coffee or whole berries are placed in heaps and undergo fermentation. They are then spread out and dried in the sun. The dried fruit flesh, shell, and silver skin are removed mechanically. These beans are known as "hard coffee."
- *Wet process.* The berries are opened by a pulping machine and the fruit flesh is removed by water during washing and the beans are fermented in water for a short time. Thereafter, they are dried and taken out of the silver skin. The washed coffee is usually considered higher quality than the unwashed.

Coffee Roasting. Roasting is necessary to develop the flavor of coffee. During the roasting process, the beans change in color from green to light or dark brown depending on the degree of roast. Coffee may be roasted to the light stage which is a light brown color, medium roast is coffee beans roasted to a dark brown color, and dark roast is coffee roasted to a very dark brown color. Roasting causes a 20 percent loss in weight. Roasted coffee attracts moisture and should be stored in airtight containers. The aroma of freshly roasted coffee is easily lost because of the volatility of the flavor esters. Since ground coffee loses its aroma and flavor much faster than the bean, coffee should be ground just before use.

Decaffeinated Coffee. Coffee contains the stimulant, caffeine. Decaffeinized coffee is popular with those persons who are sensitive to caffeine. Approximately 97 percent of the caffeine is removed before the roasting. Neither the aroma nor the taste is absolutely dependent upon the caffeine, therefore, decaffeinated coffee has become popular. The caffeine is extracted from the raw coffee with ether, benzene, and other solvents. The caffeine content of normal coffee is between 1.1 and 2.5 percent, that of caffeine-reduced coffee 0.2 percent, and 0.08 percent in so-called decaffeinated coffee.

Powdered Coffee (Instant Coffee). Instant coffee consists of coffee extract that is spray-dried or freeze-dried. The quality of the powders on the market varies with the quality of the coffee bean and the processing methods. This product is convenient to store and easily prepared. Boiling water is poured over the coffee powder.

Coffee Substitutes (Surrogate). Even though the term

"coffee substitute" is frequently used, there is in reality no such thing as imitation coffee. The stimulating effect of coffee and the fragrance of its fine aroma cannot be imitated. Nevertheless, many products have been used as replacements to make a drink similar to coffee. The most popular are:

- barley and the malt produced from it
- rye
- chicory and sugar beet
- figs
- types of sugar

The consumption of imitation coffees varies with the price of coffee. As prices increase, the consumption of coffee substitutes increases; as prices decrease, the consumption declines.

3.6.2 Tea—The

Tea comes from the leaf buds and young leaves of a tropical evergreen plant. The terminal bud and the next two leaves are usually hand plucked; however, the terminal bud and the first leaf are used for tea of superior quality. The tea plant is grown in the form of a bush, and flourishes in sub-tropical and tropical climates. After plucking, the tea is withered, rolled, fermented, dried, sifted, and graded. The best known tea-producing countries are Sri Lanka (Ceylon), China, Java, Sumatra, India (Assam), Japan, East Africa, and Formosa. During the processing, the leaf turns from green to black, but in some countries green tea is preferred. It is produced by heating the leaf to prevent fermentation. Immediately after plucking, the leaves are treated either with steam or they are placed in heated pans to induce evaporation of the juice contained in the leaves. Leaves for black tea are laid out on wire netting until they wilt. After 12 to 20 hours, the now somewhat elastic leaves are mechanically rolled under increasing pressure and then fermented. The fermentation causes the tea leaves to oxidize, develop flavor, and turn to a bright copper red color. After fermentation, the leaves are either roasted or dried in hot air, at which point the rolled tea leaves take on their black color.

Quality characteristics: Darjeeling tea, which grows at a height of 7,000 feet in the Himalayas, has a delicate and distinctive flavor. Tea grown at high altitudes is of better quality than that grown at lower heights. The Indian tea varieties, the so-called *plantation teas,* usually give a full, pleasant infusion. Assam tea is the strongest, Darjeeling the most aromatic. The tea from Ceylon, particularly that from mountainous regions, is also very aromatic. It is especially known for its light brown color. Chinese and Japanese teas, weaker flavored than Indian varieties, have an especially aromatic mild taste. Consumption of tea from Ceylon (Sri Lanka), India, Java, and Sumatra has increased substantially over the last few years.

Commercial Varieties of Black Tea

Leaf Tea

1. *Flowery-Orange-Pekoe.* The finest, most delicate leaf tips, slightly fluffy with a silky down.
2. *Orange-Pekoe.* Delicate, rolled leaves, sometimes with whitish-gray or golden tips.
3. *Pekoe.* The second leaves down from the tip of the branch.
4. *Pekoe-Souchong.* The third rough leaf, which is long and open. *Souchong.* Large, conically-shaped leaves, rolled roughly.

Broken Tea. This tea is used as a filler in blends. It is made by repeatedly rolling the leaves, so that the

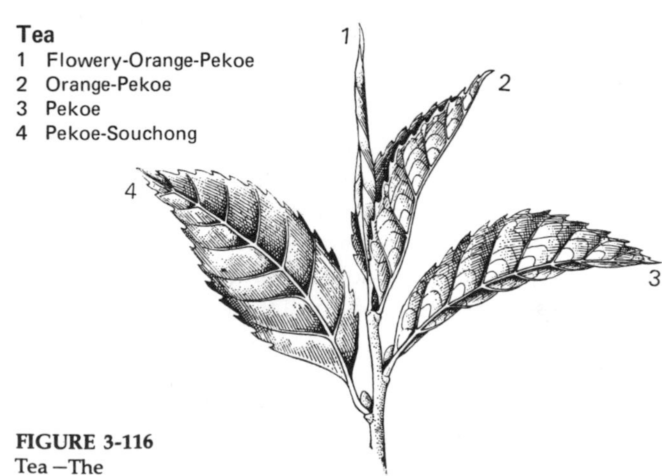

FIGURE 3-116
Tea—The

enlarged surface area speeds up the preparation of the infusion.
Scrap Tea dust and fannings. This is the waste and is less valuable. Most scrap tea is used to fill tea bags.

3.6.3 Cocoa – Cocao

The term cocoa refers both to the dried-roasted, or unroasted seeds of the cocoa tree and to the product resulting from the grinding of the original or partially defatted cocoa mass, which is then known as cocoa powder. Cocoa powder should contain a minimum of 10 percent cocoa fat for regular cocoa and up to 22 to 24 percent for breakfast cocoa. The Dutch process cocoa has the higher fat content. The cocoa mass is the basis of cocoa powder and the raw material for the manufacture of chocolate. Cocoa is not only a stimulant, but also a food. Raw cocoa beans contain 12.5 percent protein, 50 percent fat, 11 percent starch, and 12 percent other carbohydrates.

Cocoa comes from the evergreen tree of the genus Theobroma. The tree is native to Central America and the northern part of South America. It is now found in Africa, where Nigeria and Ghana have become major suppliers. The cocoa tree can reach a height of 45 feet (13 to 14 meters), and carries flowers at the same time as fruits. The fruit is a pod with a leathery shell that contains several rows of seeds. The trees require much care and an average temperature of 70°F. to 75°F. (21°C. to 24°C.), There are many varieties and their quality is affected by the soil, climate, and method of processing.

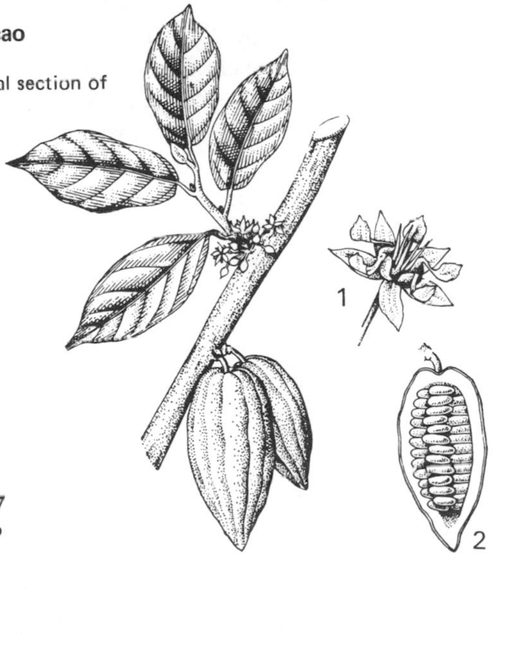

Cocoa – Cocao
1 Flower
2 Longitudinal section of the fruit

FIGURE 3-117
Cocoa – Cocao

After picking, the beans are stacked in heaps and *fermented* for a few days at 120°F. (50°C.). After fermentation, they are dried and packed in sacks for shipment to Europe or North America. On arrival in the chocolate factories, the beans are washed and then *roasted* at 210°F. to 300°F. (100°C. to 150°C.) to develop flavor and aroma. After roasting, they are *shelled* and cracked into small nibs. Depending upon the quality and the prevailing price, crushed cocoa beans are blended by the same method used for coffee and tea. These blends are then ground into a smooth liquid mash. The finer the cocoa is ground, the better the quality. *The cocoa mass consists of 50 percent fat, or cocoa butter.* Part of the fat is then removed under hydraulic pressure. The remaining residue is pulverized into a fine powder. The fat content of cocoa is about half that of chocolate. Cocoa should be stored in sealed containers in a dry area.

3.6.4 Chocolate – Chocolat

Chocolate – Chocolat. This is a mixture of cocoa mass that contains 50 percent cocoa butter fat. It is also called bitter chocolate or baking chocolate. Sugar, flavorings, almonds, nuts, milk, and other ingredients may be added, depending on the variety of chocolate. The ingredients and additives determine the taste, character, and the name of the product. Although half of the cocoa mass is cocoa butter, more may be added to improve the taste and melting qualities.
Coating Chocolate – Couverture. This usually contains a maximum of 50 percent sugar and a minimum of 33 percent cocoa mass. Cocoa butter is added to bring its content to a minimum of 35 percent. Coating chocolate is used to coat chocolate-covered candies and on pastries or cakes.
Chocolate-Covered Candies – Pralines. These are candies with a chocolate coating. One of General du Plassis's cooks by the name of Pralin is said to have been the inventor of chocolate candies.

4 Nutrition

4.1 Basic Principles of Nutrition

Balanced nutrition is necessary for maintaining the human body in good health. The body is continuously using the substances which make it up, and these must be replaced by absorbing food. A number of important factors must be considered if the process of alimentation is to be carried out correctly.

Hunger and thirst are sensed automatically by a healthy person.

Appetite is the desire for food without really being hungry. Appetite is mainly psychological. In moments of psychological stress, it is possible to have no appetite in spite of being hungry.

Variety. It is important for the human body to take on a variety of different foods. Only varied food intake can ensure balanced nutrition.

Digestion takes place in the gastrointestinal tract, and is the breakdown of the food prior to its absorption into the body.

Metabolism is the conversion of nutrients occurring in a series of processes in different parts of the body. This activity is necessary for the building and continuous functioning of cells and tissues.

Nutrients perform specific functions in the nourishment of the body. Of major importance are supplying the body with the necessary calories for energy and ensuring the continuity of the vital functions. Nutrients include protein, carbohydrate, fat, minerals, vitamins, and water.

Taste and aroma. The substances which stimulate the perception of taste and aroma are not vitally necessary from the nutritional standpoint; on the other hand, they are necessary for increasing the appetite and for stimulating the digestive glands.

Fiber is necessary for peristaltic action (example: movement of the intestines which pushes food along). Modern science has suggested other roles for dietary fiber such as a preventive measure for a wide range of disease processes.

Diet is the food consumed daily by an individual or group with an emphasis on nutrient content.

Modified diets are special regimens prescribed as measures for prevention, control, and/or treatment of certain disease states.

The above factors are important for the maintenance of health in the human body. Daily consumption of minimum servings of important food groups and recommended allowances for essential nutrients provides the basis for balanced nutrition. Other factors such as food preparation procedures affect the nutritive value of food.

4.2 Digestion

The Digestive Process

Digestion is a *complicated physical and chemical process.* It can be compared to a huge laboratory, where any malfunction can bring the whole process to a standstill.

Digestion starts in the mouth. The food is broken up and chewed with the teeth while simultaneously being mixed with saliva from the *salivary glands.* Proper chewing is extremely important for good digestion. Food is then swallowed and transported to the stomach via the esophagus.

"Carry-over" digestion from the mouth continues in the stomach. Then, further digestion occurs in the stomach when the food mass is mixed with *gastric juice from the gastric glands* by gastric contractions, a mechanical action.

The *partially liquified and dissolved food mass, or chyme,* is mixed with *bile, intestinal juice, and pancreatic juice* in the *small intestine* by additional mechanical action. The *bile* is prepared by the *liver* and concentrated and stored by the *gallbladder. Intestinal juice* is secreted by the *small intestine* and *pancreatic juice* by the *pancreas.* Digestion in the small intestine results in the complete breakdown of the food mass to the end products of digestion.

The food-absorbing villi of the *small intestine absorb the nutrients* and transport them to the cells via the blood or lymph circulation. In the *large intestine or colon* the water is extracted from the chyme, which partially solidifies. The rectum stores the feces or stool prior to the discharge from the bowels or defecation.

The following substances are excreted from the body: water, salt, nitrogenous waste, carbon dioxide, cellulose, and other undigested food substances, as well as intestinal bacteria. These substances leave the body via exhalation, perspiration, urination, and defecation. *Regular bowel movements* are important for health. Regularity can often be achieved by appropriate food and adequate fluid intake as well as by a healthy way of life including exercise.

The Digestibility of Foods

Recognizing that many foods and food preparation methods are tolerated differently by individuals, the following food list attempts to illustrate foods that may be classified as easy or difficult to digest.

Easily Digested Foods: Refined bread, crackers, and cereal; tender, lean or ground beef, veal, pork, lamb, poultry, fish, liver, and sweetbreads prepared by baking or roasting, broiling, stewing, or creaming; eggs prepared any way except fried; cooked vegetables such as asparagus tips, green and wax beans, beets, carrots, white and sweet potatoes, spinach, winter squash, and vegetable purees and juices; ripe peeled fruits such as avocado, banana, peach, pear, grapefruit and orange sections; cooked or canned apples, apricots, cherries, peaches, and pears; and fruit purees and juices; milk and milk products including mild-flavored cheese and yoghurt; simple plain desserts, such as cake and cookies, custard, fruit whip, gelatin, ice cream, and pudding; cream soup; butter, margarine, cream, smooth peanut butter, cooking fat, and vegetable oils; some seasonings, such as salt, sugar, and flavoring extracts in moderate amounts; decaffeinated coffee, cereal coffees, tea, milk beverages, cocoa, and hot chocolate in moderate amounts.

Difficult to Digest Foods: coarse or whole grain bread, crackers, and cereal products; tough, fatty meats; salted and smoked meats, fish, and poultry; fried eggs; raw and fried vegetables; gas-forming vegetables, such as broccoli, brussels sprouts, cabbage, cauliflower, and onions; raw apples, unripe fruits, fruits with tough skin and seeds such as berries; strong-flavored cheese; rich desserts, such as cake, pie, and other pastries; doughnuts; desserts with coconut and/or nuts; salad dressings; some excessive amounts of garlic, onion, pepper, and other herbs and spices; alcohol, carbonated beverages, caffeinated coffee, and chocolate drinks; and foods with high fat content.

4.2.1 The Gastrointestinal Tract

The diagram of the gastrointestinal tract identifies the major segments of the digestive tract and the organs and glands concerned with digestion. (See Fig. 4-1.)

4.3 Metabolism

The organism normally absorbs all the necessary substances from the chyme in the stomach and intestines. The remainder which cannot be digested is evacuated as waste. The nutrients taken from the chyme reach the various cells, tissues, and organs and undergo many complicated changes. Once these changes are complete, the residual products are excreted via the kidneys, lungs, intestines, and sweat glands. All these changes and conversions which the nutrients undergo during their journey through the cells of the body are collectively referred to as *intermediary metabolism.* It is extremely important that these processes maintain a state of equilibrium if the organs, tissues, and cells are to function normally, and the organism as a whole is to remain healthy. A malfunction or blockage in the metabolic pathways disrupts the normal state of balance and can result in pathological symptoms. Insufficient or excessive quantities of certain substances can be formed. If, for example, the body is not receiving enough iron, the required number of red blood corpuscles are not produced, and anemia may develop.

Breathing, thirst, and hunger stimulate the human being to ingest substances to meet physiological requirements to assure building and maintenance functions, such as *air* (oxygen), *water,* and *substances of animal and vegetable origin.* Instinct, age-old experience, tradition, habit, and a subjective sensitivity guide human beings in food selection. Foods are chosen from the available raw materials which, on the one hand, contain the necessary quantities of nutrients, and, on the other hand, have a certain amount of enjoyment value.

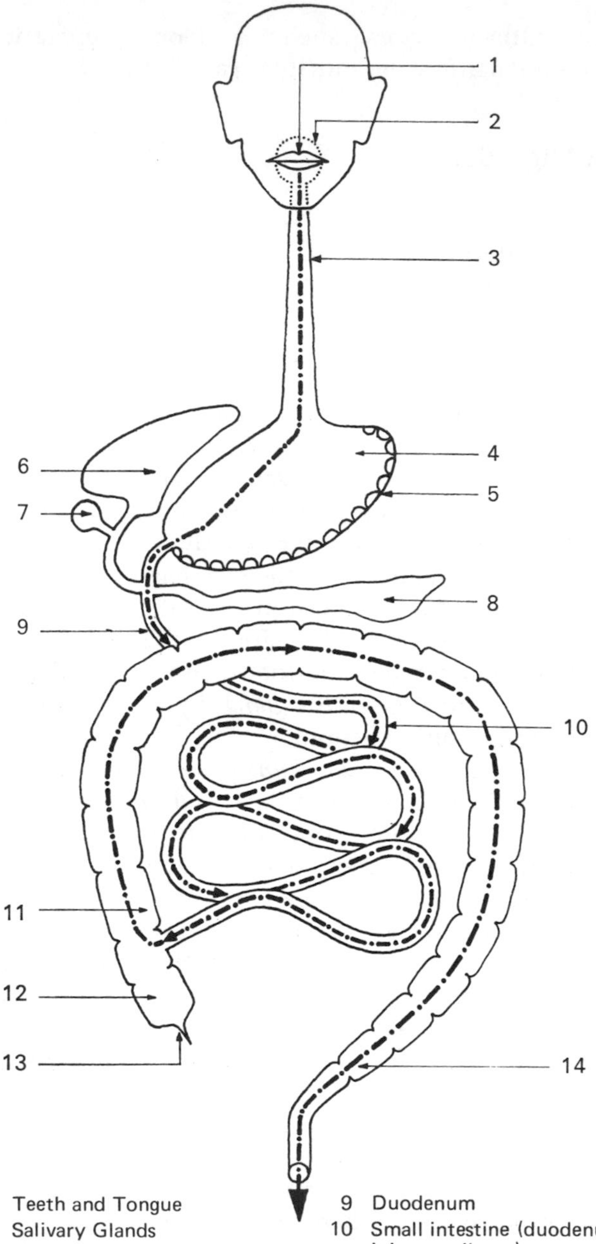

1 Teeth and Tongue
2 Salivary Glands
3 Esophagus
4 Stomach
5 Gastric Glands
6 Liver
7 Gall bladder
8 Pancreas
9 Duodenum
10 Small intestine (duodenum, jujunum, ileum)
11 Large intestine (colon)
12 Cecum
13 Appendix
14 Rectum

FIGURE 4–1
The Gastrointestinal Tract

4.4 Nutrients

Nutrients serve the organism in three ways:

- to give energy
- to build and replace the cells that make up the organs and tissues
- to regulate body processes.

Foods contain the following *basic nutrients: protein, carbohydrate, fat, minerals, vitamins, and water.* Food also contains substances which promote the perception of *taste* and which act as *stimulants.* Although these latter substances cannot actually be classed as nutrients, they are nevertheless important for total enjoyment of the diet and, hence, indirectly for the nutrition of the body.

4.4.1 Proteins

The primary function of dietary protein is the building and repairing of body tissue. Without the proteins contained in food, the cells could neither be built nor continuously replaced as they wear out. Protein also has important regulatory functions. Protein foods have energy value. The food intake, therefore, must always contain a certain amount of protein. However complete the diet might be, if no protein were included, the result could only be emaciation and finally a slow death. The American diet is rich in protein. Mean per capita consumption is over 100 grams (3.5 ounces) of protein per day. However, it cannot be assumed that intake is equally distributed among different population groups. Any extra protein is burned in the metabolic process as energy, and does not have its usual body-building effect. Extra protein intake, however, is uneconomical. Liberal protein intake is not generally considered hazardous to health except under certain circumstances such as the presence of some forms of kidney disease.

Almost all animal and vegetable products contain protein, but animal protein (meat, fish, eggs, milk, cheese, and poultry) is more complete than vegetable protein. Vegetable protein is usually consumed in the form of bread, flour and cereal products, vegetables including legumes (peas, beans, lentils, and peanuts), and nuts. Two basic measures must be considered in establishing the daily protein requirement: quality and quantity. The quality of protein is based on the essential amino acid content. This calculation is difficult because of the lack of information about the essential amino acid requirement in relation to the total nitrogen, the variations in different types of food, and the availability of amino acids in foods. The quantity of protein recommended is based on the assumption that the efficiency of utilization of proteins in the United States standard for adults has been established as approximately 0.9 gram (.032 ounce) per kilogram (2.2 pounds) of body weight per day.[1] This becomes about 45 grams (1.6 ounces) daily for a person weighing 50 kilograms (110 pounds) or 65 grams (2.3 ounces) for a person weighing 70 kilograms (143 pounds).

4.4.2 Carbohydrates

The major function of carbohydrates is to provide energy for muscular activity and the creation of warmth. The greater the physical demands on the body, the higher is the energy need and, therefore, the carbohydrate requirement. Carbohydrates occur mainly as sugar and starch in vegetable foods (flour and cereal products, fruits, and vegetables). Milk is the only animal food contributing to the daily carbohydrate intake. Pure sugar, syrups, jellies, jams, honey, and candy are a source of concentrated carbohydrate. Carbohydrates must be broken down into glucose, fructose, and galactose in preparation for absorption within the walls of the small intestine. For example, cane sugar and beet sugar (disaccharides) must first be split into glucose and fructose by the digestive juices.

The carbohydrate of refined flours and cereals, sugars, and sweets is completely or almost com-

1. Dorothea Turner, *Handbook of Diet Therapy*, 5th ed. (Chicago: The American Dietic Association), p. 16.

pletely digested; whereas that from fibrous vegetables, fruits with seeds, and whole-grain flours and cereals is less completely digested. This is partially explained by the presence of nondigestible components such as cellulose in the latter group of foods. Cellulose, which occurs in almost all vegetable products, is classified as a carbohydrate, but, contrary to starch and sugar, is not digested by man. In spite of this, cellulose, as part of the total dietary fiber, is necessary for normal gastrointestinal function (see section 4.5.5). No specific allowance has been established for the amount of carbohydrate. However, a normal diet including at least 100 grams (3.5 ounces) of carbohydrate daily will maintain metabolic processes.

4.4.3 Fats

Dietary fats are chiefly true fats or simple lipids. These include the animal and vegetable fats and oils which consist, chemically speaking, of fatty acids and glycerol. These are rendered more accessible to digestive and absorptive processes by the bile from the gallbladder. Generally speaking, vegetable sources contain more unsaturated fatty acids. Some *vegetable oils* reduce the cholesterol content of the blood when consumed in high polyunsaturated fatty diets and are, therefore, *recommended* for people with heart or liver disorders or as a preventive measure. Fats are potent carriers of energy in the body, and thus constitute valuable reserves for the body. Fats have the highest calorie value of the nutrients supplying energy. Fats are also important in the process of body maintenance and regulation. Extra fat in the diet is partially stored away in fat deposits. During periods of undernutrition, the body lives mainly on these deposits of fat. Fat comes from animal and vegetable food: milk and milk products; animal fats in such foods as meat, poultry, fish, and egg yolk; and vegetable fats including margarine, seeds and vegetable oils, fruits or vegetables (avocados, olives), and nuts. Many prepared foods such as salad dressings, cakes, pastries, gravies, and sauces contain fat. No precise levels for either the quantity or type of fat in the normal diet have been established. However, many Americans could probably benefit from some dietary modification of fat intake.

4.4.4 Calories

The above mentioned energy sources—protein, carbohydrates, and fat—create warmth during the process of metabolism. This warmth is measured in calories, 1 calorie representing the amount of warmth necessary to increase the temperature of 1 kilogram of water by 1°C. The more physical work a man does, the more nutrients are burned. Different foods produce varying amounts of energy, and for this reason it is important to know their calorific values. Foods can be evaluated on the basis that 1 gram protein creates 4.1 calories, 1 gram carbohydrate creates 4.1 calories, and 1 gram fat creates 9.3 calories of warmth. Since there are slight variations in calorie values obtained for different foods within a given group, the figures are rounded off to:

- 1 gram protein yields 4 calories
- 1 gram carbohydrate yields 4 calories
- 1 gram fat yields 9 calories

TABLE 4-1 Calorie Content. The approximate calorie content of some representative foods

Food	*Calories*
Bread, whole-wheat, soft crumb type (1 pound loaf, 16 slices)	1,093
Peas, green, immature (1 pound frozen, cooked)	275
Beef, lean with 21% fat, ground, cooked (11½ ounce yield from 1 pound raw meat)	932
Pork, light cured ham, lean with 16% fat, baked (13.1 ounces yield from 1 pound, unbaked ham without bone and skin)	1,075
Potatoes, baked in skin (1 pound, refuse: skins and adhering potato, 23%)	325
Milk, cow, fluid whole (1 quart, 3.5% fat)	634

Source: Nutritive Value of American Foods in Common Units, Agriculture Handbook No. 456, Agriculture Research Service, United States Department of Agriculture, Washington, D.C., 1975.

The daily calorie requirement, by occupation, is as follows:

• *sedentary occupations:* non-manual workers, office workers, clerks, officials, and supervisors	2,200 to 2,400
• *moderately muscular occupations:* shoemakers, bookbinders, doctors, and postmen	2,800 to 3,000
• *muscular occupations:* metal workers, painters, and carpenters	3,000 to 3,200
• *occupations involving heavy manual labor:* bricklayers, blacksmiths, soldiers, farm laborers, diggers, and longshoremen	3,200 to 3,600
• *heaviest manual laborers:* harvesters and lumberjacks	3,600 and more

4.5 Accessory Food Factors

This phrase, accessory food factors, was coined by the British in the early part of the twentieth century and used for many years to denote the vitamin content of food.

4.5.1 Vitamins

Vitamins are nutrients which are vitally important in the prevention of disease and in the regulation of body processes. Today, a wide range of different vitamins is known, which when missing from or inadequate in the diet provokes very typical deficiency diseases, such as scurvy. Vitamin deficiencies may be secondary to other diseases. In the initial stages, such illnesses may be cured by taking the vitamins which were previously missing. For this reason, special vitamin preparations are widely available. However, in general, if healthy persons consume an adequate diet, nutritional supplementation is unnecessary. Hypervitaminosis, causing toxic signs and symptoms, is caused by overdosage, or metabolic disease, or other disturbances producing a vitamin intolerance. The daily vitamin requirement is quantitatively low, but this is no reflection on the importance of these nutrients.

Vitamins are present in most animal and vegetable foods, provided losses during growth, food storage and handling, food processing, and food preparation and preserving are minimal. Some vitamin losses occur in such food processing techniques as the milling of flour and cereal products, canning and drying fruits and vegetables, and pasteurizing milk. Of the roughly thirty known vitamins, the following are especially important to include in the daily diet and are thoroughly researched at the present time:

Vitamin A: Vitamin A deficiency results initially in night blindness or diminished vision in dim light, and later, in eye diseases, skin changes, reduced rate of growth, and a lowering of resistance to infection. Vitamin A is *fat soluble* and fairly *heat stable,* but sensitive to light and air. It is only found in animal foods, mainly fish liver oils, milk, whole milk cheese, fortified margarine, butter, liver, and egg yolks. However, in many vegetable products there is a provitamin (carotene), which easily converts into vitamin A in the liver. Therefore, plant foods with carotene content are considered a vitamin A source. All leafy green vegetables, green stem vegetables (asparagus and broccoli), yellow vegetables (carrots, sweet potatoes, pumpkin, and winter squash), tomatoes, and yellow fruits (apricots, peaches, and cantaloupe) are rich in vitamin A. White and red cabbage, celery stalks, white root and bulb vegetables have a low vitamin A content.

The daily recommended allowance for adults is 5,000 International Units. The value of Vitamin A is expressed in International Units (1 iu = 0.6 microgram beta-caroten).

Vitamin D: Infants, growing children, adolescents, pregnant and lactating women, and persons who have limited exposure to sunlight are most susceptible to some form of vitamin D deficiency. It is characterized by such problems as insufficient or delayed calcification of the bones and teeth (rickets), slow rate of growth, predisposition to dental caries, and muscle twitchings and cramps.

Vitamin D is *fat soluble* and resistant to heat. In the human skin, a substance (provitamin) is present which is converted into vitamin D by the action of the ultraviolet light of sunshine. For this reason, it is not absolutely necessary for the total vitamin D allowance to be contained in the food consumed. Practically the only natural vitamin D sources, though poor sources, are milk, cream, fatty fish, fish liver oils, liver, and egg yolk. The primary sources are fatty fish, fish liver oils, and fortified foods such as milk and milk products, bread and cereal products, margarine, and infant foods.

The recommended daily allowance of Vitamin D for infants, children, adolescents, pregnant and lactating women is 400 International Units. Although no recommended allowance is indicated for adults, a dietary intake of 400 International Units for healthy adults of all ages is not risk-producing.

Thiamin (Vitamin B_1): Chronic deficiency of thiamin leads to serious disorders and damage to the nervous system and heart (beriberi disease prevalent in the Orient). A mild deficiency is characterized by such symptoms as loss of appetite, nausea, apathy, fatigue, dizziness, and numbness. Thiamin deficiency states are found in the alcoholic. Thiamin is water soluble and, therefore, is often lost in food processing, preparation, and cooking. Preparation and cooking losses depend upon preparation methods such as soaking, amount of water used in cooking and retained after cooking, length of cooking period, and amount of surface area exposed. Thiamin is extremely sensitive in an alkaline medium. The addition of baking soda or bicarbonate very quickly destroys the vitamin. Thiamin is comparatively heat-resistant in the dry form and in solution in an acid medium. Little loss occurs in cooking procedures such as baking bread and cooking breakfast cereal because the water used in preparation is consumed.

Thiamin is naturally present in an exceptionally wide range of foods such as whole-grain and enriched bread, cereal, and flour products; lean meat especially pork, organ meats and sausage; eggs; green leafy vegetables and legumes; and nuts. A daily allowance for adults of 0.5 milligrams per 1,000 calories is recommended. Older persons should maintain an intake of 1 milligram per day, even if the intake is less than 2,000 calories daily. Requirements increase during pregnancy and lactation.

Riboflavin (vitamin B_2): A severe riboflavin deficiency disease in human beings has not been identified. However, lack of riboflavin does produce signs and symptoms involving the skin, mucous membranes especially the mouth and eyes. Typical eye changes include inflamed eyelids, itching and watering, inability to focus properly, sensitivity to light, and rapid tiring.

Like thiamin, riboflavin is water soluble, reasonably heat resistant for short periods, but very susceptible to light. Small losses may occur in food processing and preparation. In general, when cooked in liquid form, precautions taken to conserve thiamin will protect riboflavin. Riboflavin is found in significant quantities in organ meats such as liver and kidney, lean meat, milk, cheese, eggs, whole-grain bread and cereal products, and leafy green vegetables.

Riboflavin allowances are computed as 0.6 milligrams per 1,000 calories for people of all ages. Recommended levels increase during pregnancy and lactation.

Niacin: Pellagra, the deficiency disease of niacin, is characterized by changes in the skin and mucous membranes, diarrhea, and mental disturbances. Pellagra in the United States is practically nonexistent today. However, incidence of the disease has been reported among chronic alcoholics and is secondary to other illnesses.

Niacin is the most stable of the vitamin B group, but because it is water soluble some may be lost in cooking water and meat drippings. Both animal and plant foods are good sources of either or both niacin and a dietary factor, tryptophan, converted to niacin. The chief sources are liver, lean meat, poultry, fish, milk, eggs, whole-grain and enriched bread and cereal products, legumes, and nuts.

The allowance recommended for adults, expressed as niacin, is 6.6 milligrams per 1,000 calories, and not less than 13 milligrams at caloric intakes of less than 2,000 calories. Increases are recommended for pregnancy and lactation.

Vitamin B_{12}: Lack of vitamin B_{12} is seldom seen in the United States because of the high protein diet consumed. However, individuals on borderline

Herbs and Spices Used for Cooking.
(See key to illustration, page 160)

Oregano
Cinnamon
Coriander
Chervil
Cloves
Marjoram
Paprika
White Pepper
Black Pepper
Aniseed
Tarragon
Bay Leaves
Caraway
Fennel
Thyme
Sage
Mace
Juniper
Ginger
Basil

Cold Snacks: Sandwiches, Salads, and Fruits
Snacks froids: sandwich, fruits et diverses salads

Fillet of Sole, Grenoble Style
Filets de sole grenobloise

Vol-au-vent with Vegetables
Vol-au-vent bouquetiere

Black Salsify with Vegetables
Salsifis frits (vegetarien)

Veal Cutlet, Valais Style
Escalope valaisanne

Vegetarian Platter
Assiette de legumes (vegetarien)

Platter, Paysanne Style
Assiette paysanne

Veal Cutlet, Hungarian Style
Escalope hongroise

Chicken, Fermiere Style
Poulet fermiere

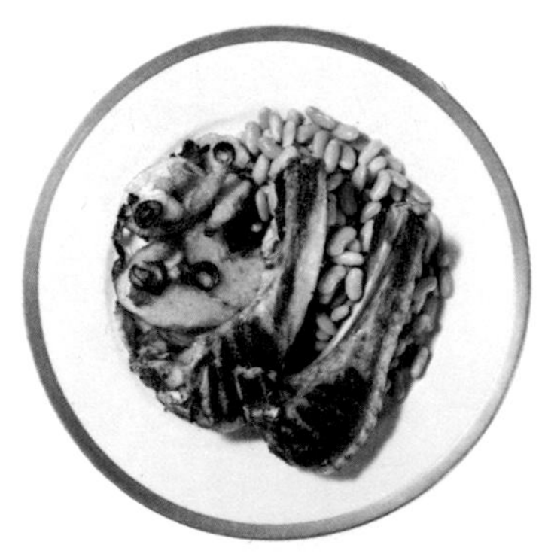

Lamb Chops with Lima Beans
Cotelettes d'agneau aux flageolets

diets, such as food fad diets and vegetarians, may show signs of lack of this vitamin. Nervous disorders and changes in mucous membranes may result. Absorption defect in some persons may cause pernicious anemia, a blood disease. Other illnesses may decrease vitamin B_{12} absorption and produce vitamin deficiency.

Vitamin B_{12} is water soluble, and could be washed out of food which is soaked too long. It is not especially sensitive to heat or air, but does lose its potency on exposure to light, strong acids, and alkali.

Vitamin B_{12} is present in large quantities in liver and kidney. Meat, fish, eggs, milk, and cheese also supply good amounts. There is very little, if any, of the vitamin in vegetable foods. The recommended daily dietary allowance for this vitamin is 3 micrograms for adolescents and normal adults. The level of 4 micrograms per day is set for pregnant and lactating women.

Ascorbic Acid (vitamin C): The classic severe deficiency state is scurvy. Lack of ascorbic acid results in abnormalities in the supporting or intercellular tissues which could result in hemorrage, bleeding gums, malformed and weak bones, degeneration of muscle fibers and anemia. Ascorbic acid deficiency is a factor involved in reduced resistance to infection and retarded wound healing. Mild deficiency produces vague symptoms such as weakness, irritability, weight loss, and pain in muscles or joints. Ascorbic acid is water soluble and chemically unstable. Therefore, undue exposure to oxygen, alkali, copper and iron (copper utensils and non-stainless steel knives), and prolonged cooking at high temperatures accelerate the rate of vitamin loss. If vegetables are finely cut up or chopped, ascorbic acid is very quickly destroyed by exposure to oxygen (oxidation) and light. If potatoes are cooked after being peeled, more ascorbic acid and B vitamins are lost than when cooked in the jackets. Baking soda also reduces the ascorbic acid level if added to green vegetables. Proper preparation and cooking methods such as short soaking and cooking times, moderate heat exposure, and minimum holding periods will reduce losses of all water soluble vitamins. Consumption of raw fruits and vegetables helps assure adequate daily vitamin intake.

Ascorbic acid is present in fair to good quantities in potatoes, vegetables, and fruits. The largest amounts are found in citrus fruits, cantaloupe, guavas, pineapple, rose hips, strawberries, broccoli, brussels sprouts, cabbage, green peppers, kale, spinach, and turnips. In nearly all cases, dried products contain no ascorbic acid. Milk and meat are practically devoid of the vitamin.

An allowance of 45 milligrams per day is recommended as an adequate supply for health in normal adults. An increased intake is recommended during pregnancy and lactation and may be appropriate during periods of continued stress and drug therapy.

4.5.2 Minerals

Minerals, mineral salts, mineral elements, or inorganic nutrients are present in the cells, tissues, and fluids, soft tissues, and hard skeletal structures such as blood, muscles, and bone. Minerals are vitally important, even if they are only necessary in minute quantities. One cannot replace another, as is the case with some nutrients. Minerals are interrelated and do not play independent roles in general body function. Any deficiency of certain minerals can, over a long period of time, be fatal. Minerals are grouped as follows: (1) major minerals or macronutrients, needed in the diet at levels of 100 milligrams per day or more, and (2) trace minerals or micronutrients, needed in amounts no higher than a few milligrams per day. About 13 different minerals are known to be needed by the body, and all must be derived from the diet. The minerals whose supply is most likely to be critical are calcium, iron, and iodine.

Calcium: A variety of illnesses such as rickets, osteomalachia (adult rickets), osteoporosis (bone thinning), and periodontal disease are associated with bone-forming materials such as calcium.

Milk and milk products are the richest source of calcium. Certain other foods make contributions to the daily diet: leafy green vegetables, fruit, eggs, canned fish, and shellfish. Drinking water also contains some calcium but varies with the water supply. The allowance of 800 milligrams per day assures an adequate supply of calcium in the diet for adult men and women. Additional dietary calcium should be consumed during pregnancy and lactation.

Iron: Iron deficiency anemia is fundamentally a dietary disease. This is probably the most widespread form of malnutrition in the United States. In iron deficiency anemia, lack of iron produces defective red blood cells and results in faulty body functioning.

Good to excellent sources of iron are liver and other organ meats, lean meat, egg yolk, leafy green vegetables, dried fruit, whole-grain and enriched cereal products, legumes, shellfish, and molasses.

Adult males have an allowance of 10 milligrams iron per day. The allowance for adult females and during lactation is 18 milligrams; during pregnancy the allowance exceeds 18 milligrams.

Iodine: Iodine is necessary for the proper functioning of the thyroid gland and regulation of basal metabolism. Lack of iodine results in enlargement of the thyroid glands and a condition known as simple goiter. Cretinism, a deficiency present at birth or during infancy, is characterized by physical and mental retardation. An increased incidence of thyroid cancer is associated with iodine deficiency.

Food and water sources of iodine are variable depending upon the soil content and composition of animal feed. Soil in coastal regions is generally richer in iodine than soil in inland areas. Seafood is the only excellent, consistent source of the mineral. Therefore, the regular use of iodized salt in food preparation and at the table is a better safeguard to assure nutrient adequacy.

The daily requirements for adults is approximately 50 to 75 micrograms. Growing children, as well as pregnant and lactating women, need more. Iodine may be restricted in certain skin conditions, such as acne.

Examples of other essential mineral elements necessary for proper body function:

Phosphorus: There is no evidence of a phosphorus deficiency in man to the extent that vital processes fail to function. Nevertheless, phosphorus assumes many widely varying roles by giving rigidity to the bones and teeth, serving as an essential component in many metabolic processes including brain and nerve metabolism, particularly in regulatory processes, and being a constituent of substances that control heredity.

Phosphorus is present in many foods especially high protein foods. Good to excellent sources are meat, milk and milk products, eggs, legumes, nuts, and whole-grain bread and cereal products. The recommended dietary allowance of 800 milligrams for adults has been established. Higher levels are set for pregnancy and lactation.

Magnesium: Magnesium deficiency is likely to occur in association with a number of diseases or stress conditions when food intake and/or absorption are altered. Since magnesium is necessary for regulatory functions such as transmission of nerve impulses and muscle contractions, a deficiency state produces neuromuscular dysfunction.

Major food sources of magnesium are dairy products, whole-grain bread and cereals, dry beans and peas, soybeans, nuts, and green leafy vegetables. Adults have an allowance of 300 to 350 milligrams magnesium per day. Allowances are higher for pregnancy and lactation.

Sodium: Sodium deficiency in humans is unlikely, but excessive retention or excretion usually related to disease or extreme environmental conditions leads to sodium imbalance. The principal source of sodium is table salt, sodium chloride, and many sodium compounds used in food processing and preparation. Animal foods, specifically milk, eggs, meat, poultry, and fish are natual sources.

Minerals are present in all basic food groups. Some food processing and food preparation methods reduce mineral content. For example, soaking foods and cooking in large quantities of water, when minerals are soluble, may decrease the mineral contribution to the diet. Therefore, the use of the liquid in which vegetables have been cooked for making dishes such as soups and sauces is recommended.

4.5.3 Water

The water content of the human body varies with age, weight, sex, and physical condition. About 65 percent of body weight of lean adults is water. Human beings consume between 4¼ to 7 pints of water daily, either in the form of liquid or food. Water is necessary as the medium in which all chemical and physical processes of the body operate. The amount of water required is dependent upon environmental conditions, physical work, and the food intake. Intake is normally regulated by the sensation of thirst.

4.5.4 Taste Agents and Stimulants

These are generally present in small quantities in food. Their function is nevertheless important: they stimulate the digestive glands, the appetite, and/or the metabolic process. This is the role played by the aromatic substances present in spices or created by special ways of preparing food (steaming, grilling, roasting, frying).

4.5.5 Dietary Fiber

During digestion most foods are not entirely utilized, and indigestible substances remain. These substances most frequently occur in plant foods and chiefly consist of cellulose (carbohydrates). In spite of indigestibility, they are very important for the peristaltic action of the digestive organs and, above all, ensure a rapid passage of the chyme into the intestine. If the food contains insufficient roughage, this can lead to constipation. Where there is too much roughage, the food passes through the intestines too quickly, and cannot be properly used by the body.

4.6 Applied Nutrition

The experience gathered during the period of classical cooking, as practiced in the 18th and 19th centuries, shows that eating too luxurious and heavy food can lead to an early death. Since the beginning of this century, many nutritional experts have tried to identify those kinds and quantities of foods which are the most suitable for people in different age groups and in varying states of health. This work has resulted in great advances in knowledge concerning the availability of suitable nutrition in normal and disease states.

Normal Food

This is generally prepared using both classical and modern cooking techniques. It should be varied and made up of both animal and vegetable foods. Special care should be taken to assure proper proportions of the key nutrients with emphasis on calorie, vitamin, and mineral content. Those modes of preparation that promote nutrient retention should be given priority. Food selected with high vitamin *and mineral content that has been prepared with care to retain nutrients for a total diet which includes raw vegetables and fruits offers a good guarantee of proper nutrition.*

Lenten Fare (Diets)

This was originally decreed by church regulations. All types of meat are sometimes prohibited. Generally, fish is accepted as a replacement. Fish dishes are complemented with fresh vegetables and fruits. Milk products are recommended because of the protein, vitamin, and mineral content. The use of vegetable fat is preferable to animal fat.

Vegetarian Food

A total or strict vegetarian diet excludes not only meat, but also foods that are derived from animals such as milk and milk products, eggs, and in some cases, even a few non-animal foods. The main elements of this type of diet are vegetables, legumes, nuts, seeds, bread and cereal products, fruits, and fats and oils. These are carefully cooked using vegetable fats and oils. Since a wide range of vegetable foods and meat analogs exist, it is possible to achieve a fairly balanced form of nutrition. In certain cases, this type of food can be used for special dietary purposes. Care should be taken to supplement these diets since certain essential forms of protein are missing in vegetable foods.

Food for Modified Diets

This is especially prepared food for those suffering from various illnesses or for preventive measures.

The food must meet the requirements of the disorder, and should never adversely affect metabolism. Many regular foods are used for dietary cooking. Special precautions such as cooking without added salt or fat may need to be taken. The main therapeutic adaptations of the normal diet are as follows: (1) provide change in consistency of foods, (2) increase or decrease caloric level, (3) modify nutrient content, (4) increase or decrease fiber content, (5) provide foods bland in flavor, (6) include or exclude specific foods, and (7) modify quantity and frequency of meals and snacks. Special dietary foods are prescribed for a variety of conditions: overweight or underweight; protein deficiency; fevers and infection; disturbances of the gastrointestinal tract; liver, gallbladder, and pancreatic malfunctions; cardiovascular and renal disorders; surgical conditions; metabolic and nervous disorders; anemias; allergic and skin disturbances; and children's diseases.

4.7 Food Value Chart

TABLE 4-2.

In 100 g of the following foods:	*Calories*	*Protein (g)*	*Fat (g)*	*Carbohydrates (g)*	*Vitamins*			*Minerals*
					A	*B_1*	*C*	
Root vegetables	32	1	-	7	III	I	I	III
Milk drinks	34	3.5	1	5	I	I		II
Fresh fruit	50	-	-	12	I	I	III	III
Cleaned leafy vegetables, salads	63	2	5	2	III	I	III	III
Whole milk	64	3	3.8	5	I	I		II
Boiled potatoes	65	1-2	-	15		I	II	III
Yoghurt made from whole milk	71	4.8	3.8	4.5	I	I	I	II
Saltwater fish (cod)	78	17	-	*				II
Cottage cheese	86	17	1	2	II	I		II
Freshwater fish (trout)	104	19	2	*		I		
Veal without fat, raw	106	20	10	*		I		I
Game (venison, hare, chamois)	123	21	4	*		I		I
Coffee cream (15% fat content)	127	3.1	10	4	I			I
Chicken	128	20	5	*		I		I
Fried potatoes	138	2	7	16		I	I	III
French Fried potatoes	167	2	10	18		I	I	III
Eggs: 2 eggs = 3-4 oz	187	13	11	1	II	II		II
Cottage cheese (creamed)	188	14	14	4	II	I		I
Whole grain bread	229	8	1	48		II		III
Turkey	230	20	14	*		I		I
Medium fat beef, raw	231	18	17	*		I		I
White bread	266	7	1	53		I		I
Cheese (50% fat content)	280	26	16	3	II	I		II
Cooked ham	283	19	20	*				I
Pork sausages	300	12	27	*		I	I	I
Duck	325	18	28	*		I		I
Cooked pork	340	15	30	*		I		I
Whipped cream (35% fat)	350	2.2	35	3	II	I		I
Raw rice (dry)	352	7	-	79		II		II
White flour	352	10	-	76		I		I
Raw pasta (egg noodles)	369	13	2	72		I		I
Full fat cheese	398	27	30	3	II	I		II
Bacon	625	10	65	*				II
Nuts (hazel nuts, almonds)	627	13	61	13	I			I
Butter	760	1	81	*	II			II
Margarine	780	1	84	*	II			I
Coconut fat	925	1	99	*				
Cooking oil	928	1	99.9	*				

III = high II = medium I = low * = none

4.8 Modified Diets

Many illnesses lead to disturbances in the metabolism, and thus are harmful to the body; on the other hand, certain illnesses may be controlled or cured by altering the metabolic process. The regulation of the food consumed by the patient is important under these circumstances. The choice of food and mode of preparation depends upon the type of illness and general condition of the patient.

Dietetics is the name given to the application of the science and art of human nutrition in helping people select and obtain food for the primary purpose of nourishing their bodies in health or disease throughout the life cycle.

The term *modified diet* refers to the choice of food as a preventive, supportive, or key therapeutic measure to meet the patient's nutritional, psychological, and aesthetic needs. In this way, the diet can be considered as part of, or the principal, medical treatment. The physician and dietitian determine the patient's dietary needs and prescribe the diet modification. The dietitian translates the diet order into palatable menus, directs the mode or preparation, evaluates the patient's response to the diet, and counsels the patient and family. The kitchen chef prepares the special dietary food according to specifications established by the dietitian and receives feedback concerning patient acceptance of the diet.

The normal menu serves as the basis for planning daily modified diets. The main principles of special dietary cooking are the same as those for preparation of the normal diet. The difference lies in the selection of food and ingredients most appropriate for the individually planned modified diet. Strict sanitation must be practiced in every respect. Only a few types of food are specially prepared for dietary purposes such as salt-free foods. The physician and dietitian determine the type and quantity of food. The diet of each patient is dependent upon the type and stage of illness, patient's condition, and food preferences. Therefore, the diet selected for patients all suffering from the same illness can vary considerably. Nevertheless, there are certain basic medical principles which form the basis for planning diets for some of the main types of illnesses.

Diets for Gastrointestinal Conditions

Many special dietary recommendations are made for the management of a number of digestive tract disorders. Traditionally, many diet modifications have been of questionable value. There should be a sound rationale and scientific basis for using a restricted diet. If not, a liberal diet modification, which is now likely to be nutritionally adequate and well accepted by the patient, is advised. The conservative approach has been to allow foods described as easily digested and non-stimulating such as bland, smooth, and low fiber foods. Cooking methods that minimize chemical, mechanical, and thermal irritation to the digestive tract are recommended. Therefore, some major considerations in menu planning and food preparation would be to identify individual food intolerances; vary daily menu plans to improve patient acceptance and nutritive content of diet; cook foods especially raw fruits and vegetables; avoid strong-flavored foods and highly-seasoned dishes; use methods of preparation least likely to cause digestive disturbances such as poaching, simmering, and steaming; use methods of preparation for maximum retention; and avoid serving food at extreme temperatures.

The more liberal approach to dietary management has been to recommend a normal diet with a few modifications primarily based on avoidance of foods poorly tolerated and flexibility to meet individual requirements. The quantity of food and meal spacing may be as important as the type of food consumed. A few foods such as coffee and alcohol may be avoided or restricted.

Diets for Liver, Gallbladder, and Pancreatic Disorders

Dietary management varies considerably depending upon the specific disease, acute or chronic stage, disease complications such as fluid retention or hemorrhage, condition of the patient such as nutritional deficiency or overweight, and food tolerance including loss of appetite, nausea, and vomiting.

In liver disease the aim is to protect the liver from stress and to aid in its proper functioning. Generally, a diet high in calories, protein, and carbohydrate with a moderate fat content is recommended. Other modifications with changes in food consistency, size and frequency of meals, sodium content, and vitamin supplements will depend upon the individual case. In the final stages of liver disease, protein intake is reduced because nitrogen-containing substances are not metabolized by the liver.

In gallbladder disease, a fat-restricted, bland diet reduces symptoms. If overweight, a low calorie diet is prescribed.

Dietary treatment in pancreatic disorders depends upon the nature and extent of digestive impairment: a typical diet in chronic pancreatitis is soft consistency with high calorie, high protein, and low fat levels divided into six small meals.

Loss of appetite may be a significant problem for patients with any of these conditions. Therefore, every effort should be made to encourage the patient to eat. For example, attractive food served in a pleasant, calm atmosphere will stimulate the appetite. Simply prepared foods that are poached, steamed, simmered, and boiled will not overtax the digestive processes.

Diets for Cardiovascular Conditions

Dietary management for these disorders varies depending upon the emphasis as a preventive or therapeutic measure, acute or chronic stage of illness, and complications.

Frequently, calorie-controlled diets are formulated to meet individual needs. The type and quantity of fat is adjusted. Usually total fat consumption is reduced, cholesterol intake restricted,and the ratio of unsaturated fats (mainly vegetable oils) to saturated fats (mainly animal fats) is increased. For some individuals, it may also be necessary to moderately restrict total carbohydrate intake and limit dietary sources of sugar.

In acute situations like heart attack or complications with infection, obesity, high blood pressure, constipation, and/or fluid retention, additional restrictions modify the diet prescription:

- sodium restriction if fluid and sodium retention
- fluid restriction if poor circulation and fluid retention
- liquid, soft, or bland diet.

Diet for Diabetes Mellitus

Diabetes is a malfunction of the metabolism. It is caused by poor utilization of carbohydrate because of insufficient or total lack of functioning insulin, a hormone secreted by the pancreas. The metabolism of protein and fat are also altered. When the disease is uncontrolled, the blood sugar becomes elevated, sugar spills over into the urine, and excessive amounts of urine are excreted to remove the sugar.

Dietary management controls but does not cure the disease. Dietary control is the central therapeutic measure. A dietary prescription is planned and adjusted periodically to control the calorie, carbohydrate, protein, and fat content of the food intake. When planning and preparing the diet, these quantities must be calculated exactly, served in measured quantities, and adhered to by the patient. The rule about choosing a food preparation method which least affects the nutritive content of food and controls caloric content is applicable for this dietary modification.

In some cases, insulin therapy or oral hypoglycemic (blood sugar lowering) agents will be prescribed in addition to dietary control. A regular, normal diet with emphasis on calorie control and liberal protein intake is recommended for the diabetic. The carbohydrate content of the milk, bread and cereal, fruit, and starchy vegetable food groups is calculated to control quantity and plan for carbohydrate distribution throughout the day. Low calorie foods such as low carbohydrate vegetables and salads without sauces and controlled amounts of salad dressing are encouraged. Simply prepared foods and raw fruits and vegetables are recommended. Mixed dishes such as casseroles are acceptable but more difficult to include in the menu plan unless an accurate estimate of nutrient content per serving is feasible.

Diabetics are prone to early signs of heart disease. Recent trends in the dietary management of these patients include such measures as fat-control.

A current theory stresses calorie-control and fat-control rather than undue concern with carbohydrate restriction in the dietary management of diabetics. However, the traditional, conservative approach recommends the reduction or avoidance of foods with high sugar content such as concentrated sweets and rich desserts and alcoholic beverages.

5 The Menu

5.1 Menu Planning

Menu planning is an art and a science that requires an extensive knowledge of foods and their basic methods of preparation and service; an understanding of the nutritive value of foods; and a sensitivity for the aesthetics in food combinations.

It was Careme who said that the success of a dinner depends on the composition of the menu, assuming, of course, that the preparation of the food is flawless.

As in any other art, menu planning requires careful planning and the observance of a few principles that are basic to meeting the objectives of the management; satisfying the customer, patient, or guest; and utilizing the skills and abilities of the available personnel. These principles are:

- type of institution
- nutritional principles
- physical facilities
- personnel
- variety of foods
- combination of flavors
- season of the year
- budget
- menu terminology
- long range planning

The type of institution is the first consideration in planning menus. The objective or purpose of a hospital will differ from that of a hotel or restaurant, while neither of these will be the same as that of a fast food establishment or a university residence hall. The menus of each should focus on the people to be served. For those persons who receive all their meals in a hospital, extended care facility, retirement home, or residence hall, the menus must be planned to meet the total nutritional requirements of the group to be served.

Restaurants, hotels, fast food establishments, industrial cafeterias, and school lunchrooms usually provide only part of the daily food intake of the client or student. Although these operations do not have responsibility for fulfilling the total daily dietary requirements of the individual, the menu should include foods that will provide selections that will meet their nutritional needs.

Satisfying the guests requires knowing them. The successful menu maker will know the age, sex, occupation, and economic status of the patrons because these factors are significant in their acceptance of certain foods. Food habits and preferences are sometimes the result of family attitudes and practices, ethnic backgrounds, regional preferences, and religious traditions and restrictions.

There is a difference in planning a menu for

Americans or Germans, for a physicians' association or a butchers' trade organization; for a country wedding or for one in a large city. The life style of the clients must be considered—their national dishes, the methods of preparation, and the seasoning must be harmonized to suit their tastes. A well-known German saying reinforces this, "What the farmer doesn't know, he doesn't eat." A real connoisseur, however, is usually curious to try dishes that are unfamiliar to him, and he particularly enjoys those foods that have been prepared with imagination, skill, and flair of the unusual.

Nutritional principles, as applied to menu planning, are the same throughout the life cycle. The activity level and the metabolic processes vary with individuals depending on age, sex, and activity and, therefore, the caloric requirements differ. Persons with physical illnesses may require a modified diet. These diets are planned by a dietitian who is qualified to adjust the normal diet to meet the nutritional needs of the patient. In recent years considerable attention has been given to the nutrition of the elderly. Their needs differ from younger adult's only in terms of calories required. The general slowing down of body processes and activity in older persons usually reduces the need for high caloric foods, such as sweets and fats. Many older people lack the physical strength and interest to prepare foods that are balanced, adequate, and easily assimilated. When an elderly person enters a retirement home or an extended health care facility, the change from a familiar environment to one that is strange often causes feelings of depression, loneliness, and insecurity. As a result of these disturbances, the clients often complain about the food and refuse to eat. Planning menus that are nutritionally adequate and appealing for this group offers a real challenge. Loss of teeth or poor fitting dentures makes chewing difficult. Individuals suffering from paralysis or blindness may have problems handling foods. It should not be assumed that people with these and other handicaps must have only ground, soft, and liquid foods. Many individuals will adjust surprisingly well and enjoy a variety of foods that differ in texture, particularly if the foods are carefully prepared and attractively presented in a form that can be handled easily.

The physical facilities available will influence the menu pattern. The amount of space and the type and capacity of the equipment will determine the variety of the products that can be prepared and the number of persons that can be served. The menu must be planned to distribute the work load between the various pieces of equipment and to utilize all the equipment.

Personnel. The number of employees available and their skills and abilities, the total number of man-hours, and the number of employees scheduled at any specific time are controlling factors in menu planning. In the small establishment where only one or two cooks are employed, the menus must obviously be quite simple with limited selections. In a larger commercial enterprise, the skill and size of the labor force affect the number of selections that can be offered on the menu. Spiraling food and labor costs in recent years have prompted the development of more simplified menus and quality-controlled food production systems.

The trend toward the use of more prepared foods, preportioned meats, poultry, and fish products, processed vegetables, mixes, and frozen foods aids the menu planner in balancing the work load between production units. The wise menu planner will avoid overloading an individual or a department with a large number of menu items that require time-consuming tasks and last minute preparation. A well-balanced work schedule is important to control the standard of quality and maintain the morale of the work force.

Variety in the menu should be introduced not only through the food items, but also in terms of methods of preparation, and the texture, color, form, and shape of the food. The planner must have a vast knowledge of foods and must also be able to plan and visualize interesting combinations of each. Variety can be achieved on the menu by offering entrees that have been roasted, fried, and braised; vegetables that have been steamed, baked, and sauteed; salads in the form of raw vegetables, molds, and combinations of fresh or canned fruit; desserts that have a good balance between pastries, puddings, and frozen items. The basic forms of preparation must offer variety not only on the single menu, but the methods of preparation should differ from day to day and from menu to menu. A Potage creme Dubarry (Cauliflower Cream Soup) followed on the next day by a Potage a l'allemande (German Cream Soup) does not offer the required variety since both are thick soups. Regardless of whether the food item is fish, meat, poultry, game, or vegetables, there must be variety in the food items and in their presentation.

Monotony can be avoided by providing foods of different sizes, shapes, and heights on the same menu. Potatoes and some vegetables may be served whole, or in cubes, diced, shredded, julienne, or thick or thin slices.

Every course in a menu must be fundamentally different from the others in terms of appearance and preparation. If the first course consists of a cold entree (hors d'oeuvre varie), the foods used in the preparation should not be repeated in any form in the courses that follow. The different kinds of sauces, which are either served with the food or separately, must differ from each other in color, taste, and seasoning. Butter sauces (Hollandaise, Bearnaise, and Mousseline) are very similar and should occur only once in a menu. Nor should two brown sauces, that have been prepared in the same way, appear in the same menu. Fish served in a White Wine Sauce should not be followed by an Allemande Sauce (thick white sauce) in the next course. A balance of red meats and white meats should be offered. Leg of lamb or mutton and beef should never be featured on the same menu, nor should the dark meat of poultry and game be served after a red meat. Whenever a soup is prepared with vegetables, the following course should include a different variety of vegetable than those in the soup. The use of fresh fruits and vegetables will add color, texture, and flavor to every menu. Deep-fat fried dishes should never appear more than once on a menu.

Variety may also be introduced through color. A menu that provides an assortment of foods with rich natural colors will have more eye appeal and be easier to merchandise than the menu that is composed of foods of all one color or colorless foods. Artificial coloring should not be used. Menus should include items with contrasting textures and consistencies. A fresh green salad served with a pasta or a cream of tomato soup with a crisp cheese wafer will increase the appeal of each item. Only one creamed dish should be offered in the same meal.

Combination of flavors is perhaps the most significant factor affecting palatability of foods. The skillful menu planner will consider not only the sweet, salty, bitter, and sour flavors but also those of spicy and highly-seasoned foods. A variety of these flavors that complement each other will be far more interesting than a duplication of the same flavors.

In the past soups were never served after a cold hors d'oeuvre, but now that fewer courses are served, a highly-seasoned soup, such as spiced tomato soup, would be appropriate.

The flavors of certain vegetables and accompaniments combine with certain meats, and some combinations have become traditional. The wise planner will use initiative and imagination in planning to avoid monotonous repetitions. *Endives with roast veal, chestnuts with ham,* and *risotto with veal and chicken* are appropriate combinations. *Pasta* is excellent with *braised beef, roast veal, stews, and game stews;* it would never be served, however, with a steak or with roast beef or leg of lamb or mutton. *Fried and roast potatoes* are suitable with *grilled or fried meats; steamed potatoes with braised meats, roasts and stews;* and *boiled potatoes* are a favorite with *poached fish and boiled meats.* A chocolate sauce would ruin an apple dish, but it is excellent with pears. Crisp cookies are good with ice cream but a softer cookie is better with stewed fruit.

The season of the year exerts an influence on food preferences. During cold weather greater quantities of heavy foods, such as chowders, roasts, and rich pastries, will be consumed. On a hot summer day, cold soups, cold hors d'oeuvre, crisp cool salads, chilled and frozen desserts, and cold buffets are usually popular. One or more hot items should also be included on the menu for those who prefer hot food.

In some locations, the availability of certain foods will vary with the seasons. Improvements in transportation and distribution systems have made it possible, however, to perk up a menu with "off season" foods. Maximum use should be made of perishable foods when they are on the local markets. During this time, they are usually at their peak of quality and at their lowest price.

Fish is of poorer quality after swimming upstream to spawn and during the spawning period. It should, therefore, not be featured on the menu during this time.

Fresh game is at its peak during the fall months. It is best to avoid serving frozen game, particularly that from furred animals.

Featured traditional foods and appropriate themes on holidays and for special events add interest to a menu. Many novel and interesting ideas can be promoted on Valentine's Day, Easter, Thanksgiving Day, and other holidays.

The budget will stipulate the projected income and the amount of this income that can be used for the purchase of food. Food sales, the major source of the potential income, must also cover labor and operation costs. The percentage of income that can be spent for each of these expenses should be determined by management.

The menu must be planned in accordance with the established food cost percentage. To maintain this percentage it is necessary to calculate daily food costs, provide and use standardized recipes, know raw food and portion costs, and adjust prices and menu selections as costs fluctuate. The daily food cost is based on storeroom requisitions and purchases.

A standardized recipe system is essential for successful food cost control. The recipes should list the total raw food cost and the individual portion cost. The menu planner must know and keep these costs up-to-date. Failure to use such a system will lead to major inconsistencies in quality and cost controls. Portion control is necessary from an aesthetic and cost standpoint. Portions should be standardized in relation to cost and appetite so that a variety of foods can be enjoyed in a meal without excessive cost or waste.

5.1.1 Diagram of a Menu Schedule

Plan from. . . . . to.	Sunday, May 15, 1977	Menu No.	Number Portions Prod.	 Sold	Price	Monday, May 16, 1977	Menu No.	Number Portions Prod.	 Sold	Price
1st course	Mushroom Omelet	1.4.2.17	10	8						
Menu A	Consomme Sevigne Chicken Saute with Chambertin wine Homemade Noodles Stuffed Tomatoes, Provence Style Florida Salad	1.3.1.4	50	35						
Menu B	Consomme Sevigne Sirloin Steak with Pepper French Fried Potatoes Stuffed Tomatoes, Provence Style Green Salad	1.1.1.15	87	85						
Dessert	Coupe Melba	1.3.1.4	30	30						
Menu alterations	Menu B/Soup from	1.3.1.4				Menu Schedules for 7 to 10 days				
Speciality of the day 1 2 3	Sliced Veal, Zurich Style Beef Stew, Farmer's Style Veal Rib Roast Lorette	17.1.3.24 17.4.2.3 18.3.4.7	10 15 15	8 10 5						
Season	Asparagus (10 varieties)	Special	14	11						
Staff lunch	Veal Cutlet Cordon Bleu Noodles, Salad	—	45	40						
Staff evening meal	Coffee, Toast Cheese Potatoes in their jackets	—	40	38						

FIGURE 5-1
Diagram of a Menu Schedule

5.1.2 Framework of the Menu

The courses of the menu should be arranged on the menu in the same sequence that they will be ordered and consumed. Appetizers and other light dishes such as soup, cold and hot hors d'oeuvre, and fish are served as separate courses preceding the main course *(grosse piece).* This course is followed with more light dishes. Technically, the complete classical menu framework usually includes the following courses:

1.	Cold hors d'oeuvre	*Hors-d'oeuvre froid*
2.	Soup	*Potage*
3.	Hot hors d'oeuvre	*Hors-d'oeuvre chaud*
4.	Fish	*Poisson*
5.	Main course	*Grosse piece*
6.	Hot entree	*Entree chaude*
7.	Cold entree	*Entree froide*
8.	Sherbet	*Sorbet*
9.	Roast and salad	*Roti, salade*
10.	Vegetable	*Legume*
11.	Sweet dish	*Entremets*
12.	Savory	*Savoury*
13.	Dessert	*Dessert*

The following are explanations of the menu courses:

Traditionally, the fish dish is called *Releve de poisson. Grosse piece* is the modern term for what was known as the *Piece de resistance* or *Releve de boucherie, -de volaille, -de gibier.* At one time there was a difference of opinion in the cooking fraternity about the appropriate time to serve the vegetable—before or after the roast. It was finally agreed that it should be served afterwards. In some establishments, *sweet dishes* (ice cream, Bavarian creams, some puddings, blancmange, stewed fruit, and mousse) are often served with cookies unless cookies have been used in the preparation of the dish. *Desserts* may consist of mixtures of dried grapes, nuts, almonds, small pastries, chocolates, and fresh fruit and cheese. In the classical French menu, however, *the cheese plate is always offered before the sweet dish.*

The thirteen course menu conforms to every aspect of the classical menu framework. Menus today, however, seldom offer such an extensive number of courses and dishes. The menu illustrates the kinds of food served in each course and the proper sequence of service. The sherbet which is shown

Menu *(in English)*

Cold hors d'oeuvre	*Oysters*
Soup	*Consomme Princesse*
Hot hors d'oeuvre	*Marrow on Toast*
Fish	*Blue River Trout*
	Whipped Butter
Main course	*Beef Tenderloin with Vegetables*
Hot entree	*Breast of Chicken with Truffles*
Cold entree	*Mousselines of Ham with Paprika*
Sherbet	*Champagne Sherbet*
Roast	*Roast Pheasant*
Salad	*Salad*
Vegetable	*Gratinated Asparagus*
Sweet dish	*Blancmange with Hazelnuts*
	Cookies
Savory dish	*Emmentaler Cheese Sticks*
Dessert	*Fruits — Dessert*

Menu *(in French)*

Hors-d'oeuvre froid	*Natives*
Potage	*Consomme princesse*
Hors-d'oeuvre chaud	*Croute a la moelle*
Poisson	*Truite au bleu*
	Beurre fouette
Grosse piece	*Filet de boeuf jardiniere*
Entree chaude	*Supremes de poulet aux truffes*
Entree froide	*Mousselines de jambon au paprika*
Sorbet	*Sorbet au Champagne*
Roti	*Faisan roti*
Salade	*Salade*
Legume	*Asperges en branches au gratin*
Entremets	*Bavarois aux noisettes*
	Patisserie
Savoury	*Paillettes d'Emmental*
Dessert	*Fruits — Dessert*

within the framework is not treated as a separate course. It serves as a refreshing dish and it also provides an opportunity for brief greetings or announcements without interfering with the continuity of service. It would be inappropriate to serve a frozen drink in the middle of a short menu, or to have speeches or toasts at that time. This menu lists all the possible courses in a menu. Choices of foods are seldom offered within a course. Occasionally, there may be a choice in the method of preparation for the sweet dishes, soups, and fish, such as a clear and a thick soup, a fried and a boiled fish course, a hot and a cold sweet dish.

Changes in the order of courses are permitted and sometimes recommended, provided the general rules are not broken. Thus, the hot entree is often served before the main course. The methods of preparation of the fish course and the main course then become extremely important.

In recent years there has been a trend toward simplification of menu patterns and fewer menu selections. The discriminating guest does not demand a large choice of foods and courses. A menu of three to six carefully selected delicacies that have been expertly prepared is more likely to be considered a culinary treasure than an extensive list of different foods. Courses are traditionally served in the order of the menu framework as shown in Examples 1 and 2.

Example 1

Soup	Potage
Main course	Grosse piece
Vegetable	Legume
Sweet dish	Entremets

Example 2

Soup	Potage
Fish	Poisson
Main course	Grosse piece
Vegetable	Legume
Sweet dish	Entremets

Menus arranged as those in Examples 3, 4, 5, and 6 may begin with a salad. In these menus, fruit and cheese may be served instead of a sweet dish.

Example 3

Cold hors d'oeuvre	Hors-d'oeuvre froid
Soup	Potage
Fish	Poisson
Main course	Grosse piece
Roast	Roti
Vegetable	Legume
Sweet dish	Entremets

Example 4

Cold hors d'oeuvre	Hors-d'oeuvre froid
Soup	Potage
Fish	Poisson
Main course	Grosse piece
Cold entree	Entree froide
Roast	Roti
Vegetable	Legume
Sweet dish	Entremets
Dessert	Dessert

Example 5

Cold hors d'oeuvre	Hors-d'oeuvre froid
Soup	Potage
Fish	Poisson
Main course	Grosse piece
Hot entree	Entree chaude
Cold entree	Entree froide
Roast	Roti
Vegetable	Legume
Sweet dish	Entremets
Dessert	Dessert

Example 6

Cold hors d'oeuvre	Hors-d'oeuvre froid
Soup	Potage
Hot hors d'oeuvre	Hors-d'oeuvre chaud
Fish	Poisson
Main course	Grosse piece
Hot entree	Entree chaude
Cold entree	Entree froide
Sherbet	Sorbet
Roast	Roti
Vegetable	Legume
Sweet dish	Entremets
Dessert	Dessert

If a savory dish is added to the menu in Example 6, the framework of the classical menu will be complete. The savory dish is served after the sweet dish (entremets).

At one time, the vegetable course was called *entremets de cuisine,* and the sweet dish *entremets sucre.* This explains why the cook responsible for preparing the vegetable is known as the *entremetier.*

Classical Menu

Hors-d'oeuvre froid
Potage
Hors-d'oeuvre chaud
Poisson
Grosse piece
Entree chaude
Entree froide
Sorbet*
Roti
Salade
Legume
Entremets
Savoury*
Dessert

Modern Shortened Menu

Cold Hors d'oeuvre†
Soup†
Hot Hors d'oeuvre†
Meat Dish with Garnish
Vegetable†
Salad†
Sweet Dish†
Dessert†

—— Courses which have not been rearranged

--- Courses which have been rearranged

* Is omitted from short menus

† Need only be offered as alternatives in modern lunch menus

FIGURE 5-2
Menu Framework

The shortened version of the classical menu, as shown in Fig. 5-2, shows how some of the courses in the longer menu can be combined or omitted. The courses should be arranged in the proper order; however, there is greater flexibility in the menu and a greater variety of foods can be offered. A cold entree, such as a mousse, may serve as a cold hors d'oeuvre; a chaud-froid or pate may be substituted for the meat dish. In more elaborate menus, fish or light hot entrees may be used as the hot hors d'oeuvre. In simple luncheon menus, the more extensive entrees with vegetables are frequently used as the meat dish rather than as a main course. A roast served with appropriate vegetables may also replace the grosse piece. Frozen drinks (sherbets) and the savories are omitted in the shortened menu, but all the other courses maintain their traditional function.

5.1.3 Types of Menu

The lunch menu. This is the midday meal, and it is generally composed of light food. Fruit juice or vegetable juice is often served instead of soup.

The brunch. The name is derived from the words "breakfast" and "lunch," and the brunch menu is usually a combination of the two meals. Some brunch menus include foods that are traditional breakfast favorites. Others provide a wide choice of fruits, hot breads, eggs, meats, coffee, and tea.

The dinner. This is the evening meal, and includes three to five courses. The dinner usually represents the main meal of the day.

The gala menu. This is a menu for festive evenings. The menu should be carefully planned for the specific occasion, and the food and service must be flawless.

The light menu. This menu is for midday or evening meals for days of fasting. Although meat is generally omitted from this menu, fish, eggs, milk and cheese products, vegetables, pasta, rice, fruit juices, and fruits may be served.

The vegetarian menu. Foods of animal origin are not permitted in this type of menu; however, eggs and milk products are used under some conditions. All kinds of plant foods and vegetable and fruit juices are of special importance in these menus.

5.1.4 Examples of Menus

The following menu was selected for a dinner for twelve persons:

Menu

Clear Oxtail Soup with Marsala
Filet of Sole, Bonne Femme Style
American Mixed Grill
Puffed Potatoes
Cardoons with Beef Marrow
Mimosa Salad
Crepes Suzette
Fruit Basket

The preceding menu is appropriate for a small group; however, it would be extremely difficult to serve the same menu to a large group of people. It would be impossible to maintain the quality and proper temperature of the mixed grill. Crepes for a small group can be prepared at the table quite easily, but it would be impractical to serve this dessert to a large group. The following menu is an example of one that could be served to a group of one hundred or more persons:

Menu

Clear Oxtail Soup with Marsala
Roast Rib of Beef, American Style
French Fried Potatoes
Cardoons with Beef Marrow
Mimosa Salad
Iced Vacherin with Fruits

The following menu was served for a conference of 800 persons:

Menu

Game Pate — Melon with Kirsch
Cumberland Sauce
Clear Soup with Diced Vegetables
Roast Spring Chicken
Potato Chips
Buttered Green Beans
Salad
Chilled Fruit with Whipped Cream

The individual courses were selected for fast service. A slice of game pate and a piece of melon were arranged on each plate and these were placed on the table before the guests arrived. The Cumberland Sauce was also placed on the table. The waiters served half a spring chicken and green beans on the prewarmed plate of each guest. The potatoes and salad were served separately on the table. The fruit, garnished with whipped cream, was served in small individual glass bowls.

The two dinner menus which follow correspond to those found in fine restaurants or hotels:

Christmas Dinner

Medallions of Rock Lobster on Tomato Mousse, Duchess Style
Real Turtle Soup with Sherry
Baby Chicken Stuffed with Goose Liver in Casserole
Truffle Sauce — Pearl Potatoes
Asparagus Tips and Green Peas with Butter and Parsley
Endive Salad
Christmas Pudding with Cognac
or
Frozen Souffle
Fruit Basket

New Year's Day Dinner

Birds' Nest Soup with Port
Slices of Poached Turbot—Rich Sauce
Duckling with Orange in Cocotte
Bigarade Sauce—Mirette Potatoes
Sauteed Brussels Sprouts
Hearts of Lettuce Salad
Chocolate Blancmange
or
Biscuit Tortoni with Maraschino Cherries
Cookies, French Style
Assorted Fruit

New Year's Eve Supper

Clear Soup, Princess Style
Beef Tenderloin Wellington
Red Wine Sauce
Straw Potatoes—Tomatoes Clarmart with Peas
Endive Salad
Ice Cream Charlotte—Melba Sauce
Candies

This New Year's Eve Supper is suitable for a supper following festive occasions or at gala balls. On such occasions (New Year's Eve and New Year's Day) light, *cold buffets* are popular.

Cold Buffet for New Year's Day

Lobster Cocktail with Caviar
Medallions of Salmon, Norwegian Style
Pate of Venison—Mousse of Goose Liver
Poularde with Truffles
Assorted Salads
Ice Coupe "New Year's Day"—Cassata, Naples Style
Plum Cake—Candies
Fruit Basket

Menus for Special Occasions

Clear Soup with Meat Dumplings
Lobster, American Style
Roast Partridge on Buttered Toast
Potato Chips
Green Peas, Bonne Femme Style.
Green Salad
Ice Cream Cake Deliciosa
French Cookies
Dessert

Shrimp Cocktail

Clear Beef Soup with Diced Vegetables
Saddle of Veal Prince Orloff
Madeira Sauce—Potatoes, Castle Style
Cauliflower, Polish Style
Salad, Elizabeth Style
Surprise Omelet with Grand Marnier
Pears with Swiss Cheese

Midnight Theater Supper

Clear Soup, Madrid Style
Salmon Steaks, Parisian Style
Glazed Galantine of Duckling
Duchess Salad
Iced Tangerines
Cookies

By today's standards the following menu may seem rather heavy; the true gourmet, however, will take only a small portion of each of the delicacies.

Menu

Cocktail Crispi
Birds' Nest Soup
Old-fashioned Pike Dumplings with Rock Lobster Medallions
Bresse Capon with Truffles in Casserole
Pearl Potatoes
Mixed Vegetables
Endive Salad
Peach Melba
Candies
Dessert and Fruit

5.2 Types of Meals

The classical and formerly common types of meals such as Breakfast—*Petit dejeuner,* Lunch—*Dejeuner,* Dinner—*Diner,* and Supper—*Souper* have as a result of changing life styles, changed both in composition and in terms of the hour at which they are consumed. The most important types of meals are therefore reclassified as follows:

Breakfast—Petit dejeuner. Depending upon nationality and local custom, breakfast may be anything from a cup of black coffee or tea with biscuits to a full-scale English breakfast. The English breakfast is considered a main meal and may include: fruit juices, fresh fruits, tea, marmalade and toast, cold cereals or porridge, egg dishes, fish dishes (haddock and kippers), ham, chicken, or lamb chops.

Lunch—Dejeuner. Usually served at midday, lunch consists of simpler foods and fewer courses than dinner. The luncheon menu often includes a light main course, fruit juice, salad, and fruit. A hearty soup served with bread and fruit is also a popular midday meal. Salads and fruit juices are sometimes served instead of a soup. Cheese, fruits, or a light frozen specialty are the usual desserts.

Snacks. Small hot or cold dishes which can be combined with salads, fruits, yoghurt, or cottage cheese are favorite snack items. Small portions of all kinds of sausages, cold meats, and sandwiches are also eaten as snacks.

Dinner—Diner. Dinner, served in the evening, is usually the principal meal of the day in most restaurants and hotels. At this time of day, the customer has more time for leisurely dining. Most dinner menus will consist of three to five of the following courses:

- Cold hors d'oeuvre
- Soup
- Fish or hot hors d'oeuvre
- Main course with garnishes
- Sweet dish or dessert

The Midnight Supper. This generally refers to a gala menu of four to six courses served late in the evening on festive occasions. The food should always be of excellent quality, easy to digest, and carefully served.

Buffet. Cold buffets in the past were usually identified with after-theater performances, balls, and other late evening occasions. Today cold, warm, and combination buffets are served at lunchtime and in the evening. Buffets provide the opportunity for the ultimate in culinary art, decor, color, variety of food, and fast service. A large group of people can be accommodated easily with a minimum of service. Cold buffets are especially popular during the summer months.

5.3 Menus for the Day

The printed menu is an important merchandiser. The customer frequently forms his first impression of the restaurant from the menu that is presented to him. It should be designed to harmonize with the decor and atmosphere, and it should be planned to function as a promotion tool that will increase sales through customer satisfaction. Whether a simple menu, listing the menu for the day or one that is more complex with a wide selection of courses and dishes, the menu should be written in a clear style and arranged on the card so that the guest may make his choices easily.

There are a variety of menu formats differing widely between establishments; there are, however, certain fundamentals that are basic to designing any menu regardless of the format. These are:

- the menu should be on durable paper stock that is stain resistant
- the size should permit easy handling at the table
- the format should be simple with adequate margins and spacing for easy reading
- the size and style of the print should be legible
- food items should be listed in the classical order or in the sequence that the food will be ordered (small cold, small hot, large cold, and large hot dishes)
- specialties on the menu may be printed in bold face type, in colored print, underlined, or attached on a colored rider or sticker
- descriptions of menu items should be worded to give a clear and interesting visual image of the food item; misleading terminology and information should be avoided
- the grammar, spelling, prices, and other information should be accurate
- the menu should be spotlessly clean, free of marks and corrections
- the name, address, telephone number, and days and hours of service should be listed on the menu

The correct order of the groups of dishes on the menu

The order of dishes on the following menu is not quite identical to that of the menu framework. Since the specialties for the day can consist of either the hot entrees or the main courses (taken from the full menu card), this group of dishes is listed after the entrees rather than after the main courses.

Cold hors d'oeuvre	*Hors-d'oeuvre froids*
Soups	*Potages*
Hot hors d'oeuvre	*Hors-d'oeuvre chauds*
Fish	*Poissons*
Hot entrees	*Entree chaudes*
Specialties of the day	*Plats du jour*
Roasts	*Rotis*
Vegetables	*Legumes*
Sweet dish	*Entremets*
Dessert	*Dessert*

In certain establishments there is a choice of vegetables and the guest selects the one he wants with the meat he has ordered. In other restaurants the vegetables and garnishes that accompany the meat are indicated on the menu, for example: "Veal Chop in Hunter Sauce with Rice," "Tournedos Rossini—French Fries and Salad," "Veal Liver, English Style."

If the hot dishes must be prepared in advance because of the required preparation time, then these dishes and the main dishes on the Menu for the Day (also previously prepared), should follow the hot entrees in a separate group as *Specialties of the Day (Plats du jour)*. These dishes are usually less expensive than the so-called "made to order" dishes. The *following menu* is an example of the *Menu for the Day*.

Menu for the Day	
Melon	Grapefruit
Tomato Juice	Orange Juice
Carte du jour	
Melon	Pamplemousse
Jus de tomates	Jus d'oranges
Cold hors d'oeuvre	*Hors-d'oeuvre froids*
Mixed hors d'oeuvre	Hors-d'oeuvre varies
Mallossol Caviar	Caviar malossol
Goose Liver Pate	Pate de fois gras
Russian Eggs	Oeufs a la russe
Soups	*Potages*
Cup of Clear Soup	Consomme double en tasse
Real Turtle Soup	Tortue claire
Cream of Asparagus Soup	Creme Argenteuil
Hot hors d'oeuvre	*Hors-d'oeuvre chauds*
Patty Shells, Queen's Style	Bouchees a la reine
Cheese Omelet Emmentaler	Omelette emmentaloise
Fried Eggs Meyerbeer	Oeufs au plat Meyerbeer
Fish	*Poissons*
Blue River Trout	Truite au bleu

Hollandaise Sauce	Sauce Hollandaise
Whitefish, Meuniere Style	Fera meuniere
Deep-fat Fried Perch, Tartar Sauce	Perches frites, sauce tartare
Entrees	*Entrees*
Tournedoes Rossini	Tournedos Rossini
Sirloin Steak, Bearnaise Sauce	Entrecote bearnaise
Veal Cutlets, Hunter's Style	Cote de veau chasseur
Lamb Chops with Green Beans	Cotelettes de mouton aux haricots verts
Calf's Liver, English Style	Foie de veau a l'anglaise
Specialties of the Day	*Plats du jour*
Roast Beef with Mixed Vegetables	Roast beef jardiniere
Osso Buco, Milanese Style	Osso buco milanese
Breast of Veal Riblets, Bourgeois Style	Tendrons de veau Bourgeoise
Roasts	*Rotis*
Spring Chicken in a Casserole	Poulet de grain en casserole
Saddle of Hare Mirza	Rable de lievre Mirza
Vegetables	*Legumes*
Asparagus, Melted Butter	Asperges en branches, beurre fondu
Green Peas with Mint	Petits pois a la menthe
Sauteed French Beans	Haricots verts sautes
Stuffed Tomatoes, Provence Style	Tomates provencale
Risotto with Saffron	Risotto au safran
Buttered Noodles	Nouilles au beurre
Boiled Potatoes	Pommes nature
Sauteed Potatoes	Pommes sautees
French-Fried Potatoes	Pommes frites
Puffed Potatoes	Pommes soufflees
Mixed Salads	Salades diverses
Sweet Dishes	*Entremets*
Choice of Ice Cream	Glaces au choix
Peach Sundae	Coupe Melba
Ice Cream Sundae, Victoria	Coupe Victoria
Souffle Rothschild	Souffle Rothschild
Crepes Suzette	Crepes Suzette
Fruit Salad with Kirsch	Macedoine de fruits au Kirsch
Assorted Tarts, Cakes	Gateaux divers
Stewed Fruits	Compotes
Dessert	*Dessert*
Fruits—Cheeses	Fruits—Fromages

Our Specialties

Scotch Smoked Salmon on Toast
Goose Liver Medallions—Chilled Melon
Pheasant Terrine, Gourmet's Style
Clear Oxtail Soup with Diced Vegetables
French Fish Soup, Marseille Style
Rock Lobster Thermidor
Stuffed Sole, Chef's Style
Mixed Grill Special
Veal Cutlet en Papillote
Stuffed Leg of Poularde, Louisette
Saddle of Venison Baden-Baden
Paella Valenciana
Chicken Curry, Bombay Style
Porterhouse Steak, Mexican Style
Frozen Souffle with Grand Marnier
Williams Pears with Chocolate Sauce
Pineapple Crepes Flambe
Baked Alaska

The same menu in French:

Nos Specialites

Toast de saumon fume d'Ecosse
Medaillons de foie gras—Melon rafraichi
Terrine de faisan a la facon des gourmets

Oxtail clair a la brunoise
Bouillabaisse marseillaise
Langouste Thermidor
Sole Farcie a la mode du chef
Mixed grill special maison
Cote de veau en papillote
Jambonneau de poularde Louisette
Selle de chevreuil Baden-Baden
Paella valenciana
Chicken curry Bombay style
Porterhouse steak mexicana
Souffle glace Grand Marnier
Poires Williams Suchard
Crepes a l'ananas flambees
Omelette norvegienne

The menu style should be simple, attractive, and easy to read. It may be designed so that specialties or daily features can be added in the form of a clip-on or sticker. Menu items are sometimes identified with a number which simplifies ordering.

5.4 Presentation of the Food

The saying "the eye eats too" is fully justified. The meal service or presentation of the food has an important effect on customer acceptance. The table settings should be coordinated with the foodservice so that the food, china, glassware, table linens, and silver are both attractive and functional. The food must be of excellent quality and at the proper temperature for palatability and safety. The table appointments should be attractive, and the food should be served by personnel who are efficient, courteous, and sensitive to the customers' needs. Serving food at the *proper temperature* is perhaps the greatest factor in controlling the quality of food that has been carefully prepared. Practices that will aid in maintaining hot foods at the proper temperature are:

- Heat food to the proper temperature before serving.
- Heat plates, bowls, and serving dishes before dishing food into them.
- Heat sauces and gravies before pouring over food or into sauce boat.
- Serve food to guest immediately after it has been dished.
- Cover all hot foods with a warm plate cover after dishing on the plate.
- Prepare deep-fat fried foods just before serving, drain and serve on a dish covered with paper.
- Avoid serving portions that are too large.

The dishes in which food is served must be appropriate for the particular food item. Not only does the properly designed serving dish enhance the appearance of the food, it also simplifies the service. Today earthenware dishes are available in shapes and sizes to suit the character of the particular food, and food served in these dishes will retain the heat better than in most any other serving dish. Rich soups, beef broths, and gratinated soups are especially attractive when served in earthenware or copper dishes. The soup should be stirred gently from the bottom so that the vegetables and other contents can be distributed evenly into the serving dish. Croutons, puffs, and crisp biscuits are usually served in a separate dish and added to the soup at the table.

If boiled potatoes are served on the same plate with poached fish, the potatoes should be arranged attractively in small quantities or they should be served separately in a vegetable dish. Blue fish should always be served with the court bouillon in a special casserole or earthenware dish to prevent changing color or cooling.

Egg dishes should be served on porcelain or glass but not on silver because it will oxidize on contact with egg.

Vegetables, served as garnishes, should be served on a plate large enough to arrange them attractively.

Fish, meat, and vegetables that are served in a sauce should not be disguised by the sauce. Roasted meat, whether white or rare, should never be covered with a sauce or gravy. If the meat is sliced and arranged on a platter, the connoisseur can admire the artistry of the cook. Since even the best sauces and

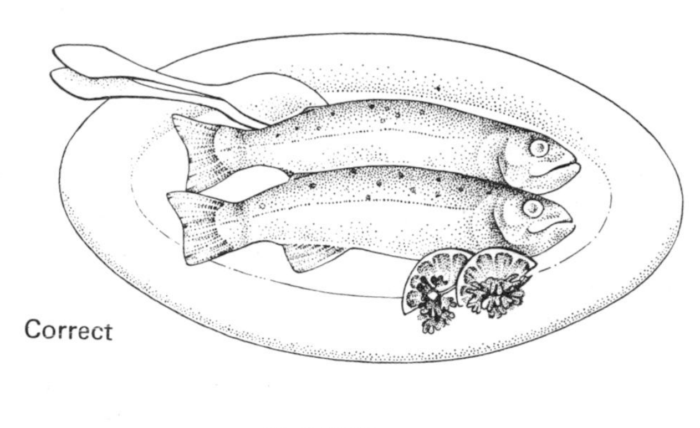

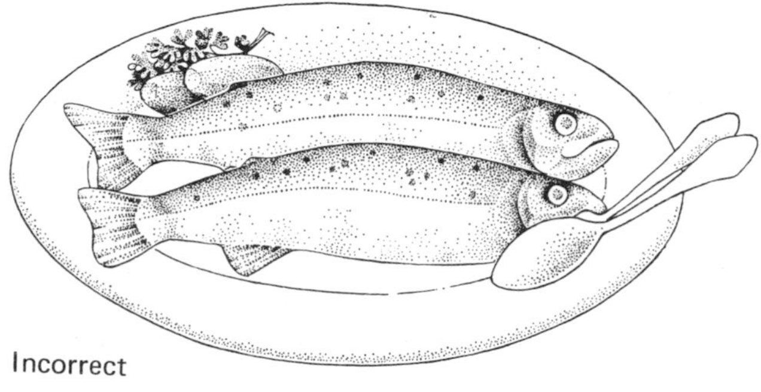

FIGURE 5-3
Presentation of Fish

FIGURE 5-4
Serve the Guest from the Left Side

gravies will change the color and appearance of the meat, they should be served separately in a sauce boat.

A bouquet of fresh watercress is an attractive garnish when a roast is served without vegetables. Scallops, steaks, and cutlets should be served with lemon and parsley if no other garnishes are available. A whole fish should be garnished by placing a cluster of parsley and lemon wedges beside the head of the fish; the garnish is placed near the bone of a chop. (See Fig. 5-3)

The cook needs to know how the waiter will present and serve the dish to the guest. He can then arrange the food on the dish so that the waiter can serve the food simply or the guest can help himself easily. The waiter should always stand to the left of the guest and present the correct side of the platter to him. For example, when serving a whole fish, it will be the side of the dish towards which the tail is pointing; and when serving slices of fish or meat, it should be the side of the dish with the last or top slice that is nearest the guest. If garnishes or vegetables are placed on only one side of the dish, they should be arranged in such a way that the guest does not have to reach over the meat to serve himself vegetables. The guest should always be served from his/her left-side. (See Fig. 5-4.)

Souffles should be prepared and timed so that they can be served without delay when removed from the oven. The alert waiter will place the necessary plates in front of the guests and serve the souffle immediately. Otherwise, the souffle will collapse. Souffle puddings and gnocchis, Parisian Style, are also very delicate items and should be served in the same way.

The preparation and presentation of *cold* dishes is an art that requires culinary skill and imagination. Complete organization of the work, an adequate supply of appropriate serving dishes, and sufficient quantities of perfectly prepared clear gelatin are basic essentials.

Bases made from semolina, rice, and butter are sometimes used, however, to be most effective they should be a pure white color. Finely diced aspic is more attractive than chopped aspic. There should always be complete harmony between the garnishes and the entree. This harmony concerns the *use* of the garnish as well as the content of the garnish itself.

Only edible substances, such as truffles, leeks, sweet peppers, eggs, pickles, capers, and radishes, should be used for decorating. Wood, paper, foil, wax, and artificial substances are not appropriate for decorating food. The so-called *pieces montees* or pompous culinary structures are now considered out-of-place and are no longer used for decorating. Today, decorations and centerpieces for tables and buffets often include ice sculptures, floral arrangements, elaborate creations made with royal icing, and artistically garnished arrays of food.

The presentation of cold dishes requires a sensitivity for the combination of colors, shapes, and textures to achieve complete harmony between the appearance of the food, the table appointments, and the decorations.

5.5 The Service

There are many types of service. Each differs from the other, and each type will differ between establishments. The goal of each is to serve quality food attractively and efficiently. To achieve this goal, certain basic requirements must be met regardless of the type of service.

5.5.1 Rules of Service

Mise en Place. Good service is dependent upon the mise en place or the preliminary preparation. This requires organizing the work. The cutlery, glasses, silence cloths, tablecloths, napkins, serving dishes, coffee and tea services, plate warmers, banquet carts, and the serving cart for flambe should be in place and ready for use.

Rules for Serving Guests. Certain rules for serving guests are valid for any type of service. These are:

- *Presenting the food.* The waiter should stand at the left of the guest and hold the serving dish close to the guest's plate with the serving cutlery pointing toward the guest so that he can serve himself more easily.
- *Serving the food from the dish.* The food is always served *from the guest's left.* The waiter should ask the guest what he would like before serving the food onto his plate.
- *Serving the food using a service table.* The dishes are served from a service table using platewarmers. This enables the waiter to have both hands free so that he can serve the food onto the plates more quickly and efficiently.
- *The placement.* The glasses, empty plates, or plates with the food, and cups and saucers are placed on the table from the right, *with the exception of the bread plates, salad plates, and finger bowls.* The latter are used on the left and are, therefore, placed from the left.
- *Clearing.* Plates are also cleared from the right. Serving dishes, bowls, sauce boats, and salad bowls are removed first, then the plates and glasses. Each time the table is cleared, any soilage or bread crumbs should be removed.

5.5.2 Types of Service

The types of service were formerly named after their country of origin. Thus one used to talk about *English, French,* and *Russian* service. Now the services are named more objectively.

The Banquet Service. This service is used for a given number of people who are to be served a predetermined menu simultaneously. The appetizer is often on the table before the guests are seated. The food is usually dished onto warm plates in the kitchen. The plates are then taken into the dining room in heated carts or on trays. The waiter removes the appetizer dishes from the table and then serves the dinner plates to the guests. In another type of banquet service, the food is prepared and arranged on heated serving platters and dishes in the kitchen. The waiter takes the platters of food and the heated dinner plates into the dining room. The waiter places an empty dinner plate in front of each guest and then serves the food from each of the serving dishes onto each guest's plate.

The waiter clears the dinner plate, salad plate, bread and butter plate, and silver from each guest before the dessert is served. The coffee cups and saucers are sometimes placed on the table before the meal is served. The waiter fills the cups from a coffee server.

The Table d'hote service. This refers to the simultaneous service of the same menu at an established price. It may offer no choices or it may provide a limited selection of items within categories, such as a juice, soup, or fruit cup for the appetizer. Each waitress or waiter should be able to serve ten or twelve guests.

The a part service. Contrary to the table d'hote service, with the *a part service* the guests are served individually. Although all the guests have the same menu, they do not all have to appear for the meal at the same time. The dishes are placed on the tables so that the guests can help themselves, or they are offered and either served by the waiter or merely held while the guest helps himself. The dish is then placed on the table.

The a la carte service. The guest selects items from the selection offered on the menu. Each item is given a separate price. The *a la carte service* is most often employed in restaurants. In some establishments, the dishes are placed on plate-warmers within reach of the guest, so that he can help himself; in others, the food is shown to the guest and then dished onto the plate and served by the waiter.

Self-service. The guest selects his own food and beverage, and collects his tray and cutlery from a service counter. He usually then pays the cashier and goes to a dining table. The cafeteria is a well-known example of this type of service. Self-service is popular in establishments where large numbers of guests arrive at the same time, and a large turnover is experienced. There are several types of cafeterias but most specialize in fast service and low cost. Some smaller establishments also use the self-service system.

FIGURE 5-5
Example for Organizing a Cold Buffet

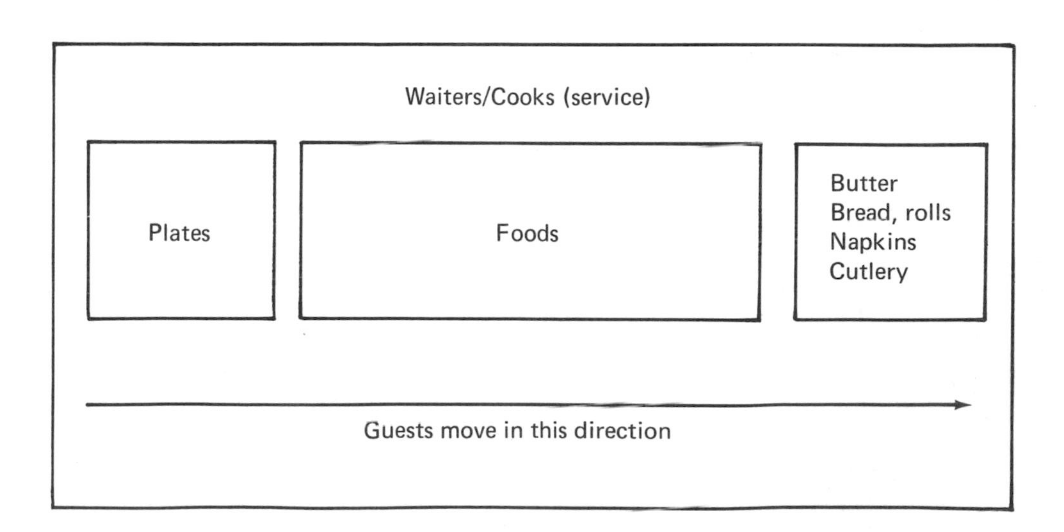

The buffet service. The best known is the cold buffet, although, this type of service may also include a complete meal from the soup to the dessert. The various foods, usually elaborate presentations, are placed upon a table from which the guests make their choice. (See Fig. 5-5.) Plates and cutlery are also on the buffet table, or on a separate table. The guests serve themselves, or the food is placed on their plates by service personnel. The guest usually pays a flat rate price, which is based on the number of choices offered.

5.6 Menu Spelling

The standard references for menu spelling are:

- *French: Larousse gastronomique* and *Larousse*
- *English: The Concise Oxford Dictionary* and *Webster's International Dictionary*

The rules for spelling which are contained in these works should be followed. The so-called *international menu language,* in which the first letter of nouns and fantasy names must be written in capitals, should in the interest of standardization *no longer be used.*

French spelling

Capitals and small letters: In French menus, except at the beginning of a line, all words are written in lower case except the first letter. Proper names, fantasy names, geographical area, and place names are written with a capital letter only when used as nouns.

Examples: Potage parisienne
but
Asperges du Valais (*area name*)
Entrecote Cafe de Paris (*place name*)
Emince Touring (*fantasy names*)
Coupe Melba (*proper name*)

The use of "a la:"

a.) The "a la" or "a la mode de" as it should be written, is used as little as possible, in order to keep repetition in the menu to a minimum. *"A la" is only used* in the sense of:

- A la facon de (du, de la)
- a la mode de
- a la maniere de

It should also be used when naming foods.

Examples: Epinards a la creme (*name of the food*)
Risotto a la turque (*a la maniere*)
Sole a l'italienne (*a la mode*)
Truite a la bernoise (*a la facon*)

The use of "a la" should be maintained where the name concerned begins with a vowel, and when its omission would result in a *phonetic dissonance.*

Examples: Ravioli a l'italienne
Peche a l'imperatrice

b.) *"A la" is not used* with proper names when used as a dedication or honor to a person.

Examples: Tournedos Rossini
Peche Melba
Poularde pochee Demidoff

c.) *"A la" is sometimes used* with names of places or regions.

Examples: a la mode de Caen
Ravioli a la milanaise
or
Ravioli milanaise

When in doubt, the "a la" should be omitted.

d.) *"A la, au, aux."* It should be remembered that the "a la" changes depending of the noun concerned.

Example: Spaghetti a la creme
Spaghetti au fromage
Spaghetti aux morilles

e.) *Adjectives (descriptive words) when the "a la" is omitted.* When the "a la" is omitted, the adjectives are expressed in the feminine, since the "a la" is being used instead of "a la mode."

Example: Potage parisienne

Exceptions: If it is the name of a food, then the adjective is expressed in the same gender as the noun. (See also paragraph d.)

Examples: Saumon fume suedois
(Swedish smoked salmon)
but
Saumon fume a la suedoise (*a la mode*)
(Smoked salmon, Swedish style)

Spelling of Russian proper names:
In order to ensure a common way of spelling Russian proper names, those ending with "ov" or "of" will all take the ending "off."

Examples: Demidoff, Malakoff, Stroganoff

English spelling:
The use of capital and small letters: Everything is written in small letters, except for proper names and geographical names.

Examples: Swiss cheese
Peter the Great

All *adjectives* derived from *proper names* are written with a capital letter:

Examples: English style, French dressing, Parisian steak, Victorian pies

Rules for the translation of "a la"

The "a la" or "a la mode de" are normally translated into English by the word "style."

Examples: Russian style
Milanese style
Viennese style
Charterhouse style

Drinks
All drinks in English and French are always written with a small letter, except for brand names, such as Grand Marnier, Campari, Canadian Club, Courvoisier, Martell.

Examples: *correct*
Omelet with rum
Omelette au rhum
but
Omelet with Grand Marnier
Omelette au Grand Marnier

Rules applicable to all languages
Spelling mistakes: these can be avoided by using the works already indicated, and the menu translation book, *Menus Translated For You,* by Eugen Pauli, Duchamp and Jenning.

Nationality: The menu should be written in the language of the country concerned; in international establishments the language is French.

Presentation of the menu: The layout and spelling should be without errors. The words should either be positioned symmetrically, or every new line should begin at the left-hand margin.

New lines: Generally the first letter of a new line will be a capital letter, except where it is a continuation of the name of a dish.

Example: *correct*
Roast saddle of venison
with game sauce
Selle de chevreuil roti
chasseur

incorrect
Roast saddle of venison
With game sauce
Selle de chevreuil roti
Chasseur

Menu in the singular: The menu texts are always based upon *one guest.*
Number of portions: If *several persons* can be served from *one piece* of food, it should be described in the singular.

Examples: *correct*
Leg of lamb, boulangere style
Gigot d'agneau boulangere

incorrect
Legs of lamb, boulangere style
Gigots d'agneau boulangere

If *at least two pieces of the food* are to be served *to each person,* then the dish should be expressed in the plural.

Examples: *correct*
Fillets of golden trout, bonne femme style
Filets de rouget bonne femme

incorrect
Fille*t* of golden trout, bonne femme style
File*t* de rouget bonne femme

Separation of the individual courses: Each course should be clearly separated from the next by means of a space or a line. See the following examples of menus.

Splitting descriptions at the end of a line: Descriptive terms that belong together should not be split up at the end of a line.

Examples: *correct*
Fillets of sole,
bonne femme style
Filets de sole
bonne femme

incorrect
Fillets
of sole, bonne femme style
Filets
de sole bonne femme

Abbreviations: No abbreviations should be used within the text of the menu, for example sc. instead of sauce or fr. instead of fresh.

Proper names: Proper names which refer to a classical type of preparation should not be translated, nor should the "a la" or "style" form of description be used.

Examples: *correct*
Ice coupe Melba
Coupe Melba

incorrect
Ice coupe Melba *style*
Coupe *a la* Melba

National dishes: Well-known national dishes can be written in their original fashion.

Examples:

	Minestrone	not: Italian vegetable soup
	Ravioli	not: stuffed noodle squares
	Welsh rarebit	not: Welsh cheese cream

Double descriptions: If the basic form of preparation is included in the description of a dish, there is no need to repeat it.

Examples: *correct*
Fere meuniere

incorrect
Fera *doree* a la meuniere

correct
Irish stew

incorrect
Irish stew *a l'anglaise*

correct
Roast prime rib of beef

incorrect
Roast prime rib of beef roti

Example of menu spelling and translation

French	English
Dejeuner	*Lunch*
Cocktail de crevettes	*Shrimp cocktail*
Cotelettes de chevreuil Baden-Baden	*Venison cutlets Baden-Baden*
Pommes dauphine	*Dauphine potatoes*
Choux de Bruxelles aux marrons	*Brussels sprouts with chestnuts*
Souffle au citron-Sauce aux abricots	*Lemon souffle-Apricot sauce*
ou	*or*
Fromage et beurre	*Cheese with butter*

Diner	*Dinner*
Consomme a la paysanne	*Clear soup, paysanne style*
Perches frites	*Deep-fried perch*
Sauce tartare	*Tartar sauce*
Filet de boeuf Parmentier	*Fillet of beef Parmentier*
Chou-fleur a la creme	*Cauliflower with cream sauce*
Salade	*Salad*
Coupe Melba	*Ice coupe Melba*

5.7 History of European Cookery

Cookery, the most ancient of the arts, dates back to the prehistoric age. Although little is known about prehistoric cookery, the discovery of the use of fire for culinary purposes during this period had a great influence on the diet of man. After fire was discovered, men gathered around the hearth and shared their meat and game. Other staple foods in the diets of these ancient peoples included roots, grains, fruit, honey, fish, milk, and eggs. Roasting was probably the first method of cooking. Meat was roasted on the hot embers of an open fire or on spits above the open flame.

Boiling, another mode of cookery in primitive times, was practiced before pottery and other cooking vessels were known. The hides and stomachs of animals were made into bags. Filled with food, water, and hot pebbles, the bags were dropped into a pit that was lined with stones and filled with water. Hot pebbles were added to the pit to maintain the cooking temperature throughout the cooking process.

More is known about cookery in Egypt than in any other ancient civilization. Although there are no books nor manuscripts of this period, pictorial records of bakers and cooks at work and inscriptions in hieroglyphics were found in tombs, pyramids, and clay tablets. Vegetables, fruit trees, vines, chicken, fish, and eggs were plentiful along the River Nile. The Egyptians were known for their breadmaking and confections, and bakers were held in high esteem.

The Persians were notorious for their lavish banquets and feasts. The Assyrian king, Sardonapalus, introduced the first cooking contests offering thousands of gold pieces and other rewards to those who produced a new dish. Marmalades made from the fabulous fruits of Persia, delicate sweets, and fine wines, served in elaborate vessels of gold, were in abundance at every feast. Some of the foods introduced by the Persians continue to be featured on menus throughout the world today.

It was from the Persians that the Greeks learned the art of cooking and dining. Until the middle of the fifth century B.C., there was little difference in the diets of the rich and poor in Greece. Barley pastes, barley gruel, and barley bread were the basic fare. The early Greeks ate four meals a day—breakfast or acratisma; dinner, ariston or deiphon; relish, hesperisma; and supper, dorpe. Later, luncheon replaced the midday dinner, and dinner was served at a later hour. The dinner soon developed into banquets or feasts for religious or social purposes.[1] The best chefs of Greece, including Thimbron, Themacides, and Archestratus, were trained in Syberius, a city famous for its cuisine. Many recipes which have been handed down to us through the Romans and French were created in this city.[2]

The Roman cuisine was based on the recipes and methods of cooking learned from the Greeks and from *De Re Coquinaria,* the first known book on cookery. This book was supposedly written by Apicius in the first century A.D.; however, the only known copies date from the eighth and ninth centuries.[3] The Romans soon developed their own cuisine which was more elaborate and more delicate than that of the Greeks. The magnificence of their banquets and gastronomical splendors continued to flourish until the end of the fourth century.

The fall of the Roman Empire brought a decline in the development of cookery, literature, and

1. Ellwanger, George H., *The Pleasures of the Table* (Doubleday Page and Company, 1902), p. 19.
2. Page, E. B. and Kingsford, P. W., *The Master Chefs,* A History of Haute Cuisine (London: William Clowes and Sons, Limited, 1971), pp. 9, 10.
3. Aresty, Esther, *The Delectable Past* (New York: Simon and Schuster, 1964), p. 20.

the arts. The monasteries, however, assumed an active role in keeping these arts alive. Large monasteries were complex communities with farms, trade schools, and commercial centers as well as religious foundations. St. Gall in Switzerland, known for its culinary delicacies, was one of the first training centers for cooks.

The Romans took many of their traditions of cookery with them to England. It was the Germanic invaders, however, who had the greatest influence on English cookery. The dishes of the Celts, Saxons, and Normans became basic culinary fare. The majority of people in England were farmers and laborers. Their food was simple and hearty. The English banquets and feasts of the Middle Ages were extravagant affairs with an abundance of food and ale. It was during the reign of Henry VIII that Christmas became a time of feasting. Great preparations were made for the twelve day period, from Christmas Eve to Epiphany. Throughout the Elizabethan period, there was an attitude of indifference toward the preparation of food, and this continued until many years later when the hotels and clubs employed chefs from France.

Until early in the sixteenth century, the cooking of France was as unimaginative as that of England. In 1533, the Duke of Orleans married Catherine de Medici, of the well-known Florentine family. She took many of the famous chefs and pastry cooks of Italy with her to France. The French learned from these Italian masters and skillfully developed their own school of cooking. The cuisine of France continued to grow, and by the end of the seventeenth century, France was known throughout the world for its classic cuisine. The classic French cuisine implies a perfectly planned menu; fresh and superior ingredients; talented cooks; simple, artistic, and perfect presentations; subtle and balanced tastes; and an appreciative audience.

5.8 Lexicon of Well-Known Connoisseurs and Food Philosophers

Bagration, Pierre (1765-1812), Prince, Russian general, fatally injured in the battle of Borodino.

Banzer, M.C. and Friebel, Carl, authors of the universal cookery book *Die Restaurationskuche.* Banzer is one of the founders of the museum of cookery in Frankfurt am Main, and he was the director of the International Association of Cooks. Friebel is mainly known as a writer for the professional journal, *Die Kuche.*

Bernard, Emile (1826-1897). A friend of Urbain Dubois. Bernard and Dubois made French cooking famous at the German emperor's palace. These were the two grand masters who propagated the then developing Russian service in central European professional circles.

Brillat-Savarin, Anthelme (1755-1826), known as the greatest French food philosopher of all time, was author of the world famous work, *Physiologie du gout (The Physiology of Taste).* As a real connoisseur, it was his true calling to found *the art of eating.*

Careme, Marie-Antoine (1784-1833), famous French head chef, chef of dukes and kings, idol of connoisseurs, writer of well-known works in the field of cookery. In these works, he founded the variety of classical French cookery in which the greatest successes were found in pompous stands, centerpieces (pieces montees) and visual representations—excesses which were suited to the period. Through his books devoted to cookery, his work as a pastry cook, and his theoretical work, Careme made great contributions to the culinary world. He is regarded by many as the founder of classic French cuisine. His well-known works include: *Le Patissier royal parisien* (1815), *Le Patissier pittoresque* (1815), *Le Cuisinier parisien* (1828), and *L'art de la cuisine francaise au XIXe siecle* (1833).

Chateaubriand, Francois-Rene (1768-1848), French writer, diplomat, and ambassador.

Colbert, Jean Baptiste (1619-1683), successful French statesman, economist, and patron of the arts under King Louis XIV.

Conde, Louis (1621-1686), Prince, named the Grand Conde, French statesman, and politician. A patron of gastronomy (Riz Conde).

Dubarry, (du Barry) Marie, Jeanne Becu (1743-1793), countess, mistress of King Louis XV of France. She was a mannequin, a lady of pleasure, and was accepted at the court. She was executed during the French Revolution.

Dubois, Urbain (1818-1901) wrote a unique book which is reminiscent of those from Honore de Balzac: *La cuisine de tous les pays* (1868), *La cuisine artistique* (1872), and other valuable works. He published *La Cuisine classique* (1856) with Emile Bernard. The book continues to be read and appreciated (the 18th impression appeared in the year 1900).

Dumas, Alexander (father) (1802-1870). The writer of the *Three Musketeers* also immortalized his name in the field of cookery with a gastronomical work entitled: *Grand Dictionnaire de cuisine* (Paris 1873).

Escoffier, Auguste (1847-1935), head chef in Paris and various foreign luxury hotels, especially in London. His greatest honors came to him through his book, *Le Guide culinaire.* This book completely reformed old French cooking (la cuisine classique). The Master Auguste Escoffier created the fundamentals of today's French cooking. When preparing his vast work, *Le Guide culinaire,* Escoffier started with the principles of old French cookery. He eliminated the pompous, poor taste of an earlier period, and introduced specialties from other countries. Thus he was the founder—and this is important—of an international art of cooking, which today is considered to be a part of French cooking. Careme was the "cook of kings and king of cooks." Escoffier was the "king of chefs and the chef of kings."

Gouffe, Jules (1807-1877) a follower of Careme and author of a complete cookery book for luxury food entitled *Le livre de cuisine* (1867), followed in 1873 by *Le Livre de Patisserie.*

Henry IV of France (1553-1610), a great conqueror in troubled times. On his best days he practiced gastronomy, and aimed at ensuring a chicken in every pot "Poule au pot" for his people every Sunday. This is the source of the "Petite marmite Henri IV."

Lucullus, Lucius Licinius (circa 110-56 B.C.), Roman general, statesman, and one who enjoyed good food.

Marie Louise (1791-1847), eldest daughter of the Emperor Francis II of Austria. She became Napoleon's wife in 1810.

Melba, Dame Nellie (1861-1931), a famous Australian singer, whose name was immortalized in cookery by the old master Escoffier with the marvelous "Peche Melba."

Metternich, Prince Clemens Wenzel Lothar (1773-1859), duke, Austrian statesman, cunning diplomat, and ambassador in Paris. Engineered the marriage of the Austrian princess, Marie Louise, with Napoleon I.

Meyerbeer, Giacomo (1791-1864), German composer, a great musician.

Murat, Joachim (1767-1815), a son of a hotel keeper, Marshal of France, brother-in-law of Napoleon, king of Naples, and later summarily shot.

Nelson, Horatio (1758-1805), English admiral, victor of the battles of Abuku (Abukir), and Trafalgar.

Parmentier, Antoine-Augustin (1737-1817), agronomist. Introduced the potato to France and Europe, developed plantations, wrote many books on food, and popularized the use of tubers for cooking.

Reyniere, Grimod de la, A.-B.-L. (1758-1838). A rich and famous gastronome. Author of the scholarly *Almanach des gourmets,* in which Grimod praised and criticized suppliers and cooks. He functioned as a kind of "cooking policeman." Every new culinary creation had to be served to and evaluated by a "jury of tasters." Many a cook awaited their verdict with bated breath. One thing is quite certain—as long as people talk about the art of cooking, the name of this connoisseur will live on.

Rossini, Gioacchino Antonio (1792-1868), an Italian who lived for a long time in Paris, a world-famous opera composer.

Sorel, Agnes (circa 1422-1450), a very beautiful woman, and mistress of Charles VII of France. She became the owner of several castles, one of which was Beaute. Eventually she became known as "Madame Beaute."

Soubise, Charles de Rohan, Prince (1715-1787), Marshal of France, statesman, and diplomat.

Vatel (1635-1671), descended from Swiss parents (from Fribourg). Famous master of the court of Prince Conde.

Wellington, Arthur Wellesley, Duke of (1769-1852), English general, policy-maker, victor over Napoleon at Waterloo.

Kitchen Accounting

6

6.1 Introduction

Cost control is one of the prime functions of sound management in any foodservice operation. Effective cost control requires a system of procedures and records that serve as guidelines for effective and successful operation within the limits of the budget.

Prior to developing a system of procedures and records, certain management functions must be in effect to ensure achieving the highest possible gross profit. These functions include:

- establishing purchasing methods in accordance with real needs
- establishing methods for receiving food and supplies, including checks on quality, quantity, packaging, and portioning
- establishing methods for menu planning, food production, storage control, and service
- establishing selling prices (initial calculation)

The calculation of the gross profit of the kitchen (final calculation) acts as a barometer of good kitchen management. Where gross profit is too high, either too much is being saved in terms of quality or quantity, or the selling price is excessive. In both cases the result may be declining sales volume. If, on the other hand, the gross profit is too low, then inadequate purchasing practices, lack of quantity control, improper utilization of purchased goods, or too low selling prices are probably the cause. To achieve the balance between maintaining profitability and good quality requires knowledge and skill. Only those who know this relationship will be rewarded with good profits and satisfied guests. Obviously, the profitability of a kitchen must be firmly based and calculated exactly and honestly.

It is not the intention here to explain accounts payable, inventories, accounts receivable, or balance sheets. The following principles for the establishment of the cost of food items have purposefully been kept simple and practical. Comprehensive teaching of this subject is a matter for the professional schools.

6.2 Initial Calculation of the Selling Price

		Amounts	*Percentages*	
The cost of raw materials includes the food cost of all goods necessary for preparing the dish.	*Cost of raw material*	$5.00	100% *(base)*	*Base*

Additional charge to the raw material costs (overhead) and net profit, as explained in left column	$9.50	190%

The additional charge to the raw material cost includes the *overhead,* i.e., all cost and expenses over and above those of the raw materials which are necessary for operation of the establishment, for example:

- salaries in cash and kind
- social benefits
- energy, heating, lighting, and cleaning
- marketing, promotion, office expenses, and supplies
- repair and maintenance costs
- interest and mortgage costs

+ *the predetermined net profit*

Calculated sales price =

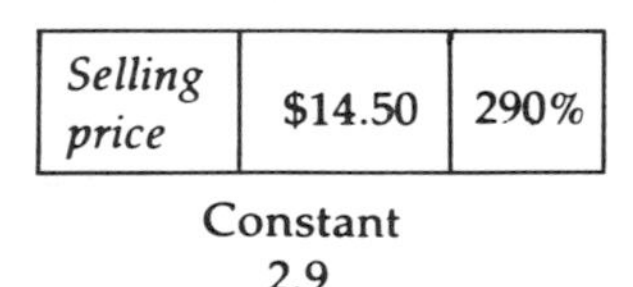

Selling price	$14.50	290%

Constant
2.9

As a rule management will determine the operational expenses to the raw material costs, which are then expressed as a percentage of the material cost. In the example given, the figure was 190% (see following explanation).

Calculation of the selling price

	Raw material cost	+	operational expenses	=	selling price
	100%	+	190%	=	290%
Example:	$5.00	+	$9.50	=	$14.50

A simplified calculation eliminates the need to add operational expenses repeatedly. The selling price is obtained by multiplying the raw material costs by a *constant.* This constant is equal to one hundredth of the selling price, which is expressed as a percentage of the raw material costs.

Example: $\frac{290}{100} = 2.9$

$\$5.00 \times 2.9 = \$14.50$

In practice the same constant is used to calculate the raw material cost when the selling price is known.

Example: $\$14.50 \div 2.9 = \$5.00$

6.3 Final Calculation of Gross Profit

If the initial calculation of the selling price is a responsibility of the chef, he must be informed of the actual operating results so that he can modify his management techniques or his initial selling price calculation if necessary. In certain cases, particularly in small establishments, the calculation of the gross profit actually obtained is the responsibility of the chef.

Applying the same figures to 100 servings at $14.50 each, we obtain the following results:

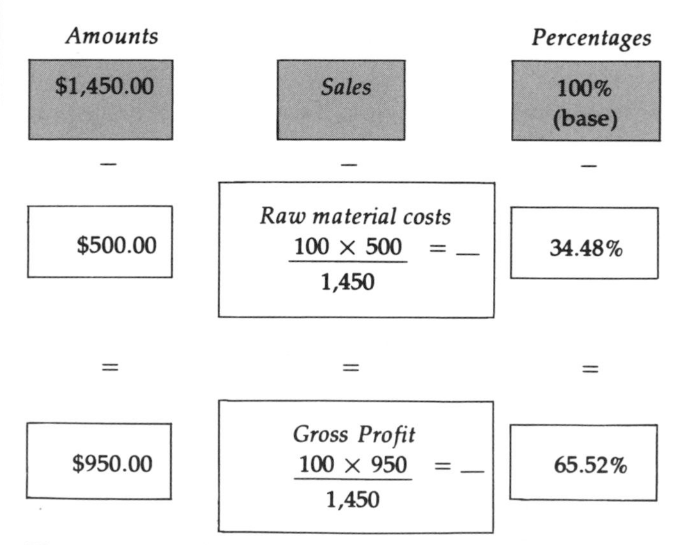

The gross profit obtained should correspond to the operational expenses.

6.4 Price Calculation for Menus and Dishes

Menu: Index No. 1.1.2.2.3 *Date:* No. of persons: 10

Scrambled eggs with tomatoes
Chilled consomme with sherry
Veal chops with mushrooms
Baked potato
Green salad
Strawberries with cream

Calculation:

Dishes	*Name of raw materials*	*Quantities for 10 persons*	*Cost* Per unit as purch.	*Per item*	*Total*
Scrambled eggs with tomatoes	Toasted bread	1¾ pounds	.69/pound	1.21	
	Butter	1 ounce	.90/pound	.06	
	Eggs	20	.07/each	1.40	
	Cream	6 ounces	.98/pint	.36	
	Spices, salt	—	—	.01	
	Tomatoes, fresh	1 pound	.45/pound	.45	
	Oil	1 ounce	.90/pint	.06	
	Onion	1 ounce	.12/pound	.01	
	Parsley	1 ounce	.50/pound	.03	$ 3.59
Cold consomme with sherry Recipe No. 12.1.2.2	Beef, slices	2¼ pounds	2.50/pound	5.62	
	Egg whites	2	.04/each	.08	
	Leeks	1 ounce	.50/pound	.04	
	Celery	1 ounce	.29/pound	.02	
	Carrots	1 ounce	.16/pound	.01	
	Tomato paste	1 ounce	.45/pound	.03	
	Onion	1 ounce	.12/pound	.01	
	Stock	5¼ pints	2.32/gallon	.73	
	Spices, salt	—	—	.01	
	Vegetable brunoise	3½ ounces	—	.10	
	Sherry	6 ounces	2.10/quart	.42	$ 7.07
Veal chops with mushrooms	Rib of veal	4 pounds	3.00/pound	12.00	
	Spices, salt	—	—	.04	
	Flour	1 ounce	.105/pound	.01	
	Shortening	2 ounces	.75/pound	.09	
	White wine	6 ounces	2.10/quart	.42	
	Cream	12 ounces	.98/pint	.74	
	Mushrooms	2¼ pounds	1.20/pound	2.70	
	Butter	1 ounce	.90/pound	.05	
	Flour	1 ounce	.105/pound	.01	$16.06
	Carry forward				$26.72

Dishes	Name of raw materials	Quantities for 10 persons	Cost Per unit as purch.	Cost Per item	Total
	Carried forward				$26.72
Baked potato Recipe No. 21.1.4	Potatoes	5 pounds	.23/pound	1.15	
	Butter	2 ounces	.90/pound	.10	
	Flour	½ ounce	.105/pound	.003	
	Parsley	1 ounce	.50/pound	.03	
	Chives	1 ounce	—	.03	
	Nutmeg, spices, salt	—	—	.04	
	Clarified butter	6 ounces	.75/pound	.29	$ 1.64
Green salad	Lettuce	3 heads	.29/head	.87	
	Salad dressing	1 pint	3.65/gallon	.46	$ 1.33
Strawberries and cream	Strawberries	3¼ pounds	.65/pound	2.11	
	Sugar	2 ounces	.18/pound	.02	
	Cream	1 pint	.98/pint	.98	$ 3.11
Rolls	Rolls	10	.02/each	.20	$ .20
	Cost of raw material				$33.00
	Selling price = Raw material costs × constant 2.9				$95.70
	Selling price per person				$ 9.57

Dish: Hungarian Goulash *Date:* *No. of persons:* 10

Calculation: Spaetzle

Dish	*Name of raw material*	*Quantities for 10 persons*	*Per unit as purchased*	*Cost Per item*	*Total*
Goulash Recipe No. 17.4.2.1	Round of beef	2 pounds	2.40/pound	4.80	
	Lard	2 ounces	.35/pound	.04	
	Onion	14 ounces	.12/pound	.01	
	Paprika	1 ounce	3.18/pound	.20	
	Tomatoes	1¼ pounds	.45/pound	.56	
	Tomato puree	3½ ounces	.02/ounce	.07	
	Beef stock	1¼ pints	2.32/gallon	.36	
	Red wine	½ pint	2.10/quart	.53	
	Spices, salt	–	–	.04	$ 6.61
Spaetzle Recipe No. 22.1.5	Flour	1 pound	.105/pound	.105	
	Milk	⅓ pint	1.23/gallon	.05	
	Water	⅓ pint	–	–	
	Eggs	4	.82/dozen	.27	
	Spices, salt	–	–	.04	
	Butter	1½ ounces	.90/pound	.084	$ .549
Rolls	Rolls	10	.02/each	.20	$ .20
	Cost of raw material				$ 7.359
	Selling price = Raw material costs × constant [2.9]				$21.37
	Selling price per person				$ 2.137

PART II
COOKERY

Basic Principles

7

7.1 The Art of Cooking

What does the art of cooking mean? It means that one knows a great deal about the practical aspects of cookery and cooking techniques. It presupposes a full and precise knowledge of food; a well-developed sense of taste and smell; a sensitivity for color, texture, and shape or form; and the ability to coordinate all the major elements into complete harmony.

Practical Aspects of the Art of Cooking

According to John Ruskin, a nineteenth century English writer and art critic, the art of cooking includes a grandmother's thrift, a knowledge of modern chemistry, a Frenchman's sense of artistry, and an Arab's hospitality. In summary, the art of cooking means providing high quality food and service to the complete satisfaction of the guest.

The Art of Classical Cooking

Classical cooking refers to French cookery that reached its zenith in the kings' palaces during the seventeenth and eighteenth centuries. French cookery is subject to continuous change, and is closely linked with changes occurring in other art forms. The goal to be achieved today is the combination of classical dishes coupled with artistic, but simple, decorative foods. Only by understanding cookery in this sense is it possible to achieve perfection in the practice of culinary art.

Classical Cookery. Classical cookery includes all the basic dishes together with those specialties and dishes adopted from the old French and international cookery. On the other hand, those "historical" monstrosities, with their pompous and unaesthetic structures or pretentious ornamentation are not a part of classical cooking. Only attractive presentations which satisfy the palate and the eye are classical. This is especially true when the name of the dish also corresponds to its actual ingredients. The names, Rossini, Colbert, a la bordelaise, a la portugaise, a la florentine, and Argenteuil are recognized classical names, and recipes for these dishes require specific ingredients.

Plain Cooking. Contrary to classical cookery, plain cooking originally started in private kitchens. The food is simpler, but nevertheless nutritionally adequate and carefully prepared. Many regions and local areas have their own particular cuisine. The climate and geographical conditions, the background of the people, and the traditions and customs of the area often influence the eating patterns and nutritional needs of the people. Many of the dishes unique to a specific region have gained widespread acceptance, as more and more emphasis is placed on nutritional and health needs of the people.

Modern Cooking. Although classical cookery must constitute the basis of all innovations, the trend today is towards safe and efficient storage, simplification of food preparation methods and service, and improved nutrition. The classical art of cooking and modern cooking are dependent upon one another. Only those innovations and classical dishes which conform to basic nutritional principles in terms of ingredients, methods of preparation, and all other culinary rules can be considered modern.

The increasing interest in nutrition and in the nutritive value of foods has greatly influenced food choices. These choices are based on foods that are rich in nutrients, low in calories, and free of synthetic additives. In an effort to reduce fat consumption, whole milk and cream are being replaced by low-fat milk and yoghurt; herbs are replacing butter as seasoning for vegetables; more fish and fresh vegetables are being consumed; and fresh fruits are substituted for desserts that are high in calories. The use of basic methods of preparation, such as blanching, poaching, steaming, and grilling, that will conserve nutrients is equally as important as providing variety. Synthesizing classical cookery with these principles that lead to the health and well-being of the individual is basic to modern cooking.

Dietary Cooking. A specific diet is based on the modifications of the nutritional components of the normal diet. Included in these changes are modifications in the number of calories; modifications in one or more of the nutrients (proteins, fats, carbohydrates, vitamins, and minerals); and modifications in texture and seasoning (liquid, bland, or low residue). Although most of the normal foods are used, they must be tailored to meet the needs of the individual and be prepared so that none of the nutritional content is lost or damaged.

7.2 Cooking Techniques

The term cooking techniques refers to the skills and methods required for the preparation of high quality hot and cold dishes. These techniques may vary to some extent depending on the types of food and the serving system, but in principle they are the same, and may be grouped as follows:

- basic information
- basic methods of preparation
- mise en place
- basic preparations
- basic elements of dishes and their garnishes
- basic elements of meals

The outline of cooking techniques shown in Figure 7–1 illustrates the structure and relationships between the individual groups and sub-groups. It is obvious that a knowledge of basic information, basic methods of preparation, mise en place, and basic preparations is absolutely necessary. This fundamental methodology and a knowledge of the basic types of preparation and of recipes are requisites for the preparation of quality food. The basic elements of meals incorporate all these cooking techniques. The individual who is responsible for the preparation of food must have an appreciation and understanding of all the techniques to insure efficiency and quality in food preparation.

7.2.1 Temperature Chart

7.2.2 Physical and Chemical Processes

7.2.2.1 The Cooking Process

Cooking generally means conducting heat into the food to change and improve it in terms of palatability, bacteriological content, and taste. If moist heat is used, such as water, the soluble substances in the food are transferred into the fluid, for example, infusing herbs, tea, and coffee. With dry heat, such as the oven, a part of the water evaporates, and the food taste becomes stronger and more concentrated. The cooking process begins at about 140°F. (60°C.). Most bacteria are killed between 140°F. (60°C.) and 150°F. (65°C.), provided that the product is held at this temperature for sufficient time. Most

Basic Information	Basic Cooking Methods	Mise en Place	Basic Preparations: For Foods	Basic Preparations: For Basic Stocks
Types of:	Blanching	*Preparation and Finishing:*	Ingredients and Additives	— white
— preparation	Poaching	Hot Dishes	Marinades	— brown
— cutting	Boiling	Cold Dishes	Meat Jellies	— game
— dressing	Steaming	Pastry	Breadings	— poultry
— carving	Deep-fat Frying		Stuffings	— fish
— preserving	Sauteing		Ingredients for	— vegetable
Temperature	Grilling (broiling)		— stocks	
Methods of Roasting	Gratinating		— sauces	
Quantities	Baking		— soups	
	Roasting		Seasoned Butters	
	Braising		*For Desserts:*	
	Glazing		Dough	
	Poeler		Mixtures	
	Stewing		Creams	
			Sauces	

↓

Basic Elements of Dishes and Their Garnishes	
Sauces	Salads
Soups	Vegetables
Hors d'oeuvres	Potatoes
Egg Dishes	Pasta/Rice
Fish Dishes	Hot Desserts
Entrees	Cold Desserts
Main Dishes	Frozen Desserts

↓

Basic Elements of Meals
Menus
Menus for the Day
Restaurant Menus

FIGURE 7-1
Methodological Structure of Cooking Techniques

TABLE 7-1 Physical-Chemical Kitchen Thermometer

	+580°F. (304.5°C.)	
	545°F. (285°C.) to 580°F. (304.5°C.)	Broiler heat (gratinating)
	490°F. (254.5°C.)	High oven heat
	340°F. (171°C.)	Medium oven heat
	320°F. (160°C.) to 475°F. (246°C.)	Sauteing
	320°F. (160°C.) to 355°F. (179°C.)	Deep-fat frying
	300°F. (149°C.) to 490°F. (254.5°C.)	Grilling
	300°F. (149°C.) to 390°F. (199°C.)	Glazing
	285°F. (141°C.) to 490°F. (254.5°C.)	Baking
	285°F. (141°C.) to 390°F. (199°C.)	Braising in oven
	285°F. (141°C.) to 320°F. (160°C.)	Poeler
	265°F. (129.5°C.) to 300°F. (149°C.)	Blanching in oil
	250°F. (121.5°C.) to 285°F. (141°C.)	Stewing/Simmering
	230°F. (110°C.) to 390°F. (190°C.)	Roasting
	230°F. (110°C.)	Low oven heat
	230°F. (110°C.)	Steaming in pressure cooker = 6.5 psi
	212°F. (100°C.)	Blanching in water.
• Water boils at sea level. Increasing altitude = lower air pressure = lower boiling point for water = food requires longer cooking period. • 539 calories required to convert 1 kilogram of water into 1 kilogram of steam	+212°F. (100°C.)	Boiling point
	200°F. (93°C.)	Natural starches gel: potatoes, cereals, rice, flour, arrowroot, tapioca, sago
	195°F. (91°C.)	Starch binding agents lose some of their thickening power
	194°F. (90°C.) to 208°F. (98°C.)	Simmer
	190°F. (88°C.) to 195°F. (91°C.)	Herb tea, coffee infusions
	185°F. (85°C.)	Rinsing temperature for dishwashing machines, killing of bacteria
	175°F. (79°C.) to 185°F. (85°C.)	Internal meat temperature of pork and poultry
	165°F. (74°C.)	Internal meat temperature for "well-done" veal
	160°F. (71°C.)	Regeneration temperature for fast food
	160°F. (71°C.)	Egg yolk coagulates
	160°F. (71°C.)	Internal meat temperature for "well-done" red meat
	150°F. (65°C.)	Starch binding agents gel
	150°F. (65°C.) to 190°F. (90°C.)	Poaching
	150°F. (65°C.)	White of egg coagulates
	140°F. (60°C.) to 150°F. (65°C.)	Killing of pathogenic agents after a certain period of time (pasteurizing)

TABLE 7-1 Physical-Chemical Kitchen Thermometer, continued

	140°F. (60°C.)	Internal meat temperature of large beef roasts for "medium"
	120°F. (49°C.)	Eating temperature for most hot dishes
	120°F. (49°C.)	Internal meat temperature of large beef roasts for "rare"
	100°F. (38°C.)	Internal meat temperature of large beef roasts for "bleu'
	50°F. (10°C.) to 120°F. (49°C.)	With moisture, bacteria develop best
	45°F. (7°C.) to 48°F. (9°C.)	Optimal storage temperature for potatoes
	39°F. (4°C.) to 43°F. (6°C.)	Optimal storage temperature for vegetables and fruits
	37°F. (3°C.) to 41°F. (5°C.)	Optimal storage temperature for boiled products
• freezing point for water. 79.7 calories are required to convert 1 kilogram of ice into 1 kilogram of water. 1 calorie = the amount of heat required to raise 1 cubic centimeter of water 33.8°F. (1°C.)	32°F. (0°C.)	
	32°F. (0°C.) to 37°F. (3°C.)	Optimal storage temperature for meat, fish, and milk products
	0°F. (−18°C.) to −8°F. (−22°C.)	Optimal storage temperature for frozen products
	−40°F. (−40°C.) to −76°F. (−60°C.)	Optimal temperature for shock-freezing
• Absolute zero = no further movement of molecules	-459°F. (−272°C.)	

proteins (simple proteins) alter their characteristics or lose moisture from about 145°F. (63°C.). Coagulation takes place between 165°F. (74°C.) and 175°F. (80°C.). This means that at about 175°F. (80°C.) the collagen in meat is transformed into gelatin. By softening the collagen, the meat becomes most tender and more easily digestible. Proper cooking will also destroy pathogenic organisms and make meat safer for consumption. Foods cooked at higher temperatures, such as in a pressure steamer, will require a shorter cooking time.

The air pressure at sea level is about 29.9 inches, and decreases with increasing height. Water also evaporates at a lower temperature above sea level and, therefore, a longer cooking time is necessary.

Microwave ovens are suitable for heating precooked or frozen foods. Most cooked foods can be reheated without dehydration or loss of flavor. Porous foods, such as rare roast beef, will have greater cooking losses and become dry and tough when cooked by microwave.

Results of excessive cooking:

- the proteins (simple proteins) toughen; food is less palatable and less digestible.
- several nutrients are partially or totally destroyed (vitamins C, B_1, B_{12}), see "Vitamins" page 173.
- the structure of some foods is reduced to a porridge-like mass.
- taste and aroma are partially or totally destroyed.
- chlorophyll (the green in leaves) and other natural

coloring substances sometimes undergo major color changes.

- sugar and other substances burn or caramelize and acquire a bitter taste.
- the moisture and fat content are reduced excessively, resulting in dry, tasteless products.
- excessive shrinkage occurs.

Boiling Potatoes. These should be covered with water and brought to the boiling point immediately. When tender, the potatoes should be drained thoroughly. If they are left too long in hot water, the starch jells on the surface and forms a hard, insulating layer that prevents the inside from becoming soft.

Boiling Sweet Rice Dishes. Since sugar turns into a syrup-like solution at high temperatures, it thickens the solution. When boiling rice or semolina dishes, the sugar should be added at the end of the cooking process. Otherwise, the sugar inhibits the hydration, or absorption of water, and the grains of rice or semolina neither swell properly nor become soft.

7.2.2.2 The Poaching Process

The poaching process is a method of moist heat cookery. Foods are immersed in liquid that is between 150°F. (65°C.) and 195°F. (90°C.). The temperature is maintained throughout the cooking period. The liquid barely bubbles, and the bubbles do not break the surface of the water.

Cooking Stocks. The basic stocks are obtained by immersing meat, poultry, or fish bones in water and heating in an uncovered container to the boiling point. The heat is immediately reduced so that the liquid barely simmers. To retain clarity and nutritive value, stocks should never be boiled. High temperatures may cause cloudiness. Stock may be clarified in two ways:

- clarifying with ice: the opaque substances clump together and precipitate to the bottom of the container.
- clarifying with egg white: one slightly beaten egg white, a crumpled egg shell, and some ice water are mixed together for each quart of stock. The mixture is stirred into the stock and it is heated very slowly. The heavy foam that accumulates is pushed to one side and the stock is simmered (never boiled) for 10 to 15 minutes. The stock is removed from the heat and after standing for one hour, it is strained through a cloth.

7.2.2.3 Gelatinization Process with Starch

Most starches are derived from cereal grains or roots. Starches are important in food preparation, and because of their different characteristics, they differ in their thickening power, clarity, and viscosity. When combined with liquid and heat, the cellulose softens and the starch granules begin to swell and absorb the liquid. This process is called gelatinization. When heated, the mixture thickens. Natural cereal, potato, sago, tapioca, and arrowroot starch begin to gelantinize or swell at 150°F. (65°C.). The first stage of binding or thickening begins at 160°F. (70°C.). At this temperature only part of the starch grains is broken and the texture of the mass is still quite grainy. Unless the starch is cooked longer, it may have a raw taste. Certain starches, such as waxy maize, reach maximum thickness at about 160°F. (70°C.). If this starch is heated above 200°F. (93°C.), the starch granules of the mixture will rupture, and the mixture will become thin.

Starch should be mixed thoroughly with cool or warm liquid before heat is applied. It may also be mixed with fat before dispersing in water. This is called *roux.* For foods with a high sugar content, such as puddings and pie fillings, the starch should be mixed with the sugar before adding to the liquid. Most starch mixtures should be heated to the boiling point and then cooked at a lower temperature to obtain the maximum viscosity and a cooked flavor.

7.2.2.4 The Gelatinization Process with Flour

Flours differ in their thickening power depending on the gluten and starch content. Pastry and cake flours thicken better because they have a higher starch content and less gluten than bread flour. Because of the starch content, flour mixtures must be heated to 200°F. (93°C.). After reaching this temperature, the heat should be reduced and the cooking continued for 20 to 30 minutes to achieve full viscosity and to remove the starch taste.

7.2.2.5 The Process of Boiling and Evaporating

Boiling, in its technical sense, refers to the conversion of liquid to gas at the *initial boiling point* of a liquid; for example, water boils when the bubbles break on its surface. Evaporation is the conversion of liquid to gas *below the initial boiling point*, for example, a street drying off in the winter after rain has fallen.

What the eye sees as steam is not vapor, but finely distributed water droplets or fog. Energy is necessary to produce vapor pressure and is measured in calories. A large *calorie* corresponds to the amount of energy needed to increase the temperature of 1 kilogram of water at 59°F. (15°C.) by 34°F. (1°C.). The greater the pressure, the higher the temperature at which the vapor forms. At a vapor pressure of 6.5 psi, required for a high-pressure steamer, the initial boiling point is 230°F. (110°C.). The higher the temperature the faster the food cooks. It should be remembered that the total mass of food, the size of the food pieces, and the temperature of the food at the onset of the cooking process will all affect the length of cooking time. Food that is to be cooked in a pressure steamer should be of uniform size. See "Heating Methods and Equipment" page 32. As shown on the "kitchen thermometer," almost 80 calories are necessary to convert 1 kilogram of ice into water at 32°F. (0°C.). Steam contains more heat than hot water. Pressure steamers are suitable for thawing and cooking pieces of food that are small enough for the heat to penetrate rapidly and evenly. If the pieces are too large, the exterior may be overcooked before the heat penetrates the inside of the food.

Freeze-drying. As air pressure is lowered, the boiling point of liquid drops. (At the top of a high mountain, water boils at a lower temperature than at sea level.) In a vacuum, therefore zero air pressure, water boils at a temperature below the normal freezing point (32°F.) (0°C.).

Freeze-drying is a process where prefrozen food is put into a vacuum chamber and heated. The ice crystals of the food boil immediately and are converted to steam. The steam must be removed as rapidly as it is formed. The food dries and is vacuum packed.

The Rising of Dough. The substance that causes a dough to rise is called a *leaven*. Dough is leavened by the formation of steam in the dough or the formation of gas in the dough. Water expands 1600 times its original volume when converted to steam. The ratio of water to flour in the dough will determine the extent of leavening that is possible with steam.

The process involving baking powder and yeast is one of fermentation. The volume increase caused by fermentation is far lower, however, than that induced by the water converting into steam. When slightly heated, the fermentation agents create carbon dioxide gas. If the temperature exceeds 140°F. (60°C.), the fermentation process stops, and any further rising of the dough is due to the production of steam from the remaining water. For this reason, dry dough will not rise properly even if large amounts of baking powder and yeast are added.

The Rising of Puff Paste. As can be seen from the diagrams on page 514, properly made puff paste is folded. There is always a layer of margarine or butter between the layers of paste. There are often hundreds of layers. These layers should never be damaged by improper handling; since butter and margarine contain 16 percent water, the water is converted to steam during baking. A steam cushion develops between each layer and causes the pastry to rise. This is the reason a product, such as vol-au-vents, rises to two or three inches with hundreds of thin, tender, and crisp layers.

The Beating of Egg Whites. Stored or older eggs have greater ability and are better for beating than fresh eggs. The egg whites become thicker during storage, and the foaming ability and stability increase with age. Unless eggs are at least three days old, they cannot be whipped to maximum volume. The egg foam should be folded into the mixture immediately after whipping. If allowed to stand or if improperly stirred, the air bubbles created by beating will burst again. These little bubbles, like miniature balloons, are filled with air. When heated in the oven, steam is created in each balloon which then expands. This is the reason a dish containing beaten egg whites rises during baking. If the heat is reduced on a souffle, or it is suddenly chilled, the steam in the little balloons condenses, the balloons shrink, and the entire mass collapses.

7.2.2.6 The Roasting Process

The basic principles of roasting are fully described in section 7.7. From a chemical and bacteriological standpoint, the following aspects are very important:

Salt should be added after roasting has begun and browning is completed. Salt is hygroscopic; that is, it absorbs water. The water in the meat is attracted to the surface and delays browning.

Meat is tenderized for roasting and braising in two ways: by mechanically destroying the cell fibers (elastin) with sharply pointed wooden meat mallets or special machines (tenderizers); by chemically altering the collagen (the basic substance forming the connective tissues). Collagen can be changed into gelatin either by moist heat, marinating in an acid solution, or by adding a chemical tenderizer. This occurs, for instance, when braising pigs' feet; after cooking, the stock has a very high gelatin content. The chemical tenderizers contain certain enzymes that break down the connective tissue. The basic substance, however, is usually papain, which comes from the papaya fruit. (See also "Foods" page 135.) In tropical countries, where this fruit is abundant, meat is often marinated with fresh papaya juice. The recommended quantity of chemical tenderizer should not be exceeded.

7.2.2.7 The Frying Process

The frying process as discussed here refers to the deep-fat frying method of cooking. This process is used extensively in large foodservice establishments because of the ease and speed of preparation. The food is immersed in fat in deep-fryers that are heated with gas or electricity and thermostatically controlled.

Edible fats and oils with a high smoke point (heat resistant) are used since they can be heated to nearly 475°F. (245°C.) without breaking down. When deep-fat frying, the high temperature of the fat converts the water content of the food into steam. A good quality fat will have large white bubbles on its surface which break rapidly during the frying process. Fats with a high percentage of free fatty acids have a low smoke temperature. Foods fried in fat with a low smoke temperature will absorb more fat than if fried in fat with a high smoke temperature. Hydrogenated vegetable fats and vegetable oils are lower in free fatty acids and have a higher smoke temperature than do butter, animal fats, and olive oil. Vegetable fats are, therefore, generally used for frying.

Fats are high in cost and should be kept in good condition. Recommended cooking temperatures and times should be followed. After the frying is completed, the heat should be reduced to 200°F. (93°C.). Suggested temperatures for deep-fat frying are given on page 268. The temperature and time will vary depending on the type of equipment, the quantity of food in the fryer, and the size of the pieces of food.

Decomposition of fat, due to excessive heating, produces undesirable flavors and indigestible substances. A white smoke known as acrolein forms as the fat breaks down. Excessive foaming and smoking of the fat and deterioration of flavor in fried foods indicate the presence of a high free fatty acid content. When this occurs, the fat should be discarded. The following practices are necessary to preserve the frying life of the fat:

- Avoid salting foods over the fryer or griddle as salt will break down the fat.
- Replace fat lost during frying process with fresh fat.
- Keep equipment clean. Sediment in the fat or on the equipment can break down the fat.
- Avoid adding fresh oil to rancid oil.

TABLE 7-2 Effect of the pH Value on Food

Acids	*pH Value*	
Very high	0	
	1	Hydrochloric acid
	2	Lemons
		Vinegar
High	3	Rhubarb
		Grapefruit
	4	Oranges
Medium		Cherries
	5	Bananas, asparagus, spinach, potatoes, coffee
Low	6	Many vegetables, butter, milk, salmon, meat
Neutral	7	Pure water
	8	Ripe olives, egg white, hard water
	9	
	10	
	11	
	12	
	13	
Alkalis	14	Caustic soda

- Avoid use of steel wool on thermostats.
- Avoid use of metal tools, and repair any exposed iron on the equipment. Metals cause a breakdown of the fat.
- Dry the food before immersing in fat.
- Store fats in a dark, dry, cool area. Rancidity develops on exposure to air or light.

Young potatoes contain little starch and they are usually moist and good for salads, steamed or creamed potatoes. Older, dry potatoes have a higher specific gravity and they are low in sugar and high in starch. These are good for baking, whipping, or deep-fat frying. The sugar in young potatoes has not converted into starch, and therefore, the potatoes are unsuitable for deep-fat frying. The potatoes will stick together, and form dark stripes on the surface due to caramelization of the sugar.

7.2.2.8 Acidity in Cooking

Acidity is expressed in *p*H. Water is neutral with a *p*H value of 7. The lower the *p*H value, the higher the acid content. The strongest acid is indicated by 0 and the strongest alkali by 14. Since the chlorophyll of green vegetables is destroyed by acidity, it is better retained by cooking vegetables in a small amount of tap water that is usually alkaline or by using a waterless method.

Baking soda should never be added to green vegetables. The alkalinity produced by baking soda destroys some of the B vitamins and the ascorbic acid, and it also has a detrimental effect on the texture and flavor of vegetables.

In order to maintain the white or light color of food, a small amount of acid may be added during the last half of the cooking period. By adding citric acid to mushrooms, the bright white color can be maintained. *Table 7–2 shows that most foods are acidic. The most important point to remember is that foods with low acidity and neutral foods are more susceptible to attack by bacteria than those with a high acid content.*

7.3 Methods of Preparation, Cutting, and Dressing

7.3.1 Fish—Poissons

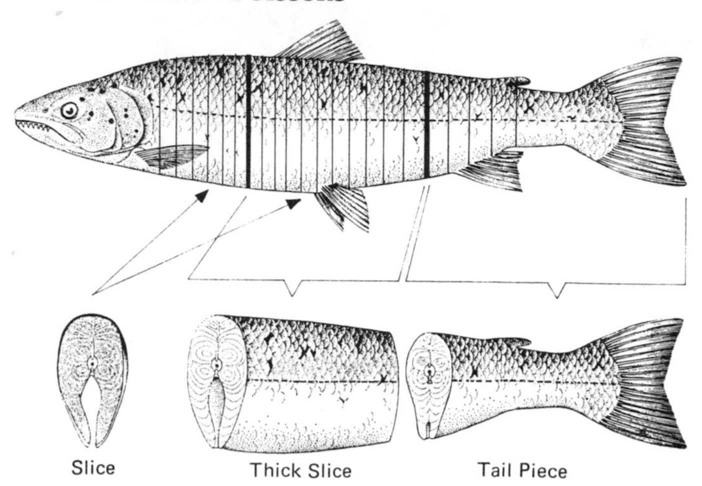

FIGURE 7-2
Salmon — Saumon

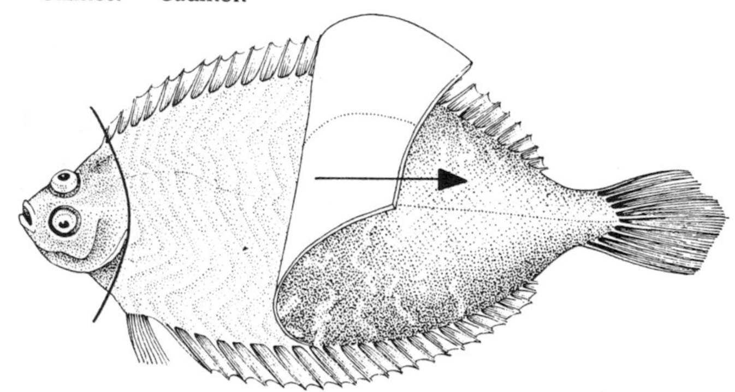

Lemon soles are skinned from head to tail.

FIGURE 7-3
Lemon Sole — Limande

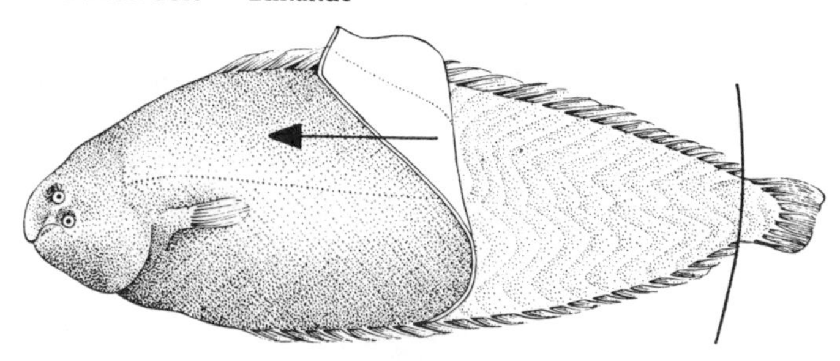

Soles are skinned from the tail to the head.

FIGURE 7-4
Sole

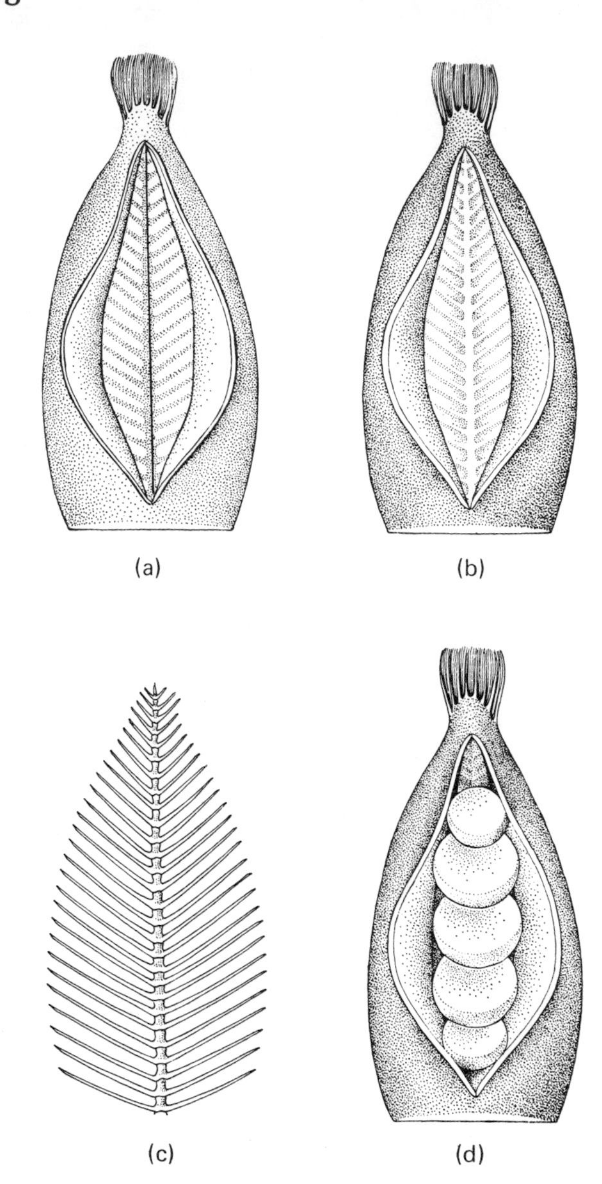

a. Loosening the fillets from the center
b. Deep-fat fried
c. Bones removed after deep-fat frying
d. The sole filled with Colbert butter

FIGURE 7-5
Sole Colbert

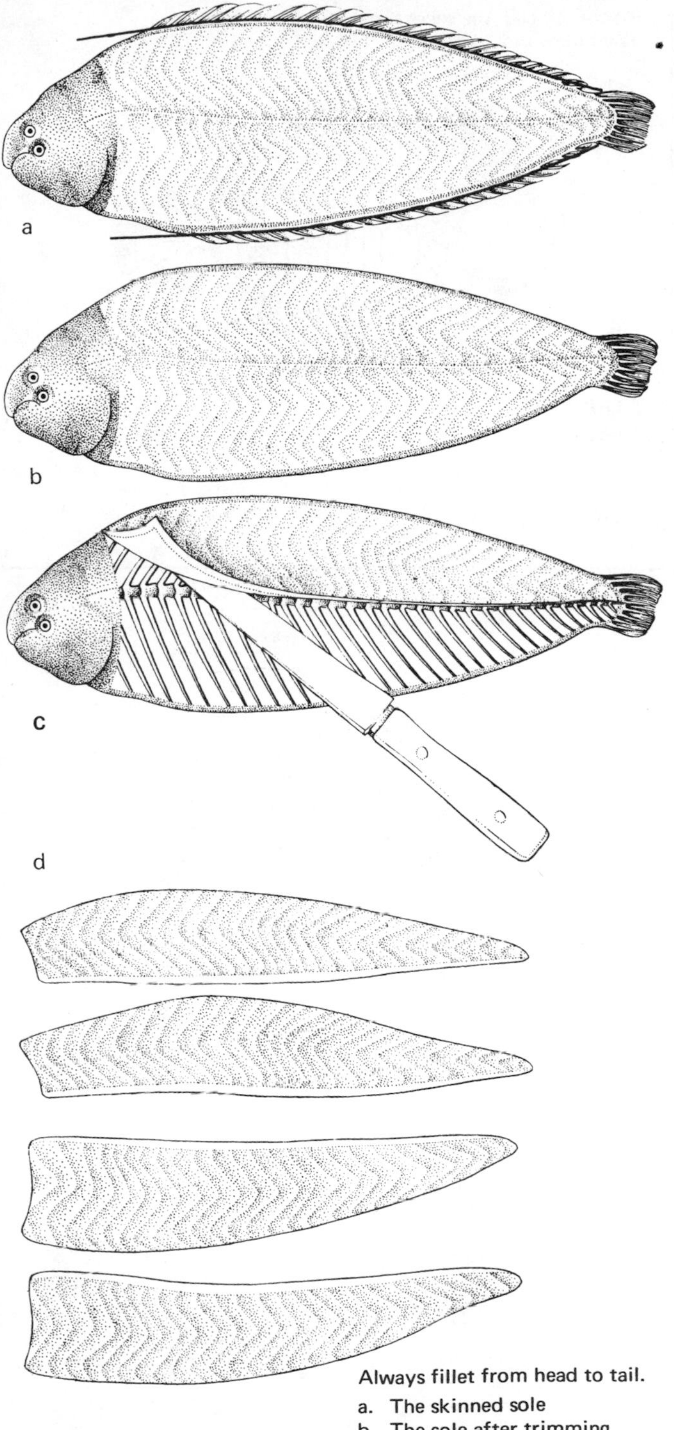

Always fillet from head to tail.

a. The skinned sole
b. The sole after trimming
c. Filleting
d. The four fillets ready for use

FIGURE 7-6
Filleting — Sole

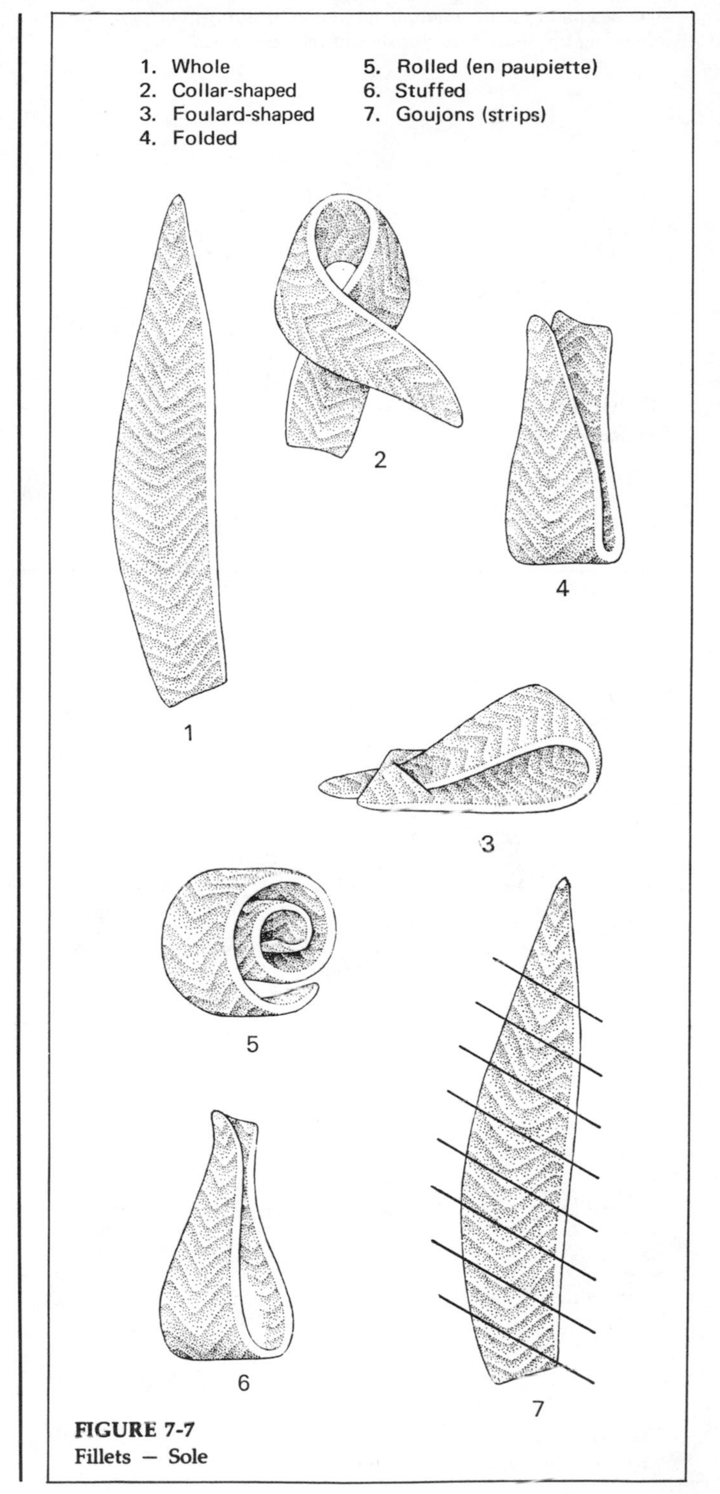

FIGURE 7-7
Fillets — Sole

The head and tail of small plaice should be cut off *without* removing the skin. The fish should then be carved.

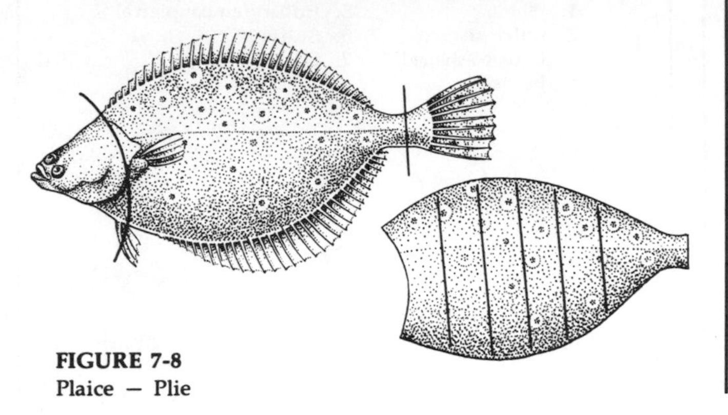

FIGURE 7-8
Plaice — Plie

At the tail end, the slices should be cut thicker. Only raw turbot should be cut in this way.

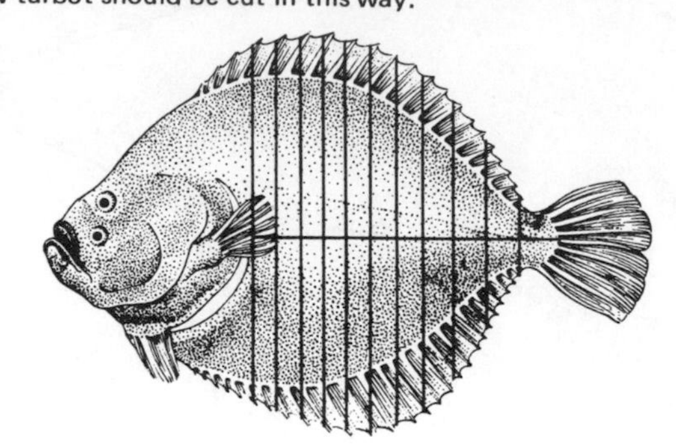

FIGURE 7-9
Turbot

a. Carved whitefish for sauteing
b. Carved trout for sauteing
c. Trout in a ring shape for poaching "bleu"
d. Whiting, English Style

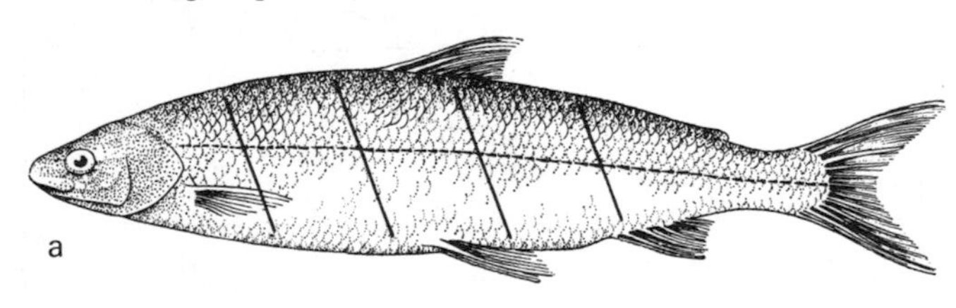

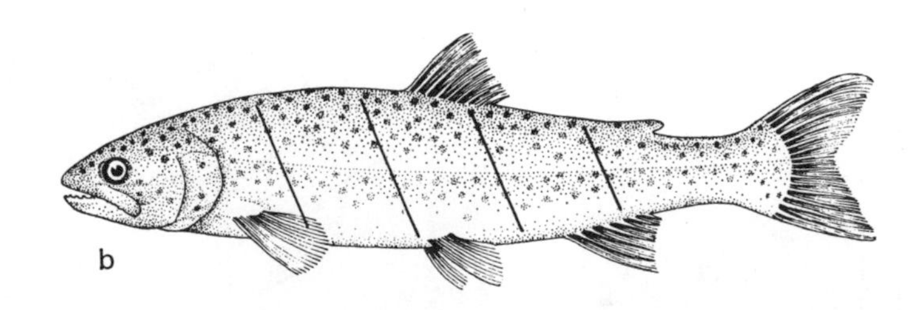

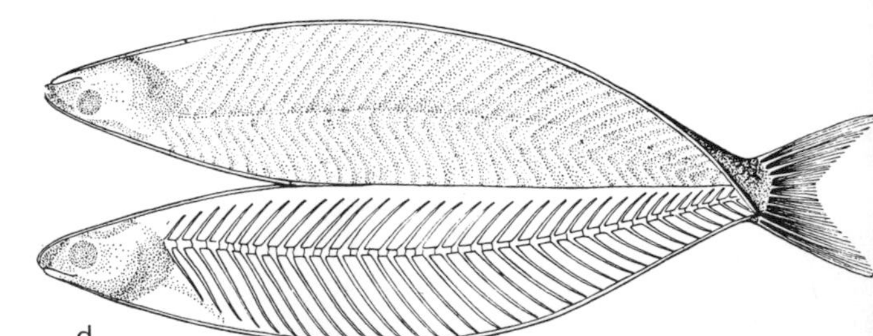

FIGURE 7-10
Various Ways of Preparing Fish

a. Loosen the skin behind the neck fins
b. Remove the skin using a towel

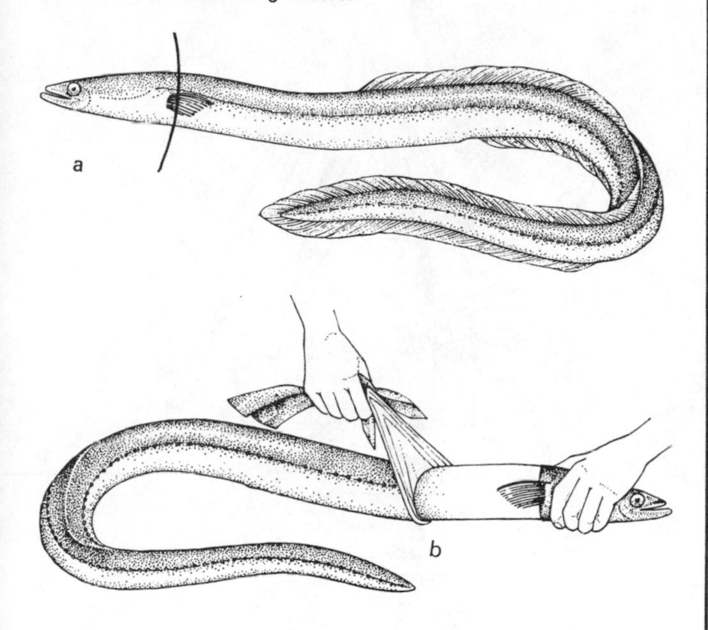

FIGURE 7-11
Eel – Anguille

FIGURE 7-12
Filleting Freshwater Fish

1. Remove the fillets from the head towards the tail
2a. Remove the backbone
2b. The fillet ready for use

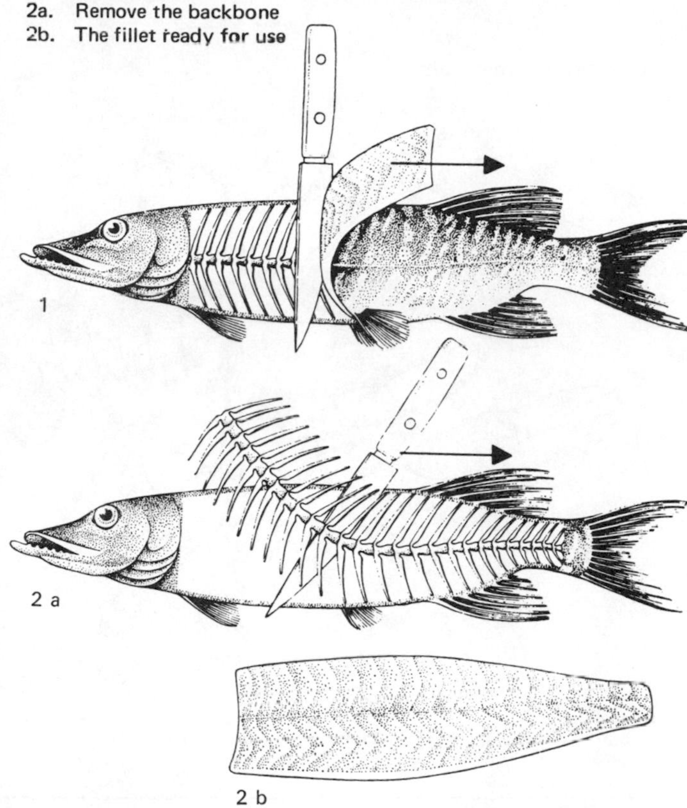

The fillets are skinned working from the tail forwards.

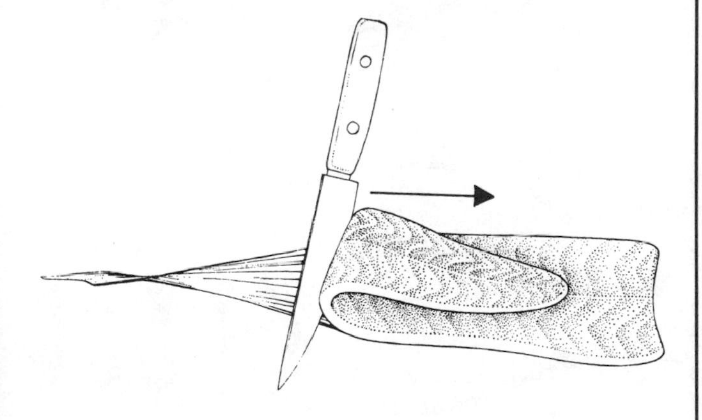

FIGURE 7-13
Skinning Fish Fillets

a. Cutting small fillets
b. Cutting larger fillets

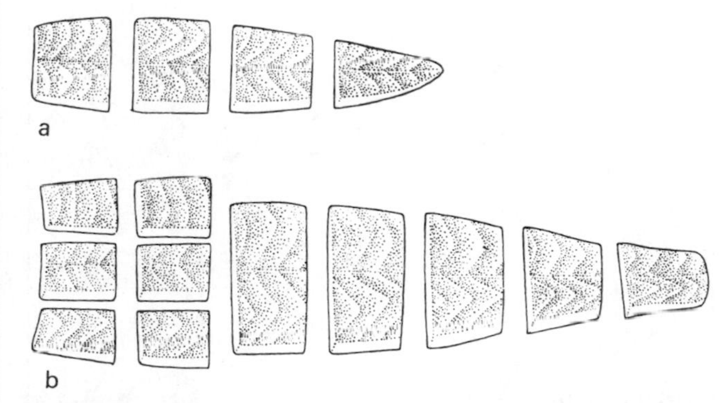

FIGURE 7-14
Cutting Fish Fillets

7.3.2 Crustaceans and Shellfish—Crustaces et coquillages

Homard à.l'américaine

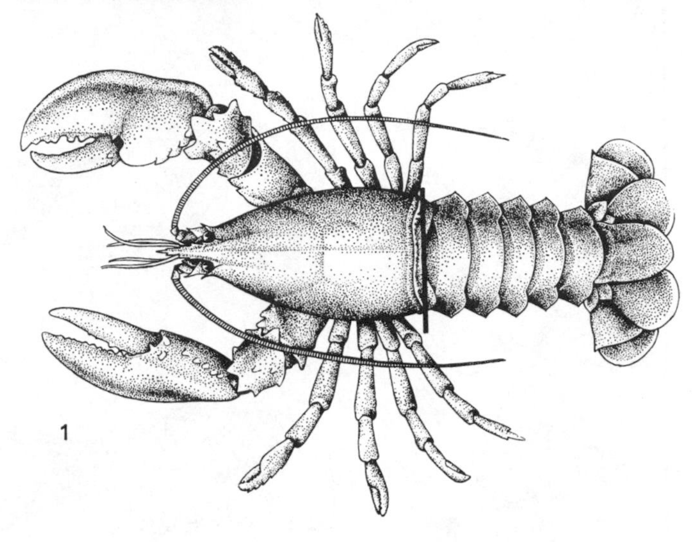

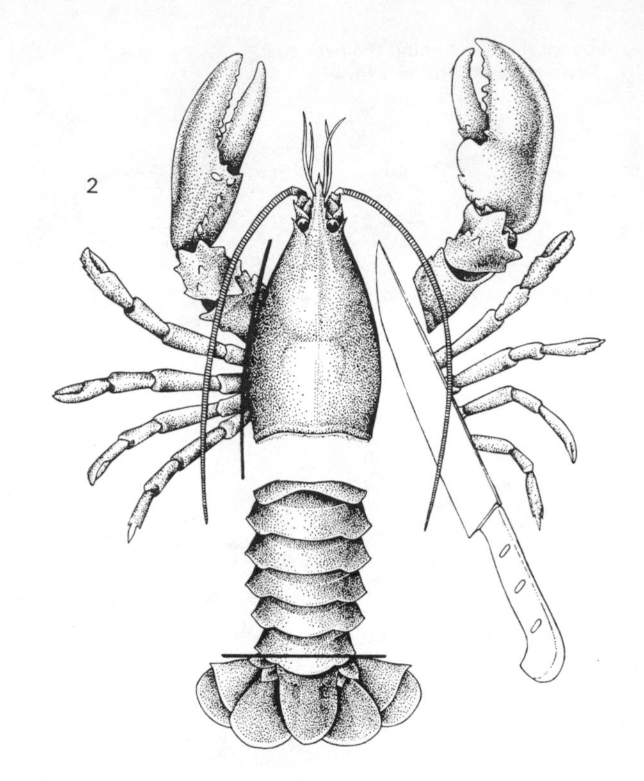

FIGURE 7-15
Lobster, American Style — Homard a l'americaine

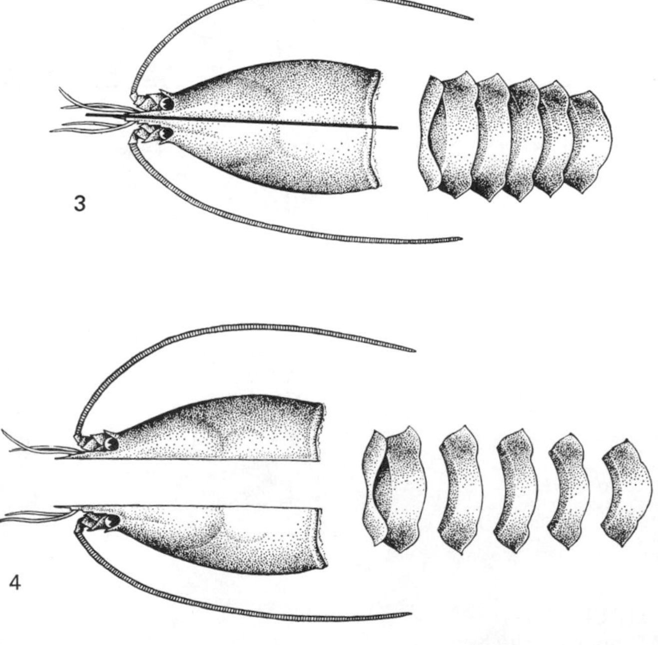

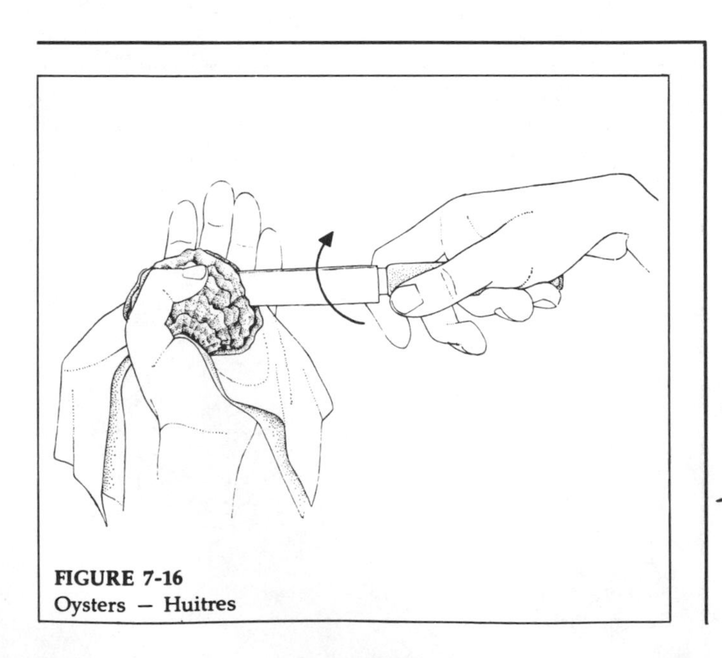

FIGURE 7-16
Oysters — Huitres

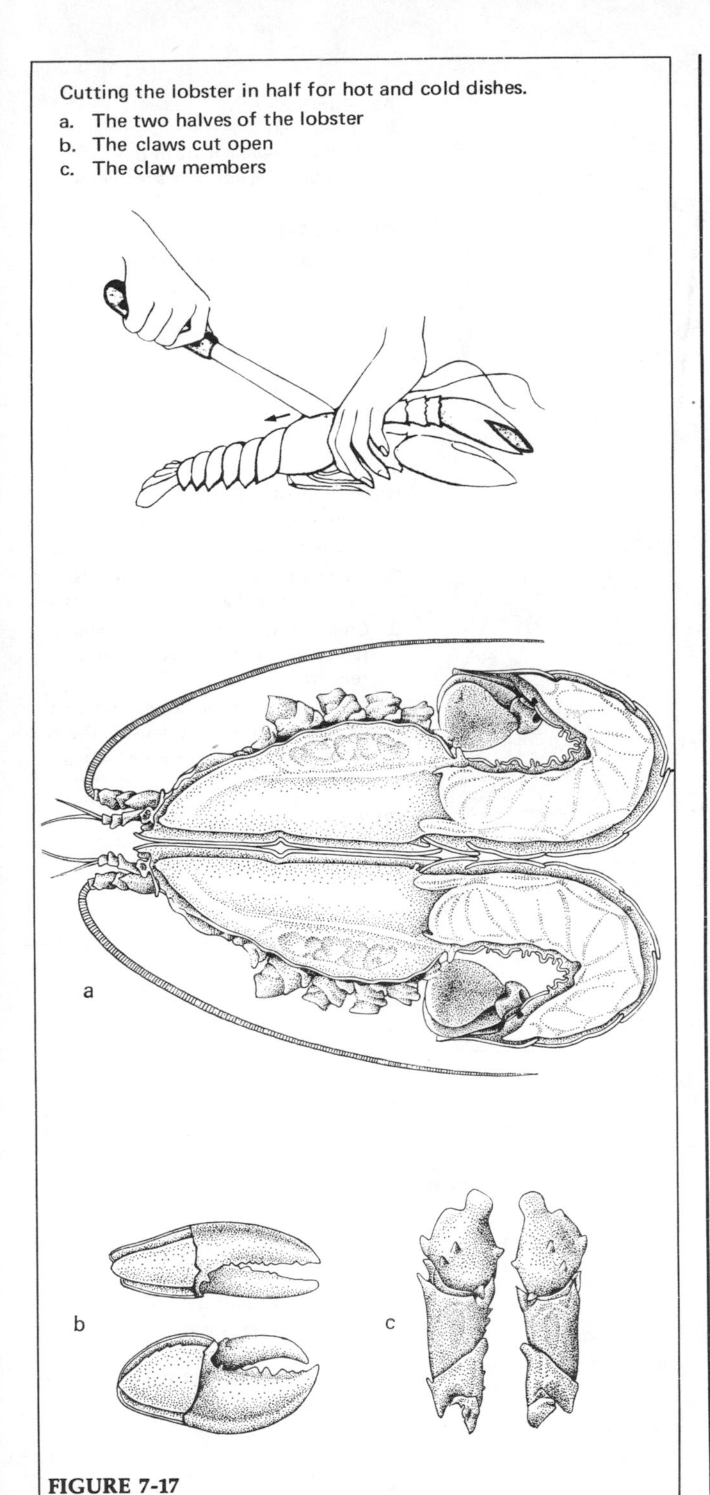

FIGURE 7-17
Lobster — Homard

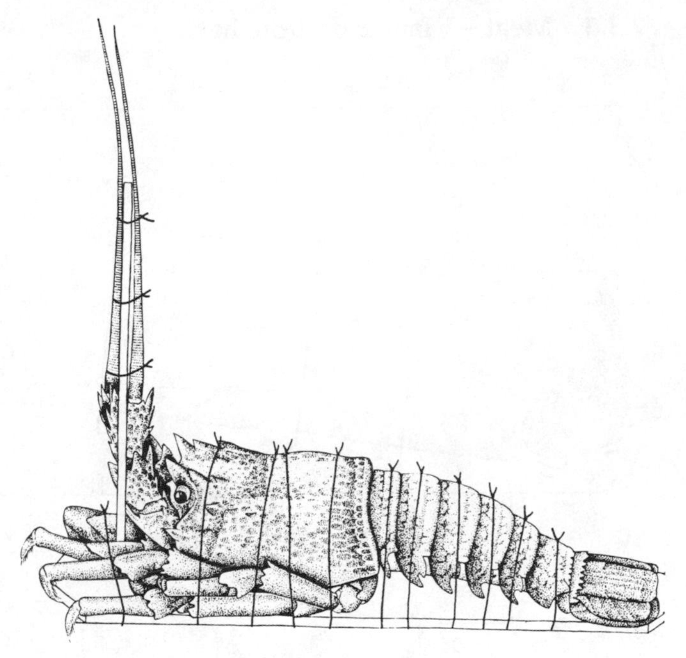

Preparation before cooking. The body is bound horizontally to a board, and the antenna vertically to a stick.

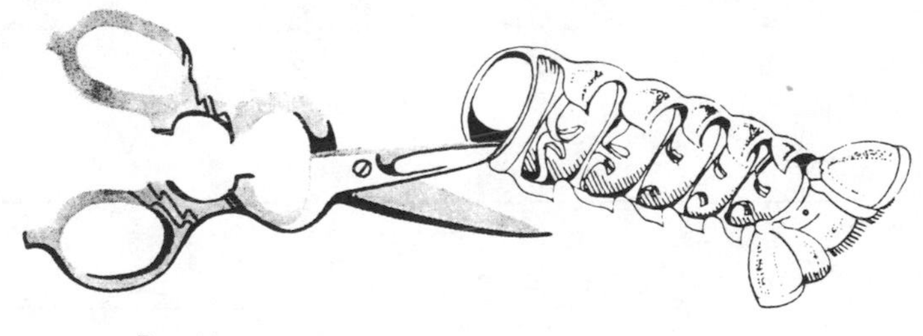

Removing the tail meat

Tail meat without shell

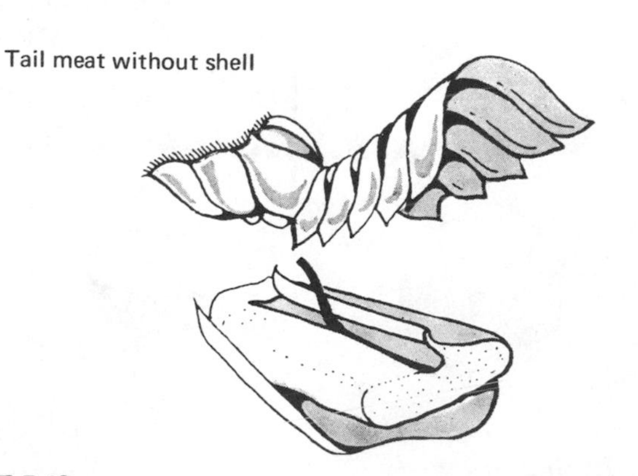

FIGURE 7-18
Rock Lobster (Langouste) — Langouste

7.3.3 Meat—Viande de boucherie

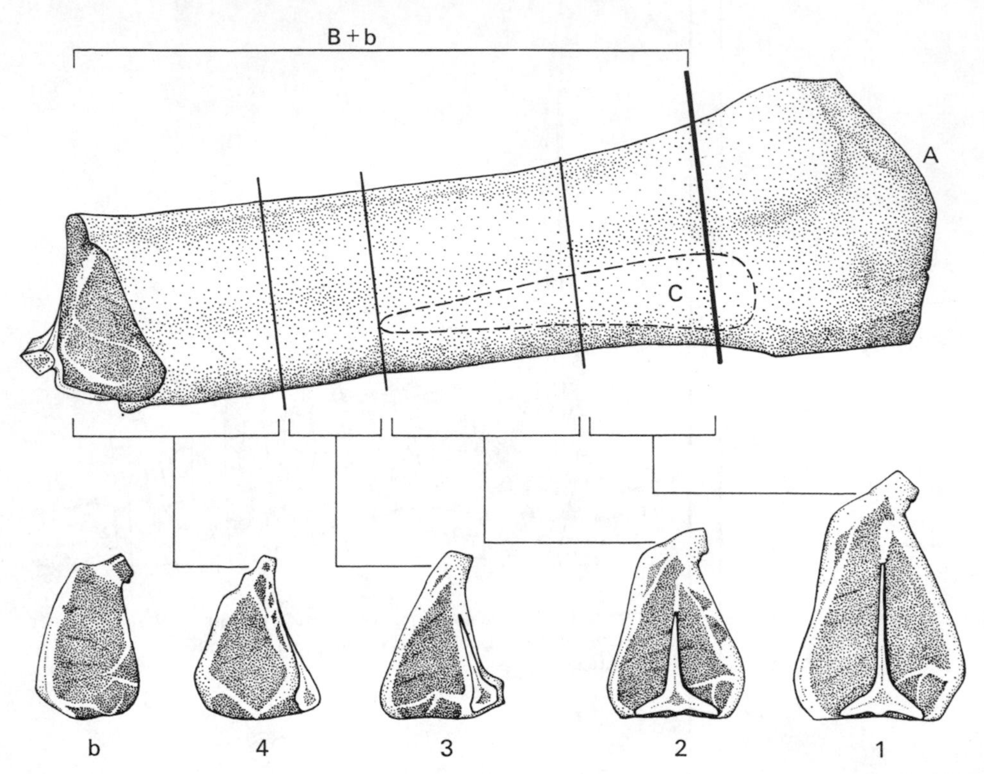

A. **Rump**
B. **Loin,** deboned
b. **Sirloin steak** cut from B
C. **Tenderloin,** for cuts see below

FIGURE 7-19
Sirloin/Strip Loin — Aloyau

The following pieces are cut **across the sirloin** including the bone:

1. **Porterhouse steak,** tenderloin, and sirloin steak cut at the thickest point.
2. **T-bone steak,** cut further forward, and thus smaller than the Porterhouse steak.
3. **Club steak,** cut at the tip of the tenderloin, but not including the tenderloin.
4. **Rib steak** with the bone. Rather than dividing into four rib steaks, the whole piece may be used as a standing rib roast.

FIGURE 7-20
Sirloin Cuts

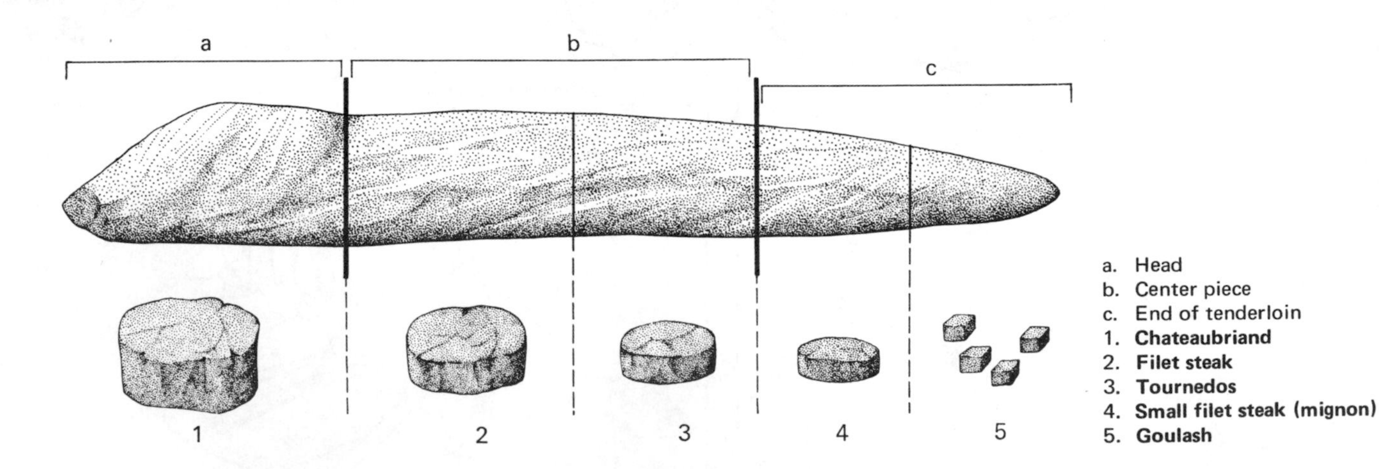

a. Head
b. Center piece
c. End of tenderloin
1. **Chateaubriand**
2. **Filet steak**
3. **Tournedos**
4. **Small filet steak** (**mignon**)
5. **Goulash**

FIGURE 7-21
Beef Tenderloin — Filet de boeuf

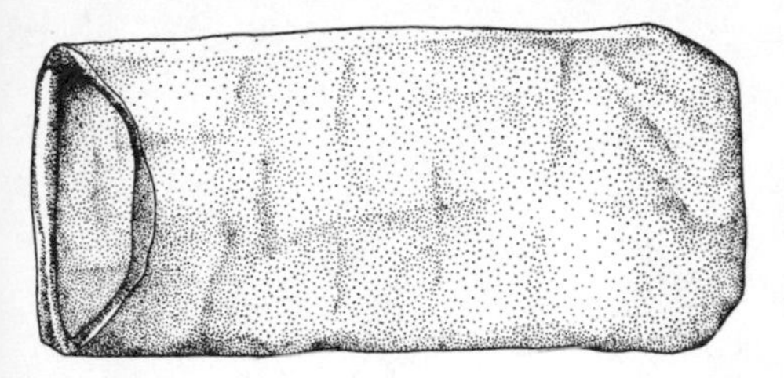

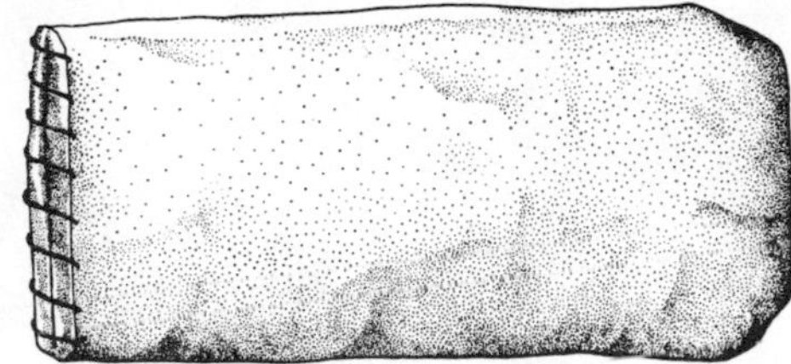

FIGURE 7-22
Stuffed Breast of Veal – Poitrine de veau farcie

1. Open the deboned breast at one end. Continue the opening to the other end.
2. Stuff the breast and sew it closed.

The riblets are cut through across the breast, folded into a U-shape, and the two ends bound together.

FIGURE 7-23
Veal Breast Riblets – Tendrons de veau

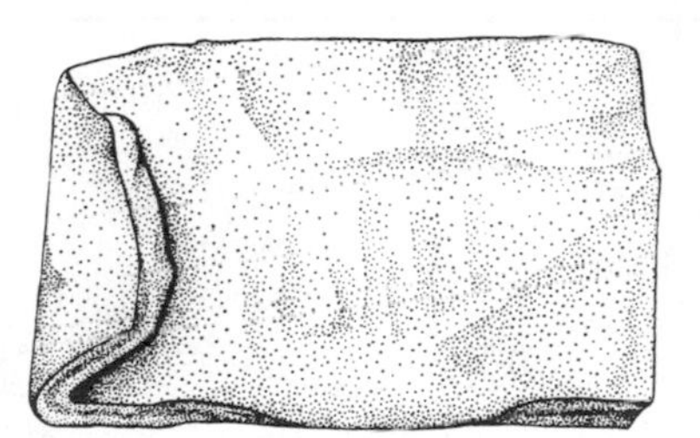

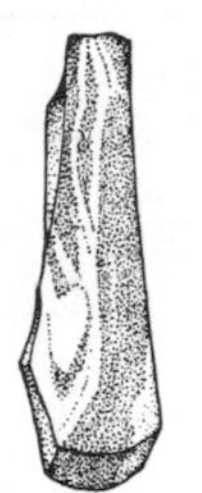

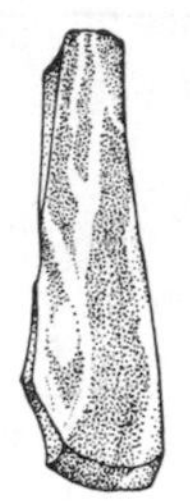

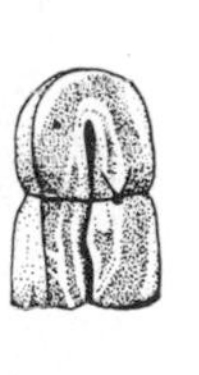

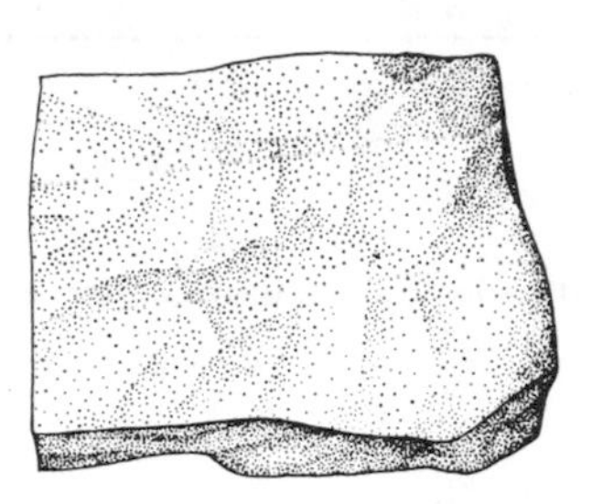

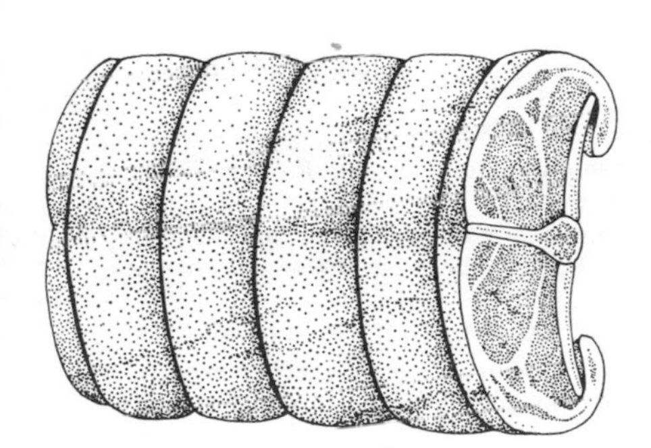

Saddle of lamb is formed by the two loin pieces. The thin ends should be pressed inward and bound.

FIGURE 7-24
Saddle of Lamb – Selle d'agneau

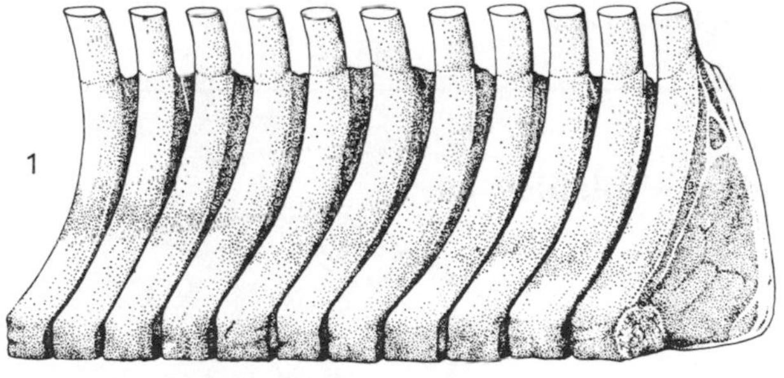

This form of preparation is used for lamb, mutton, and veal, and is very popular in English-speaking countries.

1. Prepare the meat as for roasting. Pare the ribs, uncovering about 3/4 inch of the bone. Cut slightly with the saw between the ribs from the inside of the rack.
2. Shape the whole piece into a crown with the inside facing outward and bind. After roasting, remove the string, and fill the cavity as desired.

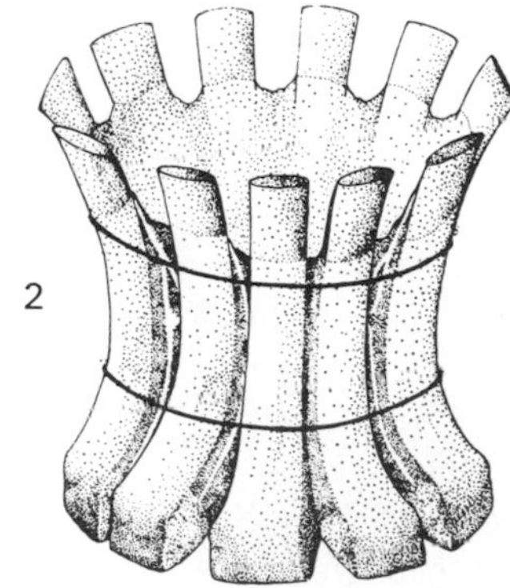

FIGURE 7-25
Lamb Crown Roast – Couronne d'agneau

Breast of lamb is first boiled, then deboned. The meat is cut into pieces, breaded, and pan-fried in butter.

1. Triangular shape
2. Square shape

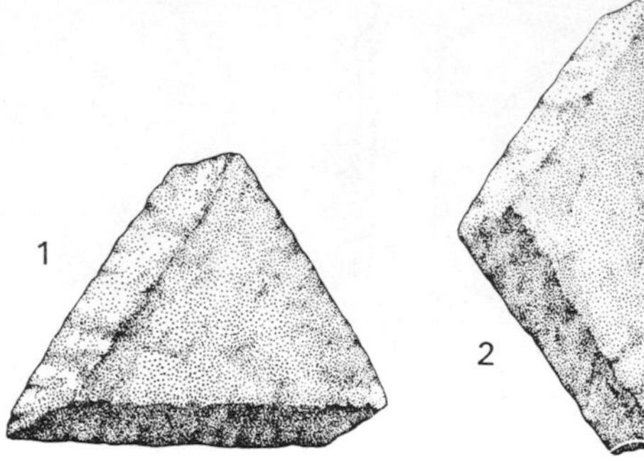

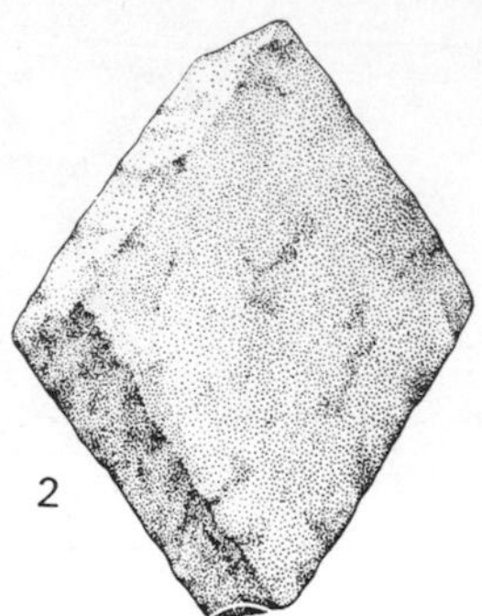

FIGURE 7-26
Lamb Epigrammes — Epigrammes d'agneau

This is used for lamb and mutton (Baron de mouton).

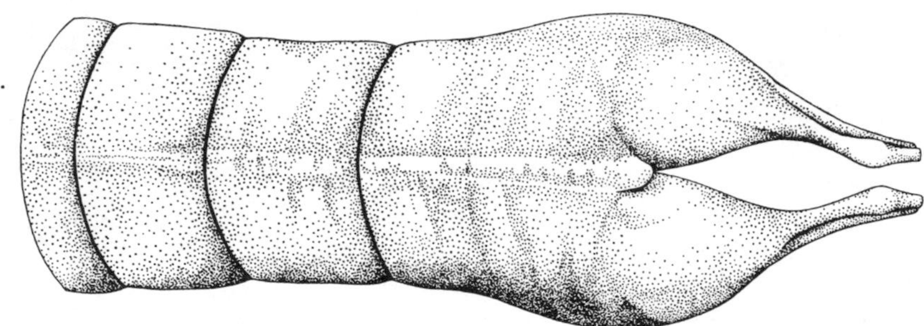

FIGURE 7-27
Baron of Lamb — Baron d'agneau

7.3.4 Poultry—Volaille

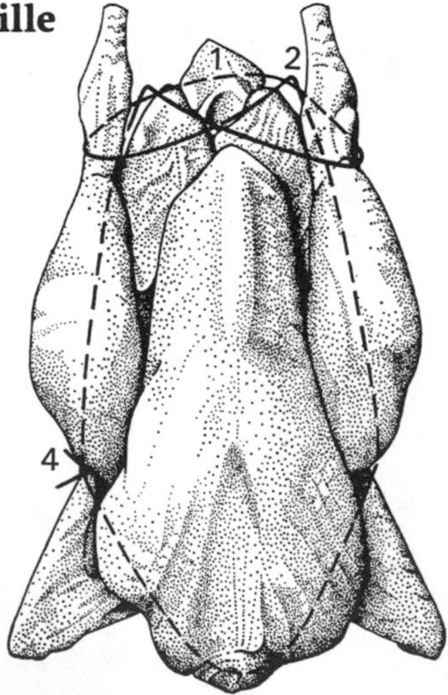

1. The string is passed under the tail end and crossed above the legs.
2. Pass the two crossed ends of the string between the legs. Place the chicken on the left side and draw the string over the left wing.
3. First cover the end of the neck with the breast skin, and then attach the string between the end of the neck and the shoulders.
4. Knot both ends of the string on the right-hand side.

Note: It is possible to begin at 3, but the string cannot be pulled as tight as when one begins at 1.

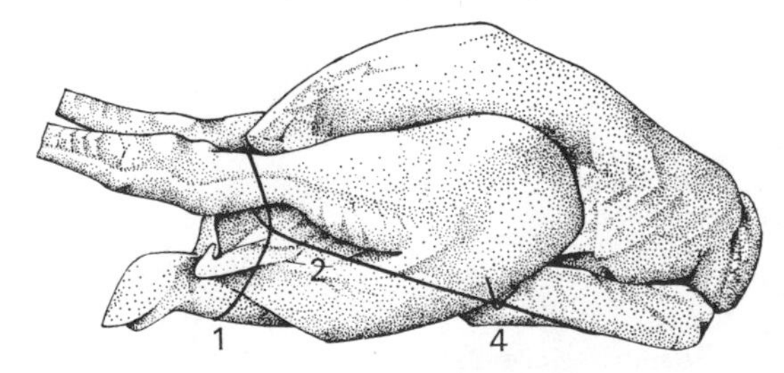

FIGURE 7-28
Trussing by Hand

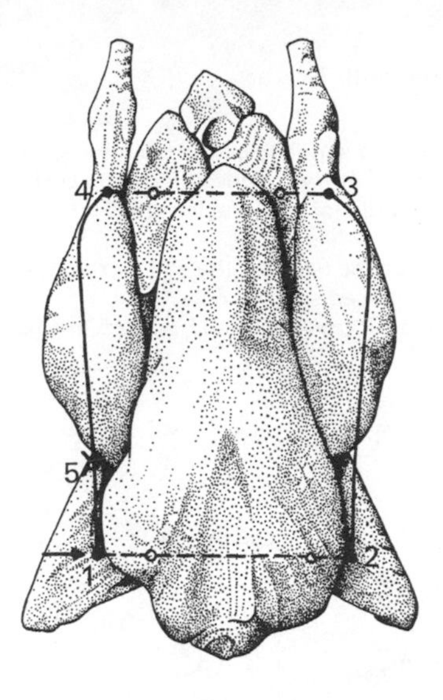

FIGURE 7-29
Trussing with Needle

1. The needle enters through the wing and passes through the breast skin and neck stump.
2. The needle comes out through the other wing.
3. The needle passes through the end of the leg and through the breast.
4. The needle comes out through the end of the other leg.
5. Tie up the two ends.

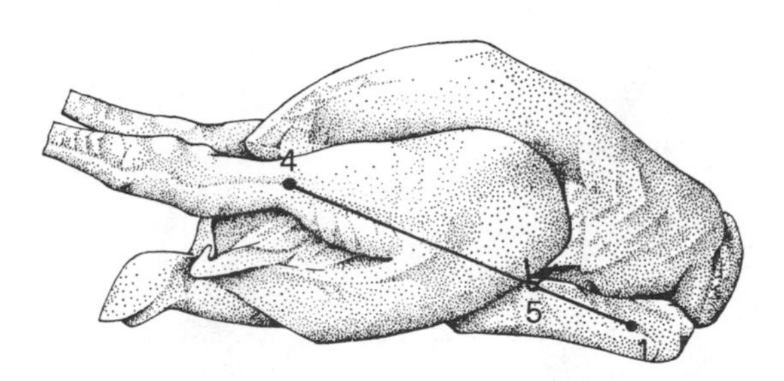

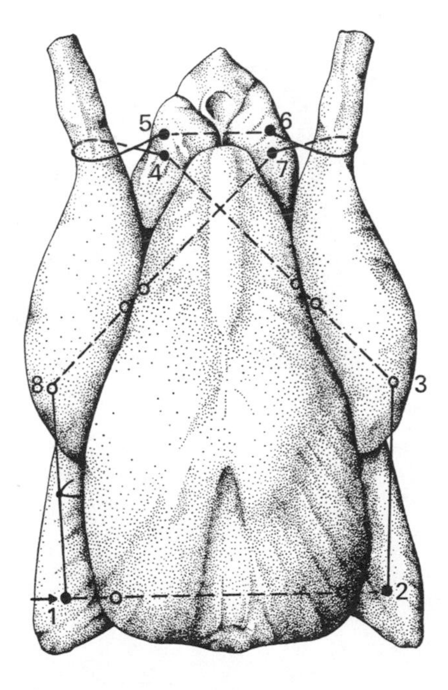

FIGURE 7-30
Crossed Trussing with Needle

1. and 2. Simple trussing.
3. Insert the needle through the middle joint toward 4, and bring it out above the leg.
4. Wind the string around the end of the leg, and insert the needle at point 5, which should be below 4.
5. Pass the needle through the end of the breast to 6.
6. The needle should exit below the end of the leg. Pass the string around the leg and insert the needle at 7, above 6.

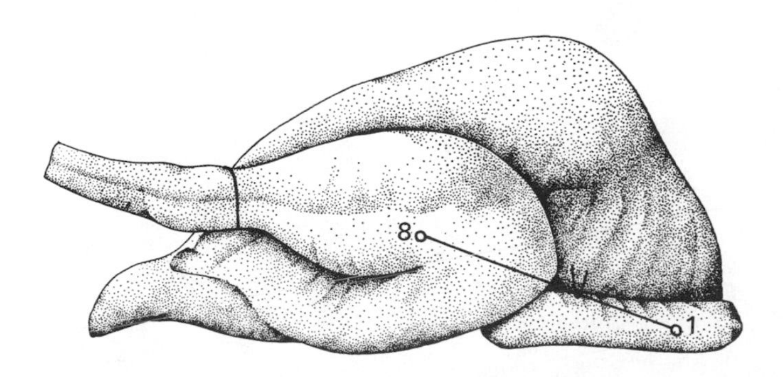

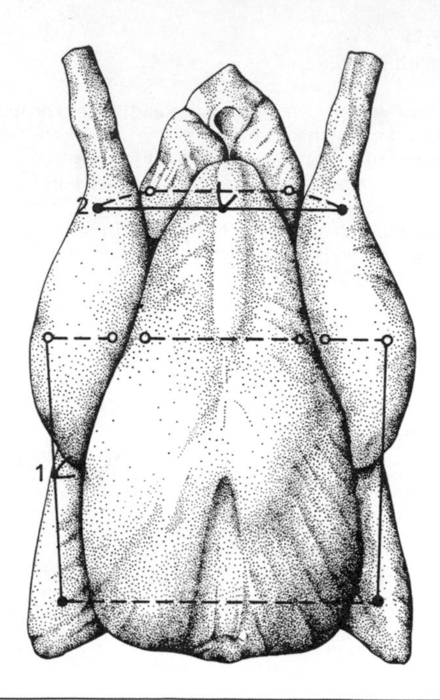

FIGURE 7-31
Double Trussing with Needle

1. First carry out the simple trussing technique, except at the third point of entry, the needle should be inserted through the middle joint of the leg, and not the end of the leg.
2. The two ends of the legs and the end of the breast must then be pierced and bound.

Note: Goose and turkey are usually trussed in this way.

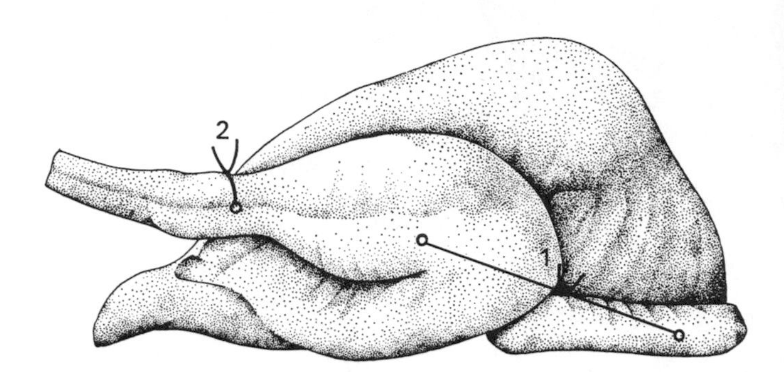

Slit the back of the chicken. Remove the backbone. Remove the legs and cut into two pieces. Separate the wings from the breast, and cut the latter into two halves.

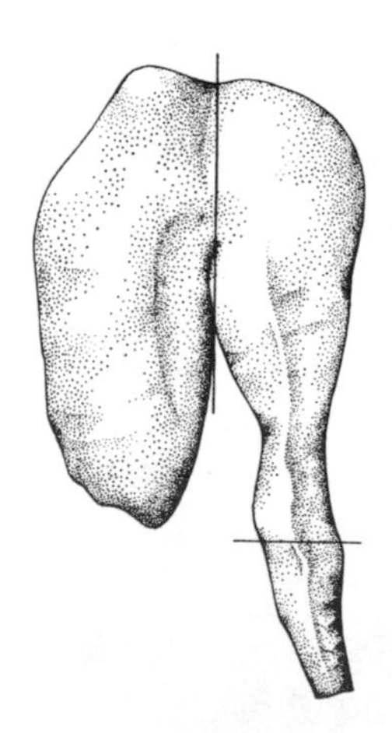

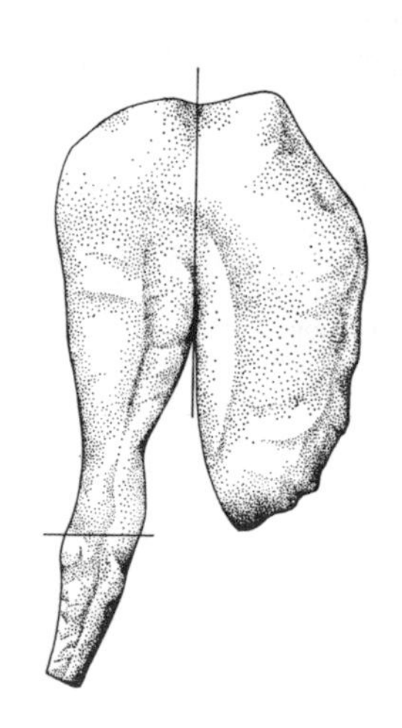

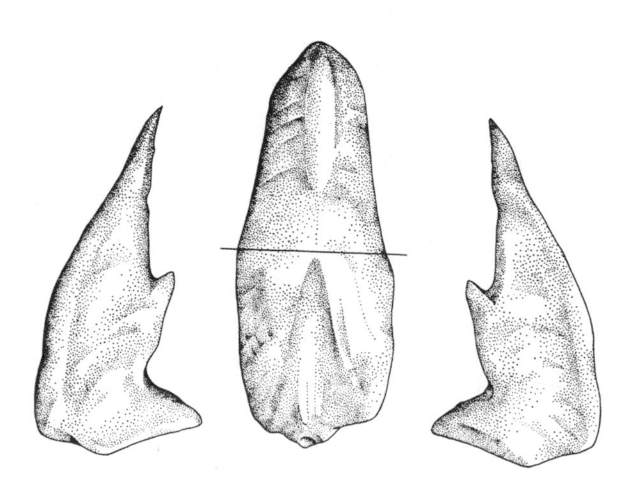

FIGURE 7-32
Cutting a Chicken for Sauteing

Slit the back of the chicken and loosen the whole backbone. Press the chicken flat, and insert the legs through the two holes cut in the skin.

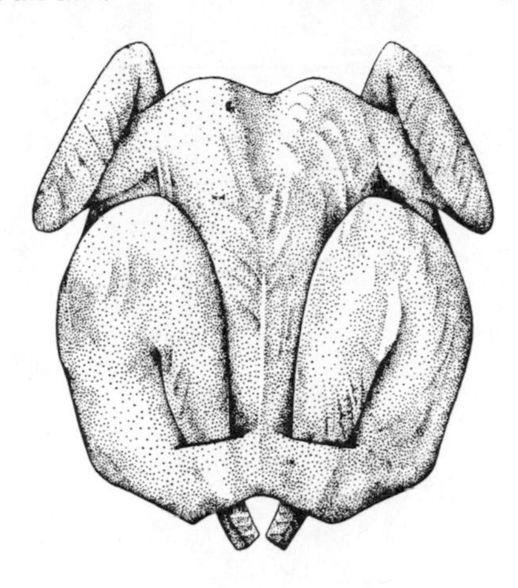

FIGURE 7-33
Preparing a Chicken for Grilling

1. Cut the legs along the back.
2. Pull out the tendons.
3. Cut off the feet and tendons.

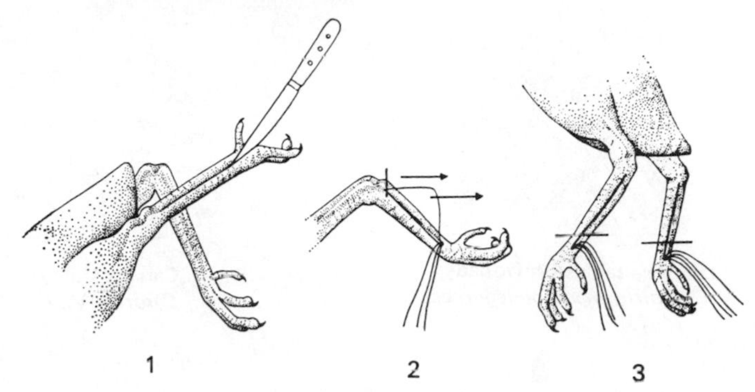

FIGURE 7-34
Removing the Tendons of Turkey

Cut fine slices of unsalted bacon, fat back. Cover the whole breast and bind as shown below.

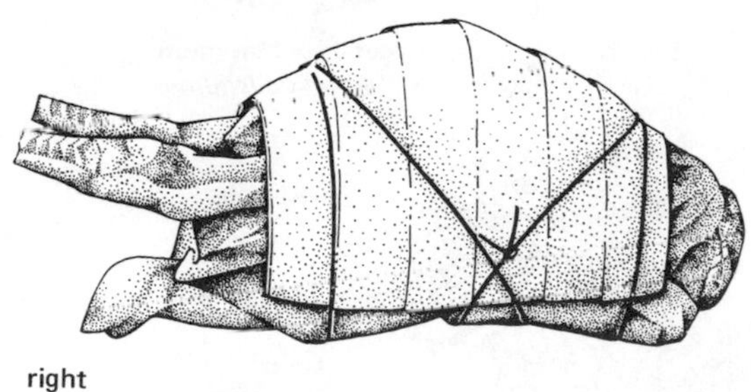

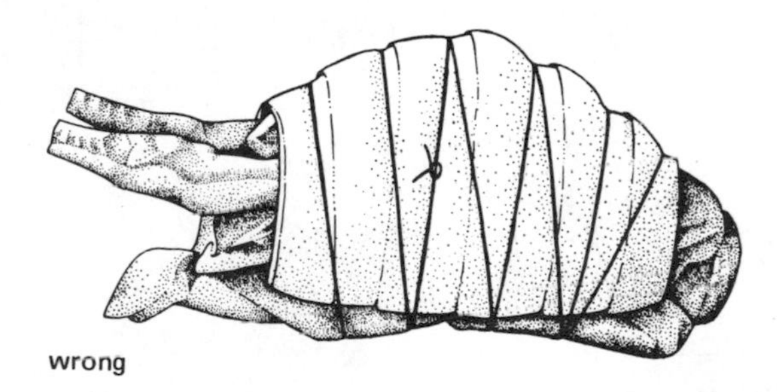

FIGURE 7-35
Barding Poultry and Feathered Game

7.3.5 Vegetables—Legumes

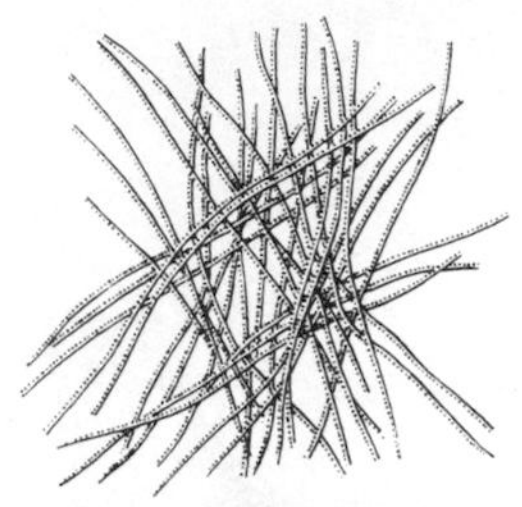

(a) **Vegetables Chiffonade**
Chiffonnade de legumes

(b) **Vegetables Brunoise**
Brunoise de légumes

(c) **Vegetables Jardiniere**
Jardiniere de légumes

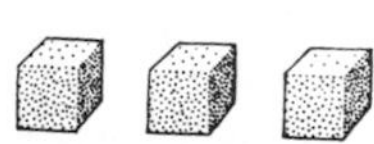

(d) **Macedonian Vegetables**
Macédoine de legumes

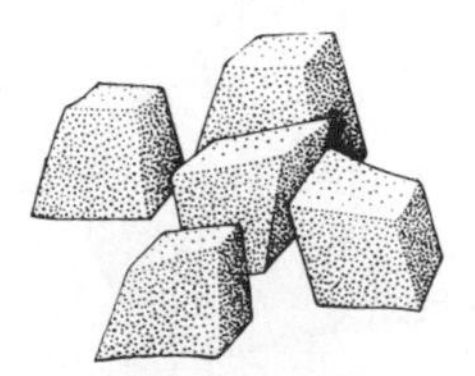

(e) *Mirepoix*

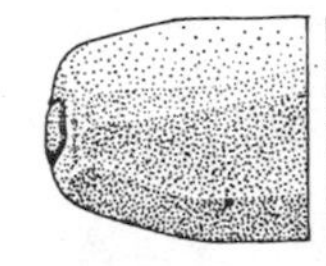

(f) **Carrots Vichy**
Carottes Vichy

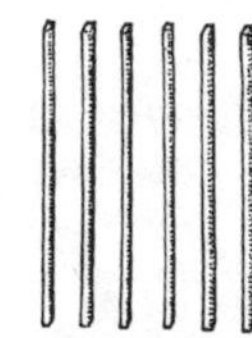

(g) **Vegetables Julienne**
Julienne de legumes

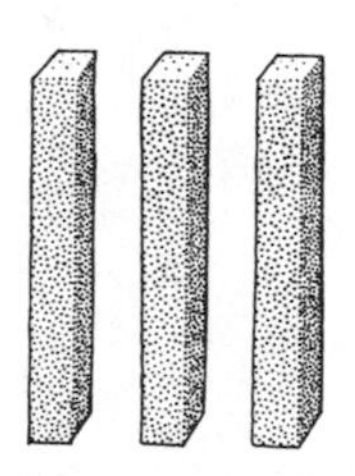

(h) **Vegetable Sticks**
Bâtonnets de legumes

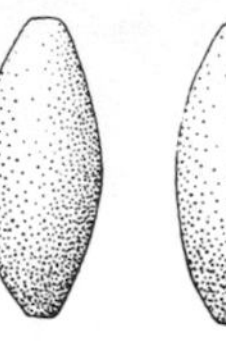

(i) **Spring and Garden Vegetables**
Printaniere et Jardiniere

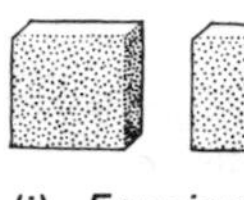

(j) *Fermiere, Minestrone*
Paysanne, croute au pot

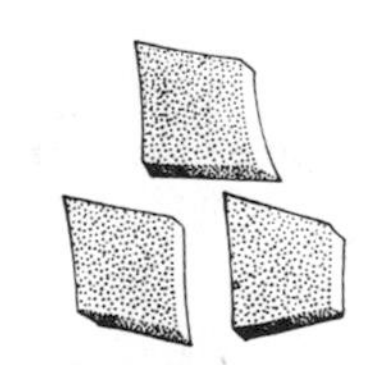

(k) **Vegetables Matignon**
Matignon de legumes

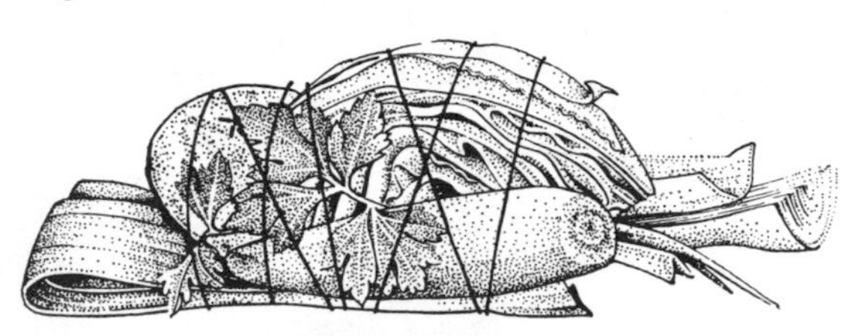

(l) **Bouquet garni**

FIGURE 7-36
Vegetables — Legumes

7.3.6 Potatoes—Pommes de terre

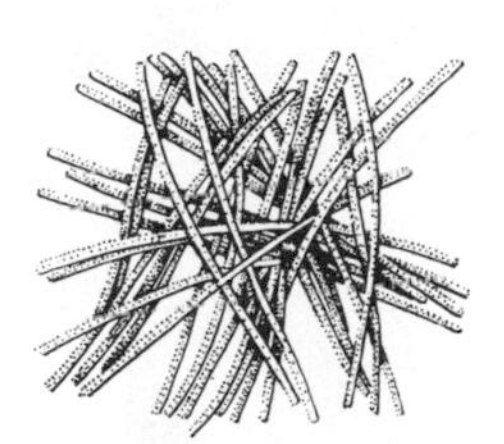

(a) **Straw Potatoes**
Pommes paille

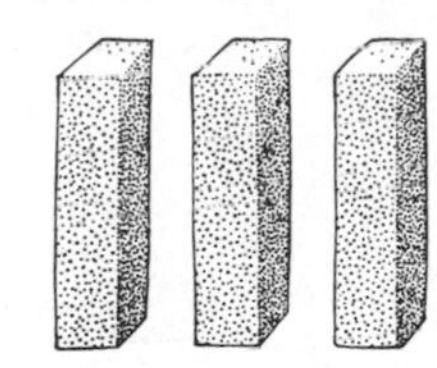

(b) **Potatoes Mignonnettes**
Pommes mignonnettes

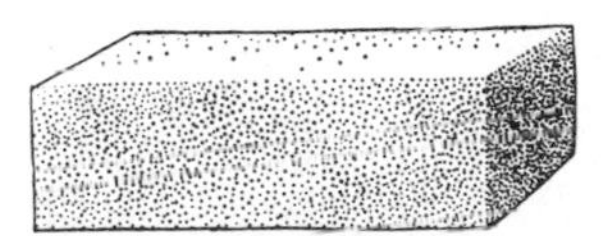

(c) **Potatoes Pont-neuf**
Pommes pont-neuf

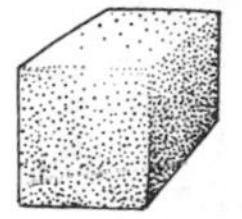

(d) **Potatoes Rissolé**
Pommes rissolees

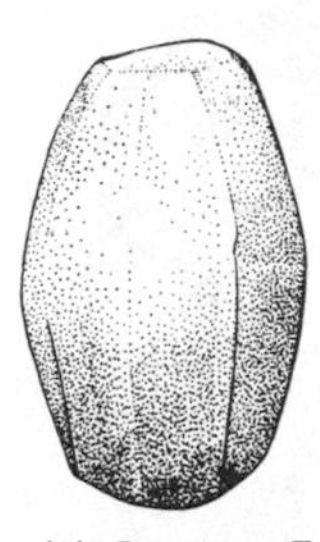

(e) **Potatoes Fondante**
Pommes fondantes

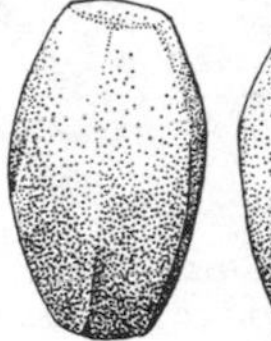

(f) **Potatoes, Chateau Style**
Pommes chateau

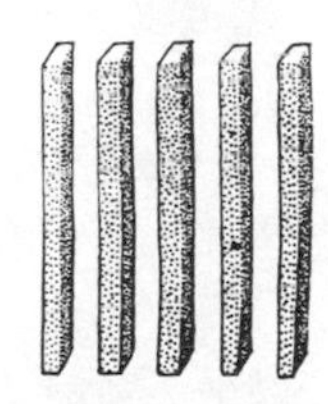

(g) **Matchstick Potatoes**
Pommes allumettes

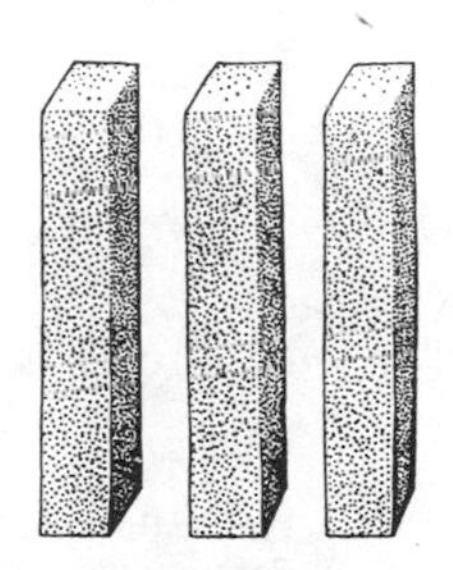

(h) **French Fries**
Pommes frites

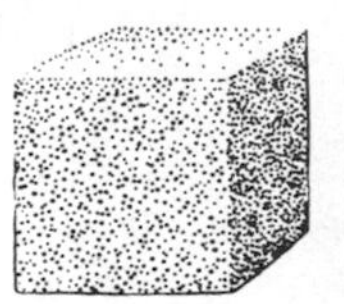

(i) **Potatoes Maxim**
Pommes Maxim

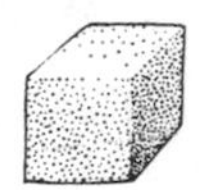
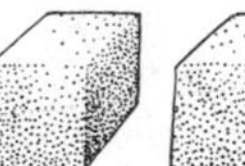

(j) **Potatoes Parmentier**
Pommes Parmentier

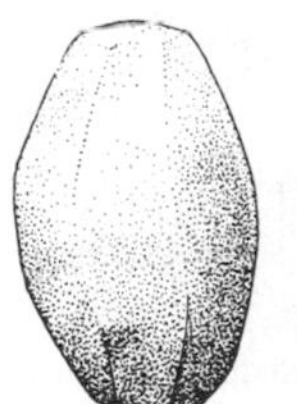

(k) **Boiled Potatoes**
Pommes nature

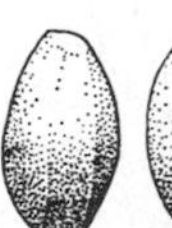

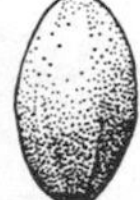

(l) **Potatoes Olivette**
Pommes olivettes

FIGURE 7-37
Potatoes – Pommes de terre

7.3.6 Potatoes—Pommes de terre (continued)

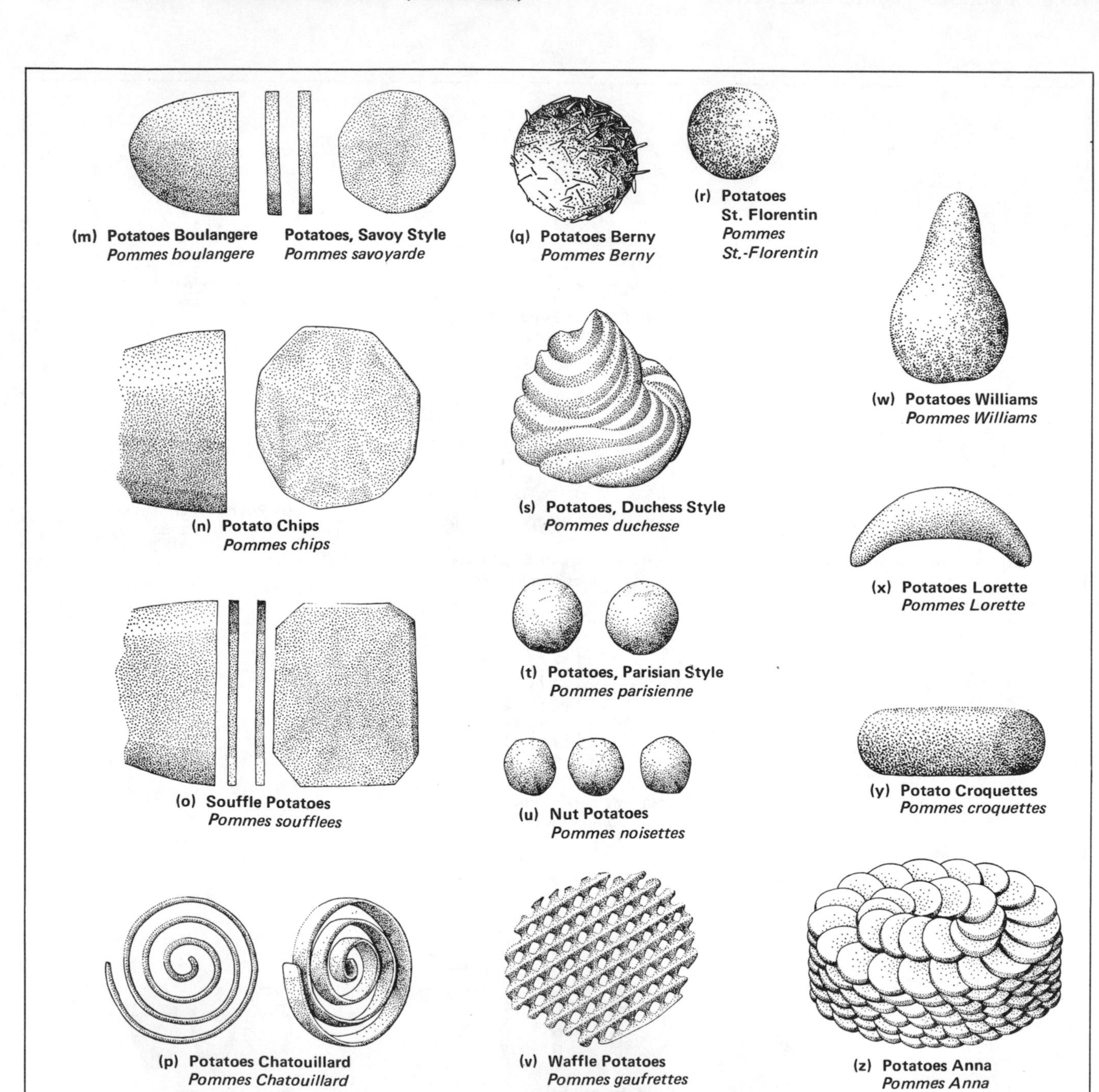

FIGURE 7-37A
Potatoes—Pommes de terre

7.3.7 Miscellaneous—Divers

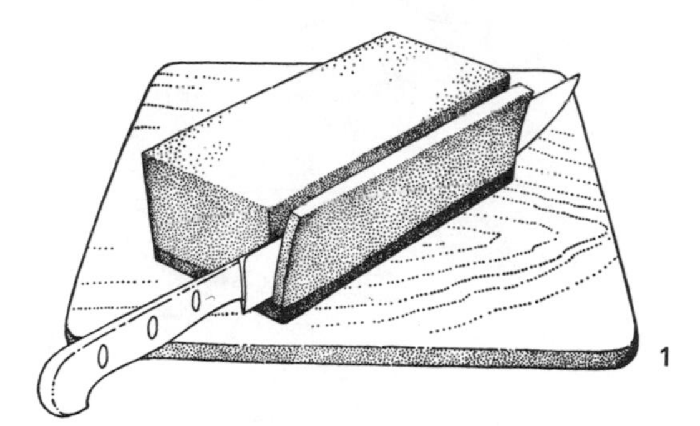

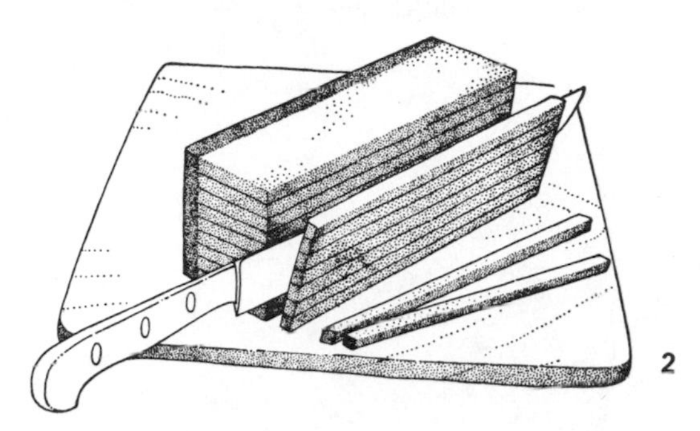

FIGURE 7-38
Cutting Larding Strips

1. Cut the slices down to the rind.
2. Place the rind on the left and cut the strips.

Using a larding needle (lardoire), dry pieces of meat are larded by passing strips of lard (1/5 to 2/5 inch thick) through the meat.

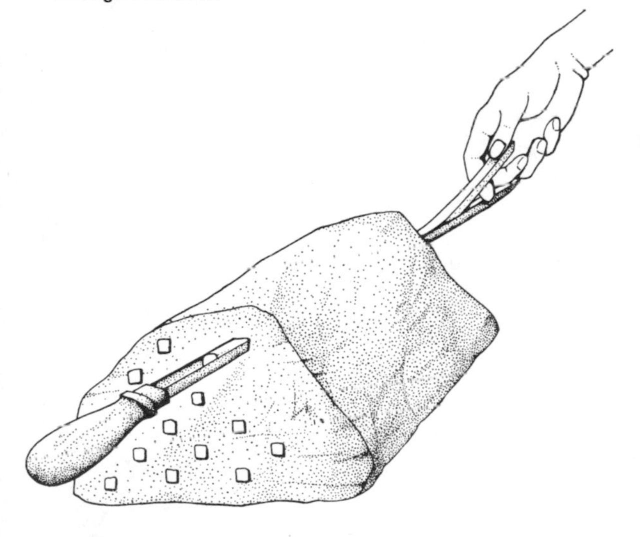

FIGURE 7-39
Larding Large Pieces of Meat

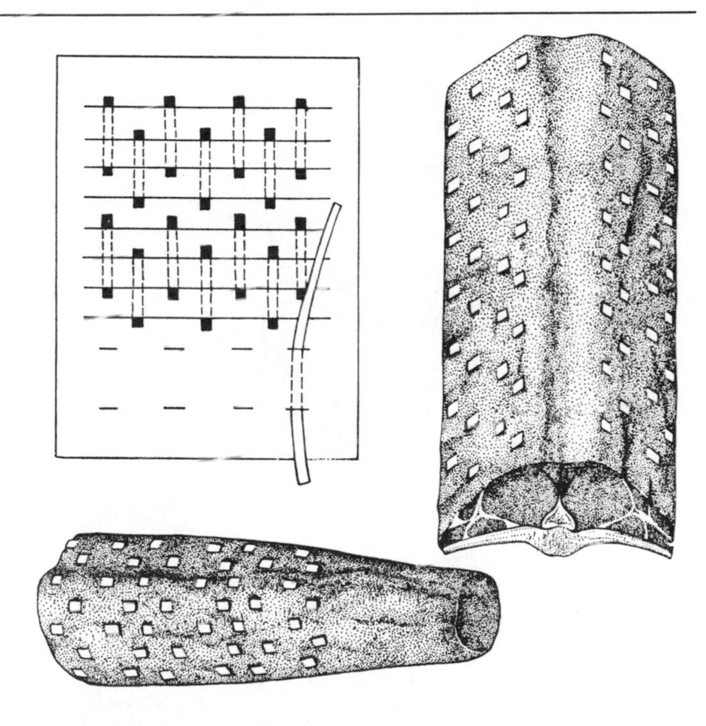

1. Diagram of larding. The rows are staggered.
2. Larding saddles. For small saddles (venison and red deer), two rows of larding are sufficient. For larger saddles (veal and mutton), more rows are necessary.
3. Larding of tenderloin and legs of lamb or mutton is done lengthwise.

FIGURE 7-40
Larding Various Pieces of Meat

1. Meat for birds is cut from the rump, top pieces, or shoulder depending on the animal and the quality.
2. Beef slices from the rump, spread with bacon slices, pork stuffing, and slices of gherkin.
3. The three birds, each bound differently.

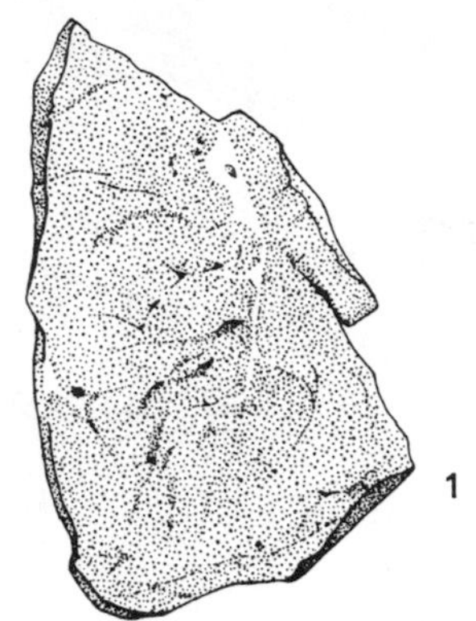

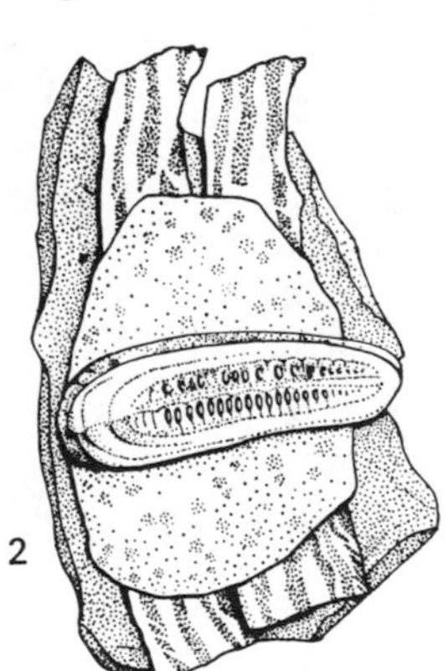

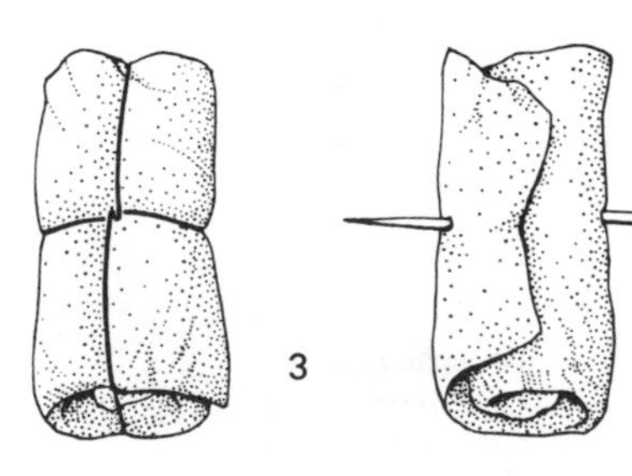

FIGURE 7-41
Birds — Paupiettes

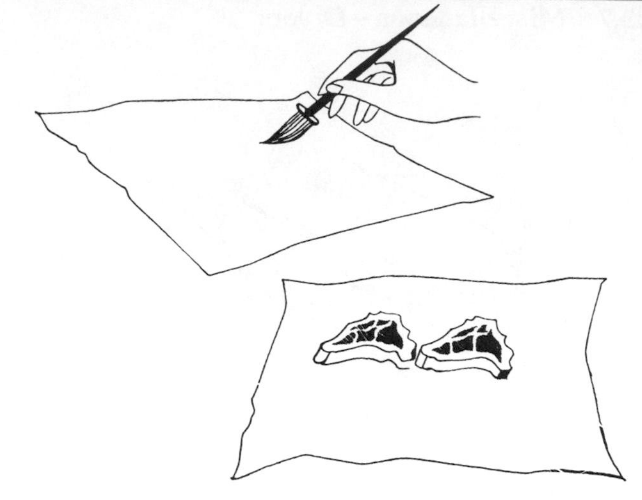

Season the meat or fish and coat the foil with oil.

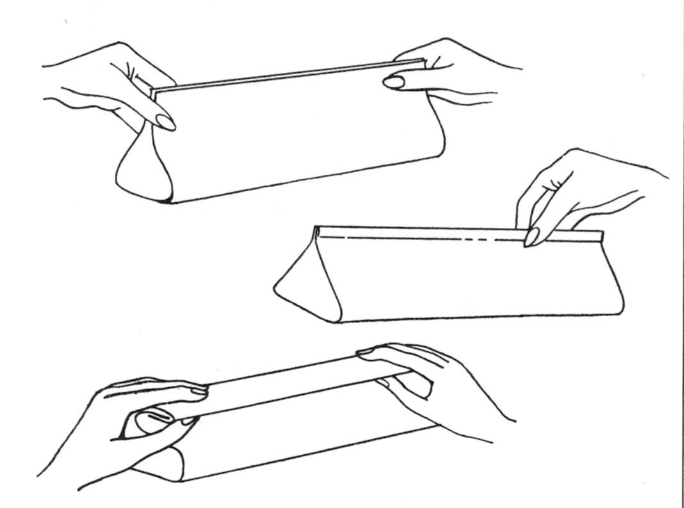

Pack loosely and fold the foil over twice.

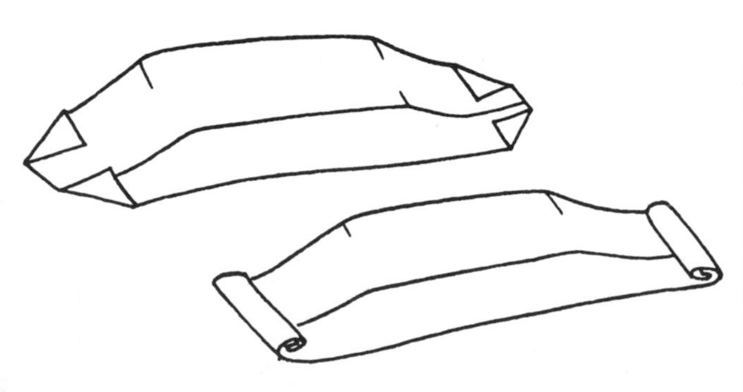

Turn the four corners inward and fold both ends twice.

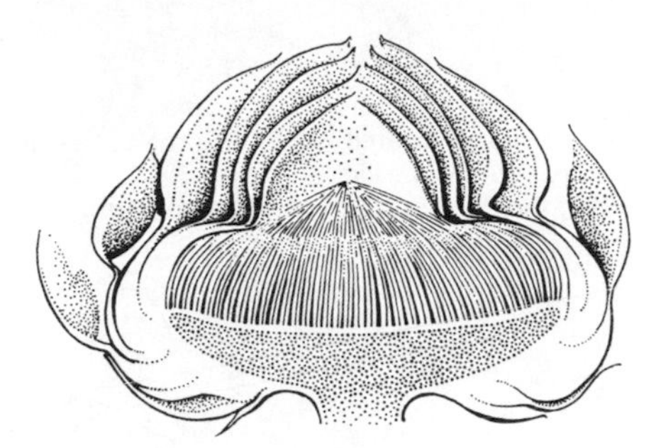

Section of unprepared artichoke.

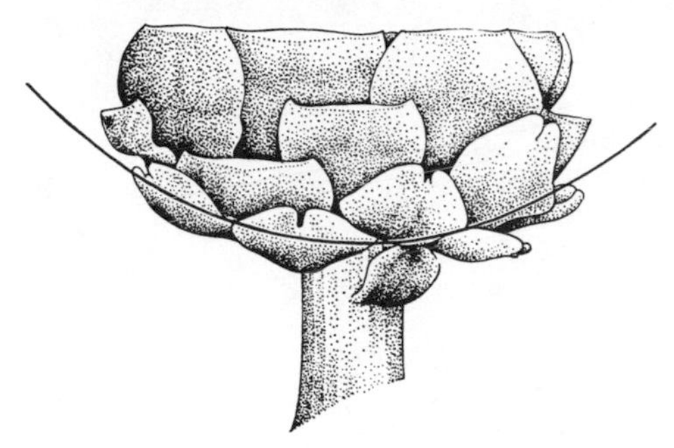

Removing the stalk and bottom leaves.

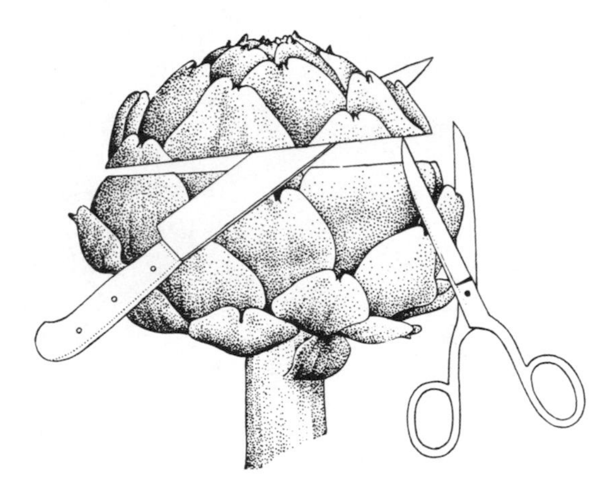

Removing the tips of the outer leaves.

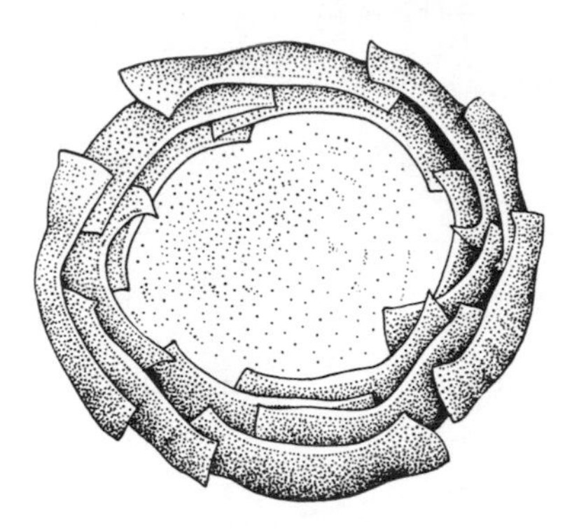

Removing the hay (beard) in the center of the artichoke.

Rubbing the heart with lemon.

FIGURE 7-42
Preparing Artichokes

1. Cutting the bread
2. Slicing into croutons
3. to 7. Different crouton shapes

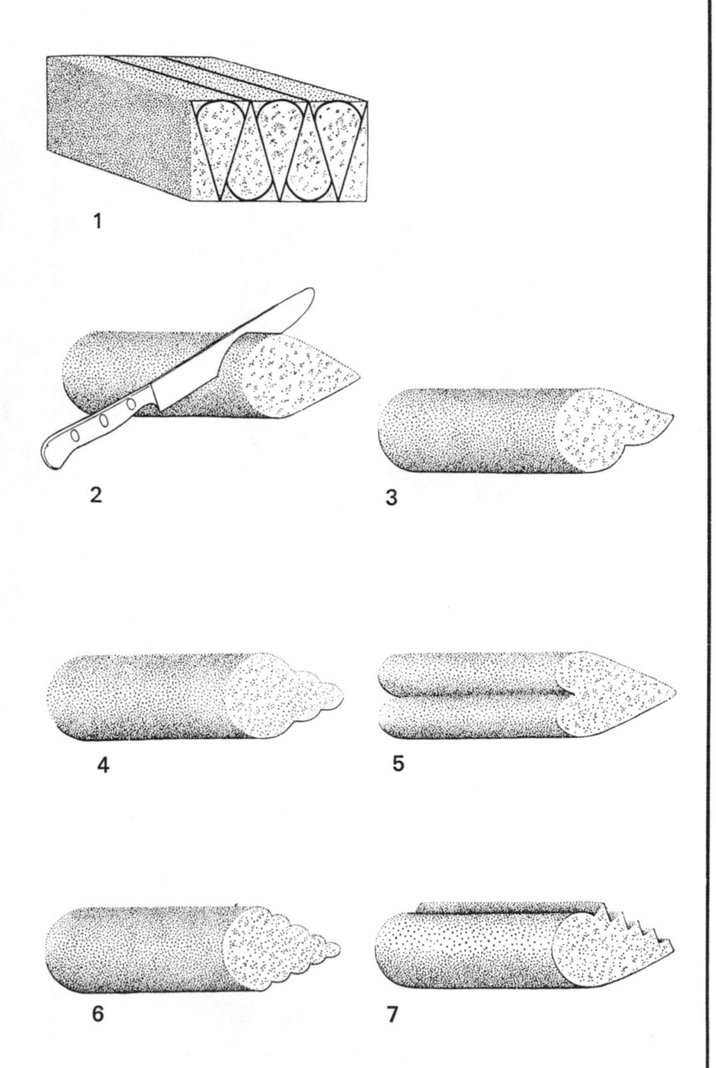

FIGURE 7-43
Cutting Bread Croutons

1. Dip the iron, previously heated in oil, into the batter up to 1/10 inch from the top edge.
2. Finish cooking the crust patties in a deep-fat fryer.

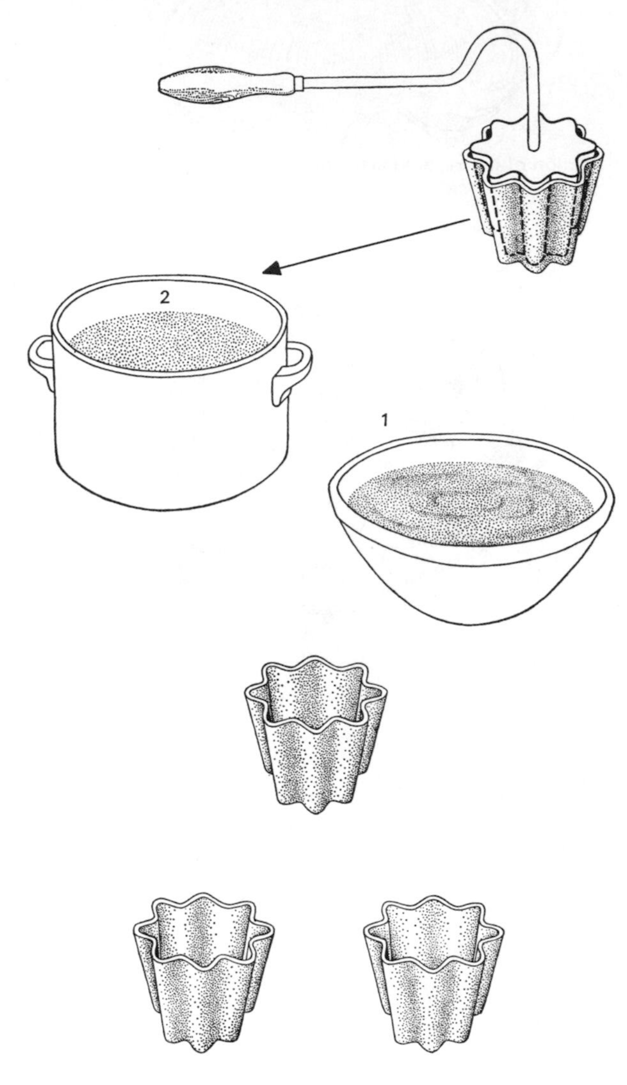

FIGURE 7-44
Crust Patties

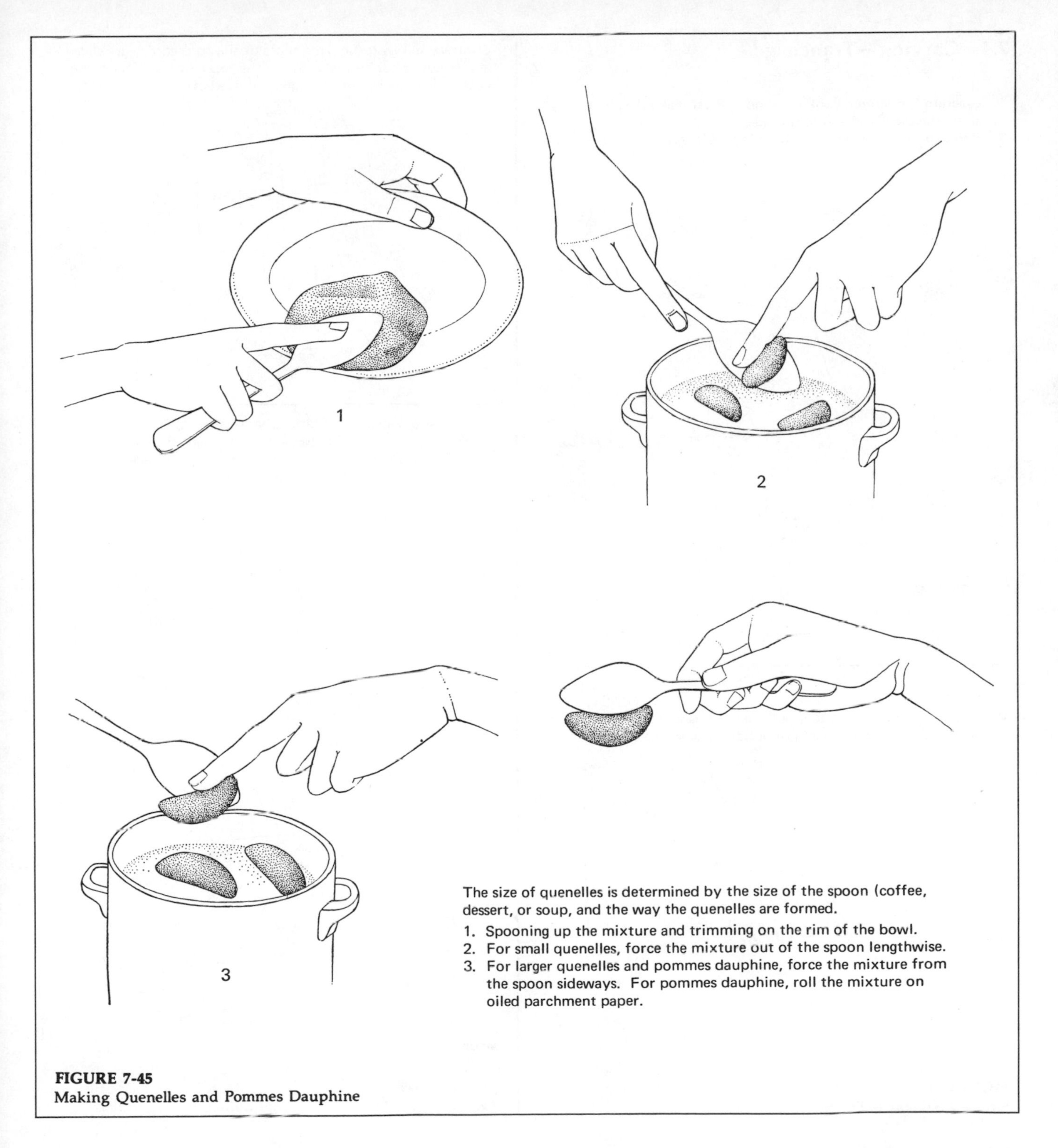

The size of quenelles is determined by the size of the spoon (coffee, dessert, or soup, and the way the quenelles are formed.

1. Spooning up the mixture and trimming on the rim of the bowl.
2. For small quenelles, force the mixture out of the spoon lengthwise.
3. For larger quenelles and pommes dauphine, force the mixture from the spoon sideways. For pommes dauphine, roll the mixture on oiled parchment paper.

FIGURE 7-45
Making Quenelles and Pommes Dauphine

7.4 Carving – Tranchage

1. Diagram for carving cooked salmon. First make deep cuts along the back and across the side.
2. Remove the slices with a fish knife and fork.

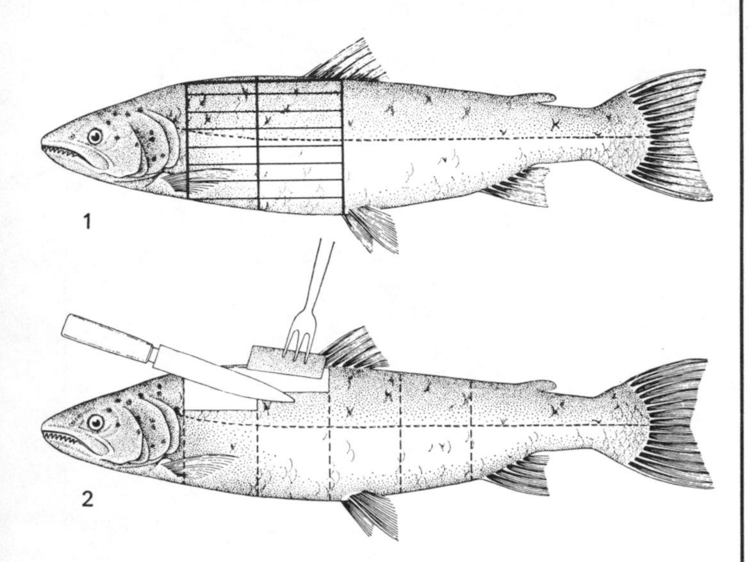

FIGURE 7-46
Salmon – Saumon

When carving smoked salmon, remove the fins and bones first. The slices are then cut (on a bias) obliquely down to the skin.

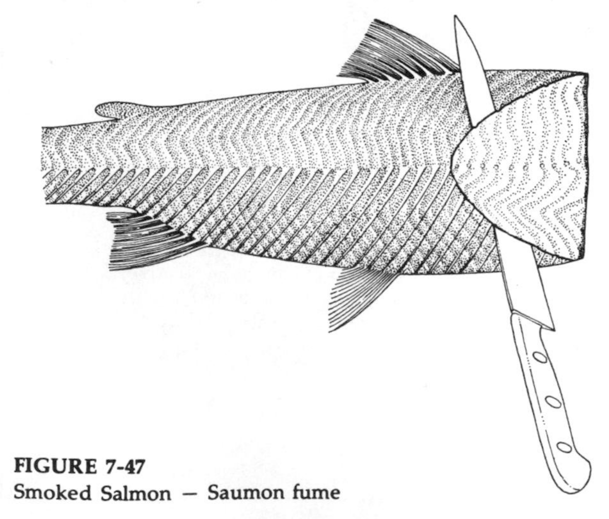

FIGURE 7-47
Smoked Salmon – Saumon fume

Contrary to raw turbot, the slices of the cooked fish are sliced and removed horizontally. After the top half is removed, the backbone must be cut through and lifted off.

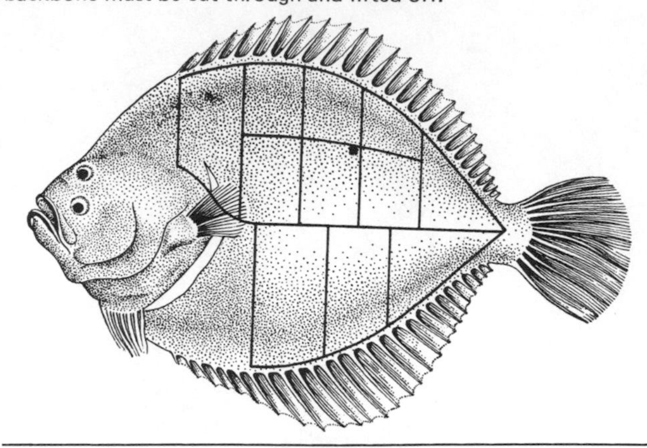

Double sirloin steak, rib steak, Chateaubriand, Porterhouse, and T-bone steak should always be cut diagonally. If possible, use a cutting board to collect the meat juices.

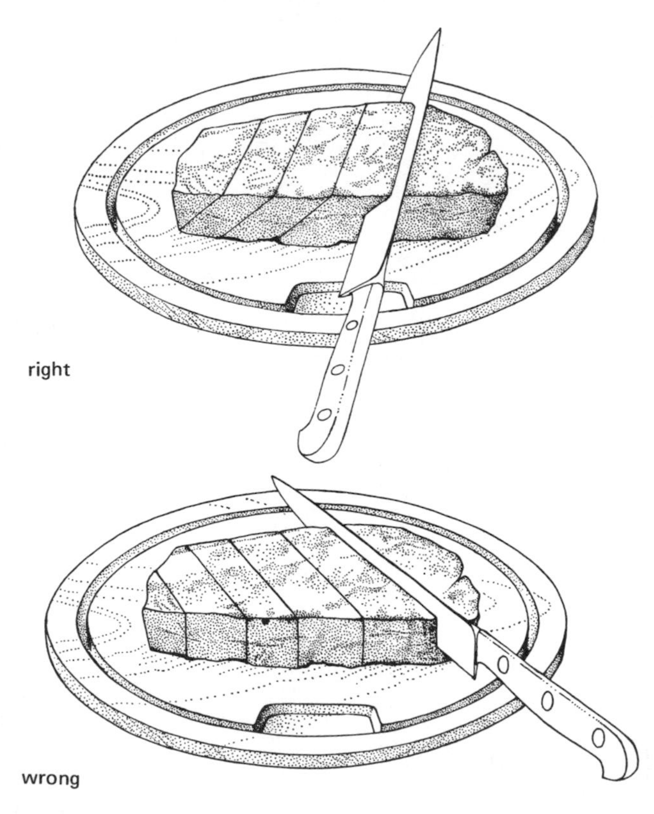

FIGURE 7-49
Double Sirloin Steak – Entrecote double

Roast beef should always be cut vertically with a carving knife.

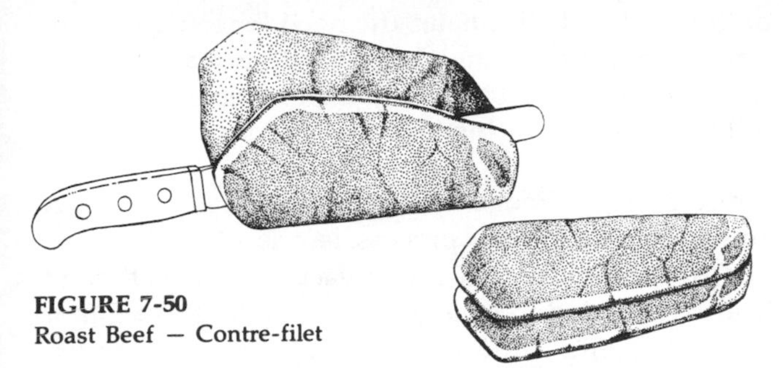

FIGURE 7-50
Roast Beef — Contre-filet

1. Diagonal cut
2. Cross cut
3. Longitudinal cut = English cut

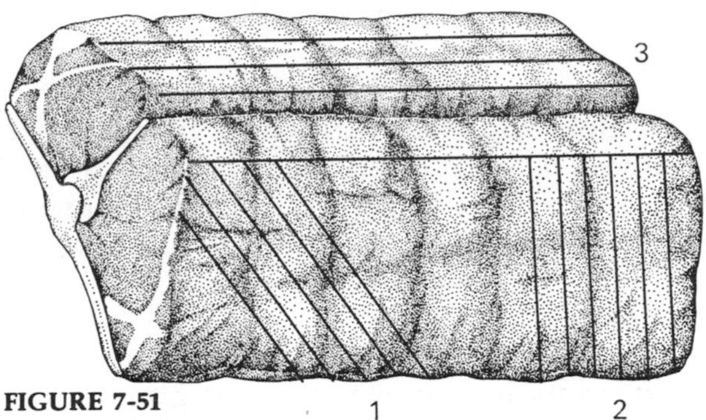

FIGURE 7-51
Saddle — Selle

FIGURE 7-52
Leg of Mutton — Gigot de mouton

At 1. Loosen the meat around the bone and cut four slices.
At 2. Place the leg so that 3 is uppermost and carve slices.
At 4. Turn the leg and remove the final slices at 4 and 5.

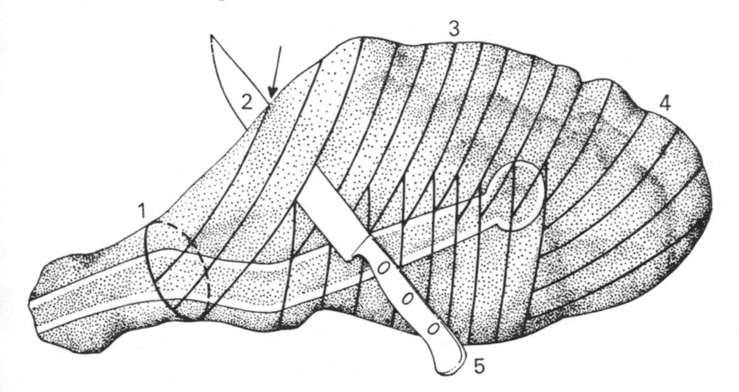

Remove and divide the legs and thighs. Carve both sides of the breast lengthwise and remove the breastbone.

1. One leg
2. Half a wing
3. Breastbone

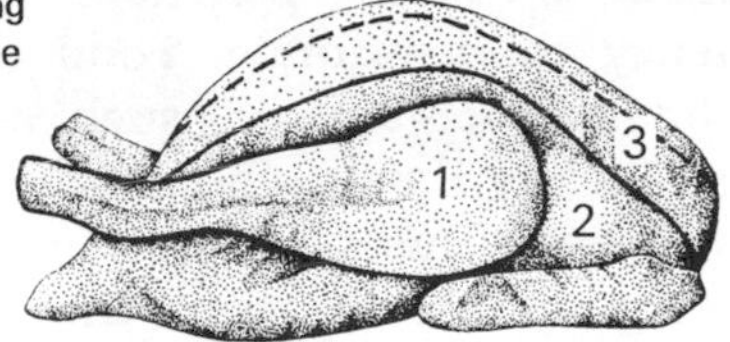

FIGURE 7-53
Chicken — Poulet

1. Remove and divide the legs and thighs.
2. Remove the wings.
3. Cut each side of the breast lengthwise into four fillets.

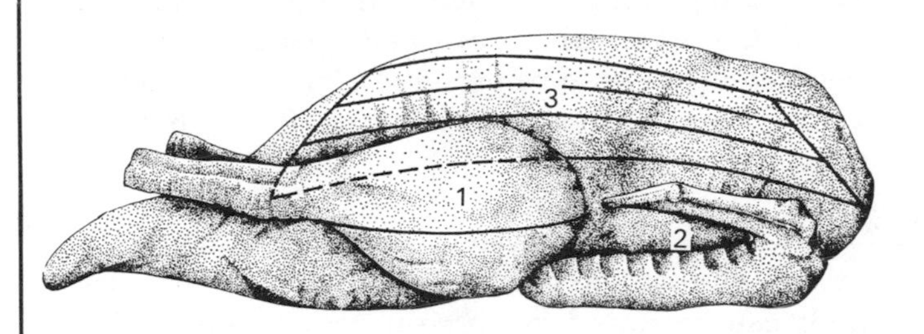

FIGURE 7-54
Duck — Canard

After removing the legs, the breast of the poularde is separated from the breastbone into two pieces and carved diagonally.

1. Leg cut into three pieces.
2. Half of the breast carved diagonally.

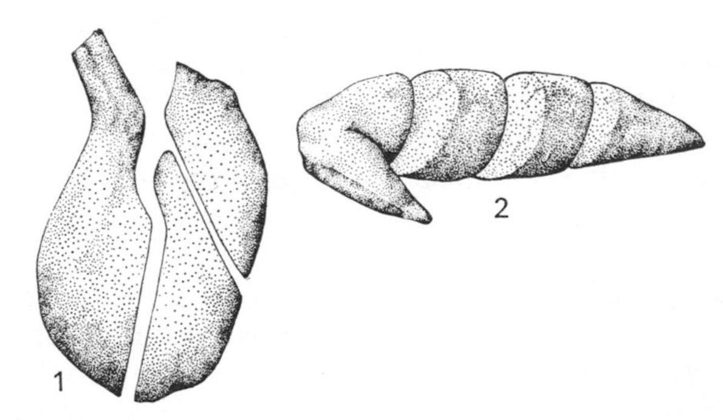

FIGURE 7-55
Poultry — Poularde

7.5 Methods of Preserving Food

Most fresh foods are highly perishable and have a natural tendency to deteriorate. Food spoilage is caused by the microorganisms, such as bacteria, yeasts, and molds; by the enzymes within the food itself; and by insects. This deterioration can be controlled by using only fresh foods that have been cleaned and stored properly. Foods can be preserved to avoid deterioration over a period of time. Modern methods of food preservation include refrigerating, freezing, canning, dehydration, freeze-drying, salting, and pickling.

Refrigerating. The action of microorganisms and enzymes can be retarded for short periods of time by refrigerating foods at temperatures as low as 32°F.(0°C.). Meats that have been partially or completely prepared can be preserved for a short time by refrigerating the food in plastic bags from which the air has been removed.

Nacka System. This system provides a method of preserving foods in plastic bags under vacuum. The foods can be stored for three to four weeks at 35°F. (2°C.) to 40°F. (5°C.). (See Section 7.5.3.)

Freezing. The flavor, color, texture, and nutritional values of many foods are preserved by freezing at temperatures as low as −60°F. (−52°C.). Vegetables, fruits, poultry, game, meats, and fish are some of the foods that can be frozen.

Canning. The foods are sealed in containers and heated. The heat cooks the food and destroys the microorganisms. Storage in sealed containers prevents further contamination. Vegetables, fruits, mushrooms, fish, and meat can be preserved by this method.

Dehydration. This process removes the water in foods. Artificial drying processes that are more efficient, more sanitary, and faster have replaced sun-drying. Among the common dried foods are fruits, vegetables, legumes, whole and nonfat milk, buttermilk, and egg solids. Dehydration is not only a method of preserving food, it also reduces the weight of the food and eliminates the need for refrigeration. These foods require much less storage space than in the natural state and have gained acceptance in the military service, in institutions, and by campers.

Freeze-drying. Foods that are freeze-dried are frozen and then dried. This process is one of *sublimation.* The frozen food is put into a vacuum and sufficient heat is provided to change the ice crystals to a vapor without going through a liquid phase. Approximately 98 percent of the moisture is removed from the food reducing the weight to 1/10 of the original. Fruits, vegetables, shrimp, coffee, and certain meats are freeze-dried and these foods can be rehydrated easily. The change in flavor, texture, and color of freeze-dried foods is minimal.

Curing. Another mode of preservation is curing. Creosotes from smoke and curing salts are both used to retard food deterioration. Food with a salt content of above 5 percent resists deterioration and that with an 8 percent content is preserved. Bacon, ham, and cod are examples of food that have been cured.

Pickling. Vegetables, such as cucumbers, beets, okra, and carrots, herring, pigs' feet, and game are examples of foods that can be preserved by a pickling process. The food is immersed in a solution of vinegar and other preservatives. The acid reaction inhibits deterioration.

7.5.1 Sterilizing

Canning Fresh Vegetables

Since vegetables have a very low acid content, the only safe way to can them is to process them under 10 pounds (4.5 kilograms) of pressure using a steam pressure canner. The United States Department of Agriculture recommends the following procedure for canning vegetables.[1].

[1] United States Department of Agriculture, Home and Garden Bulletin Number 8, *Home Canning of Fruits and Vegetables.* 1971.

- Use fresh, young, tender vegetables of uniform size.
- Wash thoroughly in several changes of water. Do not soak in water.
- Pack either raw or cooked vegetables by the following methods:

Raw pack: Pack cold raw vegetables (except corn, lima beans, and peas) as tightly as possible in a sterile jar. Cover with boiling water leaving ½ inch (1.2 centimeters) of space at top of jar. Add ½ teaspoon (3 grams) of salt to each pint (½ liter) jar.

Hot pack: Cover vegetables with water and heat to boiling point or cook as long as required for specific vegetable. Pack cooked vegetables loosely in sterile jars. Vegetables should be near the boiling point when packed. Add ½ teaspoon (3 grams) of salt to each pint (½ liter) jar; 1 teaspoon (6 grams) to quart (liter) jars. Cover with the boiling liquid from the vegetables or with boiling water. Leave head space in jars as recommended in specific recipe.

Insert a long spatula around the jar between the sides of the jar and the vegetables to release any air bubbles. Add liquid to cover vegetables if necessary.

Keep jars in very hot water while filling remainder of jars. Wipe rims of jars with a clean cloth.

Remove jar lids from boiling water and place on jars. Screw ring bands on jars tightly by hand.

Follow the directions of the manufacturer of the canner being used. These pointers apply to any steam pressure canner.

Fill bottom of canner with 2 to 3 inches (5 to 7.5 centimeters) of boiling water.

Place filled glass jars on rack so that steam can circulate around each container.

Use a rack between each layer of jars.

Fasten canner cover securely so that no steam can escape except through the vent.

When steam pours steadily through the vent, let it escape for 10 minutes or more until all air is driven from the canner. Close pet cock or put on weighted gauge.

Let pressure rise to 10 pounds (4.5 kilograms). At this moment start counting processing time. Keep pressure constant by regulating heat under the canner. Do not open pet cock.

Remove canner from heat as soon as processing time is completed.

Remove jars from canner.

Canning Fresh Fruits

Fresh fruits, fruit juices, and tomatoes are canned by the boiling water method. A canning kettle and lid are required for this process. The kettle must be deep enough so that the tops of the jars are covered by at least 1 inch (2.5 centimeters) of boiling water. Either the "raw pack" or "hot pack" method may be used. The United States Department of Agriculture recommends the following procedure:[2]

- Use fresh firm fruits without defects.
- Wash fruit thoroughly and pare if necessary.
- Cut fruit directly into a solution of 2 tablespoons (30 milliliters) of each salt and vinegar to 1 gallon (3.79 liters) of water. Do not leave fruit in solution more than 20 minutes. Rinse the fruit before putting in jars.
- Pack either raw or cooked fruit by the following methods:

Raw pack: Put cold, raw fruit into sterile jars and cover with boiling-hot syrup, juice, or water to within ½ inch (1.2 centimeters) of rim of jar. The syrup improves the appearance of most fruit and keeps them firmer. Put jars into canner containing hot but not boiling water.

Hot pack: Heat syrup or other liquid to boiling point in a large pan; add the prepared fruit, and cook as directed for specific fruit. Remove fruit from syrup and pack in sterile jars; pour syrup into jars to within ½ inch (1.2 centimeters) of rim of jar, or as directed in specific recipe; put jars into canner containing boiling water.

Add boiling water to bring water in canner an inch or two (2.5 centimeters or 5) over tops of jars;

---

[2] United States Department of Agriculture, Home and Garden Bulletin Number 8, *Home Canning of Fruits and Vegetables.* 1971.

never pour boiling water directly on glass jars. Put lid on canner.

As soon as water in canner comes to a rolling boil, start to count processing time. Boil gently and steadily for the time required for the specific fruit. Keep covered with water throughout processing.

Remove jars from the canner as soon as processing time is completed.

Proportions for Sugar Syrup

4 cups (10 deciliters) water or juice to 2 cups (454 grams) sugar equals 5 cups (12.5 deciliters) of *thin* syrup.

4 cups (10 deciliters) water or juice to 3 cups (680 grams) sugar equals 5½ cups (13.8 deciliters) of *medium* syrup.

4 cups (10 deciliters) water or juice to 4¾ cups (1080 grams) sugar equals 6½ cups (16.2 deciliters) of *heavy* syrup.

7.5.2 Freezing

What is Freezing?

Freezing is a three-step process that requires chilling, sharp freezing, and holding at low temperatures. As soon as the food is thoroughly chilled, it is frozen at −10°F. (23°C.) or below. After the food is frozen, it can be stored at a temperature of 0°F. (−18°C.) for a long period. (See Freezing Plants, page 41.)

Why Freezing?

Quality and Nutritional Value. Freezing is a process that will preserve natural flavors, colors, and nutrients. The organisms that cause spoilage and the enzymes that cause further ripening are not destroyed by freezing, but they become inactive. They do become active when the foods are thawed. Foods for freezing should be fully ripe, firm, and as fresh as possible.

A Natural Method of Preservation. There are no preservatives, taste additives, or artificial colors in frozen foods.

Cost and Labor Savings. A high percentage of the preparation tasks (cleaning, washing, and peeling) are transferred to the commercial processor. Fewer employees are needed and less supervision is required when preparation tasks are reduced.

Pricing. Production costs and portion costs are simplified and more exact because the preparation costs do not have to be calculated. Each portion cost can be easily calculated and prices can be determined on the basis of exact costs.

Portion Control. Frozen products are packaged in standard-sized containers in either bulk or individual portions. The number of portions required can be determined easily and the problems of overproduction and underproduction are reduced.

Reduced Cooking Time. The cooking time of frozen products as compared to equivalent fresh products is generally reduced by 30 percent to 50 percent. Frozen prepared dishes require even less cooking time.

Simplified Menu Planning. A wider selection of menu items can be offered because of extensive inventory of variety of frozen foods. Seasonal foods are available throughout the year in frozen form. Greater variety can be offered on the menu without increasing staff or workload.

Purchasing. An inventory of frozen foods may decrease the frequency of purchases and deliveries.

The Freezing Process and its Effects. Water is the main constituent of all perishable foods. This water is not pure, but is an unsaturated solution of salts, sugars, acids, and other soluble substances, and is, in part, found free in the cells or in the intercellular spaces. The water should be frozen as quickly as possible so that small ice crystals are formed. After the water in the food has been transformed into ice, the damaging activities of the microbes and enzymes are stopped; the gradual degeneration of the vitamins and nutrients ceases.

Best Quality Raw Materials. Only food of the best possible quality should be frozen. The freezing process maintains the original quality of the food prior to freezing; that is, if the product was initially poor, then freezing will not improve it.

Correct Preparation. Good food handling practices and procedures are necessary to guarantee safe and sanitary conditions. Food handlers should wear clean uniforms, plastic gloves, and hair protectors. All equipment must be clean.

Correct Packing. Waxed lined cardboard boxes with plastic liners; heavy plastic bags with wire tape; heavy duty aluminum foil; coated, moisture-vaporproof, laminated freezer paper; polyethylene sheets; and clear plastic adhesive wrap are good packaging materials that will protect the food from exposure to air, odors, and dehydration.

Freezing Equipment. The food must be frozen through to the center (0°F.) (−18°C.) *as fast as possible.* Both *low temperatures* and *good freezing performance* are necessary. If the freezing process is slow, large ice crystals will form and rupture the cell tissue. Instructions from the manufacturer will specify the amount of food that can be frozen at one time—usually 2 to 3 pounds (4.4 to 6.6 kilograms) of food per cubic foot (35 cubic meters) of freezer space. In case of power failure or mechanical breakdown dry ice can be placed in the freezer to help keep food frozen. The dry ice should be added as soon as possible after the power goes off.

Maintenance of the Deep-Frozen Chain. It is necessary to maintain a temperature of 0°F. (−18°C.) to −12°F. (−25°C.) from the time the food is frozen until it reaches the user. The lower the temperature, the longer the quality can be maintained.

Thawing and Cooking. Basically, frozen products are cooked by the same method as their fresh counterparts. Partially or fully thawed frozen food must be consumed quickly. Thawed food should never be refrozen.

7.5.2.1 Freezing Raw Products

The Raw Product and its Condition

Most vegetables and fruits can be frozen. Some varieties freeze better than others. Fresh meat, game, poultry, feathered game, and freshwater fish can also be frozen.

Pretreatment

The food products are first blanched, boiled, fried, or otherwise prepared and then frozen.

- *Vegetables:* wash, peel, blanch quickly in boiling water, chill, drain, and pack. The following should not be blanched: cucumber, zucchini, peppers, tomatoes, and kitchen herbs.
- *Fruits and Berries:* depending on the use of the product, these fruits can be frozen without an additive, or with the addition of sugar or syrup (possibly with a little ascorbic acid); stone fruits must be blanched.
- *Meat:* fresh, lean meat from young animals should be used. The USDA inspection stamp guarantees wholesomeness and the shield-shaped USDA grade mark insures quality. The meat should be in ready-to-use portions.
- *Fish:* freshwater fish, either whole or filleted, should be kept cold after being caught. The fish should be frozen and glazed. After freezing starts, dip the fish in cold water and complete the freezing process.

Packing

Polyethylene bags (odorless, minimum thickness 0.05 mm) and sheets, plastic containers, aluminum foil (extra strong), and aluminum containers are all suitable for packing the food. All frozen products must be *carefully* packed in moisture-vaporproof paper, preferably *hermetically* sealed, and marked with the *date, contents, and weight or number of units.* Freezer-proof sealing tape and labels should be used.

Correct Freezing

When freezing, the lowest possible temperatures should be used: −22°F. (−30°C.) and below.

Rules:

- The freezer should be set at the minimum temperature.
- Consider the capacity of the freezer; process only an amount that can be frozen within 24 hours.
- The food should be packed as flat as possible.
- Place the packages against the chilling walls or next to the freezing plates.
- Leave space between the packages so that the cold air can circulate freely.
- Stack packages after they are completely frozen.

Storage

The period of storage depends upon the type of food and its fat content. All frozen food must be stored at 0°F. (−18°C.) or lower.

- *Fruits and vegetables:* 6 to 12 months
- *Lean meat:* 6 to 10 months
- *Fatty meat:* 2 to 4 months
- *Poultry:* 8 to 10 months
- *Freshwater fish:* 2 to 3 months
- *Baked products:* 2 to 4 months

Checks and Maintenance of the Plant

- The storage temperature of at least 0°F. (−18°C.) must be checked daily.
- Absolute order and cleanliness.
- Frost should be removed at regular intervals; defrost when the frost layer exceeds ½ inch (2 centimeters).

Cooking Frozen Raw Products

The following points apply to both commercial and home produced frozen food.

- *Vegetables.* Boiling and steaming times are reduced by ⅓ to ½; a minimum of liquid should be added.
- *Fruits.* For cooking and baking purposes: fruits can be used in the frozen state; fruits for salads and desserts are best when partially thawed.
- *Meat, Poultry, Game.* Thaw large pieces at refrigerator temperature. Thaw small pieces at refrigerator temperature or use in the frozen or partially thawed state.
- *Fish.* Whole or filleted fish should be thawed until it can be sliced or separated. Breaded fish products should be cooked while still frozen.

7.5.2.2 Frozen Prepared Foods

Technological developments resulting from both food and equipment research have led to the use of more prepared foods in foodservice establishments in recent years. The shortage of skilled foodservice personnel, spiraling labor costs, and the increasing number of persons eating away from home have augmented the demand for new types and forms of foods that can be served easily with a limited labor force. The ever-increasing number of prepared foods on the market makes it possible to supplement menus and offer greater variety. Some foodservice systems are designed around foods that are prepared on the premises and then frozen and stored for later use.

The extensive use of these partially and fully prepared foods has increased the demand for new types of equipment for processing, storing, finishing, and serving the food.

Although there is a growing trend to produce prepared foods on the premises, there are many problems related to the production techniques: the development of recipes for products that require ingredients, such as anti-oxidants, emulsifiers, tenderizers, and other unfamiliar products; and the equipment required for processing, packaging, storing, and reconstituting. Because of the high cost of the equipment and the technical knowledge needed for such a system, the more common practice is to purchase commercially prepared products to meet specific needs. The use of prepared foods can provide:

- control of food and labor costs
- control over quality, quantity, and portion size of menu items
- greater variety in menu selections
- savings in labor costs because fewer skilled employees will be required
- opportunity to reduce staffing needs during slack periods or weekends by utilizing less skilled personnel
- constant availability of certain food products
- flexibility to meet needs as related to special events, increased business, staff absences, and emergencies
- simple way to feature popular specialty items daily

7.5.2.3 Finishing Methods for Prepared Foods

The finishing method depends on the type of dishes, the packaging, and the methods of heating available in the kitchen. (See Section 2.3.3, Heating Methods and Equipment.) *All* dishes can be further seasoned or garnished. A limited mise en place should always be available so the prepared dishes can be finished with a flair and merchandised attractively.

A work sheet with specific directions for thawing, heating, and garnishing should be written for each item. Using such a guideline, even auxiliary personnel are able to prepare the dish so that it can be served at any time.

Depending on the packaging, the dishes are prepared as follows:

Boiling Bags. These are polyethylene packs that are resistant to both very low and very high temperatures. Foods in boiling bags are prepared by placing them, still frozen, into boiling water and heating for the prescribed length of time (15 to 20 minutes). No losses occur, and since they are heated indirectly via the hot water, there is less danger of overcooking. Since the package is hermetically sealed, several different menu items can be heated in the same water.

Alutrays. The heating or final stage of cooking takes place in an oven, a broiler, or in an automatic convection oven. (See page 33.) Alutrays cannot be used in microwave ovens. They are generally used for dishes which are to be glazed or gratinated.

Porcelain and Plastic Containers. When heating in microwave ovens (see "Heating Methods and Equipment," pages 31-35), materials that allow energy to pass through and penetrate into the food should be used. China, ceramics, and opaque glass may be used if there is no metal trim or metal base glaze. Plastics, such as plastic wrap or freezer containers, are only suitable for warming food. Only plastics that are labeled "dishwasher proof" or "may be placed in boiling water" should be used. The cover of the containers should be placed loosely on the container to avoid splitting or bursting.

Ready-to-Cook Dishes. Gnocchi, ravioli, French-fried potatoes, and pommes dauphine should be finished in a frying pan, an oven, or in a deep-fat fryer, depending upon the cooking instructions. The following must be remembered for all dishes: do not cook excessively large quantities at one time, keep the heating equipment hot, so that the temperature does not drop when the food is placed inside.

Meat Dishes. Meat dishes which have been frozen with the meat juices or a sauce should be heated slowly in the pan, adding a little liquid. If necessary, the meat juices should be bound as soon as the meat has thawed.

Vegetable Dishes. Fully precooked vegetable dishes should be slightly thawed and then heated with a small amount of liquid.

Soups and Soup Ingredients. Fish soups or specialty soups should be thawed in the pan with a little water and then heated. Soup ingredients, such as shredded savory, pancakes (Celestine), marrow, semolina, and liver dumplings should be cooked while still frozen.

7.5.3 Nacka System

This method of preservation is a chilling system used in preparation kitchens. The preparation kitchens are located away from the main establishment and are supplied on a daily basis with the appropriate quantities of raw materials. Since this system has only limited use in the hotel and restaurant business, the description is purposely brief.

This system of preservation was originally developed in Sweden for the personnel of mining companies, and was adopted and improved by the Nacka hospital—hence the name. Before freezing, the raw materials are first prepared and cooked. The foods, which are 80 percent precooked, are then packed in vacuum-sealed plastic bags (in individual or up to five portions). A subsequent pasteurizing process is necessary for certain delicate dishes. The prepared foods must then be chilled as quickly as possible to 37°F. (3°C.) to 39°F. (4°C.) either in ice water or in a freezing tunnel. If then stored at the same temperature, the food keeps for about three weeks. For this reason, exact dating is mandatory. Opened bags must be used immediately and must not be refrozen. Any food preserved using this system must be kept chilled until it is to be prepared and served. The following dishes can be prepared using this system: soups, meat with sauce, vegetables, vegetable salads, whipped and fried potatoes, pasta, rice, and corn.

The food is heated by placing the bags in boiling water. Depending upon the size of the bag, the food is either served directly onto the plates or kept warm in bain-marie units. The main advantages of this system are independent preparation; possiblity of storage for a few days in a refrigerated storeroom; no expensive finishing equipment required; and no containers to wash. Some disadvantages are limited choice; additional fresh vegetables required to accompany the main dish component; limited storage; and danger of scalding oneself when opening multiportion bags.

7.6 Cooking Temperatures of Fats and Oils

Knowledge of the temperature ranges of various fats is necessary to be able to select the correct fat for the use. When the smoke point of a fat is reached, chemical changes occur that affect the usability of the fat. Smoke indicates that the fat is breaking down and the product being fried will absorb fat because the proper frying temperatures cannot be maintained. Rancidity in the fat affects the flavor, odor, and usability of the fat and the food fried in the fat.

Maximum Temperatures of Fats and Oils

Butter, fresh, very hot	230°F. (110°C.)
Clarified butter	320°F. (160°C.)
Kidney fat	355°F. to 375°F. (180°C. to 191°C.)
Lard	375°F. to 400°F. (191°C. to 205°C.)
Coconut oil	355°F. to 390°F. (180°C. to 200°C.)
Peanut oil	445°F. to 455°F. (230°C. to 235°C.)
Sunflower seed oil	440°F. (227°C.)
Special plant fats	475°F. (250°C.)

Required Fat Temperatures for Sauteing

Hamburger	initially 340°F. (170°C.), then 265°F. (130°C.)
Sirloin steak	initially 340°F. (170°C.), then 265°F. (130°C.)
Chateaubriand	initially 320°F. (160°C.), then 255°F. (125°C.)
Tournedos	initially 340°F. (170°C.), then 285°F. (140°C.)
Veal cutlet	initially 285°F. (140°C.), then 265°F. (130°C.)
Veal chop	initially 285°F. (140°C.), then 250°F. (120°C.)
Pork chop	initially 285°F. (140°C.), then 265°F. (130°C.)
Mutton chop	initially 340°F. (170°C.), then 265°F. (130°C.)
Breaded cutlet	initially 265°F. (130°C.), then 240°F. (115°C.)
Fish a la meuniere	initially 285°F. (140°C.), then 230°F. (110°C.)

Note: for Deep-fat Frying
Only very *heat resistant, non-foaming fats* should be used. Fats should not be mixed with oils, since this inevitably leads to foaming. Hydrogenated fats and natural fats are resistant to oxidation changes that cause breakdown. Overheating the fat can be prevented by correct adjustment of the heat controls and periodic checks of the thermostats. The fat in the deep-fat fryer should be filtered after each use. The deep-fat fryer should be covered when cool to protect it from the effects of light and oxygen. Deep-fat fryers should not be overloaded. It is better to use two or more deep-fat fryers. Oils with a high polyunsaturated fatty acid content are not suitable for deep-fat frying, since these acids combine very quickly with the oxygen in the air and oxidize. For example, sunflower seed oil should not be used for deep-fat frying, in spite of its high smoke point, because of its more than 50 percent content of polyunsaturated fatty acids. Soybean oil, sesame oil, and rape seed oil are not suitable for deep-fat frying.

Required Fat Temperatures for Deep-Fat Frying

Small fish, for one-step frying	355°F. (180°C.)
Larger fish or pieces of fish, for blanching	265°F. (130°C.) to 285°F. (140°C.)

Larger fish or pieces of fish, for frying	355°F. (180°C.)
French-fried potatoes, for blanching	265°F. (130°C.)
French-fried potatoes for frying	355°F. (180°C.)
Pommes soufflees, for blanching	250°F. (121°C.) to 285°F. (140°C.)
Pommes soufflees, for frying	355°F. (180°C.)
Croquettes and Cromesquis	320°F. (160°C.)
Choux, Beignets	320°F. (160°C.) to 340°F. (170°C.)
Vegetables, for blanching	285°F. (140°C.)
Vegetables, for frying	320°F. (160°C.) to 340°F. (170°C.)

7.7 Basic Principles of Roasting

Roasting refers to the process of cooking in an uncovered container without water.

Roasting Meats

Roasting is recommended for large tender cuts of beef, veal, pork, lamb, and for some poultry and game. The length of time of roasting must be controlled or the product will dry out. Only tender, top grade, and fine quality meats are suitable for roasting. (See pages 77-80.) Well-marbled and fat-covered meats provide better roasts. Lean meats must be larded or barded before roasting since they have little or no fat content.

Roasting Equipment

There are two methods for roasting meat: the spit (see Figure 7-56), and the oven.

Domestic ovens incorporating a spit are also available. Roasting on the spit functions only by heat conducted by radiation. Oven roasting involves heat conducted by radiation, by direct contact, or by convection. *The roasting pan or other container must be of an appropriate size for the piece of meat* to avoid burning the fat and meat juices on the exposed surfaces not covered by the meat.

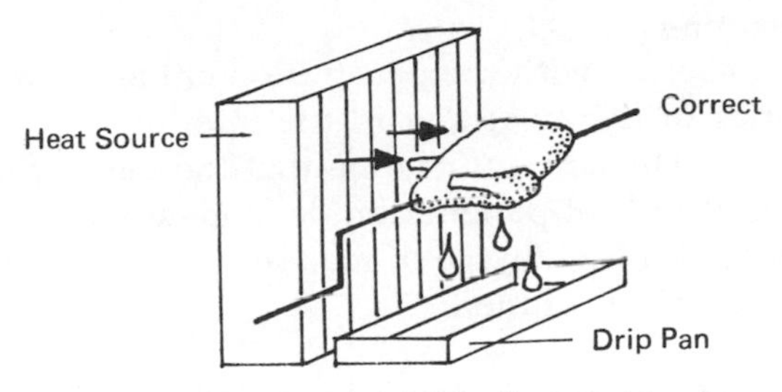

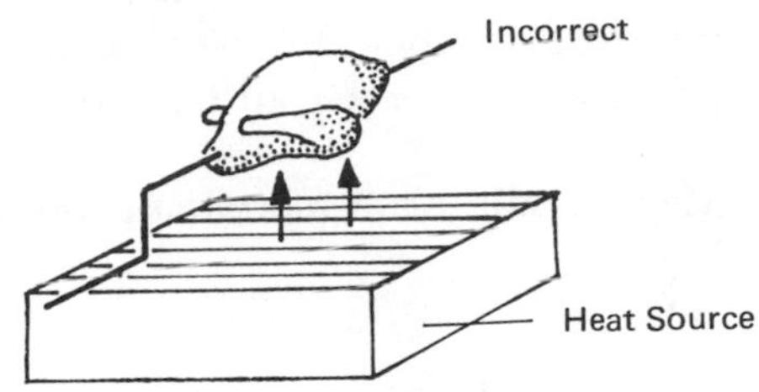

FIGURE 7-56
Roasting Equipment

When Roasting in the Oven

- Place roasts fat side up and poultry, breast side down, in an open shallow roasting pan or on a grill placed on a pan to retain the fat and juices.
- Insert a meat thermometer in the meat so the bulb is in the center of the largest muscle. The bulb should not touch the bone or fat.
- Do not cover; add no liquids.
- Roast fat-covered meats (lean meats may need to be barded or larded) in a preheated oven at 300°F. (150°C.) and maintain this temperature throughout roasting process. Roast small roasts at 350°F. (177°C.). Sear roasts with little fat covering in an oven preheated to 475°F. (245°C.). Leave at this temperature until browned, then reduce temperature to 300°F. (150°C.) and complete roasting.
- Remove the roast from the oven when the proper internal temperature has been reached. If the roast is allowed to stand before carving, remove it from the oven when the thermometer registers 5° to 10° below the desired degree of doneness.
- Allow roast to stand 15 to 20 minutes in a warm place after removing from oven.

Roasting

This occurs with the penetration of heat from the exterior of the meat toward the interior.

The amount of time that the meat will be exposed to heat penetration depends upon the type of meat and the degree of roasting required. From this it can be concluded:

- The roasting time is determined by the *thickness of the meat and the weight.*
- Should the thickness of the meat not be uniform, it must either be cut into two pieces, or the thinner part must be protected from the heat (aluminum foil).
- Meat should be at room temperature before roasting.

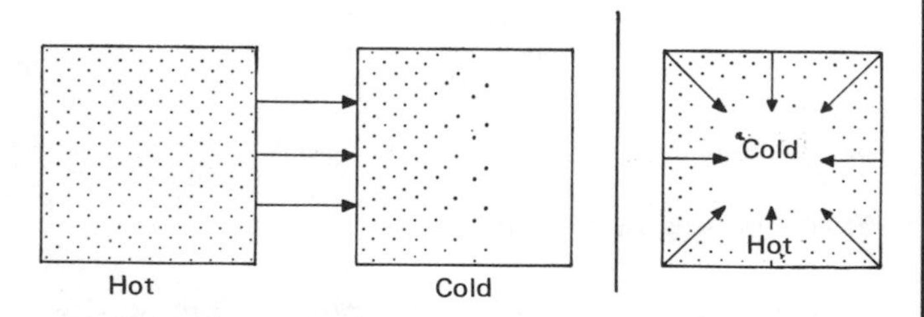

FIGURE 7-57
Roasting

Heat Flow

Our ancestors had neither thermometers nor thermostats, nor was it possible to adjust the oven and spit temperatures by operating a switch or turning a tap. Nevertheless, they were excellent at roasting meat, since they carefully controlled the flow of the heat from the oven or spit to the roast itself. The same degree of care and attention is necessary today. The size of the oven, its heating capacity, and the heat conduction techniques used must be considered. It is not possible to roast a large amount of meat in a small oven, nor in one which heats too slowly because its burners are too small. If the voltage has dropped or the gas pressure has been lowered, it will also be difficult to roast the meat properly. On the other hand, an oven can be equipped with a very fast and powerful heating system that needs to be carefully controlled. The oven can also be too large for the size of the piece of meat. *The art of roasting requires coordination of all these factors to achieve the correct heat flow.* Constant checking permits the roast cook to recognize whether the degree of heat is insufficient or excessive, and enables him to make the appropriate adjustments. The temperatures used for roasting sometimes tend to be too high because of the old theory that all the juices would be lost if the meat is not seared. It is true that meat without a fat covering may be seared. If roasting begins at 455°F. to 490°F. (235°C. to 255°C.), the temperature should be lowered to 300°F. (150°C.) as soon as the meat is brown. The beginner will soon notice that the thicker the meat, the lower the temperature required, and that the highest temperature, 490°F. (255°C.), is used only for the smallest pieces. *High temperatures during roasting cause the fat to melt and much of the meat juice to evaporate leading to a reduction in weight and volume and resulting in the formation of a bitter and inedible crust.* It is, therefore, very important to check and maintain this equilibrium of heat throughout the roasting process.

Roasting Times

The roasting time depends on the thickness, weight, size of the piece of meat, and upon the degree of roasting desired. There is *no definite rule* for the time required for roasting.

However, extensive research has made it possible to provide guidelines for average roasting times which every cook should know. (See Table 7-3.) It is, of course, necessary to *differentiate between roasting white meats, including poultry, which must be well-done, and red meats which are served more or less rare. If the bone is left in the meat, or the spit is used, the roasting time will be longer.*

Presentation of Roasts

After the roasting is completed, large roasts should stand for 10—15 minutes in a warm place. The roast should be removed from the oven when the thermometer registers 5 to 10 degrees lower than the desired degree of doneness. The meat continues to cook upon removal from the oven. The juices that accumulate in the center spread throughout the entire piece of meat. Furthermore, the meat will be easier to carve and juices will not be lost during carving. Small pieces of *feathered game or roast poultry must be served immediately.*

When roasted meat has been carved, it should be served at once. The gravy obtained by deglazing is served separately in a sauce boat.

Summary of the Principles of Roasting

- The process of roasting tender meats consists only of warming the meat and browning the exterior.
- The roasting time for a piece of meat is dependent on the weight, size, and thickness.
- The flow of heat between the heat source and the roast must be checked frequently.
- Roasted meat, except small feathered game and poultry, should stand in a warm place for 10 to 15 minutes before carving.
- Carved or whole pieces of meat should not be presented in gravy.

7.7.1 Methods for Determining the Degree of Roasting

Adjustment of Oven Temperatures
There is no definite rule for controlling the roasting time by oven temperature; however, the paragraph "Roasting Times" (page 256) and Table 7-3, "Average Roasting Times for Meats," give the possibilities.

Needle Test
The needle test is an old, well-proven method for measuring the degree to which meat of any kind is roasted. A needle is inserted into the middle of the roast. The color of the meat juices shows the degree to which the meat has been roasted.

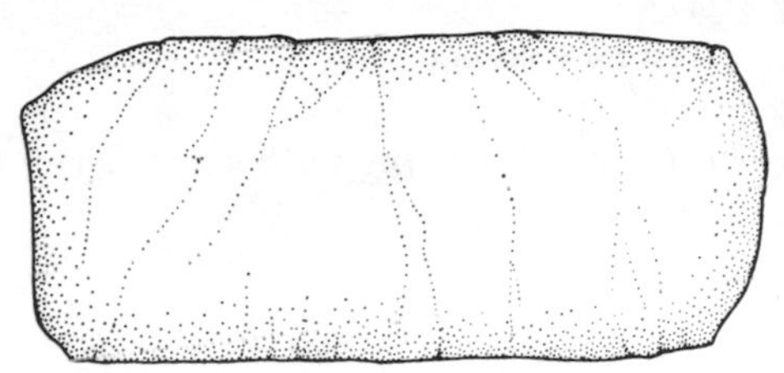

Rare Bleu — Only for red meat, the meat juices are dark red.

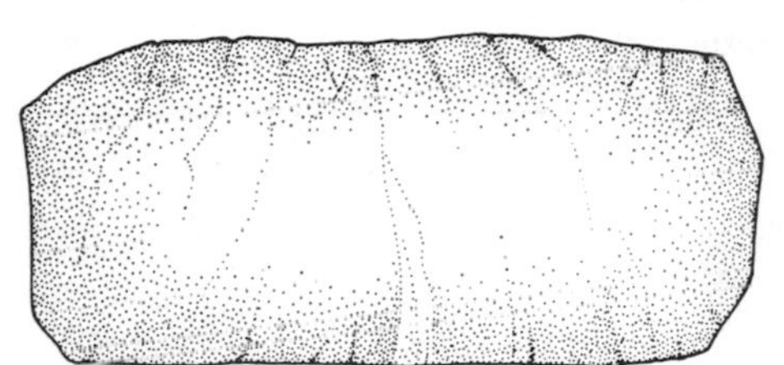

Medium Rare Saignant — Only for red meat, the meat juices are red.

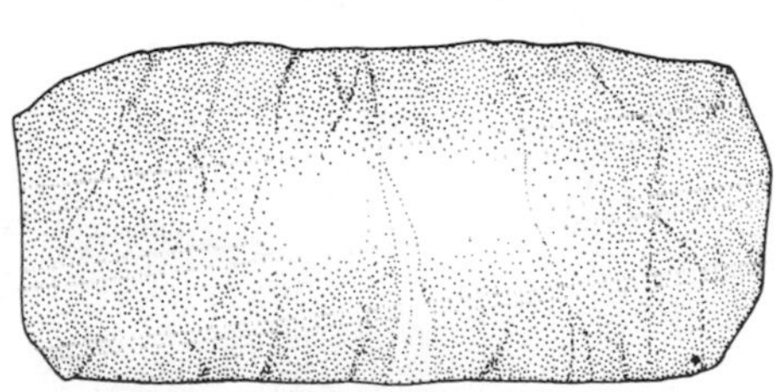

Medium A Bint — For red meat and game, the meat juices are pink.

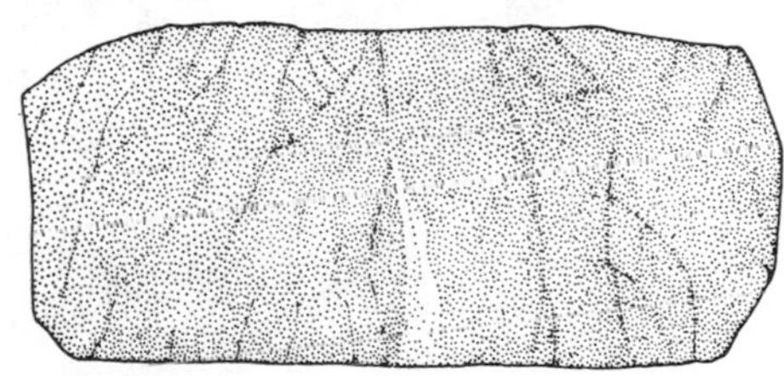

Well-done Bien Cuit — For any roast, the meat juices are clear and light.

FIGURE 7-58
Methods for Determining the Degree of Roasting

FIGURE 7-59
The Needle Test for Roasting

Testing the degree of roasting with a needle (for roasts in the oven and on the spit)

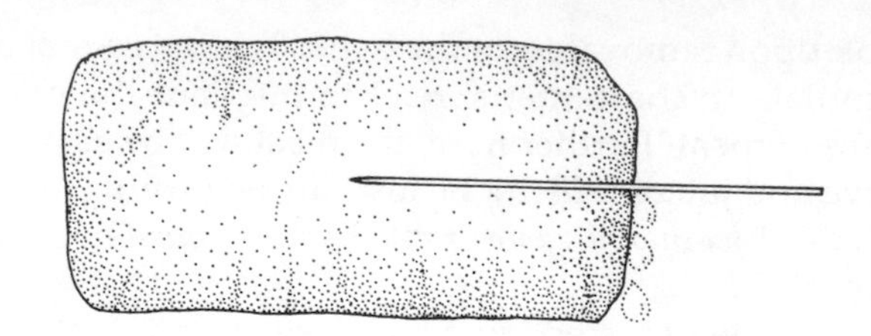

FIGURE 7-60
Meat Thermometer

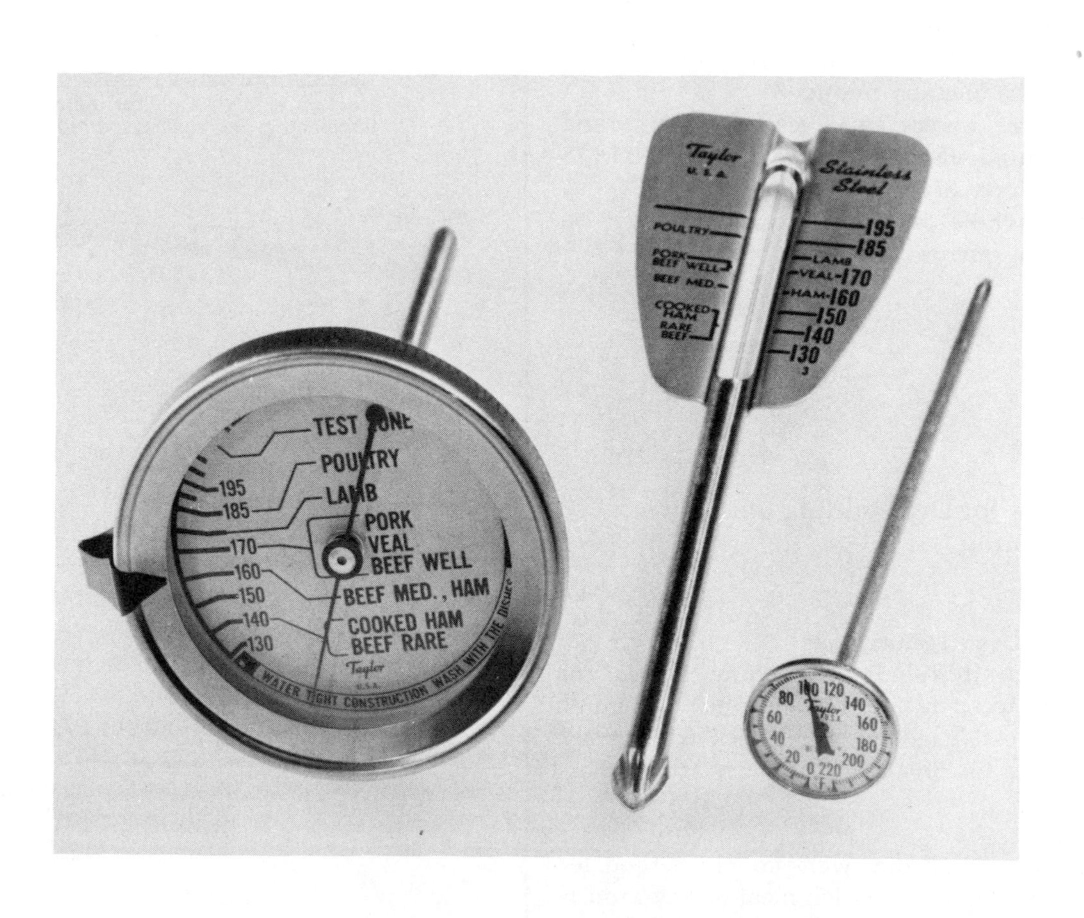

TABLE 7-3. Average Roasting Times for Meats

Beef

Degree of Roasting: *medium*

Oven Temperature: *Constant Temperature Method 300°F. (150°C.)*
Searing Method 490°F. (225°C.) to 300°F. (150°C.)

Type	*Thin (1½ inches)*	*Thick (2½ to 3 inches)*	*Extra Thick (4 inches plus)*	
Beef tenderloin, whole	5 to 6 minutes per pound	8 to 10 minutes per pound	roast at 425°F. (220°C.) for 50 minutes	
Beef sirloin	8 minutes	10 to 13 minutes	—	per pound
Rib roast	—	—	15 to 18 minutes	per pound
Saddle of lamb	8 minutes	10 minutes	—	per pound
Leg of lamb	8 minutes	13 minutes	15 to 20 minutes	per pound

Other Red Meats: *game*

Degree of Roasting: *medium to medium rare*

Oven Temperature: *490°F./455°F. (255°C./232°C.) to 390°F./340°F. (200°C./171°C.)*

Type	*Approximate roasting time per piece*	
Leg of venison	30 to 40 minutes	*Per pound:* 8 to 10 minutes
Saddle of venison	20 to 30 minutes	*Per pound:* 6 to 8 minutes
Saddle of hare	15 to 20 minutes	
Wild boar	As for pork, well done	
Woodcock	12 to 15 minutes	
Quail	8 to 10 minutes	
Wild duck	15 to 20 minutes (rare)	
Pheasant		
1¾ to 2½ pounds	20 to 25 minutes dependent upon the size	
Partridge	12 to 18 minutes	

TABLE 7-3 Average Roasting Times for Meats, (continued)

Veal and Pork

Degree of Roasting: *well-done, juicy*

Oven Temperature: *Constant Temperature Method to 300°F./325°F. (150°C./163°C.)*
Searing Method 440°F./410°F. (227°C./210°C.) to 300°F./325°F. (150°C./163°C.)

Type	*Thin* (1½ inches)	*Thick* (2½ to 4 inches)	
All cuts	10 minutes	18 to 20 minutes	per pound

Poultry

Degree of Roasting: *well-done, juicy*

Oven Temperature: *440°F./410°F.*
(227°C./210°C.) to 355°F./320°F. (179°C./160°C.)

Type	*Weight*	*Approximate roasting time per piece*	*per pound*
Capon	4 to 6 pounds	70 to 90 minutes	
Poularde	3 to 4 pounds	50 to 70 minutes	
Chicken	2 to 2½ pounds	35 to 45 minutes	
Spring chicken	1½ to 1¾ pounds	25 to 35 minutes	
Chick	14 ounces	15 minutes	
Turkey	8 to 12 pounds		18 minutes
Young turkey	5 to 8 pounds		15 to 18 minutes
Guinea fowl	1½ to 2 pounds	30 to 35 minutes	
Nantes duckling	3 to 4 pounds	35 to 40 minutes	
Duck	4 to 5 pounds		15 to 18 minutes
Gosling	3 to 6 pounds		15 to 18 minutes
Goose	6 to 12 pounds		18 to 20 minutes
Young pigeon	½ to ¾ pound	12 to 15 minutes	
Pigeon	14 to 16 ounces	15 to 20 minutes	

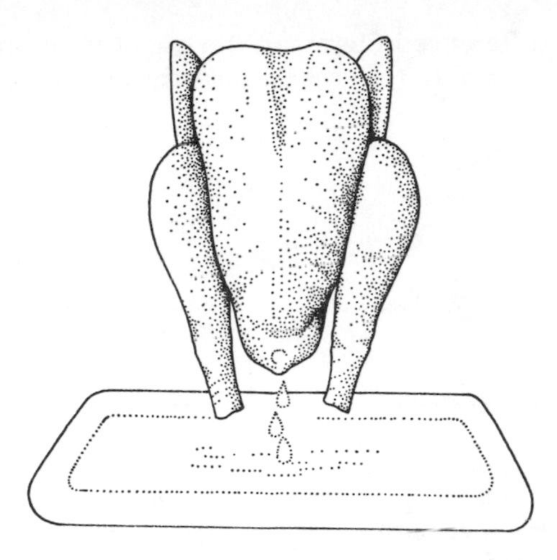

FIGURE 7-61
Test for Degree of Doneness of Poultry

There is another method for determining the degree to which poultry is roasted. The poultry is held above a white plate with the legs toward the plate. If the juices are clear and light, the bird is well-done.

Meat Thermometer
The temperature of the meat is measured using a meat thermometer. The newest and most reliable method works on the principle that each stage of the cooking process results from a definite meat temperature. The tip of the thermometer is equipped with a heat-sensitive point. Therefore, the tip should be inserted into the thickest part of the meat, and should not be in contact with any bones, fat, or equipment. The thermometer pictured in Figure 7-60 is used as follows:

- Move the red arrow until it is set to the desired degree of doneness.
- When roasting in the oven *insert* the thermometer *before starting* the cooking process.
- When the temperature-indicating needle points to the red needle, the required degree of doneness has been reached.

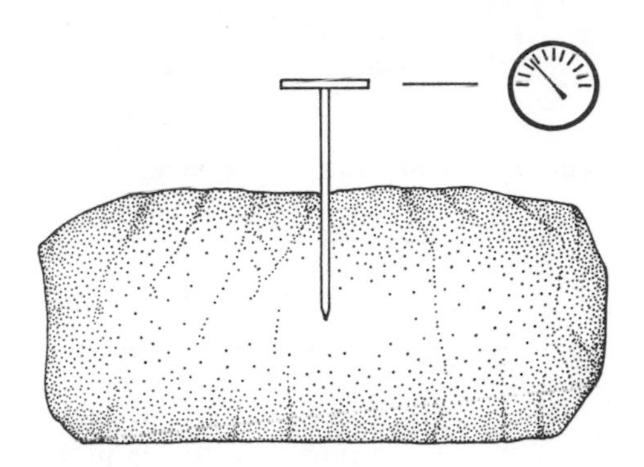

FIGURE 7-62
Temperature for Roasted Meats

Meat temperatures (for all types of roasts)

Rare *Bleu*	Only for red meat, *meat temperature of 125°F. (52°C.)*
Medium rare *Saignant*	Only for red meat, *meat temperature of about 130°F. (55°C.)*
Medium *A point*	Only for red meat and game, *meat temperature of about 140°F. (60°C.)*
Well-done *Bien cuit*	For red meat, *about 160°F. (70°C.)* For veal and lamb, *about 170°F. (77°C.)* For fresh pork and poultry, *about 185°F. (85°C.)*

7.8 Quantities/Portion Sizes

The type of establishment and the clientele exert a significant influence upon portion sizes and the quantities needed. The following information should *be considered as a general guideline.* For example, whether a braised meat dish forms part of a menu together with an hors-d'oeuvre, dessert, and an entree, or a menu with a soup as the only other dish makes a great difference in terms of the quantity of braised meat required. In the second case, the amount would

TABLE 7-4 Table of Quantities (portion sizes)

	Per person Menu	a la Carte
Soups		
Portion	–	½ pint
Plate	⅓ pint	⅓ pint
Cup	½ pint	½ pint
Small cup (for turtle soup)	2 fluid ounces	2 fluid ounces
Pasta to be added per quart	1 ounce	1 ounce
Egg dishes	2 units	2 units
Sauces		
Brown and white sauce	2 fluid ounces	4 fluid ounces
Hollandaise	2 fluid ounces	4 fluid ounces
Melted butter	¾ ounce	1 ounce
Fish (ready to cook)		
Perch	5½ ounces	9 ounces
Grayling	5½ ounces	9 ounces
Trout	5½ ounces	9 ounces
Pike	5½ ounces	9 ounces
Salmon	5½ ounces	9 ounces
Sole	5½ ounces	9 ounces
Turbot	7 ounces	10½ ounces
Pike-perch	5½ ounces	9 ounces
Perpared fillets	3½ ounces	6½ ounces
Beef (ready to cook)		
Tenderloin steak	4¼ ounces	6½ ounces
Sirloin steak	4¼ ounces	6½ ounces
Rump steak	4¼ ounces	6½ ounce
Boiled beef	5½ ounces	9 ounces
Tenderloin goulash	4¼ ounces	6½ ounce
Roast beef	4¼ ounces	6½ ounce
Braised beef/goulash	5½ ounces	7 ounces
Tongue	4¼ ounces	6½ ounce
Tripe	4¼ ounces	6½ ounce
Veal (ready to cook)		
Cutlet	4¼ ounces	5½ ounce
Cutlet for breading	3½ ounces	4¼ ounce
Roast	5½ ounces	6½ ounce
Chop	5½ ounces	6½ ounce
Sliced	3½ ounces	5½ ounce
Liver, kidneys	3½ ounces	5½ ounce
Head (without bone)	5½ ounces	9 ounces
Stew	5½ ounces	9 ounces
Pork (ready to cook)		
Chop	5½ ounces	6½ ounce
Chop, smoked, cured	5½ ounces	6½ ounce
Roast	5½ ounces	6½ ounce
Ham	3½ ounces	5½ ounce
Bacon	3½ ounces	5½ ounce
Lamb/Mutton (ready to cook)		
Cutlet	4¼ ounces	7 ounces
Stew or Irish stew	5½ ounces	9 ounces
Roast	5½ ounces	6½ ounce

be double. *Every establishment should prepare a table of quantities for its own requirements,* expressed *in gross weights* for the kitchen records, and *in ready-to-cook weights* for the preparation kitchen.

ABLE 7-4 Table of Quantities (portion sizes)

	Per person Menu	a la Carte
oat (ready to cook)	9 ounces	12½ ounces
ame (ready to cook)		
Leg of venison	6½ ounces	9 ounces
Saddle of venison	8 ounces	12½ ounces
Game pfeffer (without bones)	5½ ounces	7 ounces
Hasenpfeffer (without bones)	5½ ounces	7 ounces
Saddle of hare	7 ounces	10½ ounces
Pheasant	7 ounces	10½ ounces
Partridge	7 ounces	10½ ounces
ultry (ready to cook)		
Chicken, poularde	10½ ounces	14 ounces
Duck	10½ ounces	14 ounces
Goose	12½ ounces	1 pound
Turkey	10½ ounces	12½ ounces
Guinea fowl	7 ounces	10½ ounces
Pigeon	7 ounces	10½ ounces
sta	2 ounces	3½ ounces
ce	2 ounces	3 ounces
tatoes (peeled)	5½ ounces	7 ounces
egetables (ready to cook)	3½ ounces	5½ ounces
Asparagus	7 ounces	10½ ounces
Tomato salad (ready to serve)	3½ ounces	5½ ounces
Cold Meat Dishes (ready to serve)		
Mixed cold cuts	–	5½ ounces
Ham (without bone)	–	5½ ounces
Raw ham	–	3½ ounces
Salami	–	3 ounces
Bacon, Canadian (raw)	–	3½ ounces
Open-faced sandwich with beef	–	3½ ounces
Open-faced sandwich with ham	–	3 ounces
Open-faced sandwich with salami	–	2 ounces
Cheese and Cheese Dishes		
Cheese	–	3½ ounces
Cheese slices	2 ounces	4¼ ounces
Fondue	–	5½ ounces
Fat for Cooking Potatoes per pound		
Roast potatoes		1½ ounces
Rosti (roasted grated potatoes)		2½ ounces
French-fried potatoes (blanching and frying)		2 ounces

8 The Basic Cooking Methods

The following diagrams showing the forms of basic cooking methods deserve special attention. These methods are used separately or in combination to prepare any cooked food item. How the heat is initiated and controlled is presented for each type of preparation. There are fourteen basic methods. *Each, including convenience foods, must be thoroughly understood and properly executed for perfect cooking—cooking that will ensure highest quality in terms of flavor, color, appearance, and nutritional value.*

Diagrams of the Basic Forms of Preparation

Explanation of symbols:

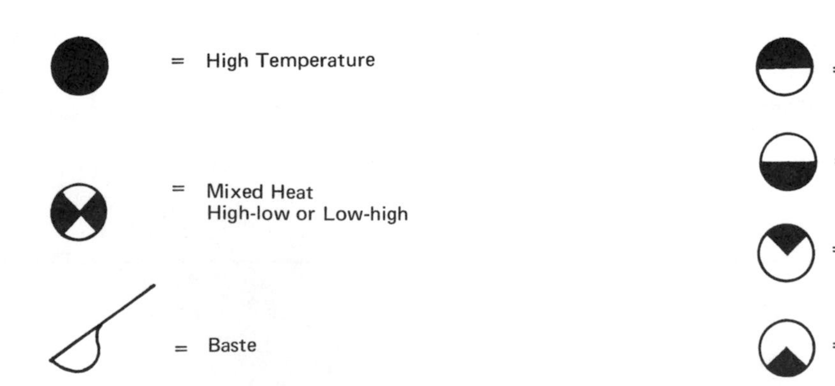

8.1 Blanching—Blanchir

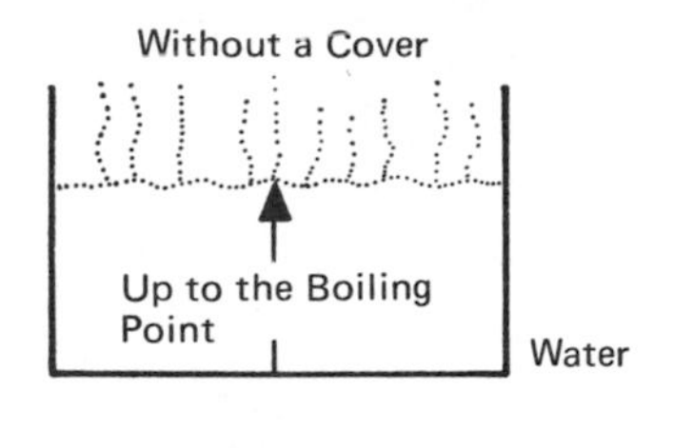

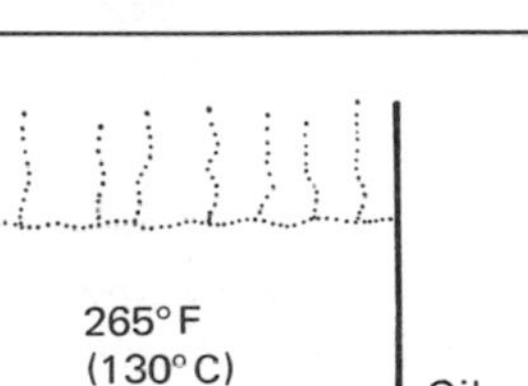

Place food in a large quantity of *cold water (1:10).* Bring to a boil slowly and boil for a short time.
Rinse and plunge into *cold water* quickly to prevent further cooking if the food is not to be used immediately.

or

Place a small amount of food in a large quantity of rapidly *boiling water (1:10).* Bring to a boil again.
Plunge food in *cold water,* drain, and refrigerate if the food is not to be used immediately.

In cold water: bones and certain cuts of meat. To open the pores and to leech out excess salt from cured ham or salt pork and to remove impurities, strong flavors, and excess blood from some foods.

In hot water: vegetables and potatoes. To close pores and to retain color and nutrients.
In hot oil: fish, vegetables, and potatoes.

Note: Blanching is often a preliminary process in many methods of cooking; in hot oil, it is equivalent to a pre-frying process.

8.2 Poaching—Pocher

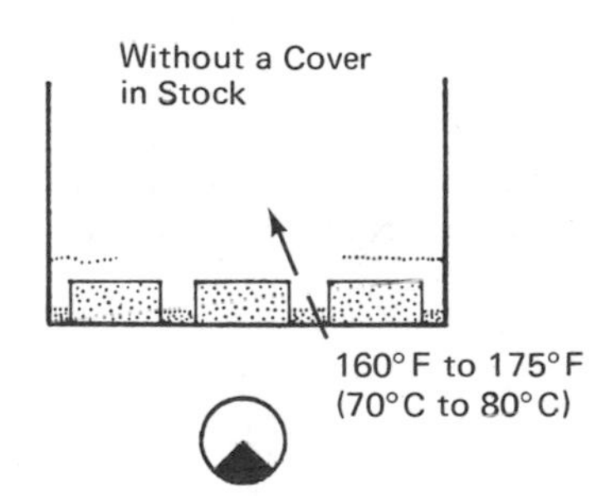

In stock or court bouillon: fish covered with aluminum foil, poultry in small amount of liquid.

Poaching, continued

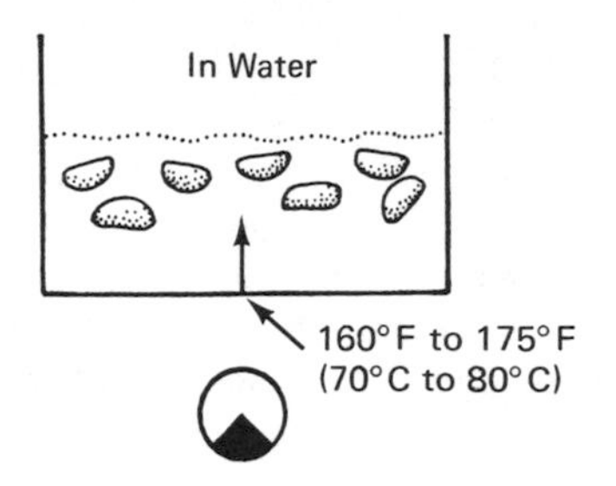

Immerse food into water, stock, court bouillon, or water bath and cook *uncovered* at 160°F. to 175°F. (70°C. to 80°C.).

In water: dumplings, variety meats, smoked pork, sausages, and eggs.

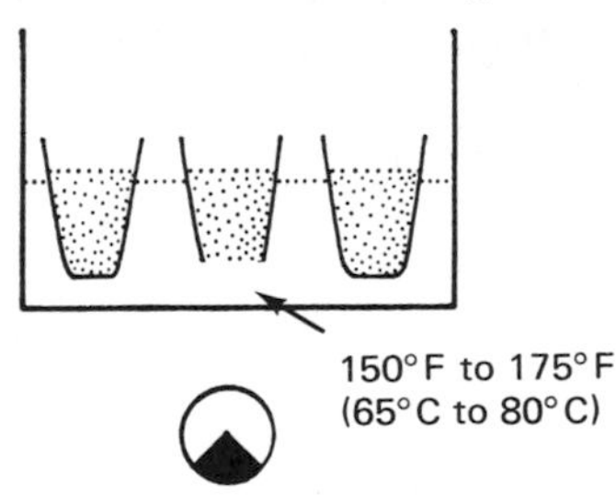

In water bath without stirring: In beakers and molds: farces, stuffings, puddings, fillings, potatoes, vegetables, timbales, sweets, and "Royale" (egg mixes).

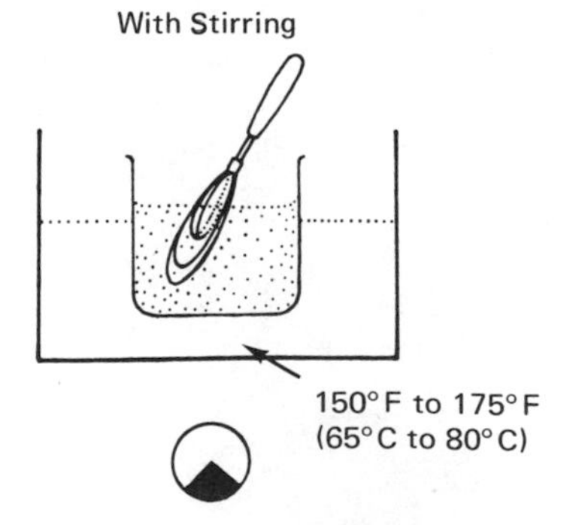

In double-boiler or in water bath with stirring: creams, sponge mixtures, and sauces.

Note: Poaching is a gentle cooking process, which prevents the food from drying out. A loss of albumin occurs at temperatures above 175°F. (80°C.).

Basic Cooking Methods	Principle/Procedure	Uses

8.3 Boiling—Bouillir

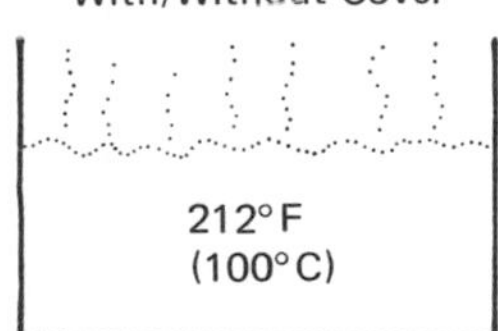

Principle/Procedure	Uses
Depending on type of food, add cold or hot water; heat to near boiling point, and allow to bubble or keep just below boiling point (simmer), with or without lid.	
In cold water with cover: *Reason:* To allow food to absorb water and cook evenly and to prevent toughness and hardness on exterior surface.	*Allow to boil:* potatoes, dried vegetables, and bones.
In cold water or stock without cover: *Reason:* Cooking at temperature under the boiling point will prevent cloudiness.	*Do not allow to boil:* clear stocks, clear broths, and meat jellies.
In boiling water with cover: *Reason:* Food cooks more quickly and retains more vitamins, minerals, and color.	*Allow to boil:* vegetables.
In rapidly boiling water without cover: *Reason:* Starch on exterior of pasta gelatinizes and boiling water keeps pieces from adhering to each other.	*Allow to boil rapidly:* pasta and rice.
In boiling water or stock without cover: *Reason:* To control simmering: first allow to bubble to close the pores. Reduce temperature and simmer gently. Add more liquid if necessary.	*Allow to boil at beginning:* blanched meat and poultry (beef, veal, mutton, lamb, chicken).

8.4 Steaming—Cuire a vapeur

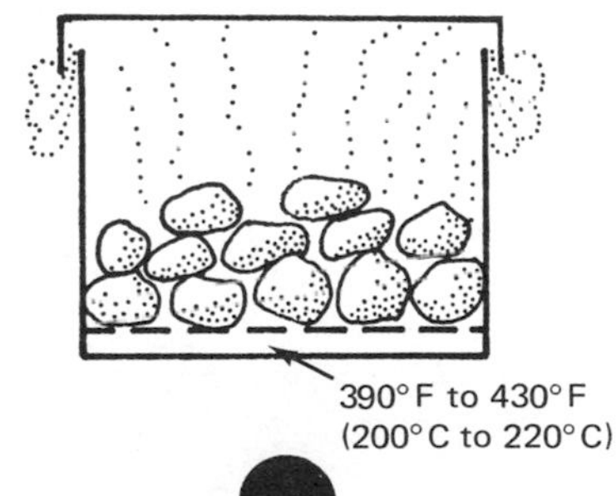

Principle/Procedure	Uses
Without pressure: Use a heavy container with a perforated base, grating, or basket, and a heavy cover. Keep boiling water at level beneath the food. Replace water lost by evaporation.	For certain soups, meats, and poultry; for vegetables, potatoes, legumes, rice; and for canning *Note:* Soups, rice, and cereals are steamed in liquid which has been superheated.

Steaming, continued

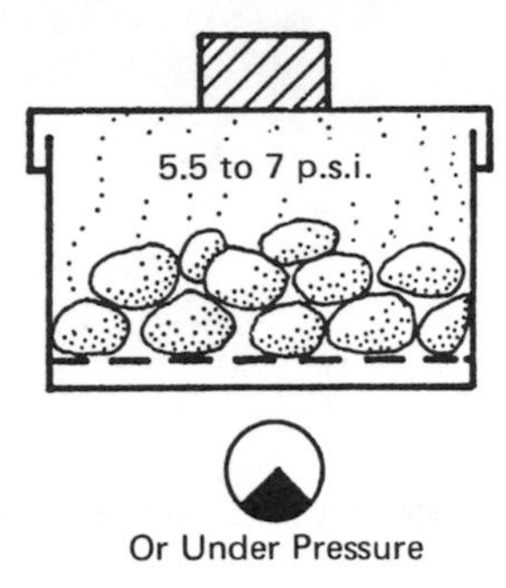

Under pressure:
Wet steam: in pressure cookers
Dry steam: in high speed steam cookers
Best working pressure: 5.5 to 7 psi
A very fast cooking method
Follow equipment manufacturer's directions.

8.5 Deep-Fat Frying—Frire

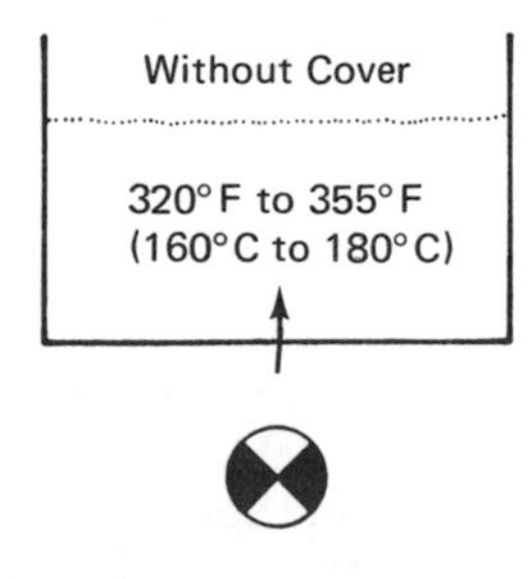

Place shortening or oil in deep-fat fryer and keep thermostat at 200°F. (93°C.) until fat is melted. Set thermostat at required temperature. Food should be dry and at room temperaure before frying. (Frozen, blanched potatoes and shrimp are exceptions.) Fry only small quantities of food at one time to avoid absorption of fat and loss of temperature. Do not salt over the fryer.

For fish, meat, poultry, vegetables, potatoes, turnovers, fritters, doughnuts, and other desserts.

8.6 Sauteing – Sauter

Without Cover

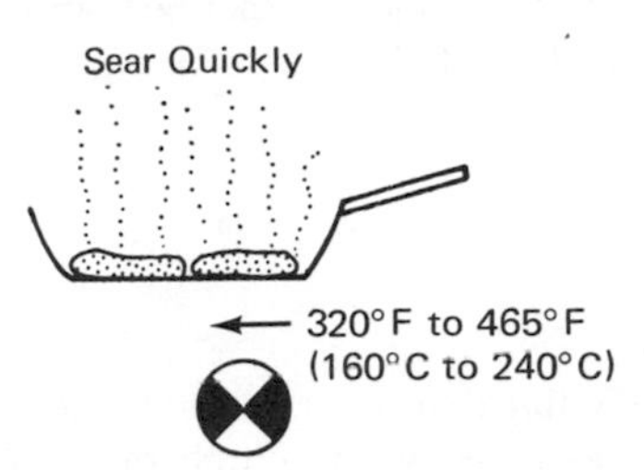

Heat small quantity of fat in a saute pan (sauteuse). Add food and saute quickly (avoid rapid loss of heat). A griddle is often used but is not suitable for finely sliced meats.

Note: The term *pan-frying* is often used interchangeably with sauteing. A larger amount of fat is used for pan-frying. Pan-frying is principally used for poultry, large fish, and other foods that are sometimes finished at low temperatures in the oven.

In saute pan (sauteuse): finely sliced meat and poultry, fish, vegetables and potatoes; saute by moving (shaking) pan constantly.
In large saute pan (sautoir): chops, cutlets, sirloin, steaks, pieces of poultry, small fish; without shaking pan, just brown and turn food.

8.7 Broiling/Grilling – Griller

Without Cover
At the Beginning

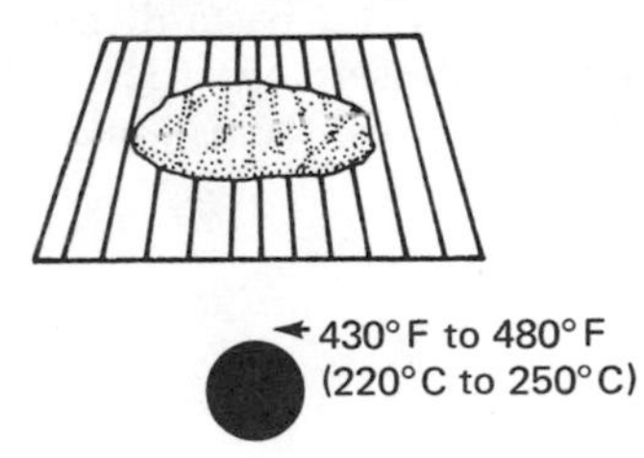

After Searing

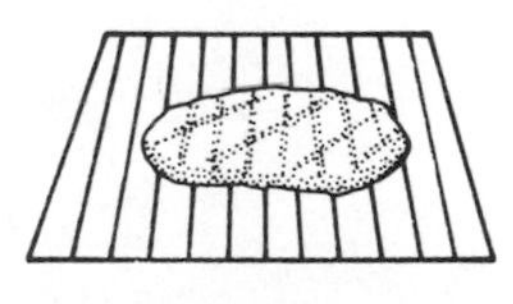

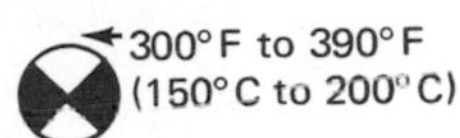

Brush food with seasoned oil and marinate for approximately 30 minutes (optional). Place on rack. The heat source may be from above, below, or both. Use high heat at beginning to seal the pores; lower the temperature and cook to desired degree of doneness. Use high heat for small pieces, and a more moderate heat for larger pieces.

For small- and medium-sized pieces of meat (chops, cutlets, sirloin steaks, Chateaubriand, mixed grill), poultry, sausages, small fish, and shellfish. Vegetables or potatoes may be wrapped in aluminum foil.

8.8 Gratinating – Gratiner

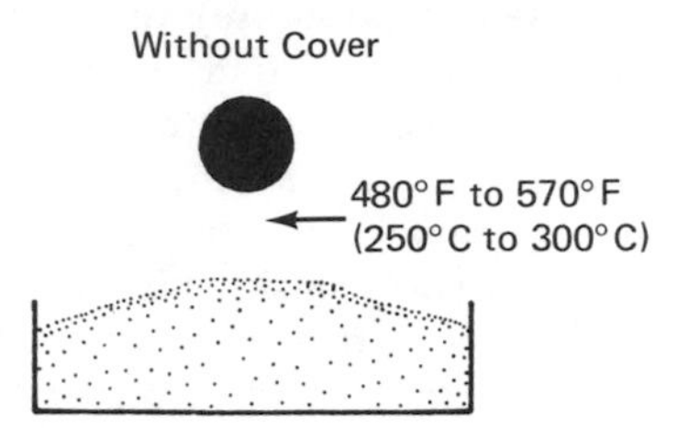

The surface of a gratin dish is covered with at least one fatty product or mixture such as fats, with butter, cheese, cream, or egg mix. The dish is placed under the salamander, broiler, or oven until a crust is formed on the top of the dish.

For fish, meat, poultry, vegetables, potatoes, pasta, casseroles, and escalloped dishes.

Follow this method using a lower temperature. The product will then be cooked at the same time.

For flat fish, thin slices of meat, and vegetables with a high moisture content (tomatoes).

This method may be applied to caramelizing the sugar.

For certain sweet dishes.

8.9 Baking – Cuire au four

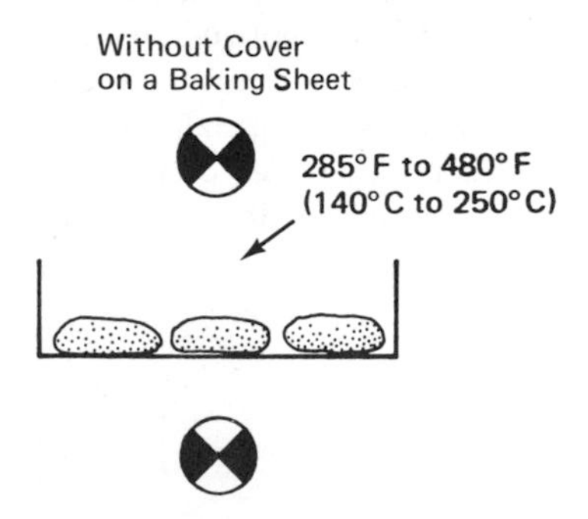

Set heat regulator at desired temperature. Place food on greased sheet or rack or use molds in oven without adding either fat or liquid and bake to desired degree of doneness. Increase or decrease heat as stated in recipe. May also be used for drying at lower temperatures.

For potatoes and pasta dishes and for many desserts, pastries, tarts, pies, and cakes; for fish and ham.

Baking, continued

Or on the Rack

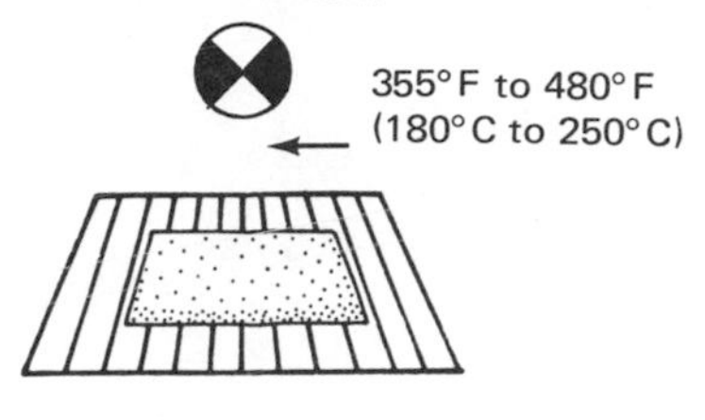

Convection Oven

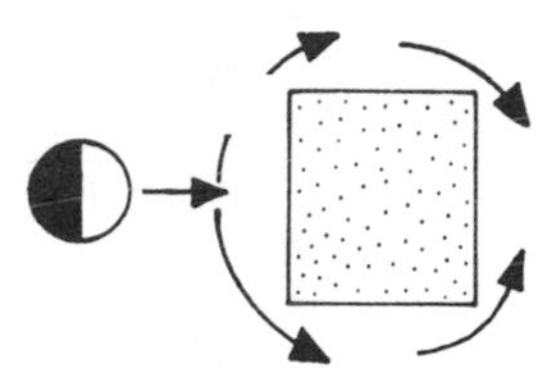

Heat Transferred by
Circulation of Hot Air

A convection oven may also be used for baking. Fans force heated air into the oven cavity for more rapid baking. A slightly higher temperature is required in a convection oven than in a conventional oven. Foods that are to be regenerated should be covered.

The foods listed above may be baked in a convection oven.
For regeneration of convenience foods.

8.10 Roasting—Rotir

In the Oven/On the Spit, without cover

Low Temperature Method. Use initial temperature and bottom heat only.

Searing Method

300° F (150° C)

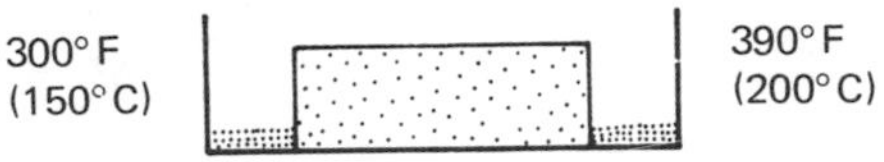

390° F (200° C)

Low temperature method for meat: Top quality meat with a fat cover is not seared. Insert a meat thermometer so the bulb is in the center of the largest muscle of the meat. Roast meat fat side up in oven at 300°F. to 350°F. (150°C. to 177°C.) until the thermometer registers the desired degree of doneness.* Do not cover and do not add liquid.

For top grades of meat with a fat covering: prime rib, rib eye, sirloin, rump roast, and turkey.

Searing method for meat: Sear meat in fat at 390°F. (200°C.). Insert a meat thermometer so the bulb is in the center of the largest muscle of the meat and place roast in oven preheated to 300°F. (150°C.). Roast and baste frequently until thermometer registers the desired degree of doneness.

For large pieces of fish, poultry, game, and meat without a fat covering and for potatoes.

Roasting, continued

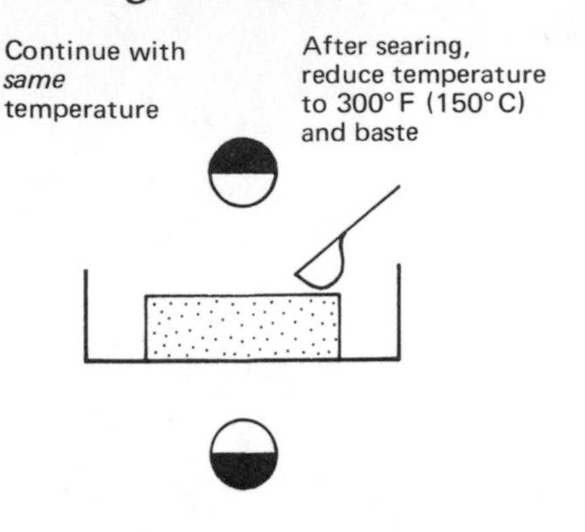

For fish: After searing, roast at 230°F. (110°C.).

For poultry, game, potatoes: After searing, roast at 335°F. to 390°F. (180°C. to 200°C.)

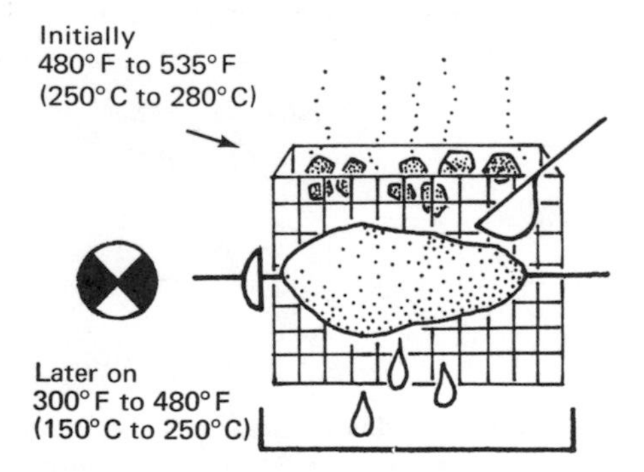

Note: The searing method is used for roasting on the spit except the initial heat should be increased slightly and more frequent basting is necessary. The larger the piece of meat, the lower the temperature required after the initial high heat.

*See Table 7-3. Average Roasting Times for Meats.

8.11 Braising—Braiser (for red meat)

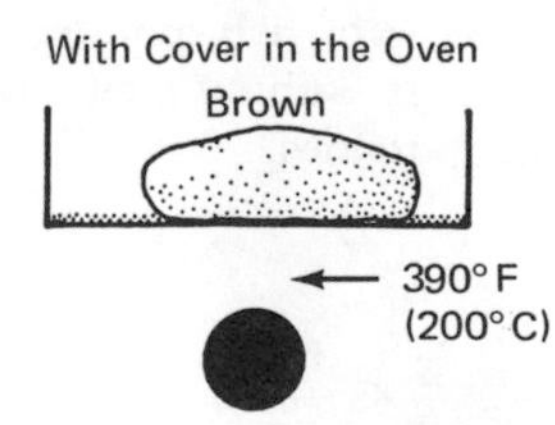

The basic forms of preparation in 8.11 are similar to 8.14. Each is a gentle form of cooking. The food is covered and heated in the oven with a small amount of liquid. The more tender the meat, the lower the heat and the less liquid required.

For beef, mutton, and lamb:
Beef: chuck, foreshank, brisket, short plate, flank, round, tip.
Mutton, Lamb: neck, shoulder, foreshank, breast, hind shank (leg).

Braising, continued

Add liquid and boil down

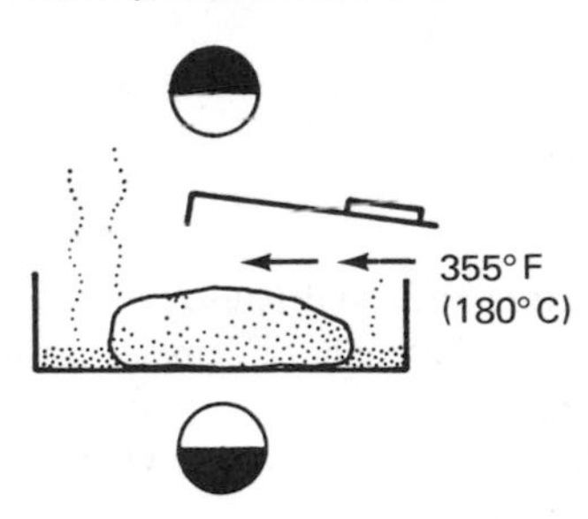

Fill 1/4 full and braise

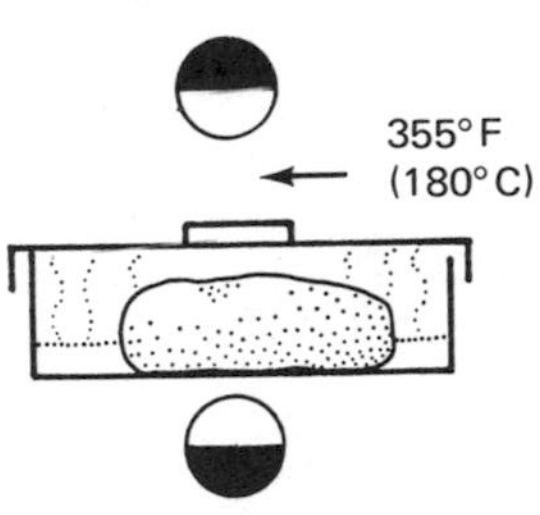

Red meat: Brown quickly in fat at a high temperature. Drain. Pour red wine or marinade over meat and reduce to a glaze. Fill pan ¼ full of brown stock and braise at medium temperature. Baste and turn meat. Reduce stock, strain, and pour over the meat. Braise uncovered until tender.

Strain stock, remove fat

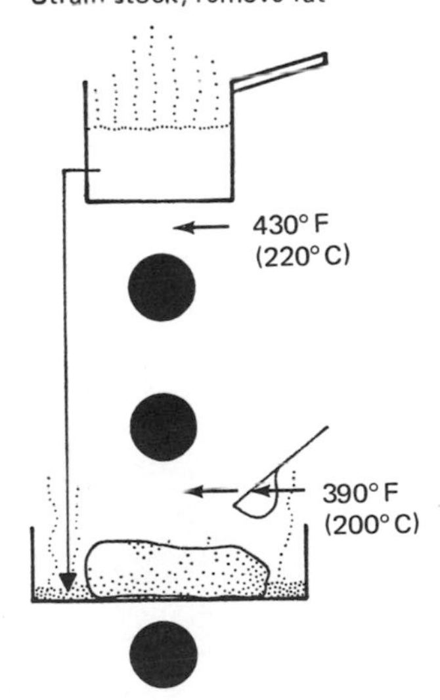

8.11.1 Glazing—Glacer (for white meat and poultry)

Follow directions in 8.11 except use lower temperature and deglaze with white wine. Add brown stock, reduce to a glaze. Add more stock until pan is 1/6 full because white meat becomes tender more quickly than dark meat. When nearly tender, glaze strongly with the syrup-looking stock. Add white wine and stock. Strain and remove fat.

For white meat and poultry:
Veal: shoulder, shank, breast, hind shank.
Poultry: poularde, turkey, chicken.

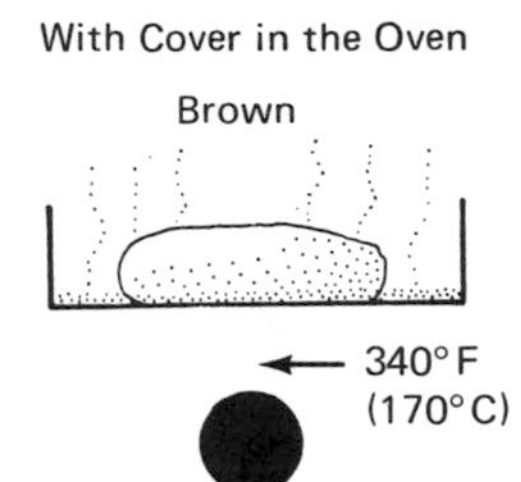

Brown/deglaze, reduce and glaze

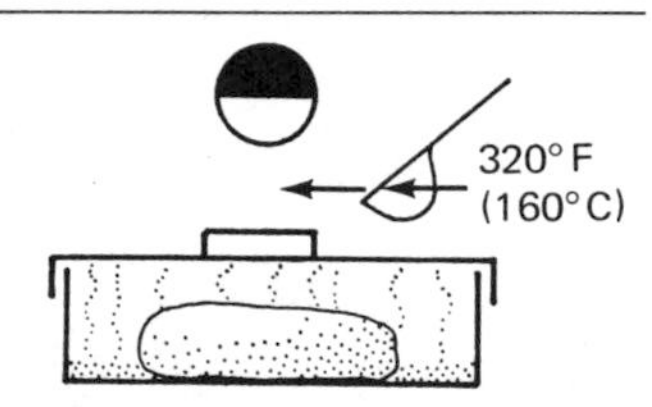

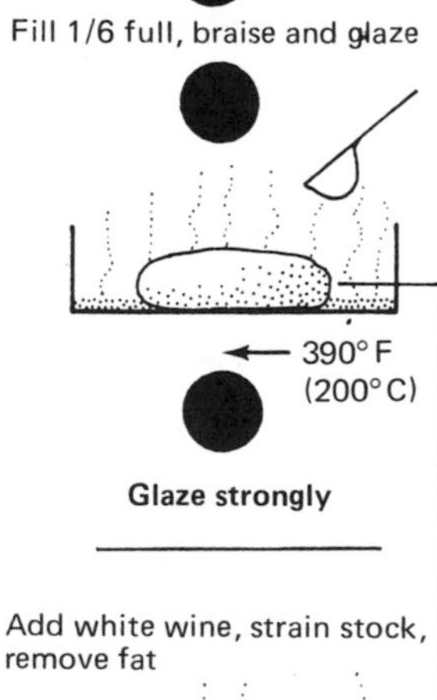

430° F
(220° C)

Note: When glazing the first time, a layer forms around the meat which prevents the loss of any juice and the drawing out of the meat. (See pages 405-406.)

8.12 Braising—Braiser (for fish and vegetables)

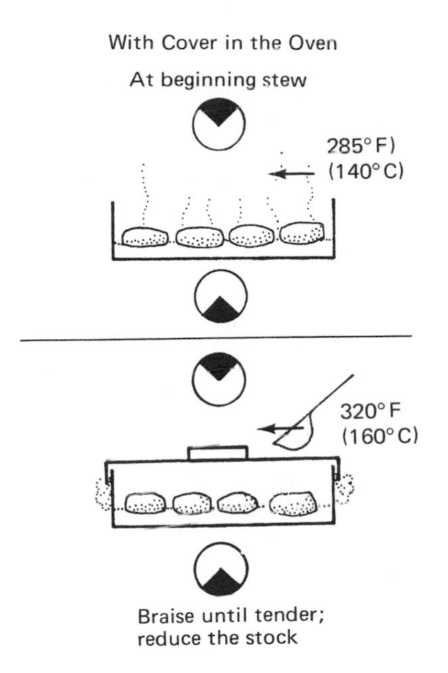

Vegetables:
Turn oven regulator to low heat. Begin by stewing ingredients. Add vegetables. Top them with ⅓ of broth, cover, and braise. Baste occasionally. Reduce the liquid. Serve in liquid or use it for making a sauce.

Fish:
Begin by adding a stewed matignon (See page 291). Add half white wine and half fish stock up to ⅓ of the fish. Cover and braise in the oven. Baste. Use liquid for making a fish sauce.

For fish and vegetables:
Vegetables: green beans, cabbage, sauerkraut, lettuce, and fennel.
Fish: salmon, carp, trout, and turbot.

8.12.1 Glazing—Glacer (for vegetables)

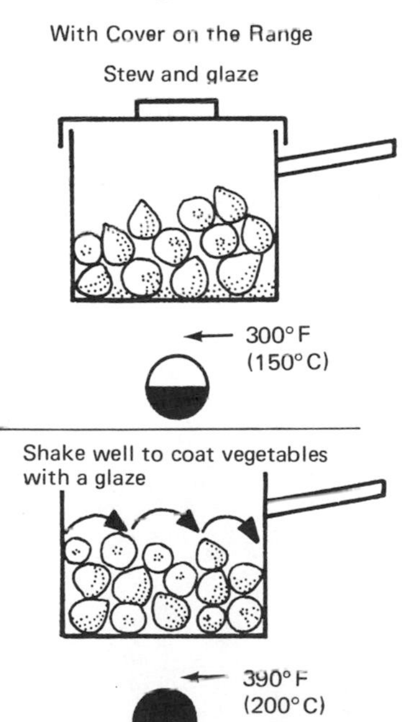

Turn oven regulator to low. Add a small amount of liquid, sugar, and butter. Cover vegetables. Reduce liquid. Remove cover and toss until the vegetables are coated with a glaze.

For vegetables:
carrots, turnips, small onions, and chestnuts.

8.13 Poeler—Poelage

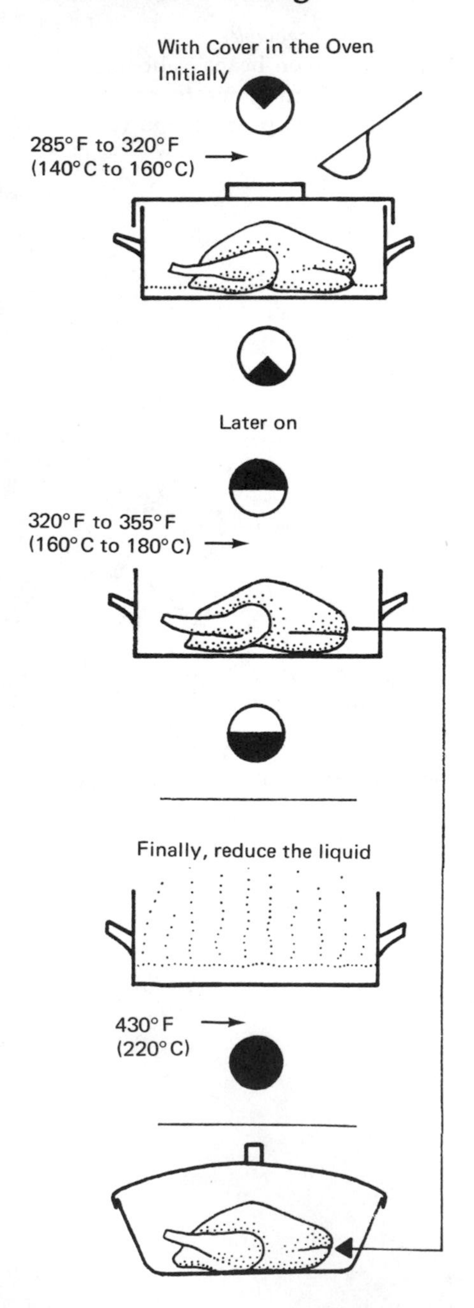

Turn oven regulator to low. Cook meat in generous amount of butter in a covered pan in the oven. Baste regularly. Remove the cover and cook until golden-colored. Remove meat and deglaze pan with wine and/or brown stock. Reduce liquid.

For poultry and tender meat pieces:
Poultry: chicken, turkey, goose, and duck.
Meat: loin and sirloin of veal, tenderloin and sirloin of beef.

8.14 Stewing/Simmering—Etuver

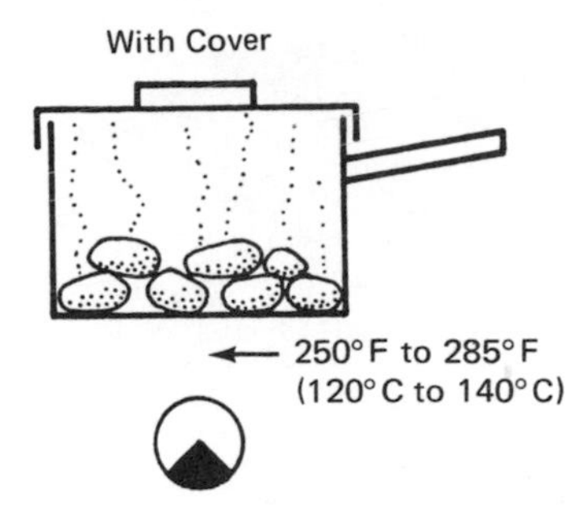

Stew the food in fat and add a small amount of liquid, or none at all. Cover the food and stew over very low heat. When liquid is formed, reduce to serving consistency or replenish the liquid with stock or water depending on the recipe (fricassee).

For fish, small pieces of meat, vegetables, and fruits.

9 Convenience Foods

9.1 Convenience Foods and their Application

The term "convenience foods" is of American origin, where it has become so common that it has spread throughout the world. The definition of convenience foods is simple: *all raw materials that are in any way processed constitute convenience foods.* Hundreds of years ago, and even to this day among certain African tribes, families transformed their grains of corn into semolina or flour using mortars or other primitive grinding implements. Even these simple processes may be described as resulting in convenience foods. The same is true for fermenting and drying tea, for roasting and grinding coffee. Be it roasted coffee, ground cereals, peeled carrots, filleted fish, portioned and breaded cutlets, ready-to-use meats, or prepared meals, all may be classified under the general term convenience foods. Recently a more specific term "ready foods" has come into use. This term refers to *preserved, prepared dishes, and prepared meals* manufactured ready-to-use. It would appear that even in earlier times people sought to make certain foods available in a semi-prepared condition. Thus the movement, as a whole, did not start with the catchwords, "rationalization," "automation," or "labor shortages"; nevertheless, there has been a meteoric expansion in the use of convenience foods over the last few years.

The application possibilities for convenience and ready foods are practically unlimited. It is important to choose applications that increase, rather than decrease, productivity and, at the same time, lower overhead costs. We must, therefore, be aware of where, how, and when convenience foods can be used.

Where:

- in all hotel and restaurant establishments
- in canteens and institutions
- in hospitals
- in the military
- at home
- for large gatherings
- in schools and colleges

How:

- as partially processed products
- as ready-to-cook products
- as ready-to-heat dishes
- as ready-to-serve products

When:

- there are staff shortages
- there is insufficient storage space
- there are supply problems for raw products
- there are storage problems for raw products
- the processing equipment available is inadequate
- the preparation and finishing areas and equipment are inadequate
- there is insufficient time

The problems of purchasing, storing, serving, and merchandising these new food products require a sound knowledge of basic food production and service. Unless the appropriate techniques and knowledge are used in handling and evaluating these products, great losses in food quality and costs can be incurred.

A continuous education program should be in effect to provide instruction to food production and service employees. There must first be an understanding of the basic principles of purchasing, food production and service, menu planning, storage, and merchandising. A knowledge of these principles is required before new systems, techniques, and methods can be understood and effectively applied to the use of the new food products.

9.2 Degrees of Preparation

As Figure 9-1 shows, there are *four different degrees to which food can be prepared.* A simple example illustrates the structure of the different degrees or stages and how they are partially interdependent: A whole poularde is purchased. It must then be cleaned, and when this is completed, the product is partially processed. If it is then cut into portions, it becomes a ready-to-cook product. When further prepared by applying one of the basic forms of preparation, such as braising, it becomes a ready-to-heat product, such as poulet saute or braised chicken. If the same food is garnished with mushrooms, vegetables, potatoes, or noodles, it is a ready food. The combination of various prepared dishes results in a prepared, complete meal. Products which are ready-to-serve, can also be partially prepared from the basic raw materials, but are usually served "as is" to the guest. The chronological order shown in Figure 9-1 illustrates the possibility of purchasing many products from industrial suppliers at any degree of preparation desired. The organization of the establishment and its kitchens will determine whether the products should arrive in raw condition or partially or completely prepared. A knowledge of *the methods of preservation* of food, as described in Section 7.5, is necessary. These can be briefly recalled as: drying, hot-packing, salting, smoking, dehydrating, marinating, pickling, sterilizing, vacuum packing, refrigerating, freezing, and freeze-drying.

The most important method of preservation in the hotel and restaurant business is freezing. The freezing process is described in Section 7.5.2. Other processes used in industry include: pasteurizing, steaming, chemically acidifying, and the Nacka system.

9.3 Methods of Preparation

Convenience foods may be heated by several different methods. The heating process should have no detrimental effect on the quality, degree of doneness, or appearance of the food. An instruction sheet, including the following information, should be prepared for each item:

- product
- unit, weight, number of portions
- supplier
- equipment to be used for preparation
- length of time and temperature for preparation
- additional ingredients
- presentation

The functions of the different systems for preparing food are described in Section 2.3.3. Following are the methods most frequently used when preparing preserved convenience foods: hot water, regeneration, and microwave.

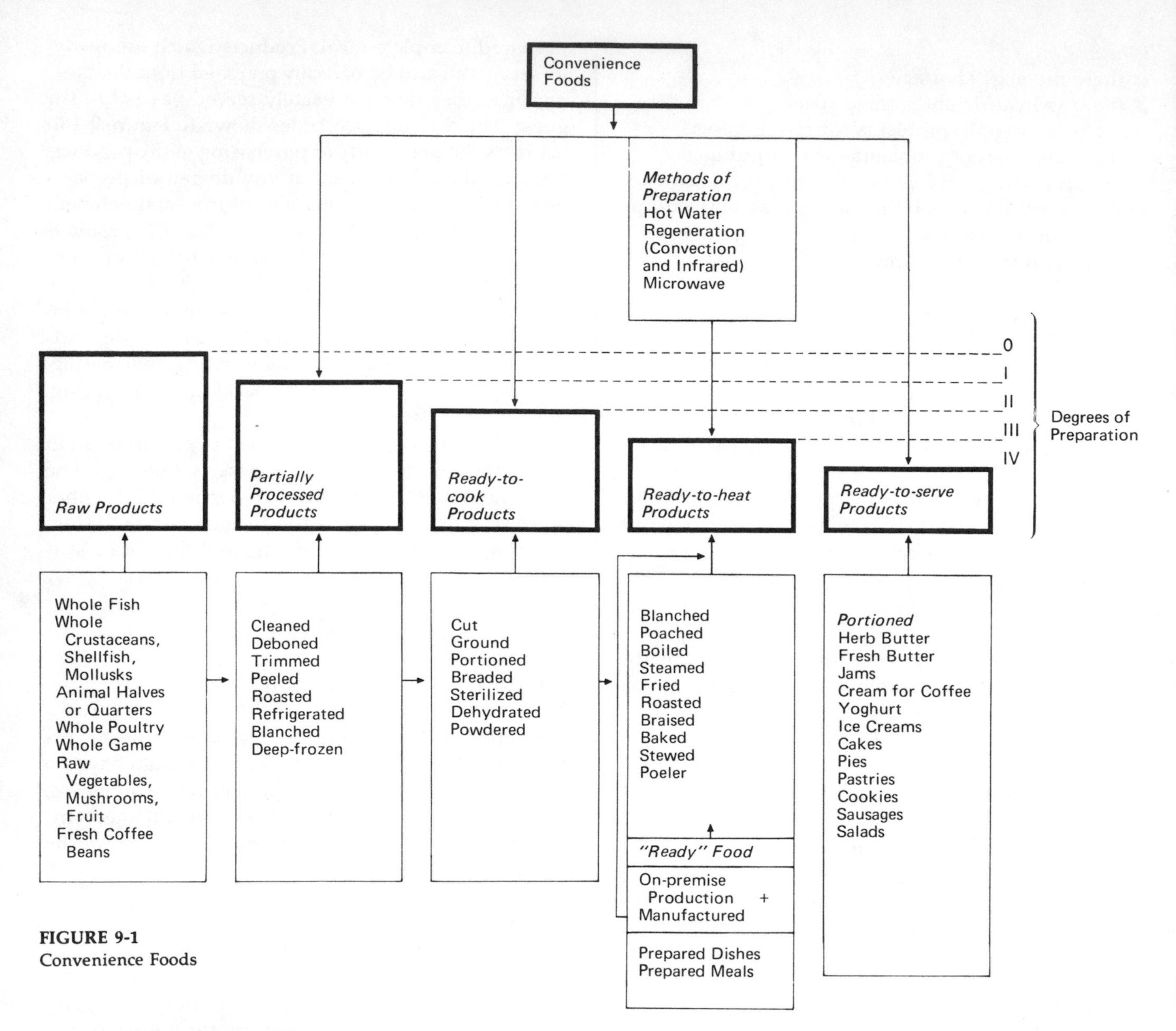

FIGURE 9-1
Convenience Foods

Hot Water. As mentioned under freezing and the Nacka system, preparation in hot water is usually used with the boiling bag process. A large quantity of water is kept at 185°F. to 195°F. (85°C. to 91°C.) in a bain-marie, in a fixed or tilting steam-jacketed kettle, or in a simple open pot. The ratio of hot water to boiling bag should be at least 20:1 by volume. When dipping the usually chilled or frozen boiling bag into the hot water, the temperature of the water should never be allowed to drop more than 10°F. (−12°C.). The length of the heating period depends upon the size and characteristics of the product in the bag. Several components of the menu can be heated at the same time. Care must be taken to avoid burning oneself when opening the bag. Depending on the size of the units, the products are either served directly or held in bains-marie.

Microwave. The principle of microwave heating is described under "Heating Methods and Equipment" (see Section 2.3.3). This is a heating process and not a basic form of preparation. Frozen prepared foods should usually be thawed before heating. Certain precautions should be taken when using a microwave oven. These include:

- metal objects should never be put in the cooking chamber.
- sauces should be heated separately when possible.
- sauced dishes splatter and the crockery should be covered with paper toweling or a paper plate.
- sealed boiling bags or closed plastic containers should be pierced before placing in the oven. This allows steam to escape during cooking.
- dishes or containers used in the oven should be heat-tempered, ovenproof clear glass containers without metal trim; china, ceramics, pottery without metal trim or metal base glaze; paper dishes.
- the preserving method for the food can cause taste changes during the heating process, therefore, each dish must be seasoned to taste before serving.
- the microwave oven must be kept spotlessly clean.
- the oven should be turned on only when the door is closed and when there is food in the oven to avoid damaging the Magnetron tube.

Almost all products need to be prepared, using one of the basic forms of preparation, before heating in the microwave oven. Microwave ovens are particularly suitable for preparing convenience foods.

Regeneration Equipment. As explained in Section 2.3.3, regeneration ovens function using either convected hot air or infrared heat. They are suitable for heating quantities of food for large groups, banquets, or parties. The previously prepared meals are portioned on plates or unitized platters, which are individually covered. The plates, arranged on mobile oven racks, can be rolled from the preparation area into the oven and from the oven to the serving area. Depending on the size of the oven, between 32 and 72 meals can be heated simultaneously in about 15 minutes. These ovens reduce cooking time and the multiple shelves spaced close together increase the oven capacity. They are useful for banquets of all sizes, for canteens, and for groups of people arriving at undetermined times, such as road, rail, and air travelers.

9.3.1 On-Premise Production of Convenience Foods

As previously stated, the term convenience foods refers to *prepared dishes and prepared meals*. In principle, they are portioned and ready-to-serve. The possible preserving techniques and methods of preparation are limited. The following are methods of preservation:

- refrigerated, ready-to-serve, packed in clear foil, keeping period of 12 to 48 hours
- refrigerated, vacuum packed, ready-to-serve, keeping period of roughly 6 days
- frozen, packed in a partitioned boiling bag, to be served only after preparation, keeping period roughly 3 months. Details on this system are found under "Freezing," Section 7.5.2.2.

The possible methods for heating the food are:

- microwave ovens
- the hot water method

The conditions governing all on-premise production of convenience foods are:

- hygienically impeccable processing and serving conditions
- standardized recipes
- observation of rules concerning storage periods
- each pack marked with production and expiration dates
- planning types of food and quantities to be produced

- safe and appropriate preparation (heating) methods
- essential equipment such as blast freezers, adequate refrigeration for safe storage and the necessary equipment for re-thermalizing the food

Examples of Foods for On-Premise Production. Farm-style sausages with onions; meat loaf with mushrooms; fricassee of veal, bonne femme style; beef, modern style with buttered potatoes; sliced beef with mashed potatoes; stuffed beef birds with pasta; beef tongue in Madeira sauce with noodles; chicken curry with rice; beef stew with red cabbage and creamed potatoes; pork stew with vegetables and homemade noodles; pork stew, bourgeois style with noodles; chopped steak with pepper sauce; roast pork with boiled potatoes and beans; tripe a la mode de Caen with buttered potatoes; piccata milanese with spaghetti; ham in Madeira sauce with ratatouille; Szigediner goulash with buttered potatoes; bisque de homard; bouillabaisse; lasagne verde; canneloni a la crema; liver dumplings with onion sauce and mashed potatoes; veal and ham pie; macaroni and cheese, creamed chicken, apple pie, and various national dishes.

9.4 Profitability

As shown in Figure 9-2, the purchase price increases progressively in relation to the degree to which the product is prepared. On the other hand, losses incurred from waste, labor, and overhead costs may be reduced. Since less space and fewer machines are required, investments, running costs, interest, and depreciation can be limited. The preparation costs of ready-to-serve foods are reduced to zero. The following comparison serves as a simple example. Establishment A makes a raspberry ice cream pie, a job that includes the following stages: cleaning and sorting the fruit, mixing a dough, preparing the ice cream and garnish, baking the crust, filling and garnishing the pie, freezing and portioning. Establishment B buys the finished pre-portioned raspberry ice cream pie directly from the supplier. This product can be placed directly into the freezer compartment of the service counter where it is plated and served. In theory, it should be possible to eliminate the kitchen and base the menu on convenience foods and ready-to-serve products. The overall costs of such a system should be thoroughly analyzed. The advantages of a totally ready-to-serve food system would include: re-

Profitability

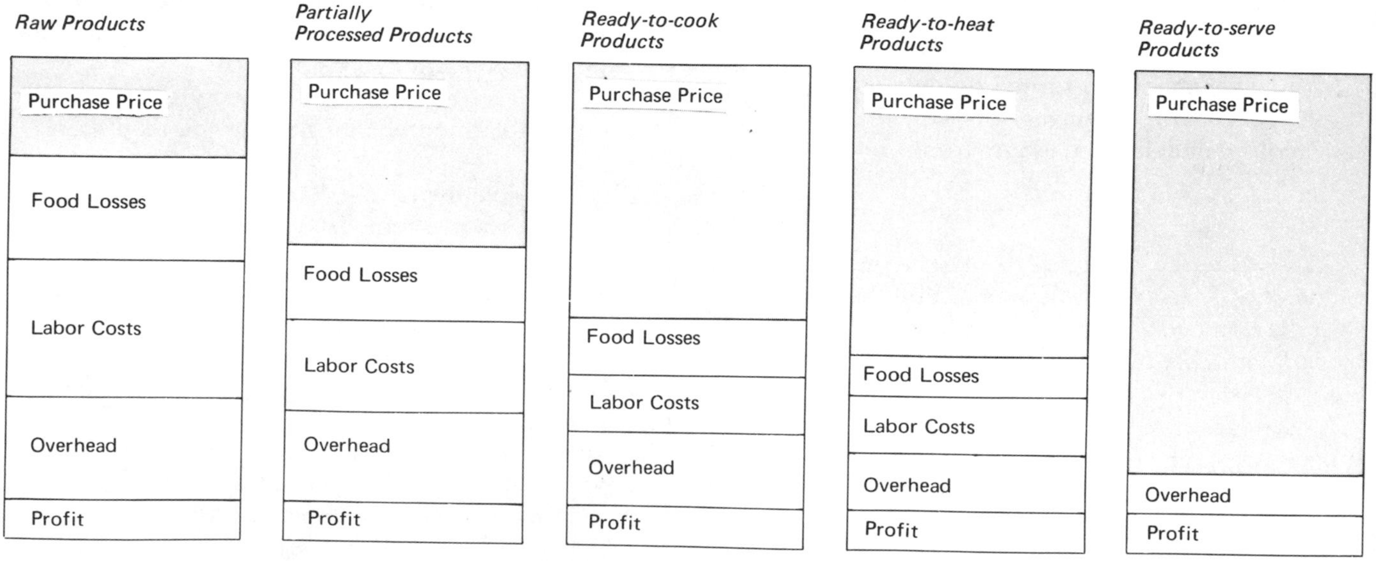

Raw Products	*Partially Processed Products*	*Ready-to-cook Products*	*Ready-to-heat Products*	*Ready-to-serve Products*
Purchase Price	Purchase Price	Purchase Price	Purchase Price	Purchase Price
Food Losses	Food Losses	Food Losses	Food Losses	
Labor Costs	Labor Costs	Labor Costs	Labor Costs	
Overhead	Overhead	Overhead	Overhead	Overhead
Profit	Profit	Profit	Profit	Profit

FIGURE 9-2
Profitability

duction in labor costs; reduction in operating costs, such as power, gas, water, and steam; reduction of waste; possible reduction in size of plant required; the food production can be equalized over a given period of time; built-in portion control; reduction in investment and depreciation of equipment.

Disadvantages of such a system are: choice of menu items limited to availability of products; lack of control over the quality of food served; lack of control of nutritional content of specific items. For example, the ingredients in a specific entree may not meet the protein requirements for a patient or those of a school lunch program.

Note: Convenience foods can maintain or increase profits only if they are used methodically as a solution to a specific problem. The above comments could lead one to the erroneous conclusion that cooks will become redundant in the future. As Figure 9-1 shows, even convenience food products must be produced at some time using one or more of the basic forms of preparation. It is even more evident that with the continuously increasing labor costs for skilled personnel, the latter must be assigned to the preparation and finishing of the more important and more expensive foods. Cooks should not devote time to preparing products that can be easily produced on an industrial basis or by less-skilled personnel. A good basic training program is absolutely necessary for all foodservice personnel.

10 The Recipes: Basic Forms of Preparation

10.1 Bases and Ingredients—Bases et Ingredients

10.1.1 Marinades

Marinades are liquids that usually contain lemon juice or vinegar and/or wine; various seasonings and spices; and oil. Marinades may be cooked or uncooked. The purpose of a marinade is:

- to permeate the meat or fish with aromatic substances
- to tenderize the fibers of certain pieces of meat
- to ensure the preservation of the product over a longer period of time

INSTANT MARINADES—MARINADES A LA MINUTE
Ingredients for fish: lemon juice, chopped herbs, and spices; for meat pates, galantines, and terrines: pate seasoning mixtures and Madeira wine and brandy; for grilled meats: salt and spice mixes, oil for basting; for lamb and mutton: various herbs and a small amount of crushed garlic mixed with oil.
Preparation of the above items: Marinate the pieces of fish and meat for 15 to 30 minutes.

Uncooked Marinade for Meats and Game (Marinades crues pour viande de boucherie et gibier)

YIELD: *U.S. — 5 quarts*
Metric — 5 liters (U.S. equiv. — 5¼ qt.)

INGREDIENTS	*U.S. Weight or Volume*	*Metric Weight or Volume*	PROCEDURE
Wine, red or white	4½ quarts	4.5 liters	1. Combine vinegar and wine.
Vinegar	1 pint	5 deciliters	

Mirepoix:			
Onion	14 ounces	400 grams	2. Saute all the ingredients slightly and add to the wine and vinegar. Mix thoroughly.
Carrots	7 ounces	200 grams	3. Place meat in a stainless steel container, crock, or bowl and add marinade. Cover with a weight to keep meat submerged.
Celery	5 ounces	150 grams	4. Refrigerate.
Garlic	2 cloves	2 cloves	
Bay leaves	2	2	
Cloves	3	3	
Peppercorns, crushed	¾ ounce	20 grams	
Juniper berries, (for game only)	¾ ounce	20 grams	
Rosemary	1 sprig	1 sprig	
Thyme	1 sprig	1 sprig	
Salt	½ teaspoon	3 grams	

Variation

Cooked Marinade. This marinade is the same as the uncooked marinade except the ingredients are heated to the boiling point.

10.1.2 Meat Jellies—Gelees

Meat Jelly (Gelee de viande)

YIELD: *U.S. — 5 quarts*
Metric — 5 liters (U.S. equiv. — 5¼ qt.)

INGREDIENTS	*U.S. Weight or Volume*	*Metric Weight or Volume*	PROCEDURE
Veal bones, chopped	8 pounds	4 kilograms	1. Blanch the bones, calves' feet, and rind. Add the cold stock and heat to the boiling point. Add the bouquet garni, salt, and cloves, and simmer 4 to 5 hours, uncovered.
Calves' feet	6 pounds	3 kilograms	
Bacon rind	1 pound	500 grams	
White stock	1¾ gallons	7 liters	
Bouquet garni	1	1	2. Skim and remove fat as it collects.
Salt	1 ounce	30 grams	3. Strain through cheesecloth.
Cloves	½ teaspoon	3 grams	
Clarification			
Lean beef, chopped	1¾ pounds	800 grams	
Egg whites	2 or 3	2 or 3	4. Add the chopped beef, egg whites, and spice sachet. Simmer for 1 to 1½ hours. Strain. Adjust seasoning and color.
Spice sachet:	1	1	
Tie in cheesecloth:			
Parsley stems, chopped	1 teaspoon	5 grams	
Thyme	¼ teaspoon	.5 gram	
Bay leaf	1	1	
Peppercorns, crushed	½ teaspoon	3 grams	
Garlic, crushed	¼ teaspoon	2 grams	

Note: If the jelly does not set properly, add gelatin (allow 1½ teaspoons gelatin per pint of stock). Madeira wine may be added to the jelly.

Variations of Meat Jelly

Fish Jelly—Gelee de poisson. Mix ground, inexpensive, sliced white fish with chopped onions, the whites of leeks, egg whites, and a small amount of white wine; add cold fish fumet; stir carefully until boiling point is reached and remove from fire immediately; allow to drain (steep) for ½ hour. Skim and strain carefully through a cloth.

Poultry Jelly—Gelee de volaille. Chicken stock is substituted for white stock.

10.1.3 Panadas—Panades

Panadas are used for binding, extending, and improving stuffings. They are always used cold. The ingredients for the various panadas are all based on 1 quart (1 liter) of liquid.

Flour Panada (Panade a la farine)

YIELD: *U.S. — 1 pound*
Metric — 1 kilogram (U.S. equiv. — 2¼ lb.)

INGREDIENTS	*U.S. Weight or Volume*	*Metric Weight or Volume*	PROCEDURE
Water	1 quart	1 liter	1. Combine water, salt, and butter in a saucepan. Heat to the boiling point.
Butter	5 ounces	150 grams	
Salt	¾ ounce	20 grams	
Flour	1¼ pounds	600 grams	2. Add the flour stirring constantly with a wooden spoon. Cook until the mixture leaves the sides of the pan.

Variations of Flour Panada

Bread Panada—Panade au pain. Follow the recipe for Flour Panada substituting 1 quart (1 liter) of milk for water and 1¾ pounds (900 grams) of white bread for flour. Remove crust from the bread and soak in hot milk. Squeeze and break up the bread. Stir constantly over heat until mixture becomes thick and quite dry.

Rice Panada—Panade au riz. Follow the recipe for Flour Panada substituting 1 quart (1 liter) of stock for water, ¾ pound (350 grams) of rice for flour, and reduce the amount of butter to 1 ounce (30 grams). Cook the rice in the stock and butter, stirring until the mixture is thick and dry.

10.1.4 Forcemeats—Farces

Forcemeat is a mixture of finely chopped meat, fish, or poultry that is combined with seasonings and spices and bound with panadas and/or eggs. Forcemeats are used to stuff fish, poultry, meat, or vegetables. They are also used in the preparation of mousses, molds, and pates. The ingredients of forcemeats should be cool when mixed to avoid curdling. Forcemeats may be made into quenelles.

Fish Mousseline Forcemeat (Farce mousseline de poisson)

YIELD: *U.S. — 1 pound*
Metric — 1 kilogram (U.S. equiv. — 2¼ lb.)

INGREDIENTS	*U.S. Weight or Volume*	*Metric Weight or Volume*	PROCEDURE
Fish, skinned and boned	½ pound	500 grams	1. Grind fish very fine.
Cream	1 cup	5 deciliters	2. Combine fish with cream and eggs. Mix thoroughly.
Eggs, whole	2	3	
Salt	½ teaspoon	3 grams	3. Add seasonings.
Pepper	¼ teaspoon	2 grams	
Parsley	1 tablespoon	15 grams	
Chives	1 tablespoon	15 grams	
Egg whites, whipped	2	3	4. Fold in whipped egg whites. 5. Refrigerate until ready to use.

Forcemeat for Fish Dishes (Farce de poisson)

YIELD: *U.S. — 1 pound*
Metric — 1 kilogram (U.S. equiv. — 2¼ lb.)

INGREDIENTS	*U.S. Weight or Volume*	*Metric Weight or Volume*	PROCEDURE
Fish, skinned and boned	½ pound	500 grams	1. Chop fish very fine and mix thoroughly with the panada.
Panada	4 ounces	200 grams	
Cream	½ cup	2 deciliters	2. Add the parsley, chives, cream, and seasonings to fish. Blend thoroughly.
Salt	½ teaspoon	5 grams	
Pepper	¼ teaspoon	2 grams	
Parsley	1 tablespoon	15 grams	
Chives	1 tablespoon	15 grams	
Egg whites, whipped	2	3	3. Fold in the egg whites.

Forcemeat for Game (Farce de gibier)

YIELD: *U.S. — 1 pound*
Metric — 1 kilogram (U.S. equiv. — 2¼ lb.)

INGREDIENTS	*U.S. Weight or Volume*	*Metric Weight or Volume*	PROCEDURE
Game meat, ground	7 ounces	400 grams	1. Grind the game meat, pork, and lard. Mix thoroughly.
Lard	4 ounces	200 grams	
Pork	2¾ ounces	150 grams	
Goose liver	2¾ ounces	150 grams	2. Saute the goose liver, apple, and shallots. Add seasonings.
Apple, chopped	1	1	
Shallots, chopped	1 ounce	50 grams	
Salt	½ teaspoon	5 grams	
Pepper	¼ teaspoon	2 grams	
Brandy	¼ cup	60 milliliters	3. Pour brandy and Madeira over forcemeat. Heat and flame.
Madeira	2 tablespoons	30 milliliters	

Note: Forcemeat made with raw meat must be cooked thoroughly before serving.

Forcemeat for Hot Meat Dishes (Farce de viande)

YIELD: *U.S. — 1 pound*
Metric — 1 kilogram (U.S. equiv. — 2¼ lb.)

INGREDIENTS	*U.S. Weight or Volume*	*Metric Weight or Volume*	PROCEDURE
Veal, ground	5 ounces	250 grams	1. Dice all the meat. Put the meat and the ice cubes through the meat grinder two or three times.
Pork ground	5 ounces	250 grams	
Ice cubes	5 ounces	250 grams	
Lard	4 ounces	200 grams	2. Blend the lard and eggs. Add to the meat and mix thoroughly.
Egg yolks	2	3	
Salt	½ teaspoon	5 grams	3. Add seasonings.
Pepper	¼ teaspoon	2 grams	
Cream	¼ to ½ cup	158 milliliters	4. Blend cream into the mixture until the right consistency. 5. Chill until ready to use.

Note: Chopped mushrooms, diced tongue, truffles, goose liver, or chicken liver may be added to the forcemeat to enhance the flavor and the color.

Mousseline Forcemeat for Fish Dishes (Farce mousseline)

YIELD: *U.S. — 1 pound*
Metric — 1 kilogram (U.S. equiv. — 2¼ lb.)

INGREDIENTS	*U.S. Weight or Volume*	*Metric Weight or Volume*	PROCEDURE
Veal	½ pound	500 grams	1. Remove fat and sinews from meat. Dice meat.
Ice cubes	4 ounces	200 grams	2. Attach the finest blade to the meat grinder and put meat and ice cubes through the grinder several times.
Cream	½ cup	3 deciliters	3. Add the cream, egg whites, and seasonings slowly. Mix thoroughly.
Egg whites	3	5	
Salt	½ teaspoon	3 grams	4. Refrigerate until ready to use.
White pepper	1/8 teaspoon	1 gram	

Plain Forcemeat for Hot Dishes (Farce simple)

YIELD: *U.S. — 1 pound*
Metric — 1 kilogram (U.S. equiv. — 2¼ lb.)

INGREDIENTS	*U.S. Weight or Volume*	*Metric Weight or Volume*	PROCEDURE
Pork, ground	4 ounces	200 grams	1. Grind the pork with the ice cubes.
Ice cubes	5 ounces	250 grams	2. Grind the fat and mix thoroughly with the pork.
Fat	¾ ounce	50 grams	
Bread or flour panada	5 ounces	250 grams	3. Combine the panada, eggs, and seasonings with the pork and mix thoroughly.
Egg	1	2	
Egg yolks	3	5	
Cream	3 tablespoons	45 milliliters	4. Add the cream gradually and stir until the mixture is very smooth. Add more cream if necessary.
Pepper	¼ teaspoon	2 grams	
Salt	½ teaspoon	3 grams	

10.1.5 Duxelles

There are two types of duxelles:

- Dry duxelles, a form of mushroom hash, used to stuff tomatoes, mushrooms, and other vegetables.
- Duxelles with added liquids, tomato sauce, stock, fish fumet, or wine, combined with other ingredients and used in forcemeats, stuffings, and sauces.

Dry Duxelles (Duxelles seches)

YIELD: *U.S. — 8 ounces*
Metric — 225 grams

INGREDIENTS	*U.S. Weight or Volume*	*Metric Weight or Volume*
Mushrooms	¼ pound	115 grams
Butter	3 tablespoons	40 grams
Onion, chopped	½ onion	½ onion
Shallots, chopped	2	2
Salt	½ teaspoon	3 grams
Pepper	1/8 teaspoon	1 gram
Nutmeg	few grains	few grains

PROCEDURE

1. Clean and trim mushrooms. Mince very fine. Put in cheesecloth, twist, and extract as much liquid as possible.
2. Saute chopped onion in melted butter until slightly brown. Stir frequently.
3. Combine remainder of the ingredients with the mushrooms and stir over high heat until all the liquid has evaporated.
4. Refrigerate or freeze.

Variation of Duxelles

Duxelles for Tart Shells—Duxelles pour tartelettes farcies. Combine an equal quantity of dry duxelles and either mousseline forcemeat or finely chopped ham.

Duxelles for Stuffed Vegetables (Duxelles pour legumes farcis)

YIELD: *U.S. — 1 pound*
Metric — 1 kilogram (U.S. equiv. — 2¼ lb.)

INGREDIENTS	*U.S. Weight or Volume*	*Metric Weight or Volume*
Mushrooms	¼ pound	115 grams
Butter	3 tablespoons	42 grams
Onion, chopped	½ onion	½ onion
Shallots, chopped	2	2
Salt	½ teaspoon	3 grams
Pepper	1/8 teaspoon	1 gram
Nutmeg	1/8 teaspoon	1 gram
Tomato puree	2 tablespoons	30 milliliters
White wine	¼ cup	60 milliliters
Brown sauce	2 tablespoons	30 milliliters
Bread crumbs	¼ to ½ cup	85 grams

PROCEDURE

1. Clean and trim mushrooms. Mince very fine. Put in cheesecloth, twist, and extract as much liquid as possible.
2. Saute chopped onion in melted butter until slightly brown. Stir frequently.
3. Combine remainder of the ingredients with the mushrooms and stir over high heat until all the liquid has evaporated.
4. Refrigerate or freeze.

10.1.6 Ingredients for Stocks, Sauces, and Soups—Ingredients pour fonds, potages

HERB BOUQUET—BOUQUET GARNI

Herb bouquet refers to a combination of parsley, thyme, and bay leaf. If fresh herbs are used, the parsley is folded around the other sprigs and all are tied with a string. Tarragon, rosemary, basil, fennel, garlic, or celery are sometimes added to the bouquet depending on the specific recipe. Bouquets for very light stocks and sauces are made of only white vegetables. Bouquets are specified as small, medium, or large.

MATIGNON

Matignon is a combination of finely minced vegetables used for garnishing meats. The choice of the vegetables is determined by the use.

MIREPOIX

Mirepoix is a mixture of vegetables, herbs, and spices with or without meat used to enhance the flavor of meat, fish, and shellfish dishes. Onion, celery, carrots, leeks, garlic, peppercorns, bay leaves, cloves, thyme, and rosemary are used in various combinations.

SPICE SACHET—SACHET D'EPICES

Various spices and herbs are tied in clean cheesecloth. The spice sachet is cooked with meats, game stews, sauerkraut, pickled beets, beans, and in soups and sauces.

ROUX

A roux is a mixture of flour and fat such as butter, margarine, oil, chicken fat, or drippings. The flour and fat are cooked to eliminate the taste of uncooked flour. There are three basic types of roux: white roux used for Bechamel or Veloute sauces and some soups; blond roux which is made with butter; and brown roux used to thicken brown sauces such as demi-glaze or Espagnole. The thickness of the sauce will depend on its use. Generally speaking, 2 ounces (55 grams) of fat and 2¾ ounces (75 grams) of bread flour are required for each quart (947 milliliters). White or blond roux may be made with butter, but brown roux is made with other fats. Flour browns to a better color in fat because most fats withstand higher temperatures than butter. The longer cooking time required for brown sauces may cause the starch in the roux to break down. The roux should be stirred constantly for 5 to 15 minutes over moderate heat.

10.1.7 Seasoned (compound) Butters—Beurres composes

Seasoned butters refer to butters that have been mixed with one or more substances. The butters are melted or cooked for varied periods of time and used as accompaniments to meat, fish, and vegetables. They are also used in sauces or as garnishes.

Seasoned Butter (Beurres composes)

YIELD: *U.S. — 1 pound*
Metric — 1 kilogram (U.S. equiv. — 2¼ lb.)

INGREDIENTS	*U.S. Weight or Volume*	*Metric Weight or Volume*	PROCEDURE
Butter	1 pound	1 kilogram	1. Whip butter.
Lemon juice	2 ounces	1 deciliter	2. Add other ingredients and mix thoroughly.
Salt	½ teaspoon	3 grams	
White pepper	1/8 teaspoon	1 gram	

Variations of Seasoned Butter—using 1 pound U.S. (1 kilogram metric) butter

Anchovy Butter—Beurre d'anchois. Add 5 ounces (300 grams) of anchovy fillets. Omit salt.
Basil Butter—Beurre au basilic. Add 2¾ ounces (150 grams) of basil.
Cafe de Paris Butter—Beurre Cafe de Paris. Add 5 cloves of garlic, 9 anchovy fillets, ¾ ounce (50 grams) of parsley, ¾ ounce (40 grams) of chives. Mix thoroughly. Add 6 beaten eggs, 2 tablespoons (½ deciliter) of Madeira, and 2 tablespoons (½ deciliter) of brandy.
Caviar Butter—Beurre de caviar. Add 2¾ ounces (150 grams) of caviar. Omit salt.
Colbert Butter—Beurre Colbert. Add ¾ ounce (50 grams) of meat extract and ¾ ounce (50 grams) of tarragon to the recipe for Maitre d'Hotel Butter.
Dill Butter—Beurre d'aneth. Add 2¾ ounces (150 grams) of finely chopped dill.
Garlic Butter—Beurre d'ail. Add 4 ounces (200 grams) of crushed garlic.
Horseradish Butter—Beurre de raifort. Add 4 ounces (200 grams) of finely grated horseradish.
Kneaded Butter—Beurre manie. Equal parts of butter and flour are kneaded together. Use to thicken sauces and soups at the last minute by dropping small (pea size) balls into liquid and stirring until thickened.
Lobster Butter—Beurre de homard. Add 5 ounces (250 grams) of cooked chopped lobster and 2 tablespoons (½ deciliter) of brandy.
Maitre d'Hotel Butter—Beurre maitre d'Hotel. Add 4 ounces (200 grams) of chopped parsley and 1/8 teaspoon (2 grams) of white pepper.
Mustard Butter—Beurre a la moutarde. Add 2¾ ounces (150 grams) of prepared mustard.
Pimiento Butter—Beurre de piment. Saute 5 ounces (300 grams) of pimientos in butter. Cool and grind. Combine with butter mixture. Add 1¾ ounces (100 grams) of diced pimiento.
Shrimp Butter—Beurre de crevettes. Add ½ ounce (350 grams) of cooked chopped shrimp and 2 tablespoons (½ deciliter) of brandy.

10.2 Basic Stocks—Fonds

A carefully prepared basic stock is essential to any quality sauce or soup. A good chef, who really knows and loves his profession, can best demonstrate his abilities in the preparation and in the use of basic stock.

Stocks must always be cooked slowly and should not be covered. Scum and fat should be removed as they accumulate.

Bones used for making brown stock should be cut into small pieces with a meat saw. After browning the bones, only a small amount of liquid need be added. This is initially reduced to a glaze to ensure that the stock has a rich brown color. Only at this point should the full measure of liquid be added and simmered gently for 4 to 6 hours. *If the stock is not going to be used immediately, to prevent spoilage, it should be cooled as quickly as possible by placing the container in cold running water. It should then be refrigerated.*

10.2.1 White Stock (Fond blanc)

YIELD: *U.S. — 10 quarts*
Metric — 10 liters (U.S. equiv. — 2.6 gal.)

INGREDIENTS	*U.S. Weight or Volume*	*Metric Weight or Volume*	PROCEDURE
Bones, veal	10 to 12 pounds	5 to 6 kilograms	1. Cut bones with a meat saw. Wash in cold water.
Water	12 quarts	12 liters	2. Place bones in stock pot and cover with cold water. Heat to the boiling point (blanch).
Bouquet garni:			3. Drain.
Onion, chopped	1 pound	455 grams	4. Cover bones with water. Add bouquet garni and spices.
Celery, chopped	½ pound	225 grams	5. Simmer for 4 hours. Remove scum as it accumulates.
Thyme	½ teaspoon	3 grams	6. Skim and strain.
Parsley	1 teaspoon	5 grams	
Bay leaf	1	1	
Cloves, whole	½ teaspoon	3 grams	
Peppercorns, crushed	½ teaspoon	3 grams	

10.2.2 Brown Stock (Fond brun)

YIELD: *U.S. — 10 quarts*
Metric — 10 liters (U.S. equiv. — 2.6 gal.)

INGREDIENTS	*U.S. Weight or Volume*	*Metric Weight or Volume*
Veal or beef bones, chopped	12 to 16 pounds	6 to 8 kilograms
Fat	4 ounces	110 grams
Water	12 to 15 quarts	12 to 15 liters
Mirepoix:		
Onion, chopped	8 ounces	200 grams
Celery, chopped	4 ounces	100 grams
Carrots, chopped	4 ounces	100 grams
Tomato puree	1 pint	0.5 liter
Pork rind	4 ounces	110 grams
Salt	1 teaspoon	15 grams

PROCEDURE

1. Place bones and fat in a roasting pan.
2. Brown in oven at 375°F. (191°C.).
3. Turn bones occasionally to brown uniformly.
4. Mirepoix is added to partially browned bones and together both are then browned to final stage. Tomato puree is optional.
5. Drain fat from pan and reserve.
6. Deglaze roasting pan with small amount of water.
7. Cover bones with deglazing liquid and water, add pork rind and seasoning, and heat to the boiling point. Simmer for 5 to 6 hours.
8. Skim surface and add more water if necessary.
9. Strain through cloth.

10.2.3 Game Stock (Fond de gibier)

YIELD: *U.S. — 10 quarts*
Metric — 10 liters (U.S. equiv.—2.6 gal.)

INGREDIENTS	*U.S. Weight or Volume*	*Metric Weight or Volume*	PROCEDURE
Game bones, chopped	12 to 16 pounds	6 to 8 kilograms	1. Place the bones, rind, and fat in a pan and brown.
Pork rind	5 ounces	140 grams	
Fat	4 ounces	110 grams	
Juniper Berries	6	6	
Mirepoix:			
Onion	8 ounces	200 grams	2. Add the mirepoix and continue browning.
Celery	4 ounces	100 grams	3. Remove bones and mirepoix and place in a stock pot.
Carrots	2 ounces	55 grams	4. Deglaze the pan with a small amount of liquid.
Water	12 to 15 quarts	12 to 15 liters	5. Pour all the ingredients into the stock pot and simmer slowly for 4 hours.
Salt	1 teaspoon	15 grams	6. Skim the fat frequently and add more water if necessary.
			7. Strain through cloth.

10.2.4 Chicken Stock (Fond de volaille)

YIELD: *U.S. — 10 quarts*
Metric — 10 liters (U.S. equiv. — 2.6 gal.)

INGREDIENTS	*U.S. Weight or Volume*	*Metric Weight or Volume*	PROCEDURE
Bones, chicken and veal	10 to 12 pounds	5 to 6 kilograms	1. Wash bones in cold water.
Water	12 quarts	12 liters	2. Place bones in stock pot and cover with cold water. Bring to a boil (blanch).
Bouquet garni:			3. Drain.
Onion, chopped	1 pound	455 grams	4. Cover bones with the water. Add bouquet garni and spices.
Celery, chopped	½ pound	225 grams	5. Simmer for 4 hours. Remove the scum as it accumulates.
Thyme	½ teaspoon	3 grams	6. Strain through cloth.
Parsley	1 teaspoon	5 grams	
Bay leaf	1	1	
Cloves, whole	½ teaspoon	3 grams	
Peppercorns, crushed	½ teaspoon	3 grams	

10.2.5 Fish Stock (Fond ou fumet de poisson)

YIELD: *U.S. — 10 quarts*
Metric — 10 liters (U.S. equiv. — 2.6 gal.)

INGREDIENTS	*U.S. Weight or Volume*	*Metric Weight or Volume*	**PROCEDURE**
Fish bones	10 to 12 pounds	5 to 6 kilograms	1. Chop and wash bones.
White mirepoix:			
Onion	4 ounces	110 grams	2. Saute the mirepoix in butter.
Celery	2 ounces	55 grams	3. Combine the fish bones, mirepoix, and water.
Garlic	2 cloves	2 cloves	4. Heat to the boiling point. Remove scum as it accumulates.
Mushroom trimmings	4 ounces	115 grams	
Bay leaves	2	2	
Cloves	3	3	
Butter	3 ounces	85 grams	
Water	10 quarts	10 liters	
Wine, white or red	1 pint	0.5 liter	5. Add wine and salt to the stock and simmer for 30 minutes. Strain.
Salt	1 tablespoon	15 grams	

10.2.6 Fish Essence (Essence de poisson)

YIELD: *U.S. — 10 quarts*
Metric — 10 liters (U.S. equiv. — 2.6 gal.)

INGREDIENTS	*U.S. Weight or Volume*	*Metric Weight or Volume*	**PROCEDURE**
Fish bones	10 to 12 pounds	5 to 6 kilograms	1. Chop and wash bones.
White mirepoix:			
Onion	4 ounces	110 grams	2. Dice the vegetables for mirepoix and the mushrooms very fine.
Celery	2 ounces	55 grams	
Garlic	2 cloves	2 cloves	
Cloves	3	3	
Bay leaves	2	2	
Mushroom trimmings	4 ounces	110 grams	
Butter	5 ounces	150 grams	3. Saute the mirepoix in butter.
Fish stock	10 quarts	10 liters	4. Combine the mirepoix, mushrooms, fish bones, fish stock, and wine. Simmer slowly for 30 minutes. Strain through cloth.
White wine, chablis or sauterne	1 pint	0.5 liter	
Salt	1 tablespoon	15 grams	

Note: The reduced stock of poached fish such as that from "filets de sole au vin blanc" is also referred to as fumet de poisson.

10.2.7 Vegetable Stock (Fond de legumes)

YIELD: *U.S. — 10 quarts*
Metric — 10 liters (U.S. equiv. — 2.6 gal.)

INGREDIENTS	*U.S. Weight or Volume*	*Metric Weight or Volume*	PROCEDURE
Fat	5 ounces	150 grams	1. Saute the onion and leeks in the fat for a few minutes. Add other vegetables and saute until transparent.
Onion, chopped	10 ounces	300 grams	
Leeks, sliced	10 ounces	300 grams	
Celery, diced	5 ounces	150 grams	
Cabbage, shredded	5 ounces	150 grams	
Tomatoes	4 ounces	100 grams	
Fennel	4 ounces	100 grams	
Garlic	1 clove	1 clove	
Bay leaf	1	1	
Clove, whole	1	1	
Water	12 quarts	12 liters	2. Add liquid and salt and simmer for approximately 1 hour.
Salt	1 tablespoon	15 grams	

Note: This stock is used primarily for vegetarian and fish items.

SECOND COOKING OF BASIC STOCK—REMOUILLAGE

The second cooking of a basic stock is called remouillage. It is used in the preparation of meat extract (glace de viande). The cooked chicken and game are added to the basic stock and a mirepoix. The stock is simmered for 5 hours.

MEAT EXTRACT—GLACE DE VIANDE

This meat extract is prepared by reducing the brown stock to a gelatinous consistency. The glaze is used to improve the flavor of sauces and to coat certain meats, game, poultry, and aspics.

The meat extract is made by straining the remouillage or brown stock into a heavy stock pot. The stock is allowed to simmer over low heat to a syrupy consistency. Towards the end, the remaining liquid should be strained into a smaller, heavy bottom saucepan. The heat should be very low, and the glaze should simmer until thick enough to coat a spoon.

The hot glaze should be poured into containers, covered tightly, and refrigerated. Glace de poisson and Glace de gibier are obtained by reducing a Fumet de poisson and a Fond de gibier, respectively.

11

Sauces—Sauces

The foundation of a good sauce is a stock that has been skillfully prepared. There are, however, some sauces that do not require stock, such as Hollandaise and Bearnaise. Sauces are used to add richness and color, and to enhance the flavor of certain foods. A sauce should have a smooth texture and a flavor and consistency that complements the food it accompanies; it should never mask the flavor of the food. There are many different preparations for the sauces, and there are distinct differences in their flavor, texture, and appearance. Sauces fall into two basic categories: warm and cold sauces. The warm sauces are derived from a few basic brown or white sauces.

The *Sauce Espagnole* was considered, at one time, the basic ingredient of all brown sauces, and as a result, the flavor and consistency of all brown sauces were very similar. The quality of the sauce was further affected by not reducing the stock sufficiently in order to obtain a greater yield. In recent years the *Espagnole* has been replaced by the delicate, reduced, and *partially-bound veal stock, Fond brun lic.* In addition to the Fond brun, there are other basic sauces with many variations. Special seasonings, garnishes, and other ingredients may be added to provide an even greater variety. The strength of the sauce is increased and the flavor improved by reducing the volume.

The preparation of fine sauces is an art, and it is usually assigned to the cooks who have had an extensive background of training and experience.

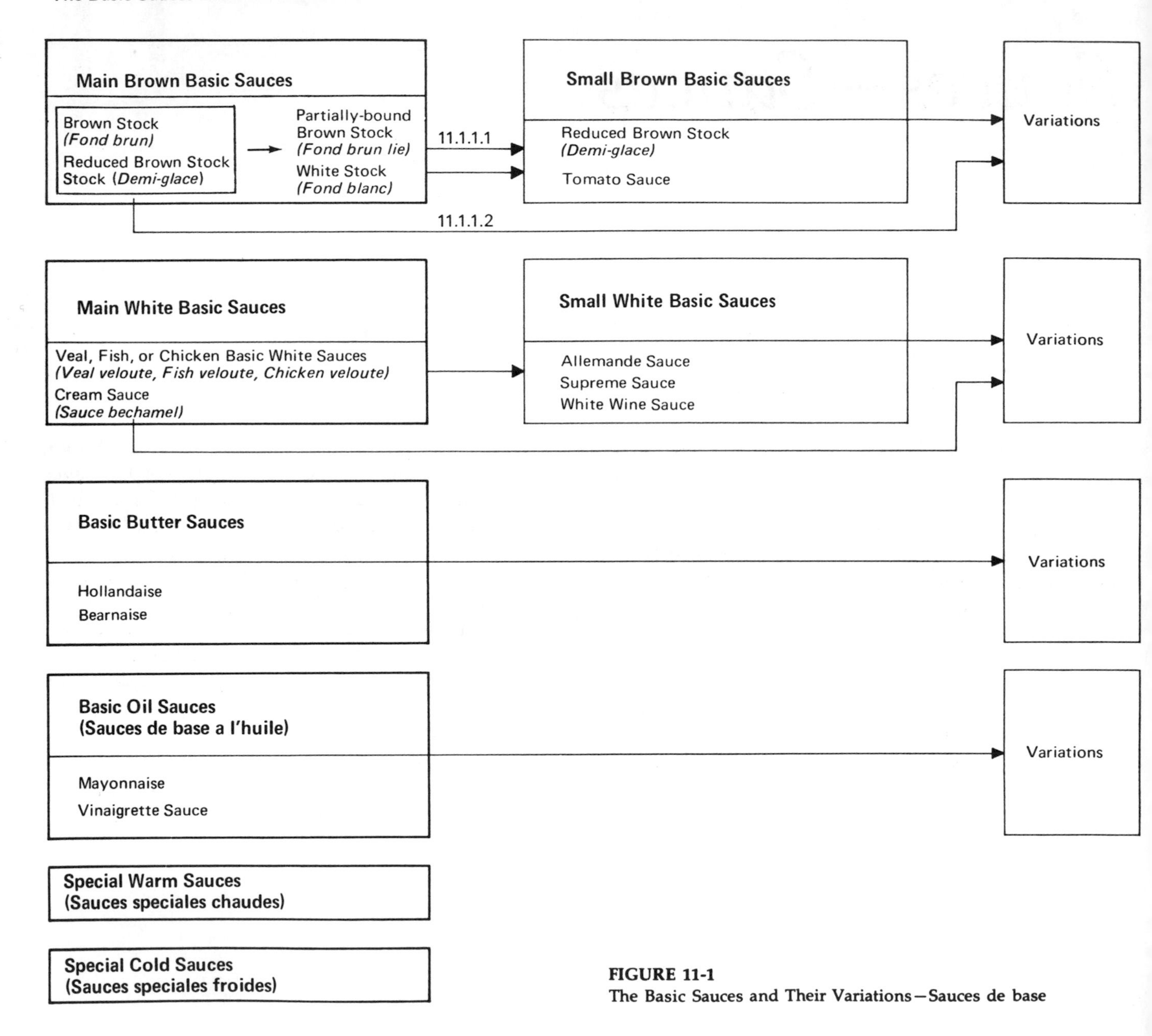

FIGURE 11-1
The Basic Sauces and Their Variations—Sauces de base

11.1 Brown Sauces — Sauces brunes

Structure of the main and small brown basic sauces and their most important variations.

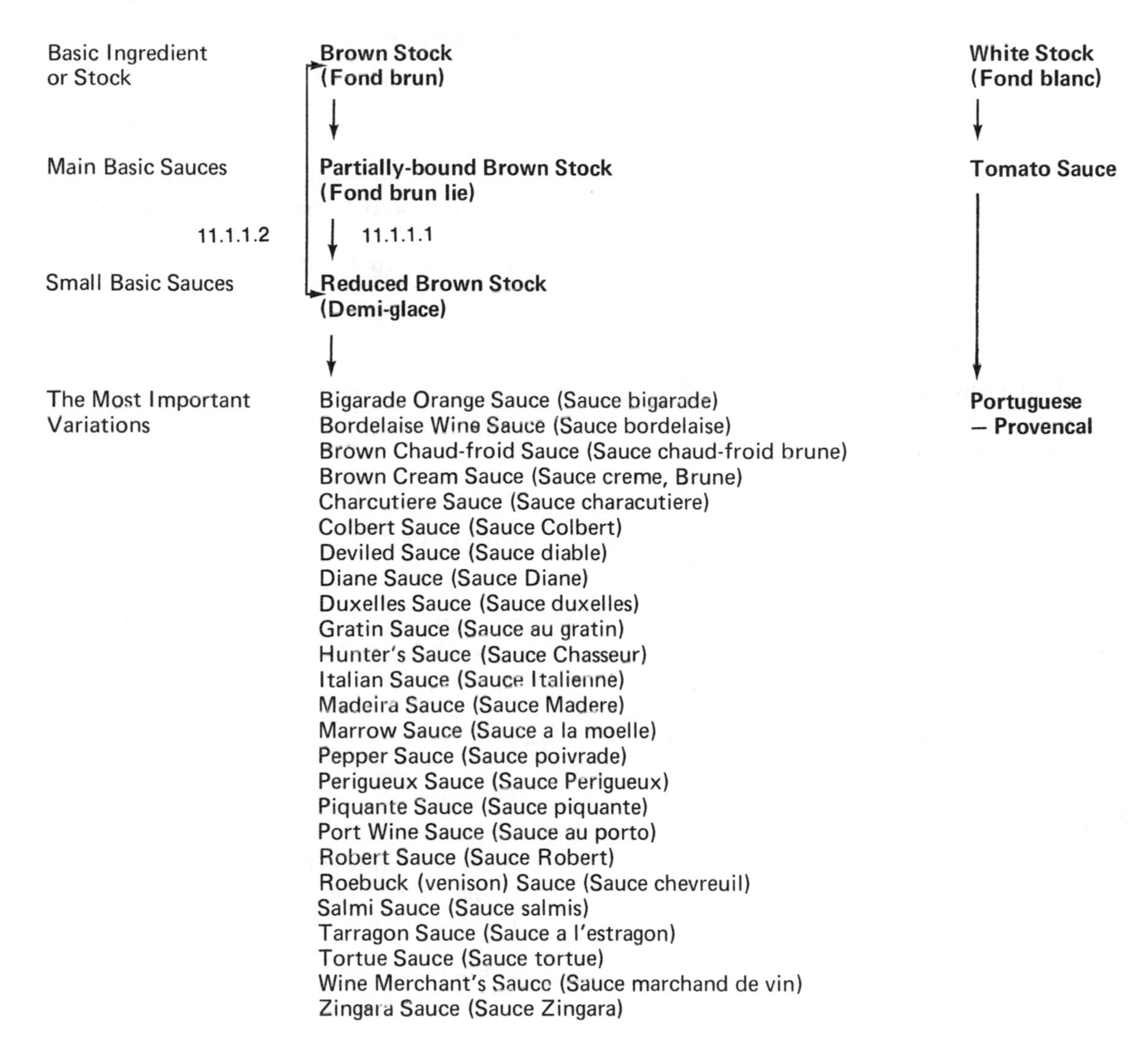

FIGURE 11-2
Brown Sauces—Sauces brunes

11.1.1 Brown Basic Sauce (Fond brun lie)

YIELD: *U.S. — 10 quarts*
Metric — 10 liters (U.S. equiv. — 10½ qt.)

INGREDIENTS	*U.S. Weight or Volume*	*Metric Weight or Volume*	PROCEDURE
Brown stock	20 quarts	20 liters	1. Dissolve arrowroot or cornstarch in 2 cups (4 deciliters) of cold stock.
Arrowroot	4 to 5 ounces	100 to 150 grams	2. Reduce the remainder of the stock to half its volume.
OR			3. Stir dissolved cornstarch or arrowroot into the reduced stock.
Cornstarch			4. Stir and cook until slightly thickened.

11.1.1.1 Veal Demi-Glace I (Demi-glace I)

YIELD: *U.S. — 10 quarts*
Metric — 10 liters (U.S. equiv. — 10½ qt.)

INGREDIENTS	*U.S. Weight or Volume*	*Metric Weight or Volume*	PROCEDURE
Butter or margarine	1 ounce	30 grams	1. Saute the mirepoix in fat. Add tomato puree and cook until vegetables are tender.
Mirepoix:			
Carrots	3 ounces	100 grams	
Celery	2 ounces	50 grams	
Onion	2 ounces	50 grams	
Bay leaf	¼ leaf	¼ leaf	
Thyme	1 sprig	1 sprig	
Tomato puree	4 ounces	100 grams	
White wine	1 quart	1 liter	2. Deglaze with wine.
Brown sauce	15 quarts	15 liters	3. Add brown sauce.
Salt	1 tablespoon	20 grams	4. Simmer for ½ hour. 5. Strain. 6. Bind with starch if necessary. 7. Adjust seasoning.

11.1.1.2 Veal Demi-Glace II (Demi-glace II)

YIELD: *U.S. — 10 quarts*
Metric — 10 liters (U.S. equiv. — 10½ qt.)

INGREDIENTS	*U.S. Weight or Volume*	*Metric Weight or Volume*	PROCEDURE
Butter or margarine	5 ounces	150 grams	1. Brown the bones in melted fat.
Veal bones, finely chopped	12 to 16 pounds	6 to 8 kilograms	
Mirepoix:			
Carrots	3 to 4 ounces	100 to 150 grams	2. Add mirepoix and continue to brown.
Celery	2 to 3 ounces	50 to 75 grams	
Onion	2 to 3 ounces	50 to 75 grams	
Bay leaf	¼ leaf	¼ leaf	
Thyme	1 sprig	1 sprig	
Tomato puree	4 ounces	100 grams	3. Add tomato puree.
Flour	4 ounces	100 grams	4. Dust with flour and brown for a few minutes.
White wine	1 quart	1 liter	5. Deglaze with wine.
Brown sauce	20 quarts	20 liters	6. Add brown sauce.
			7. Reduce volume by half.
Arrowroot	5 ounces	150 grams	8. Strain.
OR			9. Bind with starch if necessary.
Cornstarch			10. Skim off fat and adjust seasoning.
Salt	1 tablespoon	20 grams	

11.1.1.3 Meatless Brown Sauce — Fond brun maigre

The method used to prepare a basic brown sauce, using fish stock with red wine instead of brown stock, is followed to prepare this sauce.

Variations of Demi-glace

Bigarade Orange Sauce — Sauce bigarade. This sauce is prepared with a reduction of red wine, orange juice, and fine strips of orange and lemon peel (zeste). These ingredients are covered with a demi-glace, and the mixture is simmered and then flavored with Curacao and a dash of cayenne pepper. (See Young Duckling Bigarade, page 424.)

Bordelaise Wine Sauce — Sauce bordelaise. This wine sauce is made with a reduction of red wine, chopped shallots, crushed peppercorns, thyme, and bay leaf; demi-glace is added to the reduction and it is simmered for a few minutes. It is then strained and flavored with lemon juice. The sauce may be garnished with sliced or diced blanched beef bone marrow.

Brown Chaud-froid Sauce — Sauce chaud-froid brune is prepared by reducing 1 quart (1 liter) of demi-glace and a few drops of truffle essence to half its volume. 1 pint (5 deciliters) of meat jelly and ½ cup (1 deciliter) of Madeira are added. The sauce is strained through cheesecloth and cooled. *Note:* Fond de veau lie may be used instead of the usual demi-glace. The giblets and backbones of poultry may be used with the veal for brown sauce; the bones and trimmings of game may be used for game dishes.

Brown Cream Sauce — Sauce creme (for meat dishes only). It is prepared by draining the fat from the pan and deglazing with white wine. Demi-glace is added and reduced to half the volume. The sauce is bound with equal parts of veloute and cream.

This sauce may also be made for mise en place. Approximately 5½ quarts (5½ liters) of demi-glace are reduced to half the volume. The demi-glace is bound with 2½ quarts (2½ liters) of veal veloute. When ready to use, ¼ cup (56 milliliters) of white wine is added to 1 quart (1 liter) of the basic sauce. The sauce is heated to the boiling point and 1 pint (473 milliliters) of cream, a few grains of cayenne pepper, and the juice of ½ lemon are added.

Charcutiere Sauce — Sauce charcutiere. It is prepared by combining a reduction of vinegar and white wine, shallots and peppercorns with demi-glace. It is simmered a few minutes and strained. Julienne of pickles, mustard, Worcestershire sauce, and meat glaze are added.

Colbert Sauce — Sauce Colbert. It is a reduction of chopped shallots, crushed peppercorns, white wine, and demi-glace. The sauce is simmered for a few minutes and then strained. After the sauce is removed from the heat, softened butter, chopped herbs, and lemon juice are added.

Deviled Sauce — Sauce diable. It is made from a reduction of white wine, shallots, peppercorns, demi-glace, and tomato puree. The sauce is heated to the boiling point, strained, and bound with butter. It is seasoned with cayenne pepper and chopped herbs.

Diane Sauce — Sauce Diane. This is a demi-glace sauce which has been well-peppered and prepared with cream. It may be a sauce poivrade that has been prepared with double cream. It is usually garnished with hard-cooked egg whites and truffles cut into half-moon shapes.

Duxelles Sauce — Sauce duxelles. This sauce is prepared by sauteing a quantity of chopped shallots in butter and deglazing the pan with white wine. Demi-glace and tomato puree are added. Dry duxelles (see Section 10.1.5) are added and the sauce is heated to the boiling point, the temperature is reduced, and the sauce is simmered slowly. Chopped parsley is added before serving.

Gratin Sauce — Sauce au gratin. Fumet de poisson is reduced with chopped shallots. Dry duxelles (see Section 10.1.5) and brown sauce are added and the sauce is heated to the boiling point. It is garnished with chopped parsley.

Hunter's Sauce — Sauce chasseur. It is made by sauteing sliced shallots and mushrooms in butter and deglazing with white wine. After reducing, a demi-glace and a small amount of tomato puree are added. The sauce is simmered for a few minutes, and the butter and parsley are added.

Italian Sauce — Sauce italienne. It is made by sauteing chopped shallots, ham, and mushrooms in butter and deglazing the pan with white wine. Demi-glace and tomato sauce or tomato puree are added. The sauce is then boiled for a few minutes, and chopped parsley and tarragon leaves are added.

Madeira Sauce — Sauce Madere. This is a demi-glace sauce with Madeira wine.

Marrow Sauce — Sauce a la moelle. This sauce is prepared by the same method used for Bordelaise Wine Sauce. It is served with blanched beef marrow cubes, chopped parsley, and some flakes of fresh butter.

Pepper Sauce — Sauce poivrade. See Roebuck Sauce.

Perigueux Sauce — Sauce Perigueux. To prepare this sauce a reduction of Madeira wine and chopped truffles are added to demi-glace. The sauce is bound with butter.

Piquante Sauce — Sauce piquante. This sauce is a reduction of white wine, vinegar, and chopped shallots added to demi-glace and seasoned with cayenne pepper. It is garnished with chopped pickles, herbs, and tarragon.

Port Wine Sauce — Sauce au porto. This is a Madeira Sauce using port instead of Madeira.

Robert Sauce — Sauce Robert. This sauce is prepared from a reduction of chopped onions, white wine, and demi-glace. It is simmered for a short time and strained. Mustard and lemon juice are added. It is especially good with pork chops.

Roebuck (venison) Sauce — Sauce chevreuil. This game sauce is prepared by sauteing a mirepoix, bacon trimmings, crushed peppercorns, and juniper berries in butter. It is deglazed with a small amount of game marinade (made with red wine). Veal and game stock are added, and the sauce is reduced to half its volume. It is slightly bound with cornstarch. The sauce is strained and seasoned with cayenne pepper, lemon juice, and butter.

Salmi Sauce — Sauce salmis. The chopped carcasses,

neck, and skin from game being cooked is sauteed in butter with a mirepoix. It is deglazed with a little white wine and reduced. Demi-glace is added. It is simmered for 30 minutes and strained. The sauce is further diluted with the game stock and boiled down to the desired thickness. Truffle essence and reduced mushroom stock are added.

Tarragon Sauce — Sauce a l'estragon. This sauce is a reduced demi-glace with a little white wine and a sprig of tarragon. It is strained and garnished with chopped tarragon leaves.

Tortue Sauce — Sauce tortue. It is a Madeira Sauce with herbs (such as thyme, bay leaf, parsley, sage, rosemary, and basil), a little tomato sauce, and a pinch of cayenne pepper. It is garnished with diced calf's tongue, pickles, quartered mushrooms, pitted olives, and quenelles de veau.

Wine Merchant's Sauce — Sauce marchand de vin. This is a reduction of red wine and shallots that have been deglazed with demi-glace and reduced.

Zingara Sauce — Sauce Zingara. This sauce is a reduction of shallots and white wine. Demi-glace and a little Tomato Sauce are added and the sauce is simmered for a short time. It is seasoned with paprika and garnished with julienne of beef tongue, truffles, and mushrooms.

11.1.2 Tomato Sauce (Sauce tomate)

YIELD: *U.S. — 10 quarts*
Metric — 10 liters (U.S. equiv. — 10½ qt.)

INGREDIENTS	*U.S. Weight or Volume*	*Metric Weight or Volume*	PROCEDURE
Oil	¾ cup	2 deciliters	1. Heat oil. Fry bacon trimmings and mirepoix.
Bacon trimmings	5 ounces	150 grams	
Mirepoix:			
Carrots	6 ounces	200 grams	
Celery	4 ounces	100 grams	
Onion	4 ounces	100 grams	
Bay leaf	½ leaf	½ leaf	
Thyme	2 sprigs	2 sprigs	
Tomato puree OR Tomatoes, fresh	4 to 5 pounds	2 to 2.5 kilograms	2. Add the tomato puree. Continue frying and stir in the flour.
Flour	4 ounces	100 grams	
White stock	12 quarts	12 liters	3. Add the white stock. 4. Simmer for 1 to 1½ hours. Add more white stock if necessary.
Sugar	¼ cup	80 grams	5. Strain. Add sugar (optional) and salt. Adjust seasoning.
Salt	1 tablespoon	20 grams	

Variations of Tomato Sauce

Portuguese Sauce — Sauce portugaise. Peeled, seeded, and diced tomatoes are added to crushed garlic and onions that have been sauteed in oil. The mixture is simmered and combined with some reduced meat juices, a little tomato puree, and chopped parsley. It is heated to the boiling point and a few flakes of butter are added.

Provencale Sauce — Sauce provencale. It is made from a reduction of white wine, shallots, and garlic. Peeled and chopped tomatoes and tomato puree are added and simmered. It may be garnished with chopped parsley, olives, and mushrooms.

11.2 White Sauces — Sauces blanches

The basic white sauce is used in the preparation of many sauces. Some are derived from veal stock, some from fish stock, and others from stock made from poultry or vegetables. The sauces should always be derived from the corresponding stock. For example, Tarragon Sauce for fish from fish stock. *The structure of the main and small white sauces with their most important variations.*

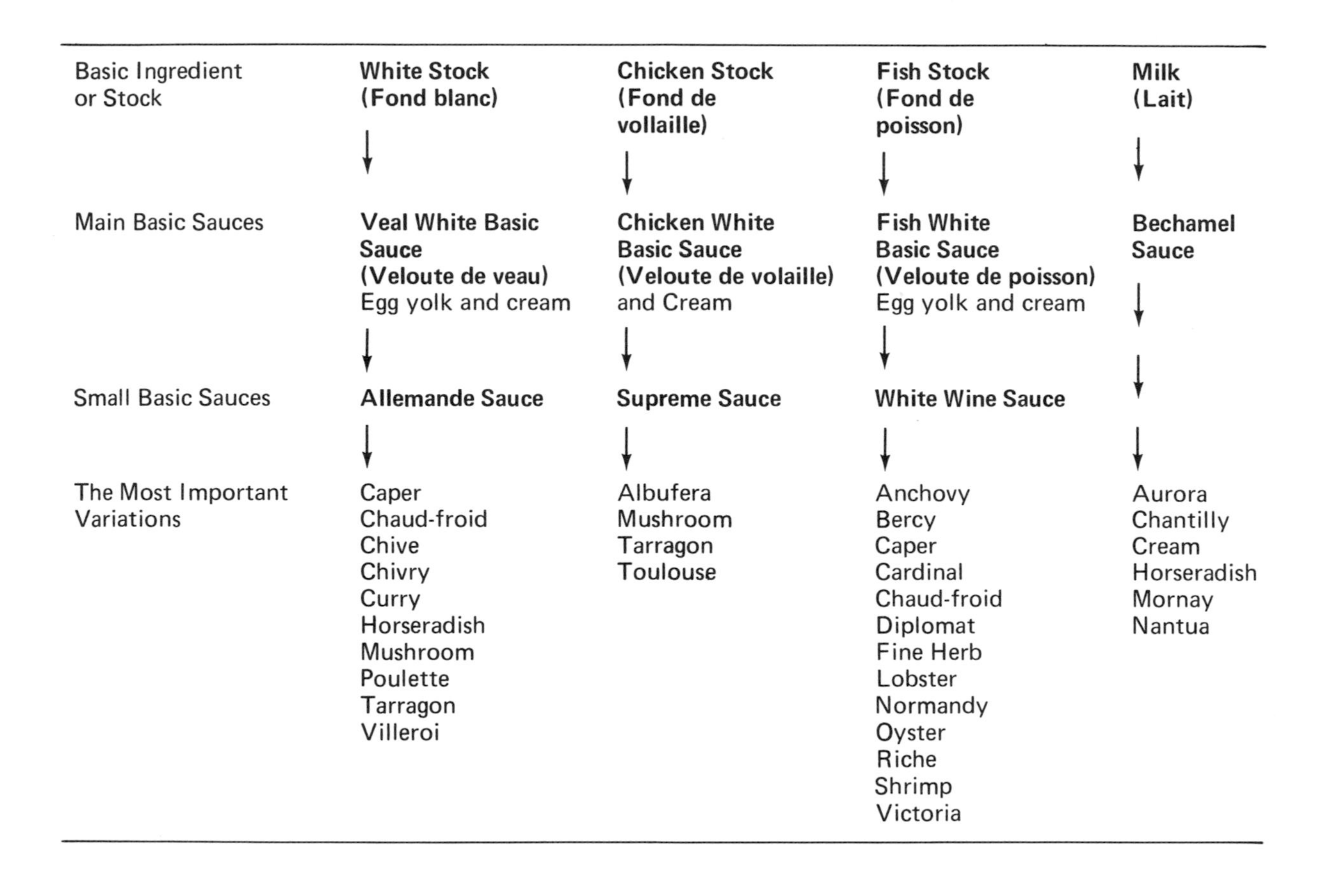

Basic Ingredient or Stock	**White Stock (Fond blanc)**	**Chicken Stock (Fond de vollaille)**	**Fish Stock (Fond de poisson)**	**Milk (Lait)**
	↓	↓	↓	↓
Main Basic Sauces	**Veal White Basic Sauce (Veloute de veau)** Egg yolk and cream	**Chicken White Basic Sauce (Veloute de volaille)** and Cream	**Fish White Basic Sauce (Veloute de poisson)** Egg yolk and cream	**Bechamel Sauce**
	↓	↓	↓	↓
Small Basic Sauces	**Allemande Sauce**	**Supreme Sauce**	**White Wine Sauce**	↓
	↓	↓	↓	↓
The Most Important Variations	Caper Chaud-froid Chive Chivry Curry Horseradish Mushroom Poulette Tarragon Villeroi	Albufera Mushroom Tarragon Toulouse	Anchovy Bercy Caper Cardinal Chaud-froid Diplomat Fine Herb Lobster Normandy Oyster Riche Shrimp Victoria	Aurora Chantilly Cream Horseradish Mornay Nantua

FIGURE 11-3
White Sauces—Sauces blanches

11.2.1 White Basic Sauce (Veloute)

YIELD: *U.S. — 10 quarts*
Metric — 10 liters (U.S. equiv. 10½ qt.)

INGREDIENTS	*U.S. Weight or Volume*	*Metric Weight or Volume*	PROCEDURE
Butter	1¼ pounds	600 grams	1. Melt butter.
Flour	1¾ pounds	800 grams	2. Add flour; stir and cook without coloring.
White stock, Chicken stock, OR Fish stock	12 quarts	12 liters	3. Add the cold stock. 4. Simmer for 1 to 1½ hours, stirring occasionally. If necessary, add more stock. 5. Adjust seasoning. 6. Strain through cheesecloth.
Salt	1 tablespoon	20 grams	

Note: If the stock used has a weak flavor, saute a mirepoix in the butter before mixing in the flour.

11.2.1.1 Allemande Sauce (Sauce allemande)

YIELD: *U.S. — 10 quarts*
Metric — 10 liters (U.S. equiv. — 10½ qt.)

INGREDIENTS	*U.S. Weight or Volume*	*Metric Weight or Volume*	PROCEDURE
Veal white basic sauce (Veloute de veau)	12 quarts	12 liters	1. Reduce the sauce to the desired consistency while stirring.
Thickening: (liaison)			
Egg yolks	8 to 10	8 to 10	2. Blend egg yolks and cream.
Cream	1 quart	1 liter	3. Add the hot sauce slowly to the thickening, stirring constantly. Heat the sauce almost to boiling point to bind.
Lemon juice	¼ cup	60 milliliters	4. Add lemon juice to taste.

Variations of Allemande Sauce

Caper Sauce — Sauce aux capres. Add capers and a dash of vinegar to Allemande Sauce.

Chaud-froid Sauce, Blond — Sauce chaud-froid blonde. Yield: 2½ cups (5 deciliters). Combine 1¾ cups (3½ deciliters) of Allemande Sauce and 1¾ cups (3½ deciliters) of chicken or meat jelly. Cook slowly for 15 minutes. Add ¾ cup (1½ deciliters) of cream and ½ teaspoon (2 grams) of salt. Cook slowly until the sauce coats the spoon. Strain the sauce and beat until cool.

Chaud-froid Sauce, White — Sauce chaud-froid blanche. Follow the recipe for Chaud-froid Sauce, Blond, with these exceptions: substitute white basic sauce (Veloute) for Allemande Sauce and add ¼ cup (½ deciliter) of cream.

Chive Sauce — Sauce aux ciboulettes. This sauce is prepared by adding finely chopped chives to Allemande Sauce.

Chivry White Sauce — Sauce chivry. This is an Allemande White Sauce combined with blanched and chopped herbs, such as tarragon, spinach, parsley, and/or chervil.

Curry Sauce — Sauce curry. Yield: 2 cups (4 deciliters). Saute a small vegetable mirepoix in 2 tablespoons (30 grams) of butter. Add ½ teaspoon (2 grams) of salt, 1 teaspoon (5 grams) of curry powder, a grated clove of garlic, 1/8 teaspoon (0.5 gram) of thyme, and a sprig of parsley. Deglaze with 1½ cups (3 deciliters) of Veal White Basic Sauce (Veloute de veau). Cook slowly for 30 minutes. Strain. Add ½ cup (1 deciliter) of cream. Add juice of ½ lemon.

Horseradish Sauce — Sauce raifort. Yield: 1 cup (2 deciliters). Add 1 tablespoon (15 grams) of grated horseradish to 1 cup (2 deciliters) of Allemande Sauce.

Mushroom Sauce — Sauce aux champignons. Yield: 2 cups (4 deciliters). Saute ¼ pound (100 grams) of peeled mushrooms in butter. Add the mushrooms to 1½ cups (3 deciliters) of Allemande Sauce.

Poulette Sauce — Sauce poulette. Yield: 1 cup (2 deciliters). Add 1 tablespoon (15 grams) of chopped parsley, 1 tablespoon (15 grams) of butter to 1 cup (2 deciliters) of Allemande Sauce. Add ¼ teaspoon (1 gram) of lemon juice. This sauce is served with vegetables or variety meats.

Tarragon Sauce — Sauce a l'estragon. This is an Allemande Sauce seasoned with tarragon vinegar and chopped tarragon leaves.

Villeroi Sauce — Sauce Villeroi. Yield: 1 cup (2 deciliters). Cook 1 cup (2 deciliters) of Allemande Sauce and ¼ cup (½ deciliter) of ham stock, and a few drops of essence of truffle until the sauce coats a spoon. Strain and garnish with julienne of chicken, sliced mushrooms, and truffles.

11.2.1.2 Supreme Sauce (Sauce supreme)

YIELD: *U.S. — 10 quarts*
Metric — 10 liters (U.S. equiv. — 10½ qt.)

INGREDIENTS	*U.S. Weight or Volume*	*Metric Weight or Volume*	PROCEDURE
Chicken White Basic Sauce (Veloute de volaille)	10 quarts	10 liters	1. Reduce the sauce to the desired consistency.
Cream	1 quart	1 liter	2. Add cream a little at a time.
Butter Lemon juice	9 ounces of ½ lemon	250 grams of ½ lemon	3. Add butter and lemon juice. 4. Adjust seasoning. 5. Strain through cheesecloth.

Variations of Supreme Sauce

Albufera Sauce — Sauce Albufera. This is a Supreme Sauce to which meat glaze has been added.
Mushroom Sauce — Sauce aux champignons. Mushroom stock is reduced and added to mushroom caps. The mushrooms are then added to Supreme Sauce.
Tarragon Sauce — Sauce a l'estragon. This is a Supreme Sauce with blanched and chopped tarragon leaves.
Toulouse Sauce — Sauce Toulouse. This is a Supreme Sauce seasoned with truffle essence, lemon juice, and melted butter.

11.2.1.3 White Wine Sauce (Sauce au vin blanc)

YIELD: *U.S. — 10 quarts*
Metric — 10 liters (U.S. equiv. — 10½ qt.)

INGREDIENTS	*U.S. Weight or Volume*	*Metric Weight or Volume*	PROCEDURE
Fish White Basic Sauce (Veloute de poisson)	10 quarts	10 liters	1. Reduce sauce and stock to desired consistency.
Fish stock (from poached fish)	1 quart	1 liter	
Thickening: (liaison)			2. Blend egg yolks and cream. 3. Add the hot sauce slowly to the thickening, stirring constantly.
Egg yolk	4 to 6	4 to 6	
Cream	1 quart	1 liter	4. Reduce slightly.
Butter	9 ounces	250 grams	5. Mix in butter and lemon juice.
Lemon juice	of ½ lemon	of ½ lemon	6. Strain through cheesecloth.

Variations of White Wine Sauce

Anchovy Sauce — Sauce aux anchois. Yield: 1 cup (2 deciliters). Add 2 tablespoons (30 grams) of anchovy butter to 1 cup (2 deciliters) of White Wine Sauce.
Bercy Sauce — Sauce Bercy. Yield: 1 cup (2 deciliters). Saute 1 tablespoon (15 grams) of chopped shallots in butter. Add ½ cup (1 deciliter) of White Wine Sauce and ½ cup (1 deciliter) of fish stock. Boil slowly until about ½ cup (1 deciliter) of liquid remains. Add 1 cup (2 deciliters) of White Wine Sauce, 1 tablespoon (15 grams) of butter, and 1 tablespoon (15 grams) of chopped parsley.
Caper Sauce — Sauce aux capres. This is a White Wine Sauce garnished with capers.
Cardinal Sauce — Sauce Cardinal. This is a White Wine Sauce seasoned with lobster butter and truffle essence.
Chaud-froid Sauce, Meatless — Sauce chaud-froid maigre. Yield: 2½ cups (5 deciliters). Combine 1¾ cups (3½ deciliters) of Veloute Sauce made with fish stock and 1¾ cups (3½ deciliters) of fish aspic jelly. Cook slowly until about 2 cups (4 deciliters) of liquid remain; continue to cook over high heat for a few minutes. Add ¼ cup (½ deciliter) of cream. Add a few drops of lemon juice.
Diplomat Sauce — Sauce diplomate. This is a White Wine Sauce mixed with shrimp butter. It is garnished with shrimp and dusted with cayenne pepper.
Fine Herb Sauce — Sauce aux fines herbes. This is a

White Wine Sauce with chopped parsley and tarragon leaves.

Lobster Sauce — Sauce homard. Yield: 1 cup (2 deciliters). Combine 1 cup (2 deciliters) of White Wine Sauce with 2 tablespoons (30 grams) of lobster butter. Add a sprinkling of cayenne. Strain. Fold in 2 tablespoons (30 grams) of diced lobster before serving.

Normandy Sauce — Sauce normande. Yield: 1½ cups (3 deciliters). Combine 1 cup (2 deciliters) of Veloute Sauce made of fish stock base with ½ cup (1 deciliter) of mushroom stock, and ½ cup (1 deciliter) of fish stock. Boil until about 1 cup (2 deciliters) remains. Mix 2 beaten egg yolks with 3 tablespoons (45 grams) of cream. Add to sauce. Add 3 tablespoons (45 grams) of butter.

Oyster Sauce — Sauce aux huitres. Yield: 2 cups (4 deciliters). Combine ½ cup (1 deciliter) of oyster stock and 2 cups (4 deciliters) of White Wine Sauce. Add 1/8 teaspoon (.5 gram) of cayenne, ½ teaspoon (2 grams) of salt, and 1/8 teaspoon (.5 gram) of pepper. Cook for 10 minutes. Garnish with 12 poached oysters.

Riche Sauce — Sauce riche. This White Wine Sauce is mixed with crayfish butter, truffle essence, and sliced mushrooms.

Shrimp Sauce — Sauce aux crevettes. This is a White Wine Sauce seasoned with shrimp butter and cayenne. It is garnished with diced shrimp.

Victoria Sauce — Sauce Victoria. This is a White Wine Sauce seasoned with lobster butter. It is garnished with diced lobster meat and truffles.

11.2.2 Bechamel Sauce (Sauce bechamel)

YIELD: *U.S. — 10 quarts*
Metric — 10 liters (U.S. equiv. — 10½ qt.)

INGREDIENTS	*U.S. Weight or Volume*	*Metric Weight or Volume*	PROCEDURE
Roux:			1. Melt butter and mix in flour. Cook for a few minutes.
Butter	1¼ pounds	600 grams	2. Allow roux to cool.
Flour	1¾ pounds	800 grams	
Milk	10 quarts	10 liters	3. Scald milk and gradually add to the roux.
Nutmeg	¼ teaspoon	1 gram	4. Add nutmeg, bay leaf, and onion.
Bay leaf	1	1	5. Simmer for a least 30 minutes. Add more hot milk if necessary.
Onion, studded with cloves	1	1	6. Adjust seasoning.
Salt	1 tablespoon	15 grams	7. Strain through cheesecloth.

Note: If the sauce is to be used to coat fish, meat, or vegetables, the consistency should be thicker than normal.

Variations of Bechamel Sauce

Aurora Sauce — Sauce aurore. This is a Bechamel Sauce seasoned with tomato puree.

Chantilly Sauce — Sauce Chantilly. This is a Bechamel Sauce blended with whipped cream.

Cream Sauce — Sauce creme. Mix a small amount of cream into a Bechamel Sauce.

Horseradish Sauce — Sauce raifort. This sauce may be prepared from a thick Cream Sauce or from a white basic sauce (veloute). Horseradish is added to the sauce.

Mornay Sauce — Sauce Mornay. This is a Cream Sauce with grated cheese, butter, and cayenne.

Nantua Sauce — Sauce Nantua. This is a Bechamel Sauce seasoned with shrimp butter. It is garnished with diced lobster.

11.3 Butter Sauces—Sauces au beurre

Structure of the basic butter sauces and their variations

Basic Sauces:

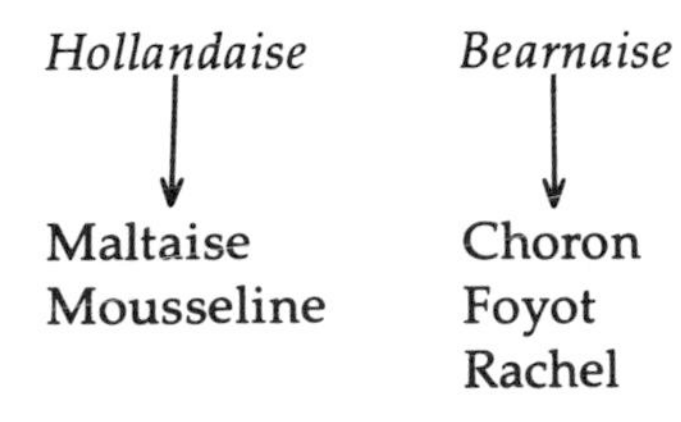

11.3.1 Hollandaise Sauce (Sauce hollandaise)

YIELD: *10 servings*

INGREDIENTS	*U.S. Weight or Volume*	*Metric Weight or Volume*	PROCEDURE
Shallots, chopped	2 ounces	50 grams	1. Reduce the chopped shallots, vinegar, and crushed peppercorns in a small saucepan until almost dry.
Vinegar	¼ cup	½ deciliter	
Peppercorns, crushed	10 to 15	10 to 15	
Water, cold	¼ cup	½ deciliter	2. Add cold water and egg yolks. Beat the mixture to a thick cream consistency using either low to medium heat or a water bath.
Egg yolks	6	6	
Butter, melted and clarified	1¼ pounds	600 grams	3. Using low heat, mix in melted butter very slowly, beating constantly.
Salt	1/8 teaspoon	1 gram	4. Add seasoning (caution if salted butter used) and lemon juice.
Cayenne pepper	few grains	few grains	5. Strain through cheesecloth.
Lemon juice	of ½ lemon	of ½ lemon	6. Keep at a moderate temperature in a water bath.

Note: For vegetables (asparagus, artichokes, cauliflower) Hollandaise Sauce is usually made with tarragon vinegar and white wine. The necessary degree of acidity can be obtained by using lemon juice.

Variations of Hollandaise Sauce

Maltaise Sauce—Sauce maltaise. This is a Hollandaise Sauce with orange juice and garnished with strips of blanched orange (zeste) peel. (A specialty for asparagus.)

Mousseline Sauce—Sauce mousseline. This is a Hollandaise Sauce to which whipped cream is added just before serving.

11.3.2 Bearnaise Sauce (Sauce bearnaise)

YIELD: *10 servings*

INGREDIENTS	*U.S. Weight or Volume*	*Metric Weight or Volume*	PROCEDURE
Shallots, chopped Tarragon vinegar Peppercorns, crushed	2 ounces ¼ cup 10 to 15	50 grams ½ deciliter 10 to 15	1. Reduce the chopped shallots, tarragon vinegar, and crushed peppercorns until almost dry.
White wine Egg yolks	¼ cup 6	½ deciliter 6	2. Add wine and egg yolks. Beat the mixture to a thick cream consistency using either low heat or a water bath.
Butter, melted and clarified	1¼ pounds	600 grams	3. Using very low heat, mix in melted butter very slowly, beating constantly.
Salt Cayenne pepper Lemon juice	⅛ teaspoon few grains of ½ lemon	1 gram few grains of ½ lemon	4. Add seasoning (caution if salted butter is used) and lemon juice. 5. Strain through cheesecloth.
Tarragon leaves, chopped	1 leaf	1 leaf	6. Garnish with chopped tarragon leaves. 7. Keep at a moderate temperature in a water bath.

Note: The container used for serving this sauce should be warm, never hot.

Variations of Bearnaise Sauce

Choron Sauce—Sauce choron. This is a Bearnaise Sauce mixed with a little tomato puree.

Foyot Sauce—Sauce Foyot. This is a Bearnaise Sauce mixed with meat glaze.

Rachel Sauce—Sauce Rachel. This is a Bearnaise Sauce mixed with both tomato puree and meat glaze.

11.4 Oil Sauces—Sauces a l'huile

Structure of the basic oil sauces and their most important variations

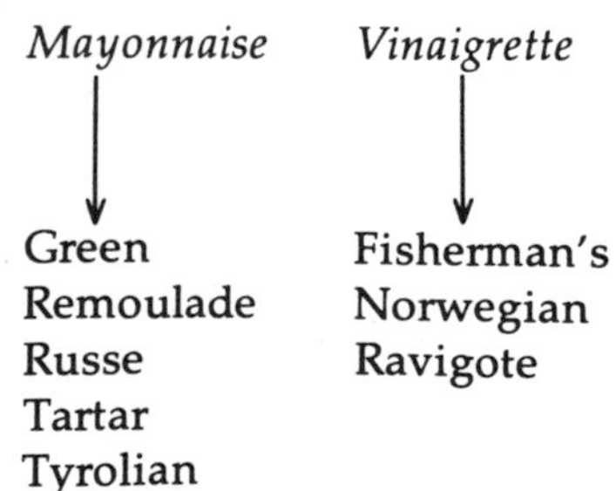

11.4.1 Mayonnaise (Sauce mayonnaise)

YIELD: *U.S. — 10 quarts*
Metric — 10 liters (U.S. equiv. — 10½ qt.)

INGREDIENTS	*U.S. Weight or Volume*	*Metric Weight or Volume*	PROCEDURE
Egg yolks	40	40	1. Beat egg yolks on second speed of mixer until well beaten.
Salt	2 ounces	50 grams	
Mustard	4 ounces	100 grams	
Cayenne pepper	¼ teaspoon	2 grams	
Vinegar	1½ to 2 cups	3 to 5 deciliters	2. Mix dry ingredients with one half of the vinegar and add to beaten egg yolks.
Oil	8½ quarts	8½ liters	3. Add oil to the eggs *gradually.* Continue beating constantly. 4. After all the oil is added, add remainder of vinegar. Continue beating for 5 minutes.
Lemon juice	4 ounces	120 milliliters	5. Season with lemon juice and Worcestershire Sauce.
Worcestershire sauce	1 ounce	30 milliliters	

Note: Mayonnaise should never be frozen.

Variations of Mayonnaise

Bagration Sauce—Sauce Bagration. This is a mayonnaise with anchovy puree and caviar added.
English Sauce—Sauce anglaise. This is a mayonnaise with English mustard added.
Green Sauce—Sauce verte. This is a mayonnaise mixed with puree of blanched spinach, parsley, and tarragon.
Gribiche Sauce—Sauce gribiche. This is a sauce made by beating crumbled hard-cooked egg yolks with vinegar and oil as for mayonnaise. It is seasoned with salt, pepper, and mustard and garnished with chopped gherkins, capers, parsley, tarragon, chives, and julienne of hard-cooked egg whites.
Mayonnaise Sauce, Russian Style — Sauce mayonnaise a la russe. This is a sauce made by beating equal parts of liquid meat jelly and mayonnaise. A dash of tarragon vinegar and some finely grated horseradish are added to the mixture which is beaten over ice until it thickens. The sauce must be used immediately. It is especially suitable for molded vegetable salad, for timbales, and for coating slices of shellfish and fish.
Ravigote Sauce — Sauce ravigote. See Vinaigrette Sauce.
Remoulade Sauce — Sauce remoulade. This is mayonnaise with chopped pickles, capers, parsley, and anchovy essence added.
Tartar Sauce — Sauce tartare. This is mayonnaise with chopped egg whites, pickles, capers, parsley, and onion added.
Tyrolian Sauce — Sauce tyrolienne. This is mayonnaise with tomato puree and chopped parsley added.

11.4.2 Vinaigrette Sauce (Sauce vinaigrette)

YIELD: *U.S. — 1 quart*
Metric — 1 liter

INGREDIENTS	U.S. Weight or Volume	Metric Weight or Volume
Onion, chopped	5 to 7 ounces	150 to 200 grams
Herbs: parsley, chives, tarragon, basil	5 ounces	150 grams
Vinegar	½ cup	1½ deciliters
Oil	2 cups	5 deciliters
Salt	½ teaspoon	4 grams
Pepper	1/8 teaspoon	1 gram

PROCEDURE

1. Combine all ingredients and mix well.
2. Adjust seasoning.

Note: The sauce should always be stirred before serving.

Variations of Vinaigrette Sauce

Fisherman's Sauce—Sauce a la pecheur. This is a Vinaigrette Sauce mixed with chopped crab meat.
Norwegian Sauce—Sauce norvegienne. This is a Vinaigrette Sauce mixed with egg yolks and anchovy fillets, both chopped.
Ravigote Sauce—Sauce ravigote. This is a Vinaigrette Sauce mixed with chopped pickles and capers. (This sauce is also frequently derived from Mayonnaise Sauce.)

11.5 Special Hot Sauces—Sauces speciales chaudes

Applesauce. This sauce is an apple puree seasoned with sugar and lemon juice. It is served hot with roast goose, duck, or pork.
Bread Sauce. This is a sauce made from milk boiled with an onion, cloves, bread crumbs, butter, nutmeg, salt, and pepper. (Especially suited for feathered game.)
Mustard Sauce—Sauce moutarde. This sauce is prepared by adding hot water to white roux to which butter and desired quantity of mustard are added. The finished sauce should be heated carefully.
Sour Cream Sauce—Sauce smitane. This is a sauce made from sauteed chopped onion moistened with white wine, reduced, and added to sour cream. It is simmered, strained, and seasoned with butter and lemon juice. (Especially suitable for game.)
Soubise Sauce—Sauce Soubise. Yield: approximately 1 quart (1 liter). Combine 1 pound (500 grams) finely cut and blanched onion, 7 ounces (200 grams) blanched rice, approximately 2 cups (5 deciliters) milk or white stock, 1 bay leaf, 1 clove, and seasoning. Cook covered in a water bath in the oven. Strain. Thicken with egg yolks and cream. (This sauce is served with lamb and mutton roasts, saddle of veal or mutton, and lamb cutlets.)

11.6 Special Cold Sauces—Sauces speciales froides

Cranberry Sauce—Sauce cranberry. Yield: 1 quart (1 liter). Combine 2 cups (4 deciliters) of sugar and 2 cups (4 deciliters) of water. Stir to dissolve sugar. Heat to boiling. Add 1 pound (500 grams) fresh cranberries. Cook until skins pop, about 5 minutes. Remove from heat. Serve warm or chilled. (Usually served with roast turkey.)

Cumberland Sauce—Sauce Cumberland. Yield: 1 quart (1 liter). Mix well with a whisk 1 pound (500 grams) red currant jelly, 1¼ cups (3 deciliters) port wine, ½ cup (1 deciliter) of both orange juice and lemon juice, a little English mustard, a pinch each of cayenne pepper and ginger. Add blanched julienne peels from 2 lemons and 2 oranges. (Usually is served with cold game.)

Horseradish Sauce, Chantilly—Sauce raifort chantilly. Yield: 1 quart (1 liter). Mix with a wooden spoon 1½ pints (8 deciliters) of whipped cream, 4 to 5 ounces (100 to 150 grams) of grated horseradish, lemon juice, and a little cayenne pepper. Adjust seasoning.

Mint Sauce—Sauce menthe. Yield: 1 quart (1 liter). Combine 2 cups (5 deciliters) vinegar, 2 cups (5 deciliters) water, 2 ounces (50 grams) chopped peppermint leaves, and ⅓ cup (85 grams) sugar. Cover and bring to a boil. Allow to cool. (This is usually served with hot or cold lamb dishes.)

Soups—Potages

12

The term *clear soup* refers to the various kinds of *bouillons* and *consommes.* Thick soups are broths and/or stocks *always thickened* with flour, grits, groats, barley, semolina, or with a vegetable and potato (also in the form of puree).

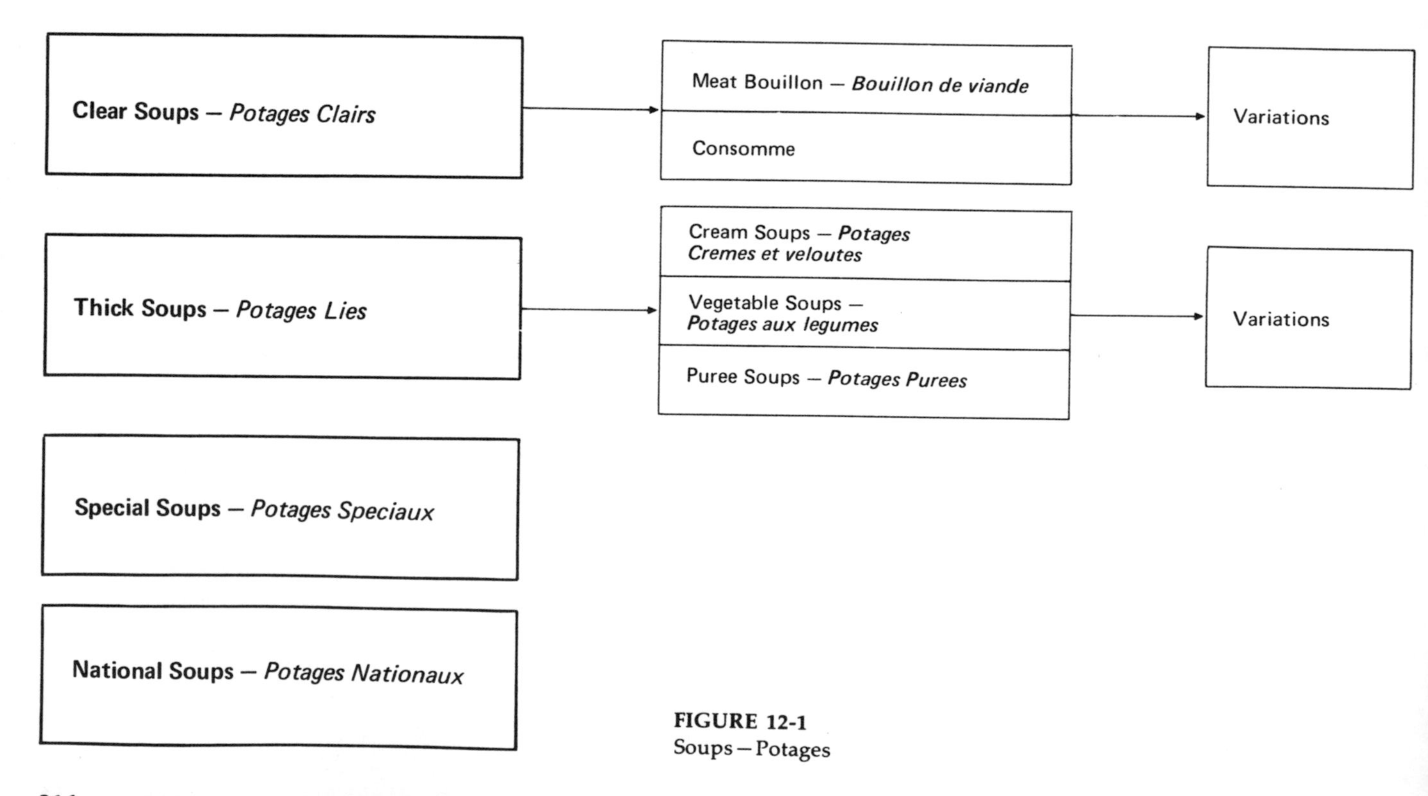

FIGURE 12-1
Soups—Potages

12.1 Clear Soups—Potages clairs

This term generally refers to bouillons or consommes made from beef. Special consommes such as poultry or fish should be identified as such on the menu. One portion normally consists of ¾ to 1¼ cups (2 to 3 deciliters).

12.1.1 Meat Bouillon (Bouillon de viande)

YIELD: *U.S. — 10 quarts*
Metric — 10 liters (U.S. equiv. — 10½ qt.)

INGREDIENTS	*U.S. Weight or Volume*	*Metric Weight or Volume*
Beef bones, chopped	10 to 12 pounds	5 to 6 kilograms
Lean beef	2 pounds	1 kilogram
Bouquet garni:		
Parsley	1 teaspoon	5 grams
Thyme	½ teaspoon	3 grams
Bay leaf	1	1
Celery, chopped	½ pound	225 grams
Onion, chopped	½ pound	225 grams
Onions, browned	2	2
Salt	1 teaspoon	5 grams
Pepper	1/8 teaspoon	1 gram
Water	12 quarts	12 liters

PROCEDURE

1. Put bones and meat in cold water. Bring to a boil and skim.
2. Add remaining ingredients.
3. Simmer for 4 hours, skimming off foam and fat occasionally.
4. Strain through cheesecloth.

Note: If the bouillon is being prepared for a dish with boiled beef, the meat should be put in boiling water. First brown the onions and add them with skins in order to give the bouillon a good color.

12.1.1.1 Marmite

This is the term for a broth or a broth with boiled soup meat.

12.1.1.2 Petite Marmite (Petite marmite)

YIELD: *10 servings*

INGREDIENTS	*U.S. Weight or Volume*	*Metric Weight or Volume*	PROCEDURE
Meat	3 pounds	1½ kilograms	1. Blanch the meat and the chicken.
Chicken	2 pounds	1 kilogram	
Leeks	7 ounces	200 grams	2. Peel and cut vegetables into sticks or thin slices.
Carrots	7 ounces	200 grams	
Celery	5 ounces	150 grams	
Cabbage	7 ounces	200 grams	
Turnips	3½ ounces	100 grams	
Stock, boiling	3½ quarts	3½ liters	3. Combine blanched meat and chicken with vegetables, boiling stock, and seasonings.
Parsley, chopped	1 tablespoon	15 grams	4. Simmer slowly. Test the meat with a fork from time to time. When it slips off the fork easily, remove it. Cut the meat into smaller pieces and put back into the soup.
Chervil, chopped	1 teaspoon	5 grams	
Salt	1 teaspoon	5 grams	
Pepper	1/8 teaspoon	1 gram	5. Season to taste.
Marrow bones, rinsed	2 to 3 pounds	1 to 1½ kilograms	6. Poach marrow bones separately. Put them in the soup just before serving. 7. Garnish with chopped parsley.

Note: Fried slices of bread, cranberries, dill pickles or grated cheese can be used as garnish. Petite Marmite should always be served in special earthenware casseroles.

12.1.1.3 Petite Marmite, Henry IV—Petite marmite, Henry IV

Made like Petite Marmite (12.1.1.2), but with more chicken than beef.

12.1.1.4 French Beef Broth—Pot-au-feu

For many years this was the name given to a Petite Marmite (12.1.1.2), but made only with beef. Today, smoked ribs, bacon, and pork sausages are often used. The use of strongly smoked pork or smoked sausages, however, spoils the excellent taste of the beef broth.

12.1.2 Consomme

YIELD: *U.S. — 10 quarts*
Metric — 10 liters (U.S. equiv. — 10½ qt.)

INGREDIENTS	*U.S. Weight or Volume*	*Metric Weight or Volume*
Lean beef, minced	3 to 4 pounds	1½ to 2 kilograms
Mirepoix:		
Leek, minced	8 ounces	225 grams
Carrots, minced	4 ounces	110 grams
Celery, minced	4 ounces	110 grams
Egg whites	4 to 6	4 to 6
Water	2 quarts	2 liters
Stock (bouillon), cold	10 quarts	10 liters

PROCEDURE

1. Mix minced beef and mirepoix. Add egg whites and water. Cover and let stand in a cool place for about an hour.
2. Add stock.
3. Heat to the boiling point, stirring occasionally.
4. Simmer slowly for 2 hours.
5. Strain through cheesecloth and skim off any fat.
6. Adjust seasoning.

Note: The green parts of leeks and celery should be included in the mirepoix.

12.1.2.1 Double Consomme—Consomme double

This is prepared as Consomme (12.1.2), except that the quantity of meat is doubled and a richer mirepoix used.

12.1.2.2 Cold Consomme—Consomme froid

This soup is prepared starting with Double Consomme (12.1.2.1) which has had the fat carefully skimmed off. It is seasoned with Madeira, port wine, and cayenne pepper. It is portioned into cups while still warm and allowed to cool. Either a mixture of sauteed vegetables (vegetable brunoise) or diced, seeded, and peeled tomatoes can be used as garnish. It can be served without any further additions. Cheese straws (paillettes de fromage) are often served separately.

Note: A cold consomme should always be strong and spicy. When cold it should gel slightly.

12.1.2.3 Chicken Consomme—Consomme de volaille

This soup is prepared using the Consomme recipe (12.1.2), adding to the meat chopped chicken trimmings (carcasses, necks, and wings) that have been lightly roasted to give a good poultry flavor.

12.1.2.4 Game Consomme—Consomme de gibier

This soup is prepared using the Consomme recipe (12.1.2) with the addition of chopped game bones and trimmings that have been cooked for a short time.

12.1.2.5 Fish Consomme (Consomme de poisson)

YIELD: *10 servings*

INGREDIENTS	*U.S. Weight or Volume*	*Metric Weight or Volume*	PROCEDURE
Fish, ground	1¼ pounds	600 grams	1. Combine fish, mirepoix, egg whites, water, and white wine. Mix well.
White mirepoix:			
Onion, chopped	2 ounces	55 grams	
Leeks, chopped	2 ounces	55 grams	
Celery, chopped	3 ounces	85 grams	
Thyme	½ teaspoon	3 grams	
Bay leaf	1	1	
Egg whites	2 to 3	2 to 3	
Water, cold	1 pint	½ liter	
White wine	¾ to 1¼ cups	2 to 3 deciliters	
Fish stock, cold	2½ quarts	2½ liters	2. Pour fish stock over the mixture. 3. Bring to a boil and simmer for 30 minutes.

Note: Fish dumplings, diced shellfish, vermicelli, rice, or croutons can be used for a garnish.

Variations of Clear Soups

Birds' Nests Consomme—Consomme aux nids d'hirondelles is a double chicken consomme flavored with brandy and garnished with cleaned, boiled, and shredded edible nests of the East Indian Salangare swallow.

Bouillon with Beef Marrow—Bouillon a la moelle (beef) is a clear soup garnished with cubed or sliced beef marrow, previously blanched.

Bouillon with Pearl Barley—Bouillon a l'orge perle (beef) is a bouillon garnished with boiled barley.

Bouillon with Semolina—Bouillon a la semoule (beef) is a bouillon garnished with boiled semolina.

Consomme, American Style—Consomme americaine (beef) is a consomme with tomato puree, seasoned with cayenne pepper and Madeira, and garnished with tapioca.

Consomme, Andalusian Style—Consomme andalouse (beef) is a consomme blended with tomato puree and garnished with julienne of lean ham and rice.

Consomme with Asparagus—Consomme aux pointes d'asperges is a clear soup thickened with tapioca and garnished with asparagus tips.

Consomme Aurore—Consomme aurore (beef) is a clear soup with tomato puree and tapioca.

Consomme, Bavarian Style—Consomme bavaroise (beef) is a consomme garnished with small semolina dumplings (quenelles).

Consomme with Beef Marrow—Consomme a la moelle (beef) is a clear soup garnished with poached slices of beef marrow. Slices of bread fried in butter are served separately.

Consomme, Belle Fermiere—Consomme belle fermiere (beef) is a consomme with sauteed julienne of cabbage and green beans garnished with pasta.

Consomme, Brunoise Style—Consomme brunoise (beef) is a clear soup with sauteed, finely diced leeks, carrots, celery, cabbage, and turnips.

Consomme Carmen (beef) is a consomme blended with tomato puree and garnished with strips of sweet peppers and dry cooked rice.

Consomme Caroline (chicken) is a consomme garnished with dry cooked rice.

Consomme Celestine (beef) is a clear soup garnished with a julienne of thin pancakes.

Consomme Chantilly (chicken) is a clear soup garnished with a julienne of cooked egg whites and dry cooked rice.

Consomme with Cheese Straws—Consomme aux paillettes (beef or chicken) is a clear soup. Cheese straws, seasoned with paprika, are served separately.

Consomme with Cheese Toast—Consomme aux diablotins (chicken) is a clear soup with small round slices of bread that have been covered with cheese, seasoned with paprika, and browned.

Consomme Croute au Pot Style—Consomme croute au pot is a Petite Marmite Consomme with finely sliced leeks, carrots, turnips, cabbage, and celery. Croutons fried in butter are served separately.

Consomme Demidoff—Consomme Demidov (chicken) is a consomme garnished with tiny chicken dumplings (quenelles) and finely diced, sauteed vegetables (brunoise).

Consomme Dubarry (beef) is a clear soup garnished with cauliflower and molded custard (royale).

Consomme, Duchess Style — Consomme duchess (chicken) is a consomme garnished with julienne of chicken.

Consomme with Egg Drops—Consomme aux oeufs files is a clear soup with beaten eggs added to the boiling consomme.

Consomme with Egg Yolk—Consomme a l'oeuf (beef) is a consomme served with one egg yolk per cup of soup.

Consomme, French Style—Consomme pot-au-feu is Consomme Croute au Pot Style (Consomme croute au pot) garnished with small cubes of boiled meat. It is served in a special pot with small slices of fried bread offered separately.

Consomme with Fried Puff Pearls—Consomme aux pois frits is a consomme with fried puff pearls served separately. (Thick pancake batter is poured through a colander over hot fat to make puff pearls.)

Consomme, Hungarian Style—Consomme hongroise (beef) is a clear soup flavored with paprika and Madeira and garnished with sauteed tomatoes (peeled, seeded, and diced).

Consomme, Hunter's Style—Consomme chasseur (feathered game) is a clear soup garnished with sliced mushrooms and tiny puff shells (profiterolles).

Consomme Julienne—Consomme julienne (beef) is a clear soup with very finely cut pieces (thin sticks) of cooked vegetables: carrots, leeks, celery, and turnips.

Consomme Leopold—Consomme Leopold (beef) is a bouillon with semolina garnished with julienne of Boston lettuce and chervil.

Consomme Lucullus—Consomme Lucullus (chicken) is a clear soup garnished with slices of boiled chicken and truffles, green peas, and asparagus tips.

Consomme Madrilene—Consomme madrilene (chicken) is a double strength consomme or chicken consomme flavored with Madeira, brandy, and cayenne pepper. It is garnished with diced tomatoes. It can be served hot or cold.

Consomme Monte Carlo—Consomme Monte Carlo (chicken) is a clear soup garnished with stuffed pancakes (crepes with goose liver filling are rolled and sliced into thin circles).

Consomme with Liver Dumplings—Consomme aux noques de foie (beef) is a consomme garnished with tiny liver dumplings.

Consomme, Paris Style—Consomme parisienne is a clear soup garnished with sauteed finely diced vegetables (brunoise), molded custard (royale), and chervil.

Consomme with Pasta—Consomme aux pates (beef) is a clear soup garnished with fine noodles.

Consomme Paysanne—Consomme paysanne (beef) is a consomme garnished with very finely sliced and cooked vegetables: leeks, carrots, celery, turnips, and cabbage.

Consomme with Pearl Tapioca—Consomme aux perles du Japon is a consomme garnished with cooked pearl tapioca.

Consomme with Poached Eggs—Consomme aux oeufs poches (beef or chicken) is a consomme garnished with small poached eggs.

Consomme, Princess Style — Consomme princesse (chicken) is a consomme garnished with molded custard (royale), cooked pearl barley, and julienne of cooked chicken.

Consomme with Profiterolles—Consomme aux profiterolles (beef or chicken) is a consomme with profiterolles, fried petite size puff shells (pate a chou, recipe 25.1.3), served separately.

Consomme with Quenelles—Consomme aux quenelles (beef or chicken) is a clear soup garnished with meat or chicken dumplings (quenelles).

Consomme with Ravioli—Consomme au ravioli is a clear

soup garnished with very small ravioli.

Consomme with Royale—Consomme royale is a consomme garnished with molded custard (royale).

Consomme with Sago—Consomme au sagou is a clear soup garnished with cooked sago.

Consomme with Semolina—Consomme a la semoule (beef) is a consomme garnished with cooked semolina.

Consomme with Spring Vegetables—Consomme printaniere (beef or chicken) is a clear soup with slightly cooked small cubes of carrots, turnips, and celery, and strips of beans and sorrel.

Consomme with Tapioca—Consomme au tapioca (beef) is a clear soup garnished with cooked tapioca.

Consomme with Three Fillets—Consomme aux trois filets (beef) is a consomme garnished with julienne of chicken, tongue, and truffles.

Consomme with Vermicelli—Consomme aux vermicelles (beef) is a clear soup garnished with cooked vermicelli (fine noodles).

Consomme, Viennese—Consomme viennoise (beef) is a clear soup garnished with square egg noodles and potato dumplings.

Consomme Xavier—Consomme Xavier (beef) is a clear soup with egg drops and chervil.

Queen's Consomme—Consomme a la reine (chicken) is a consomme thickened with tapioca and garnished with molded custard (royale) and julienne of chicken.

12.2 Thick Soups—Potages lies

12.2.1 Cream and Veloute Soups—Potages cremes et veloutes

Several decades ago there were two basic methods to prepare *cream soups.* Cream soups (potages cremes) were made with a Bechamel Sauce, the appropriate puree, and thickened with cream. Cream soups (veloutes) were made with Veloute Sauce, the appropriate puree, and thickened with cream and egg yolk (liaison) and butter. Today with the availability of very fine quality thickening flours, from many different cereals, cream soups can be prepared by one method. One can, therefore, write Cream of rice or Potage creme de riz and Puree of Potato Soup or Potage parmentier on a menu.

GRUEL (PORRIDGE)—BOUILLIES

These soups are served as easily digestible foods. The basic ingredients are cereal flour, flakes, coarsely-ground barley and cereal grains, water or slightly salted stock, and sometimes herbs. After straining, they are thickened with milk or cream.

12.2.1.1 Basic Preparation for Cream and Veloute Soups

YIELD: *U.S. — 10 quarts*
Metric — 10 liters (U.S. equiv. — 10½ qt.)

INGREDIENTS	*U.S. Weight or Volume*	*Metric Weight or Volume*	PROCEDURE
Fat	10 to 14 ounces	300 to 400 grams	1. Melt fat. Add flour and blend. Cook slowly and stir. Do not let flour brown.
Rice flour	14 to 16 ounces	400 to 500 grams	
Stock (white, chicken, fish, or other)	10½ quarts	10 liters	2. Add cold stock and simmer for about 30 minutes. If too much evaporates, add more stock.
Butter	2 ounces	55 grams	3. Bind with cream, butter, or thickening.
Cream	1 quart	1 liter	4. Strain.
OR			5. Season to taste.
Thickening:			6. Do not allow the soup to boil again if thickened with liaison.
Cream	1 pint	5 deciliters	
Egg yolks	2	2	

Note: Alternate method: Dissolve the rice flour in cold milk or white stock. Add this to boiling stock. The soup is then finished with the ingredients in the basic recipe.

Variations of Cream and Veloute Soups

Barley Soup—Orge perle is prepared by sauteing 4 ounces (100 grams) of barley and 1 teaspoon (5 grams) of flour in butter. Add 3 quarts (3 liters) of white stock and a bouquet garni. Cook soup until barley is tender.

Cream Soup Agnes Sorel—Creme Agnes Sorel is a basic cream soup made with chicken stock and sauteed mushrooms. It is garnished with julienne of mushrooms, beef tongue, and chicken.

Andalusian Cream Soup—Veloute andalouse is prepared by blending 3 quarts (3 liters) of basic cream soup recipe (12.2.1.1) with ¾ cup (2 deciliters) of tomato puree and 1¼ cup (3 deciliters) of onion puree (soubise). Without letting soup boil, bind. It can be garnished with diced tomatoes, strips of sweet peppers, and dry cooked rice.

Cream of Asparagus Soup—Creme Argenteuil is prepared using basic cream soup recipe (12.2.1.1) made with equal parts of asparagus stock and white stock. It is garnished with asparagus tips.

Cream Soup Bagration—Creme Bagration is prepared using basic cream soup recipe (12.2.1.1) made with veal stock. It is garnished with cut macaroni.

Cream of Barley Soup—Creme d'orge is prepared using basic cream soup recipe (12.2.1.1) replacing rice flour with barley flour.

Cream of Cauliflower Soup—Creme Dubarry is prepared using basic cream soup recipe (12.2.1.1) made with equal parts of cauliflower stock and white stock. It is garnished with tiny cauliflower florets.

Cream Soup Canoness—Veloute chanoinesse is a cream soup made with fish cream sauce, mushrooms, parsley, and crayfish butter. It is garnished with poached slices of fish milts.

Cream Soup Caroline—Veloute Caroline is a soup made from basic cream soup blended with almond milk and cooked rice.

Cream Soup Carmen—Veloute Carmen is a basic cream soup with tomato puree. It is garnished with diced tomatoes and dry cooked rice.

Cream Soup Choisy—Creme Choisy is a Cream of Lettuce Soup (Creme de laitue) with croutons served separately.

Cream Soup Dame Blanche—Veloute dame blanche is

prepared by adding ¾ cup (2 deciliters) of almond milk to 3 quarts (3 liters) of basic cream soup recipe (12.2.1.1) made with chicken stock. Adjust thickening. It is garnished with small quenelles of chicken and diced chicken.

Cream Soup Derby—Creme Derby is a basic cream soup made with onion, seasoned with curry, and garnished with dry cooked rice, chopped truffles, and, if desired, chicken dumplings.

Cream of Green Wheat Soup—Creme de ble vert is made using basic cream soup recipe (12.2.1.1) replacing rice flour with green wheat flour.

Cream Soup Jackson—Creme Jackson is a soup made by mixing equal parts of basic cream soup and Cream of Potato Soup. It is garnished with vermicelli or cooked tapioca and julienne of white parts of leeks.

Cream of Lettuce Soup—Creme de laitue is a basic cream soup with chopped, blanched, sauteed Boston lettuce.

Cream Soup Mary Stuart—Veloute Marie Stuart is prepared using the basic cream soup recipe (12.2.1.1) made with barley flour and chicken stock. It is garnished with sauteed finely diced vegetables (brunoise) and chervil leaves.

Cream Soup Milanese—Milanaise is prepared by adding ¾ cup (2 deciliters) of tomato puree to 3 quarts (3 liters) of basic cream soup recipe (12.2.1.1). Cook and bind. It is garnished with elbow macaroni, julienne of white truffles, tongue, and ham.

Cream of Morel Soup—Creme de morilles is prepared by adding 3½ ounces (100 grams) sauteed morels to 3 quarts (3 liters) of basic cream soup recipe (12.2.1.1). Strain and bind. It is garnished with finely cut morels.

Cream of Nettle Soup—Creme d'ortie is prepared by adding 10 ounces (300 grams) of blanched young nettle leaves to 3 quarts (3 liters) of basic cream soup recipe (12.2.1.1). Strain and bind. It is garnished with croutons.

Cream of Oatmeal Soup—Creme d'avoine is prepared using basic cream soup recipe (12.2.1.1) replacing rice flour with oatmeal flour.

Cream Soup Portuguese—Creme portugaise is basic cream soup blended with tomato puree and sliced bacon. It is strained and then garnished with dry cooked rice.

Cream of Rice Soup, German Style—Creme allemande is a soup made with sauteed rice, stock, and bouquet garni. After boiling for 10 minutes, the bouquet is removed, and the soup is thickened.

Cream Soup Rossini—Veloute Rossini is prepared by adding 7 ounces (200 grams) of goose liver butter to 3 quarts (3 liters) of basic cream soup recipe (12.2.1.1) made with chicken stock. Goose liver butter: Blend 3½ ounces (100 grams) of goose liver trimmings or puree with 3½ ounces (100 grams) of butter until smooth.

Cream of Sorrel Soup—Creme d'oseille is prepared by adding 7 ounces (200 grams) of sauteed sorrel to 3 quarts (3 liters) of Cream of Oatmeal Soup (Creme d'avoine). It is strained and then garnished with croutons.

Queen's Cream Soup—Creme a la reine is prepared using basic cream soup recipe (12.2.1.1) made with chicken stock. It is garnished with diced chicken.

Semolina Soup (Thick)—Semoule liee is prepared by sauteing 5 ounces (120 grams) of semolina in butter. Add 3 quarts (3 liters) of white stock and a bouquet garni. Cook for 20 minutes and bind.

12.2.2 Vegetable Soups—Potages aux legumes

These soups are composed of one or more types of vegetables, usually including onion, leeks, and diced bacon, which are first sauteed, then boiled, but not strained. If a vegetable soup consists of several different vegetables, only small quantities of those vegetables with a strong flavor, such as cabbage and turnips, should be used. All vegetable soups must be garnished with chopped parsley, chives, or chervil. Flour or potato is used for binding.

12.2.2.1 Basic Preparation of Vegetable Soup

YIELD: *U.S. — 10 quarts*
Metric — 10 liters (U.S. equiv. — 10½ qt.)

INGREDIENTS	*U.S. Weight or Volume*	*Metric Weight or Volume*	PROCEDURE
Fat OR butter	3½ ounces	100 grams	1. Saute onion and other vegetables.
Leeks	3 pounds	1.5 kilograms	2. Add potatoes and continue to saute.
Carrots, finely sliced	1 pound	.5 kilogram	
Onion, finely diced	2 pounds	1 kilogram	
Celery, finely sliced	1 pound	.5 kilogram	
Potatoes OR turnips	1 pound	.5 kilogram	
Stock	7 to 8 quarts	7 to 8 liters	3. Add stock and simmer until ingredients are well cooked and soup is bound.
Cream (optional) OR Milk	1 pint	5 deciliters	4. Add milk or cream (optional).
Cabbage, finely shredded	½ pound	225 grams	5. Add cabbage and simmer 10 minutes.
Salt	1 teaspoon	6 grams	6. Adjust seasoning.
Pepper	¼ teaspoon	2 grams	
Fried bread			7. Garnish with fried bread and parsley.
Parsley, chopped			

Note: If potatoes are not in the recipe, the vegetables must be dusted with flour or rice flour before deglazing with stock. Acidic vegetables, such as leeks and cabbage, must be well cooked. If not, the soup will curdle when bound with cream or cream and egg yolks (liaison).

Variations of Vegetable Soups

Bonne Femme Soup—Potage bonne femme. Yield: 10 quarts (10 liters). Use 3½ ounces (100 grams) of fat, 3 pounds (1.5 kilograms) of leeks, 5 pounds (2.5 kilograms) of finely sliced potatoes, 7 to 8 quarts (7 to 8 liters) of stock, and 1 pint (5 deciliters) of cream. Adjust seasoning. Garnish with fried bread and chopped parsley.

Cultivator Soup—Potage cultivateur. Yield: 10 quarts (10 liters). Use 3½ ounces (100 grams) of butter, 7 ounces (200 grams) of diced bacon, 7 pounds (3.5 kilograms) of finely sliced vegetables (leeks, onion, carrots, celery, turnips, and potatoes), 7 to 8 quarts (7 to 8 liters) of stock, and seasoning. Follow method in recipe 12.2.2.1. When portioned, serve grated cheese separately.

Fermiere Soup—Potage fermiere. Cultivator Soup

(Potage cultivateur) served with fried slices of bread.
Flemish Soup—Potage flamande. Yield: 10 quarts (10 liters). Use 3½ ounces (100 grams) of butter, 14 ounces (400 grams) of onion and leeks, 1¾ pounds (800 grams) of chopped brussels sprouts, 5 pounds (2.5 kilograms) of finely sliced potatoes, 7 to 8 quarts (7 to 8 liters) of stock, and seasoning. Follow method in recipe 12.2.2.1. Garnish with small brussels sprouts.
Leek Soup—Potage aux poireaux. The same as Bonne Femme Soup (Potage bonne femme) with an increased quantity of leeks.
Paysanne Soup—Potage paysanne. Yield: 10 quarts (10 liters). Use 3½ ounces (100 grams) of butter, 10 ounces (300 grams) of diced lean bacon, 7 pounds (3.5 kilograms) of finely sliced vegetables (onion, leeks, carrots, turnips, celery, cabbage, and potatoes), 3½ ounces (100 grams) of flour, and 7 to 8 quarts (7 to 8 liters) of stock. Follow method in recipe 12.2.2.1. Serve grated cheese separately.

12.2.3 Puree Soups—Potages Purees

Soups made from dried or fresh vegetables and then put through a sieve or foodmill are known as "puree soups." Vegetables with a high starch content or potatoes, rice, and flour can be used for binding puree soups. Cream is used for enriching them. These soups are garnished with chives, parsley, or croutons.

12.2.3.1 Basic Preparation of Puree Soups

YIELD: *U.S. — 10 quarts*
Metric — 10 liters (U.S. equiv. — 10½ qt.)

INGREDIENTS	*U.S. Weight or Volume*	*Metric Weight or Volume*	PROCEDURE
Fat	4 ounces	120 grams	1. Lightly saute mirepoix (or fresh vegetables).
White mirepoix: Onion, Leeks	2½ pounds	1.2 kilograms	
Potatoes OR Vegetable	6 pounds	3 kilograms	2. Add potatoes or vegetable, ham and bacon, and continue to saute.
Stock	8 quarts	8 liters	3. Add stock, a little white wine if desired, and seasoning.
Ham and bacon rinds	2 pounds	1 kilogram	4. Bring quickly to a boil, stirring occasionally. 5. Strain. 6. Bind if necessary.
Cream	1 pint	5 deciliters	7. Add cream (optional).
Salt	1 teaspoon	6 grams	8. Adjust seasoning.

Variations of Puree Soups

Puree of Carrot Soup—Puree Crecy. Yield: 10 quarts (10 liters). Use 3½ ounces (100 grams) of fat, 28 ounces (800 grams) of onion and leeks, approximately 6 pounds (3 kilograms) of carrots, 10 ounces (300 grams) of rice, 8 quarts (8 liters) of stock, and seasoning. Follow method in recipe 12.2.3.1.
Puree of Carrot Soup with Tapioca—Puree velours. Yield: 10 quarts (10 liters). Combine 7 quarts (7 liters) of Puree of Carrot Soup (Puree Crecy), and 3 quarts (3 liters) of stock. Garnish with 7 ounces (200 grams) of tapioca.

Puree of Cauliflower Soup Dubarry—Puree Dubarry. Yield: 10 quarts (10 liters). Use 3½ ounces (100 grams) of fat, 1¼ pounds (600 grams) of white mirepoix, approximately 6 pounds (3 kilograms) of cauliflower, 2 pounds (1 kilogram) of potatoes, 8 quarts (8 liters) of stock, and seasoning. Follow method in recipe 12.2.3.1. Garnish with cooked cauliflower florets.

Puree of Fresh Pea Soup—Puree de pois frais. Yield: 10 quarts (10 liters). Use 4 ounces (120 grams) of fat, 2½ pounds (1.2 kilograms) of leeks, 1 pound (500 grams) of lettuce, 6 pounds (3 kilograms) of fresh peas, a little chervil, sugar, 8 quarts (8 liters) of stock, and seasoning. Follow method in recipe 12.2.3.1. Garnish with fresh peas and chervil leaves.

Puree of Fresh Pea Soup Lamballe—Puree Lamballe. Yield: 10 quarts (10 liters). To 10 quarts (10 liters) of Puree and Fresh Pea Soup add 6 to 7 ounces (150 to 200 grams) of tapioca.

Health Soup—Puree sante. Yield: 10 quarts (10 liters). Add 1¼ pounds (500 grams) of shredded sorrel simmered in butter until water in vegetable has evaporated (chiffonade of sorrel) to 10 quarts (10 liters) of Puree of Potato Soup Parmentier (Puree Parmentier).

Potato Soup with Tapioca—Puree argentee. Yield: 10 quarts (10 liters). Add 3 to 5 ounces (100 to 150 grams) of cooked tapioca to 10 quarts (10 liters) of Potato Soup.

Puree of Lentil Soup—Puree Conti. Yield: 10 quarts (10 liters). Use 3½ ounces (100 grams) of fat, 1¾ pounds (800 grams) of mirepoix, 7 ounces (200 grams) of bacon rinds, 2 pounds (1 kilogram) of soaked lentils, 1 pound (500 grams) of potatoes, a little chervil, 10 quarts (10 liters) of stock, and seasoning. Follow method in recipe 12.2.3.1.

Puree of Pea Soup St. Germain—Puree St. Germain. Yield: 10 quarts (10 liters). Use 4 ounces (120 grams) of fat, 1¾ pounds (800 grams) of onion and leeks, 7 ounces (200 grams) of bacon rinds, 2½ pounds (1.2 kilograms) of soaked, dried split green peas, 3 pounds (1.5 kilograms) of potatoes, 10 quarts (10 liters) of stock and seasoning. Follow method in recipe 12.2.3.1.

Puree of Potato Soup Parmentier—Puree Parmentier. Yield: 10 quarts (10 liters). Use 4 ounces (120 grams) of fat, 2½ pounds (1.2 kilograms) of onion and leeks, 6 pounds (3 kilograms) of potatoes, 8 quarts (8 liters) of stock, ham and bacon rinds, and seasoning. Follow method in recipe 12.2.3.1.

Puree of Potato and Tomato Soup Malakoff—Puree Malakov. Yield: 10 quarts (10 liters). Use 3½ ounces (100 grams) of fat, 2½ pounds (1.2 kilograms) of leeks, 3 pounds (1.5 kilograms) of potatoes, 3 pounds (1.5 kilograms) of tomatoes, 8 quarts (8 liters) of stock and seasoning. Follow method in recipe 12.2.3.1. Garnish with 1¼ pounds (800 grams) of blanched sauteed chopped spinach.

Puree of Red Bean Soup—Puree Conde. Yield: 10 quarts (10 liters). Use 3½ ounces (100 grams) of fat, 1¾ pounds (800 grams) of mirepoix, bacon rind, 2 pounds (1 kilogram) of red beans, 1 pound (500 grams) of potatoes, 1 quart (1 liter) of red wine, 10 quarts (10 liters) of stock and seasoning. Follow method in recipe 12.2.3.1.

Puree of Spinach Soup—Puree florentine. Yield: 10 quarts (10 liters). To 10 quarts (10 liters) of Puree of Potato Soup Parmentier (Puree Parmentier) add 2 pounds (1 kilogram) of blanched chopped spinach.

Puree of Vegetable Soup—Puree garbure. Yield: 10 quarts (10 liters). Use 5 ounces (150 grams) of fat, 1¼ pounds (600 grams) of onion, 1¼ pounds (600 grams) of leeks, 7 ounces (200 grams) of bacon trimmings and rind, 7 ounces (200 grams) of turnips, 7 ounces (200 grams) of cabbage, 1¾ pounds (800 grams) of carrots, 4 pounds (2 kilograms) of potatoes, 8 quarts (8 liters) of stock, and seasoning. Follow method in recipe 12.2.3.1.

Puree of Watercress Soup—Puree cressonniere. Yield: 10 quarts (10 liters). Use 3½ ounces (100 grams) of fat, 2½ pounds (1.2 kilograms) of white mirepoix, 6 pounds (3 kilograms) of potatoes, 1¾ pounds (800 grams) of watercress, 8 quarts (8 liters) of stock and seasoning. Follow method in recipe 12.2.3.1. Garnish with sauteed chopped watercress leaves.

Puree of White Bean Soup Faubonne—Puree Faubonne. Yield: 10 quarts (10 liters). Use 3½ ounces (100 grams) of fat, 1¾ pounds (800 grams) of white mirepoix, 7 ounces (200 grams) of bacon rind, 2½ pounds (1.2 kilograms) of soaked white beans, 2 pounds (1 kilogram) of potatoes, white wine, if desired, and seasoning. Follow method in recipe 12.2.3.1.

Puree of Yellow Pea Soup Victoria—Puree Victoria. Yield: 10 quarts (10 liters). Use 3½ ounces (100 grams) of fat, a few bacon rinds, 2½ pounds (1.2 kilograms) of onion and leeks, 2½ pounds (1.2 kilograms) of soaked, dried yellow peas, 3 pounds (1.5 kilograms) of potatoes, 10 quarts (10 liters) of stock, and seasoning. Garnish with 3⅓ ounces (100 grams) of cooked rice.

Sport Soup—Potage sport. Yield: 10 quarts (10 liters). Garnish 10 quarts (10 liters) of Puree of Pea Soup St. Germain (Puree St. Germain) with 1 pound (500 grams) of sorrel shredded in a fine julienne and simmered in butter (chiffonade of sorrel), 10 ounces (300 grams) of cooked and cut noodles, and chopped parsley.

12.3 Special Soups—Potage speciaux

Special soups are those made with unusual ingredients and/or prepared by a distinctive method. The following are classified as special soups.

Beef Tea (Beeftea)

YIELD: *U.S. — 1 quart*
Metric — 1 liter

INGREDIENTS	*U.S. Weight or Volume*	*Metric Weight or Volume*
Beef	3 pounds	1.5 kilograms
Water	3 quarts	3 liters
Bouquet garni:		
Celery leaves	2 tablespoons	50 grams
Bay leaf	½ leaf	½ leaf
Thyme	½ teaspoon	3 grams
Parsley	4 sprigs	4 sprigs
Leek, white portion	1	1
Cloves	2	2

PROCEDURE

1. Place beef, water, and bouquet garni in an airtight container.
2. Poach for 2 to 3 hours in a double boiler.
3. Strain carefully, season lightly, and serve in small cups.

Crayfish Bisque (Bisque d'ecrevisses)

YIELD: *U.S. — 10 servings*

INGREDIENTS	*U.S. Weight or Volume*	*Metric Weight or Volume*	PROCEDURE
Fat	2 ounces	50 grams	1. Saute the crayfish and mirepoix in fat until the crayfish turn red.
Crayfish, rinsed and cleaned	3 to 4 pounds	1.5 to 2 kilograms	
Mirepoix, finely chopped	7 ounces	200 grams	
Diced tomato OR Tomato puree	2¾ ounces	80 grams	2. Add tomato and continue to saute.
Brandy	¼ cup	½ deciliter	3. Flambe with the brandy.
White wine	¾ cup	2 deciliters	4. Add the wine and reduce.
Fish stock	1½ quarts	1.5 liters	5. Add the fish stock and plain stock and simmer for 10 minutes.
Stock	1 quart	1 liter	6. Remove the tails of the crayfish. Pound the carcasses and put them back in the soup. Simmer.
Rice flour	2¾ ounces	80 grams	7. Bind the soup with the rice flour. Strain.
Egg yolks	2	2	8. Thicken with egg yolks and cream. Adjust seasonings, and garnish with diced crayfish tails and cubed tomatoes.
Cream	¾ cup	1 to 2 deciliters	

Variations of Bisque

Lobster Bisque—Bisque de homard is prepared using Crayfish Bisque recipe substituting live lobster for crayfish.

Shrimp Bisque—Bisque de crevettes is prepared using Crayfish Bisque recipe substituting shrimp for crayfish.

Crustacean Soup—Veloute de crustaces is prepared with Crayfish Bisque recipe using a variety of crustaceans.

Other Special Soups

Fish Soup—Veloute de poisson. Yield: 10 servings. Use 3 quarts (3 liters) of basic white sauce made with fish stock. (Veloute de poisson, see Section 12.2.1.1) thinned with milk. Thicken with 2 egg yolks and 1¼ cups (3 deciliters) of cream. Adjust seasoning. Garnish with cubes of fish or fish dumplings.

Germiny Soup—Potage Germiny. Yield: 10 servings. Saute 7 ounces (200 grams) of sorrel shredded in a fine julienne in 1 ounce (30 grams) of butter (chiffonade of sorrel). Add 2½ quarts (2.5 liters) of consomme. Just before serving thicken with 4 egg yolks and 1¾ cups (4 deciliters) of cream. Do not allow soup to boil. Garnish with chopped chervil leaves.

Puree of Chicken Soup, Queen's Style—Puree a la reine. Yield: 10 servings. Poach 1 chicken in 3½ quarts (3.5 liters) of chicken stock and 7 ounces (200 grams) of bouquet garni. Puree the chicken meat reserving the breast. Bind the stock with 3½ ounces (100 grams) of rice flour. Add the puree and 1¼ to 1¾ cups (3 to 4 deciliters) cream. Adjust seasoning. Garnish with diced breast of chicken.

Puree of Game Soup—Puree de gibier. Yield: 10 servings. Boil 1 pound (½ kilogram) of game meat (preferably venison) with 14 ounces (400 grams) of lentils in 3 quarts (3 liters) of game stock (fond de gibier, recipe 10.2.3) with 1 onion studded with cloves and bay leaf. Cook until meat is tender and grind. Flambe with brandy. Add ½ to ¾ cup (1 to 2 deciliters) of cream. Adjust seasoning. Garnish with cubed game meat.

Real Turtle Soup Lady Curzon. Yield: 10 servings. Heat 1½ quarts (1.5 liters) of real turtle soup (available canned) with a little sherry. Whip ¾ cup (2 deciliters) of cream. Pour soup into heated cups, garnish with whipped cream sprinkled with curry powder. Glaze under the broiler.

Real Turtle Soup Londonderry. Yield: 10 servings. Heat 1½ quarts (1.5 liters) of real turtle soup (available canned). Thicken with 3 egg yolks and ½ cup (1½ deciliters) of cream. Add a little sherry and Madeira. Do not let soup boil.

Real Turtle Soup (English Specialty). Available canned. Season with a little brandy and Madeira. If necessary, the canned soup can be extended one third with double consomme.

12.4 National Soups—Potages nationaux

The methods for preparing these soups are quite varied. The name of the soup should appear on the menu *in the language of the country of its origin.*

Basler Zwiebelsuppi (Onion Soup, Basel Style)

YIELD: *U.S. — 10 servings*

INGREDIENTS	*U.S. Weight or Volume*	*Metric Weight or Volume*	PROCEDURE
Onion	1 to 1¼ pounds	500 to 600 grams	1. Brown onion in fat. Add browned flour and blend with fat.
Fat	2¾ ounces	80 grams	
Flour, browned	7 ounces	200 grams	
Stock	3 quarts	3 liters	2. Add the stock gradually and simmer for 1 hour.
Croutons	5 ounces	150 grams	3. Adjust seasonings.
Cheddar cheese, finely diced	5 ounces	150 grams	4. Garnish soup with croutons and cheese just before serving.

Bauern-Chrutsuppe (Health Soup, Paysanne Style) Bernese Specialty

YIELD: *U.S. — 10 servings*

INGREDIENTS	*U.S. Weight or Volume*	*Metric Weight or Volume*	PROCEDURE
Spinach, finely chopped	1¾ pounds	800 grams	1. Saute spinach, onion, chervil, and marjoram in fat.
Green onion, chopped	7 ounces	200 grams	
Chervil, finely chopped	5 ounces	150 grams	
Marjoram, finely chopped	1 sprig	1 sprig	
Stock	3 quarts	3 liters	2. Add stock and simmer for 30 minutes.
Egg yolks	3	3	3. Thicken with egg yolks and cream.
Cream	1¾ cups	4 deciliters	
Bread, toasted	10 slices	10 slices	4. Place toasted bread in bowls and cover with soup. Garnish with chives.
Chives	3 ounces	75 grams	

Note: Sorrel may be used in the spring.

Berner Topf (Soup, Bernese Style)

YIELD: *U.S. — 10 servings*

INGREDIENTS	*U.S. Weight or Volume*	*Metric Weight or Volume*
Stock	3½ quarts	3.5 liters
Salt pork	1¾ pounds	800 to 900 grams
OR		
Hocks		
Yellow peas, dried	1 pound	500 grams
Leeks, fine strips	7 ounces	200 grams
Carrots, fine strips	3½ ounces	100 grams
Celery, fine strips	3½ ounces	100 grams
Chives	5 ounces	150 grams

PROCEDURE

1. Simmer stock, salt pork or hocks, yellow peas, leeks, carrots, celery, and chives for 1½ hours. Add more stock if necessry.
2. Remove pork and puree soup.
3. Cut pork into small pieces, add to soup, and heat.
4. Serve in soup bowls and garnish with chives.

Bortsch Polonais (Polish Borscht Soup)

YIELD: *U.S. — 10 servings*

INGREDIENTS	*U.S. Weight or Volume*	*Metric Weight or Volume*
Leeks	7 ounces	200 grams
Savoy cabbage	7 ounces	200 grams
Red beets	10 ounces	300 grams
Onion	3½ ounces	100 grams
Celery	3½ ounces	100 grams
Parsley roots	2	2
Butter	1¾ ounces	50 grams
Stock	2½ quarts	2.5 liters
Fennel	1¾ ounces	50 grams
Salt	2 teaspoons	10 grams
Soup meat	1 pound	500 grams
Duck, browned and disjointed	1	1
Bacon	7 ounces	200 grams
Chipolata sausage, sliced	10	10
Sour cream	¾ cup	2 deciliters
Red beet juice	1¼ cups	3 deciliters
Cloves	2	2
Bay leaf	1	1

PROCEDURE

1. Cut all vegetables into julienne pieces and saute in butter.
2. Add stock, fennel, seasoning, soup meat, duck, and bacon.
3. Simmer until meat is tender. Remove meat and cut in pieces.
4. Add meat and chipolatas to soup. Adjust seasoning.
5. Bind with sour cream and red beet juice.

Note: Meat and sour cream may be served separately.

Bouillabaisse a la Provencale (Provence Bouillabaisse) French Specialty

YIELD: *U.S. — 10 servings*

INGREDIENTS	*U.S. Weight or Volume*	*Metric Weight or Volume*	PROCEDURE
Fish (combination of red snapper, turbot, halibut, scallops, perch, pike, trout, whiting, red mullet)	7 pounds	3.5 kilograms	1. Divide the fish (large ones in slices, smaller ones whole) into two groups according to the cooking time required.
Olive oil	½ cup	1 deciliter	2. Saute the onion and leeks in the olive oil.
Onion	8½ ounces	250 grams	3. Combine all the ingredients and simmer for 20 minutes. Remove spice sachet.
Leeks	5 ounces	150 grams	
White wine	1 pint	5 deciliters	4. Add fish requiring the longer cooking time and simmer for 10 minutes.
Fish stock (10.2.5)	2½ quarts	2.5 liters	
Tomatoes, peeled	4	4	5. Add fish requiring less cooking time and continue to simmer for 5 minutes.
Garlic cloves, grated	2	2	
Parsley, chopped	2 ounces	50 grams	
Saffron	1/8 teaspoon	1 gram	
Fennel powder	1/8 teaspoon	1 gram	
Fennel leaves	¼ teaspoon	2 grams	
Spice sachet:			
Clove	1	1	
Bay leaf	1	1	
Savory	1 sprig	1 sprig	
Thyme	pinch	pinch	
Pernod	few drops	few drops	
Salt	2 teaspoons	12 grams	
Bread slices	10	10	6. Toast bread and brush with garlic butter, place on bottom of soup terrine, and pour the soup into the terrine.
Butter	5 ounces	150 grams	

Note: The fish may be served separately on a hot platter.

Variation of Bouillabaisse

Bouillabaisse a la Marseillaise—Fish Soup, Marseilles Style. Use recipe for Bouillabaisse a la provencale using water in place of white wine. When served, place slices of bread in the bowl.

Bunder Suppe (Soup, Grisons Style) Swiss Specialty

YIELD: *U.S. — 10 servings*

INGREDIENTS	*U.S. Weight or Volume*	*Metric Weight or Volume*	PROCEDURE
Fat	1¾ ounces	45 grams	1. Cut vegetables, dried beef, and fresh ham very fine (brunoise). Saute in fat and add flour.
Onion	5 ounces	150 grams	
Leeks	5 ounces	150 grams	
Carrots	3½ ounces	100 grams	
Celery	1¾ ounces	50 grams	
Grisons (dried) beef	3 ounces	80 grams	
Fresh ham	3 ounces	80 grams	
Flour	1 ounce	30 grams	
Pearl barley	3½ ounces	100 grams	2. Add pearl barley and navy beans and continue to saute.
Navy beans	1¾ ounces	50 grams	3. Add stock and simmer for 1½ hours.
Stock	3 quarts	3 liters	
Egg yolks	2	2	4. Thicken with egg yolks and cream. Adjust seasoning.
Cream	1¼ cups	3 deciliters	

Note: A special Grisons sausage, Beinwurst, may be substituted for the Grisons. It should be cooked with the soup, removed and diced, and added to the soup before serving. Grisons is an air-dried beef similar to jerky; the fresh ham is similar to prosciutto.

Busecca (Busecca Soup) Italian Specialty

YIELD: *U.S. — 10 servings*

INGREDIENTS	*U.S. Weight or Volume*	*Metric Weight or Volume*	PROCEDURE
Fat	2 ounces	60 grams	1. Saute onions and leeks in fat. Add potatoes, carrots, cabbage, and tomatoes and continue to saute.
Onion, finely chopped	5 ounces	150 grams	
Leeks, finely chopped	5 ounces	150 grams	
Potatoes	14 ounces	400 grams	
Carrots	5 ounces	150 grams	
Cabbage	3½ ounces	100 grams	
Tomatoes	3½ ounces	100 grams	
Barlotti beans, precooked	2 ounces	60 grams	2. Add beans, tripe, and tomato puree.
Veal tripe	1 pound	500 grams	
Tomato puree	¼ cup	½ deciliter	
Stock	3½ quarts	3.5 liters	3. Add stock and simmer until all ingredients are cooked.
Pesto:			4. Prepare pesto by chopping and pounding bacon, garlic, and marjoram.
Bacon	1½ ounces	40 grams	
Garlic cloves	2	2	5. Add pesto to soup at end of cooking time.
Marjoram	1/8 teaspoon	1 gram	6. Serve grated cheese separately.
Parmesan cheese	3 ounces	100 grams	

Chicken Broth (English Specialty)

YIELD: *U.S. — 10 servings*

INGREDIENTS	*U.S. Weight or Volume*	*Metric Weight or Volume*	PROCEDURE
Chicken, blanched	2 to 3 pounds	1 to 1.5 kilograms	1. Poach chicken with vegetables.
Carrots, julienne	5 ounces	150 grams	2. Season chicken stock and add poached, skinned, and disjointed chicken.
Celery, julienne	3½ ounces	100 grams	
Leeks, julienne	7 ounces	200 grams	3. Serve toasted slices of bread separately.
Turnips, julienne	1¾ ounces	50 grams	
Chicken stock	3½ quarts	3.5 liters	

Gazpacho (Spanish Specialty)

YIELD: *U.S. — 10 servings*

INGREDIENTS	*U.S. Weight or Volume*	*Metric Weight or Volume*	PROCEDURE
Cucumber, peeled and diced	3	3	1. Combine the vegetables and bread crumbs.
Tomatoes, diced	2 pounds	1 kilogram	
Onion, diced	3½ ounces	100 grams	
Green pepper, diced	3½ ounces	100 grams	
Garlic, finely chopped	2	2	
White bread crumbs	3½ ounces	100 grams	
Ice water	1 quart	1 liter	2. Add water, wine vinegar, salt, and pepper.
Red wine vinegar	½ cup	1 deciliter	3. Puree the mixture.
Salt	½ teaspoon	3 grams	
Pepper	¼ teaspoon	2 grams	
Olive oil	½ cup	1 deciliter	4. Add the olive oil gradually, whipping constantly until a smooth mixture is formed. 5. Refrigerate for at least 2 hours. 6. Whip before dipping into cups or soup terrines.

Geflugelkleinsuppe (Cream of Chicken Soup) German Specialty

YIELD: *U.S. — 10 servings*

INGREDIENTS	*U.S. Weight or Volume*	*Metric Weight or Volume*	PROCEDURE
Fat	1 ounce	30 grams	1. Saute poultry pieces in fat.
Necks, wings, hearts of chicken or geese, blanched	2½ pounds	1.2 kilograms	
Carrots, julienne	3½ ounces	100 grams	2. Add carrots, celery, leeks, turnips, and barley and continue to saute until tender.
Celery, julienne	3½ ounces	100 grams	
Leeks, fine strips	7 ounces	200 grams	
Turnips, diced	1¾ ounces	50 grams	
Pearl barley	2 ounces	60 grams	
Stock	3 quarts	3 liters	3. Add stock and simmer.
Cream	1¼ cups	3 deciliters	4. Bind with cream and adjust seasoning.

Gulyas (Hungarian Goulash Soup)

YIELD: *U.S. — 10 servings*

INGREDIENTS	*U.S. Weight or Volume*	*Metric Weight or Volume*	PROCEDURE
Fat	1¾ ounces	50 grams	1. Cut beef shoulder into ¾ inch (2 centimeters) cubes.
Onion, finely sliced	12 ounces	350 grams	2. Saute the onion and beef in fat.
Beef shoulder	2 pounds	1 kilogram	
Sweet Szegedin paprika	¾ ounce	15 grams	3. Add paprika, salt, and pepper.
Salt	½ teaspoon	3 grams	
Pepper	¼ teaspoon	2 grams	
Stock	3 quarts	3 liters	4. Add stock and simmer until meat is tender.
Potatoes, diced	2 pounds	1 kilogram	5. Add potatoes and tomatoes. Simmer until the vegetables are done. Adjust seasoning.
Tomatoes, diced	3½ ounces	100 grams	
Spaetzle	7 ounces	200 grams	6. Add spaetzle before serving.

Note: In Hungary, the term "Gulyas" always refers to the soup, Gulyas. The "Gulyas" main dish is known in Hungary as "Porkott."

Kerbelsuppe (Chervil Soup) Swiss Specialty

YIELD: *U.S. — 10 servings*

INGREDIENTS	*U.S. Weight or Volume*	*Metric Weight or Volume*	PROCEDURE
Fat	1¾ ounces	50 grams	1. Melt fat in a casserole. Add leeks and saute until light brown.
Leeks, finely chopped	1 pound	500 grams	
Potatoes, finely sliced	1¾ pounds	800 grams	2. Add potatoes and marjoram.
Marjoram	1/8 teaspoon	1 gram	3. Stir vigorously with a whisk until potatoes are broken into pieces.
Chervil	5 ounces	150 grams	
Cream	1¼ cups	3 deciliters	4. Add cream, stock, salt, pepper, and chervil. Heat and adjust seasoning.
Stock	3 quarts	3 liters	
Salt	½ teaspoon	3 grams	
Pepper	¼ teaspoon	2 grams	5. Serve croutons and grated cheese separately.
Croutons	5 ounces	150 grams	
Cheese, grated	5 ounces	150 grams	

Krautsuppe (Austrian Specialty)

YIELD: *U.S. — 10 servings*

INGREDIENTS	*U.S. Weight or Volume*	*Metric Weight or Volume*	PROCEDURE
Fat	1¾ ounces	50 grams	1. Saute onion in fat. Add cabbage and 1 pint (.5 liter) of the stock.
Onion, chopped	5 ounces	150 grams	
Savoy cabbage, julienne	1¾ pounds	800 grams	
Rice	3½ ounces	100 grams	2. Prepare a cream soup with the flour, salt, and remainder of the stock.
OR			
Wheat flour			
Stock	3½ quarts	3.5 liters	
Salt	½ teaspoon	3 grams	3. Add the sauteed cabbage to the soup and heat to the boiling point.
Egg yolks	3	3	4. Thicken soup with egg yolks and sour cream. Adjust seasoning and add paprika.
Sour cream	¾ cup	2 deciliters	
Paprika	1/8 teaspoon	1 gram	

Leberknodelsuppe (Liver Dumpling Soup) German Specialty

YIELD: *U.S. — 10 servings*

INGREDIENTS	*U.S. Weight or Volume*	*Metric Weight or Volume*	PROCEDURE
White rolls	4	4	1. Soak rolls in the milk.
Milk	1½ cups	3.5 deciliters	
Beef liver	9 ounces	250 grams	2. Grind liver, beer marrow or kidney fat, and soaked rolls.
Beef marrow	2 ounces	60 grams	
OR			
Veal kidney fat			
Eggs	2 to 3	2 to 3	3. Add eggs, flour, onion, garlic, and seasoning. Stir vigorously. Let stand for 30 minutes or longer.
Flour	1¾ ounces	50 grams	
Onion, chopped	2 ounces	60 grams	4. Shape mixture into small dumplings.
Garlic	1 clove	1 clove	5. Poach the dumplings in 3 quarts (3 liters) of simmering strong broth.
Broth	3 quarts	3 liters	6. Serve the liver dumplings in the broth. Garnish with chopped parsley.

Mehlsuppe Mit Kaseschnitten (Flour Soup with Toasted Cheese) Swiss Specialty

YIELD: *U.S. — 10 servings*

INGREDIENTS	*U.S. Weight or Volume*	*Metric Weight or Volume*	PROCEDURE
Fat	4 ounces	120 grams	1. Brown the flour in the fat. Add chopped onion and leeks immediately.
Flour	7 ounces	200 grams	
Onion, chopped	4 ounces	100 grams	
Leeks, chopped	3 ounces	80 grams	
Stock	3½ quarts	3.5 liters	2. Add stock, stirring constantly until blended. Simmer for 1 hour. Remove floating fat frequently.
Bread, toasted	10 slices	10 slices	
Emmentaler cheese	7 ounces	200 grams	3. Add more stock if needed. Adjust seasoning.
Butter	2 ounces	60 grams	4. Sprinkle cheese and drops of melted butter on toast. Float the toasted cheese slices on the soup when serving.

Minestrone (Italian Specialty)

YIELD: *U.S. — 10 servings*

INGREDIENTS	*U.S. Weight or Volume*	*Metric Weight or Volume*	PROCEDURE
Fat	1¾ ounces	50 grams	1. Saute bacon, onion, and leeks in the melted fat until tender.
Bacon, diced	3½ ounces	100 grams	
Onion, finely sliced	3½ ounces	100 grams	2. Add the onion, leeks, carrots, celery, and cabbage and saute.
Leeks, finely sliced	5 ounces	150 grams	
Carrots, finely sliced	3½ ounces	100 grams	
Celery, finely sliced	3½ ounces	100 grams	
Savoy cabbage, finely sliced	7 ounces	200 grams	
Tomato puree	1½ ounces	40 grams	3. Add tomato puree and stock and simmer for 1 hour.
Stock	3 to 4 quarts	3 to 4 liters	4. Add potatoes, rice, spaghetti, tomatoes, and Barlotti beans and continue to cook for 20 to 30 minutes.
Potatoes, sliced	7 ounces	200 grams	
Rice	1 ounce	30 grams	
Spaghetti, broken pieces	1 ounce	30 grams	
Tomatoes, diced	3½ ounces	100 grams	
Barlotti beans, precooked	1¾ ounces	50 grams	
Pesto:			
Bacon fat	1¾ ounces	50 grams	5. Make a pesto by combining the bacon fat, garlic, marjoram, and basil. Pound the ingredients together until a smooth paste is formed. Adjust the seasoning.
Garlic	3 cloves	3 cloves	
Marjoram	1/8 teaspoon	1 gram	
Basil	1/8 teaspoon	1 gram	6. Add pesto to the soup before serving.

Mock Turtle Soup (American Specialty)

YIELD: *U.S. — 10 servings*

INGREDIENTS	*U.S. Weight or Volume*	*Metric Weight or Volume*	PROCEDURE
Calf's head stock	2 quarts	2 liters	1. Simmer clear calf's head stock, brown basic sauce (Fond de veau lie, 11.1.1) and seasoning for approximately 30 minutes. Bind if necessary.
Brown basic sauce	1½ quarts	1.5 liters	
Madeira	¼ cup	½ deciliter	2. Add Madeira and sherry and adjust seasoning.
Sherry	¼ cup	½ deciliter	
Calf's head, diced	10 to 14 ounces	300 to 400 grams	3. Add diced calf's head.

Note: Small chicken dumplings may be used as a garnish.

Mulligatawny Soup (Indian Specialty)

YIELD: *U.S. — 10 servings*

INGREDIENTS	*U.S. Weight or Volume*	*Metric Weight or Volume*	PROCEDURE
Fat	2 ounces	60 grams	1. Saute the chopped onion in melted fat.
Onion, chopped	5 ounces	150 grams	
Curry powder	½ to ¾ ounce	10 to 20 grams	2. Add curry powder and continue to saute.
White basic sauce	2½ to 3 quarts	2.5 to 3 liters	3. Make white basic sauce with chicken stock. Strain and add to onion mixture.
Cream	¾ to 1¼ cups	2 to 3 deciliters	4. Add cream and adjust seasoning.
Rice	4 ounces	100 grams	5. Garnish with cooked rice and julienne of chicken.
Chicken	8 ounces	225 grams	

Note: This soup may be served hot or cold.

Mutton Broth (Scottish Specialty)

YIELD: *U.S. — 10 servings*

INGREDIENTS	*U.S. Weight or Volume*	*Metric Weight or Volume*	PROCEDURE
Fat	1¾ ounces	50 grams	1. Saute vegetables in melted fat.
Leeks	7 ounces	200 grams	
Celery stalks	3½ ounces	100 grams	
Carrots	3½ ounces	100 grams	
Turnips	1¾ ounces	50 grams	
Onion	1¾ ounces	50 grams	
Mutton stock	3 to 3½ quarts	3 to 3.5 liters	2. Add mutton stock, mutton neck or breast, and pearl barley.
Mutton neck OR Mutton breast	14 to 16 ounces	400 to 500 grams	3. Simmer for 1 to 1½ hours. Remove mutton from the broth and dice.
Pearl barley, blanched	3½ ounces	100 grams	4. Garnish the broth with the diced mutton.

Note: Lamb may be substituted for mutton.

Nudelsuppe Mit Huhn (Chicken Noodle Soup) German Specialty

YIELD: *U.S. — 10 servings*

INGREDIENTS	*U.S. Weight or Volume*	*Metric Weight or Volume*	PROCEDURE
Chicken, blanched	2 pounds	1 kilogram	1. Poach blanched chicken in chicken stock with bouquet garni.
Chicken stock	3½ quarts	3.5 liters	
Bouquet garni:			
Bay leaf	½	½	
Celery, leaves	2 tablespoons	25 grams	
Thyme	½ teaspoon	3 grams	
Parsley	4 sprigs	4 sprigs	
Cloves	2	2	
Leek, white portion	1	1	
Egg noodles	3½ ounces	100 grams	2. Cook egg noodles in salted water and drain. 3. Remove cooked chicken and bouquet garni from stock. 4. Cut chicken into small pieces. 5. Add chicken and noodles to the soup. Adjust seasoning.

Olla Podrida (Spanish Specialty)

YIELD: *U.S. — 10 servings*

INGREDIENTS	*U.S. Weight or Volume*	*Metric Weight or Volume*
Mutton breast	10 ounces	300 grams
Veal knuckle	10 ounces	300 grams
Oxtail	1 pound	500 grams
Chicken or pigeon	1¾ pounds	800 grams
Smoked sausage (chorizos)	10 ounces	300 grams
Ham	7 ounces	200 grams
Chick peas	9 ounces	250 grams
Vegetables, finely sliced: Leeks, Carrots, Celery, Savoy cabbage	2 pounds	1 kilogram
Salt	1 teaspoon	5 grams
Garlic	2 cloves	2 cloves
Parsley, chopped	1 tablespoon	15 grams

PROCEDURE

1. Simmer mutton breast, veal knuckle, oxtail, chicken or pigeon, sausage, ham, and chick peas with the finely sliced vegetables until the meat is tender.
2. Remove meat and cut into small pieces.
3. Add meat and salt to soup. Season with garlic and parsley.

Note: When serving, the soup can be presented in a bowl and the meat and vegetables on a separate platter.

Oxtail Soup (English Specialty)

YIELD: *U.S. — 10 servings*

INGREDIENTS	*U.S. Weight or Volume*	*Metric Weight or Volume*	PROCEDURE
Fat	3 ounces	75 grams	1. Season oxtail slices and brown in fat and bacon trimmings. Add mirepoix and continue to saute.
Bacon trimmings	2 ounces	50 grams	
Oxtail slices	2 pounds	1 kilogram	
Fat and bacon trimmings	1 ounce	30 grams	
Mirepoix: Onion, chopped; Celery, chopped; Carrots, chopped	10 ounces	300 grams	
Tomato puree	1 to 1¾ ounces	30 to 50 grams	2. Add tomato puree, white wine, and brown stock. Simmer slowly for 2 to 3 hours. Remove oxtail from soup and discard bones. Press meat pieces and chill.
White wine	1¼ cups	3 deciliters	
Brown stock	3 quarts	3 liters	
Flour, browned	4 ounces	120 grams	3. Bind soup with browned flour.
Brandy	¼ cup	½ deciliter	4. Skim the fat and add more stock if necessary.
Madeira	½ cup	1 deciliter	5. Strain through a fine sieve. Adjust seasoning.
Potatoes, diced	5 ounces	150 grams	6. Add brandy and Madeira.
Carrots, diced	5 ounces	150 grams	7. Garnish with chilled oxtail meat and cooked diced vegetables.

Note: For Clear Oxtail Soup, do not brown flour.

Pesto Genovese (Italian Specialty)

YIELD: *U.S. — 10 servings*

INGREDIENTS	*U.S. Weight or Volume*	*Metric Weight or Volume*	PROCEDURE
Fat	1¾ ounces	50 grams	1. Chop leeks, onion, carrots, potatoes, celery, and cabbage into very fine pieces.
Leeks	5 ounces	150 grams	2. Saute leeks and onion in fat. Add other chopped vegetables and continue to saute.
Onion	3½ ounces	100 grams	
Carrots	2¾ ounces	80 grams	
Potatoes	3½ ounces	100 grams	
Celery	1¾ ounces	50 grams	
Cabbage	1¾ ounces	50 grams	
Stock	3 quarts	3 liters	3. Add stock and tomatoes. Simmer for 1 hour.
Tomatoes, peeled and diced	3½ ounces	100 grams	
Egg noodles, fine	3½ ounces	100 grams	4. Add egg noodles and continue cooking for 20 minutes.
Pesto:			5. Prepare pesto by combining fat, garlic, marjoram, and basil and pounding until a smooth mass.
Fat	1¾ ounces	50 grams	6. Add pesto to soup. Adjust seasoning.
Garlic	1 clove	1 clove	
Marjoram	¼ teaspoon	2 grams	
Basil	¼ teaspoon	2 grams	

Note: During simmering, check thickness of soup continuously, adding stock if necessary. In Italy the soup is served quite thick. If desired, bacon rind or ham bones can be added during the cooking.

Other National Soups

Petite marmite, Henry IV—French specialty. See 12.1.1.3.

Pot-au-feu—French Beef Broth. See 12.1.1.4.

Potage aux nids d'hirondelles—Birds' Nest Soup (Chinese Specialty). Usually found canned. The dried nests, however, can be purchased. Soak swallows' nests in cold water for 2 hours. When they swell and become transparent, clean them carefully by removing bits of egg shell and other foreign matter that might be in them. Blanch for 5 to 6 minutes and drain. Put the nests in strong chicken consomme. Poach, keeping them on a gentle but sustained boil, for 45 minutes. Adjust seasoning and add a little Madeira and cayenne pepper.

Puree a la Vaudoise (Vaudoise Pot) Swiss Specialty

YIELD: *U.S. — 10 servings*

INGREDIENTS	*U.S. Weight or Volume*	*Metric Weight or Volume*	PROCEDURE
Stewing beef	2 pounds	1 kilogram	1. Blanch beef.
Leeks	10 ounces	300 grams	2. Combine the vegetables and beef and add to the boiling stock.
Carrots	7 ounces	200 grams	
Celery	7 ounces	200 grams	3. Simmer slowly until the meat is tender.
Savoy cabbage	3½ ounces	100 grams	4. Remove meat and cut the meat and sausage into small pieces.
Turnips	3½ ounces	100 grams	
Onions, small	3½ ounces	100 grams	
Stock	3½ quarts	3.5 liters	
Vaudois sausage	14 ounces	400 grams	5. Add meat and sausage to the soup. Adjust seasoning.
Chives	2 ounces	60 grams	6. Garnish with chives and chervil.
Chervil	2 ounces	60 grams	

Rahmsuppe (German Cream Soup)

YIELD: *U.S. — 10 servings*

INGREDIENTS	*U.S. Weight or Volume*	*Metric Weight or Volume*	PROCEDURE
Fat	3½ ounces	100 grams	1. Make a roux with the fat and flour.
Flour	5 ounces	150 grams	
Stock	2 quarts	2 liters	2. Combine the stock, milk, bouquet garni, caraway seed, cloves and thyme.
Milk	1½ quarts	1.5 liters	
Bouquet garni:			3. Simmer 1 hour. Strain.
Bay leaf	2	2	
Celery leaves	4 tablespoons	50 grams	
Parsley	12 sprigs	12 sprigs	
Leek, white portion	2	2	
Caraway seeds	1/8 teaspoon	1 gram	
Cloves	4	4	
Thyme	1 teaspoon	6 grams	
Cream	1¼ cups	3 deciliters	4. Add cream and butter. Adjust seasoning.
Butter	2 ounces	50 grams	5. Serve slices of fried bread separately.

Vichyssoise (American Specialty)

YIELD: *U.S. — 10 servings*

INGREDIENTS	*U.S. Weight or Volume*	*Metric Weight or Volume*	PROCEDURE
Fat	1¾ ounces	50 grams	1. Melt fat and saute leeks. Add onion studded with cloves, and bay leaf.
Leeks, finely chopped	1¼ pounds	600 grams	
Cloves	6	6	
Onion	1	1	
Potatoes, diced	2½ pounds	1.2 kilograms	2. Add potatoes and stock. Cook until potatoes are soft.
Stock	2½ quarts	2.5 liters	3. Puree (strain).
Cream	1¾ cups	4.5 deciliters	4. Add cream and adjust seasoning.
Croutons	5 ounces	150 grams	5. Garnish with chives.
			6. Serve croutons separately.

Note: This soup may be served hot or chilled.

Zuppa Mille-Fanti (Mille-fanti Soup) Italian Specialty

YIELD: *U.S. — 10 servings*

INGREDIENTS	*U.S. Weight or Volume*	*Metric Weight or Volume*	PROCEDURE
Bread crumbs, white	3½ ounces	100 grams	1. Blend bread crumbs, parmesan cheese, eggs, and parsley.
Parmesan cheese	1¾ ounces	50 grams	2. Add small amounts of the bread mixture gradually to the boiling stock stirring constantly with a whisk.
Eggs	3	3	
Parsley, chopped	1 ounce	30 grams	3. Cover and let stand 5 to 6 minutes.
Stock	3 quarts	3 liters	4. Stir before serving.

Zuppa Pavese (Italian Specialty)

YIELD: *U.S. — 10 servings*

INGREDIENTS	*U.S. Weight or Volume*	*Metric Weight or Volume*	PROCEDURE
Beef broth, strong	3 quarts	3 liters	1. Portion boiling beef broth into individual bowls.
Eggs	10	10	2. Break 1 egg into each bowl.
Bread slices, toasted	10	10	3. Place toasted slice of bread, that has been sprinkled with grated cheese, on top of soup and gratinate.
Grated cheese	5 ounces	150 grams	4. Sprinkle with meat juice.

13 Hors d'oeuvres — Hors d'oeuvres

13.1 Cold Hors d'oeuvre — Hors d'oeuvre froids

Cold hors d'oeuvre should stimulate the appetite, and, therefore, should always be served as the first course. Soup is often omitted to make way for the hors d'oeuvre. If a soup is served after the hors d'oeuvre, it should be a spicy, clear soup, such as consomme, clear oxtail soup, or real turtle soup, in order to again stimulate the palate. Formerly, the cold hors d'oeuvre was divided into three main groups: *Hors d'oeuvre a la suedoise, Hors d'oeuvre a la russe, Hors d'oeuvre a la parisienne.* Since the modern art of cooking is simplicity itself, and the world is becoming increasingly calorie-conscious, often only one dish is served such as melons, or meat or fish cocktails. It is better to offer one quality product, presented in a simple way, than a cold hors d'oeuvre made from a variety of poor quality products. Whether simple or really luxurious, an hors d'oeuvre must be attractively presented. With the exception of *hors d'oeuvre riches,* a vast choice of different hors d'oeuvre is available *a la carte.* They are listed in the form of *small snacks* (see illustration page 177), *cold specialties, specialties of the season,* or as small cold dishes on the menu. *Toast and butter should be served separately with all hors d'oeuvre dishes.*

FIGURE 13–1
Plate of Hors d'oeuvre — Assiette d'hors-d'oeuvre

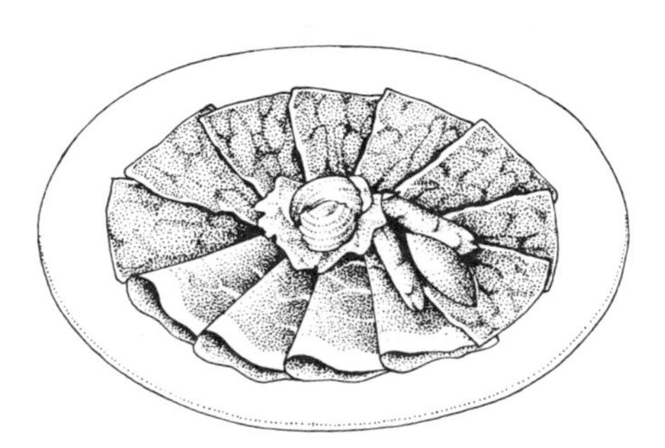

FIGURE 13–2
Grisons Platter — Assiette des Grisons

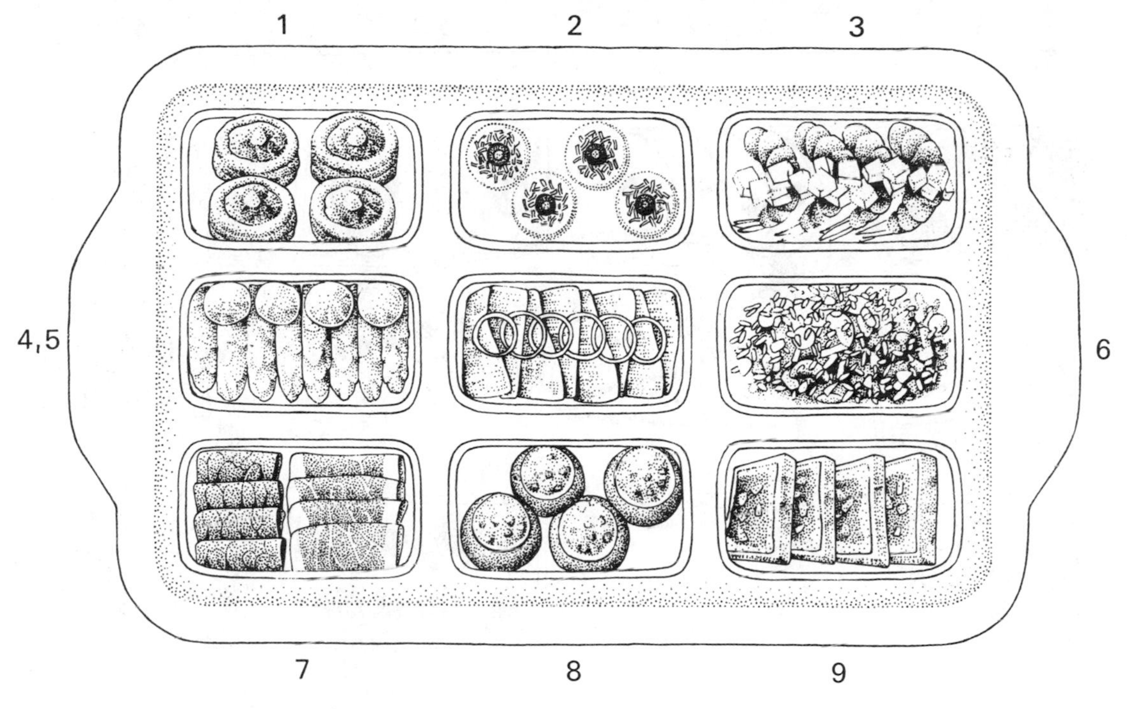

Hors d'oeuvre Platter — Hors d'oeuvre sur assiette

1 Patty Shell with Goose Liver Mousse
2 Artichoke Hearts with Waldorf Salad
3 Shrimp with Jelly
4 Asparagus Tips with Mushrooms
5 Sardines with Onion Rings
6 Italian Vegetable Salad
7 Grisons Dried Beef and Ham
8 Tomatoes Stuffed with Russian Salad
9 Chicken Loaf

FIGURE 13–3
Hors d'oeuvre Platter — Hors d'oeuvre sur assiette

Hors d'oeuvre Platter — Hors d'oeuvre sur assiette
This is a well-presented platter with a limited choice of simple or more expensive foods. The basic rule here is "small in quantity, but big in quality" and at the same time attractively served.

Assorted Hors d'oeuvre — Hors d'oeuvre varies
These can be served on special portioned platters, on large silver platters with hors d'oeuvre dishes, or even from the serving cart. A choice of 6 to 10 different items, including a spicy salad, is quite sufficient. When presenting and, particularly, when serving, care must be taken to ensure that the colors of the different items harmonize.

Rich Hors d'oeuvre — Hors d'oeuvre riches
This is still a classical form of presentation. Lobster or rock lobster (a la parisienne) should always be included. The hors d'oeuvre dish system in conjunction with a silver platter can be used, but it is also possible to arrange the center pieces on a silver platter covered with meat jelly, and to serve the accompaniments in small separate bowls. A rich hors d'oeuvre should, as the name suggests, include exquisite specialties, such as rock lobster, lobster, smoked salmon, poached salmon, caviar, goose liver pate, and shrimp. (See also illustration page 387.)

Well-known Cold Hors d'oeuvre:
Admiral's Canapes — Canapes amirale. Small toasts

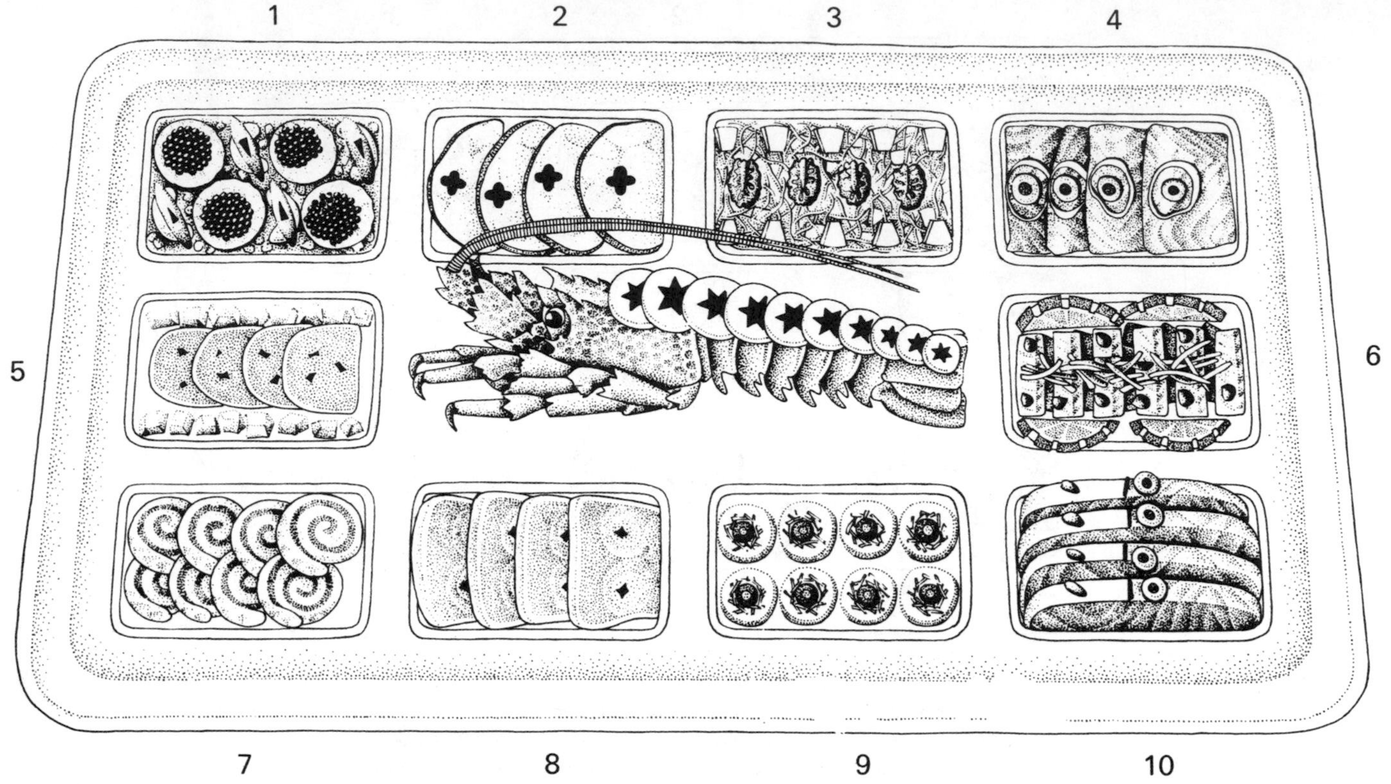

1 Tartlets with Caviar
2 Beef Tenderloin, London House Style
3 Waldorf Salad
4 Smoked Salmon
5 Goose Liver Pate with Jelly
Rock Lobster Decorated with Lobster Slices
6 Smoked Eel with Lemon
7 Rolled Fillets of Sole
8 Terrine of Game
9 Artichoke Hearts Filled with Chicken Salad
10 Poached Salmon Slices, Cold

FIGURE 13–4
Assorted Hors d'oeuvre — Hors d'oeuvre varies

are spread with shrimp butter and garnished with shrimp.

Anchovy Canapes — Canapes d'anchois. Small toasts are spread with anchovy butter and garnished with anchovy fillets and chopped hard-cooked eggs.

Anchovy Fillets — Filets d'anchois. Anchovy fillets are presented attractively and garnished with capers.

Anchovy Sticks — Batons d'anchois. Puff paste strips are spread with anchovy fillets, covered with a second strip of puff paste, brushed with egg yolk, and baked.

Artichokes, Greek Style—Artichauts a la grecque. Blanched artichoke hearts are cooked in white wine, oil, lemon juice, fennel, salt, pepper, thyme, and bay leaf and allowed to marinate in the liquid.

Asparagus Spears — Pointes d'asperges. Blanched or raw spears are marinated in a Vinaigrette Sauce (recipe 11.4.2) and garnished with hard-cooked eggs.

Assorted Canapes — Canapes varies. Different shapes of small toasts are spread with fish or meat puree mixed with butter and glazed with jelly.

Avocado Stuffed with Shrimp — Avocats aux crevettes. Avocado cups are prepared by cutting a ripe avocado lengthwise, gently twisting halves apart and remov-

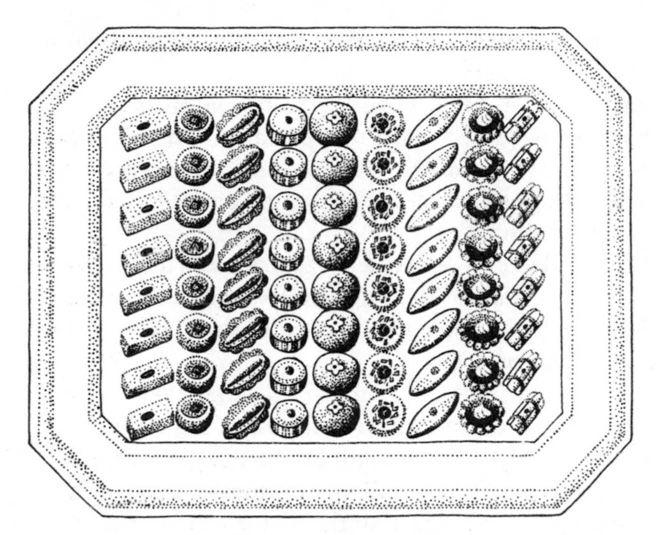

FIGURE 13–5
Assorted Canapes — Canapes varies

ing stone. Marinated baby shrimp are mixed with a well-seasoned cocktail sauce containing a little brandy. Avocado cups are filled with shrimp mixture, garnished with eggs, truffles or olives, and lemons. Toast is served separately.

Bismark Herring — Bismarck-Heringe. Fresh herring are marinated in wine, vinegar, seasoning, and onion rings.

Cantaloupe — Melon cantaloup. Cantaloupe is cut in half, seeds removed, and served on crushed ice.

Cauliflower — Chou-fleur. Cauliflower florets are cooked, marinated, and served with mayonnaise.

Caviar — Caviar. It is served in bowls on ice with toast and fresh butter accompaniments.

Caviar Canapes — Canapes de caviar. Small toasts are spread with caviar butter and garnished with caviar.

Caviar Profiterolles — Duchesse au caviar. Small round puffs (chou) are stuffed with caviar and glazed with jelly.

Celery Hearts, Greek Style — Celeri a la grecque. Blanched celery hearts are cooked in white wine, oil, lemon juice, fennel, salt, pepper, thyme, and bay leaf and allowed to marinate in the liquid.

Cheese Sticks — Allumettes au fromage. Puff paste (feuilletage) strips are rolled in egg and cheese, twisted, and baked.

Cheese tartlets — Tartelettes au fromage. (See page 465.)

Chilled Eggs — Oeufs froids. (See Cold Egg Dishes, 24.1.)

Cold Fish Dishes — Poissons froids. (See page 490.)

Crayfish — Ecrevisses. Crayfish or crayfish tails are served with mayonnaise.

Crayfish Canapes — Canapes d'ecrevisses. Small toasts are spread with crayfish butter and garnished with crayfish tails.

Crispi Cocktail — Cocktail Crispi. Pieces of peeled pears, oranges, and grapefruit are mixed with mayonnaise containing a little orange juice, orange peel, and brandy. It is served in champagne glasses and garnished with a pitted cherry and walnuts.

Fennel Root — Pieds de fenouil. Blanched fennel is cooked in white wine, oil, lemon juice, fennel, salt, pepper, thyme, and bay leaf and allowed to marinate in the liquid.

Fish Mayonnaise — Mayonnaise de poisson. Skinned and boned fish are arranged on a bed of lettuce, coated with a thick mayonnaise and garnished with anchovy fillets, capers, and slices of hard-cooked egg. (See page 490.)

Fruit Cocktail — Cocktail de fruits. Fresh ripe fruits (pears, oranges, peaches, and apricots) are cut into pieces and mixed with a mayonnaise seasoned with ketchup, brandy, and orange peel. It is served in champagne glasses and garnished with fruit.

Goose Liver — Foie gras. This is served in either sausage or block form. Butter and toast are served separately.

Goose Liver Canapes — Canapes de fois gras. Small toasts are spread with goose liver puree and garnished with truffles.

Grapefruit — Pamplemousse. Unpeeled grapefruit halves are sectioned using a special serrated knife, sprinkled with sugar and a few drops of kirschwasser. The grapefruit is served cold on a napkin.

Herring Salad — Salade d'hareng. Marinated herring fillets are arranged on a platter, coated with sauce (recipe follows), and garnished with apple slices.

> *Sauce:* Sour cream, yoghurt, (possibly mayonnaise), mustard, olive oil, sliced onions, wine vinegar, chives, parsley, paprika, and salt are thoroughly mixed to prepare sauce.

Lobster — Homard. Fresh lobster is boiled, cut in

half, garnished, and served cold. Mayonnaise is served separately. (See page 495.)
Lobster Cocktail — Cocktail de homard. This cocktail is prepared in the same way as shrimp cocktail, mixing the tail meat into the sauce and using the opened claws for decoration.
Marinated Mushrooms — Champignons marinees. Very small white firm mushrooms are sliced and sauteed in oil with chopped shallots and lemon juice. Vinegar, white wine, salt, pepper, oil, garlic, sugar, fennel, and thyme are added, and mushrooms are cooked and marinated in this liquid.
Mayonnaise Eggs — Oeufs in mayonnaise. Poached or soft-cooked eggs are coated with mayonnaise and garnished.
Mortadella Sausage — Mortadella. Sausage is sliced and served attractively.
Mousses. (See page 498.)
Ox Muzzle Salad — Museau de boeuf. This is usually purchased ready-made.
Ox Tongue Canapes — Canapes a l'ecarlate. Small toasts are spread with mustard butter and covered with fine slices of ox tongue.
Oysters — Huitres. Freshly opened oysters are served on a bed of crushed ice with a lemon wedge. Buttered slices of bread are served separately. (See page 496.)
Profiterolles — Duchesse. Small round puffs (chou) are made with goose liver, chicken or game puree, and glazed with jelly as desired.
Prosciutto Ham — Jambon cru. Sliced very thin; rolled up. Served with melon slices.
Rock Lobster — Langouste. Rock lobster or rock lobster slices are garnished and glazed with jelly. Mayonnaise is served separately. (See page 495.)
Rock Lobster Cocktail — Cocktail de langouste. Rock lobster tails, prediced and prepared like the shrimp cocktail, are placed in a champagne glass and smothered with the sauce. Top with a slice of rock lobster, cover with a slice of truffle surrounded with chopped hard-cooked egg.
Salads — Salades. Salads are prepared with fish, tongue, ham, chicken or vegetables (beets, cucumbers) attractively cut and seasoned with a thin, spicy mayonnaise, a vinaigrette, or an ordinary salad dressing. (See Salads, Chapter 19.)
Salami — Salami. The meat is cut into fine slices and attractively served.
Salmon with Mayonnaise — Saumon en mayonnaise. Salmon is coated with mayonnaise and garnished.
Sardines — Sardines. These fish are served in oil with chopped hard-cooked eggs, onions, and capers as a garnish.
Shrimp Aspic — Aspic de crevettes. Shrimp tails preplaced into a mold coated with aspic and decorated with truffles. They are covered with aspic and allowed to cool and gel.
Shrimp Cocktail — Cocktail de crevettes. Cooked shrimp are marinated in brandy and lemon juice. The shrimp are placed in a cup or champagne glass which is filled two-thirds full with sauce (recipe follows). Garnish the cocktail with shrimp tails, half-moon slices of hard-cooked egg and truffles.

> *Sauce:* Mix 1¼ cups (3 deciliters) of thick, strongly seasoned mayonnaise with a julienne of celery, 2 tablespoons (40 grams) of tomato ketchup, a little Grand Marnier, a few pinches of cayenne pepper, and a few drops of orange juice. If desired, grated horseradish and lemon juice can be added.

In the United States shrimp cocktail is often served as follows: the peeled shrimp are arranged on the edge of a special glass cup which fits into another dish containing crushed ice. In the center is a small deep cup containing a highly spiced sauce which is made of tomato ketchup, lemon juice, and cayenne pepper. Other ingredients may be added to the sauce, such as grated horseradish, diced celery, caviar, or mango chutney. The shrimp are dipped into the sauce one by one as they are eaten.
Smoked Salmon — Saumon fume. Smoked salmon is finely sliced, garnished with lemon and onion and served with toast and butter separately. To slice, see page 226.
Sole Fillet Cocktail — Cocktail de sole. Cocktail sauce, recipe given with Shrimp Cocktail but prepared without orange juice, is portioned into either a wide flat champagne glass or a glass bowl to a depth of ½ inch (12 millimeters). A soft-cooked egg is placed in the center and encircled by half slices of poached paupiettes of sole. (Paupiettes of sole are fillets of sole

spread with fish forcemeat and rolled.) The cocktail is garnished with truffles.

Stuffed Eclairs — Eclairs. Finger-shaped puffs (chou) are stuffed with goose liver, poultry or game puree, and glazed with jelly.

Stuffed Eggs — Oeufs farcis. Hard-cooked eggs are stuffed with a puree of goose liver, chicken or game, with caviar or with a butter mixture and glazed with jelly.

Stuffed Olives — Olives farcies. Pitted olives are stuffed with anchovy or crayfish butter.

Tartlets — Bouchees. Very tiny patty shells are filled with puree of goose liver, game, poultry, caviar, or fish mayonnaise.

Tomatoes — Tomates. Tomatoes are peeled, seeded, and sliced to use for a salad or halved to stuff with a vegetable salad.

Trout — Truites. Small boiled trout are served in jelly or coated with mayonnaise.

FIGURE 13–6
Trout — Truites

Tuna — Thon. Water-packed tuna is arranged on a platter, dressed with a little oil, coated with a salad dressing or vinaigrette, and garnished.

13.2 Hot Hors d'oeuvre — Hors d'oeuvre chauds

At large dinners, tiny, spicy, hot hors d'oeuvre are served between the soup and fish course. In today's shortened menus, they are often served instead of the hot entree. The size and richness depends upon the composition of the menu. Many hot hors d'oeuvre are suited for serving as *small a la carte dishes,* and are usually described as *hot snacks.*

Well-known Hot Hors d'oeuvre:

Anchovy Sticks — Batons d'anchois. Preparation is described under cold hors d'oeuvre dishes. Serve hot.

Brochettes — brochettes. Tender pieces of liver, kidneys, sweetbreads or tenderloin cubes, and bacon are threaded on a metal or wooden skewer, dipped into butter and bread crumbs, and grilled. When served, the meat can be transferred to a silver skewer. The brochette is topped with maitre d'hotel butter.

Buckwheat Pancakes — Blinis. The batter is made with yeast, milk, white and buckwheat flours, salt, and egg yolks. It is allowed to rise, and beaten egg whites and cream are added. Pancakes are served with fresh caviar.

Calf's Brain Fritters — Beignets de cervelle. Poached calf's brain is cut into large cubes, dipped in batter, and deep-fat fried. Tomato Sauce (recipe 11.1.2) is served separately.

Canapes with Cheese — Canapes aux fromage. Grated processed cheese is mixed with some cream and seasoned with paprika and nutmeg. Depending on the name to be given to the canape, it is garnished with chopped ham, anchovies, caraway seed, and chopped salami. Gratinate for a few moments until browned.

Cassolettes with Goose Liver, Aiglon — Cassolettes a l'aiglon. Small chinaware pots are filled with a salpicon (ingredients finely diced and bound with a sauce) made from goose liver and mushrooms and bound with a Madeira Sauce. (See page 302.) A goose liver souffle mix is put on top, and the cassolette is baked in a waterbath inside the oven.

Cassolettes, Modern Style — Cassolettes moderne. Small chinaware pots are filled with a salpicon (ingredients finely diced and bound with a sauce) of veal dumplings, chicken breast, and mushrooms and bound with Madeira Sauce. Cassolettes are baked in a waterbath in the oven.

Cassolettes Suzanne — Cassolettes Suzanne. Small chinaware pots are filled with alternate layers of asparagus tips and chicken fillets and topped with a Supreme Sauce (recipe 11.2.1.2) and a slice of truffle.

Cheese Fritters — Beignets de fromage. Cream puff pastry (pate a chou) is mixed with grated cheese and a little paprika and deep-fat fried. Tomato Sauce (recipe 11.1.2) is served separately.
Cheese Pancakes—Crepes au fromage. (See Pancakes, Chef's Style—Crepes a la mode, page 466.)
Cheese Souffle — Souffle au fromage. Yield: 10 servings. Prepare a white roux using 3½ ounces (100 grams) of butter and 4 ounces (110 grams) of flour. Cool slightly and add 1 pint (5 deciliters) of boiling milk. Stir vigorously over heat until mixture is smooth. Cool slightly and add 8 egg yolks, 1¾ ounces (50 grams) of grated cheese, and 1¾ ounces (50 grams) of diced cheese, ¼ ounce (5 grams) of potato flour, and seasoning (salt, pepper, and nutmeg). Just before putting into the oven, fold in 8 to 9 stiffly beaten egg whites. Fill buttered and floured souffle molds with souffle mixture. Place molds in a hot waterbath and cook on a low flame until souffle mixture is warmed thoroughly. Place mold on a baking sheet in the oven, and allow the souffle to rise with increasing heat.

Note: If a souffle mass is properly prewarmed, it will require approximately the following baking time: large molds — 30 minutes, single portion molds — 7 to 8 minutes. A souffle must be served immediately after it is cooked. To test souffle for doneness, stick a long needle into the center. If the needle is dry when removed the souffle is ready.

Cheese Pie — Quiche au frommage. (See page 464.)
Cheese Tart, Lorraine — Quiche Lorraine. Yield: 1 tart. Make dough from 10 ounces (300 grams) short crust paste (recipe 25.1.2). Line tart form with dough, puncturing the bottom in several places with a fork. For filling, use 3½ ounces (100 grams) of diced bacon (reserve some bacon slices which can be cooked and rolled to garnish tart) and 3½ ounces (100 grams) of diced onion. Saute bacon and onion and spread them over tart shell bottom. Distribute 10 ounces (300 grams) of grated Gruyere cheese evenly over the bacon and onion. Mix 1¾ ounces (50 grams) of flour, ¾ cup (2 deciliters) of milk, ¼ cup (1 deciliter) of cream, and 2 egg yolks. Fold in 2 beaten egg whites. Spread this mixture over the cheese. Bake the tart at medium heat for approximately 25 minutes. Garnish with bacon. (See illustration page 338.)
Cheese Tart Paysanne Style — Quiche au fromage a la paysanne. (See page 464.)
Chicken Croquettes — Croquettes de volaille. Yield: 10 servings. Saute some shallots in butter, add 1¼ pounds (600 grams) of cooked chicken, 3½ ounces (100 grams) of ham, and 7 ounces (200 grams) of sauteed mushrooms, all finely diced. Add 1 to 1¼ pints (5 to 6 deciliters) of thick Supreme Sauce (recipe 11.2.1.2), stirring well. Bind with 4 to 6 egg yolks and adjust seasoning. Spread mixture to a depth of about ¾ inch (20 millimeters) on an oiled sheet and allow to cool. Cut into shapes as desired. Roll pieces in flour, dip in egg wash, roll in fine bread crumbs, and deep-fat fry. Serve with an appropriate tomato sauce or brown sauce.
Note: Fish, lobster, and game croquettes can be made in the same way, except that an appropriate sauce is used for binding the croquettes.
Chicken Cutlets — Cotelletes de volaille. Chicken croquette mixture is shaped into chop form, breaded and fried in butter. Fish and game chops can also be made in the same way. A sauce is served separately.
Crusty Shells — Croustades. The shells are made of Duchess potatoes, rice, semolina, or tart pastry. Fillings for puff paste patty shells (bouchees) can be used.

Dumplings — Gnocchi. (See Pasta Dishes, 22.1.)
Eggs — Oeufs. (See Hot Egg Dishes, Chapter 14.)
Fondue — Fondue. (See page 463.)
Fritots (a type of fritter) — Fritots. Calf's brain, sweetbreads, calf's head, cauliflower, and black salsify are cooked. Halved tomatoes are added and the ingredients are dipped in batter and deep-fat fried. French-fried potatoes are arranged around the Fritots, and a Tomato Sauce (recipe 11.1.2) is served separately.
Ham Souffle — Souffle au jambon. Finely pounded and strained (pureed) ham is blended with a Bechamel Sauce (recipe 11.2.2). Egg yolks and stiffly beaten egg whites are folded in together with a little paprika and the souffle mixture is baked. Chicken and game souffles can be made in the same way.
Kromeskies of Chicken — Cromesquis. Chicken cro-

quette mixture is shaped into sausages, rolled inside thin slices of lean bacom, dipped in batter (see page 517), and deep-fat fried. Tomato Sauce (recipe 11.1.2) is served separately.

Meat on a Skewer — Attereaux. Tender pieces of meat are threaded on wooden skewers, dipped into a thick Villeroi Sauce, breaded, and deep-fat fried. It can be served on a silver skewer.

Mushrooms on Toast, Emmentaler Style — Croutes aux champignons emmentaloise. (See page 463.)

Pancakes — Pannequets. Pancakes made with unsweetened batter are stuffed with fillings for puff paste patty shells (bouchees).

Pasta — Pates. Certain special pasta dishes can be used as a hot hors d'oeuvre. (See page 457.)

Small Pastries, Homemade Style — Petits pates a la bourgeois. A small amount of meat or mushroom salpicon (ingredients finely diced and bound with a sauce) is centered on circular layer of puff paste. Another small circular layer of puff paste is placed on top. The edges are sealed, brushed with egg yolk, and baked.

Patties Diane — Bouchees Diane. Puff paste patty shells are filled with a salpicon of feathered game, truffles, and mushrooms, bound with a Salmi Sauce, and garnished with a slice of truffle.

Patties Joinville — Bouchees Joinville. Puff paste patty shells are filled with a salpicon of shrimp tails, mushrooms, and truffles, bound with a Joinville Sauce, and garnished with a slice of truffle.

Patties Montglas — Bouchees Montglas. Puff paste patty shells are filled with a salpicon (small diced ingredients bound with a sauce) made from goose liver, mushrooms, tongue, and truffles, and bound with a Madeira Sauce.

Patties St. Hubert Style — Bouchees St. Hubert. Puff paste patty shells are filled with game puree in a Pepper Sauce. A mushroom cap is placed on top.

Puff Pastry Patty Shells, Queen's Style — Bouchees a la reine. Yield: 10 servings. Saute some chopped shallots in butter, deglaze with ¾ cup (2 deciliters) of white wine, and reduce. Add a salpicon of 14 ounces (400 grams) of veal dumplings, 14 ounces (400 grams) of chicken breast, and 7 ounces (200 grams) of cooked mushrooms all finely diced. Bind with 1¼ pints (6 deciliters) of Supreme Sauce (recipe 11.2.1.2). Add a little cream, lemon juice, and adjust seasoning. Fill puff paste patty shells with mixture.

Raclette — Raclette. (See page 463.)

Ramekins — Ramequin. (See page 463.)

Ravioli — Ravioli. (See page 455.)

Rice Rings — Bordures. Rings are formed by pressing cooked rice or noodles bound with egg into buttered ring mold. The center can be filled with salpicon (a combination of finely diced ingredients bound with a sauce) or diced meat in sauce.

Risotto — Risotto. (See recipe 22.3.1.)

Rissoles — Rissoles. These are deep-fat fried small pastries made from puff paste or pastry dough cut in various shapes (circles or half moon) and filled with a cooled salpicon (ingredients finely diced and bound with a sauce) of shellfish, fish, chicken, goose liver, or game bound with appropriate sauce. The filling used determines the name of the rissole.

Sardine Fritters — Beignets de sardines. Canned sardines are dipped in batter and deep-fat fried. Sauce is served separately.

Swiss Tartlets — Tartelettes suisse. Same as for Tartlets, Oberland Style, but filled with cheese and a fine Royale Sauce.

Tartlets — Barquettes. Boat-shaped tartlets are filled with a salpicon (a combination of small diced ingredients bound with a sauce), with a puree of shellfish or sole, or with chicken puree and garnished with truffles.

Tartlets and Dumplings — Tartelettes aux gnocchi. Small tart shells are filled with Gnocchi, Parisian Style (see page 454), bound with a cream sauce, sprinkled with cheese and a few drops of melted butter, and baked in the oven.

Tartlets, Oberland Style — Tartelettes oberlandaise. Small molds, lined with short crust pastry (recipe 25.1.2), are filled with a mixture of equal parts of diced cheese and ham. They are covered with Royal Cream and seasoned with paprika. The tartlets are then baked in the oven. Royal Cream: 1 pint (5 deciliters) cream, mixed with 4 eggs, seasoned and strained.

Timbales — Timbales. Well-buttered timbal (dariole) molds, each of which has a round slice of truffle placed on the bottom, are filled with fish, chicken, or game forcemeat. They are filled with an appropriate salpicon (ingredients finely diced bound with a sauce). The name is determined by the ingredients. It is closed with forcemeat and poached in a waterbath in the oven. There are also timbales formed with yeast dough and hollowed out after baking. These are filled with a bound salpicon and the pastry lid is replaced on top.

Toasted Cheese Sandwich, Open-faced — Croutes aux fromage. (See page 463.)

Vol-au-vent, Cardinal Style — Vol-au-vent cardinal. Large puff paste patty shells are filled with fish dumplings, slices of rock lobster, mushrooms, truffles, and bound with a cream sauce.

Vol-au-vent, Toulouse Style — Vol-au-vent toulousaine. Large puff paste patty shells are filled with chicken breasts, calf's brain, sweetbreads, mushrooms, truffles, and bound with an Allemande Sauce (recipe 11.2.1.1).

Welsh Rarebit. (See page 477.)

13.3 Savories

The term savories or savory, traditionally English, refers to a course served between the sweet dish and the dessert. (See The Framework of the Menu, 5.1.2.) These are usually highly seasoned small dishes similar to those described under hot hors d'oeuvre, such as oyster tarts, cheese sticks, cheese fritters, and fish roe. Today savories are seldom served as a separate course; they are more commonly used for cocktail parties, buffets, and snacks.

Hot Egg Dishes— Oeufs chauds

14

Eggs are prepared in many different ways for breakfast or luncheon dishes; for hors d'oeuvres, snacks, and buffets. Eggs are sometimes served between the soup course and the main course. A la carte portions usually include three eggs, while an allowance of one or two eggs is sufficient for an hors d'oeuvre.

14.1 Soft or Hard-cooked Eggs in the Shell (Oeufs a la coque)

YIELD: *U.S. — 10 eggs*
Metric — 10 eggs

INGREDIENTS	*U.S. Weight or Volume*	*Metric Weight or Volume*	PROCEDURE
Eggs	10	10	1. Bring eggs to room temperature so that shells will not crack during cooking.
Water	2 quarts	2 liters	2. Place the eggs in boiling water.
			3. Reduce heat and cook to desired degree of doneness. If eggs are cooked too long, a green color forms around the egg yolk due to the formation of ferrous sulfide at the surface of the yolk. (See Section 7.2.2.2.)
			4. Serve hot in the shell.

Note: Soft-cooked eggs are cooked to order for 3 to 5 minutes, medium-cooked eggs for 6 to 8 minutes, and hard-cooked eggs for 8 to 10 minutes. If the eggs are being used for garnishes, they are simmered for 10 minutes. Hard-cooked eggs should be plunged into cold running water immediately to stop the cooking process.

14.2 Soft-cooked Eggs (Oeufs mollets)

YIELD: *U.S. — 10 eggs*
Metric — 10 eggs

INGREDIENTS	*U.S. Weight or Volume*	*Metric Weight or Volume*	PROCEDURE
Eggs	10	10	1. Cover the eggs with boiling water.
Water	2 quarts	2 liters	2. Simmer for 6 minutes and remove from hot water.
			3. Cool the eggs in cold water enough to remove shells.
			4. Tap the eggs gently on a hard surface to break the shells. Peel carefully under a stream of water.
			5. Warm peeled eggs for a minute in hot water.

Note: Soft-cooked eggs and poached eggs can be served in the same way. They are simply placed on puff paste underliners, on bread croutons, or on stuffed tartlets. A tomato sauce or a spicy brown sauce is served separately.

14.3 Poached Eggs (Oeufs poches)

YIELD: *U.S. — 10 eggs*
Metric — 10 eggs

INGREDIENTS	*U.S. Weight or Volume*	*Metric Weight or Volume*	PROCEDURE
Eggs, fresh	10	10	1. Carefully place open eggs into simmering water and vinegar.
Water	2 quarts	2 liters	2. Simmer for 3 to 4 minutes.
Vinegar	¾ cup	2 deciliters	3. Remove eggs with a skimmer. Trim off any trailing bits of white.
			4. Place eggs in cool water until needed.
			5. To reheat, place in hot salted water for about 30 seconds.

Variations of Poached and Soft-cooked Egg Dishes

Eggs Argenteuil — Oeufs argenteuil. Poached eggs in tartlet shells filled with asparagus tips and covered with Cream Sauce.
Eggs Aurora Style — Oeufs a l'aurore. Poached eggs or soft-cooked in puff paste underliners covered with Aurora Sauce (Allemande Sauce with Tomato Sauce).
Eggs Belle Helene — Oeufs belle Helene. Poached or soft-cooked eggs in patty shells filled with asparagus tips and covered with Supreme Sauce.
Eggs, Florentine Style — Oeufs florentine. Eggs arranged on a base of leaf spinach (epinard en branches), covered with a Mornay Sauce, sprinkled with cheese and melted butter, and gratinated under the broiler.
Eggs, Grand Duke Style—Oeufs a la grand duc. Poached eggs on fried bread croutons, coated with a

FIGURE 14—3
Eggs, Grand Duke Style – Oeufs a la grand duc

FIGURE 14—4
Eggs Italian Style – Oeufs a l'italienne

Mornay Sauce, sprinkled with cheese and melted butter, and gratinated in the oven. The eggs are arranged on a platter with bouquets of buttered asparagus tips placed between the eggs. Sauteed julienne of mushrooms and truffles sprinkled with Madeira Sauce are placed in the center of the plate.

Eggs, Italian Style – Oeufs a l'italienne. Poached eggs are placed on baked tartlet shells filled with a duxelles (recipe 10.1.5). Madeira Sauce is served separately.

Eggs, Piedmontese Style—Oeufs a la piemontaise. Soft-cooked or poached eggs on a base of white, braised rice, sprinkled with a julienne of truffles; Madeira Sauce is poured around the eggs.

Eggs, Swiss Style – Oeufs suisse. Soft-cooked or poached eggs are placed on a pastry shell spread with a duxelles (recipe 10.1.5) with chopped ham. Half of each egg is coated with Tomato Sauce; the other half with Cream Sauce.

14.4 Scrambled Eggs (Oeufs brouilles)

YIELD: *U.S. – 1 serving*
Metric – 1 serving

INGREDIENTS	*U.S. Weight or Volume*	*Metric Weight or Volume*	PROCEDURE
Butter	1 tablespoon	15 grams	1. Melt butter in a saute pan.
Eggs	3	3	2. Add the eggs and stir them into a thick mass using a wooden spoon and a low temperature.
Salt	¼ teaspoon	2 grams	
Cream	1 tablespoon	15 milliliters	

Note: For scrambled eggs, the temperature must be correct. If cream is to be used, it should be folded in after the eggs are cooked.

Variations of Scrambled Egg Dishes

Scrambled Eggs with Asparagus Tips — Oeufs brouilles aux pointes d'asperges. Scrambled eggs are garnished with asparagus tips.

Scrambled Eggs with Bread Croutons — Oeufs brouilles aux croutons. Scrambled eggs are garnished with triangular or heart-shaped bread croutons.

Scrambled Eggs with Chicken Livers — Oeufs brouilles aux foies de volaille. Scrambled eggs are garnished with diced chicken livers in Madeira Sauce.

Scrambled Eggs with Puff Paste — Oeufs brouilles aux fleurons. Scrambled eggs are garnished with puff paste cut into diamond shapes.

Scrambled Eggs with Tomatoes — Oeufs Brouilles a la portugaise. Scrambled eggs are garnished with diced tomatoes.

14.5 Fried Eggs (Oeufs au plat)

YIELD: *U.S. — 1 egg*
Metric — 1 egg

INGREDIENTS	*U.S. Weight or Volume*	*Metric Weight or Volume*
Egg	1	1
Butter	½ teaspoon	5 grams
Salt	to season	to season

PROCEDURE

1. Melt butter in skillet, add the egg, and season.
2. Baste the egg with hot butter over very low heat until it is done.
3. To get a firm white, cover the pan with a lid at once.
4. If a softer white is desired, pour a little water over the egg, cover, and cook for about 1 minute.

Variations of Fried Egg Dishes

Fried Eggs, American — Oeufs au plat a l'amercaine. Fried eggs served with grilled slices of bacon and grilled tomato halves.

Fried Eggs and Bacon — Oeufs au plat au lard. Fried eggs on lean strips of grilled bacon.

Fried Eggs with Brown Butter — Oeufs au plat au beurre noir. Fried eggs covered with brown butter.

Fried Eggs with Chipolata Sausages — Oeufs au plat chipolata. Small chipolatas placed between fried eggs. The eggs are surrounded with glazed pearl onions or fried onion rings.

Fried Eggs with Ham — Oeufs au plat au jambon. Fried eggs on slices of grilled ham.

Fried Eggs, Hunter's Style — Oeufs au plat chasseur. Fried eggs covered with sauteed chicken livers and mushrooms bound with Madeira Sauce.

Fried Eggs, Meyerbeer — Oeufs au plat Meyerbeer. Fried eggs with slices of grilled lamb kidney and surrounded with a ring of Truffle Sauce.

Fried Eggs, Piedmontese Style — Oeufs au plat a la piemontaise. Fried eggs with small mounds of braised rice surrounded with a ring of Madeira Sauce.

Fried Eggs, Portuguese Style — Oeufs au plat a la portugaise. Fried eggs are served with small mounds of sauteed diced tomatoes.

Fried Eggs with Shrimp — Oeufs au plat aux crevettes. Fried eggs on a salpicon (a combination of small diced ingredients bound with a sauce) of shrimp. A Shrimp Sauce is poured around the eggs.

Fried Eggs, Turkish Style — Oeufs au plat a la turque. Fried eggs with grilled chicken livers bound with a demi-glace.

14.6 Eggs in a Mold (Oeufs moules)

YIELD: *U.S. — 1 egg*
Metric — 1 egg

INGREDIENTS	*U.S. Weight or Volume*	*Metric Weight or Volume*	PROCEDURE
Egg	1	1	1. Put the egg in a buttered mold.
Butter	½ teaspoon	5 grams	2. Poach slowly in a waterbath.
			3. Serve the egg on a toasted slice of bread or an artichoke heart.
			4. Truffles, ham, tarragon, or chervil can be used as a garnish.

Note: This form of preparation is rarely used. A suitable sauce or butter can either be poured over, or served separately.

14.7 Eggs in Cocotte (Oeufs en cocotte)

YIELD: *U.S. — 1 egg*
Metric — 1 egg

INGREDIENTS	*U.S. Weight or Volume*	*Metric Weight or Volume*	PROCEDURE
Egg	1	1	1. Put cream in a buttered cocotte.
Butter	½ teaspoon	5 grams	2. Add the egg, season, and top with a piece of butter.
Cream	1 tablespoon	15 milliliters	3. Poach in a waterbath.
Salt	½ teaspoon	3 grams	

Note: A fried slice of lean bacon, a poached slice of sweetbread, or a salpicon of white meat may be placed on the bottom of the cocotte before adding the egg. The cream is often replaced with a spicy brown sauce.

14.8 Deep-Fat Fried Eggs (Oeufs frits)

YIELD: *U.S. — 1 egg*
Metric — 1 egg

INGREDIENTS	*U.S. Weight or Volume*	*Metric Weight or Volume*	PROCEDURE
Egg	1	1	1. Slide egg into medium hot fat, about 300°F. (150°C.), using 2 wooden spoons to shape the egg. The yolk should be enveloped by the white to keep it soft.
Salt	½ teaspoon	3 grams	2. Remove excess fat by placing egg on absorbent paper.
			3. Season.

Note: Deep-fat fried eggs are served on toast, croutons, or grilled tomato halves. Tomato Sauce, Italian Sauce, or Deviled Sauce may be served separately.

14.9 Omelet (Omelette)

YIELD: *U.S. — 1 serving*
Metric — 1 serving

INGREDIENTS	*U.S. Weight or Volume*	*Metric Weight or Volume*
Butter	1 tablespoon	15 grams
Eggs	3	3
Salt	½ teaspoon	3 grams

PROCEDURE

1. Beat eggs and salt moderately until whites are blended.
2. Heat butter in an omelet pan, add beaten eggs, and put over heat.
3. Mixture should begin to cook immediately at the outer edges. Lift cooked portions at the edges so uncooked portions flow underneath. Slide pan rapidly back and forth over heat to keep mixture in motion and sliding freely to avoid sticking.
4. Mixture is set when egg no longer flows freely. Let it cook 1 minute to brown slightly.
5. Fold into oval shape in front part of pan.
6. Turn omelet onto a warm plate.

Note: A properly prepared omelet should be moist and creamy inside, not cooked through. Garnishes and/or fillings can be served in various ways:

- the garnishes sauteed and combined with the eggs before cooking the omelet.
- the filling is added to the partially-cooked omelet. Care must be taken to ensure that the filling remains on the inside when the omelet is folded.
- after the omelet has been prepared, it is cut lengthwise and filled.
- when the omelet is served, it is decorated with a garnish of vegetable bouquets; or a sauce may be served separately.

Variations of Omelets

Cheese Omelet — Omelette au fromage. Grated cheese is added to the beaten eggs before cooking the omelet.
Ham Omelet — Omelet au jambon. Finely diced ham is sauteed in butter before the eggs are added. Follow method in recipe 14.9.
Mushroom Omelet — Omelette aux champignons. Sliced mushrooms, sauteed in butter, are added to the beaten eggs before cooking the omelet.
Tomato Omelet — Omelette portugaise. A prepared omelet is filled with sauteed, diced tomatoes.
Omelet with Asparagus Tips — Omelette aux pointes d'asperges. Asparagus tips, lightly sauteed in butter, are added to the beaten eggs before they are cooked. The omelet is garnished with a bouquet of asparagus tips when served.
Omelet, Emmentaler Style — Omelette emmentaloise. A prepared omelet is covered with Emmentaler cheese, quickly browned under a broiler, and served surrounded with a light cream sauce mixed with grated cheese.
Omelet with Herbs — Omelette aux fines herbes. Chopped herbs are mixed with the beaten eggs before cooking the omelet.
Omelet, Hunter's Style — Omelette chasseur. A prepared omelet is cut lengthwise, filled with sauteed chicken livers and mushrooms bound with a Madeira Sauce.

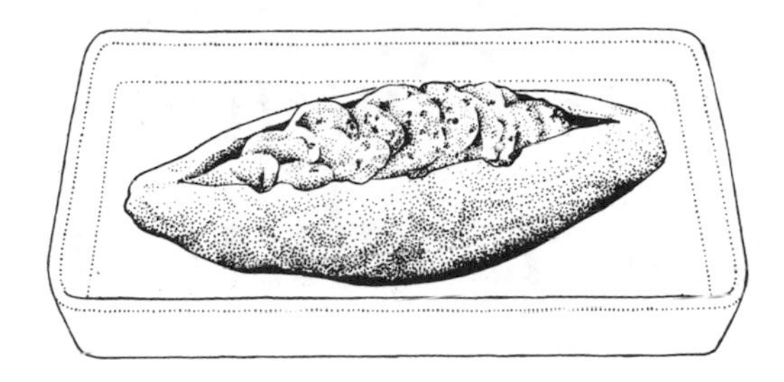

FIGURE 14–5
Omelet with Kidneys – Omelette aux rognons

Omelet with Kidneys – Omelette aux rognons. A prepared omelet is stuffed with sauteed kidneys bound with a Madeira Sauce.

Omelet, Paysanne Style – Omelette paysanne. Chopped onions, diced ham, and precooked potatoes are sauteed in butter. Diced tomatoes and chopped parsley are added. Sauteed vegetables are mixed in the beaten eggs and made into a pancake-shaped omelet.

Omelet, Queen's Style – Omelette a la reine. A prepared omelet is filled with Queen's style stuffing. (See page 351.)

Omelet Rossini – Omelette Rossini. Sauteed diced goose liver and truffles are mixed with the beaten eggs before the omelet is prepared. The omelet may be garnished with a border of goose liver and truffles. A small amount of Demi-glace Sauce is poured over the bottom of the plate.

15 Hot Fish Dishes—Poissons chauds

Formerly, when the full menu was being served, the hot fish dishes always came *before the grosse piece* (main course). Today, they are used in the following ways: *hot hors d'oeuvre, hot snacks, main courses, and a la carte dishes.*
The cold fish dishes (24.2) are mostly used as *cold snacks, cold hors d'oeuvre, and for cold buffets.*

The Basic Cooking Methods for fish are as follows:

Boiling—Cuire
- in court bouillon
- in white court bouillon
- in acidulated water (au bleu)

Poaching—Pocher
- in white wine
- in red wine

Braising—Braiser

Sauteing—Sauter
- a la meuniere
- in egg
- breaded

Deep-Fat Frying—Frire
- fried
- breaded
- in egg
- in batter
- in frying batter

Grilling/Broiling—Griller

Gratinating—Gratiner

15.1 Boiling—Cuire

Large fish are placed on a rack and immersed in cold court bouillon. Vegetables and spices are put on the bottom of the fish kettle and the rack of fish is placed over the vegetables. Once the boiling point has been reached, the fish is covered and simmered slowly. Cooking time is about 5 to 8 minutes per pound (15 minutes per kilogram). For cold fish dishes, the fish is allowed to cool in the liquid. Small fish and slices of fish are immersed in boiling court bouillon. Once the liquid returns to boiling, it is skimmed. The fish is then covered and simmered for a few minutes.

The following sauces and butter preparations are suitable for boiled fish: Hollandaise Sauce, Mousseline Sauce, melted butter (beurre fondue), noisette butter, or brown butter (beurre noir).

15.1.1 Boiling in Court Bouillon—Cuire au court-bouillon ordinaire

For lake trout (truite de lac), salmon trout (truite saumonee), and salmon (saumon).

15.1.2 Boiling in White Court Bouillon—Cuire au court-bouillon blanc

For cod (cabillaud), haddock (aigrefin), hake (colin), skate (raie), and turbot.

Basic Court Bouillon (Court-bouillon ordinaire)

YIELD: *U.S. — 5 quarts*
Metric — 5 liters

INGREDIENTS	*U.S. Weight or Volume*	*Metric Weight or Volume*
Water	4 quarts	4 liters
White wine	1 pint	5 deciliters
Vinegar	1 pint	5 deciliters
Salt	2 ounces	60 grams
White leeks, finely sliced	3½ ounces	100 grams
Carrots, finely sliced	14 ounces	400 grams
Onion, finely sliced	1 pound	500 grams
Parsley	few sprigs	few sprigs
Bay leaf	1	1
Thyme	¼ teaspoon	2 grams
Peppercorns, crushed	½ teaspoon	4 grams

PROCEDURE

1. Combine all the ingredients and simmer for 30 minutes.
2. Strain.
3. Cook fish in the stock according to the directions given in Section 15.1.

Note: This preparation can be used for poaching large saltwater fish that are suited neither for boiling in acidulated water nor for cold fish dishes. For en matelote, the white wine and vinegar are replaced by 1 quart (1 liter) of strong red wine.

White Court Bouillon (Court-bouillon blanc)

YIELD: *U.S. — 5 quarts*
Metric — 5 liters

INGREDIENTS	*U.S. Weight or Volume*	*Metric Weight or Volume*
Water	4½ quarts	4.5 liters
Milk	1 pint	5 deciliters
Lemon juice	of 1 lemon	of 1 lemon
Bay leaves	2	2
Dill	¼ teaspoon	2 grams
Salt	2 ounces	60 grams
Peppercorns, crushed	6	6

PROCEDURE

1. Combine all the ingredients and place the fish in the mixture before heating.
2. Bring to a boil, skim the liquid, cover, and simmer slowly. Allow 5 to 8 minutes per pound. (20 minutes per kilogram).

Note: This court bouillon is primarily for large, whole saltwater fish. If slices or pieces of fish are being cooked, they should not be added until the court bouillon has simmered for about 30 minutes; however, they can also be prepared in basic court bouillon.

15.1.3 Boiling in Acidulated Water—Au bleu

For carp (carpe), rainbow trout (truite-arc-en-ciel), river trout (truite de riviere), and golden trout (saibling) (ombre chevalier).

Ingredients for 5 quarts (5 liters) court bouillon (acidulated water): 4 quarts (4 liters) of water, 1 pint (5 deciliters) of white wine, approximately 2 ounces (60 grams) of salt, 7 ounces (200 grams) of finely cut white mirepoix, and 1 pint (5 deciliters) of vinegar.

Preparation: Combine all the ingredients, except the vinegar, and bring to a boil. Pour the vinegar over the *fresh,* cleaned fish and plunge into the boiling liquid. Skim, cover, and let stand in the kettle for a few minutes.

Note: Mainly for all varieties of trout, saibling, and carp. The fish should be alive when brought to the kitchen. Just before serving, the fish is killed with a sharp blow on the head, cleaned quickly, and plunged into boiling water. It is important to check that the slime on the skin of the fish is neither dried out nor rubbed off, otherwise the skin of the fish will not turn blue during cooking. Certain fish, distinguished by a high concentration of slime on the exterior when fresh will turn a light blue when poached in an acid solution. This is the preferred way of serving fresh trout and carp in Europe.

15.2 Poaching—Pocher

For whole fish, such as sand dab (carrelet) and small turbot (turbotin); for, fillets or slices of all flatfish and of cod (cabillaud), grayling (ombre), haddock (aigrefin), hake (colin), pike brochet, pike-perch (sandre), and, trout (truite).

15.2.1 Poaching in White Wine (Pocher au vin blanc)

YIELD: *approximately 10 servings*

INGREDIENTS	*U.S. Weight or Volume*	*Metric Weight or Volume*
Fish fillets	3 pounds	1½ kilograms
OR		
Fish slices	5 pounds	2½ kilograms
Butter	2 ounces	50 grams
Shallots, sliced	2 ounces	50 grams
Salt	1 teaspoon	5 grams
Pepper	¼ teaspoon	2 grams
White wine	¾ to 1¼ cups	2 to 3 deciliters
Fish stock	1 quart	1 liter
Lemon juice	from 1 lemon	from 1 lemon

PROCEDURE

1. Sprinkle sliced shallots into a buttered flat pan.
2. Place the seasoned fillets on top.
3. Pour lemon juice, white wine, and fish stock over the fish.
4. Heat but do not boil. Then cover the fish with buttered parchment paper and poach in the oven at 325°F. (163°C.) until the fish flakes. Large pieces should be basted with the stock occasionally.
5. Pour the stock off the poached fish and reduce it to the desired consistency. Use it for finishing the sauce in which the fish is served. See Sauce au vin blanc, page 307.

Note: If no Veloute de poisson is available to make the Sauce au vin blanc, the cooking liquid can be thickened with beurre manie, reduced, and finished with cream and egg yolk. All poached fish should be accompanied with boiled potatoes or rice.

15.2.2 Poaching in Red Wine (Pocher au vin rouge)

YIELD: *approximately 10 servings*

INGREDIENTS	*U.S. Weight or Volume*	*Metric Weight or Volume*
Fish fillets	3 pounds	1½ kilograms
OR		
Fish slices	5 pounds	2½ kilograms
Butter	2 ounces	50 grams
Shallots, sliced	2 ounces	50 grams
Salt	1 teaspoon	5 grams
Pepper	¼ teaspoon	2 grams
Red wine	¾ to 1¼ cups	2 to 3 deciliters
Lemon juice	2 tablespoons	30 milliliters
Beurre manie	2 ounces	50 grams
Fish stock (fond or fumet de poisson au vin rouge)	1 quart	1 liter

PROCEDURE

1. Cut the fish into pieces or slices and season.
2. Sprinkle the sliced shallots in a buttered flat pan. Place the fish on top.
3. Pour the red wine and stock over the fish. Heat.
4. Cover with buttered parchment paper and poach slowly in the oven 325°F. (163°C.) until fish flakes. It can be flambeed afterwards with brandy.
5. Reduce the stock, thicken with beurre manie and mix with a Fond de poisson au vin rouge (recipe 10.2.5). Reduce the sauce and strain. Add butter, lemon juice, and garnish as desired.

Note: This form of preparation is particularly suitable for carp, eel, and eel-pout. Glazed pearl onions, sliced mushrooms, and a ring of heart-shaped bread croutons serve as garnishes.

Variations of Poached Fish

Argenteuil Style—Argenteuil. Poached fish are covered with a White Wine Sauce and garnished with asparagus tips and fleurons (puff paste cut in crescent shape).

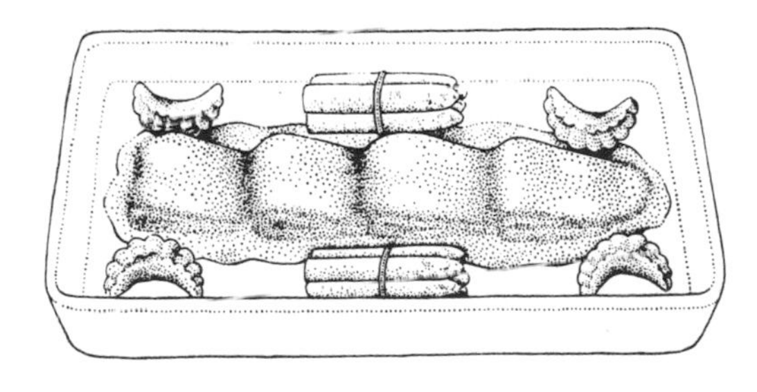

FIGURE 15-1
Poached Fish Argenteuil Style—Argenteuil

Bagration Style—Bagration. This is prepared in the same way as Mornay (see page 000) using truffle slices to garnish the sauce.

Bonne Femme Style—a la bonne femme. The fish is poached with chopped shallots, sliced mushrooms, and parsley. Reduced stock, not strained, is added to the white sauce and butter flakes are stirred in. After the sauce is poured over the fish, it is quickly browned. The dish is garnished with croutons, truffle slices, and mushroom caps.

Bordeaux Style—a la bordelaise. The fish is poached with red wine and chopped shallots. Reduced stock is mixed with a Bordelaise Wine Sauce and poured over the fish when it is served.

Byron—Byron. The fish is poached in red wine (recipe 15.2.2), covered with the sauce, and garnished with mushrooms and truffles.

with Chambertin Wine—au Chambertin. This is prepared in the same way as Byron, then browned lightly and garnished on both sides with small strips of fish fried in butter.

Choisy—Choisy. Poached fish is covered with a Mornay Sauce made with reduced fish stock and sprinkled with a julienne of mushrooms and truffles.

Duglere—Duglere. Fish is poached in fish stock with onions, diced tomatoes, and herbs. Reduced stock is mixed with a White Wine Sauce, strained, and butter added. When served, it is garnished with diced tomatoes.

Fillet of Trout, Old Bern Style—Truite de riviere "Vieux Berne." (a la carte dish for 4 persons). The trout are cleaned and marinated in lemon juice, Worcestershire Sauce, salt, and pepper. Finely chopped chives are sprinkled into a buttered cocotte. The trout is placed in the cocotte and white wine is poured over it. Covered with aluminum foil, the trout is poached in the oven for approximately 15 minutes as described in Section 15.2.1. The fish is removed and skinned from the neck towards the tail and placed on a serving platter. Strained stock is reduced and thickened slightly with kneaded butter (buerre manie). The sauce is enriched with whipped cream, chopped parsley, and tarragon. The sauce is poured over the trout which is then garnished with crayfish tails, fluted mushroom caps, puff paste diamonds, and tiny Parisian potatoes. (See illustration, page 000.)

with Herbs—aux fines herbes. Poached fish is covered with White Wine Sauce and sprinkled with finely chopped herbs.

Indian Style—a l'indienne. Fish is poached using white wine. A little curry powder is mixed with the sauce and poured over the fish. Creole rice is served separately.

Joinville—Joinville. Fish is covered with Joinville Sauce and garnished with shrimp, truffle slices, and mushrooms.

Marguery Style—Maguery. Poached fillets are garnished with mussels and shrimp, covered with a White Wine Sauce, and browned lightly under the broiler.

Marseille Style—a la marseillaise. Fish is served on slices of white bread lightly browned in butter, garnished with diced tomatoes, and covered with a White Wine Sauce seasoned with saffron.

Mornay—Mornay. (See page 368.)

Normandy Style—a la normande. Poached fish is covered with a Normandy Sauce made with oyster stock and garnished with oysters, small rolled fillets of fried fish, crayfish tails, and slices of truffles. It is surrounded with a ring of meat glaze.

Old Fashioned Style—a l'ancienne. Fish are poached in white wine, covered with White Wine Sauce, and garnished with small glazed pearl onions and mushroom caps.

Olga—Olga. This is a specialty for fillet of sole. The tops of well-formed, medium-sized baked potatoes are cut off and potatoes are hollowed out. After part of the warm potato mass is mixed with butter, cream, and a little salt, it is spread over the bottom of the empty potato shell. A salpicon of shrimp, truffles, and mushrooms is put over the potato layer. One or two poached fillets of sole are put on top and covered with Mornay Sauce made with fish stock. It is gratinated and garnished with a slice of truffle.

Portuguese Style—a la portugaise. Fish is covered with a White Wine Sauce and garnished with diced tomatoes.

Riche Style—Riche. The fish is covered with Riche Sauce and garnished with crayfish tails and slices of truffles.

Rossini—Rossini. Paupiettes of sole are cooked in white wine with chopped truffles and garnished with a salpicon of truffles. To make paupiettes, fillets of sole are spread with fish forcemeat and rolled.

Sailor's Style—en matelote. Fish is poached in red wine, covered with sauce, and garnished with mushrooms, pearl onions, crayfish tails, and croutons. (See recipe 15.2.2.)

Salmon, Riche Style—Tranche de saumon riche. Fish is poached or boiled, covered with slices of rock lobster and truffles, and garnished with crayfish tails and boiled potatoes. Riche Sauce is served separately.

Springtime Style—a la printaniere. Fish is covered with a White Wine Sauce and garnished with a printaniere (carrots, turnips, celery root, and green beans cut in various shapes).

with Truffles—demi-deuil. Fish is covered with White Wine Sauce and sliced truffles, and decorated with a ring of meat glaze.

Valentino—Valentino. (Mainly for fillets of sole.) Poached fillets are arranged with a quantity of sliced mushrooms on braised rice, covered with Mornay Sauce, and gratinated quickly in the oven or under the broiler.

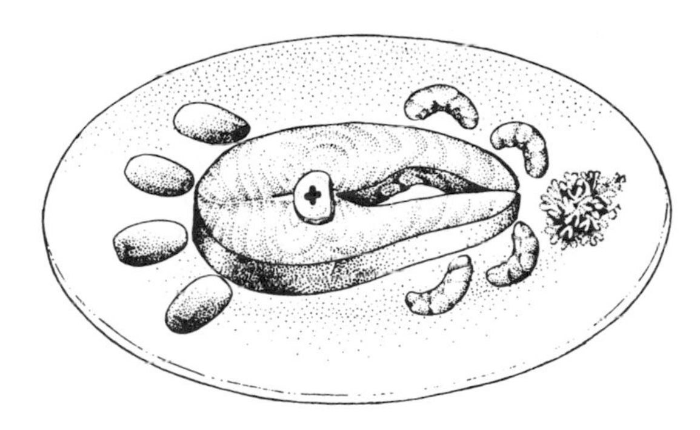

FIGURE 15-2
Salmon Riche Style—Tranche de saumon riche

with White Wine—au vin blanc. Poached fillets are covered with a White Wine Sauce and garnished with croutons or fleurons (puff paste cut in crescent shape).

15.3 Braising—Braiser

For large fish or fish pieces, such as carp (carpe), lake trout (truite du lac), salmon (saumon), sand dab (carrelet), and turbot.

Ingredients: Red or white wine, matignon (see page 291), fish stock (see page 295), sliced mushrooms (optional), and seasonings.

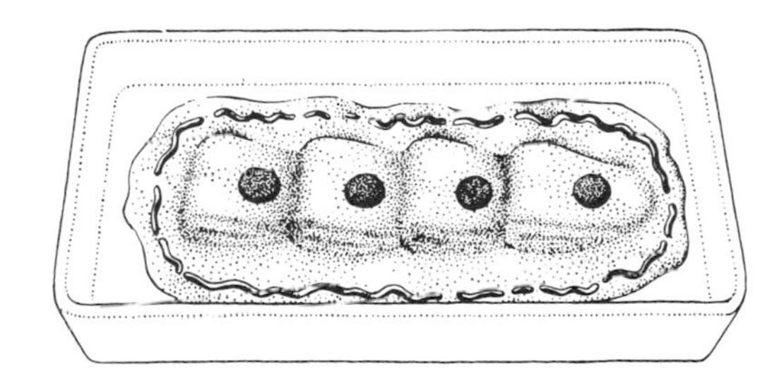

FIGURE 15-3
Poached Fish with Truffles—demi-deuil

Preparation: Butter an appropriate fish pan. Put the matignon beneath the rack where the fish is placed. Fill the pan up to ⅓ deep with red or white wine and fish stock. Cover and baste the fish from time to time with its own stock while it braises. The stock should be well reduced by the time the fish is cooked so that it can be used for enriching the corresponding sauce.

15.4 Sauteing—Sauter

For whole fish, such as golden trout (salmerin), grayling (ombre), river trout (truite de riviere), sole, (Plymouth Sole), and whitefish (fera); for fillets or slices of hake (colin), lake trout (truite de lac), pike-perch (sandre), salmon (saumon), and whitefish (fera).

15.4.1 A la Meuniere

Ingredients: Marinade: salt, pepper, lemon juice, clarified butter, butter, flour, lemon, and parsley.

Preparation: Coat the marinated whole fish, previously slashed on both sides (Carving, see page 228), or the fillets and slices lightly with flour. Heat the clarified butter over medium heat. Saute the fish golden brown on both sides. For larger fish, bake in the oven, basting from time to time. Drain the fat. Pour melted butter and lemon juice over the fish and garnish with a lemon wedge and a sprig of parsley.

Note: If the fish are sauteed in clarified butter or fat, and not garnished with hot butter, parsley, and lemon juice, they are described as *dore* on the menu. Slashing large fish along the sides permits the marinade and fats to permeate through the flesh and increases the aroma and flavor.

15.4.2 Sauteing in Egg—Sauter a l'oeuf

Ingredients: Marinade: lemon juice, salt, and pepper. Fat and butter, flour, beaten eggs, lemon, and parsley.

Preparation: Coat the marinated fish with flour, dip in beaten eggs, and saute slowly in the fat and butter until the fish is golden brown. Pour the fats and juices over the fish and garnish with a lemon wedge and parsley.

15.4.3 Sauteing Breaded Fish—Paner et sauter

Ingredients: Marinade: lemon juice, salt, and a little pepper. Flour, beaten eggs, bread crumbs, fat and butter, lemon, and parsley.

Preparation: Coat the marinated fish with a little flour, dip into beaten eggs, coat with bread crumbs, and saute in the fat and butter to a golden brown. Serve the fats and juices separately mixed with a little lemon juice. Garnish with parsley.

Note: With breaded fish, it is not necessary to make slashes into the flesh before cooking, since the taste and juiciness are retained by the bread crumbs. Cornbread crumbs can also be used instead of bread crumbs.

Variations of Fried Fish

with Bananas—aux bananes. The fish are prepared a la meunier or by broiling, garnished with bananas cut lengthwise sauteed in butter. The fish is sprinkled with chopped parsley and drenched with melted butter, together with a few drops of lemon juice. Lemons and halved tomatoes can be used as a garnish.

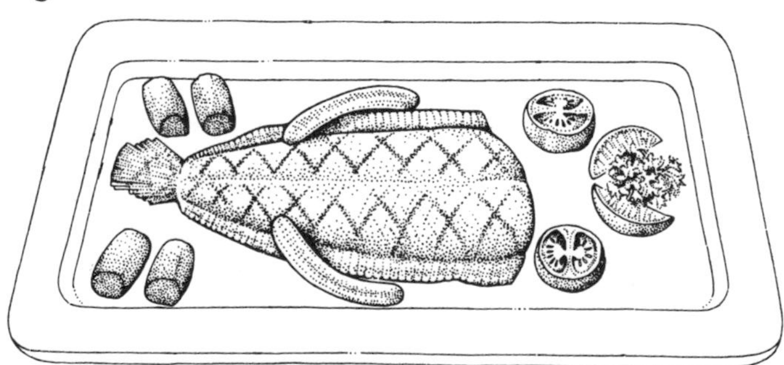

FIGURE 15-4
Sole with Bananas—Sole aux bananes

Bernese Style—a la bernoise. This variation is especially suited for perch. (See page 468.)

Colbert Style—Colbert. This is a variation for fish fillets. Fillets are prepared as described in recipe 15.4.3. A Colbert Sauce whipped with butter and lemon juice is served separately. (See Sole Colbert, page 367.)

English Style—a l'anglaise. Small fish (whiting, whitefish) are prepared as illustrated on page 226. They are prepared as described in recipe 15.4.3, sauteed in butter, covered with melted herb butter, and garnished with a lemon wedge.

Note: Fish fillets can also be prepared in this way.

Sauteed—doree. Sauteed fish are served on a platter and garnished with lemon slices.

Grenoble Style—a la grenobloise. Sauteed fish are served on a platter, and topped with mushrooms. Small, peeled pieces of lemon, capers, and fine herbs are added to foaming melted butter and poured over the fish.

Italian Style—a l'italienne. An Italian Sauce is prepared adding reduced fish stock, whipped with butter and a little lemon juice. It is served in a ring around the sauteed fish.

Jardiniere Style—a la belle jardiniere. Sauteed fish are covered with mushroom caps and garnished with beans, cauliflower, carrots, and potato straws. Hot herb butter is served separately.

Lucerne Style—a la lucernoise. Sauteed fish are served on a platter. Finely sliced onion is sauteed in butter with large cubes of tomatoes, capers, herbs, and some meat glaze are cooked together for a short while. This is poured over the fish. It is sprinkled with a few drops of anchovy essence and drenched with hot melted butter.

Meuniere Style—a la belle meuniere. Sauteed fish are arranged on a platter. Drops of lemon juice, meat glaze, and parsley are sprinkled over the fish; they are then covered with foaming melted butter and garnished with tiny sauteed potatoes, quartered mushrooms, and asparagus spears.

with Morels—au morilles. Fish are prepared a la meuniere and garnished with sauteed morels.

Murat Style—Murat. This varition is especially suited for fillets of sole. Fillets are cut into finger-sized strips, mixed with seasoning, lemon juice, and

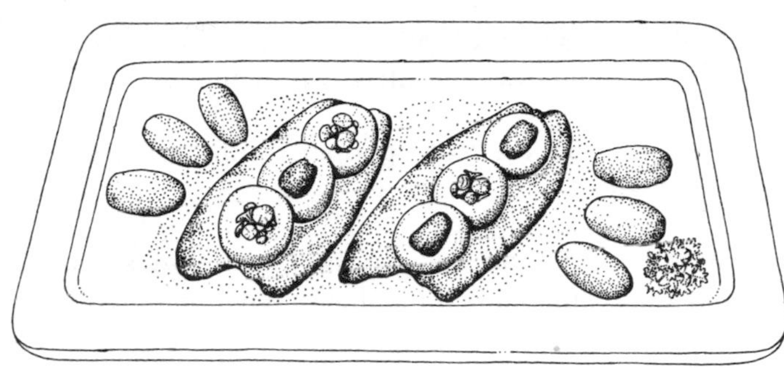

FIGURE 15-5
Whitefish Fillets, Eva Style—Filets de fera Eva

chopped parsley, coated with flour, rolled, and sauteed in butter. Sauteed tiny quartered potatoes a la parisienne and sauteed artichoke quarters are mixed with the fish fillets. All the ingredients are covered with fresh butter, or foaming melted herb butter. Slices of tomatoes are placed on top.
with Mushrooms—aux cepes. Fish is prepared a la meuniere and served with sauteed mushrooms.
Schweizerhof Style—Schweizerhof. This variation is especially suitable for whitefish. (See page 466.)
Whitefish Fillet, Eva Style—Filets de fera Eva. Fillets, which have been prepared a la meuniere, are arranged on the platter, sprinkled with lemon juice, and drenched with melted butter. Apple slices poached in white wine are filled with mushrooms (chanterelles) and sauteed tomatoes. These are placed on top of the fillets and served with potatoes.

15.5 Deep-Fat Frying—Frire

For small, whole fish or fish fillets and slices: perch (perche), pike (brochet), sole, (Plymouth) (Sole), whitefish (fera), and whiting (merlan).

15.5.1 Deep-Fat Fried—Frire nature

Ingredients: Marinade: salt, a little pepper, lemon juice, and herbs. Flour, lemon, and parsley.

Preparation: Marinate the fish, coat with flour, and fry in deep-fat at approximately 350°F. to 375°F. (177°C. to 190°C.). Place the fish on absorbent paper to remove excess fat and season with salt. Arrange on a platter on top of a paper napkin, and serve with a lemon wedge and sprig of parsley.

Note: Sometimes beer or white wine and finely chopped herbs are used for this marinade. Larger quantities should be prefried in deep-fat then completed at 350°F. to 375°F. (177°C. to 190°C.).

15.5.2 Deep-Fat Frying Breaded Fish—Frire pane

Ingredients: Marinade: salt, a little pepper, lemon juice, and herbs. Flour, egg, bread crumbs, lemon, and parsley.

Preparation: Marinate small whole fish or fillets, prepare as described in recipe 15.4.3 and fry in deep-fat at 350°F. to 375°F. (177°C. to 190°C.). Place on absorbent paper to remove excess fat, season with salt, serve on a paper napkin, and garnish with lemon and parsley.

A Variation of Breaded, Deep-Fat Fried Fish
Sole, (Plymouth) Colbert Style—Sole Colbert. On one side of a cleaned sole, a cut is made along the line of the backbone to loosen the 2 fillets slightly. (See Methods of Cutting, page 226.) The fish is prepared as described in recipe 15.4.3 and fried in deep-fat until it is golden yellow. The backbone is removed through the opening which has formed. The fish is arranged on a platter and either a few slices of herb butter are placed in the opening or melted herb butter is poured in. It is garnished with lemon and parsley.

15.5.3 Deep-Fat Frying in Egg Batter—Frire a l'oeuf

Ingredients: Marinade: salt, a little pepper, lemon juice, and herbs. Beaten eggs, flour, lemon, and parsley.

Preparation: Marinate the fish, coat in flour, dip in the beaten egg, and fry in deep-fat at approximately 350°F. to 375°F. (177°C. to 190°C.). Place on absorbent paper to remove the fat, season with salt, serve on a paper napkin, and garnish with lemon and parsley.

Note: Larger quantities should be prefried then completed at 350°F. to 375°F. (177°C. to 190°C.).

15.5.4 Deep-Fat Frying in Plain Batter—Frire en pate

Ingredients: Marinade: lemon juice and herbs. Batter made with water: 1 pound (500 grams) of flour, 1¼ pints (6½ deciliters) of water, salt, a little pepper, flour for dusting, and parsley.

Preparation: Marinate the fish, dust with flour, dip into the batter, and remove any surplus. Fry in deep-fat or prefry then complete frying at 350°F. to 375°F. (177°C. to 190°C.). Place on absorbent paper to remove excess fat and garnish with parsley.

Note: Serve a Mayonnaise Sauce or one of its variations separately.

15.5.5 Deep-Fat Frying in Special Batter—Frire a l'Orly

Ingredients: Marinade: lemon juice and herbs. Frying batter (recipe 25.1.4), flour, and parsley.

Preparation: Marinate the fish, dust with flour, dip in the frying batter, and remove excess batter. Fry in deep-fat or prefry then complete frying at 350°F. to 375°F. (177°C. to 190°C.). Place on absorbent paper to remove excess fat, and garnish with parsley.

Note: Serve a Tomato Sauce separately. The parsley can also be deep-fat fried.

15.6 Broiling/Grilling—Griller

For whole fish, such as lemon sole (limande), grayling (ombre), whitefish (fera), and whiting (merlan); for fillets or slices of pike-perch (sandre), salmon (saumon), river eel (anguille), and turbot.

Ingredients: Salt, a little pepper, flour, oil, lemon, and parsley.

Preparation: Thoroughly dry the fish before seasoning and coating with flour. Baste with oil and broil both sides of the fish. Garnish with lemon and parsley.

Note: Fish which are to be broiled should be kept as dry as possible. Usually a whipped butter sauce, herb butter, or an oil sauce is served with broiled fish.

15.7 Gratinating—Gratiner

For cod (cabillaud), grayling (ombre), haddock (aigrefin), hake (colin), pike (brochet), pike-perch (sandre), plaice (plie), sand dab (carrelet), sole, (Plymouth) (sole), and turbot.

Ingredients: Fish, seasoning, lemon juice, wine, butter, Gratin Sauce, and cheese.

Preparation: Remove the skin and bones from boiled or poached fish. Season the pieces of fish and add some lemon juice. Spread a little Gratin Sauce over the bottom of a buttered gratinating dish, place the fish in the dish, and cover with more Gratin Sauce. Sprinkle with grated cheese and drops of melted butter and gratinate in the oven.
Gratin Sauce—Sauce au gratin: Reduce fish stock (recipe 10.2.5), white wine, and chopped shallots. Add Brown Basic Sauce (recipe 11.1.1) and some duxelles (recipe 10.1.5). Then reduce the sauce slightly, beat in fresh butter, and add lemon juice and parsley.

Some Variations of Gratinated Fish
Mornay. Poached fish stock is reduced and mixed into Mornay Sauce. (See page 308.) A small part of this sauce is spread over the bottom of a buttered gratin dish. The poached fish is placed in the dish,

and covered with the remaining sauce. Cheese and melted butter droplets are sprinkled over the dish and browned either in the oven or under the broiler.

Gratinated Sole, (Plymouth)—Sole au gratin. The fillets of a skinned and cleaned sole are loosened by cutting along the line of the backbone. (See illustration on page 226.) A buttered gratin dish is sprinkled with chopped shallots, and moistened with a little white wine. The sole is placed in the dish, and seasoned with salt and lemon juice. The openings in the fish, created when the fillets were loosened, are filled with sliced sauteed mushrooms. A few mushroom caps are placed on top. The fish is covered with Gratin Sauce, sprinkled with white bread crumbs and a few drops of melted butter, and gratinated in the oven until the fish is done.

Pike Dumplings, Old Fashioned Style (Quenelles de brochet a l'ancienne)

YIELD: *8 to 10 servings*

INGREDIENTS	*U.S. Weight or Volume*	*Metric Weight or Volume*
Puree of raw boneless pike flesh	2 pounds	1 kilogram
Egg whites	5	5
Cream, chilled	1 pint	½ deciliter
Salt	1 teaspoon	5 grams
Pepper	¼ teaspoon	2 grams
Paprika	¼ teaspoon	2 grams
Anchovy fillets, chopped (optional)	4 to 6	4 to 6
Mushrooms	2 pounds	1 kilogram
Cream	½ cup	1 deciliter
Mornay Sauce	1 cup	2 deciliters
Cheese, grated	4 ounces	115 grams
Butter, melted	¼ cup	60 milliliters

PROCEDURE

1. Finely grind the deboned pike flesh.
2. Thoroughly chill this puree. Gradually work in 5 egg whites, using a wooden spatula. Add the cream very gradually and mix thoroughly.
3. Season the cold mixture with salt, pepper, and paprika. Anchovies can be added if desired.
4. Shape into nut-sized dumplings with a spoon and poach in a well-seasoned fish fumet for 8 to 10 minutes.
5. Make a duxelles of sauteed and finely diced mushrooms. Add a little cream and spread the mixture in a buttered gratin dish to a depth of about ½ inch.
6. Place the dumplings on the duxelles. Cover with a Mornay Sauce. (See page 308.) Sprinkle with cheese and melted butter.
7. Gratinate in the oven or under the broiler.

16 Crustaceans, Shellfish, and Mollusks—Crustaces, coquillages, et mollusques

Boiled Crayfish (Ecrevisses a la nage)

YIELD: *6 servings*

INGREDIENTS	*U.S. Weight or Volume*	*Metric Weight or Volume*	PROCEDURE
Fumet de poisson	1¾ cups	4 deciliters	1. Prepare a court bouillon of the fumet de poisson (recipe 10.2.5), white wine, mirepoix, and salt.
White wine	1¼ cups	3 deciliters	
Mirepoix, finely chopped	½ cup	115 grams	
Salt	½ ounce	10 grams	
Crayfish, live and eviscerated	20	20	2. Immerse the crayfish in the court bouillon. Heat to the boiling point and allow to stand for 10 minutes.
Cayenne pepper	1/8 teaspoon	1 gram	3. Add the cayenne pepper and serve in a bowl with the mirepoix. 4. Serve a Mayonnaise Sauce separately.

Crayfish Bordelaise (Ecrevisses a la bordelaise)

YIELD: *10 servings*

INGREDIENTS	*U.S. Weight or Volume*	*Metric Weight or Volume*	PROCEDURE
Mirepoix, finely chopped	½ to ¾ cup	1 to 2 deciliters	1. Saute a finely chopped mirepoix in 2 ounces (60 grams) of butter.
Butter	4 ounces	120 grams	2. Add 2 ounces (60 grams) of butter, cayenne, and the live, eviscerated crayfish. Continue sauteing until the crayfish have turned completely red.
Salt	1 tablespoon	15 grams	
Cayenne	1/8 teaspoon	1 gram	
Crayfish, live and eviscerated	30	30	
Brandy	½ cup	1 deciliter	3. Flambe with the brandy. Add the wine and reduce the liquids to ⅓ the original volume.
White wine	1¼ cups	3 deciliters	
Fumet de poisson	½ cup	1 deciliter	4. Add the fumet de poisson and the veloute de poisson. Boil briefly.
Veloute de poisson	¾ cup	2 deciliters	
Glace de viande	1 tablespoon	15 milliliters	5. Add the glace de viande, a few flakes of butter, and the chopped parsley.
Butter flakes	a few	a few	6. Pour the sauce over the crayfish and serve.
Parsley, chopped	2 tablespoons	30 grams	

Coquilles St. Jacques.

Ingredients: Cleaned scallops, white wine, shallots, some duxelles (recipe 10.1.5), finely chopped mushrooms, soft bread crumbs, and Gratin Sauce (see page 302).

Preparation: Place a layer of duxelles on the bottom of the scallop shells. Poach the scallops and the shallots in white wine and arrange on top of the duxelles with the mushrooms. Add the reduced stock to the Gratin Sauce and pour the sauce over the scallops. Sprinkle with the bread crumbs, the melted butter, and gratinate.

Note: Scallops are usually sold shucked, fresh or frozen; however, if they are not shucked, they should be placed in a warm oven to open. Use a thin knife to lift off the top shell and detach the flesh from the lower shell. In the United States they are marketed as sea scallops (large), bay scallops (medium), and cape scallops (small).

Frogs' Legs (Cuisses de grenouilles)

Frogs' Legs, Bonne Femme Style — Cuisses de grenouilles bonne femme. (See page 462.)
Deep-Fat Fried Frogs' Legs — Cuisses de grenouilles frites. These deep-fat fried frogs' legs are seasoned with lemon juice and seasonings and dipped in a batter before frying in hot fat. They are served with fresh lemon and/or Tomato Sauce.
Frogs' Legs with Herbs — Cuisses de grenouilles aux fines herbes. These are fresh frogs' legs that have been seasoned with lemon juice and sauteed in butter with chopped shallots. They are garnished with fresh parsley before serving.
Frogs' Legs with White Sauce — Cuisses de grenouilles a la poulette. These frogs' legs are prepared by the same method used for Frogs' Legs with Herbs. The legs are bound with a White Wine Sauce or a Veloute Sauce. Frogs' legs are sometimes sauteed with shallots in butter, dusted with flour, deglazed with white wine and a little stock, simmered until tender, and served with chopped parsley.

Lobster, American Style (Homard a l'americaine)

YIELD: *2 servings*

INGREDIENTS	*U.S. Weight or Volume*	*Metric Weight or Volume*
Lobsters, 1 or 2	2 pounds total	1 kilogram total
Oil	3½ ounces	100 grams
Shallots, chopped	1 tablespoon	15 grams
Garlic, crushed	¼ clove	¼ clove
Thyme	1/8 teaspoon	1 gram
Parsley	1 tablespoon	15 grams
Brandy	¼ cup	½ deciliter
Tomatoes, diced	5 ounces	150 grams
White wine	¾ cup	2 deciliters
Fumet de poisson	½ cup	1 deciliter
Glace de viande	1 tablespoon	15 milliliters
Salt	½ teaspoon	3 grams
Pepper	1/8 teaspoon	1 gram
Cayenne	1/8 teaspoon	1 gram
Butter	4 ounces	120 grams

PROCEDURE

1. After cleaning, kill the lobster quickly by splitting the front part of the body.
2. Cut up the lobster. (See page 230.) Pry open the claws.
3. Remove the innards and coral from the body and put aside. Remove the bag containing the gritty substance from the head cavity (stomach).
4. Drop the cut lobster into the hot oil and saute until it turns completely red.
5. Drain the oil.
6. Add the shallots, garlic, thyme, and parsley.
7. Heat and flambe with brandy.
8. Add the tomatoes, white wine, fumet, glace de viande, salt, pepper, and cayenne.
9. Cover and simmer slowly for 10 to 12 minutes.
10. Remove the lobster from the stock.
11. Chop the innards. Add to the coral and the stock and reduce to the desired consistency.
12. Strain the reduced stock and whip with butter.
13. When serving, place the 2 halves of the body on the pieces of lobster and cover with the stock.

Note: Sometimes only the lobster tails and claws are used, and the body is reserved for making lobster butter.

Lobster Thermidor (Homard Thermidor)

YIELD: *2 servings*

INGREDIENTS	*U.S. Weight or Volume*	*Metric Weight or Volume*
Lobster	2 (1 to 1½ pounds each)	2 (1 to 1½ kilograms each)
Oil	3½ ounces	100 grams
White sauce, medium	1½ cups	4 deciliters
Mustard, prepared spicy	1 tablespoon	15 grams

PROCEDURE

1. Split the raw lobster lengthwise down the middle. (See page 231.)
2. Saute slowly in oil.
3. Remove the tail meat from the shell and cut into slices.
4. Combine the white sauce and spicy mustard. Pour some of this sauce into the shell and arrange the slices of tail meat in the shell and in the claws.
5. Cover with sauce and brown or gratinate.

Note: Often the lobster halves are boiled in court bouillon.

Lobster Newburg

YIELD: *2 servings*

INGREDIENTS	*U.S. Weight or Volume*	*Metric Weight or Volume*	PROCEDURE
Lobster tail, cooked, cut into ¼ inch slices, or ¾ inch cubes	8 to 10 ounces	225 to 285 grams	1. In a shallow pan (sautoir) heat clarified butter, add lobster and saute without coloring.
Butter, clarified	½ ounce	15 grams	
Heavy cream	10 ounces	3 deciliters	2. Add cream to cover lobster, simmer to reduce.
Madeira	1 ounce	30 grams	3. Add Madeira to taste.
Liaison:			4. Thicken with liaison.
heavy cream	1½ ounces	50 grams	
egg yolk	1	1	

Note: This is the original recipe as it was prepared at Delmonico's Restaurant by Chef Ranhofer. Contemporary variation includes sherry instead of Madeira, brandy and the addition of coral or paprika powder to obtain pinkish color.

Variations of Lobster Recipes

Boiled Lobster. Plunge live lobster head first into large pot of boiling salted water or basic court bouillon. (*Note:* True lobster lovers prefer theirs boiled in water only, as the flavor imported from the court bouillon takes away from the natural taste.) When the water returns to boil, simmer for 6 to 8 minutes per pound of lobster. Serve lobster directly accompanied by drawn butter and fresh lemon. The claws may be disjointed and cracked or portions of the shell removed for the convenience of the guest.

Broiled Lobster. Rinse live lobster (1 pound) thoroughly in cold water. Remove claws and legs. Place lobster on chopping board with back down. Using a sharp knife and starting at the head, split the lobster in half and open flat lengthwise, but do not cut through the back shell. Remove the stomach, intestinal vein, coral (if any), and tamale. (Tamale may be used in the stuffing.) Place lobster on grill rack, shell side up and place under broiler. Large claws may be baked in the oven with a little water to retain moisture Broil 3 or 4 minutes or until shells are red. Remove from racks and fill body cavity (but not tail) with stuffing made from bread crumbs, butter, fresh chopped parsley, and a little rubbed thyme. Tamale may be added. Place on bake sheet or in roast pan and bake at 400°F. (205°C.) in oven for 15 to 18 minutes. Crack claws after cooking, for the convenience of guests. Serve lobster on platter with one claw on each side. Garnish with lemon and parsley. Serve with drawn butter.

Steamed Lobster. Place lobster in steam equipment; follow manufacturer's instructions for time. Serve as for boiled lobster.

Steamed Lobster in Seaweed. Place some seaweed in the bottom of the pot and barely cover with water; place lobster on top and cover with additional seaweed. Cover and steam 6 to 8 minutes per pound. Serve as for boiled lobster. *Note:* Lobsters are often delivered wrapped in seaweed to keep them moist. Ask your purveyor.

Mussels, Mariner's Style (Moules a la mariniere)

YIELD: *approximately 10 servings*

INGREDIENTS	*U.S. Weight or Volume*	*Metric Weight or Volume*	PROCEDURE
Mussels	7 to 9 pounds	3 to 4 kilograms	1. Wash the mussels well.
Salt	1 tablespoon	15 grams	2. Place them in a large kettle. Add the salt, pepper, white wine, and shallots. Simmer covered until the mussels open.
Pepper	1 teaspoon	5 grams	
White wine	¾ to 1¼ cups	2 to 3 deciliters	
Shallots, finely chopped	3 ounces	80 grams	3. Drain immediately.
Parsley, chopped; Thyme, chopped; Dill, chopped	Total of 2 tablespoons	Total of 30 grams	4. Add the herbs to the stock and reduce to ⅔ its volume. Stir in the butter and adjust seasoning. Add lemon juice.
Butter	7 ounces	200 grams	
Lemon juice	2 tablespoons	30 milliliters	
Parsley, chopped	as needed for garnish	as needed for garnish	5. Remove the top shell of each mussel. Place the mussels in a flat container, cover with sauce, and sprinkle with parsley.

Note: For large quantities, the stock may be extended with a fond or fumet de poisson.

Variations of Mussels

Mussels, Oriental Style — Moules a l'orientale. These cooked mussels are removed from the shells and placed on rice. Curry powder is added to the White Wine Sauce. The sauce is poured over the mussels and rice before serving.

Mussels with White Sauce — Moules a la poulette. These are Mariner's Mussels served with a White Wine Sauce that has been mixed with the stock in which the mussels were cooked.

Scampi, Bordelaise Style — Scampi a la bordelaise. See the recipe for Crayfish Bordelaise, page 371.

Deep-Fat Fried Scampi — Scampi frits. (See page 483.)

Snails, Burgundy Style (Escargots a la bourguignonne)

YIELD: *Butter for approximately 100 snails (6 to 12 per serving)*

INGREDIENTS	*U.S. Weight or Volume*	*Metric Weight or Volume*	PROCEDURE
Butter	10 ounces	300 grams	1. Whip the butter until light.
Garlic	¾ ounce	20 grams	2. Add all other ingredients except snails and mix well.
Parsley, chopped	3½ ounces	100 grams	3. Force a little butter into each snail shell.
White wine	½ cup	1½ deciliters	
Salt	1 teaspoon	4 grams	
Shallots, chopped	2 ounces	50 grams	
Lemon juice	2 tablespoons	30 milliliters	
Snails, boiled	100	100	4. Place one boiled snail in each shell and fill completely with the snail butter.
			5. Place the snails on a snail plate. Add some water and heat in the oven at 425°F. (218°C.) for 4 to 5 minutes.

Note: It is important to heat the snails in the oven until the butter is boiling. The snails may be marinated.

17 Small Meat Dishes — Entrees

In the classical menu, the term entrees referred to the courses after the grosse piece. Basically, they are divided into cold entrees and hot entrees. Today, however, the entrees are usually served as the *main dish* with suitable vegetable and salad garnishes. Both hot and cold entrees are frequently described as *single dishes* on the menu, where they appear in various categories, such as *hot snacks* (see illustration on page 493), *garnished main dishes, specialties of the day, or national dishes.* The main difference between entrees and grosses pieces is that the entrees are *cut up or jointed before being cooked,* and, therefore, do not require the same methods of preparation as the grosses pieces, which are prepared in single large pieces. It is, therefore, not possible to group the two types of dishes in the same category.

Entrees are divided into two main categories; cold entrees and hot entrees (see Chapter 24, Cold Dishes). For all types of cutting, trussing, and cleaving, see pages 232-237.

17.1 Sauteing — Sauter a la minute

As the name "a la minute" indicates, it is important that sauteed dishes are served directly out of the pan, since the quality will deteriorate (the meat will toughen), if they are held for any length of time after preparation.

The timing for such small pieces is very difficult to detemine. It depends upon the heat of the fat, the size of the saute pan, the quantity of meat, its thickness, and quality. The degree of doneness may be tested by applying light pressure with the fingers to the center or largest portion of the meat. After quickly browning the meat, press with the finger from time to time. The more yielding or spongier the meat, the lesser the degree of doneness. The greater the resistance or the firmer the texture, the greater the degree of doneness.

Rare *Bleu*	When pressed with a finger, the meat is *very soft* with a jelly-like texture.
Medium Rare *Saignant*	When pressed with a finger, the meat feels springy and resilient.
Medium *A point*	When pressed with a finger, the meat feels firm, and there is a definite resistance.
Well-done *Bien cuit*	When pressed with a finger, the meat feels hard and rough.

17.1.1 Sauteing Red Meat

Ingredients: Oil or fat with a high smoking point, salt, spices, wine, veal stock, and demi-glace.

Preparation: Saute tournedos, chateaubriand, sirloin, or rumpsteak in oil; larger pieces of meat are basted with fat from time to time. Place on a plate after the required degree of doneness has been achieved. Drain the oil and deglaze the saute pan to make the sauce which will be served with the meat. This sauce is generally derived from demi-glace or veal stock. In certain recipes, the meat is served without the stock. Sauteed beef tenderloin dishes, such as beef stroganoff, are prepared by the same method as the sliced white meat sautes (Section 17.1.2). The tenderloin is cut into small cubes and sauteed to the medium rare stage.

17.1.2 Sauteing White Meat

A clear distinction must be made between finely sliced meat, cutlets, and chops since each is prepared quite differently.

Ingredients: Peanut oil, butter, salt, pepper, chopped shallots, flour, white wine, white stock, stock or demi-glace, and cream.

Thinly sliced meat is prepared in a lyonnaise pan.

Phase I: Heat the oil in the pan. Place the seasoned and floured meat in the hot oil over high heat. Stir vigorously with a fork so that the pieces of meat are evenly sauteed; they are not browned, but a grayish color. This procedure requires only a few seconds. Saute a small quantity at a time and remove the meat from the heat before any meat juices cook out. Then place the meat on a heated platter.
Phase II: Drain any excess oil from the pan and replace it with butter. Add the shallots and saute over low heat for a few seconds. Add the white wine, reduce, and add the demi-glace or stock and the cream. Reduce once more and season to taste. Return the meat to the pan but do not allow it to cook. Arrange the meat slices on a warm platter, and pour the sauces over the top.

Cutlets and Chops: Heat the oil or butter or a mixture of the two in a saute pan. Brown both sides of the meat carefully. As soon as the meat juice is visible on the surface of the meat, remove it from the pan. Deglaze the saute pan, and prepare the sauce from a demi-glace, stock, or cream. Shallots or onion may be added. Arrange the meat on a heated platter and pour the sauce over the top.

Note: Breaded pieces of meat should not be covered with meat juices or sauce as the liquid will soften the crust. Merely garnish with beurre noisette. All sauteed white meats can be finished using only butter.

17.1.3 Variations of Sauteed Dishes

Beef Goulash Stroganoff — Filet goulach Stroganov. This is a goulash made of small cubes of beef tenderloin tips that have been sauteed in melted butter and combined with finely chopped onion and strips of cucumber that have been dusted with paprika and added to sauteed diced potatoes. The dish is deglazed with a demi-glace containing a small amount of tomato puree, removed from the heat, and thickened with sour cream.
Beef Tenderloin Goulash — Goulach a la minute. Small cubes of beef tenderloin tip and chopped onion are sauteed over high heat until partially done, seasoned, and placed on a warm dish. Finely diced boiled potatoes are sauteed in butter. The pan drippings from the meat are deglazed with demi-glace and the sauce is heated to the boiling point. Madeira is added. The meat and potatoes are reheated in the pan. Chopped parsley is scattered over the top.
Sliced Calf's Liver — Foie de veau en tranches. Thin slices of calf's liver are seasoned, coated with flour, and sauteed in butter. The liver is drenched with melted butter, and sprinkled with lemon juice and parsley before serving.
Calf's Liver, English Style — Foie de veau a l'anglaise. Thin slices of calf's liver, coated with flour, and sauteed in butter are arranged on a platter alternately

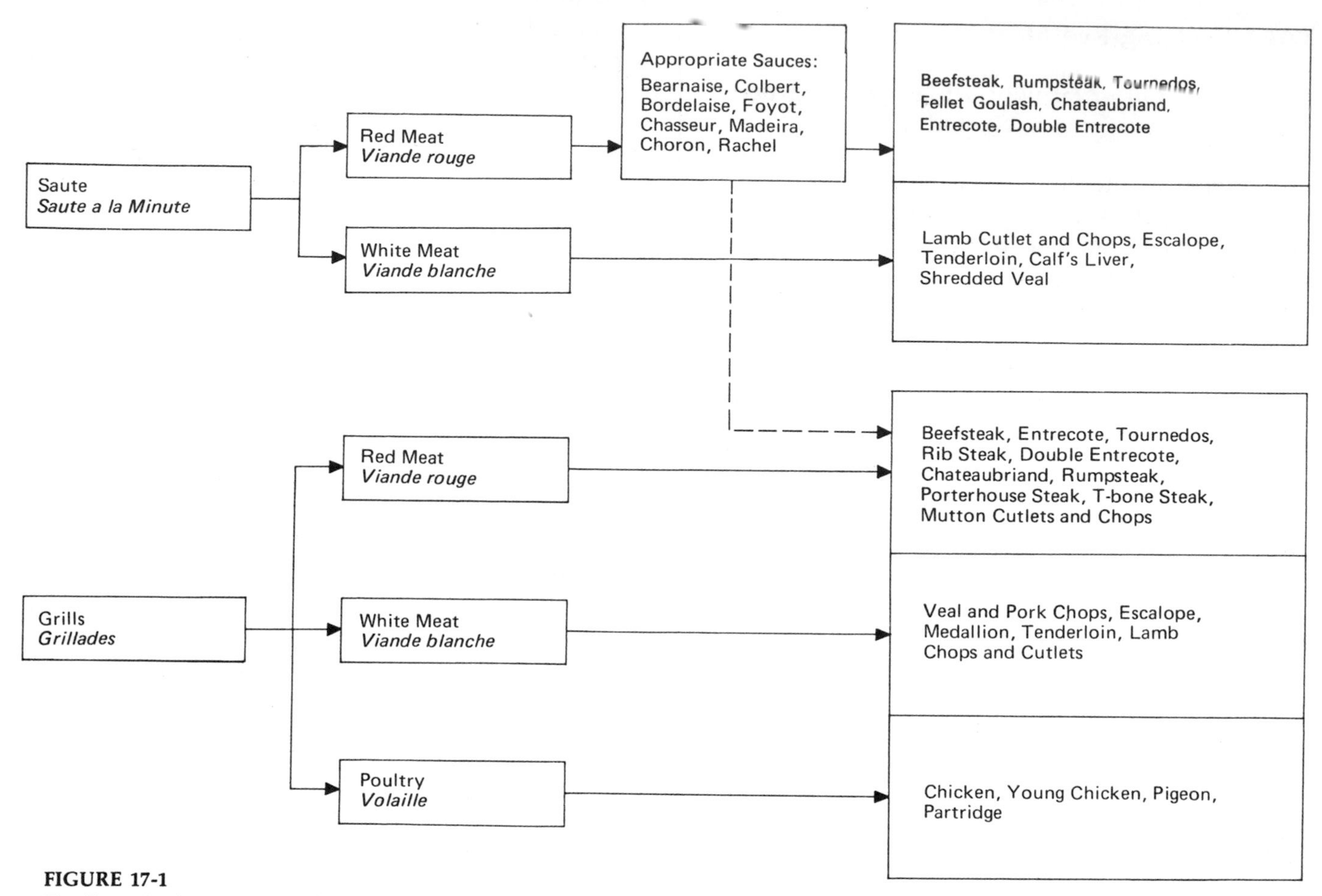

FIGURE 17-1
The Basic Cooking Methods for Hot Entrees

with strips of bacon. Melted butter is drizzled over the top of the dish.

Calf's Liver, Italian Style — Foie de veau a l'italienne. This is a platter of thin slices of sauteed liver covered with an Italian Sauce.

Sauteed Calf's Liver with Madeira Sauce — Foie de veau saute au madere. Thin slices of liver and chopped onion are sauteed in butter over high heat. The meat and onion are stirred constantly until lightly done. It is then seasoned with salt and pepper and removed from the pan. The pan drippings are deglazed with demi-glace and the sauce is heated to the boiling point. The liver is put back into the pan, and some Madeira is added. The liver is sprinkled with parsley and served immediately.

Sauteed Calf's Liver in a Rice Ring — Foi de veau saute en bordure. This liver is prepared as described under Sauteed Calf's Liver with Madeira Sauce. The meat is arranged on a platter and surrounded by a ring of rice.

Calf's Liver on Skewers — Foie de veau en brochette. Small slices of liver that have been seasoned and

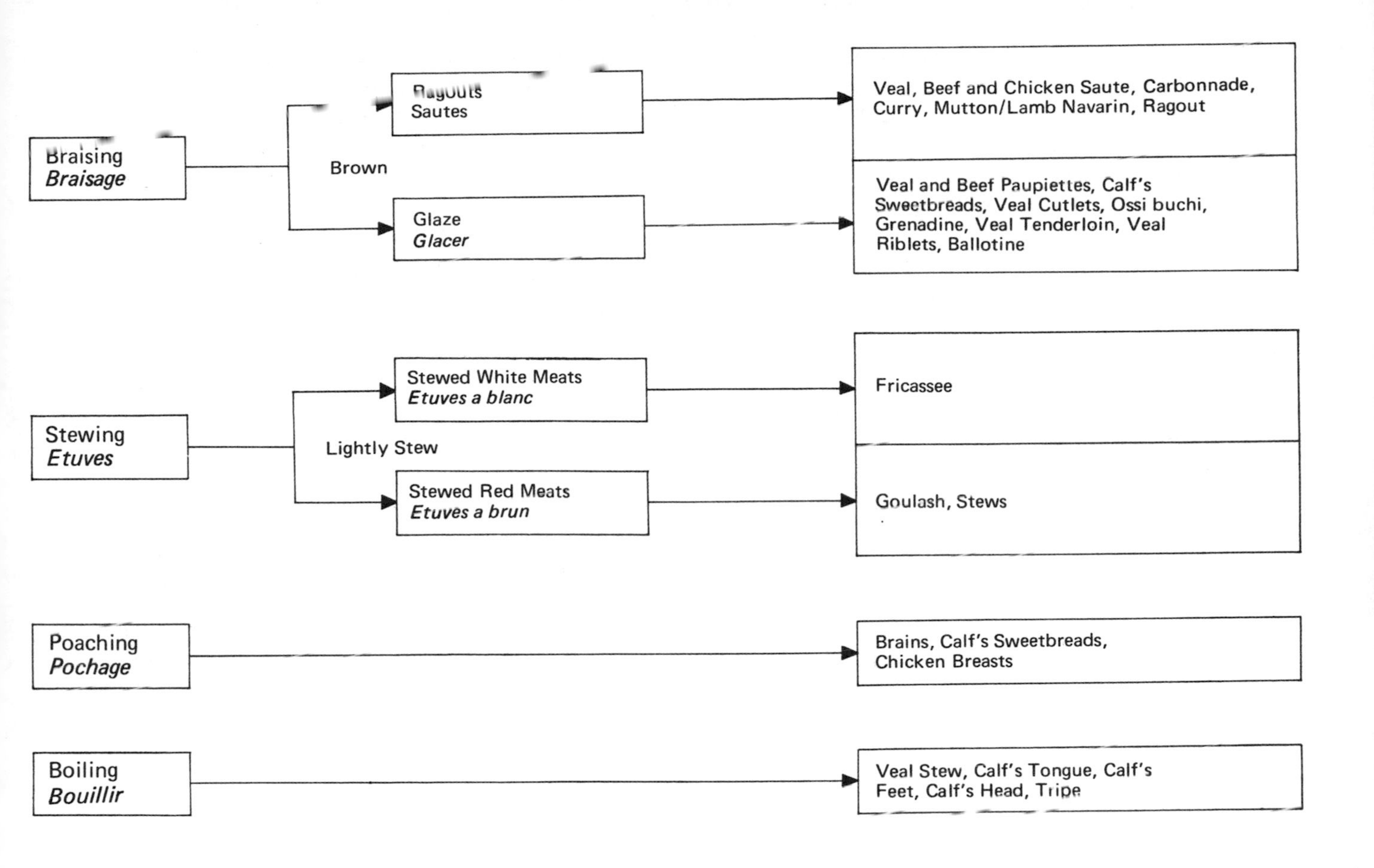

lightly sauteed in butter are arranged on skewers alternating the liver, lean bacon slices, and mushrooms. They are coated with dry duxelles, breaded, and grilled or sauteed. A Duxelles Sauce is served separately.

Goose Liver, Strasbourg Style — Foie gras a la strasbourgoise. A fresh goose liver, sliced, seasoned, and coated with flour, is sauteed quickly in butter. Thick slices of peeled apples are stewed in butter in the oven, until they are soft. Round bread croutons, sauteed in butter, are arranged on a platter and covered with the apple slices. The goose liver slices are placed on top and coated with a demi-glace seasoned to taste with port wine.

Sweetbread Medallions — Escalopes de ris de veau. Cutlets are sliced from blanched sweetbreads, seasoned, coated with flour, and sauteed in butter.

Veal Chop Nelson — Cote de veau Nelson. These veal chops are sauteed on one side and that side is spread with an onion puree (soubise). The chop is then breaded and sauteed. A Tomato Sauce is served separately.

Veal Chop Pojarski — Cote de veau Pojarski. Ground veal, sauteed onion, cream, and seasonings are mixed together and formed into chop-shaped pieces. The pieces are breaded with fine white bread crumbs, sauteed in butter and garnished with young peas and asparagus spears. Beurre noisette is served separately.

Veal Chop en Papillote — Cote de veau en papillote. A piece of aluminum foil about three times as large as a veal chop is cut as indicated in Figure 7-40. The inside of the foil is greased with oil, and one-half the foil is covered with a sauteed slice of ham topped with a duxelles. A lightly sauteed veal chop is placed on top of the ham, then another layer of duxelles and, finally, a second sauteed slice of ham. The foil is folded into an airtight bag, and the meat is baked in a hot oven.

Note: A brown sauce served in a sauce boat usually accompanies this dish.

Veal Cutlets, Bonne Femme Style — Cotelettes de veau bonne femme. The cutlets are sauteed as described on page 377. They are garnished with small onions and potato slices. The sauce and garnishes are poured over the finished cutlet.

Veal Cutlets in Cocottes—Cotelletes de veau en cocotte. This is a combination of sauteed veal cutlet served in a cocotte with small onions, potato balls, and raw mushrooms.

Veal Cutlets, Holstein Style—Escalope de veau Holstein. Unbreaded veal cutlets, sauteed in butter, are topped with fried eggs surrounded with anchovy fillets. Veal stock is served separately.

Veal Chops "Maitre Paul" — Cotes de veau "Maitre Paul". (a la carte dish for 2 persons). Season trimmed chops, dust with flour, and brown quickly as described in recipe 17.1.2. Bind grated Sbrinz and tomatoes concassees with egg, and season. Spread the mixture on top of the chop and brown under the broiler. Arrange in a serving pan and garnish with vegetables (in the Illustration on page 389 it is braised lettuce) and potatoes Anna prepared in individual timbales.

Breast of Veal, Mayor's Style — Il piatto del sindaco. (a la carte dish for 4 persons). Fold trimmed slices of calf's breast, truss, and glaze as described in Section 17.3.2. Then loosen the string, place the slices on a round serving platter and sprinkle with a sauteed julienne of sweet peppers.

Garnishes: Timbales of saffron rice, tomatoes filled with chanterelles, celery bottoms filled with sweet corn, ham, and bouquets of broccoli. *Courtesy of Rundschau: Hotel & Gastgewerbe (Zurich: Forster-Verlag AG).* (See illustration page 389.)

Veal Tenderloin Medallions "Three Musketeers" — Medaillons de veau "Trois Mousquetaires." (a la carte dish for 2 persons). Fill four uniform artichoke bottoms with creamed morels. Saute 4 tenderloin medallions and 4 slices of veal kidney in butter and place one on top of each artichoke bottom. Place the meat, garnished with tomatoes concassees and a mushroom cap, on a sword-shaped skewer. Serve thin sauteed string beans and pommes a la venitienne in clusters around the meat. (See illustration page 390.)

Venison Cutlets, Belle Forestiere Style — Cotelletes de chevreuil belle forestiere. Season trimmed venison cutlets and saute until they are rose, as described in Section 17.1.1. Flambe with gin. Saute mushrooms with shallots and season. At the last minute, add chopped parsley and a little glace de viande to the mushrooms. Arrange the mushrooms on a platter and place the venison chops on top. Garnish with brussels sprouts, marrons glaces, potatoes Williams, and peach halves filled with cranberries. *Courtesy of Rundschau: Hotel & Gastgewerbe (Zurich: Forster-Verlag AG).* (See illustration page 390.)

Veal Cutlets with Paprika — Escalope de veau au paprika. Sauteed veal cutlets are deglazed with cream and fond lie (thickened stock), reduced slightly, and seasoned to taste with lemon juice and paprika. The sauce is poured over the cutlet.

Veal Cutlets, Swiss Style — Steak de veau suisse. (See page 468.)

Veal Cutlets, Viennese Style I—Escalope de veau viennoise. These cutlets are breaded and sauteed. A slice of lemon with a ring of anchovy fillets is placed on top of each cutlet. An olive, stuffed with capers, is placed in the ring. Small heaps of chopped hard-cooked egg whites and yolks, and capers are arranged around the cutlet. Hot butter is poured over the top.

Veal Cutlets, Viennese Style II—Escalope de veau viennoise. Two connected slices of veal cutlet, from the rump, are pounded through a wet towel, breaded, and sauteed in a mixture of butter and oil. The cutlets are served on a paper napkin with a lemon wedge.

Grenadines of Veal — Grenadins de veau. These thick cutlets of veal top round are prepared as described in the basic method. Tomatoes are added to the gravy, and it is thickened slightly.

Sauteed Veal Kidneys with Mushrooms — Rognons de veau sautes aux champignons. These veal kidneys are prepared in the same way as Sauteed Calf's Liver with Madeira Sauce, substituting finely sliced calf's kidney for the liver. Mushrooms that have been sauteed in butter are served over the top.

Sliced Veal Saute — Emince de veau saute. This dish is prepared by the same method used for Sauteed Calf's Liver in Madeira. It is prepared with thin slices of fillet or top round of veal, and it is cooked to the medium or well-done stage.

Veal Steak Zingara — Steak de veau Zingara. This veal steak is seasoned with salt and paprika and sauteed in butter. The steak is cooked with a Zingara Sauce and topped with a sauteed slice of ham.

Venison Cutlets, Baden-Baden Style — Escalopes de chevreuil Baden-Baden. These cutlets are seasoned, dusted with flour, and sauteed. The pan is deglazed with white wine, demi-glace, and cream. The sauce is reduced and the fat is skimmed off. It is seasoned with cayenne and lemon juice and strained. The cutlets are garnished with pear halves filled with cranberries. The sauce is served separately.

Venison Cutlets, Hunter's Style — Escalopes de chevreuil chasseur. These cutlets are prepared exactly the same as the Venison Cutlets, Baden-Baden Style. They are garnished with mushrooms, brussels sprouts, turnips, and pommes fondantes (page 239). Sauce and red currant jelly are served separately.

Venison Cutlets Mirza — Escalopes de chevreuil Mirza. These are prepared in the same way as Venison Cutlets, Baden-Baden Style. Peeled apples are hollowed out and stewed in white wine with sugar. They are filled with red currant jelly and used as a garnish around the venison cutlets. The sauce is served separately.

17.1.4 Garnishes for Sauteed and Grilled Dishes

17.1.4.1 For Beef

Beef Steak, Tournedos, Chateaubriand, Sirloin Steak, Rump Steak

American — a l'americaine. A fried egg with slices of sauteed lean bacon. The steak is topped with the egg and bacon and garnished with peas. A demi-glace blended with tomatoes is served separately.

Belle Helene Style — belle Helene. Tournedos on toasted rounds of bread garnished with asparagus tips and sliced truffles. A sauce is served separately.

Bordeaux Style — a la bordelaise. Tournedos on round slices of toasted bread, covered with slices of poached marrow. A Bordelaise Wine Sauce is served separately.

FIGURE 17-2
Tournedos Casino

Tournedos Casino. A tournedo arranged on a base of spinach leaves, covered with a mushroom cap with dot of truffle in the center, and surrounded with a ring of stuffed olives. Madeira Sauce is served separately.

Choron — Choron. Artichoke hearts filled with peas or asparagus tips, and potato balls placed beside the

steak. A Choron Sauce is served separately. The tournedos are served on round slices of toasted bread.
Dubarry — Dubarry. A bouquet of cauliflower and potato balls that is especially attractive with a sirloin steak. A sauce is served separately.
with an Egg — a cheval. A fried egg garnish placed on top of a beef steak or tournedo. A sauce may be served separately.
Florentine Style — a la florentine. A base of spinach with semolina gnocchis arranged on each side of the meat. A Madeira Sauce is served separately.
Forestiere Style — a la forestiere. The meat is covered with a Madeira Sauce and slices of bacon and garnished with Parmentier potatoes.
Helder Style — Helder. This garnish is prepared by sauteing tomato halves, and filling them with Bearnaise Sauce. Potato balls, browned in butter, and the tomatoes are arranged on a platter with tournedos. A Madeira Sauce is served separately.
with Herb Butter — a la maitre d'hotel. Slices of herb butter. The steak is topped with herb butter. A gravy is served separately.
Hotelier Style — a la hotelier. Maitre d'hotel butter mixed with a duxelles. This is served under a sirloin steak. The steak is covered with gravy.
Lyon Style — a la lyonnaise. Onion browned in butter and a demi-glace. The steak is covered with sauteed onion and coated with a demi-glace.
with Mushrooms — aux champignons. The meat is covered with a Chasseur Sauce and garnished with a ring of mushroom caps.
Provence Style — a la provencale. Tomatoes Provence Style (see page 446) and mushrooms. The tournedos are served on toasted rounds of bread and topped with Tomatoes Provence Style and surrounded with mushrooms. A Madeira Sauce is served separately.
Rossini — Rossini. (For tournedos.) Thick slices of goose liver and slices of truffles. The tournedos are served on toasted rounds of bread and topped with a garnish of goose liver and truffles. A Madeira Sauce may surround the meat or it may be served separately.
Tyrolian Style — a la tyrolienne. Sauteed onion rings and tomatoes concassees. Gravy (jus) is served separately.

17.1.4.2 For Veal

Chops, Cutlets, Small Tenderloin Steaks, and Medallions
Asparagus — Argenteuil. Asparagus spears and potato balls. This is a garnish for sauteed veal. A gravy is served separately.
Bonne Femme Style — bonne femme. (For veal cutlets) This recipe is characterized by the simultaneous cooking of the meat and the garnish in the same pan. Season, cover, and saute the meat; then stew in butter in a cocotte or a saute pan. Garnish: peeled onions and blanched potatoes cut into rings. Add a little veal stock to the cooked meat and serve.
Note: With larger quantities, the garnish should be cooked separately.
English Style — a l'anglaise. The meat is breaded in the English fashion, sauteed in butter, and covered with slices of sauteed ham.
Milan Style — milanaise. The meat is breaded with white bread crumbs mixed with grated cheese. It is garnished with buttered spaghetti which is sprinkled with a julienne of ham, tongue, mushrooms, and truffles that have been sauteed in butter. Madeira Sauce or gravy is served separately.
Naples Style — napolitaine. The sauteed meat is garnished with Spaghetti napolitaine (recipe page 450). A sauce is served separately.
Paysanne Style — paysanne. A strip of fried lean bacon, glazed pearl onions, and fried potatoes. The

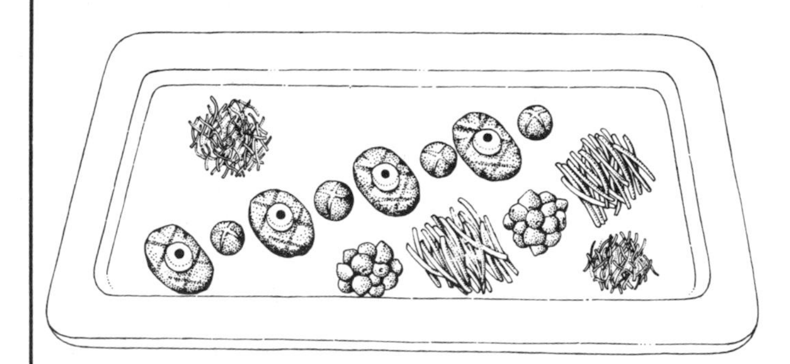

FIGURE 17-3
Veal Tenderloin Medallions with Goose Liver — Noisettes de veau au foie gras

garnish is placed on top of the Veal Saute. It is covered with gravy and sprinkled with parsley.
Veal Tenderloin Medallions with Goose Liver Pate — Noisettes de veau au foie gras. Grilled veal tenderloin medallions covered with slices of goose liver pate and truffles, served on toasted rounds of bread, and garnished with string beans, young carrots, pommes paille (julienne potatoes), and small tomatoes. A gravy (jus) is served separately.

17.1.4.3 For Pork

For Chops and Cutlets
The following are garnishes and/or side dishes: spring vegetables (printaniere), carrots and turnips, red cabbage (may be covered with apple slices), brussels sprouts with chestnuts, small stuffed cabbage rolls, spinach leaves sauteed in butter, applesauce, glazed apple slices (apple stew), baked or sauteed potatoes.
Bonne Femme Style — bonne femme. Small glazed onions, carrots, mushroom quarters, and sauteed slices of bacon. Pork chops or cutlets are covered with the garnish and served with fried potatoes. A sauce is served separately.
Brussels Style — a la bruxelloise. Brussels sprouts and fried potatoes.
Flemish Style — a la flamande. Braised chicories and deep-fat fried potatoes. Sauteed pork cutlets or chops are topped with the garnish and coated with demiglace.
Italian Style — a l'italienne. Quartered artichoke hearts and Italian Sauce. The sauteed chops or cutlets are surrounded with the garnish and covered with Italian Sauce.
Paysanne Style — a la paysanne. Sauteed slices of lean bacon, glazed onions, and fried potatoes. The chops or cutlets are garnished on both sides with the onions and potatoes, topped with a strip of bacon, and covered with gravy and a sprinkling of parsley.
Robert — Robert. The sauteed meat is covered with a Robert Sauce.
Zingara Style — Zingara. The sauteed meat is covered with Zingara Sauce.

17.1.4.4 For Mutton and Lamb

For Chops and Cutlets
Asparagus — Argenteuil. Asparagus tips and fried potatoes. The garnish is for sauteed or grilled mutton or lamb chops. A gravy is served separately.
Florentine Style — a la florentine. Buttered spinach leaves and potatoes fondantes. A Madeira Sauce is served separately.
Italian Style — a l'italienne. Artichoke hearts covered with Italian Sauce. Sauteed mutton or lamb chops are surrounded with the garnish.
Lyons Style — a la lyonnaise. Sauteed or grilled meat, covered with onion sauteed in butter. A ring of demiglace sauce is poured around the meat.
Marshall Style — a la marechal. Truffle slices and asparagus tips. Mutton or lamb chops are breaded in the English fashion, sauteed, and covered with truffle slices and served with asparagus tips.
Nelson — Nelson. Sauteed chops are coated with a soubise, sprinkled with bread crumbs, and garnished with potato croquettes. A Madeira Sauce is served separately.
Provence Style — a la provencale. Small, peeled, baked tomatoes stuffed with a duxelles and with mushrooms. The chops are surrounded with the garnish.
Shepherd's Style — a la bergere. Sauteed slices of ham, morels, and small glazed onions.

17.2 Broiling/Grilling — Griller

The red meat cuts described in the section, sautes a la minute, are suitable for grilling. To sear the meat and seal its juices, the grill is placed close to the heat. As soon as the meat is seared, the grill is placed within 3 or 4 inches (7.5 or 10 centimeters) of the source of heat, and the meat is cooked to the desired degree of doneness.

Note: Before grilling, clean the grill thoroughly and grease with oil or meat fat. Preheat the metal grill before placing the meat on it.

17.2.1 Broiling/Grilling Red Meat

Ingredients: Oil with a high smoking point, salt, pepper, and a marinade.

Preparation: Baste the pieces of meat, tied where appropriate, with oil, season, and grill on both sides so that the grill bars are branded onto the meat. Baste with oil frequently. The length of time on the grill depends on the size, cut, and quality of the piece of meat. See Section 17.1 for determining the degree of doneness.

Note: Grilled food is usually salted immediately after grilling. Larger pieces of meat should stand for a few minutes after grilling so that the heat is distributed evenly throughout the piece of meat and the juices are retained. Serve a seasoned butter sauce or herb butter with the meat.

17.2.2 Broiling/Grilling White Meat

Ingredients: Oil with a high melting point, salt, and seasoning.

Preparation: Baste the pieces of meat with oil and grill over medium heat.

Note: Breaded meat should not be grilled. Since there is much less juice in white meat than red meat, either a special sauce or a strong thickened veal stock may be served with it. Usually, however, white meat is served plain with a wedge of lemon.

17.2.3 Broiling/Grilling Poultry

Ingredients: Oil with a high melting point, salt, and seasoning.

Preparation: Cut a leaned fowl lengthwise along the back (see page 237), and remove about ⅓ or ½ inch (.8 or 1.2 centimeters) of the backbone. Tuck the legs into the slits that have been pierced through the skin and press the pieces flat. Place the chicken on the grill, skin side down, baste, and grill until tender. Remove the breastbone and carve the bird.

Note: The bird should be basted frequently during broiling or grilling.

17.2.4 Variations of Broiled/Grilled Meats

Grilled Chicken, American Style — Poulet grille a l'americaine. Cut a cleaned chicken along the back (see illustration, page 237), remove the backbone, flatten the chicken, and tuck the legs into slits in the skin. Season with salt and mustard powder mixed with a pinch of cayenne pepper. Baste with oil and grill until it is almost done. Turn and baste with butter frequently. Sprinkle with white bread crumbs (mie de pain) or bread lightly. Strips of lean bacon and halved, seeded, seasoned tomatoes are grilled and used as a garnish with potato chips. A Deviled Sauce or a hot maitre d'hotel butter may be served separately.

Grilled Chicken with Deviled Sauce — Poulet grille a la diable. This chicken is prepared as described in the method for Grilled Chicken, American Style. The chicken is served on a platter garnished with a lemon wedge and watercress or parsley. A Deviled Sauce is served separately.

Grilled Fillet of Beef, "Thirteen Stars" — Tournedos grilles "Treize Etoiles." Tournedos are grilled together with calf's liver and kidneys. The meat is arranged on skewers with chipolata sausages and mushroom caps, and placed on round slices of toasted bread. Garnishes: Tiny tartlets made of short crust pastry filled with peas, French Style; sauteed tomatoes filled with creamed morels. Fresh asparagus and potatoes venitienne are arranged on the platter with the meat.

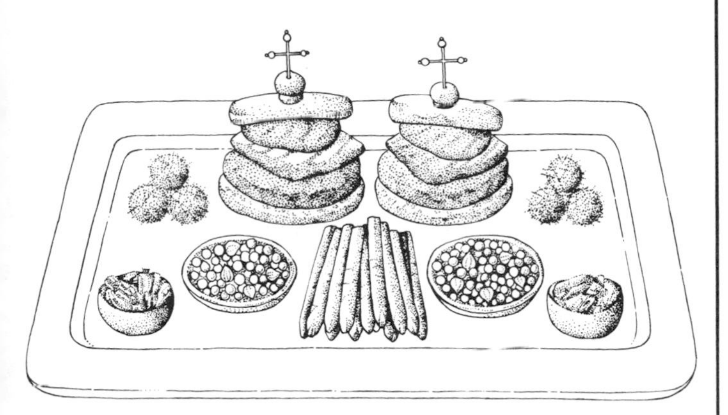

FIGURE 17-4
Grilled Tournedos, "Thirteen Stars" – Tournedos grilles "Treize etoiles"

Mixed Grill, American Style – Mixed grill a l'americaine. A mixed grill is garnished with tomatoes and crisp bacon and covered with foaming hot butter. A demi-glace sauce, with a little black pepper, is served separately.
Porterhouse Steak. An English and American cut of meat, the steak is cut at the thickest part of the sirloin close to the loin, and includes both the loin and the tenderloin. (See illustration, page 237.) The following are used as garnishes: potato chips, grilled tomatoes and bacon, sweet corn, or a black pepper sauce consisting of a demi-glace with a reduced stock of shallots, black peppercorns, and white wine. It may also be served as the grosse piece.
Rib of Beef – Cote de boeuf. Grill and garnish as for sauteed beef dishes. (See Section 17.1.4.1.) The grill is placed close to the source of heat to sear the meat and seal its juices. As soon as the meat is seared, the grill is placed within 3 inches (7.5 centimeters) of the source of heat and the meat is cooked to the desired degree of doneness.
T-bone Steak. This American cut of meat is similar to the Porterhouse steak, but cut from a piece closer to the ribs. (See illustration, page 232.) The garnishes suggested for Porterhouse steak may be used.
Viennese Minute Steak – Wiener Rostbraten. This is a sirloin steak cut from the front part of the loin, cooked on a grill, garnished with sauteed onion rings, and surrounded with a rich gravy.
Garnishes for grilled dishes, see Section 17.1.4.

17.3 Braising – Braiser

The section on sautes a la minute referred to those preparations involving fast sauteing with butter, oil, or fat. The term braising refers to preparations involving a *rapid browning* of the food, followed, however, by further braising in a stock or sauce. The two main groups are:

- ragouts – sautes
- glazed pieces of meat – viande glacee

The derivations of these categories are fully described under the basic principles of hot entrees. These groups should not be confused with stewed meat (goulashes, stews, fricassees); the latter are never browned.

17.3.1 Ragouts – Sautes

The following are the main ragout/saute preparations:

Veal Saute – Saute de veau
Beef Saute – Saute de boeuf
Chicken Saute – Poulet saute
Saute with Curry – Saute au curry
Mutton Ragout – Navarin de Mouton
Game Ragout – Civet de gibier
Carbonade – Carbonnade
The terms "saute" and "ragout" are identical, since the meat is first browned and then braised in a liquid.

17.3.1.1 Veal Saute (Saute de veau)

YIELD: *approximately 10 servings*

INGREDIENTS	*U.S. Weight or Volume*	*Metric Weight or Volume*	PROCEDURE
Veal, breast or neck, cut in 1½ ounce (45 grams) cubes	3 to 4 pounds	1½ to 2 kilograms	1. Brown the meat cubes, a small amount at a time, in the hot oil.
Oil	1¾ ounces	50 grams	2. Add the bouquet garni and garlic and continue browning for a few minutes. Drain the excess oil.
Bouquet garni	1	1	3. Place the meat in a suitable container. Season.
Garlic clove	1	1	
Salt	½ teaspoon	3 grams	
Pepper	1/8 teaspoon	1 gram	
White wine	¾ cup	2 deciliters	4. Deglaze the pan drippings with the white wine, and reduce the liquid to a syrup-like consistency (glace). Add the tomato puree, the demi-glace, and the basic stock to the meat.
Tomato puree	2 tablespoons	30 milliliters	
Basic stock	1 pint	½ liter	
Demi-glace	1 pint	½ liter	5. Cover and braise the meat for 1 hour or until it is tender. If excessive evaporation occurs, add more stock.
Madeira	¼ cup	½ deciliter	6. Remove the bouquet garni, strain the sauce, and add the Madeira. If necessary, the reduced stock can be thickened with a little cornstarch mixed with water.

Note: A mirepoix may be used instead of a bouquet garni with a saute. This is, however, time consuming and not necessary since the demi-glace was made with a mirepoix.

Variations of Veal Saute

Veal Saute, Marengo Style—Saute de veau Marengo. The finished saute is garnished with small glazed onions, sliced and buttered mushrooms, and surrounded with heart-shaped bread croutons.
Veal Saute with Mushrooms — Saute de veau aux champignons. This Veal Saute is covered with sliced mushrooms that have been sauteed in butter.
Veal Saute with Noodles—Saute de veau aux nouilles. This is Veal Saute garnished with noodles.
Veal Saute, Sailor's Style — Matelote de veau. This dish is prepared by deglazing Veal Saute with red wine and flambeing it with brandy.
Veal Saute with Spring Vegetables — Saute de veau printaniere. The finished Veal Saute is garnished with glazed carrots, turnips, celery, pearl onions, and peas.

17.3.1.2 Beef Saute — Saute de boeuf

Meat from the rump of beef is recommended for this dish. It is prepared in the same way as Veal Saute, although a longer cooking time is required.

The centerpiece pictured at right is a decorated lobster with the tail cut into attractive medallions, and the claws properly opened. The square glass dishes contain: slices of sole filled with a salmon mousse, slices of quail terrine, of poached salmon, of smoked eel, of smoked salmon, medallions of lobster and goose liver, and Russian salad with eggs and caviar. Courtesy of Rundschau: Hotel Gastgewerbe (Zurich: Forster—Verlag AG).

Hors d'oeuvre Diplomat Style – *Hors-d'oeuvre diplomate*

… Tart Lorraine – *Quiche Lorraine*

River Trout Old Bern Style – *Truite de riviere "Vieux Berne"*

Veal Chops "Maitre Paul"
Cotes de veau "Maitre Paul"

Breast of Veal, Mayor's Style
Il Piatto del sindaco

Veal Tenderloin Medallions "Three Musketeers" Style
Medaillons de veau "Trois Mousquetaires"

Venison Cutlets, Belle Forestiere Style
Cotellettes de chevreuil belle forestiere

17.3.1.3 Chicken Saute (Poulet saute)

YIELD: *approximately 10 servings*

INGREDIENTS	*U.S. Weight or Volume*	*Metric Weight or Volume*
Chicken	6 to 7 pounds	3 kilograms
Flour	8 ounces	240 grams
Oil	1¾ ounces	50 milliliters
Shallots, chopped	1¾ ounces	50 grams
White wine	½ cup	1 deciliter
Demi-glace	1 pint	½ liter
Brandy	1 ounce	30 milliliters
Salt	2 teaspoons	12 grams
Pepper	½ teaspoon	3 grams

PROCEDURE

Preparation I

1. Disjoint the chickens. **(See page 237.)**
2. Season and lightly dust the pieces with flour.
3. Heat the oil in a saute pan and *brown* the pieces of chicken on all sides. Add the shallots and saute lightly.
4. Cover the pan and complete the cooking in the oven at 350°F. (175°C.).
5. Remove the wings and breast after about 8 minutes and the legs after 15 minutes. Place in a warm container.
6. Prepare the sauce in the saute pan. Skim off the fat. Deglaze with white wine, reduce, add the demi-glace, and reduce before seasoning. Add the brandy. Add the pieces of chicken and let them simmer in the sauce for a few minutes.
7. Arrange the pieces in a serving dish and strain the sauce over them.

Preparation II

1. Disjoint the chickens. **(See page 237.)**
2. Season and lightly dust the pieces with flour.
3. Heat the oil in a saute pan and saute the pieces *only* until they turn a light gray color.
4. Cover the pan and complete the cooking in the oven at 350°F. (175°C.).
5. Remove the wings and breast after about 8 minutes and the legs after 15 minutes. Place in a warm container.
6. Prepare the sauce in the saute pan as in step 6 above, or the sauce may consist of 1 pint (5 deciliters) of Supreme Sauce, Allemande Sauce, Bechamel Sauce, or cream alone. Add the chicken to the sauce and simmer a few minutes.
7. Arrange the chicken pieces in a serving dish and strain the sauce over them.

Note: Even though served in a sauce, sauteed chicken is not a ragout. It is prepared in fat in the saute pan like a veal chop, followed by the deglazing and preparation of the accompanying sauce. The pieces are left to simmer a few minutes. If the chicken is entirely cooked in the sauce, then the dish is named differently: Chicken Curry, Chicken Fricassee, or Coq au vin. The garnishes are then usually cooked in the saute pan with the chicken, although they sometimes require longer cooking than the chicken. When large quantities are involved, the garnishes are cooked separately.

Variations of Chicken Saute

Chicken Saute, Archduke Style — Poulet saute archiduc. This chicken is sauteed without browning. It is deglazed with sherry, port, and whisky. The sauce is reduced, strained, and whipped with fresh butter. Lemon juice is added and the chicken is coated with the sauce and garnished with a julienne of truffles.

Chicken Saute Beaulieu — Poulet saute Beaulieu. Sauteed and browned chicken pieces are added to small, slightly browned new potatoes and quartered artichoke hearts that have been fried in butter. The chicken and vegetables are placed in a cocotte with pitted olives. The saute pan is deglazed with white wine and lemon juice. Reduced veal stock is added, and the sauce is boiled for one to two minutes and poured over the chicken. The cocotte is covered and heated in the oven at 325°F. (160°C.) for 15 minutes.

Chicken Saute, Hunter's Style — Poulet saute chasseur. This chicken is sauteed and browned and placed in a cocotte. Sliced raw mushrooms and chopped shallots are sauteed in butter and added to tomato concassee, white wine, and demi-glace. The sauce is simmered a few minutes and seasoned to taste. Chervil, chopped parsley, and a few drops of lemon juice are added to the sauce before pouring it over the chicken.

Chicken Saute, Piemontese Style — Poulet saute a la piemontaise. White sliced truffles, sauteed in butter, are added to the finished chicken, and it is served in a ring of rice.

Chicken Saute, Portuguese Style — Poulet saute a la portugaise. The finished chicken is garnished with sauteed sliced mushrooms and surrounded with small tomatoes stuffed with rice.

Chicken Saute Stanley — Poulet Saute Stanley. Sauteed chicken and blanched sliced onions are arranged in a cocotte. Cream, a Supreme or Bechamel Sauce, and a dash of whiskey are simmered for a few minutes and strained through a cheesecloth. The sauce is heated to the boiling point, whipped with fresh butter, seasoned to taste, and poured over the chicken pieces.The chicken is garnished with sliced truffles and croutons.

Chicken Saute with Tarragon — Poulet saute a l'estragon. A sauce flavored with tarragon is poured over the chicken and covered with blanched tarragon leaves.

Chicken saute with Truffles — Poulet saute aux truffles. Sauteed chicken is garnished with sliced truffles that have been sauteed in Madeira.

Saute of Chicken Breast — Supremes de volaille sautes. This breast of chicken is browned and sauteed with brown stock in the same way as Chicken Saute. It may be served on toasted white bread and garnished.

Rabbit Saute — Saute de lapin. This dish is prepared by the method used for Chicken Saute, using rabbit instead of chicken.

17.3.1.4 Lamb Ragout (Navarin)

YIELD: *approximately 10 servings*

INGREDIENTS	*U.S. Weight or Volume*	*Metric Weight or Volume*	PROCEDURE
Lamb, neck or shoulder, cut in 1½ ounces (45 grams) cubes	4 pounds	2 kilograms	1. Brown small portions of the meat in hot oil until all of it is browned. Add the onion and garlic. Brown all ingredients for a few more minutes. Season.
Oil	1¾ ounces	50 grams	2. Drain off excess oil.
Onion, chopped	3½ ounces	100 grams	3. Place the meat in a baking dish.
Garlic clove	1	1	
Salt	1 teaspoon	6 grams	
Pepper	¼ teaspoon	2 grams	
Red wine	¾ cup	2 deciliters	4. Deglaze the pan with red wine. Reduce the liquid to a glace.
Brown stock	1 pint	½ liter	5. Add the brown stock, the demi-glace, and the tomatoes. Pour over the meat.
Demi-glace	1 pint	½ liter	
Tomatoes, fresh, peeled, diced	1 pound	500 grams	6. Cover the baking dish and braise for 1 hour in the oven at 350°F. (175°C.). Strain the sauce and pour back over the meat.
OR			
Tomato puree	2 tablespoons	30 grams	
Onions, small, whole	10 ounces	300 grams	7. Add the small onions and potato balls. Continue braising until the meat is tender.
Potato balls, small blanched	10 ounces	300 grams	8. Serve with garnishes.

Variations of Lamb Ragout

Lamb Ragout with Spring Vegetables — Navarin a la printaniere. The ragout is prepared by the method used for Lamb Ragout. Carrots and turnips are added.

Note: The vegetables may be cooked or browned separately and served on the ragout.

Mutton Cassoulet — Cassoulet de mouton. (See page 469.)

Mutton Pilaf — Pilav de mouton. (See page 470.)

Mutton Ragout with Navy Beans — Haricot de mouton. (See page 470.)

17.3.1.5 Venison Ragout (Civet de chevreuil)

YIELD: *approximately 10 servings*

INGREDIENTS	*U.S. Weight or Volume*	*Metric Weight or Volume*
Venison, boneless breast or shoulder cut in 1½ ounce (45 grams) cubes	4 pounds	2 kilograms
Marinade:		
Red wine	1 quart	1 liter
Wine vinegar	¾ cup	2 deciliters
Mirepoix	8 ounces	240 grams
Juniper berries	4	4
Bay leaves	2	2
Peppercorns	6	6
Oil	3½ ounces	100 grams
Flour	3 ounces	80 grams
Salt	2 teaspoons	12 grams
Stock	1 quart	1 liter
Bacon, diced, browned	5 ounces	150 grams
Onions, small glazed	7 ounces	200 grams
Mushrooms, sauteed	10 ounces	300 grams
Bread, fried heart-shaped slices **(see page 244)**	10	10

PROCEDURE

1. Place the meat in the marinade for 8 to 10 days. Drain thoroughly. Separate the meat from the mirepoix.
2. Brown the meat pieces quickly in hot oil. Add the mirepoix and continue sauteing.
3. Dust with flour and saute further until the flour is browned.
4. Bring the marinade to a boil. Strain and pour the marinade and the stock over the meat.
5. Season to taste and cook until the meat is tender.
6. If excessive evaporation occurs, add more stock.
7. Remove the meat from the sauce.
8. Strain the sauce and pour back over the meat.
9. Arrange the diced bacon, onions, mushrooms, and toast on top of the ragout as garnishes.

Note: In the original recipe ¾ cup (2 deciliters) of pork blood is added to the sauce before straining it. Due to inspection and sanitation codes, this ingredient has been omitted. If sauce needs to be thickened, add 1 teaspoon of cornstarch, dissolved in water, and stir continuously.

Variations of Venison Ragout

Bonne Femme Style — Bonne femme. **(See page 470.)**
Chamois Ragout — Civet de chamois. This dish is prepared by the same method as the one used in Venison Ragout.

Hare Ragout (hasenpfeffer) — Civet de lievre. This dish is prepared by the method described for Venison Ragout. The whole animal is cut into appropriate sized pieces and braised with the bones.
Red Deer Ragout — Civet de cerf. The method described for Venison Ragout is followed for this dish.

17.3.1.6 Carbonades of Beef (Carbonnades de boeuf)

YIELD: *approximately 10 servings*

INGREDIENTS	*U.S. Weight or Volume*	*Metric Weight or Volume*
Round steak OR Boneless chuck	4 to 5 pounds	2 to 2½ kilograms
Fat	3½ ounces	100 grams
Salt	2 teaspoons	12 grams
Pepper	½ teaspoon	3 grams
Onion, finely chopped	1 pound	500 grams
Flour, browned	1½ ounces	40 grams
Dark beer	1 pint	½ liter
Brown stock	1 pint	½ liter
Bouquet garni	1	1

PROCEDURE

1. Cut the meat into 3 or 4 ounce (90 to 120 grams) pieces. Season and brown on both sides in the hot fat in a pan.
2. Brown the onion in the same hot fat.
3. In a braising pan, arrange alternate layers of meat and onion. Add the browned flour, the beer, the brown stock, and the bouquet garni.
4. Cover and braise for 1½ hours adding liquid if necessary.
5. **Drain the sauce (including the onion) off the meat. Boil the sauce. Skim the fat. Pour the strained sauce back over the meat.**

Variations of Carbonades of Beef

Carbonades, Flemish Style — Carbonnades a la flamande. The recipe for this dish is the same as the one for Carbonades of Beef; however, it may be made with either beef or pork. Vinegar is added to the

Carbonades of Pork — Carbonnades de porc. The recipe for this dish is the same as the one for Carbonades of Beef, using 3 ounce (90 gram) pieces of pork.
sauce. Boiled potatoes, steamed cabbage, and carrots are served with the meat.

17.3.1.7 Curries — Sautes au curry

All curry dishes are ragouts in which the meat has been slightly browned. Chicken, mutton or lamb, and veal curries are described under English National Dishes (Section 23.4).

17.3.2 Glazed Meats — Viande glacee

Ingredients: Vegetable fat or oil with a high smoking point, butter, salt, seasoning, mirepoix, tomato puree, wine, stock, and demi-glace.

Preparation: Cut the meat into serving portions and prefry all sides in either butter or fat. Sweetbreads should be blanched before frying. Place slices of bacon and onion, a few bay leaves, and the pieces of meat covered with butter, in a greased saute pan. Brown quickly over high heat. Pour a little veal stock over the meat, cover, and baste frequently. Reduce the stock to a glaze. Then pour on more stock until it reaches a level of $^1/_6$ of the height of the pieces of meat. Cover and braise in the oven until tender. Remove the pieces of meat, add a little stock and wine, bring to a boil, skim off the fat, strain, and season to taste, adding Madeira. For certain dishes, the gravy may be thickened with potato flour or brown sauce.

Tomato puree is often added to glazed veal, or sour cream is sometimes added to the thickened gravy. The meat pieces mentioned may be garnished by combining special garnishes or suitable flavorings with the sauce or gravy. For small quantities, the appropriate garnish is braised with the meat and served on top of the meat with the sauce. When this method is used, the slices of bacon and onion should not be placed in the saute pan before the meat.

Note: Small pieces of white meat, primarily veal and poultry, are glazed while the meat is braising. Glazing represents the braising of small pieces of white meat by stewing the meat in a small amount of stock under cover and subsequently glazing the meat in the reduced liquid without the cover.

17.3.2.1 Garnishes for Glazed Meats

- Dubarry—*Dubarry*
- Hunter's Style—*chasseur*
- Jardiniere Style—*a la jardiniere*
- with Mixed Vegetables—*a la macedoine*
- with Noodles—*aux nouilles*
- with Spring Peas—*aux petits pois*

17.3.2.2 Variations of Glazed Meats

Glazed Beef Birds — Paupiettes de boeuf glacees. These beef birds (slices from beef rump or shoulder) are prepared by the method described for Glazed Veal Birds, except a longer cooking time is required. (See page 397.)

Glazed Crepinettes (Crepinettes glacees)

YIELD: *10 servings*

INGREDIENTS	*U.S. Weight or Volume*	*Metric Weight or Volume*
Veal, lean boneless	1 pound	500 grams
Pork, lean boneless	1 pound	500 grams
Bacon, fresh, lean	1¼ pounds	600 grams
Dinner rolls	2	2
Milk	as needed	as needed
Onion, chopped and browned	3½ ounces	100 grams
Parsley, chopped	1 ounce	30 grams
Eggs	2	2
Salt	1 teaspoon	6 grams
Nutmeg	1/8 teaspoon	1 gram
Pepper	¼ teaspoon	2 grams
Butter	1 tablespoon	30 grams
Veal stock, brown	as needed	as needed
Madeira	¼ cup	½ deciliter

PROCEDURE

1. Soak the rolls in a little milk and squeeze dry.
2. Grind the veal, pork, bacon, rolls, and onion until very fine. Add the parsley and eggs.
3. Add seasonings.
4. Place the mixture on a dampened table and shape into finger-length sausages.
5. Flatten the sausages and envelope them in a suitable piece of caul (casing).
6. Saute the crepinettes in butter lightly on both sides.
7. Add brown veal stock to ½ the height of the crepinettes and baste while cooking to give them a glaze. Remove the crepinettes from the pan. Add Madeira to the gravy. Thicken if necessary before pouring over the crepinettes.

Glazed Calf's Sweetbreads—Ris de veau glace. Blanched sweetbreads are glazed according to the basic method (20 minutes). The reduced gravy is strained and whipped with fresh butter.

Chicken Legs, Stuffed — Ballotines de volaille. Boned chicken legs stuffed with a spicy mousseline forcemeat are browned lightly in butter with shallots. Veal stock is added to the pan, and the meat is braised in an oven at 325°F. (160°C.). The surface of the stuffed legs will be glazed by the reduced stock. When cooked, the chicken legs are removed, more stock is added to the pan, the fat is skimmed, the sauce is strained, and small quantities of Madeira and brandy are added. The sauce is thickened if necessary.

Chicken Wings, Stuffed — Ailerons de volaille farcis. The wings (without the bones) of capons and poulardes are used for this dish. It is prepared by the method described for Stuffed Chicken Legs.

Glazed Veal Birds — Paupiettes de veau glacees. Stuff veal cutlets (see illustration, page 242) with forcemeat (½ veal, ¼ pork, ¼ lean bacon). The birds are glazed as described in the basic method. The gravy is slightly bound and blended with Tomato Sauce.

Veal Birds with Mushrooms — Paupiettes de veau aux champignons. These veal birds are prepared by the same method as the one described for Glazed Veal Birds. Sliced mushrooms are added to the strained gravy. A mushroom cap is placed on each veal bird.

Veal Knuckle — Jarret de veau (osso buco). (See page 482.)

Glazed Veal Knuckle Slices — Rouelles de jarret de veau glacees. Veal knuckles, including the bones cut into slices 2½ inches (6.2 centimeters) thick are glazed according to the basic method. Tomatoes are added to the brown stock. The sauce is simmered, strained, and bound.

Veal Knuckle Slices, Bourgeoise Style — Rouelles de jarret de veau bourgeoise. The knuckles are prepared by the same method as the one described for Glazed Veal Knuckles. The meat is garnished with glazed carrots, turnips, and small onions.

Veal Riblets — Tendrons de veau. These individual portions of breast of veal (see illustration, page 233) are glazed as described in the basic method. The gravy is blended with tomatoes and served with the veal riblets.

Glazed Veal Tenderloin — Filet de veau glace. A trimmed and larded veal tenderloin is braised with a fine mirepoix, and a veal stock or a demi-glace. The cooked tenderloin is glazed and removed from the stock. The stock is seasoned, strained, and thickened with cornstarch.

17.4 Stewing/Simmering — Etuver

The term braising refers to methods of preparation in which the meat is quickly browned and then braised in a stock. *Viande etuvee* refers to all methods of preparation for entrees in which the meat is not browned first, but *only stewed.* The two main categories are:

- stewed white meats—*etuves a blanc (fricassees)*
- stewed red meats—*etuves a brun (goulaches et estouffades)*

17.4.1 Stewed White Meats — Etuves a blanc

Note: These include all fricassees. The meat, onion, and vegetables are placed in the pan and stewed for a short time without browning. A white stock or broth is used for deglazing. This form of preparation is especially suitable for veal and poultry. The same garnishes used for blanquette may be used. (See page 402.)

17.4.1.1 Veal Fricassee (Fricassee de veau)

YIELD: *approximately 10 servings*

INGREDIENTS	*U.S. Weight or Volume*	*Metric Weight or Volume*	PROCEDURE
Veal, boneless shoulder, breast or neck, cut in 1½ ounce (45 grams) pieces	4½ pounds	2 kilograms	1. Melt the butter in a saute pan. Add the onion and meat. Stew without browning.
Butter	1¾ ounces	50 grams	
Onion	5 ounces	150 grams	2. Dust the meat and onion with flour.
Flour	2 ounces	60 grams	
White wine	1¼ cups	3 deciliters	3. Add the wine, stock, bouquet garni, and the seasonings.
White stock	1¼ quarts	1.2 liters	
Bouquet garni	1	1	
Salt	2 teaspoons	12 grams	
Nutmeg	⅛ teaspoon	1 gram	4. Cover and simmer for about 1½ hours or until tender. Add liquid during this time if needed.
Pepper	½ teaspoon	3 grams	5. Remove the meat. Strain the sauce and reduce. Gradually add the cream and the lemon juice.
Cream	½ cup	1 deciliter	
Lemon juice	2 tablespoons	30 milliliters	6. Put the meat back into the sauce and heat.

Variations of Veal Fricassee

Chicken Fricassee — Fricassee de volaille. This dish is prepared by the method used for Veal Fricassee. The chicken is cut as described for Sauteed Chicken. (See page 237.)

Rabbit Fricassee — Fricassee de lapin. This is the same recipe as the one used for Veal Fricassee, substituting rabbit for the veal.

17.4.2 Stewed Red Meats — Etuves a brun

Note: These include the goulash dishes and simmered stews. The onion is simmered until the liquid has thickened to a glaze, then the brown stock and red wine are added. Rump and round of beef are usually used for stews and goulashes.

17.4.2.1 Hungarian Goulash (Goulache hungroise—Gulyas)

YIELD: *approximately 10 servings*

INGREDIENTS	*U.S. Weight or Volume*	*Metric Weight or Volume*	PROCEDURE
Rump, shoulder OR Round, boneless	4½ pounds	2 kilograms	1. Heat the fat in a heavy pan. Add the meat and onion. Stew, stirring occasionally until the juice coming from the meat has been completely reduced and a light glaze is formed.
Fat	2 ounces	60 grams	
Onion, finely chopped	14 ounces	400 grams	
Paprika, sweet, mild	2 tablespoons	30 grams	2. Add paprika, salt, and tomatoes OR tomato puree.
Salt	2 teaspoons	12 grams	
Tomatoes, peeled, seeded OR	1¼ pounds	600 grams	
Tomato puree	3½ ounces	100 grams	
Stock, brown	1¼ pints	6 deciliters	3. Pour in the stock and the wine.
Red wine	1¼ cups	3 deciliters	4. Cover and simmer for 1½ hours. Add the potato cubes and continue cooking until meat and potatoes are done. Add liquid during the cooking period if too much evaporation occurs.
Potatoes, cut into large cubes	1½ pounds	700 grams	

Note: In hotels and restaurants, the potatoes are usually cooked separately and added to the finished dish at service time.

Variation of Hungarian Goulash

Viennese Goulash — Goulach viennoise. The recipe for this dish is the same as the one for Hungarian Goulash, but with cubed veal from the shoulder or breast instead of beef, and white wine instead of red wine. Sour cream and lemon juice are added before serving. Cooking time: 1 hour.

17.4.2.2 Beef Stew (Estouffade de boeuf)

YIELD: *approximately 10 servings*

INGREDIENTS	*U.S. Weight or Volume*	*Metric Weight or Volume*
Beef rump, boneless cut in 1½-ounce (45 gram) pieces	4½ pounds	2 kilograms
Fat	2 ounces	60 grams
Bacon, large cubes	½ pound	250 grams
Onion, finely chopped	10 ounces	300 grams
Garlic, crushed	1 clove	1 clove
Salt	2 teaspoons	12 grams
Pepper	½ teaspoon	3 grams
Bouquet garni	1	1
Flour	1 ounce	30 grams
Red wine	1¼ cups	3 deciliters
Brown stock	1¾ cups	4 deciliters

PROCEDURE

1. Heat the fat. Add the beef, the bacon, the onion, and the garlic.
2. Cook, stirring occasionally, until the meat juices have been reduced and a glaze has formed.
3. Season the meat. Mix in the flour. Pour in the wine and stock. Add the bouquet garni.
4. Cover tightly and simmer the meat for 1½ to 2 hours until it is tender. Add more liquid during the cooking time if it is needed.
5. Remove the meat pieces from the sauce. Strain the sauce, season to taste, skim off the fat, and pour the sauce over the meat.

Variations of Beef Stew

Beef Stew with Mushrooms — Estouffade de boeuf aux champignons. The recipe for Beef Stew is used for this dish. Mushrooms are sauteed in butter and placed on top of the finished dish.

Beef Stew, Paysanne Style — Estouffade de boeuf a la paysanne. The recipe for this dish is the same as the one for Beef Stew. The stew is garnished with glazed carrots, turnips, and small onions.

17.5 Poaching — Pocher

Note: Calf's sweetbreads, brain, and amourettes (spinal marrow) are suitable for this form of preparation. The taste of variety meats is quite delicate and, therefore, simmering is not recommended.

Ingredients: **Court bouillon: water, salt, seasoning, onion, mirepoix, wine or vinegar.**

Preparation: Boil the court bouillon for 15 minutes. Add the skinned and rinsed brain or other variety meats (offal), heat to the boiling point, and then poach at about 160°F. (70°C.).

Poached Breast of Chicken — Supremes de volaille poches. The breast of chicken is poached in a reduced white (chicken) stock. A Supreme Sauce is made from the stock. Serve like Poached Chicken: with truffles, with rice, with noodles, or with tarragon (see Section 18.6.1).

Deep-Fat Fried Calf's Brain — Cervelle frite. Poached brain, cut into slices, is breaded and deep-fat fried. Remoulade Sauce is served separately.
Calf's Brain in Batter — Cervelle a l'Orly. The brain is poached, cooled in a court bouillon, and cut into four pieces. These pieces are dipped into frying batter and deep-fat fried at a high temperature. Tomato or Remoulade Sauce is served separately.
Calf's Brain in Brown Butter — Cervelle au beurre noir. The poached calf's brain is placed on a platter and sprinkled with capers, chopped parsley, and a few drops of vinegar. Brown butter is poured on the top.
Calf's Brain in Noisette Butter — Cervelle au beurre noisette. The skinned brain is poached in a seasoned court bouillon with a little vinegar. Capers, chopped parsley, and hot foaming butter are poured over the calf's brain.
Calf's Brain, Poulette Style — Cervelle a la poulette. This is a poached brain covered with a Poulette Sauce.
Calf's Sweetbreads, German Style — Ris de veau a l'allemande. The sweetbreads are blanched and then poached in white stock. An Allemande Sauce is made from the stock. The sweetbreads are covered with the sauce and garnished with diced mushrooms and cucumbers.

17.6 Boiling — Bouillir

The boiling process is used to prepare some cuts of meat. The meat may be in small or large pieces. The salted water or white stock is heated to the boiling point and the meat is added. The heat is then reduced and the meat is allowed to simmer until tender. The cooked meat can then be finished by various methods.

17.6.1 Blanquette of Veal (Blanquette de veau)

YIELD: *approximately 10 servings*

INGREDIENTS	*U.S. Weight or Volume*	*Metric Weight or Volume*
Veal, boneless shoulder, breast, or neck cut into 1½ ounce (40 grams) cubes	4½ pounds	2 kilograms
Fond blanc (white stock)	1 quart	1.2 liters
White wine	1¼ cups	3 deciliters
Salt	2 teaspoons	12 grams
Pepper	½ teaspoon	3 grams
Bouquet garni:		
Onion, chopped	1	1
Carrot, chopped	1	1
Celery, chopped	1 stalk	1 stalk
Parsley	1 ounce	30 grams
Cloves	2	2
Bay leaf	½	½
Cream OR Milk	½ cup	1 deciliter
Egg yolks	3	3
Flour	2¾ ounces	80 grams
Lemon juice	2 tablespoons	30 milliliters
Nutmeg	1/8 teaspoon	1 gram
Butter	2½ ounces	70 grams

PROCEDURE

1. Blanch the veal and cool. Add the white stock until the meat is barely covered. Add the wine, salt, pepper, and bouquet garni.
2. Cover and simmer for approximately 1½ hours or until the meat is tender.
3. Transfer the meat to a warm platter and strain the broth through a cloth.
4. Reduce the broth by ⅓. Lower the heat and stir in the cream that has been blended with the egg yolk and the flour that has been blended with some of the broth.
5. Stir constantly over low heat until the mixture thickens. Add the meat, lemon juice, nutmeg, and butter.
6. Pour some heated glace de viande over the meat and garnish with assorted vegetables.

Variations of Blanquette of Veal

Blanquette of Veal with Celery — Blanquette de veau au celeri. The basic recipe for Blanquette of Veal is used for this dish. Slightly reduced celery stock is added to the sauce and the meat is garnished with cooked celery.

Blanquette of Chicken — Blanquette de volaille. The recipe for this dish is the same as the one for Blanquette of Veal, using young chicken instead of veal.

Blanquette of Mutton, Emmentaler Style — Blanquette de mouton emmentaloise. **(See page 467.)**

Blanquette of Veal with Noodles — Blanquette de veau aux nouilles. This is a Blanquette of Veal garnished with noodles.

Blanquette of Veal, Old Fashioned Style — Blanquette de veal a l'ancienne. The recipe for this dish is the same as the one for Blanquette of Veal. Sauteed mushrooms and pearl onions are placed on top of the meat and sauce.

Blanquette of Veal in Patty Shell — Pate de veau a l'ancienne. This is a Blanquette of Veal cut into small cubes and served in a rectangular puff paste patty shell with mushrooms, chicken kidneys, and small

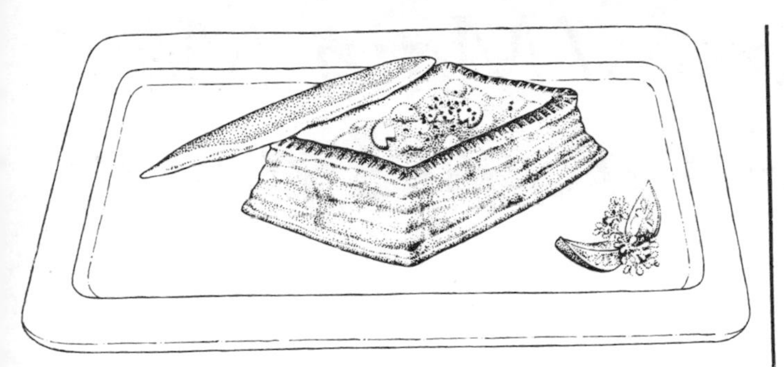

FIGURE 17-5
Blanquette of Veal in Patty Shell — Pate de veau a l'ancienne

onions.

Blanquette of Veal with Rice — Blanquette de veau au riz. The basic recipe for Blanquette of Veal is used for this dish. The veal is served on a base of white risotto or in a ring of rice.

Variations of Variety Meats

Breaded Calf's Feet — Pieds de veau panes. The calf's feet are simmered until tender in water with white wine, seasoning, and a bouquet garni. The feet are removed from the stock and allowed to dry. The joint bones are removed. The feet are dusted with flour, coated with egg and bread crumbs, and deep-fat fried. A Tartare Sauce is served separately.

Calf's Feet in Batter — Pieds de veau en fritot. The calf's feet are cut in half lengthwise, blanched, drained, and simmered in water with white wine, seasoning, and a bouquet garni. The feet are taken out of the stock and the joint bones are removed. The feet are coated with frying batter and deep-fat fried. A Tomato Sauce is served separately.

Calf's Head, Turtle Style — Tete de veau tortue. A boned calf's head is blanched and cut into large cubes. The meat is simmered in water with a little vinegar, lemon juice, an onion studded with bay leaf and cloves, carrots, bouquet garni, salt, and peppercorns. Prepare a Tortue Sauce (page 303). The drained meat is covered with the sauce and garnished with mushrooms, little dumplings, and pitted olives. Quartered hard-cooked eggs, pickles, and heart-shaped bread croutons are arranged on the platter around the meat.

Fried Calf's Head — Tete de veau en fritot. This dish is prepared by the same method described for Calf's Head, Turtle Style except the meat is dried, dipped in frying batter, and fried in deep fat. Tomato Sauce is served separately.

Calf's Head Poulette — Tete de veau a la poulette. This meat of the calf's head is simmered and covered with Poulette Sauce and garnished with mushrooms and small onions. The meat is sprinkled with parsley and surrounded with bread croutons.

Calf's Head with Tomatoes — Tete de veau aux tomates. The calf's head is simmered by the same method as described for Turtle Style. It is arranged on a platter and surrounded with tomato slices and pickles. A Tomato Sauce is served separately.

Calf's Head Vinaigrette — Tete de veau vinaigrette. The calf's head is prepared by the method described for Turtle Style. It is garnished with quartered hard-cooked eggs and pickles. A Vinaigrette Sauce is served separately.

Calf's Tongue, German Style — Langue de veau a l'allemande. The calf's tongue is simmered in a well-seasoned stock. It is carved lengthwise and covered with an Allemande Sauce.

Calf's Tongue with Madeira — Langue de veau au madere. The tongue is simmered in a well-seasoned and garnished white stock. Before serving, the tongue is peeled, carved lengthwise, and covered with a Madeira Sauce.

Tripe with Madeira — Tripes au madere. Simmered slices of tripe are marinated with chopped onion and then deglazed with demi-glace and Madeira is added.

Tripe in Tomato Sauce — Tripe napolitaine. The method of preparation for this dish is the same as the one for Tripe with Madeira except it is deglazed with Tomato Sauce.

Tripe in White Wine Sauce—Tripes au vin blanc. Simmered and sliced tripe is marinated with chopped onion. It is then sauteed lightly, dusted with flour, and cooked for ½ hour in white wine and white stock. Seasonings and caraway seed may be added before serving.

18 Main Courses/Main Meat Dishes—Grosses pieces

In the classical menu, the term grosse piece refers to the main course served before the entrees. This consists of a dish made from meats, poultry, or game. The grosse pieces differ from entrees as these *main courses are always cooked in one large piece.* Formerly, the roasts were served as a separate course following the sherbet. In the shortened menu, these two courses are combined offering a much greater variety. A grosse piece frequently consisted of meat, meaning that the roast course was necessarily poultry or game. Today, unless a classical menu is being served, the main course is *usually carved in the kitchen,* where it is also garnished and served on a platter. Carving rare roast meats in the kitchen makes it extremely difficult to provide the guest with meat that is rare and hot. Today, main courses are frequently garnished with vegetables and potatoes and are described on the menu as the *dish of the day.* Other than braised meat, these dishes should not be included under the a la carte items, since the quality both in terms of taste and of juiciness would suffer. The following basic methods of preparation and recipes form the *foundations for the main courses made from the different kinds of meats.* Today, this course is very often the only meat dish, therefore, the preparation and presentation should be faultless. Gravy or sauce should be served in a sauce boat, when possible, to keep it separate from the garnishes. Modern cookery emphasizes the importance of a variety of carefully prepared nutritionally adequate dishes in portions of appropriate size.

18.1 Basic Cooking Methods

18.1.1 Braising—Braiser

Braising smaller pieces of meat was described under entrees. The same method of cooking may be used for cuts of meats up to 4 or 5 pounds (2 or 3 kilograms). Braising is a combination of dry and moist heat cookery. In general, this method is applied to less tender cuts of meat.

18.1.1.1 Braising Red Meat

Ingredients: Fat, salt, seasoning (spice sachet), mirepoix. tomato puree or fresh tomatoes, calf's feet, bacon rinds, wine, stock, marinade, and cornstarch.

Preparation: Gently heat the fat in a braising pan of proper size. Brown the meat on all sides and remove it from the pan. Then brown the mirepoix with the bacon rinds and calf's feet, add the tomato puree, and simmer for a few minutes. Return the meat to the pan

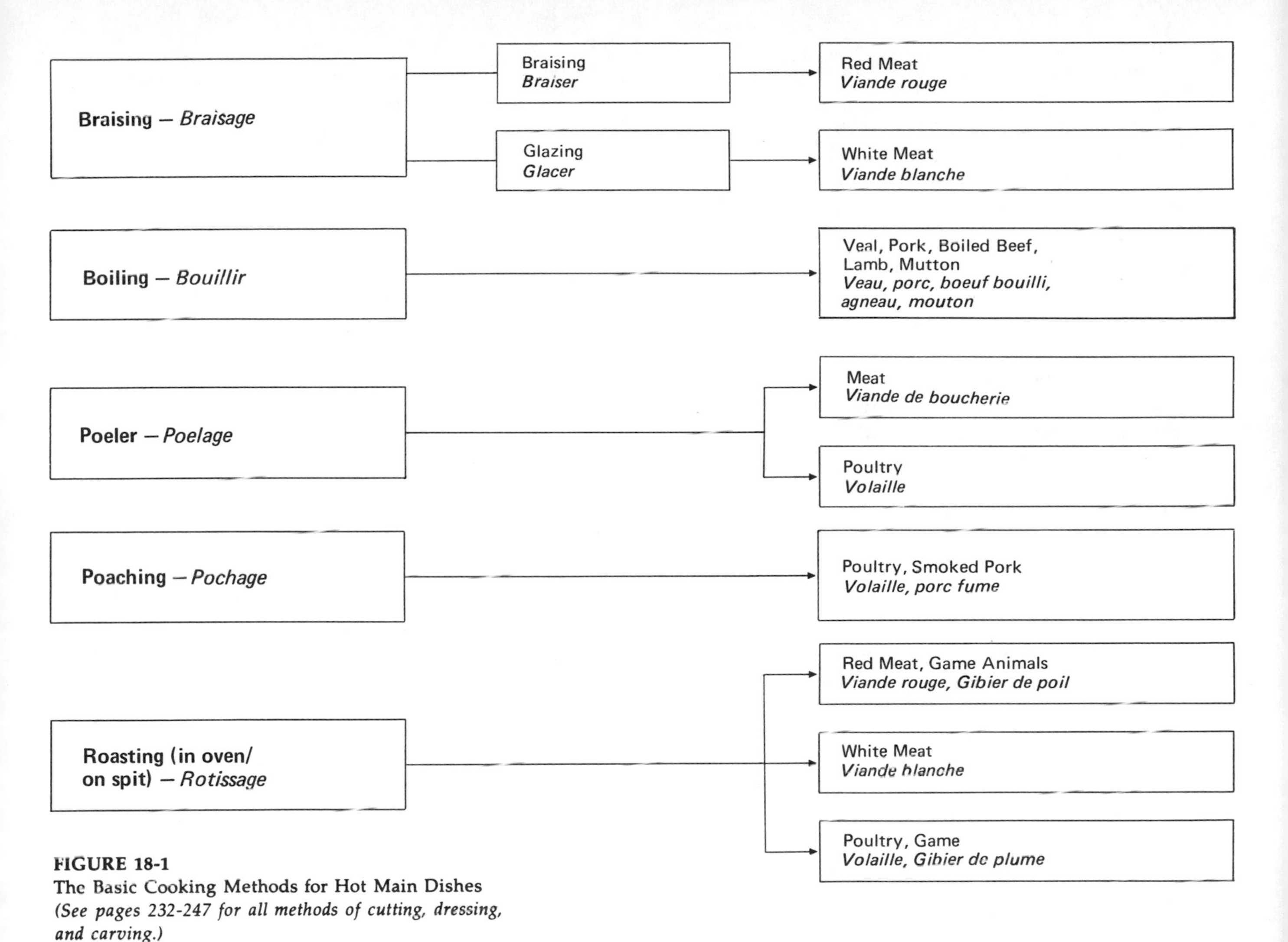

FIGURE 18-1
The Basic Cooking Methods for Hot Main Dishes
(See pages 232-247 for all methods of cutting, dressing, and carving.)

and deglaze with wine or the marinade. Reduce the liquid to a syrupy consistency and baste the meat frequently to form a slight glaze. Deglaze with a strong brown stock until the meat pieces are ¼ covered. Place a tight-fitting lid on the pan and braise in an oven at 300°F. (150°C.) until the meat is tender. If necessary, add more stock. Strain the gravy, heat to the boiling point, skim off the fat, and reduce or thicken with cornstarch as needed. Madeira can also be added.

Note: Most meats in the United States have adequate marbling and do not require larding, but larding is suggested for game (venison) which is lean. (See illustration, page 241.)

18.1.1.2 Glazing White Meat

Ingredients: Fat, salt, seasoning, mirepoix, bacon trimmings, fresh tomatoes, wine, and cornstarch.

Preparation: Heat the fat in a braising pan of the proper size. Add the meat and brown. Add the mirepoix and bacon trimmings quickly. Add the tomatoes, and continue cooking a few minutes. Deglaze with white wine, reduce, and add a sufficient amount of brown stock to cover the meat by $^1/_{16}$. Place a tight-fitting lid on the pan and braise the meat until tender, basting frequently. If necessary, add more stock. Remove the lid from the braising pan. Basting continuously, glaze the meat in the oven with the reduced stock. Remove the meat from the pan. Add a little white wine to the glaze and, if necessary, some basic stock or fond brun. Strain the stock and heat to the boiling point. Skim off the fat, thicken slightly with cornstarch, and add Madeira.

Note: All braised white meats should be glazed using a minimum of stock and small utensils. An open braising pan is the most suitable utensil.

18.1.2 Boiling—Bouillir

Ingredients: Bouquet garni, spice sachet, salt, browned onions.

Preparation: Boiling is a moist heat method of cookery. The term "boiling" is accepted terminology; however, meat should not be cooked in liquids at 212°F. (100°C.) for any extended period of time. The temperature of the liquid will be lowered when the meat is added. When the temperature reaches the boiling point again, the heat should be reduced so that the meat will continue to simmer, not boil, until it is tender. The following are examples of meat that may be boiled or simmered:

Brisket of beef, corned	Poultry
Brisket of beef, fresh	Shoulder of breast of beef or veal
Ham, cured	Smoked pork butt
Ham hocks	
Ox tongue	

The size of the pieces and the quality of the meat will determine the cooking time. Smaller or more tender pieces will cook faster and these should be removed when done. Beef bones should always be placed in cold water. After the boiling point is reached, the heat should be reduced so that the liquid simmers. Stocks should not be covered. Mutton should be blanched before simmering.

Note: The needle test is one method to check degree of doneness. Push needle through meat; if it pulls out easily, meat is done.

18.1.3 Poeler—Poelage

This is a very slow cooking method that is particularly suitable for tender cuts of meat and for poultry. The food is cooked in a container with a tight-fitting lid (casserole) and in a generous amount of butter or oil with a small quantity of stock.

18.1.3.1 Poeler Meat

Ingredients: Mirepoix, fat, spice sachet, salt, tomato puree, bacon trimmings, cornstarch, and Madeira.

Preparation: Spread a mirepoix and bacon trimmings on the bottom of the braising pan. Place the seasonings and, when appropriate, larded meat on top. Add the fat and lightly stew the meat in the oven. Then cover and place in the oven at 300°F. (150°C.), basting occasionally. Remove the lid and brown the meat in a hot oven. Then remove the meat, pour a little brown stock into the braising pan, reduce with the mirepoix to the desired consistency or thicken slightly with cornstarch. Strain and heat the stock to the boiling point, skim the fat, and add Madeira.

18.1.3.2 Poeler Poultry

Ingredients: Clarified butter, mirepoix, diced lean bacon, salt, seasoning, stock, red or white wine.

Preparation: Cover the bottom of a braising pan with mirepoix and diced lean bacon. Place the seasoned poultry, barded if necessary, on top (see page 237). Pour the clarified butter over the poultry, stew lightly, and then cover and finish the stewing in the oven, basting frequently. Remove the poultry. Deglaze with red or white wine (depending on the sauce that will accompany the dish). Add more stock and strain. Heat to the boiling point, skim the fat, and reduce before mixing in the demi-glace or Madeira Sauce.

18.1.4 Poaching—Pocher

18.1.4.1 Poached Poultry

Ingredients: White bouquet garni, spice sachet, white poultry stock, white wine, a young bird.

Preparation: Blanch the cleaned and trussed poultry. Add the bouquet garni, the spice sachet, the stock, and the white wine. Heat to the boiling point, reduce the heat, skim the stock, and poach at 160°F. to 175°F. (71°C. to 80°C.) until the meat is tender.

Note: Some of the stock is used to prepare the Supreme Sauce which is served with the poultry.

18.1.4.2 Poached Smoked Pork

Place the pork in cold water, and heat until the temperature reaches 160°F. to 175°F. (70°C. to 80°C.). Allow 20 minutes cooking time per pound (.45 kilogram).

18.1.5 Roasting—Rotir

The term roasting was originally applied to the cooking of large cuts of meat on a spit over open fires. This method of cooking is now called barbecuing or open roasting. As used today, the term roasting refers to cooking in the oven in an uncovered container with little or no added liquid. *The fundamental principles for roasting, as described on pages 255, 261 constitute the basis for all of the following roasting procedures.*

The fat content of the meat will determine whether additional fats or oils are required. Very lean cuts of meat are sometimes larded or barded before roasting. Since today there is a trend toward producing meat with less marbling or fat, the flavor and juiciness of very lean cuts of meat can be improved by larding or barding. *Larding* is the insertion of thin strips of fat back into the meat. (See page 241.) *Barding* is covering lean cuts of meat with slices of salt pork (fat back) or bacon to prevent burning or drying out of the meat. Barding is most frequently used in the preparation of poultry and game birds. (See illustration page 237.)

18.1.5.1 Roasting Red Meat

Ingredients: (Select the appropriately sized roasting pan, possibly with a rack). Fat with a high smoking point, salt, seasoning, wine, basic stock.

Preparation: Remove the roast from the refrigerator two hours before roasting. Season the roast. Preheat the oven to 500°F. (260°C.). Insert a meat thermometer into the thickest part of the muscle so that the tip does not touch fat or bone. Place the meat in the oven, fat side up, on a rack in a roasting pan. *Reduce the temperature to 230°F. to 350°F. (110°C. to 175°C.)* (the exact setting depends on the size and type of meat). Roast 18 to 20 minutes per pound (.45 kilogram) for medium rare. Baste frequently with the meat juices. When the meat is done, drain the fat carefully so that the drippings remain. Deglaze with wine and stock, and heat to the boiling point. Skim the fat and strain before seasoning. Meat roasted English style (rare) should be accompanied by a natural gravy, served separately. The degree of doneness can be determined by applying pressure with the fingers, the needle test, a meat thermometer, or time-weight ratio. (See pages 258, 261.)
Note: Beef tenderloin, roast beef, rump, leg of lamb, and game beasts (with the exception of wild boar) are the most suitable types of red meat for roasting English style (rare). English roast beef can also be roasted on the spit (see page 255) or in an automatic convection oven. Meat should be at room temperature when placed in the oven. All roasts should stand for 20 to 30 minutes before carving. Always start carving on the thinner side.

18.1.5.2 Roasting White Meat

Ingredients: Vegetable oil with a high smoking point, salt, seasoning, mirepoix, basic stock or brown stock, wine, and Madeira.

Preparation: Remove the meat from the refrigerator 30 minutes before roasting. Season the pieces of meat. Preheat the oven to 440°F. (225°C.). *Reduce the heat to between 300°F. to 360°F. (150°C. to 180°C.),* depending on the size and type of meat, and continue roasting. Baste frequently with the pan drippings.

A finely chopped mirepoix, consisting of fresh onion, celery, and carrots, is usually added to the meat during the roasting process. White meat loses more of its juices during cooking than other types of meat, therefore, a good gravy, that complements the flavor of the meat, is necessary. When the meat is done, remove it from the pan, drain the fat, deglaze the pan with wine and then with basic stock. Cook the gravy with the mirepoix. Madeira can then be added to veal. The degree of doneness can be determined by applying pressure with the fingers, the needle test, a meat thermometer, or time-weight ratio. (See pages 258, 261.)

Note: Veal, pork, lamb, and suckling pig are all considered white meat. All types of white meat should be sufficiently cooked. Pork must always be cooked well-done to kill the parasite, found in the muscle of some pork, that may be transmitted to man in the form of a disease called trichinosis. The flavor of veal is improved if it is roasted in the bottom of a roasting pan so it may "absorb" the meat juice. Fatty pieces of pork are often braised with a little hot water, instead of being roasted.

18.1.5.3 Roasting Poultry

Ingredients: Roasting fat, seasoning, salt, wine, drippings, butter, and mirepoix.

Preparation: Heat the fat and place the seasoned bird in the pan on its side. Roast in the oven, basting frequently. Draining internal juices onto a plate shows when the bird is done. The juice should be absolutely clear. A mirepoix can be added at the last moment. Remove the bird from the pan, drain the fat, deglaze with wine and drippings, heat to the boiling point, and skim the fat. Strain the gravy and season to taste. Brown butter may be poured over the finished dish. Serve the gravy separately.

Note: Young poultry is best suited for roasting. The poeler method is the preferred method for such poultry as capon, poularde, or large roasters. Roasting may be done in an oven, on a spit, or in an automatic convection oven. The bird will retain more of its juices and it will be easier to carve if it stands 15 to 20 minutes before serving.

18.1.5.4 Roasting Game Birds

Ingredients: Roasting fat, seasoning, salt, unsalted larding bacon, mirepoix, wine, brandy, game stock, and cream.

Preparation: Feathered game should be barded (see illustration page 237) to prevent the breast from drying out. Roast the bird in an oven at 455°F. to 490°F. (235°C. to 255°C.) and baste throughout the roasting time. The smaller the bird, the shorter the roasting time. Doneness may be tested with a thermometer in large birds. The hand test may be used for smaller birds. If the drumstick bone twists easily on broilers, they are usually done. The plate test may also be used. The juice and the flesh will both be a pink color when the bird is done. Remove the slices of bacon from the bird and baste at regular intervals to brown the breast. Then remove the bird from the pan, drain off the fat, deglaze with wine and game stock. Heat the cooking liquid to the boiling point, skim the fat, thicken with cream or sour cream, strain, and season to taste. The slices of bacon may be cut into strips, lightly browned, and placed on top of the bird. Serve the sauce separately.

Note: Binding with cream is not necessary; however, it does improve the flavor. Flambeing with brandy when serving is recommended.

Older game birds are better when lightly braised and prepared as "salmis."

18.2 Variations of Main Beef Dishes

18.2.1 Braised Beef (Boeuf braise)

YIELD: *approximately 10 servings*

INGREDIENTS	*U.S. Weight or Volume*	*Metric Weight or Volume*	PROCEDURE
Beef rump, round, shoulder, or shortribs	4½ pounds	2 kilograms	1. Lard the meat with strips of bacon.
Larding bacon	5 ounces	150 grams	
Fat OR Oil	1¾ ounces	50 grams	2. Brown the meat in melted fat. Brown the mirepoix and bacon.
Mirepoix	7 ounces	200 grams	
Bacon trimmings	2 ounces	60 grams	
Tomato puree	1¾ ounces	50 grams	3. Add the tomato puree, salt, and pepper.
Salt	2 teaspoons	12 grams	4. Deglaze the meat with the wine or marinade. Reduce the liquid until it is a syrupy consistency.
Pepper	½ teaspoon	3 grams	
Red wine OR Marinade	¾ cup	2 deciliters	5. Add the brown stock.
Brown stock	1 quart	1 liter	6. Cover the pan and braise the meat until tender. Turn occasionally.
Cornstarch	1 to 2 teaspoons	6 to 12 grams	7. Remove the meat from the pan. Reduce the sauce to the described consistency or, if necessary, bind with cornstarch. Strain and skim the fat. Season to taste with Madeira.
Madeira	¼ cup	½ deciliter	8. Pour a small quantity of sauce over the carved meat before serving.

Note: Most vegetables, pastas, polenta, and steamed or mashed potatoes are excellent garnishes.

Variations of Braised Beef

Braised Beef, Bourgeoise Style—Boeuf a la bourgeoise. Lard the rump and prepare initially like Braised Beef. After half the cooking time, add the garnishes (carrots, turnips, and small onions) directly to the sauce or cook separately and add when the dish is ready to serve.

Braised Beef with Noodles—Boeuf braise aux nouilles. Braise larded rump of beef and garnish with noodles.

Braised Beef, Piemontese Style—Boeuf braise a la piemontaise. Follow the method for braising beef and serve the meat with a white risotto topped with a few sauteed mushrooms.

18.2.2 Braised Beef, Modern Style (Boeuf a la mode)

YIELD: *approximately 10 servings*

INGREDIENTS	*U.S. Weight or Volume*	*Metric Weight or Volume*	PROCEDURE
Beef rump	4½ pounds	2 kilograms	1. Lard the beef rump with finger thick strips of bacon.
Larding bacon	5 ounces	150 grams	
Red wine	¾ cup	2 deciliters	2. Marinate for a few hours in the wine.
Fat OR Oil	1¾ ounces	50 grams	3. Brown the meat on all sides over medium heat. Brown the mirepoix, bacon, and calf's feet. 4. Deglaze the meat with the marinade. Reduce the liquid until it is a syrupy consistency.
Mirepoix	7 ounces	200 grams	
Bacon	2 ounces	60 grams	
Calf's feet, blanched	1 to 2	1 to 2	
Brown stock	1 quart	1 liter	5. Add the brown stock, tomato puree, and salt.
Tomato puree	1¾ ounces	50 grams	6. Cover the pan and braise until meat is ¾ done.
Salt	½ teaspoon	3 grams	
For garnishes:			
Carrots	7 ounces	200 grams	7. Strain the stock. Add the vegetables, small onions, and the stock to the meat and finish braising together.
Celery	7 ounces	200 grams	
Turnips	7 ounces	200 grams	8. Reduce the stock to the desired consistency. Season to taste.
Onions, small	5 ounces	150 grams	
Butter	3½ ounces	100 grams	9. Cut the calf's feet into strips and return to the pan.
Salt	½ teaspoon	3 grams	10. Cover the meat with the sauce and garnishes and serve.
Pepper	½ teaspoon	3 grams	

Note: The vegetable garnishes may be cooked separately and added to the braise when it is served.

18.2.3 Boiled Beef (Boeuf bouilli)

YIELD: *approximately 10 servings*

INGREDIENTS	*U.S. Weight or Volume*	*Metric Weight or Volume*
Beef short ribs, top round, or chuck	5½ pounds	2½ kilograms
Beef bones	2 pounds	1 kilogram
Marrow bones	10 pieces	10 pieces
Garniture de marmite	1 pound	500 grams
Salt, coarse	1 teaspoon	5 grams
Parsley, chopped	2 tablespoons	30 grams

PROCEDURE

1. Cut the meat into two equal portions.
2. Blanch the beef bones. Place in a stock pot in cold water and bring to a boil.
3. Add the meat pieces. Skim and add the garniture de marmite.
4. Simmer slowly and skim occasionally.
5. Cook for 2 to 2½ hours or until meat is tender.
6. Combine the coarse salt and chopped parsley.
7. Before serving, cover the sliced beef with bouillon and sprinkle the salt and parsley mixture over the top.

Note: As garnishes the following items would be excellent: various vegetable salads, gherkins, radishes, pickled cucumbers, horseradish, and mustard.

Variations of Boiled Beef

Boiled Beef, Alsatian Style—Boeuf bouilli a l'alsacienne. Garnish boiled beef with sauerkraut and cover with slices of lean bacon. Serve boiled potatoes and Horseradish Sauce separately.

Boiled Beef, Bernese Style—Boeuf bouilli a la bernoise. (See page 468.)

Boiled Beef, Flemish Style—Boeuf bouilli a la flamande. Garnish boiled beef with bouquets of carrots, turnips, and cabbage. Cover the cabbage with slices of lean bacon. Serve boiled potatoes and Horseradish Sauce separately.

Gratinated Boiled Beef with Onion Sauce—Miroton de boeuf. Coat the bottom of a gratinating dish with Lyonnaise Sauce. Place the slices of boiled beef in the dish in a symmetrical pattern *(a cheval)* and cover with an Onion Sauce. Sprinkle with bread crumbs and melted butter and gratinate in the oven.

18.2.4 Beef Tongue (Langue de boeuf)

YIELD: *approximately 10 servings*

INGREDIENTS	*U.S. Weight or Volume*	*Metric Weight or Volume*	PROCEDURE
Beef tongue, salted or smoked	3 to 4 pounds	1½ to 2 kilograms	1. Soak the tongue overnight in lukewarm water. 2. Blanch and then simmer for 3 hours until tender. 3. Remove the tongue from the kettle and plunge into cold water. Skin. Return the tongue to the stock.

Notes: 1) Tongue loses less weight and is juicier when cooked in a pressure cooker. 2) Serve a Madeira or Piquante Sauce with the meat. 3) Cook fresh beef tongue by the method used for Boiled Beef and serve it with a Caper or Mushroom Sauce.

Variations of Beef Tongue

Beef Tongue, Breton Style—Langue de boeuf a la bretonne. Cook a salted (pickled) beef tongue and serve with navy beans or lima beans. Sprinkle the beans with parsley and cover the tongue with Madeira Sauce.

Beef Tongue with Capers—Langue de boeuf aux capres. Cook a fresh (unsalted) tongue, carve, cover with Caper Sauce, and garnish.

Beef Tongue, Florentine Style—Langue de boeuf a la florentine. Cook salted (pickled) tongue, carve, serve on a platter of spinach, and cover with Madeira Sauce. Serve additional Madeira Sauce in a sauce boat.

Beef Tongue with Green Beans—Langue de boeuf aux haricots verts. Cook a salted (pickled) tongue, garnish with green beans, and cover with Madeira Sauce. Serve more sauce separately.

Beef Tongue with Spinach—Langue de boeuf aux epinards. Cook a salted (pickled) tongue and serve garnished with creamed spinach. Glaze the tongue with a little Madeira Sauce and serve more sauce separately in a sauce boat. A spicy brown sauce may be served instead of Madeira Sauce.

Leg of Lamb, Boulangere Style—Gigot d'agneau a la boulangere. Recipe 18.5.4. Reprinted, by permission, from H. P. Pettaprat, "Die feine Kuche" (Castagnola: Edizioni Rene Kramer S.A.) **(See page 439.)**

Ballotine of Mutton, Carcassone Style—Ballotine de mouton carcassonnaise. Bone a shoulder of mutton and stuff with pork forcemeat (accompaniments: diced mushrooms, sauteed lamb kidneys, sweet peppers, and truffles). Wrap the shoulder in slices of bacon and roast slowly in the oven. Remove the bacon, slice, and pour the gravy around the meat. Note: Lamb may be substituted for mutton.

Garnishes: gallette potatoes and eggplant stuffed with ratatouille.

Partridge on Canape—Perdeau sur canape. Recipe see page **426**. Reprinted, by permission, from H. P. Pellaprat, "Die feine Kuche" (Castagnola: Edizioni Rene Kramer S.A.) **(See illustration, page 442.)**

Saddle of Lamb, Imperial Style—Selle d'agneau imperiale. Trim a 4 pound (2 kilograms) saddle of lamb including the tenderloin. Truss. Spear the metal rod of the rotisserie through the center of the meat and through the backbone marrow. Roast to the medium rare stage as described in **Section 18.1.5.1.**

Garnishes: Cut 3 Italian artichokes as shown in the illustration; peel the approximately ¾ inch (1.875 centimeters) long stalks and braise the hollowed-out artichoke halves in white wine and butter, stuff with broccoli, and sprinkle with pine kernels. Stuff 6 tomato halves with garden peas, cover each with a slice of lightly poached marrow, and garnish with a halved black olive and a small mushroom. Place the tomatoes on fried slices of eggplant gratinated with a little soubise. Cut sweet peppers into boat-shaped sections and fill with soubise and gratinate to a golden brown color. Use these to crown the saddle of lamb. This is a masterpiece of fine cookery. 6 servings. **(See illustration, page 442.)**

18.2.5 Tenderloin of Beef Wellington (Filet de boeuf Wellington)

YIELD: *10 to 12 servings*

INGREDIENTS	*U.S. Weight or Volume*	*Metric Weight or Volume*
Beef tenderloin, whole, trimmed	5 pounds	2½ kilograms
Larding bacon	10 ounces	300 grams
Oil	1¾ ounces	50 grams
Forcemeat:		
Duxelles	7 ounces	200 grams
Truffles, chopped	3	3
Goose liver, pureed	7 ounces	200 grams
Pork	10 ounces	300 grams
Eggs	2 to 3	2 to 3
Port wine	as needed	as needed
Salt	½ teaspoon	3 grams
Pepper	¼ teaspoon	1 gram
Puff paste	1 pound	500 grams
Egg	1	1

PROCEDURE

1. **Use the tenderloin without the tip and without the head.**
2. Lard the tenderloin with some of the bacon. Brown on all sides in an oven at 490°F. (255°C.) for about 20 minutes.
3. Allow the tenderloin to stand until cool enough to touch.
4. Prepare the forcemeat by grinding very fine the duxelles, truffles, goose liver, and pork. Mix with desired seasoning and enough port wine to make the mixture a spreadable consistency.
5. Spread the forcemeat over the tenderloin to a thickness of ⅓ to ½ inch.
6. Wrap the tenderloin in thin slices of larding bacon.
7. Roll the puff paste into a rectangle about 1½ inches larger than the fillet in length and width. Place fillet in center of dough and seal dough around fillet. Decorate with strips of puff paste **(recipe 25.1.1)**. Brush with slightly beaten egg. Let stand a few minutes.
8. Finish baking in the oven at 400°F. (204°C.) for 30 to 40 minutes. The proper degree of doneness can best be determined by using a meat thermometer. When an internal temperature of 120°F. (49°C.) is reached, the fillet is rare.
9. Remove from oven and allow to stand 15 to 20 minutes before serving.

Note: Pie pastry which does not contain too much butter may be used instead of puff paste.

FIGURE 18-2
Tenderloin of Beef Wellington—Filet de boeuf Wellington

18.2.6 Garnishes for Beef Tenderloin, Roast Beef, Rump Roast.

Beef Tenderloin, Roast Beef, and Rump Roast are prepared by following the roasting or poeler procedures described in Sections 18.5.1 and 18.1.3.1. Tenderloins and Rump Roasts should be larded.

Andalusian Style—andalouse. Roast. Surround roast beef with stuffed eggplant, grilled tomatoes, and chipolata sausages. Serve gravy separately.

with Cauliflower—Dubarry. Roast. Surround the roast with cauliflower bouquets. Serve gravy separately.

Duchess Style—duchesse. Poeler. Surround the meat with duchesse potatoes. Serve Madeira Sauce separately.

Jardiniere Style—jardiniere. Roast. Surround the roast with bouquets of various vegetables. Serve gravy separately. (See Fig. 18-3.)

London House Style—London House. (Only for tenderloin.) Cut the larded tenderloin lengthwise to its center and fill with strips of truffles and goose liver. Then close the slit at the top, bard with thin slices of larding bacon, tie with string, and poeler (section 18.1.3.1) in the oven. Garnish with mushrooms and truffles. Serve Truffle Sauce separately. (See Fig. 18-4.)

Lorette—Lorette. Poeler. Garnish with potatoes Lorette and asparagus spears. Serve demi-glace separately.

with Mixed Vegetables—macedoine. Garnish the roast with a macedoine of vegetables. Serve gravy separately.

Nivernese Style—nivernaise. Surround the roast with bouquets of glazed pearl onions, glazed carrots, and turnips. Serve gravy separately.

Parisian Style—parisienne. Poeler. Garnish the meat with artichoke hearts and potatoes a la parisienne. Serve Madeira Sauce separately.

Portuguese Style—portugaise. Poeler. Garnish with tomatoes stuffed with a duxelles and chateau potatoes. Serve Madeira Sauce separately.

with Potato Rissoles—dauphine. Surround the meat with croquettes made of a dauphine potato mixture. Serve Madeira Sauce separately.

Provence Style—provencale. Poeler. Garnish with Tomatoes, Provence Style and mushrooms. Serve demi-glace separately.

with Spring Vegetables—printaniere. Arrange glazed carrots, turnips, pearl onions, bouquets of asparagus spears, and peas around the roast. Serve gravy separately.

Tivoli. Garnish the roast with asparagus spears and mushrooms. Serve gravy separately.

with Vegetable Bouquets—bouquetiere. Roast. Surround roast beef with bouquets of various vegetables. Serve gravy separately.

Yorkshire. (Only for roast beef.) Serve Yorkshire Pudding with the roast.

FIGURE 18-3
Garnish for Beef, Jardiniere Style—Roast beef jardiniere

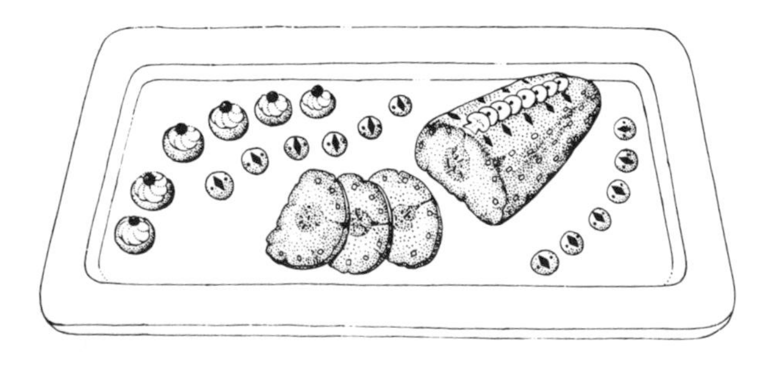

FIGURE 18-4
Garnish for Beef, London House—Filet de boeuf London House

Yorkshire Pudding

YIELD: *approximately 10 servings*

INGREDIENTS	*U.S. Weight or Volume*	*Metric Weight or Volume*
Beef kidney fat, finely chopped	8½ ounces	250 grams
Flour	14 ounces	400 grams
Milk	1¼ to 1½ pints	6 to 8 deciliters
Egg yolks	5	5
Salt	1 teaspoon	4 grams
Pepper	¼ teaspoon	1 gram
Egg whites	5	5
Drippings from roast beef (fat only)	8 ounces	240 grams

PROCEDURE

1. Combine the finely chopped kidney fat with the flour.
2. Add the milk, egg yolks, salt, and pepper to the flour mixture. Stir until very thick.
3. When ready to bake, add the stiffly beaten egg whites and work into the batter.
4. Heat a roasting pan containing the beef drippings.
5. Put batter into the pan. Batter should be no more than 1 inch deep.
6. Preheat oven to 400°F. (205°C.).
7. Bake pudding for 20 minutes. Reduce the heat to 350°F. (175°C.) and bake 15 to 20 minutes longer.
8. Cut the Yorkshire Pudding into diamond shaped pieces and use to garnish the roast beef.

Note: Individual puddings may be made in tart pans or muffin tins.

18.3 Variations of Main Veal Dishes

18.3.1 Stuffed Breast of Veal (Poitrine de veau farcie)

INGREDIENTS	*U.S. Weight or Volume*	*Metric Weight or Volume*	PROCEDURE
Breast of veal	5 to 6 pounds	2½ to 3 kilograms	1. Bone the breast of veal and remove the cartilage. Cut an opening in the meat starting on the thinner side and cut through to the clod tip. **(See illustration on page 233.)**
Forcemeat:			
Bread, white	1 pound	500 grams	2. Soak the bread in the milk. Press to remove excess milk.
Milk	¾ cup	2 deciliters	
Onion, chopped fine	7 ounces	200 grams	3. Saute chopped onion in butter. Add the bread and parsley and stir until dry. Cool.
Butter	1¾ ounces	50 grams	
Parsley, chopped	2 tablespoons	30 grams	
Raw veal or pork OR A mixture of both	1½ pounds	700 grams	4. Grind the pork and/or veal. Add eggs, salt, thyme, and pepper. Add to the bread mixture and blend.
Eggs	2	2	5. Stuff the forcemeat into the opening and then sew up the pocket with a coarse needle and thread. Rub the meat with butter.
Salt	1 teaspoon	6 grams	
Thyme	¼ teaspoon	1 gram	6. Brown the breast in the shortening. Braise the meat in a covered pan with a very small amount of moisture. Add moisture only as needed. Cook until the internal temperature reaches 170°F. (77°C.).
Pepper	½ teaspoon	2 grams	
Shortening	3½ ounces	100 grams	

Note: 1) For further explanation of braising method see **Section 18.1.1.2.**
2) Different stuffings may be used such as:
a. a bread filling
b. ⅓ panada and ⅔ forcemeat
c. a special forcemeat
3) Garnishes: ham, strips or cubes of bacon, green peppers, blanched spinach, sauteed mushrooms, or hard-cooked eggs.

Variations of Breast of Veal

Breast of Veal, Home Style—Poitrine de veau a la bourgeoise. Bone and pound the breast, season, roll, tie with string, and glaze in the oven. (See Section 18.1.1.2.) Thicken the stock and pour it onto the carved breast garnished with pearl onions, carrots, and turnips.

Glazed Breast of Veal—Poitrine de veau glacee. Bone the breast and glaze in the oven. (See Section 18.1.1.2.) Serve gravy separately.

18.3.2 Saddle of Veal Metternich (Selle de veau Metternich)

YIELD: *10 servings*

INGREDIENTS	*U.S. Weight or Volume*	*Metric Weight or Volume*	PROCEDURE
Saddle of veal	6 to 7 pounds	3 to 3½ kilograms	1. Remove the tendons of the saddle. Trim, tie, salt, and season the meat. Glaze in the oven as described in Section 18.1.1.2. After the meat is fully cooked, cool it for 15 to 20 minutes.
Fat	3½ ounces	100 grams	
Salt	1 teaspoon	6 grams	
Pepper	¼ teaspoon	2 grams	
Mirepoix	as needed	as needed	
Wine	as needed	as needed	
Brown stock	as needed	as needed	
Bechamel Sauce **(see page 308)**	1¼ cups	3 deciliters	2. Remove the fillets from the bone. Coat the backbone with Bechamel Sauce. Arrange the fillets along the backbone. Place a slice of truffle and some soubise mixed with goose liver between each fillet.
Soubise **(see page 312)**	10 ounces	300 grams	
Truffles, thinly sliced	30 slices	30 slices	
Goose liver	3½ to 7 ounces	100 to 200 grams	3. Pour the Mornay Sauce evenly over the saddle and gratinate in the oven for a few minutes.
Mornay Sauce	1 quart	1 liter	4. Garnish with glazed vegetables. 5. Serve gravy separately.

Variations of Saddle of Veal

Saddle of Veal, Forestiere Style—Selle de veau a la forestiere. Roast the saddle (see Section 18.1.5.2), remove the fillets, slice, and replace. Garnish with morels; diced, blanched, and browned bacon; and sauteed potato cubes. Serve Duxelles Sauce separately.

Saddle of Veal Orloff—Selle de veau Orlov. This is prepared by the same recipe used for Metternich. Slices of truffles and some goose liver are placed between the fillets. Pureed onion is added to Mornay Sauce and it is served separately. The meat is garnished with asparagus tips and braised cucumbers.

18.3.3 Garnishes for Saddle, Loin, Fillet, and Tenderloin of Veal

Saddle, Loin, Fillet, and Tenderloin of Veal are prepared by following the procedures described in Sections 18.1.5.2 and 18.1.3.1. Loin, Rump, Round of Veal, Loin with Kidney, Brisket and Shoulder are glazed as described in Section 18.1.1.2.

Argenteuil. Garnish with asparagus spears and noisette potatoes. Serve gravy separately.
Dubarry. Garnish with cauliflower. Serve gravy made with veal stock separately.
Flemish Style—a la flamande. Garnish with braised chicory (endive) and chateau potatoes. Serve gravy separately.
Florentine Style—a la florentine. Serve on a base of cooked spinach and surround with gravy.
Jardiniere Style—a la jardiniere. Surround with bouquets of different vegetables. Prepare a gravy with veal stock and serve separately.
with Lettuce—aux laitues. Garnish with braised lettuce. Serve gravy separately.
Lorette—Lorette. Garnish with asparagus spears and potatoes Lorette. Serve gravy made with veal stock separately.
with Mixed Vegetables—a la macedoine. Garnish with mixed vegetables (carrots, turnips, peas, and beans). Serve gravy separately.
Naples Style—a la napolitaine. Garnish with spaghetti napolitaine. Serve gravy separately.
with Noodles—aux nouilles. Garnish with buttered noodles. Serve gravy separately.
Provence Style—a la provencale. Surround with Tomatoes, Provence style. Serve gravy separately.

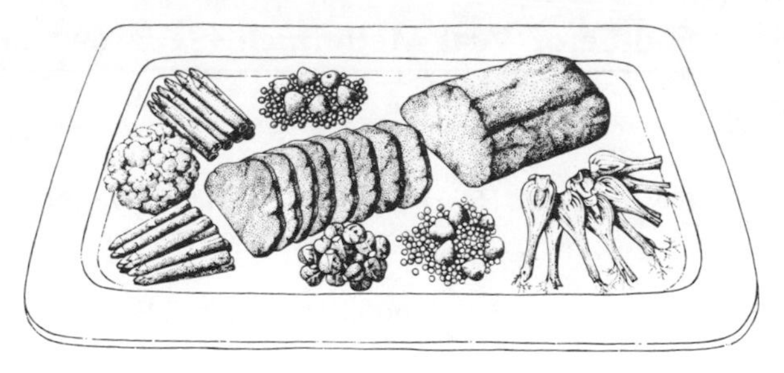

FIGURE 18-5
Garnish for Veal Loin—Longe de veau a la printaniere

Piemontese Style—a la piemontaise. Garnish with a white risotto and place sauteed mushrooms on top. Serve gravy separately.
with Spring Vegetables—a la printaniere. Surround with bouquets of various young vegetables. Serve gravy separately (See Fig. 18-5.)
with Timbales—en timbale. Garnish with individual molds of rice, spinach, and carrot puree. Serve gravy separately.

18.4 Variations of Main Pork Dishes

18.4.1 Suckling Pig—Cochon de lait

Stuff and roast. (See Section 18.1.5.2.) Served with potato sticks, glazed chestnuts, marrons glaces, mushrooms, and stewed apples. Jointed suckling pig is also suitable for roasting a la diable.

Stuffed Suckling Pig—Cochon de lait farci. (See page 473.)

18.4.2 Braised Smoked Ham (Jambon braise)

YIELD: *approximately 20 to 25 servings*

INGREDIENTS	*U.S. Weight or Volume*	*Metric Weight or Volume*
Ham	10 to 12 pounds	5 to 6 kilograms
White wine	1 pint	½ liter
Madeira wine	1¼ cups	3 deciliters
Light stock	1 quart	1 liter
OR		
Demi-glace		

PROCEDURE

1. Place ham in large kettle and cover with cold water. Cover and simmer for 2½ to 3 hours. Drain and remove rind and excess fat.
2. Braise ham another hour in a suitable pan with the wine and Madeira, turning it from time to time as described in **Section 18.1.1.2**.
3. Bring the stock in the pan to the boiling point and skim the fat. If necessary, reduce and then add the demi-glace.
4. Season the sauce as desired. Bring back to a boil and strain.

Variations of Ham

Boiled Ham with Sauerkraut—Jambon a la choucroute. Poach the ham. Garnish with sauerkraut and boiled potatoes. Serve Madeira Sauce blended with white wine separately.

Braised Ham, Burgundy Style—Jambon braise a la bourguignonne. Braise the ham and garnish with mushrooms. Serve Madeira Sauce mixed with reduced braising stock separately.

Braised Ham with Lettuce—Jambon braise aux laitues. Braise the ham and surround with steamed lettuce. Serve demi-glace sauce blended with the reduced braising stock separately.

Braised Ham, Milanese Style—Jambon braise milanaise. Braise the ham and garnish with Spaghetti, Milanese Style. Serve demi-glace sauce blended with tomate puree and the reduced braising stock separately.

Braised Ham with Spinach—Jambon braise aux epinards. Braise the ham and garnish with buttered spinach or creamed spinach. Serve demi-glace sauce blended with the reduced braising pan stock, separately.

18.4.3 Ham in a Pastry (Jambon en croute)

YIELD: *approximately 20 servings*

INGREDIENTS	*U.S. Weight or Volume*	*Metric Weight or Volume*	PROCEDURE
Ham	1-10 to 12 pounds	1-5 to 6 kilograms	1. Soak the ham for one day in lukewarm water. 2. Rinse the ham with cold water and scrub with a brush. 3. Dry the ham, and roll it into the bread dough. Garnish with the remaining dough. 4. Roll out dough and place ham in the center. Enclose the ham with the dough. Seal the edges. 5. Bake 25 minutes per pound of meat in oven at 440°F. (225°C.). Cover with aluminum foil for half the baking time.
Bread dough	4 pounds	2 kilograms	
To prepare bread dough:			
Flour	3 pounds	1.5 kilograms	1. Heat the water to 75°F. (25°C.). Add the yeast and salt and stir until dissolved. 2. Place the flour in a large bowl. Add the yeast and water mixture to flour. Stir until blended. Knead the dough vigorously for about 10 minutes. 3. Allow the dough to rise (covered) in a moderately warm place for about 3 hours before using.
Salt	1 ounce	30 grams	
Yeast	1½ ounces	40 grams	
Water	1½ pints	8 deciliters	

Note: The degree of doneness is best checked by use of a meat thermometer. (See page 258.) The following garnishes are suitable: a platter of different salads, pickles, mixed pickles, gherkins, or leaf spinach with grapes and roasted pine kernels. Serve Madeira Sauce separately.

18.4.4 Garnishes for Loin, Fillet, Tenderloin, Shoulder, and Neck of Pork

Roast as described in Section 18.1.5.2.

Boulangere Style—boulangere. Serve on potatoes boulangere. (See page 449.)
with Brussels Sprouts—au chou de Bruxelles. (See page 436.)
with Chestnuts—aux marrons. Garnish with glazed chestnuts.
German Style—a l'allemande. Serve with stewed apples or applesauce.
Jardiniere Style—jardiniere. Surround the meat with bouquets of various vegetables.
Naples Style—napolitaine. Garnish with Spaghetti napolitaine. (See page 459.)
with Creamed Potatoes—aux pommes mousseline. (See page 450.) Serve gravy separately.
with Red Cabbage—au chou rouge. Serve with braised red cabbage. (See page 437.)
Swedish Style—a la suedoise. Roast with presoaked prunes. Serve cranberry sauce separately.
with Braised White Cabbage—au chou blanc braise. Serve with braised white cabbage. (See page 437.)

18.5 Variations of Main Lamb or Mutton Dishes

18.5.1 Stuffed Shoulder of Lamb (Ballotine d'agneau)

YIELD: *6 to 8 portions*

INGREDIENTS	*U.S. Weight or Volume*	*Metric Weight or Volume*	PROCEDURE
Stuffing (see below)			1. Flatten boned shoulder. Spread with the prepared stuffing. Roll shoulder and stuffing. Tie securely with butcher twine.
Lamb shoulder	6 pounds	3 kilograms	
Oil	2 ounces	60 milliliters	2. Rub rolled lamb with oil, salt, pepper, and rosemary. Roast in oven at 325°F. (165°C.) for about 1 hour.
Salt	2 teaspoons	12 grams	
Pepper	½ teaspoon	2 grams	
Rosemary	1 teaspoon	4 grams	
Mirepoix:			
Onion, coarsely chopped	3 ounces	100 grams	3. Turn roast and add mirepoix. Roast to an internal temperature of 180°F. (80°C.).
Celery, coarsely chopped	2 ounces	50 grams	4. Remove the meat. Drain the fat into a saucepan and add flour to make a roux. Cook 10 minutes, browning lightly.
Carrots, coarsely chopped	2 ounces	50 grams	
Wine	½ cup	1 deciliter	5. Deglaze the roast pan with wine and the basic stock. Simmer until vegetables are tender. Strain.
Brown stock	1½ pints	¾ liter	6. Add strained stock to cooked roux and cook until thickened and smooth. Adjust seasoning.
Stuffing:			
Veal	7 ounces	200 grams	
Pork	7 ounces	200 grams	
Bacon, lean diced	7 ounces	200 grams	
Onion	1¾ ounces	50 grams	
Garlic	½ clove	½ clove	
Salt	1 teaspoon	6 grams	
Seasonings	as needed	as needed	
Parsley, chopped	8 sprigs	8 sprigs	
Eggs	1 to 2	1 to 2	

Note: For further explanation see Sections 18.1.5.2, 18.1.1.2 and illustration on page 439.

18.5.2 Baron of Lamb—Baron d'agneau

The baron consists of the whole of the saddle with both legs and is roasted in one piece as described in section 18.1.5.1. (See illustration page 234.) The same garnishes may be used as for leg of lamb and rib roast.

18.5.3 Leg of Lamb, English Style (Gigot d'agneau a l'anglaise)

YIELD: *approximately 8 servings*

INGREDIENTS	*U.S. Weight or Volume*	*Metric Weight or Volume*
Leg of lamb	1 leg, 5 pounds	1 leg, 2¼ kilograms
Bouquet garni	10 ounces	300 grams
Salt	1 teaspoon	4 grams
Peppercorns, crushed	6	6
Carrots	14 ounces	400 grams
Turnips	14 ounces	400 grams
Cabbage	14 ounces	400 grams
Green beans	14 ounces	400 grams

PROCEDURE

1. Blanch the lamb.
2. Simmer over low heat with the bouquet garni, the salt, and peppercorns until tender for approximately 2½ hours.
3. Cook the vegetables in stock. Arrange them in bouquets around the sliced lamb.
4. Pour a small amount of the stock over lamb and vegetables.
5. Serve Caper Sauce separately.

Note: The leg of lamb may also be served with a puree of turnips, celery, and potatoes, or beans. The vegetables may be cooked with the meat and then pureed. For further explanation of boiling method see Section 18.1.2.

18.5.4 Leg of Lamb Boulangere Style (Gigot d'agneau a la boulangere)

YIELD: *8 servings*

INGREDIENTS	*U.S. Weight or Volume*	*Metric Weight or Volume*
Leg of lamb	6 pounds	3 kilograms
Oil	2 ounces	60 milliliters
Marjoram	¼ teaspoon	1 gram
Thyme	¼ teaspoon	1 gram
Rosemary	¼ teaspoon	1 gram
Garlic	1 clove	1 clove
Potatoes, sliced	4 pounds	2 kilograms
Onion, sliced	7 ounces	200 grams
Butter	1¾ ounces	50 grams
Salt	1 teaspoon	6 grams
Pepper	½ teaspoon	3 grams

PROCEDURE

1. Preheat oven to 450°F. (230°C.).
2. Rub meat with oil, marjoram, thyme, rosemary, and garlic.
3. Insert a meat thermometer in center of meat. Place meat fat side up in a roasting pan. Reduce heat to 325°F. (165°C.) and roast 1 hour.
4. Season raw sliced potatoes with salt and pepper and place in pan with lamb. Roast until brown.
5. Add onion and continue to roast for remainder of cooking time.
6. Roast until meat reaches an internal temperature of 180°F. (80°C.).
7. Arrange the potatoes in a layer and place the carved meat on top. Coat with butter. Serve gravy separately.

Note: **For further explanation see Section 18.1.5.1 and Fig. 18-2.**

18.5.5 Saddle of Lamb—Selle d'agneau

As described in Section 18.1.5.1, roast a saddle of lamb until rare (the English fashion). Young spring vegetables (mushroom caps with glazed pearl onions, tomatoes, leaf spinach) may be used as garnishes. (See illustration, page 442; recipe, page 412.)

18.5.6 Garnishes for Saddle, Baron, Loin, and Leg of Lamb

Roast as described in Section 18.1.5.1. Legs of mature animals should be simmered or braised. (See Sections 18.1.2 and 18.1.1.1.)

Breton Style—a la bretonne. Prepare navy beans or lima beans and use as a garnish or an accompaniment for sliced mutton (roasted or braised). Serve gravy separately.
with Green Beans—aux haricots verts. Saute blanched green beans in butter and serve as a garnish or an accompaniment for roasted or braised meat. Serve gravy in a sauce boat.
with Pureed Onions—a la soubise. Roast. Serve with a soubise. (See page 312.)
with Spinach—aux epinards. Use creamed spinach or spinach timbales as a garnish or an accompaniment for roasted meat. Serve gravy separately.

18.6 Variations of Main Poultry Dishes

18.6.1 Chicken—Poulet

Poeler, poach, or roast as described in sections 18.1.3.2, 18.1.4, 18.1.5.3.

Methods of Serving Chicken, Poularde, and Capon
Beaulieu—beaulieu. Roast or poeler. Deglaze with white wine. Then add demi-glace, boil, and strain. Garnishes: artichokes, olives, and quartered tomatoes. Serve sauce separately.
Bonne Femme Style—bonne femme. Roast or poeler. Deglaze with white wine and thick veal stock. Reduce to the desired consistency, and strain. Garnishes or accompaniments: fried slices of lean bacon, glazed pearl onions, and chateau potatoes. Serve gravy separately.
in a Casserole—en casserole. Poeler (without mirepoix, only diced bacon). Just before serving, add preglazed carrots, turnips, and pearl onions to the casserole. Deglaze with Madeira and demi-glace. Serve the carved bird in a casserole covered with the sauce and vegetables. Sprinkle chopped parsley on top.
Chicken Pie, English Style—Chicken Pie. (See page 480.)
in Cocottes—en cocotte. Preparation as for "in a casserole."
in Cocottes, Grandmother's Style—en cocotte a la grand-mere. Poeler with diced bacon. For the last few minutes, add pre-glazed onions and quartered mushrooms and cook with the chicken. Deglaze with Madeira and thick veal stock. Serve the carved chicken with the garnishes in a cocotte. Sprinkle bread croutons fried in butter and parsley over the top. (See illustration, page 441.)
Demidoff—Demidov. Roast or poeler. Deglaze with Madeira or thick veal stock, reduce to the desired consistency, and strain. Garnishes or accompaniments: glazed celery, carrots, and turnips arranged in bouquets. Place slices of truffles on the top of the bird. Serve the sauce separately.
with Goose Liver Stuffing—farci au foie gras. Clean and wash spring chickens or smaller hens. Then inject goose liver puree under the skin of the breast from the front, using a pastry bag. Truss the chicken, bind a thin slice of bacon on to the breast, and roast, basting frequently. Serve a brown truffle sauce (Perigueux Sauce) separately.
Fermiere Style—a la fermiere. Roast or poeler. Deglaze with white wine, add demi-glace, heat to the boiling point, and strain. Garnishes or accompaniments: carrots, peas, lettuce, and potatoes noisettes. Serve the sauce separately.
Forestiere Style—a la forestiere. Poeler. Deglaze with white wine and thick veal stock. Reduce to the de-

sired consistency and strain. Garnish with sauteed morels or cepes over the bird, and potatoes noisettes alongside. Coat slightly with gravy and serve additional gravy separately.

Mascot—Mascotte. Roast or poeler. Deglaze with white wine and thick veal stock. Reduce to the desired consistency and strain. Garnishes or accompaniments: sauteed morels and Potatoes Parmentier together with slices of truffles placed on top of the bird. Serve the gravy separately.

with Noodles—aux nouilles. Poeler. Deglaze with Madeira. Then add demi-glace, heat to the boiling point, and strain. Garnish with noodles and serve the sauce separately.

Poached—poche. Clean the bird and then poach it, as described in Section 18.1.4. Prepare a Supreme Sauce from the stock and pour it over the carved bird when serving.

Note: Poached poultry should not be completely covered with the sauce. Additional sauce should be served in a sauce boat.

Poached with Rice—poche au riz. Poach the chicken and prepare a Supreme Sauce from the stock. Pour the sauce over the carved chicken. Garnish with white rice that has been cooked in bouillon.

Poached with Tarragon—poche a l'estragon. Poach in stock. Use the stock and prepare a Supreme Sauce flavored with tarragon. Pour the sauce over the carved chicken and garnish with blanched tarragon leaves.

Poached with Truffles—poche a la demi-deuil. Poach. Prepare a Supreme Sauce from the stock. Pour the sauce over the carved bird, and garnish with slices of truffles.

Richelieu. Roast or poeler. Deglaze with Madeira and thick veal stock. Reduce to the desired consistency and strain. Saute julienne of carrots, celery, and onions. Combine with a julienne of truffles and sprinkle over the chicken. Pour the sauce in a ring around the chicken and vegetables.

with Risotto—au risotto. Roast or poeler. Deglaze with white wine and thick veal stock. Reduce to the desired consistency and strain. Garnish with a risotto. Serve sauce separately.

with Spring Vegetables—aux premeurs. Roast or poeler. Deglaze with white wine and thick veal stock. Reduce to the desired consistency and strain. Garnish with bouquets of spring vegetables. Serve gravy separately.

18.6.2 Ducks and Geese—Canards et oies

Roast, braise, or poeler as described in Sections 18.1.3.2, 18.1.1.1, and 18.1.5.3. Older birds should be braised. (See Section 18.1.1.2.)

Duck with Olives—Canard aux olives. Poeler. Add pitted olives to the sauce (see "Poaching Poultry") and pour the sauce over the carved bird. Surround with heart-shaped fried toast. (This dish is also served under the name "Salmi of Duck.")

Braised Goose with Sauerkraut—Oie braisee a la choucroute. Braise the goose and then place it on the sauerkraut and steam for the last quarter of the cooking time. Prepare the sauerkraut using goose fat. Carve the goose, arrange on the sauerkraut, and surround with smoked sausage and lean bacon. Serve with the sauce and with boiled potatoes.

Duck with Turnips—Canards aux navets. Poeler. Serve sauce separately. (See "Poaching Poultry.") Garnish the carved duck with glazed turnips (navets).

Roast Duckling with Applesauce—Caneton roti—apple sauce. Roast the duck. Serve applesauce separately.

Young Duckling Bigarade—Caneton bigarade. Roast. Drain the fat, and then deglaze with stock. Reduce the stock and add a Bigarade Sauce. (See page 301.) Cover the carved duck with slices of sauteed oranges. Pour sauce around the bird and serve the remainder of the sauce separately.

Roast Duckling with Chestnuts—Caneton aux marrons. Roast. Deglaze with Madeira and stock. Garnish with glazed chestnuts. Serve the gravy separately.

Duckling, Nivernese Style—Caneton a la nivernaise. Roast. Surround with glazed pearl onions and carrots. Serve gravy separately.

Roast Duckling with Orange—Caneton a l'orange. Prepare by the same method described for Young Duckling Bigarade above. Substitute gravy for Bigarade Sauce. It should be served separately.

Cassoulet of Goose—Cassoulet d'oie. (See page 470.)

Roast Goose with Applesauce—Oie roti—apple sauce.

Roast the goose. Serve applesauce separately.
Goose with Chestnuts—Oie aux marrons. Roast or braise. Garnish with glazed chestnuts. Serve gravy separately.
Roast Goose with Chipolatas—Oie aux chipolatas. Roast. Garnish with chipolatas.

18.6.3 Tom Turkey or Turkey-hen —Dindon ou dinde

Roast or poeler young birds as described in Sections 18.1.3.2 and 18.1.5.3. Braise older birds. (See Section 18.1.1.2.)
Young Turkey with Chipolatas—Dindonneau aux chipolatas. Poeler the turkey. (See Section 18.1.3.2.) Deglaze with white wine and veal stock. Reduce the stock to the desired consistency and strain. Garnishes or accompaniments: glazed onions, carrots, chestnuts, quartered mushrooms, and chipolata sausages. Arrange the garnishes in bouquets around the carved bird. Pour a little gravy over the bird and serve the remainder separately. Capons, poulardes, and geese may also be served this way.

18.6.4 Guinea Fowl—Pintades

Roast or poeler as described in Section 18.1.3.2 and 18.1.5.3. Bard the bird first. (See page 237.)

Creamed Guinea Fowl—Pintade a la creme. Poeler as described in Section 18.1.3.2. Deglaze with white wine and a little demi-glace. Add sour cream, reduce to the desired consistency, and strain. Serve the sauce separately.
Guinea Fowl with Sauerkraut—Pintade a la choucroute. This dish is prepared by the same method used for "Braised Duck with Sauerkraut."

18.6.5 Pigeons—Pigeons

Use only young birds. Bard with slices of bacon. (See page 237.) Roast as described in Section 18.1.5.3. Deglaze with Madeira. Garnishes or accompaniments: young vegetables, roast or baked potatoes.

Stuffed Pigeons—Pigeons farcis. Ingredients for the stuffing: Finely chop the liver and heart of the pigeon and combine it with chopped shallots and herbs. Add 7 ounces (200 grams) of raw veal and 2 ounces (60 grams) of bread that has been soaked in milk and pressed out. Add 2 or 3 egg yolks, 1 teaspoon (6 grams) of salt, ¼ teaspoon (2 grams) of pepper and mix thoroughly. Stuff the birds with the dressing, bard with slices of bacon (see page 237), and roast in the oven, basting frequently. Deglaze with Madeira and veal stock.

18.7 Variations for Main Dishes with Game Birds

Older birds are not suitable for the following form of preparation. Game birds should always be *barded with slices of bacon* before roasting. A hot oven, 460°F. to 490°F. (238°C. to 256°C.), is absolutely necessary, especially for small birds. Roast game birds are presented on correspondingly-sized fried bread or canapes. Canapes are flat toasts, the same size as the bird, spread with a gratin forcemeat.

Small game birds should be roasted as described in Section 18.1.5.3 Carved woodcock, quail, and hazel-grouse are served on *canapes* or *fried toast*, with the gravy served separately.

Gratin forcemeat: Lightly saute chopped shallots in butter. Add diced bacon, game liver or chicken liver, and mushroom parings. Saute a little longer, strain thoroughly, and season.

Garnishes for game birds include glazed onions, chestnuts, mushrooms, truffles, and goose liver. *Sauces* include gravy, Bread Sauce **(see page 312)**, and Cranberry Sauce. Bread crumbs may also be used.

18.7.1 Pheasant and Partridge—Faisan et perdreau

Bard with bacon slices. (See page 237.)
Roast or poeler as described in Sections 18.1.5.4 and 18.1.3.2.

Creamed Pheasant—Faisan a la creme. Same preparation as Creamed Guinea Fowl. (See page 425.)
Pheasant on Canape—Faisan sur canape. Bard, roast, and deglaze with Madeira and veal stock. Place the pheasant on a serving dish on a canape. Cut the bacon used for barding the bird into strips and place on top of the pheasant. Pour some gravy on the bottom of the serving dish and serve the remainder separately. Garnish with potato chips.
Pheasant in Cocotte—Faisan en cocotte. Bard the pheasant, poeler, carve, and place in a cocotte on a canape. Garnish with mushroom caps, truffles, and potatoes noisettes. Deglaze the pan with brandy and prepare a gravy. Pour the gravy over the pheasant, cover, and heat to the boiling point. Serve hot.
Pheasant with Sauerkraut—Faisan a la choucroute. Poeler the pheasant until it is medium-done and deglaze with Madeira and stock. Place the carved bird on sauerkraut and heat to the boiling point. Surround with slices of lean bacon and smoked sausage. Serve the gravy and boiled potatoes separately.
Partridge with Cabbage—Perdreau au chou. Bard and roast a partridge until almost done. Deglaze with Madeira and veal stock. Braise cabbage (chou braise) with lean bacon and smoked sausages and cook the roasted partridge the last few minutes with the cabbage. Carve the bird and arrange on the cabbage. Garnish with the bacon and sausages. Serve gravy and boiled potatoes separately.
Partridge on Canape—Perdreau sur canape. Bard and roast using a fairly high temperature, and finish in the same way as Pheasant on Canape. (See illustration, page 442.)
Partridge in Cocotte—Perdreau en cocotte. Prepare in the same way as Pheasant in Cocotte.
Poultry Salmis—Salmis de volaille. Sear the bird very quickly, using a high temperature and leaving the meat underdone. Then remove the skin and cut the breast into slices, the legs into pieces. Chop the breastbone, trimmings, and skin and use them to make a Salmis Sauce. (See page 302.) Cover the pieces of poultry, which have been kept warm in the meantime, with the sauce and garnish with slices of truffles and mushrooms.
Note: Game birds (wild ducks, partridge, pheasant, and snipe) are generally used for Poultry Salmis; however, duck, guinea fowl, and pigeon may be used.

18.8 Variations of Main Dishes with Game Animals

The main dishes prepared using game animals are *saddle and leg of venison, saddle and leg of hare,* together with the same typical cuts of young wild boar. For roasts taken from game animals, proper aging (hanging) is essential and more effective than marinading.

18.8.1 Garnishes for Game

For Saddle of Roebuck, Leg of Roebuck, Saddle of Chamois, Leg of Chamois, Saddle of Red Deer, Leg of Red Deer, Saddle of Reindeer, Leg of Reindeer, Saddle of Hare, Leg of Hare, Saddle of Boar, Leg of Boar

Age well, lard (see page 241), roast as described in Section 18.1.5.1.

Baden—Baden. Roast with a mirepoix. Deglaze the gravy with demi-glace, white wine, and cream. Reduce the sauce, skim the fat, add a pinch of cayenne and a few drops of lemon juice, and strain. Surround the carved roast with halved pears filled with cranberries. Serve the sauce separately.
German Style—a l'allemande. Roast the larded pieces of meat. Deglaze the gravy with white wine, add demi-glace and sour cream, or cream together with a few juniper berries. Reduce the sauce to the desired consistency and strain. Skim the fat and season the sauce to taste with paprika. Coat the bottom of the serving dish with some of the sauce and serve the remainder separately. Spaetzle or noodles may be used as a garnish or an accompaniment.
Hunter's Style—Chasseur. This dish is prepared by the method used for Baden-Baden. Garnish with mushrooms, brussels sprouts, turnips, and potato fondantes. Serve red currant jelly and the sauce sepa-

rately.

Mirza. Prepare with Pepper Sauce. Fill halved, stewed apples with red currant jelly and use as a garnish around the carved roast. Serve Pepper Sauce separately.

with Pepper Sauce—a la poivrade. Roast the larded pieces of meat. Deglaze the gravy with white wine. Add crushed peppercorns and demi-glace, heat to the boiling point, and strain. Add some lemon juice and butter. Accompaniments include spaetzle, noodles, glazed onions, carrots, chestnuts, mushrooms, and winter vegetables.

19

Salads—Salades

It is difficult to define or classify salads. They are generally classified on the basis of their ingredients, or their use, or whether hot or cold. A salad usually consists of fresh greens, vegetables, fruits, dairy products, meat, fish, or poultry, served simply or in combination with a dressing. There are some exceptions. The salad may be served as an hors d'oeuvre, an accompaniment, or a main course.

Salads usually consist of four parts: the base, the body, the dressing, and the garnish. The base is nearly always lettuce or some form of salad greens; the body is made up of the ingredients that constitute the main part of the salad; the salad dressing is used to blend the salad ingredients and to add flavor; the garnish is used to add color, texture, and flavor, and it should always complement the other ingredients of the salad.

Simple salads are perhaps the most authentic of all salads. These include green salads and salads consisting of a cooked vegetable. Simple salads, especially the green salad, are served with the roast or the main course.

19.1 Salad Dressings—Sauces a salade

19.1.1 Original French Dressing—Sauce a salade francaise

Ingredients: White wine vinegar and oil in a ratio of about 1:3, depending on the strength of the vinegar, salt, and pepper.

Preparation: Mix all ingredients thoroughly.

Note: A small amount of garlic powder, finely chopped onion, and some Dijon mustard may be added. Sprinkle the prepared salad with freshly chopped parsley or chives.

19.1.2 Italian Dressing—Sauce a salade italienne

Ingredients: Red salad wine and olive oil in a ratio of about 1:4, depending on the strength of the salad wine, salt, and pepper.

Preparation: Mix all ingredients thoroughly.

Note: Finely chopped garlic may be added to the dressing. Sprinkle the prepared salad with chopped parsley before serving.

19.1.3 American French Dressing (Sauce a salade americaine)

YIELD: *U.S. — 10 quarts*
Metric — 10 liters (U.S. equiv.—10½ qt)

INGREDIENTS	*U.S. Weight or Volume*	*Metric Weight or Volume*	PROCEDURE
Mustard, dry	¾ ounce	20 grams	1. Dissolve the mustard in the water.
Water	¼ cup	½ deciliter	2. Combine the mustard, egg yolks, vinegar, paprika, garlic powder, sugar, Worcestershire Sauce, pepper, and salt in a blender or mixer.
Egg yolks	20	20	3. Add the oil slowly and whip until the dressing is smooth and thoroughly blended.
Vinegar	2 quarts	2 liters	
Paprika	¾ ounce	20 grams	
Garlic powder	½ ounce	10 grams	
Sugar	½ ounce	10 grams	
Worcestershire sauce	¼ cup	½ deciliter	
Pepper	½ ounce	10 grams	
Salt	4 ounces	120 grams	
Oil	7½ quarts	7 liters	

19.1.4 Roquefort Dressing (Sauce a salade au roquefort)

YIELD: *U.S. — 1 quart*
Metric — 1 liter (U.S. equiv.—1½ qt)

INGREDIENTS	*U.S. Weight or Volume*	*Metric Weight or Volume*	PROCEDURE
Roquefort cheese	3½ ounces	100 grams	1. Crumble the cheese and add to the dressing.
French dressing, freshly prepared (recipe 19.1.1)	1¾ pints	9 deciliters	2. Whip in a blender or mixer until smooth.

Note: Lemon juice may be substituted for the vinegar in the dressing.

19.1.5 Creamed Salad Dressing (Sauce a salade a la creme)

YIELD: *U.S. — 1 quart*
Metric — 1 liter (U.S. equiv.—1½ qt)

INGREDIENTS	*U.S. Weight or Volume*	*Metric Weight or Volume*	PROCEDURE
Cream	1½ pints	7 deciliters	1. Whip all ingredients in a blender or mixer just before serving.
Vinegar	¾ cup	3 deciliters	
Lemon juice	1 tablespoon	15 milliliters	
Salt	1½ teaspoons	8 grams	
Dry mustard	½ teaspoon	3 grams	
Sugar	½ teaspoon	3 grams	

Note: The vinegar may be replaced with lemon juice.

19.1.6 Cream Cheese Dressing (Sauce a salade au sere de lait)

YIELD: *U.S. — 1 quart*
Metric — 1 liter (U.S. equiv.—1½ qt)

INGREDIENTS	*U.S. Weight or Volume*	*Metric Weight or Volume*	PROCEDURE
Yoghurt	1¼ pints	6 deciliters	1. Beat the yoghurt and cream cheese until creamy.
Cream cheese	10 ounces	300 grams	
Salt	1 teaspoon	6 grams	2. Add seasonings, lemon juice, Worcestershire Sauce, and chives.
Pepper	1/8 teaspoon	1 gram	
Lemon juice	2 tablespoons	½ deciliter	
Worcestershire Sauce	1 tablespoon	15 milliliters	
Chives, chopped	¼ cup	½ deciliter	

Mayonnaise Sauce—Sauce mayonnaise. Thinned mayonnaise, as described in recipe 11.4.1.
Vinaigrette Sauce—Sauce vinaigrette. See recipe 11.4.2.

19.2 Simple Salads—Salades simples

Salad greens should be fresh and of good quality. They should be washed thoroughly in large quantities of water, separating the leaves to remove all the dirt and grit. The greens should be trimmed carefully, drained, refrigerated in damp cloth bags or in a colander covered with a damp cloth. Salad greens should be torn, not cut, to avoid bruising.

Salads should be presented artistically and simply so that each ingredient can be identified. The ingredients should be fresh with contrasts in color and texture, and they should be arranged attractively on the plate. Chopped chives or parsley, a sprig of watercress, sliced truffles, chopped or sliced hard-cooked eggs sprinkled over the salad will enhance the flavor and appearance.

Apple Salad—Salade de pommes. Cut peeled apples into quarters, remove the core, and slice very thin. Mix with salad dressing and sugar. Serve on crisp lettuce and sprinkle with chopped walnuts. This salad is excellent with roast poultry, game, pork, and with cold dishes.

Asparagus Salad—Salade d'asperges. Arrange cooked asparagus spears in layers in a salad bowl. Coat each layer with salad dressing or with a thin mayonnaise without covering the tips. Sprinkle with chopped truffles or parsley.

Avocado Salad—Salade aux avocats. Serve slices of avocado on crisp lettuce with a cream or Roquefort Dressing.

Beet Salad—Salade de betteraves. Wash whole beets and boil in water. Peel immediately and put back into the cooking water until cold. Heat equal quantities of wine vinegar and red wine to the boiling point with a studded onion (bay leaf and clove), a little salt, and sugar. Place the cooled beets in a bowl and cover with the hot vinegar and red wine mixture. A small amount of oil may be added if desired. Cover and refrigerate. These beets can be kept for long periods of time. Cut into slices or a rough julienne before serving.

Note: Sliced or julienne of canned beets may be used.

Breton Salad—Salade bretonne. Saute chopped onion and diced bacon in oil, add soaked navy beans, cover with stock, and cook until tender. Mix with oil and vinegar and season to taste.

Note: This salad, a good accompaniment with sausages, should always be served lukewarm.

Red Cabbage Salad—Salade de chou rouge. Prepare this salad by the same method used for coleslaw.

Carrot Salad—Salade de carottes. Slice peeled and cooked carrots. Mix with salt, pepper, finely chopped onion, and a spicy salad dressing. Sprinkle with parsley or chives before serving.

Cauliflower Salad—Salade de chou-fleur. Cut cooked cauliflower into florets. Arrange the florets in a single layer on the bottom of a salad bowl, cover lightly with thin mayonnaise, add a second layer of cauliflower and mayonnaise, and sprinkle with parsley.

Celery Salad—Salade de celeri cuit. Wash celery roots or stalks, boil in salted water, cool, and drain. Cut the roots into uniform slices and the stalks into lengths of 1½ to 2½ inches (3.7 to 6.2 centimeters), and arrange in bowls. Cover with salad dressing and sprinkle with chopped parsley.

Raw Celery Salad—Salade de celeri cru. Wash celery roots, peel, and cut into julienne strips. Mix with a thin, spicy mayonnaise, and sprinkle with chopped parsley and lemon juice.

Coleslaw—Salade de chou blanc. Wash cabbage and slice into fine strips. Mix with vinegar and chopped onion. Saute diced bacon and pour, together with the fat, over the salad. Then season with salt, pepper, and nutmeg. Add a little oil and marinate the salad for one to two hours. This salad may also be made with a spicy salad dressing. The sliced cabbage may be parboiled in hot water before the dressing is added.

Corn Salad—Salade de mache. Dress corn salad with salt, pepper, vinegar, and oil.

Note: Thick salad dressings are not suitable for this salad. Chopped hard-cooked eggs can be added, if desired.

Cucumber Salad—Salade de concombre. Cut peeled cucumbers lengthwise into two halves and remove the seeds. Cut the cucumber into thin slices, mix with some salt, place in a bowl, and press for at least 2 hours, using a plate with a suitable weight on top. Drain the juice, add the salad dressing to the cucumbers, and sprinkle with parsley.

Note: The raw cucumber may be mixed with the salad dressing without being pressed.

Elizabeth Salad—Salade Elizabeth. Pour lemon juice, seasoning, and fresh cream over Boston lettuce.

Endive Salad, Brussels Style Witloof—Salade d'endives de Bruxelles Witloof. Wash the endive, cut into strips or fine slices, wash again, and prepare with a thin mayonnaise sauce.

Note: Thin slices of apple or mandarin can be added to the endive. The salad may be garnished with walnuts. Whole leaves of endive may be served as a salad with a separate sauce.

Green Salad—Salade verte. Clean the lettuce carefully, break the large leaves, and remove any tough ribs. Break chicory and endive into strips. Wash the greens thoroughly, drain, and dry on a cloth. Toss the salad just before serving with oil, vinegar, and seasoning. (See recipes 19.1.1 and 19.1.2.)

Iceberg Lettuce Salad. This salad is made by the method described for Green Salad.

Leek Salad—Salade de poireau. Cut the white part of leeks into 2½ inch (6.2 centimeters) pieces, wash, blanch, cool, and cook in the following marinade for approximately 10 minutes: ¼ cup (½ deciliter) of olive oil, juice of 1 lemon, ½ teaspoon (3 grams) of salt, 4 peppercorns, 1 bay leaf, 2 stalks of parsley, 1/8 teaspoon (2 grams) of tarragon, and water to cover the vegetables. Serve cold on crisp lettuce.

Mushroom Salad—Salade de champignons. Cut 1 pound (.5 kilogram) of washed mushrooms into fine slices and immediately mix in lemon juice, salt, and pepper. Then add 1¾ ounces (50 grams) of chopped onion, a finely chopped garlic clove, oil, and vinegar. Sprinkle with parsley and garnish with tomato slices.

Potato Salad—Salade de pommes de terre. Cook potatoes until slightly underdone. Peel the warm potatoes and cut into fine slices. Marinate the warm potatoes for several hours in a mixture of salt, pepper, chopped onion, and bouillon. Drain thoroughly and add a spicy salad dressing, adjust seasonings, and refrigerate until thoroughly chilled. Serve on crisp lettuce and sprinkle with parsley or chives.

Spinach Salad—Salade d'epinards. Yield: 10 servings. Clean and thoroughly wash 3 pounds (1½ kilograms) of fresh spinach leaves. Arrange the leaves on a cloth, dry, and cut into strips. Just before serving, mix the spinach with a chopped onion, a chopped garlic clove, salt, pepper, oil, and vinegar. (Salad dressing may be substituted for the oil and vinegar.)

String Bean Salad—Salade de haricots verts. Remove the strings from fresh beans, blanch, cool, and drain. Cut the beans into 2 inch (5 centimeters) lengths and mix with salad dressing.

Sweet Corn Salad. Drain kernels of corn. Mix with a French or well-seasoned Mayonnaise Dressing.

Note: The salad may be garnished with pineapple wedges, sweet peppers, or Chili Sauce.

Tomato Salad—Salade de tomates. Plunge tomatoes into boiling water for a few seconds, peel, slice, and arrange attractively in a salad bowl. Pour salad dressing over the tomatoes and sprinkle with chopped parsley.

Watercress Salad—Salade cressoniere. Combine clean watercress with salt, pepper, vinegar and oil, or with a suitable salad dressing.

19.3 Mixed Salads—Salades melees

There are many categories of mixed salads. Some are composed of mixed cooked vegetables and prepared by the same method used for simple salads. Others include a variety of ingredients, such as mushrooms, truffles, and tongue in addition to the vegetables. Some of these are more elaborate preparations that may include chicken, meat, or fish. The latter are usually served as an accompaniment to cold main dishes or they may be served as an hors d'oeuvre or a snack or as a cold entree instead of a salad.

Andalusian Salad—Salade andalouse. Combine tomato wedges, julienne of sweet peppers, dry cooked rice, and a few drops of garlic juice. Fold in a salad dressing, and sprinkle with parsley.

Avocado Salad, American Style—Salade aux avocats a l'americaine. Peel the halved and pitted avocados and cut into slices. Add diced orange and grapefruit. Blend a Cream Cheese dressing into the salad or serve the dressing over the top of the salad. Garnish with toasted pecans, sprigs of water cress, or pomegranate seeds.

Flemish Salad—Salade flamande. Combine a julienne of potatoes, diced anchovy fillets, chopped onion, and bite-size pieces of crisp chicory. Toss with a salad dressing and sprinkle with parsley.

Florida Salad—Salade Florida. Cut hearts of Boston lettuce in two, cover with salad dressing, and arrange chilled canned fruits (peaches, pears, red cherries) on the lettuce.

Italian Meat Salad—Salade italienne. With the exception of game, all roasts and boiled meats are suitable for this recipe. Cut meat, pickles, apples, and a few potatoes into strips and mix with a spicy mayonnaise, chopped onions, and anchovies. Garnish with hard-cooked eggs, pickles, anchovies, capers, and olives.

Italian Vegetable Salad—Salade italienne. Mix finely diced carrots, turnips, potatoes, cut green beans, peas, and a few capers.

Jockey Club Salad—Salade Jockey-club. Arrange asparagus spears in layers on a platter and coat with a spicy light mayonnaise without covering the tips. Sprinkle with a julienne of truffles.

Russian Salad—Salade russe. This salad is prepared with the same ingredients as those used in Italian Vegetable Salad. Diced lobster is added. The salad is mixed with Mayonnaise and garnished with caviar and smoked salmon. The same salad may be bound with aspic and poured into coated and decorated molds. The molded salad should be inverted onto a serving plate and decorated with crisp lettuce or chicory.

Waldorf Salad—Salade Waldorf. Combine a julienne of crisp celery with diced apples and mayonnaise. Garnish with walnuts and cubes or wedges of chilled pineapple.

Windsor Salad—Salade Windsor. Mix a julienne of truffles, celery, chicken, tongue, and mushrooms with Mayonnaise. Decorate with watercress or parsley.

19.4 Combined Salads—Salades assorties

These salads consist of a variety of salads. Each variety of vegetable is arranged in a separate group or a bouquet. The vegetables are placed on the serving plate in many different arrangements to emphasize the differences in shape, color, and texture. Some of the salads are combined and arranged in a serving bowl and decorated with bouquets or bundles of vegetables.

Belle Fermiere Salad—Salade belle fermiere. Prepare a julienne of cooked potatoes, beets, and celery, add dressing, arrange in bouquets, and sprinkle with parsley.

Emma Salad—Salade Emma. Arrange sliced tomatoes around cucumber salad and sprinkle with chopped chives.

Lakme Salad—Salade Lakme. Combine dry cooked rice with oil and lemon juice. Place the rice in a salad bowl and surround with slices of hard-cooked egg and sliced beets. Dust with paprika.

Lorette Salad—Salade Lorette. Prepare a julienne of Romaine lettuce, celery, and beets. Add salad dressing and arrange the vegetables in bouquets on a serving plate.

Nicoise Salad—Salade nicoise. Mix equal parts of sliced cooked potatoes and cooked string beans with a Vinaigrette Sauce. Chill thoroughly. Place in a salad bowl and garnish with anchovy fillets, olives, capers, and tomato wedges. Sprinkle with chopped tarragon or chervil.

Rachel Salad—Salade Rachel. Prepare a julienne of equal parts of celery, artichoke hearts, and cooked potatoes. Mix with Mayonnaise. Arrange in bouquets and garnish with marinated asparagus.

20 Vegetables—Legumes

20.1 Basic Cooking Methods

For cutting and shaping vegetables, see pages 238-239.

20.1.1 Blanching—Blanchir

Ingredients: Water and vegetables in a 10:1 ratio, salt.
Preparation: Place clean vegetables in a wire basket and submerge into rapidly boiling water. Cover and boil for the period of time specified on the recipe. If the vegetables are not to be used immediately, drain and plunge into ice water, and cool thoroughly.
Note: Blanching is an essential part of the freezing process. All vegetables should be blanched before freezing to inhibit the enzyme action that continues after harvesting. Blanching will help preserve nutrients and color, firm the texture of vegetables, and remove bitter flavors.

Blanching in oil is a preliminary stage of deep-fat frying used for large pieces or quantities of food. (See Section 20.1.8.)

20.1.2 Boiling—Cuire

20.1.2.1 Boiling Fresh Vegetables

Ingredients: Water, salt, lemon juice, veal kidney fat, and flour dissolved in water.
Preparation: Place the cleaned vegetables in simmering salted water, and boil until tender.
Note: Lemon juice, veal kidney fat, and a little flour dissolved in water may be added to black salsify, artichoke hearts, celery roots, and cardoons to prevent the vegetables from turning black.

20.1.2.2 Boiling Dried Vegetables (Legumes)

Ingredients: Water, dried vegetables (lentils, dried peas, dried beans), bouquet garni, bacon trimmings, and salt.
Preparation: Place the dried vegetables in cold water and bring to the boiling point. Skim, reduce heat, add a bouquet garni, and continue simmering until the vegetables are tender.
Note: Dried vegetables, with the exception of dried beans, do not require soaking. These vegetables are often used for soups. When served as a side dish, the vegetables are usually bound with a sauce.

Vegetable purees are usually made of legumes, such as peas, lentils, and dried beans. After boiling, they are put through a food mill or the attachment of the electric mixer. The purees are best seasoned with cream and butter. Bechamel Sauce, butter, and cream will improve purees made from vegetables that have a high water content.

20.1.3 Steaming—Cuire a vapeur

Ingredients: Salt, seasoning, and water.
Preparation: Season and salt the vegetables, and steam until tender. The time required for cooking will depend on the type and age of the vegetables, and the equipment in which they are cooked. The variety of vegetable and the type of equipment will determine whether the vegetable should be covered during steaming. Information is available from the various manufacturers of steam equipment giving recommended steaming times and procedures for their own equipment.
Note: Pressure steaming requires less cooking time than the conventional boiling method. Nutrients, flavor, and shape of vegetables are conserved better by steaming than by boiling.

20.1.4 Braising—Braiser

Ingredients: Fat, mirepoix, bacon rind, salt, seasoning, and stock.
Preparation: Saute the mirepoix and bacon rind lightly in the fat, place the blanched vegetables in the pan in layers, salt, and season, and pour in stock up to ⅓ the height of the vegetables. The higher the water content of the vegetables, the less stock needed. Cover with greaseproof paper, weigh down. Bring to a boil, reduce heat, and braise in the oven. The stock should be reduced when the vegetables are cooked. Serve vegetables hot with a garnish or sauce.
Note: Green beans and sugar peas are first fried with diced bacon, finely chopped onion and some savory, and then braised until tender.

20.1.5 Stewing/Simmering—Etuver

Ingredients: Fat, salt, seasoning, chopped shallots, lemon juice, and white wine.
Preparation: For vegetables with a high water content, such as tomatoes (tomatoes concassees), zucchini, and mushrooms, place the fat, salt, seasoning, lemon juice, shallots, and wine in a saute pan and reduce. Add the washed mushrooms or the vegetables, cover, and simmer until cooked. The vegetables should be cooked at a low temperature to prevent evaporation of the liquid.
Note: When these delicately flavored vegetables are stewed carefully, a natural, strong stock is obtained.

20.1.6 Glazing—Glacer

Ingredients: Butter, sugar, stock or water, and seasoning.
Preparation: Blanch peeled and cut vegetables if necessary. Drain and then place them in a wide shallow pan. Add the butter, sugar, seasoning, a small amount of liquid, cover the pan and cook gently until the liquid is reduced to a light syrup. Remove the cover, and toss the vegetables in the syrup until they have a shiny, glazed appearance.
Note: The vegetables may be boiled quickly in salted water and then carefully glazed a la minute in a saute pan with butter, sugar, and seasoning. The best vegetables for glazing are those containing sugar, such as carrots, chestnuts, turnips, and pearl onions.

20.1.7 Gratinating—Gratiner

Ingredients: Mornay Sauce, Hollandaise, or demiglace (see recipes 11.2.2, 11.3.1 or 11.1.1.1 and 11.1.1.2), cheese, butter, and seasoning.
Preparation: Clean, then boil, steam, or braise the washed vegetables. Drain and place them on a buttered gratin platter, cover with the appropriate sauce, sprinkle the sauce with grated cheese and melted butter, and gratinate the vegetables in the oven or under the broiler. The vegetables may be covered with cheese, sprinkled with butter, and gratinated.
Note: Asparagus, fennel, or celery are especially suited for gratinating.

20.1.8 Deep-Fat Frying—Frire

Ingredients: Salt, seasoning, flour, egg, breading, frying batter, and frying fat.

Preparation: Season the vegetables and coat with flour. Then either dip into beaten egg, and then in bread crumbs or in frying batter, and deep-fat fry at 340°F. (170°C.). Drain the fat, salt lightly, and serve hot.
Note: Vegetables with a high water content, such as zucchini, eggplants, and tomatoes, are deep-fat fried in their raw stage. Harder vegetables, such as celery roots, black salsify, artichoke hearts, and asparagus, should be boiled or steamed before deep-fat frying. Foods that have been blanched and that are not to be used immediately should be spread out on trays to prevent further cooking.

20.1.9 Sauteing—Sauter

Ingredients: Fat, salt, seasoning, and possibly flour.
Preparation: Heat the fat, add the vegetables, season, dust with flour if needed, toss carefully, brown lightly, and saute until the vegetables are cooked.
Note: This form of preparation is especially suitable for parboiled vegetables if the cooking is to be completed a la minute. Tender vegetables, such as zucchini, peas, and eggplants, can be sauteed without parboiling.

20.2 Variations for Vegetables

The section reference of the appropriate basic cooking methods for each of the variations is given in parenthesis.

Artichokes—Artichauts. (20.1.2.1) Trim, see Figure 7-42. Artichokes lend themselves to many different preparations. The young tender artichoke may be eaten raw; artichoke hearts may be cooked, chilled, and marinated; and whole boiled artichokes may be served hot with melted butter, Hollandaise, or various hot sauces. They may be served cold with mayonnaise or other dressings. Large artichokes may be cooked and stuffed with goose liver or with a salpicon of chicken and truffles or with vegetables.
Artichokes Colbert—Artichauts Colbert. (20.1.2.1) The cooked artichoke hearts are filled with duxelles. A Colbert Sauce is served separately.
Artichokes with Young Peas—Artichauts aux petits pois. (20.1.2.1) The cooked artichoke hearts are filled with peas and seasoned with melted butter.

Asparagus—Asperges. (20.1.2.1) Boiled asparagus spears are served with Hollandaise Sauce, mayonnaise, or melted butter.
Creamed Asparagus Tips—Pointes d'asperges a la creme. (20.1.2.1) The cooked asparagus tips are bound with a light cream sauce.
Gratinated Asparagus—Asperges au gratin. (20.1.2.1 and 20.1.7) Cooked asparagus spears are arranged in layers on a gratin platter. The tips on each layer are covered with a Mornay Sauce, sprinkled with grated cheese, and melted butter.
Asparagus, Milanese Style—Asperges milanaise. (20.1.2.1 and 20.1.7) This asparagus is boiled and arranged in layers on a gratin dish. The tips are sprinkled with cheese and melted butter, and gratinated in the oven.
Asparagus—Polish Style—Asperges polonaise. (20.1.2.1) This is prepared the same as Milanese Style except the asparagus tips are sprinkled with chopped egg and parsley and topped with white bread crumbs that have been mixed with melted butter.

Brussels Sprouts with Chestnuts—Choux de Bruxelles aux marrons. (20.1.1 and 20.1.9) Brussels sprouts and chestnuts have become a traditional holiday dish. Served with turkey or goose, the brussels sprouts are blanched, drained, and sauteed in butter. The chestnuts are washed, heated, and combined with the brussels sprouts.
Creamed Brussels Sprouts—Choux de Bruxelles a la creme. (20.1.1 and 20.1.9) These are tender, slightly crisp brussels sprouts that have been blanched, sauteed in butter, and covered with a cream sauce and heated in the oven.
Sauteed Brussels Sprouts—Choux de Bruxelles sautes. (20.1.1 and 20.1.9) These brussels sprouts are especially good with roast beef, roast pork, or lamb dishes. They are blanched and sauteed in butter until just tender.

Brussels Sprouts in White Sauce—Choux de Bruxelles au veloute. (20.1.1 and 20.1.9) This dish is prepared with blanched, drained, and sauteed brussels sprouts. They are placed in a serving dish, and covered with Veloute Sauce. They should be very hot when served.

Braised Green Cabbage—Chou vert braise. (20.1.1 and 20.1.4) Braised cabbage is used as a vegetable or as a part of many garnishes. It is trimmed, cut into large pieces, washed and blanched quickly in salt water, rinsed, and drained. Chopped onion is browned with small pieces of bacon and lard. The cabbage, salt, and a spice sachet are placed in a casserole with some stock. The vegetables are covered with buttered greaseproof paper and weighted down. The dish is covered and heated to the boiling point. It is then braised in the oven for 1½ to 2 hours.

Braised Red Cabbage—Chou rouge braise. (20.1.4) For 10 servings, stew 7 ounces (200 grams) of diced lean bacon, 7 ounces (200 grams) of finely chopped onion in 5 ounces (150 grams) of lard. Add 8 pounds (4 kilograms) of finely sliced red cabbage. Continue stewing a few minutes and deglaze with 1 pint (5 deciliters) of red wine and ¼ cup (½ deciliter) of vinegar. Season, add 2 teaspoons (12 grams) of sugar and 3 finely sliced apples. Cover the cabbage, heat to the boiling point, and braise in the oven at 350°F. (175°C.) for 1½ to 2 hours. Before serving, add ¼ cup (½ deciliter) of vinegar to give the cabbage a good red color.

Braised Red Cabbage with Bacon—Chou rouge braise au lard. (20.1.4) The method of preparation for Braised Red Cabbage is followed, garnishing the cabbage with strips of bacon.

Braised Red Cabbage with Chestnuts—Chou rouge braise aux marrons. (20.1.4) The method of preparation for Braised Red Cabbage is followed. The cabbage is garnished with chestnuts.

Braised Red Cabbage with Chipolata Sausages—Chou rouge braise aux chipolatas. (20.1.4) This red cabbage is garnished with chipolata sausages.

Braised White Cabbage—Chou blanc braise. (20.1.1 and 20.1.4) The method of preparation for Braised Green Cabbage is followed.

Braised White Cabbage with Bacon—Chou blanc braise au lard. (20.1.4) The method of preparation for Braised Green Cabbage is followed, garnishing the cabbage with strips of bacon.

Stuffed Cabbage—Chou farci. (20.1.1 and 20.1.4) These stuffed cabbage rolls may be made in various sizes. (See page 441.) *To prepare:* separate the cabbage into individual leaves and blanch for 10 minutes in salted water. Spread out 2 to 4 leaves for each bouquet on the table; place an appropriate amount of stuffing on each bouquet; and wrap the leaves around the stuffing. Tighten the cabbage rolls by rolling in a cloth; place them in a saute pan with onion rings and bacon parings; add a little stock, cover, and cook in the oven. Serve with a veal stock. *Note:* A raw mousseline forcemeat or a stuffing for simple hot dishes may be used for the stuffing.

Cardoons, Bordeaux Style—Cardons a la bordelaise. (20.1.2.1) These cardoons are boiled, arranged in a dish, and covered with Bordelaise Wine Sauce.

Gratinated Cardoons—Cardons Mornay. (20.1.2.1 and 20.1.7) These boiled cardoons are sliced and arranged on a gratin platter. The cardoons are covered with a Mornay Sauce, sprinkled with cheese and melted butter, and gratinated in the oven.

Cardoons with Gravy—Cardons au jus. (20.1.2.1) The cardoons for this dish are prepared in the same way as for Bordeaux Style except they are covered with a rich veal stock instead of Bordelaise Sauce.

Creamed Carrots—Carottes a la creme. (20.1.2.1) Sliced or young whole carrots may be used. They are served in a cream sauce.

Glazed Carrots—Carottes glacees. These carrots are glazed as described in Section 20.1.6.

Carrots Vichy—Vichy carottes. (20.1.6) Thin slices of peeled carrots are sauteed in a covered pan with salt, butter, a pinch of sugar, and a little stock or water until the liquid is almost reduced. The carrots are tossed (glazed) and sprinkled with chopped parsley.

Creamed Cauliflower—Chou-fleur a la creme. (20.1.2.1 or 20.1.3) This is a dish of cauliflower flowerets that have been boiled, drained, and arranged in layers with a well-seasoned cream sauce over each layer.

Deep-Fat Fried Cauliflower—Chou-fleur frit. (20.1.2.1 or 20.1.3 and 20.1.8) Cauliflower, prepared as described under Cauliflower, English Style, is cut into flowerets, dipped in batter, and deep-fat fried. It is served with a tomato sauce.
Cauliflower, English Style—Chou-fleur a l'anglaise. (20.1.2.1 or 20.1.3) The cauliflower for this dish may be left whole or broken into flowerets. Boiled until just tender, the cauliflower is drained thoroughly, dried over very low heat, arranged in a warm serving dish, and covered with melted butter and minced parsley.
Gratinated Cauliflower—Chou-fleur au gratin. (20.1.2.1 or 20.1.3 and 20.1.7) This dish is prepared by the method used for Creamed Cauliflower. The cauliflower is arranged in a gratin dish, covered with cheese and melted butter, and gratinated in the oven.
Cauliflower, Milanese Style—Chou-fleur milanaise. (20.1.2.1 or 20.1.3) Cauliflower, prepared as described under English Style, is served with grated cheese and brown butter.
Cauliflower, Polish Style—Chou-fleur polonaise. (20.1.2.1 or 20.1.3) Cauliflower, prepared as described under English Style, is garnished with sliced hard-cooked eggs, parsley, and a mixture of bread crumbs and brown butter.

Celeriac Roots, English Style—Celeri-rave a l'anglaise. (20.1.2.1) These celeriac roots are boiled and sliced, and covered with melted butter and parsley.
Celeriac Roots, Italian Style—Celeri-rave a l'italienne. (20.1.2.1) The boiled and sliced celeriac roots are arranged on a warm dish and covered with an Italian Sauce that has been mixed with reduced celery stock and garnished with parsley.
Celeriac Roots with Stock—Celeri-rave a jus. (20.1.2.1) This dish is prepared the same as Celeriac Roots, English Style. A rich veal stock mixed with reduced celery stock is substituted for the melted butter.
Celery Stalks with Brown Sauce—Celeri en branches a la demi-glace. (20.1.4) These braised celery stalks are arranged on a dish, and covered with a demi-glace mixed with reduced vegetable stock.
Celery Stalks, English Style—Celeri en branches a l'anglaise. (20.1.1) Braised celery stalks, arranged on a dish, are covered with melted butter and sprinkled with chopped parsley.
Celery Stalks with Marrow—Celeri en branches a la moelle. (20.1.4) These braised celery stalks are covered with a bound veal stock mixed with reduced vegetable stock, and decorated with poached slices of marrow and minced parsley.
Celery Stalks with Stock—Celeri en branches au jus. (20.1.4) A rich veal stock mixed with a reduced vegetable stock is poured over the braised celery stalks.

Creamed Cucumbers—Concombres a la creme. (20.1.1 and 20.1.5) The cucumbers for this dish are peeled and cut in the same shape as potatoes chateau. The cucumbers are then blanched, drained, and stewed in butter and a small amount of stock. They are bound with a thin cream sauce.
Cucumbers, Provence Style—Concombres a la provencale (20.1.1 and 20.1.6) These are thick slices of cucumber that have been blanched and glazed. Peeled, seeded, and quartered tomatoes, slightly browned shallots, and a piece of garlic are added to the glazed cucumbers. The vegetables are then stewed in the oven until tender.

Stuffed Cucumbers—Concombres farcis. (20.1.1 and 20.1.5) This vegetable dish is prepared by hollowing the center of peeled cucumbers and cutting them into 2 inch (5 centimeters) lengths. They are stuffed with a veal sausage mixed with a duxelles and sprinkled with cheese. The stuffed pieces of cucumber are arranged in a flat, buttered dish with some stock and butter, and stewed in the oven until tender.

Deep-Fat Fried Eggplants—Aubergines frites. (20.1.8) The eggplant is peeled and cut into ¼ inch (.625 centimeter) slices. It is seasoned, coated with flour, dipped in beaten egg, and deep-fat fried at a medium temperature. Tomato or Italian Sauce is served separately.
Eggplants, Orly Style—Aubergines a l'Orly. (20.1.8) This eggplant is dipped in a light batter and deep-fat fried. A Tomato Sauce is served separately.

Braised Endive/Chicory Witloof—Endives braisees/Chicory Witloof. (20.1.4) Braised endive may be fin-

Leg of Lamb – *Gigot d'agneau boulangère*

Ballotine of Mutton, Carcassone
Ballotine de mouton carcassonnaise

Partridge on Canape
Perdreau sur canape

Saddle of Lamb, Imperial Style
Selle d'agneau imperiale

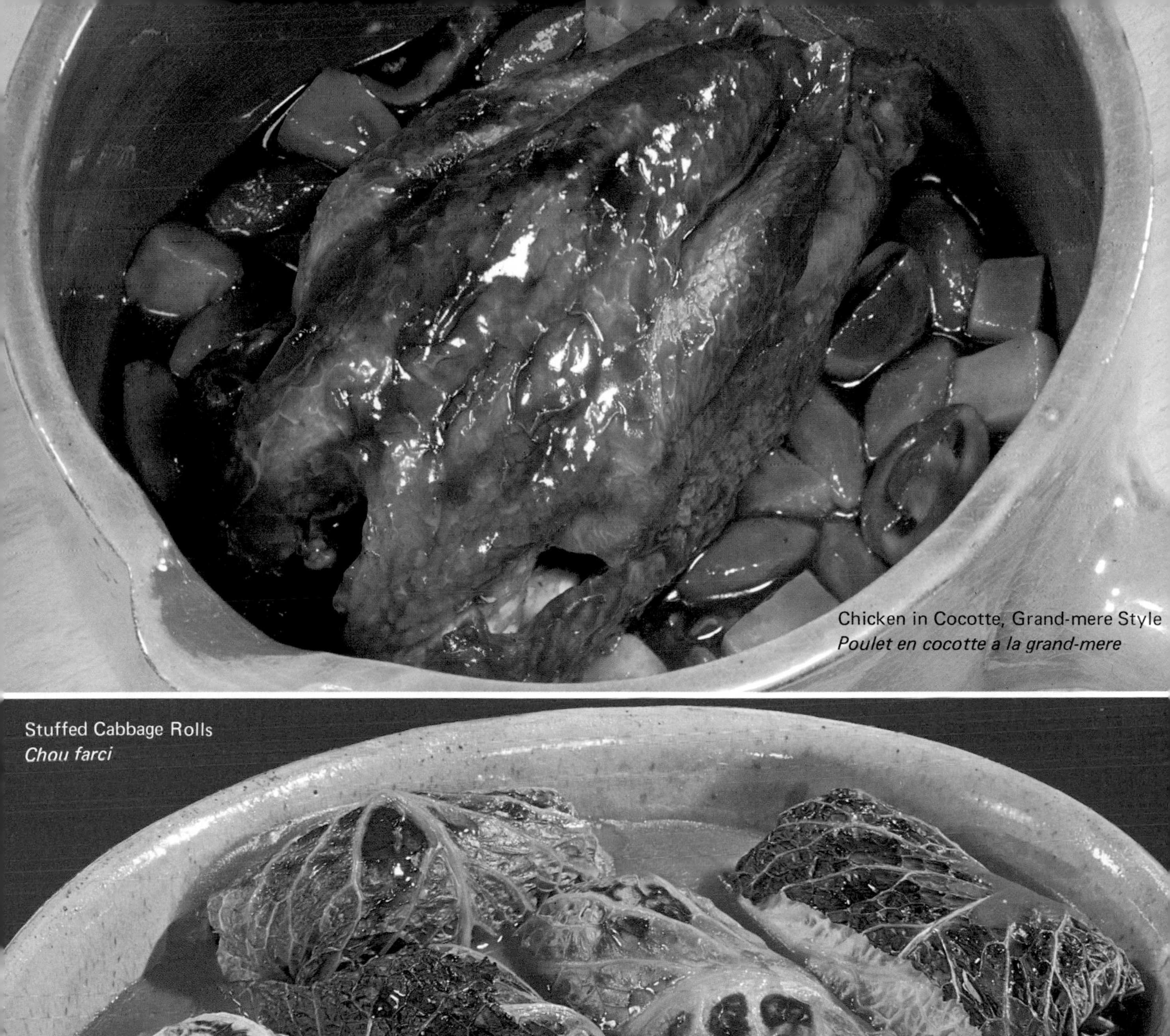

Chicken in Cocotte, Grand-mere Style
Poulet en cocotte a la grand-mere

Stuffed Cabbage Rolls
Chou farci

ished in several ways: with butter, gratinated, Milanese or Polish Style. The basic method of preparing the endive is as follows: Trim and wash the endive. Arrange the endive in layers in a well-buttered stainless steel pan. Sprinkle the endive with lemon juice, add salt, cold water, and veal kidney fat. Cover with buttered greaseproof paper, weigh down with plates, and cover the pan. Heat to the boiling point and then place in the oven at medium temperature for 30 to 40 minutes. Finish as indicated in the specific recipe.

Fennel with Brown Sauce—Fenouils a la demi-glace. (20.1.4) This dish is prepared by the method described for Celery Stalks with Brown Sauce, page 438.
Fennel, English Style—Fenouils a l'anglaise. (20.1.4) The method of preparation for this dish is exactly the same as that used for Celery Stalks, English Style, page 438.
Fennel, Milanese Style—Fenouils a la milanaise. (20.1.4) Braised fennel arranged on a warm dish is sprinkled with parsley. Hot foaming butter is poured over the fennel before serving.

Braised Green Beans—Haricots verts braises. (20.1.4) Fresh vegetables are very good when braised. The following method is recommended for braising green beans: String and wash the beans. Saute diced lean bacon in butter, add a quantity of chopped onions, and saute until they turn light yellow. Add the beans and a little stock, cover, and braise until tender and the liquid is reduced to a small quantity. Drain the beans and mix the stock with a few flakes of beurre manie. Add the beans to the stock and heat to the boiling point. Season and serve in a warm serving dish. (Dried beans must be soaked overnight.)
Note: A sprig of savory or a piece of lean bacon may be cooked with the beans.
Green Beans with Bacon—Haricots verts au lard. (20.1.4) These beans are prepared by the method described for Braised Green Beans, adding bacon to the beans before braising. The sliced bacon is arranged on the beans before serving.
Green Beans, English Style—Haricots verts a l'anglaise. (20.1.1) These beans are blanched, drained, and garnished with butter rolls, and served piping hot.
Green Beans, Paysanne—Haricots verts a la paysanne. (20.1.4) The recipe for this dish is exactly the same as the one for Braised Green Beans.
Green Beans Sauteed in Butter—Haricots verts sautes. (20.1.1 and 20.1.9) These are blanched green beans that have been sauteed in butter and seasoned.

Helvellas—Helvelles. (20.1.5) Prepare as for Creamed Mushrooms.
Creamed Kohlrabi—Chou-rave a la creme. (20.1.2.1) Boil, cut into bite-sized pieces, and bind with Cream or Veloute Sauce.

Gratinated Leeks—Poireau au gratin. (20.1.2.1 and 20.1.7) This dish is prepared by boiling and draining the leeks. They are arranged in a gratin dish, sprinkled with cheese and melted butter, and gratinated.
Note: Bechamel or Mornay Sauce may be used for gratinating.

Braised Boston Lettuce with Bacon—Laitues braisees au lard. (20.1.4) The recipe for Braised Boston Lettuce with Brown Sauce is followed. Crisp bacon strips are arranged on the lettuce, and veal stock is poured around the vegetable before serving.
Braised Boston Lettuce with Brown Sauce—Laitues braisees a la demi-glace. (20.1.4) Braised lettuce may be served as a vegetable or as a garnish. *To prepare:* remove the tough and damaged leaves, wash and drain several times. Blanch the lettuce as described in the basic recipe, page 434. Fold the leaves and arrange in a greased baking pan. Add some stock, cover, and keep warm in the oven. Pour demi-glace over the lettuce before serving.
Braised Boston Lettuce with Green Peas—Laitues braisees aux petits pois. (20.1.4) The lettuce is prepared in the same way as described for Braised Boston Lettuce with Brown Sauce. The braised lettuce is arranged in a ring in a round dish and the center is filled with green peas seasoned with melted butter. Reduced veal stock is poured over the lettuce before serving.
Braised Boston Lettuce with Stock—Laitues braisees au

jus. (20.1.4) This dish is prepared by the same method used for Braised Boston Lettuce with Brown Sauce. A slightly bound veal stock is poured over it just before serving.

Stuffed Boston Lettuce—Laitues farcies. (20.1.1 and 20.1.4) This classic French dish is served as a vegetable, and it is also used as a garnish. To stuff the lettuce, the leaves are washed, drained, and blanched. Each leaf is flattened, and a mousseline stuffing is placed in the center. The leaves are folded to enclose the stuffing. Each piece is placed in a saucepan with sliced onions, diced bacon, and some stock. The lettuce is covered and braised in the oven. The lettuce may be left whole or sliced. It is covered with a rich Veal Sauce or an Allemande Sauce.

Creamed Morels—Morilles a la creme. (20.1.5) Prepare as for Creamed Mushrooms.

Morels Poulette—Morilles a la poulette. (20.1.5)The morels for this dish are washed carefully, cut into halves or quarters, and sauteed in butter. For each pound (.5 kilogram) of morels, 2 ounces (60 grams) of butter should be used. The stock is blended with a Poulette Sauce. (See page 306.) The morels are added to the sauce.

Sauteed Morels—Morilles sautees. (20.1.8) This dish is prepared by the method described for Sauteed Mushrooms. (See this page.) The morels are sprinkled with lemon juice.

Cepe Mushrooms, Bordeaux Style—Cepes a la bordelaise. (20.1.9) In Europe the cepe is one of the favorite mushrooms. To prepare Bordeaux Style, the cepes are washed, sliced, sauteed quickly in hot oil, and seasoned with pepper and salt. Two tablespoons (30 grams) of chopped shallots and 2 tablespoons (30 grams) of bread crumbs are sauteed and added to each pound (.5 kilogram) of mushrooms. They are sprinkled with lemon juice and chopped parsley before serving.

Creamed Cepe Mushrooms—Cepes a la creme. (20.1.5) These mushrooms are first sauteed in butter and then bound with a cream sauce and seasoned with lemon juice.

Creamed Mushrooms I—Champignons a la creme. (20.1.5) The recipe for Stewed Mushrooms is used for this dish. The stock is reduced and combined with a cream sauce. The mushrooms are folded into the sauce.

Creamed Mushrooms II—Champignons a la creme. (20.1.5) The mushrooms for this dish are also prepared as described in the recipe for Stewed Mushrooms. The reduced stock is mixed with a demi-glace and cream. The mushrooms are added to the sauce.

Cepe Mushrooms, Provence Style—Cepes a la provencale. (20.1.9) The recipe for this dish is the same as the one for Bordeaux Style using onions and garlic instead of shallots.

Sauteed Mushrooms—Champignons sautes. (20.1.9) The mushrooms for this dish should be very fresh. They are sliced and sauteed in melted butter, seasoned with salt and pepper, and sprinkled with chopped parsley.

Stewed Mushrooms—Champignons etuves. (20.1.5) Many varieties of mushrooms may be used for stewing. They may be used whole, cut in quarters, or sliced. *To prepare:* Cook chopped shallots in butter in a saute pan. Deglaze with a little white wine, add the prepared mushrooms, some lemon juice, and cover. Season the mushrooms and continue cooking for approximately 10 minutes.

Stuffed Mushrooms—Champignons farcis. (20.1.5 and 20.1.7) Large mushroom caps may be stewed as described under Stewed Mushrooms, and stuffed with a duxelles, sprinkled with cheese, and gratinated in the oven or under the broiler. They may be used as a garnish for fish or meat dishes, or served as a separate dish with Madeira Sauce.

Green Peas, Bonne Femme Style—Petits pois bonne femme. (20.1.4) Fresh garden peas are preferred for this dish. To prepare the dish, finely chopped onion and diced bacon are sauteed in butter. The peas, stock, a small amount of sugar, salt, and pepper are combined and braised in a covered saucepan until the peas are tender. Then small amounts of beurre manie are added and the peas are heated to the boiling point.

Green Peas in Butter—Petits pois au beurre. (20.1.1 and 20.1.9) This dish is prepared by blanching, draining, and sauteing the peas. They are seasoned with a small amount of sugar and fresh butter.

Green Peas, English Style—Petits pois a l'anglaise. (20.1.1) These peas are blanched, drained, and arranged in a warm dish. They are garnished with butter rolls.

Green Peas, French Style—Petits pois a la francaise. (20.1.5) This is a casserole of fresh green peas, pearl onions, and a chiffonade of hearts of lettuce. The peas are seasoned and combined with a small amount of sugar, and some stock. The vegetables are covered and simmered until tender. The peas are tossed in the remaining liquid and a few flakes of beurre manie are added slowly. For each pound (.5 kilogram) of peas, use ½ ounce (15 grams) of beurre manie.

Sugar Peas—Pois mange-tout. (20.1.4) These vegetables are prepared by the method described for Braised Green Beans, page 443.

Creamed Black Salsify—Salsifis a la creme. (20.1.4) This salsify is cut into 1½ inch (3.75 centimeters) pieces, boiled, and bound with a cream sauce.

Deep-Fat Fried Black Salsify—Salsifis frits. (20.1.2.1 and 20.1.8) This salsify is boiled, drained, dipped into frying batter, and deep-fat fried. Tomato Sauce is served separately.

Grutinated Black Salsify—Salsifis au gratin. (20.1.2.1 and 20.1.7) This dish is prepared by boiling the salsify and binding it with a cream sauce. It is then arranged on a gratin dish, sprinkled with cheese and melted butter, and gratinated in the oven.

Black Salsify in White Sauce—Salsifis au veloute. (20.1.2.1) The salsify is boiled and bound with a Veloute Sauce.

Sauerkraut—Choucroute. (20.1.4) Sauerkraut is made from shredded cabbage that has fermented in a brine with juniper berries. It is often cooked with brisket of beef, roast pork, frankfurters, spareribs, and poultry. A simple method of preparation is as follows: Stew 10 ounces (300 grams) of diced lean bacon and 8 ounces (225 grams) of onion in 2 tablespoons (50 grams) of lard or poultry fat. Add 1 quart (1 liter) of fresh or canned sauerkraut, a spice sachet, 1 ounce (28 grams) of juniper berries, 1 peeled and grated potato, and ¼ cup (30 milliliters) of white wine. Cover the sauerkraut with stock and braise slowly, replacing the liquid as it evaporates. If salted or smoked meat is served with the sauerkraut, it is better to cook the meat separately without adding salt. The stock used for deglazing the sauerkraut is added.

Creamed Spinach—Epinards a la creme. (20.1.1) This dish is prepared with blanched and drained spinach that has been sauteed and combined with a cream sauce in a ratio of 1 part sauce to 5 parts spinach. It may be garnished with sliced carrots that have been buttered and flavored with dill or with sauteed mushroom slices or caps.

Spinach with Croutons—Epinards aux croutons. (20.1.1) This is a creamed spinach garnished with heart-shaped croutons.

Spinach with Chipolata Sausages—Epinards aux chipolatas. (20.1.1) This creamed spinach is garnished with chipolata sausages.

Spinach with Eggs—Epinards aux oeufs. (20.1.1) This is a creamed spinach garnished with sliced hard-cooked eggs or fried or poached eggs.

Spinach, English Style—Epinards a l'anglaise. (20.1.1 and 20.1.9) Spinach requires only brief cooking. The blanched spinach is sauteed in butter and placed in a warm serving dish.

Spinach, Italian Style—Epinards a l'italienne. (20.1.1 and 20.1.9) The spinach for this dish is blanched, drained, and sauteed in butter. Chopped browned shallots and anchovy fillets are folded into the spinach. Use 2¾ ounces (80 grams) of shallots and 2¼ ounces (65 grams) of anchovy fillets per pound (.5 kilogram) of spinach.

Spinach with White Sauce—Epinards au veloute. (20.1.1) The spinach for this dish is blanched, drained, seasoned, and combined with Veloute Sauce. The ratio is 1 part Veloute Sauce to 5 parts spinach. It may be garnished with tomato wedges and chopped parsley.

Butter String Beans—Haricots beurres. (20.1.4.) The recipe for this dish is exactly the same as the one for Braised Green Beans.

Yellow String Beans—Haricots d'asperges. (20.1.4) These beans are prepared as described in the recipe for Braised Green Beans.

Sweet Corn. (20.1.2.1) *Sweet Corn Kernels* are boiled in salted water and served with butter or with cream sauce. The kernels are also used in sweet corn pancakes and croquettes. *Sweet corn on the cob* should be simmered in salted water.

Stuffed Sweet Peppers—Piments farcis. (20.1.5) The top part of the peppers is cut off or the peppers are cut in half lengthwise and the seeds are removed. The peppers are washed and filled with a mixture of minced meat mixed with rice. They are placed in a pan on a layer of finely sliced sauteed onion with some stock and Tomato Sauce and stewed in the oven.

Deep-Fat Fried Tomatoes—Tomates frites. (20.1.8) Deep-fat fried tomatoes are used as a garnish or with fritto misto (a mixed fry of meats, or variety meats, and vegetables). The tomatoes are cut in halves, seeded, seasoned, dipped in a frying batter, and deep-fat fried.

Tomatoes, Provence Style—Tomates farcies a la provencale. (20.1.7) Yield: 10 servings. Select 5 tomatoes and cut in halves. The tomatoes are seeded, seasoned, filled with the following stuffing, and gratinated in the oven. *Stuffing:* Lightly brown 3½ ounces (100 grams) of chopped onion and ½ crushed garlic clove in 3½ ounces (100 milliliters) of oil. Mix in 7 ounces (200 grams) of grated white bread, 2 tablespoons (30 grams) of chopped parsley, 3 chopped anchovy fillets, and ¾ ounce (20 grams) of grated cheese. Continue sauteing for a few minutes and blend in ½ cup (1 deciliter) of veal stock or sauce from the braising pan.

Stewed Diced Tomatoes—Tomates concassees. (20.1.5) These tomatoes may be seasoned with various seasonings and herbs depending on the use. The tomatoes are washed, peeled, seeded, and cut into cubes. They are combined with chopped shallots that have been stewed in clarified butter. The mixture is covered and stewed slowly until the flavors are blended.

Stuffed Tomatoes—Tomates farcies. (20.1.7) Stuffed tomatoes are prepared as follows: Wash the tomatoes and cut in halves, remove the seeds, and season with salt and pepper. Place the tomatoes in a buttered pan and stuff each with the prescribed filling (see Stuffed Cucumbers, page 438), sprinkle with cheese, and gratinate in the oven for about 10 minutes.

Zucchini—Courgettes. (20.1.5) Zucchini, also called Italian squash, are stewed with a few shallots and tossed in butter.

Potatoes—Pommes de terre

21

21.1 Basic Cooking Methods

For preparation methods and cuts of potatoes, see pages 239-240.

21.1.1 Blanching — Blanchir

Preparation: Heat the water to the boiling point. Drop the potatoes into the water, bring back to the boil, and then drain. The ratio of potatoes to water should be at least 1:5. When blanching, do not add salt to the water.
Note: Blanching can be done continuously by using the wire basket from the deep-fat fryer.

21.1.2 Boiling — Cuire

Preparation: Peel and cut the potatoes into uniform size. Cover with salted water and bring to the boiling point in a tightly-covered heavy saucepan. Reduce the heat and cook until tender. Drain and return the potatoes to the heat for a few minutes to dry out thoroughly.

21.1.2.1 Boiling in Stock — Cuire au bouillon

Cut the potatoes and blanch as described in Section 21.1.1. Add other ingredients to the potatoes and treat according to the recipe. Add hot stock until the potatoes are just covered. Boil in a tightly-covered saucepan until tender and a small amount of liquid remains. Sprinkle the potatoes with chopped parsley.

21.1.3 Steaming — Cuire a vapeur

Preparation: Steam the potatoes with some salt in a pressure steamer. If a pressure steamer is not available, use an ordinary saucepan in which a 1½ inch to 2 inch (3.75 to 5 centimeters) high strainer insert can be placed. The water should not be in contact with the potatoes. The saucepan should be covered with a heavy lid.

Note: This method of cooking reduces the drawing loss and is recommended for sauteed, mashed, or potatoes cooked in their jackets.

21.1.4 Baking — Cuire au four

Preparation: Place the washed, unpeeled potatoes on a tray that has been covered with a ½ inch (1.3 centimeters) layer of salt. Bake the potatoes in an oven at 400°F. (205°C.) for 40 to 60 minutes. Serve in a napkin placed on a platter or in a special basket. Garnish with fresh butter, cream cheese, sour cream with chives, or with crisp strips of bacon.

Stuffed Potatoes. Bake the potatoes. Cut a pyramid-shaped piece off the flat side of the potatoes. Keep the cut-out piece to use as a lid. Hollow out ⅔ of the potato pulp from the shell of the bottom and the top. Whip the pulp with milk, butter, and seasonings. Stuff the shells, and serve with or without the lids. The potatoes may be gratinated.

21.1.5 Roasting — Rotir

Preparation: Blanch the uniformly cut potatoes as described in section 21.1.1. Heat the fat in a roasting pan, add the potatoes, and roast until golden-brown, turning from time to time. Drain the excess fat, cover with melted butter and parsley before serving.

Roasting is also used for *potato molds.* Slice the blanched potatoes, toss in butter (without browning), and arrange in overlapping layers in a mold. Roast in oven at 400°F. (205°C.) until tender. Invert on a serving dish.

21.1.6 Sauteing — Sauter

Preparation: Cut the boiled or steamed, peeled potatoes into thin slices. Heat the fat in a large omelet pan, add salted potatoes, and brown lightly over a low flame and turn frequently. Form potatoes into a cake shape, add butter, saute both sides of the cake until golden-brown, and carefully turn out on a round dish. Garnish with chopped parsley or chives.
Note: Onion, diced ham, bacon, or cheese may be added.

21.1.7 Deep-Fat Frying — Frire

Preparation: Cut mature potatoes into uniform strips about 2¼ inches (5.6 centimeters) long and $^3/_8$ inch (.09 centimeter) thick. Soak in cold water until ready to cook. Drain and dry on a cloth. Place a few potatoes at a time in the wire basket of the deep-fat fryer. Cook for about 2 minutes at 265°F. (130°C.). Remove potatoes, drain on paper towels, and cool. Just before serving, heat the oil to 365°F. (185°C.) and fry the potatoes until they are crisp. Drain the potatoes on absorbent paper. Keep warm in the oven, with the door open. Salt just before serving. Potato croquettes and potato fritters are deep-fat fried in oil at 375°F. (190°C.) until crisp. *During deep-fat frying, the utensil should never be covered.*

21.1.8 Gratinating — Gratiner

Preparation: Depending on the method of preparation, use raw potatoes or potatoes that have been blanched, boiled, steamed, or baked. Add stock, milk, salt, and seasoning as specified in the recipe. Sprinkle with cheese and melted butter, and gratinate. The potatoes may be covered with a Mornay Sauce (see page 308) and then gratinated.

21.2 Variations of Potatoes

The reference for the appropriate basic form of preparation is indicated in brackets for each variation.

Anna Potatoes — Pommes Anna. (21.1.5) These potatoes are cut into thin, uniform-sized, round slices and mixed with seasoning and melted butter. A thick-bottomed mold is coated with clarified butter and filled with overlapping rows of sliced potatoes. Each layer is sprinkled with clarified butter. The potatoes are covered and baked in the oven at 400°F. (205°C.) for 30 to 40 minutes. The potatoes are inverted on a pan or plate to allow the excess butter to drain.
Potatoes with Bacon — Pommes au lard. (21.1.2.1) These diced and blanched potatoes are combined with diced lean bacon and chopped onion that have been sauteed in butter. They are deglazed with stock and boiled until tender.
Baked Potatoes — Pommes au four. As described in section 21.1.4.
Bernese Potatoes — Pommes a la bernoise. (21.1.6) Boiled potatoes are grated on a course grater. They are sauteed in butter with diced bacon. The mixture is browned on one side and inverted on a serving dish.

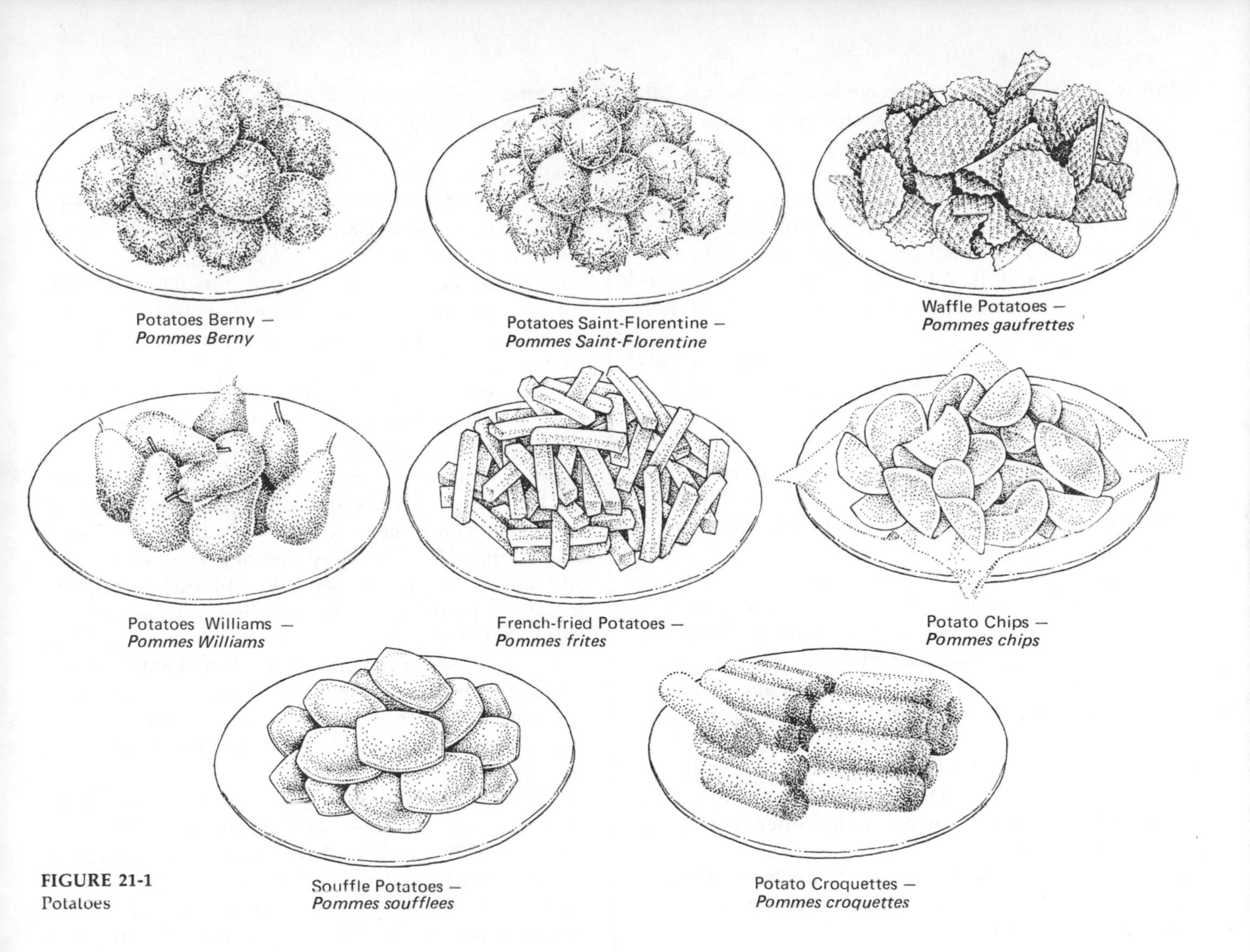

FIGURE 21-1
Potatoes

Berny Potatoes — Pommes Berny. (21.1.2 and 21.1.7) A croquette potato dough that has been mixed with chopped truffles and shaped into small balls, dipped into beaten egg, and coated with chopped almonds. The potato balls are deep-fat fried. (See Figure 21-1.)

Potatoes, Berrichone Style — Pommes berrichonne. (21.1.2.1) These potatoes are cut into olive shapes and blanched. They are combined with lean bacon and chopped onion that have been sauteed in butter. The potatoes are then deglazed with stock and boiled until tender.

Boiled Potatoes — Pommes nature. (21.1.2 or 21.1.3) These are potatoes that have been cut into oval shapes and boiled.

Boulangere Potatoes — Pommes boulangere. (21.1.5) A potato dish made of equal parts of sliced, blanched potatoes and sliced onion that are sprinkled with butter and baked in the oven.

Byron Potatoes — Pommes Byron. (21.1.8) These are mashed potatoes that have been sauteed in butter, covered with cream and cheese, and gratinated in the oven.

Potatoes, Chateau Style — Pommes chateau. (21.1.5) Oval-shaped potatoes that are blanched and roasted.

Potato Chips — Pommes chips. (21.1.7) These chips may be served hot or cold. They are made from very thin slices of potatoes that have been cut on a potato slicer, soaked in cold water, drained, and fried in deep-fat. Cold potato chips may be dusted with paprika. (See Figure 21-1.)

Potato Croquettes – Pommes croquettes. (21.1.2 or 21.1.3 and 21.1.7) Croquettes are made from potatoes that have been mashed and mixed with seasoning, butter, and egg yolk. They are formed into either oblong or ball shapes, breaded, and deep-fat fried. (See Figure 21-1.)

Dauphine Potatoes—Pommes dauphine. (21.1.7) This is a mixture of Duchess Potatoes and ⅓ Cream Puff Paste. (See recipe 25.1.3.) The mixture is shaped into dumplings and deep-fat fried.

Gratinated Potatoes a la Dauphinoise—Pommes a la dauphinoise. (21.1.8) These are prepared by the same method as Potatoes, Savoy Style using milk instead of stock.

Potatoes, Duchess Style—Pommes duchesse. (21.1.2 or 21.1.3) These potatoes are boiled, drained, mashed, and mixed with butter and seasoning. They are bound with egg yolk. The mixture is placed in a pastry bag and forced into a mound of special shape on a buttered tray. The potatoes are brushed with egg yolk or melted butter and baked.

Potatoes, Emmentaler—Pommes emmentaloise. (21.1.8) These are Duchess Potatoes topped with a slice of Emmentaler cheese, basted with butter, and gratinated in the oven.

Potatoes, English Style—Pommes a l'anglaise. (21.1.2) These potatoes are cut into oval shapes, boiled, and served in melted butter.

Potatoes, Fermiere—Pommes fermiere. (21.1.4 and 21.1.8) The pulp of baked potatoes is removed from the shell and blended with ⅔ its volume of chopped pot-au-feu vegetables. The shells are filled with the mixture and sprinkled with grated cheese and melted butter and gratinated.

Potatoes, Florence Style—Pommes florentine. (21.1.4 and 21.1.8) These baked potatoes have had some of the pulp removed. They are stuffed with sauteed spinach, covered with a Mornay Sauce, sprinkled with grated cheese, and gratinated.

Potatoes Fondantes—Pommes fondantes. (21.1.5) These are potatoes that have been cut into small egg shapes and arranged in a flat pan. They are buttered, covered, and browned slowly on both sides. They are flattened slightly with a fork and topped with fresh butter.

French Fried Potatoes—Pommes frites. (21.1.7) These are ½ inch (1.3 centimeters) thick potato sticks that have been blanched and deep-fat fried just before serving. (See Figure 21-1.)

Gratinated Potatoes—Pommes Mont d'Or. (21.1.8) Pureed potatoes, in a buttered gratin dish, are sprinkled with cheese and melted butter, and gratinated.

Potatoes with Herbs—Pommes aux fines herbes. (21.1.2 or 21.1.3) These are boiled and steamed potatoes covered with chopped parsley.

Potatoes, Hungarian Style—Pommes a la hongroise. (21.1.2.1) These are diced and blanched potatoes that have been combined with sauteed, diced lean bacon and chopped onion. They are deglazed with stock and added to peeled, seeded, and finely chopped tomatoes, paprika, and then boiled until tender.

Potatoes, Hunter's Style – Pommes chasseur. (21.1.4) The pulp of baked potatoes is combined with sauteed chicken livers and mushrooms. The top of the potato is replaced. Hunter's Sauce is served separately.

Potatoes in Jackets – Pommes en robe de chambre. (21.1.3)

Potatoes with Leeks – Pommes aux poireaux. (21.1.2.1) These are sliced and blanched potatoes. They are placed in a saucepan in alternate layers with white blanched leeks and boiled in stock.

Lorette Potatoes – Pommes Lorette. (21.1.7) These potatoes are made from a mixture of Dauphine Potatoes combined with grated cheese, shaped into crescents, and baked.

Mashed Potatoes – Pommes puree. (21.1.2 or 21.1.3) Potatoes that have been boiled and drained are mashed to a creamy consistency. Hot milk, butter, and seasonings are added and the potatoes are beaten or whipped until light and thoroughly blended.

Potato Puree with Cream – Pommes mousseline. (21.1.2 or 21.1.3) The puree is prepared with cream instead of milk.

Potatoes, Lyon Style – Pommes lyonnaise. (21.1.6) These potatoes are sauteed in butter with sliced onion.

Macaire Potatoes — Pommes Macaire. (21.1.4) The pulp of baked potatoes is mashed with butter, seasoned, and placed in a buttered pan. The mixture is formed into a round cake and browned on both sides.

Potatoes Maitre d'Hotel — Pommes maitre d'hotel. (21.1.3) These are made from steamed unpeeled potatoes. They are peeled while hot, sliced, and covered with boiling milk in a saute pan. Salt, pepper, and nutmeg are added, and the potatoes are simmered until most of the milk is evaporated. A small amount of cream and butter are added, and they are sprinkled with parsley before serving.

Minted Potatoes — Pommes a la menthe. (21.1.2.1) These oval-shaped potato slices are boiled in stock with a bouquet of fresh mint. Sprigs of blanched mint leaves are served on the potatoes.

Mirette Potatoes — Pommes Mirette. (21.1.5) These potatoes are blanched and sauteed. They are mixed with a julienne of truffles and some glace de viande.

Nana Potatoes — Pommes Nana. (21.1.5) These are cut into uniform sized potato sticks. They are mixed with seasoning and melted butter. The potatoes are arranged in baba molds and prepared by the method used for Potatoes Anna.

Nut Potatoes — Pommes noisettes. (21.1.5) These potatoes are cut from raw, pared potatoes with a round vegetable scooping spoon (melon baller) to the size and shape of hazelnuts. They may be blanched, coated with butter and roasted in the oven, or they may be sauteed in butter.

Potatoes, Old Fashioned Style — Pommes a l'ancienne. (21.1.2) These potato patties are made from a Duchess Potato mixture. The patties are dusted with flour and sauteed in butter.

Potatoes, Parisian Style — Pommes parisienne. (21.1.5) These are the same as Nut Potatoes (Pommes noisettes), but smaller in size.

Potatoes, Paysanne Style — Pommes paysanne. (21.1.2.1) These sliced and blanched potatoes are prepared by the same method used for preparing Potatoes with Bacon (Pommes au lard).

Potatoes Pont-neuf — Pommes pont-neuf. (21.1.7) These potatoes are twice as thick as French Fried Potatoes (Pommes frites). They are first blanched and then deep-fat fried before serving.

Potatoes Saint-Florentine — Pommes Saint-Florentin. (21.1.2 and 21.1.7) This is a potato croquette dough with chopped ham. It is shaped, breaded in crushed vermicelli, and deep-fat fried. (See Figure 21-1.)

Sauteed Potatoes — Pommes sautees. (21.1.6) These potatoes are boiled in their jackets, peeled, sliced, and sauteed in butter.

Potatoes, Savoy Style — Pommes savoyarde. (21.1.8) Sliced raw potatoes are arranged in a gratin dish with stock. They are covered with grated cheese, melted butter, and gratinated in the oven until cooked.

Souffle Potatoes — Pommes soufflees. (21.1.7) Souffle Potatoes require double cooking at different temperatures. Uniform-sized mature potatoes are peeled, washed, and cut lengthwise into slices $^{1}/_{8}$ inch (.3 centimeters) thick, and dried on a cloth. (See Figure 21-1.) The long even slices may be cut into ovals or fancy shapes. The potatoes are precooked in fat at a temperature of 265°F. to 320°F. (130°C. to 160°C.). Agitate the basket throughout the cooking, and cook until all the slices rise to the surface and small blisters have formed on the surface. The potatoes are drained and cooled in the frying basket. Just before serving, the potatoes are dropped into very hot deep fat at a temperature of 385°F. (195°C.) and again agitate the basket throughout the cooking. The last cooking causes the potatoes to puff. The potatoes should be drained on paper towels, salted, and served immediately. *Note:* Potatoes with too high a moisture content or those that are too mealy are not suited for this recipe.

Straw Potatoes — Pommes pailles. (21.1.7) These crisp potatoes are about $^{1}/_{8}$ inch (.3 centimeters) thick and 2½ inches (6 centimeters) long. They are fried in very hot deep fat.

Voisin Potatoes — Pommes voisin. (21.1.5) These are prepared by the same method used for Potatoes Anna with grated cheese between each layer.

Waffle Potatoes — Pommes gaufrettes. (21.1.7) The potatoes are cut with a fluted slicer (mandolin) that cuts across the width of the potato into round slices with a waffle pattern. The potatoes are deep-fat fried. (See Figure 21-1.)

Williams Potatoes — Pommes Williams. (21.1.7) These potato croquettes are pressed into pear shapes, breaded, and deep-fat fried. (See Figure 21-1.)

22 Pasta Foods, Rice— Farineux, riz

22.1 Pasta Dishes — Farineaux

Cannelloni

YIELD: *approximately 10 servings*

INGREDIENTS	*U.S. Weight or Volume*	*Metric Weight or Volume*	PROCEDURE
Ravioli dough, **(see page 455)**	2 pounds	1 kilogram	1. Roll the pasta dough to a $^1/_8$ inch (.3 centimeters) thickness. Cut into pieces 2½ × 3½ inches (6 × 9 centimeters). Dry thoroughly. 2. Pour 5 quarts (5 liters) of water, 1 tablespoon (15 grams) of salt, and 1 tablespoon (15 milliliters) of oil into a large kettle. Heat to the boiling point. 3. Drop a few pieces of pasta at a time into the water and cook to al dente stage. (See section 22.2.) Remove with a skimmer. Cool and dry.
Stuffing, **(see page 455)**	1¼ to 1¾ pounds	600 to 800 grams	4. Sprinkle grated cheese over a cutting board. Arrange the cooked pasta on the board. Fill a pastry bag with the stuffing and position the stuffing lengthwise on the pasta.
Sauce Mornay, **(see page 308)**	1 pint	½ liter	5. Roll the pasta around the stuffing. Place in a buttered gratin dish, cover with sauce, sprinkle with cheese and bake in an oven at 400°F. (205°C.) about 20 minutes until thoroughly heated.
Cheese, grated	7 ounces	200 grams	
Butter	5 ounces	140 grams	

Note: A Tomato Sauce or demi-glace may be used instead of Mornay Sauce. The term "al suago" generally refers to a demi-glace with tomato. If the cannelloni are served without baking, they are served with browned butter and a few sage leaves.

Dumplings, German Style (Noques a l'allemande)

YIELD: *approximately 10 servings*

INGREDIENTS	*U.S. Weight or Volume*	*Metric Weight or Volume*
Milk	1¼ quarts	1.2 liters
Butter	5 ounces	150 grams
Salt	½ teaspoon	2 grams
Nutmeg	¼ teaspoon	1 gram
Semolina	6½ ounces	180 grams
Eggs	8	8
Cheese, grated parmesan	5 ounces	150 grams

PROCEDURE

1. Combine the milk, 1¾ ounces (50 grams) of butter, salt, and nutmeg in a saucepan. Heat to the boiling point.
2. Add the semolina gradually and boil for 5 minutes, stirring constantly. Remove from heat and let stand until slightly cool.
3. Add the beaten eggs and half the grated cheese in small amounts.
4. Drop by teaspoonfuls into a large container of boiling salted water. Cover and simmer 10 to 15 minutes. Remove dumplings and place in a buttered baking dish. Sprinkle with remaining cheese and melted butter. Bake in an oven at 375°F. (190°C.) for 15 minutes.
5. Serve with fish or meat dishes.

Potato Dumplings, Piemontese (Gnocchi a la piemontaise)

YIELD: *approximately 10 servings*

INGREDIENTS	*U.S. Weight or Volume*	*Metric Weight or Volume*
Duchess potato mixture, without butter, **(see page 450)**	2½ pounds	1.2 kilograms
Flour	8 ounces	220 grams
Tomato sauce	1 pint	5 deciliters
Cheese, grated parmesan	3½ ounces	100 grams
Butter	3½ ounces	100 grams

PROCEDURE

1. Blend the flour into the warm Duchess potato mixture.
2. When the dough has cooled, form nut-sized balls. Groove the balls with a fork and poach for 5 minutes in gently boiling salted water.
3. Drain the dumplings.
4. Coat a baking dish with the Tomato Sauce. Arrange the dumplings in the baking dish and sprinkle them with parmesan cheese and pepper. Pour melted butter over the top and gratinate.

Gnocchi, Parisian Style (Gnocchi a la parisienne)

YIELD: *approximately 10 servings*

INGREDIENTS	*U.S. Weight or Volume*	*Metric Weight or Volume*
Cream Puff Paste, (recipe 25.1.3)	2 pounds	1 kilogram
Cream sauce, thin	1¾ cups	4 deciliters
Cheese, grated	3½ ounces	100 grams
Butter	3½ ounces	100 grams

PROCEDURE

1. Fill a pastry bag with Cream Puff Paste and form the paste into marble-sized dumplings and drop into simmering, but not boiling, salted water.
2. When all the dumplings are floating on the surface, remove them from the water, place them in a buttered gratin dish, and cover with a thin cream sauce.
3. Sprinkle with the cheese and melted butter. Place the gnocchis in the oven at 425°F. (218°C.). After 8 to 10 minutes, reduce the heat to 375°F. (190°C.), and continue baking until a golden yellow crust has formed – about 25 minutes longer.
4. Serve gnocchis immediately after removing from the oven. **(See illustration, page 493.)**

Gnocchi, Roman Style (Gnocchi a la romaine)

YIELD: *approximately 10 servings*

INGREDIENTS	*U.S. Weight or Volume*	*Metric Weight or Volume*
Milk	1¼ quarts	1.2 liters
Butter	5 ounces	150 grams
Salt	½ teaspoon	2 grams
Nutmeg	¼ teaspoon	1 gram
Semolina	9 ounces	250 grams
Cheese, grated parmesan	5 ounces	150 grams
Egg yolks	2	2

PROCEDURE

1. Combine the milk, 1¾ ounces (50 grams) of butter, salt, and nutmeg in a saucepan. Heat to the boiling point.
2. Sprinkle the semolina into the milk and stir this mixture for 15 minutes over a low flame.
3. Add 1¾ ounces (50 grams) of the grated cheese and the egg yolks. Blend thoroughly.
4. Spread the mixture to a depth of ¾ to 1 inch (1.9 to 2.5 centimeters) on a buttered sheet pan. Cool.
5. Cut round slices 1¾ to 2 inches (4.4 to 5 centimeters) in diameter. Place these in a buttered baking dish so that the edge of each slice lies on that of the last slice.
6. Sprinkle the remainder of the grated cheese and the butter over the gnocchis.
7. Bake in oven at 425°F. (218°C.) for 10 to 15 minutes until a golden yellow crust is formed.

Ravioli

YIELD: *approximately 10 servings*

INGREDIENTS	*U.S. Weight or Volume*	*Metric Weight or Volume*	PROCEDURE
Dough			
Flour	1¾ pounds	850 grams	1. Sift flour and salt. Make a well in the center of the flour.
Salt	½ ounce	15 grams	2. Combine the oil, eggs, salt, and water. Mix slightly. Pour into the well.
Oil	¼ cup	½ deciliter	3. Mix the flour in gradually and work into a smooth, firm dough. Let the dough stand for 1 to 2 hours.
Eggs	4	4	4. Divide the dough in half and roll into two very thin pieces.
Water	½ to ¾ cup	1 to 1½ deciliters	5. Place one piece of the dough on a ravioli board and cut into strips 2 to 3 inches (5 to 7.5 centimeters) wide. Place 2 to 3 teaspoons of stuffing on each square. Place the other piece of dough on top. Use a pastry cutter to separate the individual ravioli. (See Fig. 22-1.) Seal the edges and let dry about 2 hours.
			6. Heat 6 quarts (6 liters) of water, 1 tablespoon (15 grams) of salt, and 1 tablespoon (15 milliliters) of oil to the boiling point. Place 5 or 6 ravioli at a time in the water. Reduce the heat and simmer to the al dente stage.
			7. Remove with a skimmer to a buttered baking dish. Cover with a sauce or melted butter. Heat in oven at 350°F. (175°C.) for about 20 minutes. Serve immediately.
Stuffing I			
Shallots	1 ounce	30 grams	1. Brown shallots and garlic in butter.
Garlic	1 clove	1 clove	2. Add finely ground braised beef and cooked spinach.
Butter	3 ounces	85 grams	3. Add eggs and seasonings, and blend thoroughly. If too thick, add a bit of demi-glace. If too thin, reduce over heat to desired consistency.
Ground beef, braised	10 ounces	300 grams	
Spinach, cooked	10 ounces	300 grams	
Egg yolks	3	3	
Nutmeg	1/8 teaspoon	1 gram	
Salt	1 teaspoon	5 grams	
Pepper	¼ teaspoon	2 grams	

(continued on next page)

INGREDIENTS	*U.S. Weight or Volume*	*Metric Weight or Volume*	PROCEDURE
Stuffing II			
Shallots	1 ounce	30 grams	1. Brown sliced shallots in butter.
Butter	3 ounces	85 grams	
Chicken meat or livers, cooked	10 ounces	300 grams	2. Add cooked chicken meat or livers, cooked brains, and spinach.
Brains, cooked	7 ounces	200 grams	3. Grind to a very fine texture. Add seasonings and eggs and blend.
Spinach, cooked	5 ounces	150 grams	
Egg yolks	3	3	
Nutmeg	1/8 teaspoon	1 gram	
Salt	1 teaspoon	5 grams	
Pepper	¼ teaspoon	2 grams	

Variations of ravioli

Ravioli, Milanese Style—Ravioli milanaise. The ravioli are arranged in layers in a gratin dish and sprinkled with cheese. Melted butter is poured over the top, and the ravioli are heated in an oven at 350°F. (175°C.) for 15 minutes.

Ravioli, Naples Style—Ravioli napolitaine. The ravioli are arranged in layers and a Tomato Sauce is poured over each layer. The ravioli are covered with grated cheese and melted butter and heated in an oven at 350°F. (175°C.) for 15 minutes.

Ravioli, Nice Style—Ravioli nicoise. The ravioli are arranged in layers in a gratin dish. A demi-glace or a fond de veau lie (whipped with butter) is poured over the top. The ravioli are covered with cheese and melted butter and heated in an oven at 350°F. (175°C.) for 15 minutes.

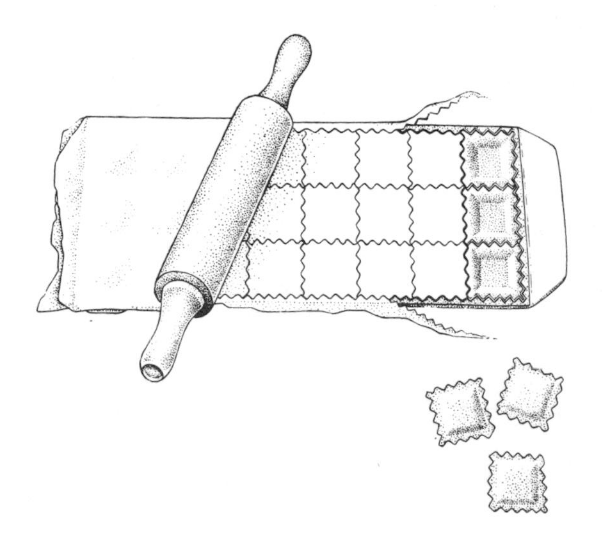

FIGURE 22-1
Stuffing the Ravioli dough. Pressing out the Ravioli on a Ravioli board.

Spaetzle (Spetzli, frisettes)

YIELD: *approximately 10 servings*

INGREDIENTS	*U.S. Weight or Volume*	*Metric Weight or Volume*	PROCEDURE
Flour	1 pound	½ kilogram	1. Sift the flour, salt, and nutmeg into a bowl. Make a well in the center.
Salt	½ ounce	15 grams	
Nutmeg	1/8 teaspoon	1 gram	
Milk and water mixture	1½ to 1¾ cups	3½ to 4 deciliters	2. Combine the lukewarm milk and water mixture with the eggs.
Eggs	4	4	3. Gradually stir in the flour until the dough takes on a thick, molasses-like consistency.
			4. Beat the dough until bubbles start to form.
			5. Pour the dough through a spaetzle colander directly into boiling salted water.
			6. When the spaetzle are all floating on the surface, remove them and prepare like pasta or saute lightly in butter.

Note: If large quantities are made, the salted boiling water must be changed frequently.

22.2 Pasta—Pates

The term pasta refers to such pasta/dough products as spaghetti, noodles, and macaroni; they are stored when dried, usually industrially produced, and may or may not contain egg.

Hard wheat flour (duram), strong in gluten content, is required for pasta products that will maintain their shape, texture, and form when cooked. The flour is kneaded into a dough with boiling water, and is then forced through special dies and comes out in various sizes and shapes. Egg noodles, an exception, must contain not less than 5.3 percent egg in the finished product according to United States government standards.

Pasta must be cooked in rapidly boiling water in a ratio of 1 pound (454 grams) of pasta to 10 quarts (9.6 liters) of water. One tablespoon (15 milliliters) of oil and one ounce (28 grams) of salt should be added to the boiling water. Pasta should be cooked uncovered.

Pasta is cooked to the *al dente* stage which means "to the teeth." This stage is reached when the pasta is still a bit resistant to the bite and it is firm, slightly chewy, and has no taste of raw flour. When the al dente stage is reached, the pasta is drained, tossed with butter, and served in heated dishes. If the pasta is not to be served immediately, it may be cooked and rinsed with cold water and heated and seasoned with butter later. Grated cheese may be served on the side.

Homemade Egg Noodles I and II (Nouilles maison)

YIELD: *approximately 10 servings*

INGREDIENTS	*U.S. Weight or Volume*	*Metric Weight or Volume*	PROCEDURE
I			
Flour	14 ounces	400 grams	1. Make a well in the flour and semolina.
Semolina, hard wheat	3½ ounces	100 grams	
Oil	¼ cup	½ deciliter	2. Mix the oil, eggs, salt, and water (or milk) in the well and gradually work in the flour until a smooth, thick dough is formed.
Eggs	5	5	
Salt	¼ ounce	7 grams	
Water	¼ cup	½ deciliter	3. Wrap the dough in a damp towel and let it stand in a cool place for at least 2 hours.
			4. Cut the dough into 5 pieces and roll and re-roll each piece until it is paper thin and translucent.
			5. Lay out the rolled pieces on a table or hang the pieces over a wooden rod to dry without allowing them to become brittle.
			6. Fold the sheets of dough lengthwise into a scroll and cut into strips.
			7. The noodles can be boiled while fresh and tossed with butter or they can be dried by spreading out on a board for at least 36 hours in a well-ventilated area.
II			
Flour	1 pound	500 grams	**1. Make a well in the flour.**
Eggs	3	3	**2. Follow procedures 2-7 for Noodles I, above.**
Salt	¼ ounce	7 grams	
Oil	¼ cup	½ deciliter	
Milk	½ cup	1 deciliter	

Variations of Noodles

Noodles, Bonne Femme Style—Nouilles bonne femme. This dish is made with boiled noodles that have been tossed with melted butter and covered with browned bread crumbs.

Buttered Noodles—Nouilles au beurre. These are noodles that have been boiled and tossed with butter.

Noodles with Cheese—Nouilles au fromage. These noodles are prepared in the same way as spaghetti. Commercial, rather than homemade noodles, should be used.

Spaghetti Bolognese and Sauce Bolognese

YIELD: *approximately 10 servings*

INGREDIENTS	*U.S. Weight or Volume*	*Metric Weight or Volume*	PROCEDURE
Spaghetti	1¾ to 2 pounds	800 grams to 1 kilogram	1. Boil the spaghetti in the salted water to the point where it is not quite cooked (al dente).
Water	8 quarts	7½ liters	2. Drain.
Salt	2 tablespoons	30 milliliters	3. Toss with the oil and butter.
Butter	¼ cup	½ deciliter	4. Serve in one of the following ways:
Oil	¼ cup	½ deciliter	a. Mix spaghetti and sauce. b. Serve sauce over spaghetti. c. Serve sauce and grated cheese separately from the spaghetti.
Sauce Bolognese (Meat Sauce)			
Oil	1¾ ounces	50 grams	1. Heat the oil in a pan.
Beef, lean, diced or ground	1¼ to 1¾ pounds	600 to 800 grams	2. Add the meat and brown.
Onion, chopped	5 ounces	150 grams	3. Add the onion, garlic, vegetables, and herbs. Cook for 5 minutes.
Garlic, finely grated	2 cloves	2 cloves	
Bouquet garni	1	1	
Vegetable brunoise	7 to 10 ounces	200 to 300 grams	
Tomato puree	1¾ ounces	50 grams	4. Add the tomato puree and tomatoes concassees.
Tomatoes concassees, **(page 446)**	7 ounces	200 grams	
Red wine	¾ cup	2 deciliters	5. Deglaze with red wine and reduce.
Brown stock	1 quart	1 liter	6. Add brown stock and season with salt, pepper, and paprika.
Salt	1 teaspoon	4 grams	
Pepper	¼ teaspoon	1 gram	7. Simmer very slowly for 2 hours.
Paprika	¼ teaspoon	1 gram	

Variations of Spaghetti

Spaghetti or Macaroni au Gratin—Spaghetti ou macaroni au gratin. This spaghetti is tossed with butter and mixed with thin cream sauce. It is placed in a buttered gratin dish, sprinkled with cheese and butter, and gratinated.

Spaghetti or Macaroni with Cheese—Spaghetti ou macaroni au fromage. This spaghetti is tossed with butter and cheese, and served with more cheese sprinkled on top.

Spaghetti, Milanese Style—Spaghetti milanaise. This is Spaghetti or Macaroni au Gratin served with a julienne of mushrooms, tongue, ham, and truffles that have been bound with a demi-glace. A depression is made in the center of the spaghetti or macaroni and it is filled with the julienne, and cheese is sprinkled over the top.

Note: If the spaghetti is being used as a side dish, the julienne is sauteed in butter and then dropped over the spaghetti.

Spaghetti or Macaroni with Tomatoes I—Spaghetti ou macaroni napolitaine I. This dish may be made with boiled spaghetti or macaroni that has been tossed with butter and arranged in layers in a baking dish. A Tomato Sauce is poured between each layer of pasta. The dish is covered with cheese.

Spaghetti or Macaroni with Tomatoes II—Spaghetti ou macaroni napolitaine II. This is another Neapolitan pasta dish made with boiled spaghetti or macaroni that has been tossed in butter. Chopped onion and tomatoes concassees are sauteed in butter, dusted with flour, deglazed with white wine and stock, and added to the tomato puree. The sauce is simmered slowly for 1 to 2 hours before it is mixed with the pasta and some cheese.

22.3 Rice—Riz

Every rice dish should be made with a top quality variety of rice (see page 111). Italian varieties of rice are especially suitable for risotto. Long grain rices are preferred for main dishes, salads, and soups where each grain should be separate, dry, and fluffy. "Siam Patna" or converted rice is good for these purposes. Short or medium grain rice is best for puddings, croquettes, and rice rings.

The ratio of rice to water varies with the type and age of the rice.

22.3.1 Risotto

YIELD: *approximately 10 servings*

INGREDIENTS	*U.S. Weight or Volume*	*Metric Weight or Volume*
Butter	5 ounces	150 grams
Onion, finely chopped	7 ounces	200 grams
Rice	1¾ pounds	800 grams
Light stock with seasoning	2¼ quarts	2.3 liters
Parmesan cheese, grated	5 ounces	150 grams

PROCEDURE

1. Saute onion in ⅓ of the butter.
2. Add rice and stir until the rice is covered with butter.
3. Pour in the boiling stock, cover, and cook the rice for about 15 minutes.
4. Remove from the heat. If necessary, add a little more stock. Stir until the rice absorbs all the liquid.
5. Add the remainder of the butter and the cheese.

Note: Risotto is best when served immediately. It should be "al dente" (see Section 22.2) and slightly sticky. If serving must be delayed, place the rice over very low heat and add a little cold stock.

Variations of Risotto

Rissoto with Chipolata Sausages—Risotto aux chipolatas. This is a risotto surrounded with chipolata sausages and topped with sauteed mushrooms.

Risotto, Milanese Style—Risotto milanaise. This risotto is prepared with rice that has been cooked in a stock with saffron.

Risotto with Mushrooms—Risotto aux champignons. This risotto is garnished with a bouquet of sauteed mushrooms.

Risotto with Tomatoes—Risotto tomate. This risotto is similar to Risotto, Milanese Style. The rice for this dish is cooked in a broth with added tomato puree and diced tomatoes.

22.3.2 Rice, Creole Style (Riz creole)

YIELD: *approximately 10 servings*

INGREDIENTS	*U.S. Weight or Volume*	*Metric Weight or Volume*
Rice	1 pound	500 grams
Water	1 quart	1 liter
Salt	½ teaspoon	3 grams
Butter	3½ ounces	100 grams

PROCEDURE

1. Wash rice thoroughly to remove excess starch.
2. Add water to rice, cover, and heat to the boiling point.
3. Reduce heat to low temperature and continue to cook for 20 minutes.
4. Separate rice grains with a fork and put rice into a buttered pan. Add salt and butter.
5. Cover rice with aluminum foil and heat in oven at 350°F. (175°C.) for 15 minutes.

White Rice—Riz au blanc. This is boiled rice that has been cooked in water or broth, drained, and sauteed in seasoned butter.

22.3.3 Rice Pilaf (Riz pilav)

YIELD: *approximately 10 servings*

INGREDIENTS	*U.S. Weight or Volume*	*Metric Weight or Volume*
Oil	3½ ounces	100 grams
Onion, finely chopped	5 ounces	150 grams
Rice, long grain	1½ pounds	700 grams
Stock	1 to 1½ quarts	1 liter
Thyme	1 teaspoon	5 grams
Pepper, freshly ground	½ teaspoon	3 grams
Parsley, chopped	3 tablespoons	45 milliliters

PROCEDURE

1. Saute the onion in the oil until transparent.
2. Add the rice and continue cooking for a few minutes.
3. Pour in the stock and seasonings.
4. Bring to a boil, cover, and simmer in the oven at 350°F. (175°C.) for 15 to 18 minutes.
5. Remove from oven. Add flakes of butter, loosen with a fork, and season to taste.

Variation of Rice Pilaf

Rice, Turkish Style—Riz a la turque. The rice used in this dish is cooked in a broth with saffron. It is then prepared as Rice Pilaf. Peeled and chopped tomatoes, peas, and dried currants are added to the pilaf. Extra stock may be needed to finish the rice.

23 National Dishes

23.1 Swiss National Dishes

Cuisses de Grenouille Bonne Femme (Frogs' Legs, Bonne Femme Style)

YIELD: *U.S. — 10 servings*

INGREDIENTS	*U.S. Weight or Volume*	*Metric Weight or Volume*	PROCEDURE
Frogs' legs	3 pounds	1.4 kilograms	1. Season the frogs' legs with salt, pepper,nutmeg, and dill weed.
Salt	1 teaspoon	6 grams	
Pepper	½ teaspoon	3 grams	
Nutmeg	¼ teaspoon	2 grams	
Dill weed	½ teaspoon	3 grams	
Brandy	½ cup	1 deciliter	2. Place seasoned frogs' legs in a bowl. Add brandy, and marinate in the refrigerator for several hours.
Butter	5 ounces	150 grams	
Shallots, finely chopped	2 ounces	60 grams	3. Heat the butter in a saute pan, add the shallots, and saute over a low flame. Add the frogs' legs, saute a few minutes, deglaze with the marinade (brandy), cover and simmer.
Lemon juice	1 tablespoon	15 milliliters	4. Sprinkle with the lemon juice.
Bread crumbs, fine and soft	2 ounces	60 grams	
Tarragon	½ teaspoon	3 grams	

Fondue

YIELD: *approximately 4 servings*

INGREDIENTS	*U.S. Weight or Volume*	*Metric Weight or Volume*
Garlic	1 clove	1 clove
White wine	1¾ cups	4 deciliters
Swiss cheese, grated	1¼ pounds	600 grams
Cornstarch	2 teaspoons	10 grams
Kirsch	2 ounces	60 milliliters
Pepper	1/8 teaspoon	1 gram
Nutmeg	1/8 teaspoon	1 gram

PROCEDURE

1. Rub a garlic clove around the inside of the fondue dish (caquelon).
2. Place the dish over the heat and pour in the wine.
3. Add the cheese gradually, stirring continuously in a figure eight pattern. Continue stirring after the mixture boils.
4. Dissolve the cornstarch in the kirsch and add to the mixture. Bring to a boil once more, stirring constantly.
5. Season to taste.
6. The fondue should continue to cook gently on the table using a small alcohol burner or hot plate under the fondue dish.

Note: If the fondue does not bind properly (the cheese may be too young or the wine too strong), add vinegar and continue stirring until it is smoothly bound. (See illustration, page 493.)

Ramequin—Cheese Gratin. Yield: approximately 10 servings. 20 slices of white bread, 20 slices of Emmentaler cheese, 5 eggs, 1 quart (1 liter) of milk, 1 teaspoon (6 grams) of salt, and ¼ teaspoon (2 grams) of nutmeg.

Preparation: (1) Place alternate slices of cheese and bread in a buttered gratin dish. (2) Mix the eggs, milk, and seasoning together, and pour over the cheese and bread. (3) Place the dish in a water bath, bake at 325°F. (160°C.), and gratinate. Sprinkle with paprika.

Note: The term "ramequin" often refers to a cheese tart. (See page 465.)

Raclette. This specialty of the Swiss Valais canton requires a special oven called a raclette and the cheese from the Alpine region. The cheese is divided and its center is exposed to heat until just the surface begins to melt. This portion is scraped off and placed on a hot plate. The raclette is served with jacketed boiled potatoes, dark bread, gherkins, and cocktail onions. The flavor is enhanced by freshly ground pepper.

Croutes au fromage—Toasted Cheese. Slices of white bread are browned in butter, covered with slices of mature Emmentaler or Gruyere cheese, dusted with paprika, baked until the cheese is melted and slightly brown. (See illustration, page 493.)

Second method: Grated cheese is mixed with a little cream or Bechamel Sauce, an egg yolk, nutmeg, and paprika. The cheese is spread on the slices of fried bread and gratinated in the oven or under the broiler.

Kaseschnitte nach Oberlander Art—Toasted Cheese, Oberland Style. Slices of bread are sauteed in butter, spread with mustard, covered with sliced ham, topped with thick slices of mature Emmentaler, dusted with paprika, and gratinated in a hot oven. Before serving, each piece is topped with a fried egg.

Champignonschnitten nach Emmentaler Art—Mushroom on Toast, Emmentaler Style. Fresh, sliced mushrooms, sauteed shallots, lemon juice, salt, pepper, nutmeg, and some white wine are covered and simmered for about 15 minutes until most of the liquid is evaporated. Bechamel Sauce and cream are added and heated to the boiling point. The mushrooms are placed on sauteed slices of bread and then covered with a slice of ham and a slice of Emmentaler cheese. These slices are gratinated in the oven and served with a fried egg on top of each.

Quiche au Fromage (Cheese Pie)

YIELD: *12 to 15 servings*

INGREDIENTS	*U.S. Weight or Volume*	*Metric Weight or Volume*	PROCEDURE
Milk	1 quart	1 liter	1. Bring the milk and cream to the boiling point.
Cream	¾ cup	2 deciliters	
Cornstarch	¾ to 1 ounce	20 to 30 grams	2. Dissolve the cornstarch in a little cold water, add to the hot milk, and bring back to a boil, stirring constantly.
Nutmeg	1/8 teaspoon	1 gram	3. Allow this mixture to cool slightly. Then season with nutmeg, paprika, and salt.
Paprika	1/8 teaspoon	1 gram	
Salt	½ teaspoon	3 grams	
Eggs, well beaten	7	7	4. Mix in the well-beaten eggs.
Emmentaler cheese, grated	10 to 14 ounces	300 to 400 grams	5. Mix in the cheese.
Short crust pastry (recipe 25.1.2)	As needed to line pans	As needed to line pans	6. Line tart pans or pie pans with short crust pastry. Pierce the bottom crust.
			7. Pour the prepared cheese mixture into the crusts.
			8. Place a few small slices of cheese on top.
			9. Bake in the oven at 350°F. (177°C.) for 45 minutes (if the pans are 8 inch (20 centimeters) diameter) until nicely browned. Serve hot. **(See illustration, page 493.)**

Kasekuchen nach Bauernart—Cheese Pie, Paysanne Style. The crust of this cheese pie is pierced and covered with diced ham or slices of bacon. It is then filled with the cheese mixture used for plain Cheese Pie. Thin slices of ham or lean bacon are arranged on top. It is baked in the oven at 350°F. (175°C.) for approximately 40 minutes.

Kasekuchen mit Krautern—Cheese Pie with Herbs. This cheese pie is prepared using the Cheese Pie recipe with the addition of 5 ounces (150 grams) of blanched spinach leaves, 1¾ ounces (50 grams) of chervil, 1 sprig of marjoram, and 1 ounce (28 grams) of parsley. The spinach and herbs are sauteed in butter and spread over the dough lining the bottom of the mold. The cheese mixture is poured into the dough and the pie is baked in an oven at 350°F. (175°C.) for approximately 40 minutes.

Tartelettes au Fromage (Cheese Tartlets)

YIELD: *20 tartlets*

INGREDIENTS	*U.S. Weight or Volume*	*Metric Weight or Volume*
Puff paste (recipe 25.1.1)	10 ounces	300 grams
Milk	1¾ cups	4 deciliters
Emmentaler cheese, grated AND Gruyere cheese, grated	10 ounces	300 grams
Eggs	3	3
Pepper	1/8 teaspoon	1 gram
Nutmeg	1/8 teaspoon	1 gram

PROCEDURE

1. Line the molds with puff paste.
2. Mix the milk, cheese, eggs, and seasonings thoroughly.
3. Fill the molds half full.
4. Bake in oven at 350°F. (177°C.) for 25 to 30 minutes.
5. Serve piping hot.

Note: These tartlets are also known as "ramequins."

Oberlander Kasetortchen (Cheese Tartlets, Oberland Style)

YIELD: *40 tartlets*

INGREDIENTS	*U.S. Weight or Volume*	*Metric Weight or Volume*
Short crust pastry (recipe 25.1.2)	as needed	as needed
Milk	1 quart	1 liter
Cream	¾ cup	2 deciliters
Cornstarch	1 ounce	30 grams
Eggs, well-beaten	7	7
Emmentaler cheese	14 ounces	400 grams
Nutmeg	1/8 teaspoon	1 gram
Paprika	1/8 teaspoon	1 gram
Onion, chopped	3½ ounces	100 grams
Butter	1 teaspoon	5 grams
Ham, finely chopped	12 ounces	350 grams

PROCEDURE

1. Heat the milk and cream to the boiling point.
2. Dissolve the cornstarch in a little cold water and add to the hot milk. Bring back to the boiling point, stirring constantly.
3. Remove from heat and allow the mixture to cool slightly and then mix in the well-beaten eggs, the cheese, and the seasonings.
4. Saute the onion in the butter.
5. Add the ham and continue sauteing.
6. Line the tartlet pans with short crust pastry.
7. On each crust, place a spoon of the onion and ham mixture.
8. Fill each tartlet with the warm cream mixture.
9. Bake in oven at 350°F. (177°C.) for 25 to 30 minutes.
10. Serve hot.

Crepes a la mode du patron—Pancakes, Chef's Style. Yield: 10 servings. Force 10 ounces (280 grams) of processed cheese through a fine sieve. Gradually mix in 1¼ cups (300 milliliters) of cream and season with a dash of nutmeg and paprika. Spread a thick layer of the cheese mixture on the pancakes and sprinkle with fresh, chopped, sauteed mushrooms and fold the pancakes twice. Spoon some Cream Sauce (recipe 11.2.2) into a buttered gratin dish. Place the stuffed pancakes in the dish and cover with more Cream Sauce. Cover with grated cheese and melted butter and gratinate the pancakes in the oven at 325°F. (160°C.).

Felchenfilets Schweizerhof—Fillets of Whitefish, Schweizerhof Style. Yield: 10 servings. Flatten and season 4 pounds (110 grams) of whitefish fillets. Spread a soubise, containing chopped and sauteed fresh mushrooms, on every other fillet (for onion puree, see page 312). Place the second fillet on top of the first one and press them together lightly. Coat the fish with flour and dip into the beaten eggs that have been seasoned with herbs. Saute the fish in butter. Before serving, cover the fish with melted butter and garnish with lemon and parsley. Serve Colbert Sauce separately.

Barschfilets nach Berner Art—Fillets of Perch, Bernese Style. Yield: 10 servings. Season 4 pounds (110 grams) of perch fillets with salt, pepper, and lemon juice. Coat the fish with flour and saute in butter. Meanwhile, prepare sauteed potatoes and place on a serving dish. Cover each fillet with Mornay Sauce and arrange the fillets on the potatoes. Sprinkle with cheese and melted butter and gratinate in the oven.

Ombre Chevalier a la Genevoise (Golden Trout, Geneva Style)

YIELD: *approximately 10 servings*

INGREDIENTS	*U.S. Weight or Volume*	*Metric Weight or Volume*	PROCEDURE
Golden trout	4 pounds	2 kilograms	1. Clean the fish and season the interiors with the lemon juice and salt.
Lemon juice	¼ cup	½ deciliter	
Salt	1 teaspoon	6 grams	
Butter	4 ounces	100 grams	2. Saute the shallot and then the herbs in butter.
Shallot	1	1	3. Add the wine and water, and bring to the boiling point.
Parsley, chopped; Chives; Thyme; Rosemary; Tarragon	Total of 1 tablespoon	Total of 15 grams	4. Poach the fish in this court bouillon, then remove it and keep it hot.
Water	¾ cup	2 deciliters	
White wine	¾ cup	2 deciliters	
Butter, kneaded	3 tablespoons	45 grams	5. Bind the liquid with the kneaded butter, and then add the egg yolks and cream.
Egg yolks	2	2	6. Season to taste.
Cream	¼ cup	½ deciliter	7. Pour the sauce over the golden trout, and serve hot with boiled potatoes.

Emmentaler Schafsvoressen (Mutton Stew, Emmentaler Style)

YIELD: *10 persons*

INGREDIENTS	*U.S. Weight or Volume*	*Metric Weight or Volume*	PROCEDURE
Mutton, breast and shoulder, 2½ ounce (70 grams) cubes	5 pounds	2.27 kilograms	1. Blanch meat and drain. Place in casserole.
Stock	1½ pints	.7 liter	2. Add stock and wine; cover and simmer for ¾ hour.
White wine	1 cup	237 milliliters	
Pearl onions	1 pound	.453 kilogram	3. Add the vegetables and simmer until tender.
Carrots	8 ounces	225 grams	
Celery root, diced	3½ ounces	100 grams	
Turnips, diced	3½ ounces	100 grams	
Cornstarch	½ teaspoon	3 grams	4. Mix the cornstarch, flour, and saffron in a small amount of water, and add to the meat.
Flour	1¾ ounces	50 grams	
Saffron	¼ teaspoon	2 grams	5. Heat to the boiling point.
Salt	½ teaspoon	3 grams	6. Serve with boiled potatoes.

Note: Lamb may be substituted for mutton.

Pieds de porc braises (Braised Pigs' Feet)

YIELD: *10 servings*

INGREDIENTS	*U.S. Weight or Volume*	*Metric Weight or Volume*
Pigs' feet	10	10
White wine	to cover	to cover
Celery, diced	1 cup	225 grams
Bay leaves	2	2
Thyme	½ teaspoon	3 grams
Parsley	¼ cup	65 grams
Onion, sliced	1 large	1 large
Garlic, crushed	2 cloves	2 cloves
Stock	1 cup	2 deciliters
Salt	2 teaspoons	12 grams
Peppercorns, crushed	8	8
Tomato puree	½ cup	1 deciliter
Madeira wine	¼ cup	½ deciliter
Mushrooms, sliced and sauteed	¼ pound	95 grams

PROCEDURE

1. Wash the pigs' feet and split them lengthwise.
2. Combine wine, celery, bay leaves, thyme, and parsley. Pour over the pigs' feet.
3. Marinate for 8 days.
4. Remove pigs' feet from marinade and saute in fat until brown.
5. Saute onion and garlic and add to the pigs' feet.
6. Add stock, salt, peppercorns, and tomato puree to the wine marinade.
7. Pour the marinade over the pigs' feet, cover, and braise in the oven at 325°F. (163°C.) until the meat is tender, about 3 hours.
8. Remove the feet and reduce the stock by one third.
9. Strain and adjust seasonings.
10. Bone the feet and add ¼ cup (½ deciliter) of Madeira wine to the gravy. Arrange the meat and gravy in individual cocottes topped with sauteed mushrooms. **Serve pasta or rice separately.**

Berne Platte—Bernese Platter. This is prepared by boiling a piece of beef with lean bacon, smoked pork chop, cured pig's knuckle, and tongue sausage until tender. The meat is sliced and arranged on a platter of braised sauerkraut or green beans. Poached marrow bones are arranged around the edge of the dish. Boiled potatoes are served separately. Cranberry sauce is a good accompaniment.

Schweizer Schnitzel (Veal Steak, Swiss Style)

YIELD: *2 servings*

INGREDIENTS	*U.S. Weight or Volume*	*Metric Weight or Volume*	PROCEDURE
Veal loin steaks	**2-2½ ounces steaks**	150 grams	1. Pound the veal steaks slightly but not too thin.
Salt	½ teaspoon	3 grams	
Egg, beaten	1	1	2. Dip the meat into beaten egg and then bread with crumbs. Saute until tender.
Bread crumbs, dry, fine, white	as needed	as needed	
Emmentaler cheese	1¾ ounces	50 grams	**3. Mix the cheese, cream or Bechamel Sauce, egg yolk, and paprika. Spread on a slice of ham.**
Cream	2 tablespoons	30 milliliters	
OR			4. Gratinate the ham in the oven or under the broiler.
Bechamel Sauce			5. Place the ham on the veal steak.
Egg yolk	1	1	6. Pour foaming hot butter over the meat and serve at once. A thickened veal gravy is served separately.
Paprika	1/8 teaspoon	1 gram	
Ham slices	2 2½ ounces	150 grams	
Butter, melted	2 tablespoons	30 milliliters	

Note: This Veal Steak, Swiss Style, was conceived to replace "Cordon Bleu."

Geschnetzeltes nach Zurcher Art—Sliced Veal, Zurich Style. This dish is prepared with equal parts of veal, veal kidney, and mushrooms that have been cut into very fine slices. The veal and kidneys are browned in butter and added to some sauteed onions. The meat and onions are placed on a dish and the drippings are deglazed with a small amount of veal stock or demi-glace, white wine, and cream. The sauce is reduced and seasoned with lemon juice and paprika. The meat is seasoned, added to the sauce, and heated. The sauteed mushrooms are arranged over the top before serving.

Other Swiss National Dishes

Basler Zwiebelsuppe, page 328.
Bauern-Chrutsuppe, page 328.
Berner Topf, page 329.
Bundner Suppe, page 331.
Kerbelsuppe, page 334.
Mehlsuppe with toasted cheese, page 336.
Potee a la vaudoise, page 342.

23.2 French National Dishes

Cassoulet de Mouton (Mutton Cassoulet)

YIELD: *approximately 10 servings*

INGREDIENTS	*U.S. Weight or Volume*	*Metric Weight or Volume*
Navy beans	10 ounces	300 grams
Water	1½ quarts	1½ liters
Bouquet garni	1	1
Garlic cloves	2	2
Salt	1 teaspoon	5 grams
Bacon ends OR Salt pork strips	10 ounces	300 grams
Lean bacon, chopped	10 ounces	300 grams
Garlic sausage OR Tongue sausage	1 pound	500 grams
Mutton, boneless (shoulder or breast, cut in cubes)	2 pounds	1 kilogram
Fat	as needed	as needed
Onion, chopped	1 pound	½ kilogram
Garlic clove, crushed	1	1
Salt	1 teaspoon	5 grams
Pepper	1/8 teaspoon	1 gram
Brown stock	½ cup	1 deciliter
Tomato puree	1 to 2 tablespoons	15 to 30 milliliters
Bread crumbs, buttered and dry	4 ounces	120 grams

PROCEDURE

1. Soak beans overnight, then boil them in the 1½ quarts of water with a bouquet garni, salt, 2 garlic cloves, and the raw bacon ends or salt pork strips tied together.
2. After boiling for 1 hour, add the lean, chopped bacon. Cook a few minutes and add the sausage. Boil until the beans and sausage are cooked.
3. Meanwhile brown the mutton in fat. Add the chopped onion and a crushed garlic clove and brown again. Add seasonings. Deglaze with stock and tomato puree. Braise as for ragout until meat is fully cooked (about 2 hours).
4. Remove the bundle of bacon ends and the garlic cloves. Combine the remaining mixture with the meat and cook together for 10 minutes.
5. Line ovenproof terrines with sliced bacon.
6. Place alternate layers of the mutton and slices of the sausage in the terrines and sprinkle bread crumbs on top.
7. Brown in the oven at 375°F. (190°C.) for about 15 minutes. Add more stock from the beans if necessary.

Note: Lamb may be substituted for mutton.

Cassoulet d'oie—Goose Cassoulet. This cassoulet is prepared by the method used for Mutton Cassoulet, substituting goose for the mutton. The legs of the goose are cut into pieces; the wings are removed from the breast and cut into two pieces; and the boned breast meat is cut into pieces.

Gibelotte de lapin—Rabbit Ragout. A Rabbit Ragout is prepared by the same method used for hasenpfeffer. **(See page 394.)** It is made with half red wine and half white stock or meat stock. To prepare Rabbit Ragout, Bonne Femme Style, follow the same procedure and add quartered potatoes.

Haricot de mouton—Mutton with Navy Beans. This mutton dish is prepared by sauteing small onions and diced lean bacon. After these are browned, they are removed from the fat and set aside. Stew-sized pieces of mutton, crushed garlic, and some flour are browned in the fat. The drippings are deglazed with water or stock, spice sachet is added, and the braising is continued for 30 minutes. The meat is removed, the sauce is strained, and the onions, bacon, beans, and meat are added to the sauce. It is simmered gently and served in terrines. *Note:* Lamb may be substituted for mutton.

Pilav de mouton—Mutton Pilaf. This pilaf is prepared by the recipe used for Navarin (Lamb Ragout) (recipe 17.3.1.4). A ring of Rice Pilaf is arranged on a serving dish, and the center is filled with the meat and sauce. (The sauce is prepared without onions and potatoes.) *Note:* Lamb may be substituted for mutton.

Civet de lievre bonne femme (Hare Stew, Bonne Femme Style)

YIELD: *approximately 10 servings*

INGREDIENTS	*U.S. Weight or Volume*	*Metric Weight or Volume*
Hare	1 (6 to 7 pounds)	1 (3 to 3½ kilograms)
Fat	3½ ounces	100 grams
Onion, coarsely cut	7 ounces	200 grams
Flour	1¾ to 2 ounces	50 to 60 grams
Spice sachet	1	1
Garlic cloves, crushed	2	2
Stock	1 pint	½ liter
Red Burgundy wine	1½ pints	7 deciliters
Bacon, lean, diced	7 ounces	200 grams
Onions, small	7 ounces	200 grams
Cream	¾ cup	2 deciliters
Brandy	¼ cup	½ deciliter
Lemon juice	2 tablespoons	30 milliliters
Salt	1 teaspoon	5 grams

PROCEDURE

1. Cut the hare into stew-sized pieces, season, and brown in fat.
2. Add the chopped onion, dust with flour, and continue cooking until brown.
3. Add the spice sachet and garlic.
4. Deglaze with the wine and the stock so that the meat is covered.
5. Cover the saucepan and braise in the oven at 300°F. (150°C.).
6. When the pieces of the hare are half cooked (after 1 hour) remove them from the saucepan, strain the gravy, reduce slightly, and then pour the gravy over the meat.
7. Saute the diced bacon and small onions and add to the meat mixture. Continue braising until the meat is tender (about 1 hour longer).
8. Add the cream and mix thoroughly.
9. Bring the dish almost to the boiling point without allowing it to boil. Keep it hot.
10. Flambe with the brandy. Add the lemon juice and salt.

Note: The original recipe calls for the blood from the hare to be mixed with the cream and added to the gravy. Due to inspection and sanitation codes, this ingredient has been omitted. If gravy requires further thickening, add 1 teaspoon of cornstarch, dissolved in water, along with the cream.

Tripes a la mode de Caen (Tripe, Caen Style)

YIELD: *approximately 10 servings*

INGREDIENTS	*U.S. Weight or Volume*	*Metric Weight or Volume*
Tripe, raw	6 pounds	3 kilograms
Beef feet, split	2	2
Onion	9 ounces	250 grams
Carrots	7 ounces	200 grams
Garlic cloves	2	2
Celery	3½ ounces	100 grams
Pork rind	7 ounces	200 grams
OR		
Salt pork		
Parsley root	1	1
Apple cider	2 quarts	2 liters
Salt	1 tablespoon	15 grams
Pepper	¼ teaspoon	2 grams
Bay leaf	1	1
Whole cloves	3	3
Thyme	½ teaspoon	3 grams
Calvados	½ cup	1 deciliter

PROCEDURE

1. Blanch the tripe. Rinse with cold water.
2. Cut into rectangular pieces about 2 × 3 inches (5 × 7.5 centimeters).
3. Place the split beef feet in the bottom of a deep earthenware pot or a braising pan.
4. Add the onion, carrots, garlic, celery, salt pork, and parsley root. Place the tripe on top.
5. Add the cider, salt, pepper, bay leaf, cloves, and thyme.
6. Bring to a boil, cover, and seal the lid hermetically, using flour paste.
7. Braise in the oven at 250°F. (121°C.) for 8 to 10 hours.
8. Take the tripe and the feet out of the stock. Remove the meat from the feet and add it to the tripe.
9. Strain the stock. Reduce to the desired thickness. Return tripe to the stock. Bring to a boil again and season to taste using cayenne pepper.
10. Flambe the dish with slightly warmed calvados.
11. Serve boiled potatoes or potatoes in their jackets separately.

Note: 1) If a pressure cooker is used, the cooking time is 1½ hours instead of 8 to 10 hours at very low heat; 2) avoid reducing the stock too much during steaming; and 3) tripe from young animals requires a shorter cooking time (about 7 hours).

Other French National Dishes

Boeuf a la mode, page 410.
Bouillabaisse a la marseillaise, page 330.
Bouillabaisse a la provencale, page 330.
Ecrevisses a la bordelaise, page 371.
Escargots a la bourguignonne, page 375.
Filets de sole Murat, page 366.
Gigot d'agneau a la boulangere, page 422.
Jambon braise a la bourguignonne, page 419.
Moules a la mariniere, page 374.
Petite Marmite, page 316.
Quiche Lorraine, page 350.
Selle de veau Metternich, page 417.
Sole Colbert, page 366.

23.3 German National Dishes

Ganseklein I. Use wings, neck, and heart of goose, cleaned well and blanched. Place in saucepan, add broth, white wine, bouquet garni and seasonings, simmer until done. Prepare a white sauce from ⅔ of the cooking liquid. Keep the giblets warm for service in the remaining stock. At service time, pour sauce over giblets and sprinkle with chopped parsley. Serve potatoes separately.

Ganseklein II. Saute the cleaned giblets of goose in fat with onions and seasoning. Dust with flour and continue browning. Deglaze with stock, white wine, and a little vinegar, and simmer covered until done. Strain the cooking liquid, thicken with cream and pour over giblets. Serve noodles or dumplings separately.

Note: The original recipe for Method II calls for goose blood mixed with cream. Due to inspection and sanitation codes, this ingredient has been omitted.

Deutsches Bifteck (German Meat Patties)

YIELD: *10 servings*

INGREDIENTS	*U.S. Weight or Volume*	*Metric Weight or Volume*
Beef, ground AND Pork, ground	2½ pounds	1.2 kilograms
Bread, white	7 to 10 ounces	200 to 300 grams
Milk	½ cup	1 deciliter
Onion	7 ounces	200 grams
Eggs	2	2
Salt	1 tablespoon	15 grams
Pepper	¼ teaspoon	2 grams
Fat	2 tablespoons	30 grams

PROCEDURE

1. Place the meat in a mixing bowl.
2. Soak the bread in the milk. Press out any surplus.
3. Chop ⅓ of the onion and saute until transparent.
4. Add the bread, cooked onion, eggs, salt, and seasonings to the meat. Mix well and shape into 10 individual patties.
5. Saute in fat until well-done.
6. Slice remaining onion and brown in fat.
7. When serving, top the meat with the browned onion and surround with some of the pan drippings.

Hamburger Steak. Yield: 10 servings. Combine 2½ pounds (1.2 kilograms) of ground beef, 7 ounces (200 grams) of chopped and sauteed onion, 3 or 4 rolls that have been soaked in ½ cup (1 deciliter) of milk, 1 teaspoon (5 grams) of salt, and ¼ teaspoon (2 grams) of pepper. The meat is shaped into hamburger patties and sauteed in fat. The hamburgers are topped with fried onion and served.

Gefulltes Spanferkel (Stuffed Suckling Pig)

YIELD: *Number of servings will depend on size of pig (Dressed pig weighing 12 pounds yields 10 servings)*

INGREDIENTS	*U.S. Weight or Volume*	*Metric Weight or Volume*
Suckling pig	1	1
Butter	1 ounce	30 grams
Shallots, chopped	1¾ ounces	50 grams
Liver	½ the liver of the pig	½ the liver of the pig
Forcemeat:		
Veal	9 ounces	250 grams
Bacon, lean, fresh	5 ounces	150 grams
Liver	½ the liver of the pig	½ the liver of the pig
Mushrooms, chopped	5 ounces	150 grams
Rolls	2	2
Milk	½ cup	1 deciliter
Cream	½ cup	1 deciliter
Eggs	4	4
Madeira	½ cup	1 deciliter
Brandy	¼ cup	½ deciliter
Salt	2 teaspoons	10 grams
Pepper	¼ teaspoon	2 grams
Butter	as needed for basting	as needed for basting
Beer	as needed for basting	as needed for basting

PROCEDURE

1. Dice half the liver and quickly brown with the shallots in butter. Cool and mix with the forcemeat.
2. Prepare the forcemeat by grinding the veal, bacon, ½ the liver, chopped mushrooms, and rolls. Stir in the milk, cream, eggs, Madeira, brandy, salt, and pepper.
3. Season the suckling pig inside and out.
4. Stuff with forcemeat and sew up.
5. Put front feet through parallel cuts made on each side of the neck.
6. Place the pig on a grill or on a layer of bread crumbs in a roasting pan. Care must be taken that both hind legs are sitting correctly, that the rear feet are fixed together using a wooden peg, and that the head is placed a little higher than the rest of the body. Wrap the ears and tail in aluminum foil.
7. During the roasting, baste the pig alternately with butter and beer. Should blisters form on the skin during roasting, pierce them.
8. Roast in oven at 325°F. to 350°F. (163°C. to 177°C.). Allow at least 30 minutes per pound.

Note: 1) This form of preparation is used when the pig is to be presented whole to the guests. If it is not to be served whole, roast the pig without stuffing. Bake the stuffing separately in a buttered mold in a water bath in the oven. 2) For garnishes, use julienne of potatoes, glazed chestnuts, and red cabbage. Serve the gravy separately.

Garnished Roast Beef and Roast Pork—Roast beef et roti de porc garnis. Roast beef and roast pork are arranged on a platter and garnished with sweet peppers and mixed pickles.

Roast Turkey, Modern Style—Dindonneau roti moderne. Medallions of turkey with a deboned turkey carcass dressed with celery salad and garnished with fresh fruit, Mayonnaise Sauce, canapes, and deviled eggs. (See illustration, page 491.)

Mushroom Pate—Pate de champignons. Prepare as described in Section 24.4.5. Stuffing: Blend ⅔ part forcemeat as used in jelly pate (see page 501) with ⅓ part pure mushroom duxelles. The pate is garnished with finely diced beef tongue, pistachios, whole cooked mushrooms, and truffles. (See illustration, page 492.)

Garnishes: Tomato wedges stuffed with fresh sweet corn blended with mayonnaise topped with green olives stuffed with almond sticks truffle slices, and cubes of Madeira jelly and gooseberry jelly. The centerpiece is a small head of white cabbage with long sweet peppers, mushrooms caps, and two ears of sweet corn.

Leg of Deer in Pastry, Lucerne Style—Gigot de chevreuil en croute a la lucernoise. (See illustration, page 492.)

Kalbshaxe Nach Burgerlicher Art (Veal Knuckle, Home Style)

YIELD: *approximately 10 servings*

INGREDIENTS	*U.S. Weight or Volume*	*Metric Weight or Volume*	PROCEDURE
Fat	3½ ounces	100 grams	1. Heat the fat in a braising pan that can be covered.
Veal shanks, large, whole	4	4	2. Place the seasoned shanks in the pan and brown on both sides over a high flame.
Salt	½ teaspoon	3 grams	
Pepper	1/8 teaspoon	1 gram	
Mirepoix, finely cut	10 ounces	300 grams	3. Add the mirepoix and tomato puree, and saute these ingredients together.
Tomato puree	1 ounce	30 grams	
White wine	¾ cup	2 deciliters	4. Deglaze the shanks with wine and reduce. Add basic stock so that only the bottoms of the shanks are covered by the liquid.
Basic stock OR Fond de veau brun	1 quart	1 liter	5. Cover and braise for at least 1 hour. During the braising, turn the shanks from time to time and baste with the liquid.
Cornstarch	2 tablespoons	30 grams	6. When cooked, remove shanks from the pan. Thin the stock slightly if necessary. Thicken with cornstarch dissolved in cold water. Bring to a boil. Add Madeira, strain, and season to taste.
Water	¼ cup	60 milliliters	
Madeira	¼ cup	½ deciliter	
Onions, small whole	7 ounces	200 grams	7. Meanwhile, glaze the small onions, carrots, and turnips separately. Toss the peas quickly in butter and arrange with the glazed vegetables over the shanks.
Carrots	10 ounces	300 grams	
Turnips	7 ounces	200 grams	
Peas	3½ ounces	100 grams	
Butter	3½ ounces	100 grams	
Parsley, chopped	as needed to garnish	as needed to garnish	8. Sprinkle with parsley.

Kalbshaxen in Rahmsauce—Creamed Veal Knuckle. These shanks are browned in fat. A mirepoix is added and browned. A small amount of stock and white wine are added and the shanks are braised until tender. The shanks are removed from the stock and kept warm. A small quantity of cream is added to the stock. It is reduced and seasoned with lemon juice and paprika, and strained. The sauce is poured over the shanks before serving. Pasta is served separately.

Bayrische Leberknodel (Bavarian Liver Dumplings)

YIELD: *approximately 10 servings*

INGREDIENTS	*U.S. Weight or Volume*	*Metric Weight or Volume*	PROCEDURE
Onion, chopped	5 ounces	150 grams	1. Saute the onion.
Butter	1¾ ounces	50 grams	
OR			
Vegetable oil			
White bread	10 ounces	300 grams	2. Soak the bread in warm milk and press out the excess milk.
Milk	¾ to 1¼ cups	2 to 3 deciliters	
Beef liver	1 pound	500 grams	3. Skin the liver and grind it with the kidney fat and the bread.
Veal kidney fat	7 ounces	200 grams	
Eggs	3 or 4	3 or 4	4. Add the onion, eggs, salt, pepper, and parsley to the liver. Mix well. If necessary, add some bread crumbs.
Salt	2 teaspoons	10 grams	
Pepper	¼ teaspoon	2 grams	5. Shape the dumplings with a large spoon or ice cream scoop and drop into the boiling stock. Cover and poach slowly in the gently boiling stock for 5 or 6 minutes.
Parsley, chopped	2 tablespoons	30 grams	
Bread crumbs	as needed	as needed	

Kartoffelknodel (Potato Dumplings)

YIELD: *approximately 10 servings*

INGREDIENTS	*U.S. Weight or Volume*	*Metric Weight or Volume*	PROCEDURE
Potatoes	3 pounds	1½ kilograms	1. Boil the unpeeled potatoes until tender.
			2. Peel and grate the potatoes.
Eggs	4 or 5	4 or 5	3. Mix the potatoes with the eggs, flour, the semolina if necessary, warm butter, salt, and pepper.
Flour	5 ounces	150 grams	
Semolina, if needed	1¾ ounces	50 grams	4. Let stand for 10 minutes.
Butter	2¾ ounces	80 grams	5. Form into dumplings and poach in gently boiling salted water.
Salt	1 tablespoon	15 grams	
Pepper	¼ teaspoon	3 grams	6. Pour browned butter over the dumplings and top with browned onion.
Onion, chopped	7 ounces	200 grams	

Note: Small fried bread croutons may be added to the dumpling mixture. For this recipe, 3½ to 7 ounces of croutons would be adequate.

Kartoffelpuffer (Potato Puffs)

YIELD: *approximately 10 servings*

INGREDIENTS	*U.S. Weight or Volume*	*Metric Weight or Volume*	PROCEDURE
Potatoes	3 pounds	1½ kilograms	1. Peel and grate the raw potatoes.
Onion, chopped	3½ ounces	100 grams	2. Add the onion, eggs, flour, salt, and pepper. Mix well.
Eggs	2	2	3. **Drop this mixture in uniformly-sized portions into hot fat. Fry until crisp on both sides and serve immediately.** immediately.
Flour	1¾ ounces	50 grams	
Salt	1 tablespoon	15 grams	
Pepper	¼ teaspoon	2 grams	
Fat	7 ounces	200 grams	

Note: 1) Chopped parsley or grated cheese may be added to the puffs. 2) When made without onion, the puffs may be served with stewed fruits and with applesauce.

Semmelschmarren

YIELD: *approximately 8 servings*

INGREDIENTS	*U.S. Weight or Volume*	*Metric Weight or Volume*	PROCEDURE
Rolls, white	8	8	1. Cut the rolls into slices.
Milk	1 pint	½ liter	2. Place in a bowl and cover with milk. Let stand a few minutes.
Eggs	8	8	3. Beat the eggs with the salt and nutmeg. Add to the soaked roll mixture.
Salt	1 teaspoon	6 grams	
Nutmeg	1/8 teaspoon	1 gram	
Butter	as needed for frying	as needed for frying	4. Heat butter in a pan and fill with the mixture to a depth of 1/5 inch. Saute each side until brown. 5. Cut the pancake into small pieces in the pan and continue to brown a little longer. 6. Repeat until mixture is all gone.
Sugar and cinnamon mixture	for garnish	for garnish	7. Sprinkle with the sugar and cinnamon.

Note: Semmelschmarren is usually served with stewed fruit.

Other German National Dishes

Dampfnudeln, page 453.
Frankfurter Pudding, page 538.
Geflugelkleinsuppe, page 333.
Leberknodelsuppe, page 335.
Nudelsuppe mit Huhn, page 338.
Rahmsuppe, page 342.

23.4 English and American National Dishes

Real Turtle Soup. This soup is usually a commercially canned product. It may be seasoned with Madeira or sherry.

Welsh Rarebit. This dish consists of buttered toast points covered with a sauce made of cheddar cheese, egg yolk, and dark beer. It is dusted with paprika and gratinated.

Cheeseburger. A beefburger is sauteed as described on page 472. The meat is covered with slices of Emmentaler or Gruyere cheese and gratinated. It is served on a hot roll. (See illustration, page 493.)

Chicken Mulligatawny. This soup is prepared by poaching a chicken in stock with a bouquet garni. The chicken is boned and cut into small slices. A cream of rice soup is made by browning sliced onion in butter, adding some curry, and deglazing with the stock. Rice flour is dissolved in liquid and added to the soup. The soup is brought to the boiling point and then cooked gently for approximately 10 minutes. Just before serving, a small amount of currant jelly, chutney, almond or coconut milk, and cream are added. The soup is strained. It is garnished with the chicken and served with rice. Sliced apples may be served instead of chutney and currant jelly. (See Mulligatawny Soup, page 337.)

Whitebait. Whitebait are small fish, 1½ to 2 inches (3.75 to 5 centimeters) long, that are cooked immediately after being taken out of the water. They are washed and drained, coated with flour, and deep-fat fried until crisp. They are placed on a cloth, sprinkled with salt, and served on a paper napkin. They are garnished with deep-fat fried parsley and lemon wedges. Whitebait are eaten whole.

Deviled Whitebait. These are prepared as described under Whitebait, and are dusted with paprika and cayenne pepper.

Curry Whitebait. These whitebait are deep-fat fried and sprinkled with a mixture of salt and curry powder.

Chicken Maryland. Seasoned chicken breasts, legs, and wings are breaded with white bread crumbs, and sauteed in clarified butter. The chicken is garnished with corn fritters, sauteed bacon, and sauteed bananas. A Horseradish Sauce, made with milk, egg yolks, and cream, may be served with the chicken.

Chicken Curry

YIELD: *approximately 10 servings*

INGREDIENTS	*U.S. Weight or Volume*	*Metric Weight or Volume*
Chicken, fryers, cut up	6 pounds (2 at 3 pounds each)	3 kilograms (2 at 1½ kilograms each)
Butter	3½ ounces	100 grams
Salt	1 tablespoon	15 grams
Onion, chopped	10 ounces	300 grams
Apples, sliced	4	4
Curry powder	2 tablespoons	30 grams
Chicken stock	1¾ pints	9 deciliters
Cornstarch	1½ tablespoons	20 grams
Cream	1¼ cups	3 deciliters
Lemon juice	2 tablespoons	30 milliliters
Rice Creole (page 461)	1 pound	½ kilogram

PROCEDURE

1. Saute the chicken pieces in butter.
2. Add the chopped onion and sliced apples and continue sauteing.
3. Dust with the curry powder and deglaze with the chicken stock so that the chicken is just covered by the liquid.
4. Braise 25 to 40 minutes until the chicken meat is tender.
5. Remove chicken pieces from the stock. Thicken the stock with cornstarch dissolved in water. Add the cream and lemon juice. Reduce the liquid to a smooth sauce. Strain. Put the chicken back in the sauce and keep it warm.
6. Serve with Rice Creole prepared from 1 pound (½ kilogram) of rice.

Note: 1) Fresh coconut milk can replace some of the chicken stock as part of the cooking liquid. 2) With variations such as Chicken Curry, Bombay Style, separate garnishes must accompany the dish. In addition to the Creole Rice, the following are suitable:

Bombay ducks	Sweet peppers
Puppadums	Diced pineapple
Kroepoek	Raisins
Chopped pan-fried onion	Mango chutney
Chopped cooked egg whites	Sauteed bananas

Variations of Chicken Curry

Lamb Curry. This curry is made from stew-sized pieces of shoulder and breast of lamb. It is prepared by the same method used to make Chicken Curry. It should cook for approximately 1 hour.

Veal Curry. This curry is made from shoulder and breast of veal cut into stew-sized pieces. It is prepared by the same method used to make Chicken Curry. It should cook for approximately 1 hour.

Irish Stew

YIELD: *approximately 10 servings*

INGREDIENTS	*U.S. Weight or Volume*	*Metric Weight or Volume*
Mutton, diced (boneless breast and shoulder)	3 to 4 pounds	1½ to 2 kilograms
Onion, sliced	1 pound	½ kilogram
Leeks	7 ounces	200 grams
Carrots	10 ounces	300 grams
Turnips	3½ ounces	100 grams
Celery	7 ounces	200 grams
Potatoes	10 ounces	300 grams
Garlic clove, crushed	1	1
Cabbage	10 ounces	300 grams
Salt	1 tablespoon	15 grams
Spice sachet	1	1
Worcestershire Sauce	1 tablespoon	15 milliliters

PROCEDURE

1. Blanch the meat quickly and return to saucepan.
2. Add the sliced vegetables, salt, spice sachet, and cover with water. Place the sliced cabbage leaves on top and simmer for 1 hour. Thicken the liquid.
3. Serve in individual casseroles and garnish with additional boiled potatoes.

Note: 1) The carrots, celery, or turnips may be omitted. Sometimes the vegetables are cooked separately. When this is done, the quantity of onion and potatoes cooked with the meat is greatly increased. 2) Lamb may be substituted for mutton.

Baked Halibut Steak

YIELD: *2 servings*

INGREDIENTS	*U.S. Weight or Volume*	*Metric Weight or Volume*
Halibut steaks	2 (8 to 10 ounces each)	2 (225 to 285 grams each)
Oil OR Butter, clarified	1 ounce	30 grams
Salt	to taste	to taste
Pepper, white	to taste	to taste
Paprika (optional)	for color	for color

PROCEDURE

1. Place fish on buttered or oiled broiler pan; brush with oil or butter and season.
2. Place under hot broiler for 2 to 3 minutes.
3. Transfer to hot oven and bake until firm to touch, approximately 8 to 10 minutes.

Serve with: lemon, parsley, butter or other compound butter, or any matching sauce such as Caper or Hollandaise Sauces.

Note: 1) This is a popular method of preparing fish in the United States either whole, cut into steaks (darne), or fillets. Swordfish, salmon, haddock, and cod may be substituted for halibut. Small whole fish, such as red snapper, pompano, shad, mackerel, and perch, may be used. 2) A very small amount of liquid (fish stock, wine) may be added to prevent the fish from drying out.

Variations of Baked Fish

Baking of Large, Whole Fish. Clean and, if necessary, scale gutted fish. With a sharp knife, make incisions crosswise through the skin, about 2 inches (5 centimeters) apart. Season fish inside and out. Place in buttered or oiled baking pan. Cover with buttered paper. Place in 300°F. to 325°F. (149°C. to 163°C.) oven and bake 6 to 8 minutes per pound or until firm to touch. Serve with matching sauce on the side.

Note: 1) A little liquid may be added (stock, wine) to prevent fish from drying or sticking to the pan. Liquid may be used to baste fish occasionally during baking. 2) Fish can be stuffed before baking with perferred filling (basic bread, forcemeat, seafood mixture); the cooking time would need to be adjusted accordingly. *Caution:* fish might overcook in order to properly cook the filling.

Chicken Pie

YIELD: *approximately 10 servings*

INGREDIENTS	*U.S. Weight or Volume*	*Metric Weight or Volume*	PROCEDURE
Chicken, frying, cut up	3 to 4 pounds	1½ to 2 kilograms	1. Season the chicken pieces with salt.
Butter	1¾ ounces	50 grams	
Shallots	1¾ ounces	50 grams	2. Saute the shallots, onion, and mushrooms in butter. Sprinkle this mixture and the parsley over the chicken.
Onion	1¾ ounces	50 grams	
Mushrooms, quartered	5 ounces	150 grams	
Parsley, chopped	1 tablespoon	15 grams	
Veal scallops, thin	10 to 14 ounces	300 to 400 grams	3. Season the veal and arrange it and the bacon on the bottom of an English pie pan.
Bacon slices, lean	7 ounces	200 grams	
Salt	1 tablespoon	15 grams	
Pepper	½ teaspoon	4 grams	
Eggs, hard-cooked	5	5	4. Cut the hard-cooked eggs in halves.
			5. Add the chicken pieces and the eggs.
Brown poultry stock	1 pint	½ liter	6. Pour in the poultry stock until the pieces are just covered.
Puff paste (recipe 25.1.1)	10 to 14 ounces	300 to 400 grams	7. Moisten the edge of the pie dish with egg yolk and place a strip of puff paste around the rim. Cover the dish with a lid made of the dough, having first moistened the inside edge with egg. Press the lid and the strip around the edge together until sealed.
Egg, slightly beaten	1	1	8. Garnish the pastry with shapes cut from the dough. Brush with beaten egg and bake the pie in the oven at 300°F. (150°C.) for approximately 40 minutes.
			9. When the cooking time is up, make a small cut at the edge of the pastry and tilt the dish to see if any liquid remains. Add stock as required.

Variations of Chicken Pie

Pigeon Pie. This is made in a cocotte, with the bottom lined with slices of uncooked bacon that have been sprinkled with chopped shallots and parsley. The halved pigeons are seasoned with salt and pepper and chopped parsley. They are placed on the bacon. Mushrooms that have been quartered and sauteed in butter and partially-cooked parisienne potatoes are added to the cocotte. The mixture is covered with veal stock. It is finished by the method used for Chicken Pie.

Steak Pie. This is a steak pie made from thin slices, ¼ inch (.6 centimeter) thick, of beef tenderloin that have been seasoned, covered with chopped shallots and parsley, and dusted with flour. The meat is arranged in a buttered cocotte in alternating layers with sauteed mushrooms. Rich stock is poured over the top. The pie is covered and finished as Chicken Pie. The baking time is approximately 1 hour.

Steak and Kidney Pie. This pie is made with thin slices of beef tenderloin and slices of veal or sauteed sliced veal kidneys. It is prepared by the same method used for Chicken Pie.

English and American Desserts

Apple Pie. This is a deep-dish apple pie. Apple slices are mixed with lemon juice, light brown sugar, cinnamon, powdered ginger or cloves, and arranged in a deep pie dish. The top is covered and sealed with a crust. The pie is baked in an oven at 350°F. (175°C.) for 30 to 45 minutes.

Custard. This custard is prepared by scalding 1 quart (1 liter) of milk with a vanilla bean. The milk is strained and added slowly to a combination of 8 eggs and 7 ounces (200 grams) of sugar. The custard is poured into individual molds. The molds are topped with bits of butter and placed in a waterbath. They are baked in an oven at 300°F. (150°C.) for 30 minutes. To test for doneness, a knife is inserted into the custard near the edge of the mold. It is done when none of the custard adheres to the knife. *Note:* All the custard may be poured into a casserole dish and baked for an hour or until it tests done. The custard may be served alone or garnished with fruit.

Other English and American National Dishes

Beef Tea, page 326.
Bread and Butter Pudding, page 540.
Bread Sauce, page 312.
Chicken Broth, page 332.
Shrimp Cocktail, page 348.
Fruit Cocktail, page 347.
Rock Lobster Cocktail, page 348.
Leg of Lamb, English Style, page 422.
Mock Turtle Soup, page 337.
Mutton Broth, page 338.
Oxtail Soup, page 340.
Plum Cake, page 575.
Porterhouse Steak, page 385.
Rice Pudding, English Style, page 540.
Semolina Pudding, English Style, page 541.
Tapioca Pudding, English Style, page 541.
Real Turtle Soup, page 328.
Veal and Ham Pie, page 504.
Yorkshire Pudding, page 415.

23.5 Italian National Dishes

Trota al chianti—Trout with Chianti Wine. The browned fish is placed on a serving platter and the oil is drained from the pan. Some chianti wine is poured into the pan and reduced by half. Tomato Sauce, chopped parsley, and lemon peel are added to the wine. The sauce is heated to the boiling point, strained, and poured over the fish before serving.

Fritto di pollo—Fried Chicken. This chicken is cut into pieces, seasoned, coated with flour, and dipped in beaten eggs that have been mixed with oil. The chicken is breaded with a mixture of white bread crumbs and cheese, and deep-fat fried. It is garnished with deep-fat fried parsley. A Tomato Sauce is served separately.

Piccata. These are small cutlets, generally cut from a veal tenderloin. The piccata is often composed of a mixture of veal and veal liver cutlets, or small cutlets of blanched sweetbreads. The cutlets are seasoned with salt, pepper, nutmeg, and marjoram. They are coated with flour, dipped in beaten eggs that have been mixed with grated cheese, and sauteed in butter. A rich, veal gravy or a Madeira Sauce is served separately. The other method is to season the cutlets, coat in flour, and saute in butter. Finely chopped lemon peel, garlic, and parsley are mixed and sprinkled over the cutlets. Lemon juice and foaming hot butter are poured over the top. They may be garnished with risotto or pasta.

Piccata milanese—Piccata, Milanese Style. This is a Piccata served with risotto and garnished with strips of sauteed tongue, ham, mushroom, and truffles. A Madeira Sauce is served separately. The cutlets may be served on spaghetti or rice with the garnishes placed on the meat.

Tagliatella alla livornese. This is a sauce served over buttered and seasoned pasta. The sauce is made of sauteed onion, peeled and diced tomatoes, Tomato Sauce, garlic, and sauteed diced beef tenderloin tips. Grated cheese is served separately.

Fritto misto—Deep-Fried Sweetbreads, Veal, and Vegetables. This Italian dish is a mixed fry or a combination of deep-fried veal cutlets, sliced sweetbreads, veal liver, veal brain, a boiled head of veal, and vegetables. The foods are coated with flour, dipped in a batter, and deep-fried. The vegetables are arranged in the center of a serving dish and surrounded with the variety meats. A Tomato Sauce may be served separately. *Note:* A variety of fruits, vegetables, fish, and meat may be used for Fritto misto. Lemon wedges are always served as a garnish.

Saltimbocca. A slice of raw ham and a sage leaf are placed on a thin veal cutlet and secured with a toothpick. The meat is seasoned, coated with flour, and sauteed. A rich veal gravy and/or a risotto are served with the meat.

Arrostino annegatto milanese. The veal for this dish is a cut from the loin that includes a slice of loin, tenderloin, and kidney. (It corresponds to the Porterhouse steak plus the kidney of beef.) A skewer is used to hold the steak together. The steak is seasoned, spiced with sage and rosemary, coated with flour, and sauteed in butter. It is placed on a warm plate, sprinkled with *gremolata* (see note below). Foaming hot butter is poured over the steak. The pan is deglazed with white wine and veal stock. The sauce is heated to the boiling point and served with the steak. *Note:* Pasta or risotto may be served as a garnish. Gremolata consists of finely chopped parsley, garlic, and grated lemon rind.

Osso Buco (Braised Veal Shanks)

YIELD: *10 servings*

INGREDIENTS	*U.S. Weight or Volume*	*Metric Weight or Volume*	PROCEDURE
Veal shanks, split	10 shanks (6 to 9 ounces each)	10 shanks (180 to 250 grams each)	1. Season the veal shanks. Coat with flour and brown on all sides in fat.
Salt	2 teaspoons	10 grams	
Seasoning	1/8 teaspoon	1 gram	
Flour	as needed	as needed	
Fat	1¾ ounces	50 grams	
Onion, chopped	5 ounces	150 grams	2. Add the onion, garlic, vegetables, and chopped herbs. Cook slightly.
Garlic	2 cloves	2 cloves	
Vegetable brunoise	10 to 14 ounces	300 to 400 grams	
Herbs, chopped	½ teaspoon	3 grams	
Tomato puree	1¾ ounces	50 grams	3. Add the tomato puree, tomatoes concassees (peeled, seeded, and crushed tomatoes), and the white wine.
Tomatoes concassees	7 ounces	200 grams	
White wine	¾ to 1¼ cups	2 to 3 deciliters	4. Cook and reduce.
			5. Add the stock and braise until meat is tender.
			6. When serving, sprinkle with gremolata (a mixture of finely chopped parsley, garlic, and grated lemon rind).

Zamponi—Pigs' Feet. The skin is removed (rinds) from the pigs' front legs and filled with a stuffing made of pork trimmings, salt, pepper, sausage seasoning, Madeira, chopped truffles, and 1 egg per pound of meat. The skin is wrapped around the stuffing and sewed at each end. The stuffed skins are marinated in brine for 3 to 5 days. They are smoked, soaked in lukewarm water overnight, wrapped in a cheesecloth, and simmered slowly for 2 hours. Hot Zamponi are served with sauerkraut. When served cold, they should be cooled in the stock.

Other Italian National Dishes

Busecca, page 332.
Cannelloni, page 452.
Cassata, page 597.
Gnocchi a la piemontaise, page 453.
Gnocchi a la romaine, page 454.
Minestrone, page 336.
Pesto genovese, page 341.
Ravioli, page 455.
Ravioli milanaise, page 456.
Ravioli napolitaine, page 456.
Risotto, page 460.
Risotto milanaise, page 460.
Spaghetti bolognese, page 459.
Spaghetti milanaise, page 459.
Spaghetti napolitaine, page 459.
Zuppa mille-fanti, page 343.
Zuppa pavese, page 343.

23.6 Austrian National Dishes

Gebackene Scampi—Fried Scampi. This Austrian dish is prepared by cooking scampi in salted water to the boiling point. The scampies are shelled, deveined, sprinkled with lemon juice, and dusted with paprika. They are dipped in flour, then in beaten eggs, and in bread crumbs. They are deep-fat fried and served with mayonnaise or one of its variations.

Wiener Rindsgulasch (Viennese Goulash)

YIELD: *approximately 10 servings*

INGREDIENTS	*U.S. Weight or Volume*	*Metric Weight or Volume*	PROCEDURE
Fat	1¾ to 2 ounces	50 to 60 grams	1. Saute the onion in the fat. Add the seasoned meat and continue sauteing.
Onion, finely sliced	1 to 1¼ pounds	500 to 600 grams	
Beef cubes, (shank and shoulder)	3 to 4 pounds	1½ to 2 kilograms	
Salt	1 tablespoon	15 grams	
Pepper	½ teaspoon	3 grams	
Garlic cloves	2	2	
Paprika, Hungarian	1½ ounces	45 grams	2. Add the paprika, herbs, and the tomato puree.
Thyme	1 small bunch	1 small bunch	
Marjoram	1 small bunch	1 small bunch	
Tomato puree	1¾ ounces	50 grams	
Vinegar	½ cup	1 deciliter	3. Deglaze with vinegar. Reduce. Add the stock. Cover and simmer until tender.
Brown veal stock	1½ quarts	1½ liters	
Cumin	½ ounce	15 grams	4. Add the cumin or caraway seeds.
OR			5. Season to taste.
Caraway seeds			

Rahmgulasch—Creamed Goulash. This goulash is prepared using the recipe for Wiener Rindsgulasch. (See page 000.) It is bound with sour cream and braised for a few minutes before serving.

Zwiebelfleisch—Beef and Onions. This recipe can be made with top round or shoulder of beef. It is prepared by slicing and sauteing several onions in fat. The fat is drained, and the beef is added to the pan with some stock and seasonings. It is covered and simmered to the medium stage. The cover is then removed, and the meat is dusted with flour. More stock is added. The meat is covered and braised until tender.

Wiener Backhendl—Fried Chicken, Viennese Style. A corn-fed chicken or a rock cornish hen may be used for this Viênnese specialty. The chicken is cleaned and trussed without removing the head and neck. The chicken is seasoned inside and outside, rolled in flour, then in beaten eggs, and finally in bread crumbs. It is deep-fat fried until the skin is crisp. The chicken is served whole on a paper napkin. It is garnished with deep-fat fried parsley and served wth lemon wedges.

Palatschinken—Austrian Pancakes. Jam (apricot is most popular) is spread between two thin pancakes. They are rolled and sprinkled with sugar.

Kaiserschmarren. Fold beaten egg whites into pancake batter. Coat the skillet with melted butter, pour the batter into the pan, and cook on one side. Sprinkle with raisins, turn the pancakes over, and allow to rise in the oven. Cut into small pieces, spinkle with sugar, and serve immediately.

Salzburger Nockerl (Austrian)

YIELD: *approximately 10 servings*

INGREDIENTS	*U.S. Weight or Volume*	*Metric Weight or Volume*	PROCEDURE
Milk	1¼ cups	3 deciliters	1. Mix the milk, vanilla, ⅓ of the sugar, and half the butter in a saucepan. Heat.
Sugar	2 ounces	60 grams	
Vanilla extract	1 teaspoon	4 milliliters	
Butter, melted	1¾ ounces	50 grams	
Egg whites	8	8	2. In a suitable bowl, beat the egg whites stiff, and carefully fold in 7 beaten egg yolks, half the remaining sugar, the flour, and the remaining butter.
Egg yolks	8	8	
Flour	1¾ ounces	50 grams	3. Shape this mixture into large dumplings with a spoon. 4. Place in the hot milk. Cover and poach. 5. When the dumplings begin to turn brown, turn them over and cook for a short while. 6. Remove the dumplings and beat the milk with an egg yolk and the remaining sugar to a creamy consistency. Pour this over the dumplings.
Sugar, confectioners'	as needed	as needed	7. Sprinkle with confectioners' sugar before serving.

Apfelstrudel (Apple Strudel)

YIELD: *approximately 10 servings*

INGREDIENTS	*U.S. Weight or Volume*	*Metric Weight or Volume*
Dough		
Flour	12 ounces	350 grams
Water, lukewarm	½ to ¾ cup	1 to 1½ deciliters
Egg	1	1
Oil	1 tablespoon	15 milliliters
Salt	1/8 teaspoon	1 gram
Filling		
Apples, peeled, cored, finely chopped	3½ pounds	1½ kilograms
Sugar	5½ to 7 ounces	150 to 200 grams
Cinnamon	1 tablespoon	15 grams
Raisins	7 ounces	200 grams
Rum	2 ounces	59 milliliters
Pine kernels	3½ ounces	100 grams
OR		
Hazelnuts		
Bread crumbs	9 ounces	250 grams
Butter	3½ ounces	100 grams
Cream	½ cup	1 deciliter
Butter, melted	3½ ounces	100 grams

PROCEDURE

Dough

1. Make a well in the flour.
2. Place the water, egg, oil, and salt in the well and mix them together. Mix the flour in gradually until a firm smooth dough is formed.
3. Cover the dough with a prewarmed bowl and let it rest 1 hour.

Filling

1. Marinate the apples with the sugar, cinnamon, raisins, and rum for a short time.
2. Brown the bread crumbs in 3½ ounces (100 grams) of butter and mix with the pine kernels or hazelnuts.
3. Spread a cloth on a table and dust it with flour.
4. Roll out the dough on the cloth as thin as possible.
5. Draw out and stretch the dough with your hands until it is paper thin. Trim the edges of the dough if thick or uneven.
6. Sprinkle the bread crumbs and nuts evenly over the dough. Distribute the apples evenly over the dough.
7. Hold the cloth on one side with both hands and lift it up little by little so that the dough rolls itself up around the filling.
8. Arrange on a baking pan.
9. Coat with cream and butter. Press dough together along the sides.
10. Bake the strudel in the oven at 375°F. (188°C.) for 30 minutes frequently basting with butter. It should be brown and crisp when done.
11. When serving, cut the strudel into slices and sprinkle with confectioners' sugar. Vanilla Sauce may be served separately.

Note: Strudels filled with plums are prepared in the same way.

Other Austrian National Dishes

Krautsuppe, page 335.
Wiener Gulasch, page 399.
Wiener Rostbraten, page 385.
Wiener Schnitzel, page 468.

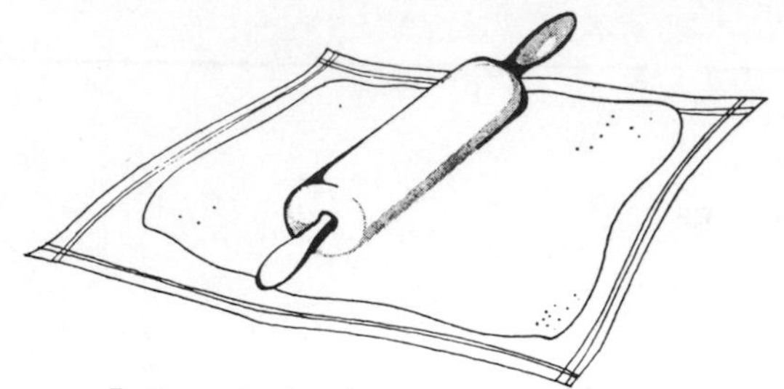

Roll out the dough very thin.

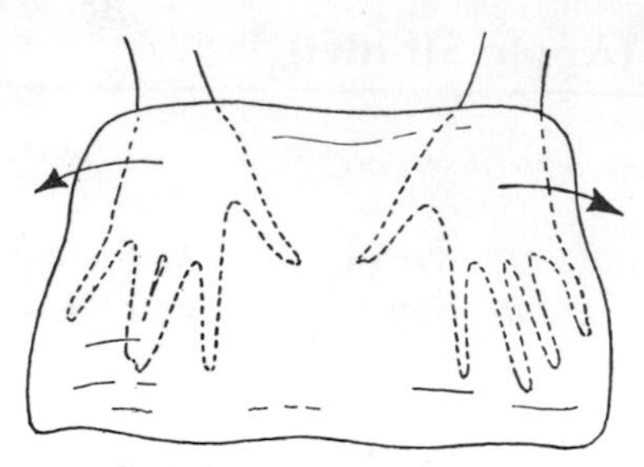

Stretch out over the back of the hands.

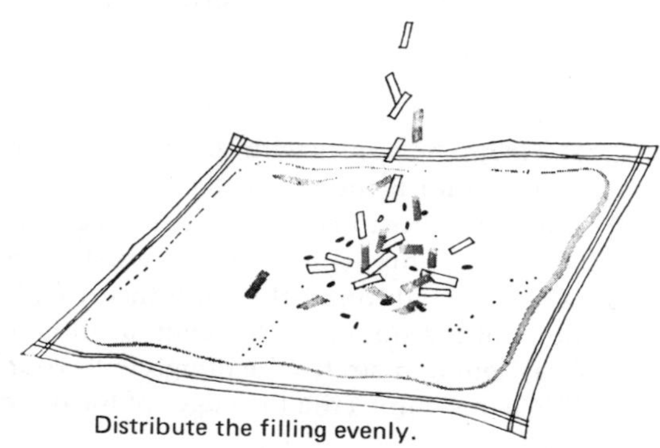

Distribute the filling evenly.

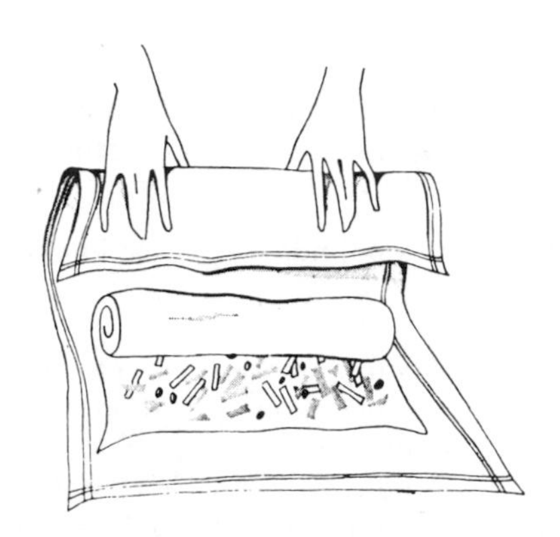

Roll the dough by lifting the cloth.

Baste frequently with cream during baking.

FIGURE 23-1.
Preparation of dough for Apple Strudel

23.7 Other National Dishes

Carp Paprika (Hungarian). This is a popular Hungarian dish. The carp is cut into slices and prepared a la meuniere. A sauce is made by sauteing chopped onion in butter, dusting them with flour and paprika, and deglazing with stock and sour cream. The fish slices are arranged in a baking dish, covered with the seasoned sauce, simmered until tender, and garnished with lemon wedges.

Esterhazy Rostelyos (Hungarian)—Braised Steaks. These are ½ inch (1.3 centimeters) sirloin or round steaks that are browned in butter and kept warm. Sliced carrots, parsnips, and celery are sauteed in the drippings and then coated with flour and paprika. Stock and capers are added to the vegetables. The steaks are added to the sauce and simmered until the meat and vegetables are tender. Sour cream is blended into the sauce just before serving.

Szegediner Gulyas (Hungarian Goulash)

YIELD: *approximately 10 servings*

INGREDIENTS	*U.S. Weight or Volume*	*Metric Weight or Volume*	PROCEDURE
Fat	3½ ounces	100 grams	1. Heat the fat. Add the onion and brown lightly.
Onion, finely chopped	1 pound	500 grams	
Lean pork, diced	3 to 4 pounds	1½ to 2 kilograms	2. Add the meat and seasonings and saute until the meat is nearly tender.
Paprika, sweet	1½ to 1¾ ounces	40 to 50 grams	
Salt	1 tablespoon	15 grams	
Pepper	½ teaspoon	3 grams	
Garlic, minced	1 clove	1 clove	3. Add the garlic, tomato puree, the braised sauerkraut, and a little stock if it is needed.
Tomato puree	1 ounce	30 grams	4. Cover tightly and continue cooking for 1 to 1½ hours.
Sauerkraut, braised	1¾ pounds	800 grams	5. Add the sour cream. Season to taste and heat just to the boiling point.
Stock	as needed	as needed	
Sour cream	½ to ¾ cup	1 to 2 deciliters	6. Serve boiled potatoes separately.
Potatoes, peeled	1¾ pounds	800 grams	

Paella Valenciana (Spanish)

YIELD: *approximately 10 servings*

INGREDIENTS	*U.S. Weight or Volume*	*Metric Weight or Volume*	PROCEDURE
Olive oil	1¾ ounces	50 grams	1. Heat the oil. Saute the garlic and then remove.
Garlic cloves, crushed	2	2	
Chicken meat, diced (mainly from legs and thighs)	1¾ pounds	800 grams	2. Brown the chicken and pork pieces on all sides. 3. Add onion and sweet peppers. Cover and cook for 10 minutes. Do not allow them to brown.
Pork, lean diced	7 ounces	200 grams	
Onion, chopped	5 ounces	150 grams	
Sweet peppers, all colors, diced	7 ounces	500 grams	
Rice	1 pound	500 grams	4. Add the rice. Heat and stir over a high flame until it becomes transparent.
White wine	1¼ cups	3 deciliters	5. Add the wine and boiling stock, the tomato puree, salt, saffron, shrimp, octopus, and sole or hake. Simmer covered for about 15 minutes.
Stock	1½ quarts	1½ liters	
Tomato puree	7 to 10 ounces	200 to 300 grams	
Salt	2 teaspoons	10 grams	
Saffron	1/8 teaspoon	1 gram	
Large shrimp OR Scampi	20	20	
Octopus	5 ounces	150 grams	
Sole slices OR Hake slices	10 ounces	300 grams	
Peas	3½ ounces	100 grams	6. Sprinkle in the peas.
Mussels	20	20	7. Arrange mussels and 3½ ounces (100 grams) of shrimp on the top. Do not stir.
Shrimp	3½ ounces	100 grams	8. Serve in the pan.

Note: 1) The rice must be cooked just done, not dry. The dish should never be served dry. Add stock if necessary. 2) Artichokes, mushrooms, julienne of beef tongue or ham, eel and/or veal can be included in the dish. 3) Diced poultry, diced veal liver, or fried diced beef tenderloin can be used to garnish the top of the dish.

Cold Dishes—Cuisine froide

24

From a technical standpoint, cold dishes were formerly divided into cold entrees and cold buffets. Today the term, cold dishes, refers to any dishes that are served cold, from cold hors d'oeuvre to the elaborately composed cold buffets.

On the *menu,* cold foods appear under the general terms, *cold dishes, cold snacks, cold specialties of the house,* or *specialties of the season.*

When cold dishes form *part of a complete menu,* they are generally used as *cold hors d'oeuvre* or as *cold main courses.* Only on rare occasions do they appear as the entree froide, a course that was formerly served between the grosse piece and the roti.

All cold dishes, with the exception of the cold hors d'oeuvre dishes, are included in this chapter. A perfect mise en place and broad knowledge of foodstuffs are important. The skilled garde-manger will distinguish himself by his methods of preparation, cutting, trussing, and carving, as well as by his use of modern arrangements. Since the appearance of cold dishes is especially important, particular attention must be given to *color combinations* and *attractive presentations.* Cold dishes include the following categories:

- Bases and ingredients
- Methods of preparation, cutting, and dressing
- Cold hors d'oeuvre dishes
- Cold egg dishes
- Cold fish dishes
- Cold shellfish
- Cold entrees
- Cold meat dishes
- Cold buffets

24.1 Cold Egg Dishes—Mets aux oeufs froids

Cold eggs are usually served with assorted hors d'oeuvre. They are also excellent served with cold fish, meat, and poultry dishes when these are accompanied by marinated vegetables and salads.

Egg Salad—Salade aux oeufs. Mix sliced hard-cooked eggs with a thin, spicy mayonnaise or with oil, vinegar, and finely chopped onion, and seasoning.

Egg and Cheese Salad—Salade aux oeufs et fromage. Arrange egg salad in a circle and place a cheese salad in the center.

Egg and Sausage Salad—Salade aux oeufs et cervelat. Arrange egg salad in a circle and place a sausage salad in the center.

Egg and Tomato Salad—Salade aux oeufs et tomates. Serve egg salad surrounded with slices of tomato.

Egg Tartlets—Oeufs en tartelettes. Fill baked pastry tartlet shells with an Italian Salad (see page 432), place a soft-cooked or poached egg on each, garnish, and glaze with aspic.

Poached Eggs on Artichoke Hearts—Oeufs poches mascotte. Spread artichoke hearts with a mousse of ham or goose liver. Place a poached egg or a soft-cooked egg on each. Garnish with truffles or tarragon, and glaze with aspic.

Poached Eggs on Tomatoes—Oeufs poches sur tomates. Stuff halved, seeded, and seasoned tomatoes with an Italian Salad. (See page 432.) Place a poached egg or soft-cooked egg on each, garnish with truffles or tarragon, and glaze with aspic.

Russian Eggs—Oeufs a la russe. Arrange sliced hard-cooked eggs on a Russian Salad (see page 433), cover with thick, spicy mayonnaise, and garnish with smoked salmon, anchovy fillets, capers, or cover a Russian Salad with a Remoulade Sauce, place hard-cooked eggs stuffed with caviar on top, and garnish with a vegetable salad around the eggs.

Stuffed Eggs—Oeufs farcis. Remove the yolks from hard-cooked, halved eggs. Puree the yolks, blend with whipped butter, and add a mousse of ham or fish, or anchovy paste. Fill the egg whites with the yolk mixture. Eggs can also be stuffed with diced tomatoes or caviar. Coat with aspic after stuffing.

24.2 Cold Fish Dishes—Mets de poisson froids

For cold dishes, fish are boiled as described on page 360 and allowed to cool in the stock. They can be presented in various ways, but, in general, simple and attractive presentations are preferred.

Fish Mayonnaise—Mayonnaise de poisson. Remove the skin and bones from cooked fish or canned salmon and marinate with seasoning and lemon juice. Place a few lettuce leaves on a dish, arrange the fish in a dome shape on the leaves, and coat with a spicy thick mayonnaise. Decorate the dome with anchovy fillets in a lattice pattern and place a caper in each square. Arrange slices of hard-cooked egg around the dome. Garnish with a few clusters of vegetable salad. Serve a Mayonnaise Sauce separately.

Lake Trout, Modern Style—Truite du lac moderne. Remove the head and tail of a cleaned trout and slice the middle section into uniform medallions. Poach the head and tail together with the slices of fish in a fish kettle. When cool, remove from the stock, skin the slices carefully, and arrange on a platter as shown in Fig. 24-1. Decorate each slice. Serve with stuffed eggs, tomatoes, and asparagus spears. Coat the entire dish with jelly. Serve a Mayonnaise or Remoulade Sauce separately.

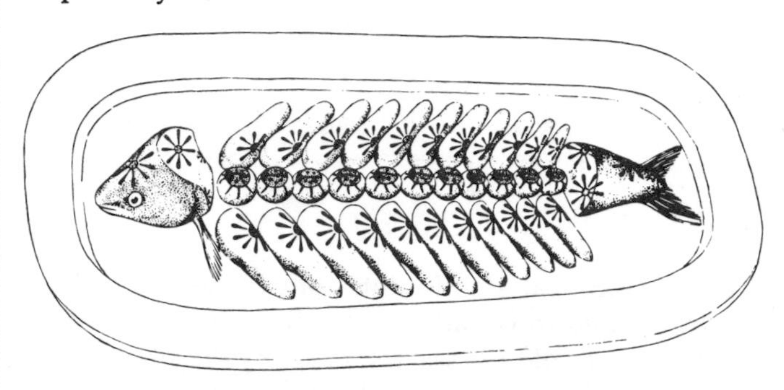

FIGURE 24-1
Lake Trout, Modern Style—Truite du lac moderne

Lake Trout with Tarragon—Truite du lac a l'estragon. Clean the trout and stuff with forcemeat. Place the fish in a fish kettle so that it need not be moved during cooking or cooling. To poach lake trout, see Section 15.1.1. When cold, remove the trout very carefully from the fish kettle and skin from head to tail. Place on a platter and decorate with blanched tarragon leaves along both sides. Place slices of hard-cooked egg and truffles along the back. Surround the fish with stuffed eggs, slices of marinated cucumber with tomatoes on top, and Russian Salad (see page 433) in timbales. Glaze the whole dish with fish jelly. Mix Remoulade Sauce with chopped tarragon and serve in a sauce boat.

Salmon Medallions, Norwegian Style—Medaillons de saumon norvegienne. Cut the salmon into medallions, poach, and cool in the stock. Place 2 shrimp on each medallion and coat with jelly. Coat a platter with jelly, place the medallions on the jelly in the original order, and surround with smoked salmon flakes,

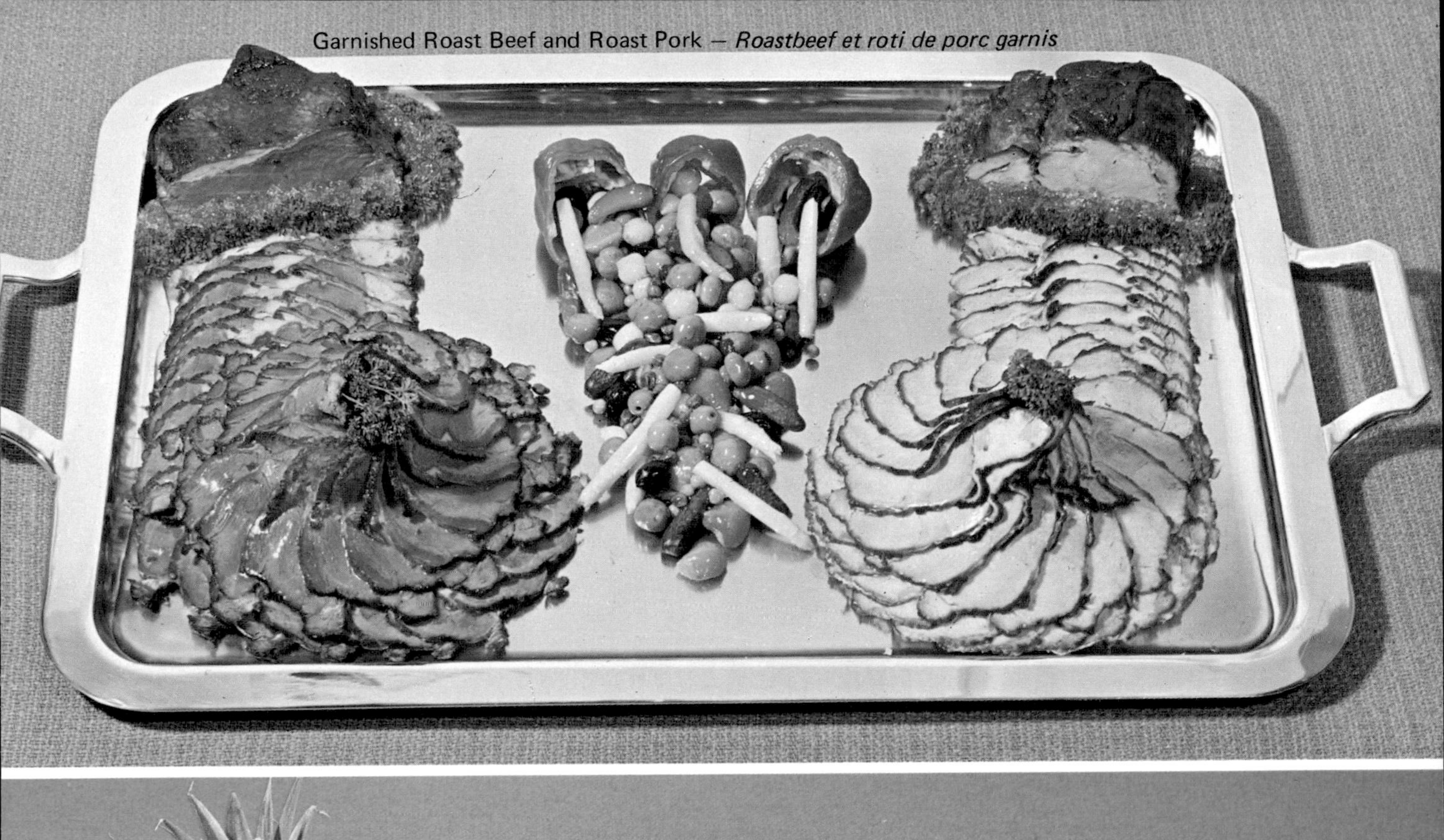

Garnished Roast Beef and Roast Pork – *Roastbeef et roti de porc garnis*

Roast Turkey, Modern Style – *Dindonneau roti moderne*

Mushroom Pate — *Pate de champignons*

Leg of Deer in Pastry, Lucerne Style — *Gigue de chevreuil en croute a la lucernoise*

Cheese Platter for a la Carte Service
Plateau de fromages pour le service

Banquet Cheese Platter
Plat de fromages pour banquet

Cheese Snack
Snack au fromage

Cheese Salad
Salade de fromage

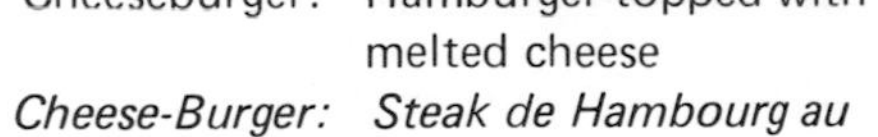

Cheeseburger: Hamburger topped with melted cheese
Cheese-Burger: Steak de Hambourg au fromage

Toasted Cheese
Croutes au fromage

Cheese Tart
Quiche au fromage

Fondue

Gnocchi, Parisian Style – *Gnocchi a la parisienne*
Pasta with Cheese – *Nouilles au fromage*

1. Little Ice Bombe
Petite bombe glacee pralinee

2. Ice Coupe Jacques
Coupe Jacques

3. Frozen Souffle Grand Marnier
Souffle glace au Grand Marnier

4. Frozen Parfait with Almonds
Parfait glace amandine

5. Ice Coupe, [illegible] Style
Coupe maison

6. Frozen Pudding with Kirsch
Pudding glace au kirsch

7. Cassata, Naples Style
Cassata napoletana

8. Ice Coffee *Cafe glace*

9. Frozen Mousse with Cassis
Mousse glacee au cassis

10. Frozen Biscuit with Chocolate
Biscuit glace au chocolat

11. Ice Coupe Romanoff
Coupe Romanoff

12. Ice Cream Cake with Nougat
Tourte glacee nougatine

blanched and marinated cucumber slices, and small peeled tomatoes.

24.3 Cold Shellfish (Crustaceans and Mollusks)—Crustaces et coquillages froids

Preparation of Crustaceans for Cold Dishes

Place live, well-cleaned crustaceans in a simmering ordinary stock (court-bouillon ordinaire, Section 15.1.1), bring to a boil, remove from the heat and let stand covered for 8 minutes per pound (.45 kilograms). Cool completely in the stock. The cooking time for crayfish is 4 minutes per pound (.45 kilograms). Just before placing in the stock, pull out the middle tail fin to remove the intestine.

Cold Crayfish—Ecrevisses froides. Remove the meat from the claws and tail of cooked, cooled crayfish or the crayfish can be left whole and the claws opened. Crayfish arranged in this fashion can be used as a garnish for hors d'oeuvre and cold fish dishes.

If the crayfish are being served as a separate dish, break open the claws and arrange the whole crayfish on a paper napkin on a platter, garnish with lettuce leaves and parsley. Serve Mayonnaise Sauce, radishes, and Sweet Pepper Salad separately.

Cold Lobster—Homard froid. Cut a cooked, cooled lobster in half lengthwise (see Fig. 24-2). Remove the tail meat, slice, garnish each slice with truffles, and coat with jelly. Fill the two lobster shells with Russian Salad (see page 433), place on a platter, and arrange the halved slices of lobster on top. Place the opened claws in front of the lobster. Serve a Mayonnaise Sauce separately.

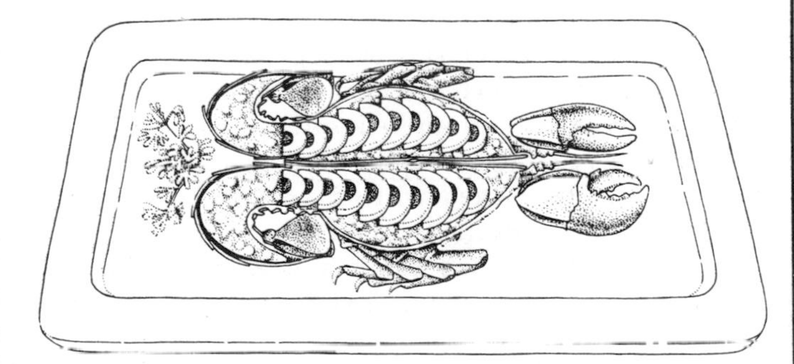

FIGURE 24-2
Cold Lobster—Homard froid

Lobster, Russian Style—Homard a la russe. Remove the tail meat from a cooked, cooled lobster. Slice, garnish with truffles, and coat with jelly. Arrange the slices on the lobster (see Fig. 24-3). Serve with eggs stuffed with caviar, tomatoes stuffed with Russian Salad (see page 433), and Lobster Mousse on small artichoke hearts. Serve Mayonnaise Sauce separately.

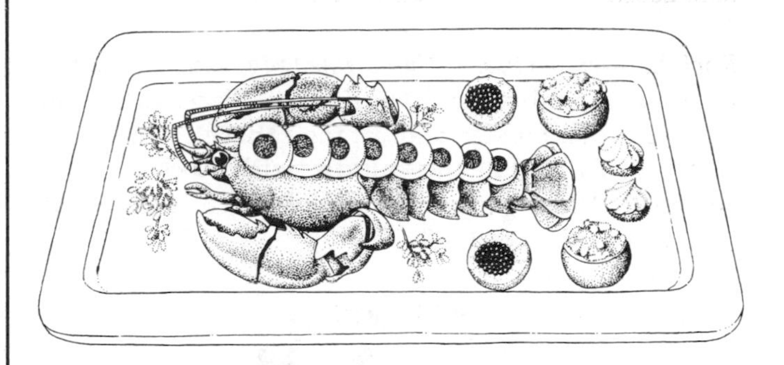

FIGURE 24-3
Lobster Russian Style—Homard a la russe

Rock Lobster Mousse—Mousse de langouste. Grind the trimmings from boiled and cooled rock lobsters repeatedly and strain using a fine sieve (or pass through the meat grinder).

Place a bowl in crushed ice. In the chilled bowl, mix ¾ cup (2 deciliters) of fish veloute and ½ cup (1½ deciliters) of liquid jelly per pint (.47 liters) of the puree. Immediately mix in ½ to ¾ cup (1½ to 2 deciliters) of whipped cream. For molds and presentation, see Section 24.4.4.

Rock Lobster, Parisian Style—Langouste a la parisienne. Cook the rock lobster as described. (See illustration page 231.) Meanwhile, bind a Russian Salad (page 433) with a spicy mayonnaise and jelly. Remove the tail meat and cut into slices. Decorate the slices with truffles and coat with jelly. Arrange the rock lobster body with the tail shell on a base of Russian Salad. Arrange the slices attractively on the tail. Serve with stuffed artichoke hearts, timbale, and stuffed eggs. Serve a Mayonnaise Sauce separately.

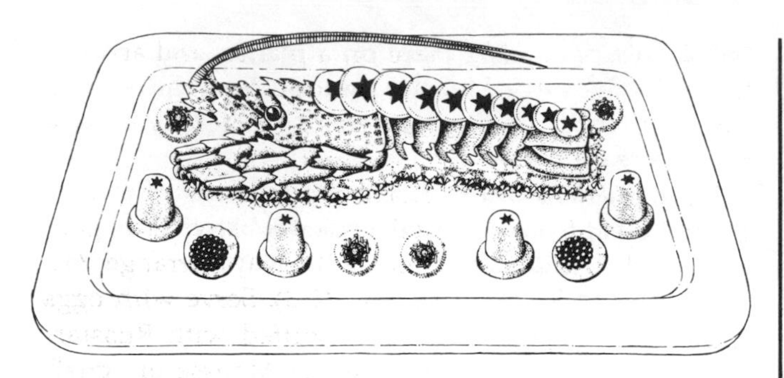

FIGURE 24-4
Rock Lobster Timbale—Timbale de langouste

Rock Lobster Timbale—Timbale de langouste. Coat the inside of a timbale mold with jelly. Place truffles on slices of rock lobster and arrange these in the mold (see Fig. 24-5). Fill the middle with Rock Lobster Mousse. Allow to set in a cool place. Serve surrounded with diced jelly.

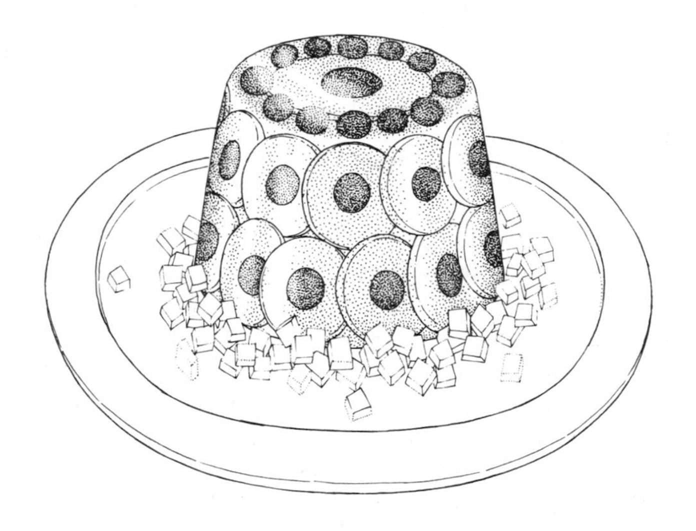

Oysters—Huitres. These are generally served cold as an hors d'oeuvre. Open the oysters just before serving (see illustration page 230) and remove the upper shell. Arrange the oysters on a bed of ice in a special oyster dish. Serve lemon wedges separately. A sauce made with wine vinegar, finely chopped shallots, and pepper or Tabasco Sauce can also be served. Slices of black bread and butter are often served with this dish.

Storage of oysters: Oysters must be alive when purchased. Fresh oysters have a tightly closed shell. Gaping shells that do not close when handled indicate that the oysters are dead and no longer fit for use. Oysters should be stored in the refrigerator at 40°F. (4°C.).

24.4 Cold Entrees—Entrees froides

24.4.1 Aspic

Line the appropriate molds with a thick layer of jelly, garnish with truffles, hard-cooked egg whites, and coat the garnish with jelly. Depending upon the name of the dish, arrange layers of goose liver slices, sliced paupiettes, or poultry fillets in the center of the mold. Coat each layer with jelly. Allow each layer to congeal before adding the next layer.

24.4.2 Chaud-froid Dishes—Chauds-froids

Chicken Chaud-froid—Chaud-froid de volaille. Poach a chicken or a poularde, cool in the stock, and use the stock to prepare a Chaud-froid Sauce. (See page 307.) Cut the chicken into attractive fillets or pieces. Arrange these in a lattice pottera and coat with a lukewarm Chaud-froid Sauce. After the sauce has set, garnish with truffles, sweet peppers, tarragon, or blanched leeks, and coat with a jelly which has cooled to the consistency of syrup. Depending upon the name of the dish, such pieces can either be arranged upon a jelly base, surrounded with a ring of jelly, or placed on a vegetable salad base. These cold specialties can also be ringed with diced jelly, marinated vegetables, or a vegetable salad.

A smooth, shiny sauce and a clear jelly are absolutely necessary to make successful chaud-froid dishes.

Stuffed Poultry Chaud-froid—Chaud-froid de volaille farci. Poach the poultry and allow to cool in the stock. Remove the fillets, coat with a Chaud-froid Sauce, garnish, and coat with jelly. Build up the trimmed carcass, including the legs, with a goose liver or ham mousse (see Section 24.4.4) in the shape of the type of fowl. If the bird was poached after being stuffed, then cut the stuffing into cubes and add to the mousse before filling the trimmed carcass. Allow to cool and set, coat with lukewarm Chaud-froid Sauce, garnish according to the description of the dish, and coat with jelly. Serve the stuffed poultry surrounded by the supremes (fillets).

24.4.3 Galantines

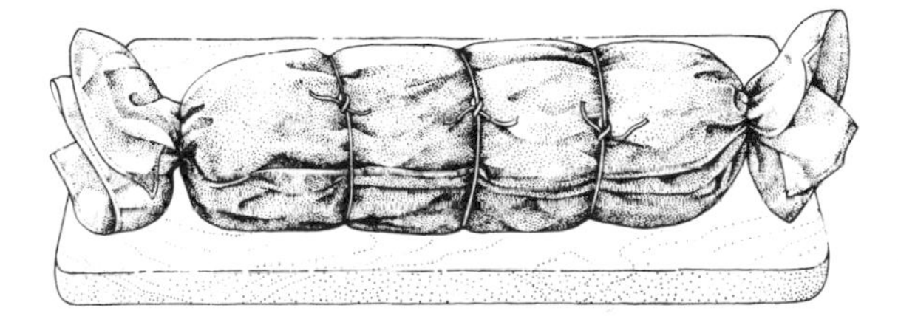

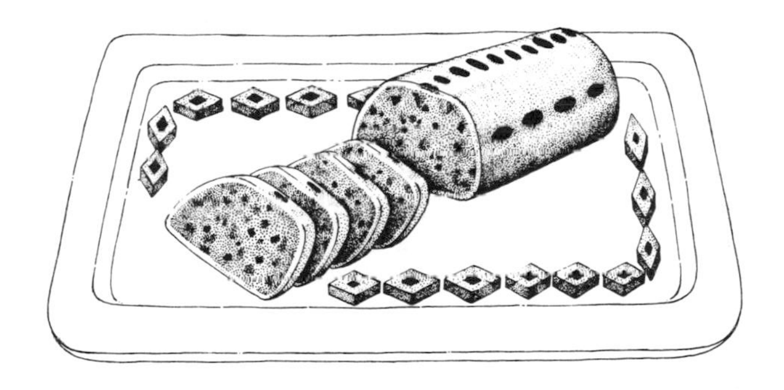

FIGURE 24-6
Galantines—Galantines

Poultry Galantine (Galantine de volaille)

YIELD: *approximately 10 servings*

INGREDIENTS	*U.S. Weight or Volume*	*Metric Weight or Volume*
Chicken	3 to 3½ pounds	1½ kilograms
Veal	10 ounces	300 grams
Pork	7 ounces	200 grams
Chicken meat, from leg of the chicken	9 ounces	250 grams
Shallots	2 ounces	60 grams
Eggs, beaten slightly	2	2
Cream	¾ cup	2 deciliters
Sausage seasoning	¼ teaspoon	2 grams
Tongue, diced	2 ounces	60 grams
Ham, diced	2 ounces	60 grams
Chicken meat, from the breast of the chicken	3½ ounces	100 grams
Truffles, quartered	2¾ ounces	80 grams
Pistachios, blanched	1¾ ounces	50 grams
Madeira	1 ounce	30 grams
Brandy	1 ounce	30 grams

PROCEDURE

1. Cut the skin open along the backbone of a cleaned chicken. Carefully remove the skin from both sides of the bird so that the meat comes away with the skin, leaving the skeleton including the leg and wing bones. Remove the leg meat and part of the breast meat, but leave a uniform layer of meat attached to the skin. (The leg meat is used in the forcemeat. The breast meat is diced for use in the galantine.)
2. Saute the shallots and allow to cool.
3. Grind the veal, pork, chicken leg meat, and shallots *very fine*. Blend the mixture thoroughly in a bowl and place in a bed of crushed ice.
4. Add the eggs, cream, and seasoning very gradually.
5. Add the diced meats, truffles, and pistachios which have been marinating in the brandy and Madeira. Add the marinade.
6. Place the whole mixture on the chicken skin to which a layer of the flesh is still attached. Form into a slightly oval shape. Sew the skin together.
7. Tie it in a cloth and poach in a rich poultry stock for 1 to 1½ hours. Do not remove from the stock until partially cooled.
8. Tighten the cloth once more around the galantine and keep it under pressure until it has completely cooled. Coat the finished galantine with jelly or chaud-froid and garnish with truffles.

Note: Use the stock to prepare Chaud-froid Sauce.

Variations of Galantine

Duck Galantine—Galantine de canard. The ingredients and method of preparation are the same as for Poultry Galantine, using duck meat instead of chicken.

24.4.4 Mousses

Goose Liver Mousse, Game Mousse, Chicken Mousse, Fish Mousse, and Tomato Mousse are prepared in the same way as Ham Mousse.

Note: When using chicken, fish, and rock lobster, poach the meat and allow it to cool in the stock. Game meat should be roasted to the rare stage. Goose liver should be braised. Leftovers and trimmings of these meats may also be used. Vegetable Mousse should be prepared with vegetables that have been blanched and thoroughly drained.

Ham Mousse (Mousse de jambon)

YIELD: *approximately 10 servings*

INGREDIENTS	*U.S. Weight or Volume*	*Metric Weight or Volume*
Ham, cold boiled	2 pounds	1 kilogram
Veloute	1¼ cups	3 deciliters
Liquid jelly	1¾ cups	4 deciliters
Salt	½ teaspoon	3 grams
Pepper	¼ teaspoon	2 grams
Dry mustard	⅛ teaspoon	1 gram
Whipped cream	1¼ to 1¾ cups	3 to 4 deciliters
Brandy	½ ounce	15 grams
Madeira	½ ounce	15 grams

PROCEDURE

1. Coat a mold with some of the liquid jelly.
2. Grind the ham very fine and cool on a bed of crushed ice.
3. Gradually mix in the Veloute, the liquid jelly, salt, pepper, and dry mustard.
4. Add the whipped cream, brandy, and Madeira.
5. Immediately pour the mixture into the mold.
6. Chill until firm. Turn out onto a serving plate just before serving.

Mousselines.

Mousselines are made the same as mousses. Whereas mousses serve 6, 8, or 10 persons, a mousseline is served individually. They can be shaped in small molds or as quenelles, garnished and coated with jelly. (See Fig. 24-8.)

Goose Liver Mousselines—Mousselines de foie gras a la gelee. Coat a flat platter with a layer of jelly and allow to congeal. Place oval-shaped mousselines on the jelly, coat with a little jelly, and allow to set. Place a slice of truffle on each and coat again. Place the dish in a cool place. Cut out the mousselines so that each is coated with jelly. When serving, garnish with jelly and radishes.

FIGURE 24-7
Ham Mousse—Mousse de jambon

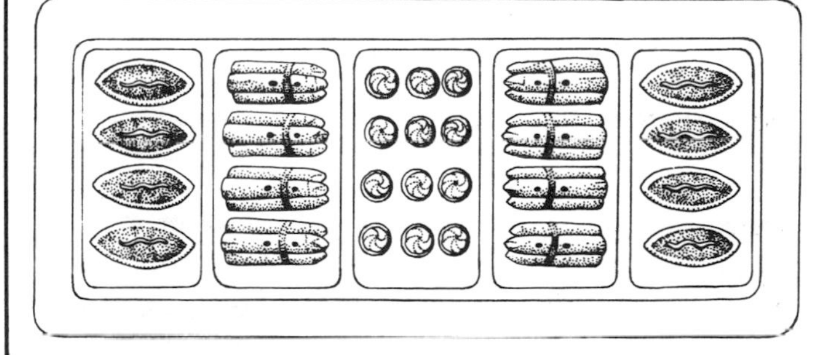

FIGURE 24-8
Mousselines—Mousselines

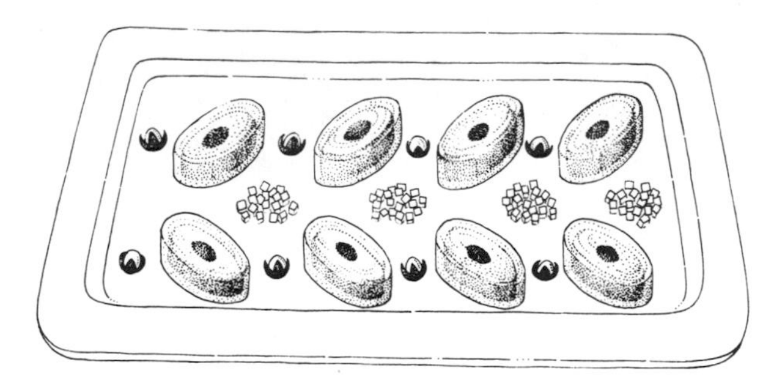

FIGURE 24-9
Goose Livers Mousselines—Mousselines de foie gras a la gelee

FIGURE 24-10
Stuffed Ham Cones with Chicken Mousse—Cornets de jambon a la mousse de volaille

Stuffed Ham Cornets with Chicken Mousse—Cornets de jambon a la mousse de volaille. Stuff the ham cornets with Chicken Mousse and place on a base of Russian Salad. (See page 433.) Arrange a mushroom cap between each cone or a rosette of mousse. Coat the dish with jelly.

24.4.5 Cold Pates—Pates froids

A pate (pie) applies to meat or fish dishes enclosed in pastry and baked. The various pates made from poultry, goose liver, game, veal, and ham form another important group of cold dishes.

Filling and finishing a pate: Line a pate mold with rolled pastry dough and line the base and sides with thin slices of unsalted bacon. Fill the mold with a prepared stuffing containing diced meat and complete with another layer of thinly sliced unsalted bacon. Close the pate with a layer of pastry dough garnished with dough shapes and brush the top with egg wash. Make a hole in the center of the top layer of dough so the steam can escape. Depending on its size, bake the pate for 1 to 2 hours. Cool and when thoroughly chilled, fill with the appropriate aspic jelly, which should be liquid though not hot. Refrigerate.

Pastry Dough (Pate pour pate)

YIELD: *U.S. — 3 pounds*
Metric — 1⅓ kilograms

INGREDIENTS	*U.S. Weight or Volume*	*Metric Weight or Volume*
Flour	2 pounds	1 kilogram
Eggs	3	3
Butter	12 ounces	350 grams
Salt	¾ ounce	20 grams
Water, lukewarm	1¼ to 1¾ cups	3 to 4 deciliters

PROCEDURE

1. Make a well in the flour.
2. Place the eggs, butter, salt, and 1¼ cups (3 deciliters) of water in the well. Mix these ingredients.
3. Gradually work the flour into the liquids and knead until a fairly firm dough is formed. Use the remaining water only if necessary.
4. Cover and let the dough stand for 2 hours before using.

Jelly Pate (Pate a la gelee)

YIELD: *approximately 10 servings*
(1 quart-sized pate mold)

INGREDIENTS	*U.S. Weight or Volume*	*Metric Weight or Volume*
Veal liver, diced	4½ ounces	125 grams
Shallots, chopped	1½ ounces	40 grams
Butter	¾ ounce	20 grams
Pork	9 ounces	250 grams
Veal	9 ounces	250 grams
Larding bacon, unsalted	7 ounces	200 grams
Apple	1	1
Cream	¾ cup	2 deciliters
Sausage seasoning	¼ teaspoon	2 grams
Ham, diced	2¾ ounces	80 grams
Tongue, diced	2¾ ounces	80 grams
Bacon, unsalted, diced	2¾ ounces	80 grams
Truffles, quartered	as desired	as desired
Madeira	1½ ounces	40 grams
Brandy	¾ ounce	20 grams
Pastry for pate **(see page 500)**	as needed	as needed
Bacon, unsalted, thinly sliced	8 ounces	240 grams
Aspic jelly (recipe 10.1.2)	1 pint	½ liter

PROCEDURE

1. Quickly brown the diced liver and chopped shallots in the butter. Cool.
2. Grind the pork, veal, bacon, liver, and the apple. Then put through a very fine sieve.
3. Cool the mixture in a bowl on a bed of crushed ice. Gradually mix in the cream and seasoning.
4. Meanwhile, marinate the diced meats and truffles in the Madeira and brandy and add these to the mixture.
5. Line a pate mold with rolled pastry dough and line the base and sides with thin slices of unsalted bacon.
6. Place the prepared filling in the mold and cover with another layer of thinly sliced unsalted bacon.
7. Close the pate with a layer of pastry dough garnished with dough shapes.
8. Brush the top with egg yolk.
9. Make a hole in the center of the top so the steam can escape.
10. Bake in the oven at 350°F. (175°C.) for about 1½ hours.
11. Allow to cool, and then fill with the appropriate aspic jelly which should be liquid but not hot.
12. Chill.

Game Pate (Pate de gibier)

YIELD: *approximately 10 servings*
(9 inch loaf pan or 1 quart pate mold)

INGREDIENTS	*U.S. Weight or Volume*	*Metric Weight or Volume*
Liver (from game or veal)	5½ ounces	150 grams
Milk	as needed	as needed
Shallots, chopped	1 ounce	30 grams
Butter	¾ ounce	20 grams
Game meat (deer or hare)	10 ounces	300 grams
Larding bacon, unsalted	7 ounces	200 grams
Pork	6½ ounces	180 grams
Veal	3½ ounces	100 grams
Apple	1	1
Juniper berries	2 or 3	2 or 3
Sausage seasoning	¼ teaspoon	2 grams
Cream	¾ cup	2 deciliters
Bacon, unsalted, diced	2¾ ounces	80 grams
Game meat, diced	2¾ ounces	80 grams
Truffles, quartered	as desired	as desired
Madeira	1 ounce	30 grams
Brandy	1 ounce	30 grams
Pastry for pate **(see page 500)**	as needed	as needed
Bacon, unsalted, thinly sliced	8 ounces	240 grams
Tenderloin of game, whole, browned, and wrapped in bacon	1	1
Aspic jelly **(see page 285)**	1 pint	½ liter

PROCEDURE

1. Soak the liver in milk. Drain it then dice and brown in butter with the shallots. Cool.
2. Grind the game meat, bacon, pork, veal, liver, apple, and juniper berries. Then put through a fine sieve.
3. Cool the mixture by placing it in a bowl on a bed of crushed ice. Gradually mix in the cream and the seasoning.
4. Meanwhile, marinate the diced meats and truffles in Madeira and brandy and add these to the mixture.
5. Line a pate mold with rolled pastry dough and line the base and sides with thin slices of unsalted bacon.
6. Place half the filling in the mold. Lay the whole tenderloin on this and then add the rest of the filling. Cover with another layer of thinly sliced unsalted bacon.
7. Close the pate with a layer of pastry dough garnished with dough shapes.
8. Brush the top with egg yolk.
9. Make a hole in the center of the top so that the steam can escape.
10. Bake in the oven at 350°F. (175°C.) for about 1½ hours.
11. Allow to cool. Then fill with the appropriate aspic jelly which should be liquid but not hot.
12. Chill.

Chicken Pate (Pate de volaille)

YIELD: *approximately 10 servings (1 quart pate mold)*

INGREDIENTS	*U.S. Weight or Volume*	*Metric Weight or Volume*
Chicken liver	4¼ ounces	120 grams
Milk	as needed	as needed
Shallots, chopped	1½ ounces	40 grams
Butter	1 ounce	30 grams
Chicken	10 ounces	300 grams
Veal	5 ounces	150 grams
Pork	5 ounces	150 grams
Larding bacon, unsalted	8½ ounces	240 grams
Sausage seasoning	¼ teaspoon	2 grams
Cream	¾ cup	2 deciliters
Larding bacon, unsalted, diced	2¾ ounces	100 grams
Chicken breast, diced	2¾ ounces	100 grams
Ham, diced	2¾ ounces	100 grams
Truffles	1¾ ounces	50 grams
Pistachios	1¾ ounces	50 grams
Madeira	1 ounce	30 milliliters
Brandy	1 ounce	30 milliliters
Pastry for pate **(see page 500)**	as needed	as needed
Aspic jelly **(see page 285)**	as needed	as needed

PROCEDURE

1. Soak the liver in milk. Drain. Then brown it with the chopped shallots in butter. Cool.
2. Grind the chicken, pork, bacon, and liver. Then pass through a fine sieve.
3. Cool the mixture by placing it in a bowl on a bed of crushed ice. Gradually mix in the cream and the seasoning.
4. Meanwhile, marinate the diced meat, truffles, and pistachios in the Madeira and brandy and add these to the mixture.
5. Line a pate mold with rolled pastry dough and line the base and sides with thin slices of unsalted bacon.
6. Place the prepared filling in the mold and cover with another layer of thinly sliced unsalted bacon.
7. Close the pate with a layer of pastry dough garnished with dough shapes.
8. Brush the top with egg yolk.
9. Make a hole in the center of the top so that the steam can escape.
10. Bake in the oven at 350°F. (175°C.) for about 1½ hours.
11. Allow to cool and then fill with aspic jelly which should be liquid but not hot.
12. Chill.

Variations of Pates

Pate, Menagere Style—Pate a la menagere. Line a pate mold with pastry dough, fill as for veal and ham pie, close with a layer of pastry dough, and finish as for pates froids. (See page 500.)

Mushroom Pate—Pate de champignons. (See Illustration, page 492.)

Veal and Ham Pie

YIELD: *approximately 10 servings*

INGREDIENTS	*U.S. Weight or Volume*	*Metric Weight or Volume*
Veal cutlets	1¾ to 2 pounds	800 to 900 grams
Brandy	3/8 cup	½ deciliter
Salt	½ teaspoon	3 grams
Pepper	¼ teaspoon	2 grams
Ham, smoked, sliced	1¼ to 1½ pounds	600 to 700 grams
Shallots	3½ ounces	100 grams
Salt	1 teaspoon	6 grams
Pastry for pate (see page 500)	10 ounces	300 grams
Aspic jelly	1 pint	½ liter

PROCEDURE

1. Marinate the veal cutlets in the brandy and Madeira with the salt and pepper.
2. Fill a baking dish with layers of smoked ham slices and veal cutlets, placing a few sauteed shallots between each layer.
3. Add the marinade and salt.
4. Cover the pie with rolled out pastry dough. Decorate as desired.
5. Brush with egg yolk.
6. Place in the oven at 350°F. (175°C.). As soon as the dough cover puffs up a little and is slightly split, pierce a hole in the center so that the steam can escape. Bake about 40 minutes.
7. Allow to cool. Fill with jelly.

24.4.6 Cold Souffles—Souffles froids

Wrap a paper sleeve around each cocotte to 1 to 1½ inches (2.5 to 3.7 centimeters) above the level of the rim. Coat the bottom of the cocottes with a small amount of jelly and allow to congeal. Fill with a mousse mixture (see page 498) to the height of the sleeve. Decorate the top of the souffles and coat with jelly. Cool the mixture and allow to set. Carefully remove the sleeves. The souffle is named according to the composition of the mousse mixture.

24.4.7 Terrines

Terrines were originally earthenware containers used for poaching various meat and poultry forcemeats in a waterbath. Today enamel containers and fireproof glass casseroles with covers are also used. The term terrine refers to any preparation put into a container lined with strips of bacon and baked. Both the dish and the contents are called terrines. The finished terrines can either be kept in the containers, as is generally the case in France, or they can be turned out of the dish into a second container that has been coated with jelly and then decorated. The terrine in this container is then covered with more jelly. When cool, the terrine is turned out, sliced, and garnished with jelly cubes. Terrines are always served cold.

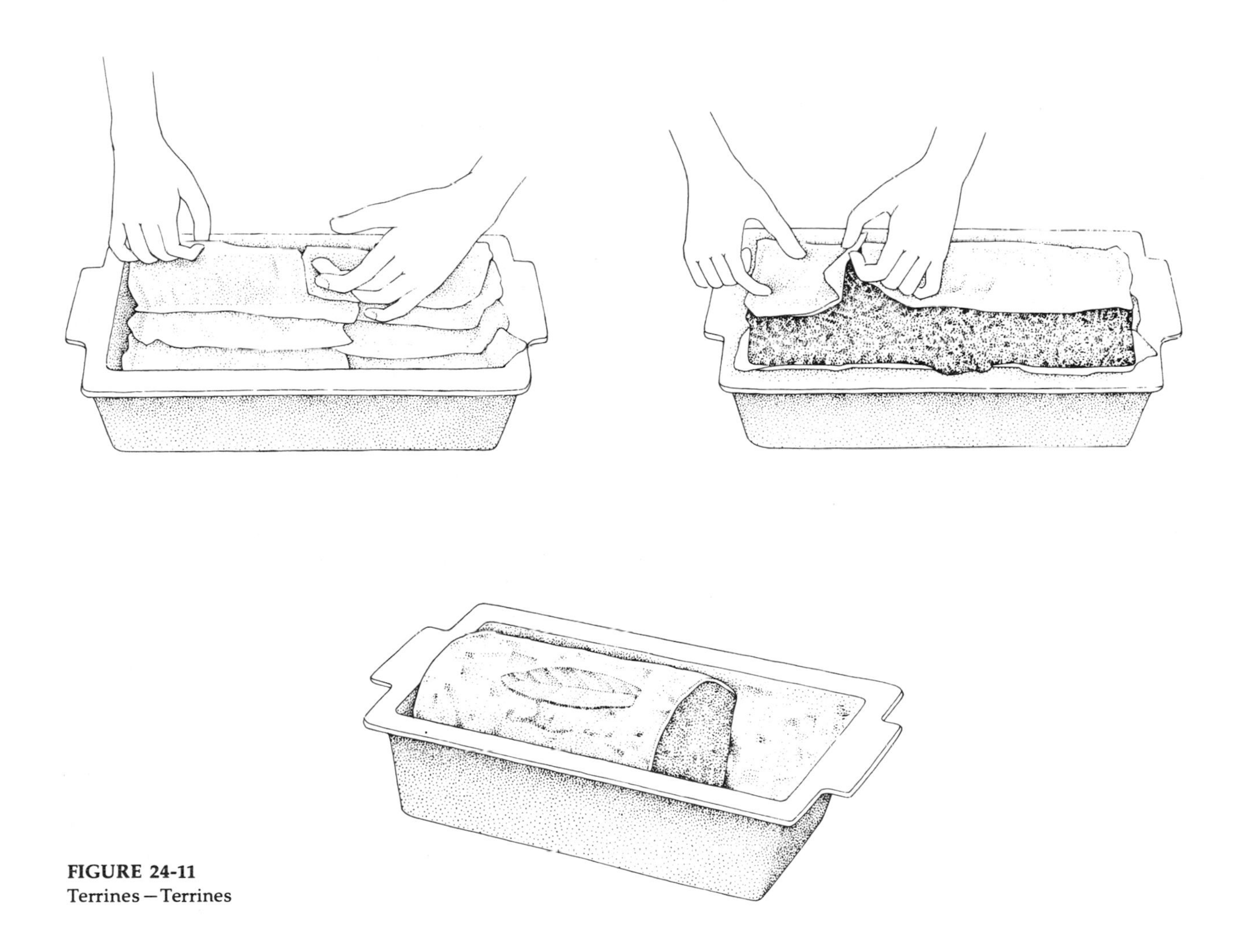

FIGURE 24-11
Terrines — Terrines

Terrine, Bourgeoise Style (Terrine Maison)

YIELD: *approximately 10 servings*

INGREDIENTS	*U.S. Weight or Volume*	*Metric Weight or Volume*	PROCEDURE
Bacon, finely ground	9 ounces	250 grams	1. Mix the ground bacon, pork, pork liver, and veal together.
Pork, lean, finely ground	14 ounces	400 grams	
Pork liver, finely ground	14 ounces	400 grams	
Veal, finely ground	5 ounces	150 grams	
Garlic, finely chopped	1 clove	1 clove	2. Lightly saute the shallots and garlic in butter and add them to the meat.
Shallots, finely chopped	1¾ ounces	50 grams	
Butter	1 ounce	30 grams	
Chicken liver	5 ounces	150 grams	3. Quickly saute the chicken liver in the butter.
Brandy	3/8 cup	½ deciliter	4. Remove the liver, deglaze the pan with brandy, and add it to the meat mixture.
Cream	3/8 cup	½ deciliter	5. Add the cream, lemon juice, egg, sausage seasoning, salt, and pepper to the meat and blend it in the mixer so the ingredients combine to form a smooth and light forcemeat.
Lemon juice	from 1 lemon	from 1 lemon	
Egg, beaten	1	1	
Sausage seasoning	½ teaspoon	3 grams	
Salt	1 teaspoon	5 grams	
Pepper	½ teaspoon	3 grams	
Tongue, boiled, finely diced	2 ounces	60 grams	6. Add the diced tongue. 7. Adjust the seasoning if necessary.
Larding bacon, thinly sliced	9 ounces	250 grams	8. Line the terrine with the bacon slices. 9. Place half the mixture in the terrine. Press down. Smooth the surface. 10. Cut the chicken liver into small pieces and place them on the surface. 11. Fold the slices of larding bacon over the top so the meat mixture is completely enveloped.
Bay leaf	1	1	12. Place the bay leaf on top. 13. Cover with aluminum foil. 14. Poach for about 2 hours in a waterbath in the oven at 350°F. (175°C.), just until the fat on the surface is clear. Remove the bay leaf. Cover with a fresh sheet of aluminum foil, weigh down, cool, and store in the refrigerator.

24.5 Cold Meat Dishes—Plats de viandes froides

These refer to cold dishes made from *meat, poultry, and game.* Although they are often combined and prepared with jelly, pickles, and salads, they can also be served individually. The primary forms of preparation are roasting, braising, and poeler. (For methods of carving, see page 246.)

24.5.1 Beef—Boeuf

Fillet, roast sirloin of beef, rib steak, rump pot roast. Roast to desired degree of doneness. Use simple decorations for whole pieces and coat with a thin layer of jelly. Accompaniments: spring vegetables, tomatoes, asparagus spears, pickles, shaped mushrooms, fruit, jelly cubes, and parsley. Sauces: variations of mayonnaise, cold Horseradish Sauce, Cream Cheese Sauce with Roquefort. (See Illustration page 491.)

Tongue—Langue. Boil, trim, dress, and cool. Use simple decorations and coat with a thin layer of jelly. Accompaniment: same as fillet but without fruits. Sauces: Horseradish Sauce and Cream Cheese Sauce with herbs.

24.5.2 Veal—Veau

Saddle, breast, fillet, filet mignon, loin, rump, round of beef. Whole pieces should be decorated simply and coated with a thin layer of jelly. Accompaniments that may be used with these meats are: vegetables a la grecque, tomatoes, stuffed artichoke hearts, asparagus spears, vegetable salad, mushrooms, fruit only as decoration. Sauces: variations of mayonnaise, cold Horseradish Sauce, and Cream Cheese Sauce with herbs.

24.5.3 Pork—Porc

Loin of pork, ham. Roast or glaze a loin. Simmer or braise a ham depending upon the type of dish. Use simple decorations for whole pieces and coat with a thin layer of jelly. Accompaniments: sweet glazed vegetables, such as carrots, turnips; fruit, such as mustard fruit, stewed apples, and prunes. Sauces: apple puree, cold Horseradish Sauce, or Cranberry Sauce. (See illustration page 492.)

24.5.4 Lamb—Agneau

Baron, Saddle, roast breast, leg. Roast the meat until rare. Use simple decorations for whole pieces and coat with a thin layer of jelly. Accompaniments: mixed pickles, vegetables a la grecque and those mentioned with veal. Sauces: Mint Sauce or cold Horseradish Sauce.

24.5.5 Poultry—Volaille

Poularde, duck, goose, turkey. Roast or poeler. Decorate according to the type of dish, coat with jelly or with Chaud-froid Sauce (see Section 24.4.2). Accompaniments for duck and turkey: stewed apples, oranges, sweet-and-sour fruits, glazed chestnuts, and spring vegetables. Accompaniments for poularde: spring vegetables coated with jelly, mushrooms, tomatoes, asparagus spears, and artichokes. Sauces for duck, goose, and turkey: Cranberry, Cumberland, and cold Horseradish Sauce. (See illustration page 492.) Sauces for poulardes: variations of Mayonnaise or Cream Cheese Sauce with herbs.

24.5.6 Game—Gibier

Woodcock, quail, grouse, pheasant, partridge, saddle and leg of roebuck, boar, saddle of hare. Roast the meat until rare. Depending on the dish, decorate, coat with jelly or with Chaud-froid Sauce. (See Section 24.4.2.) Accompaniment: stuffed apples and pears, pineapple, red cherries, oranges, mustard fruit, mixed pickles, spring vegetables a la grecque, tomatoes, asparagus spears, and mushrooms. Sauces: Cumberland, Cranberry, Horseradish, and Cream Cheese with ginger. (See illustration page 492.)

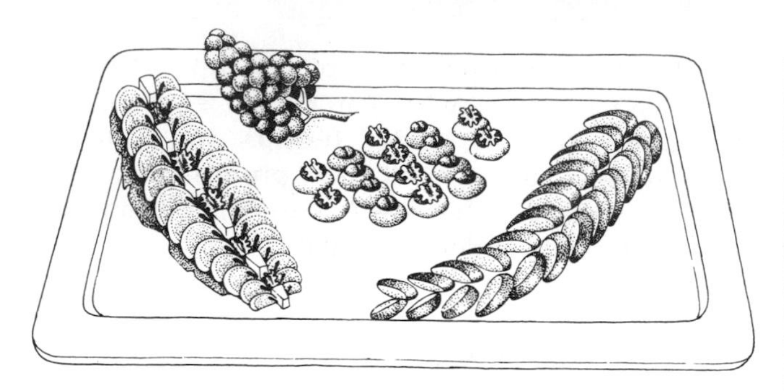

FIGURE 24-12
Saddle of Deer with Fruit—Selle de chevreuil aux fruits

24.5.7 Special Variations

Cold Boiled Beef, Southern France Style—Boeuf bouilli froid a la mode du Midi. Boil a beef rump and allow to cool. Slice and garnish on one side with spring vegetables a la grecque and on the the other side with stuffed tomatoes and cucumbers. Serve cold Horseradish Sauce and whipped cream cheese with herbs separately.

Cold Braised Beef—Boeuf a la mode froid. This dish has been handed down from the old French cuisine. Lard a beef rump roast and braise with calf's feet and vegetables, but do not bind the gravy with flour (See page 410.) Coat an appropriate mold with jelly, garnish with the braised vegetables, and fix these with a second layer of jelly. Place the braised beef in the mold and fill it with the gravy. When cold, turn out and garnish.

Cold Beef Tenderloin with Asparagus Spears—Filet de boeuf froid Argenteuil. Roast the whole tenderloin and glaze. Arrange on a dish, carve a few slices, garnish with asparagus spears, and coat with jelly.

Beef Tenderloin Chevet—Filet de boeuf Chevet. Coat a cradle-shaped mold with jelly, line with various colored, shaped, and well-seasoned vegetables, and fix these with another layer of jelly. Place the roast tenderloin in the mold and fill the mold with jelly. Refrigerate until congealed; unmold, and garnish.

Cold Beef Tenderloin with Spring Vegetables—Filet de boeuf froid a la printaniere. Roast the whole tenderloin and glaze. Arrange on a dish, surround with blanched and marinated spring vegetables which are coated with jelly.

Cold Roast Beef—Roastbeef froid. Roast the whole piece and glaze. Arrange on a dish, carve a few slices, and place them in front of the roast. Garnish the meat with vegetable salad and coat with jelly.

Duck with Tongue—Caneton a l'ecarlate. Poeler a duck and cool in the stock. Remove the two breast pieces and the skin, slice the breast meat, and rearrange on the breastbone with a half slice of orange between each slice of meat. Surround the bird with medallions of beef tongue alternating with glazed orange slices. Serve cold Horseradish Sauce separately.

Ham Souffle Marquerite—Jambon souffle Marguerite. Simmer a smoked ham slowly and cool in the stock. Remove the top part horizontally along the bone. Prepare a mousse (see page 498) with this meat and arrange on the cut surface. Cover with slices of ham and cornets. Accompaniments: ham rolls, stuffed tomatoes, and stuffed green sweet peppers, all thinly coated with jelly. Sauce: Horseradish Sauce. (See Fig. 24-13.)

Breasts of Poularde, Hawaiian Style—Supremes de poularde Hawaii. Slice the breasts of 2 roast poulardes lengthwise. Place 2 pineapple halves, cut

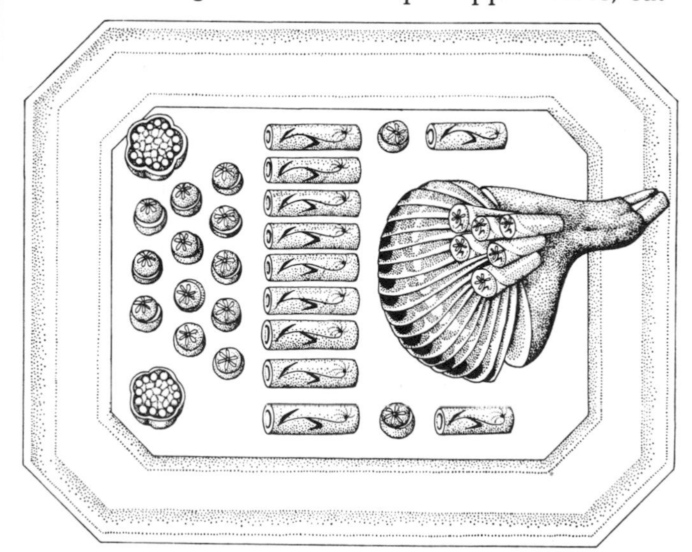

FIGURE 24-13
Ham Souffle Marguerite—Jambon Souffle Marguerite

lengthwise and hollowed out, in the center of a platter and garnish with celery salad and slices of pineapple and banana. Arrange a sliced breast half in a fan shape on each side of the two pineapple halves. Surround with small goose liver medallions garnished with truffle slices. Coat the whole dish with a thin layer of aspic. Serve Cumberland Sauce separately. (See Fig. 24-14.)

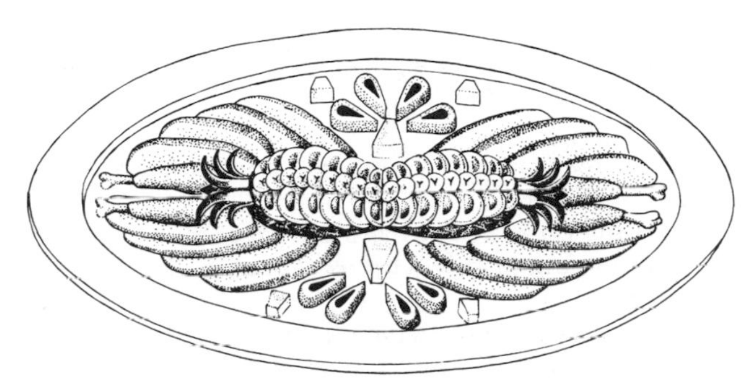

FIGURE 24-14
Breasts of Poularde, Hawaiian Style—Supreme de poularde Hawaii

Roast Turkey, Modern Style—Dindonneau roti Moderne. (See illustration page 491.)

Breasts of Turkey with Ham Slices and Truffles—Supremes de dinde au jambon saumone et truffles. Roast the turkey breasts, slice, and arrange in the original order with slices of truffles. Stuff a pineapple with celery salad and diced pineapple and surround with ham rolls stuffed with celery salad, and truffle croquettes. The truffles should be served in their natural shape. (See Fig. 24-15.)

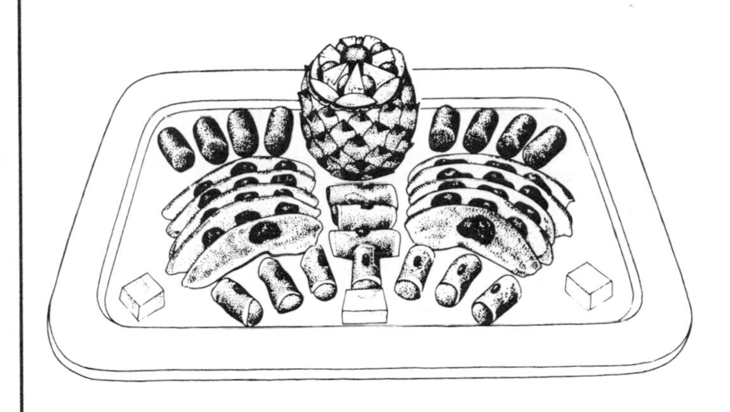

FIGURE 24-15
Breasts of Turkey with Ham Slices and Truffles—Supremes de dinde au jambon saumone et truffes

Suckling Pig, Modern Style (Cochon de lait moderne)

YIELD: *1 pig*

INGREDIENTS	*U.S. Weight or Volume*	*Metric Weight or Volume*
Suckling pig	1 at 12 pounds	1 at 5½ kilograms
Seasoned salt	2 teaspoons	60 grams
Madeira	3 tablespoons	45 milliliters
Stuffing for pig:		
Veal, lean	1 pound	500 grams
Bacon, lean and unsmoked	7 ounces	200 grams
Liver from the pig, finely diced	–	–
Shallots	2 ounces	60 grams
Butter	4 tablespoons	120 grams
Madeira OR Sherry	3 tablespoons	45 milliliters
Parsley, chopped	½ cup	150 grams
Chervil	1 teaspoon	5 grams
Thyme	1 teaspoon	5 grams
Seasoned salt	1 teaspoon	5 grams
Bread crumbs, fine, white	7 ounces	200 grams
Eggs	4 to 5	4 to 5
Butter	3 tablespoons	60 grams
Beer	1 cup	235 milliliters

PROCEDURE

1. Dry the suckling pig. Remove eyeballs and close eyelids. Sprinkle the pig with seasoned salt and Madeira wine.
2. Brown the veal, bacon, liver, and shallots in butter. Deglaze with Madeira or sherry and add all the seasonings.
3. Grind the warm meat and the herbs as finely as possible. Cool.
4. Add the bread crumbs and the eggs.
5. Stuff the pig loosely with the dressing. Sew up the opening.
6. Put a block of wood in the pig's mouth to hold it open. Pull the forelegs forward and bend the hindlegs forward under the body. Skewer the legs in place. Cover the ears with aluminum foil. Cut a crisscross pattern lightly into the rind of the pig.
7. Place in the oven at 450°F. (230°C.) for 15 minutes. Reduce the heat to 325°F. (165°C.). Baste with butter or oil every 15 minutes for the first hour. Continue basting with the pan juices and additional oil or butter. Allow a baking time of 30 minutes per pound.
8. When the pig is done, transfer it to a serving platter.
9. Drain the fat from the roasting pan. Add butter and beer to the pan. Deglaze.
10. Remove the foil from the ears and the wood block from the mouth. Place an apple or a branch of celery in the pig's mouth.
11. Surround the pig with straw potatoes and garnish with clusters of parsley or watercress, artichoke hearts stuffed with horseradish mousse, tomatoes stuffed with celery salad, stuffed mushrooms, or stewed apples stuffed with cranberries.

Note: The skin should be glazed and crisp but not dry. Rub the skin with an oil-soaked cloth before serving.

FIGURE 24-16
Suckling Pig, Modern Style—Cochon de lait moderne

Veal Cutlets with Ham Mousse—Cotes de veau a la mousse de jambon. Decorate the grilled cold cutlets and coat with jelly. Invert ham mousse in the center of a platter and surround with the cutlets. Garnish with jelly cubes. Serve Horseradish Sauce separately. Recipe for mousse, see Section 24.4.4. (See Fig. 24-17.)

FIGURE 24-17
Veal Cutlets with Ham Mousse—Cotes de veau a la mousse de jambon

Saddle of Veal, Bohemian Style—Selle de veau boheme. Stuff a roasted, boned saddle of veal with a veal stuffing mixed with pistachios and red sweet peppers. Tie, coat with jelly, cool, slice, and arrange on a dish. *Accompaniments:* artichoke hearts stuffed with beans, tomatoes and mushrooms, and thin slices of hard-cooked eggs with jelly. An elegant decoration consists of round truffles on a spit with garlands of raw carrots, cucumbers, and radishes. (See Fig. 24-18.)

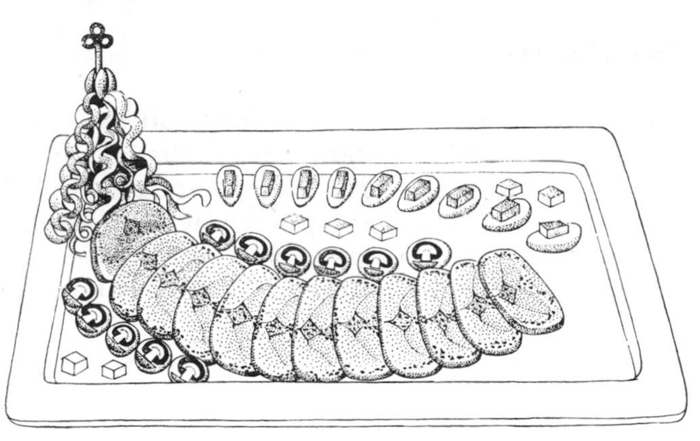

FIGURE 24-18
Saddle of Veal, Bohemian Style—Selle de veau boheme

Leg of Venison in Pastry, Lucerne Style—Gigot de chevreuil en a la lucernoise. (See illustration page 492.)

Cold Saddle of Venison St. Hubert—Selle de chevreuil froide St. Hubert. Roast a saddle of venison and allow to cool. Remove the fillets and cut into uniform slices. Spread some game mousse (mousse de gibier) over the backbone, replace the slices in their original order, and coat with game mousse to give a smooth surface. Place thin, halved pineapple slices along the top of the backbone and decorate with cherries. Garnish both sides of the saddle with quartered pineapple slices. Arrange some game mousse on poached slices of apple and place a red cherry on top of each. Coat the whole dish with jelly. Serve a Cumberland Sauce and Waldorf Sauce separately. (See Fig. 24-19.)

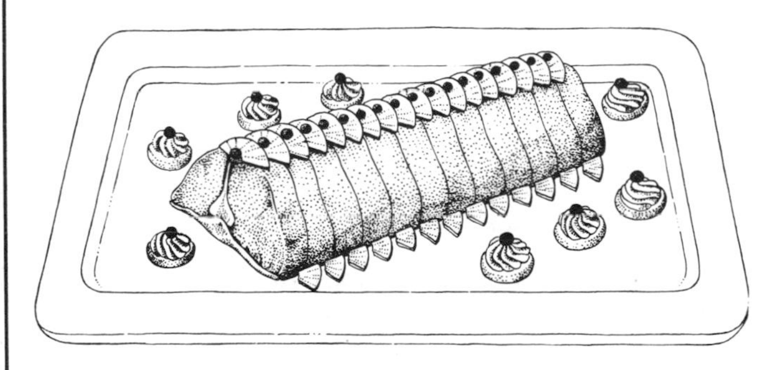

FIGURE 24-19
Cold Saddle of Venison St. Hubert—Selle de chevreuil St-Hubert

24.6 Buffets

This term refers to a choice of foods offered to the guests as a refreshing snack. The number of hot and cold dishes depends upon the type of occasion. A buffet can consist of a variety of sandwiches, a platter of cold meat cuts, fruit cakes, pies, and pastries, but can also involve the ultimate in luxury in terms of both choice of foods and the finesse of their preparation. When planning a buffet menu, one begins with the hors d'oeuvre dishes, continues with soup, then egg dishes, fish, and shellfish. Then come the various meat, poultry, and game dishes, accompanied by the appropriate salad, and the menu is completed with sweet dishes, pastries, fruit, and the dessert.

Cold Buffet

Melon—Grapefruit—Tomato Juice

Terrine of Caviar Malossol

Consomme in a Madrilene Cup

Poached Eggs with Tarragon
Medallions of Crawfish, Parisian Style
Norwegian Salmon
Fillets of Sole Calypso

Ham a la Gelee
Roast Beef with Spring Vegetables
Veal Tongue Argenteuil
Mousse de Foie Gras with Paprika
Pate of Venison, Menagere Style
Galatine of Chicken with Truffles
Chicken Vendome
Chaud-froid Pheasant
Qual Glace

Russian Salad—Hearts of Lettuce

Fruit Salad with Kirsch
Coupe Melba
Pastries
Cake, Breton Style
Sweets
Fruits

Buffet froid

Melon—Pamplemousse—Jus de tomates

Terrine de caviar malossol

Consomme en tasse madrilene

Oeufs poches a l'estragon
Medaillons de langouste parisienne
Saumon norvegienne
Filets de sole Calypso

Jambon a la gelee
Roastbeef printaniere
Langue de veau Argenteuil
Mousse de foie gras au paprika
Pate de chevreuil a la menagere
Galantine de volaille truffee
Poularde Vendome
Faison en chaud-froid
Cailles glacees

Salade russe—Coeurs de laitues

Macedoine de fruits au Kirsch
Coupe Melba
Patisserie
Gateau a la bretonne
Friandises
Fruits

Gala Buffet

Various Shellfish
Cold Salmon
Shrimp with Avocados
Cold Turbot Joinville
Zurich Stuffed Pike
Danish Stuffed Eel
Swedish Salmon
Rolls of Sole Rosita

Double Consomme with Sherry

Pate Maison
Roast Beef Nicoise
Fillet of Beef Wellington
Saddle of Veal with Garden Vegetables
Terrine with Calvados
Saddle of Venison Diana
Turkey Mexican Style
Veal and Ham Pie
Pheasant Bristol
Beef Tongue a l'escarlate

Variety of Salads

Boiled Beef Cultivateur
Country Ham in a Crust
Bollito Misto
Potato Salad—Mixed Pickles

Vacherin Mont d'Or
Emmentaler

Fruits of the Season

Charlotte Russe
Souffle Glace with Grand Marnier
Sherbet with Champagne
Sugar Kirschtorte
Sweets

Grand Buffet de Gala

Variations de fruits de mer
Saumon froid moderne
Crevettes aux avocados
Turbot froid Joinville
Brochet farci zurichoise
Anguille farcie danoise
Saumon suedoise
Calamares alla Toscana
Paupiettes de sole Rosita

Consomme double au Xeres

Pate maison
Roastbeef nicoise
Filet de boeuf Wellington
Selle de veau jardinere
Terrine au Calvados
Selle de chevreuil Diana
Turkey Mexican style
Veal and ham pie
Faisan Bristol
Langue de boeuf a l'ecarlate

Salades diverses

Boeuf bouilli cultivateur
Jambon du pays en croute
Bollito misto
Salade Parmentier—Mixed Pickles

Vacherin Mont d'Or

Emmentaler

Fruits de la saison

Charlotte russe
Souffle glace au Grand Marnier
Sorbet au Champagne
Zuger Kirschtorte
Friandises

25 Desserts/Entremets: Basic Forms of Preparation

25.1 Doughs—Pates

Flour must be sifted before measuring. Sifting removes lumps, separates granules, and incorporates air. Flour that is measured by weighing does not require sifting. For storing or resting period, doughs are wrapped in aluminum foil, polyethelene wrap, or airtight containers to prevent drying or the formation of a crust.

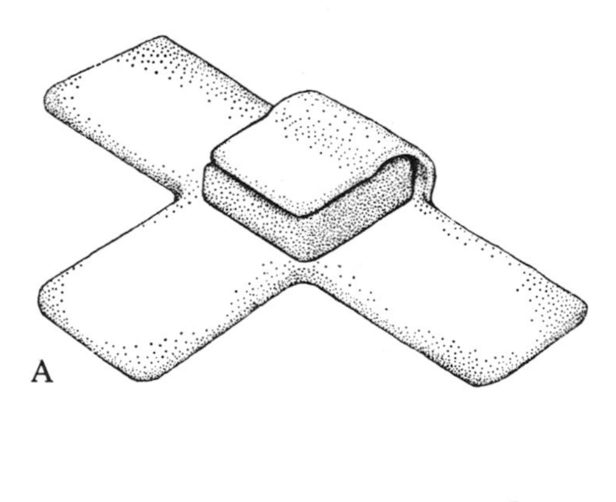

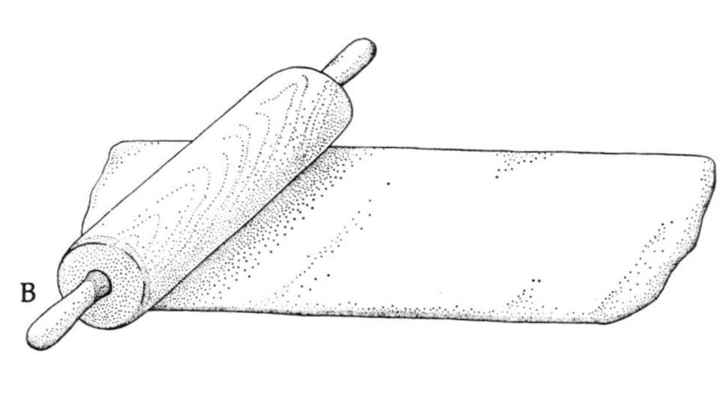

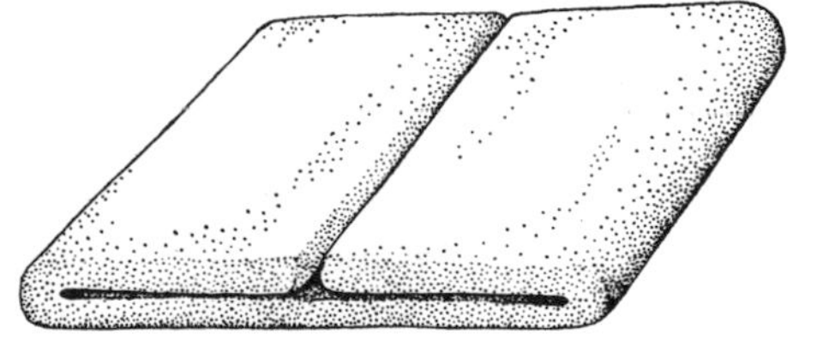

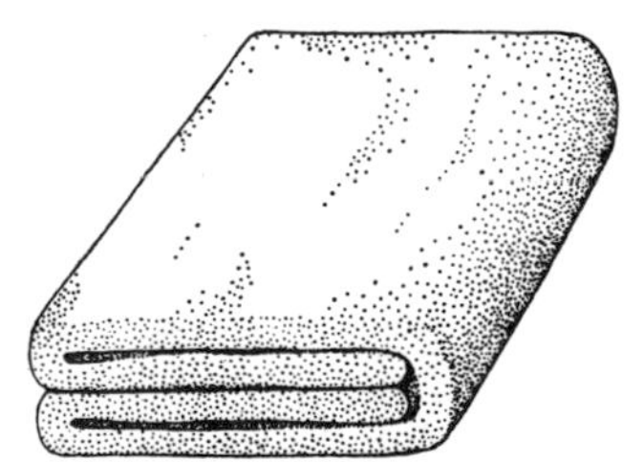

FIGURE 25-1
Doughs—Pates

25.1.1 Puff Paste (Feuilletage)

YIELD: *30 medium-sized pastries*

INGREDIENTS	*U.S. Weight or Volume*	*Metric Weight or Volume*
Flour, sifted	2 pounds	1 kilogram
Fat	1½ to 1¾ pounds	700 to 900 grams
Water	1 pint	5 deciliters
Salt	¾ ounce	20 grams
Lemon juice	1 teaspoon	5 milliliters

PROCEDURE

1. Place the flour on a table. Make a well in the center.
2. Pour the water, 3½ ounces (100 grams) of fat, the salt, and the lemon juice (if desired) into the well. Work into a ball of dough as quickly as possible.
3. Allow to rest for 1 hour.
4. Cut a cross in the top of the ball of dough and roll it out into a cross shape leaving the center four times as thick as the four ends.
5. Knead the remaining fat until soft and form into a block. Place the block on the middle of the cross and fold the four ends over it. Roll out to an oblong shape. Fold the ends to the center and then fold in half. Repeat this rolling out and folding 4 times, wrapping the dough and allowing it to rest 20 minutes in the refrigerator before each rolling.
6. Bake medium-sized pastries made from this dough in an oven preheated to 475°F. (246°C.) for 5 minutes. Reduce the temperature to 390°F. (200°C.) and continue baking about 25 minutes longer.

Note: It is important to roll the dough on a marble or other smooth surface previously dusted with flour. Any sticking should be avoided. The flour used for dusting should always be brushed off the dough before it is folded. The dough must be rolled right into the corners without flattening the edges. Margarine is generally used as the fat (a special baking margarine); butter is used only for especially fine pastries of puff paste.

25.1.2 Short Crust Paste (Pate brisee)

YIELD: *6 ten-inch crusts*

INGREDIENTS	*U.S. Weight or Volume*	*Metric Weight or Volume*
Flour, sifted	2 pounds	1 kilogram
Fat	14 to 21 ounces	400 to 600 grams
Salt	¾ ounce	20 grams
Water	1¾ to 2 cups	4 to 5 deciliters

PROCEDURE

1. Rub the flour lightly with the fat until it resembles fine bread crumbs, then form a well in the center.
2. Pour the water into the well. Add the salt. Work into a ball of dough as quickly as possible and allow to rest for 1 hour before using.

Note: When using cake pans measuring 10 inches (26.3 centimeters) across, about 10 ounces (280 grams) of this dough will be required per pan.

25.1.3 Cream Puff Paste (Pate a chou)

YIELD: *Beignets — 50 servings*
Gnocchi — 25 servings
Eclairs — 200 servings

INGREDIENTS	*U.S. Weight or Volume*	*Metric Weight or Volume*
For Beignets Souffles:		
Water or milk	1 quart	1 liter
Flour, sifted	1 pound	500 grams
Butter	7 ounces	200 grams
Salt	½ ounce	10 grams
Sugar	1 ounce	30 grams
Lemon peel, grated	as desired	as desired
Eggs	18	18
For Gnocchi Parisienne and Pommes Dauphine:		
Water	1 quart	1 liter
Butter	7 ounces	200 grams
Flour, sifted	1¼ pounds	600 grams
Salt	½ ounce	10 grams
Nutmeg	as desired	as desired
Eggs	18	18
For Eclairs and Choux:		
Milk	1 quart	1 liter
Flour, sifted	1¼ pounds	600 grams
Butter	10 ounces	280 grams
Salt	½ ounce	10 grams
Sugar	1 ounce	30 grams
Lemon peel, grated	as desired	as desired
Eggs	20	20

PROCEDURE

1. Place the water or milk, butter, salt, sugar, and lemon peel or nutmeg in a pan. Bring to a boil.
2. Add the flour and mix with a wooden spoon until the mixture no longer clings to the pan or spoon.
3. Remove from the heat and beat in the eggs one after another, beating thoroughly after each addition.

25.1.4 Frying Batter (Pate a frire)

YIELD: *U.S. — 2 quarts*
Metric — 2 liters

INGREDIENTS	*U.S. Weight or Volume*	*Metric Weight or Volume*
Flour, sifted	2 pounds	1 kilogram
Beer	1½ pints	8 deciliters
Water	1¼ pints	6 deciliters
Oil	¾ cup	2 deciliters
Egg yolks	4	4
Salt	½ ounce	15 grams
Sugar	½ ounce	15 grams
Nutmeg	optional	optional
Egg whites	8	8

PROCEDURE

1. Place the flour in a bowl. Make a well in the center of the flour. Add the beer, water, oil, egg yolks, and seasonings. Blend into the flour.

2. Beat the egg whites until stiff but not dry. Fold into the flour mixture.

25.1.5 Brioche Dough (Pate levee [a brioches])

YIELD: *40 to 50*

INGREDIENTS	*U.S. Weight or Volume*	*Metric Weight or Volume*
Yeast	1 ounce	30 grams
Water, lukewarm	¾ cup	2 deciliters
Flour, sifted	2 pounds (4 ounces + 1¾ pounds)	1 kilogram (100 + 790 grams)
Butter OR Margarine	1¼ pounds	600 grams
Salt	¾ ounce	20 grams
Sugar	1½ ounces	40 grams
Eggs	10 to 12	10 to 12

PROCEDURE

1. To prepare the starter dough, dissolve the yeast in lukewarm water and add to 4 ounces (110 grams) of the sifted flour. Mix until a thin dough forms. Allow to rise in a warm place for 1 or 1½ hours.

2. Meanwhile, knead the butter until soft and mix with the sugar until smooth. Add remaining flour, salt, and eggs. Work into a firm dough. If necessary, add a small quantity of lukewarm water. The dough should be dry and firm, not soft. Slap the dough vigorously by hand until bubbles form.
3. Mix in the starter dough and slap vigorously once more. During fermentation, fold the dough twice and slap again.
4. Fill the molds ⅓ full and allow the dough to rise at a moderate temperature until the molds are full.
5. Bake at 450°F. (232°C.) for 10 minutes or until golden brown.

25.1.6 Sugar Paste (Pate sucree)

YIELD: *50 to 60 individual tart shells or 7 to 8 nine-inch shells*

INGREDIENTS	*U.S. Weight or Volume*	*Metric Weight or Volume*
Flour	2 pounds	1 kilogram
Butter OR margarine	1 pound	500 grams
Sugar	14 ounces	400 grams
Egg yolks	8	8
Water	2 tablespoons (approx.)	¼ deciliter
Lemon rind, grated	½ teaspoon	3 grams

PROCEDURE

1. Make a well in the center of the flour.
2. Place the butter, sugar, egg yolks, water, and lemon rind in the well and mix these ingredients together before working the flour into the mixture.
3. Gradually work in the flour to give a smooth dough.

Note: Prepare this dough as quickly and with as little handling as possible, otherwise it will become tough. It is used primarily as a base for fruit tarts.

Pasta Dough—Pate a nouilles. (See page 458.)
Pie Dough—Pate pour pates. (See page 500.)
Ravioli Dough—Pate a ravioli. (See page 455.)

25.2 Mixtures—Appareils

25.2.1 Genoise Batter (Genoise)

YIELD: *2 ten-inch layers (round)*

INGREDIENTS	*U.S. Weight or Volume*	*Metric Weight or Volume*
Eggs	10	10
Sugar	10 ounces	300 grams
Flour	5 ounces	150 grams
Cornstarch	5 ounces	150 grams
Butter	3½ ounces	100 grams
Lemon rind, grated	½ teaspoon	3 grams

PROCEDURE

1. Whip the eggs and sugar either, in a pan on the range or over a warm (not boiling) water bath, to a soft foam which draws into a ribbon.
2. Remove from the heat and continue whipping the mixture until it is almost cold.
3. Carefully fold in the flour and cornstarch, and finally fold in the melted butter and lemon rind.
4. Divide the batter between 2 ten-inch layer pans.
5. Bake in oven at 425°F. (220°C.) for 25 to 30 minutes with open steam outlet.

Note: In this recipe a careful distinction must be made among whipping, mixing, and folding in. The amount of butter to be added depends on the requirements of the batter; light batters require only 2¾ ounces (77 grams) while 7 ounces (196 grams) can be necessary for heavier ones. Usually about 3½ ounces (98 grams) should be added. Sponge cake batters are generally used for cakes or for patisseries: in the latter case, they are baked in rectangular pieces approximately 1½ inches (3.75 centimeters) thick. This batter may be used for little cakes, or it may be baked in ring molds or timbales. The batter may be flavored with vanilla instead of lemon rind.

25.2.2 Cold Sponge Cake Batter (Biscuit froid)

YIELD: *2 ten-inch layers (round)*

INGREDIENTS	*U.S. Weight or Volume*	*Metric Weight or Volume*	PROCEDURE
Eggs	8	8	1. Place the eggs and water in a mixing bowl.
Water	½ cup	1½ deciliter	
Sugar	10 ounces	300 grams	2. Add the sugar and the whipping agent and mix at medium speed for 4 to 5 minutes.
Whipping agent	1½ ounces (approx.)	40 grams	3. Reduce the speed and add the sifted flour, baking powder, and the lemon rind. Mix at high speed for 4 to 5 minutes. Prepare and bake as for Genoise.
Flour	11¼ ounces	320 grams	
Baking powder	½ ounce	14 grams	
Lemon rind, grated	½ teaspoon	3 grams	

Note: Since the excellent, modern whipping agents give a sponge cake identical in quality to a Genoise, the latter is seldom used. This batter may also be used for Swiss rolls and Moor's heads (40 to 50 units).

25.2.3 Ladyfingers (Biscuit de champagne)

YIELD: *200*

INGREDIENTS	*U.S. Weight or Volume*	*Metric Weight or Volume*	PROCEDURE
Eggs	6	6	1. Whip the eggs, egg yolks, and sugar, either in a pan on the range or over a warm (not boiling) water bath, to a soft foam which draws into a ribbon.
Egg yolks	4	4	
Sugar	12 ounces	350 grams	2. Remove mixture from the heat and continue whipping until it is almost cold.
Flour	12 ounces	350 grams	3. Fold in the flour and grated lemon rind.
Lemon rind, grated	½ teaspoon	3 grams	4. Fill a pastry tube with the dough and shape into finger lengths in a pan lined with ungreased paper.
			5. Bake in an oven at 390°F. (215°C.) for about 15 to 20 minutes.

Note: See page 570 for ladyfingers used for petites-fours and desserts, such as Charlotte Russe.

25.2.4 Cornet Batter (Masse a cornets)

YIELD: *60 cornets*

INGREDIENTS	*U.S. Weight or Volume*	*Metric Weight or Volume*
Sugar	1 pound	500 grams
Hazelnuts	9 ounces	250 grams
OR		
Almonds		
Egg whites	12	12
Flour	6½ ounces	180 grams

PROCEDURE

1. Mix the sugar and hazelnuts with 2 egg whites and put through the milling machine.
2. Place the milled nut mixture in a bowl. Add the remainder of the egg whites and work in the flour. Stir vigorously until the mixture is smooth and thick. Add more flour if required.
3. Use an appropriate template or form, and arrange the dough on a buttered baking pan and bake in oven at 375°F. (200°C.) for 12 to 15 minutes.
4. While still hot, wrap around a dummy cornet made of wood, or shape as desired.

Note: If a milling machine is not available, the nuts must be finely grated. This mixture can also be used for rolls, leaves, and little tubs.

25.2.5 Japanese Meringues (Masse a japonais)

YIELD: *6 tart shells*

INGREDIENTS	*U.S. Weight or Volume*	*Metric Weight or Volume*
Egg whites	10	10
Sugar	1 pound	500 grams
Hazelnuts, finely grated	7 ounces	220 grams
Flour	2¼ ounces	65 grams

PROCEDURE

1. Beat the egg whites until stiff but not dry. Add 3½ ounces (98 grams) of the sugar and continue beating until the sugar is thoroughly blended.
2. Combine the flour, hazelnuts, and the remainder of the sugar. Fold this mixture into the beaten egg whites and sugar.
3. Place the mixture in a pastry bag with a flat nozzle. Pipe the mixture into a spiral form on buttered baking sheets.
4. Bake in oven at 360°F. (200°C.) for 15 to 20 minutes.

Note: This mixture may also be used for Japanese pastries and tarts. Replace one fourth of the hazelnuts with almonds. Spread the mixture on a buttered baking tray to a depth of 1/10 inch (.25 centimeter).

25.2.6 Praline Mixture (Masse pralinee)

YIELD: *U.S. — 2½ pounds*
Metric — 1.1 kilograms

INGREDIENTS	*U.S. Weight or Volume*	*Metric Weight or Volume*
Sugar	1¼ pounds	600 grams
Hazelnuts	10 ounces	300 grams
Almonds	10 ounces	300 grams

PROCEDURE

1. Place the sugar in a heavy pan. Stir continuously over low heat until the mixture is golden brown.
2. Brown the hazelnuts and almonds slightly. Add immediately to the sugar, and pour the mixture onto an oiled marble surface.
3. When cold, crush the praline mixture in the milling machine and sift.

Note: This mixture is used for ice cream, puddings, souffles, and cremes.

Souffle Mixture—Masse a souffle. See Souffles, Section 26.1.

25.2.7 Meringue Mixture (Meringage)

YIELD: *50 to 60 meringue shells*

INGREDIENTS	*U.S. Weight or Volume*	*Metric Weight or Volume*
Egg whites	10	10
Sugar	1 pound	500 grams

PROCEDURE

1. Beat egg whites until stiff but not dry.
2. Add 1¾ ounces (50 grams) of sugar and beat until sugar is thoroughly blended.
3. Add the remaining sugar gradually, folding it in with a wooden spoon.
4. Fill a pastry bag with the meringue mixture. Shape the meringue into shell forms on a baking sheet covered with parchment paper.
5. Preheat the oven to 225°F. (106°C.). Bake the meringue shells for 1 hour or longer.
6. If shells are not used immediately, store them in an airtight container.

25.2.8 Italian Meringue Mixture (Meringage a l'italienne)

YIELD: *approximately 50 shells*
or topping for 4 nine-inch pies

INGREDIENTS	*U.S. Weight or Volume*	*Metric Weight or Volume*	PROCEDURE
Sugar	1 pound	500 grams	1. Heat the sugar and water in a heavy pan and stir until the sugar is dissolved.
Water	1 cup	2½ deciliters	2. Cook until the syrup reaches the soft ball stage 234°F. to 240°F. (110°C. to 115°C.).
Egg whites	10	10	3. Meanwhile, beat the egg whites until stiff and fold in the confectioners' sugar.
Sugar, confectioners'	3½ ounces	100 grams	4. Add the cooked syrup slowly (in threads) to the beaten egg whites. Continue beating until the mixture is cool.

Note: This meringue may be used for shells or as a pie topping. It is cooked and may be used for a topping, or it may be placed in the oven to brown lightly.

25.2.9 Pancake Batter (Appareil a crepes)

YIELD: *U.S. — 1 quart (40 crepes)*
Metric — 1 liter

INGREDIENTS	*U.S. Weight or Volume*	*Metric Weight or Volume*	PROCEDURE
Flour	7 ounces	200 grams	1. Combine the flour, sugar, and salt.
Sugar	1¾ ounces	50 grams	2. Add the milk gradually and stir until the mixture is free of lumps.
Salt	¼ ounce	5 grams	3. Add the beaten eggs and the oil. Blend well.
Milk	1 pint	½ liter	4. Butter the pancake pans lightly and saute the crepes until yellow on both sides.
Eggs	6	6	
Oil	¼ cup	½ deciliter	

Note: If the pancakes are to be served sweet, grated orange peel, vanilla, or other flavoring may be added.

25.3 Creams—Cremes

Creams are very light and refreshing sweet dishes. They are also used as a base for many desserts. Whipped cream, fruits, chocolate, liqueurs, and/or nutmeats may be added to increase the richness and for a variety of flavors. Creams served with a colorful garnish in crystal coupes, bowls, or stemware are a simple but attractive dessert.

25.3.1 Vanilla Cream I (Creme a la vanille)

YIELD: *U.S. — 1½ quarts*
Metric — 1½ liters

INGREDIENTS	*U.S. Weight or Volume*	*Metric Weight or Volume*
Egg yolks	10	10
Sugar	9 ounces	250 grams
Milk	1 quart	1 liter
Vanilla extract	2 teaspoons	10 milliliters
Cream	1¼ cups	3 deciliters

PROCEDURE

1. Beat the egg yolks and the sugar until slightly foamy.
2. Scald the milk and add it gradually to the beaten eggs and sugar.
3. Pour the mixture into a saucepan and heat the cream just to the boiling point. Continue to cook slowly until it coats a wooden spoon. At this point, remove the cream from the heat.
4. Add the vanilla.
5. Strain.
6. Stir until cool.
7. Add the cream before serving.

Note: Never allow the cream to boil.

25.3.2 Vanilla Cream II (Creme a la vanille)

YIELD: *U.S. — 1¼ quarts*
Metric — 1¼ liters

INGREDIENTS	*U.S. Weight or Volume*	*Metric Weight or Volume*
Vanilla cream powder	¾ to 1 ounce	20 to 30 grams
Sugar	7¾ ounces	220 grams
Egg yolks	4	4
Milk	1 quart	1 liter

PROCEDURE

1. Blend the vanilla cream powder, the sugar, and the egg yolks.
2. Gradually add the scalded milk.
3. Pour the mixture into a saucepan and bring to the boiling point, stirring constantly.
4. Remove from heat and stir until cool. Strain.

Note: Cream may be added if desired.

Variations of Vanilla Cream—Creme a la vanille

Cream with Chocolate—Creme au chocolat.

Cream with Filberts—Creme aux avelines.

Cream with Mocha—Creme au mocca.

Cream with Pistachios—Creme aux pistaches.

Cream Praline—Creme pralinee.

25.3.3 English Custard Cream (Creme anglaise)

YIELD: *U.S. — 1¼ quarts*
Metric — 1¼ liters

INGREDIENTS	*U.S. Weight or Volume*	*Metric Weight or Volume*	PROCEDURE
Egg yolks	10	10	1. Blend the egg yolks, sugar, and vanilla cream powder.
Sugar	14 ounces	400 grams	
Vanilla cream powder	2 ounces	60 grams	
Milk	1 quart	1 liter	2. Gradually add the scalded milk. 3. Return the mixture to the saucepan and briefly bring to a boil, stirring constantly. 4. Remove from the heat. Stir while cooling. Strain.

25.3.4 Mousseline Cream (Creme mousseline)

YIELD: *U.S. — approximately 2 quarts*
Metric — 2 liters

INGREDIENTS	*U.S. Weight or Volume*	*Metric Weight or Volume*	PROCEDURE
Milk	1 quart	1 liter	1. Heat the milk to the boiling point.
Vanilla cream powder	1½ ounces	40 grams	2. Blend the vanilla cream powder, the sugar, and the egg yolks.
Sugar	9 ounces	250 grams	3. Gradually add the hot milk to the egg mixture.
Egg yolks	5	5	4. Pour the mixture into a saucepan and beat, stirring constantly.
Gelatin, unflavored	½ ounce	14 grams	5. Add the gelatin which has been soaked in the cold water. Stir until dissolved.
Water, cold	½ cup	1 deciliter	
Whipping cream	1½ pints	¾ liter	6. Remove from heat and cool the mixture. 7. As soon as it begins to thicken, fold in the whipped cream.

Note: Cream mousseline can be flavored with liqueur, mocha, or chocolate as desired.

25.3.5 Pastry Cream (Creme patissiere)

YIELD: *U.S. — 1¼ quarts*
Metric — 1¼ liters

INGREDIENTS	*U.S. Weight or Volume*	*Metric Weight or Volume*	PROCEDURE
Milk	1 quart	1 liter	1. Heat the milk to the boiling point.
Vanilla cream powder	2½ ounces	70 grams	2. Blend the vanilla cream powder, the sugar, and the egg yolks.
Sugar	7¾ ounces	220 grams	3. Gradually pour the hot milk into the sugar and egg mixture.
Egg yolks	8	8	4. Heat the mixture to the boiling point. 5. Stir quickly and cook only until the cream is thick and smooth.
Vanilla extract	2 teaspoons	10 milliliters	6. Add the vanilla extract.

25.3.6 Saint Honore Cream (Creme Saint-Honore)

YIELD: *U.S. — approximately 2 quarts*
Metric — 2 liters

INGREDIENTS	*U.S. Weight or Volume*	*Metric Weight or Volume*	PROCEDURE
Vanilla cream powder	2½ ounces	70 grams	1. Blend the vanilla cream powder, the sugar, and the egg yolks.
Sugar	7¾ ounces	220 grams	
Egg yolks	8	8	
Milk	1 quart	1 liter	2. Heat the milk to the boiling point. Add the milk gradually to the sugar and egg mixture. Stir constantly. 3. Heat mixture to the boiling point. Stir quickly and cook only until the cream is thick and smooth.
Gelatin, unflavored	½ ounce	14 grams	4. Add the gelatin which has been soaked in the cold water and stir until it is completely dissolved.
Water, cold	½ cup	1 deciliter	
Vanilla extract	2 teaspoons	10 milliliters	5. Add the vanilla.
Egg whites	6	6	6. Fold the beaten egg whites gently into the cream.
Whipping cream	¾ cup (more if desired)	2 deciliters (more if desired)	7. Cool until the cream begins to thicken. 8. Whip and fold in the whipping cream.

25.3.7 Butter Cream I (Creme au beurre)

YIELD: *U.S. — approximately 1 quart*
Metric — 1 liter

INGREDIENTS	*U.S. Weight or Volume*	*Metric Weight or Volume*	PROCEDURE
Eggs	8	8	1. Beat the eggs and sugar in a double boiler over a low flame or in a water bath until foamy (like a Genoise batter).
Sugar	14 ounces	400 grams	2. Remove from heat and beat the mixture until it is cooled.
Butter	1 pound	500 grams	3. Whip the butter and then gradually add it to the egg and sugar mixture, beating constantly.
Flavoring	as desired	as desired	4. Flavor as desired.

25.3.8 Butter Cream II (Creme au beurre)

YIELD: *U.S. — approximately 1 quart*
Metric — 1 liter

INGREDIENTS	*U.S. Weight or Volume*	*Metric Weight or Volume*	PROCEDURE
*Sugar syrup 28° Baume	1¾ cups	4 deciliters	1. Combine the sugar syrup and the egg yolks in a saucepan. Heat to the boiling point.
Egg yolks	5	5	2. Remove from the heat and beat the mixture continuously until it is cooled.
Butter	1 pound	500 grams	3. Whip the butter and add it gradually to the cooked and cooled mixture.
Flavoring	as desired	as desired	4. Flavor as desired.

*A 28° syrup is prepared by combining 2 pounds 6 ounces (1.07 kilograms) of sugar with enough water to produce 1 quart (1 liter). (See Section 25.5.)

25.4 Sauces

The individual portion size for sauces will vary between ¼ (½ deciliter) and ½ cup (1 deciliter) depending on the use and the consistency of the sauce. Cream sauces should be thinned with milk. The appropriate fruit juice should be used to thin fruit sauces.

Apricot Sauce (Sauce aux abricots)

YIELD: *U.S. — approximately 1 quart*
Metric — 1 liter

INGREDIENTS	*U.S. Weight or Volume*	*Metric Weight or Volume*	PROCEDURE
Apricot marmalade (jam)	1¼ pounds	600 grams	1. Combine the marmalade, sugar, and water in a saucepan. Bring to the boiling point.
Sugar	3½ ounces	100 grams	2. Remove from heat and strain or blend.
Water	1¼ cups	3 deciliters	3. Add kirsch and lemon juice.
Kirsch	2 tablespoons	¼ deciliter	
Lemon juice	1 teaspoon	5 milliliters	

Variations of Apricot Sauce

Fruit Sauce—Sauce aux fruits. Prepare as for Apricot Sauce. Use fruit, jam, or puree as desired.

Strawberry Sauce—Sauce aux fraises. Prepare as for Apricot Sauce. Use strawberry jam or puree.

Chocolate Sauce I (Sauce au chocolat)

YIELD: *U.S. — approximately 1 quart*
Metric — 1 liter

INGREDIENTS	*U.S. Weight or Volume*	*Metric Weight or Volume*	PROCEDURE
Vanilla sauce (page 530)	1¾ pints	9 deciliters	1. Prepare vanilla sauce.
Chocolate, semisweet	5 ounces	150 grams	2. Add grated chocolate to the hot vanilla sauce. Stir until dissolved.

Chocolate Sauce II (Sauce au chocolat)

YIELD: *U.S. — approximately 1 quart*
Metric — 1 liter

INGREDIENTS	*U.S. Weight or Volume*	*Metric Weight or Volume*	PROCEDURE
Chocolate, semi-sweet	1 pound	500 grams	1. Melt the chocolate with the sugar syrup in a hot water bath.
Sugar syrup	¾ cup	2 deciliters	2. Gradually add chocolate mixture to the cream and blend thoroughly.
Cream	1¼ cups	3 deciliters	

Melba Sauce (Sauce Melba)

YIELD: *U.S. — approximately 1 quart*
Metric — 1 liter

INGREDIENTS	*U.S. Weight or Volume*	*Metric Weight or Volume*	PROCEDURE
Raspberries, fresh or frozen	1¾ pounds	900 grams	1. Strain *fresh* raspberries.
OR			
Raspberry puree			
Sugar, confectioners'	7 to 10 ounces	200 to 300 grams	2. Add confectioners' sugar and the lemon juice.
Lemon juice	2 tablespoons	¼ deciliter	

Note: If raspberry puree is used, boil the puree and sugar quickly, and add the lemon juice. If frozen raspberries are used, strain them and boil quickly with the sugar. Cool and add the lemon juice.

Red Wine Sauce (Sauce Bischof)

YIELD: *U.S. — approximately 1 quart*
Metric — 1 liter

INGREDIENTS	*U.S. Weight or Volume*	*Metric Weight or Volume*	PROCEDURE
Red wine	1 pint	5 deciliters	1. Combine the wine, water, the sugar, clove, and cinnamon stick in a saucepan. Heat to the boiling point. Strain.
Water	1¼ cups	3 deciliters	
Sugar	7 ounces	200 grams	
Clove, whole	1	1	
Cinnamon, stick	1	1	
Cornstarch	¼ to ½ ounce	5 to 10 grams	2. Dissolve cornstarch in water and add to the liquid. Bring to a boil, stirring constantly.
Water, cold	as needed to dissolve cornstarch	as needed to dissolve cornstarch	
Currants, dried	1¾ ounces	50 grams	3. Add the diced currants and the almonds.
Almonds, finely sliced	1¾ ounces	50 grams	
Kirsch	2 tablespoons	¼ deciliter	4. Flavor with kirsch.

Sabayon

YIELD: *U.S. — approximately 1 quart (10 servings)*
Metric — 1 liter

INGREDIENTS	*U.S. Weight or Volume*	*Metric Weight or Volume*	PROCEDURE
White wine	1¼ cups	3 deciliters	1. Combine all ingredients and place over a steam bath on medium heat. Whip mixture continuously until the foam is stiff.
Lemon	1	1	
Marsala	½ cup	1 deciliter	
Sugar	7 ounces	200 grams	2. Serve at once.
Egg yolks	5	5	
Eggs	3	3	
Curacao, Rum, Kirsch, OR Maraschino	1½ ounces	40 grams	

Note: The brief period of beating will not coagulate the eggs, as might be expected, since the alcoholic content of the mixture lowers the boiling point.

Cold Sabayon (Sabayon frappe)

YIELD: *10 to 12 servings*

INGREDIENTS	*U.S. Weight or Volume*	*Metric Weight or Volume*
Sabayon	1 recipe	1 recipe
Gelatin	½ ounce	14 grams
Water, cold	½ cup	1 deciliter
Whipping cream	1¼ cups	3 deciliters

PROCEDURE

1. Prepare recipe for Sabayon.
2. While the mixture is hot, add the gelatin which has been softened in cold water. Stir until thoroughly blended.
3. Whip the mixture until very thick. Place over cracked ice and continue beating until the sauce is cold. Add the whipped cream.
4. Pour into dessert dishes or serve over fruit.

Vanilla Sauce (Sauce vanille)

YIELD: *U.S. — approximately 5 cups*
Metric — 1¼ liters

INGREDIENTS	*U.S. Weight or Volume*	*Metric Weight or Volume*
Vanilla cream powder	¾ to 1 ounce	20 to 30 grams
Sugar	7 ounces	200 grams
Egg yolks	4	4
Milk	1 quart	1 liter
Vanilla extract	2 teaspoons	10 milliliters

PROCEDURE

1. Blend the vanilla cream powder, the sugar, and the egg yolks.
2. Heat the milk to the boiling point, and add it gradually to the sugar and egg mixture.
3. Return the mixture to the saucepan and bring to a boil, stirring constantly.
4. Remove from the heat. Add the vanilla. Stir until cool.

25.5 Sugar Boiling—Cuisson de sucre

Sugar boiling is divided into two parts:
The preparations
The phases of sugar boiling

1. The unsaturated sugar solutions (syrup): 1° to 28° Baume
2. The saturated sugar solution: 29° Baume
3. The supersaturated sugar solutions: 84° Reaumur to 130° Reaumur or 221°F. (105°C.) to 324°F. (162.5°C.)

A solution is composed of two parts:

- *the solute* or the dissolved substance
- *the solvent* or the substance in which the solute is dissolved

In a sugar solution, the sugar is the solute, and water, unless otherwise stated, is the solvent. The degree of solubility in a sugar solution will vary with the amount and kind of sugar, the amount and kind of solvent, and the temperature. Sugars are usually more soluble at higher temperatures.

1. *An unsaturated sugar solution* (syrup) is one in which more sugar can be dissolved in the solvent at a given temperature. These solutions remain liquid when cooled. They are measured with the Baume sugar scales and can be measured when cold. In theory, hot supersaturated solutions can be measured this way; however, the sugar scale does not function properly with thick liquids. The addition of 3 to 5 percent glucose will prevent crystallization.

2. *A saturated sugar solution* (clarified sugar) at 29° Baume refers to a solution which after cooling, crystallizes slowly if no glucose is added. It is one in which the solvent can absorb no more sugar at the given temperature. Five percent glucose should be added to prevent crystallization. Saturated syrup can be stored and used when diluted with liquids, such as water or liquors. The saturated sugar solution is also the basis from which supersaturated sugar solutions are made.

3. *A supersaturated sugar solution* is one that contains more sugar than the solution would normally hold at a given temperature. After cooling, this solution will solidify into a firm, crystalline form. The excess sugar is capable of crystallizing out of the solution. Depending on the use, an addition of 5 to 20 percent glucose is necessary to prevent crystallization. These solutions are too thick to be measured by a Baume sugar scales. A Reaumur or Fahrenheit sugar thermometer should be used.

The Preparation and Boiling of Sugar

The following equipment is needed to prepare sugar syrups: Baume sugar scales, sugar thermometer, saucepan, a brush, and a container for storing the sugar solution (saturated syrups should not be hermetically sealed). Combine the water and sugar in a saucepan and, if necessary, add glucose. Stir frequently to dissolve the sugar crystals. Measure with the sugar scales or the thermometer to test the degree of doneness. Dip the brush in water and moisten the sides of the pan to wash down and dissolve any sugar crystals. The solution should be clear and colorless. A *saturated syrup* made from *3 pounds (1.36 kilograms) of sugar and 1 quart (1 liter) of water* is required for making supersaturated sugar solutions. Further boiling reduces the moisture and increases the concentration of sugar in the solution. The degree of doneness can be measured most accurately by use of a thermometer.

TABLE 25-1 The Phases of Sugar Boiling

	Basis for:
I 1° to 28° Baume = unsaturated sugar solutions (syrup) for immediate use	
1. 1-¼ pounds (567 grams) sugar in 1 quart (1 liter) boiling water = syrup at about 15° Baume	*dipping sponge biscuits*
2. 1-½ pounds (780 grams) sugar in 1 quart (1 liter) boiling water = syrup at about 20° Baume	*fruit icing*
3. 2 pounds (907 grams) sugar in 1 quart (1 liter) boiling water = syrup at about 25° Baume	*glazed fruits*
Cold solutions register about 2° to 5° Baume higher	
II 29° Baume = saturated sugar solution (clarified sugar syrup) suitable for keeping 3 pounds (1,361 grams) sugar in 1 quart (1 liter) boiling water = clarified sugar syrup at about 29° Baume	*Clarified sugar syrup for keeping and as the raw material for boiling supersaturated sugar solutions*

III a) 84°R. to 130°R. or 221°F. to 324°F. (105°C. to 162°C.) = supersaturated sugar solutions

1. Small thread	=	84°R. or 220°F. (106°C.)	According to the application, add 5% to 20% glucose
2. Large thread	=	86°R. or 225.5°F. (107°C.)	
3. Little souffle	=	89°R. or 232.5°F. (111°C.)	
4. Large souffle	=	90°R. or 234.5°F. (113°C.)	
5. Soft ball	=	92°R. or 239.0°F. (115°C.) ←	*Italian Meringue 92°R. to 97°R.*
6. Medium ball	=	94°R. or 243.5°F. (117°C.) ←	*Fondant 94°R. to 97°R.*
7. Firm ball	=	97°R. or 250.0°F. (121°C.)	
8. Soft crack	=	100°R. or 257.0°F. (125°C.)	
9. Medium crack	=	113°R. or 286.0°F. (141°C.)	
10. Hard crack	=	115°R. or 291.2°F. (144°C.) ←	*Spun sugar 115°R.* / *Pulled sugar 121°R.*
11. Caramelized sugar	=	122°R. or 306.5°F. (152°C.) ←	*Caramelized sugar 122°R.*
12. Burned sugar	=	130°R. or 324.5°F. (162°C.) ←	*Color sugar 130°R.*

III b) The finger test for supersaturated sugar solutions

1. *Small thread:* Dip the thumb and index finger into cold water, then into the hot syrup; the doneness is determined by the thread formed. Take a drop of the sugar solution between the thumb and index finger. When pulled apart a very fine thread forms.
2. *Large thread:* Repeat the test and the sugar solution will form a strong thread between the thumb and finger when they are separated.
3. *Little souffle* (blow): Dip a wire ring into the sugar solution. A thin skin forms over the ring; blow on the skin and when a bubble forms this stage is reached.
4. *Large souffle* (feather): Repeat the blow test and the bubbles will hang together.
5. *Soft ball:* Drop a half teaspoon of syrup into cold water; the sugar solution forms a small lump, and a soft ball can be formed with the fingers.
6. *Medium ball:* Follow the preceding test and the sugar solution will form a firmer lump in water than the soft stage; a firmer ball can be formed with the fingers than the soft ball test.
7. *Firm ball:* The sugar solution forms a firmer lump when dipped into cold water; a firm ball can be formed with the fingers.
8. *Soft crack:* The sugar solution tested in water breaks into threads that can be bent. The syrup sticks to the teeth when bitten.
9. *Medium crack:* The sugar solution spins threads as it flows from a spoon; very sharp crack between the teeth when bitten.
10. *Hard crack:* The sugar solution tested in water breaks into hard brittle threads that break like glass.
11. *Caramelized sugar:* The sugar solution turns golden yellow when the sweet caramel stage is reached.
12. *Burned sugar:* The sugar solution is bitter tasting, burned, and very dark brown or black. It is used as food coloring.

Fondant Icing (Fondant)

YIELD: *U.S. — approximately 15 pounds*
Metric — 6.8 kilograms

INGREDIENTS	*U.S. Weight or Volume*	*Metric Weight or Volume*
Sugar	12 pounds	6 kilograms
Glucose	1¼ pounds	600 grams
Water	2 quarts	2 liters

PROCEDURE

1. Boil the sugar, glucose, and water. Cool slightly by adding a little cold water. Skim and strain. Bring to a boil again, cool with a little water, skim and strain again. Repeat the procedure 6 times.
2. Place the syrup back over a high flame and continue boiling. Wipe the sides of the pan frequently with a wet brush to remove any sugar crystals that have formed.
3. When the sugar solution reaches 250°F. (121°C.) or 97° Reaumur, pour it onto a wet marble slab.
4. Cool. Work the fondant with a spatula by lifting and folding it from the edges to the center until it turns milky and then white.
5. Work it even more vigorously as it begins to thicken until it is very smooth and creamy.
6. Cover with a damp cloth and store in an airtight container.
7. When using, heat the necessary quantity in a bain-marie.

Note: Fondant is used to make fine pralines, candies, and icing. Flavor as desired.

Confectioners' Sugar Icing (Glace au sucre en poudre)

YIELD: *U.S. — ⅔ cup*
Metric — 160 milliliters

INGREDIENTS	*U.S. Weight or Volume*	*Metric Weight or Volume*
Egg whites	2	2
Sugar, confectioners'	½ cup	120 grams
Flavoring	as desired	as desired

PROCEDURE

1. Mix egg whites, confectioners' sugar, and flavoring until the mixture becomes glossy and can be drawn into a ribbon.

Royal Icing (Glace royale)

YIELD: *U.S. — ⅔ cup*
Metric — 160 milliliters

INGREDIENTS	*U.S. Weight or Volume*	*Metric Weight or Volume*	PROCEDURE
Egg whites	2	2	1. Combine the egg whites and confectioners' sugar.
Sugar, confectioners'	10 ounces	300 grams	
Lemon juice	few drops	few drops	2. Add lemon juice and 1 to 2 drops of acetic acid.
Acetic acid (vinegar essence)	1 to 2 drops	1 to 2 drops	

Note: The finished icing should always be white, glossy, smooth, and stiff. Keep covered until used.

Water Icing (Glace a l'eau)

YIELD: *U.S. — approximately ⅔ cup*
Metric — 160 milliliters

INGREDIENTS	*U.S. Weight or Volume*	*Metric Weight or Volume*	PROCEDURE
Sugar, confectioners'	7 ounces	200 grams	1. Blend confectioners' sugar and syrup until it becomes a thick, glossy mixture.
Thin sugar syrup at 15° Reaumur	2 tablespoons	30 milliliters	

Hot Desserts—Entremets chauds

26

26.1 Souffles

Souffles are especially susceptible to dropping temperature and are, therefore, served in the cocottes (straight-sided ovenproof souffle dish) in which they were baked. Accurate baking temperatures and proper beating of the egg whites (the stiff but not dry stage) are essential for delicate tender souffles.

Vanilla Souffle (Souffle a la vanille)

YIELD: *approximately 10 servings*

INGREDIENTS	*U.S. Weight or Volume*	*Metric Weight or Volume*
Milk	1 pint	5 deciliters
Sugar	4½ ounces	125 grams
Butter	3½ ounces	100 grams
Flour	3½ to 4¼ ounces	100 to 120 grams
Egg yolks	8	8
Vanilla extract	2 teaspoons	10 milliliters
Egg whites	8 to 10	8 to 10
Sugar, confectioners'	as needed to dust tops	as needed to dust tops

PROCEDURE

1. Place the milk and sugar in a saucepan and heat to the boiling point.
2. In a second pan, melt the butter and the flour. Mix until smooth.
3. Pour the boiling milk over the butter and flour mixture and stir constantly. Remove from the heat. Cool slightly.
4. Beat the egg yolks until light. Stir them into the cooked mixture. Add vanilla.
5. Butter the souffle dish or dishes and dust with flour. Pour the souffle mixture into the souffle dish.
6. Just before baking, carefully fold in the stiffly beaten egg whites.
7. Place the baking dishes in a waterbath and heat on the range for a few minutes to warm the mixture.

(continued on next page)

8. Place the baking dishes in the oven at 325°F. (163°C.). Halfway through the baking time increase the temperature to 350°F. (175°C.). The approximate baking times are: 10 individual souffles for 8 to 10 minutes; two 7 to 8 inch (17.5 to 20 centimeters) souffles for 20 to 30 minutes; one 10 to 12 inch (25 to 30 centimeters) souffle for 35 to 45 minutes. After the souffle has risen, test for doneness by inserting a long needle. It should come out clean.
9. When done, dust with confectioners' sugar and serve at once. A Cream or Fruit Sauce may be served with the souffle. **(See Illustration page 500.)**

Variations of Vanilla Souffle

Almond Souffle—Souffle aux amandes. Combine 3½ ounces (100 grams) of almonds that have been peeled, finely chopped, and lightly browned with 10 ounces (280 grams) of ground almonds and 1 cup (237 milliliters) of milk. Fold the almond mixture into 1 quart (1 liter) of uncooked Vanilla Souffle. Finish as described in the recipe for Vanilla Souffle.

Cherry Souffle—Souffle aux cerises. Flavor 1 quart (1 liter) of Vanilla Souffle mixture with kirsch and lemon juice and add 9 ounces (250 grams) of pitted cherries. Finish as described in recipe for Vanilla Souffle.

Chocolate Souffle—Souffle Suchard. Add 9 ounces (250 grams) of melted baking chocolate to a Vanilla Souffle. Follow procedure described in recipe for Vanilla Souffle.

Hazelnut Souffle—Souffle aux avelines. Mix 1 quart (1 liter) of Vanilla Souffle with 12 ounces (335 grams) of hazelnut praline. Finish as described in the recipe for Vanilla Souffle.

Lemon Souffle—Souffle au citron. Flavor Vanilla Souffle mixture with lemon juice and grated lemon peel. Finish as described in recipe for Vanilla Souffle.

Mocha Souffle—Souffle au mocca. Flavor Vanilla Souffle mixture with mocha extract (instant coffee). Finish as described in recipe for Vanilla Souffle.

Praline Souffle—Souffle au praline. Mix almond praline into the Vanilla Souffle, pour into the cocottes, and sprinkle with praline mixture. Finish as described in recipe for Vanilla Souffle.

Rothschild Souffle—Souffle Rothschild. Add pitted cherries and strawberries to a Lemon Souffle. Follow procedure described for Strawberry Souffle.

Strawberry Souffle—Souffle aux fraises. Flavor Vanilla Souffle mixture with lemon juice and pureed strawberries. Finish as described in recipe for Vanilla Souffle. After half the baking time, arrange a circle of strawberries on the top.

26.2 Hot Puddings—Puddings chauds

26.2.1 Molded Puddings—Puddings demoules

Molded puddings are turned out and served on a dish covered with a paper napkin. These puddings are baked and served as described in the recipes for souffles. Puddings in large cocottes should be baked about 30 minutes and those in individual cocottes about 10 minutes.

Saxon Pudding (Pudding Saxon)

YIELD: *approximately 10 servings*

INGREDIENTS	*U.S. Weight or Volume*	*Metric Weight or Volume*
Milk	1 pint	5 deciliters
Sugar	4½ ounces	125 grams
Vanilla bean	1	1
Butter	3½ ounces	100 grams
Flour	4½ ounces	125 grams
Egg yolks	8	8
Lemon rind, grated	1 teaspoon	6 grams
Lemon juice	2 tablespoons	¼ deciliter
Raisins	1¾ ounces	50 grams
Egg whites	8	8

PROCEDURE

1. Place the milk, vanilla bean, and sugar in a saucepan and heat to the boiling point. Remove from heat, cover, and steep for 20 minutes. Remove vanilla bean.
2. In a second pan, melt the butter and the flour. Mix until smooth.
3. Pour the milk over the butter and flour mixture and stir well while it is still over the heat. Remove from the heat and cool slightly.
4. Beat the egg yolks until light. Stir the grated lemon rind, lemon juice, and the raisins into the cooked mixture.
5. Butter a smooth-walled pudding mold and coat with flour. Pour the pudding mixture into the mold.
6. Just before baking, carefully fold in the stiffly beaten egg whites.
7. Place the mold in a waterbath and heat slowly on the range until the mixture is thoroughly warmed.
8. Place the pudding (still in its water bath) in the oven at 350°F. (175°C.) and bake until done, approximately 35 to 45 minutes.
9. Invert the pudding onto a dish covered with a paper doily.
10. Serve a rich fruit sauce separately or serve a cream sauce (vanilla, mocha, caramel, or chocolate) over it.

Variations of Saxon Pudding

Almond Souffle Pudding—Pudding souffle aux amandes. Blend almonds into the pudding mixture as specified under Almond Souffle. Finish as described in the recipe for Saxon Pudding. Serve a Praline Sauce separately.

Cherry Souffle Pudding—Pudding souffle aux cerises. Add 4 ounces (60 milliliters) of kirsch and 9 ounces (250 grams) of pitted cherries to the Saxon Pudding mixture. Serve a Fruit Sauce separately.

Hazelnut Souffle Pudding—Pudding souffle aux avelines. Blend hazelnuts into the Saxon Pudding. Serve Praline Sauce separately.

Regency Pudding—Pudding souffle regence. Coat the molds with caramel, fill with the pudding mixture, and finish as described in recipe for Saxon Pudding. Serve Caramel Sauce separately.

Royal Pudding—Pudding souffle royale. Line the buttered molds with thin slices of biscuits roules. Fill with Saxon Pudding mixture and bake. Serve Apricot Sauce separately.

Sans-Souci Pudding—Pudding souffle Sans-Souci. Saute diced apples in butter and add to the Saxon Pudding mixture. Pour pudding into molds and bake. Serve Vanilla Sauce separately.

Strawberry Souffle Pudding—Pudding souffle aux fraises. Add some pureed strawberries and a few sliced strawberries to the Saxon Pudding mixture. Serve a Strawberry Sauce separately.

Pudding, Diplomat Style (Pudding diplomate)

YIELD: *approximately 10 servings*

INGREDIENTS	*U.S. Weight or Volume*	*Metric Weight or Volume*
Milk	1½ pints	8 deciliters
Sugar	4¼ ounces	120 grams
Vanilla bean	1	1
Eggs	5	5
Raisins	1¾ ounces	50 grams
*Sponge cake, diced	7 ounces	200 grams
Orange peel, candied	1¾ ounces	50 grams
OR		
Lemon peel, candied		
Rum	¾ ounce	20 grams

PROCEDURE

1. Heat the milk, vanilla bean, and sugar to the boiling point. Cover and steep for 20 minutes. Remove vanilla bean.
2. Beat the eggs slightly and add the hot milk gradually.
3. In a separate bowl, mix the raisins, sponge cake, and candied peel. Pour in the rum. Then add the milk and egg mixture.
4. Butter the molds. Line the bottoms with buttered, greaseproof paper. Carefully pour in the sponge cake mixture.
5. Place the molds in a waterbath and bake the pudding in the oven at 350°F. (175°C.) for 35 to 45 minutes (if it is one large mold) or until a knife or long needle inserted into the center of the pudding comes out clean.
6. When done, turn out of mold.
7. Serve a Vanilla or Fruit Sauce separately.

*Crumbs of Ladyfingers (Biscuit de Champagne) may be used.

Note: The cake can be replaced by cubes of plain dinner rolls. In this case, add 7 ounces (200 grams) of sugar.

Frankfurt Pudding (Pudding francfort)

YIELD: *approximately 10 servings*

INGREDIENTS	*U.S. Weight or Volume*	*Metric Weight or Volume*
Butter	7 ounces	200 grams
Sugar	9 ounces	250 grams
Egg yolks	12	12
*Sponge cake crumbs, dried and sifted	7 ounces	200 grams
Almonds, unpeeled, finely grated	7 ounces	200 grams
Cinnamon, ground	½ teaspoon	3 grams
Raisins (optional)	3 to 4 ounces	100 grams
Egg whites	12	12
Bread crumbs	as needed	as needed

PROCEDURE

1. Whip the butter and sugar until creamy.
2. Add egg yolks gradually.
3. Add sponge cake crumbs, almonds, and cinnamon. Add raisins if desired.
4. Beat the egg whites until stiff but not dry and carefully fold them into the mixture.
5. Butter the pudding mold and sprinkle the mold with bread crumbs. Turn the mixture into the mold.
6. Place the mold in a waterbath. Bake in the oven at 350°F. (175°C.) for about 30 to 35 minutes.
7. Invert pudding onto plate. Serve a Red Wine Sauce (page 529) on the side.

*Crumbs of Ladyfingers (Biscuit de Champagne) may be used.

Rice Pudding (Pudding souffle au riz)

YIELD: *approximately 10 servings*

INGREDIENTS	*U.S. Weight or Volume*	*Metric Weight or Volume*
Rice	3½ ounces	100 grams
Milk	1 pint (more if needed)	5 deciliters (more if needed)
Vanilla bean	1	1
Sugar	3½ ounces	100 grams
Butter	1½ ounces	40 grams
Raisins	1¾ ounces	50 grams
Lemon rind, grated	1 teaspoon	6 grams
Egg yolks	8	8
Sponge cake crumbs	7 ounces	200 grams
Egg whites	8 to 10	8 to 10

PROCEDURE

1. Wash the rice thoroughly. Drain.
2. Combine the milk and vanilla bean and heat to the boiling point. Cover and steep for 20 minutes. Remove vanilla bean.
3. Combine the rice and milk and cook for approximately 30 minutes.
4. Add the sugar.
5. If the mixture becomes too thick, add a little more milk. Cool slightly.
6. Add the butter, raisins, lemon rind, and beaten egg yolks.
7. Butter the molds and coat with dried sponge cake crumbs.
8. Beat the egg whites until stiff but not dry. Carefully fold them into the pudding mixture.
9. Pour the pudding into the molds. Place them in a hot waterbath.
10. Bake in oven at 350°F. (175°C.) for 35 to 45 minutes (if it is one large mold) or until a long needle inserted into the center of the pudding comes out clean.
11. Remove from oven and turn out of mold.
12. Serve as quickly as possible.
13. Serve a Vanilla or Fruit Sauce separately.

Variation of Rice Pudding

Rice Pudding with Caramel—Pudding de riz au caramel. Coat the molds with caramel and finish the pudding as described in the recipe for Rice Pudding. Serve a Vanilla Sauce separately.

26.2.2 English Puddings—Puddings anglais

English puddings are served in the special pudding dishes in which they are baked. Puddings are popular in England and are usually served with fruit syrup or stewed fruit.

Bread and Butter Pudding

YIELD: *approximately 10 servings*

INGREDIENTS	*U.S. Weight or Volume*	*Metric Weight or Volume*
Bread, sliced thin	7 ounces	200 grams
Butter	3½ ounces	100 grams
Vanilla bean	1	1
Milk	1½ pints	8 deciliters
Eggs	4 to 5	4 to 5
Sugar	4¼ ounces	120 grams
Raisins	1¾ ounces	45 grams
Butter	2 ounces	50 grams
Sugar, confectioners'	1 tablespoon	20 grams

PROCEDURE

1. Coat thin slices of bread with melted butter and place them overlapping in a buttered pudding dish.
2. Combine the milk and vanilla bean and heat to the boiling point. Add milk slowly to the eggs and sugar.
3. Sprinkle the raisins over the bread.
4. Slowly pour the milk mixture over the bread.
5. Top with a few flakes of butter.
6. Place the pudding dish in a waterbath and bake in an oven at 350°F. (175°C.) for about 45 minutes until a light crust forms.
7. Sprinkle with confectioners' sugar before serving.

Custard Pudding

See page 481.

Rice Pudding, English Style (Pudding de riz a l'anglaise)

YIELD: *approximately 10 servings*

INGREDIENTS	*U.S. Weight or Volume*	*Metric Weight or Volume*
Rice	5 ounces	150 grams
Milk	1 quart	1 liter
Vanilla bean	1	1
OR		
Lemon rind, grated	1 teaspoon	6 grams
Sugar	4¼ ounces	120 grams
Eggs	2	2
Butter	1¾ ounces	50 grams
Sugar, confectioners'	1 tablespoon	20 grams

PROCEDURE

1. Wash the rice thoroughly. Drain.
2. Heat the milk and vanilla bean to the boiling point. Cover and steep for 20 minutes. Remove vanilla bean. (Lemon rind may be substituted). Add the rice to the milk and boil for about 35 minutes. If necessary, add a little more milk.
3. Combine the sugar and eggs and add to the milk and rice mixture.
4. Pour the mixture into a buttered baking dish. Top with a few flakes of butter.
5. Place the baking dish in a waterbath. Bake at 350°F. (175°C.) for about 35 to 40 minutes until the pudding is golden-yellow.
6. Dust with confectioners' sugar.
7. Serve a stewed fruit or a fruit sauce with this pudding if desired.

Variations of Rice Pudding, English Style

Semolina Pudding, English Style—Pudding de semoule a l'anglaise. Combine 1 quart (1 liter) of milk with 1 vanilla bean and heat to the boiling point. Cover and steep 20 minutes. Remove vanilla bean. Add 5 ounces (150 grams) of semolina to the hot milk. Cook for 10 minutes and finish as described in the recipe for Rice Pudding, English Style.

Tapioca Pudding, English Style—Pudding au tapioca a l'anglaise. Combine 1 quart (1 liter) of milk and 1 vanilla bean and heat to the boiling point. Cover and steep 20 minutes. Remove vanilla bean. Add 5 ounces (150 grams) of tapioca to the hot milk. Cook for 10 minutes and finish as described in the recipe for Rice Pudding, English Style.

26.3 Desserts Made with Leavened Dough—Entremets a la pate levee

Creole Savarin (Savarin au Rhum)

YIELD: *approximately 10 servings*

INGREDIENTS	*U.S. Weight or Volume*	*Metric Weight or Volume*	PROCEDURE
Dough			
Yeast	¾ ounce	20 grams	1. Dissolve the yeast in the lukewarm milk and mix in a little flour until a soft dough is formed. Cover and allow this starter dough to rise in a warm place until double in bulk.
Milk, lukewarm	½ cup	1 deciliter	
Flour	12 ounces	350 grams	
Butter, kneaded	5 ounces	150 grams	2. Combine the kneaded butter and sugar and blend. Add all the other ingredients and work into a dough. This must then be slapped by hand until bubbles form. Mix in the starter dough and once more slap the mixture hard for several minutes.
Sugar	½ ounce	15 grams	3. Butter a ring shaped mold and dust with flour. Fill ⅓ full with dough. Cover and let rise in a warm place until mold is filled.
Eggs	4	4	4. Bake in oven at 450°F. (230°C.) for 20 minutes until it is golden yellow.
Salt	¼ ounce	5 grams	5. Turn out and allow to cool.
Lemon rind, grated	½ teaspoon	3 grams	
Syrup			
Black tea	¾ cup	2 deciliters	1. Place all ingredients for the syrup except the rum in a saucepan and bring to a boil.
Water	¾ cup	2 deciliters	2. Remove from heat. Strain. Add the rum.
Sugar	9 ounces	250 grams	3. When Savarin is to be served, soak it in this hot syrup then place on a platter and coat with apricot jam.
Lemon peel	from 1 lemon	from 1 lemon	4. Serve a Vanilla or Fruit Sauce separately.
Orange peel	from 1 orange	from 1 orange	
Clove, whole	1	1	
Cinnamon, stick	¼ stick	¼ stick	
Rum	¾ cup	2 deciliters	
Apricot jam	4 ounces	120 grams	

Variations of Creole Savarin

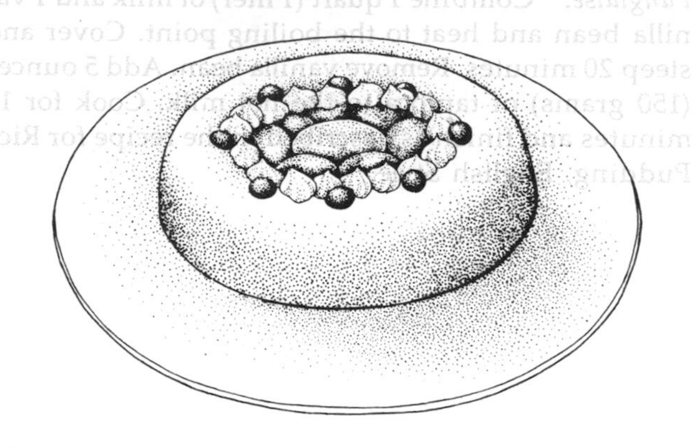

FIGURE 26-1
Savarin with Fruit (hot)—Savarin aux fruits (chaud)

Savarin Chantilly (cold)—Savarin Chantilly. Prepare the savarin as described in the recipe for Creole Savarin. After soaking in hot syrup, cool the savarin on a serving plate. Just before serving, fill with sweetened, vanilla-flavored whipped cream.

Savarin with Chocolate Pears (cold)—Savarin aux poires Suchard. Finish the savarin as described under Creole Savarin. After soaking in hot syrup, cool the savarin on a serving platter. Fill with stewed pears and coat with a creme mousseline mixed with chocolate.

Savarin with Fruit (hot)—Savarin aux fruits. Finish the savarin as described under Creole Savarin. Soak in hot syrup, arrange on a serving plate, and fill with stewed apricots, peaches, or cherries. Coat with apricot jam. Serve a Fruit Sauce separately.

Jelly Doughnuts (Boules de Berlin)

YIELD: *30 to 35 doughnuts*

INGREDIENTS	*U.S. Weight or Volume*	*Metric Weight or Volume*
Yeast	1¾ ounces	50 grams
Milk, lukewarm	1¼ cups	3 deciliters
Flour	2¼ pounds	1 kilogram
Sugar	2½ ounces	70 grams
Salt	¾ ounce	20 grams
Lemon rind, grated	1 teaspoon	6 grams
Eggs	3	3
Egg yolks	10	10
Butter	7 ounces	200 grams
Jam	1 ⅛ pounds	½ kilogram

PROCEDURE

1. Dissolve the yeast in half the lukewarm milk.
2. Place the flour in a bowl and make a well in the center. Pour the milk containing the yeast into this well and mix in some of the flour until a soft dough is formed. Dust this starter dough with a little flour and allow it to rise in a warm place until about double in bulk.
3. Mix the sugar, salt, lemon rind, eggs, egg yolks, the remainder of the lukewarm milk, and the flour with the starter dough. Beat it vigorously by hand until bubbles form.
4. Work in the slightly melted butter and beat the mixture a second time until it no longer sticks to the hands. Should the dough be too firm, it may be necessary to add more milk. Should the dough be too soft, more flour can be added.
5. Place the dough in a floured bowl, cover, and allow to rise slightly in a warm place.
6. Dust a pastry board with flour. Place dough on it and roll to ⅓ inch (.8 centimeter) thickness. Cut out rounds

(continued on next page)

about 2 inches (5 centimeters) in diameter. Place a little jam on half the cut rounds, moisten the edges with water, and cover with a second round of dough. Press edges together with fingers to seal thoroughly.

7. Place these balls upside down on a floured cloth. Cover with another floured cloth and allow to rise in a warm place until doubled in size.
8. Deep-fat fry at 370°F. (190°C.). When properly prepared, the jelly doughnuts should have a light-colored ring around the center.
9. Before serving, roll the doughnuts in cinnamon sugar. If the doughnuts are to be served hot as a sweet dish, a Vanilla or Red Wine Sauce may be served separately.

Note: A canned cherry or half a yellow plum (mirabelle) may be used as the filling instead of the jam.

Raised Dumplings (Dampfnudeln)

YIELD: *approximately 30 servings*

INGREDIENTS	*U.S. Weight or Volume*	*Metric Weight or Volume*
Yeast	2 ounces	60 grams
Milk, lukewarm	1 pint	½ liter
Flour	2 pounds	1 kilogram
Sugar	2½ ounces	70 grams
Salt	¾ ounce	20 grams
Lemon rind, grated	1 teaspoon	6 grams
Eggs	4	4
Egg yolks	4	4
Butter	6 ounces	170 grams
Cream, lukewarm	1½ pints	¾ liter

PROCEDURE

1. Dissolve the yeast in half the lukewarm milk.
2. Place the flour in a bowl and make a well in the center. Pour the milk containing the yeast into this well and mix in some of the flour until a soft dough is formed. Dust this starter dough with a little flour and allow it to rise in a warm place until about double in bulk.
3. Mix the sugar, salt, lemon rind, eggs, egg yolks, the remainder of the lukewarm milk, and the flour with the starter dough. Beat vigorously by hand until bubbles form.
4. Work in the slightly melted butter and beat the mixture a second time until it no longer sticks to the hands.
5. Form the dough into egg-sized pieces and round them slightly on a floured board. Place them in a buttered flat pan leaving $^{1}/_{16}$ inch (.15 centimeter) of space between each. Brush each dumpling with butter. Cover the pan and allow dumplings to rise in a warm place.
6. When dumplings are doubled in size, pour on 1½ pints (¾ liter) of warm cream and sprinkle with sugar.
7. Bake at 275°F. (135°C.) for 1 hour or more until they are a golden color.
8. Separate the dumplings before placing on a serving dish. Sprinkle with sugar. Serve a Vanilla Sauce separately.

Rum Baba (Baba au Rhum)

YIELD: *approximately 10 servings*

INGREDIENTS	*U.S. Weight or Volume*	*Metric Weight or Volume*
Dough		
Yeast	¾ ounce	20 grams
Milk, lukewarm	½ cup	1 deciliter
Flour	12 ounces	350 grams
Butter, kneaded	5 ounces	125 grams
Sugar	½ ounce	15 grams
Eggs	3 to 4	3 to 4
Salt	¼ ounce	5 grams
Lemon rind, grated	½ teaspoon	3 grams
Currants, dried	3½ ounces	100 grams
Apricot jam	4 ounces	150 grams

PROCEDURE

1. Dissolve the yeast in the lukewarm milk and mix in a little flour until a soft dough is formed. Cover and allow this starter dough to rise in a warm place until double in bulk.
2. Blend the kneaded butter with the sugar. Add all other ingredients and work into a dough. This must be slapped by hand until bubbles form. Mix in the starter dough and once more slap the mixture hard for several minutes.
3. Butter and flour the baba molds. Use a pastry bag to put the dough into the molds. Cover and allow the dough to rise to ⅔ the height of the mold.
4. Bake in the oven at 350°F. (175°C.) for 45 to 50 minutes until it is golden yellow.
5. Turn out on a rack to cool.
6. Soak the baba in the hot syrup (see below) and coat with apricot jam. Serve an Apricot Sauce separately.

INGREDIENTS	*U.S. Weight or Volume*	*Metric Weight or Volume*
Syrup		
Black tea	¾ cup	2 deciliters
Water	¾ cup	2 deciliters
Sugar	9 ounces	250 grams
Lemon peel	from 1 lemon	from 1 lemon
Orange peel	from 1 orange	from 1 orange
Clove, whole	1	1
Cinnamon, stick	¼ stick	¼ stick
Rum	¾ cup	2 deciliters

1. Place all ingredients for the syrup, except the rum, in a saucepan and heat to the boiling point.
2. Remove from the heat. Strain. Add the rum.

Variations of Rum Baba

Baba Chantilly (cold)—Baba Chantilly. Prepare a Rum Baba, soak in syrup, cool, place on a serving platter, and garnish with whipped cream.

Baba with Sabayon (hot)—Baba au sabayon. Prepare a Rum Baba. Soak in syrup, and serve hot, coated with Sabayon (see page 529). Serve additional Sabayon separately.

26.4 Omelets—Omelettes

Baked Alaska (Omelette surprise)

YIELD: *approximately 10 servings*

INGREDIENTS	*U.S. Weight or Volume*	*Metric Weight or Volume*
Sponge cake	7 ounces	200 grams
Liqueur	¼ cup	½ deciliter
Fruit salad mixture	10 to 14 ounces	300 to 400 grams
Ice cream	1 pint	½ liter
Candied fruit	1¾ ounces	50 grams
Omelette souffle, **(see page 546)**	1 recipe	1 recipe
Sugar, confectioners'	as needed	as needed

PROCEDURE

1. Using about half the sponge cake, place a ½ inch (1.2 centimeters) thick layer on an ovenproof platter.
2. Cut the remainder of the cake in thin slices.
3. Sprinkle liqueur over all the cake.
4. Combine and mix the fruit salad with the ice cream. Arrange on top of the cake.
5. Surround and cover the ice cream with the thin slices of cake.
6. Spread the omelet mixture over the sponge cake and decorate with some of the same mixture and with the candied fruits.
7. Sprinkle with confectioners' sugar and lightly glaze in the oven at 500°F. (240°C.). Watch carefully. Sprinkle with confectioners' sugar again and serve immediately.

Note: A meringue mixture may be used instead of the Omelette souffle.

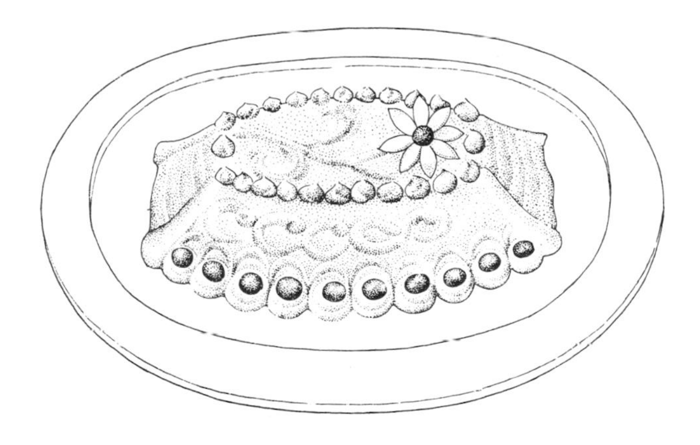

FIGURE 26-2
Baked Alaska—Omelette surprise

Omelet with Jam (Omelette a la confiture)

YIELD: *1 serving*

INGREDIENTS	*U.S. Weight or Volume*	*Metric Weight or Volume*	PROCEDURE
Eggs Salt Sugar	2 to 3 ¼ teaspoon 1 teaspoon	2 to 3 2 grams 6 grams	1. Combine the eggs, salt, and sugar and beat until light.
Butter Jam	as needed 1 tablespoon	as needed ¼ deciliter	2. Heat some butter in a pan. Add the egg mixture and stir. While still liquid, form the eggs into a long oval. Shape and continue frying for a few moments. Then fill with jam and fold over.
Sugar	½ teaspoon	3 grams	3. Turn the omelet out onto a platter and sprinkle with sugar. Then caramelize the sugar on the omelet in a lattice pattern using a red hot iron.

Omelet Souffle (Omelette souffle)

YIELD: *2 servings*

INGREDIENTS	*U.S. Weight or Volume*	*Metric Weight or Volume*	PROCEDURE
Egg yolks Sugar	6 5 ounces	6 150 grams	1. Whip the egg yolks and sugar until creamy.
Egg whites Vanilla extract Lemon rind, grated	8 ½ teaspoon ¼ teaspoon	8 3 milliliters 2 grams	2. Add the stiffly beaten egg whites, vanilla, and lemon rind. 3. Place about ⅔ of the mixture in a long oval baking platter that has been buttered and lightly floured. Form a well in the center. 4. Place the remaining ⅓ of the mixture in a pastry bag and pipe it around the well in a decorative pattern. 5. Dust the souffle with confectioners' sugar and bake in the oven at 350°F. (175°C.) for 10 minutes.
Sugar, confectioners'	as needed	as needed	6. Dust once more with confectioners' sugar and serve immediately.

Omelet Stephanie (Omelette Stephanie)

YIELD: *2 servings*

INGREDIENTS	*U.S. Weight or Volume*	*Metric Weight or Volume*	PROCEDURE
Egg yolks	4	4	1. Whip the egg yolks and sugar until creamy.
Sugar	2¾ ounces	80 grams	2. Fold in the stiffly beaten egg whites and flour alternately.
Egg whites	6	6	
Flour	1½ ounces	40 grams	3. Add cream, melted butter, lemon rind, and vanilla extract.
Cream	2 tablespoons	1/8 deciliter	
Butter, melted	¾ ounce	20 grams	4. Heat the butter in an omelet pan. Pour the omelet mixture into the pan and bake in the oven at 325°F. (160°C.) for 25 minutes or until firm.
Lemon rind, grated	¼ teaspoon	2 grams	
Vanilla extract	½ teaspoon	3 milliliters	
Butter	as needed in omelet pan	as needed in omelet pan	
Strawberry jam	1¾ ounces	50 grams	5. Combine the strawberry jam and liqueur.
Liqueur	½ ounce	15 grams	6. Cover the omelet with the strawberry mixture, fold the omelet, sprinkle with sugar, and serve immediately.

Note: The omelet can be filled with fresh strawberries that have been marinated in sugar and liqueur.

Variations of Omelets

Omelet, Norwegian Style—Omelette norvegienne. See Baked Alaska, page 545.

Rum Omelet—Omelette au Rhum. Prepare the omelet as described in the recipe for Omelet with Jam without adding the jam. Invert the omelet onto a platter, sprinkle with sugar, and caramelize. Pour rum over the top and flambe.

26.5 Pancakes—Crepes

Pancake Butter—Appareil a crepes

See page 522.

Crepes Suzette I

YIELD: *2 servings—3 pancakes each (prepared at the table)*

INGREDIENTS	*U.S. Weight or Volume*	*Metric Weight or Volume*
Sugar cubes	2	2
Orange peel	from 1 orange	from 1 orange
Sugar	1¾ ounces	50 grams
Butter	1¾ ounces	50 grams
Orange juice	¾ cup	2 deciliters
Lemon juice	1 teaspoon	5 milliliters
Grand Marnier	1¾ ounces	50 milliliters
Pancakes	6	6
Brandy	7/8 ounce	5 milliliters

PROCEDURE

1. Rub the sugar cubes over orange peel.
2. Slightly caramelize the sugar and sugar cubes in a flambe pan.
3. Add the butter (do not brown) and deglaze with the orange and lemon juice. Continue stirring until the sugar is completely dissolved.
4. Add the Grand Marnier. Dip each side of the pancakes into the sauce.
5. Fold each pancake into fourths and arrange in the pan. Pour the brandy over the crepes and flambe.
6. Moisten the pancakes once more with the liquid. Serve on plates with remaining liquid.

Crepes Suzette II

YIELD: *10 servings—2 pancakes each (prepared in the kitchen)*

INGREDIENTS	*U.S. Weight or Volume*	*Metric Weight or Volume*
Butter	10 ounces	300 grams
Sugar	10 ounces	300 grams
Orange juice	1¼ cups	3 deciliters
Orange rind, grated	from 4 oranges	from 4 oranges
Lemon juice	¼ cup	½ deciliter
Grand Marnier	5 ounces	150 milliliters
Pancakes	20	20
Sugar	2 tablespoons	30 grams
Brandy	2¾ ounces	75 grams

PROCEDURE

1. Whip the butter and sugar until creamy.
2. Add the orange juice, orange rind, lemon juice, and Grand Marnier and mix well.
3. Spread a thick layer of this cream over the pancakes. Fold each crepe twice and arrange side by side on a warmed silver platter.
4. Sprinkle with sugar. Glaze quickly in a hot oven.
5. Flambe with the heated brandy.

Variations of Crepes

German Pancakes—Pannequets. These pancakes are generally larger and thicker than the crepes, although the same batter is used. German pancakes are baked in the oven and then filled with applesauce, jam, or poached strawberries.

Pancakes, Normandy Style—Crepes a la normande. Stew sliced apples in butter, add white wine, sugar, a few drops of lemon juice, a dash of cinnamon, a few drops of kirsch, and some raisins. Roll the mixture into thin hot pancakes, sprinkle with sugar, and glaze. Serve an Apricot Sauce separately.

Pancakes, Parisian Style I—Crepes a la parisienne. Flavor apricot jam with kirsch and spread on pancakes. Roll the pancakes, arrange on a platter, dust with sugar, and glaze under the broiler.

Pancakes, Parisian Style II—Crepes a la parisienne. Fill the pancakes with a rich fruit salad bound with a thick Vanilla Sauce. Sprinkle with sugar and rum. Brown slightly.

26.6 Fritters—Beignets

Apple Fritters (Beignets de pommes)

YIELD: *approximately 10 servings*

INGREDIENTS	*U.S. Weight or Volume*	*Metric Weight or Volume*
Apples, sour	2½ to 3 pounds	1.2 to 1.5 kilograms
Kirsch	¼ cup	½ deciliter
Sugar	5 ounces	150 grams
Cinnamon, ground	1 teaspoon	6 grams
Frying batter, (recipe 25.1.4)	as needed	as needed
Cinnamon sugar	as needed	as needed
Vanilla Sauce OR Fruit Sauce	1 pint	½ liter

PROCEDURE

1. Peel and core the apples.
2. Cut the apples into thin crosswise rings.
3. Combine the kirsch, sugar, and cinnamon. Add the apple rings and marinate them several hours, turning frequently.
4. Meanwhile prepare the frying batter.
5. Drain the apple rings, dip into the batter, and fry at 320°F. (160°C.).
6. Drain well.
7. Coat with cinnamon sugar and serve immediately.
8. The Vanilla or Fruit Sauce should be served separately.

Note: Moisture or juice accumulates on the cut surface of fresh fruit that has been marinated with sugar. The fruit should be dipped in the batter only in small quantities, otherwise, the batter becomes too thin.

Variations of Fritters

Apricot Fritters—Beignets d'abricots. Cut fresh apricots in half, coat with sugar, and sprinkle with kirsch. Dip the apricots into frying batter and deep-fat fry in hot oil. Coat with cinnamon sugar before serving.

Pineapple Fritters—Beignets d'ananas. Marinate slices of pineapple in sugar and liqueur. Dip into frying batter and deep-fat fry. Coat with cinnamon sugar and serve a Fruit Sauce separately.

Souffle Fritters (Beignets souffles)

YIELD: *10 servings*

INGREDIENTS	*U.S. Weight or Volume*	*Metric Weight or Volume*
Cream puff paste, (recipe 25.1.3)	2 to 3 pounds	1 to 1½ kilograms
Fat	as needed	as needed
Cinnamon sugar	3½ ounces	100 grams
Vanilla Sauce OR Fruit Sauce	1 to 2 pints	½ to 1 liter

PROCEDURE

1. Use a pastry bag to form 1 ounce (28 grams) dumplings of the paste on oiled greaseproof paper.
2. Carefully place the dumplings in the deep-fat fryer and fry slowly at 320°F. (160°C.).
3. Drain excess fat on absorbent cloth or paper.
4. Coat the fritters with cinnamon sugar.
5. Serve at once.
6. Serve the Vanilla or Fruit Sauce separately.

FIGURE 26-3
Souffle Fritters—Beignets souffles

26.7 Rissoles (Turnovers)

Jam Rissoles (Rissoles a la confiture)

YIELD: *10 servings — 2 per serving*

INGREDIENTS	*U.S. Weight or Volume*	*Metric Weight or Volume*
Puff paste, (recipe 25.1.1)	1 to 1¼ pounds	500 to 600 grams
Jam	7 ounces	200 grams
Egg	1	1
Egg yolk	1	1
Sugar, confectioners'	as needed	as needed

PROCEDURE

1. Prepare the puff paste.
2. Roll the paste out on a marble slab dusted with flour.
3. Use a round pastry cutter and cut the dough into 3 inch (7.5 centimeters) circles.
4. Place a teaspoon (4 grams) of rich jam in the center of each disc, brush the edges with beaten egg and fold one half over the other to form semi-circular rissoles.
5. Seal the edges of each rissole.
6. Brush with egg yolk.
7. Place on a dampened baking sheet and allow to stand several minutes.
8. Deep-fat fry at 365°F. (185°C.) or bake at 400°F. (204°C.).
9. When serving, sprinkle with confectioners' sugar.

Variations of Rissoles

Apple Rissoles, Normandy Style—Rissoles a la normande. Stew finely sliced apples in butter with sugar, a little white wine, a few drops of kirsch, lemon juice, and some raisins. Fill the rissoles as described under Jam Rissoles. Serve a Vanilla Sauce separately.

Fruit Rissoles—Rissoles aux fruits. Prepare a salpicon of fresh or canned fruits. Bind with sugar, a few drops of kirsch, and some jam. Prepare the rissoles as described under Jam Rissoles and fill them with the salpicon. Serve a Fruit Sauce separately.

Strawberry Rissoles—Rissoles aux fraises. Mix fresh strawberries with some sugar, kirsch, and a small quantity of strawberry jam. Prepare the rissole as described in the recipe for Jam Rissoles, using this strawberry filling instead of the jam. Serve Strawberry Sauce separately.

26.8 Fruit Toasts—Croutes aux fruits

Pineapple Toasts (Croutes a l'ananas)

YIELD: *10 servings*

INGREDIENTS	*U.S. Weight or Volume*	*Metric Weight or Volume*
Bread, white	10 slices	10 slices
Butter	4 ounces	100 grams
Pineapple slices, canned	15 slices	15 slices
Apricot Sauce, (see page 527)	1 pint	5 deciliters
Cherries	10	10

PROCEDURE

1. Saute the bread in butter until golden.
2. Heat the pineapple in its juice.
3. Arrange 3 half slices of pineapple on a piece of bread.
4. Coat the pineapple with hot Apricot Sauce.
5. Garnish with a red cherry or strawberry and serve.

Variations of Fruit Toasts

Apple Toasts, Normandy Style—Croutes a la normande. Prepare the slices of bread or the zwieback as described in the recipe for Pineapple Toasts. Stew the peeled and sliced apples. Add white wine, a few drops of kirsch and lemon juice, sugar, and raisins. Pour hot fruit onto the toasts, arrange the toasts in a turban shape on a platter, cover with the hot apple mixture, and coat with Apricot Sauce.

Strawberry Toasts—Croutes aux fraises. Prepare the slices of bread or the zwieback as described in the recipe for Pineapple Toasts. Decorate with strawberries that have been poached in sugar syrup and coat with a Strawberry Sauce.

26.9 Hot Desserts with Fruit—Entremets chauds aux fruits

Apple Charlotte (Charlotte de pommes)

YIELD: *approximately 10 servings*

INGREDIENTS	*U.S. Weight or Volume*	*Metric Weight or Volume*	PROCEDURE
Bread, toasting Butter, melted	10 slices 4 ounces	10 slices 100 grams	1. Line the bottom of a timbale with bread that has been cut into a disc and dipped in melted butter. 2. Cut ½ inch (1.2 centimeters) wide strips of bread the same length as the height of the timbale. Dip them in melted butter to line the timbale overlapping them as they are put in place.
Butter	2 ounces	50 grams	3. Heat 2 ounces (50 grams) of butter in a saucepan.
Apples Wine, white Sugar Raisins Cinnamon, ground Cloves, ground Lemon rind, grated	3 pounds ½ cup 10 ounces 1¾ ounces 1/8 teaspoon 1/8 teaspoon ½ teaspoon	1½ kilograms 1 deciliter 300 grams 50 grams 1 gram 1 gram 3 grams	4. Place peeled and finely sliced apples in the saucepan with the wine, sugar, raisins, lemon rind, cinnamon, and cloves. Cook until slightly thickened, stirring constantly. Place the thick part of the mixture in the lined timbale and press down lightly.
Rum	¼ cup	½ deciliter	5. Reduce the remaining liquid from the apple mixture to a syrup-like consistency, flavor with rum, and pour into the mold.
Apricot Sauce, (see page 527)	1 pint	½ liter	6. Place a buttered slice of bread on top and bake in an oven at 375°F. (190°C.) for 30 to 40 minutes. 7. Remove from oven and let the charlotte rest a few minutes. 8. Turn out carefully just before serving. 9. Serve an Apricot Sauce separately.

Note: See illustration, page 500.

FIGURE 26-6
Apple Charlotte—Charlotte de pommes

Apple Roll (Roulade de pommes)

YIELD: *approximately 10 servings*

INGREDIENTS	*U.S. Weight or Volume*	*Metric Weight or Volume*	PROCEDURE
Apples Sugar Lemon juice Cinnamon, ground Butter Wine, white Currants, diced	3 pounds 3 to 5 ounces few drops 1 teaspoon 1¾ ounces ½ cup 4 ounces	1½ kilograms 100 to 150 grams few drops 6 grams 50 grams 1½ deciliters 100 grams	1. Slice the peeled apples and stew in a flat pan with the sugar, lemon juice, cinnamon, butter, white wine, and diced currants. When apples are tender, remove the mixture from the heat and cool.
Sugar pastry (recipe 25.1.6) Egg yolks	1¼ to 1¾ 1 to 2	600 to 800 grams 1 to 2	2. Roll out the sugar pastry into a long strip about 11 inches (27.5 centimeters) wide. 3. Place the apple mixture in the center down the full length of the strip. Fold the sides of the pastry over the mixture, moistening the edges with egg yolk and pressing them together to form a straight seam. 4. Place the roll on a baking tray with the seam downwards. Brush with egg yolk. Garnish with pastry cut-outs as desired. 5. Bake in the oven at 375°F. (190°C.) for about 45 minutes until the crust is golden brown.
Sugar, confectioners'	as needed	as needed	6. To serve, cut into slices and sprinkle with confectioners' sugar.
Vanilla Sauce **(see page 530)** OR Apricot Sauce **(see page 527)**	1 pint	½ liter	7. Serve Vanilla or Apricot Sauce separately.

Apple Strudel

See pages 485, 486.

Apples, Basle Style (Pommes a la baloise)

YIELD: *10 servings*

INGREDIENTS	*U.S. Weight or Volume*	*Metric Weight or Volume*
Apples, medium sized	10	10
Wine, white	¾ to 1¼ cups	2 to 3 deciliters
Sugar	3 to 5 ounces	100 to 150 grams
Butter	3½ ounces	100 grams
Jam	7 ounces	200 grams
Kirsch	¼ cup	½ deciliter
Sugar, confectioners'	as needed	as needed
Almonds, sliced and browned	1¾ ounces	50 grams
Vanilla Sauce, (see page 530)	1 pint	½ liter

PROCEDURE

1. Peel the apples.
2. Using a melon baller, remove the cores without completely cutting through the apples.
3. Place the apples in a flat, buttered dish. Add the white wine.
4. Fill the holes in the apples with sugar and top with a flake of butter.
5. Bake in the oven at 375°F. (190°C.) for 40 to 60 minutes until apples are tender.
6. When serving, fill the apples with jam mixed with the kirsch. In each serving dish, place some of the syrup-like juice from the baking dish.
7. Sprinkle the apples with confectioners' sugar and sliced, browned almonds.
8. Serve a Vanilla Sauce separately.

Apricots with Meringue (Abricots meringues)

YIELD: *approximately 10 servings*

INGREDIENTS	*U.S. Weight or Volume*	*Metric Weight or Volume*
Milk	1 quart	1 liter
Salt	¼ teaspoon	2 grams
Rice	5 ounces	150 grams
Sugar	4¼ ounces	120 grams
Cinnamon, ground	½ teaspoon	3 grams
Vanilla extract	1 teaspoon	5 milliliters
Apricots, cooked	2 to 3 pounds	1 to 1½ kilograms
Meringue, (see page 521)	1 recipe	1 recipe
Apricot Sauce, (see page 527)	1 pint	½ liter

PROCEDURE

1. Heat the milk and salt to the boiling point.
2. Add the blanched rice and cook by the method described for Rice Pudding (page 539).
3. Add the sugar, cinnamon, and vanilla.
4. Spread the rice mixture on a buttered platter.
5. Arrange the apricots on top and cover with meringue. More meringue may be used to decorate the dish if desired.
6. Sprinkle with sugar and bake at 350°F. (175°C.) until lightly browned.
7. Serve the Apricot Sauce separately.

Apples with Meringue—Pommes meringues. Prepare the rice as described in the recipe for Apricots with Meringue. Spread the rice on a buttered platter, top with stewed apples, and cover with the meringue mixture. Sprinkle with sugar and bake at a low temperature. Serve Apricot Sauce separately. See illustration page 592.

Baked Apples, Bonne Femme Style (Pommes au four)

YIELD: *10 servings*

INGREDIENTS	*U.S. Weight or Volume*	*Metric Weight or Volume*	PROCEDURE
Apples, large	10	10	1. Wash the apples. 2. Pare ¼ inch (.50 centimeter) wide strip of apple skin in a spiral pattern from top to bottom. 3. Core the apples.
Sugar Raisins Cinnamon, ground	3½ to 5 ounces 4 ounces ½ teaspoon	100 to 150 grams 100 grams 3 grams	4. Fill the centers with a mixture of sugar, raisins, and cinnamon.
Butter	5 ounces	150 grams	5. Place in a flat, buttered baking dish. Top each apple with a flake of butter.
Wine, white	¾ to 1¼ cups	2 to 3 deciliters	6. Add the wine. 7. Bake in the oven at 375°F. (190°C.) for 40 to 60 minutes until the apples are tender but not mushy.

Baked Apples in Pastry (Pommes en cage)

YIELD: *approximately 10 servings*

INGREDIENTS	*U.S. Weight or Volume*	*Metric Weight or Volume*	PROCEDURE
Apples, medium sized	10	10	1. Peel and core the apples. Fill them with a mixture of sugar and raisins.
Sugar	2¾ to 3½ ounces	80 to 100 grams	2. Roll out the puff paste very thin and cut 5½ inch (13.7 centimeters) squares.
Raisins	1¾ to 2 ounces	50 to 60 grams	3. Place some pastry cream on each square and place an apple on it.
Puff paste, (recipe 25.1.1)	1¼ to 1½ pounds	600 to 700 grams	4. Wrap each apple in the puff paste, moisten the edges with water, and seal covering each apple completely.
Pastry cream (recipe 25.3.5)	1 cup	¼ liter	5. Brush the puff paste with egg yolk, put a round leaf of puff paste on top of each apple, and brush again with the egg yolk.
Egg yolks	1 to 2	1 to 2	6. Bake in the oven at 350°F. (175°C.) for about 45 minutes. Use a needle to test for doneness.
Vanilla Sauce (see page 530)	1 pint	½ liter	7. Serve a Vanilla Sauce separately.

Cut out the squares.

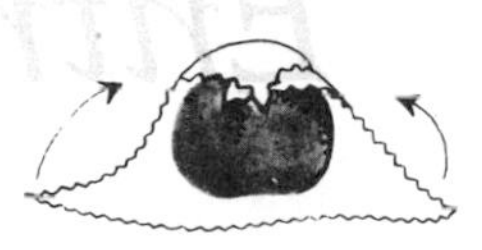

Closing the paste.

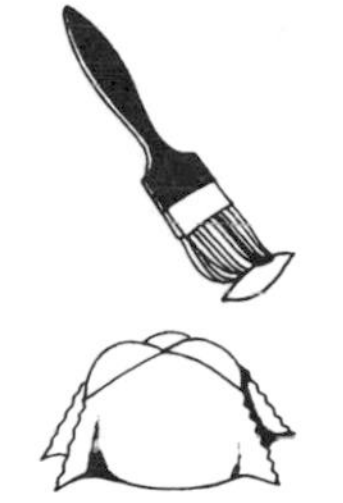

Decorate with puff paste.

Brush with egg yolk.

Test with needle.

Lift out of the dish.

FIGURE 26-7
Baked Apples in Pastry—
Pommes en cage

Pineapple Conde—Ananas Conde. Ingredients for approximately 10 persons: 1 quart (1 liter) of milk, 5 ounces (150 grams) of rice, 4¼ ounces (120 grams) of sugar, 1¾ ounces (50 grams) of butter, 1 vanilla bean, 1 pinch of salt, a little ground cinnamon, 20 small pineapple slices, 10 ounces (300 grams) of apricot jam, approximately 1 pint (½ liter) of Fruit Sauce (see page 527). *Preparation:* Prepare the rice as described under Rice Pudding (see page 539). Spread on a buttered platter, place the pineapple slices on top, and coat with hot apricot jam. Serve Fruit Sauce separately.

Plum Gratin—Gratin aux prunes. Place a round sponge cake or pudding mixture (Semolina Pudding, English Style, Section 26.2.2) in a gratin dish. Cut plums in half and arrange over the cake or pudding. Decorate with meringue or a soft ground almond paste and gratinate in the oven. Stew plums in red wine and serve separately. (See illustration page 592.)

Stewed Fruit Conde—Fruits Conde. Decorate a bed of Rice Pudding with hot stewed fruits and coat with hot apricot jam. Serve Fruit Sauce separately.

Stewed Pears Conde—Poires Conde. Decorate a bed of Rice Pudding with hot stewed pears and cover with melted pear jelly. Serve Fruit Sauce separately.

27 Cold Desserts—Entremets froids

These cold desserts include custards, jellies, puddings, mousses, tarts, cakes, and cookies. The puddings, custards, and tarts may be made in large serving dishes, molds, or pie pans. Many of these desserts may also be made in individual cups, cases, molds, or tart shells. They can be garnished with fruits, chocolate, toasted nuts, whipped cream, or sauces.

27.1 Custards—Cremes renversees

Blancmange (Blanc-manger)

YIELD: *approximately 10 servings*

INGREDIENTS	*U.S. Weight or Volume*	*Metric Weight or Volume*
Milk	1¼ pints	6 deciliters
Salt	¼ teaspoon	2 grams
Gelatin, unflavored	9 ounces	250 grams
Water, cold	½ ounce	14 grams
Almond paste	½ cup	1 deciliter
Vanilla extract	2 teaspoons	10 milliliters
Whipping cream	1¼ cups	3 deciliters

PROCEDURE

1. Heat the milk and salt to the boiling point.
2. Soak the gelatin in ½ cup cold water. Add the gelatin and the almond paste to the hot milk. Stir well until the gelatin is dissolved.
3. Strain through a cheesecloth.
4. Add vanilla.
5. Place the saucepan in cold running water. Stir mixture frequently until cold.
6. As soon as the mixture begins to congeal, fold in the whipped cream and immediately pour into the mold.
7. Chill until thoroughly set. Unmold to serve.

Note: The almond paste can be replaced by almond essence and sugar. A little kirsch may be added if desired.

Variations of Blancmange

Apricots, Favorite Style—Abricots favorite. Stewed apricots are arranged around the bottom of a ring mold. The mold is filled with Blancmange, cooled, and inverted onto a plate. An Apricot Sauce is served on the side.

Surprise Eggs—Oeufs en surprise. A Blancmange mixture is poured into a casserole and allowed to set. Stewed apricot halves are arranged, round side up, on the Blancmange. A few drops of clear syrup are poured over each apricot. A Fruit Sauce is served separately.

Caramel Custard (Creme au caramel)

YIELD: *approximately 10 servings*

INGREDIENTS	*U.S. Weight or Volume*	*Metric Weight or Volume*
Milk	1 quart	1 liter
Eggs	8	8
Salt	¼ teaspoon	2 grams
Sugar	7 ounces	200 grams
Vanilla extract	2 teaspoons	10 milliliters
For Caramel Sauce:		
Sugar	7 ounces	200 grams
Water	¼ cup	115 milliliters

PROCEDURE

1. Heat the milk to the boiling point.
2. Beat the eggs. Add sugar and salt and mix thoroughly.
3. Add the hot milk, stirring constantly.
4. Add the vanilla. Strain.
5. Coat the insides of the custard cups with caramelized sugar. (See note below).
6. Pour the custard into the custard cups.
7. Place the cups or molds on a rack in a pan of hot, but not boiling, water. Poach in the oven at 325°F. (163°C.) for approximately 30 minutes.
8. To test for doneness, insert the tip of a knife into the custard near the edge of the cup. If the blade comes out clean, the custard should be removed from the oven and the waterbath. There is sufficient heat stored in the custard and the cup to complete the cooking process after removal from the oven. The custard will be firm in the center by the time it has cooled.
9. Invert the custard cup onto a platter or individual dessert dishes. The liquid caramel will flow down the sides of the custard. If the custard is thoroughly chilled, it may be necessary to dip the cups, to the depth of the caramel syrup, quickly in hot water so that all the syrup will be released.

FIGURE 27-1
Caramel Custard—Creme renversee au caramel

Note: To caramelize sugar: Heat in a heavy pan over low heat 7 ounces (200 grams) of sugar. Stir constantly with a wooden spoon until sugar is melted. Remove pan from heat and add ¼ cup (115 milliliters) water very slowly and carefully. (Adding water quickly can be very dangerous and may cause an explosive action). Return the pan to low heat and cook until the mixture is golden brown.

Variations of Caramel Custard

FIGURE 27-2
Custard Beau-Rivage—Creme Beau-Rivage

Custard Beau-Rivage—Creme beau-rivage. This is a Caramel Custard baked in a ring-shaped mold. The center is filled with flavored whipped cream. The ring is surrounded with small cream-filled cornets (cornet batter, recipe 25.2.4).

Custard, Florence Style—Creme florentine. This Caramel Custard is poured into a mold which has been coated with caramel. It is poached in the oven, cooled, and inverted onto a serving plate. The center is filled with whipped cream flavored with kirsch.

Royal Custard—Creme royale. This is a Caramel Custard that has been poured into a buttered ring-shaped mold (without the caramel coating). The custard is poached, cooled, and inverted onto a serving dish. The center is filled with whipped cream.

Custard, French Style (Creme a la francaise)

YIELD: *approximately 10 servings*

INGREDIENTS	*U.S. Weight or Volume*	*Metric Weight or Volume*
Milk	1 quart	1 liter
Eggs	6	6
Sugar	5 ounces	150 grams
Salt	¼ teaspoon	2 grams
Vanilla extract	2 teaspoons	10 milliliters
Nutmeg	few grains	few grains
Whipping cream	as needed	as needed

PROCEDURE

1. Heat the milk to the boiling point.
2. Beat the eggs. Add sugar and salt and mix thoroughly.
3. Add the hot milk, stirring constantly.
4. Add the vanilla. Strain.
5. Pour into a baking dish or into individual custard cups.
6. Dust tops with grated nutmeg.
7. Place the molds on a rack in a pan of hot, but not boiling, water. Poach in the oven at 325°F. (163°C.).
8. To test for doneness, insert the tip of a knife into the custard near the edge of the cup. If the blade comes out clean, the custard should be removed from the oven and waterbath. There is sufficient heat stored in the cups to complete the cooking process after removal from the oven. The custard will be firm in the center by the time it has cooled.
9. Garnish with whipped cream.

Variations of Custards, French Style

Apricot Custard in Cocottes—Petits pots de creme aux abricots. This is Custard, French Style, topped with stewed apricot halves, covered with thick Apricot Sauce, and sprinkled with chopped and browned hazelnuts. Surround the apricots with whipped cream.
Fruit Custard in Cocottes—Petits pots de creme jardiniere. This Custard, French Style, is garnished with diced fruits, covered with a thick Apricot Sauce, and decorated with whipped cream.

FIGURE 27-3
Apricot Custard in Cocottes—Petits pots de creme aux abricots

27.2 Bavarian Creams—Cremes bavaroises

Bavarian Cream (Bavarois a la creme)

YIELD: *approximately 10 servings*

INGREDIENTS	*U.S. Weight or Volume*	*Metric Weight or Volume*
Prepared Vanilla Cream (recipe 25.3.1 or 2)	1½ pints	8 deciliters
Gelatin, unflavored	½ ounce	14 grams
Water, cold	½ cup	1 deciliter
Whipping cream	1¾ cups	4 deciliters
Sweet jelly (page 565)	as needed	as needed

PROCEDURE

1. Soak the gelatin in the cold water until dissolved.
2. Add the gelatin to the hot vanilla cream. Cool.
3. Whip the cream.
4. As soon as the vanilla cream begins to congeal, fold in the whipped cream.
5. Coat the inside of the molds with sweet jelly. Chill. Pour the Vanilla Cream into the mold.
6. Refrigerate until firm.
7. Dip the mold in hot water quickly and invert the mold on a chilled plate.

Note: The sweet jelly should be about $^1/_5$ inch (.5 centimeter) deep in the mold and chilled until firm. The cream is then poured into the mold.

Variations of Bavarian Creams

Bavarian Cream with Apple—Bavarois a la normande. This is Bavarian Cream combined with apples that have been stewed with sugar, rum, white wine, and lemon juice. The cream is served with a ring of stewed apple quarters. An Apricot Sauce is served separately.
Chocolate Bavarian Cream—Bavarois Suchard. Crushed chocolate is added and blended into the basic recipe for Bavarian Creams while it is still hot. Sauce Suchard is served separately.

Bavarian Cream, Diplomat Style—Bavarois diplomate. This is a Bavarian Cream combined with sponge cake and fruits that have been drizzled with rum and maraschino. It is inverted onto a serving plate and decorated with whipped cream.

Bavarian Cream with Hazelnuts—Bavarois aux avelines. This is a Bavarian Cream mixed with a finely ground praline mixture (recipe 25.2.6).

Bavarian Cream with Maraschino—Bavarois au marasquin. This Bavarian Cream is flavored with maraschino and a few drops of kirsch.

Bavarian Cream with Mocha—Bavarois au mocca. This is a Bavarian Cream flavored with mocha extract. Mocha Sauce may be served separately.

Neapolitan Bavarian Cream—Bavarois rubane. The Bavarian Cream is divided into equal amounts in three containers. Each is tinted with a different color. One is flavored with vanilla, one with chocolate, and the other with mocha. After each layer is set, the next is poured on. Vanilla Sauce may be served separately.

Charlotte Russe. The base and sides of a mold are lined with ladyfingers (see page 570). A Bavarian Cream that has been flavored with kirsch and maraschino is poured into the mold. After the cream is set, it is inverted onto a serving plate and garnished with whipped cream.

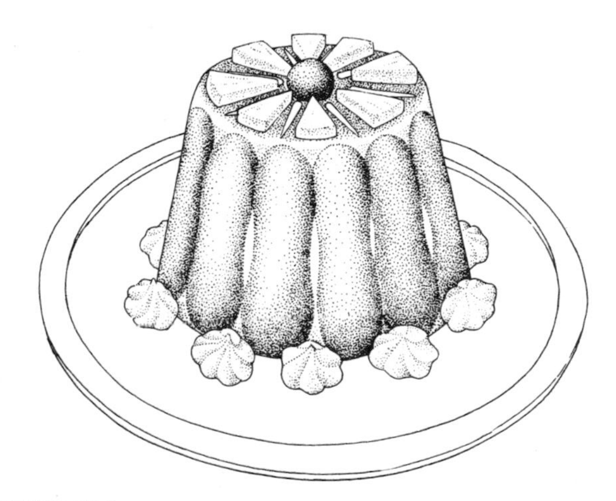

FIGURE 27-4
Charlotte Russe—Charlotte russe

Eugenia Cake with Melba Sauce—Eugenie Melba. A round Genoise sponge cake (recipe 25.2.1) is sliced into 2 layers and filled with the basic Bavarian Cream. The upper side is iced with the same cream and covered with sliced peaches and whipped cream. The cake should be cool before cutting. Melba Sauce is served separately.

Royal Charlotte—Charlotte royale. Thin slices from a 1½ to 2 inch (3.75 to 7 centimeters) thick Jelly Roll (see page 574) are used to line the base and sides of a charlotte mold. The mold is filled with Bavarian Cream that has been flavored with kirsch. After the mold is firm, it is inverted onto a serving plate and garnished with whipped cream.

FIGURE 27-5
Royal Charlotte—Charlotte royale

27.3 Desserts Made with Cream Puff Paste—Entremets a la pate a chou

Cream Puffs—Choux Chantilly. These puffs are prepared from Cream Puff Paste (recipe 25.1.3) which is forced through a pastry tube into walnut-sized balls onto a buttered baking tray. They are brushed with beaten egg yolk and baked in an oven at 400°F. (205°C.) for 15 minutes. When cool, they are slit and filled with whipped cream and sprinkled with sugar. (See illustration, page 594.) *Note:* 2 pounds (1 kilogram) of Cream Puff Paste yields about 50 cream puffs. About 1 teaspoon (5 grams) of whipped cream is allowed per each puff.

Cream Puffs with Pastry Cream—Choux a la creme. These puffs are filled with Pastry Cream or St. Honore Cream (see page 525) and sprinkled with sugar.

Chocolate Eclairs—Eclairs Suchard. These are eclairs with kirsch coated with chocolate icing. (See illustration, page 594.)

Chocolate Profiterolles—Profiteroles Suchard. These are petite cream puffs filled with whipped cream. The cream puffs are arranged in a serving dish, coated with chocolate sauce, and sprinkled with toasted almonds.

Eclairs with Kirsch—Eclairs au kirsch. These eclairs are made from Cream Puff Paste (recipe 25.1.3) which is shaped into finger-length strips and placed on a buttered baking tray. The eclairs are brushed with beaten egg yolk and baked in an oven at 400°F. (205°C.) for 10 minutes. When cool, the eclairs are slit on one side and filled with Pastry Cream or St. Honore Cream (recipe 25.3.6) that has been flavored with kirsch. The eclairs are coated with a kirsch-flavored icing. *Note:* 2 pounds (1 kilogram) of cream puff paste yield about 60 eclairs or 120 profiterolles.

Mocha Eclairs—Eclairs au mocca. These are eclairs with kirsch that have been coated with mocha icing. (See illustration, page 594.)

Saint Honore Cake—Gateau Saint-Honore. This cake is made with Short Crust Pastry and Cream Puff Paste. The Short Crust Pastry (recipe 25.1.2) is shaped into circle 8 inches (20 centimeters) in diameter. These are placed on a baking tray. Cream Puff Paste (recipe 25.1.3) is piped around the rims of the bases. The bases are pierced and baked. On a separate baking sheet, Cream Puff Paste is formed into about 2 dozen hazelnut-sized balls. These are baked in an oven at 375°F. (190°C.). St. Honore Cream (recipe 25.3.6) is spread on the bases of the puffs. The small puffs are dipped into a sugar solution boiled to 84°R = thread stage (see Table 25-1) and immediately placed around the outer ring of the cake. The cake is often garnished with whipped cream and fruits.

27.4 Desserts with Whipped Cream—Entremets a la creme

Chantilly Meringues (Meringues chantilly)

YIELD: *approximately 40 shells (20 servings)*

INGREDIENTS	*U.S. Weight or Volume*	*Metric Weight or Volume*
Egg whites	10	10
Vanilla	1 teaspoon	5 milliliters
Cream of tartar	1/8 teaspoon	½ gram
Sugar	1 pound	500 grams

PROCEDURE

1. Whip the egg whites until foamy. Add the vanilla and cream of tartar.
2. While continuing to whip, add 1 tablespoon (15 milliliters) of the sugar at a time. Whip until mixture forms very stiff peaks.
3. Cover baking sheets with parchment paper. Form meringues with a spoon or put mixture in a pastry bag and pipe onto the baking tray. Dust meringues lightly with granulated sugar.
4. Bake in the oven at 175°F. to 200°F. (80°C. to 93°C.) for 2 to 4 hours, depending on the size. The meringues should dry out rather than bake, and they should not brown.
5. After half the baking time has elapsed, dent the bottom of the meringue.
6. When done, cool. Remove meringues from baking sheet and store in a warm dry place.
7. To serve, fill 2 shells with sweetened and flavored whipped cream. Press the shells together and garnish with more whipped cream.

Note: About 1¾ ounces (55 milliliters) of whipping cream are required per portion.

Chestnuts with Whipped Cream—Vermicelles Chantilly. Chestnuts are shelled, peeled, and simmered in milk with a vanilla bean. Then they are grated and worked into a smooth puree. Sugar syrup, a few drops of kirsch, and milk are added to the puree. It is put into a pastry bag and piped into a circle on a platter. The center is filled with sweetened and flavored whipped cream.

Cornets with Whipped Cream—Cornets Chantilly. These cornets are made from an almond mixture. They are filled with sweetened whipped cream flavored with vanilla.

Whipped Cream—Creme Chantilly. This whipped cream is sweetened with sugar and flavored with vanilla extract.

Whipped Cream with Fruit—Mont-Blanc. Arrange whipped cream on a platter and garnish with fruits that have been marinated in kirsch and sugar. (Strawberries, bananas, peaches, and/or pears.)

Vacherin with Whipped Cream (Vacherin Chantilly)

YIELD: *30 to 40 portions*

INGREDIENTS	*U.S. Weight or Volume*	*Metric Weight or Volume*
Egg whites	10	10
Sugar	1 pound	500 grams
Vanilla	1 teaspoon	5 milliliters
Cream of tartar	1/8 teaspoon	½ gram

PROCEDURE

1. Whip the egg whites until foamy. Add the vanilla and cream of tartar.
2. While continuing to whip, add 1 tablespoon (15 milliliters) of the sugar at a time. Whip until mixture forms very stiff peaks.
3. Cover baking sheet with parchment paper. Fill pastry tube with meringue mixture. Pipe onto tray in lattice pattern to form *cake bases.* It should make 6 or 8 bases.
4. Bake in the oven at 175°F. to 200°F. (80°C. to 93°C.) for 2 to 4 hours, depending on the size. The vacherins should dry out rather than bake, and they should not brown.
5. When done, cool. Remove from baking sheet and store in a warm dry place.
6. To serve, fill 2 shells with sweetened and flavored whipped cream. Press the shells together and garnish with more whipped cream.

Strawberry Vacherin—Vacherin aux fraises. This is Vacherin Chantilly with a filling of whipped cream and strawberries that have been marinated in liqueur and sugar. It is covered with whipped cream and decorated with fresh strawberries.

27.5 Jellies—Gellees

Port Jelly (Gelee au porto)

YIELD: *approximately 2 quarts*

INGREDIENTS	*U.S. Weight or Volume*	*Metric Weight or Volume*
Water	1 quart	1 liter
Egg whites	4	4
Sugar	11¼ ounces	320 grams
Lemon juice	of 2 lemons	of 2 lemons
Lemon rind	from 1 lemon	from 1 lemon
Gelatin, unflavored granular	1 ounce	30 grams
Water, cold	1 cup	¼ liter
White wine	1¼ cups	3 deciliters
White port	¾ cup	2 deciliters

PROCEDURE

1. Place the water, egg whites, sugar, lemon juice, and lemon rind in a saucepan and mix well.
2. Stir continuously and cook to the boiling point.
3. Cover pan, lower the heat, and simmer gently for 10 minutes.
4. Add the soaked gelatin and stir until completely dissolved.
5. Strain the jelly through a cloth.
6. When the jelly is almost cool, add the white wine and the port.

Note: This jelly can be used for lining and coating molds and for jellied fruits. It may be tinted if desired.

Variations of Jelly

White Wine Jelly—Gelee au vin blanc. This is a jelly prepared by the same method used for Port Jelly except 1 pint (480 milliliters) of white wine is used and the port wine is omitted.

Kirsch Jelly—Gelee au kirsch. This is a white wine jelly flavored with kirsch.

27.6 Cold Puddings—Puddings froids

Rice Pudding, Empress Style (Riz a l'imperatrice)

YIELD: *approximately 10 servings*

INGREDIENTS	*U.S. Weight or Volume*	*Metric Weight or Volume*
Rice	3½ ounces	100 grams
Milk	1 pint	½ liter
Sugar	5 ounces	150 grams
Gelatin, unflavored	½ ounce	14 grams
Water, cold	½ cup	1 deciliter
Vanilla	1 teaspoon	5 milliliters
Kirsch	2 tablespoons	30 milliliters
Candied fruits	4 ounces	100 grams
Whipping cream	1 pint	½ liter
White wine jelly (page 000)	¾ cup	2 deciliters
Raspberry syrup (page 000)	as needed	as needed

PROCEDURE

1. Wash the rice thoroughly.
2. Scald the milk. Add the rice to the milk and cook to a thin, smooth consistency.
3. Soak the gelatin in cold water. Add gelatin, sugar, and vanilla to the hot rice mixture. Stir until gelatin is dissolved.
4. Cool. When the mixture begins to congeal, quickly add the kirsch, the fruits, and the whipped cream.
5. Place white wine jelly in individual molds to a depth of $^1/_5$ inch (.5 centimeter). Fill with rice mixture and refrigerate until firm.
6. Dip the molds in hot water for a moment and then invert on a serving dish.
7. Thin raspberry syrup slightly. Serve the syrup separately.

Note: This rice can be served in cups rather than molds. It is then topped with marinated fruits and whipped cream. Raspberry syrup is served separately.

FIGURE 27-6
Rice Pudding, Empress Style—Riz a l'imperatrice

Variations of Rice Pudding, Empress Style

Apricots Sybilla—Abricots Sybille. A thin sponge cake base covered with a layer of Rice Pudding, Empress Style, that has been mixed with finely chopped apricots. It is topped with thin slices of nougat and apricots. An apricot sauce with cherries and almond chips is served separately. This is an elegant and impressive preportioned dessert. (See the illustration, page 593.)

Pineapple, Empress Style—Ananas a l'imperatrice. This is Rice Pudding, Empress Style, which has been poured into ring molds that have been lined with thin slices of pineapple. It is unmolded when cool and served with an Apricot Sauce.

Semolina Victoria—Semoule Victoria. This pudding is prepared in the same way described for Rice Pudding, Empress Style, except 5 ounces (140 grams) of semolina are substituted for the rice and 1 quart (8 deciliters) of milk is used. The pudding is poured into molds that have been lined with jelly. A slightly thinned Raspberry Sauce is served separately.

Apricots, Florence Style—Abricots florentine. This is a Semolina Victoria mixture which has been poured into ring molds. When set, it is turned onto a serving plate and filled with apricot halves, covered with an Apricot Sauce, and sprinkled with chopped and toasted almonds. It may be decorated with whipped cream.

Strawberry Flummery (Flamri aux fraises)

YIELD: *approximately 10 servings*

INGREDIENTS	*U.S. Weight or Volume*	*Metric Weight or Volume*	PROCEDURE
Water	1¼ cups	3 deciliters	1. Combine the water and wine, and heat to the boiling point. Add the semolina slowly and stir constantly. Simmer until the mixture is thick and smooth.
White wine	1¼ cups	3 deciliters	
Semolina	4 ounces	100 to 120 grams	
Egg yolks, beaten	4	4	2. Remove from the heat. Add the egg yolks, sugar, salt, lemon juice, and grated lemon rind. If mixture is *very* thick, it may be necessary to thin with water. Finally fold in the beaten egg whites.
Sugar	4 ounces	120 grams	
Salt	¼ teaspoon	2 grams	
Lemon juice	2 tablespoons	30 milliliters	
Lemon rind, grated	½ teaspoon	4 grams	3. Fill buttered molds and poach in a waterbath in the oven at 325°F. (163°C.) for 40 to 60 minutes until they test done.
Egg whites	6	6	
Fresh strawberries, pureed	1¼ to 1½ pounds	600 to 700 grams	4. Cool. Turn out of molds. Puree the strawberries and combine with sugar and liqueur. Pour the puree over the molds.
Sugar	½ pound	225 grams	
Liqueur	2 tablespoons	30 milliliters	
Strawberries, marinated, fresh whole	to garnish	to garnish	5. Marinate the whole strawberries in liqueur and decorate molds as desired.

27.7 Cookies—Petits-fours

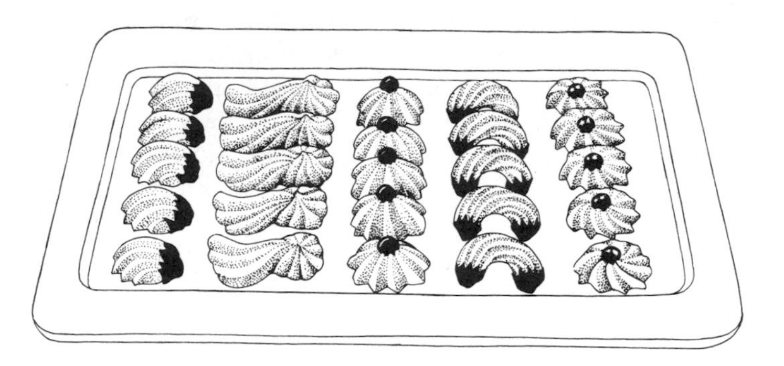

FIGURE 27-7
Cookies—Petits fours

Almond Macaroons (Macarons aux amandes)

YIELD: *approximately 60 macaroons*

INGREDIENTS	*U.S. Weight or Volume*	*Metric Weight or Volume*	PROCEDURE
Almonds, finely ground	9 ounces	250 grams	1. Combine the almonds, confectioners' sugar, and lemon rind.
Sugar, confectioners'	1 pound	500 grams	
Lemon rind, grated	½ teaspoon	3 grams	
Egg whites	3 to 4	3 to 4	2. Add the unbeaten egg whites and blend well. 3. Whip slowly until foamy so the mixture can be put through a pastry tube. 4. Line a cookie sheet with parchment paper. 5. Pipe in small mounds.
Sugar, coarse	1¾ ounces	50 grams	6. Moisten the mounds with a drop of water and sprinkle with coarse sugar. 7. Bake in the oven at 250°F. (120°C.) for 15 minutes. Increase the heat to 300°F. (150°C.) and continue baking about 15 minutes longer until golden brown.

Note: Dried and finely ground nuts may be added. The amount should always be 1 part of nuts to each 2 parts of confectioners' sugar.

Almond Sponge Cake (Biscuits aux amandes)

YIELD: *about 50 cookies*

INGREDIENTS	*U.S. Weight or Volume*	*Metric Weight or Volume*
Butter cookie dough	2 pounds	1 kilogram
Almonds, sliced and lightly toasted	4 ounces	100 grams

PROCEDURE

1. Mix the almonds with the dough.
2. Form into a roll about 1½ inches (3.75 centimeters) in diameter. Chill.
3. Cut the roll into thin slices and place on baking sheet.
4. Bake in oven at 350°F. (177°C.) for approximately 8 minutes.

Butter Cookies (Petit beurre)

YIELD: *about 50 to 60 cookies*

INGREDIENTS	*U.S. Weight or Volume*	*Metric Weight or Volume*
Flour	1 pound	500 grams
Butter	14 ounces	400 grams
Sugar, confectioners'	5 ounces	150 grams
Salt	½ teaspoon	3 grams
Vanilla extract	2 teaspoons	10 milliliters

PROCEDURE

1. Make a well in the flour.
2. Place the butter, confectioners' sugar, salt, and vanilla in the well and mix thoroughly.
3. Work in the flour gradually and knead to a smooth dough.
4. Refrigerate the dough for 1 hour.
5. Roll the dough to ¼ inch (.6 centimeter) thickness on a marble slab dusted with flour. Cut into circles and pierce with a fork.
6. Bake in oven at 375°F. (190°C.) for approximately 8 minutes or until lightly colored.

Note: The following combination of ingredients can be used instead of those given above and the same procedure followed.

Flour	1 pound	500 grams
Butter	10 ounces	300 grams
Sugar, confectioners'	7 ounces	200 grams
Egg yolks	2 to 3	2 to 3
Salt	½ teaspoon	3 grams
Vanilla extract	2 teaspoons	10 milliliters

Cuisses de dames

YIELD: *180 to 200*

INGREDIENTS	*U.S. Weight or Volume*	*Metric Weight or Volume*
Eggs	15	15
Sugar	2 pounds	1 kilogram
Butter	14 ounces	400 grams
Flour	3 pounds	1½ kilograms
Almonds, peeled and finely ground	9 ounces	250 grams
Lemon rind, grated	from 2 lemons	from 2 lemons
Kirsch	1¾ ounces	50 grams
Baking soda	1/8 teaspoon	1 gram

PROCEDURE

1. Combine and blend the eggs and sugar.
2. Cream the butter until it is soft. Add the butter, flour, almonds, lemon rind, kirsch, and baking soda to the egg and sugar mixture.
3. Mix well and knead the dough until firm on a marble slab dusted with flour.
4. Shape into finger-shaped pieces, 3½ to 4 inches (8 to 10 centimeters) long.
5. Fry in deep fat at 370°F. (188°C.).

Ladyfingers (Pelerines)

YIELD: *100 to 120 ladyfingers*

INGREDIENTS	*U.S. Weight or Volume*	*Metric Weight or Volume*
Egg yolks	12	12
Egg whites	15	15
Sugar	9 ounces	250 grams
Flour	7 ounces	195 grams
Salt	½ teaspoon	3 grams
Cornstarch	3½ ounces	100 grams
Lemon peel, grated	1 tablespoon	15 grams

PROCEDURE

1. Beat the egg yolks until thick and lemon-colored.
2. Whip the egg whites until stiff but not dry. Fold the sugar into the egg whites gradually. Whip until thick.
3. Fold in the egg yolks.
4. Sift the flour, salt, and cornstarch together. Fold the dry ingredients into the egg mixture. Add lemon peel.
5. With a pastry tube, pipe the mixture into finger-sized strips on a greased baking sheet that has been sprinkled with sugar.
6. Sprinkle the ladyfingers with sugar and bake in an oven at 375°F. (190°C.) for about 12 minutes.

Note: For drier ladyfingers, see page 519.

FIGURE 27-8
Ladyfingers—Pelerines

Madeleines

YIELD: *40 to 50 madeleines*

INGREDIENTS	*U.S. Weight or Volume*	*Metric Weight or Volume*
Eggs	5	5
Sugar	9 ounces	250 grams
Cake flour, sifted	9 ounces	250 grams
Butter, clarified	9 ounces	250 grams
Lemon rind, grated	2 teaspoons	12 grams

PROCEDURE

1. Combine eggs and sugar in a double boiler and heat *over* boiling water. Stir constantly. Remove from heat and beat until cool and very thick.
2. Fold the flour into the egg mixture.
3. Add the melted butter and lemon rind. Stir until blended.
4. Fill madeleine pans or small muffin tins with the mixture.
5. Bake madeleine forms about 8 minutes; muffin tins 12 to 15 minutes in an oven at 350°F. (177°C.).

Milanese Cookies (Petits milanais)

YIELD: *about 50 to 60 cookies*

INGREDIENTS	*U.S. Weight or Volume*	*Metric Weight or Volume*
Flour	1 pound	500 grams
Sugar	9 ounces	250 grams
Butter	9 ounces	250 grams
Egg yolks	4 to 5	4 to 5
Lemon rind, grated	from 1 lemon	from 1 lemon
Salt	¼ teaspoon	2 grams
Soda	1/8 teaspoon	1 gram

PROCEDURE

1. Make a well in the flour.
2. Combine the sugar, butter, egg yolks, lemon rind, salt, and soda in the well.
3. Work in the flour gradually and knead to a smooth dough.
4. Refrigerate the dough.
5. Roll the dough on a marble slab dusted with flour. Cut shapes as desired. Brush with egg yolks and bake in oven at 375°F. (190°C.) for 8 minutes or until golden color.

Prussian Cookies (Prussiens)

YIELD: *25 to 30 cookies*

INGREDIENTS	*U.S. Weight or Volume*	*Metric Weight or Volume*
Puff paste trimmings	10 ounces	300 grams
Sugar	3 to 4 ounces	80 to 100 grams
Sugar, confectioners'	1¾ ounces	50 grams

PROCEDURE

1. Roll out the puff paste on a sugar-coated board (instead of flour) and fold once with regular puff paste.
2. Roll to a strip 15 inches long (37.5 centimeters) and 8 inches wide (20 centimeters). Roll each long side of the dough towards the center. Place one roll on top of the other and flatten slightly.
3. Cut this double roll into slices. Place each slice on a baking tray and sprinkle lightly with confectioners' sugar.
4. Bake in oven at 375°F. (190°C.) for 8 to 10 minutes. Then turn the cookies over and sprinkle with a little more confectioners' sugar. Continue baking 8 to 10 minutes longer or until firm and golden color.

Vanilla Waffle (Bricelets a la vanille)

YIELD: *approximately 80 to 120 waffles*

INGREDIENTS	*U.S. Weight or Volume*	*Metric Weight or Volume*
Flour	2 pounds	1 kilogram
Butter	14 ounces	400 grams
Sugar	1 pound	500 grams
Eggs	8	8
Salt	½ teaspoon	2 grams
Vanilla	1 tablespoon	15 milliliters
Lemon rind, grated	½ teaspoon	2 grams

PROCEDURE

1. Make a well in the flour.
2. Combine all other ingredients and place in the well.
3. Work the flour into the mixture little by little until smooth dough is formed.
4. Shape the dough into walnut-sized balls and bake in a French waffle iron until golden color.

27.8 Cakes—Gateaux

Black Forest Cake (Tourte de la foret noire)

YIELD: *1 cake (12 to 16 servings)*

INGREDIENTS	*U.S. Weight or Volume*	*Metric Weight or Volume*	PROCEDURE
Cocoa Flour	1 ounce 2½ ounces	30 grams 75 grams	1. Combine cocoa and flour.
Eggs Sugar Cornstarch Butter Sugar syrup Kirsch	5 5 ounces 2½ ounces 1¾ ounces ½ cup 2 teaspoons	5 150 grams 75 grams 50 grams 1 deciliter 10 milliliters	2. Prepare the cake batter as described for sponge cake. (recipe 25.2.2.) 3. Bake in a 1¼ inch (3 centimeters) deep cake pan in an oven at 350°F. (177°C.) for 20 to 25 minutes. 4. When cool, cut the cake into 3 layers. 5. Combine the sugar syrup and kirsch. 6. Moisten the bottom layer and the top layer with the kirsch-sugar syrup.
Whipping cream	1 pint	½ liter	7. Spread whipped cream over the bottom layer of the cake to a thickness of ¼ inch (.6 centimeter), place the second layer on top, and spread it with whipped cream. Place the remaining layer on top. 8. Spread whipped cream over the top and sides of the entire cake.
Chocolate shavings	9 ounces	250 grams	9. Sprinkle with shaved chocolate.

Note: Pitted and marinated red cherries may be placed between the individual layers.

FIGURE 27-9
Black Forest Cake—Tourte de la Foret-Noire

Gugelhupf (Gugelhopf)

YIELD: *approximately 10 portions*

INGREDIENTS	*U.S. Weight or Volume*	*Metric Weight or Volume*
Butter	9 ounces	250 grams
Sugar	10 ounces	300 grams
Flour	1¼ pounds	600 grams
Eggs	6	6
Milk	¾ cup	2 deciliters
Baking powder	¾ ounce	25 grams
Lemon rind, grated	from 1 lemon	from 1 lemon
Almonds, sliced	as needed	as needed

Note: Raisins may be added to the mixture.

PROCEDURE

1. Cream the butter and sugar together.
2. Add the eggs and about ⅓ of the flour. Mix well.
3. Add the milk, the remainder of the flour and the lemon rind. Mix again.
4. Butter and flour a special (gugelhopf) mold and line with sliced almonds.
5. Pour the batter over the almonds.
6. Bake in the oven at 350°F. (177°C.) for 45 to 50 minutes until it is golden yellow and tests done.

Jelly Roll (Biscuits roules)

YIELD: *40 to 50 slices*

INGREDIENTS	*U.S. Weight or Volume*	*Metric Weight or Volume*
Sponge cake mixture (recipe 25.2.2)	1 recipe	1 recipe
Sugar	as needed	as needed
Jam, hot	as needed	as needed

FIGURE 27-10
Jelly Roll—Biscuits roules

PROCEDURE

1. Spread the sponge cake mixture about ½ inch (1.3 centimeters) thick in a sheet pan lined with greaseproof paper.
2. Bake in the oven at 375°F. (190°C.) for about 15 minutes.
3. Remove the cake from the oven and loosen the edges. Reverse onto a clean cloth which has been sprinkled with confectioners' sugar.
4. Spread the sponge cake with warm jam.
5. Roll the cake and place on a serving plate with the loose edge down. Cool before serving.

Note: Vanilla or Fruit Sauce may be served separately.

Loaf Cake, Menagere Style (Cake menagere)

YIELD: *approximately 20 slices*

INGREDIENTS	*U.S. Weight or Volume*	*Metric Weight or Volume*
Flour	14 ounces	400 grams
Raisins	4 ounces	100 grams
Currants, diced	4 ounces	100 grams
Butter	9 ounces	250 grams
Sugar	9 ounces	250 grams
Eggs	4	4
Milk	¼ cup	½ deciliter
Baking powder	1½ teaspoons	6 grams
Ginger	½ teaspoon	3 grams
Candied fruits	4 ounces	100 grams
Rum	¼ cup	½ deciliter

PROCEDURE

1. Sift the flour.
2. Dust the raisins and currants with some of the flour.
3. Cream the butter and sugar together until fluffy.
4. Add the eggs and flour alternately.
5. Add the milk gradually.
6. Add raisins and currants, baking powder, ginger, candied fruits, and rum.
7. Mix until thoroughly blended.
8. Line two loaf pans with greaseproof paper.
9. Fill with cake mixture and bake in oven at 350°F. (177°C.) for 50 to 60 minutes or until the needle test shows it done.

Plum Loaf Cake

YIELD: *about 50 slices*

INGREDIENTS	*U.S. Weight or Volume*	*Metric Weight or Volume*
Flour	1½ pounds	750 grams
Raisins	1¼ pounds	600 grams
Butter	1½ pounds	750 grams
Sugar	1½ pounds	750 grams
Eggs	16 to 18	16 to 18
Baking powder	1½ teaspoons	6 grams
Candied fruit	1½ pounds	750 grams
Rum	½ cup	1 deciliter
Lemon rind, grated	from 1 lemon	from 1 lemon

PROCEDURE

1. Sift the flour.
2. Dust the raisins with some of the flour.
3. Cream the butter and sugar until fluffy.
4. Add the eggs and flour alternately to the butter and sugar. Blend.
5. Add raisins, baking powder, candied fruits, and rum.
6. Line 4 loaf pans with greaseproof paper.
7. Fill the pans with the cake mixture. Bake in oven at 350°F. (177°C.) for 50 to 60 minutes or until the needle test shows it done.

Note: Instead of using baking powder, the egg whites can be whipped until stiff and folded into the mixture after all the other ingredients have been added.

Mocha Cake—Gateau au mocca. This is a sponge cake (recipe 25.2.2) with a mocha-flavored butter cream filling. The sides and top of the cake are iced with Mocha Fondant and sprinkled with chopped toasted almonds.

Filled Pastries (Tranches et tourtes millefeuilles)

YIELD: *20 slices or 1 large pastry*

INGREDIENTS	*U.S. Weight or Volume*	*Metric Weight or Volume*
Puff paste trimmings (recipe 25.1.1)	1¾ pounds	900 grams
Sugar, confectioners'	3½ ounces	100 grams
Cream filling (recipe 25.3.5 or 25.3.4)	1½ pounds	700 grams
Fondant (recipe 25.6)	7 ounces	200 grams
Kirsch	1 ounce	30 grams

PROCEDURE

1. Roll out the puff paste to a 16×25 inch (40×62.5 centimeters) oblong. Allow to rest 30 minutes.
2. Mark using a perforating roller.
3. Bake in oven at 350°F. (175°C.). After 10 minutes, dust lightly with confectioners' sugar. Continue baking 15 to 20 minutes longer.
4. Cut into 3 strips about 5 inches (12.5 centimeters) wide.
5. Spread cream filling on two of the strips and place one on top of the other.
6. Blend the kirsch into the fondant.
7. Place the third layer on top and frost it with a thin coating of the fondant mixture.
8. Cut into 1 inch (2.5 centimeters) slices.

Note: Individual pastries may be prepared if desired. Roll the dough into three 10-inch (25 centimeter) circles. Cut each into 6 pie-shaped wedges. Roll into cone shapes and bake. Various creams and fruits may be used for fillings. (See illustration, page 594.)

Pineapple Cake—Gateau a l'ananas. This is a cake made with sponge cake (recipe 25.2.2). It is filled with butter cream to which chopped pineapple has been added. The cake is iced with pineapple-flavored fondant icing and decorated with pineapple slices.

Pound Cake (Gateau quatre quarts)

YIELD: *2 cakes*

INGREDIENTS	*U.S. Weight or Volume*	*Metric Weight or Volume*
Butter	1 pound	500 grams
Sugar	1 pound	500 grams
Eggs, whole	2	2
Egg yolks	8	8
Flour	1 pound	500 grams
Egg whites	8	8
Lemon rind, grated	from 1 lemon	from 1 lemon

PROCEDURE

1. Cream the butter and sugar thoroughly.
2. Add the whole eggs, the yolks, ½ cup of the flour. Mix well.
3. Beat the egg whites until stiff. Add the remaining flour and the lemon peel to the creamed mixture.
4. Fold in the beaten egg whites.
5. Grease and flour 2 loaf or layer cake pans. Pour the batter into the pans.
6. If loaf pans are used, line them with parchment paper before filling. Bake loaves for 1 hour in the oven at 325°F. (163°C.). If layer cake pans are used, the baking time will be 20 to 25 minutes.

27.9 Tortes—Tourtes

Almond Torte (Gateau aux amandes)

YIELD: *2 tortes (12 to 16 servings each)*

INGREDIENTS	*U.S. Weight or Volume*	*Metric Weight or Volume*
Egg yolks	16	16
Sugar	14 ounces	400 grams
Egg whites	16	16
Flour	9 ounces	250 grams
Almonds, finely ground	14 ounces	400 grams
Lemon peel, grated	½ teaspoon	3 grams
Sugar, confectioners'	1¾ ounces	50 grams

PROCEDURE

1. Whip the egg yolks and sugar until foamy.
2. Beat the egg whites until stiff and fold them alternately with the flour, almonds, and lemon peel into the egg yolk mixture.
3. Pour the mixture into pans buttered and dusted with flour.
4. Bake 40 to 50 minutes in an oven at 350°F. (177°C.).
5. Sprinkle confectioners' sugar over the torte.

Variation of Almond Torte

Hazelnut Torte—Gateau aux noisettes. The recipe for Almond Torte is used for this torte. Hazelnuts are substituted for almonds.

Linzertorte (Gateau de Linz)

YIELD: *3 tortes*

INGREDIENTS	*U.S. Weight or Volume*	*Metric Weight or Volume*	PROCEDURE
Flour	1 pound	500 grams	1. Put flour on a board or marble slab and make a well in the center of the flour.
Sugar	12 ounces	350 grams	2. Place butter, sugar, and eggs in the well and blend thoroughly. Add the hazelnuts, cinnamon, salt, and rum.
Butter	10 ounces	300 grams	
Eggs	3	3	
Hazelnuts, finely grated	9 ounces	250 grams	3. Gradually mix in the flour.
Cinnamon, ground	1/8 teaspoon	1 gram	
Salt	¼ ounce	5 grams	
Rum	1 tablespoon	15 milliliters	
Milk	as needed	as needed	4. Milk is added as needed until the ingredients form a stiff dough. 5. Allow the dough to rest in a cool place. 6. Roll the dough to a ¼ inch (.6 centimeter) thickness. Line the bottoms of spring form pans with the dough. Moisten the edges and place a ½ inch (1.2 centimeters) thick strip of dough all around the sides of the rim.
Raspberry jam	as needed	as needed	7. Fill the center with raspberry jam and arrange thin strips of dough in a lattice pattern over the jam. Brush the dough with egg yolk. 8. Bake in the oven at 400°F. (205°C.) for 20 to 25 minutes.
Sugar confectioners'	as needed	as needed	9. When the torte has cooled, remove it from the form and fill the squares with more jam. Sprinkle with confectioners' sugar.

FIGURE 27-11
Linzertorte—Gateau de Linz

Sachertorte (Gateau Sacher)

YIELD: *2 tortes*

INGREDIENTS	*U.S. Weight or Volume*	*Metric Weight or Volume*	PROCEDURE
Butter	9¾ ounces	280 grams	1. Cream the butter.
Chocolate, semi-sweet, melted	9¾ ounces	280 grams	2. Mix in the cooled and melted chocolate.
Egg yolks	14	14	3. Alternate the egg yolks and sugar while adding them gradually to the butter and chocolate mixture.
Sugar	8½ ounces	240 grams	
Egg whites	18	18	4. Fold in the stiffly beaten egg whites alternately with the flour.
Flour	6¼ ounces	180 grams	
			5. Bake in two spring form pans for 50 to 60 minutes in an oven preheated to 325°F. (160°C.).
			6. Slice the tortes horizontally through the middle. Reverse the layers so the top of the cake will be flat.
Apricot preserves	1 pint	½ liter	7. Spread 1 cup of apricot jam between the layers of each torte.
			8. Cover the tortes with chocolate glaze and decorate.

FIGURE 27-12
Sachertorte—Gateau Sacher

Zuger Kirschtorte (Tourte au kirsch)

YIELD: *1 cake (12 to 16 servings)*

INGREDIENTS	*U.S. Weight or Volume*	*Metric Weight or Volume*
Sugar syrup at 29° Baume	7 ounces	200 grams
Cherries, red	7 ounces	200 grams
Butter cream (pink-colored, with kirsch (recipe 25.3.7)	10 ounces	300 grams
Japanese meringues (recipe 25.2.5)	2 layers	2 layers
Genoise cake (recipe 25.2.2)	1 layer	1 layer
Almonds, slivered	4 ounces	100 grams
Sugar, confectioners'	as needed	as needed

PROCEDURE

1. Combine sugar syrup and cherries.
2. Spread a very thin layer of thick, pink-colored butter cream over a layer of Japanese meringues.
3. Remove the upper crust from the Genoise cake and dip both sides into the sugar-cherry mixture. Place this cake on the Japanese layer that has been covered with butter cream.
4. Press the layers lightly with a flat plate.
5. Place the second Japanese layer on top and then cover the sides and the top of the cake with butter cream.
6. Press almond slivers into the sides of the cake.
7. Dust the top with confectioners' sugar and decorate in a diamond pattern.

27.10 Fruit Tarts—Tartes aux fruits

Apple Tart (Tarte aux pommes)

YIELD: *1 tart (6 to 8 servings)*

INGREDIENTS	*U.S. Weight or Volume*	*Metric Weight or Volume*
Short crust pastry (recipe 25.1.2)	10 ounces	300 grams
Apples, peeled and wedged	1¾ pounds	800 grams
Sugar	2¾ to 3½ ounces	80 to 100 grams
Apricot jam	as needed	as needed

PROCEDURE

1. Line the tart pan with the pastry.
2. Arrange the apple wedges over the pastry in a ring-shaped pattern.
3. Sprinkle with the sugar and bake about 25 minutes in an oven at 425°F. (220°C.).
4. Glaze with apricot jam before serving.

Apple Tart with Custard (Tarte aux pommes a la creme)

YIELD: *1 tart*

INGREDIENTS	*U.S. Weight or Volume*	*Metric Weight or Volume*	PROCEDURE
Short crust pastry (recipe 25.1.2)	10 ounces	300 grams	1. Line the tart pan with pastry. Prick it.
Apples, peeled and wedged	1¾ pounds	800 grams	2. Arrange the apple wedges on the pastry and sprinkle with sugar.
Sugar	2¾ to 3½ ounces	80 to 100 grams	3. Bake about 20 minutes at 375°F. (190°C.) until almost done.
Custard			
Milk	¾ cup	2 deciliters	4. Combine and mix well the milk, cream, eggs, sugar, cinnamon, and vanilla. Strain.
Cream	¼ cup	½ deciliter	5. Pour the custard mixture over the apples in the tart shell.
Egg	1	1	6. Return to oven and bake approximately 20 minutes longer.
Sugar	1¾ ounces	50 grams	
Cinnamon, ground	1/8 teaspoon	1 gram	
Vanilla extract	1 teaspoon	5 milliliters	

Note: Sugar paste (recipe 25.1.6) may be used instead of the puff paste.

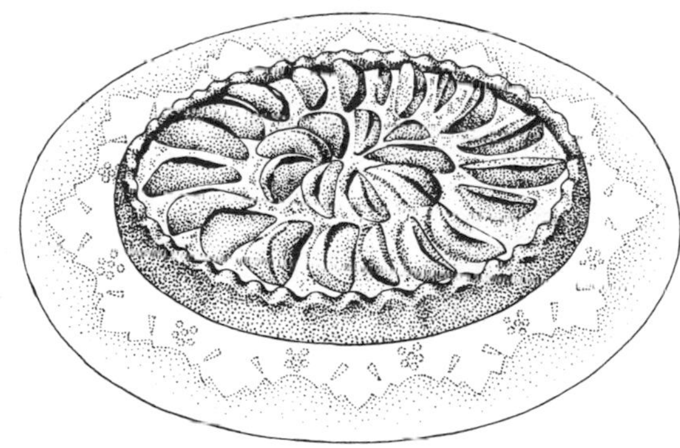

FIGURE 27-13
Apple Tart with Custard—Tarte aux pommes a la creme

VARIATIONS OF FRUIT TARTS

Apricot Tart—Tarte aux abricots. These tarts are prepared the same as Plum Tart.
Plum Tart—Tarte aux prunes. Tart pans are lined with Short Crust Pastry. The pastry is pierced with a fork, sprinkled with cracker crumbs, covered with halved plums, sprinkled with a little sugar, and baked. Additional sugar is sprinkled over the top before serving.

Strawberry Tart (Tarte aux fraises)

YIELD: *1 tart (8 to 10 servings)*

INGREDIENTS	*U.S. Weight or Volume*	*Metric Weight or Volume*
Puff paste (recipe 25.1.1)	10 ounces	300 grams
Strawberries, fresh	1 to 1¼ pounds	450 to 560 grams
Sugar	9 ounces	250 grams
Kirsch	¼ cup	½ deciliter
Jelly, strawberry OR Jelly, red currant	½ cup	1 deciliter

PROCEDURE

1. Line the tart pans with puff paste.
2. Fill the tart with uncooked rice or dried beans and bake it in the oven at 450°F. (230°C.) for 20 to 25 minutes. When baked, remove the rice or beans. Cool the shell.
3. Marinate the strawberries in sugar and kirsch.
4. Arrange the strawberries in the baked tart shell and coat them with the jelly.

FIGURE 27-14
Strawberry Tart—Tartes aux fraises

Strawberry Tart with Meringue Topping (Tarte aux fraises meringuee)

YIELD: *1 tart (8 to 10 servings)*

INGREDIENTS	*U.S. Weight or Volume*	*Metric Weight or Volume*
Puff paste (recipe 25.1.1)	10 ounces	300 grams
Egg whites	6	6
Sugar	9 ounces	250 grams
Strawberries, fresh, small or halved	8 ounces	¼ kilogram

PROCEDURE

1. Line the tart pan with puff paste.
2. Fill with uncooked rice or dried beans and bake in the oven at 450°F. (230°C.) for 20 to 25 minutes. When done, remove the rice or beans and cool the shell.
3. Beat the egg whites to the soft-peak stage. Add sugar gradually and continue beating.
4. Divide the meringue into two equal portions.
5. Add the strawberries to one part of the meringue and pour into the tart shell.
6. Decorate with the remaining meringue and sprinkle with sugar.
7. Bake in the oven at 450°F. (230°C.) until lightly browned.

Tartlets—Tartelettes. These are small pastry shells made from short crust paste or puff paste trimmings.

FIGURE 27-15
Tartlets with Fruit—Tartelettes aux fruits

27.11 Cold Desserts with Fruit—Entremets froids aux fruits

Birchermuesli

YIELD: *approximately 10 servings*

INGREDIENTS	*U.S. Weight or Volume*	*Metric Weight or Volume*	PROCEDURE
Oatmeal	4¼ to 5 ounces	120 to 150 grams	1. Soak the oatmeal in the milk for about 15 minutes.
Milk	¾ cup	1½ deciliters	2. Add the almonds and sugar.
Almonds, finely grated	4½ ounces	130 grams	
Sugar	4¼ ounces	120 grams	
Apples, grated	2 to 3 pounds	1 to 1½ kilograms	3. Combine the apples, lemon juice, and cream and add to the oatmeal mixture.
Lemon juice	½ cup	1 deciliter	
Cream or yoghurt	½ cup	1 deciliter	
Honey	as desired	as desired	4. Add a little honey and some fresh fruit if desired.
Fruits of the season	as desired	as desired	
Whipping cream	to garnish	to garnish	5. Garnish with whipped cream and pecans or almonds.
Pecans or almonds	to garnish	to garnish	

Apricots, Royal Style—Abricots royale. Tartlet molds are coated with cherry jelly (see page 565), and filled with alternate layers of well-formed stewed apricots and cherry jelly, and refrigerated. A Genoise base (recipe 25.2.1) flavored with kirsch and filled with red currant jelly is placed on a serving plate. The molds are arranged on the Genoise base. A coating of warmed red currant jelly is poured over the top. Chopped pistachios are sprinkled over the top.

Fruits in Jelly—Fruits a la gelee. Pour some white wine jelly or port wine jelly (see page 565) into attractive wine glasses (champagne glasses). Place in the refrigerator and allow to set. Fill the glasses with alternate layers of jelly and fruits or stewed fruits of different colors. Allow to set. The fruits should always be dry when put in place.

Fruit Salad—Fruits rafraichis (Macedoine de fruits). Pineapple, apples, pears, bananas, peaches, and oranges are cut into uniform-sized pieces. Strawberries or peeled grapes may be added. The fruits are combined with sugar or thick sugar syrup, kirsch, maraschino, and a few drops of lemon juice and chilled in the refrigerator. The fruits are arranged in a glass bowl and topped with various colored fruit slices. Whipped cream may be served on the side.

Strawberries, Marquess Style—Fraises a la marquise. This is a strawberry puree combined with sweetened whipped cream that has been flavored with vanilla and arranged in glass bowls. Strawberries that have been marinated in sugar and kirsch and coated with sugar are placed on top of the cream. This is served very cold.

Strawberries Romanoff—Fraises Romanov. These strawberries are marinated in liqueur and sugar. They are combined with sweetened and flavored whipped cream and garnished with additional strawberries.

Frozen Desserts—Entremets glaces

28

Frozen desserts are popular and offer variety to the menu at reasonable costs. Frozen desserts are classified in this section on the basis of the method of preparation. These classifications are *plain ice creams and sherbets,* and *fancy still-frozen specialties.* The ice creams, sherbets, and ices are frozen in a mechanical freezer that churns or stirs the mixtures and incorporates air into them as they freeze. Fancy specialties, such as bombes, frozen puddings, mousses, parfaits, and souffles, are frozen without agitation.

Ice creams are prepared by freezing a pasteurized and homogenized mixture. *The milk fat* content of plain ice cream must reach 10 percent. When *ice cream* is mixed with fruits, chocolate, nuts, or other products, the milk fat content must be at least 8 percent. All ice cream manufacturers are required to abide by the laws within the state where ice cream is produced. Manufacturers who ship ice cream across state lines must also follow federal regulations.

The facilities, equipment, and utensils used for processing, freezing, and storing frozen desserts must meet sanitation and safety regulations. All areas must be ventilated to remove moisture. Equipment that comes in contact with the ice cream mixture must be constructed of stainless steel or noncorrosive material. Equipment and utensils must be steam-cleaned or sanitized. Usually equipment is rinsed, dismantled, washed with steam or hot water, sanitized, and air-dried. Mechanical equipment should be rinsed, sterilized, and rinsed again just before it is used.

28.1 Plain Ice Creams and Sherbets—Glaces simples

28.1.1 Plain Ice Cream (Glaces a la creme)

YIELD: *approximately 20 servings*

INGREDIENTS	*U.S. Weight or Volume*	*Metric Weight or Volume*	PROCEDURE
Egg yolks	10	10	1. Combine the egg yolks and the sugar. Beat until slightly foamy.
Sugar	9 ounces	250 grams	2. Scald the milk. Add gradually to the eggs and sugar.
Milk	1 quart	1 liter	3. Pour the combined mixture into a saucepan and simmer until the mixture coats a spoon.
			4. Remove from heat and stir vigorously until cool. Strain.
Cream	1¼ cups	3 deciliters	5. Add the cream and stir until blended.
			6. Freeze.

Some Variations of Ice Cream

Chocolate Ice Cream—Glace au chocolat. Semi-sweet grated chocolate is added to the ice cream mixture before freezing—5 ounces (140 grams) semi-sweet chocolate per quart (1 liter) of ice cream.
Mocha Ice Cream—Glace au mocca. Mocha extract is added to the ice cream mixture before freezing.
Praline Ice Cream—Glace au praline. Crushed praline is added to the ice cream mixture before freezing—4 ounces (115 grams) praline to 1 quart (1 liter) of ice cream.

Tea Ice Cream—Glace au the. This is an ice cream prepared with a mixture of 1 quart (7½ deciliters) sugar syrup at 18° to 19° Baume, 1½ cups (3 deciliters) of strong, strained tea, ½ cup (120 milliliters) rum, and 1¾ cups (415 milliliters) cream. The mixture is then frozen.
Vanilla Ice Cream—Glace a la vanille. This is a vanilla ice cream made with vanilla beans. One vanilla bean is heated with the milk for each quart (liter) of ice cream mixture. The vanilla bean is removed before the mixture is put in the freezer.

28.1.2 Fruit Sherbet (Glace aux fruits)

YIELD: *20 to 30 servings*

INGREDIENTS	*U.S. Weight or Volume*	*Metric Weight or Volume*
Water	1 quart	1 liter
Sugar	3 pounds	1½ kilograms
Fruit puree	1 to 1½ quarts	1 to 1½ liters
Lemon juice	¼ cup	60 milliliters
Optional addition		
Egg whites, beaten	4 to 5	4 to 5
OR		
Cream	1 quart	1 liter

PROCEDURE

1. Combine sugar and water and cook to the boiling point, 29°Baume. Cool.
2. Add pureed fruit and lemon juice.
3. Freeze.

Note: Beaten egg whites or cream should be added after the mixture is slightly frozen.

Pineapple Sherbet (Glace a l'ananas)

YIELD: *20 to 30 servings*

INGREDIENTS	*U.S. Weight or Volume*	*Metric Weight or Volume*
Sugar syrup at 22° Baume	1 quart	1 liter
Crushed pineapple and juice	1 cup	235 milliliters
Lemon juice	1 lemon	1 lemon
Egg white	1	1

PROCEDURE

1. Combine sugar syrup, pineapple, and lemon juice. Strain.
2. Beat egg whites until stiff but not dry.
3. Check temperature and when it reaches 19° Baume, freeze the mixture.

Some Variations of Fruit Sherbet

Apricot sherbet—Glace aux abricots. This sherbet is made with pureed apricots. It is prepared by the method used for making fruit sherbet.

Lemon Sherbet—Glace au citron. This sherbet is prepared with 1 quart (1 liter) of sugar syrup at 20° Baume, the juice of 3 to 4 lemons, and thin slices of the peel of 2 lemons. The mixture should stand for 1 to 2 hours. When ready to freeze, a well-beaten egg is added. The freezing process should be continued until the sherbet turns a brilliant white color.

Orange Sherbet—Glace a l'orange. This sherbet is prepared with a mixture of 1 quart (1 liter) of sugar syrup at 23° Baume, the juice of 12 to 14 oranges, the grated peel of 2 oranges, and the juice of 1 lemon. The mixture should register 19° Baume. 1¾ cups (415 milliliters) of cream is added to the chilled mixture. It is then strained and frozen.

Peach Sherbet—Glace aux peches. This sherbet is made with pureed fresh or frozen peaches. It is prepared by the same method used for making fruit syrup.

Raspberry Sherbet—Glace aux framboises. This sherbet is made with pureed fresh or frozen raspberries. It is prepared by the same method used for making fruit sherbet.

Strawberry Sherbet—Glace aux fraises. Pureed fresh or frozen strawberries are used in this sherbet. It is prepared by the method used for fruit sherbet.

28.1.3 Liqueur Sherbets

The basic ingredient in liqueur sherbet is a sugar syrup at about 20° Baume, to which the desired flavoring is added. When the temperature of the mixture registers 18° to 19° Baume, it is ready to freeze.

Curacao Sherbet (Glace au curacao)

YIELD: *U.S. — 1 quart*
Metric — 1 liter

INGREDIENTS	*U.S. Weight or Volume*	*Metric Weight or Volume*	PROCEDURE
Sugar syrup at 18° to 19° Baume	1 quart	1 liter	1. Combine the syrup, the curacao, the orange juice and rind, and the lemon juice.
Curacao	½ cup	120 milliliters	2. Blend thoroughly.
Orange juice	of 2 oranges	of 2 oranges	
Orange rind	from 2 oranges	from 2 oranges	
Lemon juice	of 1 lemon	of 1 lemon	3. Fold beaten egg white into the syrup mixture.
Egg white	1	1	4. Pour into a mold and freeze.

Kirsch Sherbet (Glace au kirsch)

YIELD: *U.S. — approximately 1 quart*
Metric — approximately 1 liter

INGREDIENTS	*U.S. Weight or Volume*	*Metric Weight or Volume*	PROCEDURE
Sugar syrup at 18° to 19° Baume	1 quart	1 liter	1. Combine the syrup, kirsch, maraschino, lemon juice, and rind.
Kirsch	½ cup	120 milliliters	
Maraschino	½ cup	120 milliliters	
Lemon juice	of 1 lemon	of 1 lemon	
Lemon rind, grated	from 1 lemon	from 1 lemon	2. Strain and freeze.

28.1.4 Sundaes—Coupes

Ice cream served in frosted silver or glass cups or champagne glasses is an attractive dessert. Plain ice cream may be served in various ways. All varieties of plain ice cream may be served either individually or combined. The ice cream may be topped with poached fruits, fresh fruits, syrups, nuts, coconut, or a combination of any of these. The sundaes are often garnished with whipped cream.

Denise Sundae—Coupe Denise. Mocha ice cream decorated with liqueur-filled chocolates and whipped cream.

Helene Sundae—Coupe Helene. Vanilla ice cream topped with half a stewed or canned pear and covered with a light-colored fruit sauce. Whipped cream is piped around the rim of the dish. Hot chocolate sauce is served separately.

Jacques Sundae—Coupe Jacques. Lemon sherbet and strawberry ice cream garnished with a pyramid of fruit salad and covered with Fruit Sauce. Whipped cream is piped around the rim of the cup.

Melba Sundae—Coupe Melba. Peach Melba (page 590) served in a cup.

Mexican Sundae—Coupe mexicaine. Mandarin or orange ice cream topped with diced pineapple which has been marinated in kirsch and sugar. Whipped cream is piped around the rim of the cup.

Mikado Sundae—Coupe Mikado. Vanilla ice cream sprinkled with finely chopped ginger and garnished with a small cluster of pitted cherries. Whipped cream is piped around the rim of the cup.

Romanoff Sundae—Coupe Romanov. A layer of vanilla ice cream covered with a pyramid of strawberries that have been marinated in sugar, kirsch, and maraschino. Flavored strawberry puree is poured over the top, and the rim of the cup or glass is piped with whipped cream.

Singapore Sundae—Coupe Singapour. Pineapple ice cream garnished with diced pineapple and sliced bananas that have been marinated in kirsch and sugar. Whipped cream is piped around the rim of the cup.
Valais Sundae—Coupe valaisanne. Vanilla ice cream that has been flavored with kirsch and maraschino is topped with two stewed apricot halves and covered with apricot marmalade. Whipped cream is piped around the rim of the cup.
White Lady Sundae—Coupe dame blanche. Vanilla ice cream covered with a thin slice of pineapple, then with a poached or canned peach half, and a light-colored fruit sauce. Whipped cream is piped around the rim of the glass.

28.1.5 Fancy Ice Creams—Glaces fantaisie

Ice cream lends itself to elaborate forms of presentation. It can be molded in intricate forms and shapes; it can be combined with other foods to give variety of texture, color, or shape; it can be served in fruit shells, coconut shells, or attractive glassware; it can serve as a foundation for other foods such as layers of meringue, pastries, and fruit combinations; it is used as a filling for tart shells, cream puffs, and meringue shells.

Frozen Mandarins—Mandarines givrees. The top of each piece of fruit is removed near the stem end. The juice is extracted and the pulp removed. A sherbet is made using the mandarin juice (follow recipe for orange sherbet substituting mandarins for oranges). The sherbet is served in chilled mandarin shells covered with the mandarin tops which have been dusted with confectioners' sugar.

Ice Cream Charlotte—Charlotte glacee. Vanilla ice cream flavored with kirsch and maraschino and poured into a mold lined with ladyfingers. After the mold is firm, it is turned onto a serving plate and garnished with whipped cream.

Ice Cream Meringues—Meringues glacees. A dipper of ice cream is placed between two meringue shells.

The meringues are arranged on a dish and garnished with whipped cream.

Ice Cream Jardiniere—Seille a la jardiniere. Small buckets are made of Cornet Batter (recipe 25.2.4) and filled with vanilla ice cream flavored with kirsch and maraschino. The buckets are decorated with fruit and whipped cream.

Ice Cream Vacherin—Vacherin glace. Vanilla ice cream is spread between two vacherin layers. These are placed on a dish and decorated with whipped cream.

Peach Melba—Peche Melba. (See Fig. 28-1) Ripe, soft peaches with white flesh are dipped into boiling water for a few seconds and then immediately plunged into ice-cold water. The peaches are then peeled and arranged on a dish that has been dusted with sugar. Peaches that are not quite ripe should be poached in a light syrup for a few minutes, and then cooled in the syrup. The peaches are arranged on a layer of good quality vanilla ice cream and covered with sweetened raspberry puree and a few fresh sliced almonds.

Pear Melba—Poires Melba. Poached pears arranged on a layer of vanilla ice cream and covered with raspberry puree.

Pears Helene—Poires Helene. Halved, stewed or canned pears arranged on a layer of vanilla ice cream in a glass bowl are coated with a clear white wine jelly or a fruit jelly and decorated with whipped cream. Hot chocolate sauce is served on the side.

28.1.6 Wine Sherbets—Sorbets

The mixture for wine sherbets is made by combining 1 quart (1 liter) of sugar syrup at 28° Baume with 1 quart (1 liter) of sparkling wine or white wine. The mixture should register 15° Baume. Lemon or orange juice is usually added. ½ cup (1 deciliter) may be substituted for the wine. The sherbet is made in an ice cream freezer. After the mixture starts to freeze, the sides of the container should be scraped down and two beaten egg whites should be added. The consistency of the sherbet should be similar to that of slush. These sherbets are served in champagne glasses.

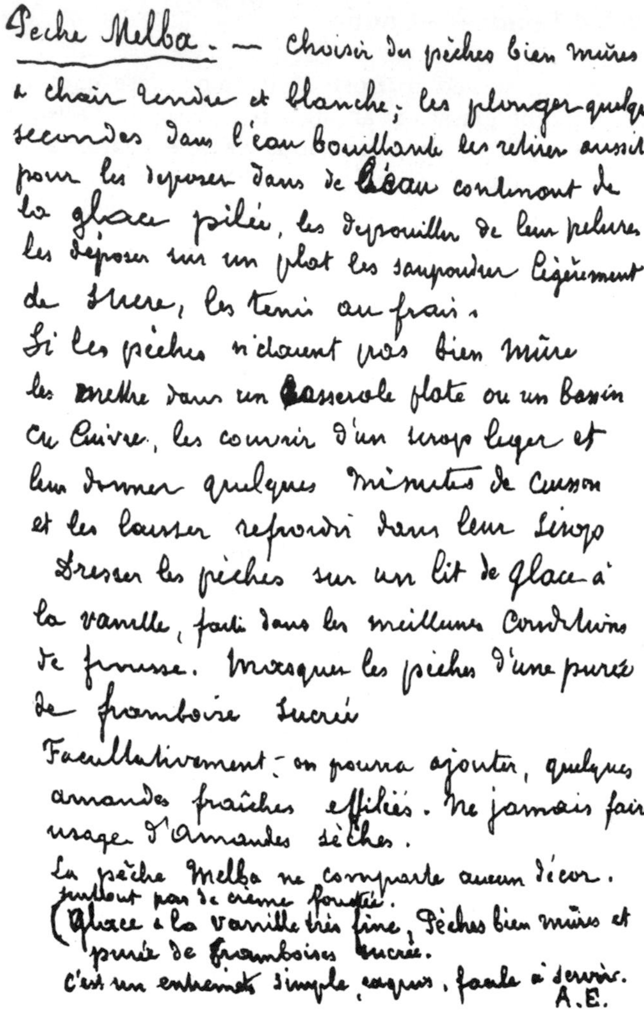

<u>Peche Melba.</u> — Choisir des pêches bien mûres à chair tendre et blanche; les plonger quelques secondes dans l'eau bouillante les retirer aussitôt pour les déposer dans de l'eau contenant de la glace pilée, les dépouiller de leur pelures les déposer sur un plat les saupoudrer légèrement de sucre, les tenir au frais.
Si les pêches n'étaient pas bien mûre les mettre dans une casserole plate ou un bassin en cuivre, les couvrir d'un sirop léger et leur donner quelques minutes de cuisson et les laisser refroidir dans leur sirop.
Dresser les pêches sur un lit de glace à la vanille, faite dans les meilleures conditions de finesse. Masquer les pêches d'une purée de framboise sucrée
Facultativement: on pourra ajouter, quelques amandes fraîches effilées. Ne jamais faire usage d'amandes sèches.
La pêche Melba ne comporte aucun décor. surtout pas de crème fouettée.
(Glace à la vanille très fine, Pêches bien mûres et purée de framboises sucrée.
C'est un entremets simple, exquis, facile à servir.
A.E.

FIGURE 28-1
Peach Melba—Peche Melba. Introduced by A. Escoffier in 1892, Peche Melba is one of the most famous ice cream specialties in the world. The original recipe, published for the first time, is shown here.

Apple Charlotte — *Charlotte de pommes*

Vanilla Souffle — *Souffle a la vanille*

Apple with Meringue – *Pommes meringuees*

Gratinated Plum Tarts – *Gratin de prunes*

Apricots Sybilla — *Abricots Sybille*

Sour Cherries Basle Style — *Les griottes baloises*

Strawberry Slices and Rolls – *Tranches et roulades de fraises*

Cream Puffs and Eclairs – *Choux et eclairs*

28.1.7 Granite Sherbet—Granites

This is a sherbet made of ⅔ sugar syrup and ⅓ raspberry, strawberry, or red currant juice or puree. Lemon juice and kirsch are added, and the mixture is adjusted to register 17° to 18° Baume. This mixture is frozen by the same method used to freeze sherbet; egg whites, however, are not used in granite sherbets. The texture has a granular appearance.

28.1.8 Soft-Serve Frozen Products

This soft-frozen dairy dessert has less total milk solids than ice cream. The product is frozen in a machine that injects up to 120 percent air into the mixture. The finished product is light and creamy. Since the mixture is usually frozen plain, the soft ice is often served with toppings such as strawberry, pineapple, and chocolate.

28.2 Fancy Still-Frozen Specialties—Glaces legeres

The mixtures used for these frozen desserts consist of the same as the one used for basic ice cream. After the mixture is whipped and cooled, approximately an equal amount of whipped cream is folded in. The mixture is poured into molds and frozen at −4°F. (25°C.) to −13°F. (9°C.).

Apricots Sybilla—Abricots Sybille
Recipe on page 567. (See illustration on page 593.)

Sour Cherries, Basle Style—Les griottes baloise
In the center. Kirschwasser flask made of chocolate and marzipan. Decoration made of nougat with a choice of chocolates and other delicacies. *Surrounded* with single-portion bowls with sour cherries, Melba Sauce, an almond macaroon dipped in kirsch, all coated with a layer of Bavarian Cream (see page 561). Decorated with chocolate drums filled with pistachios. A modern show-piece featuring individual portions.

Strawberry Slices and Rolls—Tranches et roulades de fraises. Puff paste slices and rolls filled with strawberries that have been marinated in kirsch. The slices or rolls are garnished with whipped cream or Mousseline Cream.

Cream Puffs/Eclairs—Choux
Recipe on page 562.

28.2.1 Iced Biscuit (Biscuits glaces)

YIELD: *15 to 20 servings*

INGREDIENTS	*U.S. Weight or Volume*	*Metric Weight or Volume*
Egg yolks	10	10
Sugar	12 ounces	350 grams
Egg whites	6	6
Whipped cream	1 quart	1 liter
Liqueur	1 ounce	30 milliliters
Whipped cream	as needed to decorate when served	as needed to decorate when served

Also needed
Oblong molds which can be covered or sealed

PROCEDURE

1. Beat the egg yolks and combine with sugar. Place in a warm water bath and continue beating until creamy.
2. Remove from water bath and beat until the mixture is cool.
3. Whip the egg whites until stiff but not dry.
4. Fold the egg whites, whipped cream, and liqueur into the egg and sugar mixture.
5. Pour the mixture into chilled molds. Place cover on mold and freeze.
6. Cut into slices and serve garnished with whipped cream.

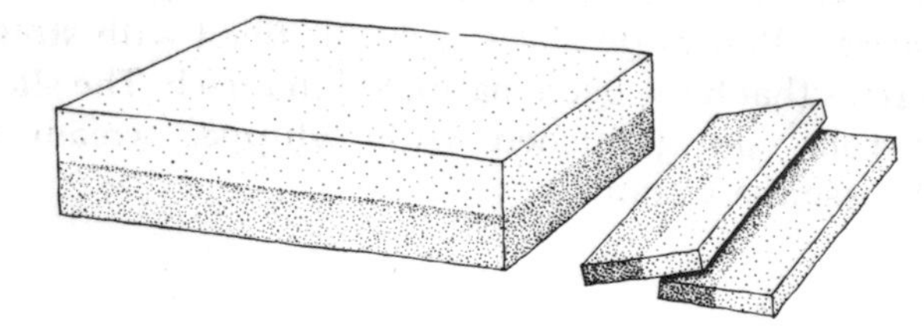

FIGURE 28-2
Ice Cream Bombe—Bombes glacees

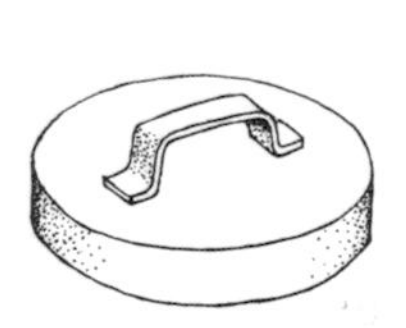
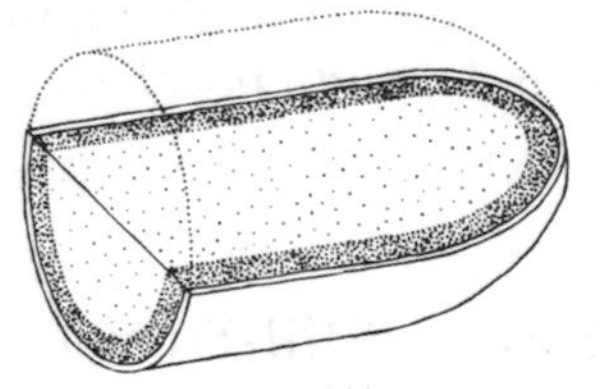

FIGURE 28-3
Iced Biscuit—Biscuit glaces

28.2.2 Ice Cream Bombes (Bombes glacees)

YIELD: *approximately 30 servings*

INGREDIENTS	*U.S. Weight or Volume*	*Metric Weight or Volume*
Vanilla ice cream OR Fruit sherbet	1 quart (approximately)	1 liter (approximately)
Egg yolks	18	18
Sugar syrup at 28° Baume	1 pint	½ liter
Whipping cream	1½ pints	¾ liter
Liqueur	1 ounce	30 milliliters

PROCEDURE

1. Chill the molds and line with the ice cream or sherbet.
2. Beat the egg yolks. Add the syrup. Place in a warm water bath and continue beating until light and creamy.
3. Fold the whipped cream and liqueur into the egg and syrup mixture.
4. Pour mixture into the lined molds.
5. Freeze.

Ice Puddings—Puddings glaces. Timbale forms are lined with ice cream and filled with alternate layers of bombe mixture and thin layers of sponge cake that have been soaked in a liqueur. Waxed paper is placed over the mixture and the timbale is sealed and placed in a freezer at −4°F. (25°C.).

28.2.3 Cassata

A chilled mold is lined with a layer of each of three flavors of ice cream—approximately 1 pint (½ liter) of each flavor. After the ice cream is firm, a filling—approximately 1 pint (½ liter)—is poured into the mold. The filling consists of Italian Meringue Mixture (recipe 25.2.8), whipped cream, vanilla extract, diced candied fruits that have been marinated in maraschino, crushed nougat pieces of macaroon, and toasted almonds. It is frozen at −4°F. (25°C.).

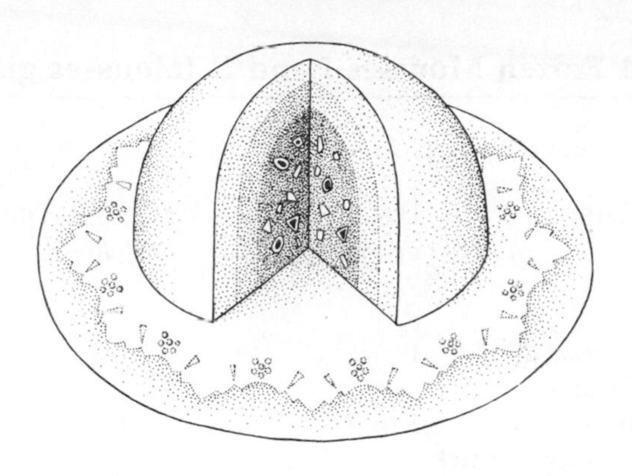

FIGURE 28-6
Cassata Naples Style—Cassata napoletana

Cassata, Naples Style—Cassata napoletana. A chilled semi-spherical mold is lined with each of three flavors of ice cream. After the ice cream is firm, a filling is poured into the mold. The filling consists of 1 quart (1 liter) of whipped cream combined with Italian Meringue Mixture (recipe 25.2.8) made with 6 egg whites, vanilla extract, candied fruits marinated in maraschino, toasted sliced almonds, crushed nougats, and small pieces of macaroon. The mold is frozen at −4°F. (25°C.).

28.2.4 Frozen Mousses I and II (Mousses glacees)

YIELD: *approximately 15 servings*

INGREDIENTS	*U.S. Weight or Volume*	*Metric Weight or Volume*
I		
Sugar syrup at 29° Baume	1 pint	½ liter
Fruit puree, unsweetened thick	1 pint	½ liter
Liqueur	1 ounce	30 milliliters
Whipping cream	1 quart	1 liter
II		
Egg whites	5	5
Sugar	12 ounces	350 grams
Water	¾ cup	180 milliliters
Fruit puree	1 pound	500 grams
Lemon juice	1 fluid ounce	30 grams
Whipping cream	1 pint	½ liter

PROCEDURE

I

1. Combine the sugar syrup, fruit puree, and liqueur.
2. Whip the cream and fold into syrup mixture.
3. Pour the mixture into chilled molds.
4. Freeze at −4°F. (25°C.).

II

1. Combine the sugar and water. Boil to the soft ball stage, 234°F. to 240°F. (112°C. to 116°C.) or 29° Baume.
2. Beat the egg whites until stiff. Continue beating while adding the hot sugar syrup very gradually. Beat until cold.
3. Add the fruit puree and lemon juice to the egg mixture.
4. Fold in the whipped cream.
5. Pour into molds and freeze at −4°F. (25°C.).

Note: Mixture II may also be used for filling ice cream bombes. If, however, it is being used as a mousse, it should be named in accordance with the variety of fruit puree used.

28.2.5 Frozen Parfaits (Parfait glaces)

YIELD: *approximately 15 servings*

INGREDIENTS	*U.S. Weight or Volume*	*Metric Weight or Volume*
Egg yolks	15	15
Sugar syrup at 36° Baume	1 pint	½ liter
Flavoring	as desired	as desired
Whipped cream	1 quart	1 liter

PROCEDURE

1. Mix the egg yolks with a dash of cold water.
2. Add the hot sugar syrup, and beat the mixture in a hot waterbath until it forms peaks.
3. Remove from the heat and continue whipping until cool.
4. Add desired flavoring.
5. Fold in the whipped cream.
6. Pour into ice cream bombe molds and freeze.

Note: Choose from a variety of flavorings, such as vanilla, chocolate, mocha, or liqueur.

28.2.6 Frozen Souffles I and II (Souffles glaces)

YIELD: *15 to 20 servings*

INGREDIENTS	*U.S. Weight or Volume*	*Metric Weight or Volume*
I		
Sugar	1 pound	455 grams
Water	1 cup	240 milliliters
Egg whites	10	10
Whipping cream	1½ pints	710 milliliters
Liqueur	1 ounce	30 milliliters
Fruit puree	1¼ pints	590 milliliters
II		
Egg whites	10	10
Sugar	7 ounces	200 grams
Whipping cream	1¾ pints	825 milliliters
Liqueur	1 ounce	30 milliliters
Egg yolks	3	3

PROCEDURE

I

1. Boil the sugar and water until they form a syrup at 92° Reaumur or 238°F. (115°C.).
2. Beat the egg whites stiff and slowly add the boiling syrup, beating constantly until mixture is cool.
3. Carefully fold in the whipped cream, liqueur, and the fruit puree.
4. Take small dishes or suitable paper molds and stick paper strips to the upper edge of the inside walls so that the strips project 1 inch (2.5 centimeters) above the rims.
5. Pour the mixture into the molds to the top of the paper strips (See Fig. 28-5) and freeze.
6. When serving, remove the paper strips and dust with chocolate powder.

II

1. Beat the egg whites adding ¾ ounce (21 grams) of sugar when they are slightly foamy. Beat until stiff. Add the remainder of the sugar gradually.
2. Fold in whipped cream combined with liqueur and egg yolks.
3. Freeze.

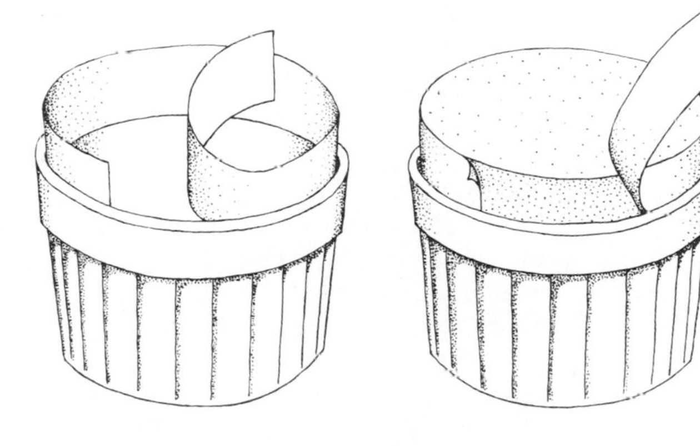

FIGURE 28-5
Frozen Souffles—Souffles glaces

Frozen Souffle Grand Marnier—Souffle glace Grand Marnier. This is a frozen souffle (recipe 28.2.6) with Grand Marnier added. It is dusted with cocoa and garnished with strawberries or cherries. (See pages 587, 589.)

Glossary

AGAR-AGAR. A gelatinous extractive of an oriental seaweed used as a stabilizer in foods.
AGING. A term applied to the ripening process of meat. The action of enzymes on the connective tissue increases the tenderness of the meat.
AGNEAU. (Fr.) Lamb.
A L'. (Fr.) According to a style. Used before words beginning with a vowel, as *a l'Andalouse*.
A LA. (Fr.) According to a style, such as *a la Francais*—meaning "according to the French way".
A LA CARTE. (Fr.) A list of menu selections with each item priced separately.
A LA KING. Foods prepared in a white cream sauce containing pimientos, mushrooms, and green peppers.
A LA MODE. (Fr.) Literally "in the fashion"; pie a la mode is pie with ice cream.
AL DENTE. (It.) Literally "to the teeth"; pasta cooked to a slightly underdone stage; there should be some resilience to the bite.
ALMOND PASTE. Mixture of ground blanched almonds, sugar, water, and flavoring.
AMANDINE. (Fr.) Prepared with or garnished with almonds.
AMONTILLADO. (Sp.) Medium dry sherry.
ANCIENNE, A L'. (Fr.) Old-fashioned.
ANDALOUSE, A L'. Andalusian style; mayonnaise combined with tomato puree and sweet pimientos or sweet peppers.
ANGLAISE, A L'. (Fr.) English style.
ANTIPASTO. An Italian combination of anchovies, olives, sardines, pickles, and other snack foods served as an appetizer.
ARGENTEUIL. District in France known for its excellent asparagus.
ARROWROOT. Starch obtained from the roots of the arrowroot plant; used in the preparation of delicate soups, sauces, puddings, and custards.
ARTICHAUT. (Fr.) Artichoke.
ASIAGO CHEESE. An Italian hard cheese made from cows' milk in the province of Vicenza.
ASPIC. Clear meat, fish, or poultry jelly used for hors d'oeuvres, salads, or desserts.
AS PURCHASED (A.P.). Food as purchased on the market before the inedible portions, such as husks, outer leaves, peels, or skins, are removed.
AUBERGINE. (Fr.) Eggplant.
AU GRATIN. (Fr.) Food sprinkled with bread crumbs and/or cheese and browned.
AU JUS. (Fr.) With natural juice.
AU LAIT. (Fr.) With milk.
AU NATUREL (Fr.) Plainly cooked or served in natural state.

BABA. (Fr.) A small yeast-raised cake soaked with rum and topped with whipped cream.
BAIN-MARIE. (Fr.) A double boiler insert or a steam table with openings to hold food at controlled temperatures for serving.
BAKING. *See* Basic Cooking Methods, 8.9.
BANNOCK. A large round scone or oatcake.
BARD. (Barding) To wrap poultry, game, or fish with thin slices of fat or salt pork to prevent drying while roasting.

BAR DE LUC. Jam made of red currants. Bar de luc, a town in Lorraine, France, is famous for its red currant jam.

BASTE. To moisten food while cooking, to add flavor, and to prevent drying. Meat drippings, melted fats, and sauces are used for basting.

BATTER. A mixture of flour, liquid, and other ingredients that is thin enough to pour; used for cakes, pancakes, and as a coating for foods.

BAUME. A scale used in hydrometers for liquids lighter than or heavier than water that indicates specific gravity in degrees.

BEAT. To incorporate air into an ingredient or a food mixture by turning the ingredients in an up and over motion using a spoon, rotary beater, or an electric mixer.

BEEF TEA. Essence of beef, extracted by long slow simmering.

BEIGNETS. (Fr.) Fritters.

BEL PAESE. Soft-textured Italian cheese made of cows' milk.

BEURRE. (Fr.) Butter.

BEURRE MANIE. (Fr.) Kneaded butter and flour used as a thickening agent.

BEURRE NOIR. (Fr.) Browned butter sauce combined with parsley, vinegar, and seasonings.

BIFTEK. (Fr.) Beefsteak.

BISQUE. (Fr.) Thick cream soup or puree of shellfish or bivalves.

BLANC. A French culinary term used to describe a court bouillon or white stock.

BLANCHING. *See* Basic Cooking Methods, 8.1.

BLANCMANGE. (Fr.) Pudding made of milk, sugar, cornstarch, and flavoring.

BLANQUETTE. (Fr.) Ragout or stew made of lamb, veal, or chicken and a rich veloute sauce.

BLEND. To combine two or more ingredients and mix to a smooth consistency.

BOILING. *See* Basic Cooking Methods, 8.3.

BOMBAY DUCK. East Indian dried fish. A delicacy served with curried dishes.

BOMBE. (Fr.) A dessert of ice cream frozen in an arch-shaped mold.

BONNE FEMME. (Fr.) Term used to indicate simple home-style or family-style.

BOUQUET GARNI. (Fr.) A combination of fresh parsley, thyme, and bay leaf tied together and used to flavor stews, soups, braised meats, and vegetables.

BOURGEOISE, A LA. (Fr.) Plain family style, such as meats served with vegetables.

BRAISING. *See* Basic Cooking Methods, 8.11, 8.12.

BRAZIER. Heavy duty stewing pan with two handles and a tight-fitting lid.

BRIE CHEESE. A soft, rich cheese from France.

BRINE. Solution of water and salt.

BRIOCHE. (Fr.) A rich raised dough made of yeast, milk, butter, eggs, sugar, and flour. Dough is usually formed into small rolls.

BROCHETTE. (Fr.) Cubes or strips of meat broiled and served on a skewer. Onion, green peppers, fresh tomatoes, mushrooms, and fruit are sometimes combined with the meat.

BROILING. *See* Basic Cooking Methods, 8.7.

BRUNCH. Combination of lunch and breakfast.

BUNUELOS. (Sp.) Fritters

CALORIE. (large or kilo-calorie) The unit used to express food energy; the amount of heat required to raise the temperature of 1 kg. water 1°C.

CAMEMBERT CHEESE. Soft, creamy cheese with an edible crust. Produced in France and in the United States.

CANARD. (Fr.) Duck.

CANDIED. When applied to fruit, the fruit or fruit rind is cooked in a heavy syrup until transparent, then drained, and dried. When applied to yams, sweet potatoes, or carrots, the vegetables are boiled and then cooked in a heavy syrup.

CANNELONI. (It.) Tubes or squares of pasta stuffed with meat, fish, or cheese and baked with butter and cheese or with a cream sauce and cheese.

CAPERS. The unopened flower buds of a plant grown in Greece, northern Africa, and southern Europe. The buds are pickled in salt and vinegar and used as a seasoning and a condiment.

CAPON. Castrated male chicken weighing between five and seven pounds.

CARAMELIZE. To heat sugar until it melts and reaches a brown color.

CARDOON. Vegetable of the thistle family. The tender stalks and roots are used in soups and as a vegetable.

CARRE DE MOUTON. (Fr.) Rack of mutton.

CASSATA. (It.) Candied fruit, chocolate, and ladyfingers.

CAUL. Web fat or membrane surrounding the paunch and intestines of animals. Used as a casing for sausages, minced meats, and salpicon.

CAVIAR. Salted roe (eggs) of salmon, sturgeon, or certain other fish. Black caviar, imported from Russia, is the most select.

CELESTINE. (Fr.) Consomme with slices of unsweetened pancakes.

CEPES. (Fr.) Species of mushroom.

CERISES. (Fr.) Cherries.

CERVELAT. Similar to salami, but more mildly seasoned.

CERVELLE. (Fr.) Brains.

CHIANTI. (It.) A light semi-dry red Italian wine from Tuscany.

CHAMPIGNON. (Fr.) Mushroom.
CHANTERELLES. (Fr.) Species of mushroom.
CHANTILLY CREAM. (Fr.) Sweetened and flavored whipped cream.
CHARCUTERIE. (Fr.) Pork butcher's meat or shop.
CHATEAUBRIAND. (Fr.) A thick steak cut from the center of a beef tenderloin.
CHAUD. (Fr.) Hot.
CHAUD-FROID SAUCE. (Fr.) A sauce used to coat cooked meat, game, poultry, or fish.
CHEF DE CUISINE. (Fr.) Executive chef or chef in charge.
CHEF DE PARTIE. (Fr.) The chef in charge of a department, such as the fry station.
CHESHIRE CHEESE. Hard yellow English cheese made of cows' milk.
CHEVREUIL. (Fr.) Venison.
CHICORY. Green leaves for salad. The roots are roasted and finely ground and used to strengthen coffee.
CHIFFONADE. Shredded or minced vegetables used for soups, salads, or salad dressing.
CHILIES. Hot red and green peppers in fresh and powdered form; used for cayenne pepper, chili powder, and for sauces, pickles, and meat dishes.
CHINA CAP. A cone-shaped strainer or seive.
CHORIZO. Spiced pork or pork and beef sausage.
CHOU PASTE. (Fr.) A cream puff or eclair batter.
CHUTNEY. Highly seasoned relish made from mangoes or other fruits, sugar, vinegar, and spices.
CILANTRO. Fresh green coriander; also called Chinese parsley.
CITRON. A yellow fruit with thick rough skin larger than a lemon but not as acid. The rind is candied and used in fruit cake, breads, and confections.
CIVIT. (Fr.) A ragout made of the meat of furred game.
COGNAC. French brandy.
COINTREAU. Trade name for an orange-flavored cordial.
COLLOPS. Cutlets.
CONCASSER. French term used for rough chopping of a substance or for breaking a substance by pounding in a mortar.
CONDE. Dessert consisting of creamed rice combined with fruit and sauce of red preserves or jam.
CONDIMENTS. Sauces used for seasonings, such as Worcestershire, mustard, ketchup, and Escoffier.
CONSOMME. (Fr.) Clear broth. May be served plain, hot, chilled, or jellied.
CONVENIENCE FOOD. Foods available in varying degrees of preparation.
COQ AU VIN. (Fr.) Chicken cooked with wine.
COQUILLES. (Fr.) Scallops or shell-shaped dishes.
CORNETS. A conical-shaped thin crisp pastry used to hold a rich cream or ice cream, or thin slices of ham or other chilled meat rolled into a horn shape.
COUPE. (Fr.) Ice cream served in a stemmed glass with fruit and Chantilly Cream.
COURT BOUILLON. Water, vinegar, herbs, and seasonings in which fish is poached.
CREAM. This term usually applies to blending a shortening and sugar mixture. The shortening or butter is beaten until soft and then the sugar is added. The mixture is beaten until light and thoroughly blended.
CREPE. (Fr.) A thin pancake.
CREPINETTES. (Fr.) A croquette mixture enclosed in a layer of forcemeat, brushed with butter, covered with bread crumbs and sauteed or baked.
CROISSANT. (Fr.) Crescent-shaped French roll.
CROUTONS. (Fr.) Butter-fried or toasted bread cut into cubes and served with soups.
CRUSTACEANS. Shellfish (crab, lobster, shrimp).
CUISINE. Style of cookery as Swiss, French, Spanish, American.
CURACAO. Liqueur made from the zest of the bitter orange; used for a flavoring in creams, icings, and jellies.
CUT-IN. To cut fat into dry ingredients with a pastry blender so that the fat remains in small particles.

DAL. (Indian) Dried beans, peas, or lentils.
DEEP-FAT FRYING. *See* Basic Cooking Methods, 8.5.
DEGLAZE. To dilute pan juices with stock, wine, or cream.
DEJEUNER. (Fr.) Lunch or mid-day meal.
DEMI. ((Fr.) Half.
DEMI-GLACE. (Fr.) Reduced brown stock.
DICE. To cut food into one-eighth inch cubes.
DIET. Daily allowance of food and drink.
DIETITIAN. One who has completed a prescribed academic program and earned a baccalaureate degree from an accredited college or university and has completed an approved dietetic internship; plans and directs foodservice programs in hospitals, colleges, and commercial establishments.
DINDE. (Fr.) Turkey-hen.
DINDON. (Fr.) Tom turkey.
DINDONNEAU. (Fr.) Young turkey.
DRAWN BUTTER. Melted butter.
DREDGE. To coat food by rolling in or sprinkling with flour.

DRUPE. A single-stoned fruit.

DU JOUR. (Fr.) The term means "of the day"; food that is ready to serve on that day.

DUSTING. Sprinkle with fine sugar or flour.

DUXELLES. (Fr.) A mushroom hash composed of finely chopped mushrooms, sauteed with onions and seasonings.

EAU. (Fr.) Water.

ECLAIR. (Fr.) Finger-shaped pastry made with chou paste and filled with whipped cream or vanilla pastry cream; usually iced with chocolate.

EDAM. Trade name for a Dutch low-fat yellow cheese that is rather dry with a red wax outer casing.

EDIBLE PORTION (E.P.). This term refers to the portion of the food that is eaten after all waste or trimmings, such as parings or rind, are removed.

EMINCE. (Fr.) Food that has been cut into a fine mince.

EMMENTALER. Swiss hard cheese with a sweet delicate flavor that is made from whole or semi-fat milk.

ENTRECOTE. (Fr.) Known as sirloin steak in the United States. Literally "between the ribs".

ENTREMETIER. (Fr.) Cook who prepares the vegetables.

ENTREMETS. (Fr.) Desserts.

EPINARDS. (Fr.) Spinach.

ESCARGOTS. (Fr.) Snails.

ESCOFFIER. (Fr.) The name of a famous French chef who is considered the master of modern classical cuisine.

ESSENCE. Extract from food substance.

EXTRACT. A concentrate used for flavoring (almond, anise, vanilla).

FAISAN. (Fr.) Pheasant.

FARCE. (Fr.) Forcemeat or stuffing.

FERMIERE, A LA. (Fr.) "Farmer's wife" style; chicken or meat poeler garnished with vegetables.

FILET MIGNON. The tenderloin of beef; very fine-textured and tender.

FILLET. Inside piece of the loin of beef, pork, lamb, veal, or game; boned fish; boned breast of poultry.

FINES HERBES. (Fr.) Mixture of minced herbs (parsley, tarragon, chervil, and chives) used for seasoning sauces, steaks, omelets, and salads.

FLORENTINE, A LA. (Fr.) As prepared in Florence; usually a spinach soup or a spinach garnish.

FOIE. (Fr.) Liver.

FOIE GRAS. (Fr.) Fat goose liver.

FOLD. Cooking term referring to a method of combining fragile ingredients, such as beaten egg whites, into a mixture without breaking or mashing.

FOND BLANC. (Fr.) White stock; the basis of white sauces.

FOND BRUN. (Fr.) Brown stock; the basis of thickened gravies and brown sauces.

FONDUE. (Fr.) Melted cheese with kirsch or wine into which pieces of French bread are dipped; also special sauces into which cooked cubes of meat are dipped.

FORCEMEAT. Chopped meats and seasonings used for a stuffing.

FORESTIERE, A LA. (Fr.) Method of preparing small pieces of meat or poultry. The dish is garnished with mushrooms and noisette potatoes.

FRAISES. (Fr.) Strawberries.

FRAMBOISES. (Fr.) Raspberries.

FRICASSEE. (Fr.) Pieces of poultry, veal, or lamb seared without browning and cooked as a stew.

FRITTO MISTO. (It.) Variety of deep-fried meats, poultry, or fish arranged around an assortment of deep-fried vegetables.

FROID. (Fr.) Cold.

FROMAGE. (Fr.) Cheese.

FUMET BLANC DE POISSON. (Fr.) White fish stock.

GALANTINE. (Fr.) Boned, stuffed, and poached fish or meat that is rolled, pressed, glazed, and served cold.

GAME. Edible wild animals such as deer, bear, hare, squirrel, and buffalo.

GAME FOWL. Edible wild birds including pheasant, partridge, pigeons, ducks, geese, grouse, quail, and squab.

GARDE MANGER. (Fr.) Pantry, larder, cold meat department or person in charge of this department.

GARNISH. A food used to enhance or decorate the dish, such as sprigs of watercress or parsley; radishes, carrots, and vegetables; lemon rind, croutons, nutmeats, or chocolate curls.

GARNITURE DE MARMITE. (Fr.) Garnish of cooked diced meat and vegetables.

GAUFRES. (Fr.) Thin sweet wafers.

GHEE. A form of clarified butter used in Indian cookery.

GIBIER. (Fr.) Game.

GIGOT D'AGNEAU. (Fr.) Leg of lamb.

GJETOST. National cheese of Norway made from the whey of goats' milk. It has a sweet caramel flavor.

GLACE DE VIANDE. (Fr.) Stock reduced to a jelly consistency and used for glazing cooked meats.

GLAZING. *See* Basic Cooking Methods, 8.11.1, 8.12.1.

GNOCCHI. Small Italian dumplings made of potatoes, semolina, or puff paste.

GORGONZOLA. A semisoft blue-veined Italian cheese.

GOUDA. A Dutch cheese.

GRAND MARNIER. (Fr.) Good quality cognac with an orange flavor often served as a liqueur.

GRANITE. (Fr.) A water ice.

GRATINATING. *See* Basic Cooking Methods, 8.8.
GRENADINE. Syrup made from the juice of the pomegranate and sugar.
GRILLING. *See* Basic Cooking Methods, 8.7.
GROATS. Hulled and coarsely-crushed grain of oats used for making porridge, gruel, and broth.
GROSSE PIECE. (Fr.) Main course of a menu.
GRUYERE. A hard, light, yellow, cooked cheese with holes. It is made in Switzerland, France, Finland, and Argentina.
GUGELHUPF. German cake made with almonds and raisins and baked in a fluted pan.

HAGGIS. A Scottish food made from hearts, lungs, and livers of calves or sheep; highly seasoned, combined with oatmeal, and cooked in a sheep's stomach.
HARICOTS. (Fr.) Beans.
HARICOTS VERTS. (Fr.) Green string beans.
HASSENPFEFFER. (Ger.) Rabbit stew.
HELVELLA. A conical-shaped fungus similar to the conical morel.
HERB BOUQUET. *See* Bouquet Garni.
HORS D'OEUVRE. (Fr.) Small canapes served hot or cold as appetizers at the beginning of a meal.
HUILE. (Fr.) Oil.
HUITRES. (Fr.) Oysters.

ISINGLASS. Very pure gelatin prepared from the air bladders of fishes, especially sturgeon; used as a replacement for gelatin in jellies and puddings, and as a clarifying agent.

JAMBON. (Fr.) Ham.
JARDINIERE. (Fr.) Fresh vegetables cut into thin strips or diced, cooked, and arranged as a garnish around meat.
JULIENNE. Vegetables or meat cut into long, thin strips.
JUS. (Fr.) Juice. The term is used in reference to the natural juices of broiled or roasted meats.

KABOB. Pieces of marinated meat, vegetables, or fruit cooked on a skewer.
KIEV. Stuffed with seasoned butter.
KIRSCHWASSER. (Ger.) Cherry cordial or brandy.
KNEAD. To fold, stretch, and press dough to incorporate air and improve its texture.
KUMMEL. (Ger.) A liqueur flavored with caraway seeds.

LAIT. (Fr.) Milk.
LANGOUSTE. (Fr.) Spiny lobster with no claws.
LAPIN. (Fr.) Rabbit.
LARD. The fat of hogs that has been melted, clarified, and hardened; used for frying or as a shortening.
LARDING. To insert thin strips of salt pork, bacon, or fat into the surface of uncooked meat, fish, or poultry to keep it moist while cooking.
LARDOON. Thin strips of salt pork or bacon inserted into dry meat, fish, or poultry.
LEGUMES. (Fr.) Fruit or seeds of leguminous plants; peas, beans, or lentils that are used either fresh or dried.
LENTILS. Small flat seeds of leguminous plants that are used in soup.
LIAISON. A binding agent, such as eggs, used to thicken sauces and soups.
LIMBURGER. A soft cheese with a strong flavor and odor.
LIQUEUR. Sweet alcoholic beverage usually served as an after-dinner drink. Available in many flavors.
LYONNAISE. Food heavily seasoned with onions.

MACEDOINE. (Fr.) Combination of various fruits or vegetables.
MADEIRA. A sweet dark, full-bodied wine originating in the Portuguese island of Madeira.
MADELEINE. Small cake baked in a mold.
MADRILENE SOUP. (Fr.) A double strength consomme that may be served jellied or hot. It is flavored with Madeira, brandy, cayenne pepper, and garnished with diced tomatoes.
MAITRE D'HOTEL. (Fr.) Person in charge of a dining room.
MAITRE D'HOTEL, A LA. (Fr.) A style of preparation. Sauce: melted butter seasoned with lemon juice, parsley, salt, and pepper.
MARASCHINO. A liqueur made from Marasca cherries grown in Dalmatia.
MARINADE. A combination of lemon juice or vinegar, wine, oil, and seasonings used to add flavor to foods. Also used to tenderize some meats.
MARINATE. To soak or steep in a marinade of vinegar, lemon juice or wine, oil, and seasonings to give added flavor, to tenderize, or to preserve.
MARRON. (Fr.) Chestnut.
MARSALA. (It.) A semi-dry wine made from grapes grown near Marsala in Sicily.
MARZIPAN. Almond paste made of ground almonds, sugar, and egg white.
MASK. To cover completely, usually with a sauce or an aspic.
MATELOTE. (Fr.) Rich fish stew

usually prepared from freshwater fish, wine, herbs, and seasonings.

MATIGNON. (Fr.) Minced raw or cooked vegetables used for garnishing meats.

MEAT EXTRACT. A preparation made by reducing a stock to a gelatinous consistency.

MEDALLIONS. Small rounds of tenderloin or foie gras.

MELBA SAUCE. Combination of pureed raspberries, currant jelly (optional), sugar, and cornstarch. Usually served over ice cream.

MELBA TOAST. Very thin slices of white bread toasted in the oven until crisp.

MERINGUE. Egg whites stiffly beaten with sugar. Used as a topping for pies, puddings, and Baked Alaska and browned in the oven; also formed into shells, baked, and used as a base for ice cream, whipped cream, and other fillings.

METABOLISM. A term used to designate the sum of all chemical and physical changes which occur to substances within the body after absorption.

MEUNIERE, A LA. (Fr.) "Miller's wife" style; lightly floured fish sauteed in butter and seasoned with lemon juice, parsley, and hot butter.

MILANAISE, A LA. (Fr.) Milan style. Method of preparing spaghetti.

MIREPOIX. A mixture of diced vegetables, herbs, and spices with or without meat to enhance the flavor of meat and fish dishes.

MISE EN PLACE. (Fr.) Literally means "put in place". Interpreted as organizing and completing, in advance, all the preliminary tasks involved in the preparation of a meal.

MIX. Combine two or more ingredients and stir until blended.

MIXED GRILL. Assorted grilled meats, such as chop, kidney, and sausage, garnished with tomatoes and mushrooms.

MOCHA. Strong coffee mainly used in blended coffee. It is also a mixture of coffee and chocolate flavors used in ice cream, frostings, cakes, and pies.

MOHN. Poppyseed.

MORTADELLA SAUSAGE. A large sausage of Italian origin but is also made in France. An excellent commercial pork product served as an hors d'oeuvre.

MOUSSE. (Fr.) A delicate, smooth dessert made from cream, eggs, or gelatin, and flavorings such as chocolate, fruits, or coffee. The term also applies to savory dishes, such as cold dishes and salads made with gelatin, ground meat, poultry, or fish, and seasonings.

MOUSSELINE SAUCE. (Fr.) Hollandaise Sauce with whipped cream.

MOUTON. (Fr.) Mutton.

MOZZARELLA. Semisoft, mild Italian cheese used in pizza and other cooked foods.

MUENSTER. Semisoft, mild-flavored German cheese.

MYSOST. A sweet caramel-flavored whey cheese popular in the Scandinavian countries.

NEUFCHATEL. A soft, creamy, mild French cheese.

NOIR. (Fr.) Black.

NOISETTE. (Fr.) Hazelnut. The term is also used to designate small round pieces of beef tenderloin or lamb; noisette potatoes are shaped with a melon ball cutter and sauteed in butter until brown.

NOUILLE. (Fr.) Noodle.

NUTRIENTS. Nutritive substances such as proteins, carbohydrates, fats, vitamins, minerals, and water.

NUTRITION. The sum of the processes by which the living organism receives and utilizes food substances necessary for maintenance of its functions and to promote growth, replace loss, and provide energy.

OEUF. (Fr.) Egg.

OFFAL. Variety meats; brains, liver, tongue.

ORGEAT. (Fr.) A nonalcoholic almond-flavored syrup used in mixed drinks or as a food flavoring.

OSHA. Occupational Safety and Health Administration.

OSSO BUCO. (It.) Veal shanks that have been sauteed, and cooked with tomato, onion, wine, and garlic; served with rice or spaghetti.

OVER-RUN. The increase in volume of a frozen dessert resulting from the incorporation of air into the mixture during freezing.

PAELLA. (Sp.) Famous Spanish dish of rice seasoned with saffron and cooked with tomatoes, peas, wine, chicken, shellfish, and other ingredients.

PAIN. (Fr.) Bread.

PAMPLEMOUSSE. (Fr.) Grapefruit.

PANADA. (Fr.) Preparation made of flour or bread cooked in water, milk, or stock; used to bind forcemeats or stuffings.

PAN-FRY. To cook in an uncovered skillet with a small amount of fat.

PARFAIT. Frozen dessert made of alternate layers of ice cream and fruits or flavored syrups.

PARMENTIER, A LA. (Fr.) Method of preparing various dishes which always include a form of potatoes.

PASTA. Products made from a hard-wheat flour dough and forced through dies of various sizes and shapes. Pastas are known by different names such as macaroni, spaghetti, vermicelli, ravioli, canneloni, and others.

PASTY. Cooked ground meat, seasonings, and potatoes encased in pastry and baked.

PATISSERIE. (Fr.) French pastry or a pastry shop.

PAUPIETTE. (Fr.) Thin slices of meat stuffed, rolled, and braised.

PAYSANNE, A LA. (Fr.) Peasant or country style; a soup or meat dish served with buttered vegetables.

PESTO. A green sauce made with oil, anchovies, herbs, and garlic.

PETIT DEJEUNER. (Fr.) Breakfast.

PETITE MARMITE. (Fr.) A rich vegetable soup with lean pieces of meat or poultry served in individual covered pots with cheese-covered toast floating on top of the soup.

PETITS-FOURS. (Fr.) Small rich cakes dipped in fondant icing and decorated; fancy cookies, such as macaroons, shortbreads, and butter cookies.

PETITS POIS. (Fr.) Fresh garden peas.

PICCATA. Small cutlets, generally from veal.

PIGNOLIAS. (Pine Nuts) Seeds of pine cones from the stone pine.

PIQUANT. Pungent, highly seasoned.

PLATS DU JOUR. (Fr.) Specialties of the day.

POACHING. *See* Basic Cooking Methods, 8.2.

POELER. (Fr.) *See* Basic Cooking Methods, 8.13.

POISSON. (Fr.) Fish.

POIVRADE. (Fr.) (1) Method of preparing ground game; (2) Pepper Sauce; (3) small artichokes eaten with salt.

POLENTA. (It.) Cornmeal.

POMME. (Fr.) Apple.

POMME DE TERRE. (Fr.) Potato.

PORT DU SALUT. (Fr.) Semisoft creamy cheese with mellow to robust flavor.

POTAGE. (Fr.) Soup.

POT-AU-FEU. (Fr.) Rich flavorful vegetable soup.

PRALINE. A confection made of pecans, sugar, and cream.

PROSCIUTTO. Italian ham (diced, salted, seasoned, and pressed pork).

PROVENCALE, A LA. (Fr.) Provincial style. Certain dishes using brown sauce, tomatoes, garlic, onion, and seasonings.

PSI. Pounds per square inch.

PUPPADUM. Round thin crisp Indian wafer served with drinks, meals, curries, and tea.

PUREE. The strained pulp of foodstuffs.

QUENNELE. (Fr.) Forcemeat dumpling.

QUICHE. (Fr.) A rich pie dough covered with a custard-like mixture. It is baked and served as an hors d'oeuvre or luncheon dish. Quiche Lorraine, the best known, is made with Gruyere cheese and diced ham or bacon.

RACLETTE. Famous Swiss dish; scraped melted cheese served with boiled potatoes and gherkins.

RAGOUT. (Fr.) Rich savory stew of meat, fish, or poultry and vegetables.

RAMEKIN. Individual shallow earthenware or china dish in which food can be baked and served.

RECONSTITUTE. To restore to the original form or condition by adding water.

REDUCTION. A process used to increase the flavor and richness of liquids and sauces. The liquids thicken during very slow simmering by the evaporation process until reduced to about one-half their original volume.

REMOULADE. (Fr.) A highly seasoned sauce made of mayonnaise, gherkins, onion, tarragon, capers, anchovy essence, and chervil.

RICE FLOUR. Flour milled from rice.

RISOTTO. (It.) Rice dish.

RISSOLE. (Fr.) Turnover made with very thin puff paste filled with forcemeat and deep-fat fried.

RISSOLER. (Fr.) To brown.

ROASTING. *See* Basic Cooking Methods, 8.10.

ROE. Mass of fish eggs. Beluga caviar is the best of the hard roes. Herring and salmon roe are soft roe and are used as a substitute for caviar and for garnishes.

ROQUEFORT. Semisoft French cheese with veins of blue-green mold and a sharp piquant flavor.

ROSE HIPS. Red fruit of the dog rose used for making jellies, sauces, and beverages.

ROSEWATER. Liquid distilled from rose petals.

ROUX. Mixture of melted butter or fat and flour used to thicken soups and sauces.

SABAYON. (Fr.) A sauce or dessert composed of whipped eggs, sugar, white wine, and flavoring.

SACCHARIN. Ortho-benzosulfimide; three hundred times sweeter than sucrose. It has no food value and is used as a calorie-free sweetener.

SAGO. Floury substance from the palm tree used as thickening agent.

SALAMANDER. A small broiler with the heat source at the top and a shelf below.

SALMIS. A roasted game stew.

SALPICON. A mixture of finely diced meat and vegetables bound with a sauce and used for canapes, croquettes, and timbales.

SAUTEING. *See* Basic Cooking Methods, 8.6.

SAUTOIR. (Fr.) Large round, shallow, heavy duty pan with straight walls and a long handle. Used for sauteing.

SAVORIES. Light dishes, such as cheese straws, tartlets, and cheese biscuits, served at the end of the meal.

SCAMPI. Large shrimp.

SCORE. Nomenclature used in the United States Standards for Grades of Butter. The score designates the grade, example: U.S. Grade AA or U.S. 93 Score is the highest quality. The score or grade is determined on the basis of classifying the characteristics of the flavor, body, color, and salt.

SCORING. To cut gashes on the fat surrounding a steak or on the layer of fat covering a ham or on the crust of a pie.

SEAR. To brown the surface of meat at a high temperature.

SEC. (Fr.) Dry, as a wine or champagne.

SEMOLINA. Fine particles of the gluten of durum wheat which are not used in the manufacture of fine flour. Used for making pastas and puddings.

SHALLOT. A mild-flavored onion. The plant produces clusters of lateral bulbs that multiply freely.

SHELLFISH. *Crustaceans* which include crab, lobster, and shrimp; *mollusks* which include abalone, clams, oysters, and scallops.

SHERBET or SORBET. (Fr.) Frozen mixture of fruit juice, sugar, and milk. Gelatin and egg whites are sometimes added.

SIMMERING. *See* Basic Cooking Methods, 8.14.

SIMPLE SYRUP. Equal portions of sugar and water boiled until the sugar is dissolved. Used as a sweetener for drinks.

SKEWER. Thin pointed wooden or metal pin to hold small pieces of meat and/or vegetables in place for broiling.

SOUBIS. (Fr.) Pureed onion and butter or cream served with various meat dishes.

SOUPER. (Fr.) Supper.

SOUS CHEF. (Fr.) Assistant to the head chef. He supervises the kitchen and the personnel responsible for certain units of the kitchen.

SOY BEANS. Vegetable that is often used as a meat substitute. The beans are used as a vegetable, for an edible oil and flour, and for a Soy Sauce served with oriental foods.

SPAETZLE. (Ger.) Small Austrian dumplings cooked in a stock and served in soups, as garnishes, or with meats.

SPICE SACHET. A variety of spices and herbs tied in cheesecloth; used to season soups, sauces, and other dishes.

SPIT. A pointed rod on which meat is held while roasting or barbecuing above or in front of open heat.

SPRING-FORM PAN. Baking pan with removable rim. A hinged clamp holds the rim and bottom together.

STEAMING. *See* Basic Cooking Methods, 8.4.

STEEP. To soak in hot liquid to extract flavor.

STEWING. *See* Basic Cooking Methods, 8.14.

STILTON CHEESE. A semisoft English cheese with veins of mold. It has a spicy flavor and is a good dessert cheese.

STOCK. A liquid in which bones and trimmings of meat, fish, game, or vegetables have been cooked.

SUET. Hard fat around the kidneys of beef, mutton, veal, and lamb. Used in steamed puddings, mincemeat, and suet-crust pastry.

SWEDE. Yellow rutabaga.

SWEETBREAD. The thymus of the calf and lamb. Calves' sweetbreads are used as a garnish or in combination with other foods.

SYLLABUB. A traditional English dessert made with stiffly beaten cream, sugar, and wine.

TABASCO. Brand name of a hot spicy condiment made of vinegar and hot peppers.

TABLE D'HOTE. (Fr.) A complete meal at a fixed price, as opposed to a la carte in which each item is priced separately.

TAGLIATELLA. (It.) A pasta.

TAHINA. A paste made from crushed sesame seeds.

TARRAGON VINEGAR. A white vinegar flavored with tarragon.

TARTAR-STEAK. Raw ground beef which is highly seasoned and garnished, and usually served as an appetizer.

TARTLET. Small tart.

TERRAPIN. Freshwater turtle.

TERRINE. (Fr.) An earthenware casserole. The term is also used to designate the food prepared in the dish, such as terrine of chicken.

THICKENING. To give body to a sauce, broth, or liquid food by adding flour, starch, arrowroot, eggs, butter, or roux.

TIMBALE. Finely ground meat, seasonings, and vegetables bound with eggs and baked in a water bath in the oven.

TIMBALE SHELLS or ROSETTES. Crisp shells or cases made by dipping a hot timbale iron into a light batter and then into deep fat. The shells are filled with creamed chicken.

TORRONE. (It.) Nougat.

TORTUE. (Fr.) Turtle.

TOURNEDOS. (Fr.) Small steaks cut from the tenderloin of beef.

TREACLE. A heavy dark syrup which is a by-product from the sugar-refining process.

TRIFLE. An English dessert made of sponge cake sprinkled with wine and combined with jam, a rich custard sauce, and whipped cream.

TRIPE. Stomach of cattle.

TRUFFLES. Round, pungent, black fungi found in France and Italy; used in sauces, pates, stuffings, and in decorations.

TRUSS. To tie or skewer the legs and wings of poultry and game in a manner to retain the shape and juices during the cooking process.

VEAU. (Fr.) Veal.

VERMICELLI. (It.) Long, very thin pasta product used in soups.

VERT. (Fr.) Green.

VESIGN. Spine marrow of sturgeon.

VIANDE. (Fr.) Meat.

VICHY, A LA. (Fr.) Vegetables cooked in water with butter and a small amount of sugar; usually refers to carrots. The water of the Vichy Springs gave the vegetables a unique delicate flavor.

VICHYSSOISE. (Fr.) Cold soup made of pureed tomatoes, finely chopped leeks, chicken stock, and cream. Served chilled and garnished with chopped chives.

VIN. (Fr.) Wine.

VINAIGRETTE SAUCE. Mixture of oil, wine vinegar, and herbs.

VITAMIN. An organic substance found in animal and plant tissues that is essential in the regulation of metabolic functions.

VOLAILLE. (Fr.) Poultry.

VOL-AU-VENT. (Fr.) A puff-pastry shell in which meat, poultry, or fish bound with a sauce is served.

WHIP. To beat ingredients, such as eggs, into a froth in order to increase volume by incorporating air.

WORCESTERSHIRE SAUCE. Brand name of a dark spicy sauce used to season meats and other foods.

ZABAGLIONE. (It.) A dessert or sweet sauce made with beaten egg yolks, marsala wine, and honey. Beaten egg whites are folded in when used as a dessert.

ZAMPONI. (It.) The stuffed skin of pig's feet.

ZEST. The outermost colored part of the peel of citrus fruit.

ZITI. (It.) A pasta.

ZWIEBACK. Hard, crisp, toasted biscuits similar to rusks.

References

American National Red Cross. *Advanced First Aid and Emergency Care.* First Edition. Garden City, New York: Doubleday and Company, Inc., 1973.

American Spice Trade Association. *What You Should Know About Cinnamon.* New York, 1961.

—*What You Should Know About Nutmeg and Mace.* 1966.

—*What You Should Know About Paprika.* 1966.

—*What You Should Know About Pepper.* 1964.

Aresty, Esther J. *The Delectable Past.* New York: Simon and Schuster, 1964.

Beck, Simone; Bertholle, Louisette; Child, Julia. *Mastering the Art of French Cooking.* New York: Alfred A. Knopf, 1965.

Bowes, Anna de Planter and Church, Charles F. *Food Values of Portions Commonly Used.* Philadelphia: J. B. Lippincott Company. *Note:* Eleventh edition revised by Charles Frederick Church and Helen Nichols Church.

Bull, Sleeter. *Meat for the Table.* New York: McGraw-Hill, 1951.

Culinary Institute of America and the Editors of Institution Magazine. *The Professional Chef.* Edited by LeRoi A. Folsom. Fourth edition. Boston: CBI Publishing Company, Inc., 1974.

Ellwanger, George H. *The Pleasures of the Table.* New York: Doubleday Page and Co.

Escoffier, A. *The Escoffier Cook Book.* New York: Crown Publishers, 1956.

Fowler, Sina Faye; West, Bessie Brooks; and Shugart, Grace Severance. *Food for Fifty,* Fifth Edition. New York: John Wiley and Sons, Inc., 1971.

Gates, June C. *Basic Foods.* New York: Holt, Rinehart, and Winston, 1976.

Guy, Christian. *An Illustrated History of French Cuisine.* Translated by Elisabeth Abbott. New York: The Orion Press, 1962.

Harger, Virginia; Shugart, Grace; West, Bessie Brooks; and Wood, LeVelle. *Food Service in Institutions.* New York: John Wiley and Sons, Inc., 1977.

Harrison, S. G.; Mansfield, G. B.; Wallis, Michael. *The Oxford Book of Food Plants.* 1969. Reprinted in 1971 and 1973. London, W1: Oxford University Press.

Hartley, Dorothy. *Food in England.* 1954. Reprinted in 1955, 1963, and 1964. London, W1: Macdonald and Company Publishers Ltd.

Johnston, Harriet. *Quality, Quantity Cuisine I.* Boston: CBI Publishing Company, Inc., 1976.

Kotschevar, Lendal H. *Quantity Food Purchasing.* Second Edition. New York: John Wiley and Sons, Inc., 1975.

Kotschevar, Lendal H. *Standards, Principles, and Techniques in Quantity Food Production.* Third Edition. Boston: CBI Publishing Company, Inc., 1966.

Krieger, Louis, C. C. *The Mushroom Handbook.* New York: Dover Publications, 1967.

Longree, Karla. *Food Service Sanitation.* Second Edition. New York: John Wiley and Sons, Inc., 1973.

Longree, Karla, and Blaker, G. *Sanitary Techniques in Food Services.* New York: John Wiley and Sons, Inc., 1971.

Lowe, Belle. *Experimental Cookery from the Chemical and Physical Standpoint.* Seventh Edition. New York: John Wiley and Sons, Inc., 1955.

Montagne, Prosper. *Larousse Gastronomique.* Edited by Charlotte Turgeon and Nina Froud. New York: Crown Publishers, Inc., 1961.

Morgan, William, J., Jr. *Supervision and Management of Quantity Food Preparation.* Berkeley, California: McCutchan Publishing Company, 1974.

National Dairy Council. *Newer Knowledge of Cheese.* Second Edition. Chicago, 1967.

National Dairy Council. *Newer Knowledge of Milk.* Third Edition. Chicago, 1968.

National Live Stock and Meat Board. *Beef Grading.* Chicago, 1976.

National Live Stock and Meat Board. *Facts About Beef.* Chicago, 1976.

National Live Stock and Meat Board. *Facts About Pork.* Chicago, 1976.

National Live Stock and Meat Board. *Lessons on Meat.* Fourth Edition, revised. Chicago, 1974.

National Live Stock and Meat Board. *Meat in the Food Service Industry.* Chicago, 1975.

National Restaurant Association and American Spice Trade Association. *A Guide to Spices: How to Buy Them—How to Store Them—How to Use Them.* Technical Bulletin No. 190, Second Revision. Chicago, Illinois, N.D.

National Restaurant Association and United Fresh Fruit and Vegetable Association. *Buying, Handling, and Using Fresh Fruits.* Chicago, Illinois, N.D.

National Safety Council. *Hand Knives.* Data Sheet 369, revised. Chicago, Illinois, N.D.

Pedderson, Raymond B. *Specs: The Comprehensive Foodservice Purchasing and Specification Manual.* Boston: CBI Publishing Company, Inc., 1977.

Richardson, Treva M. *Sanitation for Food Service Workers.* Second Edition. Boston: CBI Publishing Company, Inc., 1974.

Romans, John R. and Ziegler P. Thomas. *The Meat We Eat.* Tenth Edition. Danville, Illinois: The Interstate Printers and Publishers, Inc., 1974.

Rombauer, Irma S. and Becker, Marion Rombauer. *Joy of Cooking.* Revised Edition. Indianapolis: Bobbs-Merrill Company, 1975.

Root, Waverly. *The Food of France.* New York: Alfred A Knopf, 1958.

Simon, Andre L. *A Concise Encyclopedia of Gastronomy.* New York: Harcourt Brace and Company, 1952.

Sonnenschmidt, Frederic H., Nicholas, Jean. *The Professional Chef's Art of Garde Manger.* Edited by Jule Wilkinson. Boston: CBI Publishing Company, Inc., 1976.

Tannahill, Reay. *Food and History.* New York: Stein and Day, 1973.

Terrell, Margaret E. *Large Quantity Recipes.* Third Edition. Philadelphia: J. B. Lippincott Company, 1975.

Terrell, Margaret E. *Professional Food Preparation.* New York: John Wiley and Sons, Inc., 1971.

Todoroff, Alexander. *Food Buying Today.* Revised Edition. Chicago: The Grocery Trade Publishing House, 1938.

Turner, Dorothea. *Handbook of Diet Therapy.* Fifth Edition. Written and compiled for the American Dietetic Association. Chicago: The University of Chicago Press, 1973.

United States Department of Agriculture. *Federal Standards for the Composition of Milk Products.* Agricultural Handbook No. 51. Washington, D.C.: United States Department of Agriculture, Food Safety and Quality Service, 1977.

United States Department of Agriculture. *Home Canning of Fruits and Vegetables.* Home and Garden Bulletin No. 8. Revised 1971. Washington, D.C.: Superintendent of Documents, United States Government Printing Office.

United States Department of Agriculture. Agricultural Marketing Service Home and Garden. Washington, D.C.

—Bulletin No. 148. *How to Buy Butter.* 1968.

—Bulletin No. 193. *How to Buy Cheese.* 1971.

—Bulletin No. 201. *How to Buy Dairy Products.* Revised 1974.

—Bulletin No. 144. *How to Buy Eggs.* 1968.

—Bulletin No. 141. *How to Buy Fresh Fruits.* 1967.

—Bulletin No. 195. *How to Buy Lamb.* 1971.

—Bulletin No. 198. *How to Buy Potatoes.* 1972.

—Bulletin No. 157. *How to Buy Poultry.* 1968.

United States Department of Commerce. National Consumer Educational Services Office, National Marine Fisheries Service. *Food Fish Facts,* No. 1-56. N.D.

United States Department of Health, Education, and Welfare. *Sanitary Foodservice.* Public Health Service Publication, No. 90. Cincinnati, Ohio, 1969.

United States Department of Interior, *Guide for Buying Fresh and Frozen Fish and Shellfish,* Circular 214. Washington, D.C.: Superintendent of Documents, United States Government Printing Office, 1959.

Watson, Betty. *Cooks, Gluttons, and Gourmets.* Garden City, New York: Doubleday Publishing Company, 1962.

Wilkinson, Jule. *The Complete Book of Cooking Equipment.* Revised Edition. Boston: CBI Publishing Company, Inc., 1975.

Williams, Sue Rodwell. *Nutrition and Diet Therapy.* Second Edition. Saint Louis: The C. V. Mosby Company, 1973.

Index